W9-ABQ-647

MASTERING *the* ART *of* SOUTHERN COOKING

MASTERING *the* ART *of* SOUTHERN COOKING

Nathalie Dupree
& Cynthia Graubart

Photographs by Rick McKee

With a foreword by Pat Conroy

GIBBS SMITH
TO ENRICH AND INSPIRE HUMANKIND

First Edition
12 13 14 15 16 5 4 3 2 1

Published by
Gibbs Smith
P.O. Box 667
Layton, Utah 84041

1.800.835.4993 orders
www.gibbs-smith.com

Gibbs Smith books are printed on paper produced from sustainable PEFC-certified forest/controlled wood source. Learn more at www.pefc.org.
Printed and bound in Hong Kong

Library of Congress Cataloging-in-Publication Data

Dupree, Nathalie.
Mastering the art of Southern cooking / Nathalie Dupree & Cynthia Graubart ; photographs by Rick McKee ; with a foreword by Pat Conroy. — First Edition.
pages cm
Includes index.
ISBN 978-1-4236-0275-0
1. Cooking, American—Southern style.
I. Graubart, Cynthia Stevens. II. Title.
TX715.2.S68.D858 2012
641.5973—dc23
2012017365

To Jack,
who has gone from a two for
his palate to an eight in just
eighteen short years.
—Nathalie

To Cliff,
who never met a cornbread
he liked until mine.
—Cynthia

CONTENTS

ACKNOWLEDGMENTS

It is with humility and gratitude to those who have gone ahead that we thank them for their legacy. From the nameless slaves and cooks who tended crops and stoked fires, to those who wrote down what they cooked and what they ate, we thank you. Recipe collections begun by Martha Washington (1749), Thomas Jefferson (1780), Mary Randolph (1824), Sarah Rutledge (1864), Mrs. A. P. Hill (1867), and Mrs. S. R. Dull (1928) eventually found their way into print, providing hundreds of "receipts" of inspiration. Community cookbooks published throughout the South are a source of pride here, and for good reason. Honest food is found between their pages.

We look to our contemporaries in the field and thank them for keeping the South on the minds of cooks across the United States: John Egerton, John Folse, Damon Lee Fowler, Rebecca Lang, Dorie Sanders, David Shields, Virginia Willis, and others. We miss the nearness of Edna Lewis but know this collection would make her smile, just knowing more people will learn the true techniques of Southern cooking.

Our primary debt, however, is to those who have helped so generously along the way, starting with Kate Almand and Grace Reeves at Nathalie's Restaurant; those from Rich's cooking school, starting with Charles Gandy and Elise Griffin and ending ten years later with Carol Smaglinski and Margaret-Anne Surber; those of the first television crew, starting with Forsythia Chang, Anne Galbraith, and Gena Berry, then Ray Overton, and ending fifteen years later with Virginia Willis and Mary Moore; and those who worked so assiduously on this book, starting with Deidre Schipani for her wisdom and ending with intern Mary Katherine Wyeth, who, too, quickly became a diligent cook and recipe tester. We have credited many of their recipes here. Beth Price was our ballast when we felt we were sinking, always there to read another round of edited recipes, as well as devise and coordinate our recipe testing by outside testers. Our loyal friends and fans have helped us write a better book, especially our battery of a dozen proofreaders, including Carol Kay, Sarah Gaede, Sally Young, and Pat Royalty. We wish we could name you all.

We are grateful as well for our patient families and friends, who during the last few weeks of our editing, got nothing to eat without fixing it themselves and put up with our bleary eyes and short tempers. That said, for five years they reaped the benefits of eating well.

We could not have done this book without those at Gibbs Smith publishing: Christopher Robbins, for pushing us to do it, and most importantly, our hard-working and loyal editor, Madge Baird, and production editor/designer, Melissa Dymock. And right up to the bitter end, our talented and supremely dedicated photographer, Rick McKee, who was there to shoot a dish or ingredient on a moment's notice.

It is difficult to close the acknowledgements, fearing we have omitted someone who should appear between these covers. Whoever you may be, please accept our appreciation for your contribution to this tome, and our sincere apology for our oversight.

FOREWORD
BY PAT CONROY

In the summer of 1988, I served as best man in the wedding of Cliff and Cynthia Graubart in a civil ceremony of restrained elegance. It took place in a museum at the Campidoglio on a hill overlooking the city of Rome, Italy. The famous Southern cookbook writer Nathalie Dupree was the matron of honor.

Later that evening, I hosted a party on my rooftop terrace overlooking the Tiber River. Nathalie cooked the meal that night with me serving as errand boy and her sous chef. Nathalie prepared a wedding dinner that was one of the finest meals I ever ate under the Roman stars in my three years of magical eating in Italy. What the Italians did not know that night was that Nathalie Dupree had managed to fix a Southern feast in a kitchen with a view of St. Peters Cathedral and the Vatican in the windows behind her. Everything that Nathalie Dupree touches turns to gold. Now she has teamed up with the bride of that oft-celebrated wedding in Rome and they have produced this definitive and seminal work.

I've carried a lifetime passion for the reading pleasure I can get from Southern cookbooks and consider Southern cooking to be one of the great cuisines of the world. When they come out, I try to read them all and buy them all. I've met the Lee Brothers, and the great Frank Stitt, and Jean Anderson and Joe Dabney. I wrote an introduction to the superb novelist Janice Owens' hilarious and moving cookbook *Cracker Kitchen*, wrote one for *Southern Living's Comfort Food*, and another for my former student on Daufuskie, Sallie Ann Robinson, who published her delightful cookbook *Gullah Home Cooking the Daufuskie Way* in 2003. For many years now I've known my way around Southern letters and Southern cuisine.

Mastering the Art of Southern Cooking is the most exhaustive and well researched volume on Southern cooking ever published. It is massive in its sheer size and the audacity of its ambition. The book certainly looks like a candidate to replace Mrs. H. R. Dull's classic 1928 cookbook, *Southern Cooking*. Its range is large and its scope is encyclopedic. I had no idea there were this many recipes for Southern food popping out from ovens in kitchens below the Mason-Dixon line. But the true beauty of this book is the clarity and ease that will lend confidence to the beginning cook and expertise and knowledge to the gifted one. My piecrusts have always been mysterious messes, but not after I read Nathalie and Cynthia's cogent explanation of the art. My fried chicken has never been as good as my mother's or as bad as my grandmother's, but these two writers unlock the secrets for an impatient, itchy cook like me. They make baking cakes and pies seem simple and joyous and well—a piece of cake to me. Their recipes for vegetables are mouthwatering, and the ones for fish make me happy to be alive and living beside salt water and having access to pristine, clear water rivers flowing through the Lowcountry of South Carolina.

In a long-ago place, Nathalie Dupree was my first cooking teacher in downtown Atlanta's mythical Rich's Department Store. She was a wonderful, eccentric teacher who made cooking seem like it was one of the most wonderful ways to spend a human life. Nathalie began to invite me to her sumptuous dinner parties and her guests were always the most interesting people in Atlanta at any given time. The talk was high spirited and animated and good natured. Famous chefs and cookbook writers made their way to Nathalie's table in the eighties, and Cynthia Graubart met her future husband, Cliff, at one of Nathalie's soirées. Although I always thought Cliff was set up and that Nathalie was playing matchmaker for Cynthia, the producer of Nathalie's cooking show at that time. Cliff was a Jewish boy from Brooklyn, and the most Southern food he'd eaten when I met him was a bagel. Cynthia is a splendid cook in her own right, and the marriage has prospered as Cliff sits down to magnificent Southern meals every day of his life, though I've caught him backsliding when I find him in a deli slathering cream cheese and lox on a poppy seed bagel.

So this glorious cookbook comes into our Southern world as celebration, compendium, and almost a sacred text. I feel I have an intimate and deeply personal connection to this book. Cynthia Graubart was the beautiful bride standing on the Campidoglio in Rome as Nathalie Dupree caught the flung bouquet that Cynthia tossed in the air behind her.

I thought about that Roman wedding the whole time I was reading this book and how the arc of history has a way of inflating or repeating itself. But I still remember the pleasure of those Roman friends who raved over the quality of Nathalie's meal that night, so exotic, so original, so refined in its execution. I didn't have the heart to tell them that Nathalie waltzed into a country with one of the great cuisines of the planet humming in trattorias all around her, yet she paid homage to the food and people of the American South. She fixed one of the finest Southern meals I've ever eaten.

Mastering the Art of Southern Cooking is destined, I think, to become one of those classics of the breed like the inimitable Junior League cookbook *Charleston Receipts*. It imparts wisdom, a dash of history, a pinch of philosophy, and a wagon load of good eating. It is a splendid achievement.

—Pat Conroy

THE VERY BEGINNING

The day I met Julia Child, in June 1971, my last day at Cordon Bleu in London, she toured the school and came to see the results of our final exams. I was brought out to meet her, as I was the only American student in the Advanced Certificate class graduating that day. I had never heard of her, as I had been living in London for a couple of years and had never seen a cooking show on television. In spite of my ignorance, I was drawn to the commanding presence of this woman. Later, on Marylebone Lane in London in front of the Cordon Bleu, I ran into her and asked her what I should do with the rest of my life.

She answered, "Teach cooking. Open a cooking school. We need cooking schools in America." I never forgot the advice given to me by this stranger who had only known me five minutes. I had no idea how to teach anything, much less cooking. David, my favorite former husband, and I left London and went to Majorca, where we wound up working in a restaurant—he as bookkeeper, I as chef—without either of us speaking the language or having ever been inside a restaurant kitchen. At the end of the season and a tremendous learning curve, we returned to the United States, to Atlanta, where my father and David's parents lived. I cooked two carrot cakes a day for a restaurant until it was time to move to fifteen acres of land we had jointly purchased with his stepmother, Celeste Dupree, in rural Georgia, midway between Social Circle and Covington, Georgia, forty miles east of Atlanta, across from the Tri-County Cattle Auction Barn and Hub Junction.

There, with the help of my brother we built a kitchen and restaurant inside an old machine shop warehouse we had converted into an antique shop. There was no money for air-conditioning, but then we hadn't had air-conditioning in Majorca, either. By the next summer, we had put a window unit in the small dining room, and ultimately, one in the kitchen.

We grew as much of our own food as we could, including exotics like shallots and almost all the summer vegetables for our restaurant. Our neighbors would give us baskets of produce they couldn't use in exchange for free meals. We also grew an abundance of fresh herbs. To my knowledge, there was no other restaurant in Georgia using fresh herbs at that time except, perhaps, parsley. The majority of upscale restaurants in Atlanta served continental cuisine, while we served what we grew and what we could purchase locally in grocery stores or from local farmers. I did what I had done in Majorca: I combined the fresh produce available with classic European cooking techniques. This ultimately became the basis for what has been called "New Southern Cooking." It is a continuation of this food that we are doing in this book.

In the mid-seventies, Rich's Department Store asked me to start a cooking school in their Downtown Atlanta, Georgia, store. I called Julia and asked if I could come see her. She asked, "What do we have to speak about?" I told her she had suggested start a cooking school when we had met four years earlier. She clearly didn't remember me. I bumbled on, asking her what kind of a cooking school I should start. "Well, a full participation one, of course," she said. So I did.

Soon, I was doing what Julia had recommended—teaching. Customers at the restaurant had asked me to teach them, driving down from Atlanta, an hour each way with a few bottles of wine tucked in their cars (our restaurant was in a dry county). I formed friendships with those students that I still have today.

Rich's Cooking School contained twenty stoves, for a maximum of forty students, in a separate room on the street level of their downtown store. We rarely had that many in a class, unless it was a demonstration class. Within ten years I had taught more than 10,000 students and stopped counting.

Julia and her husband, Paul, came to the school many times, promoting her books to large audiences. We grew to know each other, particularly after serving together on the board of the International Association of Culinary Professionals (IACP), our professional organization. She read stories I wrote for *Brown's Guide to Georgia* about Southern cooking—classic techniques of biscuit making and fried chicken as well as mainstream recipes from the South.

On one of her visits we went up to the store's book department. She purchased some *Southern Junior League Cookbooks* as well as one by Mrs. H. R. Dull, *Southern Cooking.* Julia said, off-handedly, "Dearie, you should write a book about Southern cooking techniques one day like the articles you are doing." I felt uneasy, overwhelmed with a "who, me?" feeling and didn't answer her.

So, here I am, more than thirty years and twelve books later, with that book she told me to write. She didn't tell me to use the "Mastering the Art of" part of the name of her book, but out of reverence, I feel I must. It was her idea, after all.

Now I wish we had followed more of her advice. It was given to everyone as part of the introduction to *Mastering the Art of French Cooking.* As she said about culling her original manuscript, "even on Bible paper it would take a stand to hold it." It has taken a lot of winnowing over the last five years to realize what she was saying. We removed 300 pages and a hundred photographs to get it down to 720.

She had other advice: "Learn from anyone who knows one thing you don't know," and "never apologize." I have tried to do the learning but have not conquered the "never apologize." Julia was one of a kind, a master teacher. Women cooks owe her a debt because she forged a path that wouldn't have existed without her. I hope this book will pay back a little of what she did for me.

WHY DID WE WRITE THIS BOOK?

We dearly love the food of our region and the people who produce and cook it. We fantasize about Southern food, fix it for our families, and tote it to our friends.

This book is intended for people who want to know the whys and wherefores of Southern cooking, both historic and modern, and the steps towards achieving great results. It is written for those who have enough time to read the introductory information in the chapters, not the harried cook who simply has to get the food on the table in fifteen minutes for her—or, in these days, his—starving family, although we have some easy recipes, too. It uses almost no pre-packaged ingredients except those necessary in any pantry (see page 19)—canned tomatoes, rice, and a few others—although we have made good use of frozen foods on occasion, particularly those we put up ourselves. Geared towards home cooking as opposed to restaurant fare, it highlights recipes where learning a technique is required, with a bit of thought necessary. The book includes, as well, some recipes and techniques that are easily mastered using local ingredients presented in new ways, such as peaches and figs with country ham.

One of the results of the publication of my book *New Southern Cooking* (published in 1985 by Knopf and still in print twenty-seven years later by the University of Georgia Press) was the companion series for Public Television. Cynthia produced over eighty or more television shows in three series. The shows brought an outpouring from Southerners across the United States who wanted to learn to cook foods they remembered eating while growing up. They craved a taste they fondly remembered but didn't know where to start, because the techniques were no longer in daily practice. Historically, the cooks preparing Southern dishes had made them seem like magic. To them, the needed techniques were part of the rote learning of their childhoods, repeated so much they were second nature. They craved their foods of their region—grits, for instance, used in new and exciting ways as well as traditional.

New Southern Cooking on PBS was groundbreaking. It showed the country how to prepare Southern dishes. Each show featured an entire meal, from starter to dessert. Every step for each dish was shown on camera with no made-up TV magic. When we made a bread, we had a bread made for every stage in a bread's life, from yeast to slicing. The steps in the process for great Southern recipes like piecrusts, biscuits, and chicken and dumplings were demonstrated in great detail—possible mistakes and all—so the home cook could learn and then duplicate the foods dear to their hearts and memories. Like the book, it codified Southern cooking.

We traveled extensively throughout the Southeast, visiting more than eighty locations to show how our products were grown and produced—catching shrimp, going oystering, picking peaches, making hominy, watching grits being stone ground and peanut butter being made.

A new generation has grown up needing to learn the techniques of how to make biscuits, chicken-fried steak, and hoppin' John, as well as cream corn, and seed a hot pepper. They see chefs do razzle-dazzle on television but, with a few notable exceptions, not teach the basics. Exotic ingredients flash into recipes, but sadly the basics, such as separating the yolk and white of an egg, are often omitted. We have set out to change this, to codify even further the methodology we used in the television series. We gathered methods and recipes of how to cook the iconic dishes of our region, as well as how to use the available ingredients in more modern ways—such as roasting okra rather than only frying it and yet achieving a crispy, snacking-good result.

Aided by an army of assistants and testers, we culled through recipes to retain the best of the best. We have collected and treasure the historic recipes that form the basis of our cooking, and we feature some of them here to show the silver thread that binds us to our Southern heritage to the dishes we still serve today.

We couldn't include them all, so please don't bemoan the lack of one famous old cake recipe your family always made. It may be on the cutting room floor, and, most likely, the techniques it used are in another recipe. There are hundreds more recipes to be collected and tested. We have focused this book on the basics—the techniques and traditions we feel should be captured, codified, and carried on to the next generation of cooks. There are many more techniques and recipes to be studied and reproduced. We recognize that this new generation will use our book merely as a starting point, adding to it as they gain in skill and experience.

WHAT MAKES SOUTHERN FOOD UNIQUE?

Southerners lie awake at night and remember their grandmother's biscuits, their Aunt Sue's mashed potatoes and gravy, the grits from the mill down the road, and the boiled peanuts their grandfather taught them to cook in an large, well-used old can over a fire in the backyard. We crave our food and dream about it.

THE GEOGRAPHY AND THE INHABITANTS

The American South is larger than Western Europe. It is composed of the eleven states of the Confederacy, which stretch from Virginia to Texas. The region is bounded on the east by five states bordering the Atlantic Ocean: Virginia, North Carolina, South Carolina, Georgia, and Florida. Four others stretch westward from Florida, on the Gulf of Mexico: Alabama, Mississippi, Louisiana, and Texas. Two other states separated by the Mississippi River—Tennessee and Arkansas—stretch westward from Virginia to Texas. The region also includes the southern parts of the border states to the north that still allowed slavery when the Civil War began, stretching westward from Delaware across Maryland to Kentucky and Missouri. These Border States remained in the Union; West Virginia separated from Virginia over the issue of secession, becoming a new state in 1863, yet remains linked to Appalachia.

Now home to more than 100 million people, the settlers were diverse. Only remnants of Native Americans remained, but large numbers of English, ranging from minor royalty to indentured servants and former prisoners, as well as Africans, Scotch-Irish, French, Spaniards, Germans, and Welch settled early. A smaller cultural sprinkling of Italians, Jews, Chinese, and Greeks, as well as Hispanics (in Texas and later, Florida), added spice to the cultural hodgepodge of food in the South, to form a distinctive blend of Southern cuisine. They are historically linked by the common experience of shared defeat in the American Civil War in the defense of chattel slavery followed by decades of poverty that lasted well into the New Deal. This South is the only region of the United States that from the earliest beginnings was a biracial society. Chicago, Cleveland, Detroit, Los Angeles, New York City, and Washington, D.C., all have large pockets of Southern cultural infusion. These pockets intertwine and celebrate the food, music, and culture of the South, which expanded there in large part because of the mass migration of several million African Americans (called the Black Diaspora) during and after the post-Civil War period of Reconstruction. It continued to accelerate after World War II until the Civil Rights revolution significantly diminished the region's history of racial discrimination.

When we say *Southerners,* we don't mean just the people living here now. We mean all the extended family of Southerners, who write us from Oregon, saying, "My grandmother lived in Mississippi, and she made a hoecake for me every morning for breakfast when I stayed with her in the summer. It was lacy, and crisp, but solid in the middle. She's gone now, but I sure would like to make that hoecake. Do you know how?" The extended family lives all over the world now, perhaps not even having a relative here anymore.

Their family may have migrated as part of the Southern Diaspora, when African Americans went north or west in search of opportunity and greater freedom but remained segregated, either by choice or design. Both blacks and whites were lured away by the promise of cheaper, more fertile land, education, and advancement—the whites to Kansas before the Civil War or California's Central Valley during the Great Depression in search of work to feed their families. Or a grandmother had married a soldier who returned to another place from one of the many military bases that at one time dotted the South. But those families passed on the lore, some of them in the manner of African storytellers repeating generations' of oral recitations, others through diaries and letters. They reminisced about family and childhood friends. They considered themselves and their children part of the Southern culture no matter how far they roamed. It was and remained part of their identity.

Early English colonists brought cattle, chickens, and pigs as well as curries and spices, wheat, oats, and other grains, along with root vegetables and beans. Africa, through ship captains and others, contributed peas, okra, melons, eggplants, benne (sesame) seeds, and rice. Indigenous foods included the all-important "three sisters"—corn, native beans and squash (including pumpkins)—as well as poke sallet (supplemented by English and African greens), muscadine and other wild grapes, plums, wild game, and seafood. Other arrivals included tomatoes from Central and South America.

Slavery prevailed in areas that depended on large quantities of cheap labor, such as regions growing cotton or rice. Rice, once prevalent in the lower coastal South, had a symbiotic relationship with slavery. Slaves from the rice-growing areas of Africa had the skill, knowledge, and ability to grow the finest rice in the world, bringing great wealth to the South. Hurricanes and the end of slave labor did away with what was left of rice as a primary crop in South Carolina near the end of the nineteenth century, although it is now a boutique crop and continues to be grown there. Louisiana, Arkansas, and Texas continue as rice-growing states into the twenty-first century.

Southern foods vary according to the origins of the inhabitants, as well as the geography, weather, and soil content that range from the Lowcountry of Georgia and South Carolina to the mountains. We include more from some regions than others, to avoid duplication of technique as well as to avoid multiple variations of one recipe. For that reason we offer variations throughout, to hint at the ways others embellish the same recipe.

There are some decidedly Southern foods that are the buzzwords of what makes our cuisine unique. They include rice, grits, turnip and collard greens with pot likker, okra, pecans, peanuts, hot peppers, black-eyed and other peas. There are more things that make it special, such as our soft-wheat flour and our seafood and the textures of our food.

Corn, a native crop, was historically a crop of much value in the South. Grits, corn meal, and corn flour are integral by-products of corn. Cornbread is as popular as Kentucky whisky, originally called corn moonshine liquor. Corn was eaten freshly boiled and buttered off the cob, scraped to be "creamed" in a frying pan, or fried as fritters. Corn provided sustenance all year. We see it now in even more ways, modern succotash recipes contrasting with microwaved corn on the cob.

In Texas, only the eastern part remains oriented towards Southern food. West Texas is oriented towards Tex-Mex and Mexican food, as well as beef barbecue. Commercial corn products such as tortillas, along with guacamole and salsas, began finding a place in the Southern diet by the late 1980s, with Mexican and Hispanic foods gaining in the decades that followed.

Florida, too, is only part Southern in its cuisine, primarily the area where Cynthia grew up, near Jacksonville, and farther West into its boundaries with Georgia and Alabama.

Louisiana developed two distinctive cuisines, still independent of other Southern food. The Cajun cuisine, a form of country cooking created by French Acadians, is broad and flavorful. The "holy trinity"—onions, celery, and bell pepper—and "the pope" —garlic—are its base. Creole cuisine is New Orleans city food, a sophisticated, rich mélange of Spanish, French, Italian, and African dishes. In this book, we have not been able to do justice to this noble and exciting food. It is for someone else to do. We have relied on Paul Prudhomme, John Foltz, and the *Times Picayune* cookbook for our knowledge, as well as recipes we have collected ourselves.

Hot peppers and their sauces provide an important condiment all over the South. Up until the late eighties, it was common to see simple hot peppers in a jar of vinegar on the table of home kitchens; but now there is an extensive variety of commercial sauces and an astounding infusion of hot peppers of all sizes and heats.

African foodstuffs brought to the South are still beloved among the broad expanse of Southerners, without regard to color and income. The legacy of poverty suffered by both races after the Civil War, combined with the presence of black cooks (first as slaves then as servants) in white middle-class homes well into the 1960s, resulted in the broader enjoyment of comforting and filling foods that have been called "soul food" for more than forty years. The South remains definitive as a region in which upper-class whites regularly eat peas and other peasant dishes. The peanut is a significant Southern financial and nutritional asset with worldwide dietary influence. Southerners are as liable as other Americans to eat peanut butter sandwiches and salted peanuts. Only in the South, however, do newcomers wonder about "bald peanuts" when hearing native Southerners' drawl in talking about savoring them. No, they are not hairless; they are freshly harvested peanuts boiled in the shell in salted water.

Turnip and collard greens remain an important source of nutrients, and not just among low-income residents. The heat of the kitchen and traditional African one-pot cooking techniques encouraged the slow cooking of tough greens and pole beans on the back of the stove, with a slice of salted or smoked hog jowl, fatback, or streak of lean (seasoning meats to provide flavor and protein) and hot pepper. Young greens are now sautéed, braised, or even used in salads, perhaps rubbed with salt or oil to tenderize and make them malleable, but there is still a great affection at all income levels for the older style, eaten with cornbread, particularly when there is a nip in the air. The broth (called "pot likker") adds nutritional value and warmth.

IRRESISTIBLE QUALITIES OF SOUTHERN FOODS

It is the textures and flavors that are hard to separate by region. Crispy, for instance, is uniquely Southern: crisp fried chicken; crisp fried pork rinds; crisp chitlins; crisp French fries; fried steak; fried catfish and perch, bass and flounder; trout freshly fried from the streams; and even fried watermelon rind. The flavor from lard-fried foods is almost inseparable from the texture of crispy.

Crispy also results from roasting and grilling. The skin of grilled pork crackles when you bite into it. Roasted Sunday chicken, with a skin that separates from the flesh and crunches, leaves the breast moist and tender. Grilled or roasted potatoes become deep brown and crispy around the edges, and just-picked rosemary sprinkled over them takes their flavor over the top. Onions crisp up in the oven, and toasted bread snaps and crackles. Cheese straws offer a crisp introduction before they melt in the mouth.

Flaky-melting is another texture. The combination of lard (or even shortening or butter) and flour in biscuits and piecrusts is unrivaled, due to the Southern flour we have primarily used for over a hundred years, which is lower in gluten and bleached to make it more tender. The melting flakiness of biscuits in one's mouth cannot be achieved without it.

Tingle on the tongue, the little dancing in our mouth that hot red peppers give, insinuates itself in our foods, from turnip greens to hot pepper jelly.

Which brings us to sweet/sour. In hot pepper jelly, the components of sugar, cider vinegar, and hot peppers form a multipurpose condiment. It adds bite and caramelization to a pork roast (the "ah" taste) or other pig parts, or added to a sautéed piece of country ham is a finishing sauce, melting in the pan and embracing the ham. Vinegar in a cruet, splashed on cooked greens or just about anything brings dash to the daily diet. (Usually the vinegar has a hot pepper immersed in it to give that pop we want.)

Sweetness in main courses—but definitely not in cornbread, which needs no sweetening, corn bringing its own sweetness—is not unusual. Take Coca-Cola with country ham, for instance, either to finish as a reduction in a frying pan or to cook the ham long and slow as it braises. Sweet onions from Vidalia, Georgia, and Texas Sweets smoothly enhance grilled meats, tomatoes, salads, and vegetables, cooked along with, inside, and as an accompaniment, raw

THE SOUTHERN PANTRY

All of the ingredients in this book can be found in an average Southern local grocery store or market in season. Those of us who can't live European style and shop every day or two find our pantries invaluable. The modern Southern pantry is a combination of shelves and cupboards, refrigerator and freezer. Some items, like quail, may be special ordered by those who are not so fortunate to have them accessible.

Stocking a kitchen is a very individual decision. For busy families, a well-stocked kitchen, featuring most of the items on our lists, will be the quickest answer to the refrain heard every day, "What's for dinner?" For smaller families, the needs may differ, and relying on flavorful condiments such as our Tomato Conserve (page 644) or a quick Pan Sauce (page 667) made with Dijon mustard and heavy cream to quickly liven-up sautéed chicken breasts or a pork tenderloin are go-to solutions for fast weeknight meals. Singles may cook a main dish leisurely on the weekend and then package it in smaller portions in the freezer for future meals. Still others relish breads and sweets fresh from the oven. They will keep a complete baking pantry.

We have compiled the lists that follow from our recipes in this book, which represent the cooking we do regularly. We rely heavily on our pantries and spend the bulk of our weekly shopping gathering fresh and seasonal fruits and vegetables for use in our daily meals.

One caveat: every family should have a list of ten meals they can make with little effort from the pantry (including the refrigerator and freezer). These could include chili, chicken breasts, macaroni pie, rice pilaf, soups, ham and redeye gravy, omelets or other egg preparations, etc. Post the list inside the pantry door for quick reference. The ingredients for these things should be kept on hand at all times, ready for use when the cook is too tired or hungry to think, when the "cook" isn't home and the other family members need to prepare the meal, or in case of hurricanes and other emergency situations. Replace as you use so your pantry is always complete.

Nathalie's top five pantry meals: Shrimp and Grits, Sausage and Apples, Macaroni Pie, Fast Chicken Breasts with Ribboned Vegetables, lady peas, and cornbread, Vidalia Onion Tart, Biscuits with Pork Tenderloin. Fortunately salad greens are available year-round in my garden. I keep chicken breasts, sausage, and pork tenderloin in the freezer as part of my pantry staples. There are always bits and pieces for soups there as well.

Cynthia's top five pantry meals: Comforting Cheese Soup (broccoli variation), Lemon-Lime Pot Roast with Tomatoes and Garlic (always a cooked one in her freezer), Skillet Lemon Chicken Thighs (boneless, skinless thighs are a freezer staple for her), along with cooked rice from the freezer, and omelet or savory tart concoctions from the bits and pieces of leftovers on hand.

Check the expiration dates of canned goods, and keep the oldest ones handiest. If dried herbs are a necessity or preference, since they should be renewed annually, split the purchase with a friend and replenish only as needed. If there is no need to replenish after a year, strike it off the list and do without. Unlike spices, there is rarely a time when one specific herb is the only one that can be used to enhance a dish. Thyme, oregano, and marjoram, are easily interchangeable if not perfect substitutes. If choosing just one, I would choose marjoram. Rosemary lasts well on the pantry shelf, but fresh is better. The ratio of "three to one" commonly used in cookbooks is only applicable if the dried herbs are freshly purchased. Old stale herbs are no better than dust, and there is no ratio for "dust to fresh herbs."

The Freezer

Making double batches of main dishes, having a stash of flavorful stocks, and storing the best of our summer fruits and vegetables is only the tip of the iceberg for how helpful freezer storage can be to the cook. Frozen peaches, mangos, and blueberries are always in Nathalie's freezer for speedy desserts, along with pecans and peanuts. The boiled peanuts are for her husband.

Cynthia's Pantry

Being the laziest of cooks, with two children and preferring to spend my time reading old cookbooks, I've been known to take shortcuts, especially for hectic weeknight meals. My freezer has bags of frozen chopped onions (as I'm more apt to find a spoiled onion in my pantry than a Vidalia dressed in pantyhose), and my refrigerator has jarred minced garlic. My freezer is never without a bag of sliced peaches, as my favorite last-minute dessert to make for unexpected guests is Lazy Girl Cobbler (page 552), and my self-rising flour gets replenished far more often than my baking soda or baking powder. I almost never cut a recipe down in size: I'll make the full recipe and freeze some for another meal; it always feels like money in the bank to me. For my weekend cooking, I tend to use all fresh ingredients.

THE PANTRY

The Baking Pantry

- ❑ All-purpose soft-wheat flour
- ❑ Self-rising soft-wheat flour
- ❑ Bread flour
- ❑ Cornmeal
- ❑ Self-rising cornmeal mix
- ❑ Cornstarch
- ❑ Baking soda
- ❑ Baking powder
- ❑ Cream of tartar
- ❑ Breadcrumbs or panko
- ❑ Granulated sugar
- ❑ Confectioners' sugar
- ❑ Dark or light brown sugar
- ❑ Unflavored gelatin
- ❑ Active dry yeast
- ❑ Vanilla, lemon, and almond extracts
- ❑ Vanilla bean
- ❑ Unsweetened cocoa powder
- ❑ Grated or shredded coconut, preferably frozen

Staples in Cans, Jars, Boxes, and Bags on Shelf, in Refrigerator or Freezer

- ❑ Peas and beans, including black-eyed peas, butter beans, butter peas, cowpeas, crowder peas, English peas, lady peas, and white acre peas preferably frozen but dried or canned if need be
- ❑ Tomatoes—crushed, diced and whole, preferably the best brand available
- ❑ Tomato paste
- ❑ Chicken and beef stock or broth, homemade and commercial
- ❑ Pecans and peanuts
- ❑ Black olives, such as Greek and Italian
- ❑ Pimentos or jarred red peppers
- ❑ Red and white wine vinegar, cider vinegar, sherry vinegar
- ❑ Shortening, lard, and/or vegetable oil
- ❑ Olive oil
- ❑ Soy sauce
- ❑ Mayonnaise—preferably Duke's
- ❑ Worcestershire sauce
- ❑ Hot sauce
- ❑ Horseradish
- ❑ Ketchup
- ❑ Chili sauce
- ❑ Tomato conserve
- ❑ Coca-Cola
- ❑ Sorghum, maple syrup, and light or dark corn syrup
- ❑ Honey—Tupelo, orange blossom, or sweet clover
- ❑ Peanut and other nut butters
- ❑ Jams and jellies such as apricot, strawberry, raspberry, red currant, muscadine, and red pepper
- ❑ Evaporated and sweetened condensed milk
- ❑ Rice—Carolina Gold, long-grain, wild, arborio, on shelf or in freezer
- ❑ Quick grits (not instant) and stone-ground grits
- ❑ Pasta
- ❑ Garlic
- ❑ Onions
- ❑ Potatoes
- ❑ Dried fruit—apricots, candied ginger, cherries, cranberries, figs, prunes (dried plums), and raisins
- ❑ Graham crackers, gingersnaps, vanilla or chocolate wafers, and/or butter cookies for crusts
- ❑ Chocolate, semi-sweet, dark, and milk, in chips or bars
- ❑ Bourbon
- ❑ Dry sherry and/or dry Madeira, vermouth or other fortified wine
- ❑ Liquor or liqueur, such as Grand Marnier and/or Limoncello, or Cointreau

Refrigerator Staples

- ❑ Butter, salted and/or unsalted, as preferred
- ❑ Large eggs
- ❑ Whole milk
- ❑ Buttermilk—whole or dried
- ❑ Heavy cream
- ❑ Sour cream
- ❑ Clemson blue cheese
- ❑ Soft goat cheese
- ❑ Parmesan cheese
- ❑ Sharp Cheddar cheese
- ❑ Feta cheese
- ❑ Gruyère cheese, preferable Conte, or Swiss in emergencies only
- ❑ Cream cheese
- ❑ Greek or other yogurt
- ❑ Fresh herbs in season—thyme, oregano, flat-leaf parsley, basil, marjoram, cilantro, mint, lemon balm, rosemary, chives
- ❑ Meats—pork (streak o' lean, fatback, or other seasoning meat); country ham slices (thin for biscuits, thicker for sautéing for a meal)

Spices and Seasonings

- ❑ Benne (sesame) seeds—black and white
- ❑ Coriander seed and ground coriander
- ❑ Cumin seed and ground cumin
- ❑ Fennel seed
- ❑ Curry powder
- ❑ Chili powder
- ❑ Ground hot red pepper
- ❑ Hot red pepper flakes
- ❑ Hungarian paprika
- ❑ Mustard—dried and whole seed and Dijon
- ❑ Candied and ground ginger
- ❑ Rosemary
- ❑ Ground turmeric
- ❑ Whole and ground cloves
- ❑ Saffron threads
- ❑ Sesame seeds
- ❑ Poppy seeds
- ❑ Nutmeg
- ❑ Whole and ground cinnamon
- ❑ Bay leaf
- ❑ Salt—kosher, sea, table
- ❑ Pepper—black peppercorns, grains of paradise, white or other

SEASON TO TASTE

The great gift of cooking is to be in charge of the decisions made in the kitchen. Seasoning a dish is up to the cook, tasting at various points in a recipe, to determine the flavors of the finished dish. In our recipes we use the phrase "season to taste with salt and pepper." In some recipes, this direction comes at a point in the recipe where physically tasting the dish is impractical. In these cases, we mean to add salt and pepper as you normally would, to the level you appreciate. Where the direction comes later in a recipe, by all means grab a spoon and taste the goodness before deciding how much salt or pepper is needed. The cook is in charge.

SALT

Salt is salt. The basic mineral makeup of salt, no matter where it comes from or how it is packaged, is the same. The differences lie in the physical size and shape of the grains. Table salt is the most common salt used in our recipes. It is always the best for baking, as the grain dissolves well in dough. Kosher salt is a larger grain, and therefore measures differently. The grain takes up more space in the measuring spoon, allowing for more space between grains, and therefore requires a bit more to make up the same measure of table salt. We follow the formula of 1½ teaspoons of Morton brand kosher salt is equal to 1 teaspoon of table salt. For Diamond brand kosher salt, our measure is 2 teaspoons Diamond brand is equal to 1 teaspoon table salt. Sea salt contains additional minerals left behind during the evaporation process, and each measures slightly different, although much more closely to table salt than the kosher salts; so follow the "season to taste" rule.

or cooked. A little sugar on top of a baked tomato never hurt anyone, nor did brown sugar on a sweet potato. Sweet bourbon beef and Thanksgiving turkey have moved around the country from our sideboards.

Tenderness is another quality. Tender cakes and cobblers, all made from that soft-wheat flour, excel. When I studied cooking in London, my teacher wanted to know what made Southern cakes so much better. It is that combination of tenderness, lightness, and flavor that runs through our desserts and makes them memorable enough to crave when in a different country.

If a spoon did not stand up in the iced tea from its sugar content, than surely peach cobbler, pralines, divinity, and our cakes—daffodil cake, caramel cake, and coconut cake—and our pies—crispy pecans interspersed with corn syrup giving a crisp-tender rendition, sweet potato pie, fried peach pies with their crisp sweetness, and even peaches eaten over the sink as they drip from our mouths—stand up to anyone's idea of goodness.

Small wonder our food haunts us when we leave the South, following us wherever we move, emerging more and more in cuisines around the nation and the world, and winding up in the dreams of foreigners.

It isn't just popularity—it's passion. We love our food! It dominates our thoughts from early morning, when we wonder if we have time for biscuits filled with melting butter, or grits topped with shrimp, and drink our Coca-Cola (Nathalie's favorite) for breakfast. We think about it through noon, when we have cravings for fried chicken or turnip greens with cornbread. By sundown we wish we had a mint julep—or at least iced tea flavored with freshly picked mint—in our hands, and dream about peach cobbler for dessert. It starts all over again the next morning.

HOW TO USE THIS BOOK

Any book this size can be intimidating, so begin at the beginning. Reading cookbooks is a pastime enjoyed by many non-cooks, propped up in bed late at night. We only wish it was practiced by more cooks! Resist the temptation to dive right into a recipe in the middle of the book. Take the time to read the information at the beginning of each chapter. The introductory material, both here at the beginning of the book and at the beginning of each chapter, is here for a reason: it introduces the reader to the subject at hand, including an orientation to the ingredients central to the chapter, specific equipment beneficial to the outcome of a recipe, and the techniques needed to achieve success. There is something here for everyone, from the most experienced to the novice.

Always begin by reading the recipe from start to finish. Visualize the process, gather the ingredients and equipment. Don't attempt a challenging recipe when you are in a hurry. Give yourself time to work through the details of a recipe. Although the recipes have been written to stand alone, many recipes will give a cross-reference to a technique or another recipe in order to avoid being overly repetitious. Follow the trail through those references to learn more about a technique or process. The index in the back of the book is perhaps the best way to access the detailed information or explanation you might be looking for.

Some of the recipes are quite long, purposefully. We have written them so that the reader will know what to expect in each stage of the recipe. The language of the recipes is important. In spite of the length of some recipes, all recipes are written in sparse but detailed language. The nuance of the words is important. *Whisk* means to use a whisk to combine the ingredients. A stand mixer is called for in a recipe for good reason: the batter is thick, or the mixing time is lengthy; so we call for that specific equipment to make the job easier and the result better. We hope to have written in the voice that gives you confidence, as if we are standing right next to you in the kitchen!

But not all of the recipes are challenging. Many will be familiar from Nathalie's books (the beloved Lazy Girl Cobbler, Snacking Sour Cream Cornbread, Lemon Lime Pot Roast with Tomatoes and Garlic), and others so easy you'll wonder why you need a recipe. We've tried to be thorough but not intimidating. Learning techniques ultimately makes the cook's job easier and far more rewarding.

Sprinkled throughout the book are boxes of information that provide a helpful tip, or further elaborate on an ingredient or technique. We've also included historical references in these boxes—there's so much to learn by studying where we've come from.

The foods in these recipes are well known but not old-fashioned. We take the glorious goodness overflowing from our farms and markets, teach a traditional technique, and also use traditional foods in new ways (Okra Chips, anyone?). What's old is new again, and the techniques are here to enhance your skills and confidence.

The more you cook, the more successful you will be. For the most intimidating of Southern fare, like biscuits and piecrusts, practice is imperative. Give yourself the gift of a quiet morning or afternoon to sequester yourself alone in the kitchen. Make several batches of biscuits, each of different sizes and with different ingredients, to discover which one is your preference and to develop your technique. Do the same with piecrusts. Don't tell anyone what you are doing. Practicing doesn't mean perfection, but serving luscious Southern food is about as gratifying as anything I do. A Southern gourmet is one who does the best she/he can with the food at hand.

STARTERS

Southern hospitality is more than a cliché. Historically, plantations were far apart and transportation was rudimental. Guests, invited or unexpected, were welcomed and fed in good times and bad. Hard times, like the Great Depression, were times for helping each other. Even in good times, welcoming included offering something to eat or drink, to start the occasion, large or small.

In a region that has enjoyed big, mid-day farm lunches (called dinner) and three o'clock dinner in Charleston, it is hard to say when starters started, just as it is hard to say what a starter is. The word canapé is derived from the French word for "couch," for instance. Hors d'oeuvre means, according to Food Lover's Companion, *"outside the work" meal, or food outside the work. Starters is a word we have adopted to mean something we can eat anytime short of a main course.*

Starters have gone from a narrow range of options to a broad swath of foods presented in new and exciting ways. The highlights once were when one was offered a ham biscuit or cheese straws, doled out stingily to children or offered graciously to adults. On a sideboard or buffet table, shrimp was draped around the edges and on top of ice in a large punch bowl with a dish of cocktail sauce in the center.

We've had celery sticks (which I still love) filled with pimento cheese or peanut butter; roasted pecans, peanuts, or variations thereof; various dips, including artichoke, crab and onion made from packaged onion soup and sour cream, served with chips; oysters wrapped in bacon, hopefully crisp, but often not.

Some of these remain in our repertoire, but we've kept them simple and resonant to the culture. Along our coast we use fresh crab, finding the canned not worth the effort; pimento cheese is still high on every Southerner's list, and we've filled a tart with it. Rather than ubiquitous cubes of mediocre cheese, we've poured melted hot pepper jelly over logs of goat cheese. Fresh vegetables shine, such as zucchini rounds with a little bit of grated carrots.

A variety of ingredients have become available to stimulate the imagination. The English custom of tea with sandwiches and other delicacies was certainly not lost on Southerners, even after we started dumping enough sugar in our tea to make a spoon stand up unaided and enough ice to chill an igloo. Tiny grits cakes with shrimp and bacon; peaches and figs with country ham; savory tarts and custards that could replace soup or salad at the table or be served in the living room have all changed the order of meals.

Cynthia's husband, Cliff, has a habit of fixing little nibbles for the family while waiting for dinner. He might show up with a chopped-tomato-and-basil concoction or a chicken liver paté he whipped up in the food processor, with a glass of wine rather than the still popular bourbon and branch water his neighbor drinks. Many of us don't even know when we are hungry—my French son-in-law, Pierre Henri, who frowns at nibbling outside of meals and is no fan of canapés, says that when one eats, the hunger comes. So a starter should be only that—something to whet the appetite, readying one to sit down and eat a meal.

PEACHES AND FIGS WRAPPED IN COUNTRY HAM

Serves 2

TRADITIONALLY IN EUROPE, *melons are wrapped in prosciutto ham and served as a starter or appetizer. Our thinly sliced country ham is supple enough to wrap equally well and is enjoyed by all, whether with peaches, figs, or cantaloupe. Serve as a nibble on toothpicks or plated as a starter.*

1 fresh peach
6 fresh figs, stems removed
2–3 biscuit slices of country ham

Peel and slice the peach into wedges. Cut an X in the top of each fig, cutting three-fourths of the way down, keeping the sections attached at the base. Tear the country ham into strips.

Roll a small portion of country ham around a finger and insert into the X on the fig. Wrap another ham strip around each peach wedge. Cover with plastic wrap and refrigerate until serving time, not more than 2 to 3 hours.

Variation: Cut peeled cantaloupes or mangos in cubes or wedges, and wrap with country ham. May be secured with a toothpick.

COUNTRY HAM WITH BAKED STUFFED FIGS

Serves 4

The bubbling cheese and lush figs, *served on a platter of thinly sliced country ham or wrapped in it and served on plates is simple, uses what's on hand and seasonal, and is a combination of comforting and sensual.*

12 figs, stems removed
6 ounces Clemson Blue Cheese, room temperature
2 tablespoons finely chopped pecans
1/2 cup finely chopped fresh herbs, such as thyme, oregano, and/or flat-leaf parsley
4 ounces thinly sliced country ham

Preheat oven to 450 degrees.

Cut an X in the top of each fig, cutting three-fourths of the way down, keeping the sections attached at the base. Move to an ungreased rimmed baking sheet and gently open them.

Mix together the cheese, pecans, and herbs until well blended. Use a small spoon or piping bag to gently stuff each fig with filling. Bake the figs for 8 to 10 minutes, until the cheese is bubbling.

Arrange the country ham on a platter or individual plates and top with warm figs. It is a little tricky, but these can be wrapped in thinly sliced ham and toothpicked if necessary.

Clemson Blue Cheese was originally made in an abandoned railway tunnel and is now made in a year-round climate-controlled environment at South Carolina's Clemson School of Agriculture. It has worked its way into a frequent relationship with fresh figs and country ham.

FIG AND PECAN TAPENADE WITH GOAT CHEESE

Serves 20

Dried figs keep me going between fresh fig seasons. *They pep up dips and spreads. Cream cheese has long been the base for many decorative spreads, but soft goat cheese has crept up in popularity.*

1 cup chopped dried figs
1/3 cup water
1/3 cup chopped pitted black olives
2 tablespoons olive oil
1 tablespoon red wine vinegar
1/2 tablespoon chopped green olives, optional
1 1/2 teaspoons chopped fresh thyme
1/2 cup chopped toasted pecans
Salt
Freshly ground black pepper
2 (5 1/2-ounce) logs soft goat cheese, cut into 1/2-inch-thick rounds

Cover figs with water in a heavy saucepan, bring to a simmer, and cook over medium-high heat until figs are soft and water has nearly evaporated, about 7 minutes.

Move figs to a bowl using a slotted spoon and stir in olives, oil, vinegar, green olives, thyme, and pecans. Season to taste with salt and pepper.

Arrange goat cheese circles overlapping around a small platter. Spoon fig mixture over the cheese. Serve with crackers.

CHOPPING DRIED FRUIT

To prevent dried fruit from clinging together while trying to chop it, coat the metal blade lightly with cooking oil or spray. If the dried fruit is to be used in a flour-based recipe, toss the fruit in flour to coat, then chop and return the fruit to the flour. Some cooks have success with chopping dried fruit in the food processor, just pulsing the blade a few times.

SAVORY FIG BITES

Makes 24 mini tarts

JUDY BERNSTEIN LIVES ON ONE OF THE BEAUTIFUL ISLANDS *surrounding Charleston, where she serves fresh figs from her trees to make a tarted-up starter. This makes a sweet-sour combination medley served in a crispy case. The filling is best made ahead to allow the flavors to meld.*

24 mini phyllo cups, store-bought or homemade (page 515)
3–4 tablespoons butter, melted
6 ounces soft goat cheese
1/4 cup heavy cream
3 tablespoons honey, divided
Grated rind of 1/2 lemon, no white attached
1/2 teaspoon chopped fresh rosemary
Salt
Freshly ground black pepper
1/2 cup sherry vinegar
16 fresh figs, quartered

Preheat oven to 325 degrees. Lightly butter a mini muffin pan, add the phyllo cups, and brush the cups lightly with butter. Bake 5 to 7 minutes, until crisp. Remove and set aside.

Mix goat cheese, cream, and 2 tablespoons honey until smooth and creamy. Stir in lemon rind and rosemary. Season to taste with salt and pepper.

To assemble, spoon a tablespoon of the goat cheese mixture into a cooled shell. Top with a piece of fresh fig. Repeat with remaining shells and sprinkle with black pepper. This can be done several hours ahead or up to a day in advance.

Before serving, bring vinegar and remaining 1 tablespoon honey to the boil in a small saucepan; simmer until reduced by half and slightly syrupy, 5 to 7 minutes. Drizzle over each tart.

ANOTHER NOSH-ABLE IDEA FOR PHYLLO CUPS

Using 1 1/4 cups Hot Pepper Jelly (page 648), 3 ounces Brie, peeled and cut into 30 small pieces, and 3 tablespoons chopped lightly toasted pecans, fill each phyllo cup with 1/4 teaspoon jelly. Top each with 1 piece of Brie. Sprinkle all with toasted pecans. Bake in a 350-degree oven until cheese melts, about 5 to 6 minutes. Serve warm.

FRIED WATERMELON RIND

Makes 2 cups

SOME THINK SOUTHERNERS WOULD FRY ANYTHING *if given half a chance. In this case, the watermelon rind melts inside the crunchy exterior in a totally unique and fabulous way. People will hover over the cook in the kitchen, snitching the delicacy; not much will make it to the table.*

1/3 cup cornmeal
1/3 cup all-purpose flour
1 teaspoon salt
Freshly ground black pepper
Shortening or vegetable oil for frying
2 cups watermelon rind, cubed

Remove the fruit from the watermelon and reserve for another purpose. Use a sharp knife to separate the dark tough exterior of the rind from the pale green interior. Chop interior into 1-inch cubes and discard outer skin.

Toss together the cornmeal, flour, salt, and pepper. Meanwhile, heat the oil to 350 degrees in a heavy skillet. The oil should be deep enough to submerge the watermelon cubes. With one hand, roll the still damp cubed rind in the cornmeal mixture. Use a slotted spoon to add breaded rind to the hot oil, frying in batches if necessary so as not to crowd the cubes in the pan. Fry about 8 to 10 minutes, until lightly browned. Drain on paper towels and season to taste with salt and pepper. Serve hot.

STUFFED GRAPE TOMATOES

Makes 1 pint

GRAPE AND OTHER SMALL TOMATOES *have changed the party table. They are very perky and just the right size for a bite.*

1 pint grape tomatoes

4 ounces soft goat cheese, room temperature

Basil or oregano leaves for garnish

Make a cup out of each tomato by cutting the tops off and removing the seeds with a small spoon. Reserve tops. Cut a small slice off the bottom of each tomato so it will stand without falling over. Drain tomatoes upside-down on a rack over a paper towels.

Move goat cheese to a plastic ziplock bag. Cut off one corner to make a piping bag. A star or other pastry tip may be inserted if a decorative top is desired. Turn the tomatoes right side up and move the slit end of the bag over the small tomato cavity. Push from the top of the bag, using the other hand to steady the bag. Pipe the goat cheese into the tomatoes, coming up slightly over the edge. This may be made ahead of time and stored in the refrigerator for up to 1 day. Cover with the tops and garnish with basil or oregano leaves before serving.

Variation: The fillings are endless, including ham or Basic Chicken Salad (page 96) or Pimento Cheese (page 57).

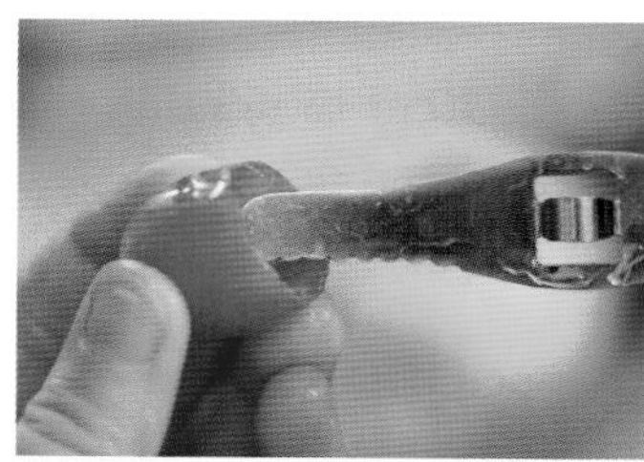

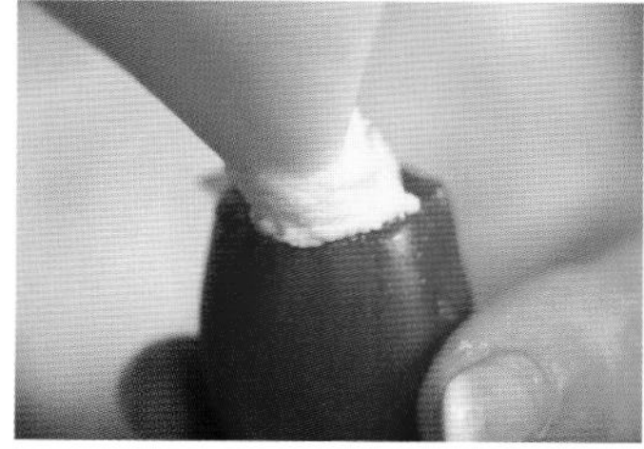

INDISPENSABLE MUSHROOMS WITH GREENS

Serves 16

PARTY FOOD SHOULD BE PRETTY, *easy to assemble, and easy to serve, as well as delicious. Button mushrooms fit the bill perfectly. They can be made ahead and reheated easily and filled with anything from beef stew to fois gras. These button mushrooms can be eaten with one bite, but please do serve with napkins if not a plate. Large mushrooms will need a plate and should be served at a sit-down meal. Any leftover filling can be frozen for another time, or it can be added to rice, couscous, or a Sunday omelet.*

3/4 pound fresh spinach or baby turnip greens, washed (page 205)
2 pounds small mushrooms, cleaned
1 cup butter, divided
2 medium onions, chopped
3 garlic cloves, chopped
1/2 cup fine breadcrumbs
1/2 teaspoon Dijon mustard
Salt
Freshly ground black pepper
1/2 cup grated Parmesan cheese

Preheat oven to 350 degrees.

Remove and discard any stems and tough leaves from the greens. Chop the leaves in a food processor. If large, blanch briefly and drain well. Remove stems of the mushrooms, chop, and set aside.

Melt 1/2 cup butter in a Dutch oven or deep skillet over medium heat, and dip the mushroom caps into it until well coated on all sides. Place them, top side down, on a greased rimmed baking sheet.

Heat remaining butter in the skillet; add the onions, garlic, and chopped mushroom stems, and sauté until very soft, about 10 minutes. Add the greens and cook a few minutes until wilted; drain off and reserve some of the liquid. Add the breadcrumbs and mustard, and mix well. Add back some of the reserved liquid if the mixture is so dry that it doesn't stick together easily. This filling can be made several days in advance or frozen and defrosted before stuffing mushrooms. Season to taste with salt and pepper.

Fill each buttered mushroom cap (up to a day in advance) with this mixture, mounding it high, and sprinkle with Parmesan cheese. Bake 10 to 15 minutes. Any leftovers freeze fine for the family, but not for company.

Variation: Add 1/2 cup finely chopped ham, crisp bacon, sautéed sausage, chopped shrimp, crabmeat, or smoked turkey. Garnish with chopped herbs or small whole shrimp.

JULIA'S KALE CHIPS

Makes about 2 cups

ONCE YOU TRY THESE BAKED KALE CHIPS, *you'll wonder why you waste your time snacking on any other chip.*

1 bunch kale, washed, stems removed
1 teaspoon salt
1/2 teaspoon freshly ground black pepper
1 tablespoon oil, cook's preference

Preheat oven to 400 degrees.

Tear the kale into bite-sized pieces and toss with the salt, pepper, and oil. Depending on quantity, spread out in a single layer on one or two rimmed baking sheets.

Bake approximately 10 minutes. Keep a close watch to see that the pieces have crisped without browning too much. If the kale has been layered on the baking sheet too much, it will take an extra minute or two.

When the chips are finished, remove from the oven and serve immediately. These do not keep well, so enjoy them in one sitting.

Variation: I enjoy the stems tossed in oil and baked as above for a cook's treat.

SAUTÉED ZUCCHINI OR SQUASH BLOSSOMS

Serves 4

SQUASH AND ZUCCHINI, *like okra, have particularly tasty blossoms. The male flowers do not traditionally bear any "fruit," but they are mouthwatering stuffed and deep-fried in a batter (page 463) or used as a pretty, flavorful garnish. The female flowers can be distinguished by the tiny vegetable protruding from the flower. The flower withers as the fruit grows.*

2 tablespoons butter
1 pint (about 12) zucchini flower blossoms, lightly rinsed and dried
Salt
Freshly ground black pepper
1 tablespoon chopped fresh thyme or basil

Heat the butter in a large skillet. Add the squash flowers and cook for just a few minutes, turning until they burst into full blossoms without browning. Season to taste with salt, pepper, and herbs. Serve immediately.

STUFFED ZUCCHINI OR SQUASH BLOSSOMS

Makes 12 blossoms

STUFFING SQUASH BLOSSOMS *with this recipe of my intern Chuck Lee and frying them in light batter results in just a kiss of crispness in the blossoms, with a melting interior. This recipe can be increased as desired. Refrigerate the leftovers for the next day. Any extra stuffing can be refrigerated and used as a stuffing for grape or cherry tomatoes.*

2 tablespoons oil, cook's preference
1/2 medium onion, finely chopped
1 garlic clove, finely chopped
1 cup goat or cream cheese or other soft variety, room temperature
2 tablespoons chopped oven-dried tomatoes
12 squash blossoms
Light Batter (page 463)
Shortening or vegetable oil for frying
Salt
Freshly ground black pepper

Heat the oil in a skillet until shimmering; add the onion and sauté 4 to 5 minutes. Add garlic and stir another 30 seconds. Remove from heat and set aside.

Beat cheese with an electric hand mixer until smooth. Stir in the onion and garlic mixture, and tomatoes until blended. Move mixture to a plastic ziplock bag. Cut off one corner to make a piping bag. Carefully open the squash blossoms and move the slit end of the bag into the blossom. Push from the top of the bag and pipe the mixture into the blossom to within 1/4 to 1/2 inch from the opening. Gently twist the top of the blossom closed. Dip into batter.

Meanwhile, fill a heavy frying pan no more than half full of oil and heat to 350 degrees. Add the blossoms one by one and fry until light brown, reducing heat if they brown too quickly. Move to a paper towel to drain. Season to taste with salt and pepper. Serve hot.

ZUCCHINI ROUNDS WITH CARROTS

Makes 12 to 15

RAW GRATED CARROTS *piled on zucchini rounds make a unique, colorful, and very refreshing appetizer, moving us toward healthy snacks with local foods. This is pretty enough for either a buffet table or for passing at a party.*

2 tablespoons olive oil
2 teaspoons red or white wine vinegar or fresh lemon juice
Salt
Freshly ground black pepper
Granulated sugar to taste
3 heaping tablespoons finely chopped fresh basil, thyme, oregano, parsley, or other mixed herbs
2 medium carrots, peeled and grated
1 medium zucchini, unpeeled and thickly sliced

Whisk together the olive oil, vinegar or lemon juice, salt, and pepper. Taste and add sugar if needed to smooth out the taste.

Chop the grated carrots slightly if necessary to be sure they will fit on the rounds. Toss the carrots lightly with the dressing, shaking off excess liquid. Mound the dressed carrots on the zucchini slices, garnish with fresh herbs, and chill. May be made up to 1 day ahead, covered tightly, and kept chilled.

Variation: Substitute cucumber for the zucchini.

LADY PEA PATTIES

Makes 24 small patties

HANDS ARE ENOUGH IMPLEMENTS FOR EATING THESE TASTY PATTIES. *Serve from the pan, stack on the buffet table, or pass with napkins.*

3 cups cooked and drained lady peas or other small peas or beans
1 large egg, lightly beaten
1 teaspoon chopped fresh thyme
1 tablespoon chopped fresh basil
1 tablespoon chopped fresh oregano
1 small red onion, chopped
2 garlic cloves, chopped
1 green onion, chopped
1/2 jalapeño pepper or other small hot pepper, roasted, peeled, seeded, and finely chopped
All-purpose flour
Shortening or vegetable oil for frying
Norman's Rémoulade (page 660) or Red Pepper Mayonnaise (page 104)

Line a rimmed baking sheet with parchment or waxed paper and set aside.

Mash the peas or beans with a fork in a large mixing bowl. Mix in the egg, thyme, basil, oregano, onion, garlic, green onion, and desired amount of jalapeño pepper.

Form the mixture by hand into 24 small patties and move to prepared baking sheet. Sprinkle the patties lightly with flour on both sides.

Coat the bottom of a large skillet with oil and heat until shimmering. Cooking in batches, cook patties about 1 1/2 to 2 minutes on the first side. Turn with a spatula and cook another 1 1/2 to 2 minutes on the second side. Remove to a warm serving platter.

Serve hot with Rémoulade Sauce or Red Pepper Mayonnaise.

Variation: Any cooked peas can be made into a similar patty, so don't feel "locked in" to lady peas just because they are my favorite!

COCA-COLA-GLAZED WINGS

Serves 6 to 8 as a starter

THIS RECIPE ADAPTED FROM *Virginia Willis'* Bon Appetit, Y'all *is an outdoors or den use-your-hands-nosh. The exact measures are not crucial. Start with fewer hot peppers rather than more. Virginia uses Scotch Bonnets.*

1 cup Coca-Cola
1/2 cup fresh lime juice or apple cider vinegar
1 1/2 cups light or dark brown sugar
1–3 red jalapeños or other small hot peppers, finely chopped
3 pounds chicken wings
Salt
Freshly ground black pepper

Bring the Coca-Cola, lime juice or vinegar, brown sugar, and peppers to the boil in a small saucepan. Reduce heat to medium-low and simmer about 30 minutes, until syrupy, and set aside to cool slightly. Prepare the wings by cutting off the tips (reserving them for stock if desired, pages 111–14) and cutting the wings in half at the joint with a sharp knife. Move the wings to a large plastic ziplock bag and season to taste with salt and pepper. Pour half the cooled glaze over the wings and stir to coat. Reserve remaining glaze.

When ready to cook, preheat the broiler. Reheat reserved glaze over low heat in a small saucepan. Line a rimmed baking sheet with aluminum foil and move a rack atop the foil. Move the wings to the rack. Broil the wings in the oven 4 inches from the heat for about 10 minutes. Turn the wings over to the other side using tongs, brush with reserved glaze, and broil 10 minutes. Remove from oven, move to a warm platter, and serve immediately.

Variation: This can be a main course for fewer people.

Coca-Cola is not only a Southern drink, it is used for cooking, its sweeteners caramelizing and transforming the mundane.

GRILLED CHICKEN SATÉ

Makes 8 skewers

SKEWERED CHICKEN PIECES MARINATED IN A SNAPPY SAUCE *are ideal for snacking on while waiting for the grill to finish cooking the main course. They can be served with vegetables and turned into a main course for fewer people.*

2 pounds boneless skinless chicken breast, cut into 1-inch cubes
1/2 cup soy sauce
1 teaspoon finely chopped or grated fresh ginger
2 tablespoons dark sesame oil
1 recipe Ginger Peanut Sauce (page 660)

If using wooden skewers, soak in water until needed.

Move chicken breast pieces to a plastic ziplock bag. Add soy sauce, ginger, and oil. Marinate 30 minutes or up to overnight.

When ready to grill, thread the chicken onto small presoaked wooden skewers and move to a hot grill or a rimmed baking sheet 6 inches from the hot broiler. Grill or broil 3 to 4 minutes; turn and cook the second side another 2 to 4 minutes, until the chicken registers 165 degrees on an instant-read thermometer. Remove from grill or broiler. Serve hot on skewers, or remove chicken from skewers to a serving bowl and serve with toothpicks. Serve with Ginger Peanut Sauce for dipping.

Variations:

- Shrimp skewers are equally tasty.
- The chicken breasts may be cut into strips and threaded onto the skewers. As the strips will be thinner, adjust cooking time accordingly.

PORK AND PEANUT HORS D'OEUVRES

Makes 6 to 8 skewers

PORK AND PEANUTS ARE A VERY COMPATIBLE COUPLE. *It's the double shot of protein that makes this dish so helpful as an hors d'oeuvre, keeping guests from being ravenous while waiting for dinner. This can also be used as a main course for four.*

- 1 cup shelled, roasted, and salted peanuts
- 1 bunch green onions, both green and white parts, chopped to make 3/4 cup
- Juice of 1 lime
- 2 tablespoons light or dark brown sugar
- 1/3 cup soy sauce
- 1 teaspoon chopped fresh ginger
- 3 garlic cloves, chopped
- 1 tablespoon coriander seeds
- 2 tablespoons hot red peppers, fresh or dried
- 1/2 cup beef stock or broth
- 1/4 cup butter, melted
- 1 1/2 pounds lean pork, cut into 1-inch cubes

If using wooden skewers, soak in water until needed.

Purée the peanuts, onions, lime juice, brown sugar, soy sauce, ginger, garlic, coriander seeds, and peppers in a blender or food processor until smooth. Add the broth and butter, and purée until well blended. Pour over the cut-up pork and marinate 8 hours or more in the refrigerator, covered.

Drain, reserving the marinade. Preheat a broiler or grill. Thread the meat onto presoaked skewers or place loose on a wire rack in a single layer; grill or broil 6 inches from the heat. Cook on one side until crisp and brown, about 5 minutes. Turn, brush with the marinade, and brown the other side. Remove to a warm serving platter.

Bring the reserved marinade to the boil, reduce heat to simmer, and cook 2 to 3 minutes. Serve the pork hot on the skewers, or remove to a platter or bowl and serve with toothpicks. Use the hot marinade as a dipping sauce.

Variation: Shrimp or chicken pieces may be substituted, adjusting cooking time accordingly.

SPICY SAUSAGE BALLS

Makes 100 to 120 balls

THIS MAKES A GRACIOUS PLENTY, *but the recipe can be cut down proportionally quite easily. Any extra sausage balls can be frozen cooked or uncooked. Chilling the dough makes it easier to work with. The self-rising flour gives it the puff that makes it special.*

- 1 pound hot pork sausage
- 1 pound grated sharp Cheddar cheese
- 1 cup self-rising flour (page 451)

Preheat oven to 400 degrees.

Mix together sausage, cheese, and flour with hands to form a dough, or move to a plastic ziplock bag to massage the ingredients together to form a well-incorporated dough, and refrigerate 20 to 30 minutes.

Divide the dough into 4 pieces. Working with one piece at a time and keeping the remainder refrigerated, take 1 tablespoon of cold sausage mixture and using hands or a melon baller, roll it into a 3/4-inch ball. Move to a rimmed baking sheet, leaving a small space between balls. Repeat with remaining dough.

Bake 15 minutes. Balls will puff slightly when cooked. Remove pan carefully from the oven, as there will be hot fat on the pan. Discard the fat and serve the sausage balls immediately. They can be refrigerated overnight and reheated, or wrapped well and frozen.

EVALUATING SAUSAGE SEASONING

Usually sausage has a sufficient amount of seasoning, but it's always a good idea to sauté or microwave a small amount of sausage to know how it tastes before proceeding to add other ingredients. It might need more salt, pepper, or spices, depending on your taste.

BABY CRAB CAKES

Makes 16 crab cakes

PAT CONROY IS A DEAR FRIEND OF OURS *and former cooking student of mine; he has written the foreword to this book. His crab cake recipe is famous, having appeared in the* Washington Post *and in his* Pat Conroy Cookbook. *This adaptation is for bite-sized crab cakes that melt in your mouth. Made larger and cooked longer, they are equally appetizing as a main course. When cooking a larger cake, surround it with a poached egg ring to hold the ingredients together before turning to cook the second side.*

1 pound lump crabmeat, picked over and cleaned, all shell fragments removed
1 egg white, lightly beaten
1 tablespoon all-purpose flour
2 tablespoons finely chopped fresh chives
1 teaspoon freshly ground black pepper
1/4 teaspoon ground hot red pepper
2 teaspoons coarse salt, divided
3 tablespoons butter, divided
3 teaspoons oil, cook's preference, divided
Lemon wedges, optional

Move the crabmeat to a large bowl and pour the egg white over the crabmeat in a slow stream, stopping occasionally to mix. When the crabmeat has absorbed the egg and feels slightly sticky to the touch, sift the flour over the crabmeat. Sprinkle with chives, peppers, and 1 teaspoon salt. Stir lightly from the bottom, but don't overhandle.

Separate the crabmeat into 16 cakes by gently rolling each portion in a flattened palm. Gently press down to form the cake and move to a large plate. Sprinkle with remaining salt. Refrigerate for 1 hour.

Melt half of the butter and half of the oil in a large skillet. Move 8 of the crab cakes to the hot fat and cook until a crust forms, about 2 minutes. Turn carefully with a thin metal or plastic spatula and cook another 2 minutes. Remove to a plate and cover loosely with foil. Wipe out the skillet with a paper towel and melt the remaining butter and oil. Cook remaining crab cakes in the same fashion. Serve hot with optional lemon wedges.

HERBED SHRIMP AND SCALLOP CEVICHE

Serves 8

Cool shrimp and scallops are enticing in a glass bowl at a buffet. *They can also be served with toothpicks for nibbles or in shells or fish plates as a first course for a sit-down meal.*

We know ceviche was served by Martha Washington in early colonial days (spelled caveach) most likely wending its way here from the Spaniards in Mexico and Latin America as well as from Barbados and other islands. This is easy, fast, and beckoning, and is best made a day or two ahead and served chilled. Poaching the seafood very quickly before marinating takes away the trepidation some people have about eating "raw" seafood.

1 1/2 pounds large raw shrimp in shells
1/2 pound raw sea scallops, sliced horizontally into 1/2-inch pieces
Grated rind of 3 limes, 2 lemons, and 1 orange, no white attached
1/3 cup fresh lime juice (about 3 limes)
1/4 cup fresh lemon juice (about 2 lemons)
1/3 cup fresh orange juice (about 1 orange)
5 tablespoons chopped fresh parsley, thyme, oregano, and basil
1/2 small red onion, very finely chopped
1/4 cup olive oil
1/2–1 teaspoon hot sauce, optional
Salt
Freshly ground black pepper
1 teaspoon commercial seafood seasoning or Creole seasoning (page 670), optional
1 large avocado, peeled and sliced

Bring 2 quarts of water to the boil in a large pot. Add the shrimp and poach just a few minutes, until tender and pink. Remove the shrimp with a slotted spoon or strainer, reserving the poaching liquid, and set shrimp aside to cool.

Return the poaching liquid to the boil. Move the scallops to a heatproof strainer or colander and dip into the boiling water for about 30 seconds, until the scallops are just cooked. Remove and set aside to cool. Peel the cooled shrimp and cut into thirds. Move the scallops and shrimp to a plastic ziplock bag. Add the grated lime, lemon, orange rinds, and the juices. Refrigerate covered, and marinate overnight, tossing occasionally.

When ready to serve, bring to room temperature and drain, reserving the juice. Add the herbs, onion, oil, and hot sauce, and toss lightly. Season to taste with salt and pepper. Taste and add optional seafood seasoning as desired. Serve chilled with the avocado. It looks smashing in a stemmed wide champagne glass with a wedge of avocado.

> *Caveach,* a noun for "pickled mackerel," is also a verb that refers to the "cooking of raw fish" using lime juice or other acid. Known in early American cookbooks as *ceviche*—also spelled *cebiche* and *seviche*, this acid "cooking" actually brings about a change of appearance and texture associated with cooked fish but, in fact, does not actually cook it. In French, Spanish, and Portuguese, *escabeche* is a similar term but refers to pickling of cooked fish.

SHRIMP AND CHEESE GRITS CUSTARDS WITH GREEN SAUCE

Serves 4 to 6

THESE RICH NUGGETS OF BEAUTY AND TASTE *unmold easily from ramekins, nonstick molds, or timbales, perfect for times when a smashing starter is required. The sauce can be made up to a day or two ahead and refrigerated, but the custards are best made just before serving. The greens add a tart piquancy and dark green beauty to the sauce. Other grits, such as stone-ground, are welcome but take longer to cook. For more information on custards, see page 618.*

Grits Custards

1 cup water
1 cup milk
1/2 cup uncooked quick grits
7 ounces soft goat cheese
1 large egg, beaten to mix
2 tablespoons finely chopped fresh basil, thyme, or oregano
Salt
Freshly ground black pepper

Green Sauce

1/2 cup heavy cream
1/2 cup sour cream
10 ounces baby spinach or turnip greens, washed (page 205)
Salt
Freshly ground pepper
1 1/2 pounds shrimp, cooked and peeled (pages 326–27)
2 tablespoons chopped basil, thyme, or oregano

For the Grits Custards: Preheat oven to 350 degrees. Generously butter 4 to 6 (1/2-cup) ramekins, molds (preferably nonstick), or timbales. To ease removal, put a piece of parchment paper on the bottom of the ramekin and butter it as well.

Heat the water and milk carefully in a heavy nonstick saucepan until there is a small boil around the edge of the pan. Slowly stir in the grits. Cover and cook over medium-low heat, stirring occasionally, for 10 to 15 minutes, until the grits are tender and creamy or cook according to package directions. Add more liquid as needed. Stir in the cheese, egg, and herbs, and season to taste with salt and pepper. Spoon into prepared ramekins.

Fold a tea towel on the bottom of a large roasting pan and place ramekins on top of the towel. Pour boiling water into the pan so that it reaches halfway up the sides of the ramekins, being careful not to get any water into the custard mixture. Move the roasting pan to the center of the oven and bake approximately 30 minutes, or until the custard is set and a knife inserted in the center comes out clean. Do not let the water boil, as the boiling will overcook the custard and create holes in it; if necessary, add cold water to the pan to prevent bubbling. Remove the pan from the oven; remove the soufflé dishes from the pan. Cool slightly before unmolding.

For the Green Sauce: Add the cream and sour cream to a heavy 4-cup saucepan. Bring to the boil around the edges of the pan, taking care that it does not boil over. Reduce heat and simmer until the liquid is cooked down by about half, about 10 minutes.

Wash the greens, draining well. Remove and discard any large veins. When the cream has reduced, add the greens and let wilt briefly. Purée with an immersion blender or move to a blender and process until well puréed and smooth. Season to taste with salt and pepper.

Toss the cooked shrimp with the herbs. Run a knife around the edge of the custards and unmold the custards onto individual serving plates, remove the parchment paper, spoon the sauce around them, and distribute the shrimp evenly among the plates.

Variation: Blanch very large turnip greens briefly and drain well before adding to the cream.

Cooking grits is most easily done in the microwave, using a large heat-proof measuring cup, stirring every 5 minutes until cooked.

BACON AND BASIL "ANGELS ON HORSEBACK"

Serves 6

WHEN I WAS YOUNGER, *the "angels on horseback" served at my parents' parties were marinated bacon-wrapped oysters. The South's plump oysters and the basil taste amazingly fresh and vibrant and make a good transition from the end of our basil season in the late fall to more robust winter oysters. The crispy bacon adds a final touch.*

24 shucked fresh oysters
2 tablespoons oil, cook's preference
1/4 cup fresh lemon juice
1 garlic clove, finely chopped
Salt
Freshly ground black pepper
Dash of hot sauce, optional
12 thin bacon slices
24 large basil leaves
4 skewers

Drain the oysters and set aside. If using wooden skewers or toothpicks, soak in water until needed.

Whisk together the oil, lemon juice, garlic, salt, pepper, and hot sauce to taste. Add the oysters. Cover and marinate for 30 minutes to 2 hours, stirring once or twice.

When ready to cook, preheat the broiler or a charcoal grill.

Meanwhile, partially cook the bacon until lightly brown but still supple enough to wrap around the oysters. Cut the bacon slices in half.

Drain the oysters well, discarding the marinade. Wrap each oyster with a basil leaf and then with a piece of bacon, securing with a toothpick or threading 4 oysters onto each skewer. Grill or broil on a rimmed baking sheet for 3 minutes, or long enough to crisp the bacon, turning if needed.

Serve one skewer per person on a plate with a fork, or as individual tidbits from a platter or tray, with toothpick intact.

OYSTER FRITTERS

Serves 4 to 6

THIS RECIPE IS AN IDEAL USE FOR VACUUM-PACKED FRESH OYSTERS *as shucking them for frying is a bit more trouble than one cook can handle. There is no reason these tasty morsels can't be served right from the paper towel to those hanging around in the kitchen (who probably won't wait for the fritters to be plated if they have a choice).*

Add the oysters to the fryer one by one so they don't bunch up. When fritters are cooked enough to be turned in the oil, they turn easily with just a nudge from a metal slotted spoon. If they balk, let them cook a minute more.

24 shucked fresh oysters and their liquor
Self-rising flour (page 451)
Salt
Freshly ground black pepper
Shortening or vegetable oil for frying

Strain the oyster juice into a bowl and set aside the oysters. Season the flour to taste with salt and pepper. Stir enough of the seasoned flour mixture into the oyster liquor to make batter enough to coat the oysters, adding water if necessary. Add the oysters and stir to coat.

Heat 1/4 to 1/2 inch oil in a heavy frying pan until the oil ripples. Carefully add the fritters to the frying pan, not touching, in batches. Fry until light brown, turn and repeat. Remove to a paper towel and keep warm. Serve hot or on a plate or with napkins. Serve with hot sauce for those who must have it.

Variations:

- Add hot pepper sauce or seafood seasoning to the batter as desired.
- Add to a green salad as a starter or lunch course.

Oysters vary in saltiness, and it is the cook's prerogative to taste before flouring and season the flour appropriately.

GRILLED SKEWERED OYSTERS

Serves 4 to 6

THE SMOKY SWEETNESS OF OYSTERS *benefits from this brief, simple cooking. Served alone, they are a worthy appetizer, but they can be "stretched" into a main course by serving with rice and vegetables.*

½ cup butter
3 garlic cloves, finely chopped
24 shucked fresh oysters, drained
Salt
Freshly ground black pepper
3 tablespoons chopped fresh parsley and/or thyme and fennel fronds, optional
Cocktail Sauce (page 658), optional

If using wooden skewers or toothpicks, soak in water until needed. Preheat the grill or broiler.

Heat the butter and the garlic in the microwave or a small pan until the butter is melted. Toss the oysters in the mixture. Thread oysters onto small presoaked wooden skewers and move them to a hot grill or a rimmed baking sheet 6 inches from the hot broiler. Cook until the oysters turn white and are starting to curl at the edges, about 5 to 8 minutes.

Season to taste with salt and pepper. Sprinkle with the optional chopped herbs. Serve with Cocktail Sauce if desired.

Leave the oysters on the skewers for an informal presentation or remove them to plates by sliding the oysters off with a fork.

An old wives' tale says to eat oysters only in the months that have an R in the name (September to April). This wasn't based on health considerations but on the difficulty of shipping oysters without spoilage in hot weather and on the spawning habits of the oyster and changes accompanying the process: oysters are drier and less tasty when spawning. Present-day oyster farming, government regulations, refrigeration, and shipping are now of such a high quality that health considerations are not a problem. Still, the environmentally conscious are reluctant to eat spawning oysters, which are the future of the industry, and aficionados disdain them.

FRIED FROG LEGS

Serves 6

LOUISIANANS IN PARTICULAR LOVE FRIED FROG LEGS, *and they cook them much as they would quail, marinating them with buttermilk. One never knows when one will find oneself confronted with frog legs in the market, so we include it here.*

12 frog legs
4 cups buttermilk
Hot sauce
1 large egg
3 tablespoons Creole mustard
1 (12-ounce) bottle or can of beer
2 garlic cloves, chopped
Salt
Freshly ground black pepper
4 cups seasoned corn flour, yellow or white
Shortening or vegetable oil for frying

Soak frog legs in buttermilk with hot sauce to taste for 1 hour.

Whisk together the egg, mustard, beer, and garlic. Season to taste with salt, pepper, and hot sauce. Move corn flour to a separate bowl.

Heat the oil in a large heavy skillet to 375 degrees.

Remove frog legs from buttermilk, give a shake, and roll in corn flour, using one hand. Dip in egg mix, and then again in corn flour.

Meanwhile, heat enough shortening in a deep skillet to cover the frogs legs, taking care it is not more than halfway up the pan. Add the legs to the pan skin side down. Fry until golden brown, turning if necessary. Remove with tongs and drain on paper towels.

SHRIMP AND OKRA BEIGNETS WITH SALSA AND CILANTRO-LIME SOUR CREAM

Serves 4

HOMINY GRILL RESTAURANT IN CHARLESTON *makes the most astonishing okra beignets I've ever eaten. May these be half as good! They will inspire rave reviews.*

1 large egg, lightly beaten
2 tablespoons heavy cream or half-and-half
3 tablespoons fine dry breadcrumbs
3 tablespoons all-purpose flour
1/2 teaspoon salt, or to taste
1/4 teaspoon freshly ground black pepper, or to taste
2 cups okra, chopped into 1/3-inch thick pieces
1/2 cup yellow onion, diced
1/3 cup green bell pepper, diced
1 jalapeño pepper or other small hot pepper, seeded and finely chopped
1/2 pound raw shrimp, peeled and roughly chopped
Shortening or vegetable oil for frying
Salsa (page 668)
1 cup Cilantro-Lime Sour Cream (below)

Whisk together egg and cream in a small bowl until combined.

Whisk together breadcrumbs, flour, salt, and pepper in a large bowl. Toss okra, onion, bell pepper, jalapeño pepper, and shrimp in breadcrumb mixture. Stir in egg mixture until thoroughly combined. Allow batter to rest at room temperature for 20 minutes.

Meanwhile, make the Salsa and Cilantro-Lime Sour Cream.

After batter has rested, stir vigorously for 2 minutes, until it has a gooey consistency. Season to taste with salt and pepper. Stir the shrimp into the batter until evenly incorporated.

When ready to cook, heat oven to 200 degrees. Move a wire cooling rack to a rimmed baking sheet lined with paper towels and set aside. Line a second baking sheet with foil and set aside.

Pour oil into a wide 3- to 4-quart heavy pot to a depth of 1 1/2 inches and heat until thermometer registers 350 degrees. Carefully add level tablespoons of beignet batter to the hot oil one at a time, and fry in batches of 10 to 12 for about 2 to 5 minutes per batch, until golden brown, turning over once. Remove with a slotted spoon to the paper towels, then transfer to the foil-lined baking sheet and move into the oven to keep warm.

Serve hot with Salsa and Cilantro-Lime Sour Cream.

Variation: Substitute 1 (10-ounce) box frozen cut okra, thawed, if fresh is not available.

CILANTRO-LIME SOUR CREAM

Finely grated rind of 1 lime, no white attached
Juice of 1/2 lime
2 tablespoons chopped fresh cilantro
1 cup sour cream
Salt

Stir all ingredients together in a small bowl; cover and refrigerate until serving.

PICKLED SHRIMP, OR "SWIMPEE"

Makes 2 pounds

I COULDN'T RESIST USING THE NAME OF THIS RECIPE *from* Charleston Receipts. *It got this name from the vendors who early-on walked the streets of Charleston calling out "swimpee" to sell their wares. The recipe, however, is my own. This recipe doubles easily.*

2 pounds shrimp, cooked and peeled (pages 326–27)
3 large sweet onions, sliced
3/4 cup olive oil
1 cup sherry vinegar
Salt
Freshly ground black pepper
Fresh herbs to taste, such as lemon thyme or lemon balm
Lemon slices, optional

Starting with the shrimp, layer shrimp and onions in a large glass bowl. Mix oil and vinegar, and season to taste with salt and pepper. Pour this mixture over the shrimp and onions, and cover tightly. Refrigerate overnight or up to 1 week. Garnish with lemon slices if desired. Serve layered from the bowl with toothpicks, or on small plates. If the mixture has become too liquid, spoon off and discard the excess liquid carefully before serving.

FRIED CLAMS

Serves 2

THESE LITTLE FRIED CLAMS *make a tasty appetizer or filling for a bun with mayonnaise or its derivative, tartar sauce. If frying other types of seafood along with the clams, remember that size matters: large pieces are fried at a bit lower temperature and a bit longer than the tiny pieces, which are nearly "in and out" in a jiffy.*

4 dozen cleaned, shucked small clams
Shortening or vegetable oil for frying
1 recipe Lemon Batter for Seafood (page 327)
1 recipe Tartar Sauce (page 659)

Remove the membrane of the clam "neck" by slitting and peeling with a small sharp knife. Pat the clams dry.

Heat a large heavy pot no more than two-thirds full of the oil to between 360 and 375 degrees. Using a fork or tongs, pick up a few clams (half dozen), dip them into the batter, then slide them carefully into the hot fat (rather than dropping from a distance), watching out for spatters. As the battered clams begin to turn a light golden brown, remove them with a slotted spoon or a round Chinese strainer to a rimmed baking sheet lined with paper towels; move to a 200-degree oven to keep warm. Repeat until all the clams are fried. Serve with Tartar Sauce or a favorite dip.

PIMENTO CHEESE AND TOMATO TART

Makes 1 (8- to 9-inch) tart

Pimento cheese spread contains mayonnaise, *which gives this tart a dainty puff that surrounds oven-dried tomatoes. It's a wonderful throw-together appetizer or luncheon dish, reminiscent of a sophisticated pizza. It is important for the pimento cheese to be cold when it goes into the oven, hence the chilling instructions.*

1 recipe (9-inch) piecrust (pages 504–10)
1 1/4 cups Pimento Cheese (page 57)
1 pint grape tomatoes

Prebake the piecrust (page 503) in an 8- or 9-inch tart pan, and set aside to cool. When cool, move to the refrigerator to chill.

Spread the Pimento Cheese on the bottom of the piecrust, no more than a third of the way up the sides of the tart pan, and chill again. If using a tart pan with a removable bottom, surround the bottom of the pan with foil to prevent the filling from possibly leaking out while baking.

While the tart is chilling, halve the tomatoes and bake cut side down on an oiled rimmed baking sheet at 400 degrees for 20 to 30 minutes, or until shrunken and most of the juice has been emitted. Remove and drain. Cool to room temperature.

Sprinkle the tomato halves over the pimento cheese, rounded side up; avoid covering completely so the cheese can rise above the tomatoes. Chill until ready to bake.

When ready to bake, preheat oven to 350 degrees. Move the filled tart to a rimmed baking sheet. Bake 20 minutes, or until puffy. Cool the tart in the pan on a wire rack.

Variations:

- An unbaked crust can be used in a pinch. Watch carefully to be sure the crust gets cooked. Begin cooking the tart at 400 degrees and reduce heat to 350 degrees after the first 15 minutes of baking; cover rim with foil if browning too quickly.
- If no tart pan is to be had, a pie pan may be substituted.

IS IT A PIE OR A TART?

A pie can have a top and bottom, or just a bottom crust. A tart rarely, if ever, has a top crust. It is baked in a pan with plain or fluted sides, most often with a removable bottom, and is not as deep as a pie.

GOLDEN VIDALIA ONION TART WITH OLIVES AND ROSEMARY

Makes 1 (8- or 9-inch) tart

VIDALIA ONIONS ARE AMAZINGLY VERSATILE—*our Georgia Vidalias being among the world's sweetest onions—and they make for a satisfying tart. But any onion will do—even red ones. I also make this free-form, just because it's faster and easier, and no special equipment, like a tart pan with removable bottom, is required. Try experimenting with shapes like rectangles and squares so guests don't just think it is an onion pizza but something extraordinarily special, which it is.*

1 recipe (9-inch) piecrust (pages 504–10)
2–3 medium onions, preferably Vidalia, sliced 1/2 inch thick
Salt
2–3 tablespoons butter or oil, cook's preference
1 cup grated Gruyère, Cheddar, or soft goat cheese
1–2 sprigs fresh rosemary, leaves stripped and chopped
Freshly ground black pepper
1/2 cup Greek or other black olives

Prebake the piecrust (page 503) in an 8- or 9-inch tart pan, and set aside to cool.

Meanwhile, prepare the onions. Heat the butter in a large heavy skillet and cook the onions slowly over low heat, stirring frequently, until they are caramelized and deep mahogany brown (page 220). This should take about 30 minutes.

Layer the onions and cheese into the tart crust, beginning with the onions and ending with the cheese. Sprinkle with rosemary and pepper. Lay the olives on a counter and swack them with the side of a large knife to loosen the pits. Remove the pits, chop the olives if desired, and sprinkle them on top of the rosemary and cheese. Move to a rimmed baking sheet.

When ready to bake, preheat oven to 400 degrees. Bake 10 to 20 minutes, or until cheese is melted and the crust is a solid brown. Remove from oven. Serve hot or cold.

Variation: For a delicate layer of onions and pastry, roll the dough into an 11-inch-long rectangle and bake it free-form (page 503). Sprinkle onions only a couple of layers thick. Cut bite-size or larger.

PITTING OLIVES

To pit olives, place on a cutting board and swack down on them once or twice using the flat side of a knife blade and a fist. The pits are then easily removed by hand.

Pastry always makes a splash at a party, particularly if it is crisp and flaky and the filling is a stand-out, with enough of a twist that it is clear it isn't from the grocer's freezer section. Although any tart can be made into mini-tarts or tartlets, a larger tart has the added advantage of giving substantial portions, particularly helpful for serve-in-the-living-room dinner parties with a small plate and fork. And it is much faster to whip up. While we have complete instructions in the "Pastry and Pies" chapter for making and pre-baking, we also confess that starter tarts—to be consumed quickly by those who have a drink in the other hand—are fine uses for grocery store pastry, particularly the name brand doughs sold rolled up in a box. Avoid frozen premade pie shells in a pan. A free-form tart is a better alternative.

BACON AND ONION PIE

Makes 1 (9-inch) pie

ANY SAVORY (NON-SWEET) PIECRUST *will do for this simple quiche-like pie. The trick is making the Flavored Milk, which gives the pie an extraordinary flavor boost. It can be omitted when time is of the essence but is worth doing whenever possible.*

1 recipe (9-inch) piecrust (pages 504–10)
6 slices bacon, cooked crisp and crumbled, drippings reserved
1 medium onion
1 large egg
1 egg yolk
2 cups grated Gruyère, Cheddar, or soft goat cheese
1 cup milk, preferably Flavored Milk (page 657)

Prebake the piecrust in a 9-inch pie pan and set aside to cool.

Preheat oven to 350 degrees.

Reheat 2 tablespoons bacon drippings in a large skillet; add onion and sauté until soft. Lightly beat the egg and egg yolk together; add milk, crumbled bacon, onions, and cheese; stir together. Ladle mixture into a partially prebaked piecrust, move to a rimmed baking sheet and bake for 30 to 35 minutes, or until a knife inserted in the center of the pie comes out clean. Remove from oven and allow to rest for 5 to 10 minutes before serving.

Variation: Omit the bacon and sauté 2 additional onions.

Save drippings from bacon, sausage, and other flavorful meats and refrigerate for use in other recipes. If none are available, any fat, such as butter or oil, can be substituted in equal measure.

If the tart pan is larger than called for in the recipe, the tart will cook more quickly, as the tart is shallower. A smaller tart pan should be filled carefully, leaving at least 1/4 inch at the top of the crust. Pour excess filling into oiled ramekins and bake as a crustless pie.

ROASTED TOMATO TART

Makes 1 (8- or 9-inch) tart

THE CHEESE SHOULD BE AS GOOD AS YOU CAN GET—*fresh mozzarella, goat cheese, or Gruyère, for instance. Serve at room temperature as a snack or appetizer. Alternately, treat this as an upscale grilled cheese and tomato sandwich and serve it with tomato soup on a rainy day. Not all tarts are round. Bake oblong, either free-form or in a tart pan, to cut easily into bite-size or larger pieces. Round tarts are usually cut into wedges. Alert: The amount of tomatoes will vary depending on the size of the tart.*

- 1 recipe (8- or 9-inch) piecrust (pages 504–10)
- $1\frac{1}{2}$ cups grated or sliced fresh mozzarella, soft goat cheese, or other cheese, divided
- 1 recipe Oven-Roasted Tomatoes (page 246)
- 2–3 tablespoons chopped fresh basil, thyme, oregano, or marjoram, optional

Prebake the piecrust in a tart pan or free-form and set aside to cool.

Preheat oven to 375 degrees.

Layer the bottom of the piecrust with the cheese, reserving $\frac{1}{4}$ cup for the top. Add the tomatoes, spreading evenly over the cheese. Move to a rimmed baking sheet.

Bake 15 to 20 minutes, until cheese is melted. Sprinkle with remaining cheese and return to oven for a few minutes. Add herbs if desired. Allow to rest 5 minutes before cutting.

Variation: Substitute roasted grape or cherry tomatoes (page 246).

Once we had extra Very Versatile Cream Cheese Dough (page 512) left over, some roasted tomatoes, and a handful of lightly cooked fresh spinach leaves. We threw it all together with some caramelized onions and goat cheese and baked as above. I swoon still with the memory of it.

NIKKI'S ROASTED TOMATO AND ZUCCHINI LATTICE TART

Makes 1 (8- or 9-inch) tart

To call this a "knock their eyes out" pie *would be fair. It's stunning. My intern Nikki Moore developed this recipe one summer from some ideas we batted around as we stared at a near-empty refrigerator. It is remarkably easy. Don't feel constrained to do exactly as we did—make another design.*

1 recipe (8- or 9-inch) piecrust (pages 504–10)
1 cup soft goat cheese, divided
8–10 slices Oven-Roasted Tomatoes (page 246)
1 medium zucchini
2 tablespoons oil, cook's preference
1–2 tablespoons chopped fresh herbs, such as thyme or basil, optional

Prebake the piecrust in an 8- or 9-inch tart pan and set aside to cool. If using a tart pan with a removable bottom, surround the bottom of the pan with foil to prevent the filling from possibly leaking out while baking.

Preheat oven to 375 degrees.

Layer the prebaked crust with the cheese, saving 1/2 cup for the top. Add the tomato slices, spreading evenly over the cheese. Sprinkle with the remaining cheese on top.

Meanwhile, slice the zucchini vertically into long strips with a vegetable peeler. Heat the oil in a small frying pan, add the zucchini, and wilt just a few minutes. Cool sufficiently to handle and form into a lattice on the top of the cheese. Make a horizontal row of zucchini, leaving space between the rows. Weave the remaining zucchini under and over the horizontal row, leaving a space again so the tomatoes and cheese show through. Moved to a rimmed baking sheet.

Bake 10 to 15 minutes, or until cheese is melted. Add herbs if desired. Allow to rest 5 minutes before cutting.

Variations:

- If no tart pan is to be had, roll the pie dough into a large piece and cut, using a guide or freehand, into a circle or square. Move to an oiled or parchment-lined baking sheet. Partially prebake. Fill as above.
- Omit the zucchini and substitute 1 1/2 cups grated or sliced mozzarella cheese for the goat cheese.

SHRIMP AND OKRA PIE

Makes 1 (9-inch) pie

This medley makes a pie fit for a queen, *a lunch, or a starter. It fits the bill with beautiful colors and flavors.*

1 recipe (9-inch) piecrust (pages 504–10)
1 pound fresh okra, sliced 1/4 inch thick
1 medium onion, chopped
1/2 red or other bell pepper, chopped
3 garlic cloves, chopped
1/4 cup oil, cook's preference
1 tablespoon vinegar
1/3 cup sliced green onions
3/4 pound raw medium shrimp, peeled and deveined
3/4 cup breadcrumbs, divided
Salt
Freshly ground black pepper

Prebake the piecrust in an 8- or 9-inch pie or tart pan and set aside to cool.

Preheat oven to 375 degrees.

Stir okra, onion, bell pepper, garlic, and oil together in a large Dutch oven. Bake 35 to 40 minutes, stirring occasionally. Add vinegar and stir; continue to bake 10 to 15 minutes more, stirring occasionally. Remove from oven to continue cooking on the stovetop on the stovetop over medium-high heat. Add green onions and shrimp, and cook 3 minutes, until the shrimp are pink. Remove from heat and add 1/2 cup of the breadcrumbs. Season to taste with salt and pepper. Fill prebaked piecrust with cooked okra and shrimp mixture. Sprinkle with remaining breadcrumbs. Move to a rimmed baking sheet. Bake 5 to 7 minutes. Serve hot.

CRAB TART

Makes 1 (9 x 12-inch) tart

SEEN FREQUENTLY AT BRIDAL SHOWERS, *seafood and custard dishes show up on Southern tables regularly because they stretch the expensive crabmeat while presenting a beautiful, rich, and tasty dish. The piecrust supports the filling as it is cut into squares and served hot or cold. Lump crab is not necessary in this recipe and would be a waste. Remember, the crab is already cooked.*

1 double recipe piecrust (pages 504–10)
2 tablespoons butter
1 cup chopped green onions or scallions, both white and green parts
2/3 cup vermouth or dry Madeira
1 pound backfin crabmeat, picked over for shells
1 pound claw crabmeat, picked over for shells
10 large eggs
1 tablespoon salt
1 teaspoon freshly ground black pepper
1/4 cup tomato paste
4 cups heavy cream
3/4 cup grated Gruyère cheese
2 tablespoons chopped fresh thyme, oregano, and/or fennel frond

Preheat oven to 425 degrees.

Roll out and line a 9 x 13-inch rimmed baking sheet with the piecrust and prebake. Set aside to cool.

While the crust is cooling, melt the butter in a frying pan. Add the green onions and cook briefly, 2 or 3 minutes. Stir in the vermouth or Madeira. Toss the crabmeat in and sauté for 2 to 3 minutes, until the liquid appears to have evaporated.

Beat together the eggs, salt, pepper, and tomato paste in another bowl until the tomato paste is thoroughly incorporated. Add the crab mixture and the cream. Spoon into the prebaked crust, taking care to distribute the entire mixture evenly throughout the pan.

Toss the cheese with the herbs and sprinkle over the tart, stirring gently to incorporate a little of the cheese in with the crab mixture. Bake about 45 to 50 minutes, until the tart is firm around the edges and fairly firm in the center. The center will firm up slightly as it cools. Cut into squares when the tart has cooled somewhat and the center has set. Serve hot or cold. This tart can be refrigerated and reheated in a 300-degree oven.

Variation: Savannah Crab Custard Tart
This more delicate and traditional tart omits the green onion, tomato paste, and cheese. It changes the ratio to accommodate a 9-inch tart pan or pie plate, which should be prebaked. Mix 2 tablespoons melted butter, 1 cup milk, 1 cup heavy cream, and 4 eggs. Add the salt, pepper, crabmeat, and vermouth or Madeira and mix. Spoon evenly into the prebaked crust and bake 30 to 40 minutes, until the custard is set.

Variation: Chopped cooked shrimp is a good substitute for all or part of the crab.

SOGGY OR CRACKED PIECRUSTS

Sprinkling breadcrumbs into a prebaked crust helps keep it from becoming soggy. Another method is to brush mustard on the inside of the piecrust before filling and baking. If a piecrust cracks while prebaking, brush with beaten egg yolk, or sprinkle the bottom lightly with grated cheese before adding filling.

PEPPER JELLY TURNOVERS

Makes 2 to 3 dozen

THE CHEESE PASTRY TAKES NO TIME TO PULL TOGETHER *in a food processor or by hand. Filled with hot pepper jelly, these bite-sized jewels sparkle in the mouth.*

- 5 ounces sharp Cheddar cheese, cut into 1/2-inch cubes
- 1 cup all-purpose flour
- 1/2 cup butter, cut into 1/2-inch cubes
- 3–4 tablespoons ice water
- 1/2 cup or 1 (4-ounce) jar Hot Pepper Jelly (page 648)
- 2 tablespoons chopped smoked or country ham, or turkey ham, or turkey, optional

Preheat oven to 375 degrees.

Pulse the cheese and flour together just briefly in the bowl of a food processor fitted with the metal blade. Add the butter and process or blend until it is about the size of garden peas. Add the ice water and process briefly until the dough starts to come together.

Turn the dough out onto a board and shape it into a flat round. Roll it out (between sheets of waxed paper if necessary) 1/8 inch thick and cut into rounds with a 2-inch biscuit cutter. Place approximately 1/3 teaspoon Hot Pepper Jelly and 1/4 teaspoon chopped ham in the center of each round and fold over. Crimp the edges well with a fork to seal or the jelly will run out.

Move the turnovers to a rimmed baking sheet and bake 10 to 15 minutes. The turnovers can be frozen before or after baking. Defrost and bake or reheat before serving.

CHEESE SAUSAGE PINWHEELS

Makes 24 pinwheels

COMBINE THE TASTE OF CHEESE *with sausage or ham, roll up and bake, and what do you have? Something pretty, oh-so-good, and easy to eat. These freeze well, too.*

- 1 recipe food processor golden cheese biscuits (page 469)
- 1 (16-ounce) roll mild or hot sausage, lightly cooked, drained and cooled

Preheat oven to 400 degrees.

Pat the dough on a floured surface into a 14 x 10-inch rectangle, about 1/4 inch thick. Crumble the lightly cooked sausage evenly over the biscuit dough.

Starting on a long side of the rectangle, use the heel of one hand and roll the dough up in jelly-roll style. Slice the roll into 1/2-inch-wide pinwheels. Move to a rimmed baking sheet, leaving space on the baking sheet for biscuits to spread, and bake 15 to 18 minutes, until lightly browned.

Variation: Cheese Pinwheels

Roll out biscuit dough to 1/4-inch thickness. Spread generously with grated cheese, sprinkle with hot red pepper, and roll up like a jelly roll. Slice the roll into 1/2-inch-wide pinwheels; move to an oiled baking sheet, and bake in a moderate oven until lightly browned. They are good hot or cold.

Variation: Ham Pinwheels

Combine 3/4 pound chopped and cooked Virginia country ham, 1 chopped garlic clove, 1 chopped medium onion, 1/2 cup melted butter, 1/2 cup mayonnaise, 2/3 cup peanut butter, and a dash of hot sauce if desired. Follow directions above, substituting this mixture for the cooked sausage.

SOUR CREAM BRITTLEBREAD

Makes 40 (1 1/2-inch) crackers

CRACKERS, BRITTLEBREAD, AND OTHER THIN, CRISPY "PLATFORMS" *are one of the miracles of Southern cooking, easily made in the food processor.*

2 3/4 cups all-purpose flour
1/4 cup granulated sugar
1/2 teaspoon salt, optional
1/2 teaspoon baking soda
1/2 cup butter, cut into 1/4-inch cubes
1 cup sour cream
1–3 teaspoons freshly ground black pepper, optional
1–2 tablespoons kosher salt

Preheat oven to 400 degrees.

Pulse the flour, sugar, salt, and baking soda together in the bowl of a food processor fitted with a metal blade. Add butter and pulse several times. Add sour cream and pepper, and pulse to a soft but not sticky dough.

Divide in half and roll out each half to 10 x 18 inches, paper-thin, on a floured board or between 2 pieces of plastic wrap. Use a pizza wheel or knife and cut into 3-inch squares. Move to ungreased 11 x 17-inch jelly-roll pans or rimmed baking sheets. Cut again into 1 1/2-inch pieces. Sprinkle with kosher salt. Bake 5 to 8 minutes. Turn off the heat and allow the bread to crisp in the oven as long as necessary. Re-crisp in the oven after storing, as our humidity is the foe of crispness.

CRACKERS, NO. 1

Rub six ounces of butter into two pounds sifted flour; dissolve a teaspoonful (level full) of soda in a wineglass of buttermilk; strain this through a fine sieve to the flour; add a teaspoonful of salt; beat well; roll thin; bake. If not crisp when first baked, put them again into a slack oven, and merely heat over.—*Mrs. Hill's New Cook Book,* 1872

HOT COUNTRY HAM-AND-CHEESE ROLLS WITH DIJON–POPPY SEED SAUCE

Makes 48 small sandwiches

THESE WARM LITTLE ROLLS *will be the hit of any party. Thinly sliced pears or apples add a little extra sweetness, although figs would also be a good addition.*

1 cup mayonnaise
4 tablespoons Dijon mustard
1 large onion, finely minced
3 tablespoons poppy seeds
2 tablespoons Worcestershire sauce
Salt
Freshly ground black pepper
1 recipe Food Processor Rolls dough (page 488) baked into 48 small rolls
2 pounds sliced Gruyère cheese
2 pounds country ham or baked ham, thinly sliced
4 apples or pears, thinly sliced

Preheat oven to 350 degrees.

Blend together mayonnaise, mustard, onion, poppy seeds, and Worcestershire sauce; season to taste with salt and pepper. Spread sauce thinly on the insides of both sides of the rolls, reserving leftover sauce.

Layer cheese, ham, fruit, and another layer of cheese on rolls, beginning and ending with cheese, which holds the rolls together when melted. This can be done ahead of time and refrigerated up to several hours. Spread or brush reserved sauce on top of rolls before baking. Wrap with foil and bake for 20 minutes, or until heated through.

Variation: Substitute 12 to 14 sliced figs for the apples or pears.

CHEESE STRAWS

Makes 100

SOUTHERN CHEESE STRAWS *are made with a short crust and cheese dough. Hand-grated cheese is preferred over packaged pre-shredded cheese. If using a cookie press, grate the cheese very finely so it won't clog the press. Make sure the butter is at room temperature but not melted, so it is soft enough to ensure that the cheese and butter mixture will be smooth and not gritty.*

1 cup butter, room temperature
8 ounces Parmesan cheese, finely grated
8 ounces sharp Cheddar or Gruyère cheese, finely grated
3/4 teaspoon Dijon mustard
2 1/3 cups all-purpose flour
1/4 teaspoon salt
1 teaspoon baking powder
1/4–1/2 teaspoon ground hot red pepper

Preheat oven to 375 degrees.

Cut the butter into thin pieces, approximately tablespoon-size, and beat with an electric hand mixer in a very large mixing bowl until butter is soft. Add all the cheese and beat with the butter until the mixture is smooth. Stir in the mustard.

Whisk together the flour, salt, baking powder, and hot red pepper. Add to the butter mixture and beat until combined. Form into a ball.

Press dough out with a cookie press into straws, following manufacturer's instructions, or use the following procedure: Divide dough into fourths. On waxed paper, roll each piece into a rectangle 1/3 inch thick. Use a pastry wheel to cut dough into 4- x 1/2-inch strips. Move straws onto a rimmed baking sheet lined with a silicone mat or parchment paper. Bake at 375 degrees for 8 to 15 minutes, until light brown. Watch carefully, as overly browned straws aren't tasty. Cool on a rack.

Every oven is different. Cook the first batch, watching carefully, and if too brown, reduce heat to 325 degrees. Rotate pan halfway through baking time. Use more than one baking sheet at a time only if the sheets may be placed in the oven without overlapping. Air must freely circulate or the bottoms will be burned and the tops unbrowned. Switch shelves and positions of the pans as necessary to prevent top or bottom from browning. Take care: white cheese will not brown as much as yellow.

Once the aroma comes wafting out of the oven, they are usually done. Cooking further may burn the cheese. Remove with a metal spatula to cool on a rack. These keep several days at room temperature in a tightly sealed container, or frozen up to 3 months. Due to the heavy humidity in the South, it may be necessary to re-crisp straws on a baking sheet in a 300-degree oven.

Variation: Use cookie cutters, a pastry bag, or an indented pizza slicer to shape cheese straws. Cut into coins, triangles, hearts, or specialty shapes for special parties.

CORNBREAD MINI-MUFFIN TOPS

Makes 5 dozen

THESE ARE LIKE CROSTINI—*Anything can be put on top of them. For a hot appetizer, top with shredded barbecue pork. For a room-temperature appetizer, top with pimento cheese, country ham, or any savory jam or chutney.*

2 cups self-rising white cornmeal mix
2 cups buttermilk
1/2 cup all-purpose flour
2 large eggs
1/4 cup butter, melted
2 tablespoons granulated sugar

Preheat oven to 400 degrees. Oil mini-muffin tins and set aside.

Stir together all ingredients in a medium bowl until the cornmeal mix is moistened. Spoon 1 tablespoon of batter into each muffin cup.

Move muffin tins to oven and bake 15 minutes, or until the muffin tops are lightly brown. Cool on a wire rack. Serve warm or at room temperature. Store in the freezer, tightly wrapped, for up to 1 month.

To reheat, remove from freezer and bake at 350 degrees for 5 minutes.

If the batter tends to stick to the spoon, wipe off excess and oil the spoon to prevent batter build-up.

GRITS CAKES

Makes 8 cakes

GRITS CAKES CAN BE SERVED HOT OR COLD, *presented on a beautiful plate for a sit-down starter or main course, or cut bite-sized and served as a stand-up snack. The variations are endless. Change herbs, top with shrimp, bacon, and tomato—whatever looks lively and tastes phenomenal. The secret is never to throw away cooked grits but to repurpose them. They can be refrigerated or frozen.*

4 cups cooked grits
1 tablespoon chopped garlic
1/2 cup grated extra-sharp Cheddar cheese
2 tablespoons chopped fresh chives
4 tablespoons butter, room temperature, divided
Hot pepper sauce to taste

Butter a 9 x 5 x 2 1/2-inch loaf pan and line it with parchment paper or aluminum foil. Stir hot grits, garlic, cheese, chives, and 2 tablespoons of the butter together. Season to taste with hot sauce. Pour the grits into the pan and refrigerate until chilled and firm.

When ready to serve, unmold the grits and slice them into 8 squares or cut with cookie cutters into shapes. Heat the remaining butter in a heavy-bottomed nonstick frying pan over medium-high heat. Cook the grits cakes for 5 minutes on each side, or until golden and heated through.

These can be frozen before or after cooking.

Variation: Cut into tiny bite-sized circles.

SHAPING FUN WITH COOKED GRITS

Cooked grits can be molded into small round cakes, hearts, pyramids, and other shapes. Spread out cooked grits on a rimmed baking sheet around 1/2 inch thick or as desired. Cool briefly or up to several days in the refrigerator, covered. Cut out with cookie cutters or just with a knife into squares or oblongs. Serve as is, or top with little tomatoes, shrimp, or crab. Another way is to heap them in a loaf pan or other mold. When cool, turn out and slice or shape. A trick is to shape into a cylinder like store-bought cookie dough, wrap with plastic wrap, and roll again to smooth. Chill. When ready to use, unwrap and slice.

OKRA GRIDDLE CAKES

Makes 16 cakes

FLAVORS DANCE IN THE MOUTH *in these batter cakes. Wait until everyone is gathered around before starting to cook them, and raves will be in store. This is an ideal starter for when guests' arrival time is uncertain, or when a kitchen gathering is the order of the day. Have everything ready ahead of time except the batter. Otherwise, a stack of the still warm cakes on the buffet table will entice those who want a dollop of sour cream. These are just enough to whet the appetite, a cross between fried okra and cornbread.*

4 slices cooked bacon, drippings reserved
1 cup cooked okra, finely chopped
1 1/2 cups self-rising cornmeal mix
1/2 cup all-purpose flour
1 tablespoon granulated sugar
1 2/3 cups buttermilk
3 tablespoons butter, melted
2 large eggs, lightly beaten
Shortening or vegetable oil for frying
Sour cream, optional

Finely chop the cooked bacon and okra.

Up to 2 hours before serving, whisk together cornmeal mix, flour, and sugar in a bowl. Stir in buttermilk, butter, and eggs until just mixed. Add finely chopped bacon and okra to batter.

Heat a griddle or large iron skillet until hot. Add enough oil to coat the bottom. Sprinkle in a bit of batter to test that the pan is hot enough to sizzle and that the batter is a pourable consistency. Add water to thin if necessary. Ladle 1/4 cup batter for each griddle cake onto hot griddle and cook until the top of the pancake is dotted with large bubbles and the bottom is light brown. Turn with a large spatula, and cook until the other side is lightly browned. Keep warm in a 200-degree oven on a rack over a baking sheet or serve immediately. Continue with the rest of the batter until all is gone.

Serve hot with optional sour cream.

Variations:

- Top the sour cream with a little chopped bacon and okra.
- Substitute a little chopped turnip greens and hot pepper, a few chopped shrimp or crab in the batter for the okra and bacon.

Griddle cakes can be made thick or thin, coin- or pancake-sized. What's necessary is a hot pan—and a watchful eye. The batter must be hot enough to rise in bubbles to the top of the pancake, indicating it is ready to turn, or a goopy mess will result.

MISSISSIPPI CAVIAR

Serves 4 to 6

THIS WONDERFUL MAKE-AHEAD DIP, *made from black-eyed peas—the South's caviar—can also be a vegetable bed for grilled or smoked chops. Cover and refrigerate for up to 4 or 5 days or freeze up to 3 months.*

3 (16-ounce) cans black-eyed peas, drained
1/2 cup finely chopped green bell pepper
1/2 cup finely chopped red bell pepper
3/4 cup finely chopped hot peppers
3/4 cup finely chopped onion
1/4 cup drained and finely chopped pimento
1 garlic clove, chopped
1/3 cup red wine vinegar
2/3 cup olive oil
1 tablespoon Dijon mustard
Salt
Tabasco sauce

In a large mixing bowl, combine the peas, bell pepper, hot pepper, onion, pimento, and garlic. In a separate bowl, whisk together the vinegar, oil, and mustard, and pour over the bean mixture; mix well. Season to taste with salt and Tabasco. With a wooden spoon or potato masher, mash the bean mixture slightly. Refrigerate until ready to serve. Drain the caviar well before serving.

SOUTHERN HUMMUS

Makes 6 cups

SOLD FRESH, FROZEN, AND CANNED, BUTTER BEANS *are often found in the Southern larder, and New Southern chefs have taken to creating "Southern hummus." Any form can be used in this recipe, with the caveat that the canned beans and frozen beans will require less cooking than fresh and should be drained before using. Seasoning will always vary according to the bean, so the measurements are just a guideline. This dip is significantly better the next day.*

2 pounds fresh or frozen butter beans, butter peas, or English peas
2 medium Vidalia or other onions, chopped
8 garlic cloves, smashed and peeled
1 tablespoon salt
1/4 cup chopped fresh cilantro
1/4 cup smooth peanut butter or tahini
2 teaspoons ground cumin seed
1/4 teaspoon ground hot red pepper
3 ounces fresh lemon juice
1/2 cup olive oil, divided
Salt
Freshly ground black pepper
Ground coriander seed
Quartered pita bread, other sturdy bread, or raw vegetables for dipping

Add the beans, onion, garlic, and salt to boiling water to cover in a large pot. Reduce heat to a simmer, cover, and simmer about 10 to 20 minutes, or until beans are tender; skim off any foam as needed (pages 111–12). Drain the skimmed bean mixture and move to a food processor bowl or strong blender. Add the cilantro, peanut butter, cumin, hot red pepper, lemon juice, and 1/3 cup of oil. Purée until smooth. Season to taste with salt and pepper. This can be made several days in advance and refrigerated. Drizzle remaining oil on top just before serving, and sprinkle with coriander.

Serve with pita bread, raw vegetables, Sour Cream Brittlebread (page 47), Cornbread Mini-Muffin Tops (page 49), or other crackers.

Variations:

- Add 1 teaspoon chopped fresh mint or dill.
- Substitute white acre peas, black-eyed peas, or peanuts for the butter beans.

FOOD PROCESSOR BLACK-EYED PEA DIP

Makes 1 1/2 cups

THE FOOD PROCESSOR MAKES THIS A 5-MINUTE DISH *if the peas are already cooked. Serve with crackers or tortilla chips.*

1/4 cup fresh parsley
1 teaspoon fresh thyme
2 garlic cloves, peeled
2 cups cooked black-eyed peas or 1 (15-ounce) can black-eyed peas, rinsed and drained, or other cooked field pea
3 tablespoons olive oil, divided
1 tablespoon fresh lemon juice
Salt
Freshly ground black pepper

Chop the herbs and garlic in a food processor fitted with a metal blade. Add peas, 2 tablespoons of the oil, and lemon juice, and process until smooth. Season to taste with salt and pepper.

Move to a bowl and drizzle remaining oil on top. Serve with Sour Cream Brittlebread (page 47), Cornbread Mini-Muffin Tops (page 49), or other crackers.

THROW-TOGETHER CORN AND FIELD PEA DIP

Makes 4 cups

UNIQUE AND VERY EASY, *this can be thrown together the night before the party or even an hour before to let the flavors meld. Fresh raw (green) corn, cooked corn, and canned kernels all work fine in this recipe.*

2 cups cooked field peas with snaps, or 1 (15-ounce) can, rinsed and drained
1 1/2 cups cooked corn or 1 (11-ounce) can white shoepeg corn, drained
1/2 cup peeled, seeded, and diced tomatoes
1 jalapeño pepper or other small hot pepper, seeded and finely chopped
1/4 cup finely chopped onion
1 garlic clove, chopped
2 tablespoons chopped fresh parsley
1/4 cup olive oil
1/4 cup red wine vinegar
2 tablespoons fresh lemon juice
Salt

Toss the peas, corn, tomatoes, pepper, onion, garlic, and parsley in a bowl.

Whisk together oil, vinegar, and lemon juice. Pour over pea mixture and toss. Season to taste with salt. Cover and refrigerate at least 1 hour or overnight.

Drain before serving with Sour Cream Brittlebread (page 47), tortilla chips, or crackers.

CHUNKY EGGPLANT SPREAD

Makes 6 cups

EGGPLANT LOVES THE SOUTHERN CLIMATE AND SOIL; *thus we have an abundance all summer long. It is difficult to brown if not degorged prior to cooking, as the eggplant contains water. If brownness is not essential, proceed as desired.*

1 large eggplant
1/2 cup oil, cook's preference, divided
1 large onion, chopped
1/2 cup diced celery
2 cups peeled whole tomatoes or 1 (15-ounce) can, coarsely chopped
1–2 tablespoons tomato paste, optional
2 tablespoons red wine vinegar
1/3 cup pitted and sliced black olives
Salt
Freshly ground black pepper
2 tablespoons roasted peanuts
1/2 cup raisins

Cut the eggplant into 1/2-inch cubes and degorge (page 200) if desired for browning. Heat 1/4 cup oil in a heavy skillet. Add eggplant and cook in batches, not overcrowding the pan. Stir while cooking and browning; drain on paper towels. Add more oil to the pan as needed.

Add the onion and celery to the oil and cook 5 minutes, or until soft. Return the eggplant to the pot. Add tomatoes, tomato paste, vinegar, and olives. Season to taste with salt and pepper. Simmer for 30 minutes, stirring occasionally.

Refrigerate covered for 30 minutes or up to several days, or freeze in an airtight container. Remove (and defrost if necessary) to a serving dish and top with peanuts and raisins.

Serve with Sour Cream Brittlebread (page 47), Cornbread Mini-Muffin Tops (page 49), or other crackers.

PORK AND THYME SPREAD

Makes 1 1/2 pints

Pork has a forceful personality, *rich and satisfying even when made into this French rillette-like spread. The thyme gives an undercurrent of flavor to the spread. The fat is crucial for spreadability.*

1 1/2 pounds pork from the back, loin, or ribs
1/4 pound pork fat from back, belly, loin, or ribs
3 garlic cloves, chopped, divided
1 tablespoon chopped fresh thyme
Salt
Freshly ground black pepper

Cut the pork into finger-length strips and the fat into 1/4-inch cubes. Cook the fatback over low heat in a large Dutch oven until it renders some fat. Add the pork and enough water to cover the meat, about 1 cup. Partly cover the pan and cook over low heat for 45 minutes without browning, stirring from time to time. Keep adding water as needed to prevent the pork from drying out and browning. When done, the meat should look white and be tender.

Remove meat to a cutting board, saving the liquid and fat. Pull the meat into shreds with two forks or shred in a food processor.

Move to a bowl and add most of the reserved liquid and fat to moisten and flavor. Mix in half the garlic and the remaining ingredients. Taste and add additional garlic as desired and season to taste with additional salt and pepper.

Spoon into pretty jars or pots without packing tightly. Cover with plastic wrap and refrigerate or freeze up to 3 months. Serve with small pieces of French-type bread, toast, crackers, or vegetables like zucchini or rolled small lettuce leaves.

Variation: If only minimal fresh pork fat is available, rinse salt pork, cut into cubes, and add as needed for softness and spreadability.

CHICKEN LIVER PÂTÉ

Serves 6

It is impossible for me to think of Burge Plantation *in east Georgia without thinking of the chicken liver pâté served there for grand summer garden parties or as a prelude to dinners for hungry hunters.*

4 tablespoons butter, divided
1 medium onion, finely chopped
1 garlic clove, chopped
1 cup chicken livers
1 tablespoon bourbon
Thyme
Salt
Freshly ground black pepper
Clarified butter, optional

Melt 2 tablespoons of the butter in a large skillet. Add onion and garlic. Cook on low heat until soft, about 6 minutes. Increase heat to medium, add the livers, and sauté 2 to 3 minutes, until firm. Remove from heat and cool. Coarsely chop the liver mixture with a knife, and move the chopped livers to a sturdy blender or a food processor fitted with the metal blade; process until smooth. Add remaining 2 tablespoons butter and beat into liver mixture. Stir in bourbon and thyme. Season to taste with salt and pepper, making certain the mixture is well flavored. Spoon into ramekins or dishes and smooth the top.

If not serving immediately, cover with optional melted clarified butter. Chill or freeze.

CLARIFYING BUTTER

Melt the butter and chill. When cold, remove and discard the top foam; save the middle clarified portion; remove and discard the bottom milk solids. Store clarified butter in the refrigerator or freezer.

GUACAMOLE

Makes 1 1/2 to 2 cups

Everyone who loves avocados loves guacamole—*and, of course, it can be store-bought, even purchased frozen. But freshly made guacamole from a ripe avocado is a treat.*

1 ripe avocado
1/4 cup chopped onion
1/2 cup finely chopped tomato
2 garlic cloves, very finely chopped
1 teaspoon chopped fresh cilantro leaves
2 teaspoons fresh lime, lemon, or orange juice
Salt
Freshly ground black pepper
1 fresh jalapeño pepper or other small hot pepper, seeded and finely chopped, optional
Hot sauce, optional

Cut the avocado in half, remove the seed, and scoop out the avocado flesh with a spoon or other gadget. Mash the flesh with the fork in a medium bowl.

Add the onion, tomato, garlic, cilantro, and citrus juice; mix well. Season to taste with salt and pepper. Stir in jalapeño and hot sauce if desired.

Cover tightly with plastic wrap and store in the refrigerator. Serve with Sour Cream Brittlebread (page 47) or tortilla chips.

AVOCADOS

Mature Hass avocados are still hard when picked, as they will never ripen on a tree. They must ripen after picking, thus making them easier to ship. (Interestingly, other varieties from the equator do ripen on the tree.) To speed ripening, move the avocados to a brown paper bag for 2 to 3 days. Do not refrigerate.

Avocados turn brown when peeled. A little acid such as lemon juice will prevent browning, but always cover tightly with plastic wrap. Alas, leaving the pit in, as lore suggests, beguiles but doesn't work!

CHARLESTON CILANTRO

"Charleston cilantro" is a commonly used name for the herb also known as "Vietnamese cilantro." It has a rounded leaf that is quite different from the leaf of a cilantro plant, but the taste is similar. Regular cilantro does not like the summer heat, so I frequently use this.

FRESH TROUT DIP

Serves 6 to 8

SOUTHERNERS RELISH SEAFOOD DIPS, *from shrimp paste to blue crab dip, and they have a long history in this part of the country. When we returned from the market with some beautiful fresh rainbow trout, it was harder than originally anticipated to find a dip recipe with fresh trout. Every recipe was for smoked trout. So we made up this recipe and served it in green onion and Gruyère cheese puffs—oh-so good! The clean, sweet taste of fresh trout in this recipe really shines. Served with crackers or on slices of cucumbers, it makes a nice light starter, or pipe into Nathalie's Cream Puffs (page 518).*

2 fresh trout fillets with skin on, deboned
1/2 cup white wine
2 teaspoons chopped fresh thyme
2 tablespoons cream cheese
2 tablespoons mayonnaise
1/2 teaspoon Worcestershire sauce
1/4 teaspoon hot sauce
1 teaspoon salt
Freshly ground black pepper
1 shallot, minced
Grated rind of 1 orange, no white attached

Rinse the fillets and pat dry. Cut each fillet into 3 or 4 pieces and move to a medium saucepan.

Add wine mixed with enough water to cover fish. Bring the liquid to just below a simmer and poach the fish uncovered over low heat, keeping temperature just below a simmer, for 4 to 6 minutes, or until skin peels off easily. Remove and set on a rack over a plate to catch the dripping and allow to cool.

For the dip, whisk together thyme, cheese, mayonnaise, Worcestershire sauce, and hot sauce until smooth. Season to taste with salt and pepper. Add shallot and orange rind.

Break fish into small flakes with fingers, discarding any small bones. Fold into the sauce mixture. Taste for seasoning, adding extra salt or hot sauce as necessary. Serve chilled. Can be made a day ahead and refrigerated.

Variation: Substitute smoked trout for the poached trout.

MARION'S CRAB SPREAD

Makes 2 pounds

MARION SULLIVAN HAS BEEN A FOODIE *for the many years I've known her. She has worked with me on half a dozen books, co-authored* Nathalie Dupree's Shrimp and Grits, *and is an excellent food writer and editor for* Charleston Magazine. *Before that, she catered. True to her style, this spread makes an elegant starter and stars on a buffet table.*

1 pound cream cheese, room temperature
1 celery rib, finely chopped
2 shallots, finely chopped
2 tablespoons fresh lemon juice
2 tablespoons Worcestershire sauce
2 tablespoons horseradish
1 cup tomato sauce or ketchup
1 pound fresh lump crabmeat, picked over and cleaned, with all shell fragments removed

Whip cream cheese with an electric hand mixer until fluffy. Fold in celery and shallots, and spread mixture onto a serving platter, making the shape of a pie with a slight ridge around the edge.

Mix lemon juice, Worcestershire sauce, and horseradish. Add tomato sauce or ketchup. Spread onto cream cheese. Top with crabmeat before serving.

Variation: Substitute 1/4 cup finely chopped fresh fennel for the celery.

COLD SHRIMP PASTE SPREAD

Makes 2 cups

THERE ARE NEARLY HALF A DOZEN RECIPES *for shrimp paste, most falling into two types: a puréed cold spread of cooked shrimp or a baked loaf of mousse-like shrimp paste that is sliced and served hot. The ingredients vary little—only the technique—and are found in most coastal Southern cookbooks like* Charleston Receipts *and* Two Hundred Years of Charleston Cooking. *Variations include celery salt, Worcestershire sauce, mayonnaise, and sherry. This paste is frequently used in shrimp-paste sandwiches, open-faced or closed.*

1 1/2 pounds large shrimp, cooked and peeled (pages 326–27)
1 1/2 cups butter, room temperature
3/4 teaspoon salt
Freshly ground white or black pepper
1/2 teaspoon ground hot red pepper
1/4 teaspoon freshly grated nutmeg
Lettuce leaves or other greens

Process the shrimp in a food processor or blender until puréed and paste-like. Remove to a separate bowl.

Beat the butter until soft and white. Stir the butter into the shrimp, season with salt, white or black pepper, hot red pepper, and nutmeg; stir until smooth.

Cover and refrigerate. When ready to serve, surround with toast points or crackers, or wrap in lettuce leaves or collard greens.

HOT OR COLD SHRIMP PASTE

Makes 3 cups

THIS IS THE OTHER OF THE TWO FAMOUS SHRIMP "PASTES," *but it's technically a terrine. My fondest memories are of it being served by a group of Charleston, South Carolina, men who gather monthly to hear scholarly lectures and discussions. Once a year, ladies are invited and the men prepare a great feast including shrimp paste. After the repast, the group gathers at the foot of the mansion's steps, next to the Battery, and proceeds to march around downtown Charleston holding flaming torches, with hired police to escort them. It is great fun to see the tourists agog at such shenanigans and know there is no meaning to the march besides just fun.*

1 1/4 pounds large shrimp, cooked and peeled (pages 326–27)
1 cup butter
Dash of nutmeg
Salt
Freshly ground black pepper

Preheat oven to 350 degrees.

Process the shrimp in a food processor or blender until puréed and paste-like. Remove to a separate bowl.

Beat the butter with an electric hand mixer until soft and white. Stir the butter into the shrimp, season with nutmeg, and salt and pepper to taste, and stir until smooth.

Instead of chilling, move to a buttered loaf pan and bake until the paste comes away from the sides and is firm to the touch. Go around the sides with a knife, cover with a plate, and invert. Tap the pan gently if needed.

Slice and serve hot, or chill overnight and serve cold. Accompany with crackers or toast, or wrapped in lettuce leaves or other greens.

GRINDING SHRIMP

The shrimp in these pastes, or pâtés, are very finely ground. In France, they would be rubbed through a fine sieve. The cooked shrimp can also be put through a meat grinder twice, cleaning out the grinder with a biscuit in between grindings, or pounded with a mortar and pestle until finely ground. Food processors now make short work of this once arduous task.

Variation: Add a bit of chopped fresh lemon thyme or fresh basil in the summer.

PIMENTO CHEESE

Makes 3 cups

AS EVERY SOUTHERNER KNOWS, *this is pronounced "pimentacheese," as if it were one word. Every pimentacheese recipe is different—some chunky, some smooth. Most favor their mother's or grandmother's recipe. My husband prefers it made with Duke's mayonnaise. It keeps at least a week in the refrigerator. Process the mixture longer for a smooth spread that can be used as a dip or piped onto crackers or celery sticks. It's not bad slathered between slices of fried green tomatoes either.*

12 ounces grated Cheddar cheese
2 (4-ounce) jars pimento, drained, or Charred Red Peppers (page 223)
1 cup mayonnaise
Salt
Freshly ground black pepper

Pulse cheese, pimento, and mayonnaise in a food processor fitted with the metal blade. Process until slightly chunky but spreadable. Season to taste with salt and pepper.

Variation: Use half sharp Cheddar and half white Cheddar, grated.

Variation: Lulu Paste
To make Richmond's Lulu Paste, add 1 small chopped onion, 1/2 cup ketchup, and a pinch of dry mustard in the food processor with the cheese, pimento, and mayonnaise.

Make a BLT using pimento cheese instead of mayonnaise.

MARINATED OLIVES

Makes 2 cups

WHEN THE TREE IN MY FRONT YARD *is brimming with the tiniest of olives, I think of the ways I can flavor them. Of course, having one's own tree is not necessary, as this works with any cured olive. There are hundreds of variations.*

2 cups brine-cured unpitted olives, such as kalamata
1/3 cup olive oil
1 bay leaf
4 sprigs fresh rosemary
4 garlic cloves, sliced
1 teaspoon grated lemon rind, no white attached

Heat the oil, bay leaf, rosemary sprigs, and garlic over very low heat in a small saucepan until just warmed through. Set aside to cool.

Move the olives to a serving bowl, plastic ziplock bag, or other container. Pour cooled oil mixture over olives. Sprinkle with lemon rind.

Refrigerate olives until ready to serve, at least 12 hours for best flavor, 2 or 3 days for better flavor, and store refrigerated up to several weeks.

BUTTERED PECANS

Makes 4 cups

BUTTERED PECAN HALVES MAKE A VISITOR FEEL WELCOME. *Salt can make pecans weepy over a period of time, so store them unsalted and then salt them shortly before serving.*

4 cups shelled pecan halves, about 1 pound
1 cup salted butter, melted
Salt

Preheat oven to 250 degrees. Line 2 rimmed baking sheets with aluminum foil or parchment paper.

Toss the pecans in a bowl with the butter. Spread pecans on the prepared baking sheets. Bake for 1 hour, stirring occasionally, until the pecans are a nice brown but not burned. Remove from the oven.

If serving right away, add salt to taste. Otherwise, cool and store tightly covered. Serve as is, or reheat briefly and add salt while hot.

Variation: Spicy Toasted Pecans
Stir together 2 teaspoons paprika, 1 teaspoon onion powder, 1/2 teaspoon hot red pepper, 2 teaspoons ground cumin, and 2 teaspoons granulated sugar. Sprinkle this seasoning mix over the buttered pecans before spreading out on prepared baking sheets. Bake at 300 degrees for 25 minutes.

LOUIS LIMESTONE'S ROASTED PEANUTS

Quantity as desired

ROASTED PEANUTS HAVE A PLACE OF THEIR OWN *in Southern hearts and on Southern tables. They stand on their own at ball games and in bars, and are added to everything from sweets to . . . nuts. Roasting in the shell gives a more intense flavor.*

Fresh peanuts, in shell

Preheat oven to 350 degrees.

Spread peanuts in a single layer on a rimmed baking sheet. Bake 30 minutes, turning frequently. Serve hot, warm, or at room temperature. If storing, remove from shell and keep airtight.

The peanut had a circuitous route from South America to Africa, then returning here with the early slave ships to feed the slaves on board. Originally only slaves planted and ate peanuts, as they were disregarded by others, who fed them to animals such as the pig. It was during the Civil War that they became revered by Southerners dependent on them as a valuable source of nutrition. Southern soldiers wrote songs about peanuts, and Union soldiers were introduced to them as well.

JULIUS'S PEANUTS WITH HOT PEPPERS

Makes 1/2 pound

Julius Waring Walker was an ambassador *to Liberia and Upper Volta, and lived in other African countries as well. He sent me this recipe, which is served there. I use canned roasted peanuts. Although they "last forever," Julius says, they won't last long on the party table. Very tasty indeed!*

- 1/2 pound dry roasted peanuts
- 2–3 dried hot peppers, seeded and finely chopped
- 1 teaspoon salt, optional

Toss the peanuts and peppers together. Move to glass jars and cover tightly. Add salt as needed before serving.

BOILED PEANUTS

These are a treat unknown in many parts of the country where perhaps pretzels reign. But my memories of fraternity parties include mainly boiled peanuts and beer. The volume of peanut shells left on the floor was a matter of honor—as in, "We had five loads of beer cans and fifteen bags of peanut shells to take to the dump."

Although I enjoy the occasional boiled peanut, I don't dream about eating them. I think mostly men dream about them. My husband will insist on stopping any time he passes the boiled peanut stand by the side of the road, particularly if an old iron wash pot is atop a fire.

Wash freshly harvested (green) peanuts in a mild solution of kitchen detergent. Rinse in clear water. Cover peanuts with a medium brine (10 ounces of salt to 1 gallon of water) in a large saucepan. Bring to the boil, reduce heat, and simmer for 45 minutes or up to 2 hours, testing occasionally, until kernels are tender. (The time may vary greatly.) Taste for saltiness. Rinse immediately or allow to sit in brine an additional 15 minutes. Pour off water and drain before serving. Peanuts are ready for shelling and eating immediately; however, they can be refrigerated for up to 5 days or frozen and reheated in the microwave. They are best piping hot. If using older peanuts, the cooking time will be longer.

SALADS

Within the last thirty years, salads have gained prominence on the Southern table, with ingredients such as corn, cherry tomatoes, and butter beans interspersed and mixed in numerous new ways. Although the South was agrarian for so long, there were those who did not view any cold meal—except some Sunday-night suppers of sliced meat and tomatoes—as a "real" meal. We learned a lot from the food renaissances that swept the nation in the late twentieth century, and our notion of salads has broadened considerably.

The salads of my youth were quite different from the ones I eat now. The once ubiquitous julienned ham salad, whose city-ham was cut in finger-thick strips, is hardly seen anymore. Green salads, mostly iceberg, were used as simple starters on restaurant tables, plunked down for the ravenous to eat while waiting for an order. Potato salads, cole slaw, and sliced tomatoes were side or picnic salads. Shrimp, tuna, and chicken salad were sandwiched between slices of white bread for serving at lunch tables and drugstore counters, or in fancy triangles for teas, parties, and weddings. Reconfigured on lettuce, they became Sunday suppers.

The Southern climate, with the exception of the mountain areas such as Appalachia, accommodates two, and on rare occasion, three plantings of many crops. Where once canned ingredients might have worked their way into our diets in foods such as ambrosia and curried fruit, now fresh and dried are available all year long, with their increased flavor and personalities.

Alice Waters introduced small lettuces and greens—such as arugula, already being used in Europe—to America in the 1970s, most notably at the first gathering of American chefs to form what became American Cuisine. With the exception of very cold and very hot months, fresh salad ingredients such as tiny sweet peas, cabbage, and lettuces in spring and fall are widely available in our cottage and market gardens, even growing in baskets swinging from our porches and piazzas, where petunias and pansies once ruled. In the lower South, lettuce, broccoli, and other greens grow from September to May with only rare touches of frost to disturb them. Bibb—originally grown in caves and shipped—still claims the heart of those of us who love a tender green with a mild, refreshing taste.

When I moved to Georgia from London, the most reliable lettuce to buy was a red-tipped, and I served it nearly year-round in my restaurant. It was a mild lettuce, as opposed to radicchio and some other completely red lettuces.

Salads are more than accompaniments to a meal. Shrimp, other seafood, cold meats, and chicken, even if pulled from a store-purchased rotisserie chicken, are added to salads with abandon. Diners feel virtuous for the alleged calorie consciousness of eating "salad." There is considerable variation and increasing cultural permission to experiment and diversify these cold plates—serving some of them with hot fried chicken or oysters on top as if to proclaim their healthiness.

Fresh is the operative word for most salads, although we've added a few old-time favorites. Some salads are made from leftovers. Don't feel constrained to relegate ingredients rigidly. I frequently sprinkle my green salads with a bit of barley, quinoa, lentils, or other ingredients to add a bit more nutrition.

AMBROSIA

Serves 8 to 10

IS THIS A SALAD OR A DESSERT? *Who cares? We put it on the holiday table with the main course, and it's usually the last thing eaten before dessert. I must confess, however, that I wait for my daughter, Audrey, to arrive and peel and segment the oranges. Reserve peels if desired, and use for Candied Orange Rinds (page 627). It is the food of the gods, but Southerners have been serving it with coconut since the late 1800s.*

15 oranges
1 pineapple
1 cup unsweetened shredded coconut
2 bananas

Peel the oranges, removing the rind and the white pith coating completely. Segment the oranges over a bowl to catch the juices, releasing the orange sections and juice into the bowl, discarding the peel, pith, seeds, and membrane (page 62).

Cut off both ends of the pineapple and remove the peel. Cut the pineapple in half lengthwise and again lengthwise. Slice off the core from each quarter section. Cut each section into chunks and add to the bowl.

Toss cut-up fruit with shredded coconut and refrigerate at least 1 hour. Peel and slice bananas; toss with the fruit just before serving.

Variation: Add sliced strawberries, grapes, or other fruit in season.

WORKING WITH CITRUS FRUITS

Segmenting—Dividing a citrus fruit, such as an orange or grapefruit, into segments removes all the unwanted elements—peel, white pith, seeds, and membrane—and leaves the beautiful segmented fruit.

Slice off the top and bottom of the orange and turn a cut surface of the orange down onto a grooved cutting board (to catch the juices). Use a serrated paring knife to slice off sections of peel, starting at the top and following the curve of the orange down to the bottom, keeping the knife as close as possible to the fruit to remove the white pith, along with the peel. Carefully check and cut off any remaining white pith.

Hold the orange over a bowl in the palm of one hand and the knife in the other hand. Slide the knife against a membrane down to the center of the orange to release the segment from the membrane. Continue slicing on either side of each membrane. Loosen any stubborn segment by slightly twisting the knife against the core of the membrane to release the segment. Continue until all the segments are removed. Discard the peel, white pith, seeds, and membrane.

Storing—Most whole citrus can be stored at room temperature for up to 2 weeks, which also yields the most aroma and juice.

Maximizing the amount of juice—To get the most juice from an orange, lemon, or lime, first soften it by rolling the fruit in or under hot water or piercing it with a knife or fork and microwaving it for up to 30 seconds. My grandmother always rolled citrus gently on the counter under her palms until the inside was soft. Turns out that works too—whether room temperature or heated as above. Chefs do fancy things, like squeezing halves of small citrus with their hands, holding them over a bowl with the cut side facing inward, trapping the seeds between their fingers and releasing the juices. I keep several things handy to juice, a small hand press with a reamer surrounded with a sieve to allow the juice go through and trap the seeds into a matching cup below, and a wooden gadget that does a quick job at juicing, but not straining. There are electric and other gadgets.

Storing fresh-squeezed citrus juice—Store, preferably refrigerated, in a glass container with a tight lid, up to three days. The vitamin C is retained for up to a day.

Peeling citrus—The peel of a citrus frequently has more flavor than the juice, so don't be quick to discard it. It is easier to secure the rind before it is juiced. The pith, although bitter, includes pectin (an aid in setting marmalade). For most dishes, gentle grating, zesting, or peeling, taking care to remove just the outer layer and not the white pith, excludes the bitterness. Excess peel stores very well, dried, frozen, or canned.

CITRUS, FENNEL, AND PEPPER SALAD TOPPED WITH GOAT CHEESE

Serves 4 to 6

PERHAPS IT WAS THE PRESENCE OF AN ORANGE *in the toe of my Christmas stocking each year that makes me crave the freshness of citrus in the winter. It is easy to find jars of roasted peppers, and the two combine to make a cheerful colorful combination as welcome in the winter months as in the summer. Another name for shaved fennel is fennel slaw.*

1 red grapefruit, peeled and segmented (page 62)
1 white grapefruit, peeled and segmented
1 orange, peeled and segmented
1 fennel bulb, shaved (page 202)
1 roasted red bell pepper, torn into 1/2-inch strips (page 223)
1 small red onion, thinly sliced
1–2 tablespoons olive oil
1–2 tablespoons fresh lime juice
Grated rind of 1 lime, no white attached
1 garlic clove, chopped
Salt
Freshly ground black pepper
Granulated sugar
1/2 cup crumbled soft goat cheese
1–2 green onions, chopped
2 teaspoons chopped fresh herbs, optional

Toss the grapefruit and orange segments, fennel, pepper strips, and onion together in a large bowl.

Whisk together the oil, lime juice, lime rind, and garlic in a small bowl. Toss the dressing with the fruit mixture. Season to taste with salt, pepper, and sugar.

Sprinkle the salad with cheese, green onion, and herbs. Cover tightly with plastic wrap and refrigerate for at least 1 hour. Serve cold.

Being a Florida girl, born in Jacksonville to a mother born in Miami and a grandmother born in Ponte Vedra, citrus has always been a big part of my culinary story. Leaving Florida behind for new ventures in Texas, California, and New York with my parents and sister during our formative years, a much-beloved Christmas tradition began when my grandfather would send a large box of Florida citrus to our homesick family, packed carefully, with the pages of the Sunday edition of the *Florida Times-Union* cradling the hand-selected jewels. Papa would head out to the farmers market near the railroad tracks downtown to begin his search for the thin-skinned, heavy globes of oranges and grapefruit selected for their near-ripeness and ability to withstand the long-distance shipping. His weekly phone call would announce that the heavy brown box had been shipped, and we would wait anxiously for its arrival, sometimes up to ten days later. Papa kept up the tradition long after my mother passed away, even sending the boxes to our college dorms, and later on, to our newlywed apartments then family homes. Knowing we could buy delicious citrus in our own markets did not deter his desire for us to keep our ties to home, and the boxes came, still hand-selected and packaged with love, until he passed away at age 85.

—Cynthia

LOG CABIN SALAD

Serves 4

Mrs. Henrietta Dull recommends this banana salad *in* Southern Cooking *(1928). It has served generations of delighted children and adults. The proportions of the ingredients can be varied as needed. This is the kind of salad I grew up loving. Any kind of sturdy lettuce will do, whether the traditional iceberg or a romaine or endive.*

2 bananas
1/2 cup orange juice
1/2 cup chopped nuts, optional
Lettuce
Fresh or dried cherries, pineapple, grapefruit, cut into bite-sized pieces, optional
1/2 cup mayonnaise, sour cream, or yogurt

Peel and cut the bananas lengthwise into fourths, move to a bowl, and allow to soak in the orange juice for 1 hour.

Roll banana pieces in the chopped nuts if desired, and then arrange log cabin–style on lettuce. Place any bite-sized fruit as desired in the center. Serve with mayonnaise, sour cream, or yogurt.

PEACH SALAD

Serves 4

Peanuts and peaches overlap in seasons, *and like cozying up in this salad. Local lettuce and spinach are woefully out of season in much of the South at peach time, so they are optional. To avoid puckering up, only the ripest of peaches should be served where there is no sweetener.*

2 peaches
Lettuce or spinach, optional
1/2 cup goat, cream, or Neufchatel cheese
1/2 cup roasted and salted peanuts
2–3 tablespoons chopped basil, mint, or lemon balm
1/2 cup Basic Vinaigrette (page 105) optional

If the peach skin is pretty, leave it on; otherwise remove it. Halve the peaches lengthwise and remove the pits. Turn the peach halves onto their flat sides and cut into wedges.

Move the peaches onto the lettuce or into a bowl. Crumble the cheese and sprinkle on top, followed by peanuts and herbs. Serve the optional vinaigrette separately.

Variation:

- Substitute 2 mangos for the peaches.
- Mrs. Henrietta Dull uses a dressing of 1 cup heavy cream and 1/4 cup French dressing, which seems to be gilding the lily.

CARAMELIZED PEACH SALAD

Serves 4

THIS SALAD IS A SOUTHERN RIFF *on Italian melon and prosciutto. I learned how to caramelize peaches from Chef Frank Lee of Charleston's S.N.O.B. restaurant, who uses them on salad. I wait all year for the freestone peaches to be perfect, so they can be split evenly and caramelized on their smooth surfaces. I try to catch every bit of peach juice I can! If clingstone peaches are all that are available, cut around the pit. I prefer using sherry vinegar in this vinaigrette for this salad.*

2–3 peaches, preferably freestone
1/4–1/2 cup light or dark brown sugar
2 cups arugula, mixed herbs, or spring mix
1/3 cup Basic Vinaigrette (page 105)
1/2 cup soft goat cheese, divided
1/4 cup Buttered Pecans (page 58), chopped or left whole
4 slices country ham (page 409), julienned

If the skin is pretty, leave it on; otherwise remove it. Halve the peaches lengthwise, or if large, cut into thirds or quarters. Pat the exposed surface of peach halves on a paper towel before smooshing into brown sugar. Move to a hot griddle, grill, or heavy pan, and cook several minutes, until the sugar melts and begins to caramelize.

Meanwhile, toss the greens with the vinaigrette. Arrange on a serving dish or divide onto individual dishes and sprinkle with a portion of the goat cheese, all of the pecans, and the ham. Move the peach halves, cut side up, on top of the salad greens and sprinkle with remaining goat cheese. Serve right away.

Variation: Omit the ham and/or substitute fresh figs for the peaches.

CARAMELIZED PINEAPPLE SALAD

Serves 6

THIS RECIPE WAS DEVELOPED FOR SERVING *inside a Crown Roast of Pork (page 401), but it will brighten up any meal when ripe pineapple is available. There are many other ways to cut a pineapple and caramelize it, so search around for a favorite. It caramelizes without added sugar, it is so sweet. I confess I don't toss away the pineapple core—I snack on it. To each his own!*

1 pineapple, peeled, top reserved
2–3 tablespoons butter, melted
1/3 cup fresh lemon juice or white wine vinegar
1 teaspoon Dijon mustard
1 cup olive oil
Salt
Freshly ground black pepper
Granulated sugar
1 cup freshly chopped mint or lemon balm, optional

Cut the pineapple into 1- to 2-inch chunks. Dab the pineapple pieces with melted butter.

Heat a griddle, grill, or heavy skillet. When hot, add the pineapple in batches, not crowding the pan, and sauté until caramelized on one side. Turn with tongs or a metal spatula to caramelize on all sides.

Whisk together the lemon juice or vinegar and mustard in a medium bowl. While whisking, slowly drizzle in the olive oil and continue whisking until emulsified (page 102). Season to taste with salt, pepper, and sugar.

When all pineapple chunks are brown on both sides, add to the vinaigrette with half the chopped mint or lemon balm if using; garnish with the rest. If using for a crown roast, pile into the center and top with the pineapple crown.

Variation: For a sweet dessert or tart, sprinkle with 1/2 to 3/4 cup of brown sugar, using half on each side of the pineapple.

ROASTING PINEAPPLE

Preheat oven to 400 degrees. Line a rimmed baking sheet with aluminum foil or parchment paper.

Cut pineapple into desired shapes. Melt 2 to 3 tablespoons butter. Dot the pineapple with half the melted butter.

Roast until golden brown, about 10 to 15 minutes, and turn with tongs. Dot with any remaining butter; return to the oven until brown on the second side, about 5 to 10 minutes. Remove, saving any rendered juices.

PREPARING PINEAPPLE

To cut off the rind, slice off the top and bottom. Stand the pineapple on one of the now flat ends and cut down the exterior of the pineapple, ignoring the eyes. Use a small knife or the tip of a vegetable peeler to flick off the eyes.

To cut into chunks or to make a pineapple boat, slice off the top and bottom of the pineapple and slice the pineapple in half. Cut the pineapple off the rind, discarding the core as desired. If making a "boat," fill the remaining boat-like rind with pineapple or other ingredients.

To cut into rings, turn the pared pineapple on its side and slice into horizontal rings. Remove the core with a small biscuit cutter or a paring knife. Cut into half-circles for tarts and other decorative uses.

To cut into long slices, stand the pared pineapple on end and slice from top to bottom in the desired thickness. Cut out the core if desired. The thinner the strips, the quicker they will brown and the easier they will "break up" when moving and turning. Long slices make an attractive garnish when used as "spokes" around a plate and topped with other ingredients.

PINEAPPLE AND CHEESE SALAD

Serves 8

WHEN I WAS A TEENAGER, *I had a wonderful friend with a gorgeous figure who insisted we both needed to diet. (I weighed 105 pounds at 5 feet 4 1/2 inches tall, and she not much more.) We ate this salad with cottage cheese, touted as a diet salad, for two weeks solid. I can't remember if we lost weight or not, but I do know it was several years before I ate it again. At the time, we ate it with canned pineapple, which held the cottage cheese securely in its ring, but the fresh is now readily available and goes well with goat cheese as it did with cottage cheese.*

1 fresh pineapple, peeled (page 66)
1/4 pound plain goat, cream, or cottage cheese
1 head leaf lettuce or 1 (10-ounce) bag spinach
1 cup mayonnaise
1 cup heavy cream
Salt
Freshly ground black pepper
Dash ground hot red pepper

Cut the pineapple into bite-sized pieces. This can be done ahead of time and refrigerated.

Crumble or beat the cheese lightly and sprinkle onto the pineapple. Just before serving, spoon onto a platter lined with the lettuce or spinach.

Mix the mayonnaise and cream. Spoon the mayonnaise dressing over the pineapple. Season to taste with salt, pepper, and ground red pepper. Serve at once.

Variation: Use caramelized pineapple, page 66.

FROZEN FRUIT SALAD

Serves 8

THIS SALAD DATES BACK TO THE MIDDLE OF THE TWENTIETH CENTURY *and was very popular in Southern tearooms, at ladies lunches, and for church suppers because it was a cooling cross between a dessert and a salad and handy for making ahead. I still like it but have updated it using dried cherries rather than maraschinos.*

1 (8-ounce) package cream cheese, softened
1/4 cup sorghum or maple syrup
1 cup heavy cream
1 (20-ounce) can crushed pineapple, drained
1 banana, sliced into rounds
1/2 cup chopped dates or figs
1/2 cup dried cherries
1/2 cup chopped pecans
1 tablespoon grated lemon rind, no white attached
Lettuce leaves
Cheese Straws (page 48), optional

Line an 8-inch square pan with plastic wrap.

Beat cream cheese and syrup in a medium bowl until well blended and fluffy.

Separately whip the cream until soft peaks form. Add to the cream cheese mixture and fold together thoroughly.

Gently fold in the fruits, pecans, and lemon rind. Spoon the mixture into the lined pan. Cover and freeze at least 8 hours, or until firm.

Remove from the dish and divide into portions. Serve on lettuce leaves with optional Cheese Straws (page 48).

NATHALIE'S WATERMELON SALAD

Serves 4 to 6

WATERMELON HAS ALWAYS BEEN A STAPLE *at Southern cookouts. This is a spectacular addition with a crumble of salty feta and a handful of fresh, sweet blueberries that are also in season. It makes a beautiful red, white, and blue salad that's ever-so-yummy and healthy. Other berries can be used, but they should be sturdy so they don't break up. Strawberries will work better than raspberries, for instance.*

1 teaspoon Dijon mustard
1 teaspoon honey
2 tablespoons red or sherry wine vinegar
1/2 cup olive oil
Salt
Freshly ground black pepper
Fresh herbs to taste, such as chopped fresh basil, thyme, or rosemary
2 cups arugula, mâche, or baby spinach
2–3 cups cubed watermelon
1 pint blueberries
6 ounces feta cheese, crumbled

Whisk the mustard and honey with vinegar in a small bowl. While whisking, slowly drizzle in the olive oil and continue whisking until emulsified (page 102). Season to taste with salt and pepper. Add fresh herbs from the garden if available.

Toss to coat the greens with the dressing (reserve any extra dressing), and divide among 4 to 6 serving plates with the watermelon, blueberries, and cheese.

If using for a cookout, assemble salad ingredients together in a large serving bowl and dress just before serving. Pass extra dressing if desired.

SELECTING AND SLICING A WATERMELON

Look for a firm, symmetrical melon that is filled out at the blossom end, has a dull (rather than shiny) surface, and shows a yellow, white, or pale green to yellow underside. A ripe melon will last 4 days in a cool place or a week when refrigerated.

My husband says his family always took their watermelons to the ice man's, where he kept it until chilled or frozen, gratis, until picked up and taken home to eat, icy cold.

The easiest way to slice a watermelon is to cut it in half horizontally, then slice each half lengthwise. Using a sharp knife, turn the blade to where the red meat of the watermelon meets the white rind and slice down the length of the watermelon. To cut into triangles, slice vertically; otherwise, cut into cubes.

WALDORF SALAD

Serves 4 to 6

MRS. DULL'S 1928 EDITION OF Southern Cooking *includes this salad, and legions of Southerners grew up thinking it was Southern, even though it originated elsewhere. Leaving the apple unpeeled, as we did at home, adds color and nutrition. Our family always added raisins, but the nuts came and went, depending on the time of year and availability. The amounts in this recipe are just general guides, as it is never the same twice, being dependent upon the size and variety of apples.*

1–2 Red Delicious apples, or any other crisp, sweet red apple
1/2 cup mayonnaise
1/4 cup heavy cream, optional
2 ribs celery
1/4 cup chopped blanched pecans, walnuts, almonds, or other nuts, optional
1/4 cup raisins
Squeeze of fresh lemon juice, optional
Lettuce or spinach leaves, optional

Cut the apples into wedges and mix with the mayonnaise in a bowl. Add a little cream if the mayonnaise seems too stiff.

String and chop the celery into 1/4-inch cubes; stir into the apple mixture along with the nuts and raisins. Taste and add a bit of fresh lemon juice if desired.

Cover and refrigerate until ready to use. Serve in a bowl, or put lettuce leaves on plates and top with the salad.

Variation: Add chunks of banana, like we always did at home. Chicken or ham, too!

CUTTING AN APPLE

There are several ways of coring and wedging an apple.

- Cut the apple in half, insert a melon baller or spoon into the center of the half, and make an indentation sufficient to remove the seeds. Make a V at either end with a knife to remove the stem and blossom ends. Put the flat side of the apple half down on the cutting board, and cut into wedges.
- Core the apple first, using an apple corer, then split the apple in half and slice it in wedges, as above. Or use an all-in-one apple corer and slicer.
- Stand the apple on the end opposite the stem (the blossom end) and cut straight down on one side of the core, then the other. Slice each half in wedges, as above. If any apple remains on the core, slice it off and cut into a wedge or two if possible.

SALAD GREENS AND LETTUCES

From tender baby lettuces to sturdy head lettuces, the greens of a salad are as varied as an artist's palette. Iceberg was once the most common green salad served, particularly in restaurants, but it has thankfully been displaced by Boston, Bibb, escarole, frisée, mâche, romaine, radicchio, red leaf, and others. By far the best tasting lettuces are those picked fresh from the garden or purchased from the local farmers market. Plastic boxes and bags of salad mixes are popular items in the produce section but must be eyed carefully for rotting leaves before purchasing and used within a couple of days once purchased. Mesclun mix is a popular mix of little wild greens and lettuces, but as there is no standard for what it contains, I much prefer combining my own.

Arugula is a new green to the South, and it thrives in our soil and heat. In England it is called rocket, and in Italy it is rucola. It can be eaten alone, mixed with other greens, or used as a bed or topping for ingredients from fish to other vegetables.

Washing salad greens—Salad greens are delicate, so they should be added to a large bowl or pan of cold water rather than being run under the faucet, where they will crack, creating teeny holes that make the salad soggy after the vinaigrette is added. After gently stirring the greens in the cold water, let them rest. Pick them up and put into a colander. There will be dirt and sand in the bottom of the bowl, so avoid dumping the whole shebang into a colander and adding the dirt back in! Usually the greens will have to be rinsed the same way a second time. Check for grit—there is nothing worse—and if necessary, repeat a third time. Salad spinners work well as long as the fragile greens are not whirred in a sudden frenzy. I usually pat them dry in a tea towel, wrap, and refrigerate. In the restaurant I would layer them in the tea towels in the refrigerator crisper. Shirley Corriher shared a marvelous trick of putting them into a plastic bag and sucking out the excess air with a straw. This helps them last much longer.

Building a salad—Salad greens are only the beginning to a great salad. Fresh herbs, vegetables, fruit, and nuts all add color, texture, and taste to a salad. Delicate herbs such as basil, parsley, and tarragon mix well in a salad, whereas woody herbs like rosemary are less pleasing due to their texture. Fresh or cooked vegetables add crunch and color. Fresh fruit (even grilled or caramelized) brings a touch of sweetness, and nuts (raw or roasted) add more crunch.

When preparing the salad greens, tear (do not cut) the leaves into pieces large enough to pierce with a fork, but not too small, as smaller pieces absorb too much dressing and wilt quickly. Cutting the leaves with a knife or scissors bruises the leaves. Count on about two handfuls of greens per person for a starter salad or one that is served with a meal. A meal salad would increase to three or so handfuls per person.

GATHERED GREENS SALAD

Serves 10

IDEAL FOR A BUFFET, *I gather greens well suited to dried fruits, especially figs, cherries, or cranberries, and fresh pears.*

1/2 teaspoon fennel seed
1/4 cup sherry or red wine vinegar
1 teaspoon Dijon mustard
3/4 cup olive oil
Salt
Freshly ground black pepper
1/3–1/2 chopped dried figs, cherries, or cranberries
1–2 Bosc pears, peeled and sliced
4 cups baby spinach, red leaf lettuce, and/or Bibb lettuce
4 cups young arugula leaves
1 cup mixed herb leaves: lemon balm, mint, thyme, and/or basil
1 fennel bulb, sliced, optional
1/2 cup toasted pecan pieces, optional
3/4 cup croutons, optional
1/2 cup sliced or roughly grated Parmesan cheese

Coarsely grind the fennel seed with a mortar and pestle or electric grinder.

Whisk together the vinegar, mustard, and ground fennel seed in a small bowl. While whisking, slowly drizzle in the olive oil and continue whisking until emulsified (page 102). Season to taste with salt and pepper.

Add figs and pears to the dressing to soften the figs and keep the pears from turning color.

Toss the cleaned and stemmed greens with the herbs and fennel.

When ready to serve, remove fruit from dressing with a slotted spoon and toss with greens. Usually this is enough dressing for the whole salad. Add enough of the remaining dressing to coat the greens and season to taste with salt and pepper. Toss well with the pecans and croutons if using, and cheese, and serve.

Variations: Arugula, Fig, and Pecan Salad
Make Honey Vinaigrette (page 105), increase figs to 8, and omit pears. Substitute the Parmesan with lemon Stilton cheese. Adding 2 cups shredded duck, chicken, or seafood makes it lunch.

ARUGULA

I use the two types of arugula that grow in my garden almost year-round. Others are available in plastic containers in the produce section of most local grocery stores. A good substitute is the herb mix available in plastic boxes in the produce section. Any crumbled cheese, particularly soft goat cheese, will be amiable. To enhance the lemon flavor, grate lemon rind into the salad.

BLUEBERRY ARUGULA SALAD

Serves 4

BLUEBERRIES MAKE A WELCOME ADDITION *when sprinkled on any salad, but arugula stands up particularly well to both the weight of the blueberries and the saltiness of the feta in this summer salad.*

1 tablespoon red wine vinegar
1/4 teaspoon Dijon mustard
1/4 teaspoon granulated sugar
3 tablespoons olive oil
Salt
Freshly ground black pepper
5 cups arugula or baby greens
1/2 cup chopped pecans, toasted
1 cup blueberries or other berries
4 ounces crumbled feta cheese

Whisk together vinegar, mustard, and sugar in a small bowl. While whisking, slowly drizzle in the olive oil and continue whisking until emulsified (page 102). Season to taste with salt and pepper.

Toss arugula, pecans, blueberries, and feta together in large serving bowl. Toss ingredients with enough dressing to lightly coat arugula, and serve.

Variation: Orange, Arugula, and Avocado Salad
Omit the pecans, blueberries, and feta cheese. Add 2 peeled and sliced navel oranges and 1 sliced ripe avocado. Drizzle with dressing just before serving.

Variation: Ham and Figs on Arugula Salad
Arrange 4 ounces of diced country ham or prosciutto and 1 cup diced fresh figs on top of the arugula. Sprinkle with 1 tablespoon fresh lemon juice.

Variation: Add 1/3 cup of shredded cooked chicken, ham, shrimp, or crabmeat to the salad for a light meal.

BLUEBERRIES

Plump, the size of dried beans, and dark blue to purple in color, highbush blueberries are the fresh and frozen blueberries you'll find in your local grocery store. Harvested by hand or machine, highbush varieties are commercially grown in 38 states, Canada, and South America. Maine's smaller wild blueberries have a more intense flavor, but harvesting them is labor-intensive, so they sport a higher price tag and, consequently, are commonly found frozen and in commercially processed foods but are rarely sold fresh outside the state.

SALAD OF BABY GREENS

Serves 6 to 8

Modern greens are frequently sold prewashed. *Since I grow most of my own, I wash them as I would any green (page 70). In making a green salad, use one or all of the following: baby turnip or spinach greens; arugula; red leaf, Bibb, Boston, or other tender lettuces; and as many whole herbs as are tasty on their own. Chop whatever herbs need chopping and add them.*

5 cups baby greens
1–2 tablespoons whole or chopped fresh basil, thyme, oregano, tarragon, lemon balm, and/or mint
1/3–1/2 cup Basic Vinaigrette (page 105)

Toss the cleaned and dried greens with the chopped herbs and vinaigrette just before serving.

DRESSING A SALAD

Dress a green salad just before serving, to prevent the leaves from wilting and browning from acid in the vinaigrette. Add the salad to a large, wide bowl and drizzle dressing on top. Toss to coat the leaves lightly in dressing. Add more dressing as needed. Remove individual portions to individual serving plates after tossing to keep the leaves from getting soggy from sitting in the extra dressing.

COLLARD OR TURNIP GREENS SALAD

Serves 2

Collards and turnip greens have varied lives. *My favorite former husband's stepmother ate both in salads in the spring and the late fall, when the greens were small and tender. She even eschewed any dressing and just ate them plain. As time goes on, they have a brief window when they can be rolled up like a cigar and shredded and added to other salads, as we do with arugula. They can also be substituted for dandelion and other bitter greens. Then they pass into the bitter vegetable stage and need to be blanched, sautéed, or long cooked. By all means, try the variations as they put the salad over the top!*

1 cup baby collard or turnip greens, washed (page 205)
1/2 cup Basic Vinaigrette (page 105)
Salt
Freshly ground black pepper

Remove any stems from the greens and toss the washed, dried greens with enough vinaigrette to coat lightly. Season to taste with salt and pepper.

Variations:

- Add 1/4 to 1/3 cup crumbled goat, cream or Boursin cheese.
- Add 1/4 to 1/3 cup Buttered Pecans (page 58) or peanuts.
- Add 1/4 to 1/3 cup slivered country ham.
- Add 1/4 cup fresh herbs such as basil, lemon thyme, or marjoram.
- Rub the greens gently all over with olive oil to make a tender, limper green.

ICEBERG WEDGES WITH BUTTERMILK BLUE CHEESE DRESSING

Serves 4

LIKE FASHION, FOOD STYLES RECYCLE. *This is now served as a "retro salad." Family steakhouses were a great treat in the late 1960s and early 1970s (a step up from the diners of the 1950s), when this salad was standard fare.*

1 head iceberg lettuce
Buttermilk Blue Cheese Dressing (page 106)

Remove any limp outer leaves from the lettuce. Whack the core end of the lettuce on the counter to loosen the core. Remove the core with a small knife. Cut the lettuce in half lengthwise from core to top. Turn flat sides of lettuce halves down. Slice each half vertically into 2 wedges and move each wedge to a small plate.

Spoon a generous portion of the Buttermilk Blue Cheese Dressing on each wedge and serve. Refrigerate any leftover dressing.

FRESH ASPARAGUS SALAD

Serves 6 to 8

PENCIL-THIN ASPARAGUS *makes a dainty starter that can also be served as a hot vegetable. The asparagus will stay green, as this recipe has no acid such as vinegar or lemon to turn the spears gray.*

1–2 pounds fresh tiny asparagus, lower stalk, peeled if necessary
1 1/2 tablespoons soy sauce
1 teaspoon granulated sugar
2 teaspoons dark sesame seed oil

Slice the stalks diagonally into 1 1/2-inch lengths to get 2 1/2 to 3 cups of asparagus, including the tips. Small stalks may be served raw. For larger ones, drop into a large pan of salted boiling water and boil for 1 minute. Drain. Briefly run cold water over the asparagus to stop the cooking and to set the color.

Mix the soy sauce, sugar, and sesame seed oil until the sugar is dissolved. Add the lukewarm asparagus and toss to coat. Chill approximately 2 hours before serving, or serve hot.

Variation: Shaved Asparagus

Shave asparagus stalks with a vegetable peeler of mandoline, beginning at the bottom of the flower down to any tough portion. Toss savings and tender flours and pieces with grated Parmesan, olive oil, and a touch of sherry vinegar or lemon juice.

ROASTED BEET SALAD

Serves 2

THIS IS A BASIC BEET SALAD *dressed with a simple vinaigrette. The variations provide endless opportunities for creativity.*

3 tablespoons red or white wine vinegar
2 tablespoons Dijon mustard
1 teaspoon granulated sugar
3 tablespoons oil, cook's preference
1 tablespoon finely chopped herbs, such as marjoram, thyme, or basil
4 medium roasted beets, preferably multicolored (page 179)
Salt
Freshly ground black pepper
2 tablespoons chopped chives or green onion ends

Whisk together the vinegar, mustard, and sugar in a small bowl. While whisking, slowly drizzle in the oil and continue whisking until emulsified (page 102). Whisk in the herbs. Slice, quarter or grate the beets, depending on size. Pour dressing over beets. Season to taste with salt and pepper. Refrigerate until chilled. Top with chives.

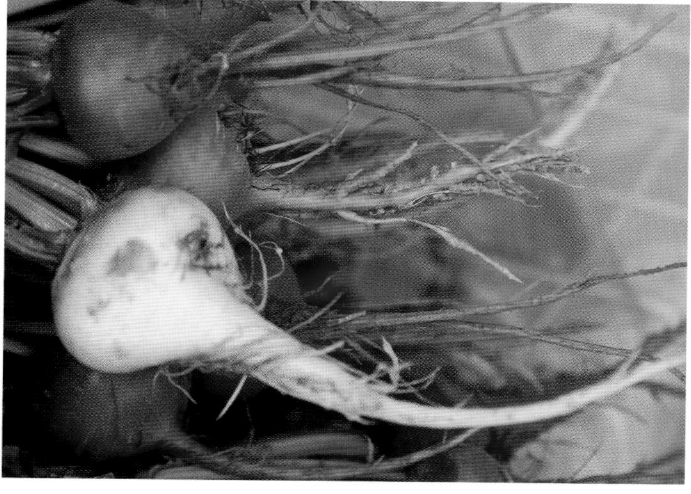

Variations:

- Add grated ginger.
- Place beets on a bed of lettuce, arugula, or chiffonade (page 208) of baby beet greens.
- Sprinkle with grated hard-cooked egg whites (page 275).
- Substitute small beets, barely roasted.
- Slice and layer with blue cheese.
- Sprinkle with cooked salmon or tuna.
- Surround with cooked baby potatoes.
- Toss with orange slices.
- Omit vinaigrette and substitute sour cream.

BROCCOLI AND ROASTED RED PEPPER SALAD

Serves 4 to 6

WHEN BROCCOLI FIRST APPEARS *in the fall, many of the other green vegetables are a memory of the past. Red peppers hang around in the garden until the very end of the season and may be available fresh. If not, use a commercial brand, either jarred or canned, or try a pimento pepper. This recipe can be a starter or a side dish.*

1 tablespoon Dijon mustard
2 tablespoons red wine vinegar
6 tablespoons olive oil
1/2 teaspoon freshly ground cumin, preferably toasted
Freshly ground black pepper
1 head broccoli, florets only, raw or cooked (page 180)
1 roasted red bell pepper (page 223)
1 small onion, thinly sliced
4 tablespoons finely chopped fresh parsley

Whisk together vinegar, mustard, and cumin in a small bowl. While whisking, slowly drizzle in the olive oil and continue whisking until emulsified (page 102). Season to taste with pepper.

Add broccoli, red pepper, onion, and parsley. Toss and serve at room temperature or chilled.

TOASTING SPICES

Many seeds, such as cumin, fennel, cardamom, coriander, mustard, and others, benefit from being toasted (also called roasted) before being ground. Add seeds to a heavy dry skillet and stir over medium-high heat until fragrant, but watching carefully to avoid burning the seeds. No oil is needed, and any heavy pan may be used, as the seeds do not stick. Once the pan begins to heat, keep the seeds moving by stirring with a spoon to avoid any hot spots in the pan. Allow the seeds to cool and then grind according to the recipe.

CRUNCHY NO-COOK BROCCOLI SALAD

Serves 4 to 6

BROCCOLI IS A TOTALLY DIFFERENT VEGETABLE *when served raw. It has crunch and fresh flavor. The other ingredients stand up well, with the bacon making it a useful starter as well as a side dish.*

1 head broccoli
1/2 medium red onion, chopped
1 cup sunflower seeds
1/2 cup raisins
1 cup mayonnaise
2 tablespoons red wine vinegar
1/4 cup granulated sugar, optional
1/2 pound bacon, cooked crisp and crumbled

Trim off the tough end of the broccoli stem. Cut the florets and stem into small pieces.

Toss together the broccoli, onion, sunflower seeds, and raisins in a serving bowl.

Mix together mayonnaise, vinegar, and sugar.

Just before serving, toss the broccoli mixture with the dressing; then sprinkle with bacon.

Variation: Broccoli Swiss Salad
Combine 1 cup mayonnaise with 1/2 cup granulated sugar and 1 tablespoon apple cider vinegar. Stir together 1 head broccoli florets with 1/4 pound grated Swiss cheese. Toss with the mayonnaise mixture. Top with 1/2 pound bacon, cooked crisp and crumbled.

WILTED COLE SLAW FOR A CROWD

Serves 10 to 15

COLE SLAW ENTERED THE AMERICAN FOOD SCENE *in the Dutch colonies (from the Dutch* koolsla, *a combination of* kool, *"cabbage," and* sla, *"salad") and has nearly as many variations as there are cooks. From early Roman times, cole slaw has been prepared with a vinegar base, and only in the last 200 years or so did the mayonnaise varieties begin to appear. It seems every Southerner has his or her own recipe and way of cutting the cabbage. In this recipe, the cabbage wilts when the hot dressing is added. Typically, it is used atop barbecue in a bun. I use the full cup of sugar.*

4–5 pounds cabbage
2–3 large Vidalia or other sweet onions, chopped
1 1/2 cups oil, cook's preference
1 cup apple cider vinegar
1 tablespoon Dijon mustard
1 tablespoon–1 cup granulated sugar to taste

Prepare cabbage as desired—shredded, chopped, sliced, or grated. Toss the cabbage and onions together in a large bowl.

Bring the oil, vinegar, mustard, and preferred amount of sugar to the boil in a saucepan. While still hot, pour the dressing over the cabbage and mix well. Chill, stirring from time to time.

Variations:

- Add chopped or grated carrots.
- My friend Elliot Mackle adds 1/2 teaspoon caraway seed per cabbage and uses less onion.

PREPARING CABBAGE

Chopped—Halve or quarter the cabbage and process in a food processor until desired size. To chop by hand, cut into thin slices, and then move knife rapidly over slices until desired size.

Finely chopped—Process quarters of the cabbage in a food processor or other machine until very fine.

Grated—Halve or quarter the cabbage and carefully rub on a grater, watching knuckles.

Shredded—Halve or quarter the cabbage and slice down with a sharp knife at the desired thickness.

TRADITIONAL COLE SLAW

Serves 10 to 15

THE DIVERSITY IN COLE SLAW *comes from the size of the cabbage pieces; very finely machine chopped for cafeterias and schools, and we've all gotten to like it on top of barbecue on a bun. Halved and quartered before slicing thickly, makes it more rustic and adds a homemade feeling, sort of "grandmother loves me." And sliced thinly is like a gourmet chef is cooking in your kitchen. Using commercial mayonnaise enables making this dish several days in advance. Some people salt, rinse, and drain the cabbage before using, to reduce the tendency of the cabbage to release water.*

4 pounds cabbage, sliced, grated, or shredded (page 77)
2 Vidalia or other sweet onions, finely chopped
1 1/2 cups mayonnaise, preferably store-bought
Dijon mustard
Salt
Freshly ground black pepper
Cider vinegar

Toss the cabbage with the onions and mayonnaise; taste. Add mustard, salt, and pepper as desired. Add a little cider vinegar for a zesty flavor.

Variations:

- Add grated carrots.
- Add a bit of hot red pepper.
- Crown with chopped salted peanuts.

Homemade mayonnaise is discouraged in all slaw recipes because it is easily diluted as the cabbage weeps. This dilutes the acid in the mayonnaise, which acts as the preservative for the egg in the mayonnaise. In a commercial mayonnaise product, the eggs are processed and therefore still have preservative properties.

WORLD-FAMOUS COLE SLAW

This recipe from Ben Moise for his World-Famous Cole Slaw shows the improvisations used by good country cooks. My husband would use his favorite mayonnaise, Duke's, however.

"Take a regular jar of Hellman's mayonnaise and remove around four heaping tablespoons of it from the center making a large hole. Into this pour a tablespoon of dill weed; a tablespoon of garlic powder; a tablespoon of black pepper; a teaspoon of salt; and two tablespoons of regular yellow mustard. Then fill it almost up to within an inch of the top with brown (cider) vinegar, cover, shake well and refrigerate overnight. Shake it again and pour this over the slaw and toss well just before putting it on the table to keep everything nice and crisp."

CARROT SLAW WITH POPPY SEED VINAIGRETTE

Serves 6 to 8

START WITH SHREDDED CARROTS, *adding favorite ingredients all along. Shredding and grating are very similar and interchangeable here. See techniques on page 77.*

6 carrots, shredded or grated
1/2 cup raisins, dried cherries, or cranberries
1/2 cup roughly chopped toasted pecans
Poppy Seed Vinaigrette (page 107)
3 tablespoons chopped fresh parsley

Toss together the carrots, raisins or dried fruit, pecans, and parsley.

Pour Poppy Seed Vinaigrette over the carrot mixture, toss, and chill. Serve on lettuce leaves if desired.

Variation: Add shredded fennel or grated zucchini.

CARROT AND FENNEL SALAD

Serves 4 to 6

THIS IS A PARTICULARLY APPEALING AND COLORFUL SALAD *that will keep a day or two. Bacon makes anything taste better.*

3 carrots, grated
2 fennel bulbs, cored and sliced
1/4 cup red wine vinegar
1 tablespoon Dijon mustard
1/4 cup olive oil
1 tablespoon finely chopped fresh herbs, such as thyme or dill
2 shallots, finely chopped
1 teaspoon granulated sugar
Salt
Freshly ground black pepper
6 slices bacon, cooked crisp and crumbled

Toss the carrots and fennel together in a large bowl.

Whisk together the vinegar, mustard, olive oil, herbs, shallots, and sugar in a small bowl until emulsified (page 102). Season to taste salt and pepper. Pour over the vegetables and let marinate at room temperature for at least 1 hour. Top with crumbled bacon just before serving.

CELERY AND OLIVES SALAD

Serves 2

This crisp, refreshing salad *is a surprisingly remarkable addition to any table for so little effort and investment. It is adapted from Kim Sunee's* Trail of Crumbs.

1–2 ribs celery
2–3 black olives, preferably kalamata
2–3 tablespoons olive oil, divided
Salt
Freshly ground black pepper

Remove tough celery strings with a knife or scrape off with a peeler. Place the celery rib flat side down and slice on the diagonal as thinly as possible.

Cut the olives off the pit in small pieces. Toss together with 1 to 2 tablespoons olive oil, adding more as needed. Season to taste with salt and pepper. Serve chilled.

Variation: Add 1 teaspoon grated orange rind, no white attached.

CORN AND BUTTER BEAN SALAD

Serves 6 to 8

An ode to the summer garden, *this salad brings amazing flavor to the table. Using fresh vegetables is always preferable; but sometimes the winter is long and I long for this succotash, so I bow to using frozen vegetables.*

1 pound shelled butter beans or butter peas, fresh or frozen
6 ears corn on the cob, preferably Silver Queen, kernels scraped from the cob; or 1 (1-pound) package frozen white shoepeg corn, or other whole kernel corn
1 green onion, sliced, white and green
8 slices bacon, cooked crisp and crumbled
3/4 cup mayonnaise
4 tablespoons white wine vinegar
3–4 tablespoons chopped fresh thyme, tarragon, or dill
Salt
Freshly ground black pepper

Add the butter beans to boiling water, reduce heat, and cook about 3 minutes. Add the corn and cook 1 minute more. Drain the beans and corn, and run under cold water to stop the cooking and refresh them. Drain thoroughly.

Gently toss together the beans, corn, onion, bacon, mayonnaise, vinegar, and herbs. Season to taste with salt and pepper.

Cover with plastic wrap and refrigerate at least 1 hour before serving for the best marriage of flavors.

CUCUMBER SALAD

Serves 4

CUCUMBER SALAD IS COOLING TO LOOK AT, *as well as to eat. Traditionally, Southern cucumber salads are dressed with apple cider vinegar or plain vinegar.*

2 cucumbers, peeled and thinly sliced
Salt
4 tablespoons granulated sugar
1/2 cup apple cider vinegar
2 green onions, chopped
2 tablespoons sesame seeds

Move the cucumber slices to a colander placed over a bowl or sink, and salt liberally. Leave for 15 to 30 minutes. Rinse and drain the cucumber slices. Squeeze water out of the cucumbers with hands or paper towels and move to a serving bowl.

Stir the sugar in the vinegar to dissolve then pour over the sliced cucumbers. Sprinkle with green onions and sesame seeds.

Perhaps it is just in my mind, but I do think raw cucumber that has had some of its juices removed by salting makes cucumbers rest easier in older tummies. We love them, but it doesn't seem to be a mutual feeling.

WILTED CUCUMBERS

Serves 4

THIS DISH IS SEEN ALL SUMMER LONG, *sliced and served at the supper table for the family or served in tomato cups for company dinners. Salting the cucumbers brings out the water, preventing dilution of the other ingredients, such as sour cream.*

2 small cucumbers, peeled and sliced
Salt
1/4 cup sour cream or yogurt
1 tablespoon fresh lemon juice or apple cider vinegar
1 teaspoon granulated sugar
Tomato cups (page 27)
Stuffed Grape Tomatoes (page 27) or sliced tomatoes

Move the cucumber slices to a colander placed over a bowl or sink, and salt liberally. Leave for 15 to 30 minutes. Rinse and drain the cucumber slices. Squeeze water out of the cucumbers with hands or paper towels and move the cucumbers to a serving bowl.

Whisk together the sour cream or yogurt, lemon juice or vinegar, and sugar. Toss with the cucumbers. Serve in tomato cups as prepared or surrounded by sliced tomatoes.

COOKED CUCUMBER CRESCENT SALAD

Serves 2 to 4

LIGHTLY COOKED CUCUMBERS *are a delightful surprise in a salad and a special treat for those whose stomachs have rebelled at the raw. The benefit of seeding cucumbers is that the remaining cucumber is pretty when sliced.*

2 cucumbers, peeled if skins are waxed
Salt, divided
1 tablespoon oil, cook's preference
2 tablespoons apple cider vinegar
Freshly ground black pepper
Pinch of granulated sugar, optional
1/2 cup sour cream
1–2 green onions, green only, chopped
2 heaping tablespoons finely chopped fresh dill, basil, or thyme
Toasted sesame seeds, optional

Cut cucumbers in half and seed. Cut the cucumbers on the diagonal into 1/2-inch crescents. Move the cucumber slices to a colander placed over a bowl or sink, and salt liberally. Leave for 15 to 30 minutes. Rinse and drain the cucumber slices. Squeeze water out of the cucumbers with hands or paper towels.

Heat the oil in a frying pan. Add the cucumbers and cook until crisp-tender, about 4 minutes. Add the vinegar, salt, and pepper, and stir in the sugar. Cook until almost all the liquid has evaporated. Remove from the heat.

Cool slightly and stir in the sour cream, green onions, and herbs. Cover and chill at least 2 hours or up to 2 days. Top with sesame seeds just before serving.

SEEDING A CUCUMBER

Run a teaspoon down the center of the cucumber half, scraping away the seeds. A crescent shape will emerge when the cucumber is sliced.

HOT MINTED CUCUMBERS

Serves 4

ELEGANT AND DELICIOUS WHEN COOKED, *there was a time when cucumbers were sharper in flavor and the seeds were more plentiful. Now, varieties like English cucumbers are seedless or have smaller seeds. This dish is especially welcome when cold, rainy weather hits unexpectedly at the end of summer.*

2 large English cucumbers, peeled
Salt, divided
1–2 tablespoons butter
1 medium onion, chopped
3 tablespoons chopped fresh mint
Freshly ground black pepper

Cut the cucumbers in half lengthwise and scoop out the seeds with a spoon if desired. Slice thinly. Move the cucumber slices to a colander placed over a bowl or sink, and salt liberally. Leave for 15 to 30 minutes. Rinse and drain the cucumber slices. Squeeze water out of the cucumbers with hands or paper towels.

Melt the butter in a skillet over medium heat. Add the onion and cook until soft. Add the cucumber slices and toss just until tender, about 2 minutes; do not overcook or they will be mushy. Remove from the heat and stir in the mint. Season to taste with salt and pepper, and serve immediately.

EGGPLANT AND PEANUT SALAD

Serves 6

EGGPLANT, AKA GUINEA SQUASH, *has a centuries-old place in Southern cuisine, as do peanuts, and the two have a surprisingly nice affinity. Vinegars were hard to come by for early colonists, which is hard to imagine, as they are now so readily available. Imagine having to use lard or some other heavy fat alone to dress a salad. Luckily, too, we have a ready supply of oils for dressing. It is important to salt and rinse the eggplant (see degorging, page 200) so the dressing is not diluted by the dark juices.*

2 eggplants, about 1 1/2 pounds each
1/2 tablespoon oil, cook's preference
2 onions, cut into 1/2-inch cubes
2 garlic cloves, chopped
1/2 cup red wine vinegar
1 cup Dijon mustard
3/4 cup olive oil
1/2 cup raisins, plumped in warm water 10 to 15 minutes and drained
1/2 cup chopped peanuts
1 tablespoon chopped fresh thyme, basil, or marjoram, optional

Peel the eggplant and cut in 1/2-to-1-inch cubes. Move the cubes to a colander placed over a bowl or sink, and salt liberally. Leave for 30 minutes. Rinse, drain, and dry cubes.

Meanwhile, heat the 1/2 tablespoon of oil in a large frying pan and add the onions. Sauté briefly, for only 1 or 2 minutes; add the garlic and cook 1 minute. Remove while the onions are still crisp.

Add the dry eggplant cubes to the pan in one layer, using more oil if necessary. Cook until lightly brown, 5 to 7 minutes. Remove while still holding its shape and soft but not mushy.

Whisk together vinegar and mustard in a small bowl. While whisking, slowly drizzle in the olive oil and continue whisking until emulsified (page 102). Stir in the still warm onions, garlic, and eggplant. Cool, cover, and refrigerate until needed.

About 30 minutes before serving, add the raisins, peanuts, and herbs, and stir. Serve at room temperature or cold.

Variation: Brush cut pieces of eggplant with oil and spread out in one layer on an oiled rimmed baking sheet. Roast in a 400-degree oven, stirring once or twice, until brown.

GREEN BEAN SALAD WITH VIBRANT VINAIGRETTE

Serves 4

SERVING COLD COOKED GREEN BEANS *in a salad was new to the South—as was cooking them al dente—starting in the mid-1970s but not commonly accepted until the 1990s. Now, however, they are frequently seen. Dressing this salad ahead of time will cause the beans to turn gray, so dress and toss just before serving.*

1 pound green beans, tipped, tailed, and cooked (page 167)
Vibrant Vinaigrette (page 107)

When ready to serve, toss the beans with the vinaigrette. Serve warm or at room temperature.

Variations:

- Combine 1 pound boiled and drained fingerling or creamer potatoes with the cooked green beans and continue as above.
- Omit orange juice and vinegar. Use 2 tablespoons grated orange rind. This salad can be tossed ahead of time, as there is no acid to turn the beans gray.

GREEN BEAN, BLUE CHEESE, AND PECAN SALAD

Serves 4

CRISP COOKED GREEN BEANS, *Clemson blue cheese, and pecans—the makings for a uniquely Southern salad.*

1 pound green beans, tipped, tailed, and cooked just 3 minutes (page 167)

4 ounces blue, feta, or soft goat cheese, crumbled

1/2 cup roughly chopped pecans, toasted

Toss the drained, warm beans with the blue cheese and pecans. For a creamier sauce, continue to toss until cheese mixture becomes a creamy consistency. The longer the beans are tossed, the more an elegant blue cheese sauce will develop. Serve at room temperature or chill until serving.

Variation: For a main course, add fingers of ham, pork, beef, or crumbled bacon—the salad can accommodate a hearty meat.

FENNEL AND APPLE SALAD

Serves 4 to 6

FENNEL HAS BEEN A CONSTANT *in my life for over forty years—it grew easily and abundantly in the garden in front of my Social Circle restaurant, reseeding itself and growing nearly wild. This refreshes throughout the fall and winter.*

1–2 fennel bulbs, cored and sliced (page 202)
Sliced fennel stalk, optional
2–3 apples, cored and sliced

1/2 recipe Sweet Southern Dressing (page 106) or Basic Vinaigrette (page 105)

1 teaspoon chopped fennel frond, optional

Combine fennel, apples, and dressing, and serve, or refrigerate up to 4 hours. Garnish with fronds if desired.

Variations:

- Substitute 3 sliced celery ribs and 5 tablespoons ground fennel seed in place of the fresh fennel bulb.
- Substitute 2 or 3 peeled and sliced blood oranges for the apples. Layer fennel and oranges in the bottom of a glass bowl, and season to taste with salt and pepper. Lightly dress with olive oil. A pound of peeled and cooked large shrimp converts this into an unusual seafood salad.

FENNEL SALAD WITH ARUGULA

Serves 4

BY THE END OF OUR HOT SUMMER, *fennel and arugula may be the only green vegetables in the garden. They combine beautifully, making a cooling salad.*

2 fennel bulbs, cored and sliced (page 202)
1 tablespoon grated orange rind, no white attached
2 teaspoons grated lemon rind, no white attached
2 tablespoons freshly grated Parmesan cheese
2 tablespoons toasted pecans
1/3 cup olive oil, plus more for drizzling
Salt
Freshly ground black pepper
1 cup arugula
1 teaspoon chopped fennel frond

Toss fennel, orange and lemon rind, Parmesan cheese, and pecans in a bowl. Drizzle with olive oil and season to taste with salt and pepper. Toss gently.

To serve, arrange arugula on a large chilled plate; top with the fennel mixture, drizzle with additional olive oil to taste, and sprinkle with fennel fronds.

Variation: The addition of peeled cooked shrimp makes a meal.

FENNEL

Fennel is a vegetable, an herb, and a spice. Some grocers call it anise.

The vegetable consists of the bulb and stalks, which are a pale green, the color of celery and having a similar crunch. The herb is the fronds held by the stalks. When the fennel blossoms begin to wither, their seeds fall and are used as a spice, green or dried, whole or ground.

The vegetables known as fennel and anise are identical in the grocery stores and can be interchanged, as can their seeds. The herbs are not the same, with fennel fronds looking more like dill and anise looking more like tarragon.

OKRA SALAD

Serves 4

IF WE HAVEN'T EATEN ALL THE OKRA *as chips (page 213), we make this cool salad from the raw okra.*

½ pound okra
2 tablespoons olive oil
1 tablespoon grated lemon or orange rind, no white attached

Barely trim the cap end of the okra. Slice okra thinly on the diagonal. Toss with olive oil. Sprinkle with lemon or orange rind.

Variation:

- Add cooked shrimp.
- Toss with grated Parmesan, salt, and freshly ground pepper.

SWEET ONION SALAD

Serves 4

SWEET ONIONS, SUCH AS VIDALIAS AND TEXAS SWEETS, *and mild red onions are the best for eating raw and in salads. The more recently picked, the sweeter. As an onion ages and dries when stored, it develops sequential layers of skin and becomes stronger tasting, so take a good look at the layers of skin before purchasing when delicacy of flavor matters.*

Long cooking dissipates any bitterness, but raw onions are another matter. Always taste an onion before using it raw. Onions are primarily served sliced, but cutting into wedges makes a nice change. Onion salads mellow when made a day or two in advance.

1 large sweet onion, sliced or wedged
Basic Vinaigrette (page 105), to coat
Herbs to taste

Toss onion in dressing and add herbs as desired.

VIDALIA ONION BREAD SALAD

Serves 4

VIDALIA ONIONS ARE SWEETER *but larger than most other onions. If substituting, use one sliced or chopped red onion. Slicing or chopping onions in a food processor causes a temporary bitterness, which subsides after half an hour or so or upon cooking.*

4 cups lightly toasted French bread torn into 1-inch pieces
4 yellow or red tomatoes, roughly chopped
1 Vidalia onion, sliced or roughly chopped
3 tablespoons sherry vinegar
1 teaspoon Dijon mustard
1 garlic clove, smashed with salt (page 204)
1/2 cup olive oil
Salt
Freshly ground black pepper

Toss the bread, tomatoes, and onion together.

Whisk together the vinegar, mustard, and garlic in a small bowl. While whisking, slowly drizzle in the olive oil, and continue whisking until emulsified. Season to taste with salt and pepper.

Toss dressing with the bread mixture and let sit at least 15 minutes or up to overnight, tossing occasionally.

COLORFUL VIDALIA ONION AND BELL PEPPER SALAD

Serves 12 to 15

FRESH BELL PEPPERS MAKE A CRUNCHY, *refreshing salad when raw and will keep up to a week in the refrigerator. This salad will also keep up to a week in the refrigerator, making an easy addition to any meal or a welcome fix-ahead starter or side. I keep it on hand throughout the summer.*

2–3 large Vidalia or red onions, sliced
3 bell peppers, cored, seeded, and sliced (mixed colors of yellow, red, and orange, or red and green)
1/2 cup red wine vinegar
1 teaspoon Dijon mustard
1/2 teaspoon chopped fresh basil
2 tablespoons chopped herbs such as lemon balm, rosemary, basil, oregano, and parsley
1 1/2 cups olive oil
Salt
Freshly ground black pepper

Toss the onions and peppers in a large bowl.

In a food processor, whisk together vinegar, mustard, basil, and other herbs, and with the motor running, drizzle in the olive oil slowly to emulsify (page 102). Season to taste with salt and pepper.

Pour enough dressing over the onions and peppers to coat. Toss once or twice before covering and refrigerating.

This salad can be eaten right away but is best made at least a day ahead. As it ages, it wilts and mellows.

Variations:

- Cut onions and peppers in triangular wedges rather than slices. This is particularly stunning when served from a glass bowl.
- Add sliced tomatoes, sweet onions, celery, fennel, or broccoli.
- Add crisp crumbled bacon.

SLICING A RAW PEPPER

Cut off the top of the pepper just below the "shoulder" to remove the entire stem end, exposing the ribs inside the pepper.

Cut off the narrow bottom.

Set the pepper on one end and make a vertical slice to open the cylinder.

Place the pepper skin side down on a flat surface and slide the knife along the inside of the pepper (with the blade parallel to the work surface), removing the ribs and seeds while unrolling the pepper so that it lies flat.

Slice the pepper into strips, then into dice if needed.

BELL PEPPER VARIETIES

Bell peppers are bred and grown in many colors, a far cry from the green bells of my youth, which became red after remaining on the plant. The paler the color, the sweeter the pepper, with yellow and orange being the mildest, followed by red. Green peppers are the harshest, and I use them less and less. The seeds should be removed, but the peel is optional. I usually do not peel fresh peppers, although they may be peeled with a vegetable peeler.

FINGERLING POTATO SALAD

Serves 8

SINCE MAYONNAISE-BASED POTATO SALADS *are frequently left out on buffet or picnic tables for several hours, when I take one to such an occasion, I use one made with a vinaigrette rather than homemade mayonnaise. I find the mayonnaise is not missed, and it is nice to not have anxiety about the salad making someone sick. (Store-bought mayonnaise has more acid, which is not dangerous when diluted by the potato and other juices, and produces a safe salad.)*

Fingerling potatoes are a recently popular variety. Previously only large potatoes, usually Idaho, were the standard, making a mushier (if beloved) salad. For this reason, we give directions for cooking the fingerlings.

2 pounds fingerling, creamer, or small new potatoes, quartered if necessary
2/3 cup red or white wine vinegar
1 tablespoon Dijon mustard
1 1/2 cups olive oil
Salt
Freshly ground black pepper
Granulated sugar
Chopped fresh herbs such as thyme or parsley, optional

Bring a large pot of salted water to the boil. Add the potatoes, reduce heat to a simmer, and cook about 25 minutes, until fork-tender. Take care the potatoes don't become mushy.

Whisk together the vinegar and mustard in a small bowl. While whisking, slowly drizzle in the olive oil and continue whisking until emulsified (page 102). Season to taste with salt, pepper, and sugar.

Toss the hot drained potatoes with enough dressing to coat lightly. Add herbs if desired.

Variation: Add crisp cooked bacon.

BOILING POTATOES

Small fresh potatoes should go into boiling water, just as green vegetables do. Larger, older potatoes, both peeled and unpeeled, usually quartered, can be substituted and should be started in cold water and brought to the boil.

TOMATO AND BASIL SALAD

Serves 4 to 6

THE SHAPE OF FOOD INFLUENCES ITS FLAVOR. *Wedges of medium or large tomatoes, or halved cherry tomatoes, not only add interest and beauty to a salad but absorb the flavor of the dressing differently.*

1 cup arugula or watercress
1 tablespoon red wine or sherry vinegar
1/2 teaspoon Dijon mustard
1/2 cup olive oil
Salt
Freshly ground black pepper
4–6 ripe tomatoes, cut into wedges, or 24 cherry tomatoes, halved
2–3 tablespoons chopped fresh basil

Wash and dry the greens, remove any tough stems, and arrange the leaves around the outside edge of a platter.

Whisk together the vinegar and mustard in a small bowl. While whisking, slowly drizzle in the olive oil and continue whisking until emulsified (page 102). Season to taste with salt and pepper.

Toss the tomatoes gently in the dressing. Remove the tomatoes with a slotted spoon and place in the center of the arugula, drizzling the remaining dressing over the arugula as needed. Sprinkle with the basil.

Variation: Crumble fresh mozzarella, soft goat cheese, or other cheese on top.

TOMATO AND WATERMELON SALAD

Serves 6 to 8

One time I took this to a covered-dish supper, *where it had a lot of competition with fabulous dishes, and it became an unexpected hit. As we talked about it, we wondered why it had taken so long for watermelon to be integrated with cheeses and other savory mixtures. Whatever the reason, we've been missing out on a refreshing salad. It is a typical New Southern dish—mixing old fruits in new ways.*

3 cups tomatoes, preferably yellow or orange, in 1-inch cubes or wedged
3 cups watermelon, cut into 1-inch cubes (page 68)
2 tablespoons fresh lemon juice, or to taste
Salt
2 slices bacon, crisped and crumbled, optional
2 ounces blue, feta, or soft goat cheese, crumbled

Gently mix tomatoes and watermelon in a medium bowl with the lemon juice and salt. Plate individually or in a serving bowl, then sprinkle bacon or other meat, and cheese.

This dish is best enjoyed the day it is prepared. No further salad dressing is needed, as the tomato and melon make a tantalizing dressing on their own.

Variations:

- If there is any left over, whir it all together, with or without the bacon, to make a refreshing soup. A little mint or lemon balm adds a refreshing note.
- Additional food companions for this salad, other than the bacon, would be tender cooked white fish broken into small pieces, or slivered chicken breast tossed together with the rest of the salad at the last minute.

TOMATO AND CUCUMBER SALAD

Serves 4 to 6

After taking a much-needed weekend getaway to the mountains, *I returned bearing beautiful fresh tomatoes and cucumbers from my friend Betty's garden. Mixed with a little sugar, some shallots, and some herbs, this cool, refreshing salad was the perfect complement to a grilled cheese sandwich for lunch.*

It also makes a lively side to grilled meats or seafood for a light supper in the summer heat. As so often happens with simple fresh dishes, they become the stars of the meal. The salt brings out the liquid in the tomatoes and cucumbers, making a wonderful "sauce." The salad will last a day or two in the refrigerator if all the ingredients are fresh.

1 pound cucumbers, peeled, quartered lengthwise, and sliced into triangles
1 large ripe tomato, cut into 1/2-inch cubes
1 large shallot, sliced into thin rings
2 tablespoons granulated sugar
1 teaspoon salt
Freshly ground black pepper
1 green onion, thinly sliced
1/4 cup finely chopped fresh parsley or other fresh herbs
1/4 cup red wine vinegar
1 teaspoon red pepper flakes, optional

Move the cucumber slices to a colander placed over a bowl or sink, and salt liberally. Leave for 15 to 30 minutes. Rinse and drain the cucumber slices. Squeeze water out of the cucumbers with hands or paper towels and move the cucumbers to a serving bowl.

Toss the tomato and shallot in with the cucumbers. Sprinkle with sugar, salt, pepper, green onion, and fresh herbs.

Pour vinegar over the salad and toss. Cover and leave 1 hour or up to 2 days. Season to taste with extra salt and pepper if necessary. Sprinkle with red pepper flakes for a little kick.

TOMATO AND MANGO SALAD

Serves 4

MANGOS WORKED THEIR WAY INTO THE SOUTH FROM SOUTH AMERICA *and south Florida by the late 1980s. Cynthia converted me to them and their many ways, and I've relished them ever since.*

1/4 cup sherry vinegar
1/4 cup olive oil
Salt

1 pound ripe tomatoes, sliced 1/4 inch thick

1 ripe mango, peeled and pitted, sliced 1/4 inch thick
3/4 cup chopped fresh basil

Whisk the vinegar and olive oil together, and season to taste with salt.

Alternate tomato and mango slices, sprinkle with the dressing, and top with basil leaves.

SLICING A MANGO

Oh, how I wish I were an expert mango slicer. I have no idea how hotels and restaurants serve beautiful slices of mangos. My grandmother Lorraine ate mangos alone at the kitchen sink, the sweet nectar dripping down her arms, as no other family members shared her passion for the fruit. Now I adore them but find cutting them for presentation to be less than rewarding, as mangos contain a large, oval, almost "hairy" seed. Here are two methods: the first method is peeling and slicing, the second is cutting and scoring.

Peeling the mango—there are two choices. Use a traditional peeler, and remove all the skin. The other choice is to slice the stem end flat, set the now flat end down on the cutting surface, and take a sharp knife to cut down close to the skin, following the contour of the fruit and cutting the skin away from the flesh, all the way down to remove the flesh. Rotate the mango as needed and continue until all the skin is removed. Now use the knife to trim slices from top to bottom off from the seed.

Cutting and scoring the mango—slice the stem end flat, and set the now flat end on the cutting surface. Use a sharp knife to cut the mango from top to bottom, beginning just off-center, and cut parallel to, and close against, the seed. Repeat on the other side of the seed. Now there are two large slices, and a seed with two short sides still attached. Follow the same method to remove the short sides. With the large slices skin side down, cut a cross-hatch pattern into the flesh, down to the skin. Pick up the slice and turn it "inside out" to make the flesh stand up away from the skin. Use a sharp knife to slice the flesh away from the skin. Repeat for the two short side pieces, although they yield just a few bites of flesh.

My grandmother clearly knew the easiest method: peel and eat alone over the kitchen sink!

—Cynthia

TOMATO ASPIC

Serves 6 to 8

GELATIN SALADS HAVE ALWAYS BEEN WELCOME *in the hot and humid South. They bring coolness as they slide down the throat, and pep up what might seem a mundane table of cold cuts as well as add dash to a glorious buffet.*

Tomato aspics are the most traditional of these. They may be made with fresh or canned tomatoes, but I find a good-quality commercial tomato juice (not vegetable juice, as sugar is usually needed to mellow it) removes any need to heat the kitchen beyond just melting the gelatin.

3 envelopes unflavored gelatin
1/4 cup water
1 quart tomato juice, room temperature
1–2 tablespoons fresh lemon juice
1 tablespoon grated onion
1 tablespoon salt
1 teaspoon granulated sugar, optional
1/4 teaspoon ground hot red pepper
1 cup mayonnaise
3 tablespoons finely chopped fresh basil leaves
Freshly ground black pepper
2 tablespoons fresh lemon juice
Fresh basil leaves, for garnish

Add the gelatin to the water in a small saucepan stirring if necessary to distribute. Whisk the tomato juice, lemon juice, and grated onion in a non-aluminum bowl. Taste and add salt, sugar, and hot red pepper as desired.

Heat the gelatin in the pan over low heat and stir until the gelatin is melted and the liquid is clear. Stir the liquid gelatin into the room-temperature tomato juice mixture. Pour into a well-oiled 1-quart mold. Let cool to room temperature then refrigerate to set, at least 3 to 4 hours.

Meanwhile, whisk together the mayonnaise, basil, pepper, and lemon juice. Chill until ready to serve.

To unmold aspic, lightly pull the set aspic away from the sides of the mold, tipping the mold slightly and pulling sufficiently from the edge to catch an air bubble. Quickly put an oiled serving dish over the mold, invert, and give a firm shake to release the aspic from the mold. Remove the mold. Slide the aspic into place if necessary. Garnish with fresh basil leaves.

USING A MOLD

Cold causes gelatin to set. If the melted gelatin is added to an already cold mixture or mold, it might head for the cold and glob up. If this should happen, reheat the whole mixture over low heat until smooth. Cool to room temperature before chilling.

When using a mold for any recipe, if the dish is to be served cold, the mold is oiled. If to be served hot, then the mold is buttered. The plate is oiled to aid in sliding the molded recipe in place.

TOMATO, AVOCADO, OLIVE, AND GREEN ONION SALAD

Serves 6

SOMETIMES A RECIPE WITH COLOR AND DASH *is needed for the table at the last minute—and this one is fabulous. If preparing ahead of time, either delay slicing the avocado until the last few minutes or sprinkle it with lemon juice to prevent it from turning brown.*

3 large ripe tomatoes, cut into 8 wedges
1 green onion, sliced
1–2 ripe avocados, halved, seeded, peeled, and cut into 1/4-inch-thick slices
3/4 cup black olives, pitted and halved, preferably kalamata
6–10 tablespoons olive oil, divided
2 tablespoons red wine vinegar
Juice of 1 lemon
Juice of 1/2 orange
1 large garlic clove, chopped
Pinch of granulated sugar
Salt
Freshly ground black pepper

Lightly toss the tomato, green onion, avocado, and olives in a large salad bowl.

Whisk together 6 tablespoons of olive oil, vinegar, lemon and orange juices, and garlic. Season to taste with sugar, salt, and pepper. Add more olive oil as needed.

Variations: Feta cheese and bite-sized pieces of cooked chicken, lamb, or ham are all good additions.

SELECTING AND STORING AVOCADOS

Gently squeeze the fruit in the palm of a hand. Ripe, ready-to-eat fruit will be firm but will yield to gentle pressure. Avoid fruit with dark blemishes on the skin or overly soft fruit.

Ripening an avocado—Put an avocado in a brown paper bag for 2 to 5 days. Adding an apple or banana to the bag will speed up the ripening, as these fruits give off ethylene gas, a ripening reagent. Unripe avocados should not be refrigerated, as the cold will prevent them from ever ripening.

Removing an avocado from its skin—Everyone has a different way of peeling an avocado. Some like to split them in half, leaving the pit in one half in order to prevent its exposure to air. Others peel them whole. There are whole and half avocado slicers available. If using an avocado skin as a "boat" for a salad, there are also scooping devices available that will leave the skin intact.

Storing or freezing avocados—Ripe fruit can be stored in the refrigerator uncut for 2 to 3 days. To store cut fruit, rub generously with lemon or lime juice or white vinegar and store in an airtight container in the refrigerator. If refrigerated guacamole turns brown during storage, it probably needed more acid, probably lemon juice. Discard the top layer or stir it in. Avocados can be puréed and frozen to use in salads and dips. Purée the flesh, adding 1 tablespoon of lemon juice for each 2 puréed avocados. Pack the purée into an airtight container, leaving 1 inch of headspace. Seal and label the containers. Freeze and use within 4 to 5 months.

GAZPACHO SALAD

Serves 4

THIS RECIPE SHOWS US *how long this kind of cooling combination has been used in the South. At a time when there was no way to chill a soup on a hot summer day, layering tomatoes and bread with cucumbers, salt, pepper and onion, then pouring some tomato juice over it along with mustard and oil, made a very cooling dish in itself, the salted tomatoes and cucumbers extracting juices that became soupy. Gazpacho salad, adapted here from* The Virginia House-Wife, *is the basis for what became a soup.*

- 1/2–1 cup biscuit or bread pieces, in 1-inch squares
- 4–5 tablespoons red wine vinegar
- 2 tablespoons finely chopped fresh parsley
- 1 tablespoon finely chopped fresh basil
- 2 large garlic cloves, chopped
- Salt
- Freshly ground black pepper
- 1/3 cup olive oil
- 3 ripe tomatoes, cut in wedges
- 1 small cucumber, peeled if skins are waxed, thinly sliced
- 1 red or yellow bell pepper, cored, seeded, and cut into strips (page 88)
- 2–4 green onions, chopped

Toss together the biscuit or bread pieces with vinegar, parsley, basil, garlic, salt, pepper, and olive oil in a medium bowl. Add the tomatoes, cucumber, bell pepper, and green onion, and stir to coat.

Variations:

- Toss with 3 cups cooked small pasta.
- Toss with 1 cup cherry or grape tomato halves.

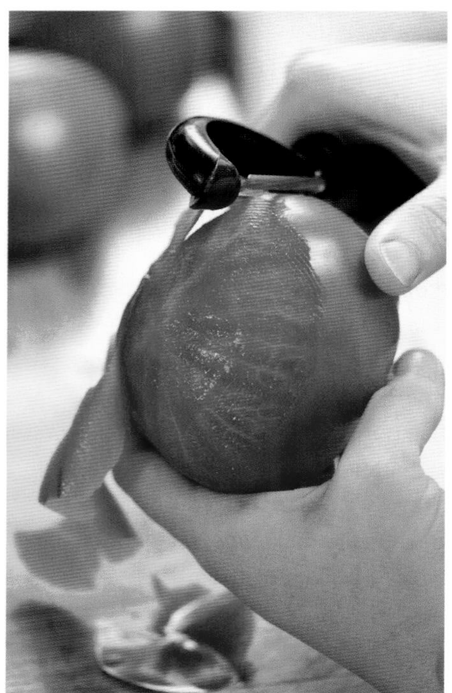

MAKING GASPACHA-SPANISH

"Put some soft biscuit or toasted bread in the bottom of a sallad bowl, put in a layer of sliced tomatas with the skin taken off, and one of sliced cucumbers, sprinkled with pepper, salt, and chopped onion; do this until the bowl is full, stew some tomatas quite soft, strain the juice, mix in some mustard and oil, and pour over it; make it two hours before it is eaten." —From *The Virginia House-Wife (1824)*

The Virginia House-Wife stresses skinning raw tomatoes. Make the judgment according to the toughness of the skin and the shape of the tomato.

PEELING TOMATOES

Some tomatoes can be peeled with a specialty tomato or other peeler. Tough-skinned tomatoes are more easily peeled by cutting a shallow X in the blossom end of the tomato. Dip into boiling water, roll, and remove with a slotted spoon to a bowl of ice water. The length of time in the boiling water—a few seconds or longer—depends on the toughness of the skin. The skin will peel back easily with fingers or a knife.

REFRESHING ZUCCHINI SALAD

Serves 4 to 6

THIS REFRESHING SIDE DISH *requires no cooking and is easy to prepare, making it ideal for a hot summer day. The zucchini ribbons are crispest when served immediately after slicing, but letting the dish sit prior to serving allows the flavors to marinate nicely. A perfectionist may prefer to work around and discard the seeds, but that is personal preference. I enjoy it when the whole zucchini is used and don't notice the seeds. Leftovers, if there are any, are delicious served atop burgers or grilled chicken.*

4 medium zucchini
1 shallot, minced
3/4 cup feta or soft goat cheese, crumbled
1 tablespoon chopped fresh mint or other herb
1–2 tablespoons olive oil
1/2–1 tablespoon fresh lemon juice, optional
Salt
Freshly ground pepper

Cut off and discard the ends of the zucchini. Ribbon the zucchini by peeling it into thin ribbon-like strips with a sharp vegetable peeler.

Toss zucchini, shallot, cheese, mint, olive oil, and lemon juice in a bowl. Season to taste with salt and pepper.

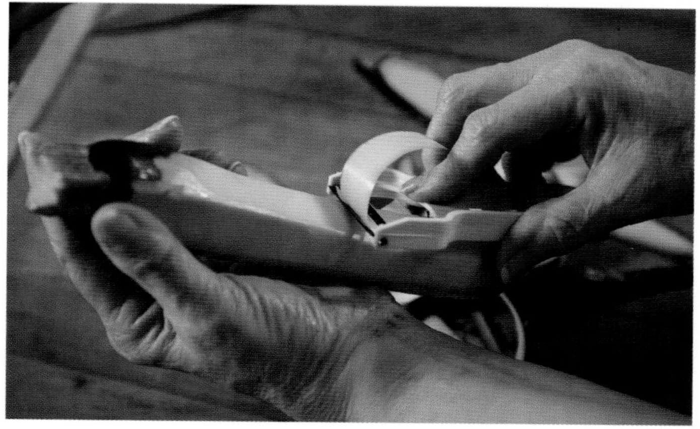

Variations:

- Add 1 to 2 carrots, ribboned in the same way.
- Add shredded chicken or peeled shrimp for a more substantial dish.

RICE AND FRUIT SALAD WITH GINGER DRESSING

Serves 6

THIS IS A RECIPE WHERE THE DRESSING *really enhances the salad. Very flexible, this salad can be made happily with any rice. When figs are in season, they are especially welcome; otherwise dried figs will do. Other dried or fresh fruits make happy substitutions.*

Ginger Dressing (page 107)
1 cup fresh or dried figs, stems trimmed, quartered
1/2 cup dried apricots
1/2 cup toasted pecans
1 cup cooked rice, room temperature
3–4 cups arugula or other tasty greens, washed and dried

Just before serving, toss the figs, apricots, pecans, and rice with a large dollop of the dressing until lightly coated; add the arugula. Taste and add more seasoning or dressing if needed. Arrange the rice mixture so the fruit is on top.

Variations:

- For a full meal, add strips of country ham, pork, chicken, or beef.
- Substitute a favorite grain such as Basmati brown rice, red rice, pearl barley, rye berries, wheat berries, farro, or the like.

EGG SALAD

Serves 4

Although egg salad is traditionally served cold, *Cynthia and I both love it freshly made and still warm, particularly in a sandwich.*

- 1/3 cup mayonnaise
- 6 hard-cooked large eggs, chopped (page 275)
- Salt
- Freshly ground black pepper

Lightly mix the mayonnaise and eggs in a bowl. Carefully add variations below, as desired. Eat warm or refrigerate at least 1 hour before serving on lettuce leaves or in lettuce cups, in Tomato Cups (page 27), or in cucumber boats. The salad keeps 1 to 2 days covered in the refrigerator.

Variations:

- Add 2 tablespoons each very finely chopped onion and celery, and 1 tablespoon Dijon mustard.
- Add 1 to 2 teaspoons curry powder.
- Add 1/4 cup chopped olives.

MAKING EGG SALAD SANDWICHES

Remove and discard crusts from thin slices of white or whole wheat bread. Spread slices of bread with mayonnaise or softened butter before spreading with the Egg Salad. Assemble and cut into triangles. This is a staple.

BASIC CHICKEN SALAD

Serves 8

Simple enough to cook on a hot day, *this is the basic chicken salad used for weddings, teas, and funerals. Chicken breasts and their white meat were once considered "special" enough to be necessary in a "company salad." Now, whole poached chicken or rotisserie chicken may suitably substitute, as the dark meat adds so much flavor. The variations include a dressed-up salad using soy sauce and curry to transport the basic to the glorious with little extra effort, as does the Swan Coach House variation.*

- 4 cups hand-shredded or chopped cooked chicken, preferably breasts
- 1 cup mayonnaise
- 1 cup very finely chopped celery
- 1–2 tablespoons very finely chopped onion, optional
- Lettuce, optional

Mix chicken with mayonnaise, celery, and optional onion. Season to taste with salt and pepper. Serve on lettuce for a plated salad.

Variation: Chicken Salad Sandwiches
Omit lettuce for sandwiches. Cut sandwiches into small triangles for special occasions. Toast bread for meals to be eaten on the spot.

Variation: Curried Chicken Salad
Omit the celery and chopped onion and add 1/2 cup of chopped green onions. Whisk 2 teaspoons of soy sauce and 1/4 cup of curry powder with the mayonnaise until smooth before adding the chicken.

Variation: Swan House Chicken Salad
The Swan House, a delightful Atlanta tearoom and gift shop, varies its chicken salad recipe by adding 1 cup of water chestnuts and 1 cup of mango chutney.

CHICKEN SALAD WITH GRAPES

Serves 4 to 6

THIS RECIPE DATES BACK TO MY RESTAURANT *in 1971. My friend Martha Summerour ate it at a ladies lunch there and nagged me for years for the recipe. I am still a bit embarrassed by all the cream, and I'm afraid to tell you how much sugar I used—but, truly, it was delicious and if only served on special occasions to thin people, it will be thoroughly welcome.*

4 tablespoons orange juice
1 cup mayonnaise
1/2 cup heavy cream
1 1/2 cups halved seedless grapes, preferably green
2 cups hand-shredded or chopped cooked chicken, preferably breasts
Granulated sugar to taste
Salt
Freshly ground black pepper
6 large lettuce leaves

Mix together the orange juice and mayonnaise in a bowl. Stir in the heavy cream.

Toss the chicken and grapes with the mayonnaise mixture. Season to taste with sugar, salt, and pepper. Refrigerate at least 1 hour before serving on lettuce leaves.

Variations:

- Substitute muscadines for the green grapes.
- Add chopped and peeled peaches, cherry tomatoes, black olives, chopped pecans, slivered almonds, or very finely chopped celery and onion.

CRAB, MANGO, AND AVOCADO SALAD

Serves 4 as a luncheon or starter course

THIS SALAD IS FLEXIBLE IN ITS INGREDIENTS. *If a spicier salad is preferred, add more red pepper. There are some excellent bottled mangos that can be substituted in emergencies. If jumbo crabmeat is not available, other parts of the crab may be substituted—but remember that jumbo is premiere. Also, it is preferable to cut the avocado at the last minute, but life doesn't always accommodate last-minute preparations. The vinaigrette prevents some discoloring, but try to avoid cutting the avocado more than an hour or two in advance.*

4 tablespoons fresh lemon juice or sherry vinegar
1/2 teaspoon Dijon mustard
3 ounces avocado oil or olive oil
Salt
Freshly ground pepper (preferably white)
1 cup crabmeat, preferably jumbo lump
1 mango, peeled and seeded
2 ripe avocados
1/8 teaspoon ground hot red pepper or to taste
1–2 tablespoons chopped fresh thyme, basil, or parsley, optional
8 Cheese Straws (page 48), optional

Whisk together lemon juice or vinegar and mustard in a small bowl. Whisk in the oil. Season to taste with salt and pepper. Set aside.

Pick through the crabmeat for any shells. Cut the mango into bite-sized pieces.

Peel the avocados, discard seeds, and cut into bite-sized pieces. If you wish to serve the salad in hollowed-out avocado shells, cut avocados in half, remove seeds, and scoop out avocado carefully before cutting it up for the salad. Set shells aside, the insides covered closely with plastic wrap to prevent them from turning brown.

If cutting mangos and avocados ahead of time, toss in sufficient vinaigrette to coat and to prevent the fruit from turning brown. Season to taste with salt, pepper, and optional herbs, reserving any pretty stems for garnish; or garnish with 2 cheese straws each.

Variations: Use bottled mangos, substitute fresh peaches or freshly chopped apple for the mangos, increase red pepper for a spicier dish, or substitute shrimp for the crab.

COLD OYSTER SALAD

Serves 6 to 8

FALL WEATHER BRINGS THE OYSTERS, *perfect in a salad. We use fresh oysters, but roasted or steamed oysters may be marinated in the same manner.*

- 1/2 cup fresh lemon juice
- 1/4 cup olive oil
- 3–5 garlic cloves, chopped
- 1/4 cup finely chopped fresh thyme
- 1/4 cup finely chopped fresh parsley
- Salt
- Freshly ground black pepper
- 2 pints freshly shucked oysters and their liquor
- 1 head leaf lettuce or 4 cups arugula

Whisk together the lemon juice and oil. Add the garlic and herbs, season to taste with salt and pepper, and set aside.

Move the oysters and their liquor to a heavy saucepan. Bring to the boil, reduce heat, and simmer a few minutes, until their edges just begin to curl. Drain, cover with marinade, and refrigerate for a few hours or overnight.

Line a serving bowl with lettuce leaves and top with oysters, drained if necessary.

MARINATED SHRIMP SALAD

Serves 6

BRIDAL AND BABY SHOWERS *are fitting occasions for cold seafood salads. I have served this to two generations of brides and mothers-to-be. This may be a gracious plenty, but because shrimp vary in size, it is important the salad not look skimpy.*

- 2 pounds shrimp, cooked and peeled, chopped if large
- 1 cup Basic Vinaigrette (page 105)
- 6 large lettuce or spinach leaves

Toss the shrimp in a cup of Basic Vinaigrette in a large bowl and marinate for 1 hour. Drain and serve over lettuce leaves on cold plates.

Variations:

- Add 1 cup feta cheese, 1 chopped red onion, 4 peeled and chopped hard-cooked eggs, and 1 to 2 tablespoons capers.
- Add 2 sliced avocados to the shrimp when marinating. Sprinkle with 1 cup feta cheese.

Variation: Shrimp Salad in Cucumber Boats

When no fresh garden lettuce is to be had in late August, halve large cucumbers, scoop out the seeds, and store in the refrigerator in water mixed with several tablespoons of white vinegar or lemon juice to preserve crispness. Drain before using.

The word *shrimp* may have its roots in the German word *schrimpen,* or "shrink up," referring to tiny, weak things. The Middle English shortened it to "shrimp."

SHRIMP SALAD

Serves 6 to 8

NEAR THE SOUTHERN SHORES, *the very best, freshest shrimp cooked in its shell, peeled, chopped, and mixed with mayonnaise, is a beach house treat ready for whoever claims they are starving.*

1 cup mayonnaise
1 tablespoon fresh lemon juice
1 hard-cooked egg, chopped
2 pounds shrimp, cooked and peeled (pages 326–27), chopped
1 tablespoon chopped fresh parsley
Salt
Freshly ground black pepper

Mix together the mayonnaise and lemon juice in a bowl. Stir in the egg, shrimp, and parsley. Season to taste with salt and pepper.

Variations:

- Add chopped fresh chives and chopped fresh parsley.
- Add up to 1 tablespoon curry powder or Creole seasoning (page 670) to the mayonnaise mixture.
- Add 1 cup chopped celery and 1/2 cup chopped green onion.
- Shrimp salad sandwiches for special occasions may be made an hour or two ahead, on sliced white loaf bread only, cut into four triangles, and covered in the refrigerator with a damp paper towel.

SWEET AND SAVORY GRILLED SHRIMP SALAD

Serves 4

A FIRE BRINGS OUT THE LUSTINESS OF SHRIMP. *They are better roasted in the shell—even with their heads on. To expedite removal of the shell, snip up the back vein of the shell. This is one time the larger the shrimp, the better. If a basket-type grill container is available, shrimp will stay on the rosemary stem, not in the fire.*

4 stems of rosemary or 4 skewers
1 1/2 pounds raw shrimp, preferably in the shell
Fresh figs, fresh peach wedges, fresh pineapple chunks, and/or whole cherry tomatoes
Oil, cook's preference, for brushing
4 cups washed salad greens, such as Bibb lettuce, red lettuce, or arugula
1/2 cup whole herbs, such as basil, lemon balm, oregano, or thyme, optional
1/2 cup lightly toasted pecan halves or quarters
1 cup Parmesan or other cheese, chopped into 1/2-inch pieces
Basic Vinaigrette (page 105)

Strip the stems of rosemary to make skewers. Soak in a bowl of water for 10 or 15 minutes. Alternate the shrimp and any of the fruit or tomato on the skewers.

Heat the grill. Brush shrimp and other ingredients lightly with oil and move to grill. Grill a few minutes on each side, until the shrimp are cooked. Remove from the grill.

Meanwhile, wash and dry the salad greens. When ready to serve, toss greens with the pecans, cheese, and vinaigrette. Divide among plates or move to a platter. Top with the warm shrimp skewers and serve.

SHRIMP AND PEA SALAD

Serves 6

Shrimp come in season *several times a year, depending on the variety. One coincides with the fresh pea season, another when the greens are at their best—in which case, use frozen white acre peas; otherwise use canned.*

- 1 cup baby spinach or other greens
- 4 tablespoons olive oil plus more for drizzling, divided
- 2 garlic cloves, finely chopped
- 1 tablespoon chicken stock or broth, or water
- 2 cups cooked fresh or frozen white acre peas, or 1 (15-ounce) can, drained
- Grated rind of 1 lemon, no white attached, divided
- Large pinch of red pepper flakes
- Salt
- Freshly ground black pepper
- 1 pound raw shrimp
- 1/4 cup shredded country ham, optional

Wash and dry the greens. Chop into 1-inch lengths.

Heat 2 tablespoons of oil in a large skillet; add garlic and sauté for 30 seconds. Add the greens, pour in a tablespoon of stock or water, toss, and cover. Cook until thoroughly wilted but not cooked all the way down, about 10 minutes. Cool.

Stir the peas into the cooled greens mixture; add half the lemon rind and red pepper flakes. Drizzle with remaining olive oil and toss to combine. Season to taste with more lemon and salt and pepper. Let rest for 30 minutes or up to 24 hours. Refrigerate if left out more than 1 hour.

Before serving, griddle, broil, or grill the shrimp until they just turn a coral-pink color. Form a nest of the salad mixture in the center of a plate, or use a ring mold if desired. Arrange 3 to 4 shrimp around the salad. Drizzle with more olive oil if desired. Serve hot, cold, or at room temperature.

Variation: Substitute butterbeans for the peas.

GRILLED SHRIMP, PEPPER, AND RICE SALAD

Serves 6

Grilled shrimp is equally good *in a salad, its dominant flavor standing up well to bell peppers.*

- 1 pound grilled shrimp (page 327), chopped if large
- 4 cups cooked and cooled white rice
- 1 cup chopped red or green bell pepper
- 1 cup chopped celery
- 1 1/2–2 cups mayonnaise
- 1 teaspoon fresh lemon juice
- Salt
- Freshly ground black pepper

Toss the shrimp, rice, bell pepper, and celery in a large bowl.

Mix the mayonnaise with the lemon juice and stir carefully into the shrimp mixture. Season to taste with salt and pepper.

Cover and refrigerate for several hours or up to 1 day.

TUNA SALAD

Serves 2 to 4

Of course, canned may be substituted, *but here in the South, where tuna are caught on long lines in the Gulf of Mexico and brought in fresh to our docks, we use leftover grilled tuna in salads as well as in sandwiches. Tuna is a sturdy fish and takes well to being tossed in a salad. Always keep leftover fish refrigerated, as you would chicken.*

1 tablespoon Dijon mustard
2 tablespoons vinegar
5 tablespoons olive oil
6 –8 ounces tuna, grilled (page 291), or canned, broken into pieces if desired
6–8 ounces green beans, tipped, tailed, and cooked (page 167)
Chopped fresh herbs, optional
1 cucumber, peeled if skins are waxed, sliced 1/8 inch thick
Anchovies, drained, optional
Salt
Freshly ground black pepper
Black olives
1 pound ripe tomatoes, quartered

Stir together the mustard, vinegar, and oil in a small bowl and set aside.

Add a layer of fish to the bottom of a bowl and a layer of green beans over it. Sprinkle with some of the optional herbs, then the cucumber. Toss with optional anchovies, the olives and tomatoes. Season to taste with salt and pepper. Drizzle with the dressing.

Variations:

- Omit the beans and add fresh halved figs, peach wedges, pineapple chunks, or other fresh fruit.
- Substitute cooked grouper or other fish for the tuna.
- Substitute cooked butterbeans or peas for the green beans.
- For a pretty variation, make a lattice of the anchovies and put the olives in the lattice diamonds. Surround with the tomatoes, rounded sides up. Brush the tomatoes with the dressing and spoon the remaining dressing over the entire salad. Garnish with more of the herbs if desired.

ROAST BEEF SALAD

Serves 6 to 8

It is always better to have too much meat *than too little for an important dinner. Leftover pieces can be recycled on bread or in a salad such as this. A variety of beet colors makes it a smashing presentation. I confess: my husband hates beets, so I replace them in this recipe with more cherry tomatoes for him.*

2 pounds rare roast beef, cut into 1/2-inch strips
1/2 pound whole cooked or canned beets, drained, cut into julienne strips, optional
1/2 pound cherry or grape tomatoes, halved or quartered as needed
1 bunch green onions, chopped
1/3 cup red wine vinegar
2 teaspoons Dijon mustard
1 garlic clove, crushed
2/3 cup olive oil
Salt
Freshly ground black pepper
3/4 pound fresh snow peas
4 tablespoons chopped fresh thyme, parsley, or oregano, optional

Toss together the roast beef, beets and/or tomatoes, and onions.

Whisk together the vinegar, mustard, and garlic in a small bowl. Whisk in the oil in a slow, steady stream. Season to taste with salt and pepper. Add to the beef and toss to coat. Refrigerate covered for 1 hour.

Meanwhile, cook the peas in boiling salted water for 2 minutes; drain. Add three-quarters of the peas to the roast beef and toss gently. Move to a serving bowl or platter and sprinkle with the remaining peas and herbs.

MAYONNAISE & VINAIGRETTE DRESSINGS

Emulsions

Mayonnaise and vinaigrette dressings are made stable using a technique called emulsion. There are two main kinds of emulsions in cooking: 1) A temporary emulsion is formed by whisking vinegar and oil together with a bit of mustard or cream. 2) A stable emulsion ensues when two or more ingredients are held together by the existence of an emulsifier, such as egg yolk or cream, as in a mayonnaise and hollandaise. At this time the particles of fat are surrounded with the molecules of the emulsifier.

Acid is important in this equation as well, which is why prepared mustard (which contains an acid), lemon, vinegar, and other acids are frequently in from the get-go. There's always the pucker quotient, however, when no more acid can be added. This is where water helps. A simplistic mental picture I conjure up is that there must be sufficient air in the emulsifier for the oil to have a place to go. This makes it clear that there has to be a lot of whisking! All the ingredients, except the oil, are whisked until they are thick and light first, then about a fourth of the oil is added, drop by drop, until the mixture has thickened. Then the rest of the oil can be added in a steady stream.

Making a temporary emulsion from vinegar and oil usually requires beating, about a fourth of the oil into the vinegar vigorously, drop by drop, as in a mayonnaise. I find it helps to whisk the vinegar and mustard together vigorously before adding the oil, just as whisking the egg, lemon, mustard, and water help in starting a mayonnaise.

A speedier process is to use a food processor or blender, adding the vinegar and mustard first and then slowly adding the oil. I find it bothersome to clean the appliance, but if someone else washes the dishes, why not?

MAYONNAISE

Makes 1 1/2 cups

Mayonnaise is an emulsified sauce. *It varies considerably with the type of oil used, so make sure the oil is one that will go well with the final product. Slaw, for instance, would be better with a neutral oil such as canola, peanut, or other vegetable oil rather than olive oil—unless adding chopped peanuts, when peanut oil would suit better.*

3 egg yolks
3 tablespoons fresh lemon juice, divided
1/4–1/2 teaspoon Dijon mustard
1 1/2 cups oil, cook's preference
Salt
Freshly ground black pepper

Whisk the egg yolks with 1 tablespoon lemon juice, mustard, salt, and 1 tablespoon water until the egg yolks are thick and lemon-colored.

Gradually whisk in one-third of the oil, drop by drop at first, until the mixture becomes cohesive. Continue whisking, adding the remaining oil in a slow, steady stream, until the mixture is thick and the oil is incorporated.

Season to taste with the remaining lemon juice, salt, and pepper. If a lighter mayonnaise is needed, add 1 or 2 more tablespoons water. Keep covered and refrigerated no longer than a week.

Variation: Aioli Mayonnaise

We made this every day in the restaurant in Spain where I was chef.

Add 4 crushed garlic cloves and 1/4 teaspoon hot red pepper after the oil is incorporated.

CAUTIONS ABOUT HOMEMADE MAYONNAISE

It is important to keep homemade mayonnaise refrigerated and to use it within a short period of time, about 1 week; otherwise discard it. Once diluted with the liquid from the potatoes, cabbage, or other common salad ingredients, homemade mayonnaise loses its low pH level and can be dangerous, particularly if left at room temperature. It is better to use a commercial mayonnaise in cases when you expect the salad to sit out for more than an hour or so, as its low commercial pH becomes a preservative to these foods rather than a detriment. The pH level of a homemade mayonnaise is too variable.

If mayonnaise breaks (curdles) or will not thicken, taste and add 1 more tablespoon lemon juice if it can use it. If not, add a tablespoon of water. This will give the oil a little more space and may thicken as well as repair a broken sauce. If not, whisk a fresh egg and a little water in a clean bowl. Slowly (drop by drop) whisk a fourth of the curdled mixture into the egg. It should be thick enough to whisk in the rest in a steady stream.

GARLIC AND RED PEPPER MAYONNAISE

Makes 2 cups

MADE IN A FOOD PROCESSOR, *this mayonnaise is an incredible bump up from regular. It's a wonderful spread for toast to accompany a soup or can be used as a regular mayonnaise. It is even good stirred into some soups.*

1 slice white bread
1/4 cup fresh lemon juice
3 egg yolks
1 tablespoon water
1/2 head garlic, about 5 cloves, peeled and crushed
3/4 cup olive oil
1 1/2 roasted red bell peppers (page 223)
1/4 teaspoon ground hot red pepper
Pinch of saffron
Salt
Freshly ground black pepper

Sprinkle the bread with lemon juice in a small bowl. Let sit until the bread absorbs the juice.

Process the egg yolks and water in the bowl of a food processor fitted with a metal blade until thick and lemon-colored. Pulse in the in the moistened bread and garlic. With the processor running, add a fourth of the olive oil drop by drop until the mixture thickens. Add the remaining oil in a slow, steady stream. When it reaches the desired consistency, add the bell peppers and hot red pepper. Process until smooth. Add pinch of saffron, and season to taste with salt and pepper.

Variations:

- Add chopped chives or other herbs.
- Omit bread for a thinner mayonnaise.
- Use clam juice or fish stock instead of lemon juice to make this like the French sauce *rouille*, which is added to fish stews.

BASIC VINAIGRETTE

Makes 1 1/3 cups

I KEEP THIS VINAIGRETTE ON HAND *in a jar on the counter, as we have salads nearly every night and we use it up quickly. Give it a few shakes or whisk it when needed. It can be varied on a whim, adding herbs, spices, or whatever else suits my fancy that day. I use extra virgin olive oil most days. Always dress a salad at the last minute, preferably at the table.*

Olive oils vary considerably, and some may be heavier than desired. If that is the case, dilute with a bit of canola or other light oil, such as grape seed. Salt and sugar take up the oily taste in a salad dressing, as does a bit of water or chicken stock. Avoid adding more vinegar than the recipe calls for, as it will just make everyone cough and still not accomplish the goal.

1–2 teaspoons Dijon mustard
1/3 cup red wine, sherry, Champagne, or other wine vinegar
1 teaspoon water
Salt
Freshly ground black pepper
1 cup olive oil
Granulated sugar, optional
Water or chicken stock or broth

For an everyday vinaigrette, whisk or shake together mustard, vinegar, water, salt, pepper, and oil. Taste and add more seasoning, sugar, and/or water or chicken stock. Refrigerate up to a week; whisk or shake as needed.

For a temporary emulsion, whisk the mustard, vinegar, water, salt, and pepper together in a small bowl. Slowly whisk in a fourth of the oil until thick. Add the rest in a steady stream while whisking. Season to taste with additional salt. Add sugar and/or water or chicken stock if still too oily-tasting. This vinaigrette will be opaque and creamy, with the ingredients evenly distributed. Store covered, in the refrigerator or on the counter.

Variations:

- For a small portion of vinaigrette, whisk together 1 teaspoon mustard, 1 tablespoon vinegar, salt, pepper, and 3 tablespoons oil. Taste for seasoning and add sugar or water or chicken stock if needed.
- Use heavy cream rather than oil for a creamy vinaigrette.
- Add 1 chopped garlic clove; a chopped shallot or green onion; a favorite chopped herb (such as thyme, oregano, or basil); a bit of curry powder, ground coriander, or cumin; or substitute honey for the sugar.

HONEY VINAIGRETTE

Makes 3/4 cup

THIS VINAIGRETTE IS ONLY SLIGHTLY SWEET. *In addition to topping salads, it makes a good marinade for chicken. Lemon balm is a member of the mint family that grows easily in the Lowcountry.*

2 tablespoons honey
1 teaspoon Dijon mustard
2 tablespoons wine vinegar
1/2 cup olive oil
Salt
Freshly ground black pepper
1 tablespoon chopped fresh lemon balm

Whisk the honey and mustard with the vinegar in a small bowl. While whisking, slowly drizzle in the olive oil. Season to taste with salt and pepper. Add lemon balm or other fresh herbs if available.

SWEET SOUTHERN DRESSING

Makes 3 cups

ADD POPPY SEEDS AND THIS BECOMES A RECIPE *popularized by the late Helen Corbitt, the famous cook for Neiman Marcus. This dressing is fabulous on fruit salads as well as on Fennel and Apple Salad (page 84). It keeps indefinitely in a covered jar in the refrigerator. If it separates, just give it a whir in a blender or food processor, and it will emulsify again.*

1 1/2 cups granulated sugar
2 teaspoons Dijon mustard
2 teaspoons salt
3 tablespoons chopped onion
2/3 cup apple cider vinegar
2 cups oil, cook's preference
3 tablespoons poppy seeds or chopped pecans, optional

Add the sugar, mustard, salt, onion, and vinegar to a food processor or blender, and blend until smooth. Pour in the oil in a steady stream and continue to blend until thick. Add optional poppy seeds or pecans. Keep covered in the refrigerator.

VIDALIA HONEY MUSTARD DRESSING

Makes about 1 1/4 cups

THIS TASTY DRESSING *is especially good for salads that have meat, chicken, or something heavy along with greens.*

1/2 onion, preferably Vidalia, quartered
2 tablespoons apple cider vinegar
2 tablespoons honey (preferably tupelo, orange blossom, or sweet clover)
1 tablespoon Dijon mustard
1/2 cup oil
1/2 teaspoon granulated sugar, optional
Salt
Freshly ground black pepper

In the bowl of a food processor fitted with the metal blade, pulse the onion until smooth.

Add the vinegar, honey, and mustard, and purée until smooth. Add the oil in a slow steady stream until the mixture is thick and emulsified (page 102). Taste and adjust for seasoning with sugar, salt, and pepper.

Store in an airtight container in the refrigerator. If dressing separates, whisk again to re-emulsify.

BUTTERMILK BLUE CHEESE DRESSING

Makes about 1 1/2 cups

6 ounces buttermilk blue cheese
1 cup sour cream
1/4 cup buttermilk
2 tablespoons finely chopped green onion or chives
Dash Worcestershire sauce
Dash hot sauce
Salt
Freshly ground black pepper

Break up the blue cheese with a fork. Stir in sour cream and buttermilk until creamy, but with bits of cheese remaining. Stir in onion or chives, Worcestershire, and hot sauce; season to taste with salt and pepper.

GINGER DRESSING

Makes 1/2 cup

1 tablespoon bottled ginger juice
2 tablespoons white wine or vinegar
1/4 teaspoon hot sauce, optional
Salt
1/3 cup olive oil

Whisk the ginger juice, vinegar, hot sauce, and a couple of big pinches of salt in a large bowl. Whisk in the olive oil but stop when the dressing takes on a slightly thick, opaque look. Set aside.

Variation: Omit the hot sauce and add up to 1 tablespoon curry powder to the vinegar.

PREPARING GINGER JUICE

Bottled ginger juice is commercially available and lasts a long time in the refrigerator, or it may be made by puréeing a 4-to-5-inch piece of ginger in a clean coffee grinder or grater and then pressing it against a strainer to extract the juice. My friend Pat Royalty showed up once with a whole container of ginger bulbs from her garden, which I divided and used to grow my own.

POPPY SEED VINAIGRETTE

Makes about 3/4 cup

2 teaspoons Dijon mustard
1 tablespoon granulated sugar
2 tablespoons finely chopped shallots
1/3 cup apple cider vinegar
3 tablespoons oil, cook's preference
2 tablespoons poppy seeds
1/2 teaspoon ground cumin
Salt
Freshly ground black pepper

Whisk together the mustard, sugar, shallots, vinegar, oil, poppy seeds, and cumin. Season to taste with salt and pepper.

VIBRANT VINAIGRETTE

Makes 3/4 cup

2 tablespoons orange juice
Grated rind of 1 navel orange, no white attached
1/2 roasted red bell pepper, torn in pieces (page 223)
2 green onions, sliced
1 garlic clove, chopped
2 tablespoons Dijon mustard
2 tablespoons red wine vinegar
1/2 cup oil, cook's preference
Salt
Freshly ground black pepper
Granulated sugar, optional

Purée the orange juice, rind, red pepper, green onion, garlic, mustard, and vinegar in a blender or food processor until smooth. Add the oil in a thin steady stream until the dressing is thick and emulsified (page 102). Season to taste with salt, pepper, and a pinch of sugar if desired.

STOCKS, SOUPS, GUMBOS, & STEWS

When soup slides down the throat, it brings with it such a sense of well-being that it frequently engenders an "ahhhh" from the eater, as if life is good. Which it is, if there is good soup to be had. The wise cook always keeps a bit of soup on hand in fridge or freezer, whether to balance out a sandwich or make or extend a meal. Soups can be served in demitasse cups or giant bowls or any size in between, so any amount is valuable. They can be stretched with a little broth, vegetables, protein foods from beans or cheese to eggs, poultry, fish or meat, serving more flavor and substance than what seemed possible at the start. They naturally pair with dumplings and all forms of bread, whether the bread is thickening the soup, used for sopping, or is an accompaniment, as a croûte or cracker. And, best of all, soups can include just about any tidbit of food or cooking liquid, making them one of the most important, nutritious, and economical foods in any home kitchen.

The basis of a memorable soup or sauce is a good broth or stock extracted from flavorful ingredients. Even if stock wasn't used for making soups and sauces and other good things, I would still probably make it just for the aroma and the process of using up all the little bits and pieces of leftovers that still have flavor and nutrition. Better yet, making stock is as easy as the cook wants it to be. Complex stocks are not the basis of average home cooking and can be ignored, except for those days when one wants to master a technique for the pleasure of it. We urge anyone who wants their food to soar above others with flavor and consistency to make their own stock. We try to make it easy.

EQUIPMENT AND PROCESSES FOR SOUP MAKING

Puréeing—Gadgets for puréeing foods include countertop blenders, hand-held immersion blenders, and food processors. Food mills and other methods of pushing ingredients through holes or sieves are useful in a pinch but are a good deal more awkward and messy.

Countertop blenders—These vary considerably in shape and quality. A heavy bottom keeps the blender from walking on the counter. If the blender does tend to walk, put the blender on top of a folded tea towel to hold it a bit. The "classic" blender container narrows at the bottom, where the blade chops any small pieces gathered there. A wide-bottomed blender container tends to leave stray bits wandering around the bottom, unable to be grabbed by the blade, so these are less likeable. The containers are sold smooth or fluted inside, with the fluted insides designed to aid in smoothing purées. Lids should fit tightly but need a removable insert on the top. Blenders with just a few push buttons work better and are easier than modern touch pads with what turns out to be irrelevant speeds.

Before puréeing in a blender, remove any solids from the pot with a slotted spoon and move to the blender. Use a ladle or cup smaller in diameter than the top of the machine to avoid spills and to ladle a small amount of liquid on top of the solids, filling no more than halfway. Not all the liquid needs to be added if all the solids are in the blender container.

Blending with still hot liquids causes a violent reaction and possible "explosion." To prevent the explosion, either drape the open container with a tea towel topped with the lid, holding the lid ajar to allow the steam to escape while blending, or top with the lid, remove the insert, and cover with a tea towel. Either way, use caution when puréeing hot liquids. There is less chance of cold ingredients exploding, so the blender can be filled a bit fuller. Emptying the blender and repeating the process is preferable to overfilling and having an explosive mess. Many times the blended liquid can be returned to the pot without any straining and whisked with any remaining unblended liquids until all the liquid is blended. If there are still chunks remaining or if the liquid is not as smooth as desired, pour through a strainer before continuing. A fine mesh strainer, preferably conical, may be needed for specialty soups.

Hand-held immersion blenders—Busy home cooks and chefs prefer immersion blenders—sturdy electric wands with permanently attached or removable blades that whir around the bottom of a pan, grabbing the cooked solids, frequently making a sucking sound, and creating an eddy that funnels the ingredients up under the blades to be puréed. The blades must be completely submerged or the mixture will splatter all over. Turn off the blender before removing from the liquid to avoid a mess. Check for any small bits that may be left on the bottom that the blades missed and remove with a slotted spoon. The blades are very sharp and should be treated with care.

Food processors—The metal blade fits loosely over a rotating stem in the clear container. If the liquid rises above the stem height, it can escape through the space around the stem and spill out from the bottom. If only solids are going to be processed with a small amount of liquid, the food processor is a good option. If there is a lot of liquid to be added, the processor will be less satisfactory. After pouring out the liquids, reinsert the blade and purée any remaining solids. It is difficult to purée every last bit, so remove any tiny pieces at the end.

Food mills or modules—These have a wide blade that rotates around the bottom of a wide sieve or colander. They strain the liquid into another container and then squash the remaining solids under the blade until they are fine enough to pass through the holes. Food mills work for the patient cook, but can be messy and time-consuming.

Stock pots and pans—Tall, narrow, lightweight pans give the water a longer time to move through the bones and vegetables, have less reduction of liquid, and are easier to keep at a low heat without boiling. Wider pots reduce the liquid more quickly and should be watched more carefully for evaporation and burning, but they will speed up the process for a casual stock without much difference in quality. Use a frying pan when a rapid stock or reduction is needed.

Dutch or French ovens—The best pans for stews are heavy, metal-lidded pots. My first one was an enameled one typical of the stew pot used for centuries. It had an indented area on the lid, which kept hot coals from sliding off the lid once they were added. The pan was pushed on top of other coals in a fireplace to create an oven. Still called "Dutch" or "French" ovens, after their countries of origin, heavy casserole pots, now rarely with indented lids, are useful on top of the stove as well as in the oven. Ovenproof handles and tight lids are important. A wide surface area, as opposed to the narrow stockpot, allows more food to be browned in less time. A heavy, enamel-lined light-colored pot is ideal, as it is easier to see the bottom of the pot to check for caramelizing or burning. Unlined cast-iron pots are inexpensive but need to be seasoned, and acids such as wine and tomatoes may pit or cause rusty off-flavors. My favorite is a round Le Creuset 6- to 12-quart pot. These pots are heavy, so ladling out the final contents in batches makes it easier on the cook.

Ladles—Ladles vary in size and use. A ladle should be long enough to reach the bottom of the pot without having to tip the pot, and its bowl should be close to the diameter of the receiving container to prevent spills. When ladling directly into individual soup bowls, a one-cup ladle is ideal. (A cup itself is awkward and messy.) To prevent the bottom of the ladle from dripping, dip the bottom of the nearly full ladle back into the pot until the pot liquid surrounds the ladle halfway. The soup grabs the exterior drippings and pulls them back into the pot.

When purchasing a ladle, buy a metal one with a long handle in an easily manipulated length and width; ideally it should have a way to hang it over a pot or rack. Metal handles can get very hot, so the width should accommodate being held with a tea towel or potholder. Wooden ladles soak in flavor and color and should be avoided, as should plastic.

Measuring and marking the ladle with a permanent marker is a good idea, as it makes it easier to know the amount of liquid being added.

STOCKS

Stocks are just flavored liquids, primarily water, but milk and a few other liquids can be stocks too. In this book, the words *stock* and *broth* are interchangeable. They can become the basis of sauces, gravies, and soups, and are excellent additions to casseroles and dressings, and much less expensive when made at home rather than purchased commercially.

Cooking—How long should a stock cook? Even a broth made from cooking a few bones in a frying pan for 10 minutes with a little water is better than none at all. As long as the bones and meat have flavor and nutritional value, they will add flavor to the water, depending on the quantity and quality of ingredients. Cooking time is usually up to 4 or 5 hours. If I am in a hurry or want a delicate stock, I cook it less time. I tend to leave it on as long as I am in the kitchen; I find it good company. Tasting is important, as it enables the cook to know how flavorful the stock is and whether adjustments should be made, such as cooking down further (reducing the liquid to concentrate the flavors) before seasoning any more. One caveat: fish bones should only be cooked for up to half an hour.

Covering/uncovering—Stocks may be simmered covered, partially covered, or uncovered. Usually I start a stock uncovered, bring to the boil, reduce the heat, and cover for the first hour or so, then uncover. An uncovered pan will speed evaporation of the liquid, so it may need more water added to keep the bones covered while cooking. A covered stock will not evaporate but may come to the boil without the cook noticing, resulting in a cloudy product. I usually half-cover the stock if I am only cooking it for a short period of time. If cooking a large quantity overnight or for many hours, I always cover the pot to ensure the liquid does not evaporate completely, and, of course, make sure the heat is low enough that there will be no danger in the long cooking. Salting all along is best, but a cook should know the saltiness of each ingredient in a soup, starting with the broth, and taste all along. (For instance, a ham broth may need no added salt.)

Skimming/non-skimming—Skimming removes the scum—the foam resulting from the blood, proteins, and

STOCK RECIPES ARE JUST VAGUE GUIDES

There's no magic to making a stock. Everyone approaches it a little differently. Stocks are flavored liquid. One friend saves every liquid from her cooking, particularly from cooking vegetables, to use as part of her stock. Traditionally, stocks are made by cooking the meat and bones of chicken, turkey, beef, veal, or pork in water with a few slices of carrot, onion, herbs, or other flavoring. Browning the ingredients intensifies the flavor, as does chopping up the bones and any meat.

A milk stock might include just carrot, onion, and celery. A court bouillon for fish might include wine, water, vegetables, and herbs. A hearty fish stock would include bones and more aggressive flavorings, such as ground fennel seed or hot peppers. A quick fish stock might include clam broth, shrimp shells, or fish bones. Vegetable stocks use no meat but substantially more vegetables.

Some chefs find carrots or onions too sweet, for instance; others think bay leaf too dominant. Calves' and pigs' feet are sometimes added by professionals to give an even more unctuous, gelatinous product but are rarely seen in a home kitchen.

Find a mix that is compatible and go with that. For instance, lemongrass, ginger, kaffir lime leaves, and other Asian ingredients are frequently added for fusion or Asian cooking. Lamb stock is primarily used for dishes to accompany lamb and is not mixed with the other meats and fowl, as it is so dominant a flavor.

Flavor is what is crucial, so a vegetable stock can have many more vegetables, for instance, or wine can be substituted for wine vinegar in a fish stock. Feel free to leave out what is not available and to add what tastes good and can enrich the flavor and texture.

A FEW TIPS FOR MAKING STOCKS

- The ratio of ingredients to water should be approximately 1 pound of combined bones and meat to 1 quart water to make a tasty, full-bodied stock. Add water to cover the ingredients. Bring to the boil, skim off the foam (composed of blood and proteins) that comes to the top, reduce heat, and simmer.
- The longer a stock is simmered, the better—within reason; nothing is to be gained by continuing to cook ingredients that no longer have flavor. A clear stock is the most desirable, visually, but is rarely essential. Ingredients should remain submerged in liquid while they are simmering. Finished broth should be strained and cooled, then refrigerated if possible; this lets the fat rise to the top to be skimmed off easily when cold.
- Tasting the broth enables the cook to know how flavorful the stock is and whether adjustments should be made, such as boiling down further (reducing to concentrate the flavors) or adjusting seasonings.
- Keep a container in the freezer for bits and pieces that add flavor to stock, including parsley stalks, extra herbs, carrot tops, Parmesan rinds, tough brown mushroom stems, etc. Cooked ingredients from meals can be easily saved and added for making stock. (I sometimes bring home the partial remains of a restaurant meal—hamburger, steak, and/or roasted chicken, for instance—to make into a broth.)
- Combining raw meats with cooked meats is tricky, as it is necessary to ensure that all are thoroughly cooked before straining. This will prevent any unhealthy bacteria in undercooked meat from contaminating the soup.
- Too many bones in any stock will make it too gelatinous for a soup, while too few will result in a watery stock.
- Onions and garlic enhance the flavor of stocks, particularly when the onion is browned.
- Parsley stems are stronger than the herb itself and should be used sparingly. Celery leaves are bitter and strong, and should never be used in a stock.
- Nothing should be wasted in the modern Southern kitchen.

vegetable residue rising to the top of the liquid. For me, it is a Zen-like experience to stand and skim. To skim, bring the liquid quickly to the boil. The proteins gather at the sides of the pan or when the pan is tipped, enabling them to be skimmed off and discarded. A long slotted flat spoon is ideal for this, but there are many gadgets that will do. Most of the time, skimming is not vital for the home cook, as the cloudiness caused by proteins is not apparent in most sauces, soups, and stews—certainly not hearty ones. If the stock is for "unknown" purposes and might wind up in a clear broth such as a chicken soup, skimming makes a visual difference.

Straining and cooling—After straining the stock, pour it into several small, wide containers and leave to cool at room temperature, uncovered. Straining the stock into a wide-mouthed container such as a bowl will cool it faster and make it easier to remove the fat.

Covering a hot liquid, particularly if it is in a tall, narrow container, prevents it from cooling and may cause it to sour. Putting hot stock in a refrigerator or freezer will heat up the other items and may cause bacteria to grow and the stock to sour as well.

Refrigerate for a few days, or cover and freeze, properly labeled. To keep it fresh, stock stored in the refrigerator should be brought to the boil every few days and cooled as above. Hopefully this won't be necessary more than once. "Bad" stock is easily discovered—it smells sour and usually doesn't need tasting to verify its unsuitability.

Reducing a stock—Once the stock is strained, the liquid may be left as it is or boiled down and reduced, making it easier to store as well as concentrate flavor and thicken. Stock reduced to a thick slurry state is called a *demi-glaze*. Stock cooked down to a viscous state produces a gelatinous consistency known as a glace de viande, which lasts indefinitely in the refrigerator. Once reduced and concentrated, stock may later be diluted by adding liquid.

Freezing and defrosting—There are many ways to freeze stock, from small amounts in ice cube trays—which are never enough for my purposes but which many people find helpful—to muffin tins lined with one-cup plastic ziplock freezer bags, filled with the tins acting as molds until the frozen stock is twisted out and moved together to a sturdy freezer bag. Although freezer containers work perfectly well, they are more difficult to store, as they vary in size radically—and, of course, they are not available for storing anything else. Try to keep containers together in an organized fashion in the freezer.

The speediest way to freeze stock (and to defrost as well) is to ladle stock into freezer bags, lay them flat on a sheet pan to freeze, remove the tray when frozen, and stack the containers. Labeling and dating is easiest before filling. Double bagging is useful in preventing leaks, in which case one bag should be facing one way and sealed, the second facing the opposite way and sealed. Expel as much air as possible. If there is any residual fat on the top of the frozen package when ready to use, it is easier to scrape it off before defrosting.

> Ingredients for soups, as well as all foods, should be free of contamination, mold, sourness, etc. Garbage in, garbage out is a good thing to remember.

Types of Stock

There are two basic colors of meat stock—white and brown. White stock is the most common stock used in the home.

White Stock—For white stocks, the meat, bones and/or vegetables are simmered without browning the meat first. They are the basis for stocks, soups, and stews when a delicate flavor is desired, or for most homemade soups.

Brown Stock—Brown stock, including veal, beef, lamb, duck, turkey, chicken, pork, and even vegetable stocks, results from first browning the meat and bones, starting with chopped meaty and bony pieces, preferably with marrow, which gives a more gelatinous quality and richness to soups and sauces. If the bones have little or no meat on them, such as neck bones, then a less flavorful, more gelatinous stock will result. A bit of meat, usually ground or cubed, will add flavor and color, as will browning any vegetables. The browning (caramelizing) of the ingredients intensifies the deep of flavor of the stock. It takes a bit of practice and attention to get the perfect color, but perfection is not required. Any caramelization adds to the stock's color and flavor. Browning vegetables adds color and flavor for a meat stock or a vegetable stock.

Ham Stock—My first ham stock was made from a ham bone I begged from the Cordon Bleu after one of my first classes. The teacher suggested I make a tomato soup from it. It was a luscious soup, and I learned how to enhance any food with a bit of leftover meat, bones, or vegetables. Ham stock can be a smoked broth made from the meat and bones from cooked smoked pork, such as the neck bone, hog jowl, ham bone, etc. Usually this broth is used to cook Southern vegetables, such as greens (see Turnip Green, page 205, or pot likker) or tomato, bean, and meat soups, when a smoky taste is desired.

Fish and Seafood Stocks—Fish and seafood usually use a white stock, made from white fish bones and/or skin, but on rare occasion the bones will be browned. If no bones are available, a "blank" bouillon is used—just vegetables cooked in water to give a little flavor. Some like adding lemongrass, kaffir lime, and/or other flavorings such as fennel seed to the water. See Country-Style Fish Broth, page 118.

Vegetable Stock—Use only vegetables and proceed as above. Corncobs are also used to make stock (page 117).

Commercial Stock or Broth—Commercial "stocks" are usually named "broths," making the two words interchangeable in modern home cooking. Technically, a stock is a base to be built upon, as in a stew or soup, where a broth is to be drunk on its own, as a bouillon. Commercial products vary widely in saltiness and nutrients. If a stock or broth is pre-salted, it makes it difficult to boil down and reduce or combine with other canned ingredients that also may be pre-salted, creating an overwhelmingly salty end product. Knowing one's stock is crucial, and tasting all the commercial stocks available is a good exercise. Barring that, purchasing canned stock or broth with the least sodium is the best guide, adding salt as needed by tasting.

Commercial broths lack the mouth-feel of homemade stocks and are relatively bland in flavor, so boost the flavor by adding a few bits and pieces of carrot, onion, celery, bay leaf, thyme, and/or other herbs, as well as seasoning with salt and pepper to taste, bringing it to the boil then reducing the heat to simmer, covered, for up to half an hour before straining and using it. There was a time when most commercial broths were canned. Now few are. Most are sold in boxes. Cubes or granules need the addition of water or other liquid and are also used by some cooks. In addition, reductions of stocks and broths are sold commercially that are dense with flavor; these can be added "as is" or made into a broth with added liquid. To determine which you prefer, have a tasting party with a few friends and blind-taste all the available products.

Bouillon is a more intense liquid with a more gelatinous flavor and is usually clarified. When reduced enough that no liquid remains, it is made into cubes and granules or thick paste-like gels.

Removing the Fat—Fat rises to the surface of a cooled liquid. Use a slotted spoon for small amounts, or if it is congealed and hard, break up and remove. Avoid removing it before the stock is finished, particularly when skimming off the foam, as it adds flavor all along. I leave the fat on when I refrigerate the stock, as it is a protective covering. I remove it before using further, as well as before freezing.

"Leftover" Stock—A stock is easily compiled of leftover pieces of meat and vegetables—from roast, steak, meatloaf, or burger to turkey, chicken, duck, or pork. Gather any bones, scraps of meat, and vegetables as well as liquids that will add a good flavor and color, avoiding those that will leave a strong taste, such as broccoli, cabbage, beets, etc. If using carcasses of fowl or meat bones, be sure to add as much meat as possible. A stock made just from bones will be gelatinous but not necessarily flavorful.

Bring the meat and/or bones to the boil with any leftover vegetables and water to cover; add any flavorings, reduce heat, and simmer, partially covered, until the desired flavor is reached—an hour or less for a small amount, up to several hours for a large amount. Strain. Taste and boil down to desired consistency and flavor. Cool. Remove fat. Refrigerate, covered, or freeze up to three months.

Household Stock—My usual time to make stock is when I am unloading groceries. I use a whole chicken, put it in a heavy pot, add water and the other ingredients below—all of which takes less than five minutes—and continue unloading the groceries. If I didn't clean out the fridge before I went grocery shopping, as a good cook would, I do it as I unload. Any suitable leftover food goes into the stockpot too, if it will add flavor, or I set it aside for use in a soup. For example: a few cooked carrots, mushrooms, onions may be added to the stock; a little broccoli, Brussels sprouts, macaroni, or cheese, spaghetti, or chili may become part of the soup.

COUNTING PEPPERCORNS

There are good reasons for using a set number of peppercorns. First, using a set number will give the cook an idea to what degree the broth is affected by the amount used. If more heat is desired, then it is easier to keep track of the flavors added. Second, on the rare occasion when the cook is careless and adds peppercorns to something that won't be strained, using peppercorns in a consistent multiple of one number (6, 12, 18) according to the quantity to be flavored, helps in counting the number to be removed, as we don't want these to end up in a bowl of finished soup. Black ground pepper can be substituted but may leave a black sprinkle in the stock.

WHITE CHICKEN OR TURKEY STOCK

Yields 6 cups

THIS FULL-FLAVORED STOCK TAKES A LONG TIME *on the stove but requires very little of the cook's time. The uncooked neck, backbones, and gizzard of a chicken or turkey, with any extraneous flesh and other bones, may be used to make a white stock. Avoid using the liver, as it will discolor the stock and make it bitter. As with any stock, use what is available, and don't worry if anything but the main ingredient is missing.*

4 pounds chicken or turkey bones and/or meat
1 medium onion, quartered
1–2 carrots, roughly sliced
1 celery rib, roughly sliced, no leaves
1 bay leaf
4–6 sprigs thyme, optional
8 parsley stems, optional
2 garlic cloves, unpeeled, optional
12 black peppercorns

Roughly chop or break up the chicken bones and pieces. Move to a large pot along with the onion, carrots, and celery, and/or any of the other available ingredients. Add enough water to cover. Bring the mixture to the boil, then reduce the heat and simmer about 45 minutes. Skim off and discard any rising fat and impurities, which come up as foam (pages 111–12).

After the foam has been removed, add the remaining ingredients. Continue to simmer half-covered for another 3 hours, or whatever is practicable, adding hot water as necessary to keep the bones and vegetables covered. Stir occasionally when passing by.

Strain the stock through a fine mesh strainer or a colander lined with dampened cheesecloth, pressing the solids to release all of the juices and extract their flavor. Cool the stock and refrigerate several hours or overnight. When cold, skim off the fat that has risen to the surface. The stock may be refrigerated up to 3 days, or it may be frozen, using containers of a size that will accommodate future needs, such as 1-quart freezer bags or containers.

Variation: Brown Chicken or Turkey Stock
Cook the chicken and/or bones and vegetables on the stovetop or roast in a baking pan in the oven until they are deep brown. Be careful not to burn, or they will add a bitter taste to the stock. When the bones are brown, add water, bring to the boil, and stir, scraping up the brown bits from the bottom of the pan. This process is called "deglazing." Pour this liquid into the stockpot and add any other stock ingredients. As soon as it comes to the boil, reduce to a simmer. Skim as impurities float to the top (pages 111–12).

USING A BOUQUET GARNI

A bouquet garni is a bundle of fresh or dried herbs added to stocks, soups, and stews. Herbs add a very subtle underlay of flavor but lose their oomph after 15 to 30 minutes. For that reason, add fresh herbs to long-cooking stocks in abundance. Otherwise, add them the last 15 minutes of cooking a stock or stew to give a final burst of flavor. Ideally, do both.

AMBER TURKEY STOCK

Makes 2 quarts

THIS IS MY FAVORITE STOCK. *Browned turkey wings and neck pieces provide a good base, resulting in a full-flavored stock that is more practical for me than chicken stock, but I use both. At holiday time, I always make a stock from browned wings and necks. I cool and then freeze it for later. The browned bones and flesh produce a beautiful amber-colored stock. It is very useful for extra gravy, dressings, and soups. Gravy made from turkey stock is substantially earthier and more succulent than chicken or many other stocks. The more the bones are chopped, the more natural gelatin will be in the stock.*

- 3 pounds turkey wings, backs, necks, or other pieces
- 1 medium onion, thickly sliced, including brown peel
- 1 large carrot, thickly sliced
- 1 celery rib, thickly sliced, optional
- 3–4 parsley stalks, optional
- 1/4 cup mushroom stems, optional
- 6 black peppercorns, optional
- 1 bay leaf
- 1/4 teaspoon dried thyme

Preheat oven to 350 degrees.

Using a meat cleaver, chop the turkey meat and bones into smaller pieces. Move the turkey pieces, onion, carrot, and optional ingredients to a heavy rimmed baking sheet and into the oven. Roast, turning occasionally. Smaller pieces will brown more quickly, so remove them as they turn a very dark brown with perhaps a small touch of black. This will take approximately 30 to 45 minutes.

Move the turkey bones and meat and all other ingredients to a deep stockpot or saucepan. Add 1/2 cup water to the roasting pan. Bring to the boil over medium heat, deglazing the pan (scraping brown bits from the bottom and sides. It's also a good way to clean the pan.) Pour into the pan along with enough water to cover the ingredients. Bring to the boil, then reduce the heat and simmer for about 2 hours, adding water as needed to keep the wings covered.

Strain the stock through a fine mesh strainer or a colander lined with dampened cheesecloth, pressing the solids to release all of the juices and extract their flavor. Cool the stock and refrigerate several hours or overnight. When cold, skim off all the fat that has risen to the surface. The stock may be refrigerated up to 3 days, or it may be frozen, using containers of a size that will accommodate future needs, such as 1-quart freezer bags or containers.

COURT BOUILLON OR VEGETABLE STOCK

Makes 1 quart

VEGETABLE STOCKS, ALSO CALLED COURT BOUILLON *(meaning, more or less, "blank broth") can be full of flavored vegetables, particularly for a soup, or more delicate, as for a liquid used in poaching fish, adding a bit of flavor but not dominating. All the ingredients are optional in their own way, and if only a few are available, there is no concern.*

- 1 small carrot, sliced
- 1 small onion, sliced
- 6 peppercorns
- 3–4 sprigs fresh thyme
- 6–8 fresh parsley stems
- 1 small bay leaf
- 1/3 cup white wine vinegar or fresh lemon juice, optional

Bring 1 quart of water to the boil with any or all of the ingredients and simmer about 30 minutes or up to several hours. Strain. Cool the stock and refrigerate several hours or overnight. The stock may be refrigerated up to 3 days, or it may be frozen, using containers of a size that will accommodate future needs, such as 1-quart freezer bags or containers.

Variation: Add kaffir lime leaves, orange rind or juice, green onions, lemongrass, or other more exotic flavorings, which grow readily in the South.

SHRIMP STOCK

Makes 6 cups

ONCE, SOME GOOD FRIENDS INVITED OVER FOR DINNER *asked if they could help, and I said they could pour the water from a bottle in the refrigerator. My table was dressed to the nines. When I sat down, I noticed an exchange of glances as they sipped their water. Lo and behold, they had poured the shrimp stock into the crystal glasses and were sure it was an exotic cold soup I was serving, it tasted so good! I use this stock in the place of fish stock or clam juice.*

36 shrimp shells
8 cups water
1 small onion, halved
1 small carrot, cut in 3 or 4 pieces
3 parsley stems
2 lemon wedges
6 black peppercorns
Salt

Crush shrimp shells with a rolling pin or in the food processor. Bring all ingredients except salt to the boil in a large pot. Reduce to a simmer and cook until the liquid is reduced by a fourth. Strain. Season to taste with salt.

Cool the stock and refrigerate several hours or overnight. The stock may be refrigerated up to 3 days, or it may be frozen, using containers of a size that will accommodate future needs, such as 1-quart freezer bags or containers.

CORNCOB STOCK

Makes 3 quarts

WHEN EIGHT OR SO CORNCOBS ARE AVAILABLE, *make this light, flavorful stock to use in chowders and soups. It freezes well for at least 3 months. For more flavor, use chicken or vegetable stock in lieu of water. The resulting broth may be boiled down to increase the flavor for a sauce or a smaller soup recipe.*

8–10 corn cobs (kernels have been removed for another use)
1 medium onion, chopped
2 large carrots, chopped
6 –8 sprigs fresh thyme
1 teaspoon salt
Freshly ground pepper

Move corncobs, onion, and carrots to a large stockpot. Add 3 to 4 quarts of water and bring to the boil. Reduce heat to simmer and cook stock about 45 minutes. Strain the stock, discarding the cobs and vegetables. Cool and use within a day or two, or freeze.

COUNTRY-STYLE FISH BROTH

Makes 4 quarts

THIS BROTH GIVES A FISH SOUP ITS FULL FLAVOR. *If using whole fish for Southern Bouillabaisse (page 146), use the bones, head, and trimmings for this broth. Or purchase them. If bones cannot be found, substitute fish fillets. (Use the cheapest available, but stay away from oily fish such as salmon and mackerel.) The broth will be flavorful, but it won't have as much body, since the bones provide gelatin.*

Fish, tomatoes, onion, garlic, and fennel all like each other and give a particularly interesting base for a broth. Hot peppers may be omitted for mild broths, or more may be added for a peppier result. As in any stock, not every ingredient is necessary, or an additional ingredient may be used to change the flavor. I usually beg the fishmonger for the bones of a large grouper, sea trout, or snapper. Flounder bones will work but are fragile.

3/4 cup oil, cook's preference
2 medium onions, sliced
2 medium carrots, coarsely chopped
1/2 cup finely chopped fresh fennel, optional
3 pounds fresh Roma tomatoes or canned Italian plum tomatoes, chopped
4 garlic cloves, chopped
3 pounds bones, head, and trimmings of a non-oily fish, well washed
6 parsley stalks
1–1 1/2 teaspoons fennel seed
2 bay leaves, optional
12 black peppercorns
Rind of 1 small orange, lime, or lemon, no white attached
1/2–1 teaspoon saffron threads
Pinch of ground hot red pepper, or 1–2 small dried peppers

Heat the oil in a heavy 12-quart stockpot. Add the onions, carrots, fennel, tomatoes, garlic, and fish bones; cook over medium heat for 10 minutes, stirring occasionally. Add remaining ingredients to the pot. Add cold water to cover, bring to the boil, reduce the heat to simmer, and cook uncovered for 30 minutes. Add water if needed.

Let the broth base cool enough to handle and then strain it through a large fine sieve or a colander lined with cheesecloth, pressing hard on the solids to extract all the juices. Taste and, if necessary, bring back to the boil and reduce to 2 quarts or less as desired, or add liquid to bring up to a desired quantity. Cool the stock and refrigerate several hours or overnight.

The stock may be refrigerated up to 3 days, or it may be frozen, using containers of a size that will accommodate future needs, such as 1-quart freezer bags or containers.

Variation: For a "standard" fish stock, leave out the carrots, fennel, tomatoes, fennel seed, orange rind, and saffron. Add the juice of 1 lemon and simmer the stock only 20 minutes.

FISHY BUSINESS

Handling fish bones requires rubber gloves. Without them, the sharp bones may sliver or cut hands. The fish should be rinsed well, with gills and any blood and detritus removed but as much flesh left on the bones as possible.

SOUPS, GUMBOS, & STEWS

Soups, gumbos, and stews are one-dish mixtures of liquids, vegetables, meat, chicken, and/or seafood. Soups are spoon- or sipping-friendly liquids—chunky, creamy, clear or somewhere in between—rather than sauce-like. Gumbos can be either spoon or fork consistencies. Stews are fork-friendly, with a thicker, more sauce-like liquid. This results from either thickening with flour or other ingredients such as arrowroot, cornstarch, rice, potatoes, or bread, as well as file and okra.

COLD AVOCADO SOUP

Serves 4

A RIPE AVOCADO IS A MARVELOUS FOOD, *full of nutrients and easy to incorporate in Southern recipes. They've been known to grow in the South from Florida up to South Carolina's Lowcountry. I even know of a ten-foot tree that was grown from seed in Charleston. Interestingly, avocados turn bitter when cooked.*

2 ripe avocados, pitted and peeled
1 cup chicken stock or broth
1 cup heavy cream or sour cream
1–2 teaspoons chopped fresh cilantro or basil
Juice of 1 lemon
Salt
Freshly ground black pepper
Ground hot red pepper

Cut the avocados up roughly and move to a blender or food processor. Slowly add the chicken stock and purée until smooth.

Transfer to a bowl and whisk in the cream and herbs. Season to taste with the lemon juice, salt, pepper, and hot red pepper. Chill in a tightly covered container or serve immediately.

BLUEBERRY SOUP

Serves 4

A PARTICULARLY REFRESHING STARTER IN HOT MUGGY WEATHER, *this may be made a day or two ahead. Ideal for serving in a beautiful teacup or small handled bowl, half of a cup is a satisfying portion.*

2 pints fresh or frozen blueberries
1 cup water
1/2 cup plus 2 tablespoons granulated sugar
1/4 cup orange juice
Heavy cream, yogurt, or sour cream to garnish

Carefully rinse the blueberries and pick out any stems.

Add the blueberries, water, sugar, and orange juice to a medium saucepan and bring to the boil. Reduce heat to low and simmer for 15 minutes.

Purée solids until smooth using an immersion blender, food processor, or sturdy blender, adding liquid as needed.

Cover and chill at least 2 hours or overnight. Just before serving, add a little heavy cream, yogurt, or sour cream to the soup. Swirl with a spoon and serve.

COLD RASPBERRY-BLUEBERRY SOUP

Serves 4

EVERYTHING HAPPENS AT ONCE. *Raspberries are on sale. Blueberries show up on the bushes just as my figs ripen. Abundance is in my garden, and there is little time to deal with it when company is calling. The two soups are made separately and joined together in the serving bowl. If only one or the other berry is available, double the ingredient of one, tasting and adjusting ingredients accordingly.*

1/2 pint raspberries
1 pint blueberries
1/2–3/4 cup orange juice, preferably fresh-squeezed, divided
1/2 cup Greek or other plain yogurt, divided
Fresh lemon juice
Salt
Freshly ground black pepper
Granulated sugar, optional
Fresh lemon balm or mint, chopped

Wash the berries, removing leaves, stems, and discolored berries. Shake dry. Purée the raspberries with 1/4 cup orange juice and 1/4 cup yogurt; set aside. Taste and add more orange juice as desired. Set aside.

Purée the blueberries until smooth with 1/4 cup orange juice and 1/4 cup yogurt until smooth. Season with lemon juice to taste, salt, and just a little ground pepper. Taste and add optional sugar if soup is too sharp tasting.

Pour the soups into individual bowls simultaneously from 2 measuring cups positioned on opposite sides of the bowl. The separate mixtures will form a mosaic. Sprinkle with chopped lemon balm or mint.

RINSING AND FREEZING BERRIES

Berries should only be rinsed just before using to avoid molding. Raspberries in particular are prone to quick deterioration so should be used promptly. Other berries are more forgiving.

To freeze, gently rinse fresh berries and allow to air-dry spread out on paper towels. Transfer the berries to a rimmed baking sheet and move to the freezer for 1 hour or so. Transfer the frozen berries to a freezer container or plastic ziplock bag, label, and freeze.

PALE PINK ICED CUCUMBER AND MINT SOUP

Serves 6 to 8

THIS RECIPE GOES BACK TO THE 1970S WITH ME. *I've served it all summer long in my restaurant and included it in two of my previous books. When my favorite former husband's father was ill, it was the only thing he craved eating. I would feel guilty about repeating the recipe here, but it's unforgettably cooling and a wonderful starter, with its seductive, pale pink color. Cynthia ranks it as just about her favorite summer soup. It requires no cooking, with the exception of the hard-cooked egg, which I have omitted from time to time, as time dictates. In fact, at one time or another, I've omitted each one of the ingredients with no deleterious effect.*

I recommend chilling all the ingredients ahead of time so the soup will already be chilled and can be served right away if necessary! If fresh local shrimp is unavailable, I use the commercially frozen tiny shrimp, as they don't have to be chopped and are already peeled. Mint is nearly a weed here, so I suspect everyone can find some to use in the summer.

3 cucumbers, peeled, seeded, and diced
Salt
1/2 cup tomato juice, fresh or canned
1/2 cup chicken stock or broth
2 1/2 cups plain yogurt
1/2 cup heavy cream
2 garlic cloves, finely chopped
1 hard-cooked egg, grated or chopped (page 275), optional
1/4 pound fresh or frozen shrimp, cooked and peeled (pages 326–27), chopped
Fresh mint, finely chopped, optional

Move the cucumber slices to a colander placed over a bowl or sink, and salt liberally. Leave for 15 to 30 minutes. Rinse and drain the cucumber slices. Squeeze water out of the cucumbers with hands or paper towels and chill.

Stir together the tomato juice, chicken stock, yogurt, cream, garlic, and egg in a large bowl until well-blended. Chill.

Add the cucumbers and shrimp just before serving. Garnish with chopped mint if desired.

CHILLED MELON SOUP

Serves 4 to 6

THIS LIGHT AND REFRESHING SOUP *is perfect for a hot summer day. Combine and chill ahead of time for a scintillating starter or even a light dessert. This recipe is a great way to use up leftover fruit. If only one or the other melon is available, double the ingredient and make one soup, tasting carefully and adjusting ingredients accordingly.*

1 1/2 cups cantaloupe cut in 1-inch pieces
5 cups seedless watermelon cut in 1-inch pieces
1–2 tablespoons white wine vinegar, optional

Purée the cantaloupe in a food processor or blender to make 1 cup of liquid. Repeat with the watermelon, making 3 cups of liquid. Taste and add the vinegar if desired. The purées can be poured separately and swirled together in the bowl for a pretty design, or they can be combined.

Variations:

- Add chopped mint, basil, or tarragon, as desired.
- A creamy goat cheese or lemon Stilton would be perfect for a savory course, while goat or plain yogurt mixed with honey and fresh mint would make a satisfying cool dessert course.

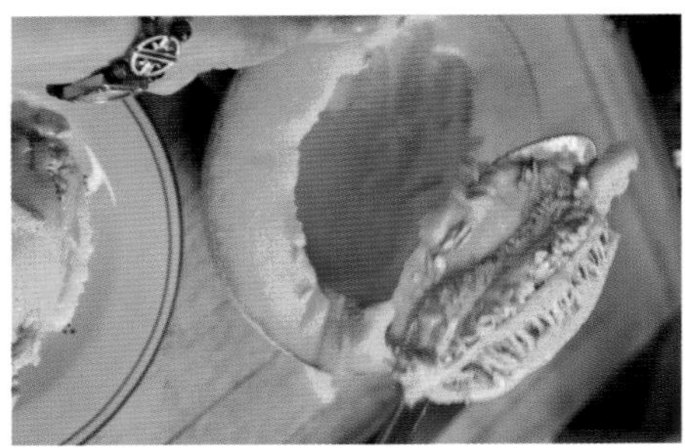

LIQUID YIELD FROM MELONS

Depending on the lateness of the season and the ripeness of the fruit, the yield of liquid from the melons may differ. Usually a melon will purée to liquid roughly based on 3 parts melon yielding 2 parts liquid; so 1 1/2 cups melon usually yields about 1 cup liquid.

BOURBON-SPIKED COLD PEACH SOUP

Serves 4 to 6

THE DAY CYNTHIA AND CLIFF LEFT ATLANTA *for their wedding in Italy, Ellis Hughes and Peter Kent hosted the couple for a bon voyage lunch. Peter served this luscious soup in honor of the couple's roots in Georgia. Cynthia still serves it each year around their anniversary. If no fresh peaches are available, use frozen or jarred.*

3 cups sliced peeled peaches
1 1/2 cups water
1 1/2 cups dry white wine
1 thin slice fresh ginger
1 1/2 tablespoons cornstarch
1 1/2 tablespoons cold water
1/2 cup granulated sugar
3 tablespoons bourbon
1–3 tablespoons grated lemon rind, no white attached
1/4–1/2 cup sour cream

Heat together the peaches, water, wine, and ginger in a saucepan over medium heat. When the liquid begins to simmer, turn the heat to low, cover, and simmer 15 minutes. Whisk together the cornstarch and cold water and add to the peach mixture. Stir in the sugar and bourbon, increase the heat, and bring the soup to the boil. Reduce heat and cook until thickened, stirring frequently. Stir frequently until thickened. Remove from heat and purée the soup. Add lemon rind and sour cream and purée the soup until smooth using an immersion blender, or purée in batches using a food processor or sturdy blender. Allow to cool, then refrigerate at least 4 hours before serving. This soup keeps a day or two, covered and refrigerated.

This soup is thickened with a cornstarch and water slurry (page 151), which is frequently used with fruit and cold soups.

BUTTERMILK-TOMATO COLD SOUP

Serves 6 to 8

THE BASE OF THIS SOUP *may be made with any color tomato and be equally stunning. There is no need to peel the tomatoes, as they are strained later. The garnish of mixed red and yellow cherry tomatoes makes it seem as if a great deal of effort was involved.*

2 pounds ripe red or yellow tomatoes
1 teaspoon salt, plus more to taste
3/4 cup buttermilk
Freshly ground black pepper
Hot sauce, optional

1 pound red and yellow cherry tomatoes, halved
3–4 tablespoons chopped fresh basil or thyme

1 tablespoon finely chopped green onion (green part only) or chives
1 tablespoon olive oil

Coarsely chop the tomatoes, reserving any juices; move to a food processor or sturdy blender as each one is chopped.

Sprinkle all the chopped tomatoes with 1 teaspoon of salt and let stand at room temperature for 1 hour to extract the juices. Purée until smooth. Strain the purée through a coarse sieve, preferably nonmetal, into a nonmetal bowl. Stir in the buttermilk. Season to taste with salt, pepper, and optional hot sauce. Refrigerate until chilled, at least 30 minutes.

Toss the cherry tomatoes with the remaining ingredients. Season to taste again with salt and pepper. Refrigerate in a closed plastic bag if not using shortly.

Just before serving, ladle the soup into individual soup bowls, spoon the cherry tomato garnish into the center of each bowl, and serve.

Variation: Quick-Cook Tomato Soup
Sauté 1 chopped onion and 2 chopped garlic cloves for 5 minutes in a large Dutch oven over medium heat. Add 3 cups chopped tomatoes, 2 tablespoons tomato sauce, and 3 cups water. Simmer 10 to 15 minutes. Garnish with chopped fresh basil.

COMBINING SOUPS

Most soups can be kept refrigerated for several days or frozen and reheated, making them a very welcome pantry or freezer staple. In fact, we have been known to mix drips and drabs of soups to stretch a meal. To test for compatibility, mix a small portion of the soups together and taste. If not compatible, serve separately in demitasse cups.

GAZPACHO

Serves 8

Gazpacho was called Gazpacha in Mary Randolph's The Virginia House-Wife (page 94). *In that recipe the dish becomes a thick salad, much like a bread salad. Mrs. Randolph combined her biscuits or toasted bread with sliced peeled tomatoes, cucumbers, chopped onion, and stewed tomato juice mixed with olive oil, salt, pepper, and mustard. At some point, the mustard was omitted and bell pepper added. I add a splash of red wine vinegar to give it some pep, but purists may omit that.*

I had a friend when I lived in Majorca, a glamorous Dutch countess, who insisted that chopped ingredients be added to the soup as garnish to aid the digestion. I've always liked this presentation, so I include it here.

2 large onions
3 large garlic cloves
2 red bell peppers, seeded and cored
1–2 small cucumbers
2 pounds ripe tomatoes, peeled and seeded, cut into chunks*
1/2 cup crumbled biscuits or bread
3 cups tomato juice, fresh or canned
5 tablespoons red wine vinegar
Salt
Freshly ground black pepper
1 cup bread cubes, fried in 3 tablespoons butter or oil, cook's preference

Cut into pieces three-fourths each of the onions, garlic, bell peppers, and cucumbers and purée in a food processor or sturdy blender, reserving the remaining one-fourth to be served as garnish.

Add the tomatoes and biscuits or bread and process again. Add tomato juice and vinegar as needed to process to a smooth texture. Remove as necessary if the container becomes too full.

Pour puréed vegetables into a bowl with any remaining juice and vinegar. If too thick, ice water or more juice may be added. Season to taste with salt and pepper.

Chop the remaining onion, garlic, bell pepper, and cucumber. Chill both the soup and the garnish ingredients. When ready to serve, ladle the soup into bowls and pass the chopped ingredients along with the fried bread cubes, to be sprinkled into each bowl. Gazpacho will last nearly a week in the refrigerator.

** If ripe, lush tomatoes are not available, use high-quality canned tomatoes*

FROM WHENCE THE TOMATO?

Tomatoes were popular much earlier in the South than the North. It may have been something as simple as the South's longer growing season that encouraged their greater consumption. It may have been the legacy of the Spanish from the 1500s. Some credit slave ships that brought tomato seeds to plant for feeding of the African slaves, already accustomed to eating them, via the Portuguese trade routes.

GOLDEN GAZPACHO WITH CHILIES AND SHRIMP

Serves 4 to 6

ADAPTED FROM CRAIG CLAIBORNE'S Southern Cooking, *I have made this many times, as much for the color as for the vibrant taste that cools and excites the palette simultaneously. Chilies vary in hotness, so we have provided a wide variation in amount.*

- 1/2–1 1/2 teaspoons finely chopped fresh hot peppers, preferably serrano
- 3/4 cup chicken stock or broth
- 1/2 teaspoon saffron threads
- 2 tablespoons fresh lime juice
- 2 pounds yellow tomatoes, peeled and seeded
- 1/3 cup chopped yellow bell peppers
- 3/4 cup chopped cantaloupe, divided
- 1/2 cup chopped mango
- 1/2 cup seeded, peeled, and diced cucumber
- 2 tablespoons finely chopped green onion, whites only
- Salt
- 1 pound small shrimp, cooked and peeled (pages 326–27)
- 1 tablespoon chopped fresh cilantro

Purée half the hot pepper, chicken broth, saffron, and lime juice in a food processor or blender. Taste and add the remaining hot pepper if desired, and purée until smooth.

Meanwhile, chop the tomatoes into small dice to make about 2 cups. Toss the yellow peppers, cantaloupe, mango, cucumber, and green onions in a large bowl. An hour before serving, add the hot pepper–broth mixture and stir to blend. Refrigerate at least 1 hour.

Season to taste with salt. Cut each shrimp crosswise in half. Roll the shrimp in the chopped cilantro. Spoon equal portions of the soup into 4 chilled soup bowls. Garnish the bowls with equal portions of shrimp.

SAFFRON THREADS

Saffron is the stigma of the purple crocus flower. Each flower has just three stigmas, so it takes nearly 14,000 stigmas to make an ounce of saffron. As it is the world's most expensive spice, luckily a little goes a long way. Avoid the powdered saffron.

BUBBLY BUTTER BEAN SOUP

Serves 6

A HEARTY SOUP, DAZZLING IN ITS PRESENTATION, *it has the added virtue of being easily made ahead until the final reheating and flourish of bubbly. This "special occasion" recipe was developed by Jimmy and Gwen Bentley when our gourmet group had gathered at their home to cook together one winter's evening. We cooked it in a kettle suspended by a crane they called a sway in an open fireplace, but I do it at home on a stove burner. Since a split of champagne (or half a bottle) is all that's needed for the soup, another split (or the other half bottle) adds merriment for wine-sipping cooks! Sparkling white grape juice may be substituted if children are joining in the fun.*

Ham bone, or 1/2 cup diced ham, or salt pork
2 celery ribs, chopped
1 medium onion, quartered
1 large bay leaf
6 peppercorns
6 whole cloves
1/2 pound fresh or frozen butter beans or butter peas
2 medium potatoes, cut into small pieces
1 "split" bottle champagne, or to taste
Chopped ham, optional
Fresh parsley, finely chopped

To prepare the broth, simmer 1 quart of water with the ham or salt pork, celery, onion, bay leaf, peppercorns, and cloves about 1 hour covered, adding water if needed to make 1 1/2 quarts. Strain the broth and skim off any grease that may have risen to the top. Set the large ham bones aside, if using, and discard the vegetables and chopped meat.

Add beans and potatoes to the broth. Bring to the boil and simmer until the both are very tender, about 30 minutes. Transfer the potatoes and beans to a large bowl and mash well with a potato masher. Return to the broth.

Chop any remaining meat from the bone and add some of it to the broth. Taste and add salt as needed. If the soup is too salty, add more water. The soup may be frozen at this point and reheated when needed.

Before serving, add 1 to 2 cups champagne to the hot soup and stir to blend over medium heat. Serve with optional garnish of the remaining chopped ham and parsley, adding a few tablespoons of champagne to each soup bowl at the table as it is served. It causes an immediate fizzle and brings exclamations of joy and praise.

GOLD AND CRIMSON BEET SOUP

Serves 6 to 8

THE ADVENT IN RECENT YEARS OF THE YELLOW BEET, *a bit milder in flavor than the red beet yet equally jewel-like in color, makes for a smashing multicolored soup when combined with the traditional red beet and similarly hued onions and cabbages. The ingredients are akin to borsch, but traditional Southern ingredients are used.*

- 3 red beets
- 3 yellow beets
- 2 tablespoons oil, cook's preference, divided
- 1 medium red onion, chopped
- 1 medium yellow or white onion, chopped
- 1/2 red cabbage, finely sliced
- 1/2 green cabbage, finely sliced
- 8–12 cups chicken stock or broth, divided
- 1 teaspoon or more white wine vinegar or fresh lemon juice
- Salt
- Freshly ground black pepper
- Granulated sugar, optional
- 1/2 cup sour cream
- 1 green onion, chopped, optional
- 3 tablespoons finely chopped fresh dill, optional

To cook the beets, remove the greens and most of the root carefully without cutting into the flesh of the beets to keep the beets from "bleeding." Wrap each color separately in aluminum foil, move to a rimmed baking sheet and bake at 400 degrees for approximately 1 hour. Remove when soft; cool, peel, and slice as desired.

Meanwhile, divide and heat the oil in two separate 2- to 3-quart pots. Add the red onion to one pot, the yellow or white to the other. Cook until soft and translucent.

Add beets to the same color onion and follow similarly with the cabbage. Cook until soft. Pour half of the chicken stock into each pot and simmer 25 minutes, or until soup is well incorporated.

Purée the yellow beet soup first; then purée the red solids before returning them to their pots. Taste for seasoning. Add vinegar, salt, pepper, and sugar to taste.

Serve the soups from 2 measuring cups, pouring simultaneously into the individual bowls so the separate mixtures form a mosaic. Serve with sour cream. Garnish soup with chopped green onion and fresh dill if desired.

ORANGE AND CARROT CURRIED SOUP

Serves 6

CURRY CAME TO THE SOUTH EARLY. *There is a chicken cooked with curry in* The Virginia Housewife, *as well as a beef soup; also* The Carolina Rice Kitchen *and old receipt books of English origin and nature, like those of Hannah Glasse, make reference to curry soup. The spices for curry were either grown here, as in the case of ground hot red pepper, ginger, and turmeric, or brought by ship via Savannah, Charleston, and Richmond from the West Indies, among other places. Curry was mixed using combinations of ground cumin, coriander, fenugreek, cardamom, cinnamon, chili, and turmeric. Each combination was different, as is still true today.*

For a hot soup, use butter. For a cold soup, use olive or vegetable oil, as the butter will coagulate when chilled.

4 tablespoons butter, or olive or vegetable oil
4–6 medium carrots, sliced
2 medium onions, chopped
1 teaspoon curry powder
2 large garlic cloves, chopped
Grated rind of 1 orange, no white attached, divided
4 cups chicken stock or broth
Juice of 2 oranges, about 3/4 cup
Salt
Freshly ground black pepper
1 teaspoon light or dark brown sugar

Heat the butter or oil in a heavy pot. Add the carrots and onions, cover, and cook over low heat for 10 minutes without browning, until the onions are soft. Stir in the curry powder and garlic, and cook 2 to 3 minutes. Add half the orange rind, the chicken stock, and orange juice. Season lightly. Continue to cook until the carrots are just tender.

Purée the solids in the pot using an immersion blender, or remove the solids to a food processor or sturdy blender and purée, adding liquid as necessary to create a smooth texture. Add the purée and the liquid back to the saucepan to reheat. Add salt and pepper to taste along with the sugar and remaining orange rind. Serve hot, or chill well if serving cold. May be refrigerated several days or frozen, preferably before adding the sugar and orange rind.

Variation: Orange and Cauliflower Curried Soup
Substitute 2 cups cauliflower for the carrots. Increase curry powder to 1 tablespoon. Replace orange juice and rind and brown sugar with 1 cup coconut milk. Garnish with freshly chopped cilantro.

CURRY FIX

When a curry's hotness is not known, be judicious. Add a little bit at a time, tasting after each addition.

If over-seasoning with curry does happen, soak some dried apricots in hot water, which are in the same color family, for about 15 minutes or so, purée them in a food processor, and add to the soup. The sweetness of the apricots will cut down on the spiciness from the curry. Add more stock or liquid, if necessary.

CREAM OF CARROT AND ZUCCHINI SOUP

Serves 8

THESE TWO SOUPS MAKE A TASTY TEAM *served side by side in a single bowl. They may be made several days ahead and served hot or cold. If serving cold, omit the butter and use 1 tablespoon oil. Two-colored soups are visually stunning and make the simplest soup appear a feat of genius. If only one or the other vegetable is available, double the ingredient and make one soup, tasting carefully and adjusting ingredients accordingly.*

2 tablespoons butter
1 medium onion, thinly sliced
1 large garlic clove, chopped
4–6 large carrots, sliced
3 medium zucchini, sliced
4 cups chicken stock or broth
Granulated sugar
Salt
Freshly ground black pepper
3/4 cup heavy cream, divided

Heat the butter in a large Dutch oven. Add the onion, cover, and sauté gently over low heat until the onion is soft but not browned, about 5 minutes. Add the garlic.

Divide the onion mixture into two 2-quart pots. Add the carrots to one pot, the zucchini to the other. Divide and stir in the stock, cover, and simmer until the vegetables are very soft, about 30 minutes for the carrots and 15 to 20 minutes for the zucchini.

Purée the solids, each pot separately, using an immersion blender, food processor, or blender, adding liquid as necessary to create a smooth texture. Return to the individual pots with the liquid, stirring. Add sugar as desired to the carrot soup, and season both pots to taste with salt and pepper. Divide the cream between the two pots, bring both just to the boil, and remove from the heat.

Pour the soups into individual bowls simultaneously from 2 measuring cups positioned on opposite sides of the bowl. The separate mixtures will form a mosaic.

Variations

- A tablespoon of chopped fresh ginger cooked with the onion adds dash to the soup.
- Winter squash such as peeled butternut can be substituted for the carrots.

COMFORTING CHEESE SOUP

Serves 6

THIS PALE AND CREAMY SOUP *can transform a rainy or cold day. This recipe is very versatile, depending on the type of stock, wine, cream, and cheese you begin with. But it is also so accommodating that adding bacon, vegetables, or other ingredients creates excellent variations. Heavy cream is best in this recipe, as it adds a natural thickness and richness. Half-and-half is an acceptable substitute for home suppers. Milk should not be substituted, as it will result in a watery, thin soup—the very opposite of what it should be. Gruyère adds a bit more of a winey flavor, whereas Cheddar takes center stage. Yellow Cheddar may be used, but the color changes and is visually less pleasing.*

3 tablespoons butter
1 medium onion, chopped
2 garlic cloves, chopped
3–4 tablespoons all-purpose flour
5 cups chicken stock or broth, divided
1 1/2 cups heavy cream or half-and-half
Ground hot red pepper
1/4 cup dry white wine
1 1/2 cups grated Gruyère or white Cheddar cheese
Salt
Freshly ground pepper, preferably white

Heat the butter in a heavy pot over medium heat. Add the onion and cook until soft, 3 to 4 minutes; add the garlic, and cook briefly. Stir in the flour and stir over the heat for a couple of minutes. Stir in the stock and cream, bring to the boil, and reduce heat to a simmer. Add hot red pepper judiciously to taste; add wine and cheese. Season to taste with salt and pepper. Add more stock if needed to achieve desired consistency. This can be prepared 1 or 2 days ahead, cooled, refrigerated, and covered until needed. When ready to serve, ladle hot soup into bowls.

Variation: Bacon and Cheese Soup
Cook and crumble 6 slices of bacon. Chop a few tablespoons of green onions or chives. Add both to each bowl at serving time for a totally different soup.

Variation: Cheese and Greens Soup
Add 1 cup slivered (see chiffonade, page 208) baby spinach or turnip greens to each bowl before adding the soup, giving the soup more dimension as well as increased nutrition.

Variation: Cheese and Broccoli Soup
Finely chop half a head of broccoli, both flowers and stems. Add to the soup for the last few minutes or upon reheating.

WINE FOR COOKING

When a recipe calls for wine, avoid the "cooking" sherry or wine that is on the grocery shelves. That wine contains salt and was invented with prohibition in mind so no one would want to drink it. Instead, buy a modest but drinkable wine.

CORN BISQUE

Serves 6 to 8

THIS BISQUE IS LIGHT IN TEXTURE *and flavor, using a stock made earlier from corncobs. For a chunkier soup, don't strain the corn at the end. Frozen corn can be substituted, using approximately 3/4 cup per cob. It will lack a bit but is still very good.*

- 5 cobs fresh corn
- 4 tablespoons butter, divided
- 8 cups Corncob Stock (page 117) or light chicken stock or broth
- 2 tablespoons cornstarch
- Salt
- Freshly ground black pepper

Shuck the corn and slice the corn from the cob into a shallow dish or pie plate. Stand each cob in the dish, and scrape the cobs, extracting the milk. Move corn and juices aside. Reserve the cobs for making more corncob stock at another time.

Melt half the butter over medium heat in a large Dutch oven and cook the corn and its milk until tender, about 5 minutes. Stir in the corn stock and bring to a simmer. Remove the solids and purée in a blender. Press the purée through a strainer with the back of a spoon, discarding any tough pieces. Return the purée to the pot, adding a little more broth or water, and bring back to a simmer over medium heat.

Move 1/4 cup of the soup to a separate bowl, whisk in the cornstarch, and then whisk back into the soup. Bring to the boil, stirring, and cook until thickened, 3 to 5 minutes. Remove from heat and add the remaining butter. Season to taste with salt and pepper

Variation: Corn and Shrimp Bisque
Add shrimp to the soup right before serving and cook for 3 to 5 minutes. Add 1/2 to 1 teaspoon saffron threads to the soup after thickening.

MUSHROOM SOUP WITH GRITS OR RICE

Serves 4 to 6

INGREDIENTS CHANGE ACCORDING TO THE WAY THEY ARE CUT AND COOKED. *When the onion and mushrooms are finely chopped and cooked briefly, they are light; when cooked long and slow until dark, they become nearly a paste. When the mushrooms are sliced, they change the soup yet again. Marjoram, lemon balm, and mint are perennials in most of the South, with basil dying out at the first December freeze.*

- 3 tablespoons butter
- 2 medium onions, chopped
- 1/2 pound fresh mushrooms, wild or cultivated, chopped
- 2 tablespoons all-purpose flour
- 5 cups chicken stock or broth
- 1 tablespoon white quick grits, long-grain rice, or wild rice
- Salt
- Freshly ground black pepper
- 1 teaspoon chopped fresh marjoram, basil, lemon balm, or mint

Heat the butter in a large Dutch oven; add the onions and mushrooms and cook until soft. Stir in the flour. Pour in the stock, stirring, and bring to the boil. Add the grits or rice, reduce the heat, cover, and simmer for 15 to 20 minutes. Season to taste with salt and pepper. Refrigerate or freeze if desired. Bring to the boil and sprinkle with herbs just before serving. This recipe doubles easily: make one to serve and one to freeze.

SHE-CRAB SOUP

Serves 6 to 8

This is an age-old recipe, *much like a bisque that was popularized by a Charleston cook Harold Dees. The technique dates back to French and English cooking and beyond.* Two Hundred Years of Southern Cooking *(the Charleston, South Carolina, cookbook) refers to the days when there were street vendors selling fresh crabs, charging more for the "she-crabs."*

Many old recipes call for cooking the soup with the crab for 20 or 30 minutes, which seems a terrible punishment for crab and diner alike. Crabmeat is rarely picked anymore from raw crabs; it now comes from crabs cooked before being "picked" and frequently includes roe scattered throughout the container. At any rate, even raw fresh crab needs only brief cooking.

4–5 tablespoons butter, divided
1 celery rib, chopped
1/2 fennel bulb, chopped, optional
1 medium onion, chopped
2 tablespoons all-purpose flour
1 1/2 cups milk
1 cup fish or shrimp stock or broth
3/4 cup heavy cream, divided
1/2 pound jumbo lump crabmeat, picked through to remove any shells
1–2 tablespoons crab roe, or what is in the container
Salt
Freshly ground black pepper
Dash hot sauce, optional
1/3 cup dry Madeira or dry sherry, warmed slightly

Melt 2 tablespoons butter in a large Dutch oven. Add the celery, fennel, and onion, and cook until soft, about 5 minutes. Add rest of the butter and stir in the flour. Cook, stirring, for a few minutes over medium heat. Add the milk, fish stock, and 1/2 cup cream. Stir until the mixture comes to the boil. Reduce the heat and simmer about 10 minutes. Strain through a fine sieve.

Meanwhile, whip the remaining 1/4 cup cream. Add the crabmeat and roe to the soup and heat briefly. Taste the soup mixture. Season to taste with salt, pepper, and hot sauce. Add a little warm Madeira or sherry to the soup bowls. Ladle in the soup. Garnish with a dollop of cream.

Variations:

- Add a sprinkle of fresh herbs or paprika.
- Use finely chopped shrimp in place of crabmeat.
- Use finely chopped cooked egg yolks if roe is not available.

VIDALIA ONION SOUP

Serves 6 to 8

AS LONG AS THERE IS ONION SOUP IN THE HOUSE, *there is a great meal ahead. Serve with a salad for a simple supper, or reduce the portion and serve it as a starter in cool weather.*

Although the recipe is titled after Georgia's famous onion, any onion may be used for onion soup. Some people prefer a mixture of onions, others just one color. The garlic in the recipe gives it a little bump of flavor.

Onion soup is a bit tricky, so keep an eye on it. The heat used under the onions must not be so high it burns and crisps them, or so low that liquid is extracted, preventing the onions from browning. A heavy pan and careful eye will make this one of the world's best soups. To speed up caramelizing the onions, use two pans, combining the contents of both (page 220) in the end.

4 tablespoons butter
2 pounds onions, peeled and sliced 1/4 inch thick (about 7 cups)
Salt
1–2 large garlic cloves, chopped
1 tablespoon all-purpose flour
8 cups stock or broth, preferably brown (if using commercial, make with 1/2 water and 1/2 stock)
Freshly ground black pepper
6–8 thick slices French bread
1 cup mixed Swiss and grated Parmesan cheese

Melt the butter over low heat in a large Dutch oven. Add the onions and a little salt; cook them slowly for 20 to 30 minutes, stirring frequently, letting the onions and the bottom of the pan become a deep rich brown, which will give the soup color and flavor. Don't hurry this recipe or the onions will burn and lose their moistness.

Add the chopped garlic and cook 1 to 2 minutes more. Remove from heat and stir in flour. Return to the heat and stir constantly for 1 to 2 minutes, or until the flour is cooked. Pour in the stock. Continue stirring until the stock comes to the boil. Reduce heat to a simmer and cook, partially covered, for 20 to 30 minutes. Season to taste with salt and pepper. Do not over-salt at this point or it may be too salty when reheated, particularly if using a commercial stock and the liquid is reduced. May be refrigerated for several days or frozen at this point.

To prepare the *croûtes,* preheat oven to 325 degrees. Arrange bread slices side by side on a rimmed baking sheet, move to the upper third of the oven, and toast about 15 minutes. Brush bread with oil or butter to add more flavor to the soup. May be kept a day or so in a plastic bag.

Reheat soup on top of stove if necessary. Preheat oven to 375 degrees. Arrange *croûtes* side by side on top of the soup and sprinkle them evenly with cheese. Alternately, ladle soup into individual bowls before adding the *croûte* to each and sprinkle it with cheese. Bake soup in the middle of the oven for 10 to 15 minutes, or until the cheese has melted and formed a light brown crust.

Variation: Super Soggy Soup
Pour the hot soup over untoasted bread and add the cheese directly to the soup for an exceptionally comforting taste.

OXTAIL SOUP

Serves 6

Just what is an oxtail, anyway? *Now referring to all genders of beef, including steers, an oxtail originally was the tail of an ox (a castrated bull). It ranges in size from 2 to 4 pounds, with the edible end weighing 1 to 1 1/2 pounds. Oxtails makes a terrific brown stock on their own and are used in many commercial brands of broth and stock. They are rarely sold intact but instead are packed presliced. This soup never lost its appeal in the South but is finally catching on up North. By nature gelatinous, oxtails make rich and unctuous stocks and soups.*

1 tablespoon meat drippings or butter
Salt
Freshly ground black pepper
1/4 cup all-purpose flour
1 1/2 pounds oxtails
1–2 celery ribs, finely chopped, divided
1 medium onion, sliced, divided
2 large carrots, sliced, divided
1 small turnip, sliced
8 cups water or beef stock or beef broth
1/4 cup Madeira or dry sherry
Salt
Freshly ground pepper
2 tablespoons chopped fresh summer savory or thyme

Heat the drippings or butter in a large heavy pot.

Add salt and pepper to the flour. Toss the oxtails in the seasoned flour mixture. Add only enough oxtail pieces to the pan that they brown without touching each other, turning as necessary. Repeat until all are browned.

Remove the oxtails and add half the celery, onion, and carrots to the pan, cooking until soft. Return the oxtails to the pot. Meanwhile in a separate pan, bring the water or stock to the boil then add carefully to the oxtail pot. Return to the boil. Reduce heat and simmer half-covered about 2 hours, until the meat is done. Skim off any scum as it is formed.

When the meat is cooked, remove meat and vegetables from the pot. Cool slightly then pull the meat off the bones and set aside, discarding the bones and cooked vegetables. Meanwhile, add the remaining vegetables and turnips to the broth, bring up to the boil, and cook about 20 minutes, or until crisp-tender.

When ready to serve, return the meat to the pot with the vegetables. Add the Madeira. Season to taste with salt and pepper, bring to the boil, reduce heat, and simmer 4 or 5 minutes. Ladle into a serving bowl or tureen and garnish with the herb.

DRIED PEAS PORRIDGE WITH CORIANDER AND MINT

Serve 6

Peas are an ancient vegetable, *going back to early Egyptian and Chinese times. Because peas are filling, a ration of a bushel of dried peas was required for every new colonist immigrating to America. Peas are protein, part of a "package," providing complete nutrition when combined with rice or whole wheat bread, among other things. In* Martha Washington's Booke of Cookery, *on which Karen Hess did such a masterful job, there is no mention of the kind of peas Martha uses for her Pease Porrage. When I went to Mount Vernon to research it many years ago, I found no indication there, either. I wish I had been able to dine at Mount Vernon when Martha was there, as her recipes show great care.*

A porrage was a mash, or pulp-like dish, made frequently of grain. The meaning has changed through the centuries. In this recipe, Martha calls for old dried peas whose husks come off in the cooking. She does cook the peas twice, perhaps the forerunner of our current method of either soaking dried peas overnight or bringing them to a boil in a covered pan, and letting sit a half-hour.

For that reason, I present my modern interpretation of Martha's porridge of peas, a fresh pea variation using white acre or lady peas, the diamonds of the pea family. (They are about the size of a 1-carat diamond or a little smaller. In this case, the smaller the better!) I love Martha Washington for adding so much butter to these peas. As much as I love adding ham or other cured pork to flavor peas and beans, I find the butter in this dish coats the peas with amazing flavor.

2 cups dried white acre or field peas
2 onions, very finely chopped or shredded, divided
2 garlic cloves, chopped
2 tablespoons ground coriander seed
Salt
Freshly ground black pepper
2 tablespoons chopped fresh mint
1/2 cup chopped parsley
1/4–1/2 cup butter
1/4–1/2 cup white wine vinegar, optional

Add the peas and half the onions to a large pot of boiling water. Cook until tender—anywhere from 30 minutes to a couple of hours, depending on the type and age of the peas. Skim off any foam as it forms and discard.

After they are tender enough to mash, remove the peas with a slotted spoon or colander and mash with a large spoon or potato masher. Return to the pot, add the garlic, coriander, salt, and pepper. Return to the boil. Lower the heat to a simmer. Add the mint, remaining onions, parsley, and butter, and simmer 15 minutes longer, or until a bit wetter than cooked oatmeal or grits. Serve with bread and butter. Pass the vinegar to be added as desired.

Variation: Butter Bean Porridge with Coriander and Mint
Substitute 8 cups of frozen butter beans. Add the beans to boiling water to cover and cook until tender—about 30 minutes. Mash as directed in the recipe and add the remaining ingredients.

PEASE

To Make Pease Porrage of Old Pease

Take 2 quarts of white pease, pick & wash y^{m} clean, y^{n} set y^{m} on in 3 gallons of water. Keep y^{m} boyling & as ye husks rise, [after] it is filled up wth cold water, scum them of into a cullender into a dish to save ye liquor & pease to put into ye pot againe. Then t[ake] up all ye pease & posh y^{m} wth a spoone; y^{n} put y^{m} in againe. & when they have boyled a while, put in 2 cloves of garlick, halfe an ounce of coriander seeds beaten, some sifted pepper & some salt, an ounce of powder of dryed spearmint. All these must be put in at ye second boyling. shread in 2 ounions & a handful of parsley very small, & put in halfe a pound of fresh butter. Y^{n} let all boyle together for a quarter of an houre. Y^{n} serve ym up with bread & bits of fresh butter put into y^{m}. & If you love it, put in a little elder vinegar.

Note: This colonial recipe can be easily read by replacing the "y" with a "th" sound.

WHITE ACRE AND GREENS SOUP

Serves 10 to 12

I dream of white acre peas, *whereas others dream of caviar. This glorious soup serves a crowd, or half can be frozen for another time. Fresh and frozen white acre peas are best in this recipe, softening after about 30 minutes; dried peas will take a bit longer.*

1/4 pound bacon or fatback, cut into 1/4-inch dice
2 tablespoons butter
1 large onion, chopped
4 large garlic cloves, chopped
6 cups chicken stock or broth
1 pound small white acre or field peas, fresh, frozen, or dried
1 teaspoon chopped fresh thyme or oregano
2 cups collard or turnip greens, washed (page 205)
Salt
Freshly ground black pepper

Fry the bacon or fatback in a large skillet; drain and set aside.

Heat the butter in a large pot. Add the onion and cook until soft. Add the garlic, stock, and peas, and bring to the boil. Reduce heat to simmer. When the peas begin to soften, add herbs.

Meanwhile, remove any stems and tough leaves from the greens; roll the greens into a cylinder shape and slice them into thin strips. Smoosh some of the peas against the side of the pot to thicken the soup, and add the greens. Continue cooking 5 minutes to wilt the greens. Season to taste with salt and pepper. May be made ahead several days and refrigerated. If freezing, omit the greens until reheating.

HERITAGE SOUP RECIPE

Originally published in London in 1727, the first cookbook published in America (Virginia, 1742) was *The Compleat Housewife* by Eliza Smith. She writes on the title page that it is "a collection of several hundred of the most approved receipts, in cookery, pastry, confectionery, preserving, pickles, cakes, creams, jellies, made wines, cordials. And also bills of fare for every month of the year. To which is added, a collection of nearly two hundred family receipts of medicines; viz. drinks, syrups, salves, ointments, and many other things of sovereign and approved efficacy in most distempers, pains, aches, wounds, sores, etc., never before made publick in these parts; fit either for private families, or such publick-spirited gentlewomen as would be beneficent to their poor neighbours."

Green Pease Soup

Make ʃtrong broth of a leg of beef, a knuckle or ʃcrag end of veal, and ʃcrag of mutton; clear it off; then chop ʃome cabbage lettuce, ʃpinach, and a little ʃorrel; then put half a pound of butter in a flat ʃauce-pan, dredge in ʃome flour, put it over the fire until 'tis brown: then put in your herbs and toʃs them up a little over the fire; then put in a pint and half of green peaʃe half boiled before, adding your ʃtrong broth, and let it juʃt ʃimmer over the fire half an hour; then cut ʃome French bread very thin; dry it well before the fire, put it in, and let it ʃtew half an hour longer; ʃeaʃon your broth with pepper, ʃalt, and a few cloves and mace. Garniʃh the diʃh with ʃpinach ʃcalded green, and ʃome very thin bits of bacon toaʃted before the fire.

—From *The Compleat Housewife*
by Eliza Smith, Virginia, 1742

Note: This colonial text can be easily read by replacing the elongated "ʃ" with an "s" sound.

PIMENTO SOUP

Serves 4 to 6

THIS PIMENTO SOUP IS A PERENNIAL STAND-BY FOR ME, *particularly at the end of summer. It can be served hot or cold. When I first moved to Georgia, pimentos were canned in a factory not too far from my home. For a long time I did not realize they were interchangeable with the bell peppers that I roasted when they turned red in my garden. If serving cold, substitute oil for butter.*

2 tablespoons butter
1 small onion, chopped
1 large garlic clove, chopped
2 tablespoons all-purpose flour
5 cups chicken stock or broth
1 cup roasted, seeded pimentos or red bell peppers (page 223), or 1 (7-ounce) jar pimentos, chopped and drained
Fresh lemon juice
Salt
Freshly ground black pepper
1 cup heavy cream, yogurt, or sour cream

Heat the butter in a large saucepan. Add the onion and cook until it is soft and translucent. Add the garlic. Stir in the flour. Add the chicken stock and pimentos and bring to the boil, stirring constantly. When the liquid has boiled briefly and thickened slightly, remove from heat.

Purée the solids in the pot using an immersion blender, or remove the solids to a food processor or sturdy blender and purée, adding liquid as necessary to create a smooth texture. Stir the purée with the remainder of the soup.

To serve, season to taste with lemon juice, salt, and pepper to taste, and top with the cream, yogurt, or sour cream. Serve hot or cold. May be made ahead several days and refrigerated.

Variation: For a quick version, purée 1 jar drained pimentos until very smooth, adding as much chicken stock as needed to purée. Whisk in the rest of the stock. Chill and serve with cream or yogurt.

PIMENTOS

Pimentos are similar to bell peppers but are pointed rather than belled at the bottom. Both are green and later turn red on the vine, which is when they develop a rich flavor. They are best roasted and peeled, but drained jarred peppers or pimentos can be used as well.

QUICK CREAMY PEANUT GINGER SOUP

Serves 10 to 12

PEANUT SOUPS ARE UBIQUITOUS ACROSS THE SOUTH, *where peanuts arrived with the slave ships. Freshly ground peanuts will yield a chunky soup with a course texture, but a smooth commercial peanut butter will produce a mousse-like and silken texture. For this soup, adapted from* Cooking Across the South (1980) *we prefer the silken texture.*

1/2 cup butter
1 small onion, chopped
2 celery ribs, chopped
3 tablespoons all-purpose flour
8 cups chicken stock or broth, heated
1 (8-ounce) jar creamy peanut butter
1 teaspoon chopped fresh ginger
1 tablespoon fresh lemon juice
Salt
Freshly ground black pepper
1/2 cup raw or roasted skinless peanuts, chopped

Heat the butter in a heavy pan until foaming. Add onion and celery, and sauté for 5 minutes, or until soft. Stir in flour and cook, stirring, until light brown. Stir in chicken broth and bring to the boil. Reduce heat and simmer 30 minutes.

Remove from the heat, strain soup, and discard vegetables. Add peanut butter, ginger, and lemon juice. Stir well and add salt and pepper to taste. Simmer 5 minutes. Sprinkle each serving with chopped peanuts. May be made several days ahead and refrigerated. Leftovers will freeze for family meals.

SQUASH PECAN SOUP

Serves 4

THIS IMPORTANT SOUTHERN VEGETABLE—*whether it is the summer yellow crookneck or zucchini that burgeons in our gardens, butternut squash, or pumpkin—has an affinity for pecans. A medley of yellow squash and zucchini has the added advantage of being served cold or hot, ideal for fall and spring weather. No need for expensive pecan halves here. If serving cold, substitute oil for the butter.*

2 tablespoons butter, or olive or vegetable oil
1 medium onion, sliced
2 large garlic cloves, chopped
2 medium yellow crookneck squash, sliced
2 medium zucchini, sliced
2 cups chicken stock or broth
1/2 cup chopped pecans
1/2 cup plain or goat yogurt
Salt
Freshly ground black pepper

Heat the butter or oil in a large pot. Add the onion and garlic cloves to the pan. Top with the squash and zucchini, cover, and cook over low heat until the onion is translucent and the squash and zucchini are softened.

Add the chicken stock, bring to the boil, lower the heat, and simmer, covered, for 10 minutes, until the zucchini is tender. Purée the solids add in the pot using an immersion blender, or remove the solids to a food processor or sturdy blender and purée, adding liquid as necessary to create a smooth texture. Return the puréed mixture to the liquid and stir.

Meanwhile, add the pecans to a small pan and toast over medium heat, 2 to 3 minutes, until lightly browned; set aside. Cool the puréed soup slightly, whisk in the yogurt, season to taste with salt and pepper, and chill until ready to serve. If serving hot, reheat without boiling, as the yogurt will separate. Serve the soup with the pecans.

Variations

- Heavy cream may be used in place of the yogurt for a richer soup.
- A tablespoon of curry powder will give a different boost to the soup. Taste to be sure it doesn't dominate the pecans, in which case omit one or the other.
- One teaspoon chopped ginger will enhance the soup.

BOURBON SWEET POTATO AND GREENS SOUP

Serves 4 to 6

THIS RICH GOLDEN SOUP IS UNIQUELY SOUTHERN, *with the sweetness of the potato enhanced by the addition of bourbon. It may be served completely smooth, but I like it partly chunky.*

3 tablespoons butter
4–5 medium sweet potatoes, peeled and roughly sliced
6 cups chicken stock or broth, divided
1/4–1/3 cup bourbon
Salt
Freshly ground black pepper
1 cup fresh greens, such as turnips, collards, or sweet potato leaves, washed (page 205)

Heat the butter in a large Dutch oven. Add a layer of potatoes. Brown on one side, turn and brown on the other. Remove and repeat until all are browned. Return all potatoes to the pot.

Add 5 cups of chicken stock to the potatoes. Cook, covered, until the potatoes are tender enough for a fork to pierce them easily. When they are tender, purée the solids in the pot using an immersion blender, or remove the solids to a food processor or sturdy blender and purée, adding liquid as necessary to create a smooth texture. Return the purée to the pot if removed.

Taste the mixture. Stir in as much of the remaining 1 cup chicken stock as is necessary for a medium-thick soup. Add the bourbon and bring to the boil. Season to taste with salt and pepper. Remove any stems and tough leaves from the greens; roll the greens into a cylinder shape and slice them into thin strips. Stir into the soup. The soup may be made several days in advance and reheated or frozen.

Variation: Omit the greens and bourbon. Add 1 tablespoon fresh chopped ginger or curry to the purée before returning to the soup.

TOMATO BISQUE

Serves 4 to 6

THERE WAS A TIME *when everyone knew the techniques of Southern cooking, so there was no need to explain in detail when using recipes. Everyone knew that bread thickened a soup. I cooked a similar recipe adaptation from a recipe of Mrs. H. R. Dull's* Southern Cooking *for many years. It is obviously a savvy way to save stale bread and to use tomatoes, either fresh or canned. It is absolutely fabulous.*

1 cup milk
3/4 cup stale breadcrumbs
1 tablespoon butter
1 small onion, chopped
6 ripe tomatoes, peeled and finely chopped, or 1 (28-ounce) can diced tomatoes with juice
Granulated sugar
Salt
Freshly ground black pepper

Rub crumbs through a mesh sieve. Heat the milk over very low heat in a large pot and add the breadcrumbs to soften.

Meanwhile, heat the butter, add the onion, and cook until soft. Add the tomatoes and their juices. Bring to the boil, reduce heat, and cook uncovered for 15 to 20 minutes over low heat, until thick. Season to taste with sugar, salt, and pepper. Stir thoroughly. Strain into the milk mixture. Reheat, stirring until combined.

TURNIP AND GREENS SOUP

Serves 4 to 6

ROOT VEGETABLES ARE GOOD BASES *for hearty soups. Beets, potatoes, turnips, parsnips, rutabagas, carrots, and sweet potatoes can all be used as the base. Any greens will do—turnip, spinach, and collard are most prevalent in the South, but sweet potato leaves, beet greens, kale, watercress, and other greens are as easily used.*

Turnips, unless noted otherwise, are usually white-fleshed and referred to as white turnips. These pink-skinned vegetables are milder than rutabagas, which are yellow-fleshed.

1 pound turnips
1 medium onion, sliced
2 tablespoons butter
2 large garlic cloves, chopped
4 cups chicken stock or broth, heated
1 pound turnip greens, washed (page 205)
Salt
Freshly ground black pepper

Peel and roughly slice the turnips. If large and strong-tasting, add them to boiling water, bring the water back up to the boil, reduce heat, and simmer 3 to 5 minutes. Drain. If the turnips are medium or small and without intense sharpness, use as is.

Heat the butter in a large Dutch oven; add the onion and cook until opaque. Add the garlic and then the turnips. Cook 5 minutes. Add the chicken stock and return to the boil. If the liquid is not covering the vegetables, add enough water to submerge any vegetable that bob up. Cover. Reduce heat and simmer until the vegetables are tender.

Remove and discard any stems and tough leaves from the greens; break the greens into large pieces and add to the vegetables. Purée the solids in the pot using an immersion blender, or remove the solids to a food processor or sturdy blender and purée, adding liquid as necessary until greens are chopped. Return the purée to the pot if removed. Season to taste with salt and pepper.

Variations

- Add 1 tablespoon chopped ginger before puréeing.
- Add 1 to 2 tablespoons curry powder before puréeing.
- Add fresh thyme, oregano, or fennel.
- Use 1 pound Jerusalem artichokes. Bring to the boil, reduce heat, and boil 5 to 10 minutes. Cool. Peel and return to the heat with the stock. Bring back to the boil, reduce heat, cover, and simmer until tender. When tender, purée as above, then add the greens and purée.

TURTLE SOUP

Serves 4 to 6

ONE OF MY LOVELIEST MEMORIES *is of cooking turtle soup with famous Southern cook Edna Lewis at a special dinner of Southern chefs. Edna was the embodiment of grace and flowed through the kitchen, effortlessly fixing the soup. This is her recipe.*

Turtle soup once frequently appeared on the Southern table. No Southern cookbook seems complete without it. Now, it is a rarity, although turtle meat is available from Internet sources and seen on a few restaurant menus, usually in Louisiana, where it is more prevalent.

2 pounds turtle meat and bones
1 small onion, chopped
Allspice
Cloves
Dried thyme
Salt
Freshly ground black pepper
1/3 cup dry sherry or Madeira
Flour
Milk
Finely chopped fresh parsley
Turtle eggs, boiled and chopped, optional

Boil turtle meat until tender with onions, spices, and water to cover. Season to taste with salt, pepper, and sherry.

Remove turtle flesh from bones. Chop finely.

Make a dumpling batter from flour and milk. Add chopped turtle, salt, and pepper to the batter. Drop dumplings into hot broth and cook until light. Garnish with parsley and optional turtle eggs.

—Edna Lewis

MIX 'N' MATCH VEGETABLE SOUP

Serves 4 to 6

THE FREEZER HAS BEEN A TREMENDOUS BOON FOR GARDENERS, *removing the need for laborious blanching and canning. Although store-bought frozen vegetables are nearly as good, certainly pulling bags of one's own vegetables from the freezer is more satisfying. This recipe is just a guide, not a mandate. Okra, spinach, turnip greens, and other good things can be added, as well as small pieces of ham, cooked chicken, turkey, or other meats and leftovers—even leftover soup.*

8 cups chicken, ham, or beef stock
1–2 cups vegetable scraps (page 113), optional
1–2 tablespoons oil, cook's preference
1 medium onion, chopped
2 large garlic cloves, chopped
1 (28-ounce) can crushed tomatoes
1 cup field peas, fresh or frozen
1 cup uncooked rice
1 cup fresh corn off the cob or frozen corn
1 cup English peas, fresh or frozen
Salt
Freshly ground black pepper

Pour stock into a large Dutch oven, add vegetable scraps if using, and simmer over low heat as necessary until broth is flavorful and reduced by about a fourth. Strain if necessary to remove the scraps.

Meanwhile, heat the oil in a small sauté pan, add the onion and cook until translucent; add garlic and sauté for another 10 to 20 seconds. Set aside.

Add sautéed onions and garlic to the strained hot broth and return to the boil. Add tomatoes and peas. Bring back to the boil and cook, stirring occasionally, about 10 minutes. Add the rice; cover and cook about 15 minutes, until the field peas and rice are cooked but not soggy. Add the corn kernels and English peas; heat through. Season to taste with salt and pepper.

Variation: One cup of cut-up or frozen okra would enhance this soup. Add 5 minutes before adding the corn kernels.

BACON, TOMATO, AND FIELD PEA SOUP

Serves 4

THIS IS A GOOD FAMILY MEAL SOUP *served with cornbread or is a fine starter. "Country" or "thick cut" bacon is best.*

8 strips bacon, cooked crisp and crumbled, drippings reserved
1 medium onion, chopped
1–2 garlic cloves, chopped
1 (14 1/2-ounce) can whole or diced tomatoes, with juice reserved
4 cups chicken stock or broth
1 pound field peas with snaps, fresh or frozen, or butter
Salt
Freshly ground black pepper
Hot sauce
2 tablespoons chopped fresh parsley, thyme, or oregano, optional
1 recipe Light and Tender Cornbread (page 477)

Reheat reserved drippings in a Dutch oven. Add the onion and cook 3 to 5 minutes. Add the garlic and cook briefly. Add the tomatoes (cutting with scissors if necessary to get bite-size pieces), reserving the juice, and add the broth. Bring to the boil and add the field peas. Reduce heat and simmer, covered, for 25 minutes.

Uncover, add reserved juice, and season to taste with salt, pepper, and hot sauce. This may be made ahead and refrigerated or frozen.

Return to the boil. Add crumbled bacon and herbs just before serving with hot cornbread.

Variation: Five minutes or less before serving, add okra, corn kernels, turnip greens, or other vegetables.

BUTTER BEAN AND SAUSAGE SOUP

Serves 6 to 8

THIS SOUP MEAL IS PARTICULARLY WELCOME *in the late fall and early spring, when the changeable nights first occur. Any sausage will do, but my particular favorite is a fennel-flavored pork or turkey sausage called "sweet Italian" in the stores. To use only one pan, cook the sausage first and remove it, reserving the fat if desired; add the rest of the ingredients to the same pan. I've cooked it the following way because it is faster to cook sausages in one pan and the soup in another. And my husband does the dishes. Either way, a nonstick pan makes for easy cleanup after sautéing sausages.*

2 tablespoons butter
1 large onion, chopped
1 celery rib, chopped
2 large carrots, sliced
5–8 cups chicken stock or broth, divided
2 cups fresh butter beans, or frozen and defrosted
1/2 teaspoon ground fennel seed
12 links pork sausage
2 large garlic cloves, chopped
Salt
Freshly ground black pepper

Heat the butter in a large Dutch oven over medium heat; add the onion, celery, and carrots, and cook until they begin to brown lightly. Add 3 cups of the stock and bring to the boil.

When the carrots have softened, purée the solids in the pot using an immersion blender, or remove the solids to a food processor or sturdy blender and purée, adding liquid as necessary to create a smooth texture. Return the purée to the pot if removed. Add the butter beans and fennel seed. Return to the boil then reduce to a simmer; cover and cook until beans are tender but not mushy, about 30 minutes. Add another 2 cups stock, or to taste.

Meanwhile, prick the sausages several times with a fork. Heat a frying pan over high heat and cook the sausages for 6 minutes, turning often. Pour off the fat and add the garlic, cooking until the sausages are lightly browned. Cut the sausages into slices and add the garlic and sausage to the soup pot. Add the remaining stock if needed. Season to taste with salt and pepper.

GARDEN VEGETABLE AND SAUSAGE SOUP

Serves 10

THIS SOUP MAY BE ADAPTED *(see variation below) to suit the most finicky vegetarian, but it may also be adapted according to what is in the garden, pantry, or freezer.*

An inexpensive soup meal like this can be prepared more easily—and feed a crowd gloriously—with a bit of organization, including cooking in stages over a day or two if necessary. For instance, fry the salt pork while preparing the vegetables. Heat the stock and fry the sausage while the vegetables are cooking. Make the garnish during the final cooking of the pasta and tomatoes. This soup may be frozen in several stages, before adding the pasta or after. Divide into smaller packages. For easier defrosting, freeze the packages flat on a tray for easy stacking.

12 cups chicken stock or broth
1 ham bone or other smoked meat
1 cup fatback or salt pork, diced
6 tablespoons butter, divided
4 medium onions, chopped
8 large garlic cloves, chopped, divided
3 celery ribs, chopped
3–4 medium carrots, sliced
1 red bell pepper, seeded and chopped
5 tablespoons fennel seed
4 medium yellow squash or zucchini, sliced
1 cup sliced mushrooms
3–4 cups small field peas such as white acre, crowder, or black-eyed peas, fresh or frozen
2 pounds Italian-flavored bulk or link sausage, pork or turkey
Salt
Freshly ground black pepper
1 cup vermicelli, spaghetti, or fettuccine
6 fresh tomatoes, peeled, seeded, and coarsely chopped, or 1 (28-ounce) can chopped tomatoes
2 cups turnip greens, washed (page 205)
1 cup chopped fresh basil leaves
2 cups freshly grated Parmesan cheese
French or Italian bread, thickly sliced

Heat the chicken stock with the ham bone in a large Dutch oven or stockpot until it comes to the boil; reduce heat and simmer 10 to 15 minutes to flavor the stock.

Meanwhile, rinse, dry, and sauté the fatback, salt pork, or other smoked pork product in another large Dutch oven. Drain off the fat, leaving the pork in the pot. Add 3 tablespoons butter and melt. Follow with the onions and half of the garlic, and cook until soft and translucent. Add the celery, carrots, bell pepper, and fennel seed. Lower the heat; cover and cook 5 to 8 minutes.

Uncover, raise the heat, and add zucchini, mushrooms, and peas. Toss over high heat for 3 minutes. Pour in the hot stock and ham bone. Return to the boil, and then reduce heat and simmer uncovered for 15 to 20 minutes. The vegetables should be fork-tender. Remove the ham bone and discard.

Meanwhile, crumble the bulk sausage or prick the links and add to a hot skillet; sauté 15 minutes, or until browned all over. Remove the sausage, drain, and add the sausage to the soup. Season to taste with salt and pepper. The soup may be made ahead to this point, cooled, and refrigerated for several days or frozen.

When ready to serve, remove and discard any stems and tough leaves from the greens. Chop the greens into rough pieces. Reheat the soup to boiling and add the pasta, tomatoes, and greens; return to the boil and simmer until the pasta is cooked. Combine the basil, remaining garlic, and cheese in a small bowl, and sprinkle over soup just before serving; serve with French or Italian bread.

Variations:

- For a tasty vegetarian soup, substitute vegetable stock, omit the pork items, and use oil to sauté.
- Add corn, okra, spinach, turnip greens, or kale.

HURRICANE SOUP WITH BREADCRUMB DUMPLINGS

Serves 6

One abnormally cold and rainy day in August, *as Hurricane Earl swirled threateningly over the Atlantic and the remnants of Hurricane Danielle were dumping buckets of rain on my house in Social Circle, Georgia, we came up with this soup from the available food in the house. We dubbed it Hurricane Soup, and it provided welcome comfort. The key to flavor in this soup is slow-cooking the onions to deep golden brown color. It will look like a lot of onions at first, but they really cook down. The aroma of the caramelizing onions will also take your mind off the weather!*

- 1/4 cup oil, cook's preference
- 5 medium onions, sliced
- 1 apple, preferably Granny Smith, cored and cut into 1/2-inch cubes
- 2 tomatoes, cut into 1/2-inch cubes, or 1 (14 1/2-ounce) can diced tomatoes
- 2 large carrots, cut into 2-inch long, 1/2-inch-wide sticks, or 20 whole baby carrots
- 10 cups chicken stock or broth
- 1/2 cup small field peas such as butter peas, white acre, or lady peas, fresh or frozen
- 2 tablespoons chopped fresh thyme
- 1 teaspoon freshly ground black pepper
- 1/2 cup watercress, arugula, or spinach, roughly chopped, optional

Heat the oil in a large Dutch oven. Add the sliced onions and cook them slowly over low heat for 20 to 30 minutes, stirring frequently, letting the onions and the bottom of the pan become a deep rich brown, which will give the soup color and flavor. Don't hurry this recipe or the onions will burn and lose their moistness.

Add the apple, tomatoes, and carrots. Cook 10 minutes over medium heat. Add the chicken stock, peas, thyme, and pepper. Stir and bring to the boil. Reduce the heat, cover, and simmer 20 to 30 minutes, until the peas are cooked and the vegetables are tender.

Meanwhile make the Breadcrumb Dumpings.

Bring the soup back to the boil and drop the uncooked breadcrumb dumplings in one at a time. Reduce the heat to medium and cook an additional 3 to 5 minutes. Stir in remaining cheese and greens, if using; season to taste with salt.

Ladle into soup bowls, add a couple of dumplings to each bowl, and garnish with additional Parmesan cheese.

Breadcrumb Dumplings

- 1 1/4 cups fresh bread or cornbread crumbs
- 1 1/4 cup grated Parmesan cheese plus more for garnish, divided
- 1 large egg
- 1/2 cup milk
- 2 tablespoons chopped fresh parsley, or oregano
- 1/2 teaspoon freshly ground black pepper

Combine the breadcrumbs, 3/4 cup cheese, egg, milk, herbs, and black pepper in a bowl. Spoon out teaspoon-size balls and move to a plate. Cover and refrigerate the balls until the soup is almost ready. Let sit at room temperature at least 5 minutes before adding to the soup.

TURNIP GREEN, BLACK-EYED PEA, AND RICE SOUP

Serves 6 to 8

THIS SERENDIPITOUS RENDERING *of the traditional Hoppin' John (page 175) and Turnip Greens (page 205), requisite for New Year's Day in the South, began as a leftover meal. It turned out to be so appetizing that I reworked it to stand alone. It's very good for a meal soup. It is rare to have fresh peas in the winter. I much prefer frozen to canned, but canned will do as well.*

3 ounces smoked pork shoulder or other seasoning meat (page 173), cut into small cubes
1–2 small hot peppers, fresh or dried, optional
1 pound turnip greens, washed (page 205)
1 pound field peas with snaps, fresh or frozen
1 cup long grain or Charleston rice (page 258)
Salt
Freshly ground black pepper
Hot sauce
1 recipe Light and Tender Cornbread (page 477)

Fill a large pot with 2 to 3 gallons of water. Add pork to the water along with the hot peppers, bring to the boil, and simmer uncovered for up to 1 hour, until a richly flavored pork broth develops. (Add water if necessary to prevent drying out). Skim off any fat or scum.

Scoop out 1 gallon of the broth and pork, add to a second pot, and return to the boil.

Remove and discard any stems and tough leaves from the greens. Cut into small pieces using scissors or two knives; add to the second pot. Reduce heat to a simmer; cover and cook 30 to 60 minutes, depending on individual preference. If the water boils down and threatens to dry out the greens, add more broth from the first pot.

Add the peas to the first hot broth and return to the boil if necessary; reduce to a simmer, and cook uncovered 15 minutes. Check the liquid to make sure there is at least 3 quarts. Add the rice and cook another 15 minutes, making sure both peas and rice are completely cooked.

Both the greens and hoppin' john (rice and beans) soups may be refrigerated or frozen at this point, separately or together. When ready to serve, remove any visible fat from the top and bring all back to the boil. Taste for seasoning; add salt, pepper, and hot sauce as desired. Ideally, each pot should have a quart of well-flavored broth. If not, add enough broth to bring up to a quart plus the vegetables in each pot.

If necessary for the sensibilities of the diners, remove any fatty pieces of meat. For a special pizzazz in serving, add the hoppin' john soup to the bowl, make a hollow in the center, and spoon the greens into the center. (Ideally there is more hoppin' john soup than turnip greens; but should the reverse be true, no matter—just put the hoppin' john in the center surrounded with the greens). Serve with hot cornbread.

Variations:

- Many Southerners break their cornbread into pieces and ladle soup on top. This is my preferred modus operandi but not my husband's; he dips his.
- The whole soup may be made in one pot, first making the broth with pork and optional peppers, and adding the greens. The beans are added to the boiling liquid 30 minutes before serving, and the rice is added 15 minutes later. The rice turns a muddier color, but otherwise there is no significant difference.

THE LOWCOUNTRY'S BEST FISH MUDDLE (SOUTHERN BOUILLABAISSE)

Serves 8 to 10

ALTHOUGH WE ARE ALL CAPABLE *of making a muddle of our lives, I've made a fish muddle that everyone loved. Because it is a long recipe full of ingredients, it looks much more difficult than it is. It's a perfect thing to cook, however, when home doing chores after fish-shopping, giving it a little attention during the day, and then a lot of attention during the last 10 minutes before serving. The fish can be substituted according to what's available. The cost seems a bit heady, so remember that it costs much less than taking 8 people to dinner. I hope you will dream of it after you eat it. What's important is making a flavorful broth full of fish bones, including a head if possible. And garlic, a lot of it. Usually a wine or liquor (in this case Pernod or other anise-flavored liquor) is added to give an extra boost of flavor at the end: the anise is not discernable but the increase in flavor is.*

The whole soup is garnished with toasted baguette croûtes *with a garlic/red pepper/tomato mayonnaise, making it absolutely scrumptious at the finish. Store-bought* croûtes *are perfectly acceptable, as is doctored-up store-bought mayonnaise. Homemade is probably better, but I have been delighted with mine. I bummed the grouper rack (that is, the head and spine of a large grouper) from the local fish market, calling ahead to be sure they saved one. With a great deal of fish clinging to it, it was enough for the broth, but additional fish with the head on would give even greater flavor. The broth may be made a day ahead, or frozen and defrosted when ready to serve. Making a marinade for the fish is a trick I learned from famous chef Anne Willan, and it makes a great deal of difference!*

Broth

1 large grouper rack (1–2 pounds)
Shrimp shells, crab shells
2 heaping tablespoons fennel or anise seed

Marinade and Soup

1/2–3/4 cup oil, cook's preference, divided
15 garlic cloves, finely chopped, divided
1–2 tablespoons saffron threads, divided
Any skins or bones from the other fish
3 pounds assorted South Atlantic fish (snapper, grouper, flounder, mahi mahi, or other local dolphin—not the mammal—sea trout, or sheepshead)
1 pound raw shrimp, in shell
2 crabs, optional
3 onions, chopped
2 leeks, white part with some green part, sliced, optional
1 fennel bulb, including fronds if possible, sliced
1 pound diced fresh or canned tomatoes
Grated rind of 1 orange, no white attached
Salt
Freshly ground black pepper
Baked bread rounds (*croûtes*) from 2 baguettes (see above)
2–3 tablespoons tomato purée
1 cup mayonnaise, homemade or store-bought
Squirt of fresh lemon juice
1 tablespoon red wine vinegar
1 small fresh hot pepper, or dash of hot sauce
1 pound clams, optional
1–2 tablespoons Pernod

Make the broth by chopping up the backbone of the grouper into approximately 2-inch pieces. Place these in a large pot. Leave the head of the grouper intact to use in the soup, as it contains wonderful meat. Remove the gills out of the head and discard. (The red "eyelashes" on either side of the head are the gills. They may be bitter when cooked.) Rinse out the empty cavity and add skin and bones to the pot. Add any shrimp or crab shells to the pot. Add the fennel seed and enough water to cover all the bones. Bring to the boil; reduce heat and simmer 20 to 25 minutes. Set aside until needed. Strain, pushing the bones enough to be sure that all the broth has been used. Discard the bones. Taste the broth and adjust seasonings. It should measure 2 or 3 quarts. If less, add water. If more, bring to the boil and boil down to 3 quarts.

Meanwhile, make the marinade for the fish by mixing 6 tablespoons of olive oil and 3 garlic cloves (chop all the garlic at one time, reserving the rest for later). Soak the saffron threads in a couple of tablespoons hot water and add to the olive oil and garlic mixture.

Cut the 3 pounds skinned and boned fish into 2-inch cubes, keeping separate according to type and thickness.

Sort out any small scraps and set aside to add last. Toss the fish in the saffron marinade and refrigerate in a plastic bag until needed. Clean the shrimp and crabs (page 326).

Heat 1/3 cup of oil in a very large pot. Add the onions, leeks, and fennel to the hot oil, and sauté until soft, about 10 minutes, taking care not to brown. Add 4 to 5 garlic cloves and sauté 1 minute more. Add the tomatoes, a bunch of the fennel fronds, and the orange rind. Bring the soup to the boil, reduce heat, and cook 10 minutes. Add the remaining saffron to a couple of tablespoons of the strained broth. Add the remaining broth and the saffron mixture to the tomato sauce. Bring the soup to the boil, reduce heat, and simmer 30 to 40 minutes, until extremely flavorful. Season to taste with salt and pepper, remembering that seafood is still to be added.

Meanwhile, make the *croûtes* and the *rouille* by toasting the bread rounds; add 1 tablespoon of tomato purée to the mayonnaise, along with the lemon juice, red wine vinegar, and pepper or hot sauce. Taste the mixture, add garlic if needed, and adjust seasonings. When absolutely delicious, set aside in a small container, cover, and refrigerate.

When ready to eat, return the soup to the boil. (If it will not cover the seafood, add enough water to cover.) Reduce the heat slightly, add the thickest pieces of fish, and cook a few minutes without letting it boil hard. Add the shrimp, crabs, and the thinner or more delicate fish, such as flounder, and cook 1 or 2 minutes in the simmering soup. Add the clams and any remaining scraps of fish. Cook until the shrimp and crabs are pink and the clams open. Remove all the seafood and put on a hot platter.

Season the soup with salt and pepper, tomato paste, and Pernod or anise liquor. Boil down quickly if necessary to increase flavor. Sprinkle fish with chopped fennel frond if desired. Serve the soup and the platter of fish separately, or mix and serve together.

PROVENANCE OF MUDDLES

There are two kinds of muddles. One is a sweet muddle made of sugar and lemon, and perhaps mint, stirred together to make a base to be added to ice tea, and, in some variation, to bourbon for mint juleps. The other kind of muddle, or "mess," is a fish muddle. Fishermen do not often have the luck to catch a whole school of a single kind of fish—or didn't prior to sonar and the other tracking devices used by present-day boats. So every cuisine that fronts a coast has some sort of stew that combines many kinds of fish.

Muddle was coined in England, centuries ago, and the name came to the colonies. Muddles are seen from Virginia to the Lowcountry of South Carolina and Georgia. Although clams are frequently seen in the ones from Virginia, along with mussels (in fact, a recipe deriving from the *Williamsburg Cookbook* including both is repeated many times on the Internet), there are many variations. There is also a muddle that originated with the Gullah people on the barrier islands off the Georgia/South Carolina coast.

HERITAGE CATFISH SOUP

The Virginia House-Wife by Mary Randolph (1824) contains this recipe for Catfish Soup that is really a muddle:

To Make Catfish Soup
(An excellent Dish for those who have not imbibed a needless prejudice against those delicious Fish.)

Take two large or four small white catfish that have been caught in deep water, cut off the heads, and skin and clean the bodies, cut each in three parts, put them in a pot with a pound of bacon, a large onion cut up, a handful of parsley chopped small, some pepper and salt, pour in a sufficient quantity of water, and stew them till the fish is quite tender and not broken, beat the yelks [*sic*] of four fresh eggs, add to them a large spoonful of butter, two of flour, and half a pint of rich milk, make all these warm and thicken the soup, take out the bacon, and put some of the fish in the tureen, pour in the soup, and serve it up.

FOOTBALL CHILI

Serves 12 to 16

THIS IS AN ALL-REGION CHILI, *accommodating those who like a multiplicity of textures and tastes. Football is a big social occasion in the South, making this perfect when tailgating for the favorite college team or throwing an at-home Super Bowl party. Use what is on hand for the meat, herbs, and spices—all of one, or a portion of each. Texans rarely use beans; many other parts of the South have a surfeit of them and always include them, heedless of the variety. Chili is so variable that it must be tasted at several points during cooking.*

2 tablespoons oil, cook's preference
2 large onions, chopped
2 1/2–3 pounds total of ground chuck, pork, or turkey, or a mixture of each
4 large garlic cloves, chopped
2 (28-ounce) cans whole tomatoes, chopped, juice reserved
3 (15-ounce) cans kidney or other beans, drained, juices reserved, optional
1/2 cup red wine vinegar
1/2 cup chili powder
2 tablespoons ground cumin
1–3 tablespoons ground coriander
2–3 teaspoons ground hot red pepper
2–4 ounces canned green chilies, chopped
1 tablespoon light or dark brown sugar
Salt
Freshly ground black pepper
Dried herbs as available, such as oregano, optional
1 package tortilla chips
2 cups grated Cheddar or Monterey Jack cheese
1 cup sour cream

Heat the oil in a large Dutch oven; add the onions and cook a few minutes before adding the meat. Lightly brown the meat and drain off excess fat.

Reduce heat; add the garlic, tomatoes, beans, vinegar, chili powder, cumin, coriander, hot red pepper, chilies, and sugar. Add reserved tomato and bean juices as needed for balancing the liquid with solid ingredients. Bring to the boil; reduce heat and simmer, stirring occasionally, for 30 minutes.

Season to taste with salt, pepper, and additional herbs. Refrigerate and remove fat if time allows. The chili may be served at one time, or divided into portions and frozen for up to 3 months. Serve with tortilla chips, cheese, and sour cream.

CORIANDER SEED AND MINT

Coriander seed, added perhaps to reduce the bilious effects—or, as Karen Hess calls it, the "cold and windy effects"—of the peas, if not scientifically sound as a theory certainly contributes a wonderful fragrance and flavor.

Mint was ubiquitous in the English cookery that was the forerunner of Martha Washington's cooking and is still used more often than any other herb in English cooking.

CRUSHING WHOLE SEEDS

Roll seeds between pieces of waxed paper, or use a mortar and pestle or a lava *molcajete,* or roll seeds in a small sturdy plastic bag. A scrupulously clean electric coffee grinder is excellent for grinding seeds.

MRS. LYNDON B. (LADY BIRD) JOHNSON'S PEDERNALES RIVER CHILI

Serves 8 to 10

THIS RECIPE, NOW IN THE LBJ PRESIDENTIAL LIBRARY, *was introduced to me in the early 1960s when Lyndon Johnson ran for the Democratic Presidential Nomination. He lost to John F. Kennedy but became vice president and, later, president. All the while, parties were held serving beef barbeque and/or chili. The Johnson daughters hosted many of these. Lynda Johnson married Chuck Robb, a high school classmate of mine; so I particularly enjoy this recipe. Texans to the core, the Johnsons do not recommend ground meat; they recommend a thick chopped meat instead. If this "chili grind" chuck is not available, try cutting raw cube steak into 1-inch pieces, or use any ground meat desired. They did not add oil, but currently beef is raised to be so much leaner that the addition of oil is often necessary.*

¼ cup oil, cook's preference
1 large onion, chopped
2 large garlic cloves, chopped
4 pounds chuck, preferably "chili grind," or cube steak cut into 1-inch pieces
2–3 tablespoons chili powder
1 teaspoon dried or freshly chopped oregano
1 teaspoon ground cumin
1 (14½-ounce) can whole tomatoes, chopped
2–6 dashes hot sauce
2 cups water
Salt

Heat the oil in a large Dutch oven and add the onion, cooking until nearly translucent, about 5 minutes. Add garlic and meat, and brown lightly. Skim the fat off the top. Add the chili powder, oregano, cumin, tomatoes, hot sauce, and water, stirring well after each addition. Bring to the boil lower heat and simmer for 1 hour. Skim fat during cooking. Season to taste with salt. May be made several days ahead or frozen up to 3 months and reheated.

CUTTING CANNED TOMATOES

Although chopped canned tomatoes are available, canned whole Roma and other tomatoes are superior. After opening a can of whole tomatoes, use a pair of kitchen scissors and cut down into the can, revolving the can to cut all the tomatoes.

VEGETARIAN CHILI

Serves 8 to 10

ADAPTED FROM MY BOOK Nathalie Dupree Cooks for Busy Days, *this is a terrific make-ahead dish. The bulgur, beans or peas, and a heady blend of spices compensate for the lack of meat. The flavors marry and develop the longer this chili sits, so cook it 1 to 2 days before consuming.*

- 2 tablespoons oil, cook's preference
- 2 medium onions, chopped
- 4 large carrots, chopped
- 2 red bell peppers, seeded and chopped
- 2 large garlic cloves, chopped
- 2 pounds frozen or canned black-eyed peas or crowder peas, rinsed and drained
- 1 cup bulgur, soaked for 20 to 30 minutes in 2 cups boiling water
- 1 (28-ounce) can whole tomatoes
- 2 cups vegetable stock or broth
- 1/4 cup chili powder
- 1 tablespoon ground cumin
- 1 tablespoon ground coriander
- 1/4 teaspoon ground hot red pepper
- Salt
- Freshly ground black pepper
- 1 cup plain yogurt
- 6 green onions, thinly sliced
- 1/4 pound Cheddar cheese, shredded

Heat the oil in a large Dutch oven. Add the onions, carrots, bell peppers, and garlic, and cook over medium heat for 5 to 8 minutes while stirring.

Add the beans, bulgur, tomatoes, stock, chili powder, cumin, coriander, and hot red pepper. Bring to the boil; reduce the heat and simmer for 30 to 45 minutes, until thickened. Season to taste with salt and pepper.

If possible, cool down, refrigerate overnight, remove any fat that accumulates on top, and reheat the next day. Serve in bowls with yogurt, green onions, and grated cheese as condiments for topping the chili. May be frozen up to 3 months.

Variation: Add lentils, farro, pearl barley, quinoa, or another grain.

BULGUR

Bulgur is a kind of whole wheat that has been precooked, dried, and cracked into particles. It is similar to couscous in that it doesn't require cooking, only adding boiling water and letting it soak. Far more nutritious than rice or potatoes, it has a slightly nutty flavor and is a versatile side dish.

GUMBOS

Gumbo is indefinable. The word, technically, is an African word meaning "okra." Logically it would seem the word gumbo means an "okra-based soup." But logic and technicalities don't apply when it comes to gumbo, because it may or may not include one of three thickeners:

Roux—may or may not include oil but always includes flour; may be thin as water or thick as mud; may be a beautiful maple brown, or a mahogany brown, or nearly black in color. (See page 655.)

Roux-based soup is usually served hot but some may be served cold. Flour and fat are cooked together, left pale or browned within an inch of black, with a liquid and flavoring product such as carrots added and cooked, solids puréed and added to the liquid, and chilled. Most can be frozen and some can be served hot or cold. A variation of this calls for cooking the food in the liquid first and the thickener added at the end of cooking, such as arrowroot or a mixture of flour and liquid, called a slurry, brought to the quick boil and cooled before proceeding.

Okra—thickens the gumbo by becoming mucilaginous when cooked a long time.

Filé powder—ground dried sassafras leaves, added at the end of cooking. It is a strong herb tasting like a bitter thyme or savory, introduced by the Native Americans. Once it boils it does not hold its thickening power. Some people insist the two ingredients—okra and filé powder—should not be combined in a gumbo, that only one should be used. Others hedge their bets and use both, or serve their okra a little crunchier than in years past and rely on filé powder for the thickening.

All three of the above—to the outrage of some purists and to the delight of others.

There are rules, but they may be broken. Seafood gumbos traditionally include okra because they are available at the same time. Tomatoes are a source of fervent debate—some say they should never be included, and some say that a seafood gumbo is worthless without them. Game-based gumbos don't usually include okra—except when they do, and then frozen okra or dried okra pods (as was thought to be done in years gone by) are used. The inclusion of filé and roux is similarly unpredictable.

A gumbo, then, is whatever the cook wants it to be.

Gumbo history dates back to the turn of the nineteenth century and probably even before that, and is closely connected to the arrival of slaves in the South. Now, however, gumbo, like many other catchall foods, is cooked by those familiar with Louisiana and Southern Mississippi cooking and has a special affinity with Cajun cooks.

CARTER/DERIAN ROUX-LESS GUMBO

Serves 8 to 10

Marion Burros of the New York Times *once stood over Hodding Carter III, a Mississippi boy, while he cooked in advance for his annual New Year's Day party so she could see how he made the family gumbo. Hodding, his family, and friends make numerous batches of gumbo, combining recipes from two or three of their favorite cookbooks, and freeze them. They reheat and serve all three on New Year's Day. I've changed the recipe in many ways, including adding more fresh seafood at the end. If an ingredient is not available, ignore it and keep on cooking. Gumbos are notoriously inconsistent but hard to ruin.*

- 1/3–1/2 cup pork fat, chicken fat, or oil, cook's preference
- 2 1/2 pounds okra, quartered lengthwise and sliced (8–9 cups), divided
- 2 large onions, chopped
- 1 red bell pepper, seeded and chopped
- 4–6 celery ribs, chopped
- 1 pound smoked sausage, peeled and cut into 1/4-inch slices
- 2 1/2 quarts fish or Shrimp Stock (page 117), heated, divided
- 2–3 cups chopped tomatoes, fresh or canned
- 8 large garlic cloves, chopped
- 1 tablespoon ground hot red pepper
- 2 tablespoons freshly ground black pepper
- 2 1/2–3 1/2 pounds peeled shrimp, cut if necessary, plus 1/2 pound to refresh if desired
- 1 1/2 quarts shucked oysters or clams
- 1 cup green onion or shallot greens or chives, chopped
- Salt
- 1–2 tablespoons fresh lemon juice
- 1 cup crabmeat to refresh, optional,
- 1/2–1 tablespoon filé powder
- Hot cooked rice
- Hot sauce
- Lemon wedges for garnish

Heat 1/3 cup of the fat or oil in a very large pot. Add 2 pounds of the okra and sauté 10 to 15 minutes, stirring often, until it is lightly browned.

Stir in the onions, bell pepper, and celery, and cook for 5 minutes, stirring occasionally and scraping the bottom of the pan to make sure nothing is burning. Remove and set aside. Check to be sure there are no burned bits; if so, remove them or clean the pan. Add the sausage to the hot pan and brown, adding more fat as necessary. Remove the sausage and set aside.

Carefully add 2 cups of stock, return the removed vegetables to the pot. Bring back to the boil and cook 5 more minutes, stirring and scraping often. Stir in the tomatoes and cook another 10 minutes, stirring and scraping as needed. Add another 4 cups of stock; cook 5 more minutes.

Stir in the garlic, hot red pepper, and black pepper. Add the rest of the stock, stirring well. Bring to the boil, add the sausage, return to the boil, reduce heat, and simmer, covered, about 45 minutes, stirring occasionally.

Add remaining okra and cook another 10 minutes. The gumbo may be frozen at this point or after adding seafood. Add shrimp, oysters, and green onions. Season with salt, and bring to the boil. Remove from the heat, skim fat from surface, and serve immediately or freeze.

If serving immediately, add lemon juice and sprinkle with filé powder, just enough to cover about 3/4 of the gumbo's surface with a sprinkling. Bring back nearly to the boil but do not let it boil.

If frozen, defrost and reheat slowly; add lemon juice and refresh with additional shrimp and the crabmeat if desired. Cook only long enough to heat through. Add the filé as above. Serve with rice and hot sauce. Garnish with lemon wedges.

THE HOLY TRINITY

Food is revered in Cajun-Creole country, so it is not irreverence that causes them to call peppers, onions, and celery "the holy trinity"—it is because they are used consistently. Cajun chef Paul Prudhomme once told me the way to get a crowd to come to a cooking demonstration was to start cooking "the holy trinity" with a little garlic and the Lord would deliver the masses to be fed. Amen.

ROAST CHICKEN GUMBO

Serves 6

THIS IS A VARIATION OF A GUMBO *by Minnie C. Fox from her book* Blue Grass Cookbook, *which has an excellent introduction by Toni Tipton-Martin. This gumbo is a light, yet still brown and flavorful, made with roasted chicken browned in fatback and butter. When I roast chicken, I roast two, using one for supper and another for the gumbo to be served a day later. I save the bones, skin, and extra flesh from any roasted chicken and use them for the stock. A rotisserie chicken may also be used in this recipe.*

1 whole chicken, about 3 pounds
2 tablespoons butter, lard, or oil, cook's preference
Salt
Freshly ground black pepper
4 cups brown or regular chicken stock or broth, divided
1 slice fatback or bacon
1 onion, sliced thinly
2 garlic cloves, chopped
1/4–1/2 cup all-purpose flour
1 (14 1/2-ounce) can whole tomatoes with juice, roughly chopped
1 small hot pepper
1/2 cup of uncooked rice
1 pound fresh okra, caps removed, or 1 pound frozen
1–2 tablespoons chopped fresh parsley
1–2 tablespoons chopped fresh summer savory

Preheat oven to 400 degrees.

Rub the chicken with butter, lard, or oil, sprinkle with salt and pepper, and move to a roasting pan. Roast for 30 minutes. Turn the chicken to brown it on the other side. Add stock as necessary to come an inch up the side of the chicken; carefully return the hot pan to the oven and roast 30 minutes more. When the chicken is browned, remove from the oven, having cooked it about 1 hour in all. Remove the chicken from the pan and cool, reserving the liquid in the pan. When the liquid is cool, remove and discard the fat.

When the chicken is cool, remove the flesh from the bones and add the bones and skin, along with any juices and liquid to the pan with the remaining stock. Bring the liquid to the boil in the pan over low heat, and scrape the bottoms and sides to deglaze the pan and release all the good brownness. Let boil to reduce the liquid slightly and add flavor from the bones to the broth.

Meanwhile, heat a large Dutch oven and add the fatback. When the fat is rendered, add the onion and cook until the onion is soft, adding the garlic for the last 1 or 2 minutes. Use a slotted spoon to remove the solids and set them aside.

Stir the flour into the residual fat until it is a medium-brown roux. Strain the liquid from the roasted chicken and add it to the flour mixture; continue to stir over heat until slightly thickened.

Add the onion and garlic to the pot, along with the tomatoes and their juice, and the hot pepper. Return to the boil; reduce heat, cover, and simmer 30 minutes. Add water as necessary to make 1 1/2 quarts of liquid. Add rice to the pot, bring back to the boil, cover, and cook until the rice is nearly done, about 11 minutes.

Meanwhile, break apart the okra with a spoon if necessary to eat easily. Add the chopped chicken back to the pot along with the okra. Return to the boil, add the herbs, and cook a few minutes, making sure the chicken has cooked thoroughly. The okra should be slightly crunchy. Taste and season with salt and pepper. Serve at once.

Variation: Any suitable vegetable can be added in place of the okra—corn, English peas, green beans, or sliced carrots—and cooked the desired amount of time.

Summer savory, which looks like thyme, is a strong culinary herb that grows nearly year round in the South. If none is available, use thyme or omit altogether.

FISH CAMP DUCK GUMBO

Serves 10

CYNTHIA AND I HAVE HAD *many magical moments taping our television series. One we talk about frequently is a dinner we had after we taped—and flew in—a crop duster planting rice in a flooded field. The dinner was held in a typical "fish camp," a rustic building in the country usually owned and run by a men's group. This was no exception. The men cooked. Cynthia and I were the honored guests, so we were served first. Knowing no different, we went and sat at the big table. Turns out it was the men's table, and all the other women were seated elsewhere. Oops! But no one asked us to move, and we had a grand time.*

Some water ducks are tastier than others. For this recipe, you have to find a hunter who knows the right type of bird to cook, where it was shot, and how it was kept until you received it. The recipe is adapted from Vintage Vicksburg *from the Junior Auxiliary of Vicksburg, Mississippi. Do not attempt this with domestic duck.*

3 large or 6 small wild ducks, skinned and cleaned
3 large onions, chopped, divided
Salt
Freshly ground black pepper
Commercial seafood seasoning or Creole seasoning (page 670), optional
1/2 cup oil, cook's preference
1/2 cup all-purpose flour
2 celery ribs, chopped
6 garlic cloves, chopped
2 bell peppers, preferably red
1 pound fresh or frozen okra, chopped
2–4 bay leaves, crumbled
2 tablespoons Worcestershire sauce
1 teaspoon ground hot red pepper
1 teaspoon chopped fresh thyme or savory
Hot sauce
Filé powder, optional
10 cups cooked white rice

Cover the ducks with water in a large pot. Add 1 onion, salt, black pepper, and Creole Seasoning to taste. Bring to the boil, cover, reduce heat, and simmer 2 to 6 hours.

Remove the ducks and let cool, saving the broth. When cool enough to handle, remove the flesh from the ducks and chop coarsely. The meat and broth may be refrigerated or frozen until ready to use. Skim the fat from the broth and discard.

A few hours before serving, make a roux of the oil and flour in a large heavy pot, cooking it carefully until it is light mahogany in color. (Some people prefer to do this in the oven.) Add the 2 remaining onions, celery, garlic, bell peppers, and okra, if you wish to add it now. Cook for 15 to 20 minutes, until the onions are soft and translucent. Bring the duck broth to the boil and pour onto the vegetables, adding water if necessary to make the pot two-thirds full. Add bay leaves, Worcestershire, hot red pepper, and thyme. Season to taste with salt and pepper. Return the gumbo to the boil, cover, reduce heat, and simmer for 1 hour. Add the duck and okra (if not added earlier), and simmer 5 minutes. Return to the boil, reduce heat, add hot sauce as desired, season to taste with salt and pepper, sprinkle with filé powder, stir, and serve over hot rice.

HOT SAUCES

There are so many hot sauces produced it is impossible to give directions on how much to use or even what color to use. Some people, like the Derian-Carters, prefer green. Others are wed to the original red. Still others combine them or use concoctions from other countries that include lime juice and garlic in addition to peppers and vinegar. Some hot sauces are peppers cooked and puréed with vinegar; others are homemade hot sauces with vinegar and hot peppers in a jar kept on the table for daily use in dousing greens, cornbread, soup, and more.

CHARLESTON SEAFOOD GUMBO

Serves 8 to 12

VERY ROUGHLY ADAPTED *from* Charleston Receipts, *this calls for a dark roux as well as okra for thickening, but no filé powder. The fish also includes local seafood—wreckfish, sea trout, red snapper, and the like. If the pieces of fish are thicker than the shrimp, add earlier, as described. If thinner than the shrimp, add after the shrimp, as they will require less cooking.*

8 tablespoons butter, divided
4 tablespoons all-purpose flour
2 medium onions, chopped
4 garlic cloves, chopped
8 cups Shrimp Stock (page 117), fish stock, broth, or water
5 fresh tomatoes, peeled, seeded, and finely chopped or 1 (28-ounce) can tomatoes with juice, chopped
2 pounds okra, fresh or frozen, sliced, divided
2 pounds fresh fish, cut into 1- to 2-inch pieces
2 pounds raw shrimp, shells removed
1 pint shucked raw oysters
1 pound crabmeat, picked through to remove any shells
Salt
Freshly ground black pepper
Hot sauce, optional

Melt 6 tablespoons of butter in a large Dutch oven. Add the flour and stir until a smooth paste forms, then continue cooking until it is a rich nutty brown but not burned, making a dark roux.

Meanwhile, heat the remaining butter in a small sauté pan. Add the onion and cook until lightly colored. Add the garlic and cook 1 minute more. Add to the brown roux. Stir in the stock, tomatoes, and half the okra. Bring to the boil, stirring. Reduce heat and cook slowly for 30 minutes, covered. Remove lid.

Fifteen minutes before serving, bring back to the boil and add the remaining okra and fish. Cook a couple of minutes. Add the shrimp and oysters, and cook just until the shrimp turn pink and the edges of the oysters just begin to curl.

Divide the crabmeat among the bowls. Taste the gumbo and season to taste with salt, pepper, and hot sauce as desired. Ladle onto the crabmeat and serve hot.

Variation:
Add chopped ham to the mixture. Add Creole spices and ground hot red pepper to taste.

BROWN ROUX

Roux is a word with many meanings. In Louisiana, it contains flour browned to the edge of being burned, usually but not always cooked in oil to brown. Roux and browned flour are sold commercially in Louisiana grocery and specialty stores. Browned (cooked) flour has less thickening capacity than uncooked flour. The French Roux on page 655 is quite a different thing, and the terminology should not be confused.

CRAB AND TOMATO STEW

Serves 4 to 6

I MADE THIS STEW *on a cold and rainy day in February. After debating running outside in the rain to gather fresh parsley and marjoram, I decided that it wasn't crucial to the stew if fresh herbs aren't available. The saffron, though one of the more expensive spices, is also unnecessary, but I love how it gives a call for seafood and really complements the crabmeat. If preferred, shrimp or a white flaky fish can be substituted for the crab.*

3 tablespoons butter
1 medium onion, chopped
2 large garlic cloves, chopped
1 (28-ounce) can diced tomatoes
4 cups chicken stock or broth
1 bay leaf
1 tablespoon chopped fresh parsley
1 tablespoon chopped fresh marjoram
1/2 teaspoon saffron threads
Grated rind and juice of 1 lemon, no white attached
Salt
Freshly ground black pepper
1 pound lump crabmeat, picked through to remove any shells

Heat the butter in a large Dutch oven over medium heat. Add the onion and garlic, and sauté until tender. Increase the heat to high, add the tomatoes and stock, and bring to the boil. Reduce heat to a simmer and add the remaining ingredients except for the crabmeat. Simmer the soup, partially covered, for 45 minutes. Remove the bay leaf.

When ready to serve, evenly divide the crabmeat and place in the bottom of soup bowls. Pour the hot stew over the crabmeat and serve immediately.

OYSTER STEW

Serves 4

CHILLY NIGHTS BEG FOR OYSTER STEW, *served with buttered toast points or oyster crackers and perhaps a green salad. I like the added crunch and flavor of the shallot and celery, and the boost the reduced chicken stock gives. Originally founded in 1737 as a private subscription music concert club, now turned elite social club (with membership passing through the men of the family), the Saint Cecilia Society has served this oyster stew at their annual balls since they began in 1822 (with the exception of the time the city was under fire during the Civil War).*

2 tablespoons butter
1 shallot or small onion, very finely chopped
2 celery ribs, or 1 fennel bulb, finely chopped, fronds reserved
1/2 cup chicken stock or broth
2 cups heavy cream
1 quart fresh shucked oysters and their strained liquid
Salt
Freshly ground black pepper
2 teaspoons chopped parsley or fennel fronds
Toast points or oyster crackers

Heat the butter in a heavy saucepan. Add the shallot and celery, and cook 1 to 2 minutes to remove the raw taste.

Add the stock, bring to the boil, and boil rapidly until the liquid is reduced to 1/3 cup. Add the cream and bring to the boiling point.

Remove from the heat and add the oysters and their liquid. Return to the stove and heat through about 2 minutes, until the oysters are warmed throughout and their edges begin to curl. Do not boil. Season to taste with salt and pepper. Pour into soup bowls, garnish with parsley or fennel fronds, and serve with the crackers.

Variations:

- Add 1 teaspoon bourbon to the heated cream.
- Substitute chopped fennel for the celery, and top with a little shredded country ham or 3 cooked and quartered new potatoes.

ST. CECILIA SOCIETY'S OYSTER STEW WITH MACE

1 quart oysters
1 cup water
1 tablespoon butter
1 tablespoon flour
2 cups cream
Salt and pepper to taste
2 blades mace

Scald the oysters in their own liquor. As soon as they are plump, remove them to another dish. Mix together the water and the butter and flour, and add to the liquor. Then pour in the cream, season to taste with salt and pepper, and add the mace. Let this become very hot; then add the oysters. As soon as the oysters are heated, remove the mace from the stew and serve. This makes eight plates of soup.

—Alicia Rhett Mayberry,
Two Hundred Years of Charleston Cooking

VEGETABLES & SIDES

Thomas Jefferson set the tone: the best way to live a long life was to eat meat as a condiment rather than an aliment. Even though Martha Washington had a ham out on the table every day for their copious number of visitors, George was fascinated by vegetables, from broccoli to rice and peas.

The Lord Proprietors, the English group that controlled Charleston from 1670 to 1720, were interested in crops not only to sustain the population but also to provide new exports. Wheat was expensive to import, and at one time community kitchens were responsible for feeding the many men brought over to work the crops. Rice was grown to capitalize on the world's demand for the finest quality of rice.

There were already vegetables, fruits, and nuts here—from corn to pecans, pumpkins, and sweet potatoes—many of their uses attributed to Native Americans, still others to the way Europeans and Africans had cooked for centuries. Thrifty from the beginning, colonists were known for their preserved and dried foodstuffs. The Civil War limited the number of available imports, with root vegetables and home gardens dictating the food.

Refrigeration, both in shipping and storing—and air-conditioning, commercial and residential—changed it all. Onions, potatoes, and sweet potatoes could be kept in cold storage until the market price was satisfactory; home cooks could purchase in quantity and freeze what they could not use. Oranges were no longer relegated just to Christmas as a special treat. Spices had a longer life due to cooler environments. Following World War II, there were other advances; new tastes for ingredients grown and developed elsewhere; and, finally, European and California produce was introduced and then grown here as well.

Chefs have currently taken the lead over home cooks in creating new and exciting dishes, utilizing new ingredients that take well to our growing climate. For example, we have lemongrass and kaffir lime growing in our gardens. Okra, once cut in thick horizontal slices or served whole, is sliced vertically or diagonally in slivers and baked or stir-fried as well as traditionally deep-fried or cooked in gumbos and stews.

Southerners still like their vegetables fresh; they still cling to the idea of growing themselves something to eat and still crave fresh foods. They have learned new cooking techniques for familiar vegetables as well as still adding pork fat to the new vegetables in an expanded cuisine.

STORING AND COOKING VEGETABLES

Microwaving vegetables—Fresh vegetables are appealing prepared in the microwave, and some studies suggest the vegetables retain more of their nutrients cooked this way. Utilizing uniform pieces and a microwave-safe container, add 1 tablespoon of water for each 1/2 pound of vegetable. Cover with microwave-safe plastic wrap or a glass lid. For 1/2 pound of vegetables, cook on high for 4 minutes. Check the tenderness of the vegetable with a fork, and continue to check in 30-second increments until the vegetable reaches desired tenderness. Tender vegetables will need only 4 or 5 minutes. Tougher, thicker vegetables will need longer. (*See* corn, page 195.)

Refreshing green vegetables—Running green vegetables under cold water stops the cooking and sets the color, causing them to look "refreshed." Chefs specify ice water, but I find ice isn't necessary with small home quantities of vegetables.

Reheating vegetables—All vegetables may be made ahead and reheated. When reheating boiled or steamed vegetables, there are several methods that may be used:

- Heat fat, such as oil, butter, duck fat, etc., in a frying pan, add the vegetables, and quickly heat, stirring rapidly. (Or use a nonstick pan with no fat added.)
- Arrange the vegetables in one layer in a heatproof pan, cover with foil, and leave in a 350-degree preheated oven until heated through. Start with 5 minutes for small, thin vegetables, or heat up to 15 to 20 minutes for thick ones, learning to know oven and pan, until confident the timing is correct.
- To blanch, add tender vegetables to boiling water for just 3 to 4 minutes, depending on size, until crisp-tender. Run under cold water and drain. Add whole root vegetables to cold water, bring to the boil, and cook for 15 to 20 minutes, depending on size and density, until nearly cooked. Drain quickly, reserve the liquid for soups if desired, and run vegetables under cold water to stop the cooking. When ready to serve, use one of these methods:
- Return the vegetables to boiling liquid briefly to heat through.
- Warm in a microwave oven.
- Steam.

Using extra produce—I'm haunted by the dribs and drabs of food in my refrigerator, and I blame the farmers market for the lush tomatoes and vivid red and yellow bell peppers that I overbuy to keep on the table—ignoring them until they are on the edge of extinction. Eggplants, with their thick skins, always seem so sturdy and indestructible that I ignore their girth when I purchase them, only to be frustrated when they take up the whole refrigerator vegetable bin. And who ever purchased one ear of corn? (These are also refrigerator hogs, by the way.) There's always one that will not fit on the grill and languishes lonely and forgotten until desperation meets dinnertime.

Fortunately, restaurants have set the stage by serving scattered bits of vegetables. So what if there isn't enough of one thing to feed everyone what would be considered a portion? A few dribs and drabs of everything will make an empty plate look like a vegetable repast.

Or stretch it—Let them eat a bit of Maque Choux (page 198), which accommodates shrimp happily, or Southern Ratatouille (page 200) tucked underneath a cooked chicken breast.

GLOBE ARTICHOKES

Artichokes are flower buds picked before they mature. A member of the thistle family, they have tough, thorny leaves that grow out of a fleshy, succulent base known as the bottom or, incorrectly, the heart. The bottom is covered with an edible, but undesirable, hairy choke that should be removed.

Baby artichokes are not babies at all, but fully mature artichokes that are smaller because they grew close to the ground and were sheltered by larger leaves on the plant. They have a tender choke and are therefore entirely edible and easier to prepare. These are often found in jars, canned, or frozen, and are also incorrectly called artichoke hearts.

Select artichokes with tightly packed leaves that are not discolored. Larger, older artichokes are tougher but make a prettier presentation. The longer an artichoke has been on the grocer's shelf, the more dehydrated it will be. Refresh it by trimming off the stem and covering the artichoke with ice-cold water for 30 minutes, or refrigerate in water up to 2 days.

TRIMMING AND PREPARING ARTICHOKES

To trim and prepare artichokes for cooking, wash with cold water and cut the stem off, leaving a level base, so that the artichoke will rest on its base. Save the stems, as they are a flavorful extension of the artichoke heart and edible when peeled. They make a good snack dipped in butter after being steamed or boiled.

Peel the tough outer leaves, snapping at the interior pale green, and discard. Cut off the top fourth of the artichoke (about an inch) with kitchen scissors, or lay it on its side and cut down across the top with a large sharp knife. Trim off the thorny tips of the remaining leaves with scissors. Artichokes will turn brown when cut. Rub the cut parts of the artichoke with a sliced lemon to prevent browning.

EXTRACTING LIQUID FROM VEGETABLES

The more liquid a vegetable naturally contains, as in the case of eggplants, the harder it is to brown. The liquid will dilute any sauce. There are two ways to extract liquid from vegetables. One is to cook them long enough to remove the liquid. The other is to degorge (page 200) with salt, which also removes any bitterness: a colander holds the produce as the liquid drains off. Rinse in cold water and pat dry.

Today, artichokes are associated with California, yet this unique member of the thistle family with Mediterranean roots was grown in Virginia as far back as the 1720s. *Martha Washington's Booke of Cookery* contains the seventeenth-century recipe "To Make Hartichoak Pie," and *The Virginia Housewife* (1825) has a recipe for boiled artichokes served with butter. Artichokes were grown in Louisiana in the eighteenth century, where the Italian influences were making stuffed artichokes a popular entrée. South Carolina was a major producer of them in the 1800s. Some grow in my Charleston garden now.

BASIC GLOBE ARTICHOKES

Serves 4

THIS IS THE MOST COMMON METHOD *of cooking artichokes, tenderizing the leaves and making them pliable and easier to remove, as well as cooking the bottom. There are many edible parts of globe artichokes—the little tender crescent of pale green that attaches each leaf to the main frame, the center portion (called the bottom) after the thistle part is scraped off, and the peeled stem.*

4 artichokes
1 cup butter or mayonnaise
Hot sauce, optional

Trim the artichokes and add them to a pot of boiling salted water. To keep them from bobbing up, spread a tea towel over the artichokes in the water and cover with a pie plate or other heatproof plate. Reduce heat, cover with a lid, and cook 30 to 45 minutes, until a leaf pulls out easily. Carefully remove the lid or plate and tea towel before removing artichokes and draining them on a plate.

Cool slightly and trim off the stems at the base so the artichokes will sit flat. Open the leaves slightly in the center, scoop out the choke with a spoon, and discard the choke. Serve hot with melted butter or at room temperature or cold with mayonnaise. Add a few drops of hot sauce to the butter or mayonnaise if desired.

Eat by pulling off the leaves, dipping the pale green bottom portion of the leaf into the butter or mayonnaise, and scraping just that portion with the teeth for a tender morsel. Proceed around the artichoke until all the leaves are gone, eating just the tender portions. In the center is the artichoke bottom, shaped like a small bowl with a furry coating inside. Spoon out and discard the furry part. To enjoy this prime piece of artichoke, cut the bowl into bite-sized pieces and dip in the sauce. The detached stem may be peeled and eaten this way as well.

Variation: Boiled Artichoke Bottoms
Cook artichokes as above, tear off leaves and set aside, remove choke and serve the bottom cut into quarters for a salad or as a "plate" for a salad.

Variation: Steamed Artichokes
Tie the artichokes together with string so they don't "bobble" around. Move to a rack in a large pot with a small amount of water inside. Cover and cook until tender, as above, monitoring the water level and adding more if in danger of boiling dry.

Variation: Microwaved Artichokes
Add trimmed artichokes to a glass dish with water to a depth of less than 1/2 inch. Cover tightly and microwave on high power for 7 minutes for 1 artichoke and up to 15 to 20 minutes for 4, checking every 4 or so minutes for tenderness.

A thick onion ring used as a base when steaming or boiling an artichoke holds the artichoke upright, and prevents the base from becoming too mushy, as the ring serves as a rack.

STUFFED ARTICHOKES

Serves 4

New Orleans restaurants serve stuffed artichokes, *based on the strong Italian influence on the cuisine in that region. The "stuffing" goes between the leaves and makes a splashy presentation. As with most restaurant preparations, it takes a bit more time than home-cooked dishes.*

1 cup breadcrumbs
1 cup freshly grated Parmesan cheese
3 green onions, chopped
2 teaspoons capers
4 garlic cloves, finely chopped
Finely chopped fresh parsley
Salt
Freshly ground black pepper
4 trimmed globe artichokes (page 160)
1 teaspoon fresh lemon juice
1/2 cup oil, cook's preference

Stir together the breadcrumbs, cheese, green onions, capers, garlic, parsley, salt, and pepper, or process in a food processor. Turn each trimmed artichoke upside down and press lightly against the counter to open the leaves. In the center of the artichoke is the choke, an inedible thistly barrier to the succulent artichoke bottom. Turn the artichoke right side up and remove the choke with a spoon, leaving the bottom intact. Fill the spaces among the leaves with the bread stuffing, using a small spoon to wedge open the space and insert the stuffing. Put any remaining stuffing into the hollow left by removing the choke. Brush the artichokes liberally with oil.

Move the artichokes to a rack in a big pot with a little water under the rack. Cover and steam for 45 minutes, or until a leaf pulls off easily. Check occasionally, being careful of steam, to be sure there is still water in the pot. Or microwave, covered with plastic wrap, on high power for 10 minutes. This may be done up to a day in advance. When ready to serve, run under the broiler until the stuffing is crisped and brown and the artichokes are heated through.

Globe artichokes are the most common of the artichokes sold in the South. They are round, as opposed to the slender artichokes sold in Europe.

GREEN ONIONS

Green onions are the early, immature onion, with a sharper, brighter flavor. The greens can be substituted for scallion greens. Vidalia green onions are larger than the average medium onion and are frequently roasted whole in season. The term "green onion" is used interchangeably by many of us for "scallions," their baby cousin.

JERUSALEM "SUNCHOKE" ARTICHOKES

These tasty knobby roots are neither from Jerusalem nor artichokes. They were so named because they taste very similar to globe artichokes. In fact, they are a type of sunflower, also known as sunchokes. They have an outer skin much like a potato, so scrub them well. They can be peeled or cooked in their skin, are delicious sautéed, baked, grilled, broiled, or boiled. Raw, they are crisp and refreshing in a salad. They can also be pickled (page 639).

SAUTÉED JERUSALEM ARTICHOKES

Serves 4

I GREW JERUSALEM ARTICHOKES *in the garden of our restaurant near Social Circle, Georgia. First I had their sunflowers, and then I had the chokes. They were a constant on our menu all summer—sautéed, baked, grilled, or broiled.*

1 pound Jerusalem artichokes, halved or quartered, if large
Butter or oil, cook's preference
Salt
Freshly ground black pepper

Heat a skillet over medium heat and melt butter to coat the bottom of the pan. Add the scrubbed chokes and sauté until tender, about 10 to 15 minutes, turning frequently.

Variation: Boiled Jerusalem Artichokes
Bring the scrubbed or peeled artichokes to the boil in enough salted water to cover. Boil until fork-tender, about 10 to 15 minutes. Drain. Peel, if necessary, and cut into pieces as desired according to size, or eat small ones whole. Season to taste with butter, salt, and pepper.

Variation: Roasted Jerusalem Artichokes
Preheat oven to 400 degrees. Toss the scrubbed chokes in butter or oil and add to an oiled rimmed baking sheet. Bake 10 to 15 minutes, as a small potato.

ASPARAGUS

When the first asparagus pokes its head up in the Lowcountry, we know it is spring. The newer varieties in the early twenty-first century include slender purple or green stalks as long as a forearm and as thin as a pencil. They are so sweet they can pleasurably be eaten raw, although rarely are.

One amazing thing about asparagus is how many personalities it has. Whether crisply cool, subtly room temperature, or hot and dripping with butter or sauce, it adds grace and refinement to a meal. While asparagus comes in many sizes, I prefer the finger-sized thin ones. If using the thin ones, allow more stalks per person. They cook quickly and are often eaten with the fingers. Larger asparagus need peeling and are best cooked standing up in a tall poacher—much like an old-time metal coffee pot—the theory being that the stems cook in the water while the tips steam.

When purchasing asparagus ahead of time, keep the stem ends moist by standing upright in about a half-inch of water in the refrigerator or lying on the refrigerator shelf in a plastic bag with the ends wrapped in wet paper towels.

Cooked asparagus can be refrigerated and served cold at a later time, or quickly heated in a microwave or under a broiler and served as a hot vegetable to accompany a meal. If not using the cooked asparagus within a few days, freeze in plastic ziplock bags. Thaw and reheat when needed. Tightly wrapped, cooked asparagus can be kept frozen for up to 3 months. It will lose its crunch but will be fine for soup or a casserole.

ASPARAGUS IN SOUTHERN HISTORY

Asparagus is a fascinating vegetable to grow. Some varieties take up to 7 years to poke their first wispy shoots up above the ground. Once up, however, they grow rapidly, and the gardener fears going away for a few days lest they have grown and gone. South Carolina was at one time a major grower and supplier of asparagus.

In a 1745 issue of *London Magazine,* the author writes that along the Georgia coast, "the good Indians regaled us and for Greens, boiled us the Tops of China-Briars, which eat almost as well as Asparagus." In *Charleston Receipts,* the recipe for "Chainey Briar" calls for 2 bunches of chainey briar (wild asparagus), cooking them as one would fresh asparagus. The top of a wild bush, Chainey Briars were considered an early substitute for asparagus.

"Sparrow Grass" was asparagus in the eighteenth century in both England and America. "Sprue," the first thinning of the growing asparagus, is the long-awaited sign of spring.

PICKLED ASPARAGUS

Martha Washington's Booke of Cookery offers a recipe for pickling "green asparagus." It instructs the reader to "hould ye roots in your hands and dip in ye green ends whilst ye water boyls. Soe doe by every bundle you have, & when yr sparragus is cold, put into a glass with verges & salt, and it will keep all ye year." Verges [also verjuice or *verjus*] is an acidic sauce based on unripe grapes with lemon or sorrel juice; vinegar would be the modern equivalent.

EATING ASPARAGUS

Traditionally, and according to Emily Post, asparagus is a finger food. Cooked properly rather than overcooked, it is still crisp and difficult to cut, shooting across the table if attempted. Cook only until its stem has the slightest bend—a decided droop is far too much. Sauced asparagus is handled with individual asparagus tongs, or hot damp cloths are passed to clean any messy fingers after eating.

BASIC ASPARAGUS

Serves 4

THE VERY TINIEST SPEARS *do not need to be peeled. Tough ends should be cut off, perhaps used for soup at a later time. Snapping is inexact and removes too much of the good part of the asparagus, so that preparation method should be avoided. It would take a very tall asparagus poacher to cook the thin asparagus—hardly suitable anyway, as they cook quickly and the stem is cooked just about the time the tip is—so I use a deep frying pan.*

1 pound asparagus

2–4 tablespoons butter or oil, cook's preference

Salt
Freshly ground black pepper

Fill a deep frying pan or chicken fryer (non-iron to avoid discoloration), large enough to hold the asparagus lying down, three-quarters full of salted water. Bring to the boil with the salt. Meanwhile, cut off any tough ends of the asparagus and, if fibrous, peel from the stem to the first little flower of the tip. If the asparagus are slender and willowy, it is not necessary to peel them, which would cause them to bend like weeping willows.

Add the asparagus to the pan, all facing the same way, in batches if necessary, with the stems in the water and the tips hanging just over the edge of the pan. Cook 3 to 5 minutes, depending on the size of the asparagus and the color. When tender, they should be crisp-tender and bend ever so slightly but still be bright green. Remove from the pot, drain, and rinse in cold water to set the color and stop the cooking. Drain again and set aside. The asparagus can be held at room temperature for a few hours or covered with plastic wrap and refrigerated for serving later. They are good hot or cold or at room temperature.

If serving cold, toss in butter or olive oil, salt, and pepper, then cover and refrigerate.

If serving hot, heat the frying pan with the butter, add the cooked asparagus, and toss quickly over the heat until heated through. (Use fingers or a pair of tongs to keep them moving so all are heated but none are overcooked). Turn out onto a platter and serve. They will turn an ugly gray if doused with citrus juice or vinegar, so use one or several of the following variations for flavor.

Variations:

- Serve with melted butter.
- Toss with grated orange and/or lemon rind for a citrus flavor. Or toss with grated ginger, buttered crumbs, herbs, roasted pecans, walnuts, or pine nuts.
- Add to salads and serve cold.
- Toss with sautéed sliced mushrooms to reheat.
- Top with 1/2 pound cooked and peeled shrimp, melted butter, or olive oil.
- Toss with olive oil, salt, and pepper. Top with slivered ham.

GRILLED OR BROILED ASPARAGUS

Serves 4 to 6

THE POPULARITY OF GRILLING *has added dimension to the table, expanding from traditional grill food such as burgers and steaks to grilling vegetables. The character of asparagus changes completely when grilled. I relish it when charred and the tips become crispy. If the asparagus are particularly thick, add to boiling salted water, cook 2 minutes, refresh, and drain before grilling.*

1 pound fresh asparagus
1/2 cup oil, cook's preference
1 tablespoon chopped fresh basil leaves, optional
1/2 teaspoon chopped fresh thyme, optional
2 teaspoons chopped fresh parsley, optional
1 green onion, finely chopped
Salt
Freshly ground black pepper

Heat the grill.

Prepare the asparagus by peeling and cutting off the bottom ends as needed. Move the asparagus to a large plastic bag or a shallow glass dish. Toss with the oil, optional herbs, and green onion. Marinate for at least 30 minutes if possible.

Shake off and discard the marinade then grill the spears about 5 to 7 minutes, turning 2 or 3 times, until no longer raw but still rigid.

If broiling, line a rimmed baking sheet with foil and broil asparagus 2 to 3 inches from the heat, turning as needed, cooking 5 to 7 minutes. Season to taste with salt and pepper.

Variation: Grilled Asparagus and Mushrooms
Cut 4 or 5 portobello or other mushrooms into quarters. Add to the marinade with the asparagus and then to the grill. Asparagus may be served whole or cut on the diagonal.

Variation: Roasted Asparagus
Preheat oven to 450 degrees. Toss asparagus in oil and spread out in one layer on a foil-lined baking sheet. Season to taste with salt and pepper. Roast for 5 to 10 minutes, according to thickness of the stalks.

ASPARAGUS AND RED BELL PEPPER STIR-FRY

Serves 4

ASPARAGUS ADAPTS WELL TO ASIAN RECIPES *and ingredients, most of which have been used in the South since they became available.*

1 tablespoon oil, cook's preference
1 tablespoon soy sauce
3 green onions, sliced
1 garlic clove, chopped
1/4 teaspoon dried hot red pepper flakes, optional
1/3 pound asparagus, cut diagonally into 2-inch pieces
1 red bell pepper, seeded and cut into triangles
1 tablespoon dark sesame oil

Heat the oil and soy sauce in a large skillet or wok until very hot. Toss the green onions, garlic, and red pepper flakes together while cooking briefly. Add the asparagus and bell pepper; cook, stirring constantly, for about 3 minutes. Reduce the heat, toss asparagus in the sesame oil, cover, and cook for an additional 1 to 2 minutes, or until just done—not too soft, not too crunchy—and still green.

Variation: Asparagus and Chicken or Shrimp
For an all-in-one dish for two people, add 1 boned chicken breast cut into 1-inch chunks or 1/3 pound peeled shrimp to the wok and stir-fry 1 to 2 minutes before adding the other ingredients.

BEANS AND PEAS

Taking their rightful place in the history of food, legumes—including peas, beans, peanuts, and lentils—are some of the oldest sources of nutrition known to man and have been equally valuable to Southerners throughout the generations, becoming one of the South's most beloved vegetables. Long a mainstay of indigent cultures, beans and peas early ensconced themselves in the class structure of the South, with Thomas Jefferson avidly pursuing different types—importing nearly 30 varieties himself for experimentation. After the Civil War, beans became as crucial a protein to both Black and White families as they were to the earliest settlers.

Technically, beans and peas are in the same family—legumes—sort of. In a sense, all peas can be beans and all beans can be peas, but we call them different things, thinking of peas as something inside the pod and calling beans the exterior package holding the pea. This only holds true so far, as many Southern beans are really peas—requiring a pod to be opened to access them—but are called beans, such as butter beans and their cousin lima beans.

Both peas and beans can be green or dried, both can be "field" or "garden"—a vague economic difference, with dried beans and peas sometimes considered a poor man's necessity available to field hands. Garden peas (called "English" peas in the South and "green" peas elsewhere) were considered a richer man's food, perhaps because they are rarely preserved.

Green beans—The typical green beans referred to in Southern nomenclature are pole green beans, bunch beans, and half runners. Green beans are considered garden food, except for pole beans, which are field vegetables, even though they can grow in the garden. Pole beans, or flat beans, are 6 to 8 inches long and 3/4 inch wide; they require diligent stringing and are tougher than other green beans. Traditionally cooked long and slow, they are frequently "put up" (canned in jars) for the winter months because they take so well to slow cooking. Bunch beans are the typical green beans found in the grocery store. Half runners are about 4 inches long and 1/3 inch wide, about the size of a lady's finger, and require only light stringing. The peas inside a half runner pod are barely present; in pole beans, they are more prominent, nearly half the size of lady peas.

Preparing Green Beans

My mother called cutting or snapping both ends of green beans "tipping and tailing." I prefer cutting to snapping, which removes too much of the bean, although many a young child was introduced to cooking by sitting in the kitchen snapping beans with their grandmothers before they could hold a knife.

Line up the beans next to each other, tough tails together. Cut off the tails. Leave the tips on if desired, or slide the beans so the tips are easily cut off as well.

Black-eyed peas—These found their way in the early pre-Christian era (1800 BCE) to Greece and India, overlapping the "cowpeas." In fifteenth-century Venice, *fagioli* were originally a black-eyed pea cooked with pork belly or fatback, a precursor to African and Southern methods of seasoning and extracting nutrition and fats for stamina. To confuse the matter, black-eyed peas in the South may be called cowpeas or field peas, and they are the best known of the Southern field peas.

Black-eyed peas, rice, and okra were no doubt brought to the New World—the Americas and the Caribbean—to feed the slaves, either en route on their horrible journey or while they were here.

As noted in Ken Abala's incredibly informative work *Beans—A History,* corn, beans, and squash (the "three sisters") were essential to the diet of early North Americans, from Aztecs to Virginians, and were described in books as varied as those by Giovanni da Verrazzano in the early 1500s to William Strachey's description in 1612 that the peas the Virginia natives ate were little, like French beans, and the same as *fagioli.* Samuel de Champlain wrote in 1613 of observing "the bean plants twine around the aforementioned corn, which grow to a height of five to six feet." This added nitrogen to the corn.

Peanuts—A rather sneaky legume, in that the plant grows under the ground and is thought of as a nut, peanuts are a mainstay of comfort and nutrition in the South. Their arrival from Africa prompted experimentation and development, from boiling and frying them in the shell, to processing them into oils and butters, to just roasting and eating them.

Cooking dried legumes—Dried peas and beans expand slowly when cooking, as the only way liquid has to enter is through the little hole called the *helium,* where the stem was attached. The addition of ingredients early on, such as ham hock, onion, and hot pepper adds to the flavor from the beginning. The hole expands with the swelling of the beans, so the initial slow penetration speeds up considerably by the end, when the bean has begun to swell up from the liquid between the layers of starch.

A cooked bean can't absorb flavor. At some point, the starch granules burst and "gelatinize," improving the bean's flavor. It is this optimum point the cook strives for—when the bean has its maximum flavor but has not burst like a balloon, losing its flavor to the broth.

To prepare for cooking, pick through the dried beans, removing all stones, and rinse the beans. The rough ratio of dried beans to water is 1 pound of dried beans to approximately 2 cups of water. The processes of soaking dried legumes are varied. Here are several:

1. The standard wisdom of soaking them overnight in a quantity of water to cover is preferable to other methods, as it helps maintain their shape and soften their skins. Drain and discard the water. Overnight soaking decreases the cooking time by 30 minutes, although it is hard for some to remember to start this process the night before.
2. The second most-discussed method is to "quick-soak" them: bring a pot of water to the boil, add the dried legumes, cover the pot with a lid, and let sit 1 hour off the heat. Drain and proceed to cook. This is a bit of a hassle, but it gives a little more bite to the beans, as the skins do not mush as much as in the previous method.
3. The third way is to cook the beans with no prior soaking.
4. My solution is to pour boiling water over the dried peas or beans when starting to gather ingredients, drain and discard the water, and proceed with the recipe.

None of these are proven to be superior to others or to have been tested scientifically to determine if the assumptions are sound. What is proven is that long, slow cooking will produce a dried bean that holds its shape and is tender and palatable.

Dried peas are not alike. The longer they are on the shelf, the longer they will take to cook. Buy them from a purveyor with frequent turnover.

Salting beans and peas—Scientists say salt toughens peas, so if the beans or peas have not been soaked, err on the side of caution and omit salt until later in the recipe. If they have been soaked, salt the water at the beginning of cooking.

The cooking time of everything depends on size and freshness. Smaller things cook quicker than larger. No one can say how long a dried legume should be cooked; it is cooked when it is "done" to the tongue and tooth. Styles of cooking beans vary radically, as the recipes will show. Cooked beans freeze exceptionally well and are frequently canned or jarred.

Dried peas and beans can be cooked without soaking, with the eater experiencing a bit more flatulence. The beans will take 1 to 2 hours longer to cook, depending on size.

PREVENTING FLATULENCE

The only proven method for preventing flatulence is a commercial flavorless product that is sprinkled on the beans just before eating. The rest is up to the bacteria in each individual's stomach. Discarding the water has not been proven to reduce flatulence, no matter how much each of us claims it does to ease our concerns of social ostracism.

BUTTER BEANS OR BUTTER PEAS

Serves 4 to 6

THE CONSTANT STARS OF THE SOUTHERN TABLE, *butter beans and the rounder butter peas, are pale green in color, the size of a pencil eraser, and are delicate, moist, tender, and flavorful relatives of lima beans. We buy butter beans in our farmers market in small sandwich-sized plastic bags, already shelled and ready to use or freeze as they are. Commercially frozen butter beans and butter peas, as well as those called "white acres," are all very good substitutes for fresh, but avoid the lima-bean-sized brownish tan ones for optimum flavor and texture. I love serving peas with Tomato Conserve (page 644), which is available in the grocery store in jars or is easy to make at home.*

4 cups shelled fresh butter beans or butter peas
1/4 cup butter or bacon fat
1/2 small onion, sliced
Salt
Freshly ground black pepper

Bring enough salted water to the boil to cover the beans in a pot. Add the beans or peas, butter or bacon fat, and onion. Return to the boil. Reduce heat, cover, and simmer 30 to 45 minutes, skimming off any foam as needed. Test to see if tender before draining. Season to taste with salt and pepper. Serve with the liquid if desired.

Variations:

- Add 2 teaspoons of chopped fresh lemon thyme, lemon balm, and basil.
- Add small baby carrots to the beans, along with 2 teaspoons of fresh herbs.
- Toss butter beans in 1 tablespoon of olive oil and serve with a few cooked fresh shrimp or 1/3 cup drained canned tuna. Season to taste with salt and pepper.

SUMMER SUCCOTASH

Serves 6 to 8

CAJUNS MAKE MAQUE CHOUX; *elsewhere we make succotash. While these dishes are similar, made with bacon drippings, sweet corn, peppers, and onions, Charlestonians add fresh butter beans, black-eyed peas, or other green field peas. Any fresh summer veggies enhance a succotash, so experiment. If there aren't any bacon drippings by the stove, use a mixture of butter and oil to sauté the vegetables. Fresh herbs from the garden can really brighten the dish.*

1 pound fresh butter beans and/or other green field peas
1 medium onion, preferably Vidalia, chopped, divided
Salt
2 tablespoons bacon or sausage drippings, or butter and oil, cook's preference
1 shallot, thinly sliced
8 ounces button mushrooms, sliced
2 garlic cloves, chopped
1 squash or zucchini, cut into 1/2-inch cubes
2 ears corn
1/4 cup chopped fresh herbs, such as thyme, basil, or rosemary
Freshly ground black pepper

Bring enough salted water to the boil to cover the beans in a pot. Add beans and half of the diced onion and return to the boil. Salt as needed. Reduce heat and simmer until beans are tender, 30 to 45 minutes, skimming off any foam as needed. Drain.

Heat drippings in a large skillet over medium heat; sauté shallot, remaining onion, and mushrooms until onion is translucent, about 10 minutes. Add garlic and sauté until fragrant, about 2 to 3 minutes. Stir in squash and cook, stirring occasionally, until tender.

Hold the corn vertically in a pie plate. Rotate and slice down the corncob with a paring knife, reserving the cobs for another use (Corncob Stock, page 117). Add kernels, cooked butter beans, and fresh herbs to the squash. When ready to serve, cook, stirring occasionally, until just heated through, the corn still a bit crispy. Season to taste with salt and pepper. Succotash may be refrigerated, covered, for 3 days or frozen up to 3 months.

GREEN BEANS

Serves 4

GREEN BEANS ARE EASILY COOKED *ahead of time and reheated. The following variations are ideas on how to broaden their use, Southern style.*

1 pound green beans, tipped, tailed, and stringed
2 tablespoons butter or oil
Salt
Freshly ground black pepper

Bring enough water to the boil to cover the beans. Add the beans and return to the boil. Reduce heat to medium and cook 5 to 7 minutes, until the beans are no longer raw but still crisp. Drain and run under cold water to refresh and set the color. Set aside. The beans may be made a day ahead and refrigerated or frozen at this point for defrosting and use later.

When ready to serve, heat the butter or oil to sizzling in a large frying pan. Add the beans and toss until heated through. Season to taste with salt and pepper.

Variations:

- Top the hot beans with Tomato Conserve (page 644).
- Top reheated green beans with warm Tomato Sauce (page 661).
- Toast 1/2 cup pecan halves in 2 tablespoons butter. Add the cooked green beans and reheat.
- Toss cooked green beans with White Butter Sauce (page 656) over high heat until beans are reheated and thoroughly coated in the butter.

Variation: Green Beans with Mushrooms and Shallots

Melt 4 tablespoons butter in a frying pan; sauté 1 pound of quartered or sliced mushrooms along with 4 chopped shallots or scallions for 1 to 2 minutes. Add the cooked green beans to the mushrooms and reheat. Add a tablespoon of chopped fresh herbs if desired.

Variation: Green Beans with Onions, Peppers, and Lime

Heat 1 tablespoon oil in a frying pan; cook 1 small chopped onion and 1/2 chopped and seeded green pepper until soft. Add the cooked green beans and 1 tablespoon lime juice and reheat.

Variation: Green Beans with Lemon Rind and Onion

Melt 2 tablespoons butter in a large frying pan. Add 1 small chopped onion and cook until soft. Add the cooked green beans and the grated rind of 1 lemon, no white attached. Toss until reheated. Like most green vegetables, green beans turn gray when doused with an acid. The lemon rind gives sufficient flavor without the unsightly change in color.

Variation: Green Beans with Tomatoes

Melt 2 tablespoons butter in a large frying pan. Add 1 small chopped onion, 1 chopped garlic clove, 3 skinned and diced small tomatoes, 1 seeded and chopped small hot pepper; cook until soft, about 5 minutes. Just before serving, add the cooked green beans and 1 tablespoon red wine vinegar and toss until reheated. (The vinegar and tomatoes will turn the beans gray if added sooner).

Variation: Green Beans with Cumin or Coriander

Heat 2 tablespoons butter or oil in a large frying pan. Add 1 teaspoon ground cumin or coriander seed, 1/2 teaspoon sugar, and the cooked green beans. Toss to combine and reheat. Season to taste with salt and pepper.

Variation: Green Beans with Sesame Cabbage
Heat 2 tablespoons butter or oil in a large frying pan. Add the cooked green beans and 1/4 head green or red cabbage (cut into 1/4-inch slices). Sauté just until the cabbage wilts but is still crisp, about 5 minutes. Mix 2 tablespoons soy sauce, 2 teaspoons dark sesame oil, 1 teaspoon granulated sugar (optional), and freshly ground black pepper to taste in a small bowl. Add to bean and cabbage mixture and toss to coat. Sprinkle with 1 tablespoon sesame seeds. Serve hot or at room temperature.

Variation: Green Beans with Sesame Seeds or Pecans
Heat 2 tablespoons butter or oil in a pan. Add the beans and toss with 2 tablespoons sesame seeds or chopped pecans.

PAN-CHARRED GREEN BEANS

Serves 4

As a young woman in my first apartment, *I had only a frying pan. So I cooked my beans in butter, slightly charring them. They were delicious as I sat on the floor and ate them from the pan. I still yearn for them on occasion.*

4 tablespoons butter
1 pound green beans, tipped, tailed, and stringed
Salt
Freshly ground black pepper

Melt the butter in a large frying pan. When very hot, add the beans and cook until dappled with dark brown. Reduce the heat, and continue cooking a few minutes more, stirring, until the beans are nearly soft. Season to taste with salt and pepper.

ROASTED GREEN BEANS

Serves 4

When a green vegetable cooks a long time, *it loses its bright color. These look slightly gray but taste wonderful, particularly with Tomato Conserve (page 644).*

1 pound green beans, tipped, tailed, and stringed
2–3 tablespoons oil
Salt
Freshly ground black pepper

Preheat oven to 400 degrees.

Drizzle the beans with oil in a large baking dish and toss. Sprinkle with salt and pepper and bake until the beans are shriveled and browned, about 35 minutes. Serve hot or at room temperature.

HOME-STYLE GREEN BEAN CASSEROLE

Serves 4 to 6

Many years ago, the Campbell Soup Company promulgated a recipe calling for cream of mushroom soup, green beans, and canned fried onions. It was extraordinarily popular in my youth and is a nostalgic and comforting dish for many Southerners to this day. This is a modern variation that may nonetheless comfort those who prefer fresh ingredients.

7 tablespoons butter, divided
2 tablespoons all-purpose flour
1¾ cups Flavored Milk (page 657)
½ cup Swiss cheese
Salt
Freshly ground pepper
1 cup mushrooms, sliced
1 pound cooked green beans (page 170)
½ cup shredded Cheddar or Gruyère cheese
4 medium onions, thinly sliced

Preheat oven to 350 degrees.

Melt 2 tablespoons of the butter in a medium saucepan. Add the flour and stir until smooth. Cook 2 to 3 minutes over low heat. Whisk in the milk all at once, stirring constantly until the mixture is thick. Bring quickly to the boil, remove from heat, and stir in the Swiss cheese. Season to taste with salt and pepper; set aside.

Melt 1 tablespoon butter in a small skillet. Add the mushrooms and cook over medium heat until softened, about 4 to 5 minutes. Mix the cooked green beans and mushrooms into the cheese sauce. Pour into a baking dish and top with the Cheddar or Gruyère.

Melt the remaining 4 tablespoons butter in a large skillet and cook the sliced onions until they caramelize and are nicely browned (page 220). Top the green bean mixture with the caramelized onions. Bake until heated through, about 15 minutes.

TRADITIONAL POLE BEANS

Serves 8 to 10

These long, tough green beans, originally Kentucky Wonders, always need stringing. The traditional long-cooking method was probably derived to incorporate the fat into the beans as an important source of energy, as well as to make them palatable and flavorful. No vitamins are lost, as the broth is eaten too. Of course, they won't melt in your mouth if you cook them for less time but will still be good. They hold their shape, just barely. Serve with Tomato Conserve.

2 ham hocks or ¼ cup white bacon, streak o' lean, or fatback, sliced (page 173)
2 pounds pole green beans, stringed, cut into 2-inch pieces
1 teaspoon granulated sugar, optional
1 medium onion, peeled
Salt
Freshly ground black pepper
1 cup Tomato Conserve (page 644)

Rinse the hocks or pork fat if necessary, and cover with water in a pot. Bring to the boil and cook for 30 minutes, skimming off the foam as needed. Remove the ham hocks from the pot of broth, add the green beans and more water if necessary to cover the beans, and return to the boil. Add sugar if desired. Put the ham hocks on top of the beans and add the whole onion to the pot. Bring to the boil, reduce heat, taking care that the pork stays on top to melt and flavor the beans. Reduce the heat and simmer until very tender, about 1 to 1½ hours, skimming off the foam as needed. Season to taste with salt and pepper. If desired, remove the ham from the bones and serve it with the beans.

Variation: Prepare pole green beans as above, adding 14 small scrubbed potatoes during the last 30 minutes of cooking.

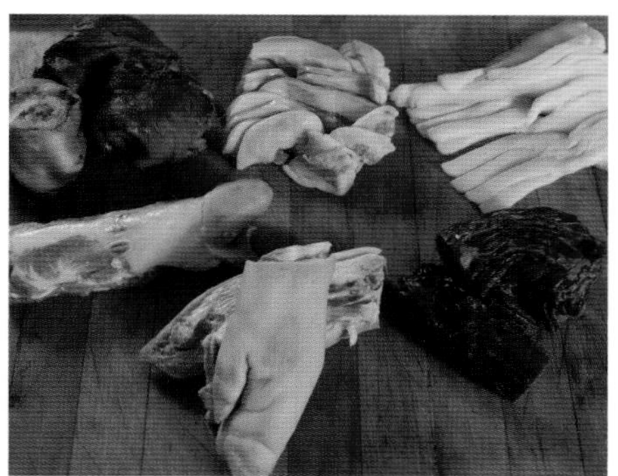

SEASONING MEATS FOR VEGETABLES

There is a long tradition of seasoning cooked vegetables with the broth of pork and other bones and meats. While "outsiders" may find these vegetables "greasy," to Southerners accustomed to them, they are full of flavor and richness. They may be eaten at a meal where no other meat is provided, which is probably the origin in an era when meat was a treat on Sunday, if then. Less fortunate people, including slaves, used the less desirable parts of the pig for their meals and seasonings. The best known of these many parts are fatback, streak o' lean, and hog jowl. Any overly salted meat should be rinsed.

Fatback—This comes from the back of the pig and can be salted, smoked, or, in some cases, left fresh. Primarily fat, it is frequently sold sliced, with just a slice going into the pan with the water and vegetables. It may also be sautéed and eaten as a "side meat." (Also called "salt pork.")

Streak o' lean—This comes from the belly of the pork and is sold salted, smoked, or in some cases left fresh. It is fattier than bacon but also may be sautéed and eaten as a "side meat." The pronunciation is run together: "streakolean."

Pork belly—For those of us used to pork belly as a seasoning meat, it is now a fearful time, as this once inexpensive piece of meat is becoming popular—fresh, sautéed, or broiled. A cured piece is sometimes called "white bacon"; it is flavorsome soaked in water and then thinly sliced, fried, and served with cream gravy.

Hog jowl—A portion or the whole hog jowl (cheek), usually just the bone and what clings to it, this is a favorite for seasoning black-eyed peas and turnip greens for New Year's Day and other holidays.

In addition to any part of cured ham, meats used for seasoning also include split pig tails, feet, hocks, and other pig parts—whether smoked, salted, or fresh. Smoked turkey necks and other smoked meats and poultry are also used as seasoning meats.

CRISP POLE BEANS

Serves 4

In the last thirty years, *it has become increasingly popular to eat pole beans in a modern way. We've found crisp garden-fresh pole beans in the summer are a yummy treat, blanched briefly to preserve their bright color and clean flavor. With garlic and shallots, the whole kitchen smells wonderful, and it's really hard to keep everyone's fingers out of the pan. Doubling the recipe is never a bad idea so that enough makes it to the table.*

1 pound pole beans, tipped, tailed, and stringed
1 tablespoon butter
1 tablespoon bacon drippings
1 large shallot, chopped
1 garlic clove, chopped
1 tablespoon chopped fresh thyme or other fresh herbs, optional
Salt
Freshly ground black pepper

Bring enough water to cover the beans to the boil in a large pot. Slice the beans on the diagonal into 2-inch pieces. Add beans to the boiling water and cook until crisp-tender, 5 to 7 minutes. Drain.

When ready to serve, heat the butter and drippings in a skillet over medium heat. Add the shallot and garlic, cooking about 2 minutes. Toss in the blanched beans and cook until warmed through. Add herbs if desired. Season to taste with salt and pepper.

BLACK-EYED PEAS WITH HOG JOWL

Serves 6

The black-eyed pea isn't really a pea at all; *it's a bean. Be that as it may, black-eyed peas are served all year long but with special emphasis to bring luck on New Year's Day. Combined with an equal amount of cooked rice, they make a traditional African dish, now called Hoppin' John, and form a complete protein—a vital source of food for what President Franklin D. Roosevelt called "the Shoeless South" during the Depression and other hard times.*

1 pound dried black-eyed peas
1/4–1/2 pound hog jowl, fatback, or other smoked meat
1 jalapeño or other small hot pepper, optional
Salt
Freshly ground black pepper

Pour boiling water over the dried peas or beans in a large pot and set aside. Meanwhile, make a broth by covering the hog jowl and optional pepper with water and bringing to the boil. Reduce heat and simmer for 1 hour to extract the juices and reduce the liquid, skimming off the foam as needed.

Pour off and discard the water from the peas. Pour the hog jowl broth over the peas, removing the jowl if desired. Simmer 30 minutes to 1 hour, or until peas are tender but still individuated, not mushy, skimming off the foam as needed.

Variation: To use fresh or frozen black-eyed peas, cook the hog jowl as above. After 1 hour, add 2 pounds fresh or frozen peas and simmer as above.

REDUCING SCUM (FOAM)

When possible, liquid added to vegetables for further cooking should be near boiling. It shocks the vegetables and reduces the amount of vegetable scum.

HOPPIN' JOHN

Serves 6 to 8

A MUST-DO DISH AT NEW YEAR'S AND OTHER HOLIDAYS, *the peas represent good luck and health. Traditionally, since this was a New Year's dish, the peas were dried, but, of course, canned or frozen are readily substituted and seen nearly all year long.*

2 cups dried black-eyed peas, lady peas, or cowpeas
1 piece fatback, hog jowl, or other smoked meat, slashed in several places
1 hot red pepper
1 medium onion, chopped
Salt
Freshly ground black pepper
1 cup uncooked rice
4 tablespoons drippings, preferably bacon

Pour boiling water over the dried peas in a large pot and set aside while preparing other ingredients. When ready to proceed, drain the peas and discard the water. Add fresh water to cover the peas. Add the fatback, hot red pepper, onion, salt, and black pepper. Bring to the boil; cover, reduce heat, and simmer until the peas are nearly tender, about 45 minutes to 1 hour, skimming off the foam as needed. Add more water as needed. Continue cooking, covered, until the peas are tender. Remove the peas with a slotted spoon, reserving enough liquid in the pot (about 3 cups) to cook the rice.

Bring reserved liquid to the boil, add the rice, and return to the boil; cover. Reduce heat and simmer until the rice is cooked, about 30 minutes. Return peas to the pot, stir together, and cook for a few minutes more. Add drippings to flavor the dish, taste, and adjust seasonings. Turn out into a large dish and serve. This may be made into a tasty salad at a later time.

Variation: Add cooked, frozen, or drained canned black-eyed or crowder peas, and cooked bacon to cooked rice and heat together.

FRESH CROWDER PEAS WITH SNAPS

Serves 6

CROWDER PEAS ARE A TOUGHER SMALL PEA *than white acres or lady peas. Even when green (fresh), they tend to be a drier pea than many others but burst with flavor. Like other zipper peas, is a rare treat to find them shelled unless frozen or canned.*

2½ pounds fresh Crowder peas to yield 1½ pounds shelled peas
3 ounces fatback (salt pork)
1 small hot red pepper, optional

Shell the peas and check for wormholes. If any pods are too tiny to shell, leave them whole or snap them in half. Cook these "snaps" with the shelled peas.

Bring enough water to cover the peas to the boil. Slice the fatback four times but leave it whole, with the rind intact. Add to the boiling water along with the peas, snaps, and optional hot red pepper. Return to the boil, reduce heat, and simmer the peas for about an hour.

ENGLISH (GREEN) PEAS

Serves 4

GREEN PEAS WERE BROUGHT FROM ENGLAND *to the New World and identified as part of English cooking merely by their name. Many people in other areas of the country call them green peas, although all peas have a "green," or raw, state. English peas are the most vibrant green of all peas and cook quickly. They have a sweetness when freshly picked and are eaten raw by many a cook while shelling them. Sugar is added by many cooks to keep English peas sweet. They freeze well when shelled.*

1/2 cup chicken stock or broth, or water
2 cups shelled fresh English peas, or same amount frozen
5 tablespoons butter
Salt
Freshly ground black pepper
Granulated sugar, optional

Bring stock or water to the boil in a large saucepan. Add peas and butter, return to the boil, cover, and cook for 3 to 4 minutes. Season to taste with salt and pepper and optional sugar.

Variation: Peas with Wilted Lettuce
Add 1 tablespoon chopped fresh thyme, romaine lettuce, and 1 bunch roughly chopped green onions to the cooked peas; heat until lettuce is slightly wilted.

Commercially frozen peas need little if any further cooking. They are also unique in that the quick freezing done commercially traps the sugar inside and keeps them from losing flavor. Fresh English peas start to lose flavor quickly once picked.

PREVENTING BOIL OVERS

Peas have a tendency to foam up while cooking and run over the top of the pot. Two ways to prevent this type of boil-over are to use a larger pot and/or add a few drops of cooking oil or butter to the water—even a teaspoon will do.

FREEZING PEAS

Fresh peas freeze very well. When purchasing fresh peas, try to purchase them already snapped—i.e., removed from the pod. Usually there will be some pods that are too small to be opened and have the peas removed. We call those "snaps" and like to have some of them in every package of frozen peas, as they add the flavor of the pod and cook simultaneously. The peas in our market are sold already snapped and in plastic bags. I freeze them as is. When freezing a bulk quantity of peas, spread out on a rimmed baking sheet and move to the freezer; when frozen, pour into plastic ziplock bags and return to the freezer. Since the peas are individually frozen, they will be easy to measure.

SAUTÉED ENGLISH PEAS

Serves 4

A very popular dish of mine, *this is a definite change from the traditional cooking of my childhood, when English peas were only cooked in water, sometimes being indistinguishable from mush.*

3–4 tablespoons oil, cook's preference
2 cups shelled fresh English peas
1–2 green onions, chopped, both white and green parts
Salt
Freshly ground black pepper
3 tablespoons finely chopped fresh basil, optional
3 tablespoons freshly grated Parmesan cheese, optional
Hot pepper flakes, optional
Granulated sugar, optional

Heat the oil in a large frying pan until it begins to shimmer. Add the peas with the green onions and sauté 2 to 3 minutes. Season to taste with salt and pepper. Add the optional ingredients to taste. Cover the pan and continue cooking 1 minute for young peas, longer for older ones. Serve hot.

CAJUN ROUX PEAS

Serves 6 to 8

Smoked sausage is a mainstay of Louisiana, *lower Mississippi, and Alabama cooking. This is a pale roux, as the flour isn't browned.*

1/2 pound smoked sausage, diced
1/4 cup oil, cook's preference
1 medium onion, chopped
1 celery rib, chopped
Half of 1 red or yellow bell pepper, cored, seeded, and chopped
4 garlic cloves, chopped
1 1/2 tablespoons all-purpose flour
2 pounds shelled fresh or frozen butter peas or butter beans, room temperature
3 cups chicken stock or broth
Salt
Freshly ground black pepper
4 green onions, sliced
2 tablespoons chopped fresh parsley
Hot sauce

Heat the oil in a large Dutch oven and add smoked sausage. Cook 3 to 5 minutes; stir in the onions, celery, and bell pepper, and cook another 3 to 5 minutes. Add garlic and heat through. Sprinkle the vegetables with the flour and stir well. Add the peas and stir in the stock. Bring to the boil and reduce to a simmer. Season to taste with salt and pepper. Cook until the peas are tender and a gravy has started to form. Add more stock as necessary to cook the peas until tender while maintaining the gravy. Season again to taste with salt and pepper. Garnish with green onions and parsley. Serve with hot sauce.

BUTTERY ENGLISH PEAS AND TOMATO

Serves 2 to 3

I ALWAYS KEEP FROZEN ENGLISH PEAS *in the freezer and grape tomatoes in the fridge (the only kind of tomato I refrigerate). The two can produce a satisfying family vegetable in a hurry.*

1 tablespoon butter
1/2 (16-ounce) package frozen green peas, defrosted
5 or 6 grape tomatoes, halved
1 tablespoon finely chopped fresh basil, optional
Salt
Freshly ground black pepper

Heat the butter in a large skillet over medium heat. Add the peas, tomato, and optional basil; toss just until warmed through; avoid overcooking, as the tomatoes will wilt and give up their juices, making the dish too soggy. Season to taste with salt and pepper.

Variation: Substitute drained canned diced tomatoes.

CREAMED ENGLISH PEAS AND POTATOES

Serves 4 to 6

"CREAMERS" IS THE NAME FOR JUST-PICKED SMALL POTATOES. *Combined with English peas and a cream sauce, they add a splendid touch to holiday or company meals, hence, "creamed" creamers and English peas. Use a large pot to prevent the potatoes from boiling over.*

12 small creamers or fingerling potatoes
8 tablespoons butter, divided
1 medium onion, sliced
2 cups shelled fresh English peas
2 tablespoons all-purpose flour
1/2 cup heavy cream
Salt
Freshly ground black pepper

Peel a band around the potatoes with a swivel peeler or knife. Cut up any large potatoes so that none are larger than 1 1/2 inches in diameter. Rinse and add to a pot of boiling water to cover. Return to the boil, reduce to a simmer, and cook until the potatoes are tender when pierced with a fork, 20 to 30 minutes, depending on size.

Meanwhile, heat 3 tablespoons of butter in a frying pan. Add the onion and sauté until tender, about 5 minutes.

Melt the remaining 5 tablespoons butter in a small saucepan. Stir in the flour to make a roux. Add heavy cream to the roux, stirring continuously to make a white sauce. Bring to the boil. Pour the sauce into the undrained potatoes and peas. Season to taste with salt and pepper.

BEETS

New varieties of beets in multicolors shimmer on the plate—diced, julienned, grated, sliced, or quartered. The small ones can be appealingly sweet and are a delight when cooked crispy. Unfortunately, my husband doesn't like beets and before we were married made me promise never to serve them to him. What a shame.

In some countries, like France, beets are sold already cooked. Farmers boil them in pots in the field, saving the hapless home cook from being covered in red dye from head to toe, as often happens here.

Select beets that are firm, with the greens attached when possible. Prepare and store the greens as you would other greens (page 205).

While cooking beet greens, add roasted and sliced beets back to their greens, which flavors both the beets and the greens.

ROASTED BEETS

Serves 4

Baking beets in aluminum foil *makes them easier to peel than boiling or steaming them. The roasting increases the flavor as well. They can be returned to the oven when peeled to roast and deepen in color.*

4–6 medium beets

Preheat oven to 400 degrees.

Wrap beets in sturdy aluminum foil. Move the wrapped beets to a rimmed baking sheet and cook 1 hour, or until beets are tender. When beets are cool enough to handle, slip off peel. Serve as is, use in another recipe, or return to oven to roast and deepen their color.

Variation: Beet Quarters with Lemon

After peeling, quarter the beets. Heat 2 tablespoons oil in a pan, add the beets, and toss until heated through. Add the juice of half a lemon. Season to taste with salt and pepper.

PREVENTING BEET JUICE STAINS

Beet juice will stain anything and everything it comes into contact with—hands, cutting board, etc. Clean the work area of anything you don't want to stain vibrant red. Use plastic gloves and plastic cutting boards when cutting the beets.

Cut off the beet stem close to, but not into, the beet. As for the root, cut close to the beet but leave a short tail. Both of these cuts will prevent excess dye from escaping the beet.

BROCCOLI

Broccoli is one of the important cruciferous vegetables, as are cauliflower and Brussels sprouts, regarded for their high nutrition. They are believed to be cancer-fighting. Cruciferous vegetable stems are more dense than the florets and should be separated before cooking. As these vegetables cook, the aroma changes and signals that the vegetables are overcooked.

Broccoli is two vegetables in one: the crisp stalk may be cut horizontally in amoeba-like slices or vertically in fingers; the flower, or head, contains delicate florets. Select firm heads with crisp stalks and avoid those that have begun to yellow. Store broccoli in the refrigerator loosely wrapped in plastic.

ROASTING BROCCOLI

To roast broccoli, toss with oil and salt and freshly ground pepper to taste. Roast, uncovered, in a 350 to 400-degree oven until slightly charred. I usually just roast the whole stalks. Another method is to peel the stalks and cut vertically into "soldiers" and roast quickly. Grated cheese added a few minutes before removing from the oven adds sophistication.

STEAMING BROCCOLI

Move a steamer rack into a pot with 1 inch of water in the bottom. Add broccoli to the steamer. Bring water to the boil, cover, and cook until broccoli is crisp-tender, about 3 to 5 minutes.

QUICK BRAISED BROCCOLI

Serves 4

THIS RECIPE SHOWS HOW TO COOK A GREEN VEGETABLE *in advance and reheat it. It uses nearly all of the vegetable, cooked in a little water and butter. When I was young, my mother cooked green vegetables in a large quantity of boiling water, turning them to a yellowish mush. Crisp-cooking insures a full-bodied green vegetable.*

1 head broccoli
4 tablespoons butter, divided
2 garlic cloves, chopped
Salt
Freshly ground black pepper

Trim off the tough end of the broccoli stalk. Peel the rest of the stalk to just below the florets; cut the stalk off and slice 1/4 inch thick. Alternatively, trim the stalk into a long rectangle, and then dice into pieces. Heat 2 tablespoons of butter in a frying pan, add the sliced stalks, and toss 3 minutes over high heat.

Meanwhile, break the head into florets. Add them, with or without stalks, with a few tablespoons water, cover, and cook 2 minutes more. This may be done up to a day in advance.

When ready to serve, heat the remaining butter in a frying pan, add the garlic, and cook briefly. Add the broccoli and toss over medium heat until coated with the garlic and butter. Season to taste with salt and pepper.

Variation: Add 1/2 cup freshly grated Parmesan cheese to the frying pan when reheating the broccoli.

BROCCOLI TREES SLATHERED WITH GARLIC

Serves 4 to 6

THERE IS SOMETHING SO ENTICING *about this manner of cooking broccoli; even children—particularly children—love it, and its name appeals to them.*

1 head broccoli
1 1/2 tablespoons butter
6–8 garlic cloves, peeled
Salt
Freshly ground black pepper

Cut the tough end of the stem off the broccoli, leaving the rest of stem attached to the florets. Cut the broccoli into florets with long spears. Heat the butter over medium-high heat in a large skillet, add the garlic, and cook 3 to 5 minutes. Add the broccoli spears, spreading so they are in one layer. Cook 1 minute. Turn the spears carefully with tongs and cook an additional minute. Reduce heat to low, cover the pan, and cook broccoli 8 to 10 minutes. Uncover and cook until any moisture evaporates, another 3 to 5 minutes, and the stem is crisp-tender but still green. Season to taste with salt and pepper.

Variation: Add 1/4 teaspoon turmeric or curry powder.

BROCCOLI STIR-FRY MEDLEY

Serves 4

PRESIDENTS DIFFER IN THEIR VIEWS OF BROCCOLI. *Virginian George Washington loved it and grew it in his garden, and Texan George H. W. Bush hated it. This colorful modern version of tossing it with other vegetables would make the crankiest president happy with his vegetables.*

2 tablespoons oil
1 red bell pepper, seeded and julienned
1 small onion, sliced
1 head broccoli, cut into florets, or the peeled and sliced stems of 1 head, optional
1 tablespoon soy sauce
Freshly ground black pepper

Heat the oil in a large skillet until hot. Add the bell pepper, onion, and optional peeled and sliced stems; stir-fry quickly for 3 to 4 minutes. Add the broccoli florets, soy sauce, and pepper to taste. Toss to combine, then cover to steam lightly until the broccoli is just done and still green, about 2 to 3 minutes.

Variation: Add 1 teaspoon chili oil and 1 tablespoon rice wine vinegar to the broccoli.

BROCCOLI WITH RED PEPPER, OLIVES, AND FETA

Serves 4

This is quick when using leftover or frozen florets. *Frozen florets need only be heated through, not pre-cooked.*

2 tablespoons oil, cook's preference
4 garlic cloves, chopped
10 Greek or Italian black olives, pitted
1 roasted red bell pepper (page 223)
1 tablespoon finely chopped fresh oregano
1 tablespoon finely chopped fresh parsley
1 head broccoli florets, cooked
4 ounces feta or soft goat cheese, crumbled
Salt
Freshly ground black pepper
1 teaspoon grated lemon rind, no white attached

Heat the oil in a large skillet. Add the garlic, olives, pepper, oregano, and parsley, and cook until heated through. When ready to serve, add the cooked broccoli to the pan, crumble the cheese over the broccoli, and heat through. Season to taste with salt and pepper. Sprinkle with lemon rind and serve warm.

CHOPPED BROCCOLI AND TOMATOES

Serves 4 to 6

My houseguest Melissa cooked this for me. *Chopping broccoli is an excellent way of encouraging everyone in the family to eat it. Braising it in a little liquid and adding tomatoes puts it over the top as a vegetable fit for entertaining as well. The broccoli may be chopped ahead and kept covered in the refrigerator for nearly a week.*

1 head broccoli
2 tablespoons butter or oil, cook's preference
1/2 cup chicken stock or broth, or water
10 grape tomatoes, halved
Salt
Freshly ground pepper

Dry the cleaned broccoli, break into stalks, and slice off the tough ends and any leaves. Cut into pieces with a sharp knife and chop roughly but relatively uniformly. Heat the butter in a large skillet, add the broccoli, and stir-fry over medium heat for 2 to 3 minutes. Add the liquid, cover, and cook until broccoli is tender yet still crisp, about 2 to 3 minutes. Remove the lid, add the tomatoes, and boil down the liquid until nearly gone. Season to taste with salt and pepper. This may be done ahead of time. When ready to serve, toss over heat a few minutes more, until any accumulated liquid is gone, and serve hot.

Variation: Add crumbled bacon, strips of ham, cooked chicken tenders, chopped fresh ginger, or grated cheese.

Variation: The spears roast and grill very nicely; see page 180 for method.

BRUSSELS SPROUTS

Brussels sprouts are another vegetable that modern cooking methods have caused to soar in popularity. It's a good-for-you crucifer and one of the first green vegetables to appear at the end of winter. My rule of thumb is if you can smell it cooking, it's cooked too much. Remove immediately from the heat, no matter what method of cooking—poaching, sautéing, roasting, or grilling.

Purchase Brussels sprouts with dark green, tightly formed heads. Those with loose leaves or that have begun to turn yellow are not fresh. Store loosely wrapped in plastic for up to 3 or 4 days, refrigerated.

SAUTÉED BRUSSELS SPROUTS LEAVES

Serves 6

WHAT A MIRACLE THESE LITTLE LEAVES ARE *when sautéed quickly in butter or oil. If removing the stem in the following way is not quick enough (see methods in sidebar, page 184), slice the sprouts thinly, removing as much of the stem as possible, and follow the directions for sautéing.*

1 pound Brussels sprout leaves

2–4 tablespoons butter or oil, cook's preference

Salt

Freshly ground black pepper

Heat the butter or oil in a large frying pan. Add the Brussels sprouts leaves and sauté quickly until they wilt. Season to taste with salt and freshly ground pepper.

ROASTED BRUSSELS SPROUTS

Serves 2

THIS HAS BECOME A FAVORITE WAY OF COOKING BRUSSELS SPROUTS. *Relishing their flavor, I fix them frequently for "just us"—along with small roasted potatoes. Very large Brussels sprouts can be sliced and cooked the same way.*

1 cup Brussels sprouts, halved or quartered

2–3 tablespoons oil

Salt

Freshly ground black pepper

Preheat oven to 400 degrees.

Toss the halved or quartered sprouts in the oil and spread in one layer on a foil-lined rimmed baking sheet. Roast 15 to 20 minutes, checking after 12 minutes, until crisp-tender. Season to taste with salt and pepper.

Variations: Fingerling or other small roasted potatoes and Jerusalem artichokes marry well with the Brussels sprouts.

TRADITIONAL POACHED BRUSSELS SPROUTS

Serves 6

THESE ARE A GRATIFYING EARLY WINTER VEGETABLE *for us in the South and they are beautiful on the plant. The right way of cooking is to produce a tantalizing gem on the plate, lightly crunchy, without the bitter taste and mushy peel of an overcooked one.*

Cutting an X in the bottom of the stem allows it to cook quickly, in keeping with the shorter time the leaves require. Peel off any tough or yellow leaves. Cut very large Brussels sprouts into quarters before cooking.

1 pound Brussels sprouts
Salt
Freshly ground black pepper
2–4 tablespoons butter or oil

Cut off the tough tip of the stem. Cut an X about 1/4 inch deep in the remaining stem. Bring a deep pan of generously salted water to the boil. Add the Brussels sprouts, return to the boil, reduce heat, and cook until a knife will pierce the sprouts, about 5 minutes. Take care that they are still firm. Run under cold water to refresh; drain. Season to taste with salt and pepper. They may be kept at room temperature several hours or refrigerated, covered, for up to 2 days before heating and serving. When ready to serve, heat butter in a large skillet, and add Brussels sprouts until heated through.

Variations:

- Brussels sprouts are particularly good with seeds, such as benne (sesame), or nuts, such as pine, pecans, and walnuts.
- The addition of raisins, dried cherries, and other sweet dried fruits is an extraordinary way to enhance Brussels sprouts. Add fruit to the sprouts when reheating.
- Substitute chicken or vegetable stock or broth for the water.

Variation: Brussels Sprouts, Apples, and Pecans
Use 2 to 3 cups boiling apple cider instead of water. Add a tart apple and cook 1 minute, covered. Add the sprouts and cook up to 3 minutes more. Drain, reserving broth for another purpose if desired. If reheating, toss sprouts and apples in 2 tablespoons butter or olive oil until warmed through. Top with 1/3 cup chopped pecans.

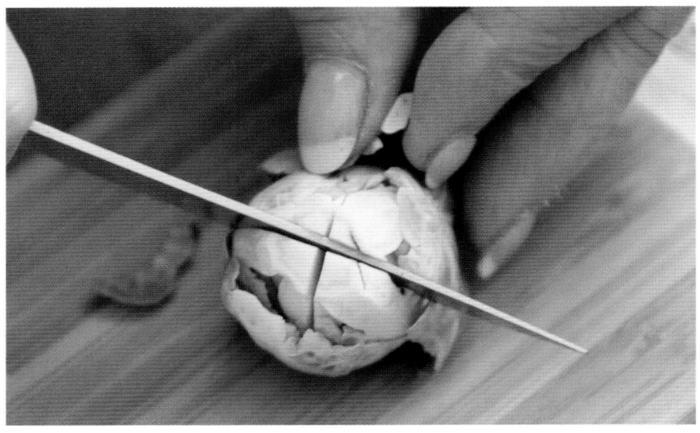

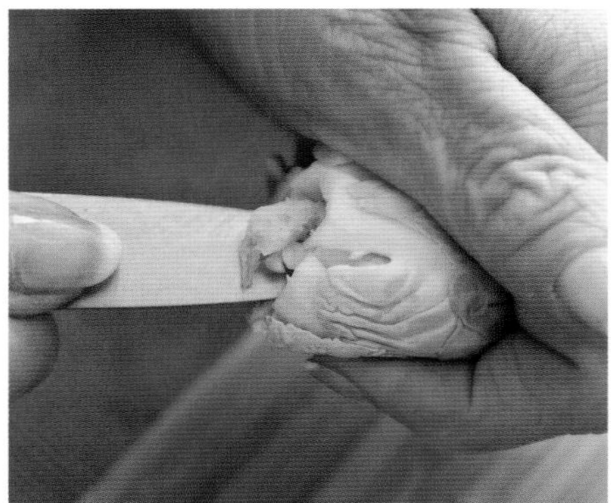

REMOVING BRUSSELS SPROUTS STEMS

Peel off the leaves from the outside and discard the stems. Or remove the stem with a knife and slice the sprouts. Or use a small sharp knife to cut a circle around the stem and remove it by digging inside the sprout. With two fingers, open the sprout and separate the leaves.

CABBAGE

Winter varieties of cabbage produce the firm, heavy heads most of us recognize. The summer varieties are sweeter and have more open leaves, producing a lighter head. Overcooking is the usual mistake, so keep the cooking times short.

Select cabbages with either firm heads or more open leaves, depending on the season as above. Cabbage stores for weeks refrigerated. Remove any loose or wilted leaves before preparing.

SIMPLE CABBAGE

Serves 6 to 8

THE PHRASE "CABBAGE-AND-CORNBREAD" *is spoken as one word, as that is the way cabbage is most often served—with crumbled cornbread in a bowl or sandwiched in cornbread. Still, it is very tasty served with meats and other vegetables. I so enjoy eating and serving it with the "pot likker." I still serve it in a bowl rather than on a plate, so everyone can have some of the broth.*

1 head cabbage, about 6 inches in diameter
2 cups water
1/2 cup butter
Salt
Freshly ground black pepper

Cut the cabbage into 6 to 8 wedges and remove the core. Bring water to the boil and add the cabbage and butter. Cover tightly with a lid, reduce heat, and simmer for 15 to 20 minutes, until the cabbage is tender but has a little "give." There should be 1 cup or so of water left in the pot. Season to taste with salt and pepper. Serve the cabbage with the liquid.

Variations:

- Slice cabbage 1/3 inch thick. Sauté 1 onion in a few tablespoons of oil and add to the uncooked cabbage. Bring enough water to cover the cabbage to the boil. Add the cabbage and onions, cover, reduce heat, and simmer for 15 to 20 minutes. Transfer the cabbage with a slotted spoon to a plate or bowl. Boil the "pot likker" sufficient to reduce the liquid down to about 1/2 cup. Garnish with chopped thyme or oregano.
- Top with Tomato Conserve (page 644).

GRILLED STEAMED CABBAGE

Serves 4

RATHER THAN LET A HOT GRILL COOL DOWN EMPTY, *add lightly steamed cabbage, which cooks quickly and can be reheated.*

1 head cabbage
2–3 tablespoons oil, cook's preference
Salt
Freshly ground black pepper
Hot pepper vinegar, optional

Remove any wilted outer leaves from the cabbage and cut into quarters. Insert a steamer rack in a pan with 1/2 inch of water in the bottom. Add the cabbage wedges to the steamer. Bring the water to the boil, cover, and cook until cabbage just begins to soften, about 5 to 8 minutes. To serve steamed, cook a few minutes longer.

To grill, cool the cabbage quarters sufficient to be able to handle them. Pat dry. Brush on all sides with oil and move to a hot grill. Cook about 10 minutes per side, checking to see that they do not burn. Season to taste with salt and pepper. Sprinkle with optional vinegar just before serving.

Variation: Serve with White Butter Sauce (page 656).

REMOVING CABBAGE CORE

Forceful people can remove the core by whacking the stem end of the whole head sturdily on the edge of a counter. The more timid of us remove the core with a knife after cutting the cabbage into wedges.

CREAMED SAUTÉED CABBAGE

Serves 2

The flavor that comes from quickly sautéing cabbage *and braising it in butter and cream is incredibly full and rich. There is a small chance an iron skillet will flavor the cream, so use a non-iron variety.*

3 tablespoons butter
1/2 medium green cabbage, cored and cut into 1/4-inch strips
1/2 cup heavy cream
Salt
Freshly ground black pepper
1 teaspoon chopped fresh tarragon, optional

Heat the butter in a large, heavy, non-iron frying pan over medium heat. Add the cabbage and sauté for 5 minutes, tossing to coat the cabbage with the butter. Pour in the cream. Bring quickly to the boil, cover the pan, and reduce the heat. Cook the cabbage over low heat for 15 minutes, or until tender but not mushy. Season to taste with salt and pepper. Sprinkle with the optional tarragon before serving.

FREEZING CABBAGE

Cabbage seems so small when still a head. Cut or shredded, it becomes abundant and generous, the parts much greater than the whole. If too abundant to use up in a short time, slice and blanch all of it and freeze a portion for a later time.

SOPHISTICATED RED CABBAGE

Serves 8

This sweet-and-sour cabbage *brings a lot of style to a game dinner featuring goose or duck on a wintry night. Use butter when accompanying turkey or quail, but use the tasty fat of a duck or goose when available.*

1/4 cup butter, duck or goose fat, or bacon drippings
2 medium onions, sliced
1 (3 1/2-pound) red cabbage, thickly sliced
2 chicken or beef bouillon cubes, crumbled
1/2 cup red wine vinegar
1 cup red wine
2 Granny Smith or Golden Delicious apples, cored and chopped or grated
2/3 cup red currant jelly
Salt
Freshly ground black pepper
2 heaping teaspoons finely chopped fresh thyme, optional
2 tablespoons chopped cooked bacon, optional

Heat the butter in a large Dutch oven. Add the onions and sauté over medium heat until soft, about 5 minutes. Add the cabbage, bouillon cubes, wine vinegar, wine, and apples, and stir with a non-wooden spoon (to avoid cabbage stains). Bring to the boil, cover, reduce heat to a simmer, and cook about 30 minutes, checking occasionally to be sure the bouillon cubes have dissolved. Stir in the jelly and cook, covered, until the cabbage is tender but not soggy. Season to taste with salt and pepper. Top with the optional thyme or bacon before serving.

CARROTS

Once upon a time, "carrot-colored" described an orange root vegetable. Now, carrots are coming out of the ground crimson, beige, bronze, and tinged with green. They can be reed-thin or finger-sized and stubby. They only need a little scraping rather than a vigorous peeling. They are sweet and delicious eaten raw or cooked. When purchasing "baby carrots," check the label. A true Baby Carrot, bred to be small, will be labeled as such. Most packaged "baby carrots" will state that they are "baby-cut carrots," or larger carrots cut down to a uniform small size.

Store carrots loosely wrapped in plastic up to two weeks in the refrigerator.

The amount of sugar needed when cooking carrots depends on the carrots' sweetness. For glazed carrots, add several teaspoons of sugar to the pot of water when cooking, and boil down the liquid until the carrots are glazed.

The time needed to cook carrots varies according to their age and thickness. Baby carrots, by their very tenderness, cook more quickly. Older carrots are tougher, and their center core requires longer cooking. Older root vegetables should go into cold water, baby carrots into boiling water.

GLAZED BABY CARROTS

Serves 4 to 6

THIS FAMILY-FRIENDLY VEGETABLE *has dozens of variations.*

1 pound baby carrots

2–4 tablespoons butter or oil, cook's preference, divided
Granulated sugar or honey

Salt
Freshly ground black pepper

Scrape the carrots and remove roots. Add to a frying pan of boiling salted water only to cover. Add 1 tablespoon butter or oil and sugar to taste. Cook 2 to 3 minutes, until crisp-tender. Uncover and boil the liquid until it becomes a glaze. Add remaining butter or oil as desired. Season to taste with salt and pepper.

Variations:
- Add chopped herbs such as thyme or parsley.
- Add a teaspoon of finely chopped or grated ginger.

SAUTÉED GRATED CARROTS

Serves 4

CARROTS AND ROOT VEGETABLES *are the answer to winter vegetable doldrums. This manner of cooking them promises of spring and is particularly suited to full-sized carrots. The optional ginger addition is a favorite of mine.*

6 carrots
1 tablespoon butter
1–2 tablespoons chopped ginger, optional
Salt
Freshly ground black pepper

Remove any greens and the stem end of the top, and peel the carrots. Put through the grating blade of a food processor or grate by hand. Melt the butter in a large skillet over medium-high heat. Add the optional ginger and grated carrots, and cook, stirring constantly, until the carrots are crisp-tender and have lost their raw taste, about 3 to 5 minutes. Season to taste with salt and pepper. Can be made ahead and reheated.

Variation: Sautéed Herbed Carrots
Use fresh herbs such as marjoram or oregano in place of the ginger.

Variation: Sautéed Honey-and-Orange Carrots
Add the grated rind of 1 orange, no white attached, 1/3 cup honey, and 1/3 cup red wine vinegar to the cooked gingered carrots. Toss over medium heat until heated through.

Variation: Add an equal amount of grated zucchini halfway through.

OUCHLESS GRATED CARROTS

Along with food processors and graters, there are many fancy graters available to grate vegetables; so scout yard sales and cookware stores. If a box grater is the only thing available, use a soft plastic bag over the grating hand to preserve knuckles.

ROASTED CARROTS

Serves 2 to 3

WITH THEIR INHERENT SWEETNESS, *these caramelized carrots cause the smallest child to swoon with delight. If you are fortunate enough to have fresh carrots, serve with their greens on. Many times carrots are used to form a rack for a roast, buttered or oiled and situated before the roast is added on top. In this case they are frequently discolored if overcooked and might be tasteless, with their essence left in the pan drippings. I eat them anyway!*

1 pound carrots, cut in pieces as desired
2–3 tablespoons butter or oil, cook's preference
Salt
Freshly grated black pepper

Preheat oven to 400 degrees.

Toss the carrots in melted butter or oil. Spread out in one layer on a rimmed baking sheet and roast 30 to 45 minutes, depending on the size, until crisp-tender and tinged with brown but not soggy. Let char slightly to caramelize and enhance the flavor.

Variations:

- Leave greens, wrapped in foil, on the carrots.
- Grilling enhances the sweetness of carrots so much that they can be eaten like candy. Brush lightly with oil before adding to a hot grill. Cook just until lightly charred and crisp-tender.

RIBBONED CARROTS AND ZUCCHINI

Serves 2 to 3

Ribboned vegetables are paper-thin strips *of firm vegetables such as beets, carrots, zucchini, turnips, and potatoes. One of their many virtues is that ribbons cook faster than almost any other shape of cut vegetables, except finely chopped. They may be cooked ahead and even used for a salad. This technique is particularly useful when there are stray vegetables in the bin. Vegetables may be ribboned in advance and kept for several days refrigerated, until ready to cook.*

1 tablespoon butter or oil, cook's preference
1 or 2 carrots
1 or 2 zucchini
1 tablespoon chopped fresh thyme, rosemary, or other favorite herb, optional
Salt
Freshly ground black pepper

Melt the butter in a frying pan. Ribbon the vegetables with a potato peeler. Add to the hot pan. Cover with a lid and cook 1 to 3 minutes. Remove lid, season to taste with herbs, salt, and pepper. Serve immediately, or cool and reheat later.

Variation: Add sliced mushrooms, ribboned turnips, potatoes, fennel, beets, and/or rutabagas if desired.

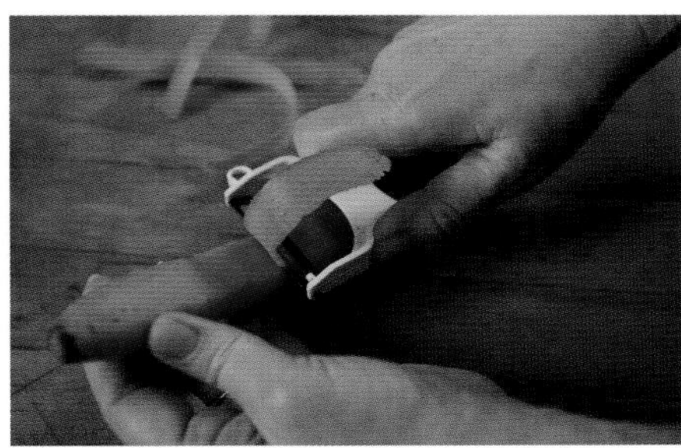

RIBBONING

Ribboned (also called shaved) vegetables are delicious raw, tossed with Parmesan or goat cheese, olive oil, and a touch of sherry vinegar or lemon juice. Peel the vegetable vertically with a good vegetable peeler or mandoline, resulting in long, slender strips of vegetables that frequently curl when sliced so thinly. I include the seeds of zucchini and summer squash because I don't want to lose the nutrients.

CARROTS AND CELERY WITH GINGER

Serves 2 to 4

These root vegetables *go a long way toward keeping vegetables on the table whether winter or summer.*

3 tablespoons butter
4 large carrots, sliced on the diagonal
4 celery ribs, sliced on the diagonal
2–2 1/2 teaspoons chopped fresh ginger
1/4 cup granulated sugar
1/4 cup fresh mint or parsley leaves

Melt the butter in a heavy pan. Add the carrots, celery, and ginger. Cover and cook over low heat until crisp-tender. Add the sugar to the pan and stir slowly and gently until the carrots and celery are well glazed and slightly browned. Top with herbs. If using mint and the leaves are small, leave whole. Otherwise, coarsely chop larger leaves.

CAULIFLOWER

Cauliflower is a cold-weather vegetable, although it is available year-round in our markets. The varieties found in the summer produce smaller heads but are often tastier. Look for firm, dense heads. Any slight discoloration can be cut off. Prevent raw cauliflower from turning brown by storing it in the refrigerator, stem side up, in an open plastic bag; poke a few holes in the bag so air can circulate. Or turn stem side down in a container of water.

CAULIFLOWER WITH HERBED VINAIGRETTE

Serves 4 to 6

CAULIFLOWER STUDDED WITH RED PEPPERS, *herbs, and onions makes a festive salad with a lot of interest and flavor and is a delectable buffet item. Use jarred peppers and pre-chopped garlic to speed the dish along. The cauliflower can be cooked up to 2 days in advance, in which case this is a snap to put together. Never again think of cauliflower as being bland!*

1 medium head cauliflower (about 2 pounds)
1 red bell pepper, roasted, peeled, seeded, and cut into strips
1 red onion, thinly sliced
3 green onions, sliced
2 teaspoons Dijon mustard
2 garlic cloves, chopped
1/4 cup white wine vinegar
1/2 cup olive oil
Salt
Freshly ground black pepper
1 teaspoon granulated sugar
2 tablespoons finely chopped fresh parsley
1 tablespoon finely chopped fresh dill
1/2 teaspoon celery seed

Break the cauliflower into florets and rinse; discard the remaining core. Cover the cauliflower with salted water and bring to the boil. Cook until crisp-tender, 4 to 5 minutes. Drain and rinse under cold water.

Toss together the cauliflower, bell pepper, red onion, and green onions. Mix together the mustard, garlic, and wine vinegar in a small bowl. Slowly add the olive oil, whisking to make an emulsion. Season to taste with salt, pepper, and sugar. Mix together the parsley, dill, and celery seed. Stir into the vinaigrette and pour over the vegetables. Serve chilled or at room temperature.

CAULIFLOWER STEAKS

Sliced thickly, drizzled with oil, and roasted or sautéed, cauliflower steaks are a great alternative for a vegetarian steak.

CAULIFLOWER AND CHEESE SAUCE

Serves 4 to 6

Crisp bits of buttered crumbs *top the luscious cheese sauce cloaking the cauliflower. Fit for a king, this cheers up any dreary cold day. If possible, flavor the milk (page 657).*

1 head cauliflower (about 2 pounds)
1 recipe Cheese Sauce (below)

Preheat oven to 350 degrees.

To cook the cauliflower, cut off the thick or discolored parts of the stem, removing all but the smallest green leaves. Make an X with a sharp knife in the remaining core, or remove core completely. (If the cauliflower is large, remove florets from the stem, discard stem, and cook florets in boiling water.) Move the whole cauliflower, stem side down, to a steamer basket over 1 cup of water. Cover and steam until tender, about 15 minutes. If microwaving, move to a microwave container, sprinkle with 2 tablespoons water, cover, and microwave until done, about 5 minutes. Drain.

Move the well-drained cauliflower to a heatproof serving bowl with the florets up. Sauté the breadcrumbs in the remaining butter until brown. Top the cauliflower with the Cheese Sauce and the remaining cheese.

The recipe may be made ahead to this point. When ready to serve, move the dish to the hot oven until the cauliflower is heated through, the cheese is melted, and the sauce is light brown and bubbling. Top with browned breadcrumbs.

Variation: Whole Cauliflower with Curry Sauce
Prepare cauliflower as above. Stir in 2 teaspoons curry powder with the flour and whisk 2 minutes, until smooth.

Cheese Sauce

Makes about 2 cups

1/4 cup butter, divided
2 tablespoons all-purpose flour
1 1/2 cups milk
1 teaspoon Dijon mustard
3/4 cup grated Cheddar cheese, divided
Salt
Freshly ground black pepper
1/3 cup breadcrumbs

To make the sauce, melt 2 tablespoons butter in a medium saucepan and stir in the flour. Add the milk and stir the mixture until it comes to the boil. Remove from the heat and add the mustard and 1/2 cup of the cheese. Stir until smooth and season to taste with salt and pepper.

CELERY

Frequently only used as an accent in salads, soups, and stews, celery is overlooked as a vegetable. It can step into service nicely, particularly when the storage bin is bare.

CELERY AND RED PEPPER BUNDLES

Serves 4

THERE ARE MANY TIMES *I have blessed celery for sitting so patiently in the bottom of the refrigerator. A red pepper is only a slight extravagance to make the mundane sublime.*

1 whole red bell pepper, seeded
1 bunch celery
1/4 cup butter or oil, cook's preference
Salt
Freshly ground black pepper

Slice the pepper into 1/4-inch rings and add to a small pan of boiling water. Cook for 2 to 3 minutes to blanch and slightly soften the flavor. Drain and set aside in a separate bowl.

Remove any tough outer ribs and string the celery as necessary. Cut each rib of celery into 3- to 3 1/2-inch lengthwise strips like thick matchsticks.

Melt the butter in a small pan. Add the celery, cover, and cook over low heat about 5 minutes, until crisp-tender. Season with salt and pepper. Divide into 4 bundles of 4 or 5 pieces of celery and slip into the rings of blanched pepper. When ready to eat, reheat the bundles about 3 to 5 minutes in a microwave or in a covered frying pan with a little butter added to it.

SLICED CELERY WITH PECANS

Serves 4

CELERY HAS A BURST OF FRESHNESS *and crispness that is unparalleled. Its flavor is malleable and accommodating, making for quixotic and surprising dishes.*

4 celery ribs
1 tablespoon soy sauce
1 tablespoon white wine vinegar
1/8 teaspoon dark sesame oil, optional
Granulated sugar
1/4 cup coarsely chopped pecans

Remove the leaves and tough ends of the celery, and string as necessary. Slice on the diagonal. Mix together the soy sauce, vinegar, sesame oil, and sugar to taste. Toss with the celery in a large bowl. Serve at room temperature, or chilled. Top with the pecans before serving.

Variation: Toss sliced celery with chopped olives. Drizzle with olive oil if desired. Serve at room temperature or chilled.

CORN

America's rich history with corn began with Native Americans, who cooked corn by roasting it in ashes until the kernels were brown and then pounded the kernels into flour or processed the kernels with water mixed with ashes (lye water) to remove the hulls for whole hominy, which was later ground. The parched corn kept indefinitely and was mixed with hot or cold water and used as needed for cooking. Today, corn is ubiquitous—from fresh corn on the cob, to high-fructose corn syrup in processed foods, to feed for farm animals.

Farm-fresh corn is practically indescribable in its taste, and it's well worth running straight home to place it in boiling water. Purchase ears with their husks still on. Feel through the husk to confirm the kernels are plump. Store ears loosely wrapped in plastic in the refrigerator. Newer varieties of corn are bred to stay sweeter once picked, so refrigerated corn lasts several days.

Fresh corn can be microwaved, as below, shucked, and frozen flat on a rimmed baking sheet. When frozen, move to a plastic ziplock bag and use as you would commercial frozen corn. The corn may also be cut from the cob and frozen in the same fashion.

Corn on the cob—Freshly cooked corn on the cob is a treat. Pulling it off the cob gives a little crunch to the teeth, a flush of sweetness on the tongue, and a feeling of satisfaction when finished. In some countries it is street food. There are three spectacular ways to cook corn on the cob:

1. Boiling Corn on the Cob
Traditionally, corn on the cob is pre-shucked (removed from its husk and silk discarded), cooked in boiling water to cover until done (approximately 5 minutes once the water returns to the boil), drained, and served with butter, salt, and pepper.

2. Microwaved Corn on the Cob
This method is clearly the easiest and, to me, the corniest-tasting method of cooking corn. Microwave up to four ears of corn, with husk and silks intact, on a glass pie plate or other shallow plate that will hold the corn easily. Cooking time is dependent on the quantity in the microwave. A little judicious testing is needed. Use 3 minutes per ear of corn for up to four ears as the guide. Remove from the microwave and let sit a few minutes in the husks until cool enough to handle. Pull the husks back but do not remove from the cob. Use a sturdy paper towel to pull the silks off the cob. Discard the silks. Leave the husks on as a "handle," or discard if preferred. Serve with butter, salt, and pepper.

3. Baked Corn on the Cob in the Husk
Preheat oven to 400 degrees. Soak the corn in its silk and husks in a shallow pan of water for 15 minutes. Spread the corn one layer deep on a rimmed baking sheet. Cook in the oven 45 minutes. Remove husks and silks carefully with a mitt or several layers of paper towel as above.

4. Grilled Corn
Remove most of the husk from the cobs, leaving the last layer (where the kernels are visible thru the husk). Cut off any silks from the end of the cob. Grill over medium heat for a total of 8 to 10 minutes, turning every 1 to 2 minutes.

EASY CORN AND SQUASH PUDDING

Serves 6 to 8

Both corn and squash puddings *are comfort foods craved at family and holiday meals. The combination of the two is suited to cure whatever ails both the able-bodied and the sick. A spoonful of corn pudding is practically medicinal in its power to restore.*

5 ears corn, shucked
3 slices bacon, cooked crisp and crumbled, drippings reserved
1 onion, chopped
3 garlic cloves, chopped
1 pound squash, such as summer yellow squash or zucchini, cut into 1/8-inch-thick rounds
2 egg yolks
2 large whole eggs
1/2 cup milk
1/2 cup heavy cream
Salt
Freshly ground black pepper
1/8 teaspoon freshly ground nutmeg
1–2 teaspoons finely chopped fresh thyme
1 cup grated Gruyère cheese

Preheat oven to 375 degrees.

Remove corn kernels from the cobs with a sharp knife as described below. Heat 2 tablespoons reserved drippings in a heavy skillet. Add the onion to the drippings and sauté, stirring as needed, until soft, 3 to 4 minutes. Add the garlic and sauté 1 minute. Add the squash slices, cover, and cook until soft and wilted, about 10 minutes.

Whisk the yolks, the whole eggs, milk, cream, salt, pepper, nutmeg, and thyme together in a large bowl until smooth. Add the cheese and the corn-and-squash mixture. Stir until well blended. Pour into a 2 1/2-quart buttered casserole. Set the casserole in a shallow pan and pour 1/2 inch of boiling water into the pan (see Bain-Marie, page 281). Bake the casserole in the water bath for 45 to 50 minutes, or until the custard is set in the center.

REMOVING CORN FROM COBS

To scrape and "milk" the corn, hold a shucked ear of corn on its end in a shallow bowl or pie dish. Using a sawing motion, slice the tips of the corn kernels from the cob with a sharp knife, turning as needed. Slice down a second time to remove all the corn and its milk.

To remove the remaining corn and "milk" next to the cob, use the blunt side of a knife to press and scrape down against the cob, turning as needed. Repeat with each ear of corn.

CREAMED OR FRIED CORN

Serves 4 to 6

CALLED EITHER "FRIED" *(since it's stewed in an iron skillet) or "creamed" (the starch from the corn milk makes a rich, thick, creamy dish), this is the quintessential home method of serving corn, as the liquid extracted is very flavorful, if scanty. Any leftovers can be reheated in the microwave or on top of the stove, or added to soup, grits, or another dish. The newer, tender sweet corn varieties combined with bacon fat and butter are fantastic though decadent.*

4–5 ears corn, shucked
2 slices thick-cut country bacon, cut into thin strips
1/2 cup water
4 tablespoons butter
Salt
Freshly ground black pepper

Remove corn kernels from the cobs with a sharp knife as described on page 196. Scrape milk from the cob as shown below.

Heat a 9- or 10-inch iron skillet or heavy frying pan and add the bacon. Cook carefully over medium heat, stirring as necessary, until crisp. Remove with a slotted spoon to a plate lined with paper towel, leaving the drippings in the pan. Add the corn with its milk to the pan of bacon drippings along with the water. Bring to the boil, stirring. Add the butter and salt, and turn down to low heat. Cook, stirring frequently, about 20 to 30 minutes. Add more water if necessary. Perfect fried corn should be thick and sticky. Season to taste with salt and pepper. Garnish with crumbled bacon.

Variation: Meri's Creamy Corn
My intern Meri made this variation because it reminded her of the corn her Southern mom, Karen, cooked for her while she was growing up. Karen started everything with bacon and onions. Her variation includes heavy cream—another definition of creamy!

Add 1 diced white onion to the bacon drippings and sauté before adding the corn. Once the corn has cooked down, add 1/2 cup heavy cream to make a creamy sauce.

Variations:

- Omit the bacon and its fat and use butter.
- Add one chopped tomato and season with 1 tablespoon chopped fresh herbs.
- Add grilled shrimp or scallops.

MILKING THE COB

To remove the remaining corn and "milk" next to the cob, use the blunt side of a knife to press and scrape down against the cob, turning as needed. Repeat with each ear of corn.

NEW-STYLE FRIED CORN

Serves 4 to 6

THE NEW VARIETIES OF CORN *allow for new methods of cooking them. This method is crunchier than fried corn and a good way to use every bit of the corn. It cooks faster and seems lighter.*

4–6 ears corn, shucked
4–6 tablespoons butter, divided
1–2 tablespoons chopped fresh thyme or basil
Salt
Freshly ground black pepper

Slice the tips off the corn kernels and scrape the corn as described for Creamed or Fried Corn (page 197), saving all the milk. Melt 3 tablespoons butter in a frying pan. Add the corn and milk, and sauté 3 to 4 minutes, stirring constantly, adding more butter as needed. Season to taste with the herbs, salt, and pepper.

MAQUE CHOUX

Serves 4 to 6

CAJUN AND CREOLE COOKS USE EVERYTHING *in their larder to great advantage. Pronounced "mock shoe," this is an exciting and colorful addition to the table and uses everything in season.*

6 ears corn, shucked
4 tablespoons butter
1 medium onion, chopped
2 garlic cloves, chopped
1 red or green bell pepper, chopped (or half of each)
1 tomato, seeded and chopped
Salt
Freshly ground black pepper

Slice the tips of the corn kernels from the cob with a sharp knife as described on page 196.

Melt butter in a large frying pan or cast-iron skillet. Add onion, garlic, and bell pepper; sauté over medium heat, stirring as necessary, until soft. Add corn and tomato, and continue cooking until heated through and corn is crisp-tender, about 3 to 5 minutes. Season to taste with salt and pepper.

Variation: Add cooked shrimp or crab to the finished dish.

EGGPLANT

Our friend and culinary scholar David Shields tells us certain vegetables that crossed the Atlantic with enslaved Africans had their African genesis recognized by prefixing the common English name of the generic item with "Guinea," the West Africa territory in which the Mandingo and Fula peoples lived: Guinea corn (*Sorghum vulgaris*), Guineafowl (*Numida meleagris*), Guinea pea (*Abrus precatorius*), and Guinea squash—the eggplant (*Solatium melongena*).

While introduced into England as a horticultural novelty at the end of the sixteenth century, the eggplant did not gain a foothold in European cuisine until the middle of the nineteenth century. In the American colonies, however, it became a fixture in those regions that used African slave labor: the West Indies, the mainland South, Central America, and Brazil. In the United States, the regions were divided about the merits of the vegetable. A northern commentator observed in an 1839 issue of *The Farmer & Gardener, and Live-Stock Breeder and Manager* magazine:

> *"This is considered a delicious vegetable; but little attention has, however, been paid to its cultivation, and it is seldom seen in our markets; but in the southern States great quantities are cultivated, and sold in their markets."*

Select eggplant that has smooth, firm, glossy skin in colors from inky black to purple, in shapes from globes to teardrops, and feels heavy for its size. Eggplant that feels light for its size is often spongy. Store eggplant wrapped in a paper towel and covered loosely with plastic. Use within 2 days to prevent bitterness from setting in.

Whether using a sharp kitchen peeler or knife, peeling the dark skin off of an eggplant is a nuisance. I peel only when I feel it is absolutely necessary, rarely for a family dish.

EGGPLANT AND RED PEPPER STEW (SOUTHERN RATATOUILLE)

Serves 10 to 12

No two stews are the same, *so don't feel constrained to duplicate this lush Southern version. With luck, all the vegetables are available at one time. Take the amount of vegetables on hand and adjust accordingly. For example, omit the tomatoes to make a zucchini, eggplant, and pepper casserole. Cut the recipe in half or double it. Just don't try to make it exact. "Go with the flow," as they say. And peeling of vegetables removes many good vitamins, so leave them unpeeled when possible.*

4 large eggplants or 6 small ones
Salt
3 red, yellow, or green bell peppers
6 medium zucchini
6 medium onions
8 tablespoons oil, cook's preference, divided
6 garlic cloves, chopped
2 cans Italian plum tomatoes with juice (totaling 28 ounces) or 2 pounds fresh tomatoes, chopped
1 cup chopped fresh herbs: preferably thyme, parsley, and basil
Freshly ground black pepper

Preheat oven to 350 degrees.

Slice the eggplant lengthwise into 1/4-inch-thick slices. Lightly score the flesh of the slices in a crosshatch pattern (like tic-tac-toe). Move the slices to a colander over a bowl or sink. Degorge the eggplant for 30 minutes.

Meanwhile, seed the peppers, and then slice the zucchini, onions, and peppers. Discard the extracted liquid from the eggplant. Rinse, drain, and dry the eggplant well with paper towels. Brush the eggplant and zucchini slices with oil and move to an oiled rimmed baking sheet. Cook in the oven until lightly browned, about 20 minutes, turning halfway through.

Heat 2 tablespoons of the oil in a heavy-bottomed pan. Add the onions, peppers, and garlic, and cook until soft, adding oil as needed, about 30 minutes. Add the cooked eggplant, zucchini, tomatoes and their juices, and half of the herbs. Season well to taste with pepper. Serve hot or cold. Freezes well and easily reheats in the microwave.

Variation: Continue to cook the ratatouille for another hour, until thick and creamy. It is savory and makes a wonderful bed for grilled pork or lamb chops or chicken breasts.

DEGORGING

Dégorger is a French cooking term meaning to use salt to draw water out of a food, such as eggplant or a cucumber. This is commonly done by sprinkling the sliced vegetable with salt and letting it sit in a colander for a period of time. After that, the vegetable is dried with a paper towel or rinsed in cold water and then dried. In this book, we use the English term *degorge*, for easy understanding.

NO-FAIL EGGPLANT LASAGNA

Serves 6

EGGPLANT LASAGNA—WHERE THE EGGPLANT SUBSTITUTES FOR PASTA—*is extraordinarily welcome towards the end of July, when Southern garden vines tumble about together, their vegetables a bit oversized but still abundant, and the cook is looking for all-in-one dishes to beat the heat. Ideally, this recipe is doubled so that one portion is frozen for a fall evening. It likes being made ahead a few days, too, refrigerated until needed so the flavors meld. Eggplant in a dish like this has become regarded as a satisfying substitute for meat.*

4–6 tablespoons oil, cook's preference
3 teaspoons finely chopped fresh basil, oregano, marjoram, and/or thyme
Salt
Freshly ground black pepper
1 large eggplant, sliced 1/2 inch thick
1 large zucchini, sliced 1/2 inch thick
1 cup freshly grated Parmesan cheese
1 cup ricotta cheese, drained
2 cups Marinara Sauce (page 661)
2 tablespoons fennel seed, crushed or ground
8 ounces grated mozzarella cheese

Stir the oil with the herbs, salt, and pepper. Brush it onto both sides of the eggplant and zucchini. Lay the eggplant and zucchini in single layers on separate rimmed baking sheets, or move to a grill, using a grill basket if needed. Broil or grill 2 inches from the heat for 4 or 5 minutes, until light brown. Turn, brush the other side with the herbed oil, and broil until lightly brown, and soft. Remove from broiler or grill.

Preheat oven to 350 degrees. Layer half of the eggplant slices in a wide, shallow 2- or 3-quart baking dish. Top with half of the zucchini. Layer in half of the Parmesan and ricotta, spaghetti sauce, and fennel seed. Repeat the layers with the remaining ingredients, finishing with the mozzarella. Cover and bake 20 to 25 minutes, or until hot and bubbly.

This dish freezes well. To reheat, defrost, covered, in the refrigerator and bake in a 350-degree oven for about 30 to 40 minutes, until heated through.

Variation: Blanch, sauté, and drain turnip greens, preferably small but cutting as necessary, and substitute for the zucchini.

STUFFED EGG-PLANTS A LA CREOLE

Parboil the egg-plants; cut them in halves; scoop out the inside, being careful not to break the outside skin, which you refill later with the following stuffing: Mix up the inside of the egg-plant with a slice of boiled ham chopped very fine, breadcrumbs, butter, salt, and pepper—shrimps if you have them, make a delicious addition; bind this stuffing with the yolk of an egg and fill your egg-plant skins; sprinkle with powdered breadcrumbs, put a small lump of butter on each piece, and bake.

—Mrs. Washington, *The Unrivalled Cook-Book and Housekeeper's Guide*, 1886

FENNEL

Cooked fennel is very different from raw fennel. Raw, it is crisp and crunchy with an anise or licorice flavor. Cooked, its flavor mellows. Fennel and "California Anise" are the same bulb sold under different names.

Purchase fennel with a tight, compact bulb. Often the stalks and fronds are attached, which are edible as well. Store in the refrigerator loosely wrapped in plastic and use within 3 or 4 days, before the bulb begins to dry out.

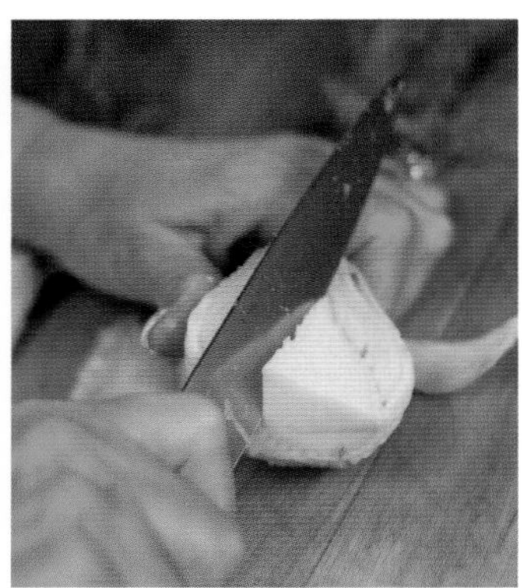

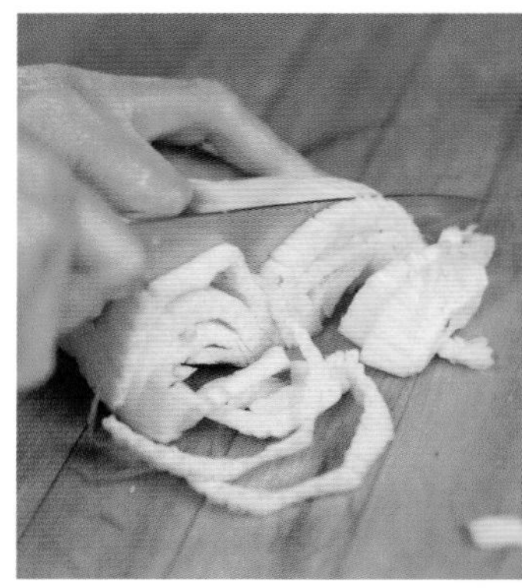

Preparing Fennel

Remove excess fronds, stalks, and tough exterior as necessary. Scrape the outer layer if necessary to remove any bad spots or stringy fibers. Cut the bulb in half lengthwise. Cut out the core, reserving it as a snack for the cook if desired. Put the flat side down on a board and slice as any other vegetable. Reserve the tops and fronds for the recipe if desired.

Sliced fennel—Move the fennel cut side down to a chopping board and slice as you would an onion; see page 217 for technique.

Shaved fennel—move the fennel to a chopping board. Use a sharp knife to shave the bulb vertically in 1/8-inch slices or thinner.

CRISP-TENDER FENNEL AND ZUCCHINI

Serves 4 to 6

TEXTURE IS TANTAMOUNT TO PLEASURE; *the contrasting colors of the pale green/white bulb of fennel and the deep green zucchini skin add even more. The crisp-tender vegetables are cooling and satisfying, whether served hot or cold.*

1 tablespoon oil
2 fennel bulbs, thinly sliced, fronds reserved
3–4 medium zucchini, sliced
1 tablespoon red wine or sherry vinegar
1 tablespoon chopped fresh oregano or marjoram, optional
Salt
Freshly ground black pepper
1/4 cup toasted chopped pecans

Heat the oil in a large skillet. Add the fennel and cook 3 to 4 minutes. Add zucchini and cook, stirring constantly, until the vegetables are crisp-tender, another 5 to 6 minutes. Stir in the vinegar and herbs, and season to taste with salt and pepper. This can be made ahead and reheated when ready to serve. Add the pecans and toss over medium heat for 2 minutes to serve hot or cold. Strip the fennel frond from the stalks and chop. Sprinkle over the finished dish.

FENNEL GRATIN WITH PARMESAN CHEESE

Serves 4

BLANCHED FENNEL QUARTERS *covered with a cheese sauce and broiled until lightly browned are as enticing as they are exciting. They accompany lamb, turkey, and other roasts with elegance.*

1–2 fennel bulbs
5 tablespoons butter
3 tablespoons all-purpose flour
2 cups milk, preferably Flavored Milk (page 657)
1/2 cup freshly grated Parmesan cheese
Pinch of ground hot red pepper
Salt
Freshly ground black pepper

Remove the fennel frond and stalk and set aside. Cut off any tough exterior and strings and remove the core. To blanch, quarter the fennel and add to a pan of enough boiling salted water to cover the vegetable. Return to the boil and cook until nearly tender, about 8 to 10 minutes. Drain very well.

Meanwhile, chop enough of the frond to make 1 to 2 tablespoons. Melt the butter in a saucepan, add the flour, and stir briefly to make a roux. Add the milk and bring to the boil, stirring. Add the cheese, hot red pepper, and chopped fronds. Season to taste with salt and black pepper. The sauce and the fennel may be cooked ahead to this point.

Lay the blanched fennel in a buttered heatproof baking dish. Use a large metal spoon to spoon just enough of the sauce over the fennel to cover, reserving extra sauce for another use. If making ahead, cover the dish. When ready to serve, remove the cover and run the dish under a preheated broiler until the cheese is browned and the fennel is heated through. May be made 1 to 2 days ahead.

GARLIC

Purchase firm, heavy bulbs and store in a well-ventilated space. Do not refrigerate. Garlic keeps for up to a month, but toss any that are soft or mildewed.

Preparing and measuring—Smash a garlic clove in its skin to pop out the clove. Chop the garlic clove finely, discarding the tough end piece. Measure with a measuring spoon. Move to the hollow of a cupped hand. This is one garlic clove, chopped. Try to use the hollow of a hand to measure salt, garlic, and other regular condiments, to save time in measuring. If that is too difficult, use a measuring spoon set. If more garlic is preferred, up the number of garlic cloves to suit your taste.

To separate the garlic cloves lay a knife horizontally across the top of the garlic head and smash the knife down on the head, breaking apart the cloves. To peel an individual clove, lay a knife flat on top of the clove and swack it, or use one of the gadgets available in cookware stores.

Making garlic paste—Sprinkle a wooden board with salt; add peeled garlic cloves, and scrape the garlic and salt together with the end of a small knife. The salt's abrasiveness will turn it into a paste. This paste can be made several days in advance and kept tightly wrapped in the refrigerator.

Cooking garlic—When cooked whole, garlic cloves are sweet and become smooth and spreadable. There are two ways to achieve this. One is to cook the whole head; another is to cook the cloves only. Whole garlic may be cooked in the microwave. The cloves tend to pop open and splatter, so cook, covered, and on medium power for 1 minute; check and cook a bit more if necessary. Garlic cloves also soften when boiled, sautéed, or baked.

Alternatively, remove only the papery exterior from whole garlic, rub with oil, wrap with foil or place in another ovenproof container, and roast at 350 degrees for approximately 1 hour, depending on size; check after 30 minutes. Garlic also takes to being boiled in water or stock.

GREENS

Greens are beloved by Southerners, feeding them in hard times and good. The origins of their popularity come from African as well as European cooks. An important source of calcium and other nutrients, greens enjoy flavor enhancement and gain protein from the addition of "seasoning" meat. Seasoning meat includes rinsed and sliced salt pork, ham hock, streak o' lean, other pieces of cured pork (page 405), and other smoked meats.

The most popular types of greens in the South are collard and turnip greens, and it is these that are generally meant when "greens" are referred to. There are numerous varieties of turnip tops and turnip greens. When cooking its tops, the turnip is frequently added to the greens. Turnip greens are preferred by those who like to add other vegetables, such as potatoes, to a cooking liquid.

Collards—cabbage-like leaves—have no root vegetable but do have a pungent odor when cooked. Their stalk is tough and is removed before cooking. Smaller varieties are now being grown that have less odor.

I never thought of kale as a Southern vegetable until my husband said he grew up with it. Chard is a recent addition to the table. Rainbow chard, with its bright red stems, has a sharp spinach-like flavor. Remove the stems and set aside. Tear the greens as with any other green, and steam, sauté, or roast the stems as with asparagus.

Poke sallet is a wild indigenous green that can grow six feet tall but is usually eaten like turnip greens when it is a smaller plant and has a mild taste. Like other greens, it becomes bitter and tough as it ages. Small stems of poke sallet can be cooked much like asparagus, but its roots and berries are inedible. It is called poke sallet, or poke, allegedly because it was put into a sack, or poke, when picked.

Other greens include cabbage, sorrel, rape, dock, beet tops, and lambs quarters. Cressi (also spelled *cresse*) grows wild near the banks of streams and is much like watercress.

Purchasing greens and storing—Buy greens that are crisp and have a bright green color. Avoid wilted or yellowing greens. Store unwashed greens in the refrigerator for up to 3 or 4 days.

One and a half pounds of fresh leaves yields one cup of cooked and drained leaves.

Washing greens—Prewashed greens are widely available, but care should still be taken to be sure they are free of dirt; it can take up to two or three washings to get them clean. Collard greens still on the stalk are sturdy enough to be held under running water, turned, and washed on the second side. Continue going through the leaves until all are well rinsed.

For other greens, remove leaves from stalks, discarding any tough greens and stalks (tender stalks may be tossed with oil and roasted). Fill a basin with cold salted water, add the loose greens, stir several times in the water, and soak. Remove from basin before tipping off the water, making sure not to pour dirt back over the greens still in the basin. Rub the greens and see if any grit is left on the leaves. If so, rinse again.

De-stemming and preparing greens—Fold the large leaves lengthwise at the stem. Pull the tough portion of the stem away from the leaf starting where the leaf meets the stem at the bottom, and discard the stem. The stem may also be cut away with a knife.

Stack several de-stemmed leaves together and roll. Use a sharp knife to cut down the roll in 1-inch pieces.

A MESS OF GREENS AND "POT LIKKER"

Serves 6 to 8, including "pot likker"

A "MESS" OF GREENS, AS COOKED GREENS ARE CALLED, *is an armful of bundles of turnips or collards that cook down to a quart of greens in addition to the broth. Regarded as a comfort food, greens can be a meal, eaten just by themselves or with cornbread or biscuits, as well as part of a larger meal. When meat was a rarity, the seasoning meat in greens was an important dietary supplement, with the fat giving energy for long days and cold nights. Greens are best when picked after the first frost, customarily around hog-butchering time, when there is a snap in the air, or in early spring; but there is hardly a time anymore when they are not available.*

1/3 pound sliced, rinsed salt pork or streak o' lean, smoked neck, or other cured pork
1–2 slices onion, optional
1 small hot pepper, optional
5 pounds turnip, collard, poke sallet, or kale greens, washed
Salt
Freshly ground pepper
Hot sauce, optional

Bring 1/2 gallon of water to the boil; add the pork, optional onion, and hot pepper and return to the boil. If time is available, cook half an hour or so to flavor the broth.

Meanwhile, tear off and discard from the greens the stalks and any tough veins. Tear or cut the remaining greens into pieces and add to the broth. Return to the boil, reduce the heat to a simmer, pushing any bobbing greens down into the liquid, and cover. Cook 50 minutes to 3 hours, as desired. Take a pair of large scissors and cut any pieces larger than bite-size. Taste and season with salt, pepper, and hot sauce as desired. Serve with the broth (pot likker), or strain, reserving the broth for another time. Cooked greens will last covered and refrigerated for several days. They freeze up to 3 months.

Variations:

- When the greens have returned to the boil, add peeled and cut-up turnips or beets, and cook until the vegetables are done, about half an hour, depending on size.
- Add small pieces of potatoes to the boiling greens and cook until the potatoes are done, about 30 minutes, depending on size.
- Break up pieces of cornbread and add to bowls of pot likker as desired.

Many Southern homes used to keep a bottle of vinegar infused with peppers on the kitchen table (the closer to Louisiana, the hotter the concoction). Greens were sprinkled with vinegar or hot sauce before eating.

POKE SALLET WITH GREEN ONIONS AND BACON

Serves 4

WHEN POKE SALLET MATURES, *it develops purple colorations on its stalk, flower stem, berries, and seeds. It is considered toxic and poisonous and should be avoided. Young plants are safe, as is the juice, but avoid eating the roots.*

3 pounds young poke sallet leaves, washed, stems removed
1 small hot pepper, optional
6 strips bacon, cooked crisp and crumbled, drippings reserved
2 green onions, chopped
Salt
Freshly ground black pepper

Add the poke sallet and hot pepper to a pot of boiling water. The poke will wilt quickly. Push any recalcitrant leaves into the liquid. Cook until the desired doneness—as little as 3 minutes or up to an hour or more. Drain, rinse in cold water, and squeeze well.

Reheat 2 tablespoons reserved drippings in a heavy skillet. Add the onions to the bacon fat, and cook briefly. Add the poke sallet and heat through. Top with crumbled bacon.

Variation: Poke Fritters
Cook and drain young poke leaves; tear in half if too large. Make a cornmeal batter. Use coarse cornmeal, 1 lightly beaten egg, and just enough water to make a batter, not too runny. Dip the leaves in the batter. Meanwhile, heat oil to 360 degrees in a frying pan. Add the leaves one by one, turning as necessary. Reduce heat if browning too quickly. Drain on paper towels. Season to taste with salt and pepper.

SIMPLE SAUTÉED GREENS

Serves 4 to 6

ALL GREENS CAN BE COOKED THIS WAY *when tender. Larger ones need blanching (page 159), their tough stems removed first. My beloved Celeste Dupree, my favorite former mother-in-law, grew turnip greens in her annual garden. She would eat the tender baby ones in a salad or cook them as a quick sauté.*

2 pounds small greens, washed (page 205)
2–4 tablespoons butter
Salt
Freshly ground black pepper

Remove any tough veins, stalks, or stems from the greens. Melt the butter in a large frying pan. Toss the still damp greens in the butter until well coated. (If dry, add ⅓ cup water). Cover the pan and cook 3 to 5 minutes, until wilted. Season to taste with salt and pepper.

Variations:

- Add 1 cup heavy cream to the pan after removing the greens, bring to the boil, and let boil down to about ⅔ cup.
- Cook the butter until it turns a nutty brown before adding the greens.
- Substitute oil for the butter and add chopped garlic to the pan.
- Substitute frozen spinach, collards, or kale, defrosted and well drained.
- Top sautéed mushrooms, onions, garlic, and/or tomatoes with the still damp greens before covering and wilting.

CHIFFONADE OF TURNIP, COLLARD, KALE, OR BABY BEET GREENS

Serves 4 to 6

NEW, LESS BITTER VARIETIES *of greens in the last twenty years, as well as recent use of smaller and younger greens, have led to exciting, dashing dishes like this.*

2 teaspoons butter or oil
2 cups chiffonade or ribboned greens
2 garlic cloves, chopped
1 teaspoon finely chopped fresh ginger
1 pound cooked beets or
 1 (16-ounce) can beets, drained and coarsely chopped
2 tablespoons fresh lemon juice or cider vinegar
Salt
Freshly ground black pepper

If large and bitter, remove stems and blanch greens. Melt the butter or oil in a large skillet and add the greens, garlic, and ginger. Cover and cook until the greens are wilted, just a few minutes. Stir in the chopped beets and lemon juice or vinegar. Season to taste with salt and pepper. Heat through for 1 to 2 minutes and serve hot or at room temperature.

CHIFFONADE

To chiffonade is to roll into several layers and cut into very thin strips, as with greens or basil. Stack washed and deveined greens. Roll into a cigar shape. Lay flat on the board and slice horizontally 1/4 inch thick, or thinner for herbs.

FRIED GREENS

Serves 4

I SERVED THESE GREENS, *which are easily made ahead of time, as garnishes in my restaurant in Social Circle, Georgia. Although Cynthia's husband says we will fry anything in the South, these are deservedly exceptional.*

1 pound turnip or collard greens, washed
Shortening or vegetable oil for frying
Salt, optional
Freshly ground black pepper, optional
Ground hot red pepper, optional

Stem the greens and remove the veins. Chiffonade (above) into 1/2-inch-wide ribbons. Dry very well with paper towels. Pour enough oil to reach the halfway mark into a heavy skillet or deep-fat fryer, and heat to 350 degrees. When hot, add the dry greens by the handful—the fat will boil up considerably. Fry until crisp, about 5 minutes. Remove all the greens with a Chinese-type or slotted strainer and drain on a paper towel. Continue to fry in batches until all the greens are cooked. They will last several hours unsalted. Just before serving, season to taste with salt, pepper, and hot red pepper if using.

MUSHROOMS

Whether eaten by themselves, on top of a steak or fish, or tossed over pasta, rice, or vegetables, mushrooms are a handy part of our cuisine. Many kinds of wild mushrooms grow naturally in the South, although only experts know where to find them anymore. From South Carolina to Virginia, morel and shiitake hunters closely guard their secret places. Only the trained should search for and eat wild mushrooms. For the rest of us, cultivated must do. Cultivated mushrooms have been grown sporadically in the South since at least the 1970s, perhaps even earlier.

Dried mushrooms are a convenient resource. Soak in boiling liquid, which itself becomes flavorful. The broth should always be strained before using in soups, stocks, sauces, or grain dishes.

Purchasing mushrooms—Buy mushrooms that are dry and firm. Avoid any that are slimy. Wrap mushrooms loosely in paper towels and refrigerate for two or three days.

Preparing mushrooms—After years of saying otherwise, authorities now say that washing and soaking mushrooms does not cause them to absorb more water. But I still prefer brushing or wiping them clean: use a damp paper towel that has been dipped in salt, or a mushroom brush, to brush away any dirt. Another way to clean without soaking is to spray them rapidly with a sink water sprayer. Mushrooms are harder to chop when soggy.

Slice off the end of the stems if tough or wizened. They have nutrition and flavor, so save them to flavor broth.

MUSHROOM DUXELLES

Makes 2 cups

DUXELLES, THE FRENCH TERM FOR THE PASTE *that results from cooking mushrooms, shallots, and herbs, is good by itself but is particularly excellent as a condiment for rice and grains as well as a wide variety of green vegetables. It forms a base for dishes used as stuffing, on its own or mixed with spinach, shrimp, cheese, breadcrumbs, etc., and stuffed into fish, tomatoes, mushrooms, squash, zucchini, and eggplant. It is traditionally cooked until all moisture is gone, but if desired for another purpose, it is tasty with more moisture. I've added garlic, which is not traditional but is divine. The food processor makes chopping a snap.*

1/4 cup butter
1 pound fresh mushrooms, cleaned and finely chopped
1/4 cup finely chopped onion or shallot
2 garlic cloves, chopped, optional
3–5 tablespoons finely chopped fresh parsley, thyme, or other herb

Melt the butter in a large heavy skillet over medium-low heat. Add the mushrooms, onion, and garlic if using, and cook until nearly all the moisture has cooked out—about 15 minutes—or until it is almost a paste—about 20 to 30 minutes. Add the herbs and store, covered, in the refrigerator for up to 1 week, or freeze for up to 3 months.

SAUTÉED MUSHROOMS

Serves 2 to 4

SIMPLE SAUTÉED MUSHROOMS CAN BE EATEN ALONE *or added to most any dish, whether fresh or reconstituted (see below). They add variation and flavor and are now easy to have on hand.*

$1/2$–1 pound fresh or reconstituted mushrooms, cleaned
2 tablespoons butter
Salt
Freshly ground black pepper

Remove any brown or tough stems and put them aside for another purpose. Slice the mushrooms if large, or leave whole if small. Heat the butter in a frying pan. Add the mushrooms and sauté 3 to 5 minutes, until tender but cooked. Season to taste with salt and pepper. Serve hot. May be refrigerated or frozen and reheated.

Variation: Sautéed Mushrooms, Sesame Seeds, and Vegetables
Ideal to perk up leftovers, sautéed mushrooms can enhance cooked asparagus, broccoli florets or stalks, butter beans, carrots, zucchini, green beans, snow peas, and more. Cook mushrooms separately, then combine and reheat with the vegetable of your choice and top with a tablespoon of sesame seeds.

Variations:
- Sauté 2 chopped garlic cloves, 1 chopped shallot or 1 small onion, and chopped fresh herbs or ginger. Add mushrooms and cook as above.
- Cut an equal weight or a little more of okra, slice diagonally, add to the hot butter, and sauté 2 to 3 minutes. Reheat with the mushrooms.

GRILLED PORTOBELLO MUSHROOMS

Serves 4 to 6

PORTOBELLO MUSHROOMS (A LARGER VARIETY OF THE CREMINI MUSHROOMS) *are now grown all over the United States, including the South. They may be treated like a steak—served whole, or sliced and added to another dish.*

4–6 medium-sized portobello mushrooms, each about 4 inches across
Salt
6 garlic cloves, finely chopped
4–6 tablespoons olive oil
Freshly ground black pepper
Fresh herbs, optional

Clean the mushrooms; remove the stems and reserve them for another use. Shake the salt, garlic, olive oil, and pepper in a plastic bag. Add the mushrooms, seal the bag, and turn to coat the mushrooms in the oil. Marinate up to 1 hour.

Grill top side up for 4 to 5 minutes, or broil the mushrooms on a broiler pan. Flip the mushrooms and cook 4 more minutes. The mushrooms should be well cooked on the outside but creamy and tender on the inside. Sprinkle with fresh herbs if using. Serve whole or sliced.

Variations:
- Add sliced cooked mushrooms to a salad or green vegetable.
- Serve in a crusty burger bun with Cheddar cheese, lettuce, ripe tomato, and a slice of red onion.

Variation: Stuffed Mushrooms
Remove and chop all the stems from a batch of mushrooms, such as cremini, portobello, or button, and sauté in butter; add chopped garlic and cook briefly. Add breadcrumbs, chopped spinach, cooked shrimp, and/or cheese. Up-end the caps and fill the underside of the caps from which the stems have been removed with the mixture, Move to a rimmed baking sheet or another ovenproof dish and cook in a 350-degree oven for 15 minutes, until cooked through. May be made ahead and reheated.

OKRA

Okra, a flowering plant like its cousins cotton, cocoa, and hibiscus, loves poor soil, unpredictable rains, and heat. It does not like frost, which is why many living above the Mason-Dixon Line are unfamiliar with its goodness or view it with suspicion—odd, since so much of the world relishes it. In India it is called "lady fingers," its graceful pods curving into a slender tip much like a lady's finger. Africans frequently call it "gumbo," a term that has taken root in Louisiana and other Cajun areas as well as in the Gullah region of South Carolina and Georgia.

Okra's origins are iffy. The earliest report of it was in the 1200s by a Spaniard visiting Egypt, where it had most likely originated from Ethiopia. It spread to the Americas in the mid-1600s, with Thomas Jefferson viewing it as commonplace by the late-eighteenth century. Most likely it came to the South by way of slave traders. It is improbable that Africans themselves brought it over, regardless of the apocrypha about poking seeds in their ears or hair arrangements.

The worst thing about okra is picking it—its fibrous exterior has a fuzziness that clings and can cause itching, and the plant is aggressive in the way it protects the flowers from which the okra emerges. Both the flower and the okra are edible, as are the leaves. The flower is stuffed or fried; the leaves are cooked like beet or other greens.

Okra's multiplicity of seeds are reluctant to leave the pentagon in which they are nestled—it's rare for an okra seed to spill out, even when stir-frying. Stir-frying, frying, roasting, and grilling deter the mucilaginous quality inherent in okra. So, too, does acid, which is why it is so frequently paired with tomatoes or citrus, or put up as a pickle. It has a crisp texture when eaten raw, and its mild flavor is well suited to cooking alone or with other vegetables.

Buying and storing okra—When buying okra, look for the smallest pods. By the time larger pods are cooked, they are much less palatable. If the smaller ones are not available, slice the larger ones on the diagonal before preparing.

To freeze okra, spread it out separately on a flat surface during an initial freeze, then collect and keep in a freezer container. It is sold fresh, frozen, and canned. Canned okra is pressure-cooked, so it has a pronounced mucilaginous quality.

STIR-FRIED OKRA

Serves 2 to 3

Simply cooked okra is welcome *in the middle of the hot summer, when heating up the kitchen is undesirable.*

2–4 tablespoons butter

1 pound okra, sliced diagonally, caps discarded

Salt

Freshly ground black pepper

Heat the butter in a large skillet. Add the sliced okra and sauté 3 to 4 minutes, until crisp-tender. Season to taste with salt and pepper. Serve hot. May be reheated.

Variations:

- Top okra with a small portion of White Butter Sauce (page 656).
- Sliver okra by removing the caps and thinly slicing the okra vertically for a completely different look. Continue as above in Stir-Fried Okra.
- Add to other sautéed vegetables, such as corn or grape tomato halves.

PAN-FRIED OKRA

Serves 6

THE QUANTITY OF LIGHTLY COATED CRISP OKRA *in this recipe may seem excessive for the number of people, but experience has taught me that it has a popcorn quality, inviting nibblers by its aroma and texture, and the first batch will be eaten before the second is done. If crisp enough, it can be reheated in a 350-degree oven, but watch carefully to prevent burning. Smaller okra may not need slicing, but remove the tough caps. (Pre-battered frozen okra sold commercially is inferior.) As a friend of mine said, stirring fried and delicate foods is a temptation of the devil. Stirring okra while it fries accomplishes nothing except knocking off the coating, which causes it to burn easily. Turn the okra if necessary (the okra should turn itself when brown, but use a slotted spoon to turn it if necessary). Practice "benign neglect." Removing it should be the only time it is disturbed.*

2 pounds okra
3/4 cup cornmeal
3/4 cup all-purpose flour
3 teaspoons salt
Shortening or vegetable oil for frying, cook's preference
Salt
Freshly ground black pepper

Line a rimmed baking sheet with paper towels. Wash and lightly drain okra in a colander so it will retain enough moisture for the flour mixture to adhere. Cut off and discard caps, and slice okra into 1/2-inch slices or pieces. Toss together the cornmeal, flour, and salt, and toss with a portion of the okra. Remove the okra and spread on waxed paper to dry for a few minutes. Toss again in cornmeal and flour to coat thoroughly, avoiding clumping. Repeat with remaining okra. The okra can be left up to several hours in the meal mixture to gather a thicker crust.

Meanwhile, pour enough oil into an iron skillet or deep frying pan to reach halfway up the side, and heat to 350 degrees, medium. To be sure the oil is hot enough, add a test piece of okra. Bubbles should sizzle around the okra. Add the floured okra in batches, leaving enough room in the pan to turn the okra. Brown lightly on both sides. Resist the temptation to turn the okra too soon; give it a chance to turn itself. If stirred too much, the cornmeal will fall to the bottom of the pan and burn. When brown and crisp, remove okra to paper towels to drain. If necessary, carefully drain the oil into a bowl and wipe the bottom of the pan clean of browned bits. Pour the drained oil back into the pan and repeat with the second batch. Season to taste with salt and pepper.

Variation: Omit the flour and just use cornmeal.

ROASTED OKRA CHIPS

Makes 2 cups

Familiar to those raised in warm-weather *or tropical climates, this pentagonal-shaped vegetable is harvested in the summertime from a hibiscus family tree that can grow 6 to 8 feet high. When asked to describe one characteristic of this vegetable, people will usually mention something about it being slimy, perhaps the main motivation when preparing these chips. The results were crispy tiny chips that became irresistible and blessedly "slime free." Julia Regner, who interned with me, roasted every green vegetable that came into the kitchen that summer.*

One large okra yields about 8 to 10 slices, and a small one about 5 to 7 slices. Try slicing the okra from tip to tip on a diagonal to get a 2-inch-long slice.

20 okra (about 3 cups, sliced vertically or horizontally)
2 tablespoon oil, cook's preference
1/2 teaspoon salt
1/2 teaspoon pepper

Preheat oven to 350 degrees.

Toss sliced okra gently with oil, salt, and pepper in a large bowl. Move okra onto a rimmed baking sheet and bake for approximately 10 to 15 minutes. Turn okra to the other side halfway through the cooking time. Total time to cook the okra depends on the thickness of the slice, so adjust baking time accordingly. Remove from oven when crispy and transfer to a paper towel. Any leftovers can be refrigerated. They will lose their crispiness but may be reheated.

Variation: Cynthia roasts her okra whole, following the method above, and keeps them on hand for snacking.

Variation: Grilled Okra
Slice okra or leave whole. Toss gently with oil, salt, and pepper in a large bowl. Preheat a grill pan on the stove, or preheat the grill to medium. Add the okra to the hot pan or grill and cook 5 to 6 minutes per side. Remove when crispy.

MARGARET LUPO'S DEEP-FRIED OKRA

Serves 6

THIS CRISP, THICK EXTERIOR *was developed by Margaret Lupo, longtime owner of Mary Mac's Tea Room in Atlanta. She was a dear friend, independent, competent, a mixture of tender and tough herself. Neither Cynthia nor I have deep-fryers.*

- 2 pounds okra, well rinsed
- 1 egg, beaten
- 2 tablespoons water
- 2 cups buttermilk
- 4 teaspoons salt, divided
- 2 cups all-purpose flour
- 2 cups crushed cracker meal or saltines, crushed to the consistency of cornmeal
- Freshly ground black pepper
- Shortening or vegetable oil for frying

Line a rimmed baking sheet with paper towels. Cut the stem ends off the cleaned okra and slice 1/4 inch thick. Mix together the egg, water, buttermilk, and 2 teaspoons salt in a large bowl. Toss the okra in the mixture.

Mix the flour, cracker meal, remaining salt, and pepper in another bowl. Remove okra from the buttermilk with a slotted spoon and add by spoonfuls to the flour. Toss lightly to coat, then move to a cake rack to remove excess flour.

Meanwhile, heat the oil in an electric skillet, wok, or deep frying pan to 350 degrees. Add the okra by large spoonfuls and fry until golden brown, turning only as necessary. Move with a slotted spoon to the paper towels to drain. Keep warm in a 250-degree oven while frying the remaining okra. Serve hot.

COATING OKRA

The two methods mentioned here and on page 212 allow the coating to stay crisp, and the okra can be reheated or snacked on at room temperature. A lighter batter quickly wilts on fried okra.

OKRA AND TOMATOES

Serves 4

Some genius, *long before the* Virginia Housewife *was written, realized that acid countered the mucilaginous quality of okra. With this discovery, okra and tomatoes became the basis of many vegetable dishes and soups. I prefer adding onions and garlic to my basic recipe. I usually make it with canned tomatoes, but my husband was brought up with fresh ones. His South Carolina family always served this dish over rice.*

- 3 tablespoons butter
- 1 small onion, chopped
- 1–2 garlic cloves, chopped
- 2–3 cups canned diced tomatoes with juice
- 2 cups okra, caps removed and sliced
- Salt
- Freshly ground black pepper
- Granulated sugar, optional

Melt the butter in a heavy saucepan. Add the onion and cook until soft, about 3 to 5 minutes. Add the garlic and cook 1 minute more. Add the tomatoes and okra, and bring to the boil. Reduce heat to a simmer and cook uncovered until thick, about 45 minutes to 1 hour, stirring as needed. Season to taste with salt and pepper. If the tomatoes taste "tinny," add a little sugar to smooth out the flavor.

Variation: Fresh Tomatoes and Okra
Peel and seed 4 to 5 large tomatoes to substitute for the canned tomatoes.

Variation: Okra with Corn and Tomatoes
Scrape corn off the cob and add to the pot 5 minutes before serving.

MARINATED OKRA

Serves 4

For an unusual finger food, *these still crunchy okra take the place of pickled okra (page 640). Leave the cap on or, if necessary, trim carefully, leaving a minimum of cap on.*

- 1 pound okra
- 1/4 cup red wine or sherry vinegar
- 1/2 cup olive oil
- 1 tablespoon Dijon mustard
- Grated rind of 1 small orange, no white attached
- 3 tablespoons fresh orange juice
- 1–2 teaspoons ground cumin
- Salt
- Freshly ground black pepper

Add uncapped okra to a pan of boiling water for 30 seconds. Drain and run quickly under cold water to stop the cooking. Set aside to cool.

Whisk together the remaining ingredients. Pour over the okra in a bowl and cover; marinate several hours or overnight. Drain and arrange on a serving platter to be eaten as a finger food, or on individual salad plates.

Variation: Season with coriander or fennel seed, either whole or grated, as desired.

ONIONS, LEEKS, AND SHALLOTS

There are an endless variety of uses for the onion—from freshly chopped white ones in cucumber salad, to deeply caramelized ones for tarts, soups, and steaks, not to mention crispy fried ones for a side dish. Each way they taste a little different, bringing something else to the table.

Onions are the most forgiving of friends in the kitchen. They rarely need to be measured accurately, as they are ever-changeable themselves, varying with the amount of cold storage they have had, their growing region, their color, and, of course, their size. Onions can be sweet enough to eat raw (Vidalia onions are one Georgia version) or so sharp and bitter, they can make you cry. The aroma warms a cold house as they sauté in a pan, caramelizing for a rich onion soup or to top a steak. They can be so mild they can hardly be tasted, as in a homemade tomato sauce.

There are two categories of onions: spring-summer fresh onions and fall-winter storage onions.

All fresh onions—red, yellow, and white—emerge from the ground in the spring and summer, March through August. Fresh onions have a thin layer of skin and are sweeter than onions that have been stored. Spring-summer onions are best for salads, sandwiches, and light spring and summer dishes. While some do not like caramelized spring and summer onions, I think they are the best because they are indeed sweeter.

After the spring and summer onions are past their moment, all varieties are stored, usually in cold storage in the South. Called fall-winter storage onions, these are available from August to March. As they dry out, they develop layers of thick, light brown, brittle skin. Their flavor is intense, their odor is sharper, and they are more likely to make the cook cry when chopping them. They keep their flavor when cooked for a long time.

When an onion is first picked, the outside is moist. I've seen onions pulled and laid on the ground or rack to dry, and then returned to find an outside layer of their skin dry. Each subsequent dry layer is an indication of an onion's age and treatment. They get wet and gummy inside if they age too long outdoors, and if not stored properly, will turn gray-black and rotten, their odor a far cry from enticing.

According to the onion council, the greatest percentage of harvested onions are yellow; they are the kitchen workers and are adaptable to almost anything. Red onions comprise only around 10 percent of those harvested; they add color to salads and sandwiches and grill very prettily. White onions are only 5 percent of the harvest; they are sweeter and are primarily used in specialty cuisines, such as Mexican.

Storing onions— Store onions uncovered in a basket or other airy place, separated from potatoes and other vegetables, and avoid refrigeration.

Shallots

Depending on the variety, shallots have one or several bulbs. One shallot can be whatever amount the cook wants it to be. Measure a typical shallot and use that as a consistent amount. It can be blue-gray (French) or rusty colored (American), and the exterior varies.

Tasting like a cross between onion and garlic, shallots did not become widely available in the South until the late 1970s to early 1980s, although they were readily available in Europe. Some cooks substitute scallions for shallots, but I prefer combining a small amount of onion and garlic to substitute.

Now grown larger, one chopped shallot is approximately 2 tablespoons.

Preparing Onions

Some definitions are in order that apply to home cooking rather than the rigid definitions of a culinary school. It is important to know that every one of these will yield a different measure of onion to start, although once cooked and the water extruded, they will wind up roughly the same in volume but not in flavor or texture.

The macho manner the chefs use—Cutting off both ends of the onion and then proceeding is silly in that the greatest source of the enzyme that causes tearing of the eyes is in the root end of the onion. For this reason and to keep their mascara on, home cooks are especially encouraged to retain the root until the onion has been chopped or sliced.

The first step for either chopping or slicing:

Cut the onion in half from stem end to root, leaving the root intact. Peel the onion and discard the peel or save for stock or dying fabric or Easter eggs. Lay the flat side of both halves of the onion down, so the cut surface is not exposed and the flat surface enables a firm grasp.

Chopping—This method is preferred when small pieces are desired, perhaps for cooking, as in a soup, or when they are to be combined, as with tomatoes for a salsa. Chopped onions may be purchased frozen and are very handy in emergencies (which in Cynthia's house is sometimes the difference in putting a stew on the stove or not.)

Holding the peeled and halved onion with the fingers of one hand (as in the photo series, frame 4), cut into the peeled onion half at regular intervals parallel to the work surface, working from the stem end to a quarter of an inch from the root. Holding the cut portions together with one hand, slice down perpendicular to the cut portions, keeping the slices parallel and roughly the same size. Stop when about 1/4 inch from the root of the onion.

Dicing—Smaller than chopped, this method is preferred when absolutely uniform product is required. Dicing is used for garnishing as well as in the uses noted above for chopping. Other words instructions may note are "minced" or "very finely chopped" to describe a similar product. Dicing is rarely used in this book.

Slicing—Hold the peeled onion half with the fingers of one hand, knuckles toward the knife and fingers tucked under. Move the knife up and down on the peeled onion half, starting at the stem (not root) end and moving toward the root, in a steady back and forth motion, trying to maintain the same distance between slices. Stop a quarter of an inch or so from the root and save the remainder of the onion for stock or discard.

Sliced 1/2 inch thick or more is preferred by some for fried onion rings and for raw onions on hamburgers.

Sliced 1/3 to 1/2 inch thick is the ideal size for caramelizing, cooking long and slowly until all the natural sugars come out. Also called "sliced roughly" these may take up to an hour to caramelize, but it is well worth it.

Sliced somewhere around 1/4 inch thick, the onion is most often cooked over medium or low heat until it is translucent. Caramelizing is tricky but can be done if a low heat is used along with a great deal of patience.

Sliced about 1/8 inch thick, the onions are transparent and are usually served raw, as on a hamburger, in a salad, or as a garnish. It is difficult to cook very thin onions, as they may burn quickly and lose all their juices, becoming dry and hard.

Measuring Onions

Chop an onion the size and color most frequently purchased. Measure in a dry measuring cup. That equals one onion for the recipes used in your home. When larger onions are purchased, estimate accordingly. If recipes taste a little bland or less "oniony" than desired, up the amount considered as one onion.

Cooking onions—Although an onion may certainly be cooked in the microwave, without fat in a nonstick frying pan, or in water until the water evaporates, these methods do not render the most flavor.

The preferred method is to heat a heavy frying pan. When very hot, add a teaspoon of butter or other fat such as oil or drippings. There should be a sizzling and a singing in the pan. A mixture of butter and vegetable oil will take a higher heat without burning than if butter alone is used, and vegetable oil alone takes an even higher heat.

Add 2 onions, sliced or chopped, depending on the need. After the great sizzling subsides, salt the onions as liberally as desired, reduce the heat, and continue cooking over low heat until some of the onions' water is extruded by the salt.

TO SAVE A MARRIAGE

I've never heard of a man divorcing his wife because she didn't cook onions, but I've heard of plenty of marriages cooked onions saved. I once had a cooking student who attended only one cooking lesson, making it clear when she arrived that the only reason she was there was because her husband wanted her to be a good cook, and he had a fantasy of her staying home and cooking all day. She believed her hands were meant to hold charge cards, not a knife. When I ran into her several months after her solo class, I asked her why she had not returned. She looked at me, stunned. "Well," she said, "I learned everything I needed to know—I learned that if I cooked onions and garlic the second I hit the house, he thought I had been home cooking all day."

In fact, according to an onion source, men do eat more onions than women do. I've never measured my consumption of onions in poundage, but they have always been a necessity for my cooking. They would be my first choice for the "what would you take to a desert island" question. I decided this long ago when I found out they prevented scurvy and I wanted to be a pirate. Now it turns out they have many more antioxidant and medicinal uses.

ROASTED ONIONS

Serves 6 to 8

While I prefer roasting Vidalia onions, *I find any white or yellow onion does fine. They stretch a meal and may even steal the show. If serving the onions hot, use butter. If serving cold, use oil.*

6–8 medium onions, halved or quartered
8–10 tablespoons butter or oil, cook's preference
Salt
Freshly ground black pepper

Preheat oven to 400 degrees.

Arrange the onions in an oiled baking dish, dot with butter or drizzle with oil, and bake for 45 minutes to 1 hour, adding more butter or oil as necessary to keep onions moist. Season to taste with salt and pepper. Serve hot or cold.

Variations:

- Toss cut onions in the oil and, cut side down, move to a hot grill or under a broiler. Turn when lightly charred. May be made a day or two in advance and served cold.
- Top with herbed breadcrumbs, browned first in butter.
- Use 1 1/2 pounds peeled whole shallots rather than onions, and reduce cooking time.
- Top cooked onions with goat or other soft cheese and oven-dried tomatoes and return to the oven for a few minutes.

Variation: Roasted Onion Flowers

Peel 6 onions, leaving the roots intact. Move each onion root-end down onto a cutting board. Cut each onion nearly in half, still leaving the root intact. Continue to cut each onion in half by rotating the onion, cutting, and creating wedges, still attached to the root. Oil a baking dish and move the onions to the dish, root-end down. Drizzle with 1/2 cup melted butter. Bake 60 to 90 minutes, basting as desired. Remove from oven and season to taste with salt and pepper.

CARAMELIZED ONIONS

Serves 6 to 8

CARAMELIZED ONIONS ARE THE BASIS *for many dishes, and learning how to do them is important, as onions have a high water content and are somewhat reluctant to brown. Cooked too low, they will extrude water and never brown. Cooked too high, they will lose too much water and be crisp rather than tender.*

8 tablespoon butter or oil, cook's preference
6 medium onions, sliced
Salt
Freshly ground black pepper

Heat the butter or oil in a large skillet. Add the onions to the hot fat, reduce the heat, and cook slowly until the onions are soft and a golden caramel brown, about 30 to 45 minutes. Stir frequently. If the onions become watery, turn up the heat a bit, taking care not to burn them. Season to taste with salt and pepper.

Variations:

- Add a bit of sugar to the onions at the end of cooking.
- Add balsamic or flavored vinegar at the end of cooking, bring to the boil, and serve.

CARAMELIZING ONIONS

Cook onions, stirring every few minutes, until the bottom of the pan becomes brown. If liquid from the onions gathers in the bottom of the pan, rather than browning, turn up the heat to remove the liquid, taking care not to burn the onions. Alternatively, heat another pan with some oil and butter, and move half the onions to the hot pan so there is not a deep layer of onions, which has a propensity towards "steaming" rather than caramelizing. When the bottom of the pan begins to brown, stir the onions so the brown goodness transfers to the onions. Continue cooking over low to moderate heat until caramel colored. There should be no excess liquid in the pan, but the onions should not be burned.

Hot water or stock may be added to remove the brown from the bottom of the pan, a process called "deglazing," which adds brown goodness to a gravy or soup. Sugar may be added at any time in the process, but a white onion in particular should not need any to be flavorful and rich.

Variations:

Caramelized onions are welcome in several ways:

- Spread over cooked green beans or inside a hot grilled cheese sandwich.
- As a condiment surrounding a roasted chicken, lamb, duck, or beef roast.
- For topping a pizza dough.
- By themselves, as a side vegetable, or accompanying liver or steak.
- Sprinkled with parsley or another herb, they can be a lively garnish.

STORING ONIONS

In recent years, the sweet Georgia Vidalia onion has been joined by Texas Sweets, Walla Wallas, and other onions developed for their sweetness and mild flavor. I particularly like them caramelized, as they are mellower than other onions.

Many Southerners purchase sweet Vidalia onions in 25-pound sacks. To feast on them all year round, keep the onions in a pair of clean pantyhose, knotting between each onion. The point is to keep the onions from rubbing together and potentially rotting at the point of contact. As the onions are bred smaller, they fit nicely into the toe.

SAUTÉED GREEN ONION, SCALLION, OR LEEK GREENS

Serves 2

ONE SPRING, MY FRIEND SUE HUNTER *insisted I cook the green stems of a green onion. Since I had previously either slivered or used them for garnish, I was dubious. As seen here, I was wrong. They are heavenly.*

1 bunch green onions, green only, 1 bunch scallions, green only, or 1 bunch leek greens, green only
1–2 tablespoons butter
Salt

Discard any damaged greens and cut off top ends if dry and unattractive. Melt the butter in a large skillet. Spread out the greens in one layer and cook 10 minutes, until brown and stiff. Remove to brown paper or paper toweling. Sprinkle lightly with salt if desired.

Variation: Roasted Green Onion and Leek Greens
Toss green onion and leek greens with oil or butter and spread out on a foil-lined rimmed baking sheet. Bake at 450 degrees for 10 to 15 minutes, checking frequently and stirring as necessary, until greens are crisp.

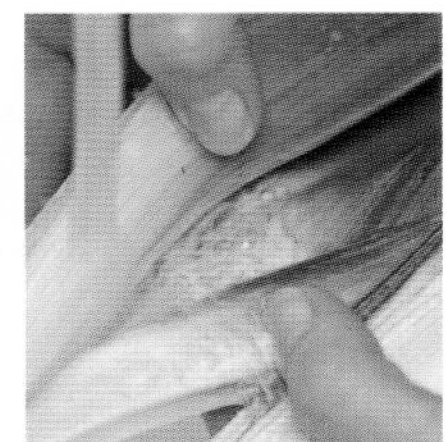
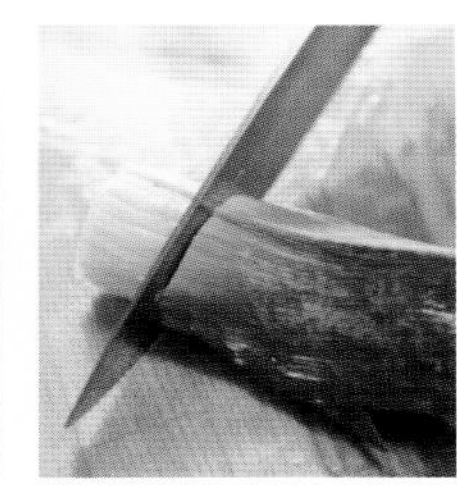

LEEKS

Leeks have a distinctive taste somewhere between a green onion and a mature onion. They are used in French, Chinese, and other ethnic cuisines. The greens are frequently discarded in Southern homes, as they have a bitter flavor, although some cuisines use them, and they are excellent roasted (see variation above).

Wild leeks are known as ramps, looking like small green onions with wider leaves, and are usually found in Appalachian areas, Virginia, West Virginia, and the northern Georgia mountains. West Virginia has a yearly Ramp Festival, where they are eaten raw, cooked, pickled and every other way imaginable. It is said the townspeople smell noxious for some time after, an unforgettable experience.

Cleaning leeks—Cut off the roots and the tough green tops, then cut 1 inch or so into the pale green end of the leeks. Cut the leeks lengthwise into 2 pieces. Run under cold water, fanning and separating the leaves to make sure all dirt and grit are removed.

BRAISED LEEKS

Serves 4 to 6

IN FRENCH CUISINE, *leek broth is used as a weight-loss aid. Adding bacon defeats this purpose but makes a succulent addition to this side dish.*

6 slices bacon
4 leeks, white and pale green only, cleaned and julienned
1 bay leaf
1 sprig fresh parsley
1 sprig fresh thyme
1/2 cup chicken stock or broth
Salt
Freshly ground black pepper

Cut the bacon into small bits and move to a medium-size saucepan. Add leeks, bay leaf, parsley, thyme, and chicken stock; bring to the boil. Reduce the heat to a simmer and cook for 20 minutes, until soft and tender. Remove herb stems before serving. Season to taste with salt and pepper.

For those who hate cleaning leeks and having the big fat greens take up the room in the fridge, frozen leeks have become a godsend.

STONE-GROUND-GRITS-FRIED ONION RINGS

Serves 4

THERE ARE MANY WONDERFUL THINGS TO DO WITH GRITS—*and this use is unexpected. The onions and batter may be prepared ahead, but the frying should be done just before serving.*

2–3 large onions
1 teaspoon salt
1/8 teaspoon freshly ground black pepper
3/4 cups all-purpose flour
1/3 cup stone-ground grits
1 1/3 cups buttermilk, plus a little more
Shortening or vegetable oil for frying

Line a rimmed baking sheet with paper towels. Slice the onions between 1/2 and 3/4 inch thick, and separate into rings. Mix together the salt, pepper, flour, and grits. Whisk 1 1/3 cups buttermilk into the dry ingredients.

Fill a deep frying pan three-fourths of the way full with oil and heat until it reaches 350 to 375 degrees.

Add a handful of the rings to the batter and coat each one completely. Spear the rings out of the batter with a long fork and allow the excess batter to drip off. Add to the oil until the pan has one layer of onions. Fry until golden and turn as they brown. Remove from the oil and drain on the paper-towel-lined pan; move the pan to a 200-degree oven to keep warm until ready to serve.

The buttermilk batter will thicken as it sits out. Add more buttermilk a teaspoon at a time until it is back to the correct consistency. Continue frying onion rings in batches, adding cooked onion rings to the lined baking sheet in the oven. Serve hot.

THE CORRECT AMOUNT OF OIL

The fat in a pan or fryer should be minimal enough to avoid bubbling over when the ingredients are added and the water from them is pushed into the fat while cooking, but deep enough to prevent the fat from lowering its temperature too much when the ingredients are added.

BELL PEPPERS

Traditionally, red bell peppers were well-ripened green bell peppers. Now new varieties of bell pepper come in a vibrant array of colors—from white and yellow to deep purple—and are sweeter than green bell peppers, which have a harsher "raw" taste. A mix of peppers makes a stunning presentation.

Purchasing and storing bell peppers—Purchase bell peppers with smooth, unwrinkled skin and no soft spots. Store wrapped in plastic in the refrigerator for up to a week.

Once the peppers are roasted, they can be kept tightly wrapped for up to a week in the refrigerator. They will last several weeks longer covered with oil or vinegar, also refrigerated. They can also be frozen in plastic ziplock bags.

Although commercial jars or cans of roasted red peppers may be purchased in Italian specialty shops or gourmet food stores, hand-peeled peppers seem better. Try to avoid no-name canned brands. Drain before chopping.

CHARRED RED PEPPERS

Makes 2 cups

WHETHER SERVED LAYERED IN A PLATTER *or cut into strips, there is nothing with flavor comparable to a red pepper.*

4–6 whole or halved and seeded red bell peppers

Preheat a broiler or grill.

Move peppers to a foil-lined or nonstick rimmed baking sheet or broiling pan. Cook 3 inches from the heat until charred, turning so all sides are nearly black, about 30 minutes. Remove to a plastic bag. The heat and moisture generated from the bag aid in lifting the skin, making it easier to remove. Cool enough to handle. Peel off the skin with fingers; some prefer to do this under running water. Remove the stem, cut the pepper in half, and remove any seeds. Leave whole or tear into strips or chop.

Another way to char peppers is to push a large grilling fork into a pepper and hold over a flame, rotating it until the pepper is charred all over. This demands more of the cook's attention but is faster overall, although the stovetop has to be cleaned.

Variation: Roasted Red Pepper Salad
Roast the peppers as above and cut peppers into strips. Toss strips in a Basic Vinaigrette (page 105).

Variation: Roasted Red Pepper Purée
Purée roasted, peeled, and seeded peppers in a food processor or chop until mushy. Press through a sieve to smooth completely. Serve as is, or add to mayonnaise, hollandaise, beurre blanc, or tomato or other sauces. Red Pepper Purée even enhances bean dips.

POTATOES

Not all potatoes are the same. They vary depending on the season, when they were harvested, how they were stored, and which of the thousands of varieties they are. The Russet potato, what we think of as the typical big Idaho potato, is the best for mashing due to its high starch content. A typical Russet, or Idaho, potato cooks up dry and fluffy, lapping up and holding the liquid without becoming runny.

Newer cookbooks tout the yellow varieties of potatoes, which have medium starch. Yukon Gold is the best known. Yellow Finn is growing in popularity. The yellow color indicates their richer flavor, and that plus the color enables the cook to reduce the amount of liquid and fat added. The Yukon Gold is my favorite variety for mashing, even though the Idaho is technically better.

Old recipe books frequently refer to small red potatoes as new potatoes and have confused generations of cooks. The times I've been able to dig up and cook fresh potatoes are vivid in memory. Here's how to distinguish between different types of potatoes:

New potatoes—are newly dug and can be any size. They are sweeter than comparably sized ones that have been dug up sometime previous. The best of these are tiny—anywhere from the size of a fingertip to an inch in diameter.

Creamers—are the very small, early spring and fall potatoes that are newly dug.

Fingerlings—are a variety of small potato about the length of a finger. They come in many colors, from white to blue.

Purchasing and storing—Purchase firm, earthy-smelling potatoes. Avoid any with soft spots. Potatoes turn green when exposed to sunlight, so store potatoes away from the light, but with ventilation. Do not refrigerate.

Cleaning potatoes—Potatoes should be washed individually under running water before being cooked. Use a small brush or a specially designed scrubber as needed to remove any caked-on dirt, especially around the eyes. Small potatoes have delicate skins and should be treated accordingly. Large potatoes can be tough, and big eyes should be cut out with the tip of a knife or a pointed peeler. Resist soaking potatoes except to specifically remove the starch or to prevent discoloration after they have been cut.

Peeling raw potatoes—Peel the potatoes under running water and move to cold water to cover as they are peeled; keep cold—even refrigerated if necessary—until ready to cook, or they will turn brown (I usually peel just before cooking).

Peeling parboiled potatoes—Score around the middle of a potato. Cook in boiling water 15 minutes. Drain then immerse in ice water. They should peel easily and can be further cooked as necessary.

Techniques for Mashed Potatoes

We don't know anyone who doesn't love mashed potatoes, and it's hard to make a batch that is a failure. But making them perfectly flavorful and fluffy is a technique that should be in every home cook's repertoire. Besides the potatoes, the main ingredients are fat, liquid, and seasonings:

Fats—Use the best butter available, but goose and duck fat are delicious, as is cream cheese. An Italian chef I know uses olive oil and mascarpone, the cream cheese of Italy.

Liquids—In order to keep the starch in the potatoes from seizing and getting gluey, potatoes need to be prevented from cooling during the mashing process, so the liquid needs to be hot when it is added to the potatoes. Add the boiling water back in for family meals, but for special occasions try whole milk, half-and-half, buttermilk, or cream. Heavy cream will give a richer product. Skim milk will do a moderately successful job. "Hot" is the operative word.

Seasonings—The other common ingredients are salt and pepper. Salt has become so important to gourmets that they disdain common table salt, pointing out its harsh iodine-like taste. Use kosher salt in the original water to boil the potatoes, then taste after the initial mashing. Taste again before adding the hot liquid, adding more salt if necessary. Pepper should be freshly ground for so sacred an occasion. Freshly ground white pepper is ideal because it can't be seen in the finished product and won't sully the potatoes, but freshly ground black pepper is just fine. Just try to avoid stale old pepper shaken out of the box or can.

Cooking—There are two things to know about time. First of all, mashed potatoes can be cooked ahead of time and reheated. And next, how long to cook the potatoes varies according to their size and age. For that reason, they should be cooked ahead of time. It is simply too stressful to be waiting for the potatoes to be done when everything else is finished. And unnecessary. To speed up the cooking time, cut the potatoes smaller and cook in a large quantity of boiling water. If time is no problem, leave them larger.

Boiling is a misnomer. It is, as my teacher once said, "too violent" a term. Cover the potatoes in salted water, bring to the boil, reduce to a simmer, and cover the pot to speed up the process.

Testing—When the potatoes appear done, pull out one and cool it enough to hold a small piece, testing to see if done. Rub it between fingers. Does it feel smooth, or is there a tiny or larger lump? Take the potatoes off the heat and drain them if satisfactory. Otherwise cook them longer. Drain in a colander. Return to the pot over heat and let "dry" a few minutes. Once rid of the excess water, the potatoes will absorb more of the yummy stuff, and be lighter and fluffier.

What kind of mash or whip is desired?
This is where memories of mother come in. If a mother had lumps in her mashed potatoes, they are craved; if she didn't, they may be abhorred—or vice versa. There are lumpy mashed potatoes that are delicious, smooth mashed potatoes that are satisfying, and even smashed mashed potatoes that are out of this world. Mashed potatoes can hold their shape stiffly enough to be piped on top of a shepherd's pie or so loose they run all over the plate (called "mousseline" potatoes). They can be mashed with a ricer, pushed through a fine sieve, or whipped (called whipped potatoes) with an electric hand mixer. So, the cook determines how lumpy and how runny they are.

Expectations contribute to happiness. If the texture doesn't suit, switch apparatus next time. But don't experiment at Thanksgiving when hosting guests. Save new methods of mashing for a family meal.

Mashing or whipping—A few minutes after "drying" the cooked potatoes, start to beat them with a potato masher or an electric hand mixer. A ricer also works. Insert the cooked potatoes in the ricer and press to extrude the potatoes. But avoid both a mouli-type sieve (one of those gadgets with a rotary handle over a disc with holes) and a wooden smasher, as both may result in gummy potatoes. Beat briefly, still over the low heat, until they start to fluff. If burning is a concern, add some butter to the pan at any time. Season to taste with salt. Add the hot liquid a little at a time and continue beating or whipping over the heat. Add butter, taste again, add salt and pepper, and the cook's work is done.

Keeping and reheating—Cover potatoes in the pan with some more hot milk or cream—about $1/3$ inch. Apply foil or plastic wrap to prevent a skin from forming. When ready to serve, remove the foil and reheat carefully in the pan over low heat, stirring in the liquid as it heats.

If cooking the potatoes a day in advance, cool and store in a well-sealed heavy-duty plastic bag. Move the potatoes to a bowl, cover with plastic wrap to keep a skin from forming, and reheat in the microwave until very hot. Or heat a pan with some butter, add the potatoes, and stir over heat continually until hot.

Freezing—I don't freeze my stellar, remember-me-forever potatoes, but I have frozen dishes that include mashed potatoes, like shepherd's pie.

Dried potatoes—One caveat: remember the rules. Use butter and cream, and don't tell anyone the truth.

WHIPPED, MASHED, OR RICED POTATOES

Serves 4

CERTAIN MEALS DEMAND MASHED POTATOES—*certainly Thanksgiving is one. But to have perfect holiday potatoes, practice makes perfect. Knowing the right pan, how much to make, and what family members like all take practice.*

2 pounds Idaho or Yukon Gold potatoes, peeled and cut into 1/2-inch cubes
Salt
2 tablespoons butter
1/2–1 cup milk, buttermilk, skim milk, or potato water, heated
Freshly ground black pepper

Add enough cold water to the potatoes to cover them by 1 inch in a heavy pot. Add 1 teaspoon salt and bring to the boil. Reduce the heat, cover, and simmer until soft, about 20 to 30 minutes. Drain well in a colander, reserving water as needed to add to mashed potatoes.

Add the butter to the empty pot and melt over low heat. Return the potatoes to the pot over a low heat and whip, mash, or rice as below to incorporate the butter. If the potatoes are more watery than desired, before adding the hot liquid, cook the potatoes with the butter until some of the liquid evaporates. Add some of the hot liquid and butter, and blend well. Continue adding milk, mashing or whipping constantly, until the desired consistency is reached. Season to taste with salt and pepper. If not serving immediately, cover with plastic wrap or foil, and see reheating instructions on page 225, then whip, beat, or mash as described on page 225 and below.

PERFECT MASHED POTATOES

There are three crucial steps in achieving this ideal: 1) cooking the potatoes sufficiently, 2) adding fat to the hot potatoes to coat the starch molecules, and 3) adding hot liquid to the potatoes over heat to let the starches swell. To check the doneness of the potatoes, remove a cube, cool enough to rub between two fingers, and see if lumps are gone. If not, cook the remaining ones longer. To finish the potatoes, select one of these methods:

- Mash or whip in the fat, then add the liquid over heat using a small electric hand mixer or sturdy whisk.
- Use a flat-bottomed masher or other heavy object to mash down the drained potatoes in the pan before stirring in hot liquid.
- Push the cooked potatoes through a ricer into the still hot pan with melted butter.

Variations:

- Substitute heavy cream, cream cheese, or mascarpone for rich mashed potatoes.
- Leave peel on and smash potatoes in the pot with a heavy object.
- Add roasted garlic or chopped fresh herbs.

ROASTED POTATOES, ONIONS, AND TURNIPS

Serves 6 to 8

THE EARTHY RICHNESS OF ROOT VEGETABLES *makes them an attractive fall and winter dish. When I grew up, all the meat drippings were saved, usually in a metal can next to the stove. The drippings were mixed willy-nilly and no one was concerned. While drippings add an enormous amount of flavor and color, nut butter or oil works as well. This recipe technique calls for browning the vegetables first on top of the stove. Note the variation calls for oven roasting.*

3 turnips, peeled
3 medium potatoes, peeled
3 medium carrots, peeled
3 medium onions, peeled
4–8 tablespoons meat drippings, butter, or oil
Salt
Freshly ground black pepper
1 tablespoon rosemary

Preheat oven to 400 degrees.

Cut the vegetables into quarters. Cover the turnips with water in a saucepan, bring to the boil, and boil 5 minutes.* Drain and dry on paper towels.

Meanwhile, heat the drippings in a large, heavy flameproof pan. Add enough of the potatoes to cover the bottom of the pan, brown on one side, and remove. Follow with the drained and dried turnips, also browning on one side. Cook the carrots briefly, browning lightly. It is not necessary to brown the onions, as they cook quickly; but if time is available, they will be a bit better if also browned on one side.

Return all the vegetables and juices to the pan and roast in the oven about 1 hour, turning every 15 minutes, until browned and crisp all over. Season to taste with salt and pepper. Crumble rosemary on top and serve hot.

**Root vegetables become bitter when old or larger than a baseball, so they should be blanched (page 159). They add so much to the flavor of the dish that it is worth the effort.*

Variations:

- Add quartered fennel bulb and cook as above.
- Green onions and shallot bulbs can be used as well.

RIBBONED POTATOES

Serves 4

WITH THE ADVENT OF NEW KITCHEN TOOLS, *there are many more methods of preparing and serving vegetables available to the home cook. The thinner a food is, the quicker it cooks. These ribboned potatoes are about as thin as one can get; once ribboned, they will cook quickly. Ribboned potatoes go farther than baked ones, so this amount should be sufficient for four people. These are pretty on the plate, quick cooking, and light eating.*

2–3 potatoes, peeled
2 tablespoons butter
2 tablespoons chopped fresh parsley
Salt
Freshly ground black pepper

To make ribbons, pare strips from the peeled potatoes with a vegetable peeler. Move strips to a bowl of cold water as peeling. Drain in a colander.

Heat the butter in a large skillet over medium-high heat. Add the potato ribbons and cook until tender, about 5 minutes, stirring constantly. Add the parsley, season to taste with salt and pepper, and serve hot.

Variation: Substitute sweet potatoes or try a vegetable mixture, such as potatoes and carrots.

STRETCHING FOOD

Singular units, like baked potatoes, are hard to serve to more than one person without seeming stingy or skimpy. The same unit cut into small pieces will serve more people. It's like the loaves and fishes parable. Perhaps it is because there is less waste—each person eats only what he or she truly want.

ROASTED FINGERLING POTATOES

Serves 4

FINGERLING (CREAMER) POTATOES *are magical accompaniments to almost anything, from a vegetarian meal to hearty steaks and chops. Their crisp brown exterior and soft interior make them beautiful and scrumptious. They are a repeat dish in our homes, winter or summer.*

1 pound small fingerling or creamer potatoes, well scrubbed and halved
1 1/2 tablespoons oil
Salt
Freshly ground black pepper
Chopped fresh rosemary, optional

Preheat oven to 350 degrees. Oil a 15 x 10-inch rimmed baking sheet, or spray with nonstick spray.

Toss the potatoes with enough of the oil to coat; season liberally with salt and pepper. Spread the potatoes on the baking sheet, allowing room between them. Roast in the oven, tossing once or twice with some rosemary, until the potatoes are soft in the center and a rich brown on the outside, 30 to 45 minutes, depending on size. Sprinkle with more rosemary.

Variations:

- Chop 4 garlic cloves and add to the oil before coating potatoes. Sprinkle generously with fresh rosemary before and after roasting.
- Cut Yukon Golds or other potatoes into 1 1/2-inch chunks and proceed as above.
- Toss the hot potatoes in 1 tablespoon mustard seed and return to the oven for another 5 minutes. Remove and add 2 tablespoons Dijon mustard, tossing with a spoon to coat the potatoes lightly. Season to taste with salt and pepper.

GARLIC-FLAVORED GIANT POTATO CAKE

Serves 6

ONE LARGE POTATO CAKE *is infinitely easier to cook than a number of smaller ones. It has an exterior crispness and brownness that far exceeds fried potatoes. Weighting down the potatoes in this recipe, and in the Anna's Potato Cake recipe (page 231), aids in pushing out the moisture from the potatoes, causing the potato cake to stick together as well as crisping the bottom of the cake. Potato cakes cut more easily with kitchen scissors or a pizza cutter than with a knife.*

2 pounds Yukon Gold or other medium-to-large potatoes, peeled
3–4 garlic cloves, chopped
2 tablespoons finely chopped fresh parsley
1 tablespoon finely chopped fresh oregano
Salt
Freshly ground black pepper
4–5 tablespoons butter or oil, cook's preference

Preheat oven to 450 degrees.

Use a sharp knife, food processor, or mandoline to cut the potatoes into julienne strips similar in size to a long grate. Toss with the garlic, parsley, oregano, salt, and pepper.

Heat the butter until sizzling in a heavy nonstick 9- or 10-inch pan or preferably a well-seasoned iron pan with a heatproof handle. Spread the potatoes over the bottom of the pan. Cover with buttered aluminum foil. Press down the foil with the bottom of another pan or heavy weight. Cook over medium heat until the bottom is brown, about 10 minutes. Move to the oven and bake 20 to 25 minutes, until the potatoes are tender and the bottom is crisp. Remove the foil and bake an additional 5 minutes. Place a heatproof serving dish over the pan. Using oven mitts, carefully flip the cake out onto a serving dish.

MANDOLINES

Mandolines, ultra-sharp kitchen slicers, used to be relegated to professional kitchens. I've always been a bit afraid of their ability to slice off a finger in no time. Now there are many safer varieties available in cookware stores that offer more slicing options to the home cook.

OVEN-PROOFING HANDLES

Know the maximum temperature of your specific pans—check the directions. Most will take up to 450 degrees. Wrap any nonmetal handle in layers of aluminum foil. *Avoid using wooden-handled pans in the oven.*

OVEN-CRISP POTATOES

Serves 4 to 6

THINLY SLICED POTATOES BRUSHED WITH OIL *and oven-crisped rival most fried ones. There is no pot of oil to deal with or discard, and these can be reheated or even served at room temperature. Don't bother freezing this dish.*

4 baking potatoes, peeled and sliced 1/8 inch thick
2 tablespoons oil
Salt
Freshly ground black pepper

Preheat oven to 400 degrees.

Slightly overlap the sliced potatoes in 2 large, well-oiled or nonstick cake or square pans. Brush with oil and sprinkle with salt and pepper. Bake 15 minutes, remove from oven and flip potatoes to the other side. Return to oven and bake 15 more minutes, until lightly browned and crisp on both sides. Slide carefully onto a serving dish, gathering any stray potatoes back on top. Cut with scissors or a pizza cutter to serve.

Variations:

- Sprinkle with 3 tablespoons chopped fresh herbs before or after baking.
- Arrange 5 slices of potato in an overlapping flower design about 4 inches across. Top with 3 smaller slices. Repeat as necessary until all potatoes are used and in a floral pattern. Brush with oil and continue with recipe as above.

SNACKING POTATOES

Serves 8

THE FRIEND WHO GAVE THIS RECIPE TO ME *always kept a container of these potatoes in the refrigerator for her teenage children to snack on rather than chips or dips. These can do double duty at picnics or on the buffet table.*

2 1/2 pounds fingerling or creamer potatoes, peeled if desired, cut into 1 1/2-inch cubes
1/2 cup chopped fresh parsley, chives, thyme, and/or basil
2 garlic cloves, chopped
1/4 teaspoon Dijon or dry mustard
1/2 cup olive oil
1/4 cup red wine vinegar
Salt
Freshly ground black pepper

Add the potatoes to a large pan of boiling water to cover. Return to the boil, cover, and reduce heat. Simmer 30 minutes, or until done. Drain well and move to a bowl. Whisk together the herbs, garlic, mustard, olive oil, and vinegar. Pour over the potatoes and toss gently. Season to taste with salt and pepper. Marinate at least 4 hours or up to a week, covered and refrigerated, preferably in a glass jar with a lid, stirring occasionally. Serve cold or at room temperature for a picnic, or reheat quickly in a frying pan or microwave for a buffet.

ANNA'S POTATO CAKE

Serves 4 to 6

ADAPTED FROM A FRENCH DISH *called Pommes Anna (Potatoes Anna), the exterior layers are buttery and crunchy and the interior moist and tender. For many of us, this is better than fried potatoes because the potatoes yield such a full flavor. Yum.*

1 1/2–1 3/4 pounds baking potatoes, peeled and sliced 1/8 inch thick*
Salt
Freshly ground black pepper
5–8 tablespoons butter, cut in pieces

Preheat oven to 400 degrees.

Thickly butter a 6-inch heavy, nonstick, well-seasoned frying pan or cake tin. Arrange the potatoes in overlapping circles to cover the base of the pan, making a pretty design. Add a second layer, continuing to overlap, and season with salt and pepper; dot with 4 to 5 pieces of butter. Continue to fill the pan with layers of potatoes (the first two layers and the last layer are the only ones that need to be pretty—the rest can be haphazard), seasoning and buttering every other layer. Butter a piece of aluminum foil and cover the potatoes and the pan. Put an ovenproof plate or heavy saucepan on top of the foil to press down on the potatoes.

Cook the potatoes on the stove over medium heat for 10 to 15 minutes to brown the bottom, checking to be sure it is not burning. When medium brown—the color of light caramel—move the pan to the oven, leaving the ovenproof plate on if it fits. Bake about 30 minutes, or until the potatoes are soft, depending on the number of potatoes. May be made ahead to this point and set aside if necessary, but it will suffer a bit. Reheat 10 minutes. Using oven mitts, turn out upside down on a serving dish, crust side up. To serve, cut with a knife or scissors.

**Thicker slices will work, but the melting quality of the interior layers of the cake will suffer a bit. A food processor or mandoline are handy tools for the nonprofessional cook.*

LAZY POTATO JEWELS

Serves 4

THESE JEWELS OF BEAUTIFULLY BROWNED CRISPY POTATOES *have the added virtue of being cooked ahead and reheated. No doubt a thrifty cook developed this way to get more life out of both the potato and the cook's time.*

1 pound potatoes, cut into 1–1½-inch chunks
2–3 tablespoons butter
2 tablespoons oil, cook's preference
2 garlic cloves, finely chopped
1 tablespoon ground fennel or coriander seed, optional
Salt
Freshly ground black pepper

Preheat oven to 250 degrees.

Bring a medium pot of water to the boil. Add the potatoes, reduce heat to a simmer, and parboil the potatoes until barely tender, 5 to 10 minutes, depending on the size. Drain. The boiled potatoes can be refrigerated for a day or so.

When ready to serve, add the butter and oil to a large roasting pan and melt in the preheated oven. Add the drained potatoes and cook, tossing occasionally, for 20 minutes, or until well browned. Remove from the oven, quickly stir in the optional fennel or coriander, return to the oven, and turn up the heat to 400 degrees. Continue roasting, stirring from time to time. Remove when golden and crisp, about ½ to 1 hour, depending on type of potato. Serve immediately when hot to get the most crunch.

SIMPLE BAKED POTATOES

Serves 6

THERE ARE TIMES *when a good baked potato is the best part of a day. Satisfying on its own, a favorite condiment can lift it to heavenly. If time is of the essence, insert a metal skewer through the potato before baking to speed up the baking time.*

6 baking potatoes
Salt
Freshly ground black pepper

Preheat oven to 500 degrees.

Prick the clean, dry potatoes several times with a fork and move to a rimmed baking sheet or oven rack. Bake for 1 to 1½ hours, until done. Cut a vertical slit down the top of the potato to release the steam (which keeps the potato light and fluffy) and season to taste with plenty of salt and pepper. Although potatoes lose some quality when baked ahead a few hours, they still are satisfactory reheated at 350 degrees for 15 minutes. Wrapping in aluminum foil makes them soggy.

Serve with butter, salt and pepper, sour cream, chives, yogurt, soft goat cheese, mascarpone, cream cheese, or grated Cheddar, as desired.

Variations:

- If time is short, cook the potatoes according to individual microwave directions. Move to a 500-degree preheated oven and bake for 10 minutes to crisp the skin before serving.
- Hundreds of recipes for twice-baked potatoes exist. They call for scooping out the center of the potato, mashing it with cheese or other ingredients, and re-baking it. Make up your own recipe and you can't go wrong.

ROBBINSVILLE FRIED RAMPS AND POTATOES

Serves 4 to 6

IN HIS BOOK SMOKEHOUSE HAM, SPOONBREAD, & SCUPPERNONG WINE, Joe Dabney writes that a sure sign of spring in the southern Appalachian Mountains is the deep green leaves of the ramp shooting up through the warming ground. A relative of the onion and garlic family, this wild leek is known for its pungent taste and aroma that lingers like a cloud around the eater for hours. Celebrated with festivals in West Virginia, Tennessee, North Carolina, and Georgia, the ramp is used in small amounts as one would an onion in salads, or in larger quantities, as below, with potatoes and eggs as a meal-in-one. Look for them in local greenmarkets.

1 quart ramps
3 tablespoons bacon drippings or oil, cook's preference
3 medium potatoes
3 large eggs

Wash the ramps, including the leaves, and cut into 1-inch pieces. Peel and chop the potatoes into 1-inch cubes. Heat the bacon fat in a heavy pan; cook the ramps and potatoes until the potatoes are brown and cooked through. Beat the eggs together lightly, pour over the potatoes, and stir. Cook for 2 minutes, until the eggs begin to set on the bottom; turn and fry on the other side for 2 to 3 minutes, until the eggs are cooked.

PICKLED RAMPS

Makes 1 pint
1 cup rice wine vinegar
1 cup water
1 cup granulated sugar
1 teaspoon coriander seed
1 teaspoon peppercorns
1 pound ramps

Mix together vinegar, water, and sugar in a saucepan and bring to the boil. Stir occasionally until the sugar is dissolved. Remove from the heat and add coriander and peppercorns.

Clean the ramps and remove any greens where the green begins on the stalk for another use (excellent pan-sautéed to serve with meats or chicken). Cut off the root end of the ramp. Move the ramps to a pot of boiling salted water to blanch 1 minute. Transfer ramps to a bowl of ice water to stop the cooking.

When both the ramps and the vinegar mixture are cool, combine them in a 1-pint jar and refrigerate. Ramps will be ready to eat in about 5 days.

SUMMER SQUASH

Summer squash grow during the warm months and can seem to overtake a garden. They include pattypan, crookneck yellow, straightneck, and zucchini. Small to medium-size squash are preferable to large ones. The larger squash tend to have more seeds and are more watery, and therefore have less flavor. Look for squash with firm, glossy skin. Store squash loosely wrapped in plastic in the refrigerator.

Every Southern gardener thrills to see the first zucchini of the season, and loathes picking it by the end of summer. As one of the South's most prolific home-garden crops, zucchini grows well in our soil and climate and has kept Southern cooks on their toes inventing new ways to bring the bounty to the table.

Similar to crookneck and yellow squash, zucchini can be substituted in most recipes calling for those squashes, although zucchini has a more distinctive taste. Salting (degorging, page 200) the sliced zucchini before using in casseroles intensifies the zucchini's flavor and causes it to shed about 20 percent of its water. Salting is a must to batter-fry or brown zucchini. Smaller zucchini contain less water, and needn't be salted, but by the end of the summer, the larger ones can't be avoided.

ZUCCHINI AND CELERY SAUTÉ

Serves 4

THESE CONTRASTING GREENS *add crunch and unexpected excitement to a meal. Shaping these vegetables into sticks (batons) enhances their flavor.*

1 tablespoon oil, cook's preference
1 tablespoon butter
4 celery ribs, sliced into 1/2-inch diagonal slices
3 small zucchini, cut into 1 1/2-inch-long sticks (batons)
2 garlic cloves, chopped
1 tablespoon chopped fresh parsley
Salt
Freshly ground black pepper

Heat the oil and butter in a large frying pan. Add the celery slices and sauté for 2 minutes. Add the zucchini sticks and sauté with the celery 2 minutes longer, or until crisp-tender. Reduce the heat to medium, add the garlic and parsley, and sauté 1 minute longer. Season to taste with salt and pepper. Serve hot. May be made a day or two ahead and reheated.

SPICY YELLOW AND GREEN SQUASH SAUTÉ

Serves 4

THIS EARTHY, SPICY DISH *is a dashing accompaniment to strongly flavored main courses. While having its own distinct flavor, squash easily accommodates other flavors such as garlic and hot peppers. It also changes its flavor as juices concentrate while the vegetables brown.*

2 tablespoons oil, cook's preference
1 small onion, thickly sliced
1 garlic clove, chopped
1/2 jalapeño or other small hot pepper, seeded and chopped, divided, optional
2 yellow squash, cut into 1/2-inch slices
2 zucchini, cut into 1/2-inch slices
Salt
Freshly ground black pepper

Heat the oil in a large skillet. Add the onion, garlic, half of the jalapeño if using, yellow squash, and zucchini. Sauté over medium heat until the vegetables are tender and just beginning to brown, about 10 minutes. Season to taste with remaining jalapeño, salt, and pepper.

SEEDING A HOT PEPPER

Wearing rubber gloves or small plastic bags on both hands, cut the pepper in half. Use the tip of a knife and fingers to remove and discard the seeds and membrane they're attached to. Store any remaining pepper for a later use or discard.

SOME LIKE IT HOT

The size of a pepper is an indication of its spiciness. As a rule of thumb, the smaller the pepper, the hotter. Scotch bonnets are small and very hot peppers popular in Florida and the Islands, and one-fourth of one would be a very peppy ingredient.

GRATED ZUCCHINI

Serves 6

GRATED VEGETABLES BECAME FASHIONABLE *in the 1980s. Until then, the idea of grating any vegetable except cabbage and potatoes was unknown. Interestingly, grating a vegetable changes both its texture and its flavor, a near-total personality transformation.*

4–6 medium zucchini, grated
6 tablespoons butter, divided
2–3 tablespoons minced shallots, scallions, or onions
Salt
Freshly ground black pepper

Move the grated zucchini to a colander placed over a bowl or sink and sprinkle liberally with salt. Let rest 15 minutes. Rinse, squeeze, and dry the zucchini with paper towels.

Melt 3 tablespoons butter in a large skillet. Add shallots and then zucchini. Toss for 4 to 5 minutes over high heat, until tender but crunchy. Season to taste with salt and pepper. May be prepared to this point several hours ahead of serving. Shortly before serving, toss it in the pan over high heat with the remaining 3 tablespoons butter. Transfer to a hot dish and serve immediately.

Variation: Mix equal amounts of grated carrots and zucchini and proceed as above.

OVEN-BAKED SQUASH ROUNDS

Serves 4

IF THE OVEN IS ALREADY HOT, *these tasty rounds make a congenial, crunchy side dish with little effort.*

4 yellow or zucchini squash, sliced into 1-inch rounds or on the diagonal
1 tablespoon oil, cook's preference
1 garlic clove, chopped
Salt
Freshly ground black pepper

Preheat oven to 350 degrees.

Toss the squash, oil, and garlic together in a bowl. Season to taste with salt and pepper. Spread the squash on a large rimmed baking sheet and bake until tender but still slightly crunchy, 20 to 25 minutes.

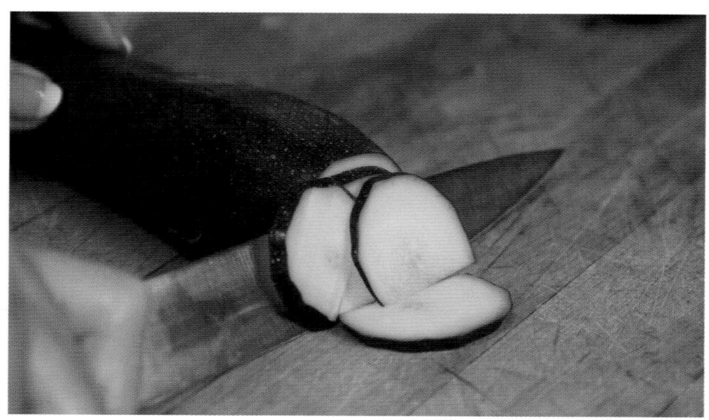

BROILED OR GRILLED ZUCCHINI AND RED PEPPER

Serves 4

IN ONLY 30 OR 40 YEARS, *these two vegetables have overtaken the use of yellow crookneck squash and green bell peppers on the grill and broiler. Perhaps it is our predilection for red and green; more likely it is the sweetness of the ripe red pepper compared to the near acrid flavor of the green bell pepper, and the shape of the zucchini makes it easier to cut. Even more water is extruded than usual when grilling zucchini, so the flavor is particularly intensified.*

- 3 zucchini, cut lengthwise into 1/4-inch slices
- 1/2 red bell pepper, cored, seeded, and cut lengthwise into 2-inch wedges
- 1/2 tablespoon oil, cook's preference
- 1/2 tablespoon red wine vinegar
- 1 tablespoon freshly grated Parmesan cheese
- Salt
- Freshly ground black pepper

Heat the broiler or grill. Brush sliced squash and red pepper with oil. Grill about 4 minutes per side. Remove to a large bowl and toss with vinegar and Parmesan. Season to taste with salt and pepper. Serve warm or at room temperature.

Variation: Whole Baked Squash
My mother-in-law Celeste would remove a small wedge from the top of the squash and insert an equal-sized slice of onion. Dot with butter, or drizzle with oil and bake at 350 degrees for 30 minutes, until squash yields to the touch but is not soft.

LAYERED ZUCCHINI AND TOMATOES

Serves 2 to 4

THERE'S A NATURAL AFFINITY *among vegetables that ripen in the same time period. The marriage of zucchini and tomatoes is one of the best. Degorge the zucchini (page 200), regardless of its size, to remove extra liquid, rather than the usual removal of bitterness.*

2 small zucchini, trimmed and sliced lengthwise into 1/4-inch slices
2 tomatoes, sliced horizontally into 1/4-inch slices and drained on paper towels
1/2 teaspoon salt
1/2 teaspoon freshly ground black pepper
1/2 cup dry breadcrumbs
1/2 tablespoon chopped oregano
1/2 cup grated Swiss cheese
1/2 cup freshly grated Parmesan cheese
1 1/2 tablespoons butter

Preheat oven to 400 degrees. Butter a 9 x 9 baking dish.

Sprinkle the sliced zucchini with salt and move to a colander placed over a bowl or sink. Let rest 15 minutes. Rinse and dry the zucchini.

Layer half the zucchini in the baking dish. Follow with half the tomatoes. Sprinkle with salt and pepper.

Mix together the breadcrumbs, oregano, and cheeses. Sprinkle half over the zucchini and tomatoes. Repeat layering one more time, ending with cheese mixture. Dot with butter, and bake until golden brown and bubbly, about 20 to 25 minutes. May be made several days ahead and reheated. Leftovers freeze fine for the family.

STUFFED SQUASH AND ZUCCHINI BOATS

Serves 6

NO RECIPE FOR A STUFFED VEGETABLE *can be exact, as none of the vegetables are consistent in size time after time. It is better to have extra stuffing than not enough, and the extra can be refrigerated or frozen for another time, or baked in a ramekin for a cook's treat. This recipe will also work for those canoe-sized, end-of-season zucchini; cook them longer.*

6 small zucchini or yellow squash
6 tablespoons butter, divided
1 onion, chopped
2 garlic cloves, chopped
1 cup grated cheese, preferably Gruyère and fresh Parmesan
2–3 tablespoons chopped fresh herbs such as thyme, oregano, or basil, optional
Salt
Freshly ground black pepper
1/2 cup breadcrumbs

Preheat oven to 350 degrees.

Halve the squash and scoop out the pulp, leaving the inside walls of the vegetable intact to form boats. Set aside; chop any broken ones and add to the pulp as necessary to fill the other boats. Cook the "boats" in the microwave until soft, just a few minutes; or add to a pot of boiling water and cook until soft, approximately 10 minutes, and drain.

Meanwhile, melt 3 tablespoons of butter in a heavy saucepan. Add the onion and chopped squash, and cook until the onion is translucent. Add the garlic and cook a few minutes more. Cool slightly and add the cheese. Taste for seasoning, add the herbs, and season with salt and pepper.

Move the boats to a rimmed baking sheet and fill with the mixture. Top the boats with breadcrumbs and dot with remaining butter. Bake 15 minutes, or until heated through. Serve hot. May be refrigerated or frozen, wrapped well. Defrost and reheat until heated through, approximately 15 minutes.

SQUASH CASSEROLE

Serves 6 to 8

SOUTHERN SIDEBOARDS GROAN *under the weight of luscious casseroles like this classic dish. This is without a doubt the most popular recipe I've ever included in a cookbook. The squash will taste better if sautéed first.*

- $1\frac{1}{4}$ cups butter, divided
- 2 medium onions, chopped
- 1 green bell pepper, seeded and chopped
- 1 red bell pepper, seeded and chopped
- 2 garlic cloves, finely chopped
- 2 pounds yellow crookneck or zucchini squash, sliced
- 2 cups grated sharp Cheddar cheese or Gruyère, divided
- 4 large eggs, beaten to mix
- $1\frac{1}{2}$ cups chopped pecans, divided
- Dash hot sauce or Tabasco, optional
- 1 cup breadcrumbs

Preheat oven to 350 degrees. Butter a large casserole dish and set aside.

Melt $\frac{1}{4}$ cup of the butter in a large skillet and sauté the onions and peppers until soft. Add the garlic and cook 1 minute then set aside.

Bring to the boil a pot filled with enough water to cover the squash, and add the squash. Cook until tender, about 10 minutes. Drain and return squash to the pot. Mash the squash until thoroughly broken into small pieces. Add $\frac{1}{2}$ cup butter, 1 cup cheese, eggs, onion mixture, and 1 cup pecans. Season to taste with hot sauce if desired, and stir well to mix.

Move mixture into the prepared casserole dish. Combine the breadcrumbs with the remaining cheese and pecans. Spread evenly over squash mixture. Dot with remaining butter and bake 45 to 60 minutes, until bubbly. Serve hot. Dish can be made ahead several days, covered and refrigerated, or frozen. Defrost before reheating.

Summer squash, such as zucchini and yellow crookneck are harvested and eaten while the vegetable is still in an immature state. Left to grow on the vine, they develop a tough outer skin, as does winter squash.

WINTER SQUASH

Numerous varieties of winter squash are available in the South, including acorn, butternut, and spaghetti. Grown in the summer, winter squash take longer to mature and are harvested when the cooler fall weather begins.

Select heavy, firm squash, as they will have moist, dense flesh. Store in a cool, dry place. If out on the counter on display, use within a week.

SORGHUM OR SWEET MOLASSES ACORN SQUASH

Serves 4 to 6

THICK SORGHUM-SWEET MOLASSES *was prevalent as table syrup during World War II, but is seen less frequently today, although the plant itself is a leading food grain. Maple syrup is a good substitute. Do try to get 100 percent maple syrup and not corn syrup with maple flavoring, which is quite a different syrup.*

- 2 acorn squash, seeded and cut into 3/4-inch rings
- 1/4 cup butter
- 1/4 cup sorghum, molasses, or pure maple syrup
- 1/2 teaspoon freshly grated nutmeg

Preheat oven to 400 degrees.

Overlap the squash rings slightly in a baking dish. Melt the butter in a small saucepan, add the syrup, and cook 1 minute, just until bubbly. Pour over the squash and sprinkle with nutmeg. Cover the pan with foil and bake for 30 minutes. Uncover and bake 10 minutes more, or until the squash is tender.

Both summer and winter squash take well to roasting, becoming fuller and richer in flavor. Roast whole or halved at 350 degrees. To roast whole, leaving skin on, prick a few times to prevent splitting, or slit as on page 237. Bake until fork-tender. To roast halved, dot with butter, salt, and freshly chopped herbs. Or top with grated cheese and continue to roast until melted, 5 to 10 minutes. Serve with roasted pecans.

SWEET POTATOES

Sweet potatoes are available year-round and especially in the fall or winter after the first freeze. They are not botanically related to yams but are frequently called yams, particularly when canned, causing great confusion. Canned "yams" can be used like sweet potatoes. Sweet potatoes should be stored in a cool place but not refrigerated. They should be firm and uniformly shaped.

The skin is full of nutrients, so use it when possible. Scrub the skin with a soft brush under cold running water to remove any dirt.

SAUTÉED SWEET POTATOES WITH PECANS

Serves 4 to 6

THIS IS EVEN BETTER *than sweet potato chips because of the caramelization around the edges. It is the first way I cook sweet potatoes when they come into season, anticipated for weeks.*

3 sweet potatoes
6–8 tablespoons butter, divided
1/2 cup chopped or halved pecans

Peel the sweet potatoes and slice as thinly as possible. (A mandoline will work to slice younger sweet potatoes but will frequently balk at tougher ones.) Heat 3 tablespoons of butter in a large heavy skillet. Add enough potatoes to cover the bottom of the pan. Cook until lightly browned and "puffy," with perhaps a speck of black in them. Turn gently and brown the other side. Remove to a serving dish. Repeat with 3 more tablespoons of butter and the remaining potatoes, cooking until lightly browned. Add the remaining 2 tablespoons of butter to the skillet, toss in the pecans, and brown lightly. Pour over the potatoes. Serve hot, but these are also delicious at any temperature.

SKILLET-COOKED BROWN SUGAR SWEET POTATOES

Serves 4

THE FAMED SOUTHERN SWEET TOOTH *is bared for all to see when it comes to sweet potatoes and brown sugar. This is certainly a family or holiday favorite.*

4 medium sweet potatoes
Water
1/2–1 cup light or dark brown sugar
1/2 cup butter
1 teaspoon salt
1/2–1 cup roasted chopped pecans

Peel the potatoes, cut them into 2-inch-thick slices, and move to a wide, heavy skillet. Add water to a quarter of the way up the sides of the pan, cover, and cook slowly until they can be pierced with a fork.

Remove from the heat and drain water from the pan. Sprinkle the sugar over the potatoes, add butter and salt, and return to low heat. Cook slowly, uncovered, until the liquid is sticky. Toss in pecans and serve hot. May be made in advance and reheated.

BAKED SWEET POTATOES

Serves 2

THE SWEET POTATO *has been a godsend to Southerners. During hard times, a cold baked sweet potato might be lunch for a schoolgirl or supper for a single person.*

2 large sweet potatoes

Salt
Freshly ground black pepper

Butter

Preheat oven to 450 degrees.

Remove any blemishes from the potatoes with a knife. Pierce the potatoes in several places with a fork. Bake 45 to 60 minutes, until a fork can penetrate the flesh of the potatoes. Split with a knife just before serving. Season to taste with salt, pepper, and butter.

Variation: Season to taste with butter, brown sugar, and ground cinnamon.

Boiling sweet potatoes is like boiling any other potato: cover peeled and cubed sweet potatoes with water and bring to the boil. Reduce heat, cover, and simmer until tender when pierced with a fork.

TWICE-BAKED STUFFED SWEET POTATOES WITH GREENS

Serves 8

GREENS AND SWEET POTATOES *arrive in the kitchen at around the same time in the fall as hog-killing time. In celebration of their compatibility, this dish dolls up the potatoes with bacon and sweet potato or other greens.*

4 medium sweet potatoes, unpeeled and washed
6 slices bacon, cooked crisp and crumbled, drippings reserved
4 green onions or scallions, sliced

1 cup cooked chopped greens, fresh or frozen, drained
1/4 cup butter, softened
1/2 cup heavy cream, heated
1/2 cup freshly grated Parmesan cheese

Ground hot red pepper
Salt
Freshly ground black pepper
1 cup finely grated Gruyère or Swiss cheese

Preheat oven to 350 degrees.

Pierce the sweet potatoes with a knife several times. Bake 60 to 75 minutes, until soft. When cool, slice each potato in half lengthwise. Hollow out the center with a spoon, taking care to leave the skin intact. Move the flesh to a bowl.

Reheat 2 tablespoons reserved drippings in a heavy skillet. Add the green onions and sauté briefly over medium heat. Add the crumbled bacon and greens. Stir and set aside.

Whip the sweet potatoes with an electric hand mixer or mash them with a potato masher in a large bowl until smooth, adding the butter, cream, and Parmesan. Season to taste with hot red pepper, salt, and black pepper. Fold the bacon-onions-greens mixture into the potatoes. Divide the mixture evenly among the 8 potato shells, mounding the mixture; top with the cheese. The potatoes can be made ahead to this point. Bake the room-temperature potatoes on a rimmed baking sheet until the cheese is melted and the potatoes are heated through, about 20 to 30 minutes.

SWEET POTATO AND TURNIP GRATIN

Serves 10 to 12

An exciting alternative to a potato gratin, *turnips and sweet potatoes complement each other beautifully, particularly when large turnips are blanched to remove their bitterness.*

2–3 pounds white turnips, peeled and sliced 1/4 inch thick
2–3 pounds sweet potatoes, peeled and sliced 1/4 inch thick
1/2 cup butter
1–2 tablespoons finely chopped fresh thyme, oregano, or tarragon
Salt
Freshly ground black pepper
1 1/2 cups grated Parmesan and/or Gruyère cheese
1 cup breadcrumbs
2 cups heavy cream

Preheat oven to 350 degrees. Butter a 3-quart casserole.

To remove their bitterness, add turnips to a pot of boiling water, cook 5 minutes to blanch them, and then drain thoroughly.

Gently combine the turnips and sweet potatoes. Cover the bottom of the casserole with a layer of the vegetables and dot with butter. Sprinkle generously with half of the herbs, salt, and pepper, and cover with half the cheese. Make another layer, finishing off with the herbs, butter, and cheese. Pour the cream around the sides. Cover with foil.

Bake until the vegetables are soft but not mushy, about 1 hour. Remove the foil and bake an additional 30 minutes. May be made several days ahead or frozen up to 3 months. Defrost in the refrigerator and reheat for 30 to 45 minutes in the oven, or reheat in the microwave, uncovered.

Variations:

- Use turnips and no sweet potatoes for Turnip Gratin.
- Use sweet potatoes and no turnips for Sweet Potato Gratin.
- Use a combination of zucchini and/or white potatoes.

TOMATOES

Ripe tomatoes are ones that make a tomato sandwich taste like a tomato sandwich ought to taste. When ripe, they leave white bread slightly soggy with juice. They taste like summer, lush and fulsome. Who can forget their first ripe tomato of the season? Tomatoes can be beautiful or funny-looking—bifurcated, scalloped, black, nearly blue, deep red, yellow and red, striped red and green, oval, or fat and bumpy.

Tomatoes prefer not to be refrigerated and are best when allowed to sit a day or two after being picked.

There are over five thousand varieties of heirloom tomatoes. Their names are exotic, and some, like the Brandywine, are as generic as "Chablis" is to white wine, with many permutations. Although the name "heirloom tomatoes" was supposed to mean seeds that have been passed down and are not hybrids, the category is much vaguer than that, and not all heirlooms are heirlooms. Most recently, there are new versions coming in from Russia and the Eastern Bloc, for instance.

Using fresh tomatoes is very easy. Just follow these guidelines:

Slicing a tomato—Cut tomato in half. Turn cut side down. Slice in desired thickness either horizontally or vertically.

Chopping a tomato—Cut tomato in half. Turn cut side down. Cut into tomato horizontally, from blossom end to stem end, parallel with the board, going up to, but not through, the stem end. Cut down vertically as in slices above, also not going through stem end. Cut down vertically again, perpendicular to the previous cuts, creating cubes.

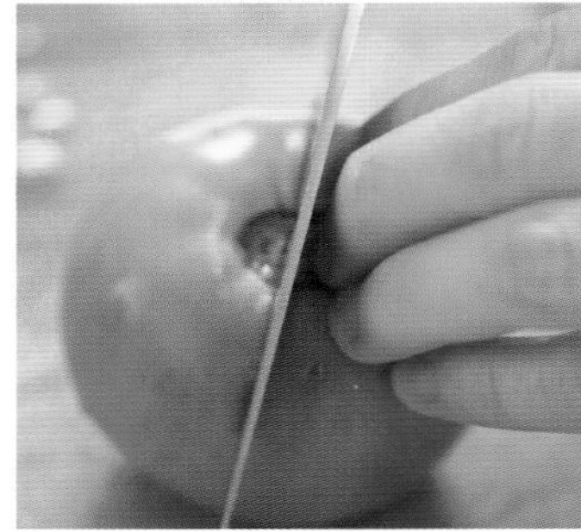

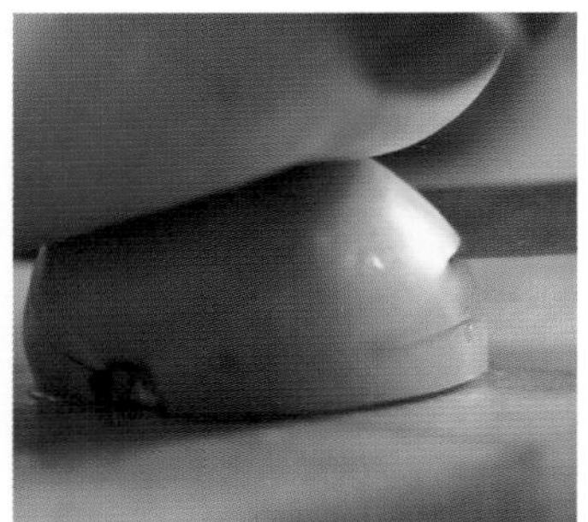

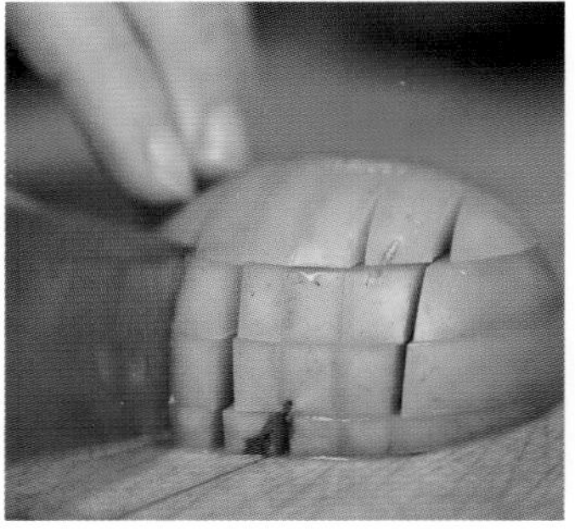

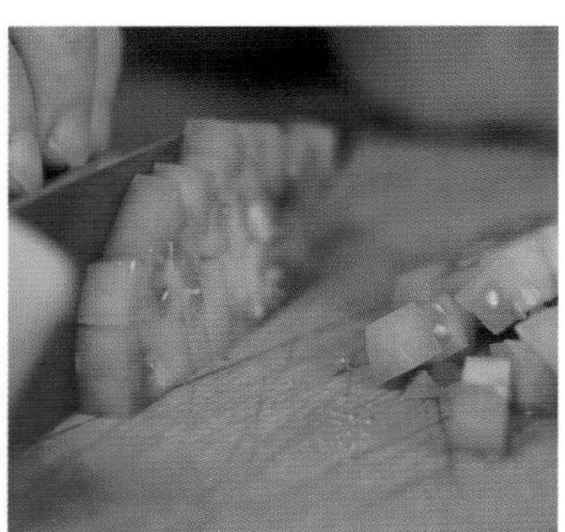

Seeding a tomato—This is a true nicety. Halve or quarter a tomato. Slip fingers or a small spoon under the "throat" and push seeds out into a strainer over a bowl, reserving juice if needed and discarding seeds. You may remove the throat (core) altogether using a knife.

Storing a cut-up tomato—Chop up a half-used tomato, sprinkled with a little salt and vinegar, cover, and refrigerate. The tomato will marinate in its own juices and make a perfect accompaniment to a piece of mozzarella, a nice addition to a salad, or a delicious snack on its own. It will last a day or two longer this way.

Freezing tomatoes—When too many tomatoes present themselves and there's no time to cook them, move clean whole tomatoes to a rimmed baking sheet and freeze. When frozen, move them off the sheet into a freezer-type plastic bag. They will stay there quite happily until time to use. They will be easy to peel, and although not suitable to serve raw or in a salad, they are a welcome addition to a conserve (like a ketchup), spaghetti sauce, soup, or a cooked dish.

TOMATO SANDWICHES

We would be remiss if we didn't mention tomato sandwiches. Spread a piece of white loaf bread with mayonnaise or butter. Slice the ripest, juiciest tomato available and place on the bread. Top with another slice of bread spread with mayo or butter. To serve for a starter or special function, leave open-faced, removing crusts, and cut into triangles. Best peeled for a fancy occasion, but certainly not for a private sandwich.

ROBERTA'S TOMATOES AND CUCUMBERS

Serves 4 to 6

Roberta O'Neill Salma and I worked together when we were young women, and we've kept our friendship alive. She is a painter and she makes simple ingredients look like art, her food tasting as good as it looks. Her husband shops for the fruit and vegetables and is very picky.

Salt brings out the liquid in the tomatoes, making a mouthwatering tomato juice. The vinegar is not needed if the tomatoes are ripe and juicy.

2 pounds ripe tomatoes cut into 1/2-inch cubes
1–2 teaspoons salt
Freshly ground black pepper
1/2 cup finely chopped fresh parsley or basil
Up to 1/4 cup red wine vinegar, if needed
2 pounds cucumbers, cut into 1/2-inch cubes
2 tablespoons chopped fresh basil, or other fresh herb, optional

Sprinkle the tomatoes well with salt and pepper, and toss with the parsley. Cover and leave 1 hour or up to 2 days to extrude the juices. Taste and add vinegar if necessary.

Sprinkle the cucumbers with salt and let sit in a colander over the sink for 30 minutes. Rinse well and drain. Stir into the tomatoes. Add chopped herbs if using, stir, and pour into a serving bowl.

Variation: Add a few thin slices of red onion.

TOMATO ROSES

To make a tomato rose, peel off the skin from a tomato using a special tomato or vegetable peeler, preferably in one long strip. Roll the skin conically, and then loosen one end to open as a rose.

OVEN-ROASTED TOMATOES

Makes ½ cups

OVEN-ROASTED TOMATOES *are the twenty-first-century replacement for the sun-dried tomatoes of the 1980s. Roasting them takes advantage of tomatoes in season for future use and also fortifies the flavors when they are not at their peak by evaporating moisture from the tomatoes and concentrating their tomato essence. I also roast them when my tomatoes are almost too ripe and nearly over the hill, rather than tossing them out. Select most any kind of herbs.*

As the tomatoes caramelize, they may get a little black around the edges. To many tomato aficionados, like us, this can only make them better.

2 pounds tomatoes
2 tablespoons oil, cook's preference
Salt
2–3 tablespoons chopped basil, thyme, or oregano

Preheat oven to 450 degrees.

Slice large tomatoes into ¼-inch-thick slices, or in wedges if small. Oil or foil-line a rimmed baking sheet. Add the tomatoes in a single layer, not touching each other. Sprinkle with salt and herbs. Drizzle the tops of the tomatoes with the oil. Bake for 30 minutes to 1 hour, or until the liquid has evaporated and the tomatoes are curled around the edges.

Cool tomatoes, move to a container, and top with 2 tablespoons of oil. Use as directed in a recipe or freeze for future use.

Variation: Slow-Roasted Tomatoes
Cook 4 to 5 hours at 275 degrees.

Variation: Charred Tomatoes
Heat a large frying pan until very hot, adding 1 tablespoon oil and 2 pints cherry or grape tomatoes. Sauté 2 to 3 minutes, until barely charred. Season to taste with salt and pepper.

Variation: Roasted Grape Tomatoes
Halve the tomatoes and move cut side down onto an oiled or foil-lined rimmed baking sheet. Bake at 400 degrees 30 minutes, and follow directions above, taking care to check often, as these cook more quickly.

Pale pink tomatoes (usually store-bought) rarely taste like a tomato ought to taste. They have been bred to be uniform in size for easy packing and shipping, their skins tough enough to prevent cracks. They are picked green, gassed, and never really turn red. Avoid them.

BASIL AND CHEESE-STUFFED TOMATOES

Serves 4

The only way tomatoes were baked *and stuffed when I was young was with an onion and bread stuffing. This is a more modern way.*

4 medium tomatoes
2 tablespoons chopped fresh parsley and/or thyme
2 tablespoons chopped fresh basil
1 garlic clove, chopped
1/4 cup oil, cook's preference
Salt
Freshly ground black pepper
4 slices Fontina, Gruyère, mozzarella, or good Cheddar cheese
Basil leaves and parsley sprigs for garnish

Preheat oven to 450 degrees. Oil an ovenproof casserole dish.

Slice the stem ends off the tomatoes (reserve for decoration) and scoop out the inside pulp and seeds (page 27). Drain completely, upside down on a rack.

Mix the parsley, basil, garlic, and oil. Season to taste with salt and pepper.

Move the tomatoes, open side up, to the oiled casserole. Divide the herb filling among the drained tomatoes. Bake for about 5 minutes. Top each tomato with a slice of cheese and return to the oven for another 10 minutes. Serve hot, garnished with basil leaves and parsley sprigs. If pretty, set the stem ends back on top of the tomatoes like caps.

Variation: Add crabmeat or chopped shrimp for a simple lunch.

Variation: Stuffed Cherry Tomatoes
Slice tops off cherry tomatoes and remove seeds with a grapefruit spoon. Fill tomatoes with herb filling as above. Bake at 350 degrees, checking every few minutes, baking only until still barely firm.

FRIED GREEN TOMATOES

Serves 4

THERE ARE MANY VARIETIES OF FRIED GREEN TOMATOES, *with batter-fried the most prominently presented due to the movie* Fried Green Tomatoes. *My friend Cynthia Hizer was the food stylist for the movie and has stories of the many she had to make during the course of filming. Quite a lot!*

For me, the tomatoes star, and their combination of firmness and sharpness are enhanced when lightly dipped into flour or cornmeal—or, in this case, both together. Crisp sautéed crumbs trap in the juiciness to let it explode in the mouth.

Since the tomatoes are not dipped in a wet batter before being dredged in the mixture of flour and cornmeal, the mixture will not adhere to the skin part of the tomato slice. This is not a problem, but it can be avoided by peeling the tomatoes prior to slicing.

2–3 green tomatoes, preferably peeled
1/3 cup all-purpose flour
1/3 cup cornmeal
Salt
Freshly ground black pepper
Shortening, butter, or oil for frying

Slice tomatoes in 1/2-inch slices. Mix flour and cornmeal together on a piece of waxed paper. Season flour to taste with salt and pepper. Coat both sides of tomato slices in flour mixture, dusting to remove excess. Set aside.

Meanwhile, heat enough oil to coat the bottom of a frying pan or cast-iron skillet until it shimmers when a drop of water is added. Coat the tomatoes again before adding them to the hot oil, in batches as necessary. Cook until golden brown, flip, and cook until the second side is lightly browned. The second side will not be as beautiful as the first. Drain the cooked tomatoes on a paper towel while frying any remaining slices. Serve hot.

ROASTED TOMATO CORNBREAD CRUMBLE

Serves 6

MY APPRENTICE ERIN SIMPSON *originated this recipe one day when we had too many tomatoes. We enjoyed it the first day and refrigerated the remainders in the dish. We found ourselves reheating what was left over the next few days, and each day it was better. This is definitely an ideal make-ahead-and-reheat dish, though it can be served right away. A rough-textured breadcrumb can be substituted for the Crumb Topping.*

- $2^{1}/_{2}$ pounds ripe plum tomatoes, cored and quartered
- 2 garlic cloves, chopped
- 2 teaspoons chopped fresh thyme, optional
- 1 tablespoon chopped fresh rosemary
- Salt
- Freshly ground black pepper
- 1 tablespoon oil, cook's preference

Crumb Topping

- $^{1}/_{2}$ cup all-purpose flour
- $^{1}/_{2}$ cup cornbread or breadcrumbs
- 2 tablespoons cold butter, cut into small pieces
- $^{1}/_{2}$ cup freshly grated Parmesan cheese

Preheat oven to 300 degrees. Oil a baking dish or pan.

Move tomatoes to the oiled dish. Sprinkle garlic, thyme, and rosemary over the top. Season to taste with salt and pepper, and drizzle the oil over the tomatoes. Cover with a layer of parchment or waxed paper topped with foil. Bake for 1 hour.

Meanwhile, make the crumb topping by pulsing the flour, breadcrumbs, and butter in a food processor or by cutting in the butter until it is in pea-sized bits. Stir in the Parmesan. This can be made ahead of time and kept chilled until ready to use.

Remove the roasted tomatoes from the oven. Using a slotted spoon, transfer the tomatoes to an oiled 1-quart oval gratin dish; reserve tomato liquid for another use or discard. Top tomatoes with crumb mixture, pressing it down gently with fingers. Bake for 10 minutes, until heated through and golden brown.

TURNIPS

Small spring turnips with the greens still attached are a delightful vegetable needing only minimal cooking. The larger "storage turnips" are best peeled and blanched (page 159) before continuing with a recipe.

Spring turnips can be stored for a few days in the refrigerator, and storage turnips will last a few weeks.

GRATED AND SAUTÉED TURNIPS

Serves 6

The grated turnips are a snappy base *by themselves, but with other ingredients (as in the variations), they become even more glamorous on the plate.*

1 pound turnips, peeled and grated
4 tablespoons butter
Salt
Freshly ground black pepper
1/2 cup pecan halves, sautéed in 3 tablespoons butter

If the grated turnips are small, they do not need blanching for this recipe. If they are larger than a golf ball, bring a large pot of water to the boil and blanch the grated turnips by cooking 1 to 2 minutes to remove the strong taste. Drain well and dry with paper towels.

Heat the butter in a large skillet or frying pan. Add the drained turnips and toss in the butter for 5 minutes. Taste and add salt and pepper as desired. May be made ahead to this point. When ready to eat, add the sautéed pecans and toss over high heat 2 to 3 minutes.

Variations:

- Use 1/2 pound grated turnips and 1/2 pound grated zucchini or carrots. Add 3 tablespoons fresh herbs if desired, preferably mint, basil, and lemon balm.
- Add sliced onion, 2 chopped garlic cloves, and a quarter-sized slice of fresh ginger, chopped, along with the turnips and any of the other ingredients in the above variations. Sprinkle with hot sauce or soy sauce before serving.

GINGERED VEGETABLE MEDLEY

Serves 4

Julienned *and grated vegetables cook very quickly. Stray vegetables in the bin can be mixed together, accommodating the thrifty cook with a medley worthy of an artist. The zucchini will extrude water, so keep the pan hot to aid the evaporation.*

1 1/2 tablespoons butter or oil, cook's preference
1/2–1 tablespoon finely chopped fresh ginger
1 large carrot, julienned or grated
1 white turnip, julienned or grated
2 zucchini, julienned or grated
Salt
Freshly ground black pepper

Heat the butter or oil in a large frying pan until hot. Add the ginger and cook 1 to 2 minutes. Add the carrot and turnip to the ginger and cook 2 to 3 minutes, until just beginning to soften. Add the zucchini and cook 2 to 3 minutes more. Stir to mix well. Season to taste with salt and pepper.

TURNIPS AND CREAM AU GRATIN

Serves 10

THIS IS ONE OF THOSE UNFORGETTABLE DISHES—*make sure it goes into your permanent repertoire. If I don't serve this at Thanksgiving, I see dour faces. Casseroles like this one are easily adapted when more or less ingredients are available than called for. Eyeball the amounts available, and adjust the ratios accordingly.*

3 pounds white turnips, peeled and sliced 1/8 inch thick
Salt
Freshly ground black pepper
2 tablespoons chopped fresh parsley, thyme and/or oregano
3 garlic cloves, finely chopped or crushed with salt
1 cup grated Gruyère cheese
1 cup freshly grated Parmesan cheese
1/3–1/2 cup butter
1 1/2–2 cups heavy cream
1/2 cup breadcrumbs or panko

Bring a large pot of water to the boil, add the sliced turnips, and return to a slow boil. Simmer young and small turnips for 3 minutes and larger ones for 8 to 10 minutes to remove excess sharpness but still leaving a bit of pep in them. Drain and pat dry with paper towels.

Butter a long casserole dish that will accommodate 3 layers of sliced turnips and the cheese—preferably no more than 3 inches deep. Spread a layer of parboiled turnips to cover the dish (they may overlap slightly) and sprinkle with salt and pepper. Mix the herbs with the garlic and sprinkle a third over the turnips. Combine the 2 cheeses and sprinkle the turnips with a third of the mixture. Dot with a third of the butter.

Continue to layer until all the turnips are added to the dish, finishing with cheese on top of the third layer. Pour cream over the entire dish until it barely covers the top layer of turnips. Sprinkle with breadcrumbs or panko and the remaining butter. May be made ahead to this point.

When ready to serve, preheat oven to 400 degrees. Add the dish, reduce the heat to 375 degrees, and bake 45 minutes, or until the cheese is melted and the breadcrumbs are nicely browned. Serve hot. This freezes up to 3 months. Defrost and reheat in a 350-degree oven for about 30 minutes, or until bubbly.

TURNIPS AND RED PEPPERS

Serves 4

Turnips meld well with bell peppers *and make a striking contrast that is particularly good with quail and turkey. This may be made ahead a day or so and reheated.*

1 pound red bell peppers
1 pound small white turnips, peeled
6 tablespoons butter, divided
2 garlic cloves, finely chopped
Salt
Freshly ground black pepper

Seed and slice the peppers. Cut the peeled turnips into quarters if the turnips are golf-ball sized, or into eighths if the turnips are larger. (Smaller young turnips can skip the next step.) Add larger turnips to a pot of boiling water and cook a few minutes to blanch (page 159); drain.

Meanwhile, melt 3 tablespoons of butter in a frying pan, add the peppers and young turnips or parboiled larger turnips, and the garlic, and cook over medium heat until the turnips are tender when pierced with a knife and peppers are still crunchy; add more butter if necessary. Season to taste with salt and pepper.

Variation: Turnips and Apples
Substitute any firm cooking apple for the peppers. Cut into wedges, leaving skin on for family, and proceed as above.

ALMOST-STEAMED VEGETABLES

Serves 2 to 3

This recipe affords the table color and dash *when the larder is discouraging. In fact, this is a favorite way to serve vegetables all winter in my home. Cooked long on low heat, the vegetables extrude their own juices and are soft and tender. Cooked quickly, they are crisp. It's a long way from the dreadful peas and carrots of the 1950s that my family ate. It's hard to remember sometimes that carrots, much less peas, were not always available fresh year-round.*

2 tablespoons butter
1 medium onion, thinly sliced
1 carrot, thinly sliced
1 celery rib, thinly sliced
Salt
Freshly ground black pepper
Herbs, as desired

Heat a saucepan with the butter and add the onion, carrot, and celery. Season with salt and pepper. Cover and cook over low heat until the vegetables are cooked. Add herbs as desired.

CHARCOAL-BROILED VEGETABLES

Serves 6 to 8

THESE VEGETABLES ARE WONDERFUL *with any simple grilled meat or fish. They are best right off the grill but may also be cooked under the broiler—they just won't pick up that smoky charcoal flavor. The vegetables are cooked sequentially, so add to the grill as each one is prepared, and remove when cooked, working as fast as possible. Leftovers can be kept a few days in the refrigerator for snacking. Serve hot, lukewarm, or cold. Gas grills perform the job as well.*

2 medium eggplants, halved lengthwise
Salt
2 large onions, quartered
Oil, cook's preference, for brushing
3 green or red bell peppers, quartered and seeds removed
3 large, firm ripe tomatoes, quartered
4 zucchini, cut into 1/2-inch-thick slices
2–3 garlic cloves, chopped
2–3 tablespoons fresh herbs
Freshly ground black pepper
Olive oil, optional

Make shallow crosshatched cuts into the cut side of the eggplant, about 1 inch apart. Sprinkle with salt and move to a colander placed over a bowl or sink for 15 minutes.

Toss the onion quarters in oil and move to a hot grill, turning until the onion has browned. Add the peppers. Turn the peppers until all the skin is charred. Remove any vegetables to a bowl as they are done.

Remove the onions, cut off the root end, and separate the layers. Remove the cooked peppers, cut into strips, and add to the bowl. Add the tomatoes to the grill cut side down, and turn when slightly charred. Remove from the grill, cut into strips, and add to the bowl.

Rinse and dry the salted eggplant. Brush the cut side with oil and move oiled side down on the grill. Cook until tender. Remove from the grill, slice, and add to the bowl. Add the zucchini slices to the grill and cook until lightly browned on both sides. Remove to the bowl and toss together with garlic and herbs. Season to taste with salt, pepper, and olive oil if desired.

LAYERED OVEN-ROASTED VEGETABLES

Serves 4–6

OUR FRIEND JENNET ALTERMAN, *a treasure to Charleston, makes this heartwarming winter dish.*

1 pound turnip greens, washed (page 205)
2 medium onions, sliced
2 large tomatoes, sliced
Salt
Freshly ground black pepper
Chopped fresh thyme, rosemary, or basil

Tear off and discard from the greens the stalks and any tough veins. Tear or cut the remaining greens. Coat a casserole dish with oil and alternate layers turnip greens, a few sliced onions, and sliced tomatoes, sprinkling with salt and pepper to taste. Bake 30 minutes, top with optional herbs, and serve hot.

Variation: Add quartered or halved baby potatoes or sliced broccoli stems.

GRITS

Good grits are like good wine. They enhance the foods around them, but can be consumed on their own with delight and pleasure. I've been known to eat stone ground grits standing up over the stove. When my mother was living with me in her last few months, the one food she craved was grits, adding to their special place in my heart.

As far back as biblical days, *grits* (or *grist*) was a catchall word for any kind of ground cereal gruel, just as the word *corn* was a word that was used for any number of cereal plants. Over the centuries, *corn* was refined to what we now know as corn that grows on a cob. These cereal plants were necessary for subsistence.

Grits didn't become common as a Southern cereal until the middle of the nineteenth century. They started as poor people's food but gradually worked their way into the middle and upper classes as a hot breakfast cereal. Hot Southern grits were eaten with butter, not with sugar and milk. Over time, other liquids were used to cook the grits, particularly milk products to help tenderize them and to enrich them. Much later they became popular for other meals.

By the mid-1970s, grits were gaining in popularity, and this accelerated with the election of Jimmy Carter. I was director of Rich's Cooking School when Carter received the Democratic nomination for president, and it was decided to hold a grits contest. I devised a grits roulade, made with half yogurt and half milk, egg yolks, and whipped egg whites that was baked flat and then rolled and filled with mushrooms. When I had run out of milk and my favorite former husband did not want to go to the store to get more, I used the yogurt at his insistence. To start off the contest, we invited some food editors who were in town for the National Chicken Cooking Contest. One of them wrote about the contest and used my recipe in her newspaper, the *Charlotte Observer*. Months later, a contest was held by Seagram's for the best appetizer recipe. Someone from Charlotte sent in my identical recipe and won the large cash prize. Rich's did not let me sue for the money or the prize, as not only did ladies not sue, but Rich's was afraid the winner would have already spent the money and we would look like greedy bullies.

Grits are so celebrated there is even an award-winning film, *It's Grits*, produced by South Carolina filmmaker Stan Woodward, capturing the love and enthusiasm of Southerners for eating grits. There are poems, songs, and stories written about the virtues of grits. Grits, says insightful Southern writer John Edgerton in *Side Orders*, "are an all-purpose symbol for practically anything of importance to Southerners. They stand for hard times and happy times, for poverty and populism, for custom and tradition, for health and humor, for high-spirited hospitality. They also stand for baking, broiling, and frying. After a bowl of grits, we half expect to find the day brighter, the load lighter, the road straighter and wider."

Southern grits are dried ground corn. Historically, the corn was dried and treated with lye made from fireplace ashes. The lye was necessary to preserve the corn and keep it from spoiling. The kernels of corn puffed up from the lye and were called hominy. When the kernel was ground, it was called grits. Grinders ranged from small hand grinders used in the home to large water-driven stone mills. The first grinding was for grits, the second for cornmeal, and the third and final grinding was for corn flour.

Although most commercial products—including real grits, traditional grits, quick grits, and instant grits—are still lye-treated, there are grits that include freshly dried and ground corn and require refrigeration, as they include parts of the corn that are liable to become rancid.

The flavor and texture of grits vary according to the color, type of corn, chemical treatment (if any), and method of grinding. A boutique industry has grown up around the production of grits, and gourmets hotly debate which are their favorites. Grits come in yellow, white, blue, and even a mix of white and yellow, with larger pieces of corn stirred in. There is no regional consensus. The people of one county may prefer yellow grits and the neighboring one white.

Cooking grits—Grits can be steamed, boiled, baked, grilled, cooked with any number of ingredients and used as a base for foods from tomatoes and bacon to the finest steaks and chops.

Grits are personal. Some prefer their grits thicker, not wanting them to spread all over their plates. Others want them so runny that they have to be eaten with a spoon. Some like more grittiness; others want them finely ground and meltingly tender. The normal ratio of grits to liquid is 1 part grits to 4 parts liquid (water, milk, cream, or stock.

More milk and cream is needed than stock). This may differ with some of the boutique brands. The liquid is brought to the boil, then the grits are slowly stirred in and cooked as designated on the package directions, or are stirred continually until they are the desired texture. Salt is added halfway through or near the end of cooking, as some people say salt toughens grits if added before cooking, and it is very difficult to add salt at the end of cooking grits, kind of like stirring sand into mud. More liquid may be stirred in and the grits cooked further than directions designate; a more tender product will ensue the longer they cook. Butter may be added anytime during the process or after cooking.

To speed up the cooking of grits, particularly stone-ground and boutique grits, they may be added to boiling liquid, removed from the heat, and soaked overnight. This speeds up the cooking considerably, the same way it does oatmeal. Some people cook grits in slow cookers or rice cookers, with a little experimentation for time. The grits will form a thin skin on the bottom, which may be discarded.

The new varieties of stone-ground and other grits are incredibly delicious, and many cook in less than 30 minutes. Still, in a pinch, quick grits—not instant—make a good grit. My favorite method of cooking grits is in the microwave in a two- or three-quart measuring cup called a "batter bowl." The reason I like it so much is that I don't have to stir the grits continually, and because I think the microwave gives the grits a little boost. I bring the requisite amount of liquid to the boil, stir in the grits, and set the microwave for 5 minutes. After 5 minutes, I add salt and stir vigorously to make sure there are no lumps or clumps, pushing the grits against the side of the bowl if necessary to smooth them out. I continue to cook and stir at 5-minute intervals, adding liquid as needed, until they are cooked. (Cooking in the microwave depends on volume, so the timing changes with the amount of food.) I have cooked grits halfway and then gone back to them at a later time and cooked them completely. Covering the bowl will speed the cooking but may create steam that can cause a severe burn. Microwave-safe plastic wrap should have an open space for steam to escape, hot pads should be used, and the grits should be removed from the bowl with care, particularly if cooking 30 minutes or more.

Storing cooked grits—Cooked grits may be stored covered in the refrigerator for several days, or frozen. Grits like to form a skin on top, so keep them covered once cooked. I prefer storing them in a plastic bag and spreading them flat, as they reheat more quickly than if in a dense clump. I also prefer reheating in the microwave. They can be reheated over the stove by stirring in hot liquid and continuing to stir over heat until they are heated through. They can also be heated in the oven at 350 degrees in a covered pan with additional liquid.

Using cooked grits—Grits are good with just about any additions—melted butter, all sorts of cheeses (as in the Cheese Grits Soufflé, page 286), bacon, ham, eggs, shrimp, salted herring (my mother-in-law's specialty), pork tenderloin, beef, and all sorts of vegetables. Adding fresh corn enhances the flavor of grits tremendously.

Like their cousin polenta, grits are mainstream, found in restaurants and homes nationwide. The corn is treated differently for grits and polenta, although they may be cooked and served in very similar ways. Some Southern restaurant chefs prefer polenta but cheat and refer to it as grits. Most of us are comfortable with grits being called "Southern polenta" or polenta being "Italian grits."

Shrimp and grits has become a hot restaurant item and is likely to remain so for years to come; in 2011 it was the most popular dish served at weddings across the United States. Cold grits can be patted flat and cut into squares, circles, or other shapes, reheated lightly by sautéing or in the oven and topped with anything that would go on rice. See Grits Cakes (page 49). See my book *Nathalie Dupree's Shrimp & Grits Cookbook* for more ideas.

GRITS *ARE* VS. GRITS *IS*

Grits, the ground corn that is the kissin' cousin of polenta, can be expressed as singular and plural. Some say, "Grits is good," just as we say, "Polenta is good." Craig Claiborne, the famous food writer for the *New York Times,* contended that the word "grits" is a plural noun. Maybe grits are, but Claiborne acknowledged that some of his fellow Mississippians insisted that grits is good, even better than oatmeal is. Whether grits is singular or plural varies according to the speaker and the use.

FRESH HOMINY

Craig Deihl, Executive Chef of Charleston's Cypress Lowcountry Grille, has created a heritage food for his menu: freshly made hominy. Making it is an arduous task. He uses Anson Mills' yellow hominy corn, Southern hardwood ash (either pecan, hickory, or oak) from his grill and smoker, and a time-honored process. This recipe makes 3½ or 4 cups of hominy, which will be eaten in no time.

The pot that the hominy is made in must be stainless steel or enamel-coated cast iron, not aluminum. The utensils must be either wood or stainless steel, and the measuring cups glass. The ratio of water to ash should be 2 to 1. The cook should wear gloves. At this strength, the lye will not burn the skin, but without gloves it will not be a pleasant experience.

Craig uses 1 gallon of water and 8 cups of ash to make a wet, sludgy ash mixture, combining the water and ash in a large stainless steel or enamel-coated pot and letting it sit for a day so the soot settles to the bottom. Strain carefully to eliminate big pieces. There will still be some ash in the water. Discard the pieces of ash. Add this water to 2 pounds of dried yellow corn. The kernels will gradually turn from yellow-orange to grayish black, which indicates that the process is working. Cover and put in a cool place, but do not refrigerate. Let sit for at least a day.

A day later, begin to heat the kernels slowly and bring to 180 degrees, making sure it never boils and the water doesn't exceed 180 degrees. Stir every half hour. After 3 hours, start stirring the kernels every 5 minutes over the heat as the mixture begins to thicken. The hulls should start popping off. The skin starts to melt off the kernels by the time the mixture is sludgy. When all of the hulls seem to be off, rinse the kernels well to remove the hulls completely, removing them with a slotted spoon if necessary. Return the kernels without any hulls to the pot and add enough water to cover them by ½ inch. Cook over low heat until the kernels begin to soften and absorb the water. They should feel almost like raw field peas.

When the kernels start to puff up, rinse them again. Return the kernels to the pot and add enough water to cover the kernels by ½ inch. Add ¼ cup salt. Cook the kernels over low heat for about 30 minutes. Taste one every few minutes. When the kernels are tender, they are done. Drain, rinse, and add the kernels to salted ice water to "shock." Drain again. If any little hulls still remain, rub the kernels between two hands to remove them completely. Keeps refrigerated for up to 2 days.

HOMINY OR GRITS?

In this book, as in most of the South, *hominy* has come to mean the whole kernels, usually found dried in the Mexican section of the grocery store and sold as "posole," or in the canned section as "hominy" or "whole hominy." This book refers to all the whole kernels as "hominy" and the dried ground corn as "grits." When you find an old recipe that calls for hominy grits, it most likely means grits, but read through the recipe to be sure, particularly if it is a recipe from Charleston, where grits are still called hominy—and only occasionally called "hominy grits."

GRITS WITH GREENS

Serves 4 to 6

THIS VARIATION OF GRITS IS MY ALL-TIME FAVORITE, *and variations of it appear in several of my cookbooks. That does not take away from its decadence, which makes it a special-occasion dish. These can be served on their own, as a base for shrimp and grits, or accompanying ham, eggs, or other delicacies. A chafing dish helps for a party.*

2 cups milk
2 cups water
1 cup grits
1 garlic clove, chopped
1 cup heavy cream
1/4–1/2 cup butter
1–2 cups freshly grated Parmesan cheese
1 cup baby spinach, or chiffonade larger spinach leaves
Salt
Freshly ground black pepper

Bring the milk and water to a simmer in a heavy-bottomed nonstick saucepan over medium heat. Add the grits and garlic, and bring just to the boil. Cook until soft and creamy, adding heavy cream as needed to make a loose but not a runny mixture. Add as much butter and cheese as desired, stirring to make sure the cheese doesn't stick. Fold in the greens and remove from the heat. The greens will cook in the hot grits. Serve in individual dishes or in a bowl. This dish also freezes well.

Variation: "Corn" on "Corn"
Add enough cream to make the grits "dip" consistency. Chop the greens before adding. Serve with crisp tortilla scoops or chips.

For Shrimp and Grits with Greens: Add small pieces of peeled shrimp to the hot grits or cook separately and add. Finish with greens. Leftovers freeze or can be spread to desired thickness and cut, then reheated as desired.

TOMATO-BACON GRITS

Serves 4 to 6

IT'S NOT NECESSARY TO BE EXACT ABOUT THIS RECIPE, *which makes it a good one to remember when time is of the essence. The bacon garnish adds crunch, and the whole dish, including the green onions, is pretty enough to serve to company. If green onions are not available, garnish with chives.*

2 cups cooked grits, cooked in Shrimp Stock (page 117) or water
2 tablespoons butter
6 strips bacon, cut in 1/4-inch slices
2 garlic cloves, chopped
2/3 cup sliced green onions, white and green parts separated
1/4 cup all-purpose flour
2 medium tomatoes, peeled, seeded, and sliced into strips
1 1/2 cups half-and-half or milk
Salt
Ground hot red or black pepper

Stir the hot grits and butter. Sauté the bacon until crisp. Remove a third of the bacon, drain on paper towels, and set aside for garnish. Add the garlic and green onion whites to the remaining bacon and grease. Sauté about 2 minutes. Sprinkle in the flour and stir until incorporated. Add the tomatoes and half-and-half, stirring until incorporated. Bring to the boil, then reduce to a simmer, stirring occasionally until the sauce thickens. Season to taste with pepper. Divide into individual bowls, spoon the sauce over the grits, garnish with the onion greens and crumbled bacon, and serve.

Variation: Add cooked shrimp and/or a handful of baby or chiffonade turnip greens or spinach to the garnish.

RICE

Cynthia and I made several trips filming Southern rice for television. We went to Louisiana and had the thrill of planting rice seed in flooded fields from a crop duster. We ate wild ducks that fed on the rice fields; we were fed boiled crawfish, plump from eating the rice leavings, on a picnic table in perfect weather in the garden of a farmer's home. In Arkansas we saw fields leveled by laser beams to expedite the planting of rice and flooding of the fields. Here in Charleston, I've seen vintage rice seeds planted by hand and harvested by hand and scythe at Middleton Plantations; the rice was then threshed and winnowed in sweet grass fanning baskets to remove the loose husks, dust, and stalks. I have some of the dried stalks, taller than I am, in a vase in my living room.

Rice has a long history in the South. It arrived in South Carolina in the late 1600s from Madagascar and was also an important crop along the Mississippi River as early as 1720. It was seen as important in feeding the African slaves, who knew how to grow and cultivate it, and as a significant cash crop, aided by those same slaves with their knowledge of the growing and cultivating of rice. Thomas Jefferson brought a hundred kinds of rice to be cultivated from one continent alone. Knowing of his interest, people sent him new varieties and even stuffed them casually into his pockets, which he then sent on to planters so haphazardly they begged him to stop, as they were afraid they would intermix with the already successful crops they were planting.

Carolina Gold rice—The first crop of Carolina Gold rice was planted in the late 1600s, and it was the number-one cash crop in South Carolina for more than 200 years, exported all over the world and providing the planters of the Lowcountry with extraordinary riches. The Civil War and then the hurricane of 1911 ended the reign of this very special rice.

As a crop grown on the backs of African slaves, Carolina Gold was hand-pounded to remove the hull, then winnowed until it was a sleek white rice. The broken pieces, called middlins, were not exported and were favored by locals, as the rice in this broken form soaked up more of the flavor of the dish in which it was prepared.

A group of dedicated historians, scientists, and food historians began to grow Carolina Gold in coastal Carolina near Charleston in the late 1990s. A small amount of rice is grown, milled, and sold commercially, heralded by the Slow Food movement and championed by farm-to-table chefs.

There is an old saw that says that Charlestonians, called "rice eaters," are like the Chinese: they eat rice and worship their ancestors. Fabulous pilafs, rice breads, waffles, pancakes, and other dishes were developed around this industry.

Louisiana rice—Called "Creole rice," Louisiana rice was considered inferior until the mid-1800s, when an Italian immigrant, Angelo Socola, became interested in it and developed a superior rice that increased production from 30,000 sacks to millions of rice sacks annually. After the Civil War, Louisiana and Texas became prime rice-growing regions. Mechanization developed for wheat farming was transferred to the cultivation and harvesting of rice. Konriko Rice Mill in New Iberia, Louisiana, is the nation's oldest continuously operating mill. It is said that "a Cajun will eat anything, but is most proud to eat what is homegrown," and that still applies to Louisiana rice.

Even though classified as a cereal, rice was used from morning to night—as breakfast on its own, with peas as in South America to this day, in rice cakes, in stuffed sausages like Boudin, in soups and stews as an addition and thickener, in pilafs, in puddings and sweets, and in breads, waffles, and other recipes as a substitute for flour.

Ways of Cooking Rice

Measuring rice—The normal ratio of liquid—stocks, bouillons, milk, or water—to rice is two cups liquid to one cup rice.

Cooking rice—The primary methods of cooking rice are steaming, sautéing and then adding broth (as in a risotto or pilau), simmering, and baking. Some prefer an explicit ratio of liquid to rice (see above); others prefer adding rice to a large quantity of boiling water and draining it when done.

Steaming rice—Essentially double boilers, devices that steam rice can be stovetop or electric. The directions for steaming are a little vague, as each one seems to be a bit different. Charleston has its own very popular traditional home rice steamer, but now many prefer little Chinese rice cookers that make smaller portions at home.

My friend Conrad Zimmerman, who gave me my first rice cooker, says, "Put shrimp water, chicken stock, milk or water in the bottom. Put equal amounts of rice with a pinch of salt in the basket, without rinsing. (He likes the stickiness.) Add water to the bottom of the steamer and add the basket at the top of the water. Turn on high. When the steam comes out, turn it down, and let cook for a few minutes more. Water may always be added. When done, fluff with a fork."

Making perfect rice—The *Episcopal Watchman* of September 29, 1832, gives directions to cook rice, which are exactly like those I learned when I was young but with a slight difference in timing and washing rice. They direct the cook to "scrub and rinse the rice in several waters until the floury particles, which are often sour or musty, are entirely removed." This is not necessary for most commercial rices, although many of the boutique and specialty rices require it. (Check package directions about rinsing, both before and after.)

The *Watchman* and I both suggest throwing a bit of salt into a large quantity of water and bringing it to the boil. Add the rice and boil steadily 10 or 11 minutes. Remove a few kernels of rice and split in two with a knife or fingernail. There should be the smallest white dot in the center when it is done. The *Watchman* recommends it is done in 12 minutes; I think 11 is better. That is the end of our differences. We both recommend pouring off or draining the rice after cooking, as in boiled rice, below.

Alternatively, drain the cooked rice in a metal colander, rinsing if desired. Put the colander over a same-size pan, add water to the pot, enough as to not allow the water to evaporate, take a wooden spoon and punch some pockets or holes in the rice to let the steam come through, cover the colander with foil, bring the water to a simmer, and let steam 10 minutes or so. Always fork rice to fluff it, and avoid spooning it.

When cooking rice, cook more than is needed. Freeze the extra in 1-cup freezer containers. Reheat in the microwave, adding a dash of water to keep the rice from drying out.

BOILED RICE NUMBER II FROM *TWO HUNDRED YEARS OF CHARLESTON COOKING*

Wash one cup of rice in several waters. Have two quarts of water salted and boiling hot. Sift the rice in and boil for 30 minutes. Put it into a strainer, rinse in hot water, and set over a kettle to dry. Serve very hot. —William's Recipe

BAKED RICE AND MUSHROOMS

Serves 4

THIS TECHNIQUE OF COOKING RICE IS VERY HELPFUL *when cooking several dishes simultaneously in a heated oven. It guarantees a fluffy rice with little work. Dried, reconstituted mushrooms are appropriate here.*

1 tablespoon butter
1/2 medium onion, chopped
1 1/2 cups long or medium-grain white rice
3 cups water
1/2 tablespoon salt
1/2 pound small button or other mushrooms, quartered
Freshly ground black pepper

Preheat oven to 350 degrees.

Heat the butter over medium heat in an ovenproof pot with a lid. Add the onion and cook until soft and slightly brown, 5 to 7 minutes. Add the rice and stir a couple of minutes to coat the grains with the butter. Add the water and salt, and bring to the boil. Stir in the mushrooms and cover with a tight-fitting lid. Bake for 17 minutes. Fluff with two forks, add pepper to taste, and serve.

Variation: To prepare on top of the stove, bring to the boil after adding the mushrooms, cover, reduce heat to a low simmer, and cook for 17 to 20 minutes, until the rice is cooked and the water has evaporated.

CREOLE DIRTY RICE

Serves 6 to 9

ACCORDING TO THE *ENCYCLOPEDIA OF CAJUN & CREOLE CULTURE, from which we adapted this recipe, when liver and giblets are added to the rice, it makes a dirty-looking dish, hence its name. For those of us who love butter-soaked rice and chicken livers as well as the "holy trinity" of Cajun cooking—onions, celery and bell peppers—this is a special treat.*

1/2 pound chicken giblets
Salt
1/2 cup butter
1/2 pound chicken livers
1 cup finely chopped onion
1 cup finely chopped celery
1 cup finely chopped bell pepper
2 tablespoons finely chopped garlic clove
1 cup chicken stock or broth
6 cups steamed rice
1/2 cup sliced green onions
1/2 cup chopped parsley
Freshly ground black pepper

Cover the giblets with lightly salted water, bring to the boil, reduce heat, cover, and simmer 45 minutes, until tender. Remove the giblets with a slotted spoon, reserving the liquid. Chop the giblets, removing all tough membranes.

Meanwhile, melt the butter in a large heavy sauté pan, add the livers, and sauté 1 to 2 minutes, until golden on all sides. Remove with a slotted spoon and coarsely chop. Add the onion, celery, bell pepper, and garlic to the pan and sauté 3 to 5 minutes, until slightly soft. Return giblets and liver to the pan, pour in the chicken stock and 1/2 cup of the giblet broth. Bring to the boil, stirring, making sure nothing is stuck to the bottom of the pan. Reduce heat, and cook until the liquid in the pan is reduced to 1/4 cup. Fold in the steamed rice and garnish with green onions and parsley, and season to taste with salt and pepper.

MRS. DULL'S STEAMED RICE

Serves 4

Mrs. Dull calls for washing rice well. *She is clear that a rice cooker or rice steamer must be used, and these are her directions. Once again, she cooks longer than I do. Her rice is, of course, already wet, so less water is needed.*

1 cup rice, washed well
1 1/2 cups water
1/2 tablespoon salt

Pour rice into the top of the rice steamer, sprinkle with salt, and add 1 1/2 cups water. Add water to the bottom of the rice steamer, bring to the boil and boil rapidly until the rice is done and fluffy, about 1 hour, checking for doneness after 40 minutes.

MUSHROOM PILAU

Serves 4 to 6

A pilau *(pronounced "pur-loo"), or pilaf, is the South's answer to risotto, with roots going back to early history of rice production.*

2 ounces mixed dried mushrooms, such as porcini, black Chinese, shiitake, or button
4 cups boiling water
3 tablespoons butter
1 tablespoon oil, cook's preference
1 medium onion, finely chopped
1 pound Carolina Gold, Arborio, or other short- or medium-grain rice
1 cup chicken stock or broth
1/3 cup freshly grated Parmesan cheese
Salt
Freshly ground black pepper

Cover the dried mushrooms with boiling water in a bowl or glass measuring cup. Soak for 30 minutes. Remove the plumped mushrooms with a slotted spoon. Squeeze to remove excess liquid. Strain and reserve the resulting liquid. Roughly chop the mushrooms, removing any hard pieces.

Heat the butter and oil. Add the onion and mushrooms. Sauté until the onions are transparent but not browned. Add the rice and stir until thoroughly coated, 1 to 2 minutes.

Meanwhile, bring the reserved mushroom broth and chicken broth to the boil. Stirring constantly, add 1/2 cup of the hot stock to the mushroom-rice mixture and continue to stir over medium-high heat until liquid is absorbed and the rice appears to be dry. Add another 1/2 cup of the stock, following the same method. Repeat over a 20-minute period, being careful not to "drown" the rice, and cook the pilaf until it has reached a creamy consistency and is al dente.

When the pilaf is done, stir in the cheese and season to taste with salt and pepper. Serve immediately.

TOMATO PILAU (AKA RED RICE)

Serves 4

HERE IS ANOTHER RECIPE *from* Two Hundred Years of Charleston Cooking, *which is a recipe of William Deas, Mrs. Rhett's butler, and is made the same way as the Okra Pilau but without okra, and using salt pork.*

5 slices salt pork, diced
1 small onion, chopped
2 cups canned tomatoes
1/2–1 cup water or chicken stock or broth, divided
Salt
Freshly ground black pepper
1 cup rice
3 tablespoons butter

Rinse the salt pork, add to a skillet with the onion, and fry until brown. Add the tomatoes, cut them with scissors, and cook over low heat for 10 minutes. Add 1/2 cup water or stock and season with salt and pepper to taste. Stir in the rice, cover tightly, and let the pilau cook slowly, about 12 minutes more, until all the liquid is absorbed, adding the remaining liquid if the rice does not seem cooked. Just before serving, stir in the butter.

Variation: Terry Thompson's Red Rice or Pilau
Terry Thompson was one of those students of mine who far exceeded me in skill. Living in Louisiana, she arrived at Rich's Cooking School with a bottle of Tabasco in her apron pocket and used it whenever I wasn't looking.

In Terry Thompson's book *Taste of the South*, the recipe calls for a chopped medium green bell pepper and 4 chopped green onions, along with poultry stock rather than water. She adds bay leaf, basil, black pepper, oregano, salt, and Tabasco, of course, along with the tomato, discarding the bay leaf before serving.

VARIATIONS ON PILAU

Pilau is pronounced as many ways as it is spelled. I've seen one spelling of *pileau*, many of *purloo*, and *pilaf*. It is featured in many historic cookbooks with several variations of ingredients: chicken seems primary, as do tomato and smoked pork, such as bacon or fatback. This Tomato Purloo is also called Red Rice, depending on the region, or is known as Mulatto Rice, which Damon Lee Fowler suggests is more for the color of the rice than a racial allusion.

OKRA PILAU

Serves 4

This recipe from Two Hundred Years of Charleston Cooking *gives great credit to Sally Washington, an African-American woman who was "a genius in her own right or else Charleston was gifted by the Gods," and was Mrs. Rhett's cook. We have adapted it here.*

8 slices bacon, diced
1 cup okra, sliced into small pieces
1 cup rice
2 cups water

Brown the bacon in a heavy frying pan. Remove and set aside on paper towels to drain, reserving fat. Add okra to the hot fat over low heat. Add the rice and 2 cups water, cover and let cook until done, about 40 minutes. Remove from heat, toss in a bowl, top with the bacon dice, and serve.

Variation: Okra Pilau II
Add 1 chopped onion and 1 tablespoon chopped green bell pepper to the bacon fat and sauté until light brown. Add 2 cups stewed tomatoes and 2 cups thinly sliced okra to the hot pan. Cook over medium heat until the tomatoes are reduced, about 15 minutes. Add 2 cups cooked rice and 1 teaspoon of salt; turn into the top of a double boiler or rice steamer, and let steam for 15 or 20 minutes. Top with crumbled bacon just before serving. Serves 6.

STUFFINGS AND DRESSINGS

Stuffings and dressings seem to have geographical dividing lines and can lead to confusion as well as Thanksgiving debates, at least in my family. Originally, in England, the breadcrumb-type mixture that went into turkey and other fowl was called forcemeat, whether or not it had any meat in it. (It was "forced" through a grinder and stuffed into boned fowl.) It might or might not contain breadcrumbs.

We started out here making stuffings, too, like they did in England and New England. These were called stuffings because the mixtures were used to stuff turkeys before roasting.

As time went on, however, we realized that our temperate Thanksgiving weather necessitated removing the stuffing from a turkey immediately. The stuffing never reached 165 degrees, the temperature necessary to kill the bacteria from the turkey juices. To guard against any unpleasant repercussions from the holiday meal, the alternative was to put the stuffing in a dish alongside the turkey—maybe even in the same pan or under the turkey. From that, it was called dressing (not to be confused with salad dressing) because it dressed the turkey. Some still call it stuffing, referring to the original mixture.

There are many glories in making dressing. The turkey cooks much more quickly with an empty cavity than with a full one. Several dressings can be made to suit a household divided between cornbread dressing and bread dressing or pecans and peanuts—all contentious issues when discussing Thanksgiving dinner.

Eggless dressings may be made in advance and frozen, defrosted, and reheated, with no extraordinary health concerns if they do not contain raw eggs. They may be basted with a stock made ahead of time from turkey parts or even from store-bought chicken stock. They may also be cooked in a rice cooker, using the stock from the turkey or chicken to replace the water. This dressing remains particularly moist and tender, while the baked dressings have more flavor from the caramelization that ensues after the aluminum foil is removed.

STUART WOODS' PECAN BISCUIT DRESSING

Serves 12 to 16

SOUTHERN AUTHOR STUART WOODS *took classes at the Cordon Bleu when he lived in London and is a terrific cook. His mother and I took trips to France and Italy together. This is an amalgam of his family recipe incorporating one of his favorites from James Beard. The biscuits make a softer, more delicate dressing.*

- 1 pound butter, divided
- 4 large onions, or 2 dozen shallots, finely chopped to make 2–3 cups
- 3 garlic cloves, chopped
- 15 cups biscuit crumbs or breadcrumbs
- 2 cups chopped pecans
- 1 cup chopped parsley
- 2 tablespoons chopped fresh tarragon
- 2 teaspoons chopped fresh thyme or 1 teaspoon dried
- Salt
- Freshly ground pepper
- 10 sausage links
- 2–3 cups turkey or chicken stock or broth

Preheat oven to 350 degrees. Butter a 9 x 13-inch baking dish.

Heat 1/2 cup of the butter in a heavy skillet; add the onions and cook until soft. Add the garlic and cook a minute more. Add the biscuit crumbs and nuts. Melt the remaining butter and add to the breadcrumb mixture along with the parsley, tarragon, and thyme. Season to taste with salt and pepper, and toss well. Meanwhile, brown the sausages in a frying pan. Drain and set aside. Move the dressing to the baking dish, top with sausages, cover, and bake 1 hour. Add stock as needed. The dressing may be baked ahead and refrigerated or frozen.

SOUTHERN CORNBREAD DRESSING (CUSH)

Serves 12

Over the years, *former students and employees have added more and more recipes to my repertoire. Cindy Morgan from Covington, Georgia, worked for me as a teenager in the 1970s. I moved, she moved, and twenty years later we ran into each other at a swimming pool, far from home. We sat by the pool and talked recipes and she gave me this one.*

5 cups crumbled cornbread
4 cups toasted bread cubes
1 1/2 cups chicken stock or broth
1/2 cup butter, divided
1 1/2 cups chopped onion
1 1/3 cups chopped celery
1 red or green bell pepper, seeded and chopped
1/3 cup chopped parsley
1/2 teaspoon dried or chopped fresh sage
1 teaspoon dried or chopped fresh thyme
Salt
Freshly ground black pepper
2 large eggs, beaten
2 hard-cooked large eggs, chopped

Preheat oven to 400 degrees.

Soak the cornbread and bread cubes in the broth. Heat 2 to 3 tablespoons butter in a large frying pan. Add the onion, celery, and bell pepper, and cook until tender. Add the soaked cornbread and bread cubes to the cooked vegetables. Melt the remaining butter and add to this mixture along with the parsley, sage, and thyme. Season to taste with salt and pepper. Stir in the raw and cooked eggs. Bake the dressing in an oiled casserole dish, uncovered, for 45 minutes.

Variation: Oyster Dressing
Simmer 1 pint oysters in water or their liquor until their edges curl. Drain and add to the dressing before baking.

Variation: Double the recipe and stuff half under the skin of the turkey before roasting.

Leftover dressing can be used for sandwiches, or spread 1-inch thick and cut into rounds, etc. Cover with a sprinkling of cheese if desired. Reheat in oven or microwave. Add to a shallow soup plate and surround with hot soup such as Vidalia Onion Soup (page 133).

Some Southerners refer to their dressing mixture as *cush,* the shortened version of the Gullah's *kushkush.* Some suggest that the original word came from the Arabian *couscous* and still others think it Native American in origin.

DETERMINING THE VOLUME OF A CASSEROLE DISH

Casserole dishes vary in depth and width. If a casserole's size is not indicated on the bottom, fill with water and pour into a measuring cup. Mark the volume with a permanent marker on the bottom. Remember, deep dishes take longer to cook, wide ones less time.

APPLE, SAUSAGE, AND FENNEL BISCUIT DRESSING

Serves 8 to 10

One of my favorite combinations is apple and sausage. *Combined with pecans and herbs, it is very sought-after on my holiday table.*

- 1/2 cup butter, divided
- 1/2 pound sweet Italian pork or turkey sausage
- 1 large onion, chopped
- 1–2 fennel bulbs, or 3 celery ribs, finely chopped
- 3 garlic cloves, chopped
- 3 tablespoons chopped fresh marjoram and/or thyme
- 1 tablespoon chopped fresh fennel frond, optional
- 1–2 red or other cooking apples, cored and cut into wedges
- 1/4 cup apple juice
- 1 cup chopped pecans
- 3/4–1 cup turkey or chicken stock or broth
- 4 cups broken biscuits

Preheat oven to 350 degrees. Butter an 11 x 13-inch baking dish.

Melt 3 tablespoons of butter in a large skillet. Prick the separated sausage links and add to the hot pan. Brown on all sides and remove from pan. Cool and chop roughly.

Meanwhile, add the chopped onion and fennel or celery to the pan, adding more butter if necessary, and cook until soft. Add the garlic, herbs, and apple, and cook a few minutes, until the apple is slightly soft as well. Add the rest of the butter to the hot pan and melt. Cool slightly. Toss with the sausage, apple juice, pecans, 3/4 cup stock, and biscuits, until the bread is well moistened, adding more stock if necessary.

Move the mixture to the buttered baking dish and bake 20 to 30 minutes, until the bread is lightly browned. It may be refrigerated several days or frozen. Defrost in microwave or refrigerator and reheat in 350-degree oven for 20 minutes.

PECAN RICE DRESSING

Serves 12 to 15

LARGE SILVER RICE SPOONS *are regular implements in South Carolina, used to spoon this dressing out of fowl, particularly turkey. The variation from Louisiana includes seafood and the "holy trinity" again.*

1/2 cup butter
Giblets and liver from turkey
1 cup chopped onions
1 cup chopped celery
2–3 garlic cloves, finely chopped
6 cups steamed white rice
1 cup chicken or turkey stock or broth
1/2 cup chopped pecans
1/2 cup chopped fresh herbs such as parsley, thyme, and sage

Melt the butter in a large pan. Add the giblets and liver and sauté until golden brown, about 15 minutes. Remove with a slotted spoon and set aside. Add the onions and celery and cook until translucent. Add the garlic and cook 1 minute more.

Meanwhile, remove any membranes from the giblets and liver, chop roughly, and return to the pan. Stir in the rice, adding stock as necessary to make moist, then the pecans and herbs. Serve as is, or as a stuffing or dressing for turkey.

Variation: Creole Oyster Dressing

Sauté 1 cup diced green bell pepper and 1/4 cup red bell pepper along with the onions and celery. Cut 1 pint oysters roughly with scissors or a knife and stir them and their liquid into the cooked vegetables. Add rice, stock, pecans, and herbs as above.

SOCIAL CIRCLE MACARONI PIE (CUSTARD MACARONI AND CHEESE)

Serves 4 as a main course, 6 to 8 as a side dish

"PIE" IS CERTAINLY A MISNOMER *for this cheesy, light macaroni-and cheese-custard. My mother-in-law Celeste Dupree served this as a main course for the noon meal along with a salad. She insisted that spaghetti was macaroni. I tried to get the exact recipe from her when she was alive, but she was hard to pin down, as she never measured anything. It was only later that I was able to figure it out and get it to my satisfaction. It may be made ahead and reheated, and leftovers freeze satisfactorily for the family.*

Tip: Cooking time varies according to the container, but with custards it is important to take care the mixture doesn't boil, as that will cause the egg to break and the mixture to separate. Metal conducts heat and cooks faster than ceramic and glass, for instance. A deep dish will take much longer to cook through than a shallow one. Make a note on the recipe what dish was used, and how long it took to cook through, so there is a record to refer to the next time.

3 cups cooked and drained spaghetti (macaroni)
4 tablespoon butter, melted
4 large eggs, beaten to mix
3 cups milk
$1\frac{1}{2}$ teaspoons Dijon mustard
2 teaspoons salt
Freshly ground black pepper
1 teaspoon ground hot red pepper, optional
1 pound sharp Cheddar or Gruyère cheese, grated

Preheat oven to 350 degrees.

Roughly cut the cooked spaghetti into 3-inch pieces and toss with half the butter. Lightly whisk the eggs with the milk in a large bowl. Add the mustard, salt, peppers, and half the cheese. Put half the spaghetti into a greased 3-quart baking dish, sprinkle with cheese to cover and 1 tablespoon of the butter. Ladle on half the egg/cheese mixture, top with the rest of the spaghetti. Ladle on the remainder of the mixture and enough cheese and the remaining butter to cover the top. If the dish is deep, it may not need all the cheese.

Move to the preheated oven. If the dish is less than three inches deep, bake for 30 minutes; if deeper, bake for about 45 minutes. Check and reduce the heat 25 degrees if the cheese is browning too much or the custard is bubbling. Cover lightly with foil and continue to cook until a fork inserted in the custard comes out clean and the top is golden brown, up to 40 minutes more, depending on the thickness of the baking dish.

COOKING SPAGHETTI

Harold McGee, author of *On Food and Cooking,* has disputed the need for large quantities of water for cooking pasta. I think this is particularly true for pasta that will be further cooked, as in baking in a casserole like Macaroni pie. Use a wide pot, which will come to the boil quicker than will a traditional tall pot. To cook pasta ahead, cook, drain, and rinse the pasta under cold water. Toss in olive oil to coat, cool, move to a plastic ziplock bag, and refrigerate until needed, or freeze for later use. To reheat, move pasta to a colander and dip into a pot of hot water.

All pasta was called macaroni in colonial days, and the name has carried over with older generations. Pasta is used in the South in the same ways it is used nationally, but we just didn't have room to include these national variations and types of pasta. Children seem to particularly enjoy the excitement of all the different shapes of pasta.

MACARONI PIE (MACARONI AND CHEESE)

Serves 6

THIS IS THE ORIGINAL *Macaroni Pie from* Two Hundred Years of Charleston Cooking, *whose name came from its being cooked in a pie dish. It was served as a side dish. Spaghetti was commonly called macaroni through the first half of the twentieth century and was the typical pasta used. In many homes, Macaroni Pie was the "real" macaroni and cheese rather than the typical white sauce and breadcrumbs version (below).*

1/2 pound macaroni
1 tablespoon butter
1 egg, well beaten
1 teaspoon mustard
1 teaspoon each black and red pepper
2 cups grated cheese
1/2 cup milk

Boil the macaroni in salted water until tender. Drain; stir in the butter and egg. Mix the mustard with a tablespoon hot water and add it with the other seasonings. Add the cheese and milk, mix well, and turn into buttered baking dish. Bake in moderate oven (350 degrees) until the cheese is melted and the dish brown on top, about half an hour.

—Martha Laurens Patterson

MACARONI AND CHEESE

Serves 6 to 8

THIS MACARONI AND CHEESE *is based on the traditional white sauce and topped with breadcrumbs. True comfort food. If at all possible, use Flavored Milk; it will make this dish so stupendous diners will dream about it later.*

2 cups butter, divided
1/4 cup all-purpose flour
2 cups milk, preferably Flavored Milk (page 657)
Salt
Freshly ground pepper
1 3/4 cups grated sharp Cheddar cheese, divided
4 cups cooked spaghetti (macaroni)
3/4 cup breadcrumbs

Preheat oven to 375 degrees.

Melt half the butter in a heavy saucepan. Add the flour, stirring until smooth. Pour in the milk and bring to the boil, stirring constantly. After the milk thickens, season to taste with salt and pepper. Remove from the heat and blend in 1/2 cup of the cheese. Move a layer of the cooked macaroni to a buttered 6 x 12-inch oblong baking dish and top with some of both the sauce and the cheese. Repeat until all the macaroni is layered, finishing with the cheese.

Melt the remaining butter in a large frying pan, add the breadcrumbs, and toss. Sprinkle on top of the casserole, which may be made ahead to this point. When ready to serve, bring the casserole to room temperature. Bake until heated through, about 20 to 30 minutes. This recipe freezes well and can be defrosted and reheated in the microwave.

EGGS

The best way to learn to move from cook to magician is to learn about the egg, the secret weapon of any good cook. That's doubly so for Southerners, who keep the historic poverty of war and the Great Depression in their folklore. If you have eggs, you have abundance. Without the egg and the thousands of ways to cook it, all cuisines would be completely different. Traditionally part of breakfast in farm kitchens, the egg has moved into its own at the dining room table. A sunny side up or poached egg may top foods from asparagus to pizza. A tender scrambled egg with melted cheese and cream may woo a suitor as an after-theater supper. A soufflé, so easily mastered, excites even the dullest luncheon of strangers.

The egg leavens, binds, coats, emulsifies, retards crystallization, moisturizes, dries, thickens sauces, sets custards, creates form to tighten sauces and soufflés, and much more.

The eggshell alone reminds me of those publicity events where a car sits on top a cup made of fine china, perfectly balanced. The shell is a marvel of engineering. It protects the little chick inside—porous enough for it to breathe, delicate enough for the chick to peck its way out, and strong enough for a hen forty times its size to roost on it. The shell has its own miraculous powers and helps clarify stocks and aspics. My grandmother used eggshells in her flower bed and coffee percolator. No wonder it is said that "the egg is the backbone of cooking, the cement that holds the castle of cuisine together." Amen.

THE MAGICAL EGG

The whole egg operates as three different entities: the whole egg, the egg white, and the yolk. All three are "cooked" (technically, coagulated) when they reach a different temperature. A whole egg is considered cooked at 160 degrees; the egg white is considered cooked at 140 to 150 degrees; and the yolk is considered cooked at 150 to 160 degrees. That's why hollandaise and lemon curd are best using only yolks rather than whole eggs: the egg white cooks too fast and white specks appear.

Adding other ingredients such as milk, flour, cornstarch, acid, and sugar also changes an egg.

Dilute an egg with milk, sugar, or cream, as in a custard, and it raises the coagulation temperature to 180 to 185 degrees.

Mix whole egg with a starch (usually flour or cornstarch), and a liquid, as in a pastry cream, it must be brought to the boil and boiled for 2 minutes. The starch raises the coagulation temperature.

Acid, such as from wine, citrus, or vinegar, reduces the coagulation temperature to around 150 to 160 degrees, depending on the ratio of acid to egg. It's frustrating that cookbooks have a habit of saying "not to boil" a custard or a hollandaise sauce, when actually it is overcooked long before 212 degrees.

Temperature, stirring, and the egg—Always whisk or stir when adding sugar to an egg yolk; otherwise the yolks will thicken partially without solidifying.

Heat affects the texture of an egg dish. A stirred custard is influenced by the air that is circulated as it is stirred, cooling and slowing down the cooking to keep the custard from solidifying. A baked custard like crème brûlée or crème caramel, which bakes undisturbed, will be firm.

If an egg mixture is rushed over the heat, it is more liable to curdle (and burn), and will also be thinner and runnier.

The nutrition and composition of a whole egg—No other food is known to match all of the egg's functions and capabilities, soluble vitamins, and minerals. There are seventy-five calories in one large egg, a package of nutrition almost complete in itself. A good (and cheap) source of protein, it provides vitamins, minerals, and "good cholesterol." Egg whites contain no fat and are essentially composed of protein, water, water-soluble vitamins, and minerals. Egg yolks have almost as much protein and far less water. They supply fats, fat- and water-soluble vitamins, minerals, cholesterol, and emulsifiers.

Only Grade A large eggs, preferably stamped USDA, are used for recipes in this and most other cookbooks. The content of 1 large egg measures 2 liquid ounces. Any other size of egg will require recipe adjustment. When a recipe calls for room-temperature eggs and time is of the essence, immerse the whole egg in its shell in warm water for 30 seconds. The color of the eggshell has nothing to do with the flavor or "goodness" of the egg. Brown- and white-shelled eggs are equal in nutrition, flavor, function, and capability.

Measuring eggs—About 8 whites or 12 yolks equal 1 cup. One white is roughly 2 tablespoons (1 ounce), a yolk a little less.

FROM HEN TO TABLE

There is an allure to the freshly laid egg that an older egg doesn't have, and for good reason. Eggs are laid warm. As they cool, their contents contract and the inner membrane separates from the outer membrane, creating a vacuum wherever the top of the egg is, whether stored small end down or on its side.

Fresh eggs have very little air between the shell and the membrane covering the white and yolk of the egg. They are best used for sunny side up, over-easy, and poached eggs, where the yolk is rounder and the white coagulates quickly and stays together. (As it ages, the white tends to wander away from the yolk.) Omelets also coagulate better and turn out more easily when the eggs are fresh.

While commercially sold eggs are coated lightly with food-grade waxes, "farm-fresh" eggs are not coated. Eggs should be wiped with a cloth before use. They should not be washed, as they are porous, and anything on their surface will be absorbed with the water. Discard any egg with a crack in its shell. A blood spot discovered once the egg is cracked open does not mean it is contaminated. Remove with the tip of a knife.

Eggs are best kept refrigerated, standing on their small end until needed. If unsure whether a refrigerated egg is cooked or raw, twirl the egg on the counter. A hard-cooked egg will spin on its end without wobbling.

Peeling eggs—As eggs age, they become more alkaline, which makes peeling cooked ones easier. They also shrink, leaving a greater vacuum between the shell and the egg, which also makes peeling easier. (The membrane and the shell are evident at the top of the egg when a hard-cooked egg is peeled.)

Cracking and separating eggs—Always use three bowls: a small bowl over which to crack the eggs, another bowl to hold the yolks; and another bowl to hold the egg whites. First, crack the egg on its side on the counter (the edge of a bowl may cause the shell to splinter). Hold the egg in two clean hands and open the egg at the crack. Move the yolk to one hand, letting the white slip through the fingers into the bowl, and move the yolk back to the other hand. Put the yolk (hopefully intact) into the second small bowl. Check the white for any yolk. Move the egg white from the small bowl to the larger third bowl. Proceed with the next egg, always cracking the egg over an empty bowl to catch the whites and always moving the whites to the larger bowl with the other whites. This will keep yolks and whites sequestered, and will ensure that no egg yolk from a newly cracked egg gets into the larger batch of whites.

An egg separator gadget is useful. Moving the yolks back and forth between two eggshells, as I did for years, is no longer recommended, as the shells may be contaminated and also might pierce the yolk. Cold eggs separate more easily than room-temperature eggs.

Keeping egg whites—Egg whites may be kept refrigerated and covered for several days or frozen separately in an ice cube tray. Gather the frozen ones together in a freezer bag or other container marked "egg whites." After defrosting, bring to room temperature for at least 20 minutes to get the optimum boost.

COOKING VARIOUS TYPES OF EGG DISHES

How many eggs—We're assuming one egg per person, except with scrambled eggs and omelets. There is no logic in this abstemiousness, except that a single scrambled egg will be hard and nasty, and a single-egg omelet is virtually impossible to ordinary people. Have as many eggs as you like, and always make extras when cooking for a crowd.

Sunny-side up eggs—There is more mastery to cooking a sunny-side up egg than one would imagine. This is partly because the white is right on the hot pan, while the yolk is protected by the white. Between the pan heat and the difference in coagulation and cooking temperatures between the white and the yolk, getting a perfect sunny-side up egg is a feat. Some want a cooked egg white with no crispy bottom, the white cooked on top and the yolk ready to run perfectly when punctured; I like the crispy bottom. A cold egg cracks more cleanly than a room-temperature egg.

Crack the still cold egg on the counter to avoid splintering the shell. Open it up into a cup, bowl, or metal spoon. Heat the butter in a heavy, well-seasoned or nonstick frying pan. When the butter has foamed and bubbled, slide the egg from the cup into the hot fat. The heat rises slowly up, thickening the white, then the yolk. When done, aficionados prefer a fluid yolk. A little practice will help the cook know what works best. Cover the pan to speed cooking without raising the heat. Of course, if you like the bottom crispy brown from the butter, do as you wish.

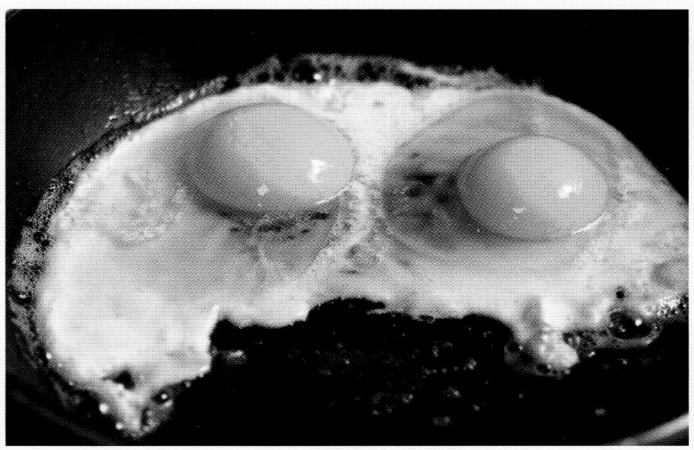

Over-easy eggs—For those whose idea of a yolk running into the hollows of an English muffin is abhorrent, the perfect solution is an over-easy egg, turned over with a spatula and slipped back into the pan yolk-first. This stops the white from cooking on the bottom and getting hard and crisp, ensuring the top portion of the white and the yolk are at 158 degrees and firm. It takes only a few moments for the rest of the yolk to catch up and harden without toughening.

Butter-poached eggs—Another method of speeding up the cooking of the yolk is the "butter-poaching" method, which is very decadent, particularly when served with bread fried in butter. After sliding the egg from the cup into the hot butter, give the eggs a minute or so to set slightly. Gently spoon hot butter on top of the yolk, repeatedly, until a membrane coats the yolk, the top is firm, and the white is tenderly cooked. Cook longer for a well-done yolk.

Soft-cooked eggs in the shell—Use a pot large enough to hold the eggs but not so large they will rattle around and bump each other. Add water to cover the eggs. Add a little white vinegar if desired, which helps coagulate any escaping egg white. Prick the shells at the large end with a tack or needle. Use a large spoon to transfer the eggs one by one ever so gently to the pan, bring just to the boil; remove from the heat, cover the pan, and let eggs sit in the hot water 4 to 5 minutes, or until cooked to personal preference. Remove eggs with a slotted spoon. Make notes of cooking time to reproduce results. The easiest way to eat is to hold the slightly cooled egg in one hand and rap sharply with a knife to open up on a piece of toast or into a shallow bowl.

These are easier to cook than eat when served in eggcups, because we have so little practice eating out of the tiny eggcups. Place the egg in its shell in the eggcup, large end down. Rap a knife or a spoon sharply on the egg to crack off the top third of the shell, or use an egg topper gadget. Season to taste with salt, pepper, and herbs as desired. Proceed to eat the egg with a teaspoon or other small spoon. Easier said than done, but oh, so elegant when managed correctly.

Coddled eggs—These eggs are so gently cooked that they remain tender. They may be coddled in the shell (as is done for the original Caesar Salad), or they may be cooked in the specially designed china egg coddlers that are secured by a metal cap with a ring.

Lay a folded dishtowel on the bottom of a saucepan large enough to hold all the china coddlers being used. Add enough water to reach the rims of the egg coddlers, but do not add the coddlers until the water comes to the boil.

Meanwhile, butter the insides of the coddlers well. If there is room, add a little sautéed mushroom or artichoke heart to the bottom of the coddler before adding the egg. Break in one egg per coddler and top with a little butter, a couple of teaspoons of cream, a little salt, a little pepper, and/or an herb of choice—tarragon or thyme are the usual. Grated cheese or a little cooked bacon or ham may also be added. Screw on the tops and set the filled coddlers onto the towel in the water-filled saucepan. Reduce heat to a simmer for 6 to 8 minutes for a medium-set egg, where the white is fully set and the yolk is slightly runny. Remove the coddlers by the ring and unscrew carefully by holding the hot lids (not the rings) with a potholder. If underdone, re-cover carefully and return to the pan for 1 to 2 minutes more. Serve with buttered toast and bacon.

Poached eggs— A very fresh egg will poach more easily

than an older egg, as the yolks and white will stay closer together. An older egg's white will be more watery and tend to stray away from the yolk. Since eggs are fragile, it is a good idea to use more eggs than needed, particularly for special occasions, removing any broken ones and using them for another purpose or discarding them altogether.

I learned how to poach eggs when I went down one weekend to work at Commander's Palace when Paul Prudhomme was the chef there. I was stunned to learn that eggs could be cooked in advance. Commander's served thousands of eggs at their Sunday brunch, and their system was a marvel to behold. There was a chef in front of a steam table of three pans. One was a pan of simmering water, into which eggs were cracked. The second was a pan of fine ice. The third was another pan of simmering water. He had his routine down perfectly. He had a 36-egg crate to the side, full of eggs that were as fresh as possible so the yolks would mound. He cracked dozens of eggs into the first pan, one after the other, with no concern if the occasional one broke. He went back to the first one, and then, one after the other, moved them with a flat spoon with holes to the pan of ice. When an order was placed, he moved a cooked egg from the ice into the barely simmering water, letting it pause—1, 2, 3 seconds—until it was warm throughout, and then patted his spoon on a piece of clean towel. It was moved to the English muffin or toast and was ready to go. Perfect!

Eggs can be poached in liquids other than water. Try red wine, tomato sauce, tomato juice or soup, gravies, etc.

POACHED EGGS

1 large still cold egg per person plus a few extras as needed
1 tablespoon vinegar per egg up to 4 eggs, optional

Grease the bottom of a frying pan (or use a nonstick pan) large enough to poach the amount of eggs needed. Add water twice the depth of an egg. Add the vinegar to help coagulate the whites. Crack the still cold egg on the counter and open it into a large metal spoon or shallow metal container. Slide the egg directly from the container into the water, or immerse the container, such as a spoon, and let cook on the spoon. Set timer for three minutes. When done, the white should be firm and the yolk soft.

Use a slotted spoon or skimmer to move each to a roasting pan of shaved ice, removing each in the order in which it was cooked, discarding any broken eggs or reserving them for another purpose. Trim off any streamers of egg white. The eggs may be stored together in the roasting pan of shaved ice and refrigerated for up to 24 hours. To reheat the eggs, slide the slotted spoon or skimmer under the egg and dip into simmering water for a few seconds, sufficient to reheat the egg thoroughly. Drain over a clean towel or paper towel. Serve hot.

Variation: Poached Eggs, Really Fancy

I have to admit I no longer think this is worth the trouble. I am in awe of cooks who can mound the perfectly fresh egg into a spiral of white but wonder if it takes a year or more to learn how to do it. For my money, I'd rather use the method above and learn how to master the perfect omelet. Nonetheless, here's how to do fancy poaching:

Add water twice the depth of an egg to a pan and heat with the vinegar and bring to the boil. Crack the egg on the counter and then open into a metal or other heatproof-handled measuring cup, metal spoon, or another pan. Reduce the water in the pan to a simmer. Gently immerse the container in the water for 5 to 10 seconds to set the outside of the egg. Remove. Make an eddy (like a whirlpool) in the water with a large spoon and slide the egg into the eddy with the other hand. (A very fresh egg will form a swirl on top.) Reduce the heat. Simmer 3 to 4 minutes or let stand off the heat for 8 minutes. By this time, the white should be firm and the yolk soft.

Variations for Poached or Sunny-Side Up Eggs

Toss blanched asparagus spears (page 164) in olive oil or melted butter. Drizzle with buttered breadcrumbs or chopped nuts, top with egg and let the golden yolk form a sauce over the asparagus. Top a pizza with the cooked egg. Use blanched asparagus spears or "bread soldiers" (toasted bread cut into strips) to dip into the runny yolk.

Remove egg with a skimmer and drain. Trim off any streamers of egg. If not using immediately, plunge into a pan of shaved ice or cold water. Store this way refrigerated for up to 24 hours. Reheat as above.

Hard-cooked eggs—Store the eggs, small end up, for 24 hours to center the yolk, particularly for fresh eggs; or roll the eggs gently with a metal spoon in the pan several times as the water comes to the boil. The Georgia Egg Council's preferred method of cooking is exactly as in soft-cooking, but it also suggests piercing the top of the egg with a thumb tack or needle before cooking, and leaving the eggs in the water covered for 15 minutes after the pot is removed from the heat. Adding a little vinegar to the water will help any exposed or cracked egg to coagulate. Adding 1 tablespoon baking soda to the boiling water helps fresh (uncoated) eggs peel more easily, but this does not affect commercially coated eggs. Still, there's no harm in trying! (See page 271, "From Hen to Table.") To prevent the egg yolk from turning green, immediately run cold water over the eggs or cool them in ice water.

My method is to add the pierced eggs one by one, gently tipping off the side of a large slotted spoon into boiling water to cover. Roll the eggs briefly to center the yolks. Simmer 11 minutes. Remove the eggs to ice water to cool. Drain. Tap the top of each egg on the counter. Roll on the counter to crack the shell. Under cool running water, start peeling at the large end to catch the air bubble. Pull off the shell, working down to the tapered end. Remember eggs in a carton of eggs do not come from the same hen, and the hens may not have eaten the same. Hence, some eggs will peel more easily than others. Cook more eggs than needed for special times.

CLASSIC OMELET

There are various opinions about what makes a perfect omelet, as there are for all egg cooking methods. In a class at a French cooking school, I was taught that omelets should be free of any specks of brown. To me, a bit of brown gives flavor. Some like them moist and slightly runny in the center. Others don't. Make your own decisions. Water makes the omelet lighter. Milk toughens an omelet. Add salt at the end, as it also toughens.

2 tablespoons butter
3 eggs
1–2 tablespoons water

Heat the butter in a very heavy 8-inch frying pan until it sizzles and sings. Whisk the eggs with the water until frothy. Pour into the hot fat to cover bottom of the pan. Use a heatproof rubber spatula to give the eggs a good stir. Season with pepper. Remove spatula. Let the eggs cook and set 1 or 2 minutes. Quickly push aside the set portion of the eggs with the spatula, simultaneously tipping the pan so the raw portion runs under the cooked portion. Let eggs set again, and repeat, pushing and tipping the pan. Repeat the process one or two more times. Fluffy, soft layers of the egg will build up. Holding the handle of the pan in one hand, with a plate in the other, tip the pan and slide one-half of the omelet out of the pan onto the plate. (If filling the omelet with grated cheese or other fillings, add them now.) Turn the pan in a slow, flipping motion so the remaining eggs form a half moon on the plate.

For a traditional omelet, after practicing with the two-flip omelet, try putting one-third on the plate, cover with the second third, and slide the third side under, jiggling the plate.

Variations abound, including adding herbs and other ingredients to the eggs, and filling with grated cheese, ham, chicken, etc. The sky is the limit.

DECADENT TOAD IN A HOLE

Serves 1

MY FAVORITE EGG IS ONE COOKED INSIDE A HOLLOW OF BREAD *fried in butter—my mother called it Toad in a Hole. For me, the best time to eat it is a rainy day when I have a cold and am languishing alone in bed. Although the recipe is for one, I usually eat two—using a larger pan. I like it even better if the butter browns to the color of a pecan.*

2–4 tablespoons butter
1 slice bread
1 large egg
Salt
Freshly ground black pepper

Melt butter in a frying pan.

Tear a hole in the center of a slice of bread that will hold the whole egg (or use a biscuit cutter for a perfect center hole).

Add the bread to the butter in the pan and fry until golden on one side. Turn with a spatula. Add more butter to the pan if needed.

Crack the egg on the counter and open over a cup. Slide the egg into the hole, not minding if it overlaps the bread a bit. Spoon butter from the pan over the egg while cooking the egg 2 to 3 minutes, until white and bottom of egg are softly firm, and the top of the egg yolk and white are cooked from the heat of the butter as well.

Remove with a spatula and eat while warm. The yolk should run all over the bread. Season to taste with salt and pepper if desired. Drink orange juice and plenty of hot tea.

EGGS BENEDICT

Serves 4

IT WAS 1893 OR 1894 AT THE WALDORF. *Or was it Delmonico's? Well, we do know it was in New York City. One story about the origin of Eggs Benedict is that a hung-over Wall Street broker named Lemuel Benedict ordered bacon and poached eggs on buttered toast and topped it off with hollandaise sauce one morning at the Waldorf Hotel in 1894. Oscar Tschirky, the famous maître d'hôtel, tweaked the "recipe" by using English muffins and Canadian bacon, and then added it to his breakfast and lunch menu.*

History also reveals that Mrs. Le Grand Benedict, a regular customer at Delmonico's, could find nothing to please her on the menu, so the chef, Charles Ranhofer, created the dish for her. His recipe, Eggs à la Benedick, appears in his cookbook The Epicurean, *a 3,500-recipe cookbook published in 1894.*

Whoever can stake a claim to the dish, it was certainly characteristic of the fashionable, rich dishes served in fancy restaurants and hotels in the late-nineteenth century. The South claims Eggs Benedict as part of a proper Sunday brunch, made enormously popular by the brunch-loving crowds in New Orleans. Possibly the hangover remedy part of the story is true after all . . .

This recipe is easy to assemble once all the pieces are prepared. Remember, the eggs may be poached ahead of time and reheated quickly, the ham (or Canadian bacon) only has to be at room temperature, and the hollandaise will hold for an hour.

2–4 English muffins, split and toasted
4 tablespoons butter, optional
4 thin slices country ham or Canadian bacon
4–6 poached large eggs (page 274)
Hollandaise Sauce (page 652)
Salt
Freshly ground black pepper

Spread the toasted muffin halves with butter as desired and move to a serving plate. Top with thin slices of ham, sometimes called biscuit slices. Reheat the poached eggs in simmering water for a few seconds, drain, and move on top of the ham. Use a large spoon to ladle the hollandaise on top. Season to taste with salt and pepper.

SOFT SCRAMBLED EGGS

Serves 4

PEOPLE CAN BE VERY PARTICULAR ABOUT THEIR SCRAMBLED EGGS. *In fact, there are many ways to serve them. The traditional way is to scramble eggs in bacon or sausage grease over high heat until they are cooked hard. Not for me! I'm a butter person. The following recipe is a method of producing creamy, big-curd scrambled eggs, terrific over buttered toast.*

2–3 tablespoons butter
7 large eggs, divided
1/4–1/2 cup heavy cream
Salt
Freshly ground black pepper

Melt the butter over low heat in a heavy saucepan, the top of a double boiler, or a pan using a water bath (Bain-Marie, page 281).

Whisk six eggs lightly in a small bowl. (The more they are whisked, the lighter they will be.) Tip eggs into the melted butter. Stir occasionally over low heat until they start to cook and thicken. Add the cream and continue stirring until eggs start to form large curds. (Some chefs do this for up to half an hour.) When the eggs are still soft but nearly done, remove from the heat. Whisk the last egg and stir it in gently to cook in the eggs' heat. Season to taste with salt and pepper.

Variations:

- Add 1/2 cup grated Gruyère or goat cheese halfway through. Continue stirring until cheese is melted.
- Add chopped fresh herbs with the last egg.

Variation: Hard Scrambled Eggs

After adding the eggs to the butter, turn up the heat a bit and whisk to break up the curds. Cook 1 to 2 minutes more.

CARAMELIZED PEACH OR MANGO OMELET

Serves 2

THIS IS A TREAT FOR TWO. *Juggling two pans is difficult, so this results in one glorious omelet. For omelet tips and directions, see page 275. For an omelet soufflé, see page 286.*

1–2 peaches or 1 mango, peeled
4 tablespoons light or dark brown sugar or confectioners' sugar
2 tablespoons butter
6 large eggs
1 tablespoon water
Salt
Confectioners' sugar

Heat a griddle, grill, or frying pan for the fruit.

Slice the fruit. Toss in the brown sugar. Add to the hot pan. Cook until sugar is melted and starting to caramelize.

Meanwhile, heat the butter until sizzling hot in a nonstick medium frying pan. Whisk the eggs with water until frothy. Pour into the butter and give a good stir. Let the eggs cook and set 1 to 2 minutes, then push aside the set eggs and tip the pan so the raw portion runs under the cooked portion. Repeat several times until eggs are just set but not overcooked.

Scatter half of the fruit over one half of the omelet. Holding the pan in one hand, tip the pan slightly to slide the omelet down and flip the other half over the fruit-covered half. Top with remaining fruit and sprinkle with sugar.

DEVILED EGGS

Makes 12

The pretty glass dish I have had for many years *holds 12 deviled egg halves. Always cook more eggs than needed if perfection is desired, as some yolks may not be centered properly or the eggs may peel imperfectly. Those eggs can be used for Egg Salad (page 96). A real Southern girl should have a strand of pearls, an iced tea pitcher, and a deviled egg dish.*

- 6–8 hard-cooked large eggs (page 275)
- 1/4 cup mayonnaise
- 1/2 teaspoon Dijon mustard
- 2 tablespoons finely chopped green onions, green portion only
- 1 tablespoon finely chopped capers, optional
- 1/8 teaspoon ground hot red pepper
- Salt
- 2 teaspoons finely chopped fresh thyme

Slice the cooked eggs in half lengthwise and move the yolks to a small mixing bowl. Mash the yolks well with a fork or whisk. Add the mayonnaise, mustard, green onions, capers, hot red pepper, and salt to taste. Mix well. Spoon or pipe decoratively back into the halves. Garnish with finely chopped thyme.

Variation: Use tiny quail eggs in place of chicken eggs for a whimsical appetizer. They are worth the extra effort. Quail eggs are not coated as commercial eggs are, so they readily peel if a bit of baking soda is added to the cooking water.

CHEESE CUSTARDS

Makes 6 starters or luncheon dishes

These rich custards are delicious alone or with a complimentary sauce. *A little goes a long way. For an elegant luncheon, the perfect accompaniment is a green salad followed by a light fruit dessert.*

- 3/4 cup heavy cream or milk
- 3 large eggs
- 1 1/4 cups grated Gruyère cheese
- Salt
- Freshly ground black pepper

Preheat oven to 300 degrees. Butter 6 custard cups and set aside. Cut 6 waxed paper rounds to fit. Butter the rounds.

Lightly mix cream or milk and eggs in a medium-sized bowl. Stir in the grated cheese and season to taste with salt and pepper.

Spread a kitchen towel in the bottom of a deep baking pan to prevent over-baking. Arrange the custard cups or soufflé dishes on top of the towel. Ladle or pour custard mixture evenly into the six cups. Move rounds of buttered waxed paper to the top of each mixture to prevent skins from forming.

Fill the baking pan with water to halfway up the sides of the custard cups and carefully move to the oven. Bake until the centers of the custards are set and a knife comes out clean, approximately 30 to 40 minutes, depending on the size; avoid boiling the custards. Remove from the water and set aside.

When ready to serve, remove the waxed paper rounds and serve in the dish, or run a knife around the sides of the dish, invert a plate on top of the custard cup, flip, and carefully remove the cup. Either way, custard can be re-warmed in a 250-degree oven if necessary.

Variation: Add chopped thyme or other herbs.

Variation: Cheese Custard with Crabmeat Sauce
Bring 3/4 cup heavy cream to the boil in a heavy saucepan and boil until reduced to 1/3 cup. When ready to eat, reheat cream, remove from heat, and gently stir in 1/3 pound of crabmeat, shells and membrane removed, and 1 to 2 tablespoons butter. Ladle over the Cheese Custards.

FRESH CORN CUSTARDS

Makes 8 custards

A HOT PUFFY CUSTARD COMBINED WITH FRESH CORN *is one of summer's many pleasures. These light custards make a special appetizer or side dish. My husband loves them with meatloaf.*

6–9 ears fresh corn, shucked
3 large eggs
1/3 cup milk
1 cup heavy cream
2 tablespoons butter, melted
1 tablespoon granulated sugar
1 teaspoon salt
Freshly ground black pepper

Preheat oven to 350 degrees. Oil or butter 8 (4-ounce) ramekins and set aside.

To cut the corn off the cob and get its precious "milk," hold a shucked ear of corn on its end in the center of a low Bundt pan, shallow bowl, or pie dish. Using a sawing motion, slice the tips of the corn kernels from the cob with a sharp knife, turning as needed. Slice down a second time to remove all the corn and its milk. Use the blunt side of a knife to press and scrape down against the cob, turning as needed, to remove the remaining corn and "milk" next to the cob. Repeat with each ear of corn.

Whisk the eggs, milk, cream, butter, sugar, and salt lightly, just until well mixed. Season to taste with pepper. Stir in the corn and its "milk." Ladle into the prepared ramekins, distributing corn and batter evenly. Leave a 3/4-inch space at the top of each so the custard can rise; do not overfill.

Add a clean tea towel to the bottom of a large shallow baking pan to prevent overcooking. Move the filled ramekins to the tea towels and pour boiling hot water into the pan until the water reaches halfway up the sides of the ramekins. Carefully move the water bath with the ramekins to the preheated oven. Bake for 20 to 30 minutes, or until the custards are set and golden brown and a toothpick inserted into the center comes out clean. Remove the custards from the roasting pan and serve immediately.

Variations:

- If corn is out of season, use a 1-pound bag of frozen white corn instead.
- Separate eggs, whisking the egg whites until stiff and folding in before adding corn.
- Whip the cream and fold in after adding corn.
- To prevent browning, cover each filled ramekin with a buttered round of waxed paper.

SOUFFLÉS

Soufflés are not difficult to make or magical, but they seem that way to the uninitiated. Soufflés are really just sauces to which egg yolks and beaten egg whites have been added. The trick is to avoid overcooking a soufflé, as the bubbles will grow like a balloon and burst, and the soufflé will fall. An undercooked soufflé, on the other hand, may be removed from the oven and served, then placed back in the oven if need be, as the egg will continue to rise. It is important to have serving plates and guests ready and waiting.

The sauce, or soufflé base, may be made a day or two in advance, with the egg whites folded in and baked when ready to serve. Refrigerate the sauce if holding more than 1 hour, and try to bring it back to room temperature before adding the egg whites. If made ahead more than a few hours, use 1 extra egg white to assure maximum volume. Be sure to remove the top rack from the oven so the soufflé has optimum space to rise.

One word about the center of the soufflé: the French call a perfect center *baveuse,* which translates as "drooling." They want it a little runny and sauce-like. The soufflé continues to cook once it is removed from the oven, so if the center is totally dry, it is probably overbaked and will collapse quicker. If the center is runnier than preferred, eat around the edges of the soufflé. Probably the center will be cooked by the residual heat from the dish before it is reached; or dish up the cooked part and put the overly runny portion back into the oven. Remember, soufflé ingredients are inexpensive, so feel free to experiment.

Panko Vs. Breadcrumbs—Panko is a special type of breadcrumb formulated in Japan. Now available from American companies and others, it is preferred by many chefs over regular breadcrumbs. At any rate, lining the soufflé dish with dry breadcrumbs (toasted or stale bread made into crumbs, or crumbs left to dry in the air or on low heat in the oven) or panko will enable the soufflé to climb equally well. The panko does give a slightly different crust.

TECHNIQUES FOR SUCCESSFUL SOUFFLÉS

The Soufflé Dish

What's the right size dish? This is one of the difficult things about making a soufflé, because soufflé dishes are like people: they can be short and squat or tall and lean. Their shape determines how long they need to be baked, and this can vary up to 5 or 10 minutes.

I use a glass bowl with volume indicators on its side for the final folding of the egg whites into the soufflé base. The final soufflé volume should be approximately 1 cup less than the size of the soufflé dish. The dish should be filled from within an inch to the rim of the dish. Using a dish that is too large makes a perfectly good soufflé, but the soufflé will not appear to rise. A smaller dish requires a paper collar, which I prefer, because it makes the soufflé appear to have risen more when baked, as it will be "over the top"! Filling the dish higher than the rim will cause the collar-less soufflé to topple when baked. Better to bake the excess in small soufflé dishes or cups the next day.

I can't stress enough how different soufflé dishes are from one another. They range in size dramatically. The cooking time will have to be adjusted according to the size of the dish. It is very disappointing when a soufflé dish is too large and swallows the soufflé, overcooking it and making it appear it didn't rise. Better to err with a too-small dish and build up the capacity by putting on a paper collar.

Beating the Egg Whites

How well the egg whites are beaten determines how much volume the soufflé will have. As the novice becomes an expert, the resulting volume will be more consistent. Egg whites are best beaten in a stand mixer with a rotary whisk; beating by hand in a copper or non-plastic bowl will yield the most volume. If all that is available for beating is another type of mixer, the soufflé will still rise, but the volume will be less. The mixing bowl must be thoroughly clean to start. Any trace of residual oil, butter or other fat will interfere with achieving the maximum volume.

Any yolk, or fat, in the egg whites will prevent them from beating properly. A small amount of the yolk may be removed by using the eggshell or a spoon as a scoop, provided the egg shell is clean. If the yolk cannot be removed, save the whole egg for another purpose, or discard.

Reheating Leftovers

Leftover soufflé can be reheated quickly in 1-minute increments in the microwave, or in a 350-degree oven for 10 to 15 minutes, until heated through, depending on the volume. Usually the soufflé miraculously rises. No matter the rise, it is certainly delicious! See the recipe for Twice-Baked Soufflé, (page 283).

Making a Paper Collar

A paper collar extends the capacity of the dish and supports the soufflé when it rises above the rim of the dish. Cut a piece of parchment or waxed paper or aluminum foil large enough to surround the soufflé dish with a slight overlap. Fold the paper in half horizontally. If the soufflé dish has a small ridge under the lip, as most do, fold the folded edge down 1/2 inch so it will fit under the exterior ridge of the dish. This helps hold the paper and the rising soufflé, straight. The paper should be buttered and sprinkled lightly with panko, as shown below.

After folding the paper as above, wrap it onto the exterior of the dish, with the 1/2-inch fold snugly under the ridge, holding the paper straight. Have ready a length of twine half again as long as the paper. Wrap the string around the paper surrounding the dish and make a loop. Pull one end of string through the loop then tie the two ends together. Situate the string just below the ridge so the paper is secure.

Soufflé Tips

- It is better to separate the eggs (page 272) when cold and let them come up to room temperature.
- Some commercial eggs developed with lower cholesterol do not whip the way standard eggs do.
- Don't worry about opening and closing the oven. In modern ovens, doing so once or twice to check won't hurt the soufflé. They fall from overcooking, not a draft.

Bain-Marie (Water Bath)

A bain-marie, or water bath, is usually a larger pan of water in which a baking dish is placed (containing custard, soufflé, and the like) to allow for long and slow cooking. Baking egg dishes in a bain-marie allows the eggs to cook evenly, preventing overheating, which causes the overcooked eggs to curdle and separate.

To make a bain-marie, place a clean tea towel (to prevent slipping and over-browning of the bottom of the dish) inside a large shallow baking pan. Move the filled baking dish (soufflé dish or ramekins, for instance) to the tea towel–lined pan. Put into the preheated oven and pour boiling hot water into the pan, avoiding splattering the dish, until the water reaches halfway up the side of the baking dish. (Using boiling hot water speeds up the time it takes to heat the pan water back to 212 degrees.)

CHEESE SOUFFLÉ

Serves 4 to 6 for lunch

LIGHT, DELICATE, BUT FILLING, *a soufflé makes a grand lunch or even a light supper. Add a green salad and a small dessert for a near-perfect meal. Comte, a type of Gruyère cheese, mixed with Parmesan cheese, makes a delicate soufflé. For a more robust flavor, use white or yellow Cheddar, but almost any combination of cheese will do. Change the amount of mustard accordingly. Freshly grated nutmeg (avoid pre-grated nutmeg altogether) enhances but must be used sparingly or it dominates. If in doubt, omit it altogether.*

For best results, read the information about soufflés preceding this recipe. Remember, a soufflé is a breath of air, not an ordeal. Enjoy making it!

4–5 tablespoons butter, divided
Breadcrumbs or panko
4 tablespoons all-purpose flour
1 1/2 cups milk, preferably Flavored Milk (page 657)
1 1/2 cups grated cheese
1 teaspoon Dijon mustard
Dash of freshly grated nutmeg (optional)
Dash of ground hot red pepper
Salt
Freshly ground pepper
6 large eggs, separated
2 additional egg whites
1/8 teaspoon cream of tartar

Preheat oven to 400 degrees. Position a rimmed baking sheet in the center of the oven with no racks above so the soufflé may rise unimpeded. The hot metal will give the soufflé a boost from the bottom as well as catch any dribbles.

Butter a 4- or 5-cup soufflé dish with 1 to 1 1/2 tablespoons of the butter and dust it with fine dry breadcrumbs or panko. Wrap a buttered and crumbed parchment, waxed paper, or aluminum foil collar (page 281) around the outside of the dish if the dish appears to be too small to hold all the soufflé mixture. Put a serving plate next to the stove area, to put under the finished cooked soufflé dish so it is easier to move.

Melt the remaining butter in a heavy saucepan. Add the flour and stir briefly until smooth. Add the milk all at once. Stir with a wooden spoon until the mixture comes to the boil and is smooth. Add the cheese, mustard, nutmeg, and hot red pepper, and mix together. Remove from the heat and add the 6 egg yolks one at a time, mixing well after each addition. Season to taste with salt and pepper, and add liberally, remembering the egg whites are yet to be added.

The sauce may be prepared in advance to this point and stored in the refrigerator or frozen. If letting the mixture rest, cover with plastic wrap or coat with a light sprinkle of grated cheese to avoid a film forming on top. If refrigerating or freezing, reheat sauce gently before proceeding.

Beat the 8 egg whites and cream of tartar in a clean, dry bowl of a stand mixer with a rotary whisk, such as a KitchenAid, or by hand with a whisk until they are shiny and form a firm peak. If using a smaller mixer, use as large a bowl as possible, circling the mixer around the bowl. Stop after the peaks just begin to form and beat the last few minutes by hand if possible. Underbeating the eggs is better than overbeating them and causing the air bubbles to burst. Stop beating before the eggs look rough and "rocky."

Use a spatula or large metal spoon to fold about 1 cup of the beaten egg white into the warm sauce to soften. Pour the sauce over the remaining egg whites, folding it in until nearly completely integrated. The last few pockets of egg whites will disappear as the soufflé bakes. (This may be done up to several days in advance, with the soufflé brought up to room temperature before baking.)

Pile the soufflé carefully into the prepared dish. It should fill the dish within an inch of the top. Smooth the top. Run a knife quickly around the inside of the dish to help release it later. If desired, make a circle in the middle of the top of the soufflé to form a "cap." This will rise separately and enhance the presentation.

Move the dish to the middle of the hot baking sheet. Immediately turn the oven down to 375 degrees. Bake 20 minutes, or until the soufflé has risen. Open the oven door, reach in and touch the top of the soufflé. If it is soft on top, close the oven door and continue to bake. Check again in 5-minute increments. When it is done, it will be lightly firm on top, and a skewer inserted into it will have a small amount of soufflé on it when removed. Remove the soufflé dish from the oven and put the dish on the serving plate. If using a collar, snip off the string and remove the collar carefully. If it starts to stick, hold a knife outside the collar to use as a firm guide, and move it around the dish while peeling off the paper. Discard paper and string.

After quickly showing off the soufflé, immediately use 2 large spoons inserted back to back in the dish to "open" the soufflé. It should have a small pool of *baveuse* in the center. If the soufflé is moderately runny, start serving, moving around the outside edges of the soufflé dish. The center will continue to cook and should be perfect in a few minutes. If the soufflé is still very runny, it may be returned to the oven until it firms a bit, just a few minutes, before or after serving the outside edges.

If the soufflé falls, the soufflé has been overbaked, causing the air bubbles so carefully beaten into the eggs to overexpand and burst. Run a knife around the inside rim of the collar-free soufflé dish. Invert the serving plate over the soufflé dish and flip the soufflé and the dish over. Give a quick, firm shake. If properly buttered and crumbed, the bottom and sides will release. Serve on the dish. No need to tell anyone it fell. It will be slightly denser than a regular soufflé and more like a light custard. Call it a twice-baked soufflé, or say nothing and just enjoy the raves.

FROM ROUX TO SOUFFLÉ

A cheese soufflé is a perfect example of putting a lot of simple techniques together that are used over and over in the kitchen and finishing with something spectacular. It is first a roux, then a white sauce, then a cheese sauce, then a cheese custard, and then, after whipping and folding in the egg whites and baking it, a soufflé with a custardy sauce.

Variation: Twice-Baked Soufflés

Butter 6 (5- or 6-ounce) ramekins and preheat oven to 375 degrees. Make soufflé as directed, and ladle evenly into the prepared ramekins. Place a clean tea towel in the bottom of a large shallow baking pan. Move the filled ramekins, to the pan lined with a tea towel. Move to the oven and carefully, without splashing the ramekins, add boiling hot water to the pan until the water reaches halfway up the sides of the ramekins. Using boiling hot water speeds up the time it takes to heat the pan water and start the cooking. Lower the heat to 350 and bake 20 minutes, depending on the size of the ramekins. The soufflés are done when the tops are lightly firm and a skewer inserted in the soufflé still has mixture clinging to it. Remove the soufflés in the water bath carefully from the oven, remove the soufflés from the bath, and let collapse and cool. Cover with plastic wrap and refrigerate up to 3 days or leave at room temperature up to 1 hour.

To serve, preheat oven to 350 degrees. Top soufflés with 1 cup grated Parmesan cheese. Bake minutes 15 to 20 minutes, until soufflés have risen again and turned slightly golden brown. Remove from oven and serve immediately.

Variation: Twice-Baked Soufflés with Tomato-Cream Sauce

Heat 1 cup heavy cream, 3 seeded and chopped tomatoes, and 1 tablespoon chopped fresh tarragon. Season to taste with salt and pepper to make a sauce. Butter a dish large enough to hold the unmolded soufflés together in a single layer. Run a knife around the insides of the ramekins, turn out the cooled, baked soufflés into the prepared dish. (If one comes out unevenly, don't worry; just push it back together.) Divide the sauce and 1 cup grated Parmesan cheese evenly over the soufflés. Bake 15 to 20 minutes, until soufflés have risen again and turned slightly golden brown. Remove from the oven and spoon each soufflé onto a warm plate. Spoon any leftover sauce on top.

CLASSIC SPOON BREAD

Serves 4

The South's answer to an everyday soufflé, *this can be served anytime. It is more a soufflé than a bread. Light and airy and requiring only a spoon, it is usually eaten with a fork. A salad is an enjoyable accompaniment for a small lunch or Sunday supper, but spoon bread can also be served with a full meal. This recipe is adapted from Damon Lee Fowler's* Classic Southern Cooking. *When I want a truly classic Southern recipe, I turn there for inspiration.*

3 cups half-and-half, preferably Flavored (page 657)
1 cup fine cornmeal, white, yellow, or mixed
3 tablespoons unsalted butter, melted
1 teaspoon salt
3 large eggs, separated

Preheat oven to 350 degrees. Butter a 7-inch round casserole or soufflé dish.

Scald the half-and-half in a heavy pan by bringing it almost to the boil, creating tiny bubbles around the outside. Pour a steady stream of cornmeal into the half-and-half, whisking constantly. Continue cooking until it forms a thick mush. Remove from heat and stir in the butter and salt. Let cool slightly.

Beat the egg yolks until pale yellow and stir them into the corn mush.

Whisk the egg whites with a stand mixer until they form stiff peaks. Gently fold the whites into the corn mush.

Pour the corn batter into the prepared dish and bake in the center of the oven for 35 minutes; at this point, feel the top and see if it is wobbly or runny. If it is, return to the oven until cooked, up to 10 minutes or so longer.

The surface should be puffy and golden brown and resemble a soufflé. Serve hot. Can be reheated in the microwave.

MAKING HALF-AND-HALF

Mix milk or water with heavy cream to a consistency thicker than whole milk. Substitute evaporated milk (not sweetened condensed) if necessary.

GREENS AND HAM SPOON BREAD

Serves 4 to 6

LIKE MOST SPOON BREADS, *this is not a bread at all but a light soufflé. Very pretty and full of good things to eat, this spoon bread serves well as a Sunday-night supper, particularly on the heels of heavy holiday meals.*

4 tablespoons unsalted butter, divided
1 medium onion, chopped
2 garlic cloves, chopped
1 (10-ounce) package frozen turnip, collard, or kale greens, thawed and squeezed dry
3 ounces smoked country ham, diced
2 cups water
1 teaspoon salt
1/2 teaspoon freshly ground black pepper
1 cup cornmeal
1 cup milk
4 large eggs, separated
1/4 cup freshly grated Parmesan cheese
1/4 cup grated Swiss cheese

Preheat oven to 350 degrees. Butter a 2-quart soufflé dish.

Melt 2 tablespoons butter over medium heat. Add the onion and cook until soft, 5 to 7 minutes. Stir in the garlic, greens, and ham, and set aside.

Bring water, salt, and pepper to the boil in a medium saucepan over moderately high heat. Stir in the cornmeal. Reduce the heat and cook 1 to 2 minutes, stirring with a wooden spoon or electric hand mixer, until the sauce base is very thick (the consistency of mashed potatoes) and almost comes together in a ball, leaving the bottom of the pan clean. Remove from the heat and beat in the remaining butter and the milk with a wooden spoon or electric hand mixer. Beat in the egg yolks. Stir in the reserved greens, ham mixture, and cheeses.

Beat the egg whites in a separate, clean bowl until stiff but not dry (page 281). Stir a fourth of the egg whites into the cornmeal and greens batter to lighten it, then fold the batter into the remaining whites. Pour the batter into the buttered dish and bake in the middle of the oven for 50 to 55 minutes, until puffed and lightly browned. It will be soft in the center and crusty around the edges. Serve immediately.

CHEESE GRITS SOUFFLÉ

Serves 8

One of the most popular ways *of using cooked grits is to make them into soufflés with beaten egg whites. A once prevalent recipe for this called for adding a commercial cheese product that came in a tub; now we use the best cheese we can find. While called a soufflé, it is traditionally baked in an ovenproof dish and frequently made ahead and reheated, collapsed.*

- 4 cups cooked grits, cooked with milk
- 1 pound grated sharp Cheddar cheese
- 1/2 cup butter
- 1 tablespoon Dijon mustard
- 1/8 teaspoon mace
- 1 teaspoon salt
- 1/4 teaspoon ground hot red pepper
- 6 large eggs, separated

Preheat oven to 350 degrees. Generously butter an 8 1/2 x 13-inch ovenproof baking dish.

The grits should have the consistency of a sauce. If they are very thick, add more milk and heat until absorbed. Stir in the cheese, butter, mustard, mace, salt, and hot red pepper. Cool slightly. Taste for seasoning and add more salt if desired.

Lightly beat the egg yolks in a small bowl. Stir 1/2 cup of the grits into the yolks to heat them slightly, then add the yolks to the grits mixture and combine thoroughly.

Beat the egg whites until soft peaks form, and fold into the grits. Pour into the baking dish. The soufflé may be made several hours ahead to this point, covered, and refrigerated. When ready to bake, return to room temperature.

Bake the soufflé for 40 to 45 minutes, or until it is puffed and lightly browned. Remove from the oven and cover lightly; serve while hot. If the soufflé collapses, no matter—it is appetizing and no apologies are necessary. It can be cooked several days ahead of serving. Reheat as a casserole. Leftovers can be frozen.

SAVORY OMELET SOUFFLÉ

Serves 2

Savory Omelet Soufflés *can be served alone as a main dish or paired with soup and salad as a larger meal. They have the virtues of being quick to make as well as exciting to serve. They are ideal for a hot summer's day in the South. Omelet soufflés are simple egg yolks lightened with beaten egg whites and flavoring, cooked in the oven, and filled with sweet or savory fillings, depending on the occasion.*

- 6 large eggs, separated
- 1/2 teaspoon salt
- Freshly ground black pepper
- 1/2 teaspoon cream of tartar
- 2 tablespoons butter

Preheat oven to 375 degrees.

Whisk the egg yolks, with salt and pepper to taste, until thick.

Whip the egg whites and cream of tartar to a soft peak. Gently fold in a large spoonful of the yolk mixture to soften the egg whites. Fold this mixture into the rest of the yolks until incorporated. Be careful not to overmix, as doing so will deflate the whites.

Melt the butter in an 8-inch nonstick, oven-safe skillet. Pour in the egg mixture and immediately move to the oven. Bake 10 to 12 minutes, or until the soufflé is fluffy and golden brown. While the soufflé is cooking, prepare any filling.

Immediately after removing the soufflé from the oven, loosen the edges of the omelet with a spatula. Slide the omelet onto a heated plate; add the filling, fold over the top, press lightly with the bottom of the pan. Top with a sprinkle of the filling if desired. Serve immediately, dividing in two at the table.

Fillings: For a savory filling, try 1/2 cup grated Cheddar cheese, or 1/2 cup soft goat cheese, or sautéed mushrooms, or a crisp fresh vegetable. For a sweet omelet soufflé, use fresh sliced strawberries or peaches mixed with 1 tablespoon of warmed red currant jelly. Omit the black pepper.

BASIC CHEESE SOUFFLÉ CASSEROLE

Serves 8

THE SOUTH IS A LAND OF CHURCH SUPPERS, *where toting food is an honored tradition. So is fixing food ahead of time to be heated or cooked later, particularly dishes than can fill in at breakfast, lunch, or dinner. I have known people as well as restaurants to pass this off as a soufflé—and why not? It is amazingly light and fluffy. Different breads will give different flavors, from biscuits to rosemary pecan or other flavored breads. Dijon mustard brings out the flavor of bland cheeses. In measuring the cheeses, plan to use a bit less for a strong sharp Cheddar or blue, but the full 4 cups for a Gruyère or Swiss. Feel free to experiment. I have frozen the casserole after baking with good success, and have also baked it, refrigerated it up to three days, and reheated it.*

6 tablespoons butter
3 cups torn biscuits or favorite bread
9 large eggs
4 cups grated cheese
1 1/2 tablespoons Dijon mustard
Dash of ground hot red pepper
3 cups milk
Salt
Freshly ground black pepper

Melt butter in a large skillet over medium heat and stir in biscuits to coat with the butter. Remove from the heat and let stand for 5 minutes, until the butter is absorbed. Move the biscuit pieces to a large plastic ziplock bag.

Whisk together eggs, cheese, mustard, hot red pepper, and milk in a large bowl. Season to taste with salt and black pepper. Transfer the mixture to the plastic ziplock bag containing the biscuits or bread. Place the bag inside a larger plastic ziplock bag with the zipper facing another direction in order to prevent leaks. Refrigerate at least 2 hours, preferably overnight or up to 2 days.

When ready to bake, preheat oven to 350 degrees. Pour mixture into a buttered 13 x 9 x 2-inch baking dish or divide between 2 (1 1/2-quart) casseroles. Cover and bake 30 minutes. Uncover and bake another 30 minutes, until eggs are set and the center measures 200 degrees on an instant-read thermometer.

Variation: Overnight Sausage and Apple Casserole Fry 2 pounds bulk sausage in a skillet, breaking it up as it cooks, and drain on a paper towel. Reserve the fat and let the sausage cool. Sauté 2 sliced tart apples into the reserved fat, remove from pan, and let cool. Move 6 cups torn biscuit pieces to a large plastic ziplock bag. Whisk together 9 large eggs, 3/4 teaspoon Dijon mustard, 1 1/2 cups grated sharp Cheddar cheese, and 3 cups milk in a large bowl. Stir in the sausage and apples. Season to taste with salt and pepper. Transfer the mixture to the plastic ziplock bag. Place inside a larger plastic ziplock bag with the zipper facing another direction in order to prevent leaks. Refrigerate at least 2 hours, preferably overnight or up to 2 days. When ready to bake, preheat oven to 350 degrees. Pour mixture into a buttered 13 x 9 x 2-inch baking dish or divide between 2 (1 1/2-quart) casseroles. Cover and bake 30 minutes. Uncover and bake another 30 minutes, until eggs are set and the center measures 200 degrees on an instant-read thermometer.

Variation: Substitute other cheeses and 1 to 2 cups of cooked ingredients, such as bacon and asparagus.

FISH & SEAFOOD

The combined Southern Seaboard, including the Atlantic and Gulf Coast, covers three-fourths of the entire East Coast, from Maine's border with Canada to Brownsville, Texas, on the Gulf border with Mexico. The inhabitants of the Southern coasts, more than any others, know about waking up and walking out to toss a line for flounder or a net for blue crab, or, in Louisiana, to gather crawfish from rice stubble. Trawlers pull up to Southern docks to unload the freshest of fish in an astounding variety of sizes and species.

South Carolinians and others on the lengthy coastline may pull their boats over on a small tidal shoal covered with oysters, jump out, and pry open the freshest and most tender of oysters to slurp and slide down their throats, letting the tangy juices dribble down their chin. They know how the taste of the oysters varies from cove to cove, as well as from state to state.

Shrimp and grits—beginning with those made by the people who went out early in the morning to their feeder creeks to catch tiny breakfast shrimp, returning to cook them in butter and pour them over their grits—has become an important restaurant and home dish.

The blue crab, called the "beautiful swimmer," is unique to the Southern waters. It offers startling contrasts: vibrant orange when steamed in its shell, cracked open to reveal delicate white meat, and the soft-shell crab, cooked after shedding its shell. Yet both taste of the sea—one tender, one crisp.

Ironically, for years Southern coastal fish dominated what was sold in the Northern and other markets to the point that what went to the North was fresher than what was sold in interior areas of the South. That changed after interstate highways and airlines provided regional transportation and demand increased.

This lack of coastal fish, however, provided catfish, freshwater bass, mountain trout, and other freshwater fish an exalted place on the rest of the Southern table. Mississippi is famed for its readily available farm-raised catfish, delicate in flavor compared to its wild bottom-feeding cousins.

ABOUT SALTWATER FISH

The Ultimate Guide to Fishes of the Southeast Atlantic Coast, by Dr. Bob Shipp (available at www.foldingguides.com), categorizes the fish available in Southern waters—from Cape Hatteras, North Carolina, to the Florida/Georgia border—and notes which of the 61 species are the best for eating. It divides the best-rated fish for eating into five groups. Here are the best-rated, along with some of my favorites.

1. Groupers, snappers, grunts, porgies, and sheepshead—The most revered are the red and gag groupers along with other members of the grouper family, black sea bass, scamp, and Atlanta perch. Quintessentially Southern fish, with tender, moist flesh, they're usually eaten as fillets and steaks, although grouper cheeks are prized.

Snappers, including the vermilion, red, and gray, are ideal for cooking whole, in steaks, or as fillets. The red porgy (often called a pink snapper, or just pinkie) is better for pan-frying. Finally, the sheepshead, with its huge head and body, is a less-expensive fish but tricky to cook.

2. Jacks, drums, spotted sea trout, and kingfish.

3. Shortfin mako shark and ray fish (skates).

4. Game fish—Dolphin (mahi mahi), wahoo, bluefin and yellowfin tuna, and cobia are the most coveted. They are followed by king and Spanish mackerel.

5. Miscellaneous species—Flounders, mullet, and wreckfish.

There are basically two shapes of fish—flat and round:

Flat fish (like flounder) are traditionally white-skinned on the bottom and gray-skinned on the top, with a center bone (spine) and rib bones attached (all can usually be removed in one piece). Flat fish swim at the bottom of their habitat, their skin color helping to camouflage them from their enemies. Some have two eyes on one side of their head. Their skin isn't very tasty, so it is usually removed before or after cooking Their fillets are either double fillets, which are one-half of the whole fish, or two single fillets slimly attached with a thin membrane. The double fillets may also be separated and sold as single fillets, depending on the thickness of the fish.

Round fish are more difficult to bone. They can be almost any color, and the skin (scales removed) is more frequently left on when served.

BUYING FRESH FISH

Whenever possible, buy fresh fish. Fresh fish has a perfume that is subtle and enticing, smelling fresh, like the sea. Avoid overpowering and fishy-smelling fish. The eyes should be clear and translucent, not cloudy. Ideally, the fish should rest on paper atop ice at the store. Know the fishmonger and be able to trust that the market is willing to spend the time and money storing fish correctly. The word *fresh* has changed in meaning; there is no standard definition for *fresh* except that the fish cannot have been frozen and must not be in a state of decomposition, according to the Georgia Department of Agriculture. Realistically, if it smells strong, it will taste strong. Oily, fatty fish smell even stronger when they are more than a couple of days old. Some properly frozen fish are comparable to fresh. Certainly there are some excellent varieties of frozen American wild-caught shrimp.

The closer to a frozen state a fish stays, the fresher it will seem. That is why fish are iced down when caught and can be kept over and under ice on a ship for as long as a couple of weeks. The constant flow of ice and fresh water from the melting ice keeps the fish fresh, stopping bacteria from multiplying, thus reducing odor and decomposition.

There are three ways fresh fish is sold: steak, fillet, or whole. A steak is a thicker piece of meat made by cutting across the fish and may include a bone. A fillet is boneless. Whole fish, one of my favorite dinner party foods, is spectacular when served at the table.

When fish is a little older, soak it in milk 15 minutes or so to get rid of some of the overly fishy flavor and odor. (Rinse before proceeding with the recipe.)

HOW MUCH FISH TO SERVE

In deciding how much fresh fish to serve, keep a quarter pound of hamburger in mind. Men usually need a bit more food than that, while women usually are satisfied with that amount. Since fish loses water and weight when cooked, figure on 6 ounces for a main course and 7 ounces when a steak has a bone. A starter course can be almost any size these days, from 2 to 4 ounces. Whole fish is usually half bone, head and innards, so double the amounts needed when buying whole fish. "Big-headed" fish, such as grouper are trickier to gauge.

STORING AND PREPARING FISH

Freezing Fish—The best way to keep a fish longer than two or three days is to freeze it. Surround it with water so the fish is in the middle of a thin block of ice. If this is too bulky to fit in the freezer, dip the fish in water, lay it flat on freezer wrap or a tray, place in the freezer, and when a thin layer of ice encloses the fish, dip it again in water. When the second layer is frozen, wrap tightly and freeze.

Preparing Fish—Most fish sold today is cleaned and dressed and ready for cooking, be it a whole fish, fillets, or steaks. If you happen to be the recipient of a fisherman's bounty, gut the fish and remove the gills—the red "eyelashes" on the head. Rub the sharp edge of a knife along on the skin of the fish to check for scales and remove. Cut off any small bones protruding from the body of the fish, such as fins, and pull out any visible interior small bones. Complete boning is optional according to the recipe and style of cooking, but remember, it is always rude to surprise the eaters with unexpected bones that may choke them.

STUFFING FISH

Preparing a whole round fish for stuffing—Rinse and dry the fish then move it to a plastic board. Snip off any fins. With a very sharp knife, cut down the spine in the center of the fish, leaving both the head and tail intact. Make a perpendicular cut at the head end of the fish to form a T. This cut will facilitate opening the pocket.

To remove the spine, keeping the fillets whole, slide the knife against the backbone on either side of the incision. Leave the skin attached. With scissors, snip down the outer edges of the exposed small bones and through the top and bottom of the backbone. Sliding the knife under the backbone, wedge the bone out. The backbone should be clean of flesh. This leaves a pocket for the stuffing, with the thicker top fillets still in place and the fish whole but boneless. Refrigerate until ready to cook.

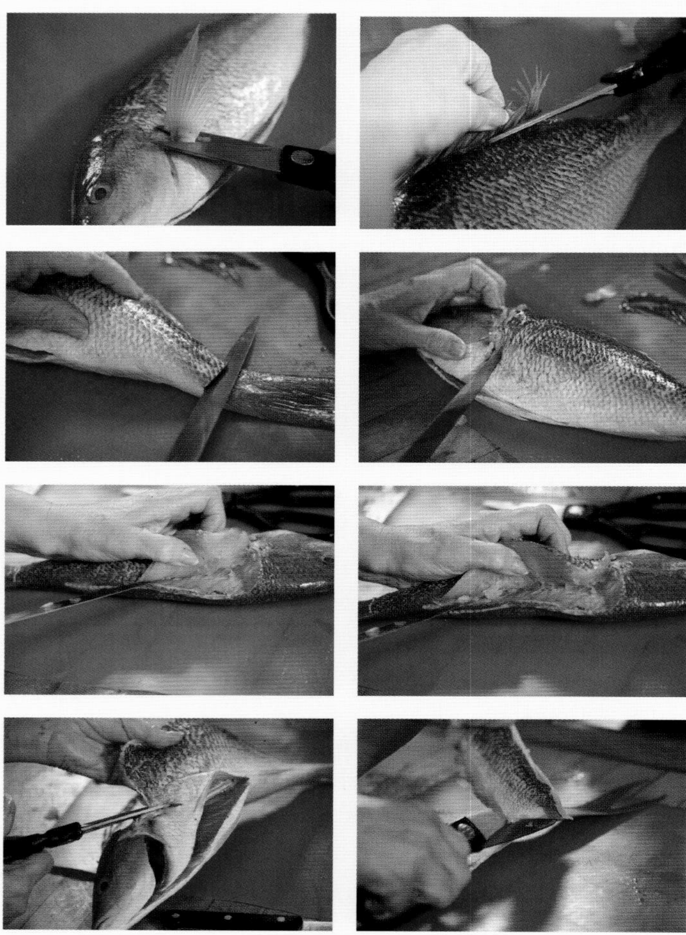

Stuffing fish fillets and flat fish—Fish fillets are frequently slit horizontally and the pocket stuffed with a filling, such as spinach and mushrooms, and served with a sauce, while very thin fillets are also spread with a similar filling and rolled up prior to cooking. Both these efforts produce "thicker" fillets, but to me the fish is frequently overcooked, particularly with thin fillets. I prefer putting the boned fillet on top of the stuffing.

Stuffing a whole flat fish—This makes a grand presentation. To remove the bone before stuffing without damaging the presentation is tricky for the novice, so follow these instructions carefully:

At the "collarbone" of the head, where the head would be removed, cut across the width of the fish, down to the bone but not through the bone. Cut down the center of the fish to the bone, going from the "collarbone" slit down to the tail in one firm cut.

Holding the knife at a slant, insert it down to the center bone. Slide the knife on top of the bone under one of the top fillets. With the other hand, peel back the fillet while working, to provide access to the bone. Stop short of the plump edge of the fillet, making a hinge. Repeat the process on the other top fillet.

Using scissors, snip down the bone on either side of the fish and sever it from the fish. If possible, cut out any little bones at the side. Discard the bone or use it for stock.

Put the stuffing in the center of the now boned fish and flip the hinged fillets back over the stuffing.

The opening will spread during cooking, so, if necessary, improve the fish's presentation with a garnish down the center; try cucumbers, cooked shrimp, zucchini, fennel, rosemary, or other herbs.

SKINNING FISH

To skin or not to skin is an individual choice, as is whether to use the fish skin and/or bones to make a broth. Once I took a group to a cooking class at a premier French cooking school. They had two chefs, one upstairs and one downstairs, both teaching the same menu. The upstairs chef was saying to skin the fish and use the skin in the broth; the other was saying to leave the skin on or discard it. My thought is this: if the skin is tough, remove it; otherwise, leave it on as a protection when cooking, then remove it later.

SKINNING A FISH FILLET

The colder the fish—even half frozen—the easier it is to skin. With the fillet skin-side down on a board, salt the fingers of the left hand to prevent them from slipping. Hold up the bottom of the fillet slightly at the tail and wedge a very sharp knife at a slight downward angle between the skin and the flesh. Pushing the knife away, work the blade between the flesh and skin until the flesh is removed. The quicker this is done, the better. (It may take several times to perfect this technique, so practice it when cutting the fillet in pieces for skewers, salads, etc.).

COOKING FISH

Fish is cooked accordingly to thickness, not weight. Measure it vertically, including its stuffing if applicable, at its thickest point. The rule of thumb is to cook the fish 10 minutes per inch of thickness at 400 degrees. For higher temperatures, 9 minutes per inch of thickness is sufficient. For lower temperatures, 11 minutes per inch is a good guide.

When a fish is flaky, it is overdone—It should "cling lightly to the bone with the suppleness of an arching cat," says one friend. Just before it flakes, the moisture is trapped inside the flesh, becoming steam ready to push the flakes apart to be released as it is cut. Fish should register 135 degrees on an instant-read thermometer when inserted into the thickest part of the fish, as gently as possible to avoid tearing the fish. A warning about the habit of testing by flaking: swordfish, among others, does not flake. Ever.

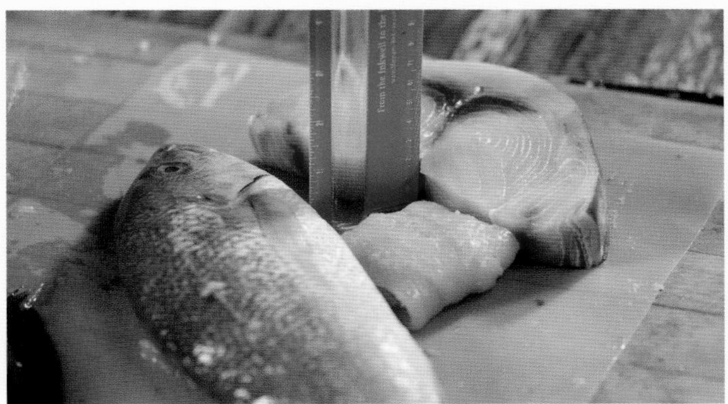

Broiling or grilling—Measure the fish at its thickest point and move to a buttered or oiled baking pan, or onto a sturdy rack on top of the pan. If it is a very thin fillet, fold it to make it thicker, or do not turn during cooking. Baste with melted butter, oil, mayonnaise, or other sauce, and add a little lemon or wine. The timing of the cooking depends on the distance from the heat and the temperature of the coals or broiler. When the fish has cooked on one side—test by pressing to see if it feels firm but has a slight "give"—turn and brush again with the butter or sauce and continue to cook. The total time is based on thickness.

Grilling small or delicate foods on a grill can be tricky. "Baskets" of varying sizes are available to hold the fish and keep it from dropping onto the coals. Made of heavy-gauge metal, frequently with a nonstick coating, these baskets are hinged on one side to allow opening and closing. Turning the contents of the basket is as simple as turning over the basket to cook the other side. Fitted with long handles, these baskets make grilling fish, kabobs, cut vegetables, and other small foods much easier.

If the fish is particularly thin, heat a pan before adding the fish. It should cook quickly on that side and not need turning when the side exposed to the heat is cooked.

Sautéing or pan-frying—Heat a thin layer (approximately 1⁄4 inch) of butter with a bit of oil in a heavy frying pan to sizzling hot—it should be 500 degrees or more. Cook fish 9 minutes to the inch of thickness, turning once after the first side is golden brown. The butter and oil might need to be changed if it burns after cooking one batch of fish.

It's usually hard to do more than one good-sized fish in a pan at one time. Adding all the fish at the same time to one skillet reduces the heat in the pan, and the fish will take longer to cook. If necessary, cook each fish individually or cook in small batches, keeping the cooked fish warm on a platter in a 250-degree oven.

Roasting or baking—Measure thickness of the fish, move to a rack or an oiled rimmed baking sheet in a preheated 450-degree oven, and roast 9 minutes to the inch, not turning.

Braising or poaching—When cooking the fish in a warm, flavored liquid—such as fish, vegetable, or shrimp stock—begin timing the cooking of the measured fish once the liquid has returned to the boiling point, and then reduce heat to a simmer and cover. Cook for 11 minutes to the inch of thickness. Remove and leave fish to continue cooking in the poaching liquid 1 or 2 extra minutes if close to being cooked.

Steaming—There are many gadgets for steaming. Fish can be steamed easily on an ovenproof plate atop a metal or steamer rack holding it above, not in, simmering water. Electric woks or skillets are easier to regulate than a pan on the stovetop. Steam covered fish for 8 to 10 minutes per inch of thickness once the steaming liquid has come to the boil. Lower heat to a simmer after adding fish.

Deep-frying—Heat oil to 360 to 375 degrees. Measure thickness of fish, add it carefully to the hot fat, and cook 10 minutes to the inch of thickness, whether it is floured and crumbed or not. If the fish is heavily battered, the batter acts as an insulator and the time might vary slightly. Test one small piece of battered fish first to see how fast it cooks and if the batter is hot. Don't mix fish of various thicknesses. Cook thick fish first then add the thin fish. When frying larger pieces, reduce the heat so the fish doesn't over-brown before the inside cooks. As with all frying, do not add so much food that it causes the temperature to drop.

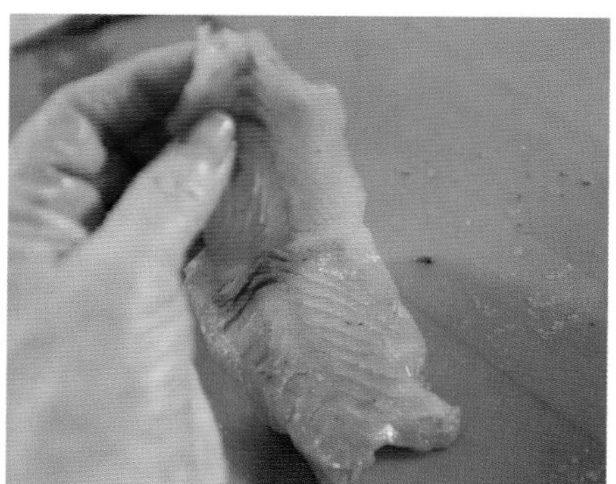

"THICKENING" FISH

Thickening very thin fish fillets can help prevent them from being overcooked. One method of thickening up is to use a batter (which not only coats but expands if it contains eggs), or a sauce such as mayonnaise (which also contains eggs), or even a non-egg product (such as a bit of Dijon mustard mixed with cream and smeared on the top), and surrounded with sliced potatoes or other vegetables.

Another method is to fold a skinny fillet in two or three folds, which allows the fish to knit together a bit while cooking, making a fatter fillet. The skin should be removed. The prettiest side is considered the bone side, so "skinned-side inside" is the rule.

BASIC BROILED, GRIDDLED, OR GRILLED FISH FILLETS WITH LEMON OR LIME

Serves 4

Broiling, griddling, or grilling *is the quickest way to cook fish. Thin fillets such as flounder are tricky, as they cook in just 2 to 4 minutes, requiring constant attention unless folded. Thicker pieces, such as grouper, tuna, salmon, or monkfish steaks or fillets stay moist longer. For grilling or broiling, leave the skin on the fish to make turning the fish easier. Score the skin in several places to prevent the fish from curling as the skin cooks. If the fillet is skinless and tearing or breaking is a concern, don't turn it at all, but protect the fillet with a thin coating of oil or butter so the side closest to the heat doesn't dry out. Another method to avoid turning is to put a thin fish on an already very hot pan, which cooks it on the bottom, and heating further only from the top using direct heat, as under the broiler, or indirect heat, as on the grill.*

- 4 flounder, snapper, grouper, or other white fish fillets (1 1/4–1 1/2 pounds total), skinned
- 2 tablespoons butter or oil, optional
- Salt
- Freshly ground black pepper
- 1/4 cup fresh lemon or lime juice
- 1 tablespoon chopped fresh herbs, such as rosemary, thyme, oregano, basil, or chives, optional
- 1/2 teaspoon paprika, optional

Rinse and pat the fish dry with paper towels.

Dip the fillets in the butter or oil. Move to a foil-lined baking pan.

Measure the fillets' thickness. If less than 1/2 inch, fold in half to double, skinned side to the inside. Broil the fish with the bone side closest to the heat until done, 9 minutes to the inch of thickness, turning over halfway through the cooking time. The fish is done when the thickest part registers approximately 135 degrees on an instant-read thermometer.

When done, use a spatula or pancake turner to transfer fish to a warm platter, and season to taste with salt and pepper. Drizzle the lemon or lime juice over the fillets and sprinkle with the herbs and paprika if using.

To griddle or pan-sear, heat pan and add fish to hot pan, and cook using the timing as above.

To grill, preheat an oiled grill to 500 degrees, add fish to hot grill or oiled fish basket (page 291), and grill using the timing as above.

Variation: Mint and Yogurt Pesto

Combine 1/2 cup plain yogurt (Greek yogurt gives an extra tang), 1 roughly chopped small onion, 1 seeded and finely chopped small jalapeño pepper, and 1 cup fresh mint or lemon balm leaves in a food processor fitted with the metal blade. Process until smooth, stopping to scrape down the sides as necessary. Season to taste with salt and pepper. For more tang, stir in 1 teaspoon lemon juice. Serve atop any simply prepared fish or chicken.

Flat fish, such as flounder, has two kinds of fillets, called double fillets, the more desirable fleshier ones located on top of the spine. The smaller ones on the bottom are best prepared folded. Very thin fish fillets retain moisture if folded in half, skinned side toward the inside.

GRILLED FISH FILLETS MARINATED IN BARBECUE SAUCE

Serves 4

AMBERJACK HAS INCREASED IN POPULARITY SINCE THE LATE 1980S; *prior to that, it was ignored. Any firm fish can be substituted. The purpose of marinating this fish is to flavor it and keep it moist on the grill.*

- 1 1/2–2 pounds amberjack, porgie, or other firm-fish fillets, skinned
- 1/2 cup Vinegar-Based Barbecue Sauce (page 664)
- 1/4 cup soy sauce

Rinse and pat the fillets dry with paper towels.

Mix the Vinegar-Based Barbecue Sauce with soy sauce. Add the fish fillets and sauce to a plastic bag and marinate up to 30 minutes.

Meanwhile, preheat the grill to 500 degrees. Shake the fish lightly, reserving the marinade separately. Add the fish to the grill bone side down, or move to an oiled broiling pan. Grill the fish 9 minutes per inch of thickness, measured at the thickest point, turning the fish halfway through the cooking time. The fish is done when the thickest part of the fish registers approximately 135 degrees on an instant-read thermometer.

While the fish is cooking, heat the marinade in a heavy saucepan and bring to the boil. Boil until the liquid is reduced by about half. Remove from the heat to a warm plate. Serve grilled fish with or on top of the warm sauce.

To griddle or pan-sear, heat pan to 500 degrees, add fish to hot pan, and cook using the timing as above.

To broil, preheat broiler, move fish to a foil-lined rimmed baking pan, and broil, using the timing as above.

Variations: Snapper, scamp, pompano, sea trout, and red drum are all pleasing in this recipe.

GRILLED TUNA STEAK

Serves 4

THESE MASSIVE FISH CAUGHT IN THE GULF *are weighed and judged on the docks. Their quality is determined by an expert who inserts a cutter to pull out a plug of the fish to judge it for texture, color, and suitability before shipping all over the world. Its popularity for sashimi is a good indicator that it's better undercooked than overcooked. Undercooked tuna steak resembles beefsteak.*

- 2 tuna steaks, 1 1/2–2 inches thick
- 1/4 cup oil, cook's preference
- Juice of 2 lemons
- Salt
- Freshly ground black pepper

Rinse and pat the fish dry with paper towels. Mix together the oil and lemon juice and marinate the steaks in the mixture for up to 30 minutes.

Preheat the grill or broiler to 500 degrees, oiling pan or grill. Season the tuna to taste with salt and pepper. Cook on the grill over very hot coals or under the broiler 9 minutes per inch of thickness, turning once. The fish is done when its thickest part registers approximately 130 degrees on an instant-read thermometer. The steaks should be brown on both sides and moist inside. Move to a warm platter and serve hot.

To griddle or pan-sear, heat pan and add fish to hot pan, and cook using the timing as above.

Variation: Marinated Tuna Steak

This recipe is from Annabelle Stubbs, the daughter of the long-time food editor of the *Atlanta Journal Constitution.* Mix together 1/2 cup oil, 1/2 cup white wine, 2 tablespoons each chopped fresh parsley and mint, and 2 chopped garlic cloves. Pour over tuna and marinate 3 to 4 hours. Reserve marinade and cook tuna as above. Boil reserved marinade for 3 minutes and serve with the hot fish.

GRILLED FISH STEAKS

Serves 4

SOY SAUCE WITH GINGER IS THE PERFECT MATCH FOR THESE FISH STEAKS, *bass, and other Southern fish. Grilling steaks is very different from grilling fillets. The density makes them more variable, with the heat searing the outside and leaving the inside moist. As with grilled meat, there is nothing worse than an overcooked fish steak.*

2 grouper or tuna steaks, 1½–2 inches thick, skinned
2 tablespoons soy sauce
1 slice fresh ginger, chopped

Rinse and pat the fish dry with paper towels. Move the fish steaks to a shallow bowl.

Mix together the soy sauce and fresh ginger and pour over the steaks.

When the grill is very hot, shake marinade from the fish and move steaks to the hot grill rack, skin side closest to heat. Grill approximately 4 to 5 minutes per side for each inch of thickness, depending on the heat of the coals. When the outside is cooked, move the fish to a warm platter, leaving it a few minutes to let the carryover heat finish cooking the fish. The fish is done when its thickest part registers approximately 135 degrees on an instant-read thermometer. Move to a warm platter and serve hot. Grouper tends to break up into large flaky chunks, so be prepared to remove it to a serving platter with a slotted spatula or fish spatula.

To griddle or pan-sear, heat pan to 500 degrees, add fish to hot pan, and cook using the timing as above.

To broil, preheat broiler, move fish to a foil-lined baking pan, and cook using the timing as above.

Variation: Honey Ginger Fish Steaks

Add 4 (½-pound) amberjack, swordfish, or tuna steaks, 1 to 1½ inches thick, to a plastic ziplock bag. Mix together 2 tablespoons finely chopped ginger, 4 tablespoons finely chopped whole green onion or scallion, 1 cup soy sauce, 2 tablespoons oil (cook's preference), 2 tablespoons honey, and 2 tablespoons sherry or gingered sherry (page 671). Follow cooking directions as above, saving marinade. Bring marinade to the boil and pour over one side of fish steaks.

FISH STEAKS VS. FILLETS

Fish steaks are cut horizontally across a large fish, usually with the bone and skin intact. Steaks are necessarily thicker than most fillets available for sale. Since steaks and fillets have different flavor as well as texture, opinions vary on which is best. I prefer fillets; my husband prefers steaks.

To justify the use of soy sauce in Southern cooking, I have done some research. Soy sauce has been a condiment in China for over 2,500 years. It is lighter than the commonly available Japanese soy sauce (each of the Asian countries has its own variation). The Chinese have a long presence in the South, starting in the 1700s when a group of Chinese deserted a Spanish ship and settled in the Louisiana bayous, intermarrying extensively. By the mid-1800s, another influx of Chinese was brought over as a hopeful substitute for slaves, a number of them settling in the Mississippi Delta. The low wages paid them, as well as poor Blacks, discouraged further recruitment. Others were brought to build the railroad and to Augusta, Georgia, to build its canals, with equally discouraging results. In the 1940s, there were more Chinese grocery stores in Augusta than any other kind. Augusta's Chinese Americans were well accepted, and Augusta had a Chinese American mayor at one time.

GRILLED STUFFED SEA TROUT

Serves 4 to 6

FRESH SEA TROUT AND RAINBOW TROUT ARE QUITE DIFFERENT, *but both are delicious. Coauthor Cynthia Graubart was born in Florida, surrounded by zealous fishermen in her family and amongst her closest family friends. This recipe comes from Ben Russell, known as "Uncle Ben," a most avid fisherman.*

1 (4- to 5-pound) whole fresh sea trout, head on, cleaned, scaled, and boned (page 290), or 4 small trout (2/3–3/4 pound each)
1 teaspoon chopped fresh dill
Salt
Freshly ground black pepper
2 tablespoons bacon fat or drippings
1 medium onion, chopped
1/2 cup chopped celery
1 cup sliced mushrooms
1 cup crumbled cornbread
1/2 cup chopped ripe black olives
1/2 cup sour cream
1/4 cup butter, melted
8 thin slices lemon

Preheat the grill to 500 degrees.

Rinse and pat the fish dry with paper towels, taking care to ensure the cavity is clean. Sprinkle the outside and inside of the trout with the dill, salt, and pepper.

Heat the bacon fat in a medium skillet and add the onion, celery, and mushrooms, and sauté until soft. Add the cornbread, olives, sour cream, and butter. If necessary, moisten slightly with water to make the stuffing hold together. Open the cavity of the fish, stuff with the mixture, and close securely with toothpicks.

Move the trout to an oiled fish basket. Arrange 4 lemon slices on each side of fish. Move the basket to the grill and cook until done, 9 minutes per inch of thickness, including stuffing. The fish is done when the thickest part of the fish registers approximately 135 degrees on an instant-read thermometer.

To griddle or pan-sear, heat pan and add fish to hot pan, and cook using the timing as above.

To broil, preheat broiler, move fish to a foil-lined baking pan, and broil using the timing as above.

Variation: Roasted Stuffed Sea Trout

Move the fish to two oiled rimmed baking sheets, arrange lemons as above, and roast at 400 degrees for 9 minutes per inch of thickness including stuffing.

SPICE-RUBBED ROASTED FISH FILLETS

Serves 4

THE SOUTH'S CULINARY HISTORY *was greatly enriched by the sea traders at ports such as Charleston's, who brought in a bounty of spices from around the world; the influence of these products is still seen today. Rubbing mild fish with spices or herbs boosts its flavor. The spices here aid in making their own saffron-y sauce.*

4 (6-ounce) flounder, snapper, grouper, or other white fish fillets
1/2 teaspoon ground ginger
2 tablespoons ground coriander seed
1 teaspoon ground cumin
1 teaspoon ground fennel seed
2 tablespoons chopped fresh parsley or cilantro
Juice and grated rind of 1 lemon, no white attached, divided
1/2 teaspoon saffron threads
1/4 cup butter, melted, optional

Rinse and pat the fish dry with paper towels.

Mix together the ginger, coriander, cumin, fennel, parsley or cilantro, 2 tablespoons of the lemon rind, and the saffron. Rub the mixture onto both sides of the fillets and move to a flat dish. Cover with plastic wrap and marinate in the refrigerator for at least 2 hours or up to 6 hours.

Preheat oven to 400 degrees.

Move the fillets and any juice to an oiled baking dish large enough to hold the fillets in a single layer. Sprinkle with lemon juice and roast uncovered for 9 minutes per inch of thickness. The fish is done when its thickest part registers approximately 135 degrees on an instant-read thermometer. Move to a warm platter. Serve hot with optional butter.

DAUFUSKIE ROASTED FISH FILLETS

Serves 4

FAMOUS FOR THE SLIGHT COVERING *puff of mayonnaise that keeps it moist, this simple baked preparation, made originally on the Gullah island of Daufuskie, is so easy it is one of the five things my husband can cook.*

4 grouper, flounder, or other fish fillets (about 1 1/2–2 pounds), skinned
1/2 cup mayonnaise
2 tablespoons Dijon mustard
1 tablespoon fresh lemon or orange juice
Paprika to taste

Preheat oven to 400 degrees.

Rinse and pat the fish dry with paper towels and move them bone side up to an oiled rimmed baking sheet large enough to hold the fillets in one layer.

Mix the mayonnaise, mustard, and juice, and stir until smooth. Spoon this mixture over the fish.

Roast 9 minutes per inch of thickness. The fish is done when its thickest part registers approximately 135 degrees on an instant-read thermometer.

Remove from the oven and move under the broiler for 2 minutes to barely brown the sauce. Move to a warm platter and sprinkle with paprika before serving.

Variations:

- Thinly slice a medium onion and spread over the fillets before topping with the mustard-mayonnaise mixture.
- Add a dash of ground hot red pepper or other hot pepper, and/or chopped fresh herbs such as tarragon, parsley, or basil to the mayonnaise.
- Substitute Pimento Cheese (page 57), which contains mayonnaise, for the mayonnaise.
- Whisk together 1/2 cup Dijon mustard with 1/4 cup heavy cream instead of the mayonnaise, and omit the lemon juice.

ROASTED FISH FILLETS WITH CREOLE SAUCE AND PECANS

Serves 4 to 6

SEVERAL TIMES, TALENTED CAJUN CHEF *Paul Prudhomme taught classes at Rich's Cooking School; other times I traveled to New Orleans to work with him at Commander's Palace Restaurant. He taught me a variation of this recipe, which uses a gracious plenty of seasoning. I am much more modest, so no amount is given. Note that there are two butters used—one melted and one not.*

6 (6-ounce) fresh sea trout or mahi mahi fillets, bones reserved to make stock for sauce
Commercial seafood seasoning or Creole Seasoning (page 670)
2 large eggs
1 cup milk
2 cups all-purpose flour
1/2 cup butter, melted
2 tablespoons oil

Pecan Butter

1 cup roasted and chopped pecans, divided
3 tablespoons oil, cook's preference
1/4 cup butter
Juice of 1/2 lemon
1 teaspoon Worcestershire sauce
1 teaspoon hot sauce
1 recipe Creole Brown Fish Sauce (page 657)

Preheat oven to 350 degrees.

Rinse and pat the fish dry with paper towels. Sprinkle the trout with the seasoning mixture. Lightly mix the eggs and milk together. Toss the flour on a plate with more Cajun Seasoning to taste, and dredge the trout fillets with it, using only one hand and keeping the other clean. Dip each fillet in the egg wash and then dredge with the flour again.

Preheat a 9-inch ovenproof skillet and add 1/2 cup melted butter and oil. Heat the butter to foaming and add the fillets. Brown one side, then turn over and move the skillet to the oven to finish cooking the fillets, about 5 minutes, cooking in batches if necessary. Remove the skillet from the oven and set the hot trout aside on a warm platter.

To make the pecan butter, purée 1/2 cup pecans with oil in a blender or food processor. Add the butter, lemon juice, Worcestershire sauce, and hot sauce, and blend well. Brush the Pecan Butter over the trout; top with the remaining chopped pecans and the Creole Brown Fish Sauce.

OVEN-ROASTED PECANS

Toss the shelled pecans in enough melted butter or oil to just cling to the pecans. Spread the pecans evenly in a single layer on an oiled rimmed baking sheet. Bake in a 350-degree oven for 5 to 7 minutes, or until the aroma starts to waft from the oven. The second you smell them, open the oven and test one. If it needs a little bit longer for the flavor to become complex and rich, and the pecan is, well, pecan-shell brown, shake the pan or stir quickly and return to the oven for no more than 1 minute. They roast very quickly, so be alert the entire time they are in the oven.

Browning on the stovetop in a nonstick pan is an alternative method. If roasting pecan pieces, be watchful, as they brown very quickly. Shake or stir over the heat for 2 to 3 minutes for small pieces, up to 5 minutes for pecan halves.

Almost any sauce used on one type of cut may be adapted for other cuts and fish.

WHOLE ROASTED SNAPPER

Serves 2 to 4

THERE ARE NUMEROUS KINDS OF SNAPPERS *in the South Atlantic waters, from pink to vermilion and deep red ones. There are, however, many masqueraders with tough skins and scales hard like tiddlywinks that are usually over seven pounds. These should be avoided, as should those that are overfished in a region.*

Snapper is a succulent, light, white fish with a clean taste. It is best when fresh or flash-frozen and cooked immediately upon defrosting. It should smell like the sea, its eyes should be bright and slightly protruding, and its flesh should be firm and bright but not iridescent. Its skin and scales should not be tough. Any white fish may be substituted with this method. This recipe can be used as a guide for larger fish.

1 (2-pound) whole snapper or other whole white fish, head on, cleaned and scaled
4 tablespoons melted butter or oil, cook's preference
Salt
Freshly ground black pepper
1/4 cup fresh lemon juice, optional

Preheat oven to 400 degrees.

Line a rimmed baking sheet with oiled aluminum foil, or oil an oven-to-table baking dish. Rinse and pat the fish dry with paper towels, taking care to ensure the cavity is clean.

Move the fish to the prepared pan or dish and make 2 to 4 diagonal slashes in the skin of the fish (top side only). Brush both sides with butter or oil. Season to taste with salt and pepper. Pour on the lemon juice.

Measure the thickness of the fish from the foil to the top side of the fish at its thickest part. Roast uncovered for 9 minutes to the inch of thickness, until meat is firm to the touch and springs back. The fish is done when its thickest part registers approximately 135 degrees on an instant-read thermometer.

Slide the fish off the foil using two large spatulas or any number of fish gadgets. Peel off the skin. The top will be prettier than the bottom so serve any guests first. Use two large implements to slide the flesh off the bone and onto the plate. When top flesh is removed, flip over the body of the fish and serve the bottom flesh, using the same method. The cheek is regarded as particularly desirable, as it is tender and flavorful.

Variations:

- Stuff the cavity with lemon slices and herbs.
- Stuff the cavity with stalks of lemon grass and broken kaffir lime leaves (discard before serving).
- Stuff with Pepper and Olive Filling (page 304).
- Serve with Marinara Sauce (page 661).

WHOLE ROASTED FISH WITH SPINACH

Serves 8 to 10

THIS ALL-IN-ONE DISH *makes a spectacular presentation for company. Everything can be prepared ahead of time and then put in the oven when guests arrive. When entertaining, it is especially important to have an instant-read thermometer, as it is tension-inducing to try to guess if the fish is done. With a large fish the top portion will obviously flake long before the inner portion is ready. There is carryover cooking with a large fish as with any large piece of food, and it will go up five or ten degrees before it gets to the table. This recipe takes longer to cook than most fish dishes because of the layered vegetables.*

Remove the foil and pour juices over the fish. Serve in the baking dish or transfer to a warm platter.

- 1 whole sea bass, sea trout, red snapper, or small salmon (3–5 pounds), head on, cleaned and scaled
- 3–5 tablespoons oil, cook's preference, divided
- 3 medium onions, chopped
- 3 garlic cloves, chopped
- 2 pounds fresh spinach, or 4 (10-ounce) packages spinach, defrosted and drained
- 3 tomatoes, peeled and cut into 1/2-inch cubes
- 1/2 cup chopped fresh cilantro, thyme, and/or parsley
- Juice of 2 lemons or 1 orange, plus the grated rind, no white attached
- 1 teaspoon salt
- 1 teaspoon freshly ground black pepper

Oil a large baking dish. Rinse and pat the fish dry with paper towels.

Heat 3 tablespoons of oil in a large frying pan. Add the onions and garlic, and sauté in the oil until the onions are soft, about 5 minutes. Add the spinach to the frying pan and wilt briefly, or defrost frozen spinach and add to mixture. Cover the bottom of the prepared baking dish with the mixture and top with the tomato. Sprinkle with herbs, lemon juice and rind, salt, and pepper. This may be done several hours in advance to this point.

When ready to bake, preheat oven to 400 degrees. Measure the thickness of the fish and move the fish on top of the layered vegetables. Make 2 to 4 slashes in the top skin. Cover lightly with oiled aluminum foil. Roast for 11 minutes per inch of thickness, plus 5 minutes more, approximately 30 minutes in all. The fish is done when its thickest part registers approximately 135 degrees on an instant-read thermometer.

Cut down the spine of the fish and remove the flesh in portions using a large fish knife and fork if possible. Divide the remaining fish into portions. Serve with a portion of vegetables.

WHOLE ROASTED FLAT FISH STUFFED WITH SHRIMP

Serves 2

WHEN YOU CUT IN AND DISCOVER *the secret pocket of shrimp and sauce, it is a wonderful surprise! A flounder's two eyes are disconcerting to some, so the head—considered a delicacy by many cultures—may be removed if desired. This dish may be prepared using two smaller flounders, adjusting the time. The sauce may be refrigerated without the shrimp for several days and then reheated when adding the shrimp. The fish may be stuffed and refrigerated 2 hours before cooking. Bring to room temperature before cooking, for accurate timing.*

1 large whole flounder or halibut, cleaned and scaled
8 tablespoons butter, divided
1/4 cup mushrooms, sliced
1 tablespoon all-purpose flour
1/2 cup Flavored Milk (page 657)
2 ounces raw shrimp, peeled
3 tablespoons heavy cream
Salt
Freshly ground black pepper
Dash ground hot red pepper
2 tablespoons chopped fresh thyme, optional
2 tablespoons breadcrumbs

Preheat oven to 400 degrees.

Rinse and dry the fish, and move it (dark skin, or top side, down) to a plastic board. Snip off any fins. With a very sharp knife, cut down the spine in the center of the fish, leaving both the head and tail intact. Make a cut at the head end of the fish perpendicular to the center cut to form a T. This cut will facilitate opening the pocket.

To remove the spine, keeping the fillets whole, slide the knife against the backbone on either side of the incision. Leave the skin attached. With scissors, snip down the outer edges of the exposed small bones and through the top and bottom of the backbone. Sliding the knife under the backbone, wedge the bone out. The backbone should be clean of flesh. Check to be sure no bones remain. This leaves a pocket for the stuffing, with the thicker top fillets still in place and the fish whole but boneless. Refrigerate the flounder until ready to cook.

Melt 2 tablespoons of butter in a frying pan. Toss the mushrooms in butter over high heat; remove mushrooms. Add 2 more tablespoons butter and the flour; stir briefly, and add the milk. Bring to the boil, stirring. Add the mushrooms to this sauce.

Chop the shrimp if they are large; add with the cream to the sauce. Return to the boil. At this point, the shrimp will be only partially cooked.

Remove the sauce from the heat and season to taste with salt, pepper, hot red pepper, and thyme. Spoon the shrimp sauce as filling inside the pocket of the fish. Carefully use a spatula to turn the fish over, with the uncut side up, and move to a well-buttered baking and serving dish.

Melt the remaining 4 tablespoons of butter in a saucepan. Brush the fish with half of the melted butter and sprinkle with the breadcrumbs. Pour on the remainder of the butter.

Measure the thickness of the fish including the stuffing. Roast, basting occasionally, 10 minutes for every inch of thickness. The fish is done when its thickest part registers approximately 135 degrees on an instant-read thermometer. Serve flounder hot in its baking dish.

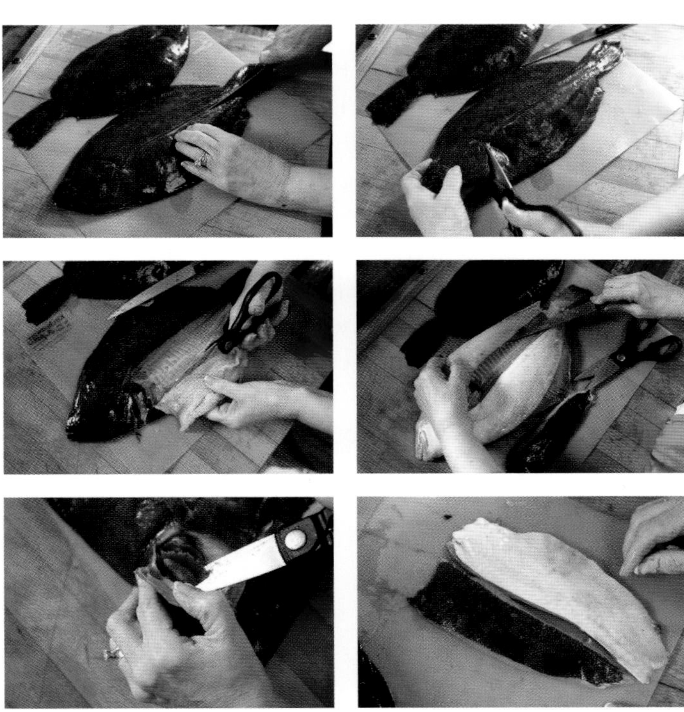

MOIST FISH IN A POUCH

Serves 2 to 4

Baking in a pouch of parchment *or aluminum foil is a form of oven-poaching. Its virtue is a dramatic presentation resulting from a dish that is assembled in advance and foolproof. Small whole fish make a glorious impression at the table, but any fish fillet will do, such as sea and fresh water trout, flounder, pompano, vermilion snapper, etc. Another glory is that it is easily diversified, getting away from the humdrum of every day cooking.*

2–4 filleted or small whole fish, cleaned and scaled
Salt
Freshly ground black pepper
1 cup dry vermouth or other white wine
2 tablespoons water

Preheat oven to 400 degrees.

Rinse and pat the fish dry with paper towels, taking care to ensure the cavity is clean. Season to taste with salt and pepper.

Using an oiled sheet of parchment, waxed paper, or aluminum foil, form a pouch for each fish or fillet by folding the paper in half, oiled side to the inside, and folding each side over about 1/2 inch twice to tightly seal the edges, leaving the top open. If using a small paper bag, oil the inside of the bag.

Move the pouches to an oiled rimmed baking sheet large enough to hold the pouches in one layer, and divide the fish between the prepared pouches. Mix wine with water, and carefully divide the liquid among the pouches. Seal top of each pouch tightly to enclose the fish and the liquid.

Cook the fish 10 minutes to the inch of thickness (add 4 to 5 minutes to the total cooking time if using aluminum foil, to give time for the heat to penetrate the foil). The fish is done when its thickest part registers 135 degrees on an instant-read thermometer.

The fish may be bagged ahead of time, leaving the top unsealed, and refrigerated. Allow to come to room temperature before adding the vermouth and placing the pan of pouches in the hot oven.

To serve, move each pouch to the dinner plate and snip open the bag with scissors, making an X in the side of the pouch. Pull open the slits and eat from the bags; the fish will be bathing in the cooking juices.

Variations:

- Serve with White Butter Sauce (page 656), or Hollandaise Sauce (page 652).
- Rub or sprinkle the fish lightly with curry powder, seafood seasoning, ground ginger, fennel seed, coriander seed or cumin before folding pouch.
- Stuff the cavity of a whole fish with fennel fronds, or mix a few tablespoons each of sautéed fennel bulb and onion and make a bed for or top the fish with it before folding pouch. Alternately, wrap the whole fish in fresh fennel fronds.
- Make a bed or top the fish with baby spinach, turnip greens, kale, or collards. If large, make a chiffonade (page 208). Season with salt and pepper and/or top with ribbons of vegetables (see below), a bit of sautéed onion, cooked peas, etc. Wrap in pouch. The vegetables will be cooked enough to wilt and be tender.
- Peel carrots, zucchini, cucumber, or other firm vegetable (even potatoes) with a potato peeler into very thin ribbons that will wilt when cooked. Drizzle with butter or oil if desired. Top the fish with any or all before wrapping in the pouch.

- Make a bed of cooked rice, plain or mixed with chopped almonds or peanuts, curry powder, etc. Top with the fish, and seal pouch as above.
- To use fish fillets in this recipe, fold each fillet in half, skinned side to the inside, layering some fennel fronds in between the folds. Move the fillets to individual pouches and continue as above.

Variation: Fish Baked in Fig or Banana Leaves

Soak unsprayed fresh fig or banana leaves in water for 10 minutes. Wrap fish in leaves, vein side in and brushed with butter, tucking any loose edges under, and bake as directed in recipe above. The fig leaves fill the kitchen with the aroma of late summer. Organic grape leaves, or commercial frozen banana leaves as found in Asian markets, can also be substituted. I use the banana and fig leaves from my trees.

Variation: Spicy Lime Sea Bass

Prepare a single pouch as above for a 5-pound sea bass. Stuff the bass with 1 lime cut into small chunks. Seal the pouch and bake the fish for 10 minutes per inch of thickness. While the fish is baking, melt 1/2 cup lime marmalade with 1 teaspoon hot sauce. Glaze the cooked fish with the melted marmalade. Thinly slice another lime and decorate the top of the fish, finishing with another coating of the melted marmalade. Oranges and orange marmalade make another variation.

WHOLE ROASTED FISH FILLED WITH PEPPERS AND OLIVES

Serves 2

Stuffing a fish need not be relegated only to rich cream sauces, as it was in the early days of the South, mimicking European cooking. Instead, boaters and fishermen developed ways using what was on hand and fresh, as Susan Puett, wife of an avid sailor, did with this recipe.

1 (3-pound) whole round fish, head on, cleaned and scaled
2 tablespoons oil, cook's preference
Salt
Freshly ground black pepper

Pepper and Olive Filling
3 tablespoons butter
4 or 5 green onions chopped
1 red, yellow, or green bell pepper, chopped
1 medium red tomato, chopped
3 tablespoons chopped fresh parsley
2 teaspoons chopped fresh herbs, such as marjoram
1 teaspoon chopped fresh basil, optional
4 black olives, pitted and sliced
Salt
Freshly ground black pepper
Juice of 1 lemon

Preheat oven to 350 degrees.

Line a baking pan with oiled aluminum foil, or oil an oven-to-table baking dish. Rinse and pat the fish dry with paper towels, taking care to ensure the cavity is clean.

Move the fish to the prepared pan or dish and make 2 to 4 diagonal slashes in the skin. Brush both sides with oil. Season to taste with salt and pepper.

Melt the butter in a frying pan and add onions and bell pepper. Cook until the onions are nearly soft and the pepper still crunchy. Add the tomato, herbs, olives, and salt and pepper to taste. Remove from the heat and spoon the stuffing into the cavity of the fish.

Measure the thickness of the fish, from the foil to the top side of the fish, at its thickest part. Roast uncovered for 10 minutes to the inch of thickness, until meat is firm to the touch and springs back. The fish is done when its thickest part registers approximately 135 degrees on an instant-read thermometer.

Scoop out and reserve the stuffing, and slide the fish off the foil onto a large, warm platter using two large spatulas or any number of fish gadgets. Peel off the skin. Pour lemon juice over the fish. The top will be prettier than the bottom, so serve any guests first. Use two large implements to slide the fillet off the bone and onto the plate. When top flesh is removed, flip over the body of the fish and serve the bottom fillet, using the same method. Top with the stuffing. The cheek is regarded as particularly desirable, as it is tender and flavorful.

OVEN-ROASTED PECAN-CRUSTED FISH FILLETS

Serves 4

MANY DIFFERENT CRUSTING MIXTURES ARE USED FOR ENHANCING FISH. *Nuts are the trickiest, as they burn easily. The egg whites help the crust adhere. Refrigerating the unbaked crusted fillets solidifies the topping, and the chilled nuts are less likely to burn.*

1 cup roasted chopped pecans
2 tablespoons all-purpose flour
1/2 cup fine dry breadcrumbs or panko
Salt
Freshly ground black pepper
4 (6-ounce) mahi mahi fillets
3 egg whites with 2 teaspoons water

Preheat oven to 400 degrees. Oil a rimmed baking sheet and set aside.

Mix together the pecans, flour, and breadcrumbs on a plate, seasoned with salt and pepper to taste; set aside.

Rinse and pat the fillets dry with a paper towel.

Beat the egg whites with a fork in a shallow bowl, incorporating 2 teaspoons of water. Using one hand only, dip the dry fillets into the egg white mixture, then into the pecan crumb mixture, pressing lightly so they will adhere. This may be done ahead to this point and the fillets refrigerated on a wire rack up to 24 hours.

When ready to cook, move the fillets to the prepared baking pan and cook 10 minutes per inch of thickness if the fillets are still cold going into the oven. Otherwise, 9 minutes per inch is sufficient. The fish is done when its thickest part registers approximately 135 degrees on an instant-read thermometer.

Variations:

- Add 1 tablespoon grated lemon rind and 2 teaspoons chopped fresh rosemary to the crumb mixture.
- Substitute cornbread crumbs for the breadcrumbs and add chopped herbs. Prepare with or without nuts.

ONION-TOPPED ROASTED FISH FILLETS

Serves 6

SOME FISH ARE ENHANCED BY ROBUST FLAVORS *such as rosemary, garlic, and vinegar. This is an ideal recipe to serve to people who are timid about, or unfamiliar with, fish, but it also pleases fish lovers. The slices of onion offer a protection for the fish and keep it moist. The recipe is easily adapted to any whole fish or fish fillets by adjusting the baking time.*

6 red snapper, grouper, rainbow trout, or catfish fillets, skinned
2 tablespoons oil, cook's preference
24 garlic cloves, peeled
1 medium onion, sliced
6 sprigs fresh rosemary, or 6 tablespoons chopped fresh rosemary
2 bay leaves
2 tablespoons olive oil
3 tablespoons red wine vinegar
Salt
Freshly ground black pepper

Preheat oven to 400 degrees.

Lightly oil a 9 x 13-inch baking dish or a rimmed baking sheet large enough to hold the fillets in one layer. Rinse and pat the fish dry with paper towels.

Heat the oil in a frying pan and cook the garlic and onion until they begin to brown but are not burned, about 8 to 10 minutes, stirring frequently.

Measure the fish fillets. Fold the fillets, skinned-side inside, if necessary to make each fillet as close to 1 inch thick as possible, and move them to the prepared dish or sheet. Top the fillets with rosemary and bay leaves. Cover with the sautéed onion and garlic.

Whisk together the olive oil and the vinegar. Pour half of this mixture over the fish, roast 5 minutes, then pour the remaining mixture over the fish and finish roasting. The total roasting time should be 9 minutes per inch of thickness. The fish is done when its thickest part registers approximately 135 degrees on an instant-read thermometer.

Move the fish to a warm platter. Remove and discard the bay leaves and serve hot. Season to taste with salt and pepper. Garnish with additional rosemary if desired.

Variation: Add sautéed spinach (page 207) and/or chopped mushrooms to form a bed for the fish.

SALT-CRUSTED WHOLE ROASTED FISH

Serves 4

SALT-CRUSTING IS A TIME-HONORED METHOD *of cooking fish that has seen a resurgence. It's exciting to crack the crust at the table, although the less confident can do it in the kitchen. The fish is flavorful but not over-salted. The substantial crust steams the fish in its own juices for a very moist result.*

1 large box kosher (coarse) salt

1 (2- to 3-pound) whole pompano, cleaned and scaled but not skinned, fins trimmed

Freshly ground black pepper

Preheat oven to 350 degrees. Cover a rimmed baking sheet with a 1/4-inch layer of kosher salt.

Rinse and pat the fish dry with paper towels. Season to taste with pepper on each side. Move the fish on top of the salt on the baking sheet. Cover the fish entirely with more coarse salt.

Roast until done, about 25 to 30 minutes, or 11 minutes to the inch of thickness (including the salt crust). The fish is done when its thickest part registers approximately 135 degrees on an instant-read thermometer. Remove from the oven and let cool slightly in the pan on a wire rack.

Crack the salt layer with a knife and remove it. Move the fish to a warm serving platter using two large spatulas or any number of fish gadgets. Peel off the skin with two forks or knives. The top fillet will be prettier than the bottom one, so serve any guests first. Use two large implements to cut and slide the fillet off the bone and onto the plate. When top flesh is removed, flip over the body of the fish and serve the bottom flesh, using the same method.

Baking under a moisture-retaining crust prevents a thick fish from overcooking. Many other crusts are used that are edible, such as herbed mashed or thinly sliced potatoes or zucchini slices, or a layer of mustard, mayonnaise or pimento cheese, or even sliced fresh tomatoes.

STEAMED SOUTHERN-CHINESE FILLETS

Serves 2

THIS RECIPE GIVES A NOD *to our immigrant Chinese population—in particular Augusta, Georgia, and parts of Mississippi during the late-nineteenth century. Their influence has endured, and nearly every small Southern town has a Chinese restaurant. This is particularly dramatic as a starter, although it may be used as a main dish. The technique of steaming assures a very moist fish.*

1 1/2 pounds fresh farm-raised catfish fillets
1 teaspoon chopped fresh ginger
1 small green onion, sliced into very small pieces
1 tablespoon soy sauce
1 tablespoon dry sherry
1 teaspoon red pepper flakes
1 tablespoon oil, cook's preference

Rinse and pat the fish dry with paper towels. Move to an oiled rimmed heatproof plate.

To make the sauce, whisk together the remaining ingredients. Pour the sauce over the fish and move the plate to a Chinese steamer or to a rack over water in an electric skillet or wok.

Bring the water to the boil, cover, reduce heat, and steam the fish 9 minutes for every inch of thickness. Reduce the time if the fish is less than 1 inch thick. The fish is done when its thickest part registers approximately 135 degrees on an instant-read thermometer. Move to a warm platter and serve.

Variation: Steamed Lime and Cilantro Fillets

Add the juice and rind of 1 lime, no white attached, 1/2 teaspoon dark sesame oil or soy sauce, 1 tablespoon chopped fresh cilantro or chopped fresh ginger.

Cover the fillets with this mixture and steam as above.

Variations:

- Pare long strips from 2 zucchini, carrots, and/or cucumbers. Season with salt and pepper and mound on a platter or plates. Top bed with fillets and grated lime rind.
- To serve the vegetables hot, heat a bit of butter, add the vegetables, season to taste with salt and pepper, and put on top of the fish for the last 2 to 3 minutes of cooking. Remove vegetables first, making a bed, and top with the cooked fish and any juices from the dish.
- This method works well with whole snapper and other fillets.

If a Chinese steamer is not available, put a heatproof rack in the bottom of an electric or other large non-iron frying pan. Pour the water in, keeping it below the level of the rack, and move a rimmed heatproof pie pan to the rack. Cover and follow cooking directions.

FRIED CATFISH

Serves 6

THERE IS A RHYTHM TO BATTERING AND FRYING CATFISH—*shake, drop, toss, and move—that is beautiful to watch. There are still extraordinarily popular rural fried catfish restaurants, although I know almost no one who still fries it at home. I frequent several—one in an old mill village outside Covington, Georgia, as well as one in Social Circle, Georgia, and a grocery outside of Oxford, Mississippi. (The one outside Covington still fries chitterlings on Friday nights.) This bottom-feeding freshwater fish is not noted for its beauty, but those that love it, love it.*

6 small whole catfish or 12 fillets
2 cups buttermilk
2 cups white cornmeal
1 teaspoon salt
1 teaspoon freshly ground black pepper
Shortening or vegetable oil for frying, cook's choice

Rinse and pat the fish dry with paper towels, taking care to ensure the cavity is clean. Soak the catfish in the buttermilk for at least 30 minutes or as long as overnight.

Mix cornmeal, salt, and pepper in a bowl. Shake off the catfish and drop into the bowl, one at a time, tossing in the mixture until coated, using only one hand and keeping the other hand available for maneuvering the bowl.

Pour $1\frac{1}{2}$ inches of oil into a skillet, or fill a deep-fryer half full with oil; heat to 360 degrees.

Measure the thickness of the catfish. Add the catfish, one by one, remembering which went in first. The fat should cover the fish. For each inch of thickness, fry 4 minutes, until golden brown. The fish is done when its thickest part registers approximately 135 degrees on an instant-read thermometer. Avoid adding too many at once, as they will lower the frying temperature. Drain on a paper towel. Move to a warm platter and serve hot.

FRYING IS PHYSICS

When the fat stops bubbling, the liquid from the interior of the fish is gone and the fat will enter the fish, making it greasy. Watch for the lessening bubbles, and when they slow down, test the internal temperature of the fish and remove it from the pan as soon as it hits 135 degrees. If exterior browns too quickly, reduce heat of fat.

CATFISH

My husband would miss catfish terribly if he couldn't have it. Found wild, catfish has a muddy taste loved by aficionados, but some of us prefer the milder, more delicate taste of farm-raised catfish. It is usually sold in fillets except when fried. I served it at my restaurant, Nathalie's, in Richmond, Virginia.

Catfish and freshwater trout are perhaps the two most popular inland Southern fish. Catfish are now increasingly farm-raised. Other sport fish include bass (smallmouth and largemouth) and bream (pronounced brim)—carp, perch, and other species.

SAUTÉED FLOUNDER STRIPS WITH RAISINS AND PECANS

Serves 4 to 6

THIS RECIPE IS VERY USEFUL *for very small flounder or the two bottom fillets. Learning to lightly flour and sauté fresh fish strips widens one's repertoire considerably. The hot vegetables will reheat the fish sufficiently, as will the sauce. This all-in-one dish came courtesy of Barbara Nevins many years ago.*

2 pounds fresh flounder fillets
3 teaspoons salt, divided
2 teaspoons freshly ground black pepper, divided
2 tablespoons all-purpose flour
1/2 cup plus 1 tablespoon oil, cook's preference, divided
1 medium carrot, chopped
2 medium onions, chopped
1 fennel bulb, chopped
1/3 cup raisins
1 3/4 cup dry white wine
3/4 cup white wine vinegar
1/2 cup roasted chopped pecans
1 cup arugula or watercress leaves

Rinse and pat the fish dry with paper towels. Flatten the fillets of fish very lightly with a pounder between pieces of waxed paper until 1/2 inch thick. This not only gets the fish a consistent size but also meshes the delicate flesh into a firmer piece.

Cut flattened fillets into strips about 1 inch wide. Toss 1 teaspoon each of salt, pepper, and flour together on a plate. Lightly dust the fish strips on both sides with this mixture.

Heat 1/2 cup oil in a large heavy frying pan. Add the fish strips and cook for about 30 seconds, turn carefully with a slotted metal spoon, and cook 30 seconds more. Carefully remove the fish, drain on paper towels, set aside on a warm rimmed platter, and lightly cover with a piece of foil or waxed paper.

Add 1 tablespoon of oil, the remaining salt, carrot, onions, and fennel to the pan juices. Sauté, stirring occasionally, for about 10 to 12 minutes, or until the onions begin to brown.

Meanwhile, soak the raisins in the white wine to plump.

Remove the vegetables from the pan with a slotted spoon and spread on top of the cooked fish. Add the raisins, wine, and vinegar to the pan juices and boil to reduce volume by half. Add the pecans. Season to taste with salt and pepper.

Move the hot fish to a bed of arugula or watercress leaves. Top with the raisin sauce, or refrigerate up to 24 hours before serving cold.

Variations:

- Add 2 teaspoons curry powder to the flour mixture or to the sauce.
- Prepare with shrimp instead of fish, omitting the flour.

WHOLE SAUTÉED TROUT IN BUTTER PECAN SAUCE

Serves 4

FRESHWATER TROUT IS FREQUENTLY "SEEDED" IN THE SOUTH, *where many regions are too warm to spawn fish. It is a delicate, clean-tasting fish, which some liken to chicken because it is so un-fishlike. This is a classic preparation for small fish whose basis is a French* meunière *sauce, with pecans added. Browned butter adds even more flavor, but the procedure is tricky to do, so this recipe does not require it but is happy when it is serendipitous. Pan sautéing a large whole fish is exceedingly difficult and not recommended, as the fish doesn't turn easily in the pan or cook thoroughly. Avoid using a larger whole fish.*

4 (8–10 inch) small, head-on mountain trout, cleaned
1/4 cup all-purpose flour
Salt
Freshly ground black pepper
9 tablespoons butter, divided
4 tablespoons chopped pecans
Juice of 1/2 lemon
Salt and freshly ground pepper to taste
1 tablespoon chopped parsley
1 teaspoon chopped fresh chives or thyme

To sauté the trout, two large frying pans are needed, or the fish will have to be cooked in two batches.

Rinse and shake the fish dry, taking care to ensure the cavity is clean. Season the flour to taste with salt and pepper on a shallow plate. Roll the damp fish in the seasoned flour using one hand, keeping the other hand clean.

Melt 3 tablespoons of butter in each of two frying pans. When the butter foams, add 1 or 2 fish, without touching or crowding, and cook about 10 minutes to the inch of thickness, half the time on each side. The fish is done when its thickest part registers approximately 135 degrees on an instant-read thermometer. Do not worry if the butter browns. Remove fish to a warm serving platter.

Wipe out one of the skillets or frying pans with paper towels. Add the remaining butter and pecans, and cook slowly until the butter is nut-brown. Add the lemon juice, seasonings, and herbs to the pan at once and reheat quickly. Pour the foaming butter sauce over the trout. Serve immediately.

OVEN-POACHED FISH FILLETS WITH LIGHT PECAN SAUCE

Serves 4 to 6

1 1/2 pounds flounder, catfish, or red snapper fillets, skinned
1–2 cups warm fish stock or broth, or water

Light Pecan Sauce
6 tablespoons butter
1/2 cup chopped pecans
1 tablespoon chopped fresh tarragon and/or parsley
3 tablespoons fresh lemon juice
1/2 teaspoon grated lemon rind, no white attached

Preheat oven to 400 degrees.

Lightly oil a baking dish large enough to hold the fish in a single layer; arrange the fillets in the dish, folding in half or thirds if necessary for thin fillets, skinned side to the inside. Add enough warm stock to come halfway up the fish. Cover the fish with a greased piece of waxed paper. Bake 11 minutes for every inch of thickness. The fish is done when its thickest part registers approximately 135 degrees on an instant-read thermometer. If the fish is not quite done, leave in the liquid a few minutes more to allow carryover heat to finish cooking it rather than returning it to the oven. Transfer fish to a hot platter.

While the fish is baking, prepare the sauce. Melt the butter in a small frying pan over low heat. Add the pecans and sauté for 1 to 2 minutes, until the nuts are lightly toasted. Add the herbs and lemon juice, and heat quickly. Spoon the sauce over the hot fillets, sprinkle with lemon rind, and serve immediately.

BLUE TROUT

Serves 4

SEVERAL TIMES A YEAR, *we drive to the mountains and return with mountain trout. These trout have a natural slick coating formed by the tiny microbes in the water, which turns a brilliant blue when the fish are poached quickly in a pan of acidulated water. To ensure the success of the transformation, great care needs to be taken not to disturb this natural coating when handling and cleaning the trout.*

For a party long ago, I rented a van with an aeration tank to keep the trout alive in lake water so I could poach them while perfectly fresh and have them turn the brilliant blue. Since the van was parked in the basement of a tall condominium building, I had to carry the trout on a tray, a few at a time, up the elevator. Then I cooked each individually. It was a heroic effort and received great praise, but I looked for another way to do the same with less effort!

When cleaned and cooked properly, the trout will automatically right itself in the pot so that it appears to be swimming with its tail curved, emerging triumphantly. Some catch their trout from ponds, others from brooks and streams, just before cooking. Restaurants may have a fish tank.

- 4 freshly caught and cleaned, head–on, whole rainbow trout (each 8–10 inches long) in a holding pail of lake water
- 1 cup fresh lemon juice
- 2 lemons, halved and cut decoratively
- 1 recipe White Butter Sauce (page 656) or Turnip Green Sauce (page 655)

To ensure the fish will not touch, bring enough large pots three-fourths full of water to the boil. Add 3 tablespoons of lemon juice per fish to each pot.

Remove the fish from the pail of lake water. Sprinkle each with lemon juice at this time to ensure that they turn blue.

Measure the trout for thickness. Add the fish to the boiling water, belly down. Let the water return to a simmer. Cook a 10-inch-long by 1/2-inch-thick trout. (In brief, cook 10 minutes to each inch of thickness. The eyes bulge when done.) Remove carefully with a slotted spoon or Chinese strainer. Drain. Serve on hot plates with lemon halves. Serve with optional sauce.

CLEANING TROUT

With one hand, hold the live trout securely from the underside, placing fingers in the gill cavity without letting the fish rub against anything, including hands. With the other hand, club the fish using a meat tenderizer or rolling pin. Insert a small knife in the anal cavity and cut along the underbelly to the head. Pull out the gills and innards in one tug. Rinse and dry the cavity gently; avoid splashing fresh water on the skin. Return the fish to a pail of lake water until ready to cook or freeze.

FREEZING TROUT

Dip the cleaned trout in reserved lake water and move the trout to a rack in the freezer, freezing the surface briefly. Dip the trout again in the lake water and freeze again. When completely frozen, move to a plastic freezer bag.

SIMPLE BROILED SHAD

Serves 2

SHAD IS USUALLY SOLD BONED, *with each fish seller having his own secret method of removing its awkward bone. Typically, it is sold by the side—a wide center piece attached to the skin and two narrow side pieces. The male shad is preferred to the female, which is less tasty when carrying the roe. Care should be taken to keep the shad from drying out. The roe is equally prized and is sold separately.*

2 shad fillets
2–3 tablespoons butter, melted
1 tablespoon chopped fresh herbs, such as tarragon, rosemary, and/or parsley
Salt
Freshly ground black pepper
Fresh lemon juice

Preheat the broiler.

Rinse and pat the fish dry with paper towels. Dip the shad in the butter and move to an oiled rimmed baking sheet or broiler pan, skin side toward the heat, enclosing the narrow side pieces in the center flap.

Broil the fish for 9 minutes to the inch of thickness, turning once during cooking. Sprinkle with herbs and season to taste with salt, pepper, and lemon juice. Serve immediately.

To griddle or pan-sear, heat pan to 500 degrees, add fish to hot pan, and cook using the timing as above.

To grill, preheat oiled grill, add fish to hot grill or oiled fish basket (page 291), and grill using the timing as above.

In the foreword to the 1976 edition of *Two Hundred Years of Charleston Cooking*, Elizabeth Hamilton wrote that she enjoyed slow-roasting shad using a 300-degree oven, as it provided enough heat to cook the shad without drying it out, and the longer cooking time presented the advantage of dissolving some of the bones.

SAUTÉED SHAD ROE

Serves 2 to 4

SHAD ROE IS MUCH PRIZED *by those who have cultivated a taste for its curiously contained package of tiny eggs. Fresh, it has no fishy odor and only a slight fishy flavor. It is available only once a year, in the spring, as the shad swims up inland rivers, like the James, Ogeechee, and Altamaha, to spawn.*

1 tablespoon butter
1 teaspoon oil, cook's preference
1 single or double shad roe (6–8 ounces), divided
Juice of 1–2 lemons

Melt the butter and oil in a large heavy frying pan and heat until very hot.

Season the shad roe with salt and pepper, add to the hot pan, and slash the top with a knife to prevent blistering. Immediately reduce the heat to low and cook for 3 to 4 minutes, depending on size. Turn and cook the other side until brown, a few minutes longer. The roe should still be pink inside. Pour the lemon juice over the roe and serve on a hot plate.

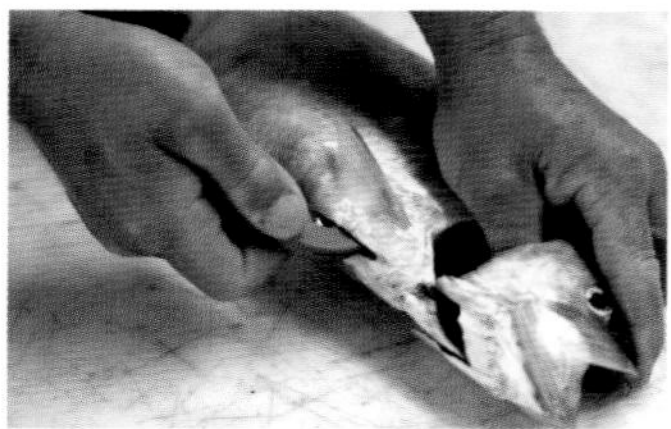
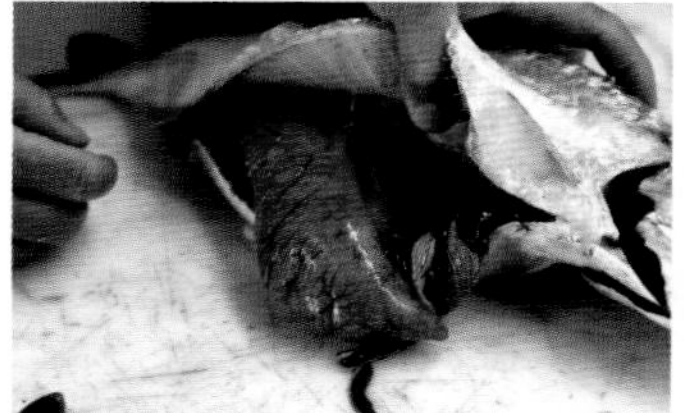
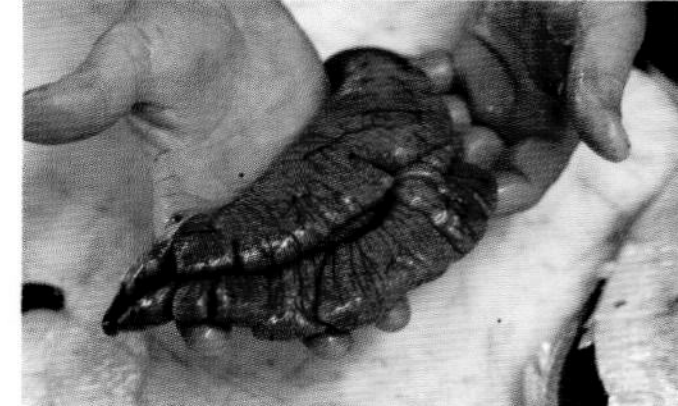

HARVESTING AND COOKING SHAD ROE

The female shad produces a large double roe held together by a thin membrane. These are usually sold singly, but when sold as a double, should be separated gently into two singles, removing the membrane joining them. Each lobe is also covered with another thin membrane that holds the eggs together. The membrane may burst, scattering the roe, if not dealt with. Here are four ways to deal with it:

1. Slash the top of the roe diagonally a few times when in the pan.
2. Parcook the roe as some do sweetbreads, adding to a solution of salted water and lemon, poaching just enough to be able to peel off the membrane when cool. Brown in a pan or on grill.
3. Firm up the roe in salted ice water and then cook.
4. Poach in a large quantity of butter.

ROASTED SHAD WITH ITS ROE AND CORN BUTTER SAUCE

Serves 4 to 6

SHAD IS AN ACQUIRED TASTE; SOME FIND IT DRY. *Roasted shad served with roe makes a dramatic presentation. It is one of those fish that should be purchased skinned and boned; the boning process is onerous for the novice. The male fish does not, of course, have the roe. The two parts—shad and roe—are cooked simultaneously.*

1¼–1½ cups butter, divided
2 single roe (6–8 ounces)
Salt
Freshly ground black pepper
2 tablespoons oil, cook's preference
2 shad fillets (2½ pounds each), boned and skinned
2 cups all-purpose flour
Salt
Freshly ground black pepper
1 teaspoon ground hot red pepper, optional
Juice of 1 lemon

Corn Butter Sauce

1–2 hot red peppers, seeded and chopped
5 tablespoons fresh corn off the cob
Juice of 2 limes
2 cups heavy cream
2 tablespoons butter
Salt
Freshly ground black pepper

Preheat oven to 400 degrees.

Melt 1 to 1½ cups of the butter in a large heavy frying pan and heat until very hot.

Season the shad roe with salt and pepper, add to the hot pan, and slash the top with a knife to prevent blistering. Immediately reduce the heat to low and cook for 3 to 4 minutes, depending on size. Turn and cook the other side until brown, a few minutes longer. The roe should still be pink inside.

To prepare the shad, toss the fillets in flour seasoned with salt, pepper, and a dash of hot red pepper if desired. Melt 2 tablespoons butter and pour onto a rimmed baking sheet. Move the floured shad to the sheet, dot with 2 more tablespoons butter, and sprinkle with lemon juice. Roast 8 to 9 minutes per inch of thickness, about 7 minutes.

For the Corn Butter Sauce, bring the hot peppers, corn, and lime juice to the boil in a large saucepan; boil briefly, until the juice is reduced by half. Add the cream and the 2 tablespoons butter, return to the boil, and cook until the cream is reduced and thick. Season to taste with salt and pepper.

Move the shad to a hot serving platter, surround with the roe, and top with Corn Butter Sauce.

When ordering shad, specify the male for a better tasting, moister fish.

CRAB

South Atlantic Blue Crabs, their habitat ranging from Maryland's shore to Florida and the Caribbean, are considered the best crabs of the world's 1,000 species. Their meat is succulent and tender. Crab shell adds great flavor to any broth as well as the crabs themselves as they cook. Their formal name means "beautiful tasty swimmers." Their vibrant blue color and gliding motion enhance crabbers' love for them. Many times, crabber and diner are the same person, as blue crabs are easily caught from floating docks, creek banks, and marshes abutting inlets, as well as from boats and mesh-wire crab traps.

Fresh South Carolina crab has the clean, bright taste of the sea and a succulence that excels any that is imported. One taste is enough to tell it is as good as any crab you will ever eat.

The drawback to the eating is the picking. A top crab picker in a packinghouse may pick a cooked crab in a minute, but ordinary mortals take longer to extract the meat. Diners confronted with the cooked crab take even longer, headily pulling claws and fins through their teeth to savor the last morsel, cracking and removing shells, and relishing the tender lump meat. No wonder crabmeat is expensive.

Those of us fortunate enough to live close enough to eat fresh crabs are also able to save from $12 to $15 a pound just by picking the crabs ourselves. Two people picking cooked crabs together, sitting and talking about the day, at a table covered with newspaper for easy cleanup, can pick 12 large crabs in less than an hour, resulting in a pound of meat. When reserving claw and other meat for another purpose, 24 large crabs will make 1 pound of lump crabmeat. A pound of crabmeat is a generous amount for four people, since crab is rarely eaten by itself due to its richness. Usually it is mixed with other ingredients, such as in a salad, pie, casserole, or soup. Many times, fresh local cooked shrimp is added to compensate for a lack of sufficient crab.

Crabmeat, since already cooked, is just heated rather than re-cooked, by being added to finished soups, such as She-Crab Soup (page 132), or to a delicate sauce for the cheese custards. In casseroles or pies, the crab is best combined with other ingredients just before the final heating or baking.

Picked cooked crab is happily added to uncooked ingredients, like fresh mango and/or avocado salad, where the coolness of the avocado and the mango are subtle enhancements to the crab.

Purchasing crab— When feeling flush, purchase fresh lump crabmeat, those prime pieces of moist and tender crab. Otherwise, purchase claw meat, back fin, or a mixed version that frequently contains some she-crab roe, making it nice for She-Crab Soup.

Most, if not all, of the commercial crab sold nowadays is steamed as soon as possible after being caught, picked out of the shells by skilled workers, and quickly vacuum-packed. Usually sold in a clear plastic tub, it will last a month or longer before opening. After opening the container, cover the crab with milk and freeze within a few days if not using immediately. The milk will keep the crab tender and prevent it from drying out.

Always purchase crabmeat from a good fish store or the supermarket, knowing the reputation of the person who sells it, being sure to read the label. An American-sounding name is no guarantee of local crab. It should be marked according to its origin, even if the information is in fine print. Asian crab can be from any—or several—Asian countries. Read the ingredients on the back and avoid purchasing any chemically laced product, indicating a non-local product. Chemicals ruin the taste of crab, and there is no sense in purchasing anything that doesn't taste good, even if it is slightly less expensive than the real thing.

Crabs vary in size according to their age, from "small" to "large" to "jumbo." The pincers closest to the body of a male crab are sturdier, and the tab on its base is long and narrow. The female crab has a wider body and a rounded tab. Three large or two jumbos make a good dinner portion. Fresh soft-shell crabs are superior to frozen.

STEAMED HARD-SHELL CRABS

Serves 4

CRAB-CRACKING CALLS FOR SERVING THE WHOLE CRABS *on newspaper-covered tables and providing hammers or mallets to the diners, who then pull out the tender meat with their fingers, tiny forks, or even nut picks. One such crab-cracking I attended was particularly glorious. It was a photo shoot for Matt and Ted Lee, held at the home of their longtime friends Josephine Humphreys and Tom Hutcheson. Other author friends of Josephine's flanked the long table—Dorthea Benton Frank and Mary Alice Monroe among them. Everyone was up to their elbows in dripping butter, crab on their chins, while we laughed in the sunshine next to the pier where the crab were caught, under the shade of a massive live oak tree.*

12 live blue crabs

Melted butter

Move a steaming rack to the bottom of a large pot. Add 1 to 2 inches of water and bring to the boil. Add live crabs in layers. Bring to the boil and cover. Reduce the heat to low and steam 15 to 20 minutes, until the crabs turn from blue to red. Serve the crabs with plenty of melted butter or other dipping sauce. Some prefer spiced crabs, although I love them just steamed.

Variation: For spicy crabs, use 1/2 to 3/4 cup commercial seafood seasoning or Creole seasoning (page 670). Sprinkle each layer with some of the seasoning mix.

INTERN CRAB CAKES

Makes 4 small cakes

THIS RECIPE BY INTERN NIKKI MOORE *is a testament to the fact that simply exquisite food such as crabmeat is best left alone. Lacking the heavier breading of most crab cakes, these are fragile, and it may be necessary to cook them in a ring to preserve their shape. Don't fret if they break while cooking or moving—just push them back together.*

Crab cakes should be loosely combined pieces of crab, preferably lump, that barely hang together when briefly sautéed. (There is a schism between bread/panko crumbs and non-crumb crab cake eaters—some people are inured to a lot of crumbs to hold the crab in place, others wanting none or just the barest minimum to brown.) Held together when cooked by a ring (or old tuna fish can), it may fall apart, but every taste of crab will linger on the tongue.

1 egg, lightly beaten
1 tablespoon mayonnaise
1/4 cup torn bread, crust removed
8 ounces lump crabmeat, picked over and cleaned, with all shell fragments removed
Salt
Freshly ground black pepper
Ground hot red pepper
2 tablespoons butter
Lemon wedges for garnish

Mix egg and mayonnaise together with a fork in a medium-sized bowl. Stir in the bread. Gently mix in crabmeat. Season to taste with salt, pepper, and hot red pepper to taste. Form four small cakes and set aside.

Heat butter in a medium-sized sauté or frying pan. Using your hands, add crab cakes gently to the hot pan, or slide the cakes individually onto a thin metal spatula or pancake turner before sliding into the pan. Quickly put a ring around it as used in poached eggs. Cook for 2 to 3 minutes, or until lightly browned. Flip over the cakes gently using a thin metal spatula, and cook on the other side until lightly browned. Serve immediately with lemon wedges.

Variation: Omit egg and bread and make a very loose crab cake.

Crab cake rings can include tuna fish cans with top and bottom removed, biscuit cutters, and egg-poacher rings.

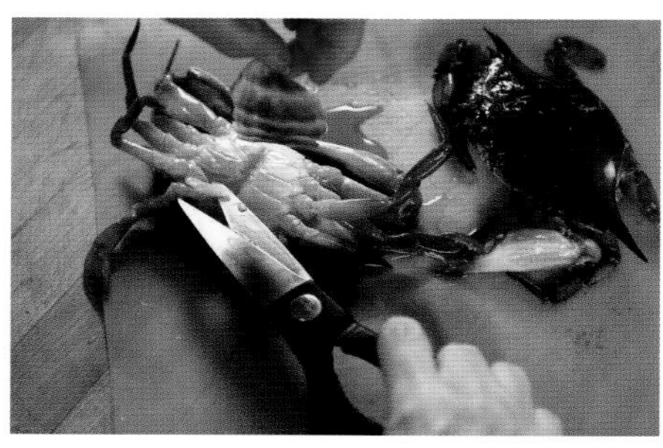

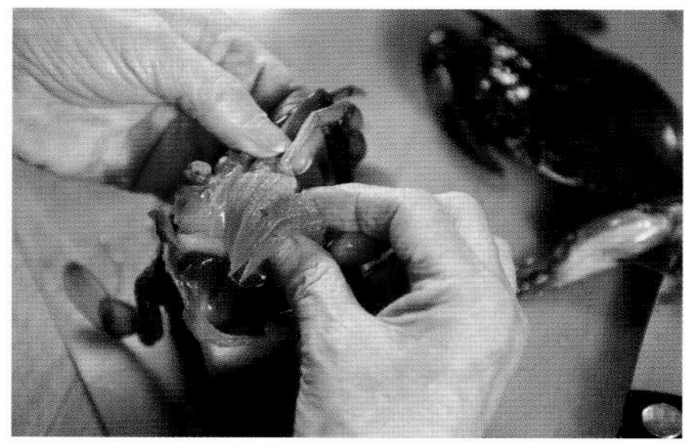

SOFT-SHELL CRAB

From Maryland to Florida, Southerners wait eagerly for the first full moon of the spring, when the weather is finally warm enough to spur the crabs into stretching in their shells and a bit of romance is in the air. They shed their shells, the female is cradled by the male, and a new generation is on the way.

During their brief time without a shell, the soft-shell crab is highly sought after, as nearly the whole crab is edible without the ordeal of picking it out of a shell. It brings an incredible crispy outside, with spurts of juices accompanying each bite.

Frozen soft-shell crabs are available commercially, but they lack the clean, fresh, flavor of the sea. They must be deeply battered to convey any of the most desirable qualities.

Cleaning Soft-Shell Crabs

Usually soft-shell crabs are sold cleaned and ready to cook. Rinse the crab under running water. If not already done, cut off the eyes and mouth, then the sand sac behind the mouth, remove the "dead men" (the spongy gray gills) from each side of the crab, and pull off the apron (the tail flap).

GRILLED OR BROILED SOFT-SHELL CRABS

Serves 1

THIS METHOD OF COOKING SOFT-SHELLS *obviates the need for a batter and leaves them crisp outside and with an amazing burst of moisture from each crab, the taste shines through. The recipe can be increased proportionately.*

2 jumbo soft-shell crabs, cleaned
Juice of 1 lemon
2–3 tablespoons oil, cook's preference
Salt
Freshly ground black pepper

Cut each crab in quarters and drizzle lemon juice and oil over all. Season to taste with salt and pepper. Add to a hot grill or an oiled rimmed baking sheet under the broiler, top side of the crab towards the heat. Cook a total of 3 to 5 minutes, depending on the size. Serve hot or cold in a salad.

SAUTÉED SOFT-SHELL CRAB

Serves 1

This recipe has never failed me *and was the first way I prepared soft-shell crab; it remains my favorite way of cooking them. The moisture flooding out from the crust of the cooked crabs, with the flavor of the sea shining through, is pure bliss. The nuts add crunch and enhance the crabs. This recipe may be multiplied for more people in the same proportions. Do not use frozen and defrosted soft-shell crabs, for they have an iodine-like taste that will come through.*

2 jumbo soft-shell crabs, cleaned
1/2 cup all-purpose flour, divided
Salt
Freshly ground black pepper
4 tablespoons butter, divided
1 teaspoon oil, cook's preference
2–3 tablespoons pecan pieces or slivered almonds

Clean the crabs, as described on page 319, and remove their apron. Season the flour to taste with salt and pepper.

Heat 2 tablespoons of butter and the oil in a heavy 10-inch skillet. Coat the crabs with the flour mixture, shake off the excess, and add to the hot butter. Sauté a few minutes on each side, no more than 2 at a time, until brown and crisp. Remove to a warm plate lined with paper towels. Meanwhile, brown the pecans or almonds in 2 tablespoons of butter. Move the cooked crabs to a serving plate and top with the buttered pecans.

SHALLOW-FRIED LEMON SOFT-SHELL CRAB

Serves 2

When I fry soft-shell crabs, *I shallow-fry them and keep the coating light without dominating the succulent crabs themselves. This is the only time I use frozen defrosted crabs, as the lemon masks any flavor loss. For more crabs, increase the ingredients proportionately.*

Shortening or vegetable oil for frying, cook's preference
1 cup all-purpose flour
Salt
Freshly ground black pepper
6 soft-shell crabs, cleaned
1 recipe Lemon Batter for Seafood (page 327)

Heat 1 inch of oil in a heavy 10-inch skillet.

Season the flour to taste with salt and pepper on a plate. Using one hand, coat the crabs in the flour on each side. Shake off the excess and dip into the Lemon Batter. Slip the crab into the hot fat, no more than 2 at a time in the pan, and fry 2 minutes on each side, watching for splatters. Turn when brown and crisp. Remove to a platter lined with paper towels and serve hot with preferred sauce.

CRAWFISH

Southern crawfish, similar to crawfish found in Australia and New Zealand, grow in ponds and freshwater, many times farmed symbiotically with rice, eating the residue once the rice is gone. Crawfish have most of their flavor in their heads and shells, which is why they are cooked with their heads on. Crawfish zealots suck the flavorful goodness from the heads. Other countries have crawfish or crayfish that can vary in size from the smaller size found in Louisiana to the lobster-sized crawfish found in the Caribbean Islands.

Since the tastiest crawfish are cooked alive and in their shells, they may cause the cook (and transporter) a bit of aggravation. They are frisky and can poke under surfaces, from fingers to Styrofoam. Once, Cynthia and I brought back several containers of live crawfish from Louisiana on a commercial airplane (probably illegal, but it was a different era). The crawfish forced their way out of the vulnerable Styrofoam chest, leaving a trail of live red objects on Hartsfield Airport's concourse. We had no choice but to ignore the wriggling creatures. Unfortunately, the taxi driver insisted we remove them from the trunk of his cab when they escaped there as well. They were so energetic, in fact, that they subsequently escaped from the cooking pot on the television set as we were taping the show!

CRAWFISH OR SHRIMP BOILS

Serves 8 to 10

LOWCOUNTRY SHRIMP AND CRAWFISH "BOILS" *are exactly the same except they use different shellfish. Also known as Frogmore Stew, they were first credited to the Gay family of Saint Helena Island, South Carolina.*

Plan on 3 pounds of crawfish (yielding 1/3 to 1/2 pound of tails) or 2 pounds of raw, headless, unpeeled shrimp (yielding 1 pound of meat) per person. It's hard to cook them all at once; instead, cook them in batches, removing the barely cooked crawfish to an empty insulated cooler, which allows them to continue cooking to just the right degree. I do not like to junk up my shellfish with seasoning mixes, but I am in the minority here.

2 pounds hot country sausage, preferably links (optional)
16 pounds crawfish, or 12 pounds raw shrimp, in their shells
1/2 pound commercial seafood seasoning or Creole seasoning (page 670)
4–5 onions, peeled and quartered
24 small new potatoes, well-scrubbed and halved
12 ears corn, shucked

Cook the sausage over medium heat until done. Set aside.

Rinse the shellfish. Bring a large pot (preferably one with a removable colander) of water to the boil with the seafood seasoning and boil a few minutes to increase the flavor. (If one large pot is not available, 2 or 3 smaller pots will work. Watch the timing, however, as adding the ingredients will reduce the water temperature and take longer to re-boil.) This can be done up to a few days ahead and be removed.

Add the cooked sausage, onions, and potatoes; return to the boil, cover, and boil until nearly tender, about 15 minutes, depending on the size of the pot. Add the corn and then the shellfish, and cook for 3 to 4 minutes, drain, and transfer to an empty insulated cooler to finish cooking.

Any sausage will do; a kielbasa or other sausage is easier to prepare outdoors or on boats, but a link sausage adds more flavor; or leave it out altogether. In fact, change the ingredients to suit the occasion. This dish resembles similar ones brought by the Portuguese to Rhode Island. But who am I to say?

CLAMS

Clams are seen in many places up and down the South Atlantic Seacoast. Discard any clams that are cracked. Rinse well. Clams love to be cooking in a lightly wined broth. Serve around a newspaper-covered table.

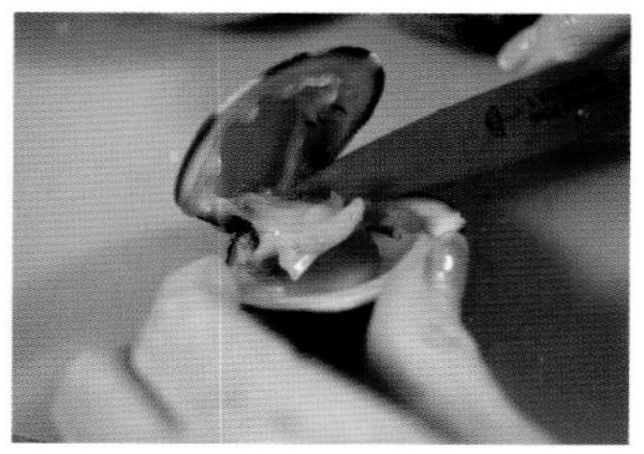

STEAMED SOFT-SHELL CLAMS

Serves 4

SOUTHERNERS USED TO CALL ALL SOFT-SHELL CLAMS BY THE NAME "MANINOSE." *All soft-shell clams (also called "steamers," "softs," and "gapers") have brittle oval shells, but their necks stick out so much that the shells can't close when removed from the water. They usually need to soak a few hours while the clams will purge themselves, preferably overnight in a mixture of 1 part cornmeal, 1 part salt, and 3 parts cold water.*

2 garlic cloves, finely chopped
1 large shallot, finely chopped
1 cup dry white wine, vermouth, or sherry
3–4 pounds (about 2 dozen) soft-shell clams, cleaned
3 tablespoons chopped fresh parsley
1 tablespoon chopped fresh thyme
Freshly ground black pepper
1 cup butter, melted
1 loaf French bread

Bring the garlic, shallot, and white wine to the boil in a large Dutch oven. Cover, reduce heat, and simmer 3 to 5 minutes. Remove the cover and add the clams, arranged in one even layer, cover, and bring back to the boil. Reduce the heat and simmer until the shells open wide, about 3 to 5 minutes. Use a slotted spoon to remove the clams. Discard any that did not open.

Strain the liquid through a very fine strainer into a bowl. Add the parsley, thyme, and pepper. Serve the broth and butter in two separate bowls.

The diners remove the clams from the shells, dip them in the broth, then in the melted butter. Serve with plenty of napkins and a bowl for the empty shells. Mop up extra liquid with the bread.

Variations:

- After straining the broth, if necessary, bring to the boil and boil until reduced to 1/2 cup. Add 1/3 to 1/2 cup heavy cream, return to the boil, and boil until slightly thickened.
- Saffron, curry powder, coriander seeds, and chopped cilantro are all possible additions to the cooking broth.

There are about 8 to 10 soft-shell clams per pound. Clams may be steamed and then stuffed, but home cooks rarely have the patience needed for this time-consuming task.

GRILLED OR OVEN-STEAMED HARD-SHELL CLAMS

Serves 4 as a starter

ALSO CALLED "LITTLENECK" CLAMS, *these are the sweet ones that are most seen in the South. Sipping the juice from their tiny shells is a treat.*

2–4 pounds cleaned littleneck or butter clams
4 garlic cloves, chopped
2 onions, chopped
1/2 cup fresh lemon juice or dry white wine
4 tablespoons chopped fresh parsley
4 tablespoons chopped fresh basil

Heat a grill or preheat oven to 450 degrees.

Cut 8 pieces of heavy-duty wide aluminum foil into 18-inch squares. Divide the cleaned clams between the foil squares.

Combine the remaining ingredients and divide among the 8 foil packets. Fold the foil loosely over the clams to allow them to open and puff up, and then fold the edges together to seal the 8 packets. Move to a rimmed baking sheet to collect any leaks and refrigerate if desired up to several hours.

When ready to cook, move the clam packets to the hot grill, or move the rimmed baking sheet to the middle rack of the oven and cook until the clams open, 15 to 30 minutes. Check by opening a package to see if the clams have opened. Size as well as temperature of the clams going into the oven will affect the cooking time. Serve 2 packets per bowl, and let everyone open their own. The clams emit a juice tasty enough to sip from the shell.

CLEANING HARD-SHELL CLAMS

Clams are quite simple to clean, the clams in their opened shells making a stunning presentation. Cover the clams with cold water in a large bowl or sink. Scrub well with a vegetable brush to remove any dirt. Toss the clams with your hands and shake off any excess grit. Lift the clams out of the water, discard the water and rinse the bowl. Repeat this procedure once or twice more, until no grit or sediment is seen on the bottom of the bowl. If absolutely necessary to remove any more sand after stormy weather, soak 10 to 15 minutes more in salted water—fresh water will kill them.

James Peterson, my mentor in things fishy and author of *Fish and Shellfish,* says that "bad" clams are usually discovered when being scrubbed clean, as they break apart and have an odor. Clams that don't open when cooked are rarely "bad" but are more reluctant to open. Remove the open, cooked clams and let the unopened ones cook a little longer. Other authorities agree, some going so far as to say that opening is not a guarantee of live clams, and that the question is moot.

ALL-IN-ONE CLAMS WITH GREENS AND TOMATOES

Serves 2

CLAMS LOVE OUR TOMATOES AND GREENS, *such as tender small turnip greens or spinach. Clams are now farm-raised off the Southern Atlantic Coast.*

1 tablespoon oil, cook's preference
1 tablespoon butter
1 medium onion, thinly sliced
1 large red, yellow, orange, or green bell pepper, cored, seeded, and cut in thin strips
2 garlic cloves, chopped
1 bay leaf
1/2 pound fresh or canned tomatoes with liquid, broken up
1 (4-ounce) can tomato sauce
2 dozen littleneck or other small clams, scrubbed clean
1 (10-ounce) package fresh baby spinach or turnip greens, washed (page 205)
Salt
Freshly ground black pepper
Granulated sugar
1 cup cooked rice
1/4 cup coarsely chopped fresh Italian parsley
1 loaf French bread

Heat the oil and butter in a large Dutch oven over moderate heat; add the onion and bell pepper, and sauté until soft, about 10 minutes. Add the garlic, bay leaf, tomatoes and their liquid, and tomato sauce. Bring the mixture to a simmer, cover, and simmer for 10 to 15 minutes. This may be made in advance then refrigerated or frozen.

When ready to serve, remove the bay leaf from the sauce, add the clams, cover tightly, and cook over medium heat, shaking occasionally until the clams open, about 10 minutes, checking frequently to see if opened. Add the greens, cover, and cook for 1 to 2 minutes, until wilted. Season to taste with salt, pepper, and sugar. Divide the rice between 2 shallow bowls, ladle the clam mixture over the rice, and sprinkle with parsley. Serve with French bread.

Variations:

- Add 1/3 cup white wine or chicken stock to thin the sauce. May be served over pasta or rice.
- Add 2 ounces of cubed ham or chopped cooked bacon with the tomatoes for a more substantial meal.

Bay leaves bring a lot of flavor to many stews, especially tomato-based ones. Care must be taken to prevent the tough center vein from lodging in a throat; therefore, crumble when adding, or diligently remove before inadvertently serving.

SHRIMP

Fresh local shrimp is something to dream about, and when the season starts, a lot of good eating is about to begin. Those who have never eaten wild-caught fresh shrimp are stunned when they eat it, saying they never ate "real" shrimp before. We know it is different, and it is the best shrimp in the world.

Most shrimp are born out in the ocean, invisible to the naked eye. They ride on top of the waves, inexorably pulled inland to our local waters—marshes, inlets, and tidal creeks. There they sink to the bottom, where they feed and grow until they ride out to the ocean again to breed, As they grow, they develop a flavor dependent to some degree on the food they eat and to some degree on the depth where they live, as well as the water they live in. Traveling down from North Carolina to Georgia and South Carolina, then to Florida and the Gulf States of Mississippi, Alabama, Louisiana, and Texas, and comparing shrimp from different warm-water regions of the South, it becomes obvious that each of these things—food, water salinity, water content, and depth—makes a difference.

As the shrimp grow and head back to the ocean, they live and feed in deeper water, and the water temperature changes as well. As this happens, they develop different flavors, from the marsh sweetness to the deep ocean "iodine" flavor. In between are all ranges of flavor, texture, and color. Different people prefer the different stages of the shrimp, just as they prefer various sizes and types. The shrimp that feed in the bayous clearly have a different flavor from those of the Lowcountry. Which shrimp you prefer may, like your taste in coffee, depend on what you are used to, what you grew up with, or the depth of your palate.

The sweetest of the shrimp are those caught by seines and nets near the shore. Called "creek shrimp," they are young shrimp whose shells are barely formed. (It is now illegal to catch these baby shrimp in South Carolina. This is not true everywhere; in Louisiana some are allowed to be caught in their bayous and are sold as "popcorn" shrimp, for instance.)

Eating a new food is a moment of epiphany. Usually that moment is so clearly etched in memory it is impossible to duplicate. So it is with shrimp and me. Fresh shrimp was a costly product as I grew up, having to be trucked up to Virginia and in later years to Atlanta. I had two moments with shrimp, however, that convinced me I had to search for fresh shrimp whenever possible.

The first was when I moved to New York as a young woman and craved Southern food. I would go on occasion to a place way on the West Side called the West Boondocks, part beer joint/ part restaurant, which served them as well as collards, turnip greens, and cornbread. And I would have shrimp parties in my small apartment.

As difficult as it was to get good fresh shrimp in Virginia and Atlanta, it was impossible to get what I called "fresh shrimp" in New York. I went to the Fulton Fish Market, my sole purpose to get fresh shrimp in the shell. Going there was always an experience. In the cold, dark early morning, the market teeming with hollering men rolling dollies stacked with boxes of fish, live lobsters in wooden crates snapping out at any passerby with a bare limb, and, finally, fresh Southeast Atlantic shrimp in the shell. I purchased as much as I could afford and made my way back to my small apartment.

Later that day, I cooked the shrimp in the shell, spreading out newspapers on the floor, my ex-pat Southern friends hanging around until the butter was sizzling hot, then descending on the shrimp, butter, and hot sauce, peeling and laughing as we ate shrimp until we were reclining, backs on the floor, knees in the air, stomachs full to bursting and only the shells left on the soggy paper. Those shrimp tasted as good as shrimp ever did and taught me a lesson. Good food is worth seeking out, and fresh is the best!

In the mid-eighties, Cynthia and I had another epiphany. We drove down to Darien, Georgia, in my 1975 Vega, a hangover from my former marriage. Cynthia had arranged for our first shrimp boat trip. At dawn the next morning, we and our camera crew were shivering on the shrimp boat *Georgia Bulldog,* a research boat for the University of Georgia. Not real shrimpers at all, the scientists had all the sonic gear necessary to track the shrimp, but nonetheless it took hours to find them. The large trawling nets on either side, which make shrimp boats look like mosquitoes to some, were out and brimmed with a catch. The shrimp was thrown on the deck, and we were allowed to scoop up as much as our coolers could hold. It was a glorious day, and we drove back to Atlanta revitalized and with great anticipation of eating the shrimp packed in ice in the cooler on the back floor of the Vega.

We arrived home and pulled out the cooler, which spilled onto the floor of the Vega. After a bit of scooping and effort, the shrimp were back in the cooler and shortly cooked and devoured. Shrimp so fresh it still has its whiskers on its head has no odor except that of the sea. Its taste is not fishy but clean and sweet. Correctly cooked, preferably in the shell, its flavor lingers but doesn't dominate, and the flesh melts without vigorous chewing. There is no comparison between fresh wild American shrimp and imported or farm-raised shrimp; it is as if they are different species.

The Vega carried the odor of shrimp until I sold it a year later. I thought so much of that extraordinarily fresh shrimp that I searched out fresh shrimp whenever possible, and volunteered many years later to do a media tour for the Wild American Shrimp Consortium, promoting fresh wild American shrimp, when my book was published.

SHRIMP BASICS

Fresh shrimp should be shiny and the meat firm against the shell. (As it ages, it separates from the shell, much like an egg does from an eggshell.) There should be no ammonia or fishy odor. When in doubt, buy commercially frozen, preferably in the shell.

Evaluating the shrimps' condition: Fresh shrimp have no odor. If their heads are intact, the feelers will frequently still be attached if they have been stored over ice or frozen immediately and properly. Shrimp that have not been treated with a preservative will frequently have a dry look. These are preferable to those treated with a preservative but requires knowing the seller's habits.

Buying Shrimp

If the shrimp are large, buy more to avoid portions looking "skimpy," as there will be fewer. Always purchase shrimp in the shell when possible. When buying shrimp without the shell, purchase about 25 percent less than is called for in a recipe using shrimp in the shell.

- Raw, headless and unpeeled shrimp—1/3 pound per serving
- Peeled shrimp—1/6 pound per serving
- Two pounds of raw headless, unpeeled shrimp—is equal to 1 pound of cooked, peeled shrimp.

Getting the Better Value

It is difficult to determine which is the better value—head on or head off—when buying fresh shrimp. Obviously, if you intend to eat the heads or make stock from heads and shells, buying them whole is economical. If not, buying them with the heads removed is usually most economical.

Cleaning Shrimp

It is not necessary to remove the vein from shrimp, but do cook and eat one test shrimp to see if it is sandy. If it is, clean the whole batch. This is particularly true if they were caught just after a storm. Shrimp may be veined and peeled before or after cooking, using one of the gadgets to remove shell and vein. Many times, carefully pulling the head off the shrimp will also remove the vein.

When serving shrimp in the shell, use a long needle or toothpick (taking care to keep it from being lost in food and being ingested) and insert it in the black vein on the back of the shrimp before cooking, threading between the sections of the shell. It should pull out in one long piece. If not, repeat the process.

Chefs "butterfly" the shrimp before cooking, cutting down the back firmly. It's an easy matter to remove the shell and the vein when the shrimp have been butterflied.

Freezing Shrimp

Move one layer of shrimp to a dated plastic ziplock freezer bag that is flat on a baking pan. Add water to cover the shrimp and freeze. Repeat. The bags will stack easily. (Take care no tails or hard shells are poking through the bag, allowing air to enter). Another method is to dip each shrimp individually in water, move to a rimmed baking sheet, and freeze. When the shrimp are frozen, remove them to a dated plastic ziplock freezer bag.

Keeping shrimp warm when serving a crowd— Remove shrimp from water or grill and move to an empty insulated cooler to keep warm. Cover and proceed with another batch.

Broiled shrimp—Move the shrimp onto an oiled foil-lined broiler pan and broil about 3 to 4 inches from the heat for 4 to 5 minutes, turning once.

Sautéed shrimp—Melt 3 tablespoons butter in a heavy skillet. Add the shrimp in a single layer, cooking in batches if necessary. Cook the shrimp for 1 minute. Reduce the heat to medium-high, and cook the shrimp until pink on both sides, about 3 minutes, turning each shrimp over at least once.

Steamed shrimp—Move a steamer basket to a pot with water just touching bottom of basket. Cover pot and boil water. Add shrimp to basket and sprinkle with spices as desired. Steam shrimp, tightly covered, for 4 to 5 minutes, or until just firm and cooked through.

LEMON BATTER FOR SEAFOOD

Makes 1 cup

Seafood always welcomes citrus, it seems. *This citrus batter welcomes shrimp, oysters, and even soft-shell crabs.*

- Juice of 3 lemons
- 1 cup all-purpose flour
- Grated rind of 1 lemon, no white attached

Add enough water to the lemon juice to make 1 cup of liquid. Move to a large bowl and slowly whisk in the flour until smooth. Stir in the lemon rind. Cover if setting aside.

Coat the seafood by dipping briefly in the batter and adding it to hot oil in a skillet. Follow recipe directions for timing.

NEW ORLEANS–STYLE BARBECUE SHRIMP

Serves 2

THIS TYPICAL NEW ORLEANS-STYLE RECIPE *was originally to be prepared with the tiny bayou or marsh shrimp that were eaten completely, fragile shell and all. Barbecue in this case means a garlicky semi-hot sauce abundant enough to allow for dipping both shrimp and bread. See photos with Pickled Shrimp (page 39).*

2 pounds large head-on shrimp
2 tablespoons commercial seafood seasoning or Creole seasoning (page 670), divided
1 tablespoon oil, cook's preference
1 large garlic head, cloves chopped
2 tablespoons chopped fresh rosemary
3 tablespoons Worcestershire sauce
3 tablespoons hot sauce
1 lemon, quartered (juice removed and reserved)
1/3 cup beer
Salt
Freshly ground black pepper
1/2 cup butter, room temperature
Food Processor Quick-Rise Crusty Bread (page 486)

Sprinkle shrimp with 1 tablespoon of seasoning. (This may be done up to an hour ahead).

Preheat a large skillet over high heat; add the oil and heat briefly. Add the garlic and rosemary to the pan and stir to lightly brown garlic, watching carefully to prevent burning.

Add the shrimp, Worcestershire sauce, hot sauce, and lemon juice and quarters. Lightly stir the shrimp and the ingredients, just enough to mix.

Pour in the beer, stirring to release any bits clinging to the bottom of the skillet, and boil the mixture to reduce while shaking the pan. Cook shrimp 2 to 2 1/2 minutes, depending on size, and add remaining seafood seasoning and salt and pepper to taste. When shrimp are finished cooking, the liquid should have a sauce consistency.

Quickly whisk in the butter, turning the heat down as necessary, until it is melted into the sauce, leaving it thick and emulsified. (If it melts, see White Butter Sauce instructions, page 656.) Taste and add salt and pepper if desired. Remove lemon quarters. Serve with crusty bread, lots of napkins, and fingerbowls. Garnish each serving with a lemon piece.

This dish is cooked very fast, so advance preparation of all the ingredients is key. Take great care the garlic is not burned while cooking the shrimp. Other fresh herbs—marjoram, thyme, etc.—may be added, as well as plenty of ground pepper.

ACADIAN PEPPERED SHRIMP

Serves 6 to 8

STOVETOP BUTTER-POACHING OF THE SHRIMP *allows for the possibility that small bayou and marsh shrimp, available in Louisiana and entirely edible due to their tender shells, might be used. If the shrimp used are large, licking fingers while peeling one's own is permissible.*

This is not to be made by the tender of tongue or heart, as it is spicy. The pepper must be freshly ground, causing a few damp blinks on its own. From Terry Thompsen, this is another wonderful bread-and shrimp dipping sauce.

2 cups butter
1/2 cup fresh lemon juice
2 teaspoons chopped fresh basil
1–2 teaspoons ground hot red pepper
2 teaspoons chopped fresh oregano or marjoram
5 garlic cloves, chopped
1 bay leaf, crumbled
1/2 cup freshly ground black pepper
2–3 pounds raw shrimp, in shells
Salt
Crusty French-style bread

Melt the butter in a large deep-sided frying pan over low heat. Increase the heat to medium and add the lemon juice, basil, hot red pepper, herbs, garlic, bay leaf, and black pepper. Stir often and cook about 10 minutes, until browned to a rich mahogany color but not burned. This may be made up to several days in advance, covered, and refrigerated.

Add the shrimp stirring to coat well with the butter. Cook about 10 minutes, until the shrimp have turned a rich deep pink. Season to taste with salt.

SHRIMP CREOLE

Serves 4

THIS RECIPE IS ADAPTED *from Craig Claiborne's* Favorites from the New York Times, *having wended its way up from Louisiana. Nonetheless, I have seen variations of it and other shrimp creoles in venerable Southern Junior League cookbooks, which claim it as their own since it has lingered so widely and long in the Southern kitchen. The Pernod adds a dash of New Orleans to the dish and is reminiscent of Oysters Rockefeller and other favorites from Commander's Palace. Red bell pepper is smoother tasting than the traditional green bell pepper.*

1 1/2 pounds raw shrimp
5 tablespoons butter, divided
2 medium onions, chopped
1 rib celery, chopped
1 red or green bell pepper, seeded and chopped
3 garlic cloves, chopped
2 pounds fresh tomatoes, chopped, or 1 (28-ounce) can diced tomatoes
3 tablespoons chopped herbs, such as fresh basil and marjoram
1 bay leaf, crumbled
Hot sauce to taste
1 teaspoon grated lemon rind, no white attached
Salt
Freshly ground black pepper
1 teaspoon all-purpose flour
3 tablespoons chopped fresh parsley
Juice of 1/2 lemon
1 1/2 tablespoons Pernod, optional
1–2 cups cooked rice

Peel the shrimp and set aside.

Melt 4 tablespoons of butter in a saucepan. Stir in the onions and cook until soft. Add the celery, bell pepper, and garlic. Cook about 3 minutes, stirring occasionally. The vegetables should stay crisp. Add the tomatoes, herbs, bay leaf, hot sauce, lemon rind, and salt and pepper to taste, and cook 20 minutes, or until thick. Add the shrimp, cover, and cook 3 minutes.

Blend the remaining butter with the flour and add bit by bit to the simmering pot. Cook about 1 minute. Add the parsley and lemon juice. Add the Pernod, heat, and serve over rice.

OVEN-COOKED NEW ORLEANS SPICY SHRIMP

Serves 8

I LEARNED THIS RECIPE WHEN I BRIEFLY LIVED IN NEW ORLEANS *as a young woman. It was served in a local casual restaurant, where I was told that the bayou and marsh shrimp had shells so fragile they could be eaten. The butter is mixed with oil to raise the temperature of the butter and the shrimp is cooked so the shells are crisp to chew. I doubt many of those shrimp are available for home cooks, so prepare to discard the shells. Once again, on a newspaper-covered table or the floor is the best place to eat this meal. Plenty of napkins are a necessity.*

2 pounds butter
1/4 cup oil, cook's preference
3 garlic cloves, chopped
2 tablespoons chopped fresh rosemary
3 teaspoons chopped fresh herbs, such as basil, thyme, and oregano
1 small hot pepper, chopped, or 1–2 tablespoons ground hot red pepper
2 teaspoons freshly ground black pepper
2 bay leaves, crumbled
1 tablespoon paprika
2 teaspoons fresh lemon juice
2 pounds raw shrimp in their shells (about 30–35 per pound)
Salt to taste
Crusty French-style bread

Melt the butter and oil in a flameproof baking dish. Add all ingredients except the shrimp, salt, and bread. Bring to the boil. Turn the heat down and simmer 10 minutes, stirring frequently.

Remove the dish from the heat and let the flavors marry at least 30 minutes. This hot butter sauce can be made up to several days in advance and refrigerated.

Preheat oven to 450 degrees. Reheat the sauce, add the shrimp, cook over medium heat until the shrimp just turn pink, and then bake them in the oven about 15 minutes or so, until shrimp are pink and cooked through. Taste for seasoning, adding salt if necessary. Serve with the sauce and plenty of bread.

SHRIMP AND CUCUMBERS WITH PEANUT BUTTER SAUCE

Serves 2

WHERE WOULD WE BE WITHOUT PEANUTS IN THE SOUTH? *They are seen everywhere, but in this case, peanut butter and soy sauce combine to make a peppy, zesty sauce to accompany the cool cucumber, shrimp, and green onions.*

1/2 cup peanut butter
1/2 cup soy sauce
1 1/2 tablespoons rice or white wine vinegar
1/4–1/3 cup granulated sugar
1–2 teaspoons hot sauce
1 thin slice fresh ginger, chopped
1 tablespoon freshly ground black pepper
3 garlic cloves, chopped
1 long cucumber, sliced thinly
Salt
1 pound shrimp, cooked and peeled (pages 326–27)
6–8 green onions, thinly sliced

Blend together the peanut butter, soy sauce, vinegar, sugar, hot sauce, ginger, black pepper, and garlic in a blender or food processor. Arrange the cucumber slices along the outside rim of a serving platter. Move the shrimp to the center of the platter and pour the sauce over. Top with green onions.

SHRIMP AND OKRA IN A TANGY BUTTER SAUCE

Serves 6 to 8

SHRIMP and okra like each other. In this case, the okra can be briefly sautéed ahead of time, added back when the shrimp is cooked, and reheated, making an all-in-one meal with the rice.

1 pound okra
1 cup butter, divided
3 large garlic cloves, chopped
1 teaspoon ground hot red pepper
1–2 tablespoons chopped fresh basil, marjoram, oregano, and/or rosemary
2 pounds raw large shrimp, shells removed
Salt
Freshly ground black pepper
3 cups cooked rice, hot

Remove the top and bottom tips of the okra and slice the pods lengthwise. Melt 1/4 cup of the butter in a large skillet, add the okra, and sauté over high heat for a few minutes, until wilted. Remove and set aside.

Add the remaining butter and melt. Add the garlic, hot red pepper, and herbs, and cook a few minutes without browning, until as hot as possible. This may be done several hours ahead—the butter will gather flavor as it sits.

When ready to serve, reheat the butter. Add the peeled shrimp and cook until pink on the first side. Turn and cook until nearly pink. Add the okra and cook 1 minute, just to reheat. Remove, season to taste with salt and pepper, and pour over hot cooked rice.

SHRIMP PILAU

Serves 4

PILAU, OR PURLOO, IS A CONSTANT IN THE LOWCOUNTRY *and places where rice is still routinely eaten. The combination of the shrimp with the zesty seasoning and crispy bacon suits just about anyone—family, friends, or special company. Those who love it spicy should add the Worcestershire sauce and ground red pepper to taste.*

4 slices bacon, cooked crisp, drippings reserved
4 tablespoons butter
1/2 cup finely chopped celery
2 tablespoons chopped red or yellow bell pepper
2 cups medium raw shrimp, peeled
1 tablespoon Worcestershire sauce, optional
1/4-1 teaspoon ground hot red pepper, optional
1 tablespoon flour
Salt
Freshly ground black pepper
3 cups cooked white rice, hot

Crumble the bacon and set it and drippings aside. Melt the butter in a large saucepan. When hot, add the celery and bell pepper. Cook until soft, about 5 minutes.

Meanwhile, sprinkle the shrimp with the optional Worcestershire sauce. Mix the optional hot red pepper and flour together with the salt and freshly ground pepper. Toss the shrimp lightly with the flour and add to the still hot butter mixture. Stir until the shrimp are cooked, about 3 to 5 minutes. Taste and re-season with salt and pepper. Reheat the drippings, combine with the shrimp, hot cooked rice and crumbled bacon. Serve hot.

Variation: Add 1 small diced tomato.

COLD CURRIED SHRIMP

Serves 2 as a starter

My recipes usually come from Southern friends. *This recipe, a standby of our friend Barbara Morgan, is an exquisite ladies luncheon dish or buffet party dish. And I do love a one-pot dish that looks glamorous.*

3 tablespoons butter
1 Gala or Golden Delicious apple, chopped
1 medium onion, chopped
2 garlic cloves, chopped
1 tablespoon curry powder, divided
2 tablespoons all-purpose flour
1 cup Tomato Sauce (page 661)
2 cups mayonnaise
1 tablespoon fresh lemon juice
1–1½ pounds shrimp, cooked and peeled (pages 326–27)
Salt
Freshly ground black pepper
6 lettuce leaves, optional
2 cucumbers, thinly sliced
¼ cup slivered almonds, toasted
1 green onion or scallion or chive, green part only, chopped

Melt the butter in a skillet. Add the apple, onion, garlic, and 2 teaspoons of the curry, and sauté until the onion is golden. Stir in the flour and then add the tomato sauce. Bring to the boil, taste, and add remaining curry powder if desired.

Remove the sauce from the heat, let cool slightly, and stir in the mayonnaise, lemon juice, and shrimp. Season to taste with salt and pepper. Chill.

When ready to serve, add the shrimp and sauce to the lettuce leaves and serve surrounded by cucumbers. Top with the almonds and green onion.

GRACE'S FRIED SHRIMP

Serves 4

This is one of my favorite stories about cooking, *and why I tend to give detail in my directions and ingredients. Grace Reeves, a mountain woman who lived in a trailer on our property, started working with me when we opened our restaurant midway between Social Circle and Covington, Georgia, and worked there until we closed. Grace had never seen shrimp before she married Bill, but he was from the shore and loved both fishing and eating seafood, and made regular fishing trips. One day early in their marriage, Grace wanted to surprise him and began frying shrimp for his supper. Bless her heart, when he walked in and saw what she was doing, he said, "Grace, honey, you must peel shrimp before you fry it."*

⅔ cup all-purpose flour
¼ cup cornmeal
2 teaspoons salt, plus more to taste
½ cup milk, or more as needed
1 egg
½–1 teaspoon ground hot red pepper
Shortening or vegetable oil for frying, cook's preference
2 pounds raw medium or large shrimp, peeled and deveined
Freshly ground black pepper

Mix together the flour, cornmeal, and salt in a medium bowl. Stir or whisk in the milk, egg, and hot red pepper, adding an additional 1 to 2 tablespoons of milk if needed to make a loose but not runny batter. Cover with plastic wrap and set aside. (This may be done in advance several hours.)

When ready to serve, heat an iron skillet over medium heat with enough oil to come halfway up its sides to 375 degrees on a deep-fat thermometer. Using tongs, dip the shrimp into the batter and immediately into the hot oil, without crowding the pan. Fry 2 to 3 minutes, or until done, turning midway, when the first side is pink. Remove with a slotted spoon or flat strainer and drain on paper towels. Keep cooked shrimp on a foil-lined baking pan in a 200-degree oven to keep warm while frying the remaining batches. Season to taste with salt and pepper. Serve hot!

NANA STUFFIE'S FRIED SHRIMP

Serves 2 to 4

WHEN CYNTHIA WAS GROWING UP, *her grandmother, known to all as Nana Stuffie due to her short stature, would go to the docks at Mayport in Jacksonville, Florida, for fresh shrimp. Once home, she would put the shrimp into clean, empty milk cartons, top with water, and freeze. Cynthia's sister Phylecia requested this double-battered fried shrimp for dinner at every visit home and later, whenever she visits Cynthia. Thank goodness for frozen shrimp.*

1 pound shrimp, peeled and deveined
1 large egg
1 cup milk
2 cups self-rising flour
1 teaspoon commercial seafood seasoning or Creole seasoning (page 670)
1/2 teaspoon salt
Freshly ground black pepper
1 teaspoon lemon pepper
Shortening or vegetable oil for frying, cook's preference

Pat shrimp dry with paper towels. Whisk together the egg and milk and add shrimp to mixture. Stir together the flour, seasoning, salt, and pepper in a wide bowl. Dunk the shrimp from the milk mixture to the flour mixture and then move to a wire rack set over a plate. Let sit for a moment, then return the shrimp to the flour mixture a second time. Move to a colander and shake well to remove excess flour.

Fry in small batches, as in Grace's Fried Shrimp (facing), about 3 to 4 minutes per batch, or until golden brown. Remove with a slotted spoon to paper towels. Continue with remaining shrimp in batches. Serve hot.

THE ORIGINAL BREAKFAST SHRIMP AND GRITS

Serves 4

WHEN MARION SULLIVAN AND I *were writing our book* Shrimp and Grits, *we searched diligently for the first printed copy of the original recipe and were very frustrated because we could not locate it, although we both knew we had seen it somewhere. Finally, we located the recipe in the 1930 edition of* Two Hundred Years of Charleston Cooking, *titled "Shrimp and Hominy." Because Charleston used the terminology "hominy" for what was called grits elsewhere in the South, we kept flipping past the recipe. The man who contributed the 1930 recipe said he had been eating shrimp and hominy for seventy-eight years during the fresh shrimp season. Now, it is eaten at any meal. He would not have cooked the grits in milk, as we do, but would have used water as they did in the book. By the 1976 edition, it was titled "Breakfast Shrimp and Grits."*

1 cup uncooked grits
4 cups water, milk, or broth
1/2 cup butter, divided
1 teaspoon salt
1 pound raw shrimp

Slowly stir the grits into simmering liquid in a heavy saucepan, preferably nonstick, and cook as package directs, stirring constantly. Do not let it "blurp" loudly, and watch the evaporation of liquid, adding more if necessary. When fully cooked to the desired texture, remove from heat and add 2 tablespoons of butter and the salt.

Meanwhile, heat 4 tablespoons butter in a frying pan and sauté the shrimp in the butter until they turn pink. Peel the shrimp before or after cooking; however, if people want to cook shrimp in the shell, they usually simmer it rather than sauté it. Add the rest of the butter to the pan and melt. Top the grits with the shrimp and pour the butter on top.

Variations:

- Use half water and half milk for the cooking liquid.
- I frequently cook grits in the microwave. For further directions, see page 255.

SHRIMP BURGERS OR SLIDERS

Serves 4

A LITTLE-KNOWN TREASURE OF SOUTHERN SHRIMPING TOWNS *is the shrimp burger. Essentially a more budget-friendly version of a crab cake, the methods of preparation are numerous. Aficionados will debate the merits of each ingredient, but the home cook will settle on the family's favorite taste and texture. The proportions are very flexible—add more or less mayonnaise or breading. Cut the shrimp into chunks or cut them more finely.*

1 pound shrimp, cooked, peeled, and deveined (pages 326–27)
2 green onions, chopped
2 tablespoons fresh lemon juice, divided
1 teaspoon grated lemon rind, no white attached
1 tablespoon chopped fresh parsley, thyme, or lemon balm
1 teaspoon commercial seafood seasoning or Creole seasoning (page 670), optional
3 tablespoons mayonnaise
1 cup breadcrumbs (cornbread, cracker, or panko)
Salt
Freshly ground black pepper
1 large egg, lightly beaten
2 tablespoons oil, cook's preference
Tartar Sauce (page 659), optional
Cocktail Sauce (page 658), optional

Chop shrimp roughly into 1/4-inch pieces and set aside.

Combine onion, 1 tablespoon of lemon juice, lemon rind, parsley, optional seasoning, and mayonnaise in a large bowl. Toss in the shrimp and breadcrumbs, and mix well. Season to taste with salt and pepper. Stir in the egg. Mixture will still be loose.

Form shrimp mixture into four patties. Wrap patties in waxed paper or plastic wrap and refrigerate 30 minutes or up to 1 day.

When ready to cook, heat oil in a large skillet over medium-high heat. Add burgers and cook 3 to 4 minutes, until lightly browned on the underside. Use two spatulas to turn the burgers over, and continue cooking on the other side another 3 to 4 minutes. Serve on buns, with optional sauces if desired.

Variation: Cook burgers on the grill in a grill basket 4 to 5 minutes per side.

OYSTERS

The South has long been known for its succulent, sweet oysters. It's no surprise, then, that oysters differ in taste according to the waters where they are grown and the nutrients they consume. The water determines their saltiness, shape, and flavor. They are bivalves, producing more prolifically in warm waters, where they are able to change their sex from male to female, become plumper and creamier, grow faster, and spawn. Cold water slows their growth, postpones their sexual maturity, and produces a leaner, crisper texture.

For these reasons, the majority of oysters in the United States come from Southern waters. The species is named for where they are grown, so all Southern oysters, ranging from the Chesapeake Bay down the Southeast Atlantic to the Gulf, are of the species *Virginia*. The waters change them, and their given names change—to Apalachicola (Florida), Breton Sound (Louisiana), and even "13"—named after a Gulf oyster "farm" where the baby organisms (spats) are transplanted and finish growing. Aficionados know down to the cove where their favorite oyster is harvested.

Some oysters are more difficult to open or eat, with extraordinarily strong protective shell muscles. South Carolina's Double Oysters, for example, are either roasted to open the shell or pasteurized and processed to be sold in bulk. Processed oysters are the source for fried, casserole, and soup oysters. Although there is a preponderance of recipes for oysters, ranging from Mary Randolph's "Oyster and Sweet Bread Pie" to the stuffed baked oysters on the half shell, my inclination runs to the simple methods—fresh on the half shell, steamed, roasted, fried, or in simple creamy soups.

Oyster Basics

Buying oysters—One pint of shucked oysters equals about two dozen plump oysters. Preshucked oysters sold in vacuum-sealed containers may be kept several weeks and usually freeze quite well.

Shucking oysters—Wash and rinse the oysters thoroughly in cold water.

Lay an oyster on the table, flat shell up, so the cup can hold the juices. Hold oyster with one hand and force an oyster knife between the shells at the hinge at the near or thin end with the other hand. Twist the knife to cut the large adductor muscle (which holds the oyster closed) close to the flat upper shell in which it is attached, and remove the shell. Slide the knife to the lower end of the same muscle that is attached to the cup half of the shell.

Leave the oyster loose in the shell if it is to be served on the half shell, or remove and keep cold. Check oysters for bits of shell, paying particular attention to the muscle where pieces of shell will sometimes cling.

An oyster will shuck more easily if it is frozen—some people like to freeze them for 10 to 15 minutes or so before shucking.

Freezing oysters—Oysters may be frozen in the shell. Lay flat on a tray for two or three hours in the shell. Remove from the tray to a plastic ziplock bag, removing as much air as possible. Freeze up to 2 months. They are better for soups, stews, stuffings, and casseroles than eating on the half shell.

Recycling oyster shells—Environmentalists encourage us to save the shells and recycle them whenever possible, since oysters frequently attach themselves to another oyster shell to grow. There are recycling centers in South Carolina and Georgia as well as other seacoast areas. Make sure there is no debris with them so the water won't be contaminated.

Oysters are amatory food. —Bryon, Don Juan II

It took millions of years to evolve man from the oyster, but it takes only a few seconds to transfer the oyster into a man. —Unknown

CICERO'S OYSTER ROAST

Makes 1 croaker sack

THERE IS PROBABLY NO OTHER TREAT IN THE WORLD *like my friend Cicero's fresh steamed oysters, plump and full in the mouth, drenched in butter, contrasted with the crisp crackers underneath, lending their salt to the oyster.*

They remind me what it means to be a true gourmet. My alma mater, the London Cordon Bleu, said a gourmet was someone who did the best possible with the food at hand. To my way of thinking, it is someone who makes sure the best possible food is at hand, and then prepares it in the best possible way. In this case, simple is the best, and simple oysters are sure gourmet.

I now live in Charleston, where there are many annual oyster roasts. We love Bowen's Island Restaurant, where they are cooked on brick in front of our eyes, covered with a steaming croaker sack, and shoveled, literally, onto the wooden table. An opening in the table allows the eating of the oysters and the pushing of the discarded shells into the trash can underneath. The shells are then used off the coast as a breeding place for more oysters to come. The oysters at Bowen's Island are "doubles"—gnarly bumpy shells make them difficult to open, and each bivalve comes from so much effort from the eater—no shuckers here—that they taste even better.

1 croaker sack (1 bushel) oysters
Butter, melted
Saltine crackers

Heat two turpentine burners (or any heavy-duty propane or outdoor burner), or make a wood fire pit. Move a sheet of heavy steel, 3 feet x 4 feet x 1/8 inch thick, over the fire and heat until very hot.

Wash the oysters if they are muddy and place on hot steel. Place a croaker sack or burlap bag on top of the oysters. With a water hose or spray bottle, spray the sack with enough water to create steam. Continue steaming until the oysters open just slightly. (If they open all the way, they will be too dry). Shovel the oysters onto plywood serving tables, and serve with butter and saltine crackers. Use oyster knives to finish opening.

An alternative method is to use a thin lard can. Pound a hole in the top with an ice pick. Fill an 8-ounce Coke bottle with water, then pour the water into the bottom of the can. Fill the can half full with oysters, replace the top, and set on the burner. When steam starts escaping through the ice-pick hole, they're ready.

There is now a process to separate and wash double oysters, honing down their shells, before returning them to the ocean for a couple of weeks. It makes them more expensive but definitely easier to eat and popular with restaurants that buy them in quantity and serve them on the half shell.

BROILED OYSTERS WITH AMERICAN CAVIAR

Serves 6

The tributaries and beds of the James River *have long been held in reverence for their fine oysters.* The Smithfield Cookbook, *1970, produced by the Junior Women's Club of Smithfield, describes putting on heavy boots and walking halfway across the James River when the tide is low and a strong wind is blowing to gather oysters at the Oyster Rocks off Mogart's Beach, full of anticipation of grand breakfasts and suppers of oysters.*

Collecting oysters is a thrill the first few times each season, walking in heavy boots and carrying a bucket. After that, one is full of admiration for those who take out their "John boats" and gather a load full to bring back to sell. It is arduous work.

3 dozen oysters in the shell

1 recipe White Butter Sauce (page 656), replacing shallots with 2 julienned leeks

6 ounces fresh American or Osetra caviar

Arrange each oyster in the cupped half of its shell, and move as many of them as possible to a large rimmed baking sheet. Run under the broiler just until the edges curl. Repeat with the rest if necessary. Serve 6 oysters in their shells on a dinner plate and top with White Butter Sauce and caviar.

In 1971, Georgetown, South Carolina, still had a few shops that sold an American black sturgeon caviar processed in Winyah Bay. The sturgeon are depleted and the caviar is no longer processed there, but any good caviar will do. (I do not use the dyed black lumpfish; not only will it "bleed," but it adds an unsavory fishiness.)

FRIED OYSTERS

Makes 24

Eaten raw or steamed, *oysters are heavenly. Fried oysters are a special treat, especially when served as the variation, an Oyster Po' Boy.*

24 freshly shucked oysters, drained
1 cup plus 1 tablespoon milk
1 tablespoon water
1/4 teaspoon ground hot red pepper
2 large eggs
1 cup all-purpose flour
1/2 cup cornmeal
Salt
1/2 teaspoon freshly ground black pepper
Shortening or vegetable oil, for frying, cook's preference

Add the oysters to a bowl with 1 cup milk and soak 15 minutes. Whisk together the 1 tablespoon milk with water, hot red pepper, and eggs. Move the flour, cornmeal, salt, and pepper to a brown paper sack or large wide bowl. Shake the bag to mix, or whisk together in bowl.

Heat enough oil to reach halfway up the sides of a large deep skillet until the oil reaches 360 degrees.

Drain the oysters from the milk and dip 5 oysters at a time into the egg mixture; then toss into the sack or bowl to coat. Remove to the hot oil and fry about 2 minutes, turn with a slotted spoon, and cook on the second side about 1 to 2 minutes. Remove cooked oysters to a paper towel-lined rack and repeat until all the batches have been cooked. Season to taste with salt and pepper. Serve hot.

Variation: Oyster Po' Boy

Cut 4 small sandwich loaves in half horizontally. Spread a generous amount of a favorite rémoulade sauce (page 659 or 660) on inside; add lettuce leaves and 5 or 6 cooked oysters. Sprinkle oysters with fresh lemon juice just before serving.

POULTRY

Poultry is such a constant in the South that were it not for pork and seafood, it could easily be the mainstay of the Southern table. We have become fortunate enough as a society to eat it several times a week; there were times when it was so expensive it was special occasion fare. Turkey was a once-a-year occasion, chicken once-a-week, and quail and duck were what you shot and brought home. Our primary poultry in the South is still the chicken, followed by turkey. Trailing along are local and commercial quail, wild duck, and geese. Commercial duck and geese produce enough fat for gluttony and are valuable additions to the cuisine, with a particular affinity for rice, potatoes and fresh field peas. Since wild duck and geese lack fat and can be tough, many cooks and hunters focus on cooking the breasts or make braises, sausages, and pâtés. It's not unusual for hunters to save up their bounty, invite their hunting friends to clean out their freezers as well, and have a giant bash.

All poultry is built much the same—legs, wings, and body—making them easy to carve and serve. Learning how to cut up one aids in learning to cut up another.

It is odd how poultry sizes have morphed over the years. Chicken is bred larger and larger; turkey is bred smaller and smaller. They almost meet in the middle of the weight range.

So, too, with taste. Commercial chicken and turkey have lost flavor and need to be seasoned well. This lack of taste, plus concerns about their feed, has led to a small but increasing sector of people who prefer locally raised, free-range chickens and turkeys. Free-range chickens have tougher but more flavorful legs and smaller breasts, making it easier to get around the yard to eat.

Chicken parts can add a lot to a meal. Chicken and duck livers are relished fried or in pâtés; giblets and hearts enhance gravy. Necks are tasty and take well to smoking. We have not quite become the French, serving cock's combs, but surely that is to come. Meanwhile, we credit the French and the English with chicken fricassee.

CHICKEN

I always think of chicken as Southern, because the South—particularly Georgia and North Carolina—was saved by a man called Jesse Jewell during the Depression when he found an innovative way to increase his sales of chicken feed. Jewell gave poor farmers baby chicks and chicken feed on credit, and then bought back the full-grown chickens at a profit to both the farmer and Jewell. He turned his feed and seed business into one of the largest international poultry corporations. He sold his business to investors in the 1960s, having the satisfaction of knowing he had saved many families during the hard times of the thirties and forties.

A virtue of chicken is its affordability. The South has reveled in plentiful, inexpensive chicken for forty years, and by the early 2000s, chicken was the most popular protein, with Americans eating more than 90 pounds per person a year. Many Southerners flocked to white meat, giving up the tastier dark meat. Chickens have now been bred to yield larger, more tender breasts. Their less-strong flavor accommodates sauces and spices well, and with less fat, they are easier to grill. Old-timers, however, still prefer dark meat, and that includes me.

Chicken was a different bird until the 1980s or 1990s when consumer tastes and habits changed. Although there were many varieties of chickens, a dressed fryer or broiler, usually a male, was less than 3 pounds; a pullet, a young chicken, was also used as a fryer or broiler. A hen was 4 or 5 pounds, usually eaten when it stopped laying; and the rooster lived a long life, as long as he was serviceable and because he was so very tough to eat that his only place was in a soup or stew. Now, with mass production, it is hard to find a chicken that is less than 4 pounds. (There is a recipe in *Charleston Receipts* for a 5-pound rooster, which would hardly be duplicable today in the average home. Yet it was certainly plausible then.)

PURCHASING CHICKEN

"All-natural" chicken means nothing is added, including coloring, and the bird is only minimally processed: cleaned, dressed, and cut up if sold in parts. By law, it may have been treated with antibiotics. Chickens are given feed, as they cannot digest grass, but are free of hormones and growth steroids.

If chicken is chilled below zero degrees, it *must* be labeled frozen. No label? Chances are it was kept between 0 and 26 degrees, thawed as necessary, and sold to appear fresh. Anything inside, however, will probably still be frozen, like the neck, liver, and gizzard. Parts like these are not necessarily from the same chicken; they are put randomly into the chicken after initial processing by large growers.

CHICKEN PARTS

A common mistake is to buy a package of already cut-up chicken parts of the same weight as the whole chicken called for in a recipe. Alas, packaged cut-up chickens contain parts that may not even be from the same chicken. It is rare to find wings, breasts, thighs, backbone, and legs in a cut-up chicken package. It might contain just one huge leg and one breast, the package totaling the same weight as a neighboring whole chicken. Usually the pieces are from much larger chickens, omitting the backbone, the same weight as the whole chickens in the case. This changes the cooking time and number of servings from eight in a whole chicken that is cut up, to four in the pre-packaged cut-up chicken. If stuck with mismatched parts, cut into smaller pieces of about the same size with a cleaver or very sturdy knife, especially if pan cooking, so the skin won't burn before the interior is cooked.

The best way to use a cut-up chicken is to buy a whole chicken weighing close to 3 pounds in size and cut it up oneself. (Those lucky enough to have a full-service butcher can ask him or her to do it for them, but they are rare and becoming rarer.)

FAVORITE BUTTERMILK SKILLET-FRIED CHICKEN

Serves 4

There are hundreds of ways to make skillet-fried chicken, which is more usual than deep-frying in home cooking. Because chicken was prepared in a certain manner during one's formative years, the manner in which chicken is fried is personal, as is the desired amount of crunch. Some people prefer a batter, with or without hot pepper sauce added. Others prefer a less crusty chicken, not wanting crunch and splintering. And still others like using a flour-egg-flour method. This Alabama recipe for pan-fried, medium-crust chicken can be altered by re-flouring for a thicker crust or knocking off any excess flour for a lighter one.

I ran across some tips for fried chicken and found one tip that was so simple I couldn't believe I had not thought of it myself: to save time and heartache when cleaning up the stove, cover the stovetop with aluminum foil to catch the oil splatters. We tried this when testing the recipe and cleaned up in half the time! Read the information on frying chicken (facing) before starting.

3 cups buttermilk or whole milk
1/4 cup salt
1 whole chicken (2 1/2–3 pounds), cut into 8 frying pieces (page 344)
1–1 1/2 cups shortening
1/2 cup butter
Freshly ground black pepper
Finely ground hot red pepper
1–1 1/2 cups all-purpose flour

Pour the buttermilk and salt into a nonreactive container or a plastic ziplock bag. Add the chicken pieces. Close the bag and refrigerate for 1 to 2 hours.

Remove the chicken from the buttermilk brine, lightly shake, and move to a colander over a bowl or sink so that the excess buttermilk drains off yet leaves the skin moist enough for the flour to adhere. Larger chickens take longer to cook, so they should be rinsed to prevent burning. If there is not time to brine, sprinkle the damp chicken lightly with salt, then add salt, freshly ground pepper, and hot red pepper to the flour.

Meanwhile, melt shortening in a 9- to 10-inch heavy-bottomed or cast-iron skillet. Add the butter in increments to the melted fat, making sure that the melted mixture will go only halfway up the chicken and that the skillet is no more than half full. While the fat is heating, pepper the chicken on both sides with the two peppers. Spread flour on a rimmed baking sheet and lightly add a bit of black pepper. Pat the still damp chicken in the flour on both sides. Knock off any excess flour by lightly tapping the bone-edge of the chicken on the counter and arrange around the sides of the colander in a single layer.

A bit before the fat registers 375 degrees on a deep-fat thermometer (or sizzles when the exposed end of the leg bone is inserted in the fat), flour the individual chicken pieces again, tapping the bone-edge of the chicken pieces on the counter to remove excess flour as desired. After each piece is floured, start adding the largest pieces to the hot fat, usually the dark meat, skin side down, to the hottest spot in the skillet, reserving the white meat for cooler spots, small pieces in last. It is helpful to add them in a pattern, such as clockwise, so removal is guess-free, with first pieces in/first pieces out. Try not to crowd the chicken in the skillet, as too much chicken in ratio to the fat will cool down the fat. The pieces may touch but not overlap. The rule of thumb is that the bottom of the pan should be visible in places. Keep a watch on the chicken, moving the pan as necessary over the heat so that all the pieces of the chicken are browned evenly. This is particularly important if the pan and burner are different sizes, as they usually are, and the heat is concentrated in one area.

Carefully maintain the heat of the fat while chicken is being added to the pan, preferably with the help of a deep-fat thermometer.

Partially cover the pan with a lid for 6 minutes. The temperature of the fat should be at least 325 degrees; remove the lid and continue to cook 3 to 4 minutes more, until the pieces are deep golden brown on the bottom. Turn the browned chicken with tongs and cook uncovered to brown the second side for 8 to 10 minutes more. Listen and look for the sizzle around the chicken pieces. Smaller pieces will finish cooking before larger pieces, so remove these from the pan as needed. The internal temperature of the chicken should register 165 degrees when an instant-read thermometer is inserted into the flesh of the chicken, not touching the bone.

The juices of the chicken will run clear and the sizzling sound will have greatly diminished.

Drain the chicken on crumpled paper towels on a rack. Perfect fried chicken is divine either hot or cold.

Variations:

- Add a chunk of bacon or other pork fat to the oil for more flavor, removing it if it seems to be burning.
- Omit brining, just soaking in buttermilk or milk, or omitting both if in a hurry. In this case, rub with salt, pepper, and ground red pepper as well as adding additional seasonings to the flour.

FRYING IS PHYSICS

Listen and look for the sizzle. My friend Shirley Corriher says frying is physics. The process of the juices pushing into the fat prevents the fat from coming in. When the meat is first added to the hot fat, it will produce little juice bubbles around the chicken from the moisture hitting the fat. As the meat cooks, the bubbles will get larger. Finally, when it is totally cooked—or most likely overcooked—the bubbles will dissipate. By then all the chicken should have been removed. When fried foods sit in fat without bubbles or any sizzling, the food is soaking up the fat rather than pushing out water, making it greasy.

FRYING CHICKEN

This is my number-one favorite skillet-fried chicken recipe. It is one of the longest recipes in the book because frying chicken is a challenge to fledgling cooks. It contains all the techniques important for achieving a perfect fried chicken. Once mastered, the cook can omit or choose his/her own brine, as well as coating and fat for frying.

Begin by looking for the smaller whole chickens to cut up (page 344). If a small chicken is not available, increase skillet size to 12 inches (from 9- or 10-inch in the recipe) and increase the amount of shortening to 1½ to 2 cups. Otherwise, cook the chicken in batches or use two skillets. It will take longer to cook to an internal temperature of 165 degrees in a smaller pan and needs more careful watching. Large chickens over 3½ pounds tend to brown too much on the outside and be raw on the inside. It is important to cut large chickens into as many smaller pieces as possible to insure even browning and properly cooked chicken.

Brining—I have adapted this recipe by adding salt to the buttermilk to brine the chicken. Modern buttermilk does not tenderize as much as it did in the past, but it adds a distinctive quality. The salt increases the moistness of the chicken and insinuates flavor into the chicken's flesh rather than just resting on the surface. Brining can be tricky. Both time of brining and amount of salt impact the saltiness of the final product. Remove the chicken after 2 hours at the most. If time of removal is uncertain, cut the salt in half, just soak the chicken in buttermilk, or avoid brining or soaking altogether. If no buttermilk is available, either plain milk or milk with a spoonful or two of plain yogurt whisked in is better than water. The amount of salt added is sufficient for the entire process. Other ingredients, like hot pepper sauce, can be added to the brine to add more flavor.

Fat—Jean Sparks, who gave me the technique for this recipe, was adamant that Crisco made the best fat for frying, second only to leaf lard, the finest kind of lard. All lard is difficult to come by unless one makes one's own, but it is worth using, as lard is very light and adds a unique flavor. To get this flavor when lard is not available, some cooks add bacon, fatback, or other pig fat. Other combinations of fats, such as shortening and butter, blend the lightness of the shortening with the extraordinary flavor as well as color of the butter.

Pan size and type matter—At one time, the traditional pan for frying chicken was an iron skillet with a high side. It retains heat without the hot spots a stainless steel or aluminum pot may have. The fat should reach no more than halfway up the side of the pan. The addition of chicken pieces causes the fat to bubble and rise. The butter has a tendency to foam up, so if the level of the fat is very close to the top of the pan, remove some of the fat and set aside. Return some of the fat back to the pan as needed.

The name "Country Captain" came up in journals all during the 1800s and included a rudimentary, tomato-less curry in *Miss Leslie's New Cookery Book* by Eliza Leslie, published in 1857. It came into its own after Mrs. William Bullard, who had homes in Warm Springs and Columbus, Georgia, hosted future President Franklin D. Roosevelt on his first visit to Warm Springs for polio treatment. It was in her home in Columbus that he later announced for governor of New York via radio. The family, including their daughter, Ms. Hart, became close friends.

For that first dinner, Mrs. Bullard had ordered *The International Cookbook: Over 3,300 Recipes Gathered From All Over the World, Including Many Never Before Published in English,* a two-volume set by the former chef of Delmonico's, Alexander Filippini, published in 1914. Country Captain appears as a luncheon dish. Mrs. Bullard selected the recipe and gave it to her cook, Arie Mullins, who served it to Roosevelt, who loved it. When the Little White House and the treatment facility were completed, another cook, Daisy Bonner served it to patients there. One wheelchair patient wrote of a grueling trip to Warm Springs in 1926—mostly in a boxcar, as there was no other way for him to get there,—and being served Country Captain when he arrived. Never did a dish taste so good. Ultimately, Daisy was FDR's favorite cook and cooked his last meal, something she wrote on the wall of his Warm Springs kitchen.

Mrs. Bullard also served her version to General George Patton, who became enamored of the dish. Years later, in honor of General Patton, it became an MRE (Meals Ready to Eat) for the troops. While traveling to the military base in Columbus, Georgia, Patton allegedly asked Mrs. Bullard to meet the train with some Country Captain. Various Columbus cookbooks have renditions of these recipes. Carson McCullers even wrote a letter describing this fashionable "new" dish she had eaten in Columbus. All this was before *Charleston Receipts* published the recipe in 1950.

Mr. Filippini's recipe was later promulgated by Cecily Brownstone, a formidable newspaper columnist for Associated Press from 1947 to 1986. She became a zealot on the subject after publishing her version in a cookbook for the benefit of the Florence Crittenden League, Specialty of the House, criticizing any other version. Her version called for dredging the chicken in flour seasoned with salt and pepper, as one would a pan-fried chicken before browning. Molly O'Neill detailed much of this in an important article in the *New York Times.*

Cecily Brownstone and I agree totally on one thing: making Country Captain with chicken breast alone is heresy. And so is making the sauce separately and adding fried chicken, as some do now in Columbus, Georgia, where it is still considered "their" dish, both in restaurants and homes. I use red bell peppers rather than green and am happy with raisins if currants are not available.

COUNTRY CAPTAIN

Serves 4 to 6

THIS IS ONE OF MY MOST BELOVED RECIPES, *in part because I served it in my restaurant in the early 1970s. It was from a recipe my second cousin in Macon, Georgia, sent me from a Columbus, Georgia, newspaper at the same time she gave me a huge electric cooker on a stand to cook it in. My stepfather, who had worked in the Roosevelt White House, came to the restaurant and told me of eating Country Captain at the Little White House on a trip to Warm Springs. My father, who had worked for General George Patton, remembered eating Country Captain from having eaten it with Patton in Columbus, Georgia.*

Here is the way I made it in my restaurant all those years ago. (I pay homage to Filippini, Miss Leslie, Cecily Brownstone, and James Beard.) Browned chicken on the bone produces an incredible underlying flavor to this dish that cannot be obtained otherwise. Because modern diners have a hard time dealing with chicken on the bone when it is heavily sauced, I remove it from the bone and add it back into the sauce. It is a messy process, but it makes a truly wonderful fork-friendly, make-ahead dish. While it is possible to cook a half recipe with just one chicken, it is not much more work to cook a whole recipe, or even double it, and refrigerate or freeze half. The kitchen is clean as a pin when the guests arrive, and I feel calm and relaxed, knowing an enchanting meal is ready to be reheated in the microwave oven or on the stovetop.

- 2 whole chickens (3 1/2–4 pounds each), cut into 8 pieces each (page 344)
- 4 tablespoons butter
- 1 tablespoon oil, cook's preference
- 1–2 onions, chopped
- 2 red bell peppers, seeded, cored, and chopped
- 4 garlic cloves, finely chopped
- 1/4–1/2 teaspoon ground hot red pepper
- 2–3 teaspoons curry powder
- 2 (28-ounce) cans Italian plum tomatoes, liquid reserved
- 1/2–1 cup chicken stock or broth, optional
- Salt
- Freshly ground black pepper
- 1 cup currants or raisins
- 8 cups cooked rice (page 259)
- 1 cup blanched toasted, sliced almonds
- Shredded coconut, optional
- 6 slices bacon, cooked crisp (page 413), optional
- 1 teaspoon dried thyme, optional
- 1/2 cup chopped fresh parsley, optional
- Chutney, optional

Pat the chicken dry with paper towels.

Heat the butter and oil over medium heat in a 10- or 12-inch heavy skillet or large Dutch oven until it shimmers. Add the chicken skin side down, dark pieces first, to the hottest part of the pan. Continue adding pieces in a clockwise fashion, to know which went in first, in batches or two pans if necessary, and cook to a deep golden brown on the bottom, about 5 minutes. Turn the chicken pieces with tongs, and brown for 2 to 3 minutes on the second side. Take care to reduce the heat or rotate the pan if there are hot spots so all the chicken browns evenly. Remove the chicken.

Add the onions, peppers, garlic, hot red pepper, and curry powder to the pan and cook until soft, stirring up all the good bits in the bottom of the pan. Add the tomatoes, cutting them into chunks, and stir some more. Return the chicken to the pan, skin side up; cover and simmer until tender, about 30 minutes. Add reserved tomato liquid or a little chicken stock if available. If runny, uncover and cook a little longer until liquid is reduced. Cool and remove any fat from the surface of the sauce. Season to taste with salt and pepper, and additional red pepper or curry as needed. Remove the chicken, cool and remove the chicken from the bone. Discard the bones and skins. Return the chicken to the now cool sauce. This may be made ahead several days and refrigerated covered, or frozen up to 3 months.

Bring the chicken and sauce to the boil quickly, stirring; reduce heat and cook as necessary until heated through. Stir the currants into the sauce, and serve the chicken and sauce on hot rice. Garnish with toasted almonds.

Mrs. Leslie served Country Captain with the coconut. Mr. Filippini draped the dish with the bacon, added the thyme and parsley, and served the dish with chutney, none of which I do.

CUTTING UP A WHOLE CHICKEN

Remove the chicken from the packaging. Move the chicken, breast side up, to a clean cutting board and dry the chicken with paper towels. Save any parts inserted in the cavity for stock or another purpose. Pull off any visible fat from the large opening. Grasp a leg in one hand and hold it away from the body. Use a sharp knife or poultry shears and cut through the skin to reveal the joint between the leg and the body. Grasp the body with one hand and the leg with the other and push the leg up from underneath to pop the leg out of the joint. Look for the space between the joint and cut the leg away by cutting through that joint. Repeat with the other leg. Separate the thigh from the drumstick of each leg by feeling where the joint is and cutting through the skin, flesh, and joint. Repeat with the other leg.

Using the same technique, hold a wing away from the body and slice through the skin to reveal the joint where the wing attaches to the body. Cut the wing away from the body by cutting through the joint. Repeat with other wing.

Turn the chicken over so the breast is now facedown. Remove the backbone by using sturdy kitchen shears to cut up each side of the backbone through the skin and ribs, completely removing it. (Some people prefer to cut up the middle of the backbone, leaving a portion attached to each side.) Save the backbone for stock.

With the breast still facedown, split the breast in half down the center, cutting through bone and cartilage. If the breast is particularly large, cut each half into two pieces by cutting the breast horizontally through the skin, flesh, and bone.

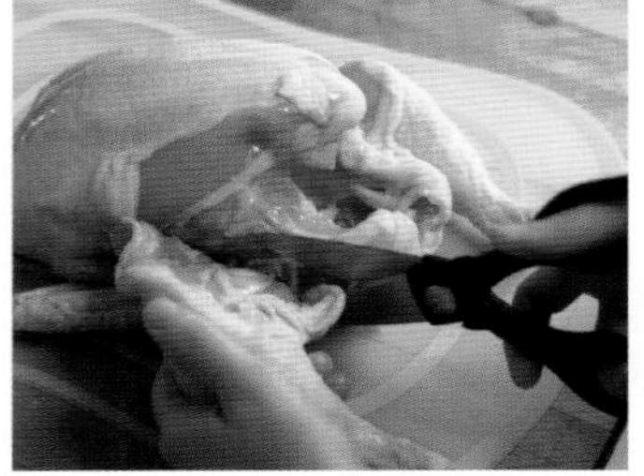

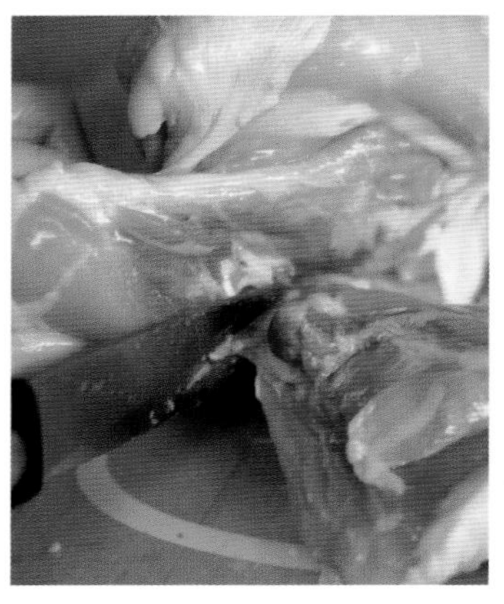

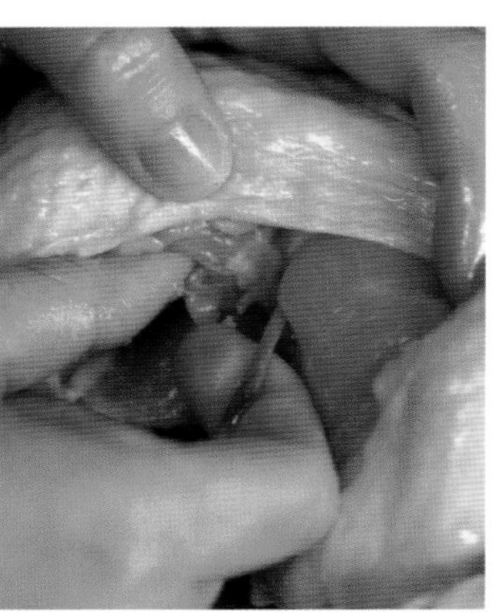

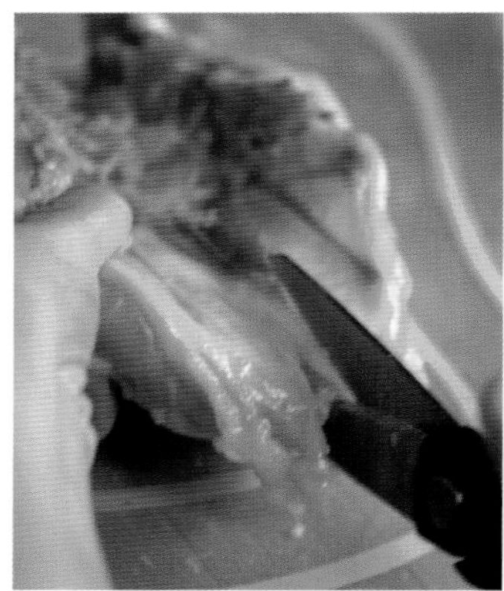

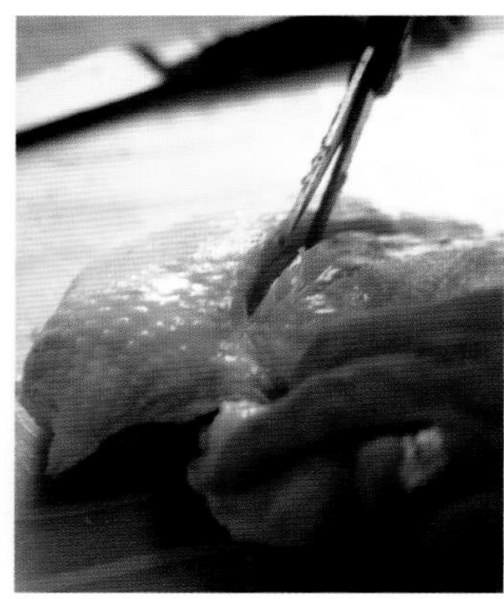

Kate, who worked for me for thirty-five years, give or take, from the early 1970s until I moved full-time to Charleston, South Carolina, in 2006, also raised her own chickens as a farm girl. Although Kate and Celeste (my favorite former mother-in-law) grew up within 10 miles of each other, they were miles apart culinarily: Kate was a cook, Celeste a banker. Both of them were adamant, however, that frying the present larger chickens was a very different thing than the chickens they used to know, or the chickens that restaurants are fortunate enough to receive in quantities after specifying them to their purveyors. One fried chicken, usually 1½ to 2½ pounds, would fit nicely, cut up, into an 8- or 9-inch iron skillet. Now, it takes two full batches or two pans to cook a whole chicken. The large chicken also takes longer to cook, making it trickier to keep from burning. (My mother, bless her heart, could never fry chicken, burning it with great regularity. We did have a roomer, Lamoine, when I was ten or eleven, who made a mean fried chicken. It was golden brown, and the little bits in the pan were worth fighting over—and worth agreeing to do the dishes for. One can imagine how yummy they were when a child is happy to clean the frying pan as part of the swap.)

CHICKEN, ORANGE, AND TOMATO CASSEROLE

Serves 6

I RUE THAT COMPATIBLE FOODS *don't always ripen in the same season. When the oranges in my garden appear, the fresh tomatoes are long gone. Using good-quality canned plum tomatoes enhances the flavor of the oranges. The chicken absorbs the medley of flavors and is tenderized by all the acid, making a succulent, never-to-be-forgotten casserole.*

1 whole chicken (3½–4 pounds), cut into 8–10 pieces (page 344)
Freshly ground black pepper
3 tablespoons oil, cook's preference
1 pound onions (approximately 2 cups), sliced
4–6 garlic cloves, chopped
1 (28-ounce) can Italian plum tomatoes, drained and coarsely chopped
1–2 tablespoon fennel seeds, roughly ground
½ teaspoon ground hot red pepper
2 teaspoons grated orange rind, no white attached
2 cups chicken stock or broth
1 cup fresh orange juice
Salt
Granulated sugar, optional
2 tablespoons coarsely chopped fresh basil, parsley, or thyme

Pat the chicken dry with paper towels. Sprinkle with freshly ground pepper.

Heat the oil over medium heat in a 10- or 12-inch heavy skillet or large Dutch oven until it shimmers. Add the chicken, skin side down, dark pieces first, to the hottest part of the pan. Proceed, adding pieces in a clockwise fashion to know which went in first—in batches if necessary, or using two pans—and cook to a deep golden brown on the bottom, about 5 minutes. Turn the chicken pieces with tongs, and brown for 2 to 3 minutes on the second side. Take care to reduce the heat or rotate the pan if there are hot spots so all the chicken browns evenly.

Remove chicken from the pan and add the onions. Cook until soft, about 5 minutes. Stir in the garlic, tomatoes, fennel seeds, hot red pepper, orange rind, and chicken stock. Bring to the boil. Return chicken to the skillet skin side up, reduce the heat, cover, and simmer 30 to 35 minutes, until the chicken is tender and its thickest part registers 165 degrees on an instant-read thermometer. Remove any fat on the surface. This may be made ahead several days, covered, and refrigerated, or frozen up to 3 months.

When ready to serve, add the orange juice to the hot chicken and ingredients, and cook uncovered about 5 minutes longer, allowing some of the liquid to cook off. Season to taste with salt, pepper, and optional sugar. Garnish with chopped basil.

DEGREASING

There are a number of ways to remove grease from the top of food:

1. While cooking, move the pan and tilt it slightly to allow all the fat and any scum to gather together at one place, making it easier to skim or spoon off.
2. Run strips of paper towel over the top of the liquid. The fat on top will come off with the towel.
3. Hold an ice cube and slide it over the top of the liquid. The fat will congeal on the outside of the cube.
4. Use a special cup with a pouring spout located near the bottom of the cup; the fat will remain in the cup as the degreased portion of the sauce is poured out.
5. Chill. The fat will come to the top and congeal, ready to be scooped off.

HUNTER'S STEW

Serves 6

IT'S A SOUTHERN TRADITION *to put something on the back of the stove to cook long and slow, and hunters are certainly known for their rabbits stews that greet people when they visit their cabins. Those who prefer catching their rabbits in the city may find all-white-meat rabbits, which are usually skinned. Frankly, I doubt many will find rabbits (not to be confused with hares) in their grocery store, so we felt we had to use chicken as a base in this recipe.*

1 whole chicken ($3^1/_2$–4 pounds) or 2 rabbits, cut into 8 pieces (page 344)
Freshly ground black pepper
2 tablespoons chicken fat or drippings
1 medium onion, sliced
3 garlic cloves, chopped
6 celery ribs without leaves, cut in half
6 carrots, peeled and cut in half
6 potatoes, peeled and cut in half
4 cups chicken stock or broth, to cover
Salt

Dry the chickens or rabbits and season with pepper. Heat the fat or drippings over medium heat in a 10- or 12-inch heavy skillet or large Dutch oven until it shimmers. Add the meat skin side down, dark pieces first, to the hottest part of the pan. Proceed, adding pieces in a clockwise fashion, to know which went in first, in batches or two pans if necessary, and cook to a deep golden brown, about 5 minutes. Turn the meat pieces with tongs, and brown for 2 to 3 minutes on the second side. Take care to reduce the heat or rotate the pan if there are hot spots so all the meat browns evenly. Remove the meat.

Add the onion to the pan and cook 5 minutes, or until soft. Add the garlic, celery, carrots, and potatoes. Return the meat to the pot and add chicken stock to cover. Bring to the boil, reduce heat, cover the pan, and simmer for 1 to 2 hours, until the meat reaches 165 on an instant-read thermometer inserted into the thickest part of the flesh. Remove any fat on the surface (Degreasing, page 345). This may be made ahead several days, covered, and refrigerated or frozen up to three months.

Variation: Remove solids to a bowl. Remove skin and bones; tear the meat into bite-sized pieces and return to the pan. Add Dumplings (page 371) if desired.

CHICKEN MAQUE CHOUX

Serves 4

MAQUE CHOUX (PRONOUNCED MOCK-SHOE) *is a traditional dish of Southern Louisiana. This version, which omits the long browning of the roux and includes the "holy trinity" of celery, onion, and sweet red pepper, along with tomatoes, is as good as it gets. The day we tested the recipe, we were unable to contain ourselves, it smelled and looked so heavenly, and we ate it standing at the stove! A bit of ground red pepper goes a long way in this dish. Double the recipe, as the maque choux is so tasty that one batch will be gone in no time; the other can be frozen.*

The trick with any dish where rice or another grain is added while cooking is to get the balance of liquid and rice correct, so add the last bit of stock carefully. If the stock is homemade and unsalted, add an additional teaspoon of salt to the rubbing mixture.

1 whole chicken (3½–4 pounds), cut into 8 pieces (page 344)
¼–¾ teaspoon ground hot red pepper
Pinch of freshly ground black pepper
1 tablespoon oil, cook's preference
1 garlic clove, finely chopped
1 medium onion, finely chopped
1 red bell pepper, seeded, cored, and finely chopped
¾ cup chopped canned whole tomatoes with liquid
2–3 cups chicken stock or broth, divided
1 cup uncooked rice
1 celery rib, peeled and chopped
½ cup frozen corn niblets, defrosted, optional
Salt

Pat the chicken dry with paper towels.

Season the chicken to taste with hot red and black peppers. Move to a plate and chill uncovered in the refrigerator, if possible, while chopping the various ingredients.

Heat the oil over medium heat in a 10- or 12-inch heavy skillet or large Dutch oven until it shimmers. Add the chicken skin side down, dark pieces first, to the hottest part of the pan. Proceed, adding pieces in a clockwise fashion, to know which went in first, in batches if necessary, and cook to a deep golden brown, about 5 minutes. Turn the chicken pieces with tongs, and brown for 2 to 3 minutes on the second side. Take care to reduce the heat or rotate the pan if there are hot spots so all the chicken browns evenly.

Add the garlic, onion, and bell pepper; cook 5 minutes before adding the tomatoes with liquid and 1 cup of chicken stock to the frying pan. Bring to the boil, reduce the heat to low, and simmer about 10 minutes. Add the rice and an additional cup of stock, bring to the boil, reduce the heat, cover, and cook until the rice is tender, about 15 minutes. Midway through, add the celery and corn if using.

If the chicken has reached an internal temperature of 165 degrees before the rice is cooked, remove the chicken from the pan and set it aside. Cover the pot and continue cooking the rice and vegetables. Once the rice is done, add the chicken back to the pot and heat through for a flavorful skillet dish. Season to taste with salt and pepper. This may be made ahead several days then covered and refrigerated, or frozen up to 3 months.

THE GENERATION OF THE CASSEROLE

Many people in Charleston insist that casseroles were invented there. Historically, the gentry ate at 3:00 pm, when the men came home for dinner and a nap. Their cooks made a meal of soup, an entrée, two vegetables, and a dessert. Simultaneously, a casserole was made that could be reheated for supper later. That way, the family had their privacy and the help their time off, since they came early to fix breakfast. Others say the custom of eating dinner at 3 o'clock gave rise to the cocktail party, as the table was cleared and the food moved to a buffet before the cook left. The family then snacked on the leftovers for their supper. I tend to doubt this, as cooks usually had "toting" privileges, being allowed to take home any uneaten food, which would have spoiled by the next day anyway without refrigeration.

SAUTÉED CHICKEN WITH MUSHROOMS AND GREENS

Serves 6 to 8

THIS FRESH-TASTING, COLORFUL SAUTÉ *is best served straight out of the pan. It's amazing how quickly greens shrink in cooking; they hog the space when first added, but a few minutes in the pan and they lessen in quantity; hence the recipe calls for what seems like a large amount.*

1 whole chicken (3½–4 pounds), cut into 8 pieces (page 344)
Salt
Freshly ground black pepper
Ground hot red pepper
½ cup all-purpose flour
2–3 tablespoons butter, divided
2–3 tablespoons oil, cook's preference, divided
½ cup wine vinegar, preferably red or sherry, divided
½ cup water, divided
1 pound mushrooms, sliced
4 garlic cloves, chopped
1 pound turnip, collard, or spinach greens, washed thoroughly

Leaving the chicken pieces slightly damp, season with salt and pepper and a dash of hot red pepper. Toss the flour, salt, and black pepper on a piece of waxed paper. Using the fingers of one hand, move the chicken pieces individually to the flour, pressing the chicken lightly into the flour. Turn and press as needed to fully coat the chicken pieces. Shake off any additional flour.

Heat half the butter and half the oil over medium heat in a 10- or 12-inch heavy skillet or large Dutch oven until it shimmers. Add the chicken skin side down, dark pieces first, to the hottest part of the pan. Continue adding pieces in a clockwise fashion, to know which went in first, in batches if necessary, and cook to a deep golden brown, about 5 minutes. Turn the chicken pieces with tongs, and brown for 2 to 3 minutes on the second side. Take care to reduce the heat or rotate the pan if there are hot spots so all the chicken browns evenly. Remove when browned and set aside.

When all pieces are browned, add ¼ cup vinegar and ¼ cup water to the pan and bring to the boil, stirring and scraping to get all the good bits off the bottom. Heat the remaining butter and oil in a separate pan, add the mushrooms and garlic, and sauté, stirring, until the mushrooms are lightly browned. Return the chicken to the pan with the vinegar and water and surround with the mushrooms. Cover and simmer 30 to 45 minutes, until the thickest part of the chicken registers 165 degrees on a meat thermometer. This may be made ahead several days and refrigerated covered, or frozen up to 3 months.

Tear off the stalks and any tough veins from the greens and discard. Tear or cut the remaining greens into pieces or chiffonade (page 208).

Remove the hot chicken and mushrooms to a hot platter. Add the greens to the still hot pan, cover, and let wilt a few minutes; remove to the platter. Add the remaining ¼ cup vinegar to the pan and scrape as before. Bring the broth to the boil for a few minutes. Taste and add the remaining ¼ cup water if the sauce is too sharp. Pour the sauce over the chicken, or serve separately.

CHICKEN WITH TURNIPS AND SWEET POTATOES

Serves 4 to 6

Many of the first free blacks *arrived in the South after a Haitian revolution, when the free blacks sided with the planters, who lost. Our culture still has some of the Haitian flavor, including this dish seasoned with allspice.*

This marinated and baked chicken has a crisper skin from sitting 24 hours in the refrigerator, seasoned. The initial water drawn out by the salt and seasoning has dried off, enabling a beautiful brown skin. Be sure to taste the stock to see if it is salty before seasoning further.

3 garlic cloves, chopped
1 medium onion, finely chopped
1–2 jalapeño or other small hot peppers, seeded, chopped
3 tablespoons soy sauce
2 tablespoons fresh lime juice
2 tablespoons fresh lemon juice
3/4 tablespoon ground allspice
1 teaspoon freshly ground nutmeg
1 tablespoon dry mustard
1 tablespoon light or dark brown sugar
1 tablespoon chopped fresh thyme or summer savory
1 whole chicken (3 1/2–4 pounds), cut into 8 pieces (page 344)
1 large or 2 medium turnips, peeled, cut into 1-inch pieces
3 sweet potatoes, peeled, cut into 1-inch pieces
1 cup chicken stock or broth
Salt
Freshly ground black pepper

For the marinade, mix together the garlic, onion, jalapeño peppers, soy sauce, lime juice, lemon juice, allspice, nutmeg, mustard, brown sugar, and thyme.

Rub the chicken pieces all over with the marinade and leave uncovered on a rack (over a tray or rimmed baking sheet to catch drippings) in the refrigerator up to 24 hours, but at least 30 minutes.

Preheat oven to 400 degrees. Lightly oil a 13 x 9 x 2-inch baking dish.

Spread the turnips and sweet potatoes in the prepared baking dish. Add the chicken stock. Season with salt and pepper. Move the chicken pieces on top of the vegetables, making sure the pieces don't overlap. If there is too much chicken, roast in a separate pan and move to the baking dish later. Roast on the middle rack 25 to 30 minutes, until the vegetables are tender and the chicken is nicely browned, its thickest part registering 165 degrees on a meat thermometer. If the chicken is not brown, move to a higher rack and turn up the heat to 500 degrees. Cook 5 or 10 minutes more, until brown. This may be made ahead several days and refrigerated covered, or frozen up to three months, but the skin will need re-crisping in the oven.

Variations:

- Marinate a whole chicken with three-fourths of the marinade. Stir the remaining marinade into the vegetables before baking.
- Substitute rutabagas for the turnips, and Yukon gold potatoes for the sweet potatoes.

BARBECUED CHICKEN

Serves 4 to 6

LET'S JUST BE HONEST. *Cynthia and I are sexist and think barbecuing is men's work. It falls in the category of "outside jobs"—like mowing the lawn, washing the car, and taking the trashcans to the street. Therefore, I know little about barbecuing, or grilling in general. Luckily, many great books have been written on the subject.*

What we do know is that barbecued chicken is often dry and the skin burnt to a crisp from the flames lapping the sauce, so we use the indirect-heat method of cooking. This method of slow-grilling the chicken and saucing near the end of cooking insures both moist meat and few flare-ups. Although this is our basic barbecue sauce and we swear by it, there is no reason another cannot be used. My godfather has been known to use bottled Italian salad dressing. We've added a version for oven-cooking as well.

The Abercrombie Sauce is the Bentley family's secret recipe, which they bottle and give away at holidays.

2 cups Abercrombie Sauce (see below)
1 whole chicken, cut into 8 serving pieces (page 344), and patted dry

Prepare the grill and heat to medium. Oil the cooking grate. If using coals, stack them to one side of the grill. If using gas, heat only one side of the grill.

When the grill is hot, dry the chicken pieces and move skin side down onto the grill rack directly over the heat. Brown the chicken over the heat for just 2 to 3 minutes to sear the outside; turn the chicken to sear the other side for 2 to 3 minutes. Move the chicken off the direct heat to the other side of the grill. Close the grill and cook 20 minutes.

Pour 2 cups of the Abercrombie Sauce into a bowl. Baste the chicken with the sauce, close the grill, and grill another 20 minutes. Baste again and continue to cook the chicken until its thickest part registers 165 degrees on an instant-read thermometer. Discard remaining sauce. Remove chicken from the grill and serve with a fresh bowl of sauce on the side.

Variations:

- Spatchcock the chicken (page 369). Bake at 400 degrees on a rimmed baking sheet without turning until the thickest part of the chicken reaches an internal temperature of 165 degrees on a meat thermometer, about 50 minutes. If the skin is not crispy, move the chicken under the broiler to crisp and brown the skin. Let rest 10 minutes for the heat to rise. To serve, cut up the center of the chicken through the breastbone. Cut each half into 2 pieces. Move to a platter and serve hot. This can be made ahead and reheated, but it loses some of its crispness.
- Use Georgia Peach Barbecue Sauce (page 664) to baste the chicken and to serve separately on the side.

ABERCROMBIE SAUCE

3/4 cup butter
1 quart apple cider vinegar
1 cup water
2 teaspoons Dijon mustard
1 medium onion, chopped
1/2 cup Worcestershire sauce
1 cup tomato sauce
1 cup chili sauce
Juice of 1 lemon
Grated rind of 1/2 lemon, no white attached
2 garlic cloves, finely chopped
1 teaspoon granulated sugar

Mix all the sauce ingredients together in a large pot. Stir cook over medium heat for 30 minutes. Pour into clean, airtight containers and keep refrigerated.

BONE-IN CHICKEN BREASTS

While boneless skinless chicken breasts are the easiest part of the chicken to cook, there is no doubt that skin-on bone-in chicken breasts are infinitely more flavorful.

Chicken breasts vary widely in size and nomenclature. They may either be the whole chest, also called whole breasts, or the split chest, also known as single or split breasts. (I try to avoid saying a "whole chicken breast" as that should mean two breasts, which may or may not have belonged to the same chest and therefore vary in size. Usually these are split down the sternum bone before sale.) When they are sold in large family packs with the bone in, the breasts tend to be from larger birds. Bone-in breast meat is hard to cook evenly as it is, because there are so many variations in thickness and bone structure.

Increasingly, as larger birds are bred and sold, there are only three single breasts, including the ribs and their flesh, in a package. It is very difficult to cook these huge chicken breasts and keep them moist. For ideal presentation, the ribs should be clipped off and used for another purpose, such as stock.

Rushed as I am on family meal nights, however, I do not want to fool with cutting off the excess flesh and rib bones, and tidying up the chicken breast. In fact, the flesh on the ribs is quite tasty. Nothing will be lost if the breast, ribs and all, is cooked as it emerges from the packet.

Any method of evening out the flesh of the breast will help, including butterflying or spatchcocking, which is the same thing as butterflying.

CHICKEN TENDERS

The tender, or fillet, is the long, thin piece of meat attached to the breast by a membrane next to the rib. It cooks far more quickly than the rest of the breast, as it is smaller and has no bone. If no other use is seen for it, it can be browned after all the breasts are browned, set aside, and returned to the pot shortly before the cooking is finished. If left on, it will delay, and perhaps prevent, even and thorough cooking, as it adds to the convoluted shape of the breast.

As the size of the birds grows, so does this fillet. It needs to be pulled off—a simple task—and set aside. Better yet, do it while unloading the groceries and add to a freezer container holding others. When enough are stockpiled, use them to make a wonderful stir-fry. These chicken tenders are sold in bulk as well and are ideal for kebabs, a stir-fry, and other quick dishes. Kids really like them grilled or fried—a healthy homemade alternative to fast food.

SIMPLE SAUTÉED BONE-IN CHICKEN BREASTS

Serves 4

THIS IS A POPULAR, EASY MEAL *for family or light entertaining of friends. Add a vegetable such as ribboned zucchini, potatoes, carrots, spinach, or just a salad with vegetables, and it is a meal in one. Sometimes it is easier to slide the chicken into a 400-degree oven once browned, since it doesn't require any attention. A pan on top of the stove needs to be checked periodically, as the chicken may burn easily, particularly in a large pan with a small amount of liquid.*

4 single split chicken breasts, bone-in
1–2 tablespoons oil, cook's preference, divided
1–2 tablespoons butter, divided
Salt
Freshly ground black pepper
1/2 cup chicken stock or broth, optional
Dry white vermouth, dry sherry, or Madeira, optional
2 tablespoons red wine vinegar or fresh lemon juice, optional

Move the chicken breasts to a cutting board to tidy up, using scissors or a knife to remove excess fat, skin, and bones as desired. Crack the breastbone, if included, by pushing down on top of the breast with the heel of a hand until a snap is heard. Pat the chicken dry with paper towels.

Heat 1 tablespoon each of oil and butter over medium heat in a 10- or 12-inch ovenproof heavy skillet or large Dutch oven until it shimmers. Add the chicken in a clockwise fashion, to know which went in first, in batches if necessary, and cook to a deep golden brown, about 5 minutes. To ensure even browning, press down firmly on the breasts with tongs or a heavy pan, and hold down during the initial sizzle from the liquid in the chicken hitting the fat.

After 4 or 5 minutes, peek underneath and look at the skin. Holding the sternum side of the breast up, push down and brown the side rib portion. When all the skin is brown, turn and cook briefly to brown on the second side. When all the pieces are browned and turned, sprinkle with salt and pepper, and cover.

Move to a 400-degree oven or continue cooking over medium heat, skin side up, until the thickest part of the chicken reaches 165 degrees on a meat thermometer.

Remove the chicken and return the skillet to the stove over medium heat. Deglaze the pan by adding the stock or another liquid such as wine; scrape to get all the good bits off the bottom and sides, bring to the boil, boil until liquid is reduced and slightly syrupy and thick, add the vinegar or juice if needed, and cook a few minutes more. Serve alongside the chicken.

Variations:

- To self-baste the bone-in chicken breast with skin on, stuff the desired ingredients—butter, lemon slices, pesto, etc.—under the skin of the chicken and continue as above.

- If skinless, increase the butter and oil to the largest amount.
- Add 1/2 cup heavy cream to the deglazed pan and reduced liquids, return to boil, and boil until reduced and thickened. Delicious. Decadent.

BONELESS CHICKEN BREASTS

Boneless breasts seem to have no resemblance at all to bone-in breasts. They are more like veal scaloppine (also called escalope) only thicker, readily absorb the flavor of the ingredients around them as they cook, and cook in the blink of an eye.

Boneless, skinless chicken breasts are without a doubt one of the speediest things to cook and require only a modicum of attention once you know a few tricks. For a family, one chicken breast per person will suffice. When serving guests, I figure two chicken breasts for hearty eaters, just so the meal doesn't appear skimpy. The addition of one more or less chicken breast in a recipe does not matter.

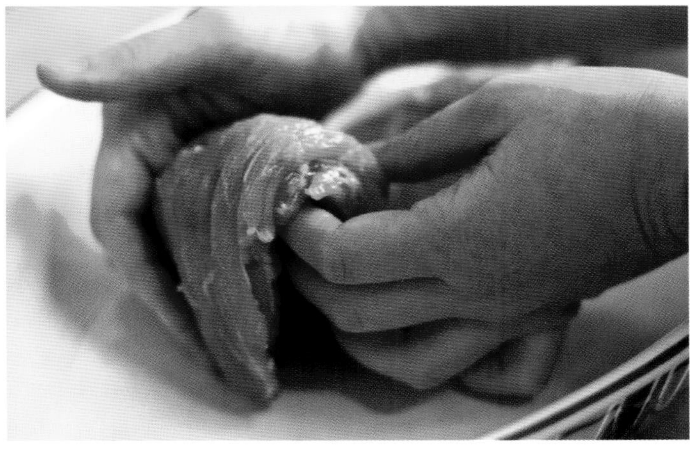

Boning chicken breasts—I prefer boning my own chicken breasts, using the bones in stock and saving that tender. It goes speedily when there is a quantity. Following are two ways to bone the breast. Leave the skin on or pull it off. The "tender" and the skin may be removed before or after boning.

Chicken breasts vary widely in size, sometimes going from small to large in one package, with each one cooking a little differently. They like moisture—before, during, or after cooking. And, finally, they are very adaptable and will take the lead from the ingredients cooked with them.

Method 1—Turn the chicken breast skin side down. Loosen the rib bones, if any, with fingers or a knife. Slide the knife towards the center bone, if any, by keeping the knife flat against the ribs. Never slide a knife towards a hand. If necessary, hold the chicken steady with a hand on top while sliding the knife to separate the flesh from the bone. Either crack the sternum bone and remove it, or slide the knife under the bone to remove.

Method 2—Turn the chicken breast skin side up. Insert the knife at the sternum bone and slide the knife, holding it firmly against the bone, to separate the flesh from the bone. It's really easy if there's no sternum bone—fingers are all it takes to remove the flesh from the ribs.

Remove the tender (page 351) and remember the filament under the skin prevents the absorption of fat, so leave it on. The skin will add flavor to the dish, so remove it after browning if the dish requires it.

Don't worry about the amount of meat left on the bone. That will add flavor to a stock (pages 111–14).

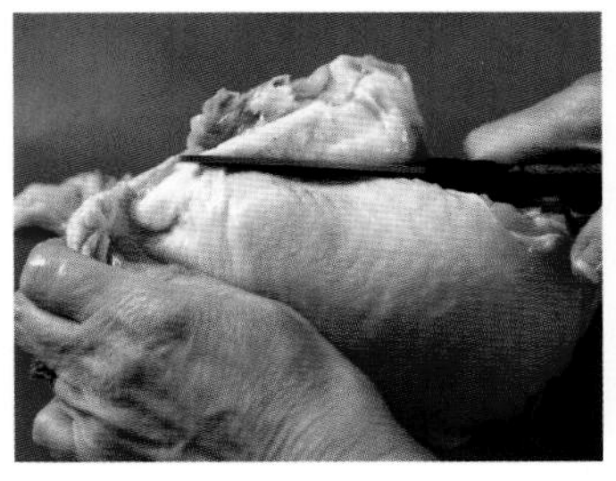

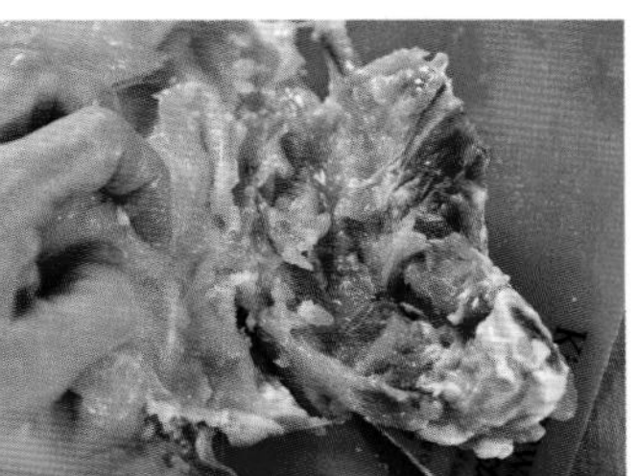

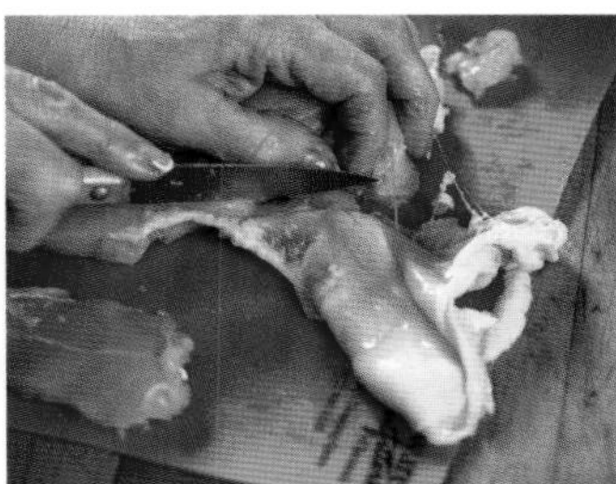

Storing boned chicken breasts—The easiest thing to do is to bone breasts immediately after bringing them home from the store. Spread out on a flat surface such as a rimmed baking sheet. Cover with foil or plastic wrap if there is a possibility they will be forgotten. Freeze. When frozen, remove and put in a freezer container or bag for easy removal later, or wrap individually before or after freezing. I freeze tenderloins separately.

MOIST AND FAST CHICKEN BREASTS

Serves 4 to 6

THIS IS PROBABLY MY FAVORITE WAY *of cooking boneless chicken breasts. The flavor is intensified rather than diluted as with a poached chicken breast. It keeps the breasts moist, allows for them to be white or brown (see variation), the white giving a fresh delicate flavor, which appears more sophisticated, the browned version giving a somewhat earthy, nearly malty flavor to the dish. It can be varied infinitely, adding vegetables to make it an all-in-one dish, or serving over rice or mashed potatoes with an accompanying vegetable. It can have crispy potatoes by its side very happily, particularly when browned. Unlike many chicken breast recipes, this can be cooked ahead and reheated, an added bonus. I usually cook a few extra to use for another dinner, or perhaps a salad. Experiment with different liquids—juices, wines, and even sherry or white wine vinegar in a pinch.*

4 boneless, skinless chicken breasts
4–6 tablespoons butter
1/4–1/2 cup chicken stock or broth
Salt
Freshly ground black pepper
1/4 cup fresh lemon juice or orange juice, white wine, dry vermouth, or dry sherry
1 cup heavy cream or 1/2 cup plain yogurt, optional
2 tablespoons chopped fresh parsley or thyme, optional

Pat the chicken dry with paper towels and remove the little pieces of meat called the tenderloin (page 351), and set aside for another time. If the breasts are plump, briefly flatten them on a board with a heavy pan, rolling pin, or mallet to aid in cooking all the meat evenly.

Heat the butter over medium heat in a 10- or 12-inch heavy skillet or large Dutch oven until it shimmers but does not brown. Add the chicken smooth (skinned) side down in a clockwise fashion, to know which went in first, in batches if necessary, and cook 2 minutes, until flesh turns white. Turn the chicken pieces with tongs, and cook the second side 1 to 2 minutes, until white. Cover and cook 3 to 5 minutes over medium heat, until the chicken breasts bounce back when touched lightly and the thickest part of the chicken registers 165 degrees on a meat thermometer. Season to taste with salt and pepper.

Remove the chicken breasts and keep warm. Add the chicken stock, salt, pepper, and juice to the pan and boil down with the remaining juices until syrupy, making sure any tasty bits have been included. (This sauce may be served as a simple sauce for family.)

For a richer, company sauce, add the heavy cream to the juices, bring to the boil, and boil rapidly until thick. If using the yogurt, add to the juices but bring just to a simmer without boiling, as it may separate.

Taste the sauce. Move the chicken breasts to a hot plate and top with a little of the sauce and the optional herbs. Serve immediately with any remaining sauce.

Variations:

- Brown the breasts on one side, then the other, for a rustic flavor and look, rather than leaving white.
- Pare 2 carrots, 1 potato—either sweet or medium Yukon gold—and 2 zucchini using a potato peeler to peel from top to bottom into a thin strip, or "ribbon." Include the skin and seedy part of the zucchini. Top the partially cooked chicken breasts with the vegetables and cover the pan. Cook 3 to 5 minutes over medium heat, until the chicken breasts bounce back when touched lightly and the thickest part of the chicken registers 165 degrees on a meat thermometer, and the vegetables are wilted. Season to taste with salt and pepper. Remove the vegetables with the chicken breasts and keep warm. Proceed with recipe, adding stock as above.
- An 8-ounce container of prewashed baby spinach wilts in approximately the same amount of time as the ribboned vegetables when added to the top of the chicken as above. A few sautéed mushrooms enhance the dish as well.

Variation: Chicken with Tomato and Herbs

After removing the chicken breasts to a hot platter, add 1 tablespoon butter, 1 finely chopped medium onion, and 1 peeled, cored, seeded, and chopped tomato to the pan. Toss over heat for 2 or 3 minutes. Add 1/2 cup sherry, tarragon or white wine vinegar, and 1/4 cup chicken stock or broth, and stir over medium-high heat to deglaze, scraping up the pan juices and bits in the skillet. Return the breasts to the skillet, turn to coat with the sauce, and heat until cooked through, about 4 minutes. Stir in 2 tablespoons chopped fresh basil, marjoram, or tarragon. Taste for seasoning, adding a bit of sugar if necessary, and serve immediately.

CHICKEN BREASTS WITH BACON AND ZUCCHINI

Serves 4

WHETHER FRYING A CHICKEN OR COOKING A CHICKEN BREAST, *Southerners love the combination of chicken and pork. If possible, purchase slab bacon and cut the strips of bacon from that. Freeze part for another time. The French call these* lardons *and sell them in the grocery stores.*

3 slices bacon
1/2 onion, finely chopped
4 boneless, skinless chicken breasts
Salt
Freshly ground black pepper
2 tablespoons chopped fresh thyme or oregano leaves
1/3 cup small black olives, preferably pitted
4 zucchini, sliced on a diagonal 1/8 inch thick
1 1/2 cups cooked rice

Preheat oven to 350 degrees.

Slice the bacon crosswise into 1/4-inch strips and add to a hot 10- to 12-inch heavy skillet. Cook, stirring or turning as necessary, until the strips brown, about 5 minutes. Watch carefully to be sure the bacon doesn't burn. Remove with a slotted spoon and set aside. Add the onion and cook briefly. Remove and set aside with the bacon.

Pat the chicken dry with paper towels and remove the little piece of meat called the tenderloin (page 351). Set it aside for another time. If the breasts are plump, briefly flatten them on a board with a heavy pan, rolling pin, or mallet to aid in cooking all the breasts evenly.

Add the chicken to the hot bacon fat, placing the smooth side (skinned side) down in a clock-wise fashion, to know which went in first, in batches if necessary, and cook 3 to 5 minutes to seal and form a nice crust. Turn the chicken pieces with tongs, and cook the second side 3 to 5 minutes, until the thickest part of the chicken registers 165 degrees on a meat thermometer. Remove the chicken.

Add the thyme, olives, and zucchini. Return the bacon mixture to the pan, top with the chicken, cover, reduce the heat, and simmer 8 to 10 minutes, until the thickest part of the chicken registers 165 degrees on a meat thermometer. Serve over rice.

Variation: Finely chop a slice of country ham and sauté until crisp, adding oil or bacon fat to ham fat if available; add to onions cooked in bacon fat or oil in place of the bacon. Add 1 to 2 cups of tomato wedges with the thyme, olives, and zucchini.

KEEPING FOOD WARM

One trick to serving food warm is to preheat oven to 200 degrees and move the cooked food—like these chicken breasts—to the warm oven after cooking. Another is to move them to the lid of a hot pan, which will keep them warm as well.

CHICKEN SCALOPPINE

Serves 2 to 3

ANN WILLAN IN HER WONDERFUL BOOK The Good Cook *gives these complete instructions for pounding chicken breasts until they are thinner, wider, and longer. These are also called cutlets, escalopes, paillards, and scaloppine. The word* scallops *is also used, but it is a bit inaccurate, as scallops are usually thicker if sea scallops and in small "squarish" pieces if bay scallops, so I avoid the term to prevent confusion.*

2 boneless, skinless chicken breasts
1/4 cup all-purpose flour
Salt
Freshly ground black pepper
2 tablespoons butter
2 tablespoons oil, cook's preference
4 ounces sliced mushrooms
2 garlic cloves, chopped
3 tablespoons white wine
3 tablespoons water
1 tablespoon chopped fresh parsley

Pat the chicken dry with paper towels. Butterfly the boneless breasts on a sheet of plastic wrap or waxed paper by slicing each breast almost in half horizontally and opening outward like a book. Cover the chicken with another sheet of plastic wrap or waxed paper and pound the chicken with a heavy pan, rolling pin, or mallet until 1/4 inch thick. Don't be distressed if overly vigorous pounding caused the flesh to tear, but try to avoid it.

Toss the flour, salt, and pepper on a piece of waxed paper. Using the fingers of one hand, move the flattened breasts individually to the flour, pressing the chicken lightly into the flour. Turn and press the second side. Shake off any additional flour.

Heat the butter and oil in a 10- to 12-inch heavy skillet. Add the chicken and cook 1 to 2 minutes on one side. Turn the chicken pieces with tongs, and cook the second side and additional 1 to 2 minutes, until the thickest part of the chicken registers 165 degrees on a meat thermometer. Move chicken to a warm plate.

In the same skillet, cook the mushrooms and garlic until tender, about 2 to 3 minutes. Stir in wine and water, stirring up any bits in the pan, until heated through. Taste to adjust the seasoning and return the chicken to the pan. Sprinkle the chicken with parsley and warm through an additional 1 to 2 minutes. Serve hot, immediately. Scaloppine is far from its best when reheated but does make a pleasant cold filling in a sandwich the next day.

Variation: Sautéed Chicken and Tomatoes
Remove the chicken and keep warm. Add a pint of cherry tomatoes for every pound of chicken and sauté until lightly charred and popped. Mix 1 tablespoon basil, a teaspoon or two of chopped fresh garlic, and 1 teaspoon grated lemon rind, no white attached, for each pound of chicken. Arrange the cutlets on a plate, top with the tomatoes and basil-garlic mixture, and serve hot.

What's the skin side when there's no skin? A chicken breast has two sides—the one with the skin is rounder and fuller than the inner side (the tenderloin, or fillet, should be removed). When breading or browning, the smooth side should be cooked first, pushing the juices through to the second side. The first side is always prettier, as no liquid has pushed through.

APPLE AND CHEESE–STUFFED CHICKEN BREASTS

Serves 4

STUFFING BONELESS BREASTS *is a good way to add flavor and dash to a chicken breast. The tart flavor of Granny Smith apples boosts the pleasure quotient of this dish, which is particularly nice when there's no time for languid conversation over cheese and apples before or after dinner. The sauce is really rich and splendid.*

4 boneless, skinless chicken breasts
1 apple, such as Granny Smith, Cortland, Ginger Gold, or Golden Delicious, thinly sliced
4 slices white hard cheese, such as Cheddar or Gruyère
1/2 cup all-purpose flour
Salt
Freshly ground black pepper
2 tablespoons butter, divided
2 tablespoon oil, cook's preference, divided
1 small onion or shallot, finely chopped
1 garlic clove, chopped
1 cup apple juice
1 tablespoon chopped fresh thyme, parsley, or oregano
1 cup chicken stock or broth
1/2 tablespoon cornstarch

Pat the chicken dry with paper towels. Remove the little piece of meat called the tenderloin (page 351) and set it aside for another time.

Butterfly the boneless breasts by slicing each breast almost in half horizontally and opening outward like a book. Cover the chicken with another sheet of plastic wrap or waxed paper and pound the chicken with a heavy pan, rolling pin, or mallet until 1/4 inch thick. Don't be distressed if overly vigorous pounding causes the flesh to tear, but try to avoid it. Move 2 thin slices of apple to the lower half of each breast. Top with a slice of cheese and flip the top half of breast over the cheese. Secure with toothpicks if desired.

Toss the flour, salt, and pepper on a piece of waxed paper. Using the fingers of one hand, move the chicken breasts individually to the flour, pressing the chicken lightly into the flour. Pat some of the mixture on top of the chicken breast and press again. Shake off any additional flour.

Heat 1 tablespoon each of the butter and oil in a 10- to 12-inch heavy skillet. Add the chicken and cook 3 to 5 minutes on one side. Turn the chicken pieces with tongs, and cook the second side 3 to 5 minutes, until the thickest part of the chicken registers 160 degrees on a meat thermometer. Do not overcook. Remove the cooked chicken to a warm platter. The temperature of the chicken will continue to rise to 165 degrees.

Heat the remaining tablespoon of butter and oil in the same skillet over medium heat. Add the onion and cook until soft and translucent, about 3 to 5 minutes. Add the garlic, apple juice, and herbs, and stir to scrape up the browned bits to deglaze the pan. Bring to the boil and cook over high heat until reduced by half. Whisk the chicken stock and cornstarch together. Whisk into the reduced apple juice, bring to the boil, and simmer about 2 minutes, or until thickened. Pass the sauce separately.

Variation: A slice of country ham with the Gruyère would be divine.

DEGLAZING

"Deglazing" a pan after cooking meat of any kind creates a tasty sauce of cooking juices that can be served with the meat as is, or can be boiled down with a little cream, vinegar, dry wine or citrus juice, and spices to make a sauce. This type of sauce may be poured over side dishes of rice or potatoes as well.

To deglaze the pan, add about 1/2 cup of liquid, preferably stock or wine, to a pan in which the meat has been browned. Heat the pan of liquid over a burner and scrape a wooden spoon around the pan to loosen the fat and juices that have dried along the sides. To intensify the sauce, boil the original liquid down and add another cup or so of extra liquid, bring back to the boil, and reduce again. All of the goodness from the pan will come together and thicken up as the liquid evaporates.

SESAME AND TURMERIC CHICKEN

Serves 4

THERE ARE MANY WAYS TO COAT CHICKEN BREASTS, *from seeds to breadcrumbs. This gives the chicken an exterior, adding a bit of protection from drying out, and adds flavor and "finish." Although sesame seeds grow in the South, imports far exceed any domestic production. White sesame seeds are more common that black ones. Either works with the sunny yellow turmeric.*

1/2 cup sesame seeds
1 teaspoon ground ginger
1 teaspoon ground turmeric
4 boneless, skinless chicken breasts
Salt
Freshly ground black pepper
2 tablespoons oil, cook's preference

Toss together the sesame seeds, ginger, and turmeric, and spread over a sheet of waxed paper.

If the breasts are plump, briefly flatten them on a board with a heavy pan, rolling pin, or mallet to aid in cooking all the breasts evenly. Season breasts with salt and pepper as desired. Add the still damp pieces to the sesame mixture individually, using one hand and keeping the other clean. Press to adhere the seeds. Turn and press the second side. May be refrigerated uncovered on a rack atop a plate (to catch the juices) for up to one day.

Heat the oil over medium heat in a 10- or 12-inch heavy skillet or large Dutch oven until it shimmers. Add the chicken smooth (skinned) side down in a clockwise fashion, to know which went in first, in batches if necessary, and cook 3 to 5 minutes to seal and form a nice crust. Turn the chicken pieces with tongs, and cook the second side 3 to 5 minutes, until the thickest part of the chicken registers 165 degrees on a meat thermometer. Serve hot. This dish does not reheat well.

Variation: Baked Cornmeal-Crusted Chicken
Season 1 cup of plain cornmeal with salt, pepper, ground red pepper, or other spices on a plate. Using one hand, dip the still damp breasts individually, breast side down, into the cornmeal mixture. Pat to coat. Turn and repeat with second side. Add to a greased rimmed baking sheet or pan and bake in a 350-degree oven until the thermometer inserted in the thickest portion registers 165 to 170 degrees, about 15-20 minutes, depending on size.

Variation:

- To bake, add seed-covered breasts to an oiled rimmed baking sheet or pan, not overlapping, and bake in a 400-degree oven until a meat thermometer registers 165-170 degrees, about 15 to 20 minutes, depending on size. Check to be sure the seeds are not over-browning; if so, reduce the heat to 350 and cook longer.
- Use a mixture of ground nuts and proceed as above.
- Use a mixture of breadcrumbs and spices and proceed as above.

OVEN-FRIED CHICKEN BREASTS WITH PECAN CRUST

Serves 4 to 6

THIS RECIPE IS ADAPTED FROM MY FORMER ASSISTANT *Virginia Willis and her wonderful cookbook* Bon Appetite, Y'All. *This technique calls for brining the boneless breast, then adding breadcrumbs as a layer. The fresh bay leaves add a fresh taste, and if only dry are available, omit them or chop them with some parsley to freshen up. This recipe requires a bit of planning and time to assemble, but it and the one for Sesame Turmeric Chicken and its variations (facing) are interchangeable in that they can be marinated or not, a lighter coat is achieved without egg, and a thicker "more fried" texture is achieved when brining and then using an egg to adhere the dry ingredients. Whenever brining something as thin as a chicken breast, do not take any chances of over-saltiness and mushiness by leaving it longer than the period of time indicated.*

1/4 cup salt
2 tablespoons granulated sugar
1 tablespoon sweet Hungarian paprika
4 garlic cloves, smashed
2 bay leaves, preferably fresh, optional
4 cups buttermilk
4–6 (8-ounce) boneless, skinless chicken breasts
1/2 cup breadcrumbs or panko
3/4 cup finely chopped pecans
2 tablespoons oil, cook's preference
2 large eggs
2 tablespoons Dijon mustard
1 teaspoon chopped fresh thyme
Freshly ground black pepper
Vidalia Honey Mustard Dressing (page 106)

Preheat oven to 350 degrees. Brush a rimmed baking sheet with oil or line with aluminum foil, and then set a large wire rack on the foil.

To make the brine, mix the salt, sugar, paprika, garlic, and optional bay leaves in a large nonreactive container. Add the buttermilk and stir until the salt is completely dissolved. Immerse the chicken breasts in the brine and marinate at room temperature for 30 minutes. (Do not brine any longer or the chicken will be too salty.)

Meanwhile, toss the breadcrumbs and pecans together in a shallow dish. Add the oil and toss well to coat. In a second shallow dish, combine the eggs, mustard, and thyme. Season both mixtures with pepper.

Using one hand, remove a chicken piece from the brine and shake off any excess liquid. Dip the chicken into the egg mixture, coating both sides, move the breasts to the bread-crumb mixture, sprinkle with crumbs to cover, and press so the coating adheres; turn the chicken over and repeat the process. Gently shake off any excess crumbs. Repeat with the remaining chicken.

Move the coated breasts to a rack set on the baking sheet. This may be done ahead of time and refrigerated an hour or so. Bake until the chicken is golden brown and the juices run clear, 20 to 25 minutes, until the thickest part of the chicken registers 165 on a meat thermometer. Serve each breast with a spoonful of Vidalia Honey Mustard Dressing.

STIR-FRIED GREENS, CHICKEN BREASTS, AND PEANUTS

Serves 4

STIR-FRYING CAME INTO POPULARITY *in the 1970s in the South, a welcome respite from standing over the hot stove and frying chicken. They cook in no time, so have everything organized and prepped in advance. Greens are a perennial accompaniment with chicken, and they certainly add color, while the nuts add crunch.*

4 boneless, skinless chicken breasts or 12 chicken tenders
1 pound turnip, spinach, or collard greens
3 tablespoons oil, cook's preference
1 tablespoon butter
1/3 cup chopped roasted peanuts
Salt
Freshly ground black pepper
Hot sauce, optional

Cut the chicken breasts into 1-inch pieces, or cut the tenders in half lengthwise. Pat dry with paper towels.

Tear off and discard the stalks and any tough veins from the greens. Tear or cut the remaining greens into 2-inch pieces.

Heat the oil in a 10 or 12-inch heavy skillet with lid until it shimmers. Add the cut-up chicken and toss over medium heat for 3 to 5 minutes, until the thickest piece registers 160 degrees on a meat thermometer.

Add the greens to the skillet and toss until coated with the juices of the chicken. Cover the pan and let the greens wilt. The chicken is done when it registers 165 degrees.

In a separate pan, melt the butter and stir in the peanuts. Sprinkle over the chicken and greens. Season to taste with salt and pepper. Pass the hot sauce.

Variations:

- Substitute pecans for peanuts.
- Slivered okra, ribboned or sliced zucchini, English peas, and other green vegetables that cook rapidly are good substitutions for the greens.
- The mood and flavor of this can be changed completely by adding a slice of ginger the size of a quarter, chopped, and 2 tablespoons of soy sauce rather than the hot sauce, and sesame seeds rather than peanuts.

BASIC GRILLED, GRIDDLED, OR BROILED CHICKEN BREASTS

Serves 4

THIS IS MY BASIC RECIPE FOR GRILLING CHICKEN BREASTS *as well as other thin meats and poultry. It's an indispensable building block for fast meals and has many uses. Serve warm with a favorite chutney, tomato conserve, or salsa on the side, on a bed of vegetables, topped with a white butter or other sauce, accompanied by a pilaf with peppers, or sliced and at room temperature in a salad. Be sure everything else is ready to serve once the chicken is started, as it cooks in no time.*

4 boneless, skinless chicken breasts
1 tablespoon oil, cook's preference
1 tablespoon fresh lemon juice
1 tablespoon ground cumin, curry, ginger, or fresh chopped herbs, optional
Salt
Freshly ground black pepper

Preheat grill, griddle, or broiler.

Spread the chicken breasts in a shallow dish. Whisk together the oil, lemon juice, spices or herbs, and salt and pepper to taste. Pour over the chicken breasts and turn to coat well on both sides. Shake off excess moisture.

Move the chicken breasts to the hot grill, a griddle, or a pan under the broiler; cook 3 to 5 minutes, turn, and cook the second side another 3 to 5 minutes, depending on the size, until just opaque throughout and the thickest part of the chicken registers 165 degrees on a meat thermometer. Do not overcook or they will be tough.

CHICKEN WITH TOMATO SALSA

Serves 6

SALSA, WHICH LOOSELY MEANS "SAUCE" IN SPANISH, *is relatively new for the South, having appeared about 25 to 30 years ago. Now, however, a great number of our citizens are Hispanic, and salsa has become part of our culture.*

This recipe may be assembled at the last minute, or it may be made ahead and reheated, as it becomes more tender and moist after a day. Either way, the bubbling hot cheese is a delight. I use a homemade or commercial salsa, depending on my time. If cilantro is not available, create an entirely different flavor by substituting fresh basil, oregano, or thyme. Hand-grated cheese is less expensive, not waxy, and more flavorful than pre-grated commercial cheese.

4 boneless, skinless chicken breasts
2 tablespoons oil, cook's preference
Salt
Freshly ground black pepper
1 cup fresh Salsa (page 668) or bottled salsa
1 cup grated Monterey Jack cheese
2 tablespoons chopped fresh cilantro

Preheat oven to 350 degrees.

Pat the chicken dry with paper towels. Rub the chicken breasts with oil and move to a baking dish. Season both sides with salt and pepper. Pour the salsa over the chicken.

Bake 15 to 20 minutes, until the thickest part of the chicken registers 160 degrees on a meat thermometer. Remove from the oven.

Change the oven setting to broil. Top the chicken with the cheese, return to the oven, and broil until bubbly and light golden brown, about 3 minutes, until the thickest part of the chicken registers 165 degrees. Just before serving, sprinkle with cilantro.

Variation: Tomato Conserve (page 644), Cranberry Relish (page 642), or chutney work just as well as salsa, but omit the cheese.

SKILLET LEMON CHICKEN DRUMSTICKS OR THIGHS **Serves 4 to 6**

THERE ARE THOSE OF US *who prefer dark meat for its full flavor and being infinitely more forgiving in cooking than breast meat. Thighs and drumsticks work very well in any of the preceding breast recipes but should be cooked slightly longer.*

This meal-in-one has an earthy flavor from browning the chicken and potatoes, with an underlying brightness from the grated lemon rind and juice as well as depth from the rosemary. A heavy skillet is a necessity for this dish.

3 tablespoons oil, cook's preference
1 tablespoon butter
6 chicken drumsticks or thighs
1 pound fingerling potatoes
10 whole garlic cloves
Juice and grated rind of 1 lemon, no white attached
2–3 tablespoons fresh or dried rosemary, divided
Salt
Freshly ground black pepper
2–3 cups chicken stock or broth, divided
12 ounces fresh baby spinach

Heat the oil and butter over medium heat in a 10- or 12-inch heavy skillet or large Dutch oven until it shimmers. Add the chicken skin side down, alternating the drumsticks top to bottom to create sufficient space in the skillet. It is helpful to add in a pattern, such as clockwise, so removal is guess-free, with first pieces in/first pieces out. Press down with a hand or heavy pan to speed the browning. As the sizzle decreases, the chicken is getting brown. If the pan is larger than the burner, it may be necessary to rotate the pan to brown all the pieces. Using tongs, turn the chicken when sizzling subsides, reduce heat, and brown the second side, checking to be sure the drippings in the bottom of the pan are no deeper in color than mahogany brown.

Meanwhile, cut the potatoes in halves or quarters and remove the outer peel from the garlic cloves. Turn the chicken when brown and sprinkle the upper side of the chicken with lemon juice and rind. Tuck the cut potatoes and the whole garlic cloves between and under the chicken pieces, and sprinkle half of the rosemary over the pan. Season the chicken and vegetables with salt and pepper to taste. If at any time the fat starts to darken too much, add 1/2 cup of chicken broth and stir the bottom of the pan, lifting the pieces as necessary.

Cover the pan, reduce the heat, and simmer 10 to 20 minutes, checking occasionally, adding enough stock to cover the bottom of the pan if it appears dry. Cover and cook until the thickest part of the chicken registers 165 degrees on a meat thermometer, about 20 minutes. Add the spinach. Cover and cook 1 minute more, until the spinach is wilted. Season again to taste with salt and pepper if needed. Serve from the skillet or move immediately to a hot platter.

Variations: Thinly sliced or ribboned zucchini, slivered okra, or another quick-cooking green vegetable can be substituted for the spinach.

DARK MEAT SUBSTITUTION

There are those of us who prefer dark meat for its full flavor and being infinitely more forgiving in cooking than breast meat. Thighs and drumsticks work very well in any of the preceding breast recipes but should be cooked slightly longer.

FRUITY CHICKEN DRUMSTICKS OR THIGHS

Serves 4

Browning the curried chicken thoroughly *until it is a deep mahogany color, then surrounding it with colorful good-for-you dried fruits, sweet potatoes, and well-chopped broccoli makes this as healthy as it is beautiful, and it's a one-skillet meal. All curry powders are different, so be judicious when deciding how much to mix with the flour. More can be stirred in after cooking.*

2 tablespoons butter
1 tablespoon oil, cook's preference
1/2 cup flour
3–4 tablespoons curry powder
Salt
Freshly ground black pepper
6 chicken drumsticks or thighs
2 sweet potatoes, peeled and diced
2 carrots, peeled and slice in 1/4-inch pieces
I cup mixed dried fruit (such as dried apricots, cherries, cranberries, prunes, and raisins) roughly chopped
1 cup chicken stock or broth
1 1/2 cups English peas, fresh or frozen

Heat the butter and oil over medium heat in a 10- or 12-inch heavy skillet or large Dutch oven until it shimmers.

Shake the flour, curry, and salt and pepper to taste in a plastic bag; add still damp chicken and shake to coat.

Add the chicken to the hot fat skin side down and cook 8 to 10 minutes on one side, until deep brown. It is helpful to add in a pattern, such as clockwise, so removal is guess-free, with first pieces in first pieces out. Turn the chicken pieces with tongs, and cook the second side an additional 8 to 10 minutes, until browned.

Stir in sweet potatoes, carrots, and dried fruit, along with the chicken broth. Cover and simmer 20 minutes, until vegetables are tender and the thickest part of the chicken registers 165 degrees on a meat thermometer. Season to taste with salt and pepper, sprinkling with more curry if desired. Stir in the peas, bring back to a simmer, and cook 1 minute. Serve from the skillet.

Variation: Slivered okra would be a welcome addition to this dish. Add as you would peas.

TUCKER THIGHS

Serves 4 to 6

This recipe came from a friend *in Tucker, Georgia, who knew I would like its combination of ingredients. I sometimes pick the coriander seeds in my garden when they are still green and smush them for this dish but ground coriander seeds do the job marvelously.*

2 pounds chicken thighs
1 1/4 cups plain yogurt
2 teaspoons finely chopped fresh ginger
1 1/2 teaspoons ground coriander seeds
2–3 garlic cloves, finely chopped
Ground hot red pepper
Grated rind of 1 lemon, no white attached
1/4 cup fresh lemon juice

Preheat oven to 350 degrees.

Pat the chicken dry with paper towels. Line a rimmed baking sheet with foil or oil well.

Whisk together all remaining ingredients. Move to a plastic ziplock bag or refrigerator container. Add the chicken thighs and turn to coat well. Marinate while preheating the oven or up to 24 hours in the refrigerator.

When ready to cook, remove the chicken thighs from the marinade, shake off to remove extra moisture, and move to the foil-lined rimmed baking sheet. Discard the marinade. Bake until cooked through, light brown, and bubbly, 25 to 30 minutes, and the temperature of the thickest part of the chicken measures 165 degrees on a meat thermometer.

POACHED CHICKEN

Makes about 4 cups shredded chicken and 6 cups broth

POACHED CHICKEN *produces tender, moist, and delicate flesh. For this reason, it is best taken off the bone after cooking and added to soups, where a bite of chicken almost slides down the throat, and in salads. It produces a wonderful broth, aka stock, which can be used for soup, sauces, and aspics. We give the recipe here but refer to it in the stock section (page 113). We brown the vegetables to give the broth and chicken more flavor, but it is simpler and faster to omit this step and just add the vegetables to the liquid when the cook is in a hurry or perfectly white breast meat is desired.*

Chicken can be poached in many liquids, including milk and wine, but water is the standard. All the optional ingredients may be omitted. I have a tendency to put on a chicken to poach when I first remove the cold ingredients from the grocery bag. While putting the rest of the purchases away, I add bits and pieces from my refrigerator that I think will taste good in it and that I don't want to waste—wizened baby carrots or peelings, cooked onion, onion or tomato skins, a bit of spinach or turnip green left over from dinner few days ago. By the time the groceries are unpacked, I have a cooked chicken ready to go with any other leftovers or to grace a salad or soup. This would be a good recipe for Guinea hen as well.

1 whole chicken (3½–4 pounds)
2 tablespoons oil, cook's preference
2 medium onions, diced, optional
1 large or 2 small carrots, sliced into ½-inch rounds, optional
1 celery rib, diced into ½-inch strips, optional
3 garlic cloves, chopped, optional
2 quarts chicken broth or stock, optional
6 sprigs fresh thyme, or 1½ teaspoons dried thyme, optional
Bunch of parsley stems
1 bay leaf, optional
6 peppercorns

Remove any fat from inside the chicken and remove any innards. Rinse the chicken if desired.

Heat the oil in a large heavy stockpot. Add the onions, carrots, and celery, and cook until soft and lightly browned, about 10 minutes. Add the garlic and cook briefly. Pour in the chicken stock. Add the thyme, parsley, bay leaf, and peppercorns.

Add chicken, breast side up. If necessary, add sufficient water to cover the chicken but not come more than three-quarters up the sides of the pot. The chicken breast may rise above water level by an inch. Poaching the chicken whole, covered, with the breast out of the water, keeps the breast from being overcooked, as it cooks much faster than the legs. Cook over medium-high heat until liquid is simmering, and then reduce heat to low. Cover the pot with a lid and simmer until the legs can easily be pulled off the bird, about 1 hour, or until the thigh reaches approximately 165 degrees on an instant-read thermometer.

Remove the pot from the heat and set the chicken on a plate to cool. When cool, remove the flesh and skin from the chicken and pull it into shreds. Discard the skin. This should yield approximately 4 cups of shredded chicken to use as desired.

Return the bones to the liquid in the stockpot. Bring to a simmer and reduce liquid to 6 cups, about 30 to 45 minutes. Strain through a fine-mesh sieve and discard vegetables, as they have probably lost their flavor. Remove any fat from the broth, either with strips of paper towel or by chilling until the fat comes to the surface, hardens, and can be removed. The broth may be refrigerated up to several days or frozen. Divide into smaller quantities to defrost quickly.

Variations:

- *To poach cut-up chicken*—Add the legs first, wait 15 minutes, and then add the breasts.
- *To poach chicken breasts alone*—A frying pan makes this easier. Heat water separately, with or without flavorings, and pour it on top of the chicken breasts in the pan to cover. Cook covered over medium heat 15 to 45 minutes, depending on the thickness of the chicken. The chicken is cooked when the thickest part reaches 165 degrees on an instant-read thermometer.

GUINEA HENS

Originally African hens, similar to a featherless pheasant, the guinea hens were domesticated and raised for some time in Charleston as well as other parts of the South. They are tough birds, so most usually poached and served in soups, stews such as Chicken and Pepper Dumplings, or in pot pies.

TASTY POACHED CHICKEN

A poached chicken will increase in richness and diversity in flavor according to the ingredients in the broth. These ingredients are, however, just a suggestion. There is no need to rush to the grocery store to find a celery rib or a parsley stem. That said, there are certain things that make a difference:

1. Too much onion and carrot can make a broth sweet.
2. Celery leaves are stronger than celery stalk, so these should be avoided.
3. Parsley stalk is stronger than the herb itself.
4. Bay leaf adds depth and a certain underlying woodsyness.
5. Boiling the liquid leads to a cloudy broth.
6. Vegetables and bones create foam on the top of the broth that should be removed with a spoon or skimmer if perfection is desired. Straining of the broth achieves some of this. The foam and fat will gather near the edge of the hottest part of the pot, and is most easily removed there.
7. To increase the flavor of a broth, simmer it; do not boil until after the bones are removed.
8. For a pure white chicken, rinse the cavity thoroughly and do not brown the vegetables; they increase flavor, however, so in a simple recipe like this they are best browned.

TEXAS CRISPY GRILLED OR ROASTED CHICKEN

Serves 4

In the mid-1970s, *the Tex-Mex cooking of my college days started moving to other parts of the South and has spread practically worldwide. This spatchcocked chicken gets its crisp skin from resting overnight in the refrigerator, uncovered. The recipe was developed by Texan Mary Nell Reck, an early founder of the International Association of Culinary Professionals.*

A smaller 2½- to 3-pound chicken is preferable, but if a larger one is all that is available, add more time to the cooking process and turn down the heat if it gets dark brown before the interior is cooked.

1 whole chicken, about 2½–3 pounds
Juice and grated rind of 2 limes, no white attached
3 garlic cloves, chopped
2 tablespoons freshly ground black pepper
2 teaspoons ground hot red pepper
2 tablespoons sweet Hungarian paprika
4 tablespoons butter, melted

Spatchcock the chicken (page 369).

Mix together the lime juice, rind, garlic, black and red peppers, and paprika; rub the chicken with the mixture. Let the chicken sit refrigerated overnight, uncovered, on a rack over a rimmed baking sheet to allow the spices to adhere and coat. Bring back to room temperature before cooking.

Prepare the grill. Brush the chicken with the butter. Cook the chicken on the hot grill breast side up so the seasonings don't fall off. Cover the grill and cook the chicken for 50 minutes, until the skin is crisp and the thickest part of the chicken reaches an internal temperature of 165 degrees on a meat thermometer.

If foregoing grilling for roasting, preheat oven to 400 degrees and bake the chicken on a rimmed baking sheet until the thickest part of the chicken reaches an internal temperature of 165 degrees on a meat thermometer, about 50 minutes, without turning. If the skin is not crispy, move the chicken under the broiler to crisp and brown the skin, watching carefully so that it doesn't burn. Let rest 10 minutes for the heat to rise.

To serve, cut up the center of the chicken through the breastbone. Cut each half into 2 pieces. Move to a platter and serve hot. This can be made ahead and reheated, but it loses some of its crispness.

ROASTED (BAKED) CHICKEN

Serves 4

THE EASIEST WAY TO ROAST CHICKEN *is to rub the skin with butter or oil, throw it into a hot or cold oven, roast it at 425 or so until the meat hits 165 degrees, and pull it out and eat it. I do this when life is frantic. But a perfect roasted chicken is another question altogether. A perfect roasted chicken has a crisp skin, a moist, tender breast, drumsticks and thighs that are so flavorful they make one want to jump up and down in praise, and a backbone with its "oysters" there for the discerning (I've always called it "the cook's treat"). I'm fondest of small chickens, but this method works for up to a 5-pound chicken, as well as for Cornish hens, adjusting the roasting times accordingly and cooking until the thickest part of the leg registers 165 degrees on a meat thermometer.*

1 (2½–3½ pound) roasting chicken
2 tablespoons oil or melted butter, cook's preference
3 or 4 sprigs rosemary, thyme or marjoram
1 lemon, pricked all over with a fork
4 carrots, peeled, optional
2 cups chicken stock or broth, optional

Preheat oven to 400 degrees.

If a crispy skin is imperative, leave chicken uncovered in the refrigerator overnight to dry the skin. If possible, remove the chicken from the refrigerator 30 minutes before cooking. If the chicken is cold when placed in the oven, it will take longer to cook. Carefully insert a few fingers under the skin of the chicken wherever it seems willing to part with the flesh, to burst the membrane attaching the skin to the flesh. The skin will collapse against the flesh and will become crisper when cooked. Take special care to keep the skin intact when at the breast and going in from the backbone to the thigh and leg. (In Ethiopia and some other countries, this is done by blowing air in with a reed or straw.)

Gently brush the outside of the chicken with the oil or melted butter. Insert rosemary, thyme or marjoram and the lemon in the cavity. Move the carrots to a roasting pan just larger than the chicken and place in a crosswise fashion to create a rack that will keep the chicken slightly elevated to aid in browning the skin on the sides. Move the chicken on top of the carrots. Add a bit of stock to the pan to keep the juices from burning.

Roast breast side up until the skin begins to brown (35 to 40 minutes). Turn the chicken breast side down with tongs or two large spoons, and continue baking 15 to 20 minutes to brown the bottom skin. Turn the chicken again breast side up and continue to cook until the thickest part of the leg measures 165 degrees on a meat thermometer. Remove from oven and turn upside down to let the juices run to the breast and rest 10 minutes before carving (facing). The temperature of the meat will continue to rise as it rests.

Discard the carrots. Add the stock to the juices in the pan and bring to the boil, stirring to get all the goodness off the bottom and sides of the pan. Let boil down until loosely thickened. Skim off any undesired fat (pages 111–12) and pour into a gravy boat and, serve with the chicken.

Variation: Stuff herbs or sliced lemon under the skin of the chicken (page 376).

Variation: Roasted Chicken on Vegetables

3 pounds fingerling potatoes, halved lengthwise
2 tablespoons chopped fresh rosemary
2 chopped garlic cloves
1 pound carrots, cut into fingerling-sized lengths
1/4 cup oil, cook's preference
Salt
Freshly ground black pepper

Toss all ingredients until well coated in oil. Season to taste with salt and pepper, and move the vegetables into a roasting pan with sides. Position the chicken breast side up on top of some of the vegetables, the vegetables forming a rack for the chicken. Roast as above, tossing the potatoes occasionally and basting the chicken with the pan juices.

CARVING A CHICKEN

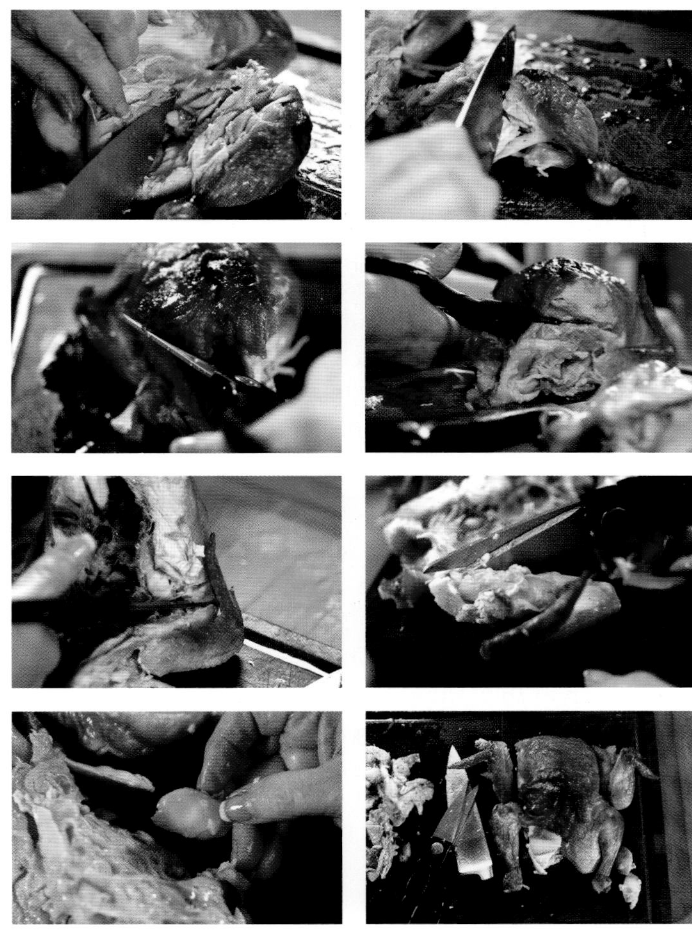

Place the chicken on a clean board or surface and hold the chicken firmly with one hand. Cut the skin between the leg and the breast to separate the leg from the body using a sharp knife. Pressing the flat of the knife against the carcass, using the other hand to grab the leg and bend it back until the bone breaks away from the carcass. Slide the knife around the leg joint, cutting down toward the tail of the chicken, keeping the knife between the oyster (that succulent little piece of meat sitting in the middle of the lower back) and the backbone. The leg is now separated from the carcass with the oyster attached. Remove the other leg in the same manner. For full servings with some of the breast attached to each wing, make a 45-degree cut with a knife or scissors diagonally across the breast, through the bone, to below the wing. Pull the wing and its breast piece away from the backbone. Repeat with the other wing. Pull off the remaining breast meat in 1 or 2 pieces, leaving the ribs and backbone. Divide the legs by cutting through the joint, leaving a portion of the thigh attached to the drumstick. Reassemble on a serving platter to look like an uncarved whole chicken.

An alternate way to serve the breast and wings is to cut the wings at the joints attached to the body of the chicken. Use a knife to wedge one side of the chicken breast off the bone; repeat with the second side.

A third way is to use the scissors to make a diamond of the breasts. Starting from the bottom, make a diagonal cut through the delicate small bones surrounding the breasts. Halfway up, reverse the slant and cut to the pulley bone (or wishbone), a tougher bone. Give a vigorous cut. Repeat on the other side of the breast. (Many people snip the pulley bone before roasting the chicken, as they do a duck, but in my family we use it to see who gets the longer piece and avoids doing the dishes.)

FINGER-LICKING JERK SKILLET CHICKEN WINGS AND SWEET POTATOES

Serves 4

EVERYTHING IN THIS RECIPE *is tasty eaten with the fingers, so put out the paper plates and napkins. The children will love it and not even realize it is good for them!*

Slices of zucchini and okra do equally well in this recipe. My husband and I were married in Jamaica, and jerk chicken was served at our wedding. While there is a Caribbean influence in the coastal areas of the South, jerk seasoning was not prominently used here until the mid-'80s.

8 chicken wings, little tips removed
1 1/2 tablespoons Jamaican Jerk Seasoning (page 670)
1 tablespoon oil, cook's preference
2 tablespoons butter
1 or 2 sweet potatoes, thinly sliced
1/4 cup all-purpose flour
Salt
Freshly ground black pepper
2–4 zucchini, peeled and sliced, or 1 pound okra, sliced or slivered

Pat the chicken dry with paper towels. Line a rimmed baking sheet with paper towels. Rub the chicken with jerk seasoning.

Heat the oil and butter over medium heat in a 10- or 12-inch heavy skillet or large Dutch oven until it shimmers. Add the chicken skin side down and cook 8 to 10 minutes on one side, until deep brown from the heat and spices. Turn the chicken pieces with tongs, and cook the second side an additional 8 to 10 minutes, until browned and the thickest part of the chicken registers 165 degrees on a meat thermometer. Remove chicken to paper towels to drain and keep warm.

Add sweet potatoes to the residual hot fat in the pan and cook 2 to 3 minutes per side, until golden brown. (They'll puff up a bit and may have darker, delicious sweet spots.) Remove and add to sheet pan with chicken.

Toss flour, salt, and pepper to taste together in a medium bowl, and toss in zucchini or okra. Shake to remove excess flour and add to hot pan and cook 2 minutes, turn, and continue to cook on second side 1 to 2 minutes. Remove to the paper towels. Return the wings and sweet potatoes to the hot pan, cover, and reheat quickly just a few minutes. Top with the fried vegetable and serve hot from the skillet.

LEMON-ROSEMARY CHICKEN

Serves 6

CYNTHIA AND I LAUGH *about and love this recipe. When she and Cliff were married in Rome, I offered to cook dinner the night before for the wedding couple, Pat Conroy, the best man, and his then wife, Lenore, and me as maid of honor. Unknown to me before I arrived in Rome, Lenore had invited nearly a hundred people. They had a very large, high-ceilinged apartment in a beautiful section of Rome, but the kitchen had a typical small European wall oven. I had planned to serve three kinds of birds—chickens, Cornish hens, and quail. So we went to the market and purchased a big quantity of all of them. I spatchcocked and broiled them, thinking they would cook faster in the small oven. They would have, if the oven hadn't kept knocking out the fuse. We got them all ready, somehow, and had a wonderful party on the rooftop, with stars shining in a midnight blue sky.*

Whether butterflied (spatchcocked) or split, this is a memorable way of cooking chicken that is very hard to top. Leftover roasted chicken is good cold, used in salads or added to casseroles—but not reheated.

1 whole chicken, about 3 1/2–4 pounds
Juice of 1 lemon
1/2 tablespoon oil, cook's preference
1 tablespoon chopped fresh rosemary, divided
1/4 cup butter
Salt
Freshly ground black pepper

Preheat oven to 425 degrees.

Spatchcock the chicken (see below) then move to a roasting pan. Whisk together lemon juice, oil, and 2 teaspoons rosemary and drizzle over chicken. Place foil over chicken and move a heavy weight (such as a marble slab or a heavy pan with a brick) on top of the chicken so it becomes flat and level. Refrigerate for several hours or overnight.

When ready to cook, remove the weight and foil. Melt butter and brush over chicken. Season to taste with salt and pepper. Move to oven and bake until the thickest part of the flesh registers 165 degrees on a meat thermometer. Remove from oven and let sit for 10 minutes before cutting down the breastbone. Garnish with remaining rosemary.

Variations: Purchase "split" chicken—usually two halves of a chicken in a package.

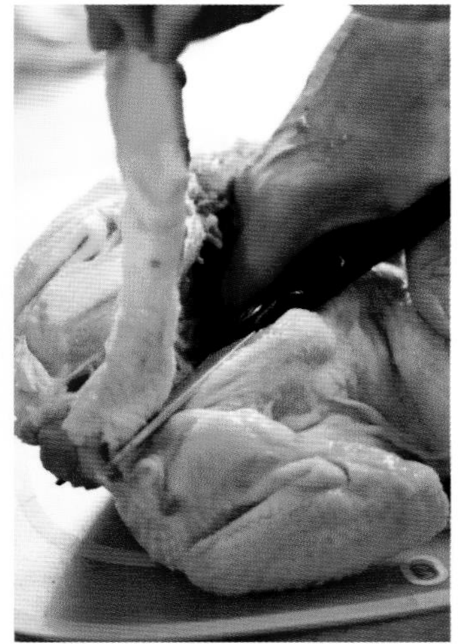

SPATCHCOCKING

To spatchcock poultry, move it to a cutting board, breast side down. Split the hen by cutting down either side of the backbone and remove it (save for stock, page 113). Turn the chicken over and press down on the sternum with the heel of one hand until it snaps. Crack the hen on either side of the breastbone by pressing down until it will lie flat.

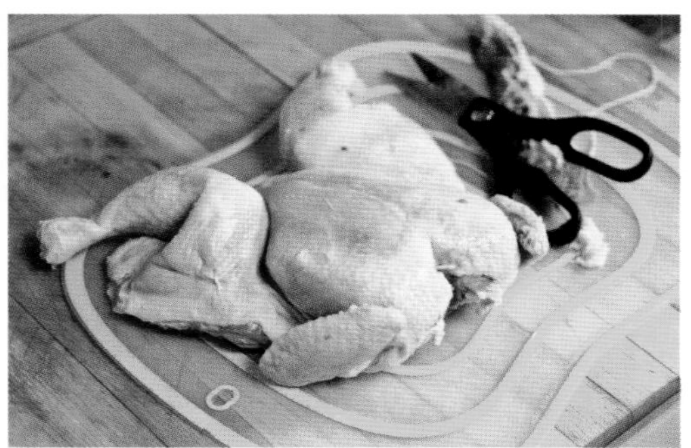

CHICKEN AND RICE PILAU

Serves 4

Pronounced purloo, *this incredible pilau is from* Two Hundred Years of Charleston Cooking, *by Blanche Rhett.*

1 roasting chicken (about $3^1/_2$–4 pounds), or cut-up chicken
$^1/_2$ cup butter, divided
1–2 teaspoons curry powder
3–4 cups cooked rice
Salt
Freshly ground black pepper

Preheat oven to 375 degrees.

Rub the chicken with half of the butter. Move chicken to a roasting pan several inches larger all around than the chicken.

Mix the curry powder with a cup of water and pour around the chicken in the pan. Move the chicken to the oven and check every 15 minutes, adding more water as needed. Baste the chicken with the water. After 30 to 45 minutes, the chicken should be brown but not fully cooked. Remove the roasting pan and chicken from the oven and set the chicken aside on a plate.

Stir the rice into the pan juices (there should be 2 cups; if not, add more water) along with the remaining butter. Spread over the pan so it will form a nice crust. Replace the chicken, cover the roasting pan, and return to the oven. When the rice has a brown crust on the bottom and the chicken is cooked to 165 degrees on a thermometer, remove the chicken to a platter and smother it in the rice, putting the crisp, brown crust on top. Season to taste with salt and pepper. Carve the chicken (page 367) as it is served with the rice. It is best served right away but can be wrapped, refrigerated, and reheated. It will lose its crisp crustiness.

Variation: Add 1 cup each of almonds and raisins to the rice, omit the curry powder, season with black pepper and add 1 to 2 chopped onions. Cook 4 or 5 slices of bacon and add to the rice.

TO TRUSS OR NOT TO TRUSS

I was trained to truss a chicken and did it that way for many years. But that was before these big-breasted chickens came on the market. In trussing, one is to pull the legs down and tie them together. It is much easier to get the interior of the thigh when it is trussed. It is also easier to carve.

CHICKEN BOG

Serves 6 to 8

Chicken Bog is a comfort food *for those who ate it sitting at their mother's kitchen table. As comforting and memory-evoking as it is, it has a less than illustrious name. A bog is slightly squishy underfoot, a good place to raise cranberries, cloudberries, and a few other things, chickens not being among them. Its name is applied because it is neither a soup nor a stew, but a moist, juicy dish in between the two. It originated in South Carolina, where the boggy nature of the Pee Dee River could be the source of the name.*

6 cups chicken stock or broth
4 cups shredded cooked chicken
1 cup uncooked rice, preferably Carolina Gold or long grain
Salt
1–2 tablespoons ground black pepper
2 tablespoons butter
3 tablespoons chopped fresh parsley

Bring the stock to the boil in a pot along with the 4 cups of chicken. Stir in rice, salt, and pepper, and reduce heat to a simmer. Simmer uncovered, gently, until rice is tender and broth has thickened, stirring occasionally. The bog should be thick and moist enough that when pressed with a heavy spoon there will be liquid. Remove from heat and stir in butter. Garnish with parsley. Serve hot. The bog refrigerates for 1 or 2 days, or freezes up to 3 months. Reheat in microwave or over gentle heat.

CHICKEN AND PEPPER DUMPLINGS

Serves 8

CHICKEN AND DUMPLINGS *is the ultimate belly warmer for hungry souls. Everything may be cooked ahead except the dumplings, which should be prepared when the chicken is ready to be reheated and served. The pepper in the dumplings is a nice surprise.*

1 whole chicken, about 3–4 pounds
4 cups chicken stock or broth
1 hot pepper, whole
1 large carrot, chopped
1 large onion, quartered
1 cup milk
Salt
Freshly ground black pepper

Move the chicken to a large Dutch oven. Add the chicken stock and vegetables, cover, and bring to the boil. Reduce the heat and simmer until the chicken is tender, 1½ hours.

Remove the chicken from the pot and set to cool. Remove the vegetables and discard. Skim the fat off the broth and boil down until tasty. When chicken is cool, remove the meat and tear into bite-size slivers, discarding the skin and bones. Return chicken to the broth and set aside while making the dumplings. The dish may be done ahead to this point, refrigerated or frozen, and reheated later. Fifteen minutes before serving, add the milk and bring to the boil. Taste for seasoning, add salt and pepper as desired, and then add the dumpling mixture. Cover, reduce heat, and simmer 10 minutes. The dumplings will swell and break up a bit. Serve hot from the pot.

DUMPLINGS

1¼ cup all-purpose flour
1 teaspoon baking powder
1 teaspoon salt
1 tablespoon freshly ground black pepper
¼ cup shortening
⅓ cup milk

To make the dumplings, combine the flour, baking powder, salt, and pepper. Cut in the shortening with two forks or a pastry blender until it resembles coarse meal. Add the milk to make a very soft dough. Drop the dumplings, 1 teaspoonful at a time, into the boiling chicken broth.

WHOLE CHICKEN

My favorite chicken is a whole chicken, preferably a small one, close to 3 pounds. It can be turned with no stress; the breast is small enough to enable the whole chicken to cook fairly evenly; and the ratio of skin to flesh is such that the skin adds flavor and dimension to all of the chicken. The bone is closer to the meat, adding its goodness as well. Life is not perfect, however, and we must cook what is available. When cooking a large chicken, it will take longer, and should be cooked at a lower temperature so the skin doesn't burn and the breast overcook.

CHICKEN POT PIE

Serves 4 to 6

Chicken pot pie is quintessentially Southern, *incorporating all sorts of textures and flavors in an exciting yet comforting way. The golden roux gives a nutty flavor to the pie. The better the crust, the better the sauce, the better the pie. But I have successfully used ready-to-roll piecrusts, puff pastry, and prebaked chicken. This should be done in stages whenever possible; cook the chicken up to 2 days ahead; cook the peppers and sauce up to 2 days ahead; roll out the piecrust several hours to a day before serving. The term* pot pie *started appearing in the early 1800s.*

1 recipe Basic Piecrust (page 507)
1 whole chicken, about 3 pounds
2 carrots, sliced
2 medium onions, divided (one is quartered and one is sliced)
1 teaspoon chopped fresh thyme
Small bunch parsley stalks
6 peppercorns
2 red bell peppers or (1 green, 1 red), cored, seeded, sliced thinly
5 tablespoons butter, divided
1 cup sliced mushrooms
2 garlic cloves, chopped
5 tablespoons all-purpose flour
1/3 cup tablespoons heavy cream
Salt
Freshly ground black pepper
1 large egg
1 tablespoon water

Roll the pastry out on a floured board into a round piece 1/8-inch thick and 3 inches wider than a 9- or 10-inch deep-dish pie pan, preferably with a ridge. Cut off 1 (1-inch) strip from the circumference of the round. Put strip aside. Cut out decorations from any excess pastry: leaves, flowers, and so forth. Wrap and chill until ready to use.

To cook the chicken and make the stock, remove any excess fat from the chicken. Place the chicken in a large pot and cover with water. Add the carrots, 1 quartered onion, the herbs, and peppercorns. Bring to the boil then turn down to a simmer. Simmer partially covered until the thickest part of the chicken registers 165 degrees on a meat thermometer, about 1 to 1 1/2 hours. Remove the chicken to cool. Strain the stock and return it to the pot; discard the solids. Bring the stock back to the boil and cook until reduced to 1 1/2 cups. Skim fat from the stock by chilling in the refrigerator and spooning off, or removing with ice cubes, or running a paper towel across the top. Set aside. After the chicken has cooled, remove the meat off the bones and shred into bite-size pieces.

Bring a small pot of water to the boil and blanch the peppers in the boiling water for just a few minutes. Drain. Meanwhile, melt 2 tablespoons butter, add 1 sliced onion and cook a few minutes; add the mushrooms and garlic and cook for several minutes, until tender.

Melt the remaining 3 tablespoons butter in a separate pan then add the flour. Stir together until smooth, and then cook slowly until a deep golden color. Add the broth and bring to the boil. Add the cream and cook rapidly to a thick, syrupy consistency. Remove from the heat and add the shredded chicken, peppers, and mushrooms. Season with salt and pepper and cool sufficiently that the crust doesn't melt. Ladle into the pie dish. Clean the rim of the dish.

Dip a finger into water and run it along the rim of the pie dish to dampen. To keep the crust of the pie from caving into the pie dish, place 1-inch strip of pastry around the rim. Dampen strip with water. Move the round of pastry on top. Press down with two fingers to push the two doughs together, and flute all around the rim. Remove excess dough with a sharp upright knife, slicing away from the pie, using the pie plate as a guide. Make a 1-inch hole in the center for the steam to escape.

Prepare a glaze by mixing the egg with water. Brush the dough with the glaze. Add any decorations, setting aside at least one to cover the hole. Brush the top and decorations with glaze. Bake the pie on a rimmed baking sheet to collect any drippings that may bubble over while it cooks. Move extra decorations to a piece of waxed paper, foil or parchment paper on the pan next to the piecrust for easy removal, as they will take less time to cook.

After 15 minutes, turn the heat down to 350 degrees, checking to see if the decorations need to be removed, and bake 25 to 30 minutes more, until the dough is puffed and brown. When the pie is done, remove from oven, cover the hole with the reserved decoration, and let the pie cool a few minutes to make it easier to serve. The first piece may not come out very prettily, particularly if the crust is too hot.

PAN-FRIED CHICKEN LIVERS WITH CARAMELIZED ONIONS AND COUNTRY HAM

Serves 4

CHICKEN LIVERS FROM CYNTHIA'S CHILDHOOD *were always eaten with caramelized onion. Country ham takes this dish over the top. Note that the onions are already cooked, as the livers cook so quickly.*

- 2 cups chicken livers (about 1 pound)
- 1/2 cup all-purpose flour
- 1 teaspoon salt
- 1 teaspoon freshly ground black pepper
- 2 tablespoons oil, cook's preference
- 6 ounces thinly sliced country ham, optional
- Caramelized Onions (page 220)

Preheat oven to 350 degrees.

Trim any fat or sinew from the chicken livers. Rinse under cold water, and leave in a bowl of cold water for 5 minutes to remove any residual blood. Remove the livers from the water and move them to paper towels to drain. Any excess water will splatter when the chicken livers are moved to the hot oil.

Toss the flour, salt, and black pepper on a piece of waxed paper. Dust the chicken livers with the seasoned flour, making certain to cover them completely so there are no wet spots showing. Shake off any excess flour so it does not burn in the pan.

Heat the oil over medium heat in a 10- or 12-inch heavy skillet or large Dutch oven until it shimmers. Gently add the livers to the hot oil. They will spit and spatter in the oil. Cover with a lid or spatter guard. Sauté them on one side for 1 to 2 minutes, until golden. Uncover the pan, flip the livers over and shake the pan. If all of the oil has been absorbed, add a little more, 1 teaspoon at a time.

Move the livers to a rimmed baking sheet and bake in the preheated oven 3 to 4 minutes, or until they are firm and their centers are cooked through. While the livers are baking, sauté the ham until the edges curl up. Add the Caramelized Onions to the frying pan to reheat while the livers are baking.

When ready to serve, remove the livers from the oven. Move them to a plate and arrange the ham around them. Mound the onions in the center.

TURKEY WITH GRAVY

Serves 8 to 10

I RARELY COOK A TURKEY LARGER THAN 14 POUNDS *and find it easier to roast two smaller ones than one larger one. My reasoning is that a large turkey takes longer to cook, is more difficult for the home cook to handle, and is difficult to store. Using two small turkeys allows for one of them to be roasted and carved ahead of time, even the night before, and one to be the "show piece" on the table. The carved turkey takes up less space in the refrigerator, and there are all those wonderful bones for stock.*

Carving a turkey at the table is a needlessly difficult task; it should be done in the kitchen. The "show" turkey can be carved up after the meal for leftovers. Rather than stuff the turkey, which also contributes to a dry breast, I flavor it with an onion, carrot, and a few herbs placed in the cavity. If fresh herbs are not available, omit them. If a rack is not available, the onions and carrots can form a resting place for the turkey. I add stock to keep the bottom from burning and to ensure a scrumptious gravy. This creates a bit of steam, so take care when opening and closing the oven.

1 (12- to 14-pound) turkey, fresh or thawed
3 onions, quartered, divided
3 carrots, divided
Chopped fresh herbs to taste, such as rosemary, sage, thyme, optional
1/2 cup melted butter or oil, cook's preference
4–6 cups turkey or chicken stock or broth
Salt
Freshly ground black pepper
1/2–1 cup heavy cream, optional

Preheat oven to 450 degrees.

Defrost turkey, if frozen, in the refrigerator, which may take several days. Unwrap fresh or frozen turkeys for several hours in the refrigerator to crisp the skin. Oil a large roasting pan and rack, if using, and set aside.

Clean the turkey of any parts at the neck or the cavity. Add half the onions and carrots with the herbs to the cavity of the turkey. If using a rack, put the remaining vegetables underneath in the roasting pan. If not, put the carrots in the center of the pan, with the onions surrounding them. Tie the turkey's legs together, and move to the rack or on top of the vegetables in the prepared pan. Brush turkey with butter or oil, particularly the breast. Add enough stock to come 1 to 2 inches up the sides of the turkey. Turn the turkey breast side down and roast for 1 hour. Open the door carefully to remove the turkey from the oven, watching out for steam. If the stock has boiled down to less than 1 inch up the sides, add enough to bring it up to 2 inches. Turn the turkey breast side up and return it to the oven and roast for 1 hour more. Cover with foil if browning too much.

Remove the turkey and check for doneness. An instant-read thermometer inserted in the thigh should read 165 degrees; or the juices should run clear when a knife is inserted into the flesh of the thigh. Let stand 30 minutes before carving. There will be some wonderful pan juices. If the juices seem fatty, skim off the fat with a paper towel or use a fat separator (page 345). Add any remaining stock to the pan. Move the pan to a burner and bring the juices to the boil over high heat, stirring constantly, and boil down to reduce until rich and flavorful. Season to taste with salt and pepper. Use the juices alone as a light sauce, or make traditional gravy (facing). For a richer sauce, add the cream and boil until thick.

A good instant-read thermometer is a must for judging accurately when a turkey is done.

Rubbing a defrosted turkey with 1 tablespoon salt per 5 pounds of turkey 2 or 3 days in advance and massaging with the salt a couple of times a day will result in a tastier turkey. In addition, leaving the turkey out of the oven for an hour to let get to room temperature before baking and allowing the skin to dry out a bit, in the refrigerator or out, will result in a crisper skin.

TRADITIONAL TURKEY GRAVY

Makes 4 cups

Making gravy at the last minute *is maddening and unnecessary. I make my gravy the night before Thanksgiving from the juices of the extra turkey (facing). I keep it refrigerated covered, and reheat it in the microwave. If there aren't enough juices, boil up some of those extra turkey bones to make additional stock. See the Amber Turkey Stock recipe (page 116) if an additional turkey is not available, and make ahead so that there will be sufficient stock to make enough gravy. Both stock and gravy freeze well.*

4 tablespoons fat from the pan juices, divided
Giblets, cut up, optional
4 tablespoons flour
2–3 cups turkey or chicken stock or broth, degreased (page 345)
1 cup heavy cream, optional, divided
Salt
Freshly ground black pepper

Heat 3 tablespoons of the fat in a 2-quart saucepan over high heat. Add the giblets if using, and brown. Stir in the flour and let turn a light brown to make a roux, stirring. Stir in the stock, and continue to stir or whisk until boiling and thickened. If it is lumpy, strain it and return to the pan. If using the cream, add half to the hot pan and whisk over heat until thickened and reduced. (It is okay to boil the cream, provided the pan is a sufficient size to hold stock and cream.) Taste and add more cream if desired, return to the boil, and boil until reduced slightly. Season to taste with salt and pepper. Cover with plastic wrap to prevent a skin from forming on the top of the gravy. Refrigerate up to 3 days or freeze. Reheat in microwave or on stovetop.

SINFUL DUMPLING GRAVY

Serves about 8

Leftover turkey stock makes the most homey, *flavorful gravy and dumplings anyone can imagine. People that eat this are catapulted into a comfort zone. A wonderful Sunday-night supper.*

4 cups turkey or chicken stock, or 1 cup butter
Salt
Freshly ground black pepper
1 recipe Dumplings (page 371)
1 cup milk

Bring stock to the boil in a large heavy pot. Add butter and season to taste with salt and pepper.

Meanwhile, prepare the dumplings. Drop the dumplings by rounded tablespoons into boiling stock. Reduce heat to simmer, cover, and cook about 5 minutes, turning dumplings as needed, until they have swelled up through the stock and are puffy and cooked through. Stir in the milk. Bring back to the boil and serve hot. Try to avoid swooning.

ROASTED CORNISH HENS

Serves 6

I LOVE PREPARING THIS *when the lemons are full and lush on my trees and the rosemary in my garden reaches several feet high. This ideal combination of goodness can be duplicated in chickens (page 352) as well as Cornish hens, but it has more of an impact on the smaller bird. A whole Cornish hen is too much food for some people, myself included. But skimpy portions can be embarrassing when serving guests. I roast an extra hen for every few people, and then cut the extras in quarters, available for second (or third!) helpings. More marinade is not needed for one or two extra birds.*

Several things make it better than average. One is loosening the hen's skin and pushing the stuffing under it, which aids in crisping the skin and intensifying the taste of the hen.

4–6 tablespoons oil, cook's preference
1 cup fresh lemon juice
3 tablespoons chopped fresh rosemary, divided
4–6 Cornish hens (1–2 pounds each), split
1/4 cup breadcrumbs
16 ounces ricotta cheese
4 tablespoons grated lemon rind, no white attached
8 garlic cloves, chopped
Salt
Freshly ground black pepper
3–5 cups chicken stock or broth

Preheat oven to 400 degrees.

Mix together the oil, lemon juice, and half the rosemary. Marinate the hens, skin side down, overnight or as long as possible.

Toss together the breadcrumbs, ricotta, lemon rind, remaining rosemary, and garlic. Season to taste with salt and pepper. Gently slide fingers under the skin of each chicken to release the skin from the surface. Spread the mixture evenly underneath the skins of the chickens. Season the hens' surface with salt and pepper. Move the hens to a rack over a rimmed baking sheet to catch the drippings. Drizzle with lemon juice and move to the refrigerator uncovered to dry the skin for an hour or so.

Distribute the hens skin side up, without overlapping each other, in a baking pan, and roast 1 hour. Check and turn birds as needed to brown all over. The hens are cooked when the thickest part of the meat registers 165 degrees on an instant-read thermometer. Remove from the pan. (Hens may be done ahead to this point and later reheated under a broiler until crisp.) Degrease the juices with a paper towel, by skimming, or by using a specialty cup (page 345).

To make a sauce, add the stock to the pan and bring to the boil, stirring the sides and bottom to deglaze (page 357) the pan. Bring to the boil again and boil until reduced to 1/2 cup per bird, tasting occasionally until flavorful, about 20 minutes. I prefer this sauce without further thickening, but if desired, thicken with flour dissolved in water. Add some of the stock to the flour/water mixture, whisk until smooth, then pour the mixture into the pan and stir over heat until it comes back to the boil. Moisten the birds and pass the remainder of the sauce.

CORNISH HENS

Cornish hens are an immature hybrid from the Cornish chicken, developed in the mid-1950s for their breasts and size. Five or six weeks old, weighing about two pounds ready to cook, even though they are called hens, they can be either male or female. Names include Rock Cornish hens, poussin, Cornish hen, and Cornish chicken. Cook as with any chicken, adjusting for size.

STUFFING UNDER THE SKIN

North Carolinian Richard Olney was a brilliant chef, writer, and editor. His adaptation of a famous old French recipe of stuffing truffles under the skin of a chicken is adapted to ingredients more available for the home cook, such as sliced lemons, grated zucchini, onions, cream cheese, eggs, basil, and garlic. Heavenly! In the early 1970s, Richard Olney's sister-in-law, Judith, brought his recipes for stuffing poultry under the skin to the South, where she taught cooking classes.

FRIED QUAIL

Serves 2

IF THERE IS ANYTHING BETTER THAN FRIED CHICKEN, *it would be fried quail. In fact, learning to fry quail is a help in learning how to fry chicken. My husband and I can each eat two quails for supper. To use as a starter, quarter after cooking and pass on small plates, or serve just the legs without a plate but with plenty of napkins.*

1 cup buttermilk
Hot sauce to taste, optional
4 quail
1 cup all-purpose flour
Salt
Freshly ground black pepper
Ground hot red pepper
Shortening or vegetable oil for frying
1/4 cup apple-cider vinegar

Pour buttermilk into a container with a cover or a plastic ziplock bag, and add hot sauce as desired. Split each quail in half, cutting down the backbone and breastbone. Move the quail to the bag and marinate 30 minutes or overnight.

Toss the flour, salt, black pepper, and hot red pepper on a piece of waxed paper. Using the fingers of one hand, move the quail pieces individually from the buttermilk to the flour, pressing the quail lightly into the flour. Turn and press as needed to fully coat the pieces. Shake off any additional flour.

Fill an electric frying pan with enough shortening to cover the quail but no more than half full, and heat to 350 degrees. Add the floured quail skin side down and fry, turning once, until crispy and browned and fork-tender.

Combine the vinegar with hot sauce as desired and serve with the hot quail.

The native wild quail in the South is the bobwhite. The Pharaoh quail is European in origin but is now commercially raised in South Carolina. Sold frozen, it is usually available four to a package.

The quail brought home by hunters has been skinned in the field, so a bit of hot sauce bumps up the flavor.

Variations: Serve with Lazy Corn Fritters (page 464).

Variation: Grilled or Broiled Quail
Remove quail from the buttermilk as above and move to a hot grill, skin side down. Season well with salt and plenty of freshly ground pepper. Cook 6 to 8 minutes, turn to the other side, and cook another 5 minutes, until the juices run clear. Remove from grill and baste with Hot Pepper Jelly (page 648) or Muscadine Sauce (page 666), or equal parts of bourbon and apricot jam before serving.

Variation: Herbed Quail
Omit soaking. Mix together 1 tablespoon each chopped fresh rosemary and thyme with 2 tablespoons oil. Rub onto each piece of quail. Season to taste with salt and pepper. Heat a heavy skillet with 1 tablespoon oil until it shimmers. Dry and add split quails and cook until brown, 6 to 8 minutes. Turn the birds over and cook another 5 to 8 minutes, until it registers 165 on an instant read thermometer.

DUCKLING WITH MINT AND LEMON

Serves 2

One of my neighbors is raising ducks, *which are very happy here in the Lowcountry and legal for backyards in Charleston. The major ducks for roasting are Peking and Muscovy, with Peking being most available frozen in our grocery stores and Asian markets, should a backyard duck not be in the works. Duck reheats very well, both in a hot oven and if crisping the skin under the broiler, so is a good fix-ahead dish. It does not need to be baked on a rack.*

Wild ducks are nowhere near as fatty, and their taste depends on where they were caught and what they ate, so I recommend moist-heat methods for those (see Braising, page 415). It's really important to remove the fat as it accumulates while cooking, as oven fires are dangerous.

Because domestic ducks and geese seem larger than they are, many people over-anticipate the number of people it serves. One duck is a little too much for two people and a bit too little for four. Leftover duck makes a fabulous salad.

1 duckling (5–6 pounds)
2 1/2 cups whole mint or lemon balm sprigs, divided
Juice and grated rind of 2 lemons, no white attached, divided
Salt
Freshly ground black pepper
1/2 cup duck stock (page 113)

Defrost duck overnight in the refrigerator.

Preheat oven to 500 degrees. Lightly oil a roasting pan large enough to hold the duck and several cups of fat.

When duck is defrosted, pull out any visible large pieces of fat from the cavity. Set aside to render at a later time. Wipe the inside and outside with paper towels to remove any excess moisture. Snip out the wishbone with scissors if desired, for easier carving later (facing).

Insert 1 1/2 cups whole sprigs of the herbs into the cavity, along with half of the grated rind. Tie the legs together with kitchen twine and snip off the end of the wing tips. The duck wing, like the chicken wing, has three parts. Remove the wing tip if present; removing the second bone is optional. Always cut right at the joint—wiggle the wing to find the joint. Move the duck to the prepared pan. Prick the skin with a large kitchen carving fork, but avoiding bruising the flesh. Salt the duck just before moving it to the oven; if it sits before cooking, it will extrude water, which will deter the browning. Cook 20 minutes.

Remove the duck from the oven and move to a steady surface. Ladle or spoon out the fat into a non-plastic bowl and reserve it for another time. Turn the duck onto one side in the pan. Reduce oven heat to 400 degrees and return the duck to the oven. Cook 20 minutes more, remove, and ladle or spoon out any fat. Turn duck onto its other side and cook another 20 minutes. For the last 20 minutes, after removing fat as above, turn the duck breast side up, and roast until the skin is brown and crisp and the thigh is tender when pierced with a fork (and the thermometer registers 170 at the thigh). The duck may be refrigerated at this point, to be reheated later.

To make the sauce, remove as much fat as possible from the roasting pan, leaving just the hard bits and a light coating of fat. Move the pan over medium-high heat, pour in 1/2 cup duck stock (page 113), and bring to the boil, scraping up the bits from the bottom of the pan. Season to taste with salt and pepper, and strain. Chop the remaining mint or balm and add with the rest of the grated rind.

Since a duck serves only 2 people, it is cut on either side of the backbone, from tail to wishbone, and the backbone is removed. Remove the wishbone if not done already. Cut down the breastbone so the duck is in 2 pieces, each with a breast and leg. If desired, cut the legs away from the breast, but the presentation will not be as splashy. Cool if too hot to handle. Wrap a kitchen towel around the fingers of one hand and pull off the breastbone and rib cage to facilitate carving the duck. Reheat the duck on a rimmed baking sheet with sides (about 15 minutes under the broiler or in a 500-degree oven) until hot and crispy. Serve with the sauce. If four people are being served scantily, cut at the leg joints as well.

Variations:

- Substitute 1 lime for one of the lemons.
- Omit herbs and citrus. Baste with Muscadine Sauce (page 666) during the last 20 minutes of cooking.

Variation: Grilled Duck with Muscadine Sauce

I do love crispy duck, and grilling or broiling is a fabulous way to ensure this, as long as the cook is watchful and prevents burning. Care should be taken to catch any fat and prevent it from flaring up or burning. I am most comfortable grilling and broiling the duck in a pan with sufficient sides to catch the rendered fat and removing it periodically.

That said, there are people who cut out the backbone and move the duck skin side down, without pricking, to a slow to medium grill. Keep a spray bottle of water handy for any flare-ups. Cook until the skin is browned and crisp, then turn and cook on the other side. Brush occasionally with 1/2 cup Muscadine Sauce (page 666) or red currant jelly. Allow 45 minutes for the duck to cook over medium heat. If possible, avoid flare-ups and keep the lid on the grill. Test for doneness by cutting into the leg. I like mine a little pink. When the duck is done, remove from the grill to a cutting board. Follow serving directions on facing page.

Variation: Duck Breast Sandwich

Conrad Zimmerman of Charleston cooks duck breast on a burner in a duck blind when he goes duck hunting. I've never been duck hunting, so I cook mine in a civilized kitchen. Eat it, chasing with brandy, as Conrad does (especially when outdoors).

Melt 1/2 cup butter in a large heavy skillet. Cook 4 duck breasts skin side down until well-browned. Turn, season to taste with salt and pepper, and cook until barely pink inside. Sauté 8 slices of French or rye bread in the remaining fat. Serve each breast between 2 pieces of hot bread.

DUCK BREASTS WITH MUSHROOMS AND SOUR CREAM GRAVY

This recipe from Ben Moise, a former South Carolina Game Warden, is just as he wrote it. It's a hunter's way of doing, and the duck breasts are delicious.

"Breast out and skin any kind of duck breasts. Slip them into a heavy plastic ziplock bag and gently pound with the edge of a cutting board or kitchen mallet until they are fairly flattened. Carefully remove them from the bag, move to a bowl, cover with buttermilk, and refrigerate for three or four hours. Dry the flattened fillets and dredge in a mixture of flour, salt and pepper. Add a little touch of garlic powder or ground red pepper or both to the flour mix if desired. Fry in a pan with a little olive oil and butter at medium heat until the breasts are just browned. Mince a couple of cloves of garlic and finely chop one small onion. Sauté these in a pan with a little butter and olive oil and add around a cup of chopped shiitake mushrooms and stir for a bit. Then add a can of chicken broth and a little white wine, probably around a half a cup or so. Mash together with a stout fork about one quarter stick of cool butter, which has been cut into thin slices, with around two tablespoons of flour until it forms a paste and roll into a cylindrical shape and chill. This is called in the trade a French Roux. Reduce the cooking liquid down to just below half of what you started with and add the French Roux about a half an inch at the time, stirring well. When all is thickened stir in a small container of sour cream. Put in the duck breasts and bring up to heat for around 4 or 5 minutes, turning once. Carefully remove the duck breasts and put them on a plate upon a bed of rice and pour the remaining sauce over them. This is a lot easier than it sounds and is a pleasant departure from the usual fare of grilled or roasted duck."

REMOVING THE WISHBONE

Take a scissors and go to the top of the neck. There is a long piece of flesh over the top of the wishbone. Snip the bone where it joins or cut out the wishbone altogether. It's worth it to make carving easier later.

DIXIE CASSOULET

Serves 15 to 20

THIS IS ADAPTED FROM A TRADITIONAL *French cold-weather dish, primarily beans with meat added. Our nutritious dried peas and beans are especially suited to this dish. It cooks, occasionally attended, for a few hours in the oven. Its aroma will drive everyone crazy with hunger all day. The beans melt in the mouth, sodden with stock and seasonings. Hundreds of recipes for cassoulet exist, and no two people agree, so there is no need to be totally dependent on the recipe. It is best made over several days with sporadic attention but can be made in three hours if necessary. A good stock is essential, as it is the stock that will enrich and enhance the flavor of the beans.*

Cassoulet, most likely the basis for the word "casserole," is traditionally baked in an earthenware pot and served with a gratin of breadcrumbs on the top. I use a sturdy enamel pot to make sure it doesn't cook too rapidly. It is easily made ahead and reheated, or frozen and reheated.

2 pounds dry field peas, black-eyed peas, lady peas, or other small peas
4 cups pork, duck, goose or other flavorful fat
6 large onions, chopped
1 fennel bulb
8 garlic cloves, finely chopped
2 quarts strong chicken, turkey, duck, or goose stock, preferably homemade
Salt
Freshly ground black pepper
1 cup finely chopped fresh parsley, divided
1/2 cup chopped fresh thyme, divided
3 tablespoons tomato purée
3 cups white wine (optional)
24 sweet Italian-style sausage links, pork or turkey
2 tablespoon coriander seeds
2 tablespoon fennel seeds
1–2 teaspoons cumin seeds
6 cups fresh breadcrumbs or panko

Soak the beans in water to cover overnight, or cover with water in a pan, bring to a boil, cover, and set aside for 1 hour. Drain the water. Meanwhile, melt enough of the fat in a large, heavy frying pan to cover the bottom of the pan. Add the chopped onions and cook until soft. Remove the exterior layer of the fennel—the stalky portions coming out from the bulb—and some of the fronds and set aside. Chop the bulb and add to the onions. Add the garlic a few minutes before completed. Add half the onions, fennel, and garlic mixture to the beans, and reserve the rest in the frying pan.

Cover the bean mixture with some of the stock in a heavy 6-quart pan; cover and cook over medium heat, stirring occasionally, until the beans are soft, about 1 1/2 to 2 hours. Add stock to cover as needed. When soft, season well with salt and pepper. Add half the parsley and half the thyme. Add the tomato purée along with the wine to the second half of the onion-garlic mixture still in the frying pan. Bring to the boil, and boil until reduced by half, just a few minutes.

Meanwhile, prick the sausage links and sauté in a little of the fat. Cut into fork-sized pieces and add to the tomato mixture along with half of the remaining parsley and thyme. Crush the coriander, fennel, and cumin seeds using a mortar and pestle or rolling pin. Season the tomato mixture with a portion of the crushed seeds, tasting as necessary. Add salt and freshly ground pepper to taste.

Add a portion of the crushed seeds to the beans, along with salt and pepper to taste.

Layer the beans and the tomato/sausage mixture in a 6-quart pan, starting with a third of the beans then half of the tomato/sausage mixture. Repeat, finishing with the last third of the beans. Taste again to be sure there is enough salt. Add stock to barely cover the beans.

Mix the breadcrumbs with remaining parsley and thyme. Layer the top of the casserole with a portion of the breadcrumbs. Dot with some of the fat.

Bake uncovered on a rimmed baking sheet to catch the drippings, in the middle of a 350-degree oven until the crumb gratin is golden brown. Push the gratin down into the beans with a large spoon. Cover again with a layer of the breadcrumb mixture. Dot with more fat. Return to oven. Repeat as often as desired, completing up to 8 gratins but no fewer than 2. Each gratin takes 30 to 60 minutes to be ready to be pushed into the beans. Be sure to taste after each gratin layer, adding any seasoning as desired. When ready, either leave in the oven to serve warm, or remove from the oven, let cool to moderate, and store covered in the refrigerator for 1 or 2 days, until ready to use. Several hours before serving, move the casserole to the countertop and let get to room temperature. Place on a baking sheet and reheat 1 hour or so. The cassoulet may be frozen when cool enough, and even reheated when frozen, which will obviously take a much longer time.

Variation: Fresh or frozen lady, white acre, and other field peas can be used to great effect. They do not need the presoaking.

FLAVORFUL FATS

The best-flavored fats are pork, duck, and goose. To use pork fat, thoroughly rinse salt pork or fatback and sauté briefly to render fat.

Duck and goose fat may remain from cooking, or can be purchased at specialty stores or online. To render the fat of ducks and geese, pull off any excess fat from the poultry. Put in a pan with water to cover, reduce heat, and simmer until water is boiled out; continue cooking without burning until fat is melted. Strain out any pieces of skin. Store refrigerated up to 1 month. This is delish for cooking potatoes and eggs and enhances any cooked food that uses bacon fat or lard.

MEATS

Gone with the Wind *opens with a lavish pork pit barbecue and a groaning table of its accoutrements. Pork has long been favored by Southerners for its flavor and versatility, and perhaps also because raising pigs didn't require much land and they were easy to feed. Every part of the pig was used, from the head to the tail. Vegetables were cooked with savory pieces of pork fat. Africans were skilled in using its fat for cooking and Europeans for preserving. This combined background brought high salting, seasoning, and smoking from bacon to country hams.*

The wealthy and those with access to grazing land for beef enjoyed it. But by and large, beef meant milk cows eaten only when no longer of service, the meat being cooked long and slow to get it tender. Some farmers were reluctant to deal with beef or give up any expensive land or energy to raise cattle. Consumption was much less than in other regions of the States, where grazing land was plentiful. But whether it was pan-fried steaks smothered in gravy, brisket, or tender veal on rare occasions, many Southerners liked their beef.

There are seven recipes for lamb in *The Virginia House-Wife*, but it has waned in popularity since WWII. Its staying power is in areas where it has historically had a stronger following than in the Deep South. Land available for game is dwindling. Where once squirrels and possums might have been a good portion of a stew, now they are more the source of tall tales and fireside stories. Venison is more readily found and relished, whether as game or farm-raised.

PORK

Pork has a long-established place in Southern cooking. The Spanish explorer Hernando de Soto brought the first pigs with him when he arrived at what is now Tampa Bay, Florida, in 1539. Thirteen pigs escaped their confines, never to be caught. These became the breeding stock that later produced the razorback and other feral pigs throughout the United States. In the early days of the colonies, pigs were kept on "Hog Island," a little island in the James River just across from Jamestown, Virginia, to provide natural confinement and prevent devastation of crops on the mainland. Native Americans showed the settlers how to smoke venison, and the settlers adapted this technique to pork. With the addition of the salting and curing techniques already in use by the colonists, country ham was born.

Hog-killing time came after the first true drop in temperature in the late fall to ensure it was cold enough to hang the meat. Most families slaughtered two pigs to put up a year's worth of meat, lard, and soap. Neighbors helped neighbors and children waited impatiently to be deemed old enough to participate. The entire pig was used in one way or another, and all the farm's resources were in use for several days—from the fires stoked to boil the huge vats of water for scalding, to every counter surface in the kitchen for sausage making.

John Egerton writes of hog-killing day in his *Southern Food: At Home, On the Road, and in History,* 1987:

> *On most Southern farms the first cold snap harkened the end of summer vegetables and the annual hog slaughter. Livers, cracklings and chitterlings (small intestines), were eaten immediately. Globs of hog fat were boiled in a gigantic black pot to be rendered into lard. Scraps of meat were ground up into sausages. Ribs were slowly steamed (as in the method recommended by Confederate general Stonewall Jackson, who oversaw the pork preparation for his men in gray). Sides of bacon, hog jowls, shoulders, and hams were cured in salt for weeks. Then they were hung in the smokehouse along with a variety of sausages, ham hocks, and knuckles to be smoked over hickory or pecan wood, peanut shells, or corncobs (known as meat cobs). Some farmers cured their meat with red pepper to prevent infestations of fly larvae in the era before refrigeration.*

COOKING TEMPERATURE FOR PORK

Although trichinosis is no longer a worry in the United States, doneness is more a matter of preference than concern. While rare pork is not beloved the way beef is, a pale, juicy pink interior is acceptable to most. Juiciness is dependent on not overcooking.

All meat should rest before carving to let the juices set. During that time, the meat will continue to rise in temperature, up to 10 degrees for larger pieces of meat. Thinner cuts cool quicker, just as they cook more quickly, and do not rise as much in temperature.

All sorts of pig breeds have come back into fashion and are being raised on boutique farms, catering to restaurants and other discerning customers, who may even want them to be fed peanuts to revive the marvelous meat of the past. Called "heirloom pigs," this new pork has better flavor than those raised in the last of the twentieth century, which were bred to have little fat and consequently lack flavor.

ROASTED PORK TENDERLOIN

Serves 2 to 3

TRUSSING A TENDERLOIN *prior to roasting (page 421) keeps the tenderloin's shape and leaves ridges, making it easier to slice. Lay the meat on the counter and tie at regular intervals. When reaching the thin tail, fold it up to make a thicker piece, and tie. The flesh knits together nicely during cooking. For home cooking, tying is only necessary when the meat needs to be beautifully sliced at intervals, as for a formal or restaurant presentation. Roast pork tenderloin 20 minutes per pound.*

1 pork tenderloin (approximately 1 pound)
2 tablespoons Dijon mustard
1 tablespoon oil, cook's preference
2 tablespoons butter
Salt
Freshly ground black pepper

Preheat oven to 400 degrees.

Trim the tenderloin of silver skin, fat, and membrane, removing the chain if desired (see below), and pat dry. Truss if desired. Rub with Dijon mustard.

Meanwhile, heat the oil and butter in a heavy pan until sizzling. Season the tenderloin to taste with salt and pepper, add quickly to the pan, and brown on the first side. Using tongs, turn and brown on the second side. Use the tongs to hold the meat and brown all over.

Move to an oiled roasting pan, tuck the tail under if not trussed, and bake 20 to 30 minutes, until the thickest part of the meat registers 145 degrees on a meat thermometer.

Remove from oven, let stand at least 3 minutes as it

PORK TENDERLOIN

The tenderloin, a lean and lazy muscle tucked along the underside of the loin, is prized for its tenderness and versatility. The way it is cooked seems to change its personality: it is different in each form both in taste and presentation but never varies in its tenderness. It can be roasted whole, cut into chunks and sautéed for biscuits, grilled on a kebab, sliced thinly for medallions or scaloppine, or cut into strips for satés or stir-fries.

Part of the tenderloin's popularity is also its size, weighing somewhere between 3/4 and 1 1/2 pounds. (They are getting bigger and bigger as our pigs are raised to be larger.) Usually sold two to a package, one will usually feed 2 1/2 people; the two tenderloins will feed 6. If both are not needed, the second should be wrapped well and refrigerated or frozen.

The tenderloin has a thin exterior film called the silver skin and also a "chain" running down part of the side, separated by membranes and fat. Professional cooks remove every bit of white, but I am not as particular. The chain may be left on or removed and used separately in a sauté, but the silver skin, membrane, and fat should be mostly removed by pulling off with a sharp knife.

Tenderloins are larger at one end, tapering down to what is called the tail. If an even width is required, cut it off or fold under when roasting. It can be flattened to be a wider piece by putting a knife or cleaver on top of the cut part and pushing down. It is an appetizing piece sliced for stir-fries and leftovers, or cooked strips can make a very nice addition to a salad or vegetables.

rises in temperature. If the tail was not tucked under, it will be well done compared to the still pink butt end of the tenderloin, but will still be a tender, flavorful piece of meat. Slice the tenderloin as desired.

Variations:

- Add rosemary, garlic, and ginger or 2 tablespoons fennel seed to the mustard.
- For stovetop whole tenderloin, lower the heat after browning, cover the pan with aluminum foil, and then a tight lid to prevent the liquid from escaping as steam. Cook over low-to-medium heat for 15 to 20 minutes, until the thickest part of the meat registers 145 degrees on a meat thermometer. Let stand at least 3 minutes as it rises in temperature.

BASIC SAUTÉED PORK TENDERLOIN BISCUIT SLICES

Serves 2 to 3

A "BISCUIT SLICE" WAS SO NAMED *because it was the width of a biscuit. With the increasing size of pigs, the tenderloin is larger, and it fits better when cut into chunks. A special treat during hog killing was to set aside the tenderloin for breakfast. Fried and sandwiched into biscuits, this is perfection in its simplicity and a treat for the farm butchers.*

I think of slices or small chunks of tenderloin tucked in a biscuit as a "to go" dish—to go on a hiking or fishing trip, or before a long walk, particularly in the era when children walked long miles to school. Now I imagine drivers eating them in the morning on the way to work, school, or golf.

1 pork tenderloin (approximately 1 pound)
1 tablespoon oil, cook's preference
3 tablespoons butter
Salt
Freshly ground black pepper

Trim the tenderloin of silver skin, fat, and membrane, removing the chain if desired (page 384). Cut the meat on the diagonal into 1/2- to 3/4- inch pieces and pat dry.

Meanwhile, heat the oil and butter in a heavy pan until sizzling. Season the tenderloin to taste with salt and pepper, add quickly to the pan, and brown on the first side. Turn, using tongs, and brown on the second side. Use the tongs to hold the meat on each side so it browns all over, cooking a total of about 4 to 5 minutes, until the thickest part of the meat registers 145 degrees on a meat thermometer, leaving the meat slightly pink inside. Remove from heat, let stand at least 3 minutes as it rises in temperature, and serve. May also be served cold or reheated.

Variations:

- Add prewashed baby spinach to the pan, with or without the meat, season with salt and pepper, cover, and let steam 1 or 2 minutes, until wilted. Serve with the meat.
- After removing the meat from the pan, add 1/2 cup Coca-Cola and 2 tablespoons brown sugar to the hot pan, stir well, and boil down to a glaze. Add a bit of cider vinegar to smooth out the sweetness.
- After removing the meat from the pan, add Hot Pepper Jelly (page 648) to the hot pan, stir well, and melt into a sauce. Pour over the meat.
- For each thick slice of raw tenderloin, add a slice of bacon to a hot pan. Cook bacon until still flexible but close to being done. Remove from the pan and drain quickly on a piece of paper towel. Wrap the flexible pieces of bacon around each piece of meat, cutting off any extra. Secure with kitchen twine. Sauté as in recipe.

CHERRY-STUFFED PORK TENDERLOIN

Serves 6

A STUFFED TENDERLOIN IS A SMASHING MAIN COURSE. *In classic European cooking, passed on to America and England, pork tenderloin was filled with dried prunes or apricots—perhaps because pork was slaughtered in autumn and fresh fruit wasn't available, or because of the more intense flavor conveyed by the dried fruits. The rich flavor of the dried cherry-and-peanut paste is incredible, and the mixture doesn't tumble out when the pork is cut as whole prunes do. The presentation is stunning.*

As with any stuffed or sliced meat, resting after cooking is crucial. Slicing is much easier when the meat is roasted ahead, cooled before slicing, and reheated. It is also delightful served cold.

2 pork tenderloins (1–1 1/2 pounds each)
1 cup dried cherries
1–2 biscuits or slices white bread, broken or torn
1/2 cup unsalted peanuts
1/4 cup red wine
Salt
Freshly ground black pepper
3 tablespoons butter
2 tablespoons oil, cook's preference

Preheat oven to 350 degrees.

Trim the tenderloins of silver skin, fat, and membrane; remove the chain if desired (page 384); and pat dry.

Purée the cherries, biscuits or bread, and peanuts using a food processor or a blender, adding sufficient wine to make a paste. Season to taste with salt and pepper.

Stuff the tenderloin following your preferred method (facing).

Once stuffed, heat the butter and oil in a large ovenproof pan or skillet sufficient to hold the two tenderloins when baking without touching but not so big as to have the juices burn. When sizzling, add the pork and cook one tenderloin at a time if necessary. Brown on one side, turn with tongs, and brown the other, using the tongs to brown all over.

Pour off excess fat if necessary; then move the pan with the two tenderloins to the oven. Bake until the thickest part of the meat registers 145 degrees on a meat thermometer (depending on preference), about 30 minutes.

Remove from the oven and let stand at least 3 minutes as it rises in temperature before slicing. (Or cool completely and slice. To serve warm, cover with foil and reheat in a 350-degree oven.) Serve with the pan juices. The dish freezes well enough for family leftovers but not for company.

Variations:

- Substitute dried cranberries for the cherries; for dried peaches, reconstitute by adding to boiling water, and soak 30 minutes, until tender. Remove, drain, chop roughly, and proceed as above.
- Stir 1 to 2 tablespoons red currant jelly into pan juices.

Variation: Pork Tenderloin Stuffed with Figs

Combine 1 cup dry white wine or vermouth, 2 tablespoons fig or other brandy, 1 cup dried figs, and soak, preferably overnight. To use fresh figs, split and sauté or roast them until nearly caramelized before being puréed with a small amount of the wine and brandy mixture.

When ready to use, remove the figs with a slotted spoon and purée in a food processor or blender, reserving the liquid for the sauce. Stuff this fig mixture into the prepared tenderloins and follow baking directions above. Slice the pork and serve with the sauce, or slice pork when cool, cover with foil, and reheat in a 350-degree oven; reheat sauce and serve.

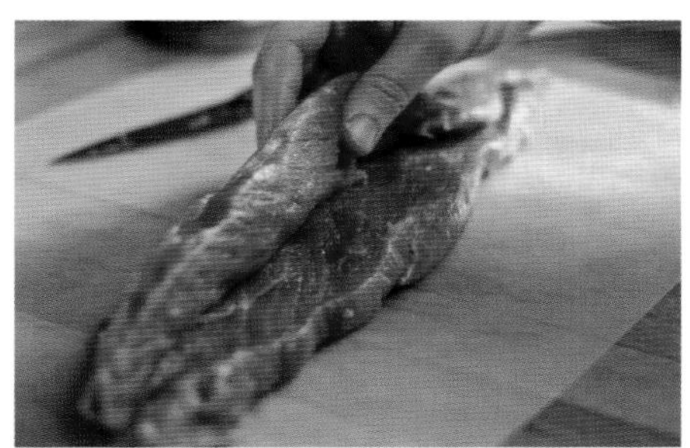

STUFFING A TENDERLOIN

Method 1—"Core" the center of each tenderloin by twisting a skewer or a long narrow knife from one end of the tenderloin almost to the other end, making a pocket for the stuffing. Pat the exterior of the meat dry and season with salt and pepper. Push the stuffing into the center with a wooden spoon handle or other long round object. Truss the meat (page 421).

Method 2—Lay the tenderloin flat on a counter or board. With a hand on top of the tenderloin to steady it, insert a knife halfway through the middle of the thick end of the tenderloin, and slide the knife down from the thick end to the thin end to butterfly the meat. Pat the exterior of the meat dry and season with salt and pepper. Transfer the stuffing into the pocket, fold over, and truss the meat (page 421).

Method 3—Open one butterflied tenderloin and spread topping over, and top with the second butterflied tenderloin, cut side down. Sew together as one.

FIGS

Figs are abundant in the South, with trees that grow to immense proportions. Even the most devout fig-eaters, such as my family, cannot consume all of a bumper crop. They are dried, made into jams, jellies, and preserves, or wrapped with country ham, sautéed, and grilled, as well as eaten fresh from the tree. Figs are in much higher regard here than in Majorca, or at least with the maître d' of the restaurant where I cooked, who sneered at them, calling them "pig food" when I put them on the tables of the restaurant as a little treat when our guests sat down. I cannot help but think of his rigid back and self-important walk when I serve them now—particularly with pork—and my guests swoon with delight.

PORK MEDALLIONS, CUTLETS, OR SCALOPPINE

Serves 2 to 3

Evocative of thin pieces of veal and chicken breast, *these change their names according to the butcher and the cookbook writer. Scaloppine, cutlets, paillards, and schnitzel recipes, to name a few, can all be converted to pork rather than veal or chicken.*

1 pork tenderloin (approximately 1 pound)
1 tablespoon oil, cook's preference
2 tablespoons butter
Salt
Freshly ground black pepper

Trim the tenderloin of silver skin, fat, and membrane, removing the chain if desired (page 384). Slice the tenderloin on the diagonal into 1/2-inch-thick slices, and pat dry. Move to a board and flatten the meat (facing).

After pressing or pounding the meat thin, pat each piece dry. Heat a large skillet, and add the oil and butter. Season the medallions to taste with salt and pepper. When sizzling, add the medallions without them touching each other. They may be cooked in batches, so have a warm plate nearby. Brown on one side, turn, and brown on the second, cooking a total of 2 or 3 minutes. Remove to the plate and keep warm.

Variations:

- Roll the just-cut damp slices in flour seasoned with salt and pepper and proceed to add to the skillet as above.
- After sautéing, remove meat and keep warm. Add 2 tablespoons of lemon juice and 2 tablespoons chicken stock or broth to the pan. Bring to the boil quickly and cook just 1 minute or so, until the sauce thickens slightly. Pour the buttery lemon sauce on top of the medallions.
- Add 1/2 cup of roughly chopped pecans sautéed in butter on top of the lemon sauce and scaloppine.
- After sautéing, remove the meat from the pan, add 1/3 cup white wine, dry vermouth, Madeira, or Marsala to the hot pan juices. Boil down slightly. Add 2/3 to 1 cup heavy cream and boil until reduced to a thickened sauce, scraping to remove browned bits. Add strained broth if desired. Serve with the meat.
- Sauté 1 cup of sliced mushrooms in 2 tablespoons butter. Remove and set aside. Add oil and butter as above and sauté medallions. Remove medallions to a warm plate. Add the mushrooms back to the pan. Add 1/4 cup brandy, rum, or bourbon. If desired, 1 or 2 tablespoons Dijon mustard may also be added at this point. Bring to the boil and boil a minute or two. Add 1 cup of sour cream and heat thoroughly without boiling the sour cream. Return the medallions to the pan and heat through. Serve hot.
- Add spinach to the hot pan, and cover. It wilts in 2 to 3 minutes over heat.
- Add ribboned carrots, turnips, and other vegetables to the pan, cover, and wilt briefly.

THINLY SLICED MEAT

To slice pork tenderloin thinly, put the tenderloin in the freezer briefly to firm up enough to avoid slicing without tearing the meat.

"Cozying up" pieces of meat until ready to serve, preferably on a hot platter, keeps everything warm. I have a bit of space between the burners on my stovetop; Cynthia uses her oven on very low; my mother had a heating tray. See what works.

FLATTENING MEAT FOR CUTLETS

Method 1—Lay a knife or cleaver flat on the cut side of each slice; press down until the meat is 1/8 to 1/4 inch thick.

Method 2—Put a hand flat on the cut side of the tenderloin slice. Carefully slide the knife through the middle of the tenderloin slice, going only 3/4 of the way through the piece, taking care to go slowly so the knife will not aim towards your hand. Open up the meat at the "hinge" like a book and lay a knife or cleaver flat on the cut side of each slice. Press out to make a "butterfly" and pound slightly with a rolling pin or other heavy implement, but avoid tearing the meat.

Method 3—Cover with plastic wrap (or move to a plastic bag) and use a mallet or frying pan to pound the meat thin.

OVEN-BARBECUED PORK TENDERLOIN

Serves 4 to 6

TENDER, SMALL MEATS SHOULD BE COOKED QUICKLY *rather than long and slow on a barbecue. These tangy, sweet, and spicy flavors envelop the pork, contrasting with the citrus, honey, and hotness.*

1 medium onion, finely chopped
2 garlic cloves, chopped
3 tablespoons tomato paste
3 tablespoons honey
3 tablespoons Worcestershire sauce
3 tablespoons red wine vinegar
1/2 cup orange juice
1/4 cup fresh lemon juice
1/4 teaspoon ground hot red pepper
2 pork tenderloins, 1–1 1/2 pounds each

Preheat oven to 350 degrees.

Purée all ingredients, except the tenderloins, until thick.

Trim the tenderloins of silver skin, fat, and membrane; remove the chain if desired (page 384); and move to a plastic ziplock bag. Pour purée over the pork and marinate at least 6 hours if possible. Remove from marinade, shake off the excess, and move to an oiled pan a bit longer and wider than the tenderloins, without the tenderloins touching. Fold the tails under to make a thicker cut. Reserve the marinade in a small saucepan.

Bake about 25 to 30 minutes until the thickest part of the meat registers 145 degrees on a meat thermometer. Remove from the oven and let stand at least 3 minutes as it rises in temperature while preparing the sauce.

To make the sauce, bring to the boil over medium-high heat. Reduce the heat and simmer until the mixture is thick, about 10 minutes. Pass separately with the pork tenderloin, warm or at room temperature.

HOT PEPPER-AND-PEANUT-ROASTED PORK TENDERLOIN

Serves 4 to 6

HOT PEPPERS AND PEANUTS *have an affinity for each other as well as for pork. Pigs were fed with peanuts in Virginia for much of the eighteenth and nineteenth centuries and into the twentieth, resulting in tender, moist, richly flavored meat. Although this practice is rare today, we pay homage to their combination with this sumptuous recipe.*

1–2 hot red peppers
1 1/2 cups roasted unsalted peanuts, skinned
2 pork tenderloins (1–1 1/2 pounds each)
4 tablespoons butter
2 tablespoons oil, cook's preference
Salt
Freshly ground black pepper
6 tablespoons white wine vinegar
Juice of 1 lemon
Juice of 1 lime
1 teaspoon ground coriander or cumin
1 1/2 cups butter

Preheat oven to 400 degrees.

Coarsely chop the peanuts. Seed and chop the peppers and mix the peppers and peanuts together. Trim the tenderloins of silver skin, fat, and membrane.

Melt the butter and oil in a large ovenproof skillet. Add the tenderloins, brown on the first side, and turn with tongs to brown on the second side. Use the tongs to move the meat so that the whole tenderloin is browned on all sides.

Remove the pork from the skillet, shake dry, and pat some of the peanut mixture onto it, coating lightly. Reserve the rest for the sauce. Season the pork to taste with salt and pepper. Return pork to the skillet and move to the oven.

Roast 20 to 30 minutes, or until the thickest part of the meat registers 145 degrees on a meat thermometer. The tail will be more well done. Remove from the oven and let stand at least 3 minutes as it rises in temperature while finishing the sauce.

To make the sauce, bring the reserved peanut-and-pepper mixture to the boil in a saucepan with the vinegar, juices, and coriander. Boil down until the liquid is nearly evaporated. Add any pan juices from the skillet and boil down briefly. Whisk in the butter, piece by piece, over low heat. Serve sauce with meat.

PORK LOIN BASTED WITH HOT PEPPER JELLY SAUCE

Serves 8 to 10

THE LOINS ARE ON EITHER SIDE OF THE BACKBONE. *For a thick roast, the loins and backbone can be cooked together, making what is called a saddle; or both sides may be boned, the backbone used for another purpose, and the loins tied together. The same recipe may be used for one side of the loin with the time considerably reduced. If a loin with backbone is desired, it may need to be special ordered.*

1 (10 to 12-pound) center pork loin saddle, bone in, tied; or 4 pounds boneless pork loin if two sides are tied together

Marinade

2 cups dry white wine or apple juice

1 cup Hot Pepper Jelly (page 648), preferably red

Glaze

3/4 cup Hot Pepper Jelly (page 648), preferably red

1–3 cups breadcrumbs or panko

Sauce, if needed

1 cup dry white wine or apple juice

1/2 cup Hot Pepper Jelly (page 648), preferably red

Make a few 1/2-inch slashes in the pork fat with a sharp knife.

To make the marinade, heat the wine or apple juice and jelly together until the jelly melts, and pour over the pork. Move to a plastic ziplock back and set in a pan in the refrigerator. Marinate overnight or as long as possible.

Preheat oven to 400 degrees. Remove the pork from the marinade, reserving marinade. Move the pork to a large roasting pan. Roast without basting until the thickest part of the meat registers 145 degrees on a meat thermometer, about 1 1/2 to 2 hours. Remove from the oven, boil marinade to cook any pork juices, and pour the marinade over the pork. Let stand 30 minutes before slicing.

To make the glaze, mix jelly and breadcrumbs together. Coat the sliced meat evenly all over with the mixture. Place under the broiler until crisp and lightly browned, about 10 minutes. To make additional sauce, reheat the marinade and boil 5 minutes, until thick. If most of the marinade has been used, add additional jelly and wine or apple juice just before boiling down.

If reheating, put sliced and glazed pork, surrounded by the unreduced sauce, in a 350-degree oven for 20 minutes. When heated, remove pork and make sauce as above. Pour the sauce on the dish or in a separate serving bowl. Serve hot or cold.

TYING PORK LOINS

Pork loins and tenderloins are frequently seen tied together and roasted. Move the two pieces to a board. With the flatter sides together (where the bone was), tie the two pieces together with cotton butcher's twine to form a whole roast. Tie as on page 421.

ZIPPY PORK LOIN ROAST

Serves 10

THIS IS ONE OF THE MOST POPULAR RECIPES *from my previous cookbooks. Ric Lands worked for me on seven books and seven television series. A Princeton graduate, he was an invaluable editor and advisor as well as a confidante and friend. He died younger than he should have, and I miss him every day. This was his recipe, which was included in* Nathalie Dupree Cooks for Family and Friends.

The roast can be cooked in two ways—roasted long and slow, making a melted barbecue-like meat; or roasted at 350 degrees, making more of a typical roasted meat. The meat becomes very dry if cooked past 145 degrees since it has so little fat, so avoid overcooking.

- 2 cups honey
- 4 tablespoons Dijon mustard
- 4 tablespoons prepared horseradish
- 4 tablespoons rosemary, crushed
- 10 garlic cloves, crushed
- 2 teaspoons freshly ground black pepper
- 2 tablespoons chopped fresh ginger
- 1 (4- to 5-pound) boneless pork loin roast

Mix together all ingredients except the pork. Place the loin in a sturdy plastic ziplock bag, and pour the marinade over the meat; let marinate in a pan in the refrigerator for 30 minutes or up to overnight.

Preheat oven to 500 degrees.

Remove the pork from its marinade and shake off the excess; reserve the marinade. Tie the two sides of roast together, if necessary, to make 1 piece. Move to a roasting pan and place in the oven.

After 15 minutes, reduce the heat to 250 degrees. Roast until the thickest part of the meat registers 145 degrees on a meat thermometer, about 5 hours. Turn the roast over in the pan every hour or so. Remove from the oven and let rest 15 to 30 minutes before slicing. Slice and move to a serving platter.

Meanwhile, bring the marinade to the boil and reduce by about half. Pour the reduced marinade over the meat. Serve hot, or refrigerate and serve cold or at room temperature.

Variation: Cook 2 hours in a 350-degree oven, until the internal temperature of the meat reaches 145 degrees. Let rest 15 to 30 minutes.

PORK LOIN ROAST WITH DRIED FRUIT

Serves 4 to 6

THIS BRAISED PORK ROAST IS VERY MOIST. *It is browned first in a hot oven, then surrounded by dried fruit, covered, and returned to the oven for roasting.*

1 (3-pound) boneless pork loin roast
3 cups chicken stock or broth
1/4 cup dried cherries, cranberries, currants, and/or raisins
1/2 cup dried figs, apples, and/or pears
2 tablespoons chopped candied ginger
1 cup heavy cream

Preheat oven to 500 degrees.

Move the meat to a large metal roasting pan and roast 30 minutes, until lightly browned. Remove from the oven and reduce the heat to 350 degrees.

Mix together the stock, fruits, and ginger, and surround the pork in the pan with the mixture. Cover loosely with aluminum foil. Return to the oven and continue cooking until the thickest part of the meat registers 145 degrees on a meat thermometer, about 1 1/2 hours, taking care to avoid steam when removing foil to test the temperature. Remove the roast to a cutting board and let stand at least 3 minutes as it rises in temperature.

Move roasting pan to the stovetop, bring the juices to the boil, and reduce by half, about 10 minutes. Add the cream and boil until thickened, about 7 minutes. The meat and sauce may be made ahead to this point, refrigerating as necessary up to several days, and reheated. Slicing is easiest when the meat has cooled. Cover with foil to reheat. If using butter, add room-temperature pieces to the warm sauce and do not re-boil. Slice the roast and serve the sauce over the pork, or pass it separately.

Variations:

- *Sauce*—Substitute 1/2 cup water for the cream, and add room-temperature butter to the reduced and warm pan liquids and serve immediately.
- If necessary, this roast may be browned first in 2 tablespoons each of oil and butter, or even cooked on the stove. It is difficult however, to find the right size pan and burners that will provide heat to the whole pan.

PORK CHOPS

Pity the pork chop. Even the earliest Southerners, with their fatty peanut-fed pigs, rarely cooked pork chops without smothering them in sauces or gravy to compensate for the meat's dryness. The bone is wider than the accompanying flesh, so the flesh can quickly become overcooked and dry when the bone is at its succulent best. A good butcher can help if instructed to cut the meat as thick as the bone. In pork chops, thicker is better, preferably at least 3/4 inch. The bone is tasty to chew on in the privacy of one's home.

Thinner pork chops are frequently sold in large multi-chop packs and require a quick browning over high heat, followed by braising in liquid.

Marinating improves all pork chops considerably. Brining does too, but should be done with thick chops to avoid over salting. Smoking thick chops combined with brining ensures moistness and tenderness. Commercially smoked chops are available in grocery stores.

Cuts of pork chops include the following:

1. **Rib chops**—the bone from the top part of the rib bone—are the most preferred, as they are the meatiest, with fat to keep them flavorful and prevent drying out.
2. **Loin chops,** like T-bone steak, include both a piece of the tenderloin and a piece of the loin. The two kinds of meat don't always cook evenly. If cut thick (1 1/4 to 1 1/2 inches), they will have a better chance of remaining moist, and do very well brined, as do rib chops. Thinner chops have little chance of remaining succulent, as they are too thin to brine, running the risk of being salty and drying out rapidly unless cooked in a sauce or liquid.
3. **Top loin chops,** or pork strop chops, are the center-cut loin chops. When boneless, they are called pork loin rib fillets.
4. **Blade chops** are tasty but tougher, are good brined or marinated, and have a bit more fat than other chops.
5. **Country-style ribs** are butterflied, or split blade chops, and are more economical than many other chops. They are usually browned and then braised (cooked in a liquid), grilled, or broiled as opposed to pan-fried.
6. **Butt (shoulder) chops** are sold as pork blade or pork steaks and are a favorite of mine. They are tougher but pack more flavor per bite, so marinating really enhances them.

Pork chops are available from grocery stores and meat counters in various types and sizes. Almost all are tender. Choose chops that have a high proportion of meat to fat and bones:

One center-cut 1/2-inch loin chop with bone in weighs approximately 5 ounces. A package of those chops weighing 2 or 2 1/2 pounds contains 6 to 8 chops.

One boneless 1/2-inch loin chop weighs approximately 4 ounces. A package of those chops weighing 1 1/2 to 2 pounds contains 6 to 8 chops.

Breakfast chops are a thinner loin cut and cook in 3 to 5 minutes *total*; they are not specified here but may be used if time is adjusted to prevent overcooking.

Counter-intuitively, bone-in chops cook slightly faster, as the bone conducts the heat. But there is little difference in the time it takes to cook bone-in or bone-out—it is the thickness that matters.

ORANGE-GINGER PORK CHOPS

Serves 4

PORK CHOPS, WHICH COME BONE-IN OR BONELESS, *are highly variable, depending on the part of the animal from which they are cut (facing). The thicker they are, the easier to grill or oven-cook. This is a luscious marinade for loin chops.*

1 cup orange juice
Finely grated rind of 2 oranges, no white attached
1 garlic clove, finely chopped
3 tablespoons finely chopped fresh ginger
1 tablespoon red pepper flakes, optional
2 tablespoons oil, divided, cook's preference
4 center-cut pork loin chops, approximately 1/2 inch thick
Salt
Freshly ground black pepper
2 tablespoons butter

Combine the orange juice, rind, garlic, ginger, red pepper flakes, and 1 tablespoon oil in a plastic ziplock bag.

Remove any excess fat from the chops and add meat to the marinade. Marinate in the refrigerator 1 hour or overnight if possible. Remove the pork chops from the marinade, reserving marinade, and dry. Season with salt and pepper.

Heat the oil with the butter in a heavy pan until sizzling. Add the chops without crowding the pan. Cook on each side and the edges until brown and the thickest part of the meat registers 145 degrees on a meat thermometer.

When the chops are cooked, remove to a warm plate and let stand 3 minutes as they rise in temperature. Meanwhile, add the marinade to the pan, bring to the boil, and boil several minutes, until reduced. Add salt and pepper. Serve over chops.

CIDER-BRINED PORK CHOPS WITH CARAMELIZED APPLES AND ONIONS

Serves 2

THE APPLE CIDER IN THIS BRINE *gives the pork a tint of sweetness and calls for the flavors of the apples and onions, which are natural complements to those of pork.*

2–4 tablespoons salt
1 tablespoon freshly ground black pepper
2 cups apple cider
2 (2- to 3-inch-thick) pork chops, bone in
3 tablespoons oil, cook's preference, divided
Caramelized Apples and Onions (page 402)

Dissolve the salt in 1 quart of warm water. Add the pepper and cider. Add the pork chops to the brine, cover, and refrigerate overnight or at least 8 hours or up to 3 days. After brining, remove chops and pat dry.

Preheat oven to 400 degrees. Rub the chops with 1 tablespoon of oil and season with salt and pepper.

Heat the remaining oil in an oven-safe skillet. Add the pork chops and brown on each side. Move the pan to the oven for 8 minutes, until the thickest part of the meat registers 145 degrees on a meat thermometer. Remove from the oven, cover with foil, and let stand at least 3 minutes to rise in temperature.

Variations:

- Substitute Coca-Cola or pineapple juice for the cider.
- Add a bit of sage or rosemary.

It is nearly impossible to use brining liquids for another purpose. Adding them to a sauce will usually cause the sauce to be too salty when it boils down. For that reason I sometimes prefer a marinade that can be used later as a sauce, as in the Orange-Ginger Pork Chops (above).

GRILLED OR BROILED MUSTARD PORK CHOPS

Serves 6

MY FRIEND ELLIOTT MACKLE *says this is one of his favorite recipes of mine, so I repeat it here. Pork and mustard have an affinity, the mustard-based rub getting crusty and lightly caramelized, the pork staying moist and tender under its protective crust. No sauce is necessary.*

½ cup Dijon mustard
2 tablespoons oil, cook's preference
2 teaspoons Worcestershire sauce
2 teaspoons dried rosemary
½–1 teaspoon ground cumin or coriander seed, optional
Salt
Freshly ground black pepper
8–12 (½-inch-thick) center-cut pork loin chops

Spray the grill with nonstick spray. Preheat the broiler or grill.

Whisk together the mustard, oil, Worcestershire, rosemary, and cumin in a small bowl. Season to taste with salt and pepper.

Brush chops on both sides with the mustard mixture. Grill or add to a rimmed baking sheet and broil 3 to 4 minutes per side, until bubbly with a few dark brown spots and the thickest part of the meat registers 145 degrees on a meat thermometer. Let stand at least 3 minutes as it rises in temperature. Serve hot or at room temperature.

MARINATED SMOKED PORK CHOPS ON MISSISSIPPI CAVIAR

Serves 4

IN THE MID-1980S, THE MARRIOTT HOTEL *in Richmond, Virginia, asked me to open a restaurant named Nathalie's. We had an exciting Southern menu that included this dish. My friend Marion Sullivan helped me train the chefs, worked with the baker night after night, and selected the appropriate Southern wines.*

Pre-smoked pork chops are available in grocery and specialty stores. The bed of Mississippi Caviar adds to the specialness of this dish.

2 tablespoons oil, cook's preference
2 tablespoons red wine vinegar
2 tablespoons fresh lemon juice
1 teaspoon soy sauce
1–2 teaspoons chopped fresh thyme
Salt
Freshly ground black pepper
4 large center-cut pork loin chops, fresh or smoked
1 recipe Mississippi Caviar (page 50)

Whisk together the oil, vinegar, lemon juice, soy sauce, thyme, and salt and pepper to taste. Rub the mixture on the pork chops, cover, and marinate in the refrigerator 1 to 2 hours or overnight.

Prepare a grill or broiler. Drain the chops and move to the grill or a sided pan; place under the broiler until browned, 8 to 10 minutes per side, depending on the thickness of chops, and the thickest part of the meat registers 145 degrees on a meat thermometer. Remove when browned and heated through, and let stand at least 3 minutes as it rises in temperature.

Arrange ½ cup Mississippi Caviar on each of four plates, top with a grilled chop, and serve immediately.

MEMPHIS BARBECUED RIBS

Serves 4 to 6

Barbecued ribs are a specialty of Memphis. *There are two world-famous restaurants there. We lived a little more than an hour away in Oxford, Mississippi, and had to go through Memphis to get—well, anywhere, it seemed, particularly on the airplane. We became experts on these restaurants.*

The Rendezvous is one of those restaurants that is so full all of the time that the floor is never seen. A trip to Memphis is not worth it if you don't eat there—or take some ribs home. They use baby back ribs.

The other restaurant, Corky's, is newer but no less popular. I've meshed the two rub recipes together and added what is reputed to be Corky's mopping sauce, for basting and for those that love the mopping sauce.

This can be made ahead up to 2 months and kept tightly wrapped. The recipe doubles easily. I always ate my Rendezvous ribs un-sauced, perhaps because they were my introduction to barbecue rubs. But others love their mopping sauce.

4 pounds baby back ribs, about 3 racks

Memphis Dry Rub

8 tablespoons paprika, preferably Hungarian
4 tablespoons garlic powder
4 tablespoons chili powder
3 tablespoons freshly ground black pepper
3 tablespoons salt
2 teaspoons dried mustard
1 tablespoon crushed celery seed
1 tablespoon whole celery seed
1 tablespoon dried oregano
1 tablespoon dried thyme
1 teaspoon ground cumin
1 tablespoon whole coriander seed
1 teaspoon ground coriander seed
2 tablespoons light or dark brown sugar, optional

Memphis Mopping or Barbecue Sauce

1 cup cider vinegar
1/2 cup tomato sauce
2 tablespoons fresh lemon juice
2 tablespoons molasses
2 tablespoons Worcestershire sauce
2 teaspoons hot sauce

Chill—or even half-freeze—the ribs. Make a slit down the outside membrane on the back of the rack on the left, the right, and across the very top of the membrane, across all bones. There are two ways to pull the membrane off: 1) dig fingernails under the top of the membrane and pull down (with luck it will all come off), or 2) use pliers and pull off membrane from one side of the rack to the other.

Move the ribs to a broiler pan, shallow baking pan, or rimmed baking sheet. Combine all the rub ingredients in a small bowl. Rub both sides of each rack with the rub mixture.

Meanwhile, combine the sauce ingredients in a pan. Bring to the boil and boil 1 to 2 minutes. Remove from heat.

Brush the ribs with the sauce and bake 30 minutes, brushing again after 15 minutes. Turn the ribs over and brush again, baking another 30 minutes, brushing after 15 minutes. The ribs are done when the meat is tender and starting to pull away from the bone.

Spoon the sauce liberally over the ribs and turn the oven to broil. Broil the ribs 5 to 7 minutes per side, spooning with the glaze again after turning over the ribs.

Bring any remaining sauce to the boil once again before serving with the ribs.

It is said that all politics are local; so, too, is all Southern barbecue. The debates about whose 'cue is best has spawned competitions that bring in big bucks for the winners—and that still doesn't resolve the question.

North Carolinians are adamant about their barbecue, and there is no town more boastful than that of Lexington, North Carolina. It is perhaps this town that makes scholars say that barbecue is the indigenous food of North Carolina. The most famous of these sauces is vinegar-based.

South Carolinians claims mustard-based, ketchup-based, and vinegar-based ones.

PORK RIBS

There are three kinds of ribs in the pig. Turning to Bruce Aidells' *The Complete Meat Cookbook,* which I keep on my shelf, ribs are described in four ways, which I've synopsized here.

Spareribs—These are the 13 ribs of the belly of the pork. The remainder of the belly is the bacon. A slab, or rack, of spareribs weighs 2 to 3 pounds and is particularly meaty at the larger end of the slab (the rear end). Bruce recommends rejecting any slabs that have more than a little fat and asking the butcher for a heavier slab with less fat. Figure on 2 to 3 servings per slab.

Baby back ribs—I didn't even see these ribs until I was an adult, perhaps because the pigs were smaller then. For a while I even thought they were from baby pigs. Also known as back ribs, they are from the upper portion of the rib section of the loin after the boneless meat is removed. With less meat than spareribs to begin with, depending on the butcher, these may have had most of their meat removed, sold with the seemingly pricier loin. Whatever meat there is, however, is tender and sweet because it is loin meat. Bruce Aidells says that once the bone and fat are accounted for, baby back ribs are probably the most expensive part of the animal. It takes a whole slab to feed one or two people. They take less time to cook because they don't have to be slow-cooked, and they are very good nibbles for hors d'oeuvres and stand-up parties, where spareribs are too big and awkward.

Country-style ribs—Country ribs are also new since I learned to cook—they came onto the scene in the late 1970s. These fatty, meaty ribs are the least expensive of the ribs; they are butterflied or split pork chops from the blade end of the loin. They like long, slow grilling or braising and have enough fat to keep them moist the whole time. Some find them the most appealing of the chops.

Cooking ribs—I used to know people who boiled spareribs to tenderize them before cooking. Boiling is the enemy of any good meat, and ribs are no exception. When precooking ribs in liquid, poach them in a large roasting pan, barely covered with water and seasoning, on top of the stove, with the water at about 165 to 170 degrees. Don't discard the liquid, as it is essentially a stock. Use it for another purpose, such as a soup or sauce.

I usually avoid precooking and instead rub or marinate these ribs, wrap them in double sheets of heavy-duty aluminum foil, and put them in a low oven or on a grill.

Bruce Aidells cooks them on a rack over moist heat. After marinating, lay them meaty side up on a rack in a shallow pan in the top third of the oven. Add a baking pan of water to the lower third of the oven to add humidity. Roast at 300 degrees for 1½ hours, basting occasionally with marinade, until the meat shrinks away from the bone.

COCA-COLA RIBS

Serves 4 to 6

WHEN VIRGINIA WILLIS'S *beautiful cookbook* Bon Appétit, Y'all *came out, I fell in love with the recipes, especially her Coca-Cola ribs. Virginia was an intern with me and worked for me after she had lived in France, helping on books and television series. When I told her how tasty they were, she laughed. "That sauce," she said, "is your recipe—you did it with chicken wings." She jazzed it up with a Scotch bonnet pepper, but I am falling back on my own recipe with this by reverting to hot pepper flakes. I admit it—I find it hard to measure the heat of individual fresh peppers, and I like to add a little at a time to make sure I don't botch it. I also like to buy one of those huge bottles of Coca-Cola and use the whole thing up, rather than opening it and having it go flat. And, finally, I use this recipe more for spare ribs than baby backs, as I rarely serve baby backs for dinner since my husband prefers spareribs. No recipe is original, and we all borrow from each other.*

4–6 pounds spareribs

Coca-Cola Rib Sauce
1 (2-liter) bottle Coca-Cola
2 cups apple cider vinegar
12 cups light or dark brown sugar
2 teaspoons red pepper flakes

As noted when making a crown roast or a rib roast, the membrane on the back of the ribs needs to be removed from both baby back ribs and spareribs. Half-freeze or chill the meat so it becomes very firm. Make slits down the outside membrane on the back of the rack on the left, the right, and one across the very top of the membrane, across all bones. There are a couple of ways to pull the membrane off: 1) dig fingernails under the top of the membrane and pull down (with luck it will all come off), or 2) use pliers and pull off membrane from one side of the rack to the other. (It is always easier to pull one way than the other, but of course it changes with the side of the animal the ribs are from. Just give it a try and see which way it yields easily. Dig fingernails under the slit side rib and pull from one side of the ribs to the other.)

Bring the Coca-Cola to the boil over high heat and boil until reduced in volume by half (about 20 minutes). Stir in remaining ingredients. Reduce heat to medium-low and simmer at least 10 minutes. Reduce heat again, to low, and let sauce sit while ribs are cooking. This sauce can be prepared, covered, and refrigerated for several weeks.

Preheat oven to 325 degrees.

Season both sides of the ribs to taste with salt and pepper. Move the ribs to a broiler pan or shallow baking pan **or** rimmed baking sheet. Brush the ribs with the sauce and bake 30 minutes, brushing the ribs again after 15 minutes. Turn the ribs over and brush again, baking another 30 minutes, brushing after 15 minutes. The ribs are done when the meat is tender and starting to pull away from the bone.

Spoon the sauce liberally over the ribs and turn the oven to broil. Broil the ribs 5 to 7 minutes per side, spooning with the glaze again after turning over the ribs. Bring any remaining sauce to the boil once again before serving with the ribs.

Ribs are usually rubbed or marinated to intensify the flavor, according to the part of the South where they are served.

Before broiling or grilling until crisp, most ribs are precooked in some way to a temperature of 165 degrees.

CROWN ROASTS

Crown roasts are made from the ribs of an animal; the backbone (called the chine bone) is removed with a saw, preferably by the butcher, enabling the roast to be manipulated into a round or, ideally, a half-round, to be matched with an identical roast from the other side of the animal. Without the chine bone removed, each vertebrae must be cut through—an arduous process—in order to turn the meat into a circle.

Although these exotic roasts may be made with just one side of an animal, using almost all the ribs, the most exquisite of them are made from the center rib cuts of two loins, what we think of as a "rack" of lamb or a standing rib of beef. Make a beef crown roast of four "racks" if true majesty is required. Curving easily once that pesky chine bone is removed, the two roasts are sewn or tied together, forming the crown. (A single loin crown is a little kattywhompus because the ribs vary in length, and there is too much flesh to turn the loin into a crown without shaving off an enormous amount of the meat. It will do for family or an outside barbecue, but not for real company.)

The most well-known crown roasts are made of lamb and pork. Beef, however, makes a spectacular crown roast as long as one has an oven large enough to handle it. I've even used goat, which has a spectacular rib, making a totally different kind of crown.

Roasting is easy, with the only caveat being that times may vary from a standard roast of the same size if the flesh meets in the center. Some, like the National Pork Board, stuff a crown roast prior to cooking. Not I! Stuffings shrink and make the whole thing take longer to cook, causing the meat to be dry.

If serving a big stand-up crowd, roast a separate boneless loin, slice it, and surround the crown with the sliced meat on a platter. This enables easier service of the meat.

PREPARING A CROWN ROAST

Have the butcher remove the chine bone (the backbone) of two similar-sized center-cut rib roasts of 5 or 6 ribs each. If desired, have the butcher cut between the ribs to facilitate easier carving. I prefer having the "cap" removed, that bunch of flesh separated by a skin-like material. The butcher charges for it anyway, and the meat is easily used for a stir-fry later or can be ground for some other purpose.

Join the two pieces of meat end to end, and turn the meat into a circle so the rib ends face outward, in a crown. Where the ends meet, make little holes in the meat, insert butcher's twine, and tie securely. Wrap the crown on the outside with the butcher's twine to hold the rib roasts while roasting.

"French" (scrape) the bones on the remaining rib section by cutting out a 2-inch web between each pair of ribs down to the fleshly part of the meat; scrape the bones, starting at the end of the rib farthest away from the backbone.

I insert a ball of aluminum foil in the center of the formed crown to keep the meat in a circle, and to help transfer heat to cook the interior of the crown.

Cook crown roasts ahead of time, checking with a thermometer periodically (135 to 140 degrees for beef, 145 degrees for pork). Roasts should stand outside the oven at least 10 minutes to allow the juices to return to the meat, during which time the temperature of the meat rises about 10 degrees before it starts to cool. Serve the roast cold, at room temperature, or reheat it if hot meat is required. Before serving, slice between the bones of the meat and push it back together to form the crown. The slices in the meat will be barely visible.

Many times the butcher will sell the raw roast with booties on the bones. Take care to remove the booties before roasting, and to avoid contamination, do not reuse them. If the crown is filled with the scraps, remove and use them for another purpose, as they will shrink when cooking and distort the shape of the roast. The scraped bones look beautiful as they are, or Brussels sprouts, potatoes, chestnuts and other round foods may be pushed onto the bone ends if desired.

CROWN ROAST OF PORK

Serves 8 to 10

A CROWN ROAST IS A STUNNING PIECE OF MEAT, *made from two or more rib roasts that are turned inward to make a round and tied end to end, the tip of the ribs forming a crown. It is jaw-dropping to serve for company, and well worth any effort.*

1 crown roast of pork (made from the center 6 ribs of two pork rib roasts and tied into a crown roast)
Salt
Freshly ground black pepper
2–4 garlic cloves
Rosemary, optional
Caramelized Pineapple Salad (page 66), optional

Preheat oven to 350 degrees.

Salt and pepper the meat, insert slivers of garlic. Rub with rosemary inside and outside the crown.

Cover the bone ends of the crown roast with foil. Make a round ball of aluminum foil that fits securely in the center of the roast to help keep its shape. Move to a shallow pan, not on a rack, and roast about 20 minutes to the pound, or until the internal temperature is 145 degrees.

To cook outdoors, move the pan to a prepared grill, cover, and cook until the thickest part of the meat registers 145 degrees on a meat thermometer. Let rest 10 minutes so the juices can return to the meat.

Remove the fat from the roasting pan. Add a little water to the pan if necessary, and bring to the boil, scraping the bottom of the pan to get all the flavor and color into the juices. Strain the juices into a small pan or cup and remove the fat as necessary. Return the juices to the roasting pan and bring to the boil; boil until slightly thickened.

When ready to serve, move to a platter or round plate, fill the center of the roast with optional pineapple salad, or garnish with rosemary. Serve the sauce separately.

Variation: In summer, adorn the pork with pineapple in a simple vinaigrette. In the winter, dress up with vegetables such as Brussels sprouts, baby glazed carrots, and/or baby potatoes piled in the middle and spilling over the sides slightly.

SAUSAGE AND APPLES

Serves 4

This is my go-to meal when we need a quick supper. *It is also the base for quiches, overnight casseroles, dressings, and other dishes.*

- 2/3 pound bulk sausage or sausage links
- 2 red or green cooking apples

Fry the sausage in a large skillet until cooked through, with no pink remaining.

Core the apples and slice into 1/2-inch wedges. Add the wedges to the sausage and sauté until apples are soft and caramelized but not mushy. Drain sausage and apples on a plate lined with paper towels. Serve hot.

COOKING SAUSAGE

Links—prick the skins before adding to a hot pan, and cook until brown; turn and repeat until brown all over. If more than 1/2 inch in diameter, add a bit of water to the pan after initial browning to keep links from burning before the sausage is cooked through.

Ground sausage—break up as much as possible. Add to a hot pan, reduce heat, and cook until light brown, stirring constantly.

Patties—add to a hot pan, cook until desired brown color, turn and cook on the second side. They should register at least 150 degrees on a meat thermometer when cooked.

CARAMELIZED APPLES AND ONIONS

Serves 4 to 6

I can never decide *whether serve just apples with my pork chops or a combination of apples an onions. Here is a variation that is both savory and sweet.*

- 6 tablespoons olive oil, divided
- 4 large apples, cored and cut into wedges
- 2 sage leaves, divided, optional
- 2 tablespoons butter
- 3 large sweet onions, thinly sliced
- Salt and pepper

In a large skillet, heat 3 tablespoons olive oil over medium heat and add the apples and 1 sage leaf. Sauté for 5 to 10 minutes, or until the apples are golden brown. Remove from the heat and remove the sage leaf.

Meanwhile, in another large skillet, heat the rest of the olive oil and the butter over medium heat and add the onions and remaining sage leaf. Season with salt and pepper to taste. Continue to cook over low to medium-low heat for 30 minutes, or until the onions are mahogany in color. Remove from heat and discard the sage leaf. Add the apples to the onions and serve immediately with pork chops or slices of roast.

FRESH HAM VS. FRESH SHOULDER

For many regions, the preferred barbecue meats are fresh pork hams and shoulders. Fresh ham is a fall and early winter meat, as it is eaten when the pig is slaughtered rather than waiting months until it is cured. These cuts are cooked long and slow, basted with a Vinegar-Based Barbecue Sauce (page 664), chopped up, and served on white bread with sauce and coleslaw. The cuts only require salt and pepper—rubbing either of them would be a fruitless exercise, as the rub would not penetrate. (I'm not even sure rubbing them with salt and pepper does anything, but it is traditional.)

Shoulders—the front leg of pork from the shoulder to the leg—are really two parts of the pig: "Boston butt," a misname if ever there was one, as it is not the butt but the upper, meatier part of the shoulder; and the "picnic ham," which is the front leg of the pork, not the ham, which is the rear.

Butts were so named because they were packed into casks or barrels also known as "butts" in pre-Revolutionary times and were sold whole, cut in half, sliced, cubed, or ground. They now range from 8 to 12 pounds, with the lesser weight being the leaner and better choice. I have to preorder the "whole butt" in advance from my grocery store; the stores assume everyone wants smaller cuts. Not only is it cheaper, it can be cut in half easily, ultimately producing two cuts—a triangular-shaped piece that contains the blade bone, and a boneless piece that can be cut into steaks, ground meat, sausages, and stir-fries. Hopefully the butcher will cut it.

Cutting the pork butt—Divide the butt in half by cutting along the edge of the bone that is partially visible on two sides of the roast. Keep the blade of the knife along the bone, scraping the bone as necessary to push the meat away, until the knife has cut through to the bone on the other side releasing the bone from the meat.

SLOW-COOKED PORK SHOULDER (AKA BOSTON BUTT AKA PICNIC HAM)

Serves 8 to 10

IDEAL FOR BARBECUE SANDWICHES, *this is so moist and succulent it can be pulled into pieces yet the skin will be crunchy.*

1 (4- to 5-pound) pork shoulder (Boston butt or picnic ham)
4–5 garlic cloves, slivered
Salt
Freshly ground black pepper
Cider vinegar
1 recipe Vinegar-Based Barbecue Sauce (page 664)
Cole slaw
Loaf bread or buns

Preheat oven to 275 degrees.

Put the pork in a sturdy pan. Pierce holes in the flesh and add slivers of garlic. Rub the skin with salt and freshly ground pepper. Move the pan to the lower part of the oven. Mix equal amounts of water and vinegar. Start basting after the first hour, and baste occasionally. Cook 6 hours and check the temperature: it should register 160 on a meat thermometer. If necessary, cook 1 more hour. Take care not to cover meat in the oven, as it will make the skin chewy. Do not baste the last hour.

Remove from oven and let rest up to 10 minutes. Carve the meat off the bone in big pieces, either reserving the crispy skin or including it in the large pieces of the meat. Tease and tear apart the meat with fingers, two forks, or two knives into edible pieces, or chop roughly. Serve hot, with barbecue sauce and coleslaw, on loaf bread or buns.

BRAISED PORK SHOULDER (PICNIC HAM)

Serves 6 to 8

IMPOSING AND AROMATIC *when served at a table laid with china, this dish is equally at home in the backyard, where one can lick one's fingers. It is heavenly either way, with crisp skin and tender, rich flesh.*

- 1 (4–5-pound) fresh pork shoulder roast (picnic ham)
- 4–5 garlic cloves, slivered or chopped
- Salt
- Freshly ground black pepper
- Rosemary sprigs, optional
- 1–2 cups chicken stock or broth, or pork broth

Shave off a bit of the pork fat with a knife and add it to a large heavy pan with a lid. Cook (render) the fat until some fat is extruded. Add the roast and cook on one side until it is crisply brown; turn and brown on successive sides until it is completely brown. Push the roast aside and remove the excess fat with a large spoon.

Cool enough to cut small slits in the meat and insert garlic cloves into the slits as desired. Rub with salt, pepper, and optional rosemary. It will make the house smell good whether or not it can penetrate the meat to flavor it. Pour in half the chicken or pork stock. Cover the pot with aluminum foil and then a lid. Cook over low heat on the stovetop or move to a preheated 325-degree oven and cook for 1½ hours.

Carefully remove lid and foil, baste with the liquid in the pan, and add stock only as needed to keep liquid in the bottom. Cover and cook heat another 30 to 60 minutes, testing temperature of meat as needed, until the thickest part of the meat reaches 145 degrees on a meat thermometer. Remove roast; let sit 10 minutes before slicing.

Skim off any fat, and bring the juices to the boil, boiling down steadily until reduced to a sauce consistency.

Variations:

- Rather than stock, mix ½ to 1 cup cider vinegar and ½ to 1 cup water. Use 1 cup of this in place of 1 cup of the stock. Cook as above.
- Mix together ½ to 1 cup of Coca-Cola, ¼ to ½ cup cider vinegar, and ½ to 1 cup water.
- Serve with Abercrombie Sauce (page 350) or a favorite barbecue sauce.
- Add 2 or 3 large carrots cut into thirds, a dozen small creamer or other small potatoes, some quarters or eighths of onion, fennel bulb, etc., around and under the roast ½ hour before serving. Cook until the potatoes and other vegetables are done, removing the roast beforehand if necessary.

FRESH PORK LEG (HAM)

Serves 20

THIS IS AN AMAZINGLY SUCCULENT PIECE *of meat with a skin that crispy-skin lovers like me adore pulling off and crunching on, with the small amount of moist flesh that clings underneath. Before cooking, it can be boned like a leg of lamb (see below), which is scary the first time but easy after that. Available weighing 10 to 25 pounds, it is impressive on the table, particularly since it is not frequently served.*

1 fresh pork leg, 10–15 pounds
10 garlic cloves, chopped
Salt
Freshly ground black pepper
Water, cider vinegar, or wine as needed

Preheat oven to 350 degrees.

Remove the exterior membrane of the ham by sliding the knife under the membrane and pulling it off. Shave off any excess fat with a knife. Rub the ham with the garlic, salt, freshly ground pepper, and any other seasoning desired, remembering that the seasoning will hardly penetrate the thick meat and any extravagant rubs will be wasted.

Move to a large roasting pan. (I have used a large paella pan and a large metal-handled wok when necessary, taking care to watch carefully lest there be dripping in the oven.)

Cook 15 to 18 minutes to the pound, until the ham reaches 145 degrees, checking frequently with a meat thermometer.

Carefully add water or vinegar or wine mixed with equal amounts of water if the juices are in danger of boiling away and the residue burning. Let rest at least 10 minutes before carving. Slice and serve, hot or cold, seasoned to taste with salt and pepper. Skim off and discard any fat from the juice and serve as is, or bring to the boil and reduce until thick.

Variations:

- Rub the fresh pork ham with ground cumin or coriander seed, rosemary, thyme, or other favorite seasoning. When chopped, add to the meat as well.
- Add Hot Pepper Jelly (page 648), red currant jelly, Dijon mustard, soy sauce, or other condiment to the juices as desired.
- Serve with a favorite barbecue sauce.
- I love marinating a fresh ham overnight in the Lechon Marinade (page 406), then boiling the marinade and serving it with the ham—incredibly delicious.

BONING LEGS OF FRESH RAW, COOKED, OR CURED PORK

All animals are built roughly the same as we are. So a hind leg would have a large ham, with a joint where it attaches to the body and the upper part of the leg. Occasionally, the butcher cuts these hams into two or three parts.

The first thing to do is to figure out which part you have. Pick it up, find the bone, and wiggle it. The slant of the bone will give a rough idea of which part it is, as will the size of the meat in relation to the bone.

Cut into the meat until the end of the bone—either top or bottom—is determined. Hold a sharp knife (I like a knife a bit larger than a paring knife; others like a boning knife) to the bone, scraping the bone and pushing the flesh away from it. Work around to the other side. Snap any sockets if possible. If not, look for a streak of fat that shows where the bone goes and sever the joint there. (Lines of fat are there to help ease the motion of the bones and joints, so they are good indicators to follow.)

When finished, the chances are there will be a pocket in the ham. This can be stuffed if desired or opened up into a butterfly.

To butterfly a fresh uncooked ham, cut down the smallest side of the ham and spread the ham out so it is reminiscent of a butterfly shape. This can be either roasted or broiled flat, smooth side up, and then turned. (Watch for flames and drips from the fat.)

When rolling a fresh ham after stuffing, which I rarely do, it is particularly important to remove the exterior membrane and shave off any fat.

LECHON DE NATIVIDAD (SUCKLING PIG, WHOLE PIG, OR HAM)

Serves 8 to 10

This is a traditional Cuban dish *used for a suckling pig, whole pig, or fresh ham. Two of my very special friends prepared this recipe—Pat Portal and Carmen Sanders, both children of immigrants from Cuba via Florida to Atlanta. Carmen prepared it for me first with grilled fresh ham (page 403). Pat, living in a suburban apartment development, and her brothers fashioned a grill using bricks and a large rack, and cooked a whole pig. I've found that both a suckling pig and a whole fresh leg are very doable for me at home. Both ladies used olive oil and I wouldn't dream of changing it. Charleston has sour oranges, as does Florida, but if they are not available, Valencia oranges do just fine.*

1 (10- to 12-pound) suckling pig, or
1 (8-pound) fresh pork ham

Lechon de Natividad Marinade

5–6 garlic cloves
1 tablespoon salt
3 sour or Valencia oranges
3 limes
3 grapefruit
3 tablespoons crushed rosemary
1/4 cup olive oil

Lechon de Natividad Sauce

6 garlic cloves
1 tablespoon salt
1/2 cup olive oil
1 cup sour orange or lime juice
Marinade (above)
1 tablespoon hot sauce
Salt
Freshly ground black pepper

Make several gashes in the pork so the marinade will soak into the meat. Move it to a large sturdy plastic ziplock bag, and put into a pan that will fit in the refrigerator.

To make the marinade, crush the garlic with the salt to make a paste (page 204).

Juice the oranges, limes, and grapefruit, reserving the shells. Stir the juices and rosemary with the garlic paste. Pour over the pork and place the shells of the fruit on top of the pork to cover. Seal the plastic bag and marinate the pork in the refrigerator up to 3 days, turning occasionally, keeping the plastic ziplock bag secure inside the pan.

When ready to cook, remove the pork from the refrigerator several hours in advance; pour off and reserve the marinade and discard the bag. Preheat oven to 350 degrees. Pat the pork dry. Brush with olive oil and move to the oven. Roast about 18 to 22 minutes per pound, basting with the marinade occasionally and brushing with olive oil, until the thickest part of the meat registers 145 degrees on a meat thermometer. Let stand at least 10 minutes as it rises in temperature.

To make the sauce, crush the garlic with the salt to form a paste. Heat the olive oil in a skillet. Stir in the juice, reserved marinade, crushed garlic, and hot sauce. Reduce the heat and cook 5 minutes. Remove from the heat, let stand 15 minutes, strain, and taste for seasoning. Serve with the pork.

Variation: Add 1/2 to 3/4 cup rum, curaçao, Grand Marnier, or Triple Sec to the marinade if desired.

SUCKLING PIGS

Suckling pigs should be ordered scraped and cleaned. Do order with the head on, but be sure to put an apple in its mouth so the mouth stays open while being cooked.

Fresh pork hams yield more meat, even though smaller, as suckling pig is not a fleshy animal and has a high ratio of bone to meat.

PORK FROM HEAD TO TAIL

Betty Talmadge, wife of a United States senator, friend of many presidents and their wives, witty and wise as well as a country ham producer, taught me a lot about the pig. She could cook anything from pickled pig's feet to the ears and the tail, and, of course, the chitlins, which reside in the middle, so to speak. Betty hosted grand stars like Lucille Ball in her Lovejoy, Georgia, home. She always had pigs and chickens, freshly scrubbed it seemed, in the front yard with bows tied around their necks to greet her guests. We had a group of "foodies" that cooked together and enjoyed barbecues on the farm every Fourth of July. There would be a Dixieland band and a table of cakes, as well as the cooked pig ready to be picked when the guests arrived, after a long night of slow cooking (page 403).

In addition to the more commonly used pieces of pork used throughout the chapter, here are some definitions of the more exotic:

Chitterlings (aka chitlins)—small intestines of the pig. Cooked alone, or stuffed with sausage meat (page 402).

Cracklings (aka cracklins)—what's left in the pan when pork fat has been rendered; added to cornbread for crunch and flavor (page 479).

Headcheese—odd bits of boiled meat and fat from "parts," like pig's heads, hearts, and tongues, seasoned and chilled; usually eaten as an appetizer.

Hog maw—tripe.

Knuckles (aka pork hocks)—the ankle bone just above the hoof.

Lights—pig lungs.

Liver sausage (aka liverell)—ground meat from parts such as liver, tongue, heart, and pig's head.

Panhas—mush made of the broth from pig parts, combined with cornmeal.

Pickled pig's feet—cleaned pig's feet, pickled (page 408).

Pig's feet—aka Trotters.

Pork hocks—pig's knuckles.

Pork tails—yummy pork from pig's tails, often cooked with greens (page 205).

Souse meat—cold jellied pressed pork from pig's tails, feet, knuckles, or heated and served as an appetizer for a luncheon or dinner.

Sweetbreads—lobes of the thymus gland.

Tom thumbs—small pieces of cooked chitlins cut, coated with flour or cornmeal and fried.

Tripe (aka hog maw)—inner lining of a pig's stomach.

A pig is a small hog; a hog weighs over 125 pounds.

CHITLINS

Makes 5 pounds

LONG CONSIDERED JUST AS CHEAP FOOD FOR RURAL BLACKS AND WHITES. *(My assistant Kate made them for her mother once a month.) They are seen less these days, rarely cooked at home; but soul-food restaurants sell them both fried and boiled, covered with a brown sauce, and they're considered a delicacy. I purchase chitlins in our local grocery store, sold cleaned and frozen, both cooked and uncooked. The cooked ones are sold in the sauce, the uncooked salted and coiled in the frozen package. This is Betty Talmadge's recipe from her book* How to Cook a Pig. *There is an annual Chitlin Strut in Sallie, South Carolina.*

5 pounds raw, frozen chitlins
1 quart water
1 teaspoon salt
1 large onion, quartered
Ground hot red pepper to taste
1–2 garlic cloves, chopped
1/4 cup cider or white vinegar
2 whole cloves

Soak the chitlins in cold water to thaw and remove the salt. Turn inside out to pick out excess fat with fingers. Move to a fresh pot of water and add salt, onion, hot red pepper, garlic, vinegar and cloves. Bring to the boil and simmer 2 to 2 1/2 hours. Remove chitlins, boil down stock. Add two cups of strained stock to a dark roux made of 2 tablespoons butter cooked with 2 tablespoons flour. Bring to the boil, season, and serve with the chitlins.

To fry: drain chitlins from stock. Cut into short lengths, pepper heavily and coat with cornmeal. Add to hot fat and cook until brown and crisp. Drain well. Serve with champagne, or, if not available, vinegar.

PIG'S TAILS

Boil as above. Brown in the oven before serving on a bun with barbecue sauce.

PIG'S EARS

Boil in salt water and vinegar or Coca-Cola until they can be pierced with a fork. Dry, move to a broiler or grill, and cook until crisp. Cool, slice thinly, and serve in a lettuce wrap or bun with a hot sauce.

PICKLED PIG'S FEET

SOLD IN JARS *in gas stations and country stores, these are still popular.*

1 pound salt
1/4 pound granulated sugar
1/4 ounce saltpeter
2 quarts water

Clean feet. Meanwhile, dissolve salt, sugar and saltpeter in 2 quarts water. Add the feet to the brine and soak refrigerated at least 2 weeks or up to 3 weeks.

HAM

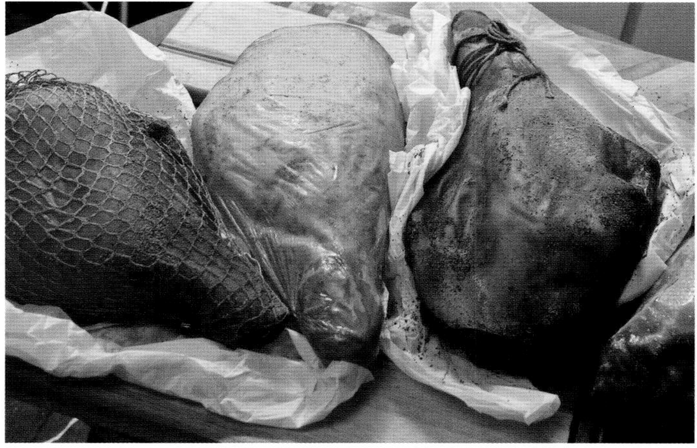

Ham is the rear leg of a hog. From there, a different image comes to each of us. I think of a fresh pork ham, like the *Lechon de Natividad* (page 406). Others might think of their mother's table groaning under the weight of a huge cured ham studded with cloves and burnished with brown sugar, which cooked all night and tasted of salt and sugar. There are those that stand in front of the meat counter and look at the variety of cured, cured and smoked, canned, ready-to-eat, partially cooked, boiled, picnic (not a ham at all), spiral-sliced, and many more types of hams, their different names and prices confusing; so they close their eyes and grab whatever comes to hand. I'll try to sort them out here. Do remember, however, to check package directions for cooking any ham, and do not assume all are the same. The USDA requires that all cured hams have cooking and safe-handling instructions on the label. Some hams have the appearance of ready-to-eat, but they will always be labeled with cooking instructions.

All hams, fresh or cured, can be sold bone-in, partially boned, or completely boned. Partially boned have the hip and/or shank bones removed. I was always told that hams with the bone left in are more flavorful, but boneless are much easier to carve. Cuts differ according to the bone. The top half of the ham is the butt. The "butt end" is the upper cut of the hind leg. It is meatier, has more fat, and is more expensive. The "butt half" has the center ham slice; the butt portion does not. The "shank half" is the lower cut of the hind leg. It is sweeter, is harder to cut, has less meat (because it has more bone), and is less expensive. The shank half includes the center cut; the shank portion has the center slice removed. The "center slice" is considered the best cut, and is up to 1 inch thick and found where the shank and butt are separated. Another bone-in ham is the "spiral-cut" ham. Precooked, it is cut around the bone with machinery that allows it to be done in one continuous cut around the ham. It makes consistently even slices from one end to the other. All of these can be glazed and reheated.

Cured Hams

There are two main types of cured ham: "country," which are dry-cured and aged, and "city," which are wet cured, and refer to almost all the other hams found in the grocery store.

Country Hams—These are delightful dry hams, cured and aged with a minimum of 18% moisture, usually by a dry-cure mixture of salt and other ingredients such as sugar or pepper, and most likely but not always smoked long over a low fire. Smoke does not penetrate deep into a ham. The curing process already draws out most of the moisture that would be affected by the smoke. Smoking does give added color. Originally, black pepper was rubbed onto hams to prevent insect infestation. Today it is a tradition rather than a necessity, as is brown sugar in the rub. If you are unused to the taste, country hams may surprise with their saltiness and dry texture.

Six to twelve months is the traditional processing time for a country ham, but it may be more or less. The producers follow USDA feed guidelines, allowing these hams to be eaten "uncooked" like the Italian prosciutto and Spanish Serrano ham, or further cooked. They may include the full shank bone or a variety of other types that include cooked and glazed, spiral-cut, and boned. Because the final product contains little water, bacteria can't multiply in them, and they are safely stored at room temperature.

At one time, hogs for the famous Smithfield, Virginia, hams were allegedly peanut-fed and had special guidelines for their feed to be called "Smithfield"—in addition to being produced within certain geographical boundaries. There was also a time when a ham with a long shank bone differed in name from one sold with a sawed-off shank bone; the longer ham designated a longer curing time. Although a few producers and regions still follow that practice, the shank-bone length/curing-time relationship can no longer be accepted as a certainty.

Country hams are produced all over the Southeast, with regions as well as states vying for the qualities they most value. Some like them sweeter, some saltier, and some milder. These seasoning recipes are guarded as family treasures; a normal one might have twice as much salt as pepper and a fourth as much brown sugar. It's all in the taste of the producer. Once processed only in the fall and cold months, year-round processing using modern technology is now the norm for ham producers. "Newcomers" are garnering recognition as ham producers, if one can consider a newcomer someone like S. Wallace Edwards & Sons, Inc., which has been making quality country ham since 1926. Their all natural product line featuring Berkshire pork is free of artificial growth stimulants, animal protein by-products and antibiotics.

Cooking a country ham—When a dried country ham arrives, usually in a burlap bag, check to see if refrigeration is required; it is only mandatory for a reconstituted and cooked ham. A dried ham will weigh between 10 and 20 pounds and can be safely kept for up to a year or two without quality diminishing by following the producer's guidelines. (It is "safe" to eat even longer than that.) There is perhaps nothing more foreboding for the cook than one of these behemoth legs, with its natural spots of green mold, perhaps, and a thick skin. In fact, the mold is typically harmless and is the signature of a country ham. Although my preference for this jewel is to serve it sliced thinly without cooking, there are those that love it cooked.

The refrain for cooking country ham can be reduced to "scrape—soak—simmer—bake." The process is best done over a span of three days, expending a little bit of time each day:

Scraping—The first step is scraping the ham, using a wire or other sturdy brush to remove any unattractive spots.

Soaking—The second is soaking the ham to reconstitute as well as de-salinate. Put the cleaned ham in a cooler, second refrigerator, or other place that will keep the ham at about 40 degrees for several days. Add ice as necessary to keep at that temperature. Change the water several times, preferably every 8 hours. Soak as little as overnight or up to 3 days.

When through soaking, discard the water and thoroughly scrub the ham and mold with a brush until satisfied the mold is removed and the exterior is satisfactory. (Please note: some country hams are shipped with instructions to cut off part of the shank bone. This is fine if there is a hacksaw nearby. But I don't have one, so I leave it on.) If soaking and cooking a country ham sounds daunting, order one already cooked. Keep cooked hams refrigerated until ready to use. Glaze and heat through, or just serve cold with no further attention.

Simmering and grilling—A country ham needs to be cooked with moisture after soaking. That may be in the oven, on top of the stove, or on the grill. For oven or stovetop cooking, surround the ham with liquid in a large pan: I prefer something sweet, like Coca-Cola, pineapple juice, apple juice, cider, or 7-Up. Cover with a lid or tight foil. Simmer—don't boil—or cook at 325 degrees for about 20 minutes per pound, or until it registers 148 degrees on a meat thermometer and comes off the bone in nice slices, about 6 to 8 hours. Check and add liquid if it has evaporated while cooking. If oven cooking, move the soaked ham to a pan with sides and surround with liquid as above and cook at 325 degrees for 6 to 8 hours. Remove from oven and discard the liquid before slicing. Taste. If it is still too salty, change the liquid and cook a bit longer, taking care it does not get cooked to shreds.

Baking and broiling—The ham may be sliced and served as above, or baked or grilled and glazed for a prettier presentation. Cook as above. Remove from oven. Move to a clean pan coming partially up the sides. Coat the ham with a favorite glaze, such as brown sugar and cloves, pineapple or peach slices, etc., which will also add sweetness. Bake at 475 degrees, then broil or grill for 15 minutes or until the glaze is melted and attractive. Country ham should—let's change that to *must*—be served in thin slices.

City Hams—"City" hams, as they are known by culinary professionals, are the familiar grocery store "wet-cured" hams, where sodium nitrate, salt, and sugar are combined with water to form a brine, sometimes called a curing solution. For a commercial cure, this is injected or pumped evenly into the ham, which is then washed and cooked. It may be smoked or not, or injected with a liquid smoke solution. (These nitrates are safe food additives approved by the USDA and are monitored for quantity. Further information can be found at www.USDA.gov. Brine-cured hams are the ones most commonly found in grocery stores. They vary enormously in quality, taste, and price.)

City hams are sold totally cooked (reaching 147 degrees for 2 to 5 minutes and needing no further cooking) or partially cooked (heated to 137 degrees to the center.) Partially cooked hams and leftovers should be heated to 160 degrees. Both partially cooked and totally cooked city hams may be sold glazed, or glazed at home after purchase.

"Cooked" Ham—This is boneless, cured, processed ham, steamed in water to cook, that needs no further cooking to be served sliced or in pieces. It is frequently referred to as "boiled" ham, which is not a USDA-permitted label. It's usually bland and non-smoked. I hate to say this, but this is what we ate when we were children, and we loved it.

Canned Ham—My mother's favorite ham, since she was of Danish heritage, was an imported boneless Danish canned ham. Served at parties as well as on holidays, she glazed it, if need be, and just reheated it, since it was already cooked. I used to love to eat the pink aspic around the hams—the tasty juices of the ham mixed with the gelatin added before processing in the can. There are so many canned hams now, I don't know how she would figure out the best one unless she spent some time studying the ingredients, which is, perhaps, when discussing any of these, the best thing to do. All canned hams are boneless but may be "composites"—i.e., made from pieces of ham—or from a whole boneless ham. Some canned hams need to be refrigerated, and some may be kept on the shelf according to package directions.

COUNTRY HAM

Serves 16

Country ham is a real treat. *Soaking and scrubbing are important to rid the ham of the excess salt and the mold formed on the outside during curing (the mold is harmless). Follow the directions on the facing page for preparing the ham for cooking.*

1 (12- to 15-pound) country ham, scrubbed, and soaked (page 410)
10 quarter-sized slices of ginger
1 teaspoon peppercorns
1/2 gallon apple cider
1 gallon water
1 cup chunky applesauce
3 tablespoons Dijon mustard
1 tablespoon prepared horseradish
1 cup light or dark brown sugar, divided
1 cup breadcrumbs

Preheat oven to 350 degrees.

Move the soaked ham to a large pan, fat side up. Add sliced ginger, peppercorns, and enough water to come 2 to 3 inches up the side of the ham. (Reserve remaining cider/water to add to pan as liquid evaporates.)

Cover pan, move to the oven, and cook about 20 minutes per pound, or until internal temperature on a meat thermometer registers 160 degrees. Remove from oven halfway through cooking and turn ham over. Return to oven and continue cooking. When done, remove ham to broiler rack and let rest 10 minutes. Discard liquid.

Remove skin and fat. Taste at this point. If still tough, cook in fresh liquid an additional 1 to 2 hours. If ham is still terribly salty, it may safely be immersed in more apple cider and water to draw out more of the salt. Let sit a couple of hours. Taste again and proceed. Drain.

To glaze, increase oven temperature to 400 degrees. Combine the applesauce, mustard, horseradish, and 1/2 cup of the brown sugar. Spread over the ham. Bake 20 minutes, or until ham is heated through and sauce is bubbly. Remove from oven and turn on broiler. Mix together remaining 1/2 cup brown sugar and breadcrumbs, and spread on ham. Broil 5 minutes, or until crisp.

Ham bone makes a good stock, so follow directions for stock (page 113) and add any scraps to the stock that are not usable for meatloaf or some other purpose.

REDEYE HAM WITH COCA-COLA REDEYE GRAVY

Serves 2

THIS DISH GOT ITS NAME *from the cut of ham that has a small bone in the center, which looks like a red eye. The story goes that water or coffee was tipped into a pan over an outdoor fire, boiled up, and poured over the ham. Now, any slice of ham works, and Coca-Cola has supplanted the coffee in my house. This ham may cry for a biscuit.*

2 (1/4-inch-thick) slices country ham

6 tablespoons (3 ounces) Coca-Cola

Trim some of the fat off the ham slices and melt it in a large heated frying pan. Add the ham, fat part down, the ham draping up the side of the pan if the piece is large.

Fry slowly until the fatty edges are soft and brown. Turn and cook until lightly browned. Remove from the pan and keep warm.

Add the Coca-Cola to the pan and bring to the boil, stirring, to get the bits off the bottom. Pour over ham.

Variation: Substitute 1/2 cup (red) Hot Pepper Jelly (page 648) and 2 tablespoons apple juice for the cola. Heat until the jelly melts in the boiling juice and the sauce thickens.

GLAZED HAM STEAK

Serves 6

THE CENTER CUT OF THE HAM *is also called ham steak. It is a tender, moist piece of meat. I serve it for brunch as well as for Sunday supper.*

1 (3-pound) precooked ham steak, 1 1/2–2 inches thick

1/2 cup sorghum or maple syrup

Lightly brush the steak with the syrup and broil on a pan 3 inches from the heat, or place directly on the grill.

Broil or grill 3 or 4 minutes. Turn and cook second side. Brush with syrup during broiling.

Tip the pan juices, if any, into a pan with the remainder of the syrup. Bring to the boil and boil 1 minute. Serve the ham with the syrup.

Variations:

- Substitute 1/2 cup barbecue sauce for the maple syrup.
- Omit maple syrup and brush with 1/4 cup honey mixed with 1/2 cup Dijon mustard. Broil as directed above.

Variation: Ham Steak in Mustard Cream

Add ham steak to a hot skillet with 2 tablespoons butter and cook 3 to 4 minutes on each side. Move to a rimmed baking sheet and keep warm in a 300-degree oven. Add 2 tablespoons finely chopped shallots, 2 tablespoons chopped fresh tarragon, and 1 tablespoon Dijon mustard to the remaining butter in the skillet. Stir in 2 tablespoons dry Madeira or dry sherry and 1 cup heavy cream. Cover and cook until the cream reduces by half, about 5 to 7 minutes. Remove ham steak from oven to a warm serving platter and coat with mustard cream.

OVEN BAKED BACON

Makes 1 pound

THE EASIEST WAY TO COOK BACON IS TO BAKE IT, *as it requires so little attention and comes out crisp, even and brown.*

1 pound bacon

Preheat oven to 400 degrees. Line a rimmed baking sheet with aluminum foil. Spread bacon slices on the foil. Bake for 15 minutes. Remove from oven. Pour off excess bacon fat carefully and turn the bacon strips with tongs. Return to oven until crisp and brown, checking frequently, about 5 to 10 minutes. Do not let burn. Remove with tongs to paper towels.

Variation: Caramelized Bacon
For those, like Cynthia, who love their sweets with salt, it simply doesn't get any better than caramelized bacon. Satisfying on its own, this bacon is a versatile topping chopped into small pieces to sprinkle on salads or stir into ice cream!

Pat bacon with 1 cup light or dark brown sugar. Proceed as above, but after 15 minutes drag the bacon slices in the melted sugar and goo. Remove to a rack over another pan to cool. (Paper towels will stick.)

CRACKLINS

Makes about 1/3 pound

STORE-BOUGHT CRACKLINS ARE FREQUENTLY CALLED PORK RINDS. *This is a misnomer as they rarely include the tough skin, or rind. There are now novelty "Cracklins" products that can be microwaved or fried. In Southern Louisiana there is a "Cracklin Trail" (and map) to help those with good digestion to find the best-rated places for cracklins.*

1/2 pound fatback, rinsed

Cut the fatback into slices and then cut the slices into thin strips. Stack the strips and cut them into small cubes.

Move the cubes to a small skillet, spreading out in one layer, and barely cover with water. Bring to the boil and cook until the water evaporates. Continue cooking until the cubes have rendered their fat and are crispy and well-browned. Remove with a slotted spoon to a plate lined with paper towels.

BEEF

Like all farm-raised animals, beef has changed considerably since Colonial days. Reading old recipes brings real awareness of the necessity of cooking all but the best parts of the animal (tenderloin, standing ribs, a few steaks) with long, slow cooking, vigorous pounding, or as ground meat. (This is excluding innards, such as brains, liver, and sweetbreads.) A smaller animal was the norm in days gone by, although Mrs. Dull (*Southern Cooking,* 1928) doesn't mention the weight of most of the cuts of meat she describes cooking, but she also hasn't much range in the cuts she prepares.

Mrs. Annabelle Hill, however, whose wonderful 1872 book was annotated by Damon Lee Fowler, stuffs many of her meats as we do flank steak today. From Georgia, as was Mrs. Dull, Mrs. Hill had more extensive and exotic preparations of beef, from stuffing rounds and sirloins to *daubes* and *à la modes,* as she called them. She also encrusted her meat in pastry, later discarded, that was solely for the purpose of keeping the meat moist.

I always josh and say that we are built like other animals, except we walk on only two feet. Still, comparison to our bodies helps understand what types of meat to purchase and how to cook them. Meat is a muscle composed of fat, collagen, protein, sugar, and water. How a meat tastes as well as its color and texture is determined by the arrangement and quantity of the muscle filaments, fat, and connective tissue. The more the muscle moves or works, the tougher the tissue. These are the cuts that should be wet-cooked, marinated, dry-rubbed, stewed, pot-roasted, steamed, poached, or slow-cooked. Muscles from the rib, plate, and loin will be more tender, with good flavor. They can be cooked by dry-heat methods, such as broiling, grilling, sautéing, roasting, stir-frying, and deep-frying.

Muscle is composed of protein, and as the muscle is cooked the heat "denatures" the protein. What this means is that the molecules unwind or separate; this is known as denatured proteins. The protein molecules are then attracted to each other and begin to coagulate, or cook. Up to 120 degrees, they shrink in width; after 120 degrees, they shrink in length. In doing all this shrinking, they "squeeze" the water out of the strands, which is why well-cooked meat is dry. This is where fat is the savior. Fat melts, basting the fibers and drenching the meat with flavor.

Meat muscle also contains collagen (Harold McGee says this means "glue producing," from the Greek) and elastin (also known as "sinew and gristle"). Collagen melts and turns into gelatin, which gives the slippery mouth-feel to slow cooked meats. Elastin, on the other hand, can only be broken down by physical means. This occurs in grinding meat or pounding cutlets ("swissing").

In the early twenty-first century, American beef-cutting styles were changed radically to accomplish the American desire for more tender beef and quicker cooking meals, particularly the desire for steaks. The meat was cut along the muscles, excising tender parts that had once been lumped along with tougher cuts. For instance, the shoulder chuck has yielded a piece called "petit tender" that rivals the tenderloin for tenderness. Only 9 to 12 ounces, this petit tender was initially sold only to restaurants and is still hard to find. Other "new" cuts were the "tri-tip roast," from which comes the

MRS. HILL'S BEEF À LA MODE

Remove the bone from a round weighing ten or twelve pounds; keep it until tender. The day before it is to be cooked, spread over it a mixture of two teaspoons salt, two of fine black pepper, one of pulverized saltpeter. One teaspoonful of cinnamon, the same of ginger, mace, allspice, cloves, and coriander seed, all beat together and sifted, then moistened with vinegar and spread over the meat. Ten o'clock next morning, fill the space from which the bone was taken with a rich stuffing, seasoned highly with thyme, parsley and onion. Roll the piece in a good circular shape, and bind tightly with a broad tape; lard it well with narrow strips of fat bacon. Put a small trivet in the bottom of a pot, or deep oven; pour in a pint of warm water; place the meat upon the trivet; put it to baking, and as soon as it warms, begin to baste with good sweet lard; rancid, strong lard should never be used for basting, it spoils everything it touches. Continue the basting with the gravy. Half an hour before the meat is done, baste and dredge with flour; bake a light brown color. Thicken the gravy very little with brown flour; pour in half a teacup of boiling water; let it boil up once, and pour into the gravy boat. If too greasy, remove the superfluous grease. This is excellent cold, and will keep well. It will require at least four hours' baking.

—*Mrs. Hill's New Cook Book,* 1872

"culotte steak," and "flatiron" (shaped like an iron). These are all flavorful and delicious as steaks. My friend Bruce Aidells, who has a number of excellent books on meat, stresses that the "chuck mock tender steak" is in fact not tender, and that names of meats are not the same all over the United States, so it may be confusing when shopping in another area of the country. Talk to the butcher and ask where the piece of meat is from and what needs to be done to make it flavorful and pleasantly edible. After all, they are charging for it and there is no reason to cook a piece of meat blindly.

RECOMMENDED INTERNATIONAL COOKING TEMPERATURES FOR BEEF

Rare	130 degrees Fahrenheit
Medium Rare	140 degrees Fahrenheit
Medium	150 degrees Fahrenheit
Well Done	160 degrees Fahrenheit

Marinating and rubbing meat—Marinades and rubs add tremendous flavor to meat. Cynthia is so dedicated to the benefits of marinating that she comes home from the grocery store and immediately prepares various marinades, moves her bounty of meat to plastic ziplock bags, adds a marinade, and puts the bags in the freezer. She says the beef and chicken spend the freezing and thawing time more productively. When reusing a marinade to serve as a sauce, bring it to a full boil for 2 or 3 minutes, then simmer until reduced to desired consistency.

Rubs are classified as wet or dry. "Wet" rubs have liquid added to make a paste and are slathered on before cooking, sometimes sitting awhile before being cooked. Dry rubs are usually a mix of dry spices rubbed into the meat, sometimes sitting before cooking, or cooked right away.

Browning—The surface of the meat should be dried with paper towels before browning.

Salting—There are many schools of thought about salting meat long before cooking or just before cooking or after cooking. Moisture follows salt. If meat is salted long before cooking, browning is more difficult due to the moisture having been extruded, making the meat less juicy. Chefs frequently season just before cooking and have a different time schedule. When the pan or grill is ready, they season quickly and sear before the liquid develops. It is easier for the home cook to brown the meat first, then season it. Avoid salting meat for stews and braises. Frequently the other ingredients, particularly commercial stocks and some canned tomatoes, are already salty enough. Since I recommend cutting the meat into large cubes; nothing will be lost, as when it is cut down to bite size and the accompanying ingredients are tasted, judicious salting can be done.

Brining—Brining is a method of salting, marinating, and flavoring. Brining may be done in any number of liquids, from water to Coca-Cola, and is supposed to add moisture and flavor to the product brined. Herbs and other seasonings are added to offer even more punch. There is also a method of injecting flavorings, including salt, into meat by hypodermic needle, but it is cumbersome for the home cook. When storing a liquid in a plastic ziplock bag in the refrigerator, be sure to double bag it, with the seals facing the opposite ways to minimize leaks. I learned this the hard way. The most commonly brined beef is the brisket.

Braising beef—Braising is a cooking technique that comes from the French word *braisier,* meaning "smoldering coal." The term originated in the eighteenth century. Like the word *sauté* in French, it is both a recipe and a technique. The traditional French pot for braising had a depressed lid, and coals were placed on its surface to surround the foods with heat. John Mariani reports on pot-roasting in the United States in 1881, and a "pot oven" (a three-legged pot with a depressed lid) was used in the hearth for cooking. Today, a heavy Dutch oven is used for braising. Meats, poultry, fish, vegetables, and fruits can be braised.

The terms *braising* and *stewing* are used interchangeably. However, braising technically differs from stewing in that there is less liquid for braising, and it uses whole pieces; stew meats are smaller. (I much prefer two-inch pieces to smaller ones.) Usually braising and stewing are done to tenderize tough cuts of meat. Meats are usually, but not always, browned first to develop color and flavor.

The amount of liquid (as a rule of thumb) should come halfway up the sides of what is being braised. The liquid is used to transmit the heat. The liquid is used to transmit heat and keep moist. Any marinating liquid should be boiled separately on the stove to kill all surface bacteria before adding it to the pan with the meat.

Liquids include water, milk, stock, beer, wine, Coca-Cola, tea, and puréed fruits and/or vegetables. (Tomatoes are frequently used, particularly canned, with their juices.)

A successful braise uses an oven temperature of 200 degrees or slightly below (180 degrees is supposed to be "the perfect temperature," which is difficult for us home cooks.) Modern sources, such as *Cook's Illustrated* magazine, may recommend an oven temperature of 300 degrees and an internal temperature of 200 to 210 degrees.

To prevent steam from escaping, which ultimately affects the amount of liquid in the pot, cover the pot with foil then a lid. Braises and stews are both better cooked a day or two ahead, as cooling results in the re-absorption of liquid lost in cooking. Meats should cool in the liquid they are cooked in to reabsorb the liquid for storing. Before serving, reheat the meat and remove from the liquid. Boil the liquid to reduce or concentrate to form a sauce.

Braising and stewing can both be done on top of the stove, keeping the temperature in mind, but most authorities prefer oven braising and stewing. In the South, however, the top of the stove may be preferable to heating up the house. A slow simmer is fine.

The beef shanks, shoulders, and cheeks are rich in collagen and gelatin and give body to braises, stews, soups, stocks, and sauces. Other cuts suitable for braising include chuck (shoulder, arm blade, shoulder steaks, short ribs), the round (bottom, rump, eye of round, bottom round), the shank and the brisket.

The appearance of red color throughout a braised meat is caused by the action of slow heating. This allows the enzymes to tenderize the meat and preserve good flavor. The myoglobin pigment remains intact, not broken down, and therefore the red color remains.

Gray meat indicates overcooking.

Stewing—By definition, *stewing* means long cooking. Use a heavy-bottomed pan to prevent burning, or brown in a pan before moving to a slow cooker. Stew meats vary considerably in quality. Ideally they should have a bit of fat for flavor and have the tough connective tissue removed. The best choices for stewing are beef chuck, lamb shanks, ox tails, osso bucco, and lamb leg or shoulder. By the same token, use sturdy vegetables in the stew, preferably root vegetables. For instance, onions, sweet potatoes, potatoes, carrots, parsnips, turnips, and beets are excellent choices.

A stew likes a flavorful base of sautéed vegetables; the classic French *mirepoix* is one onion, two stalks of celery and two carrots; Louisianans use "the holy trinity"—onion, peppers and celery. Latin cooking relies on a *sofrito,* an aromatic purée of tomatoes, peppers, cilantro, onions, and garlic. Others use fennel in place of the celery, shallots or leeks in place of—or along with—the onions. Oil is a better vehicle for a stew than butter, but pork fat, whether pure lard or bacon grease, is a popular and succulent Southern substitute. Fat from chicken, beef, or lamb may all be used.

Flour is frequently but not always used to coat the meat, giving the meat a thin crust. It helps to brown and adds thickening. A nice deep brown gives more flavor and color. Stews can also be thickened by the use of a cornstarch and water slurry (page 651), *beurre manié,* flour, or mashed potatoes (page 224). The pan liquids may also be boiled to reduce the quantity. Wine or other liquid can be added and reduced again.

Liquids vary, from liquors ranging from bourbon to wines, to stocks, or even water. The more flavor, the better the stew. Liquids are used to deglaze the pan (page 357) by adding the liquid to the pan after the meat has been browned and set aside, and stirring until all the good bits are off the bottom of the browning pan. After deglazing, the meat and mirepoix or sautéed aromatic vegetables are returned to the pot and covered with liquid.

The stew should be brought to the boil, the heat reduced to a simmer, and cooked covered until shortly before the meat is cooked. I like to remove the aromatics (herbs or vegetables that give off deep flavors and aromas in cooking) at this point, as they have "surrendered" their full flavor to the liquid. The cubed vegetables are added, and the stew is cooked until the vegetables are as tender as desired—but not mushy. The smaller the meat or vegetables, the faster they will cook. Larger pieces of both are better if using a slow cooker for many hours, as they will not dry out; smaller pieces tend to dry out much more quickly.

The final cooked temperature of the meat should be 160 degrees (well done). It should be firm to the touch but tender if pierced with a carving fork, preferably not stringy. Oven temperature, if using, should be 300 degrees. Allow 6 to 8 ounces meat per person. Pot roasts like a day or two in the refrigerator while flavors mellow and blend. Reheat in the sauce. Stews freeze well up to six months.

Broiling and grilling—These are "kissing cousins" in Southern parlance—dry-heat cooking with the source of the heat reversed: grilling cooks from the bottom; broiling cooks from the top. Knowing one's oven and broiler or grill is important. Closeness of the rack to the heat will determine the degree of caramelization, hence, flavor. Both should be preheated according to directions.

Pan-frying, griddling, and sautéing—Fast, easy, and toothsome meat comes from these methods. The meat should be dry, and if salted, salted only immediately before the meat hits the hot pan. Know the heat source: the pan should fit over the burner with no flames or hot coils licking around its side, because even cooking is the key. For this reason a heavy frying pan or griddle are recommended; it is a temptation to use a nonstick pan, but since they should not be heated over 450 or 500 degrees and don't make a good crust anyway, avoid them. All that will result is gray meat and a lot of released liquid in the bottom of the pan. Preheat the pan or griddle before adding the meat. Rub the meat with oil if desired, or put oil in the hot pan. Butter will burn, but a combination of butter and oil will take a higher heat than butter alone.

When meat is added to a hot-enough pan, it will not stick in any event. A cold pan reaches out and sucks the collagen of the meat into its pores, making it a mess to clean as well. If there is water coming from the meat, the pan is not hot enough. Take a close look at the part of the meat farthest from the heat when cooking; if the heat of the bottom is pushing water out the top, turn it as quickly as possible (much like watching for bubbles on top of a pancake). To deglaze a pan, add liquid—water, stock, wine, etc.—bring to the boil, stirring, until reduced to sauce consistency. This should help clean the pan, too.

RACK OR NO RACK?

We rarely use a rack in our roasting pans. Occasionally I'll use one for a crown roast or rib roast.

TENDERLOIN BASICS

A tenderloin, or fillet of beef, can vary widely in size, depending on the size of the animal. There are three major parts: the large end; the middle, which is the heart of the meat; and the tail, which is thinner than the rest of the tenderloin. Running alongside the middle portion is a thin piece of meat encased in fat called the "chain." The chain should be removed by either the butcher or the cook. It is delicious eaten on its own once the fat is scraped off, used for dishes like beef stroganoff, or ground for spectacular hamburgers.

The larger fat end, the butt (also called the head) is from the rump or sirloin end and is the least desirable piece but is still quite nice. The middle portion is the porterhouse-steak section and includes the chateaubriand and fillet-steak sections. This is the best part of the tenderloin and is about 8 to 10 inches long. The end, or tail section, is the rib end and includes meat for tournedos and filet mignon. (Not everyone agrees on the names for these parts, either. Some call the butt the chateaubriand, smashing it down with a cleaver and reshaping it.) I frequently remove the butt and use it as a separate roast, as it is a different size from all the rest and has a membrane going down it that indicates where to cut. Many times a tenderloin is sold without the butt and the butt sold separately.

Tenderloin is sold both untrimmed and trimmed and peeled. The average untrimmed beef tenderloin is 7 to 9 pounds, including the butt. Rarely are those large tenders sold peeled and trimmed. "Peeled" tenders are usually smaller tenders that weigh 3½ to 4 pounds when sold. Before peeling and trimming, these small tenders weigh 5 to 7 pounds. Most tenders that are sold unpeeled will include ¾ inch of fat as well as the chain. "Cow" tenders are less expensive though not as wonderful as the beef tenderloin; but they are more than satisfactory for casual grilling, large parties, hors d'oeuvres, or any time when people are drinking. Tenderloin is tenderloin, no matter the animal. I have cooked tenderloin from bulls, buffalos, beef cattle, and cows to great satisfaction.

The variance of diameter in different parts of the meat means the doneness of the meat ranges from very well done (at the tail) to rare (for the large butt) and medium rare (for the center). To achieve some degree of uniformity, fold about 2 inches of the tail underneath, making it all nearly the same diameter as the center portion. Stripped of its fat, the tenderloin needs some fat for cooking. Brush it with olive oil or butter, or lay some of the removed fat over it for part of the cooking. Zealots may lard it with narrow strips of salt pork.

The tenderloin may also be cut into pieces as desired, from steaks to smaller roasts. Some people prefer tying their meat at 1½- to 2-inch intervals. This keeps it shaped but creates lines on the meat after cooking showing where the string was. (To truss with a trussing needle, use a cotton [as opposed to plastic] twine or even uncoated dental floss. Sew in a basting stitch—over, under, over, under—without a knot at either end.) Others wrap tenderloin in dampened cheesecloth, something I find unnecessary and messy, complicating an otherwise easy process.

Butchering tip: The tenderloin of beef is wrapped in a mass of fat and membrane that needs to be completely removed with a sharp knife. Nestled next to the tenderloin is a long, thin piece of meat wrapped in fat and membrane called the "chain," which should be removed for the roast beef but can be used elsewhere. One-third of the meat weight is lost when the fat and chain are removed, whether at home or by the butcher. There is very little price savings when buying trimmed (peeled) vs. untrimmed tenderloin when all calculations are finished, so buy the best thing for convenience. The difference in size of tenderloins and the unknown amount of fat (some are also sold "partially trimmed") makes it difficult to do a price comparison. The cost of the fat is computed once all fat and membrane are removed and there are two pieces of meat (the smaller one is called the chain). If possible, get the butcher to trim it; be sure, however, to ask for the chain.

Purchasing tip: Be sure to purchase the whole tenderloin. Some stores sell pieces of the tenderloin, also untrimmed, in packages just marked beef tenderloin. It may not be a whole tenderloin at all but the less desirable part of the tenderloin—the butt, with its higher ratio of fat. It appears to be cheaper but is in fact more expensive.

TENDERLOIN STUFFED WITH COUNTRY HAM AND PARMESAN CHEESE

Serves 10 to 15

WHENEVER I MAKE THIS, *I realize it is an exceptional entrée and worth the little effort it requires. Our country ham excels as part of this dish, as it flavors the meat but does not dominate. The cheese holds everything together while adding its unique and extraordinary nuttiness. Be sure to use the best available Parmigiano-Reggiano; it is worth the extra expense. Tenderloin is clearly the most expensive cut of beef and merits good accompaniments and embellishments. The butt end of the tenderloin is removed and used to make a separate, smaller roast. It may also be stuffed, sliced, and served with the larger portion, or saved for a romantic meal* pour deux. *Freeze before or after cooking.*

This is another method of stuffing a fillet, making it a wide, flat piece of meat by "double-butterflying"—slicing into but not through each of the butterfly "wings" and layering it with the cheese and ham before rolling it up. A less than glamorous comparison is the way we used to wash sweaters, spreading out a big towel, putting the damp sweater on top, and then rolling it all up.

1 beef tenderloin, stripped of silver skin, fat and gristle, chain removed (about 3–5 pounds)

1/2 pound Parmigiano-Reggiano cheese

1/2 pound thinly sliced country ham

Oil, cook's preference for brushing

Use a large sharp knife and follow the line of fat to separate the butt from the rest of the tenderloin. (There is a "line" of fat in the meat that is easy to follow.) Cut the butt, if filling and roasting alongside the tenderloin, and the remaining tenderloin as follows: with the meat positioned lengthwise, cut down the center of the meat (butterfly), leaving the meat hinged in the center. With the knife parallel to the cutting board in the middle of one of the sides, cut again lengthwise down the meat, again leaving a hinge. Repeat on the opposite side. Now there are three parallel hinges making one wide piece of meat. Cover with plastic wrap and pound to become a thin piece of meat about 1 1/2 inches thick.

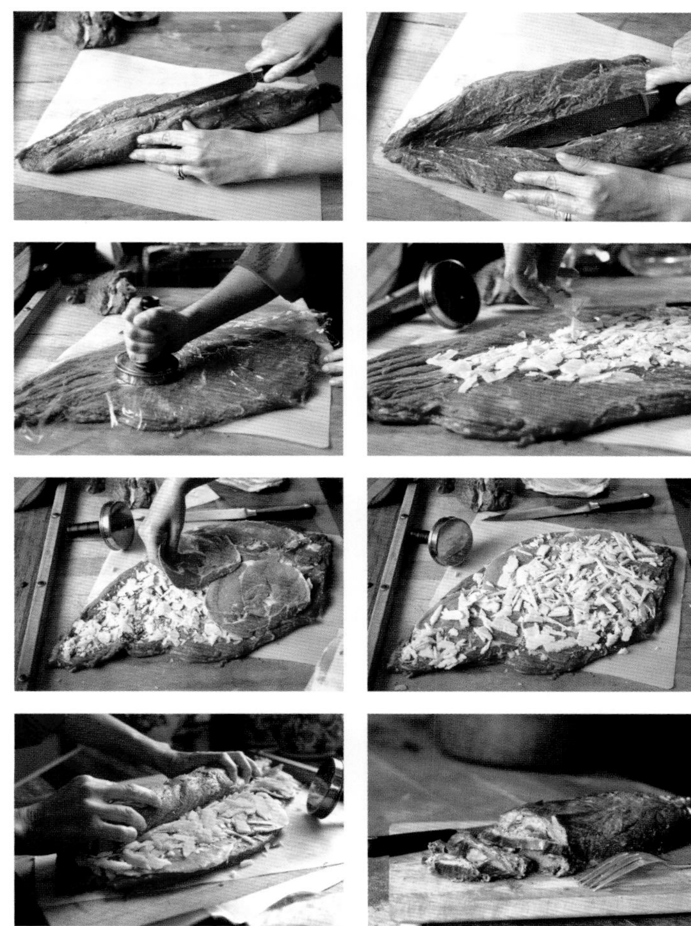

Cover the meat with a layer of sliced Parmigiano-Reggiano, then a layer of thinly sliced ham, then another layer of Parmigiano-Reggiano. Roll the beef, starting from one side and continuing to the other. Tie securely with butcher's twine. This may be done in advance, up to about 24 hours. When ready to cook, bring to room temperature and rub with oil.

Preheat oven to 425 degrees.

Move the meat to a roasting pan and cook until a meat thermometer registers 130 degrees for rare and 140 degrees for medium-rare. Remove from the oven and let rest at least 10 minutes, preferably longer. The temperature will increase 10 degrees during the 10-minute resting. Chill if possible, as it is much easier to slice when cold. Slice thinly and serve with pan juices. Serve hot or at room temperature. It may be made several days in advance and reheated, wrapped in foil.

ROASTED BEEF TENDERLOIN

Serves 8 to 10

Beef tenderloin is a miraculous meat, *fork-tender and perhaps the easiest of all meats to cook after trimming. It is often seen at Southern parties, as it is the ideal special-occasion meat. The tricks are in purchasing it and trimming it if necessary. Once that is done, anyone can cook it! Plan on 1/4 to 1/3 pound of trimmed meat per person for dinner, with a little left over for seconds. A good meat thermometer relieves much of the anxiety surrounding cooking an expensive cut of meat.*

1 beef tenderloin (about 3–5 pounds), stripped of silver skin, fat, and gristle, and chain removed
Oil, butter, or fat, cook's preference
Salt
Freshly ground black pepper
1 recipe Vidalia Onion and Vinegar Sauce (page 665)

Preheat oven to 500 degrees.

Rub tenderloin with the oil. Move to a roasting pan and season with salt and plenty of pepper. Tuck the bottom end, or "tail," underneath the meat.

Immediately reduce the heat to 400 degrees and roast the tenderloin 18 to 20 minutes, until its thickest part registers 130 degrees on a meat thermometer for rare, 140 for medium-rare. Season as needed with salt and pepper when done. Let rest 10 minutes before carving. Served hot or cold with Vidalia Onion and Vinegar Sauce. May be made ahead and wrapped in foil, then reheated for 15 minutes in a 350-degree oven. It is easiest to slice when cold.

Variations:

- Grill by moving oil- or butter-rubbed tenderloin to a charcoal grill over low fire. Cook until rare, turning as necessary.
- Serve with mustard butter. Mix together Dijon mustard, room-temperature butter, and a bit of cream.
- Cut the tenderloin in half for four people. It will take only a little less time to cook, as it is cooked by its diameter not its weight.
- Sauté with Marinara Sauce (page 661), Hollandaise Sauce (page 652), or White Butter Sauce (page 656).

Variation: Cocktail Party Tenderloin

Slice the tenderloin in half from butt to tail; rub each half with oil or All-Purpose Rub (page 673), and roast or grill until rare. Let rest. Slice thinly and use to stuff small rolls. This will make 50 slices of roast tenderloin.

Variation: Chuck Roast with Vinegar Sauce

For a chuck roast or sirloin tip, preheat oven to 325 degrees and melt 2 tablespoons butter in a heavy frying pan. Brown the meat on both sides and move to a large sheet of aluminum foil with 1/2 cup of the Vidalia Onion and Vinegar Sauce underneath the meat and 1/2 cup on top. Wrap tightly in the foil, place in a roasting pan, and cook until tender, about 25 minutes per pound. To serve, slice and top with the remaining sauce.

Filet, fillet, tenderloin, and *a tender* are interchangeable terms:
Filet = French spelling
Fillet = American spelling
Tenderloin = common term
A Tender = abbreviated form for what is technically the "whole short-loin tenderloin"

TRUSSING (TYING) MEAT

Using about 5 feet of cotton butcher's twine, rest the roast down across a portion of the twine, leaving about 12 inches from one end of the twine. Tie the string around the roast about 1/2 to 2 inches from one end of the roast and secure in a knot. Taking the long end of the string, move the string down 1 inch from the original tie and secure another loop around the roast. Continue moving down the roast at about 1-inch intervals, securing another loop each time. Tie securely in a knot at the last loop, ending about 1 1/2 to 2 inches from the other end of the roast.

FILLET STUFFED WITH BASIL AND GREENS

Serves 6 to 8

Stuffing meat gives it a whole other dimension, *and a tenderloin is particularly suited to spectacular presentation. A stuffed tenderloin also has more flavor. The filling may be cooked up to several days ahead, refrigerated, and added to the meat later. This fillet is delightful when served cold. This is the technique for a simple butterflied tenderloin.*

- 1 beef tenderloin, stripped of silver skin, fat, and gristle, chain removed (about 3–5 pounds)
- 7 tablespoons butter, divided
- 2 onions, chopped
- 5 garlic cloves, finely chopped
- 3–4 pounds fresh spinach or turnip greens, washed (page 205)
- 4 cups cooked rice
- 3 cups freshly grated Parmesan cheese
- Salt
- Freshly ground black pepper
- 6 tablespoons chopped fresh basil

To butterfly the fillet, make a long vertical slash down the middle, stopping one inch from edge to open it up, like a book, into a butterfly shape. Flatten slightly (page 419).

Meanwhile, melt 4 tablespoons of butter in a large frying pan with a lid, and add the onions and cook until soft, about 5 minutes. Add the garlic.

Roll up the turnip greens like a cigar and chiffonade (page 208). Place on top of the onions and garlic, and cover with a lid to sweat. When the greens have wilted, remove lid and cook briefly uncovered to remove any excess liquid in the bottom of the pan.

Mix the greens mixture, rice, and cheese. Season to taste with salt and pepper. Stir in the basil. Move a portion of this stuffing mixture into the split fillet. Close the fillet, encasing the stuffing, and tie it with string every 3 inches, or sew with a trussing needle using a basting stitch (over, under, over, under). Rub with the remaining butter. Season with salt and plenty of pepper.

Preheat oven to 425 degrees.

Move the trussed tenderloin to a roasting pan and roast about 20 to 25 minutes, until the internal temperature reaches about 130 degrees for rare, 140 for medium-rare. Remove and let rest at room temperature. If possible, cook this ahead so the meat may be sliced when cold, which is much easier than slicing it when it is hot. If serving hot, bring the meat to room temperature, cover with foil, and heat in the oven for 15 minutes at 350 degrees. Heat the remaining stuffing, arrange around the tenderloin, and serve. The stuffing may also be served at room temperature, as a rice salad would be.

BONELESS RIB-EYE

Serves 4 to 6

A WONDER OF AROMA AND BEAUTY, *a boneless rib roast is a perfect Sunday dinner. Selling roasts without the rib bones enables the butcher to sell the bones separately. The rib-eye adjoins the rib bones and is so tender that some people prefer it to the tenderloin, as it is more flavorful. It needs no tenderizing but can use a boost of flavor from a marinade or rub. Both the rib-eye (without the bone) and the bone-in rib steak are popular steaks requiring no marinating for tenderness, although cooks are always eager to use rubs and marinades for meat, making up their own recipes.*

Beware: do not confuse the eye of round, a tough piece of meat, with a tenderloin or rib-eye. Eye of round is very difficult to cook, tough, and recalcitrant, with little to excite the eater.

2½ pound rib-eye roast
Salt
Freshly ground black pepper
Rosemary, optional
Garlic cloves, chopped, optional
Fennel or other ground seed, optional
Sage, optional

Preheat oven to 400 degrees.

Rub the roast with seasonings as desired and move to a roasting pan. If the pan is much larger than the roast, add a little liquid—water, stock, red wine mixed with a bit of water—to prevent the juices from burning. Roast until a meat thermometer registers 130 degrees for rare or 140 degrees for medium-rare. Remove from oven and let rest 10 minutes. The meat will rise in temperature 10 degrees as it rests. Serve with the juices or another sauce as desired.

Variation: Beef Rib-Eye Roast with Savory Sauce
Mix 2 chopped garlic cloves, 1 teaspoon each of salt, pepper, thyme, and tarragon in a small bowl until it makes a paste. Spread over roast and cook as above.

After roasting, remove meat and set aside. Add 1 small chopped shallot to the juices in the pan; cook over medium heat for 2 or 3 minutes. Add 1 cup beef stock or broth and 1 tablespoon tomato paste. Stir over heat until pan juices and ingredients are all combined and bring to the boil; boil until the liquid has been reduced to ¾ cup, about 5 to 10 minutes. Serve sauce separately.

Variation: Add root vegetables—carrots, onions, fennel, and celery. Remove when cooked. Reheat when ready to serve.

RIB ROASTS

Rib roasts, bone in or bone out, usually are sold with the "caps" (aka "deckle" or "shell") on top. The cap is a tender piece of meat, covered with fat that turns crispy when cooked, but it is separated from the roast by a membrane. It is a different kind of meat and cooks more quickly than the rest of the roast, usually having turned gray when the rest is rare. Remove it if desired, and save it for another occasion. To remove the cap, chill the meat or freeze 30 minutes. Put the roast on its side, the fat facing away. If desired, shave all or part of the fat off the top with a sharp knife. Look for the membrane between the cap and the roast, and slice down across the membrane until the cap is removed. Set the cap aside for another purpose, cover, and refrigerate or freeze.

BOURBON-FLAMED RIB ROAST

Serves 6 to 10

RIB ROASTS ARE IMPRESSIVE *and tantalizing. Seeing them standing proudly on a platter, surrounded by roasted vegetables or mashed potatoes, makes meat-lovers swoon. The exterior should be crusty and brown, the interior rosy red. The whole rib roast is the most imposing, even small roasts express stature as well. The process is the same whether cooking a large or a small roast. Meat is cooked according to its thickness, not its weight, but both are good indicators of the time to be roasted. Some people prefer to cut between the ribs, serving everyone an extravagant piece of meat as is done in steak restaurants. Others first slide a long sharp knife between the ribs and the meat, then slice thinly. Rib meat is more flavorful than the tenderloin, if not quite as tender. There are many ways to add flavor if desired, or just serve it plain.*

1 standing rib roast (6–7 pounds)
Salt
Freshly ground black pepper
Rosemary or other herbs, optional
Garlic cloves, chopped
Fennel or other ground spices
Commercial seafood seasoning or Creole Seasoning (page 670), optional
1/2 cup bourbon, optional

Preheat oven to 500 degrees.

Rub the roast with seasonings as desired, fat side up, standing on the bones and move to a roasting pan. If the pan is much larger than the roast, add a little liquid—water, stock, or red wine mixed with a bit of water—to prevent the juices from burning.

Move to the oven and reduce the temperature to 400 degrees. Roast until the internal temperature reaches about 130 degrees for rare, 140 for medium-rare, about 1 1/2 hours. Remove from the oven to a warm heatproof serving platter, and let stand 30 minutes. It will increase 10 degrees during the first 10 minutes of resting. Carve. Serve with juices or flame with bourbon. To flame, carefully pour bourbon into a metal-handled saucepan. Bring to the boil and light carefully with a long fireplace-style match. Step back and pour from the pan over the roast and serve while flaming.

FLAMING

Any alcohol will ignite. Alcohol emits fumes when it comes to the boil, and the match is actually lighting the fumes. Even wine should be poured from a wide-mouthed container to prevent the bottle from exploding. Any alcohol should be diluted when going into the oven. The flame is not as dangerous as it seems; fancy restaurants can make the flames run over tablecloths, suit jackets, etc. It's fun to see done by the knowledgeable and skilled. It is a bit tricky, however.

Variation: Lemon-Rosemary Standing Rib Roast

Rub the exterior of the roast with a mixture of 2 teaspoons grated lemon rind (no white attached), 2 chopped garlic cloves, 1 teaspoon freshly ground black pepper, 1 teaspoon dried rosemary leaves, and 1 teaspoon salt. Roast as above.

Variation: Turned-off Rib Roast

An old method of cooking rib roast, developed by Anne Serrane in the 1960s and promulgated by Southerner Craig Claiborne, is to start the roast on high and then turn off the oven. It's not my favorite, as I like control, but here's the technique: Remove the roast from the refrigerator and let come to room temperature—from 2 to 4 hours. Move the roast to a shallow roasting pan, fat side up. Sprinkle the fat with flour and rub the flour in lightly. Season to taste with salt and pepper.

Move the roast to a preheated 500-degree oven and roast 25 to 30 minutes for a 2-rib roast, 40 to 45 minutes for a 3-rib roast, and 55 to 60 minutes for a 4-rib roast. Turn off the oven at the end of cooking time and do not open the oven at any time during the cooking or resting period. Keep the roast in the oven until the oven is lukewarm, about 2 hours. The roast will have a crunchy brown crust and an internal temperature suitable for serving.

PEPPERED TRI-TIP ROAST

Serves 6 to 9

THE TRI-TIP IS A "NEW" ROAST, *really a cross between a steak and a roast, carved out of the bottom sirloin into a triangular-shaped roast. It bursts with flavor and has a toothsome "chew" to it—tender but not soft.*

Figure about 4 servings per pound for a tri-tip roast, which may vary between 2 and 3½ pounds. Leftovers keep well, so there is no problem in cooking too much; the meat excels in sandwiches as well. It is important to cook this meat only to 140 degrees, as it goes up at least 10 degrees while resting. It should never be cooked more that. The tip ends are well done for those who prefer it, and the center is succulently rare.

The tri-tip does well without marinade or seasoning, so try it that way sometime when just serving family.

- 1 (2- to 3½-pound) beef tri-tip roast
- 1 tablespoon oil, cook's preference
- 1 tablespoon light or dark brown sugar
- 1–2 teaspoons freshly ground black pepper
- 2 garlic cloves, crushed with salt
- 2 teaspoons fresh or dried thyme and rosemary

Preheat oven to 425 degrees.

Rub the roast with a mixture of the oil, brown sugar, pepper, garlic, and herbs. Move to a roasting pan and roast 20 to 25 minutes, until a meat thermometer registers 130 degrees for rare and 140 degrees for medium-rare. Remove from oven and let rest 10 minutes. Move roast to a board, and slice thinly against the grain.

Variation: To grill, move roast to a grill rack over medium heat. Grill uncovered 30 to 40 minutes, checking temperature occasionally. Remove roast when a meat thermometer registers 130 degrees for rare or 140 degrees for medium-rare. Let rest 10 minutes. The temperature will continue to rise. Slice, working from the pointed end across the grain towards the round end.

GRAINS OF PARADISE

This old spice is newly discovered. Tasting like a cross between coriander seed and pepper, it has a real affinity for beef and lamb. Use it in place of pepper. This West African pepper is available online and through specialty shops.

OXTAIL STEW

Serves 4

THIS RECIPE, *attributed to a longtime Southerner whose ancestors were Caribbean freemen and freewomen of color, is similar to older recipes found all over the South. Oxen were one of the early Southern animals, but these oxtails are really from beef.*

2–4 pounds oxtails, cut up
4 slices fatback or bacon, preferably sugar-cured
1/4–1/2 cup all-purpose flour
Salt
Freshly ground black pepper
2 large onions, sliced
1–2 large carrots, sliced
2 large garlic cloves, chopped
1 (28-ounce) can whole tomatoes with juice
4 cups beef stock or broth
Pinch of granulated sugar, optional
1/4 cup chopped fresh thyme or summer savory, divided
1 cup shelled and cooked fresh or frozen butter beans or butter peas
Ground allspice to taste

If the oxtails are particularly fatty, add to a pan of boiling water, bring back to the boil, simmer a couple of minutes, drain, and dry.

Meanwhile, heat a frying pan or skillet, add the sliced fatback or bacon, and fry until crisp, rendering the fat. Remove, reserving all but 1 tablespoon of fat, and set aside on paper towels to drain.

Toss the damp oxtails in the flour and season well with salt and pepper. Add to the still hot fat in batches without overcrowding the pan. The bottom of the pan should be partly visible. If not, remove some of the meat and brown in batches. Brown on all sides before removing and repeating with the remaining pieces. When all are browned, add the onions and carrots, and cook until soft. Add the tomatoes, breaking up as needed.

Add the stock. Bring to the boil, add the oxtails back to the pot, reduce the heat to a simmer, and cook covered with foil and then a lid over low heat about 1 hour. Add water as needed if the liquid in the pot gets low. When the oxtails are tender, taste, adding salt, pepper, and sugar as desired. Add a small portion of the thyme or summer savory. Add the butter beans and cook 5 to 10 minutes more. Serve hot, garnished with the remaining thyme or summer savory and allspice to taste.

Allspice is a dried berry that comes from an evergreen tree indigenous to South and Central America. The finest allspice comes from Jamaica. The berries are picked green and dried to a dark brown color; sometimes they are confused with peppercorns, although they are larger. Their name comes from their combined flavors of cinnamon, clove, and nutmeg.

BROWNING MEAT

Heat the fat enough to sizzle or shimmer, so it will sear and brown the meat as quickly as possible. Since the temperature is reduced when ingredients are added, the fat and the bottom of the pan must be hot enough to start the cooking process.

When meat is browned, it adds a succulent flavor resulting from the caramelizing of its surface areas. This flavor seeps into the stew or soup liquid and is what boosts the flavor. The meat, deprived of its juices, is fairly tasteless, but the juices cover it when eaten, and it balances out at the end of cooking and eating. If cooked long enough, any meat will brown, but usually not enough to add the fully caramelized flavor as when the meat is cut up.

BEEF STEW WITH FENNEL, PECANS, AND ORANGE

Serves 6 to 8

Certainly beef stew is a staple of country cuisine. *Stews are usually made with the toughest of meats, which frequently contain the most flavor.*

When buying meat for a stew, I prefer getting a roast and cutting it up myself, working around the fat and sinews to extract substantial hunks of meat when possible. I prefer browning large 2- to 3-inch pieces of meat and cutting them into bite-size pieces after cooking, as opposed to buying small pieces of meat and taking the chance they will no longer be juicy when cooked, winding up with a large quantity of small chunks of stringy meat. If purchasing stew meat that is already cut up, with meat smaller than 1 inch, do not brown as heartily. This recipe doubles easily and freezes well. It reheats nicely in the microwave as well as on the stovetop.

3 pounds chuck, round, or sirloin tip roast
3 tablespoons bacon fat or drippings
2 medium onions, sliced
4 tablespoons all-purpose flour
1/2 cup dry red wine
2 tablespoons chopped fresh rosemary
1 teaspoon chopped fresh thyme
1 garlic clove, finely chopped
Juice of 1 lemon
2 1/2 cups beef stock or broth, divided
Salt
Freshly ground black pepper
2 tablespoons butter
1 fennel bulb or 3 celery ribs, sliced
1 cup toasted pecan halves
1 orange rind, julienned, no white attached

Cut the pieces of meat as close to 2 inches square as possible, using the membranes and interior fats as guides to cutting up, understanding that they are not going to be even or identical. Really tiny pieces can be set aside to grind or to use for chili, brown stock, or another purpose.

Heat the fat in a large Dutch oven and add the beef. Do not crowd the pan; the cubes should not touch each other and the bottom of the pan should be visible in spots. If not, remove some of the meat and brown in batches. Brown on one side to a deep mahogany color, then turn with tongs and continue browning all the sides. If the fat is good and hot, this process shouldn't take more than 10 minutes for all the meat.

When the meat is browned, remove it and add the onions to the pan. Cook 3 to 4 minutes, until the onions just start to brown. Remove from the heat and drain off all but 4 tablespoons of fat.

Add the flour, stir well, and return to the heat. Add the wine, stirring until it comes to the boil. Remove from heat and add the browned meat, rosemary, thyme, garlic, and lemon juice, and only enough of the stock so that the liquid covers the meat. Season to taste with salt and pepper. Stir all together, return to the heat, and bring slowly to the boil. Cover with aluminum foil then a lid, reduce to a simmer, and cook gently 1 to 2 hours, until tender. (This may also go into a 350-degree oven to cook.)

Meanwhile, make the garnish by melting the butter in a large frying pan. Add fennel or celery slices and sauté over medium-high heat for 5 minutes. Remove fennel, add pecans, and sauté a few minutes more. Blanch orange rind in boiling water for 30 seconds, drain, and reserve.

Remove stew from the heat, cool, and refrigerate until ready to serve. When cool, cut into smaller pieces if necessary, remembering it is hard to slice the meat when hot.

When ready to serve, return the fennel to the pan with the pecans to reheat, add to the stew, and top with the rind. Reheat the stew and juices on top of the stove or in the microwave and serve immediately with garnish.

Variation: Add spinach or other greens the last 10 minutes of cooking.

> A stew can be a pot roast or a pot roast can be a stew. The only significant difference is how the meat is cut. Leave the piece whole and it's a pot roast. Cut the meat into cubes and it's a stew. Whole roasts take longer to cook than cubes. Cubes take more attention to brown. Pick out a recipe, choose the form of meat according to what kind of time is available, and re-title the recipe accordingly.

LEMON-LIME POT ROAST WITH TOMATOES AND GARLIC

Serves 4 to 6

WHEN WE SERVED THIS BRAISED MEAT *on the television set to the crew, they raved and swore it was "the best thing they'd ever eaten." Cynthia says this recipe, from my* New Southern Cooking, *is one of her all-time favorites and couldn't imagine it could be improved. So be it.*

1 (2- to 3-pound) chuck, round, or sirloin tip roast
4 garlic cloves, chopped
Juice and grated rind of 3 limes, no white attached
Juice and grated rind of 2 lemons, no white attached
4 tablespoons bacon fat or drippings, or oil
1½ cups beef stock or broth
1 (14½-ounce) can diced tomatoes with juice
1–2 tablespoons chopped fresh rosemary
1–3 tablespoons chopped marjoram, lemon thyme, or other fresh herbs, optional
Salt
Freshly ground black pepper

Remove any tough pieces of fat or sinew from the roast.

Mash the garlic together with half the grated rinds and rub over the meat. Add enough of the lime and lemon juice to cover the meat, and set the rest aside. Marinate in a plastic ziplock bag or covered container 1 to 8 hours in the refrigerator, turning occasionally.

Remove the meat, reserving the marinade, and pat dry with a paper towel. Heat the drippings or oil in a large Dutch oven. Add the meat and brown on one side. When mahogany brown, turn and brown on second side. Continue until all sides are browned. Remove the meat and set aside. Reserve all but 1 tablespoon of the fat if desired.

Add the stock, reserved marinade, and tomatoes, and bring to the boil; boil for 1 or 2 minutes. Reduce the heat to a simmer and add the meat back to the pot. Cover with foil then a lid, and cook covered until the meat is tender, 1½ to 2 hours on the stovetop or in a 350-degree oven.

Remove the roast and allow to cool. Remove any obvious grease from the top of the sauce. Bring to the boil and boil until thick, about 15 minutes. If possible, chill to remove all the grease when it comes to the top (preferably after sitting overnight).

Slice the cold meat and return it to the sauce. When ready to eat, add herbs, season to taste with salt and pepper, and reheat on the stovetop. Serve hot, topped with the remaining grated rind of limes and lemons.

Mashed or smashed potatoes; white rice or wild rice; or noodles make cozy beds for stews and pot roasts.

BRAISED BEEF WITH CARAMELIZED ONIONS AND GARLIC

Serves 4 to 6

THIS BRAISED BEEF IS A MIRACLE. *It goes into the pot just as it comes home from the store, with no pre-browning, no liquid, and only bacon and onions. It emerges brown and moist after long cooking, ready to be topped with its juices and the onions that infused it. It is especially welcoming on a cold winter's night. It takes little work, but since it cooks for so long, it is a good idea to make it ahead rather than depend on a set finishing time. Leftovers are ideal for sandwiches.*

2–2½ pounds boneless chuck or round roast
½ pound bacon, cut in slivers
4 medium onions, very thinly sliced
5 garlic cloves, chopped
2–3 tablespoons chopped fresh rosemary, optional
Salt
Freshly ground black pepper

Preheat oven to 325 degrees.

Dry the roast with paper towels. Heat a large Dutch oven big enough to accommodate the meat snugly. Sprinkle the bottom with the bacon slivers, top with the sliced onions and garlic, move the meat on top; season with rosemary, salt, and pepper. If the pot is too large, liquid may need to be added later if the juices begin to burn.

Cover tightly, move to the oven, and cook for 2½ to 3 hours, checking and turning the meat after the first hour and every half hour after that, until the meat is very tender and brown and the onions are deep caramel. The meat will shrink considerably. Season with salt and more pepper if necessary.

Remove the meat to a cutting board and let rest for 10 minutes. If for some reason the onions are not brown, remove the lid and cook the onions until well browned.

Chill overnight if desired. Slice the meat very thinly, top with the onions and juices, and serve hot. May be made several days ahead and reheated in the juices on the stovetop or in the microwave.

Variations:

- If desired, this recipe can be increased to serve 20 to 25 people, by using 1 (10-pound) sirloin tip, ½ pound bacon, 10 garlic cloves, and 10 onions. Proceed as above, but cook 5 to 6 hours.
- Carrots, turnips, fennel, and other vegetables are equally good sliced and added to the pot. The only drawback is their volume may prevent the onions from caramelizing. In this case, the onions can be caramelized before adding the other ingredients.

GRANDMOTHER RHODA'S POT ROAST

Serves 6

MY SIBLINGS AND I ALWAYS SPENT A FEW WEEKS *in the summer with my grandmother. She cooked simple dishes but enjoyed food and seasoned it well. She was a big fan of potatoes to "fill you up," her favorite leftover being a sandwich of sliced cold potatoes. If they were flavored by cooking with the beef, all the better. She used any old vinegar that was around, probably white distilled, to tenderize, along with a bouillon cube and water. A better vinegar makes it tastier.*

1 (3-pound) beef chuck roast
Freshly ground pepper
3 tablespoons drippings or oil
2 onions, sliced
2 garlic cloves, chopped
2/3 cup red wine vinegar
1/3 cup beef stock or broth, divided
6 medium potatoes, peeled and quartered
4–6 carrots, peeled, optional
2 tablespoons all-purpose flour
Salt

Dry the roast with paper towels and season with pepper as desired.

Heat the drippings or oil in a large Dutch oven until sizzling. Add the meat and brown on one side, turn, and brown on the other; if thick, brown quickly on all sides. Remove and set aside. Reserve all but 1 tablespoon of fat.

Add the onions and cook until soft. Add the garlic and return the meat to the pan. Pour the vinegar over the roast and add half of the stock. Bring to the boil. Add the potatoes and carrots to the pot. Reduce to a simmer, cover with aluminum foil and a lid, and cook on stovetop or move to a 350-degree oven. Cook approximately 20 to 25 minutes per pound for well done, less for rare, testing with a meat thermometer occasionally. More or less time may be required, depending on the shape of the meat. If potatoes are not cooked when meat is done, remove meat and cook potatoes longer, covered.

When ready to serve, remove meat and potatoes, and stir in the flour until smooth. Add the remaining stock. Bring to the boil and boil rapidly until liquid is reduced somewhat and the gravy is thick. Strain if necessary. Taste and season further with salt and pepper if desired. This dish reheats well and is best made in advance.

Variations:

- Substitute Burgundy wine for the vinegar, add 1 pound sautéed sliced mushrooms and some cooked bacon for a variation of Beef Burgundy, the classic French bistro dish.
- Add 2 chopped red or green bell peppers, omit stock and all but 1 tablespoon of vinegar, and substitute 2 pounds chopped Italian tomatoes.

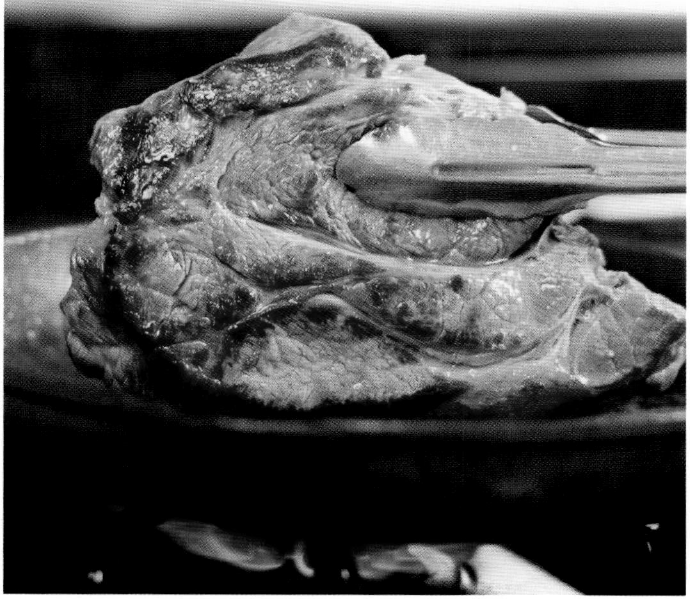

Drippings were very important during World War II, when butter and oil were both scarce. My family kept an old shortening or other can on the stove, sometimes with a piece of cheesecloth to strain, other times not bothering to strain at all.

Drippings from bacon, sausage, and other meat add an enormous amount of flavor well beyond their calories, and, of course, save money. After cooking meat, pour the fat through a strainer and reserve.

BASIL-LEMON POT ROAST WITH VEGETABLES

Serves 4

Using a roasting bag or tightly wrapping *the ingredients in heavy-duty aluminum foil and roasting in a slow oven is a good alternative to pot cooking. It's particularly handy in the summer when all the ingredients are fresh and a storm has come up, making the house chilly inside and out. This is as doable in an ill-equipped vacation home as it is in one's own home.*

2 tablespoons all-purpose flour
2 zucchini, sliced
2 yellow squash, sliced
1 onion, sliced
1/2 large eggplant, sliced
2 garlic cloves, peeled and chopped
Grated rind of 1 lemon, no white attached
10 whole basil leaves
1 tablespoon lemon pepper, divided, optional
Salt
Freshly ground black pepper
1 (2 1/2-pound) chuck, sirloin tip, or round roast
3 tablespoons chopped fresh basil
1 garlic clove, peeled and chopped
Grated rind of 1 lemon, no white attached

Preheat oven to 325 degrees.

Dust the inside of a large roasting bag with flour, as directed by manufacturer, shaking if necessary, or spread two long sheets of heavy-duty aluminum foil in a large roasting pan. Add the zucchini, squash, onion, eggplant, and garlic. Add the rind, toss to mix, and then spread out inside the bag or in the pan. Arrange basil leaves evenly over the vegetables. Rub the roast with the lemon pepper if using, or rub it with salt and pepper. Move it on top of the basil and vegetables. Seal the bag or fold over the aluminum foil and tightly seal, and roast 2 1/2 hours.

Remove the roast and let rest 10 minutes. Slice thinly across the grain. Arrange the slices on a platter and surround with the vegetables, discarding the basil leaves.

For garnish, mix together the chopped basil, garlic, and lemon peel, and sprinkle over the vegetables.

Lemon pepper is a handy ingredient to have on hand when spices are not available in a large variety. Grains of Paradise (page 424) is equally good.

MARINATED AND SMOKED BRISKET

Serves 4 to 6

BRISKET REQUIRES LONG, SLOW COOKING *but serves up a phenomenal flavor, particularly if marinated. Cooking brisket is an inexact science. The smoky taste gives it a special dash, but if unable to smoke, don't spoil the flavor by adding liquid smoke.*

1 (4-pound) untrimmed beef brisket
1 cup red wine vinegar
1 cup water
1 onion, sliced
2 garlic cloves, chopped
1/2 cup chopped fresh parsley
2 bay leaves, crumbled
1 teaspoon chopped fresh thyme
2 teaspoons chopped fresh rosemary
2 teaspoons chopped fresh basil
1 tablespoon light or dark brown sugar
1 recipe Sweet Barbecue Sauce (page 663)
Salt
Freshly ground black pepper

Move the brisket to a plastic ziplock bag or other nonaluminum container. Mix together all other ingredients except the Barbecue Sauce, and pour over brisket. Marinate in the refrigerator up to 2 days, turning occasionally. Remove from the refrigerator 1 hour before cooking to let come to room temperature.

Preheat a water smoker or a charcoal or gas grill for indirect cooking. Remove the meat from the marinade; combine water with the marinade to fill a water pan on the grill. Move the brisket to the highest rack. Cover and smoke-cook, keeping the temperature between 190 and 250 degrees, until the meat is tender enough to cut with a fork, about 6 to 7 hours. Remove from the heat and let sit at room temperature 10 minutes. Slice on the bias or pull (shred) and add Sweet Barbecue Sauce. Season to taste with salt and pepper. May be refrigerated up to 3 days, wrapped well; serve at room temperature or reheat in foil with sauce. Leftovers can be frozen.

Variations:

- Move the uncovered meat and marinade in the pan to a rack. Cover with foil and cook over indirect heat 5 hours, replenishing coals as needed. Open foil at one end to allow smoke to permeate the meat, and cook 1 to 2 hours more, until tender.
- Move meat and marinade to a heavy pan with sides. Cover tightly with foil and then a lid. Bake at 250 degrees for 5 hours, then move, still in the pan, to a hot charcoal grill. Remove lid, but keep covered with foil, and cook over indirect heat 1 to 2 hours, until tender, or continue baking in oven another 2 hours.

CYNTHIA'S BRISKET

Serves 4 to 6

Brisket is a favorite of many cultures—*the Irish are widely known for their Corned Beef, and Jewish people love their brisket. It's a cheap, tough piece of meat from the front "belly" of the beef, and can run up to 12 pounds. I mostly see ones that are 4 to 6 pounds. Marinating brisket in an acid, such as wine, vinegar, or Coca-Cola, tenderizes and adds flavor. Browning the meat after it has marinated is tricky, as wet meat is hard to brown; but anything that cooks this long will brown in the process, so many people omit browning and just throw everything into the pot. Slicing the meat part way through the cooking is crucial.*

2 tablespoons vegetable oil
1 (4-pound) untrimmed beef brisket
Salt
Freshly ground pepper
Paprika to taste
2 onions, sliced
1 cup water
1 cup red wine, or more to taste
1 (28-ounce) can diced tomatoes with juice
Beef stock or broth, optional

Heat oil in a large Dutch oven.

Dry the brisket with paper towels and season with salt, pepper, and paprika. Add brisket to hot pan and brown on both sides. Remove brisket. Sauté onions in drippings. Return meat to pot. Add water, red wine, and tomatoes. Bake covered 4 to 5 hours at 275 degrees or 2½ to 3 hours at 325 degrees. Remove the beef, reserving the sauce. Cool and refrigerate. Discard chilled fat, slice me, and cover with sauce in the same pot, adding water, wine, or beef stock if needed. Return to a 325-degree oven or over medium heat on the stovetop for 1 hour or more. May be refrigerated up to 3 days covered, or frozen 3 months.

BOURBON ROSEMARY BEEF ROUND TIP ROAST

Serves 4 to 6

Another recipe developed by our assistant Erin Simpson, *this slow-cooked roast braises in its own juices flavored with bourbon. The roast marinates 1 hour in bourbon and 2 more hours in the herbs and other flavorings.*

½ cup bourbon
1 (3-pound) beef round tip roast
2 tablespoons chopped fresh rosemary
4 garlic cloves, chopped
6 black olives, pitted and chopped
2 plum tomatoes, seeded and chopped
1 teaspoon prepared horseradish
½ cup oil, cook's preference, divided
Salt
Freshly ground black pepper

Preheat oven to 325 degrees.

Pour bourbon over the top of the roast and marinate covered for 1 hour or up to several hours in the refrigerator. Remove and pat the roast dry with paper towels.

Mix together the rosemary, garlic, olives, tomatoes, horseradish, and 2 tablespoons of the oil. Season to taste with salt and pepper. Rub this mixture over the roast and refrigerate in a plastic ziplock bag or covered container. After 1 hour, turn and let marinate another hour at room temperature. Remove roast from the mixture, setting mixture aside. Dry the roast with paper towels, removing any bits of mixture. Heat remaining oil in a large Dutch oven as needed to cover the bottom of the pan. When sizzling, add meat, brown deeply, turn and brown other side. Add back garlic-olive mixture.

Cover the pot with a layer of aluminum foil and then the lid. Bake 2 to 2½ hours, or until the meat is tender. Remove, let cool at least 10 minutes, and slice on diagonal.

Serve sauce over the roast. May be made several days in advance and reheated. The beef freezes well.

> Degrease the sauce by using a spoon to skim the top, dragging a paper towel over the top, or chilling and then removing the solid fat from the top.

CARPETBAG STEAKS

Serves 4 to 6

THIS RECIPE CALLS FOR THE NEW YORK STRIP STEAK, *which in my area of the country is a boneless steak from the "top loin," part of the "short loin." It has a terrific flavor, and its firmness allows for stuffing and/or marinating without becoming mushy. The secret to a good steak is the sizzle as the meat hits the hot fat. Mrs. Annabelle Hill was very casual when she described boning a brisket of beef and stuffing oysters into its cavity. This is perhaps a better use of both.*

2 New York strip steaks (1 1/2 pounds each)
12 ounces shelled and drained fresh oysters (about 12 oysters)
Salt
Freshly ground black pepper
4 tablespoons fresh lemon juice, divided
2 tablespoons chopped fresh fennel bulb or fennel fronds
Hot sauce, divided
1/3 cup oil, cook's preference
4 tablespoons butter, melted
Oysters Rockefeller Sauce (below), optional

Cut a horizontal slit along the side of each steak to make a pocket.

Season the oysters with salt, pepper, 2 tablespoons of lemon juice, fennel, and hot sauce to taste. Stuff about 6 seasoned oysters into each steak. Close with toothpicks or skewers, or sew with a trussing needle and string.

Heat a griddle pan, grill, or broiler. Rub the steak with oil. Season to taste with pepper. When pan is hot, add the steaks. Cook until desired doneness, about 6 to 8 minutes on each side for medium rare.

Mix the melted butter, remaining 2 tablespoons lemon juice, hot sauce, and salt to taste. Slice the steaks diagonally across the grain. Serve with the lemon-butter hot sauce or Oysters Rockefeller Sauce. Let the oysters spill out onto the plates.

OYSTERS ROCKEFELLER SAUCE

Makes about 5 cups

1/4 cup butter
1 small onion, finely chopped
2 garlic cloves, finely chopped
3 cups heavy cream
1 pint oysters, drained, reserving 1/2 cup juice
1–1 1/2 teaspoons commercial seafood seasoning or Creole Seasoning (page 670), optional
2 teaspoons Worcestershire sauce
Salt
Freshly ground black pepper
1 pound fresh spinach or 1 (10-ounce) package frozen chopped spinach, thawed and drained

Melt butter in a heavy saucepan. Add the onion and garlic. Sauté until soft, about 5 to 7 minutes. Add cream and reserved oyster juice, and bring to the boil. Boil over high heat 5 to 10 minutes, until liquid is reduced by half. Season to taste with Creole Seasoning, Worcestershire sauce, salt, and pepper. Move half the sauce to a blender or food processor and purée with half the spinach until smooth. Return this mixture to the saucepan. Add remaining spinach to saucepan. Heat thoroughly.

Bring a shallow pan of water to a simmer. Add oysters and cook 2 to 3 minutes, just until their edges begin to curl. Drain and add to sauce. Spoon some of the sauce over the steaks and pass the rest.

After the Civil War, former Northern soldiers and other adventurers carried their belongings in satchel-like suitcases made of carpet. These carpetbags expanded on the sides when stuffed with spare clothing and other possessions. Considered profiteering interlopers by local whites, who saw them as seeking to benefit from the spoils of war, they became known as "carpetbaggers." This recipe is so-named because it is a fine piece of meat that is stuffed and expanded.

HERB-CRUSTED PAN-SEARED TENDERLOIN STEAKS

Serves 4

TENDERLOIN MAKES A HEAVENLY STEAK. *The highest rated is the chateaubriand, but all of it except the thin part of the tail makes wonderful steaks. Rubbed with herbs it becomes magical. Serve with optional sauces.*

1 tablespoon chopped fresh thyme
1 tablespoon chopped fresh rosemary
1 tablespoon chopped fresh oregano
1 garlic clove, peeled and finely chopped
Salt
Freshly ground black pepper
4 (1–1½-inch-thick) tenderloin or filet mignon steaks
3 tablespoons butter
3 tablespoons oil, cook's preference
Salt
Sauce of choice

Mix together the thyme, rosemary, oregano, and garlic. Season to taste with salt and pepper. Rub the steaks on both sides with the herb mixture.

Over high heat, heat enough of the butter and oil to cover the bottom of a griddle or frying pan. When sizzling hot, add the steaks, leaving enough room between them to see the bottom of the pan, and cook 3 to 5 minutes. Turn the steaks and cook the other side for 3 to 5 minutes, until the steak reaches 130 degrees for rare, and 140 degrees for medium-rare. Season with salt.

When ready to serve, use one of these sauces to embellish the steaks:

- Béarnaise Sauce (page 653)
- Hollandaise Sauce (page 652)
- Peanut Sauce (page 660)
- Mustard Sauce (page 667)
- Red Pepper Sauce (page 440)

SIRLOIN STEAKS WITH FRESH SPINACH

Serves 4

THESE STEAKS ARE POUNDED THIN, *like a Swiss steak (page 435), and sautéed quickly. This one-dish meal can be assembled in another way by cooking the onion and bell pepper sauce first, and then sautéing the meat quickly at the end. It's up to the cook and how many pans the dishwasher is ready to tackle.*

⅓ cup oil, cook's preference
4 (4-ounce) thin boneless sirloin steaks, pounded to ⅓-inch thickness
1 onion, sliced
1 red bell pepper, seeded, cored, and sliced
4 garlic cloves, peeled and chopped
1 (14½-ounce) can whole peeled tomatoes with juice, broken into large pieces
1 tablespoon red wine vinegar
12–16 ounces fresh spinach, washed and stems removed
Salt
Freshly ground black pepper

Heat enough of the oil to cover the bottom of a large griddle or skillet until the oil shimmers. Add the steaks and brown on one side, about 2 minutes; turn and brown on the second side. Set them aside on a plate and cover with foil to keep warm.

Add the onion and bell pepper to the same pan, reduce the heat to medium, and cook until soft, about 10 minutes. Add the garlic, tomatoes, and vinegar, and cook until thick and most of the liquid has cooked out, about 7 minutes. Add the spinach. Cover until the spinach is wilted and the rest is heated through, 2 to 3 minutes.

Return the meat to the pan. Cover and reheat quickly until the meat is hot. Season to taste with salt and pepper, and serve at once.

GREENS AND CHORIZO-STUFFED FLANK STEAK

Serves 4 to 6

Over the years, *I have been blessed with a number of assistants. One of these, Elise Griffin, came up with this recipe years ago when we taught it at Rich's Cooking School. For nearly forty years, students have told me frequently how they saved the recipe and used it for dress-up dinner parties. It can be assembled in advance and cooked later or cooked completely ahead. Like brisket, it is better sliced when cold and reheated to serve. It doesn't need marinating because it has been butterflied, stuffed, and braised in a vinegar/stock mixture, all of which add to its tenderness.*

- 1 (1½–2½-pound) flank steak
- 6 tablespoons butter
- 2 garlic cloves, finely chopped
- 2 shallots, chopped
- 1½ cups finely chopped and toasted breadcrumbs
- ¼ cup finely chopped fresh parsley
- 1½ cups blanched, chopped, and drained turnip greens
- 1 egg, beaten
- ½ cup freshly grated Parmesan cheese
- ½ cup grated Swiss cheese
- Salt
- Freshly ground black pepper
- 1–2 tablespoons Dijon mustard
- ¼ pound chorizo or other hard cured sausage, cut into ¼-inch strips
- 3 tablespoons oil
- ½ cup red wine vinegar
- 12 ounces beef stock or broth
- 2 cups Tomato Sauce (page 661), optional

To butterfly the steak, make a horizontal cut the length of the flank without severing it, cutting within ⅓ inch of the edge. Open up flat like butterfly wings and move the steak between sheets of plastic wrap. Using a meat pounder or rolling pin, or even the edge of a sturdy plate, pound until the meat is ¼ inch thick.

For the greens mixture, melt the butter, add garlic and shallots, and cook until soft but not browned. Add breadcrumbs, parsley, and greens. Stir and add the egg and cheeses. Season with salt, pepper, and mustard.

To stuff the flank steak, spread the greens mixture over the opened steak. Arrange rows of the sausage strips down the length of the filling, pressing them into it. Roll up lengthwise (as with a jelly roll) and tie securely with string.

Preheat oven to 350 degrees. Heat the oil in a large nonaluminum Dutch oven until the oil shimmers. Add the stuffed meat and brown on all sides. Remove to a plate. Add the vinegar and stock to the juices in the pan and bring to the boil. Remove from the heat and return the stuffed meat to the pot. Cover with aluminum foil then a lid. Bake for 1½ hours, or until the beef is tender.

Remove the meat from the liquid. Save the liquid for another time or discard it. Move the meat to a large container with sides and weight it down with a marble slab, brick, or heavy pan to press the meat together and facilitate carving. Refrigerate until firm. Slice diagonally across the grain into ½-inch slices. May be served hot or cold. If reheating, move to a 350-degree oven for 15 minutes, and serve with Tomato Sauce if desired.

Originally, London broil was a marinated and grilled flank steak. Butchers saw an opportunity and substituted far less satisfactory meats. Some lack the flavor of flank, skirt, and hanger steaks and are frequently tasteless, chewy, and dried out. The moral is, know your butcher and always ask.

SWISSING

A means of tenderizing a tough steak, swissing is accomplished by dusting the meat with flour and pounding it with a meat mallet, rolling pin, or the rounded edge of a heavy plate or other solid object.

FLANK STEAK WITH MUSHROOM DIJON GRAVY

Serves 4 to 6

THE POPULARITY OF FLANK STEAK *lies in its ease of cooking and relatively low fat content. Grilled or broiled, flank steak is a quick-cooking steak, making it ideal for any night of the week. Flank, skirt, and hanger steaks are very popular because they are so much more flavorsome than many of the other cuts. They need marinating overnight to become tender when broiled or grilled, and should always be cooked to no more than medium-rare and sliced thinly on the diagonal. Flank steak has a longitudinal grain; hanger steak is from the same general part of the animal (called the flank), and skirt steak is from the "plate," which is a bit forward on the stomach of the beef. They usually can be interchanged.*

1 (1 1/2-pound) flank steak
8 garlic cloves, peeled
2 tablespoons fresh ground black pepper
1/3 cup oil, cook's preference, divided
2 tablespoons butter
1 onion, sliced
1 1/2 cups mushrooms, sliced
1 tablespoon prepared horseradish
1–2 tablespoons chopped fresh rosemary
1–2 tablespoons Dijon mustard
1 tablespoon red wine vinegar
2 cups beef stock or broth
Salt
Freshly ground black pepper

Rub the meat with 2 of the garlic cloves and then press the pepper evenly onto both sides. If possible, refrigerate for 3 hours or overnight.

Heat 1 teaspoon of the oil and the butter in a large skillet until hot and singing. Chop the remaining 6 garlic cloves. Add the garlic, onion, mushrooms, and horseradish, and cook over medium heat until soft, about 5 minutes. Stir in the rosemary, mustard, vinegar, and beef stock; bring to the boil, then lower heat to a simmer and reduce by half, until the sauce is thick and creamy, about 5 to 10 minutes. Season to taste with salt and pepper. Tightly covered, the sauce can be refrigerated for several days.

Meanwhile, dry the steak and dab with the remaining oil as needed. Heat the griddle pan, grill, or broiler and add the oiled steak. Cook the meat in the pan, over hot coals, or broil 4 inches from the heat about 7 minutes per side, or until a meat thermometer registers 130 degrees for rare. Remove to a board and let the meat rest for 3 minutes and then slice thinly on the diagonal across the grain. Stir any accumulated juices into the warm sauce and serve it with the meat.

GRIDDLE COOKING

I much prefer a hot griddle pan or skillet to a grill. The juices stay in the pan rather than dripping into the grill. Some go so far as to put a griddle on the grill to achieve a smoky flavor but keep the juices.

MARINATED FLANK STEAK

Serves 2 to 4

THIS MEAT IS GOOD FOR ENTERTAINING *and for family meals,as it is assembled and cooked so easily. The aroma coming from the oven announces its presence and whets all appetites. It can be served rare or medium-rare. Slice on the diagonal and serve immediately to keep tender. Avoid cooking and reheating, as the sliced meat will toughen. Instead, enjoy it in a salad or on a small sandwich.*

- 1/2 cup red wine
- 2 tablespoons chopped fresh ginger
- 1 garlic clove, chopped
- 1 teaspoon salt
- 1 tablespoon freshly ground black pepper
- 1/4 cup oil, cook's preference
- 1 (1 1/2- to 2 1/2-pound) flank steak

Mix together the wine, ginger, garlic, salt, and pepper, and put into a plastic ziplock bag. Add the steak and marinate 30 minutes or more.

Preheat a broiler or grill. Remove the steak from the marinade, reserving the marinade. Dry the steak with paper towels and rub oil on both sides. Heat a griddle, grill, or broiler. When hot, add steak and brown on one side 5 minutes. Turn, brown on second side, and cook steak to an internal temperature of 130 degrees for rare, 140 degrees for medium-rare. Remove to a board and let rest 3 minutes.

Slice diagonally across the grain and serve immediately. The marinade can be heated and poured over the sliced steak if desired.

SOUR CREAM SWISS STEAK

Serves 4 to 6

SWISS STEAK WAS A TRADITIONAL MEAL *once or twice a month in my home as I grew up. Money was scarce, and cheap meat was tough. Sometimes we lacked some of the ingredients: spices and condiments such as soy sauce were not always replenished speedily. Sour cream was a come-and-go product as well, particularly when there were no longer deliveries by milkmen and a trip to the store was needed. Still, I loved it, particularly when served with mashed potatoes. I prefer chuck meat, with its full flavor and fat. Mother used garlic salt for more options.*

- 2 pounds boneless chuck steak or top round, cut 1/4–1/2 inch thick
- 2 tablespoons all-purpose flour
- 1 teaspoon salt
- 1/2 teaspoon freshly ground black pepper
- 1/2 teaspoon paprika, optional
- 1/2 teaspoon dry mustard
- 1/4 cup oil
- 3 tablespoons butter
- 1 medium onion, chopped
- 1 garlic clove, chopped or crushed
- 1 cup water
- 3 tablespoons soy sauce, optional
- 3 tablespoons light or dark brown sugar, optional
- 3/4 cup sour cream, optional

Preheat oven to 300 degrees.

Dry the roast with paper towels. Cut the meat into serving-size pieces. Dust with flour on both sides and pound 1/4-inch thick. Sprinkle with salt, pepper, paprika, and dry mustard just before browning to prevent moisture from being extruded from the meat by the salt.

Heat the oil and butter in a Dutch oven until it shimmers. Add the meat without crowding the pan—the bottom of the pan should be visible between the pieces of meat—and brown it on all sides. Add onion, garlic, water, soy sauce, brown sugar, and sour cream if using. Cover with aluminum foil then a lid, and bake 30 to 40 minutes, until tender. The thin sauce is delectable served with the meat or separately over potatoes.

Variation: Red wine vinegar can replace the water, soy sauce, and sour cream in the dish, making a very tender and tasty dish on its own.

CHICKEN-FRIED STEAK WITH FLANNEL SAUCE

Serves 6 to 8

CHICKEN-FRIED STEAK *is steak fried in the manner of chicken. Merle Ellis, a butcher turned television and cookbook food authority, was famous in the latter part of the twentieth century for his easy explanations of meat cookery. We cooked together several times, and his food was as top-notch as his writing. We debated such things as salting or not salting meat ahead of cooking, and he was obdurate about salting first, always. We both agreed salting and peppering flour is an excellent way of flavoring meat and chicken.*

2/3 cup all-purpose flour, divided
1 teaspoon salt
Freshly ground black pepper
2 pounds boneless top round or chuck steak, cut 1/4–1/2 inch thick
2 large eggs
2 tablespoons heavy cream
2 cups crushed saltine cracker crumbs
1/2 cup oil, cook's preference

Flannel Sauce

1 onion, sliced
1/2 cup heavy cream
About 2 cups chicken stock or broth
Dash Worcestershire sauce, optional
Dash hot sauce, optional

Reserve 3 tablespoons flour for the gravy; mix the remaining flour, salt, and pepper together and move to a plate. Pound the mixture into both sides of the meat with a mallet, rolling pin, or the edge of a heavy kitchen plate. Cut the meat into serving pieces as necessary.

Beat eggs together with the cream and put on a second plate; move the cracker crumbs to a third.

Heat the oil in a large heavy skillet over moderately high heat until the oil shimmers. Using one hand, to keep the other clean and free to turn the meat, dredge the steaks in the plate of flour, dip into the egg mixture, and then into the cracker crumbs.

Add the steaks to the hot oil and brown well on one side. Turn and brown other side. Reduce heat to medium, cover the skillet, and cook for 15 to 20 minutes, turning occasionally, until the steaks are cooked through and tender. (Chicken-fried steak should be well done but not dry.) Remove the steaks from the skillet and drain on brown paper bags. Keep warm.

To prepare the sauce, add the onion slices to the pan and sauté quickly. Pour off all but 3 tablespoons of the fat from the skillet and stir in the 3 tablespoons reserved flour. Stir to incorporate any particles on the bottom of the pan, and cook for 1 to 2 minutes. Stir in the cream then the broth. Season with Worcestershire and hot sauce if using. Slice the meat across the grain and top with the sauce.

Variation: Substitute self-rising flour to yield a crustier coating.

MOTHER'S MEATLOAF

Serves 8 to 10

MEATLOAF WAS ONE OF THE THINGS *my mother made with great regularity. We would have it for supper one night, with near-ritualistic English peas and mashed potatoes, and then the next day for sandwiches for lunch. The rest was frozen for later. We always loved it. I've fiddled with the recipe some and list the variations below. In short, this is just a base for meatloaf—I change it around, and so should the cook. The ingredients are adaptable. Don't rush out and buy anything before checking to see if it is possible to just use what is available in the pantry. Meatloaf can be free-form or baked in a mold.*

This recipe can be cut in half or even thirds quite easily, as nothing needs to be exact. The virtue of this large recipe is the extra meals for the freezer.

Meatloaf

2 1/2 pounds ground beef
1 1/4 pounds ground pork or additional ground beef
2 slices bread made into crumbs, or panko
1/3 cup rolled oats
4 large eggs, beaten to mix
1 tablespoon prepared mustard, yellow or Dijon
2 cups tomato sauce or ketchup, divided
1 medium onion, chopped
1 1/2 cups milk
2 teaspoons salt
Freshly ground black pepper
1–2 tablespoons fresh herbs, such oregano, marjoram, thyme, or basil

Sauce

1/3–1/2 cup light or dark brown sugar
1 cup milk
1 tablespoons Dijon mustard
1/2 cup red wine vinegar
2 cups tomato sauce or ketchup

Preheat oven to 400 degrees. Oil 3 loaf pans or 1 sided roasting pan.

Mix the meatloaf ingredients, using just 1 cup of tomato sauce or ketchup, and pull together in a mass. Remove a few tablespoons and sauté briefly in a nonstick pan to determine if texture or taste needs adjusting. Divide between the loaf pans or shape into 1 or more oval or rounds and move into a roasting pan. Add water to come up the loaf about an inch when using a roasting pan, so the juices won't burn.

Bake for 45 to 60 minutes, basting occasionally with the pan juices, until the center of the loaf registers 165 degrees on a meat thermometer. Spread the top with remaining 1 cup ketchup the last 10 minutes of cooking. Leave in the pan in the juices to rest for 10 minutes. Cool enough to slice without it breaking up. Move to a board or a serving dish.

Heat the sauce ingredients in a small saucepan. Slice meatloaf in the kitchen or at the table and serve with the sauce if desired. For a speedy tomato sauce, mix equal amounts of tomato paste and water.

Variations:

- Make an indention down the center of the meatloaf before baking. Fill with tomato sauce the last 10 minutes of baking.
- Sometimes I use just bread and no oatmeal, sometimes no bread and a little more oatmeal or all saltine crackers. I've used whole milk instead of evaporated milk, and once I used cream. My brother likes his without the ketchup inside, only using it to spread on the top of the loaf. So when he is coming to dinner, I omit one of the eggs and use just ketchup to top the meatloaf.
- Substitute a third of the meat with ground veal.

Over the years, I've fiddled with my mother's basic meatloaf. I wonder if she would even recognize this version. I've also left out the evaporated milk and added a Southern touch—cornmeal, cornbread, or crumbled tortilla chips as a different emphasis. I think of it as "Southern *pâté*" as it is reminiscent of French *pâté* in its shape. This makes 1 or 2 free-form meat loaves or 3 made in loaf pans. The free-form loaf will be looser than one baked in a loaf pan. Be sure to reserve half the sauce for each loaf. A variety of ground meats is always better but far from necessary. As above, top with just tomato sauce the last 10 minutes of baking, or use the above sauce with the meat after slicing.

KATHY'S MEATLOAF

Serves 4 to 6

CYNTHIA AND HER SISTER PHYLECIA *learned to cook out of self-preservation, as their mother, Kathy, was not much of a cook. Although they longed for the fantasy of growing up cooking next to mother's apron strings, they both were very proud of being reared as independent and self-sufficient young women. Frequently they would arrive home from school to a note attached to a defrosting package of ground meat saying only "meatloaf." The girls knew just what to do.*

1 "heel" of bread
1/4 cup milk
1 large egg, beaten
1/3 cup tomato sauce or ketchup
1 teaspoon Worcestershire sauce
1/4 cup finely chopped celery
1/4 cup finely chopped onion
1 1/2 pounds ground round
Salt
Freshly ground black pepper

Red Pepper Sauce

1 garlic clove
1 small onion, chopped
1 red bell pepper, seeded, cored, and chopped
1 cup chicken stock, broth, or water
3 tablespoons tomato paste
1/2 teaspoon salt
1/2 teaspoon freshly ground black pepper

Preheat oven to 350 degrees.

Crumble bread into a large mixing bowl. Add milk, egg, ketchup, and Worcestershire sauce, and mix well. Stir in celery and onion. Add meat and mix thoroughly. Season to taste with salt and pepper. Move to a loaf pan and form a nice loaf.

To make the sauce, add the garlic to a food processor with the metal blade running. Stop the processor and add the onion, bell pepper, stock, tomato paste, salt, and pepper. Pulse until smooth. Pour half of sauce over the meatloaf before baking. Heat the remaining sauce in a saucepan on low.

Bake 1 hour. Pour off excess fat and return to oven for 15 minutes more. Serve remaining sauce with the meatloaf.

PURCHASING AND STORING GROUND MEAT

It is important to know the standards of anyone selling ground meat. The smartest way to purchase it is to select the meat desired and have it ground when purchasing or to grind it at home. That said, packaged ground meat is ready to go and, in a reputable store, safe for consumption.

Each type of meat has a different fat component and varies in flavor and texture according to the cut of meat ground as well. Always keep ground meat refrigerated and use as quickly as possible—certainly by the "use by" date on the package. Well wrapped, ground meat freezes up to 3 months. Defrost overnight in the refrigerator, or if necessary in the microwave. Never leave on the counter or sink to defrost.

Many times I've just used what is sold as ground meat in my grocery store for these recipes. But when I see packages of ground pork or ground veal, I snap them up, rewrap them as needed, and freeze them for meatloaf day. Of course, ground turkey can be used, but I find it a bit dry.

BETH'S MEATLOAF

Serves 6

Beth Price, who was responsible *for supervising much of the final testing of this book, is a quick study—she easily adapts recipes according to what she has in the house. She loves this for a hot leftover meatloaf sandwich for lunch with provolone cheese and mayonnaise.*

2 pounds lean ground beef or a combination of beef, veal, and pork
1 large onion, finely chopped
1 cup crumbs (bread, biscuit, or cornbread)
2 large eggs, beaten
3/4 cup milk
1 tablespoon prepared horseradish
1/4 cup plus 2 tablespoons chili sauce, divided
1/4 cup Dijon mustard
2 teaspoons salt
1 tablespoon freshly ground pepper
1/2 cup chopped fresh parsley

Mix the meatloaf ingredients, reserving the 2 tablespoons chili sauce, and pull together in a mass. Remove a few tablespoons and sauté briefly in a nonstick pan to determine if texture and taste need adjusting. Divide between two loaf pans or shape into 1 or more oval or rounds and move into one high-sided roasting pan. Add water to come up the loaf about an inch when using a roasting pan, so the juices won't burn.

Bake for 45 to 60 minutes, basting occasionally with the pan juices, until the center of the loaf registers 165 on a meat thermometer. Spread the top with the reserved chili sauce the last 10 minutes of cooking. Leave in the pan in the juices to rest for 10 minutes. Cool enough to slice without it breaking up. Move to a cutting board or a serving dish. Slice in the kitchen or at the table. Serve with Meatloaf Gravy if desired.

MIXING MEATLOAF

It was standard in my family to combine the meatloaf with our hands. With the advent of plastic bags, it is easier—and cleaner—to put each hand into a small supple plastic bag while shaping the meatloaf. The bags can be tossed away, just as disposable kitchen gloves would be.

Meatloaf Gravy

Makes 1 cup

Already tasty, *the fat and juices in the pan make a fabulous gravy for mashed potatoes or other accompaniments.*

Juices from a cooked meatloaf
2 tablespoons flour
1 cup milk or Flavored Milk (page 657)
Salt
Freshly ground pepper
Other herbs or seasonings, optional

After resting the meatloaf 10 minutes in the pan and then removing the meatloaf, put the pan over the heat. Stir in flour and cook for 1 or 2 minutes. Add milk and stir until it comes to the boil. Taste and add salt and pepper or other seasonings as desired. Cover with plastic wrap to prevent a skin from forming until ready to serve. Remove wrap and reheat gently.

OVEN-COOKED MEATBALLS

Makes 24

Meatballs will never go out of style, *whether for a main course or in a chafing dish with toothpicks. (I've seen men stand around the table unwilling to relinquish their toothpicks until the dish was replenished.) This recipe can be doubled or tripled, and probably should be. It is the only dish that Cynthia, who has years of gracious entertaining under her belt, ever ran out of while feeding a large crowd of hungry rare-book dealers in her home. Be gentle with the meatballs while shaping.*

1/3 cup milk
3/4 cup cubed day-old loaf bread, crusts removed
1 pound ground beef or turkey
1 small onion, very finely chopped or grated
2 tablespoons minced fresh flat leaf parsley, not dried
1 teaspoon minced fresh thyme, not dried
1 egg, beaten
1/4 cup grated Parmesan cheese
1 teaspoon salt
1/2 teaspoon freshly ground black pepper

Preheat oven to 350 degrees.

Pour the milk over the bread in a small bowl. Let stand about 3 minutes and then squeeze the bread dry. Discard the excess milk and move the bread to a large bowl. Add the remaining ingredients and mix gently, gently, gently, with your hands. If possible, cover and chill the meat mixture for 20 minutes to help better form the meatballs during the next stage; this is entirely optional, though.

Lightly grease a rimmed baking sheet. Gently roll mixture into 24 (1- to 2-inch) meatballs. Move to the prepared pan, leaving about 1 inch between meatballs. Bake for 20 minutes, until the meatballs become a nice golden brown. Serve hot.

Variation: Serve in a favorite tomato or marinara sauce.

HOMEY SHORT RIBS WITH POTATO DUMPLINGS

Serves 6 to 8

The mere sight of braised short ribs *causes some people to start swooning. Slow-cooked to tender perfection, short ribs fall from the bone at the slightest nudge of a fork. Some people prefer running the ribs under the broiler or grill at the end of cooking to brown and crisp, rather than browning them at the first. Either method is fine.*

4 pounds bone-in beef short ribs
1/4 teaspoon freshly ground black pepper
1 tablespoon salt
2 cups small peeled onions
6 carrots, roughly chopped
3 tablespoons all-purpose flour

Potato Dumplings

2 cups mashed potatoes
1 egg, lightly beaten
1/2 teaspoon salt
1/8 teaspoon freshly ground black pepper
1 tablespoon all-purpose flour

Heat a large Dutch oven. Add meat and brown on all sides in its own fat. Pour off excess fat. Add seasonings and 1 quart of water to the ribs. Cover and simmer for 2 hours. Add onions and carrots during the last 20 minutes.

Measure broth from the Dutch oven and add enough water to make 6 cups. Move the flour to a bowl and add small amounts of the liquid as needed from the pan to form a paste. Stir the paste back into the stew. (This method of thickening is called "making a slurry.") Keep hot while making the dumplings.

Alternatively, reserve some of the excess fat, heat in a large saucepan, add the 1 tablespoon flour, stirring to make a roux. Add 6 cups liquid, and stir until it comes to the boil and thickens. Return the thickened liquid to the pot covering the meat and continue below.

To make the Potato Dumplings, stir together the potatoes, egg, salt, and pepper. Drop by heaping tablespoons on top of the stew. Cover and steam the dumplings for 4 to 6 minutes on low simmer.

LIME AND BEER SHORT RIBS WITH MUSTARD SAUCE **Serves 4 to 6**

THIS IS WHAT WE CALL A "GOOD OL' BOY" RECIPE *to please the ball game watchers. Marinating tenderizes those sometimes very tough ribs before slow cooking. The ribs are crisped up at the end under the broiler or grill. No need to add expensive key limes or even good beer. I've made this with nonalcoholic as well as "flat" beer, and the difference in taste is hardly discernible.*

4 pounds meaty beef ribs
1 cup beer
1/2 cup lime juice

Mustard Sauce
3 egg yolks*
2 1/2 tablespoons fresh lemon juice
1/4 cup Dijon mustard
1/2 cup olive oil
2 tablespoons chopped fresh oregano or thyme
2 teaspoons finely chopped chives
Salt
Freshly ground black pepper

Preheat oven or grill to 250 degrees.

Move the ribs to a large, shallow glass or ceramic dish. Mix together the beer and lime juice, and pour over the ribs. Refrigerate in a sturdy plastic bag for 6 hours or overnight, turning occasionally. Bring to room temperature 2 hours before cooking.

Remove the ribs from the marinade and spread out separately on 2 sheets of heavy-duty aluminum foil large enough to enclose them, avoiding overlapping. Sprinkle 1/4 cup of the marinade over the ribs and seal the packets tightly. Set aside the remaining marinade.

Move the packets to a rimmed baking sheet for oven cooking, or to the heated grill and cover. (Add more coals to the grill as necessary.) Cook 1 1/2 hours, until tender. Remove ribs from the foil and drain. This can be done up to a day ahead.

Half an hour before ready to serve, preheat oven or grill to 400 degrees. Return ribs to the oven on a large pan with sides. Baste once with the reserved marinade. Cook until crisp, 15 to 20 minutes.

To make the Mustard Sauce, beat egg yolks with the lemon juice and mustard until thick, about 5 minutes. Slowly add the olive oil, continuing to mix until the consistency of a thin mayonnaise. Add herbs, and season to taste with salt and pepper. Serve chilled with the ribs.

**Raw eggs may pose a health risk, particularly to pregnant women, children and the elderly.*

MARINATED SHISH KEBABS **Serves 4**

SHISH KEBAB NEEDS A GUTSY-FLAVORED *and marinated meat to stand up to grilling.*

1/4 cup oil
1/2 cup red wine vinegar
1 teaspoon Dijon mustard
1 tablespoon fresh chopped thyme, or 1 teaspoon dried thyme
2 teaspoons Worcestershire sauce
Salt
Freshly ground black pepper
1 pound beef or lamb, cut in 1- to 1 1/2-inch cubes
2 medium tomatoes cut into eighths, or 16 cherry tomatoes
1 small yellow squash, cut into 1-inch chunks
Cooked rice

Soak wooden skewers in water to prevent burning.

Mix together the oil, vinegar, mustard, thyme, and Worcestershire sauce in a plastic ziplock bag. Season to taste with salt and pepper. Move the meat to the bag and refrigerate at least 4 hours or up to overnight, turning occasionally. Remove the meat from the marinade, pat dry with paper towels, and thread onto skewers, alternating with the tomatoes and squash.

When ready to cook, heat the griddle, grill, or broiler. Cook over medium-high heat, turning, for a total of 8 to 12 minutes, depending on meat size, until meat reaches 130 degrees for rare, 140 degrees for medium-rare. Serve hot on rice.

CALF'S LIVER WITH ONIONS AND BROWN BUTTER

Serves 3 or 4

LIKE MEATLOAF AND MASHED POTATOES, *I find liver and onions comforting when I am in a "whiney" mood, particularly in the winter. I have used both calf's and beef liver for this, as I enjoy the flavor of both. Most people, however, prefer the milder flavor of calf's liver. It is usually sold pre-sliced in the package. Soak beef liver in milk for half an hour or so to tone down the strong flavor. Drain, rinse, and dry before proceeding. The onions may be cooked up to several days in advance.*

1/2 cup butter, cut into tablespoons, divided
2–3 onions, thinly sliced
1 tablespoon oil, cook's preference
Salt
Freshly ground black pepper
4 tablespoons all-purpose flour
4 slices calf's liver (about 1 pound), each about 1/4 inch thick
1/4 cup red wine, sherry, or cider vinegar

Heat 2 tablespoons of the butter in a large nonaluminum or iron frying pan. Add the onions. Cook, stirring occasionally, over low to medium heat until they are very soft and lightly colored, about 20 to 30 minutes. This may be done in advance.

Heat another tablespoon of butter and the oil in another skillet. Add a little salt and pepper to the flour on a large plate. Using one hand, to keep the other clean and free for turning the meat, lightly dredge the liver slices in the flour, shake off excess, and add to the hot pan in batches if necessary to avoid crowding the pan. Cook 2 to 3 minutes on the first side, until brown and slightly crisp. Turn and quickly brown the other side. Cooking time will vary, depending on the thickness of the meat. Move the cooked liver to a plate.

Pour off or remove excess grease from the pan. Add the vinegar to the skillet, bring to the boil, stirring any juices into the vinegar, and cook to reduce slightly. Pour over the warm onions. Wipe out pan with paper towels.

Melt the remaining butter in the pan and cook carefully until it turns a nutty brown. Arrange the liver on the platter, pile on the onions, and drizzle them with the brown butter.

Variation: Cut meat into 1/2-inch slices.

LAMB

Thomas Jefferson loved lamb—even mutton—and served it often at Monticello. Damon Lee Fowler quotes Ellen Coolidge, writing her mother at Monticello from Jefferson's retreat, Poplar Forest: ". . . you will be astonished to hear lamb has become such a rarity."

The heat of the Deep South was not conducive to breeding and raising wooly animals, and the meat, primarily mutton, was deemed heavy for a people who mostly ate dinner at three in the afternoon and then took a nap. (This tradition went on through the 1950s and 1960s in some regions.) Ideally, a lamb is slaughtered when it is three to five months old—at one time still milk-fed by its mother. The older a sheep gets, the stronger the lanolin flavor the lamb has, which is that strong muttony flavor at the back of the mouth. It is flabbier. Age, after all, is age, and it's accompanied by loss of body tone. A young lamb has neither a musk gland nor a fell (the thin skin covering the fat).

Lamb tastes better according to what the animal eats, just as chicken does. One reason lamb is a traditional spring dish is because the first grasses that come up contain garlic and onion grass, and mint and rosemary are some of the first herbs to appear. Most American lamb is grass-fed for a longer period of time, so it benefits from doesn't have the same flavor that European, English, New Zealand, and Australian lambs have.

The average American lamb is both larger and older than spring lambs used to be. It's larger because it is a larger breed of lamb, usually Suffolk, and is allowed to grow older, usually a year, before it is slaughtered. Contrast the now familiar nine-pound leg of lamb that is sold with the less-than-five-pound leg that was sold in the mid-1900s. It is a mild meat compared to mutton, but it lacks the richness that good lamb has.

I try to find specialty producers of lamb, even if the meat is more expensive, because it is so satisfying. Two of the top names in specialty lamb production are Jamison Farms and Neiman Farms. Other farmers have joined in, and there are many more coming into existence.

Most lamb is best served rare or medium-rare, unless stewed. The most popular cuts of lamb are the leg and the ribs.

Leg of lamb—A whole leg of lamb is almost a thing of the past in grocery stores. There's a reason for that: an average American leg of lamb is 9 pounds, and it used to be less than 5. It takes a family of giants to eat 9 pounds, even after the bone is removed, so more and more it is sold halved.

If there is a 5-pound leg of lamb in a grocery store, it is most probably New Zealand or Australian legs of lamb, usually frozen. One of the virtues of a leg of lamb is that since there is so much variety in the thickness of the leg, the meat is cooked unevenly. Hence, the rare meat in middle of the larger portions and well done in the narrower, which pleases everyone.

The "fell" or outer membrane should be removed. Pry enough of the thin covering away that, using a knife or fingers, you can give it a good yank and pull it off. Discard.

I usually prefer serving a leg of lamb butterflied, as it is easier to carve and cooks in less than half an hour.

It is hard to know which part of the boned leg is being sold in the grocery store, as it comes in a netting inside the package. There are three muscles in a butterflied leg (where the bone is removed and then the flesh is cut open to resemble a butterfly):

- The top, or mini-round, which we might even call the rump roast with the eye of round in another larger animal.
- The sirloin with the mini-tenderloin.
- The sirloin tip.

Steaks are from the center cut of the leg. Kebabs come from all parts of the leg.

To serve a previously boned leg of lamb, remove netting and spread out, smooth side down, and arrange like a butterfly. If the meat forms a pocket, slit the small end of the pocket and spread it out.

GRILLED BUTTERFLIED LEG OF LAMB

Serves 8

THIS IS ABSOLUTELY MY FAVORITE WAY *of serving lamb. I didn't originate the recipe, nor is it particularly Southern; it is an adaptation of one that Julia Child developed in the 1970s. Since I've been teaching it for more than thirty years, I'm going to pretend it is Southern. One of the prime times in the South for grilling is in the spring. The summer is just too hot for the sane to stand outside over a hot grill. In late spring, when the seeds of the cilantro plant are still green and forcing their way out, I like to use them in the variation. When dry and brown, the seeds are called coriander, and I crush them between waxed paper or in my Mexican lava rock* molcajete *(mortar and pestle) with the cumin seed from my garden.*

4 pounds leg of lamb, boned and butterflied
1 cup Dijon mustard
2 teaspoons Worcestershire sauce
2 tablespoons chopped fresh rosemary
2 tablespoons chopped fresh garlic
2 tablespoons chopped fresh ginger
2 tablespoons soy sauce
1–2 tablespoons oil, cook's preference, optional
Pinch of salt
Freshly ground black pepper

Trim off any excess fat and membranes from the meat.

Mix together the mustard, Worcestershire sauce, rosemary, garlic, ginger, soy sauce, optional oil, salt, and pepper. Rub onto both sides of the meat. Refrigerate in a large plastic ziplock bag or covered container, overnight if possible.

When ready to cook, remove and shake slightly, and move to a heated oiled griddle, grill rack, or oiled pan if going under the broiler, reserving any marinade separately. Cook at medium-high approximately 5 inches from the heat for approximately 15 minutes, or until mustard coating is slightly dappled with charred bits. Turn the meat and cook on second side until the meat registers about 130 degrees in the thickest part.

Allow to rest 10 minutes, during which the temperature will rise about 10 degrees. The thinner portions will be well done and the center rare.

Slice the meat against the grain. Bring any remaining marinade to the boil and serve with the lamb. Leftovers freeze well or are good cold or hot in a sandwich or salad.

Variation: Leg of Lamb with Coriander and Orange Marinade and Sauce

Whisk together 1 cup Dijon mustard, 2 tablespoons whole coriander seeds, roughly crushed, 1 tablespoon ground cumin seed, 4 large garlic cloves, peeled and crushed to a paste, and 1/2 cup orange juice. Marinate lamb overnight; drain off the marinade and bring it to the boil in a saucepan. Reduce heat and simmer 5 minutes. Cook lamb as above and serve with sauce.

What happened to the shank that used to come with all legs of lamb? People got interested in it as a separate piece of meat because it forms an attractive triangle on the plate and is a good flavoring for bean and lentil stews (and, of course, at Passover celebrations, the shank of lamb is used). So the shank is rarely sold as part of the leg anymore.

BUTTERFLYING A LEG OF LAMB

Trim off the excess fat and the shiny silver skin, or fell, from the meat. Since it is not cooking long enough for the fibers to become tender, I like to marinate overnight, but if you decide you want lamb at the last minute, 1 or 2 hours will do.

Pretend the meat is a book. Place one hand on top and make a slit with a sharp knife along the side as if you are slicing open the book. Continue cutting through the center of the meat while applying pressure to the top until almost reaching the other side, stopping 1 to 2 inches from edge. Do not cut all the way through. "Open" the meat so each side is even. Trim the gristle and set aside.

BROILED OR GRILLED LAMB WITH HERBS

Serves 4

THIS RECIPE WAS DEVELOPED BY INTERN ASHLEY STRICKLAND *and is quick and easy to fix. The top round is an ideal size to feed a family of four that includes a heavy eater or two, or six dainty eaters.*

2 tablespoons chopped fresh rosemary
1 tablespoon chopped fresh thyme
1 garlic clove, minced
1 tablespoon oil, cook's preference
Salt
Freshly ground black pepper
1 (2-pound) top round of lamb

Preheat the broiler or grill.

Stir together the herbs, garlic, and oil, and season to taste with salt and pepper. Rub all over the lamb, making sure to fill all the crevices.

Move the lamb with herb mixture to a broiling pan and let it sit for at least 30 minutes. After it has marinated, broil or add to a hot grill for about 5 minutes. Turn and cook for another 5 minutes, or until brown. Let the meat rest for about 10 minutes and then slice and serve.

LAMB CHOPS WITH MINT-MUSTARD SAUCE

Serves 2 or 3

THICK LAMB CHOPS ARE EXTRAORDINARILY SATISFYING, *especially when accompanied by a cold or room-temperature sauce, particularly one that may be made in advance and refrigerated so all the cook has to do is cook the chops. Fresh mint is a must.*

6 (1- to 1/2-inch-thick) lamb chops
2 garlic cloves, chopped
2 heaping tablespoons finely chopped fresh mint
1/4 cup oil, cook's preference
2 tablespoons fresh lemon juice

Rub the chops with chopped garlic and mint. Mix oil with lemon juice. Drizzle on the chops. Move to a plastic ziplock bag and marinate up to 2 hours at room temperature or longer in the refrigerator. Move the chops to a preheated griddle or grill, and cook 5 to 6 minutes on each side, or until desired doneness. Serve with Mint-Mustard Sauce.

MINT-MUSTARD SAUCE

2 tablespoons Dijon mustard
1 tablespoon fresh lemon juice
1 garlic clove, chopped
3/4 cup oil, cook's preference
2 heaping tablespoons finely chopped fresh mint
2 tablespoons heavy cream or sour cream
Salt
Freshly ground black pepper
Granulated sugar

Blend together mustard, lemon juice, and garlic in a blender or food processor. Slowly add the oil and blend until emulsified (page 102) and thick. Add the mint. Quickly blend in the cream. Season to taste with salt and pepper, and add sugar as necessary. Pour some sauce over the meat and pass the rest separately.

RACK OF LAMB WITH MUSCADINE SAUCE OR RED CURRANT JELLY

Serves 2

LAMBS, LIKE PEOPLE, VARY IN SIZE, *so use a thermometer when testing for doneness. Be sure to purchase a rack of lamb large enough to feed two. Have the butcher remove the chine bone (backbone). Muscadine or red currant jelly is a miraculous addition—it colors the sauce and adds a delicate sweetness as well as thickening the sauce.*

- 1 (1½- to 2-pound) rack of lamb, trimmed with backbone removed
- 3 garlic cloves, chopped
- 1–2 heaping tablespoons finely chopped fresh basil
- 1–2 heaping tablespoons finely chopped fresh mint, thyme, or oregano
- 1–2 tablespoons oil, cook's preference
- Salt
- Freshly ground black pepper
- ¼–⅓ cup Muscadine Sauce (page 666) or red currant jelly, heated

The bones are normally scraped when purchased. If not, make a firm slice across where the meat is flat on the bone, a few inches from the end of the bones, and slide off this small piece of meat, set aside. Slide a small knife between each pair of ribs and remove the adjacent meat. To scrape further, hold knife on one side of the bone, position the thumb firmly on the other side, and scrape with the knife. If icy cold, it is possible to pull the membrane off with fingernails.

Mix the garlic, basil, mint, olive oil, salt, and pepper. Rub on the lamb, and marinate in a plastic ziplock bag for 1 hour or up to 2 days in the refrigerator.

Preheat oven to 375 degrees.

Bake the rack of lamb in a shallow baking pan 25 to 30 minutes for rare, or to an internal temperature of 125 degrees; 40 minutes for medium-rare, or 135 degrees. To present, cut down between the ribs. Arrange on the platter, crossing the bones; or serve on the plates. Pour melted sauce or jelly onto the plate.

Variation: Pan-Roasted Rack of Lamb
Heat 1 tablespoon oil in an oven-proof skillet. Salt and pepper a trimmed rack of lamb and brown, fat side down, about 3 minutes. Turn over and brown other side 2 minutes. Move the skillet to a 400-degree oven and roast 15 minutes, or until desired doneness.

Variation: For a crown roast of lamb, follow directions for Crown Roast of Pork (page 401).

The Deep South has historically had a high proportion of men in the armed forces, perhaps because the South had very powerful representatives in the U.S. Congress by the mid-twentieth century, bringing military bases to their home states as financial ballasts.

Mutton, much stronger tasting and smelling than lamb, was fed to those legions of Southern men on ships and in mess halls during World War II, and they returned vowing never to eat it again, spreading their prejudice to their families.

As time went on, lamb was reserved for special occasions such as Easter, Passover, and other spring holidays, and it had to be specially ordered.

LOLLIPOP LAMB

Serves 4

Beth Price has a real affection for capers—*enough that, after avoiding lamb for twenty years, she cooked it with capers and fell in love with it all over again.*

1 (5-ounce) jar capers
3 tablespoons grated lemon rind, no white attached
4 garlic cloves
4 tablespoons oil, cook's preference, divided
1 (8-rib) rack of lamb, frenched, fat removed, and cut into chops
Salt
Freshly ground black pepper

Roughly chop the capers, lemon rind, and garlic cloves in a food processor fitted with a metal blade. With the blade running, slowly pour in up to 2 tablespoons of oil to form a chunky paste.

Season the chops to taste with salt and pepper. Lightly press the paste onto both sides of the chops. Heat the remaining oil in a heavy frying pan until it shimmers. Add the chops and cook until brown, about 6 minutes; turn and cook until they are medium-rare (135 degrees) and the crust is nicely browned, up to 10 minutes. Serve hot; pick them up and eat like a lollipop.

PURCHASING THE LAMB

The butcher should be willing to remove the fat and cut the rack into chops. "Frenching" is scraping off the meat, fat, and membranes that connect the rib bones. It makes them pretty to view and easy to hold if they are passed as a nibble at a cocktail party.

BREADS

Hot bread is the hallmark of Southern meals, from beignets sprinkled with confectioners' sugar at the Café du Monde in New Orleans or biscuits straight from the oven eaten on the way to the barn, to cornbread with clabber or buttermilk served for a Sunday-night supper.

Because they are the easiest, we start with batter breads, then move on to simple quick breads, the most prevalent breads in the South. They usually include baking soda and/or powder. They are, as described, "quick" to make, and include biscuits and cornbread. Heat up the oven, mix together the ingredients, and a short while later, hot bread is on the table. We finish with yeast breads. The process for making yeast breads is nearly opposite from making quick breads. Yeast breads want to be kneaded and prefer a sturdier flour, while quick breads like a softer flour and light handling. The two methods are separated in this chapter. We've tried in each section to move from simplest to most complicated, talking about all the modern machinery available and how to make life simpler by doing as much as possible ahead and utilizing refrigerator, microwave, and freezer.

To begin, the Southern baker needs to understand the differences between the ingredients used here versus elsewhere. We have a different flour in the South. Carefully reading the factual information on flour and other ingredients in this chapter will be well worth the time and will boost the baker's skill enormously.

FLOUR FACTS

Where there is grain, water, and fire, there is bread. Bread has sustained humanity from the earliest days. It requires the least effort to make of any food product and has a primary spot in our cuisine. "Hot bread" was considered an integral part of any meal, from sunup to sundown, for most of my lifetime.

Any finely ground grain can be called flour. Wheat, rice, and corn flours are all available in the South, as are rye, barley, and potato flours. But wheat and corn are the primary grains. Historically, Southern wheat was either "winter wheat" or "spring wheat." Winter wheat, known as "soft wheat," was planted in the fall and harvested in the spring. Spring wheat, known as "hard wheat," was planted in the spring and harvested before the frost.

Gluten is the important part of the wheat that makes breads and biscuits light and airy. Moisture and manipulation cause gluten to perform like a rubber band. Combined with yeast, manipulation and heat, gluten allows bread to rise and stay aloft.

Flour is categorized by its protein content. The protein content of flour helps the baker know which type of flour is best for each purpose. The higher protein flours, made mostly from hard wheat, contain higher gluten and are used when stretching and developing gluten strands is desired—vital for yeast breads to rise. The lower protein flours, made from soft wheat, with lower gluten content, are used to keep quick breads, biscuits, cakes, and piecrusts tender and flaky. English wheat is softer than European wheat, and Southern colonists became accustomed to the softer wheat. Now, all sorts of flours are mixed to give specific results, and many varieties can be grown in the region. Bleaching the flour snowy white also tenderizes it, thus bleached flour produces a lighter biscuit. Whole wheat's gluten is not accessible, so it cannot stretch and is not part of the South's baking tradition.

Lower gluten flour is better for biscuits and quick breads. Bread flour contains more than 12 grams of protein per cup, some Northern brands up to 15 grams. The protein helps develop the gluten, which also gives the bread its chewy texture and crisp crust.

National brands of all-purpose flour contain 11 to 12 grams of protein per cup. This flour is suitable for most baked goods but not for the lightest biscuits. The combination of national brand all-purpose flour and baking soda or powder produces a sturdy biscuit. In the South, we use a soft-wheat flour with baking soda or baking powder. When the leavening is already added, it is called self-rising flour, known for producing a more tender and fluffier biscuit. Southern flour traditionally has 10 or fewer grams of protein per cup.

HOMEMADE SELF-RISING FLOUR

To make homemade self-rising flour, add 1/2 teaspoon salt and 1 1/2 teaspoons baking powder to 1 cup all-purpose flour.

Storing flour—Flour should stay fresh for a couple of months when stored in an airtight container at room temperature, up to 3 months in the refrigerator, or 12 months in the freezer. Bring the flour to room temperature before using.

Measuring flour—Measuring correctly is an art worth cultivating. Professional bakers weigh their ingredients to make a consistent product. The home cook relies primarily on feel and cup measurements.

Purchase a set of dry measuring cups and at least one wet measuring cup, preferably more of each. A dry measuring cup allows the cook to fill the cup to the rim before leveling off the contents with the blunt side of a knife. A liquid measuring cup (preferably glass or see-through) has a spout above the measuring mark that allows the liquid to come up to the mark without spilling over. In a dry measuring cup, a full measure of liquid would overflow.

Using a wet measuring cup will cause dry products, particularly flour, to pack in the cup. Using a dry measuring cup for the liquids will result in skimpy measurements. To see if they are both correctly manufactured, measure a cup of water in the wet measuring cup and pour it into the dry. It should come dangerously close to the brim. Unfortunately, giveaway and cheap measuring cups may be off the mark and should be discarded. A cup of Southern flour should weigh 4 ounces, if measured correctly. When a bag of flour is shipped, the flour settles in the bag. A cup of flour that is packed in the cup can weigh 5 ounces.

Clearly, weighing ingredients is preferable, but as it is sometimes awkward for the home cook, we recommend measuring flour in the following manner: Use a whisk or long spoon to stir the flour while still in the bag or storage container. Lightly spoon the flour with a large spoon into the dry measuring cup and level off the top with the back of a knife. When emptying the cup into the mixing bowl, notice if the flour breaks up or stays in the shape of the cup. If it is cup-shaped, remove 2 or 3 level tablespoons of flour, as that is a sign the flour was too tightly packed—it's always easier to add flour to a dough than to take it away.

INGREDIENTS

Baking Soda or Baking Powder—Some recipes call for baking soda while others call for baking powder, depending on the other ingredients in the recipe. Baking powder contains an acid and a base, plus a cornstarch filler. It has an overall neutral effect in terms of taste when it is free of aluminum. Recipes that call for baking powder often call for other neutral-tasting ingredients such as milk.

Sodium bicarbonate is the source of the leavening power in baking powder and in baking soda. In fact, baking soda is pure sodium bicarbonate and needs to be mixed with an acidic ingredient—such as chocolate, honey, molasses, citrus juice, sour cream, buttermilk, or brown sugar—to release the carbon dioxide that leavens the dough and prevents a bitter aftertaste. This is why recipes that already contain acidic ingredients may call for baking soda rather than for baking powder. The baking soda neutralizes any acidic ingredients in the recipe, such as yogurt, buttermilk, or sour cream. Since baking powder already contains the acid component to react with the sodium bicarbonate, it is not necessary to have acidic ingredients in the recipe.

One teaspoon of baking powder contains 1⁄4 teaspoon of baking soda, meaning that baking soda is four times more powerful than baking powder. Some recipes will call for both baking soda and baking powder. In this case, baking powder is used for its reliability—guaranteeing the acid matches the amount of soda, and the double-acting process will help give a good rise.

Baking Powder—The acid in a baking powder may be either fast-acting or slow-acting. A fast-acting acid reacts in a wet mixture with baking soda at room temperature. A slow-acting acid will not react until heated in an oven. Baking powders that contain both fast- and slow-acting acids are double-acting; those that contain only one acid are single-acting. By providing a second rise in the oven, double-acting baking powders increase the reliability of baked goods by rendering the time elapsed between mixing

TESTING BAKING SODA AND POWDER

To test baking soda for freshness, add 1/4 teaspoon baking soda to 2 tablespoons vinegar. To test baking powder for freshness, add 1 cup hot water to 2 teaspoons baking powder. Both should immediately begin to hiss and foam up. If not, discard the container and replace it with a new one.

and baking less critical. Recipes using single-acting baking powders need to be baked right away.

Nonaluminum baking powders, such as Argo, Rumford, Bakewell Cream, and Red Star, are preferable, in that order. Calumet and Clabber Girl contain aluminum and leave a metallic aftertaste. Baking powder usually should be replaced if much more than six months old, as it loses its leavening capacity over time. Make a habit of writing the date of purchase on the container.

Eggs—Eggs are a natural leavener. Used less often in yeast breads, they are found in pancakes, crêpes, cream puff doughs, popovers, Yorkshire puddings, and the like. They count as a liquid measure, substituting for other liquids for purposes of measuring. They provide color, structure, leavening, and flavor. Grade A large eggs are the standard for all recipes in this book.

Egg Wash—Egg washes are brushed onto breads before baking to give them a shine and sophistication. They can include milk, melted butter, whole eggs, egg yolks, and/or egg whites beaten with a pinch of salt to break up the strands and provide even application.

Glazes—Brushed on after baking, they include confectioners' sugar and water, milk, or butter, further tenderizing and flavoring as they soak into the bread.

Butter and Fat—Butter and fat add tenderness and flavor to bread products and aid in browning. One trick for softening cold or frozen butter is to grate it on a box grater or other grater. Melting and cooling the butter to semisolid and using softened butter makes lighter doughs. Melted butter makes the dough slightly denser.

Bakers prefer unsalted butter. If only salted butter is available, reduce the amount of salt in the recipe slightly. Shortening, oil, and lard may substitute for butter and vice versa, but each will bring its distinctive characteristics.

Liquids—Liquid activates leavening and creates steam. Water and milk are the most dominant liquids in yeast breads, but other liquids may range from sodas to beer in both quick breads and biscuits. Buttermilk, yogurt, sour cream, and other acidic liquids give an added boost of fluffiness and a tarter flavor, as they combine acid with leaveners (baking soda and baking powder).

The thinner the liquid, the less is needed. Use what is available, but whole milk and buttermilk make a better biscuit.

QUICK BREADS

Quickly combined flour and liquid will make many types of bread. Easy examples would be crackers, hardtack, beaten biscuits, griddle breads such as pancakes, hoecakes, and even some corn pones.

In the late 1700s, potash was used to leaven bread without yeast. By the mid-1800s, baking powder (albeit harsh) was developed. By the end of the 1800s, self-rising flour had been introduced and was widely accepted in the South. And this brought about the biscuit, a cousin of the English scone.

Often a cook's first bread, a quick bread rises without the mystery of yeast but rises instead with the help of leaveners such as baking soda or baking powder. Quick breads are nearly foolproof and inspire baking confidence. Mixtures for quick breads vary in thickness, from the thin batter of pancakes, to drop batters as in muffins and cornbread, to soft doughs for biscuits and scones.

Quick to mix, these breads are baked as soon as they are mixed and poured into a pan. Some are eaten right from the oven or griddle, but others, such as banana bread, are sliced more easily when cool.

If using a national-brand flour for these recipes, remove 2 or so tablespoons of flour at the start to be sure the dough does not become too dry. Certain brands of Southern flours, like White Lily Flour and Martha White, are made exclusively from soft wheat and contain closer to 9 grams of protein per cup. Cake flour is a specialty flour with 6 to 8 grams of protein per cup.

HOMEMADE CAKE FLOUR

To make cake flour, mix together 3/4 cup all-purpose flour and 2 tablespoons cornstarch.

CHEDDAR MUFFIN BITES

Makes 6 dozen mini muffins

WHETHER AT A LADIES LUNCHEON *or special party, bite-sized muffins are a hit. I often pop them out of the freezer as a light, tasty accompaniment to soups and salads as well. The muffins can be made ahead to give as gifts. These freeze beautifully; just reheat in the oven.*

- 6 tablespoons cold butter, cut into 1/4-inch cubes
- 3 cups self-rising flour
- 3/4 pound extra sharp Cheddar cheese, coarsely grated
- 1 1/2 cups milk

Preheat oven to 425 degrees. Oil mini-muffin tins.

Scatter the pieces of chilled butter over the flour and work in by rubbing fingers with the fat and flour as if snapping thumb and fingers together (or use two forks or knives, or a pastry cutter) until no pieces remain larger than a pea.

Stir in the cheese and add enough milk to make a sticky dough. The dough may be covered and refrigerated at this time if desired. Bring to room temperature. Spoon dough into tins until individual cups are three-fourths full. Cover remaining batter and leave at room temperature, repeating for each batch as needed.

Bake in the middle of the oven 10 to 15 minutes, until pale golden brown. Remove the muffins from tins and cool on a rack. If the muffins brown too much on the bottom, adjust rack, or add a baking sheet underneath the muffin tin for insulation under the next batch.

The muffins may be frozen, wrapped well, up to 3 months.

YORKSHIRE PUDDING POPOVERS

Makes 8 popovers

I WAS ALWAYS HARD ON MYSELF *about popovers because I wanted them to be perfect, with sides straight up to the mushroom-shaped tops towering over the cups, deep brown but not burned, and crisp. Then I went to a wedding in a very posh hotel, where there were various stations offering cuisines from several countries. In the room where roast beef was being served, it was accompanied by popovers. To my delight, they were kattywhompus things, the tops at an angle, and the sides of different heights. So I can say with surety: enjoy popovers, crisp outsides and airy insides, no matter how regal they look.*

Although muffin tins may be used, proper popover tins are heavier and give a nicer rise and shape. Popovers are made from Yorkshire pudding batter, though I imagine it was probably once a leftover batter a cook frantically added to a pan that had been put under the beef to catch the fat and juices from the roast beef as it cooked, rather than letting the fat burn.

1 1/3 cups bread flour
Scant teaspoon salt
3 large eggs
2/3 cup milk, divided
1 1/3 cups water, divided
8 teaspoons beef drippings or oil, cook's preference

Sift the flour with the salt into a bowl. Whisk together the eggs, 1/3 cup milk, and 2/3 cup water. Stir the egg mixture into the flour carefully until the batter is smooth. Combine the remaining 1/3 cup milk and 2/3 cup water together, add half to the batter, and whisk several minutes with a wire whisk or electric hand mixer. Stir in the rest of the liquid, cover, and let rest at least 1 hour or as long as overnight. Bring the batter to room temperature before using.

Preheat oven to 450 degrees. Divide drippings or oil among the cups of an 8-cup popover pan. Move the pan to the oven to heat.

When the pan is very hot, remove from the oven and fill each cup halfway full with batter. Bake until puffed, very firm to the touch, and brown on both the top and bottom, about 20 to 25 minutes. To test for doneness, check the area above the lip of the pan and below the risen top. A white area indicates that the popover is not fully dry and may collapse. Cook until brown and sturdy. Turn out on a serving platter and serve hot.

Variations: Add cheese, herbs, or finely chopped nuts to the batter.

ONE-POT BANANA BREAD

Makes 1 loaf

CYNTHIA WROTE *the very successful kitchen primer* The One-Armed Cook, *designed in particular for new parents. (Trying to cook dinner with a baby on your hip makes you a one-armed cook!) But the book is useful for anyone trying to get dinner on the table. This banana bread is a favorite from that book. If the bananas are very ripe, the recipe can be made with just a sturdy whisk. If less so, mash the banana with a fork before adding to the bowl. "Over the hill" bananas may be peeled, wrapped, and frozen to collect for this recipe or to use in smoothies.*

1 cup granulated sugar
1/2 cup oil, cook's preference
2 large eggs
1 teaspoon vanilla extract
3 large bananas, very ripe
2 cups all-purpose flour
1 teaspoon baking soda
1 teaspoon salt
1 cup chopped pecans

Preheat oven to 375 degrees. Oil a 9 x 5 x 3-inch loaf pan. Line with 2 pieces of parchment or waxed paper—one cut to the width of the pan and the other to the length of the pan plus 4 inches of overhang to use as handles to lift the loaf from the pan.

Whisk together the sugar, oil, eggs, and vanilla; whisk in the bananas. Add the flour, baking soda, and salt, whisking well to combine; whisk in the pecans.

Pour batter into prepared loaf pan. Bake until the loaf is golden brown, about 45 to 50 minutes. The bread is done when a toothpick inserted in the center comes out clean.

Remove the loaf from the oven and place on a wire rack to cool in the pan for 10 minutes. Lift the bread out of the pan, remove the paper, and let cool on a rack. The loaf cuts cleaner when completely cool.

FOOD PROCESSOR ZUCCHINI BREAD

Makes 1 loaf

IT'S A GOOD SNACKING BREAD, *useful for tea or serving to company, and can even be called a sweet, as it has a gracious plenty of sugar. Zucchini bread soared to popularity in the 1970s when the food processor was invented, for both the shredding and the beating could be done with the machine. And thus zucchini became an everyday Southern staple. Using a microplane or a good box grater will also do the job of grating, and an electric hand mixer can be used for the batter.*

2 small zucchini, ends removed
3/4 cup granulated sugar, optional
2 tablespoons grated lemon rind, no white attached
1/2 cup unsalted butter
2 large eggs
1/2 cup shelled pecans
1 3/4 cups self-rising flour

Preheat oven to 350 degrees. Oil a 9 x 5 x 3-inch loaf pan. Line with 2 pieces of parchment or waxed paper—one cut to the width of the pan and the other to the length of the pan plus 4 inches of overhang to use as handles to lift the loaf from the pan.

Shred zucchini in a food processor fitted with the grating disc, or shred by hand. Remove and dry with paper towels.

Add sugar, lemon rind, butter, and eggs to a food processor or mixer bowl. Process or mix only until blended. Add a third of the pecans and a third of the shredded zucchini. Process or mix, and then repeat for remaining two thirds of ingredients only until shreds disappear. Add flour and mix or process, pulsing on and off only until dry ingredients are incorporated.

Pour batter into prepared pan. Bake on center rack of the oven for 55 to 60 minutes, or until bread shrinks slightly from the sides of the pan and a toothpick inserted in the center comes out clean. Cool in the pan on a wire rack for 10 minutes. Lift the bread out of the pan, remove the paper, and let cool on a rack.

SWEET POTATO TEA LOAF WITH GINGER

Makes 1 loaf

ADAPTED FROM SUSAN FULLER SLACK'S *East Tennessee grandmother's recipe, this warmly spiced loaf offers a triple play of ground, fresh, and candied ginger. She would bake the sweet potatoes until very soft and the natural sugars began to caramelize. This seems to enhance the bread's flavor and moisture. I sometimes add 3/4 cup of fresh seasonal cranberries (cut in half) or freshly chopped soft Medjool dates. The chopped nuts create a crunchy, attractive loaf top, and dark chocolate chips are a touch of indulgence. Spread the slices with cream cheese, plain or flavored with orange zest. A crack in the dome of the bread is normal.*

1 2/3 cups all-purpose flour
1 teaspoon baking powder
1/4 teaspoon baking soda
1 cup baked and well-mashed fresh sweet potato
1 cup light or dark brown sugar
1/2 cup orange juice
1/3 cup oil, cook's preference
2 large eggs
1 teaspoon vanilla extract
1/2 teaspoon salt
1/2 teaspoon ground cinnamon
1/2 teaspoon ground nutmeg
1/2 teaspoon ground cloves
3/4 teaspoon ground ginger
1 rounded teaspoon grated fresh gingerroot, optional
2 tablespoons minced candied ginger, optional
About 21 large dark chocolate chips
3 tablespoons chopped pecans

Preheat oven to 350 degrees. Oil a 9 x 5-inch loaf pan. Line with 2 pieces of parchment or waxed paper—one cut to the width of the pan and the other to the length of the pan plus 4 inches of overhang to use as handles to lift the loaf from the pan. Oil the paper.

Whisk flour, baking powder, and baking soda a full 30 seconds. Set aside.

Whisk together sweet potato, brown sugar, orange juice, oil, eggs, and vanilla. Stir in salt, spices, grated gingerroot, and candied ginger.

Pour dry ingredients on top of the sweet potato mixture; stir together only until thoroughly combined. Pour batter into prepared pan, arrange chocolate chips evenly over the top, and sprinkle with nuts. Bake 50 minutes. The bread is done when a toothpick inserted in the center comes out clean. If necessary, bake 5 to 10 minutes more, covering loosely with foil to prevent excess browning.

Remove pan from oven and cool 10 minutes on a wire rack. Lift the bread out of the pan, remove the paper, and let cool on a rack.

Properly wrapped, the bread can be stored at room temperature for 3 days or frozen for longer storage. For the best texture, bring to room temperature before serving.

KELLY'S BANANA CHOCOLATE CHIP MUFFINS

Makes 12 muffins

I CAN KEEP MY FINGER ON THE PULSE *of what is actually being cooked at home through what my assistants are cooking for their families, what's practical and what's not. This is one of the "children love it" and "I can make it blindfolded" recipes Kelly Skelly brought in. Well, she's right. What's not to love?*

- 2 1/2 cups all-purpose flour
- 1 cup light or dark brown sugar
- 1 1/2 teaspoons baking powder
- 1 teaspoon baking soda
- 1/2 teaspoon salt
- 2 large eggs
- 1/3 cup oil, cook's preference
- 1 teaspoon vanilla extract
- 1 cup buttermilk
- 1 cup mashed bananas
- 3/4 cup chocolate chips

Preheat oven to 375 degrees. Oil a 12-cup muffin tin.

Whisk together the flour, sugar, baking powder, baking soda, and salt in a large bowl.

Whisk together the eggs, oil, vanilla, buttermilk, and mashed bananas, in a separate bowl.

Pour the egg mixture over the flour mixture, sprinkle with chocolate chips, and stir just until dry ingredients are moistened. Spoon into prepared muffin cups until individual cups are three-fourths full.

Bake for 20 to 25 minutes, until a toothpick inserted in the center of a muffin comes out clean. Remove from oven and cool 10 minutes; remove muffins from cups and cool on a wire rack.

PEACH COFFEE CAKE

Makes 1 (12-cup) Bundt cake

DELIGHTFUL WITH THE FIRST PEACHES OF THE SEASON, *this coffee cake provides a warm welcome to a weekend breakfast. No need to wait for fresh peaches, however; frozen peaches work as well.*

- 3 cups Homemade Refrigerator Biscuit Mix (page 472) or commercial biscuit mix
- 3/4 cup granulated sugar
- 2 large eggs
- 2 teaspoons vanilla extract, divided
- 1/4 cup butter, melted
- 2 cups sliced fresh or frozen peaches (defrosted) and their juice
- 1 cup sour cream
- 1/2 cup finely chopped pecans
- 1 cup confectioners' sugar
- 2 tablespoons water

Preheat oven to 350 degrees. Oil a Bundt pan and set aside.

Fork-stir or whisk together the biscuit mix and sugar in a large bowl.

Stir together the eggs, 1 1/2 teaspoons vanilla, and butter; pour over biscuit mix.

Break up peaches into large chunks and stir into biscuit mixture. Add sour cream and pecans, and stir together until well combined. Pour into prepared pan and bake on the middle rack for 55 minutes, or until a toothpick inserted in the center comes out clean (there may be a few crumbs). Move to a rack and cool 15 minutes. Turn coffee cake out on the rack and cool completely.

Stir together confectioners' sugar, water, and remaining 1/2 teaspoon vanilla, and drizzle over cooled coffee cake.

STOVETOP BATTERS

Batters are a mixture of flour with liquid and usually include a leavening agent such as baking soda, baking powder, eggs, or even beer. Batters can be thick or thin and neutral, savory, or sweet. Heat then changes them miraculously into varying thicknesses and lightnesses, whether for a crepe, a waffle, or to coat fish or vegetables for deep-frying.

The essential technique involved in a successful batter is allowing the batter to rest before cooking. Sometimes this is just ten minutes; for other recipes it's an hour, and still others, refrigerated overnight. Thin batter with a little water or milk if it is too thick after resting.

Heat is of the essence. Without sufficient heat, the batter will stick, the pan grabbing onto the protein and making it stick. Griddles, pans, and waffle irons should always be preheated for batters. If well seasoned—i.e., not previously rubbed with an abrasive or left to rust—they may not need additional butter or oil to cook in them. I like the color a little butter gives, however. Remember, the first one cooked is always a test one. Taste it, then discard it or give it to the dog.

BASIC PANCAKES

About 10 (6-inch) cakes

Pancakes are very personal. *Some like them thick, some thin, some pale tinged with brown, some golden all over. This batter is best made ahead of time, then covered and refrigerated. I much prefer whole milk, but I list the alternatives, recognizing that so many households use only skim or low-fat milk.*

1 1/2 cups all-purpose flour
3 tablespoons granulated, light, or dark brown sugar
1 1/2 teaspoons baking powder
1/2 teaspoon salt
1 1/2 cups whole, low-fat, or skim milk
3 –5 tablespoons unsalted butter, melted
2 large eggs, beaten to mix

Preheat the griddle. Preheat oven to 200 degrees.

Whisk together the flour, sugar, baking powder, and salt then make a hole in the center of the flour, down to the bottom of the bowl. In another bowl, whisk together the milk, butter, and eggs. Pour the wet ingredients into the hole in the dry ingredients, whisking the wet gently but thoroughly into the dry. Circle around the bowl with the whisk to pull in the flour. Use right away, or cover tightly and keep in the refrigerator up to several days. Whisk well before using, adding 1/2 cup of berries, nuts, bananas, cheese, bacon, and the like if desired, and thin with more milk or water if necessary to achieve desired consistency.

Test the griddle with a little water to be sure it is hot enough. The water should sizzle. Ladle or pour 1/3 cup batter onto the griddle per pancake, pushing it into rounds if necessary. If they run together, push apart or separate them when they are done. Cook until the top of the pancake is sprinkled with large bubbles, some of which are bursting; then turn and cook until the other side is lightly browned. Keep warm as directed below, or serve immediately. Continue with the remaining batter.

To keep pancakes warm and tender, layer the pancakes as they are done onto a sheet of aluminum foil or an ovenproof plate or pan, covering loosely with foil, and keep in a 200-degree oven for up to 20 minutes. For a phenomenal pancake, brush each side with a little butter before layering. (The same thing is true for reheating frozen pancakes—a little butter brushed on the ones reheated in the oven makes them truly special. Obviously this will not be appropriate for a toaster.)

The first side (down) of a pancake is always the prettiest. To tell when the pancake should be turned, look for the bubbles coming to the surface of the pancake; then turn and cook until the second side is done. An average pancake is usually 1/3 cup of batter. The size of pancakes can vary, of course, from very small to extra grand.

CRÊPES

Makes 2 cups batter, about 16 to 20 (6-inch) crêpes

THERE ARE MANY WAYS *to make crêpes and many recipes. This is the recipe I used in my restaurant. There can be more eggs or no eggs and a "crêpe" will still emerge from the pan. Water makes a lighter crêpe. Oil raises the smoking point, and butter improves flavor and color. Novices need to spend a little time practicing. "Messed up" crêpes can be discarded or fed to the dog. The first crepe is always a test one. Using two or three nonstick pans will speed up the process. The number of crêpes depends on their thickness. To hold substantial food, thicker batter is better. The gossamer lemon-filled crêpes melt in the mouth.*

1 cup whole milk
1 cup all-purpose flour
1 large egg
1 egg yolk
1/2 teaspoon salt
1–2 tablespoons granulated sugar, optional
1–2 tablespoons oil or butter, cook's preference, optional

Whisk together all ingredients except oil. Let sit 1 hour or up to overnight in the refrigerator to rest the batter. Thin with milk or water as necessary to make desired crêpe.

Heat one or more small nonstick skillets, or add a small amount of butter or oil to a seasoned pan. Add any residual oil or butter to the batter. Pour a small ladle-full of batter into the pan, swirling to cover the bottom of the pan, moving the pan as if rolling a marble around the inside rim. Don't go back and fill in, as that will make the crêpe thick. Pour off any excess batter.

When lightly browned, about 1 minute, turn over with a nonstick spatula or with fingers. Let the second side brown slightly, 30 to 45 seconds, to prevent it from being doughy. Serve right away or turn out onto a rack to cool. (The rack will help prevent the crêpes from sticking together.) Repeat with remaining batter.

Cooled crêpes may be refrigerated or frozen, separated by parchment paper or plastic wrap and wrapped tightly. Defrost, serve at room temperature, or reheat briefly in oven, filled or unfilled.

LEMON BUTTER FILLING

Makes 1 1/2 cups

1 cup granulated sugar
1/2 cup butter
8–10 tablespoons grated lemon rind, no white attached
2 teaspoons lemon juice

Mix sugar, butter, lemon rind, and juice in a bowl. Spoon 1 tablespoon filling onto each crêpe, roll, and move to an oiled baking sheet. This amount of filling should fill about 20 crêpes. Bake in a 350-degree oven 15 minutes. Crêpes may be filled up to 3 months in advance, frozen, and reheated.

Variation: Anything may be wrapped in a crêpe, from leftover meatloaf to sliced strawberries and cream. They may be served hot or cold, depending on the filling.

FOR PERFECT CRÊPES

Heat is a major factor in crêpe making. If the pan is too hot, the crêpe may stick, become hard and crisp, or burn. If too low, the crêpe batter will slide right back out or take too long to cook. The correct temperature "pushes" the crêpe off the pan so it doesn't stick.

Nonstick pans have sped up the process, but the quality of nonstick pans varies widely. Brownness is an individual preference. I know French chefs who insist that crêpes, like omelets, should be without any tinge of brown, and I know those who insist that a near-mahogany color is best. I prefer somewhere in between—a sprinkling of medium brown. I also know chefs who do not cook the second side, but a gummy crêpe is just that, and who wants to eat it?

BUTTERMILK WAFFLES

Makes 8 to 10

Of all the things in my house, *it seems to me my husband values the heavy electric waffle iron he brought to the marriage the most. It has both griddle and waffle plates. He makes Elvis Presley's grilled banana and peanut butter or grilled cheese and apple sandwiches when it is his time to cook lunch on Saturday. On rare occasions, if I make the batter ahead of time and have it ready when genius strikes, he will make waffles. The iron plates crisp both waffles and sandwiches perfectly, burnishing them with color and easing their removal. Waffle batters, like pancake batters, are best made half an hour or more before cooking.*

1¾ cups all-purpose flour
1 teaspoon baking powder
1 teaspoon baking soda
½ teaspoon salt
2 cups buttermilk
⅓ cup melted butter or oil, cook's preference
2 eggs, beaten to mix

Preheat waffle iron. Preheat oven to 200 degrees.

Whisk together flour, baking powder, soda, and salt in a bowl. In another bowl, mix buttermilk, melted butter, and eggs. Whisk together both mixtures and beat until smooth.

When the waffle iron is hot enough for a bit of oil to sizzle, ladle or pour the batter directly into the center of the lower half until it spreads to within an inch from the edges. Close and cook according to manufacturer's directions. Do not lift cover during baking. Steam will escape from the sides of the waffle iron, so take care not to get burned. When the steam subsides, the waffle is nearly ready.

When the waffle is done, lift the cover. Loosen waffle with a fork and remove. Keep warm in oven as directed on page 459, or serve immediately. Meanwhile, close the waffle iron to reheat quickly. When ready, pour in the batter for the next waffle. Thin the batter as needed with more buttermilk.

Variations:

- Self-rising flour may be substituted in equal measure for the flour, omitting baking powder, baking soda, and salt.
- For "sweet" milk waffles, use 1 tablespoon baking powder and substitute milk for the buttermilk.

RICE WAFFLES

"Boil two gills [¼ pint] of rice very soft; mix with it three gills of flour, a little salt, two ounces of melted butter, two eggs well beaten and as much milk as will make a thick batter; beat it till very light, and bake in waffle-irons."

—*Mrs. Porter's New Southern Cookery Book,* 1871

WAFFLE POCKETS

Waffle making is a very ancient craft, with the waffle irons having varying patterns and depths. The deeper "pockets" were originally designed for Belgian Waffles (which were traditionally a yeast waffle), but it works for all kinds. Many feel that the pockets of waffles are only there to hold sorghum or maple syrup. I do love both, but I also love sugar and butter, and the Lemon Butter Filling for crêpes (facing page) is fabulous spread on the waffles.

GOLDEN BROWN SOUTHERN GRITS WAFFLES

Makes 8 to 10 sturdy waffles

Cooked grits refrigerate and freeze well *and are delicious reheated or added to other products. Sorghum syrup, which was popular during World War II, gives a gratifying flavor as well as the sought-after golden color. The waffles make a substantial meal. This recipe won a White Lily contest in 1940, which paid $1 to the winner, Mrs. Edgar Langston, of Brunswick, Georgia.*

2 large eggs
1 1/2 cups milk
2 teaspoons sorghum, Georgia cane syrup, or other syrup
1 cup cooked grits (pages 254–55)
1 cup self-rising flour
1 teaspoon baking powder
5 tablespoons butter, softened

Preheat waffle iron. Preheat oven to 200 degrees.

Whisk together the eggs, milk, and sorghum in a small bowl. Crumble grits and stir into the egg mixture. Whisk together the flour and baking powder in a separate bowl. Beat the flour mixture into the egg mixture until smooth. Stir in butter.

When waffle iron is hot enough for a bit of oil to sizzle, ladle or pour batter directly into the center of the lower half until it spreads to 1 inch from the edges. Cover and bake as directed. Do not lift cover during baking. Steam will escape from the sides of the waffle iron, so take care not to get burned. When the steam subsides, the waffle is nearly ready.

When waffle is done, lift cover and loosen the waffle with a fork. Keep warm in the oven or serve immediately. Meanwhile, close the waffle iron to reheat quickly. When ready, pour in the batter for the next waffle. Thin batter as needed with more milk.

LIGHT BATTER

Makes 2 1/4 cups

Fine and thin, *like the tempura batter used in Japanese cooking, this batter should be icy cold and made at the last minute. It is ideal for frying delicate goods such as squash blossoms or thinly sliced vegetables like squash and zucchini, mushrooms, green beans, and the like, as well as shrimp.*

1 cup all-purpose flour
1 tablespoon cornstarch
1 teaspoon baking soda
1 1/4 cups ice water
Shortening or vegetable oil for frying

Whisk flour, cornstarch, and baking soda together in a bowl. Add ice water and gently whisk together without overmixing. The batter will be thin and may have some lumps. Batter will be thin. Set aside until ready to use.

BATTER-FRIED VEGETABLES

Put a cooling rack on top of a rimmed baking sheet lined with paper towels.

Pour oil into a large deep pan to a depth of about 1 1/2 inches, coming up no more than halfway up the side of the pan. Heat to 375 degrees as indicated on a candy thermometer.

Dip sliced vegetables into the batter and allow batter to drip until just a thin coating remains. Dip the edge of the vegetable into the hot oil and swirl in a circle for a second or two before allowing it to slide gently into the oil. Vegetable will sink at first and then float to the top. If needed, hold under the surface of the oil for a few seconds to brown. When cooked light to golden brown, remove with a slotted spoon to cooling rack and repeat with other vegetables. Serve warm.

LACY CORN FRITTERS (HOECAKES)

Makes 15 fritters

Native Americans introduced the settlers *to the wonders of corn, and corn cakes baked on the back of a garden hoe became a staple of American food. Still popular in the South, a corn fritter, or hoecake, is a palate-pleasing treat for breakfast with butter, jam, or maple syrup. Served alongside pan-fried fish or nestled with a dollop of black-eyed pea hummus or Mississippi Caviar (page 50), an excuse can be made for eating these with any meal of the day. I love them when they are so thin that they look like lace cookies. Well, actually, I love them thin, thick, or in-between.*

9 tablespoons cornmeal mix, (page 477)
4 1/2 tablespoons self-rising flour
1–1 1/2 cups water
Shortening or vegetable oil for frying

Whisk together the cornmeal mix and flour. Add water as needed to keep batter thin, and whisk until smooth.

Heat a thin layer of oil in a large skillet over medium heat. Using a half-full 1/4-cup measure, drop the batter into the hot skillet. Cook each cake until brown and crisp on the bottom; turn with a spatula and then brown the other side. Add more oil and water to the batter as needed to keep the batter thin. Remove to a plate lined with paper towels.

NELLY CUSTIS LEWIS'S RECIPE FOR HOECAKES

". . .The bread business is as follows if you wish to make 2 1/2 quarts of flour up-take at night one quart of flour, five table spoonfuls of yeast & as much lukewarm water as will make it the consistency of pancake batter, mix it in a large stone pot & set it near a warm hearth (or a moderate fire) make it at candlelight & let it remain until the next morning then add the remaining quart & a half by degrees with a spoon when well mixed let it stand 15 or 20 minutes & then bake it—of this dough in the morning, beat up a white & half of the yilk [*sic*] of an egg—add as much lukewarm water as will make it like pancake batter, drop a spoonful at a time on a hoe or griddle (as we say in the South). When done on one side turn the other—the griddle must be rubbed in the first instance with a piece of beef suet or the fat of cold corned beef . . .

—Excerpt from a letter written by Nelly Custis Lewis, Martha Washington's youngest granddaughter

MRS. PETERS' CORNMEAL BATTER GRIDDLE CAKES

Makes about 20

THIS RECIPE IS FROM Southern Cooking *by Mrs. H. R. Dull. It combines cooked rice with cornmeal and is cooked on the griddle.*

1 1/2 cups cornmeal
1 teaspoon granulated sugar
1 tablespoon butter
1 teaspoon baking soda
1 cup cooked rice
2 cups boiling water
1 large egg, beaten to mix
1 1/2 cups buttermilk

Mix the cornmeal, sugar, butter, soda, and cooked rice together in a large bowl. Pour boiling water over the rice mixture, stirring constantly. Let cool slightly and then whisk in the egg and buttermilk. Ladle or pour individual "cakes" onto a hot, lightly oiled griddle or onto a hot iron skillet. Add more water or buttermilk if the batter does not pour easily.

MRS. DULL ON PANCAKES

As Mrs. Dull says about pancakes and griddlecakes, "All flours and meal differ, so that quantity is hard to give. If batter is too stiff, cakes will be tough; if batter is too thin, they will be sticky. A pour batter is necessary. It is not necessary to oil the griddle if the right kind is used. A thick material cooks better. Have hot enough to sizzle when batter is poured. Too much heat causes smoking and burning. When using white flour, part meal makes a better cake. When using cornmeal, no other flour is necessary. Cold hominy may take the place of the cornmeal with white flour. Cold hominy and rice used in batter cakes with flour make good cakes and a nice way to use left-overs. Use one cup to two of flour."

—*Southern Cooking,* 1928

GRIDDLECAKES

Makes about 15, depending on thickness

AS CORNMEAL'S ANSWER TO PANCAKES, *these are perfect for Sunday-night suppers or anytime with eggs and bacon.*

2 large eggs, beaten to mix
2 cups buttermilk
1 cup cornmeal
2 cups all-purpose flour
2 tablespoons melted shortening or bacon drippings
1 teaspoon salt
1 teaspoon baking soda
1 teaspoon baking powder

Whisk all ingredients together in a large bowl until batter is light and foamy and thin enough to pour and shape the cakes.

Meanwhile, heat the griddle. When sizzling hot, ladle on griddlecakes. When bubbles come to the top indicating the bottom is cooked, turn and cook other side. Remove to plate and serve hot.

Using a round implement such as a ladle to add batters to a pan helps keep the cakes round. Note our wonky ones.

HUSH PUPPIES

Serves 6

HUSH PUPPIES ARE SYNONYMOUS WITH ANY SOUTHERN FISH FRY. *Fish camps range from shacks to estates, close to fishing spots where men can gather, make noise, drink beer, and catch and cook fish. Sometimes women are invited. Hush puppies are always on the menu.*

2 cups cornmeal
1 tablespoon all-purpose flour
1/2 teaspoon baking soda
1 teaspoon baking powder
1 teaspoon salt
3 tablespoons finely chopped green onions
1 cup plus 3 tablespoons buttermilk
1 large egg, lightly beaten
Shortening or vegetable oil for frying

Sift together the cornmeal, flour, baking soda, baking powder, and salt into a large bowl. Stir in the onions, buttermilk, and egg until thoroughly mixed. Heat the oil to 375 degrees and drop the batter by spoonfuls (about 2 teaspoons) into the hot oil. Fry until golden brown. Move to a plate lined with paper towels and serve hot.

ORIGIN OF HUSH PUPPIES

Finding the first appearance in print of a hush puppy has been confounding. In the first edition of Southern Cooking, Mrs. H. R. Dull has a corn fritter, but there is no mention of hush puppies. In the 1941 edition, she writes, "Hush puppy is a Southern dish cooked at all fish frys and hunting trips. At first they were made to feed the hungry, howling hounds or hunting dogs to keep them quiet, hence 'hush puppy.' Later they were more carefully made and eaten by the entire party. This old colonial custom has been handed down to the present day. Hush puppy Red Horse Devil No. 2 is used today to serve with barbecues."

There is a mullet named red horse once found in Florida and other states east of the Rockies going up to Maryland. It was small—finger-sized—and it is possible the first hush puppies were served with them, and the redhorse fish were, like salamanders, called puppies or dogs and served with a Redhorse Devil sauce. Wherever the name came from, if making hush puppies and a fishy flavor is desired, fry them in the fat after the fish are fried. Otherwise, consider frying them first and serving them to keep the eaters—as well as the dogs—quiet while waiting for the fish.

Marjorie Kinnan Rawlings sums it up nicely in her 1946 book *Cross Creek Cookery:* "Fresh-caught fried fish without hush puppies are as man without woman, a beautiful woman without kindness, law without policemen."

WHO IS MRS. DULL?

Today's modern food writer juggles many different hats during a career, perhaps dabbling in catering, teaching cooking classes, being a spokesperson for a product or company, writing a food column, and/or writing a cookbook. Seems like some things never change, as this career path also describes the life of Mrs. S. R. Dull, the author of *Southern Cooking,* published in 1928. After a time as a caterer, she became a spokesperson for the Atlanta Gas Light Company, demonstrating the advantages of cooking with gas, and her sessions were in high demand. She became the home economics page editor for the *Atlanta Journal,* writing a regular column for more than 25 years with recipes and tips that became the gospel to Southern cooks. At the age of 65, Mrs. Dull published *Southern Cooking,* which contained more than 1,300 recipes and became "the standard by which regional cooks have been measured since," says cookbook author Damon Lee Fowler.

BISCUITS

Biscuits are the quintessential Southern bread. They come in all shapes and sizes, whether delicately holding a bit of jam or butter or sturdily encasing ham. We dream about them, praise them in stories, legends and song, and bake endless variations.

Equipment

Scrapers—These flexible plastic gadgets, about 4 x 6, are curved on at least one side, or perhaps all around, or have one side curved and one side straight. They are a godsend for scraping out biscuit bowls. They scoop the dough out of a bowl easily. A few swipes around the bowl and it is free of ingredients and ready to go again. And it prevents leaving gunk in the bowl to clog up the dishwasher or sink.

Bench scraper—A rather fancy name for anything with a flat edge sharp enough to scrape off the counter and cut through the dough to divide it. Just about any sharp edge will clean the counter from the back of a knife to a long metal spatula, but the professional bench knives are easy to handle and store in a drawer ready to be pulled out the next time.

Flour shaker—Keeping plain all-purpose flour in a shaker (a salt shaker on steroids) is a must for baking breads and biscuits, making it easy to flour surfaces, the tops of doughs, whatever needs a helpful dusting of flour to prevent stickiness. Avoid keeping self-rising flour in one, lest it get mismarked and substituted for doughs that want only plain flour. Plain flour is fine for dusting and shaping biscuit doughs. Shirley Corriher feels self-rising flour makes the outside of a biscuit dough bitter. While we don't insist, we do think that it is a better habit to use only plain flour in a shaker.

Plastic sheets—When Cynthia and I wrote our book *Southern Biscuits,* we thought we knew just about every trick to making a successful biscuit. Then we went on the road for our book tour. In packing and unpacking our ingredients and equipment dozens of times, finding ourselves at huge women's shows where we followed one chef after another, with no time to get organized on-stage, we discovered that the flexible plastic sheets sold in the grocery store in sets of three made forming, shaping and folding our doughs much easier. Cynthia rediscovered her grandmother's old Tupperware plastic dough sheet—about 18 by 24—that even had circles on it to guide intrepid bakers. Recently she purchased one for me in a discount store for less than ten dollars.

Ingredients

Using fats and liquids—A little fat tenderizes, moistens, and adds flavor to biscuits. Butter tastes best, but lard and shortening make a lighter, flakier, more layered biscuit. The lightest fats are leaf lard, shortening, and goat-milk butter. Butter produces heavier biscuits but gives the most flavor, color, and layering.

Lard and shortening were integral in biscuit making before refrigeration was common because they did not melt, separate, or puddle as butter may when left at a hot room temperature. Lard and shortening are more easily combined with the flour, making lighter and softer biscuits.

Modern cooks cut cold butter into small cubes or pieces, and quickly mix it in by hand or with the food processor to increase the flakiness and produce a fabulous biscuit. So when we say butter is heavier, it can overcome obstacles if handled correctly. Combine two or even three fats to come up with a product combining lightness, color, flakiness, and flavor.

Flour—The best flours for biscuits include Southern Biscuit, White Lily, Martha White, and Midstate Mills. Very good substitutes include mixtures of cake flour and all-purpose flour.

Techniques

Three things activate and toughen flour—liquid, manipulation, and heat. The fat tenderizes the dough as well as sheeting it and making layers, depending on the amount that is worked into the dough. The liquid moistens the dough and activates the baking powder. The lighter the fat and the lower the gluten content of the flour, the lighter the biscuit. The less watery the liquid, the more it tenderizes the dough. Thus, cream produces a much lighter biscuit than milk, and milk produces a much lighter biscuit than water. Acidic dairy products—such as clabber, unpasteurized buttermilk, sour cream, or yogurt—boost the baking soda to lighten the product.

Kneading the dough—Rather than vigorous kneading as for yeast breads, gentle manipulation is all that is required for biscuit dough, which becomes tough when over-manipulated or kneaded. It gets its rise from trapping the gases of the leavenings (primarily baking soda).

Manipulation should develop the gluten in biscuits just enough to smooth the dough, letting the flour "hold" the fat in suspension and causing sheets of the fat to make a flakier dough.

We recommend two kinds of manipulation for biscuits:

1. Folding the dough—We pat out and fold the dough in half twice before a third patting out and cutting out the biscuits. Some people fold a dozen times, others fold in thirds, like a letter. We stick with our two-time, two-fold method for the novice. As a baker develops skill in biscuit baking however, more folding may increase the flakiness and thus the rise.

2. Hand shaping—Rolling the dough between the palms of both hands rather than patting and cutting develops the gluten, allowing a higher rise in the dough. This comes to the baker through experience and touch. We hope each baker gets to this point and hope our recipes aid this process.

Shaping the dough—Shaping the dough is the most difficult element for some. There are numerous ways to shape dough. Our friend Kate Almand used some of the self-rising flour left in the biscuit bowl, as do I. Hand-rolling and -shaping takes practice. There are several methods we find helpful for shaping:

Hand-shaping #1—Flour hands, pull a biscuit-sized piece of dough from the mass, dip the exposed (wet) part of the dough into flour, and then roll the bottom in one floured cupped palm, simultaneously turning with thumb and pinkie while smoothing the top with the other palm. Give the dough a final pat. It sounds like patting one's head while rubbing one's stomach, but once the motion is clear, it gets easier each time.

Hand-shaping #2—Pat out the dough into a round of the desired height; divide the dough into four pieces. Divide each of those into three more pieces. Roll each section between two palms to make a round. It is okay for it to be rough and bumpy.

Cutting—After folding the dough, pat it out on a floured board and then cut with a biscuit cutter, being careful not to twist the cutter. For a biscuit that splits open easily, fold the dough in half before cutting through the two layers.

Scooping—Shirley Corriher, my student from many years ago at Rich's Cooking School, has gone on to fame for her biscuits and two best-selling books. She now uses a nonstick or floured ice-cream scoop, dipping it into the flour before scooping out a very wet dough, much like a drop biscuit dough, dropping it into a greased cake pan and proceeding to fill the pan with biscuits right next to each other. This technique of putting them in a cake pan allows the biscuits to be held up on all sides, supported by the pan and each other, enabling the dough to be wetter and yet keeping them from spreading out, which would make them thinner and crisper.

Dropping—Drop biscuits can be made from a much wetter dough. Use a large floured spoon or ice-cream scoop to scoop the un-kneaded wet dough and drop the biscuits onto a greased pan, a hot soup, or a casserole as if it were a dumpling (page 371).

Cutting the biscuits—Using a biscuit cutter makes new cooks feel more secure. Biscuit cutters are sold individually or in sets, ranging from 1/2 inch to 4 inches in diameter, and ideally are at least 1 inch tall, to accommodate even the tallest biscuits, with straight, sharp edges. Round-edged items such as a glass lack a sharp edge and may squoosh the exterior, preventing the layering around the edges. Beware of twisting the cutter as it presses down on the dough. This creates an irregular exterior as well as pushing down the sides, which prevents the biscuit from rising.

Of course, in a pinch anything from a clean empty can to a shot glass may be used to cut out a biscuit.

"To dock" the dough means to pierce it, allowing for steam to escape. Docking is far from crucial in making biscuits, while with pies and tart bottoms it can be very important. Some home bakers dock the top of a biscuit once with the tines of a fork or by patting the top lightly with two or three fingers in the center of the dough. Professional bakers dock the dough to vent the steam and prevent the dough from puffing and billowing while baking. A professional dough docker looks like a small (3- to 4-inch) spiked rolling pin, or a medieval torture item. It cuts even rolls of holes to prick the bottom of biscuits and pie and tart shells to vent steam. I have never owned one, and think it is an indulgence for the home baker.

Using the right pan—Whether using a rimmed baking sheet, cake pan, pizza pan, or ovenproof iron skillet, use the same pan over and over again to become familiar with it and to "season" it. Avoid scrubbing harshly or washing in the dishwasher, as this will reduce or eliminate the "seasoned" coating. It will need to be greased occasionally. Initially, greasing the pan results in "frying" the bottom of the biscuit, but this procedure is necessary if the pan is unseasoned. For more tender or lighter colored biscuit bottoms, layer two baking sheets or two cake pans, top with parchment paper, and add the shaped dough. Baking in an iron skillet gives a crustier bottom.

A dark pan tends to burn more quickly than a light one. A round pan is preferred to a traditional cookie sheet for soft-edged biscuits because it allows the biscuits to snuggle closer together. The pan should accommodate the number of biscuits. Oversized or deep-rimmed pans slow the browning of the biscuits because the hot air takes longer to reach them.

Placing the biscuits—Placing biscuits close to each other keeps the sides from browning, making the biscuits more tender, and they prop each other up. Separating them on the pan makes a crisper biscuit, with the biscuits spreading and becoming thinner. Using an 8- or 9-inch cake pan, pizza pan, or ovenproof skillet keeps them tight enough together so that they help each other rise, the sides where they touch sheltered from browning.

USING SCRAPS OF DOUGH

Reworked scraps of dough may not be perfect for company, but they're a special treat for the cook and cook's helpers if sprinkled with cinnamon sugar before baking. Don't bother making into regular shapes—enjoy the strange shapes remaining after cutting the rounds. Scraps should be patted together, not gathered into a ball or kneaded.

FUN VARIATIONS

These variations can be used with any of the biscuit recipes:

- For golden cheese biscuits, pulse 1/2 cup shredded Cheddar cheese with the flour before adding the milk.
- For pimento cheese biscuits, pulse 1 cup shredded Cheddar cheese with the flour. When adding the liquid, mix in 1 (4-ounce) jar pimento or chopped roasted red bell peppers and, if desired, 1/4 cup finely chopped onion.

REHEATING BISCUITS

Method 1—Preheat oven to 400 degrees. Wrap leftover or baked-ahead biscuits, scones, or muffins in a single layer in aluminum foil and heat until hot, about 10 to 15 minutes.

Method 2—Split and spread the biscuits with butter and toast them in the broiler until they're hot and lightly browned; or, before toasting, spread them with shredded cheese, cream cheese, pimento cheese, jelly, poppy seeds, or sesame seeds.

MAKING BISCUITS AHEAD OF TIME

Biscuit dough will last 1 to 2 days in the refrigerator in a plastic bag or wrapped tightly. When ready to bake, pat or roll out the dough, cut out, and bake.

TWO-INGREDIENT BISCUITS

Makes 14 to 18 (2-inch) biscuits

IT'S MIRACULOUS TO MAKE A BISCUIT *with only two ingredients, particularly when making such an impressive biscuit, light and tender, capable of convincing anyone that the cook was born holding a biscuit bowl. This recipe is a good fallback for anyone who hasn't made a biscuit for a while or has to hurry up and get some baked. If using a cream with less fat (heavy cream has 36 percent) start with less and use only what is needed to make a moist, slightly sticky dough. Half-and-half just doesn't work well enough to use by itself. This is really a hurry-up recipe, but the directions are detailed.*

2¼ cups commercial or homemade self-rising flour (page 451), divided

1¼ cups heavy cream, divided

Butter, softened or melted, for finishing

Preheat oven to 450 degrees.

Select the baking pan by determining if a soft or crisp exterior is desired. For a soft exterior, use an 8- or 9-inch cake pan, a pizza pan, or an ovenproof skillet where the biscuits will nestle together snugly, creating the soft exterior while baking. For a crisp exterior, select a baking sheet or other baking pan where the biscuits can be placed wider apart, allowing air to circulate and create a crisper exterior. Brush selected pan with butter or oil.

Fork-sift or whisk 2 cups of the flour in a large bowl, preferably wider than it is deep, and set aside the remaining ¼ cup. Make a deep hollow in the center of the flour with the back of your hand. Slowly but steadily stir 1 cup of cream, reserving ¼ cream, into the hollow with a rubber spatula or large metal spoon, using broad circular strokes to quickly pull the flour into the cream. Mix just until the dry ingredients are moistened and the sticky dough begins to pull away from the sides of the bowl. If there is some flour remaining on the bottom and sides of the bowl, stir in just enough of the reserved cream, to incorporate the remaining flour into the shaggy, wettish dough. If the dough is too wet, use more flour when shaping.

Lightly sprinkle a plastic sheet, a board, or other clean surface with some of the reserved flour. Turn the dough out onto the board and sprinkle the top of the dough lightly with flour if sticky. With floured hands, fold the dough in half and pat it into a ⅓- to ½-inch-thick round, using a little additional flour only if needed. Flour again if sticky and fold the dough in half a second time. If the dough is still clumpy, pat and fold a third time. Pat dough into a ½-inch-thick round for normal biscuits, a ¾-inch-thick round for tall biscuits, or a 1-inch-thick round for giant biscuits. Brush off any visible flour from the top. For each biscuit, dip a 2-inch biscuit cutter into the reserved flour and cut out the biscuits, starting at the outside edge and cutting very close together, being careful not to twist the cutter. The scraps may be combined to make additional biscuits, although they will be tougher. For hand shaping and other variations, see pages 468–69.

Using a metal spatula if necessary, move the biscuits to the pan or baking sheet. Bake the biscuits on the top rack of the oven for a total of 10 to 14 minutes, until light golden brown. After 6 minutes, rotate the pan in the oven so that the front of the pan is now turned to the back, and check to see if the bottoms are browning too quickly. If so, slide another baking pan underneath to add insulation and retard the browning. Continue baking another 4 to 8 minutes, until the biscuits are light golden brown. When they are done, remove from the oven and lightly brush the tops with softened or melted butter. Turn the biscuits out upside down on a plate to cool slightly. Serve hot, right side up.

Variations:

- For Sour Cream or Cream Cheese Biscuits, substitute 1 cup sour cream or cream cheese for the heavy cream. Bake 8 to 10 minutes. This makes a moist biscuit.
- For Yogurt and Cream Biscuits, use ½ cup yogurt and ¾ cup heavy cream or half-and-half.
- For Yogurt Biscuits, add 1 teaspoon salt to the flour and 1 cup plain yogurt for the heavy cream. Add a bit of milk or cream to moisten if a "drier" yogurt is used. Yogurt biscuits are a bit "bouncy."
- For Strawberry Shortcake, add 1 or 2 tablespoons sugar to the dough. Line a cake pan with parchment paper. Pat the dough into the lined cake pan. Bake as above. Remove from the oven, brush the top with butter, and turn upside down on a rack to cool slightly. When cool, slice in half horizontally. To serve, sandwich with sugared strawberries and cream or serve a bowl of each separately.

BASIC SOUTHERN BISCUITS

Makes 12 to 18 (2-inch) biscuits

THIS IS THE BASIC RECIPE *most of the biscuit makers we know use, with our technique for shaping. For instance, Rebecca Lang's grandmother Tom had hands that could pull biscuits out of anything and could shape them by hand as if by magic. She would just kind of fondle the dough and it would come together. We use two different fats, for the lightness of one and the flavor of the other.*

2 1/4 cups commercial or homemade self-rising flour (page 451), divided
1/4 cup chilled shortening, lard, and/or butter cut into 1/4-inch pieces

AND
1/4 cup chilled butter, shortening or lard cut into 1/2-inch pieces
1 cup milk or buttermilk, divided

Butter, softened or melted, for finishing

Preheat oven to 425 degrees.

Select the baking pan by determining if a soft or crisp exterior is desired. For a soft exterior, use an 8- or 9-inch cake pan, a pizza pan, or an ovenproof skillet where the biscuits will nestle together snugly, creating the soft exterior while baking. For a crisp exterior, select a baking sheet or other baking pan where the biscuits can be placed wider apart, allowing air to circulate and create a crisper exterior; brush selected pan with butter.

Fork-sift or whisk 2 cups of flour in a large bowl, preferably wider than it is deep, and set aside the remaining 1/4 cup. Scatter the 1/4-inch pieces of chilled fat over the flour and work in by rubbing fingers with the fat and flour as if snapping thumb and fingers together (or use two forks or knives, or a pastry cutter) until the mixture looks well crumbled. Scatter the 1/2-inch pieces of chilled fat over the flour mixture and continue snapping thumb and fingers together until no pieces remain larger than a pebble. Shake the bowl occasionally to allow the larger pieces of fat to bounce to the top of the flour, revealing the largest lumps that still need rubbing. The quicker, the better. If this method takes longer than 5 minutes, move the bowl to the refrigerator for 5 minutes to chill the fat.

Make a deep hollow in the center of the flour with the back of your hand. Slowly but steadily stir 3/4 cup milk into the hollow, and with a rubber spatula or large metal spoon, using broad circular strokes, quickly pull the flour into the milk. Mix just until the dry ingredients are moistened and the lumpy, sticky dough begins to pull away from the sides of the bowl. If there is some flour remaining on the bottom and sides of the bowl, stir in 1 to 4 tablespoons of the remaining 1/4 cup milk, just enough to incorporate the remaining flour into the shaggy, wettish dough. If the dough is too wet, use more flour when shaping.

Lightly sprinkle a plastic sheet, a board, or other clean surface using some of the reserved flour. Turn the dough out onto the board and sprinkle the top of the dough lightly with flour. With floured hands, fold the dough in half and pat it into a 1/3- to 1/2-inch-thick round, using a little additional flour only if needed. Flour again if necessary and fold the dough in half a second time. If the dough is still clumpy, pat and fold a third time. Pat dough into a 1/2-inch-thick round for normal biscuits, a 3/4-inch-thick round for tall biscuits, or a 1-inch-thick round for giant biscuits. Brush off any visible flour from the top. For each biscuit, dip a 2-inch biscuit cutter into the reserved flour and cut out the biscuits, starting at the outside edge and cut close together, being careful not to twist the cutter. The scraps may be combined to make additional biscuits, although they will be tougher. For hand shaping and other variations, see page 468–9.

Using a metal spatula if necessary, move the biscuits to the pan or baking sheet. Bake the biscuits on the top rack of the oven for a total of 10 to 14 minutes, until light golden brown. After 6 minutes, rotate the pan in the oven so that the front of the pan is now turned to the back, and check to see if the bottoms are browning too quickly. If so, slide another baking pan underneath to add insulation and retard browning. Continue baking another 4 to 8 minutes, until the biscuits are light golden brown. When they are done, remove from the oven and lightly brush the tops with butter. Turn the biscuits out upside down on a plate to cool slightly. Serve hot, right side up.

HOMEMADE REFRIGERATOR BISCUIT MIX

Makes 10 cups

IF MAKING SEVERAL BATCHES OF BISCUITS A MONTH, *or one biscuit at a time, make a flour-and-fat base mixture to add the milk to at a later time. It will keep several months in a tightly covered container in the refrigerator. Combine one part milk or buttermilk with two parts mix for any quantity of biscuits from 4 to 40! Once again, more salt and baking powder are added. This dough can also be used in making coffee cakes, pancakes, waffles, and the like.*

10 cups self-rising flour
3 teaspoons salt
5 teaspoons cream of tartar
4 teaspoons baking powder
2 cups chilled shortening, lard, or butter, roughly cut into 1/2-inch pieces

Fork-sift or whisk the flour, salt, cream of tartar, and baking powder in a very large bowl. Scatter the shortening over the flour and work in by rubbing fingers with the shortening and flour as if snapping thumb and fingers together (or use two forks or knives, or a pastry cutter) until the mixture is well crumbled, with no piece larger than a pebble. Shake the bowl occasionally to allow the larger pieces of fat to bounce to the top of the flour, revealing the largest lumps that still need rubbing.

Store the mix in the refrigerator in an airtight container until ready to use.

FREEZING BISCUITS

Unbaked shaped biscuits freeze very well. Freeze unbaked prepared biscuits on a baking sheet covered loosely with plastic wrap. When frozen, move the biscuits to plastic ziplock bags and keep in the freezer for up to 1 month. With yeast products such as Angel Biscuits (page 474), it is best to bake them before freezing, as unbaked products may become tough and have poor texture and volume. When freezing yeast products unbaked, add 1/2 teaspoon more yeast to compensate for any loss of rise from freezing.

To bake the frozen unbaked biscuits, preheat oven according to the recipe. Move frozen biscuits to a baking sheet and bake for 5 minutes longer than the recipe directs.

FOOD PROCESSOR BISCUITS

Any of these biscuit recipes may be made in the food processor and there is no doubt that using the food processor is the method most modern biscuit makers prefer. It takes just a few minutes and little if any muss or cleanup, and it works time after time. I still recommend learning to make biscuits by hand first, just to get the feel of them—but any of the recipes in this book can be adapted to this method.

Pulse 2 1/4 cups flour 2 or 3 times in a food processor fitted with the knife or dough blade; set aside the remaining 1/4 cup. Scatter the chilled 1/4-inch shortening pieces over the flour mixture and pulse 2 or 3 times. Scatter the chilled 1/2-inch shortening pieces over the flour mixture and pulse 2 or 3 times, until mixture is well crumbled, with no piece larger than a kernel of corn. Slowly but steadily pulse in 3/4 cup buttermilk and pulse briefly to incorporate into a shaggy, wettish dough.

When the blade fully stops, remove the lid and feel the dough. Add some of the 1/4 cup reserved milk or flour as needed to make a slightly wettish dough. Pulse 1 or 2 times more until the dough looks shaggy but together.

Lightly sprinkle a plastic sheet, a board, or other clean surface using some of the reserved flour. Carefully remove the top and blade, and turn the dough out onto the board and sprinkle the top lightly with flour. Proceed as with Basic Southern Biscuits (page 471).

KATE'S UNFORGETTABLE WOODEN BOWL BISCUITS

Makes 12 to 18 biscuits

Kate Almand worked for me—*or I worked for her—from 1972 until about 2000. She was kind and curmudgeonly as well as an excellent home cook. She started making biscuits for her large family when her mother went to the hospital to have another of what turned out to be thirteen children. Large families were the norm in the era when Kate was growing up, and so small biscuits were the norm, just to have enough baked for everyone by the time the family came down for breakfast. Then another batch or two would be baked, some for eating then, and some for taking to school or the field. She was horrified by large short-order food biscuits.*

I never saw Kate Almand measure the ingredients for biscuits. She just opened a flour sack into her wooden bowl, made a well, packed it, poured in whatever kind of milk she had, grabbed a handful of lard or Crisco (which she kept on hand when lard was no longer easily available), worked it into the milk with the fingers of one hand, then made a maneuver that pulled in the flour in a whirlpool of motion, and suddenly she shaped a wet biscuit in her floured hands. It took me years to get every single step down correctly. Kate passed on just as we were finishing this book, and it is in remembrance of her that we add this recipe from our book Southern Biscuits. *Kate's hands were magic, her heart was big, and her wisdom immeasurable—like her biscuits.*

1 (5-pound) bag self-rising flour, to use 2 1/2 cups flour
1 portion sweet (fresh) milk, approximately 1 cup
1 handful room-temperature lard, hard shortening, or butter, approximately 1/3–1/2 cup
Butter, softened or melted, for finishing

Preheat oven to 500 degrees.

Fill a wooden biscuit bowl 2/3 full with as much of the bag of flour as possible. Use the back of a hand to form and simultaneously pack an 8-inch well in the center of the flour, leaving a small amount on the bottom.

Gently pour the milk into the well-packed center of the well. Scoop 1/3 cup of fat into the milk. Using the fingers of one hand, mush together the milk and fat until it looks like thick, lumpy pancake batter. Making a massaging motion with the fingers of one hand, slightly akin to playing the scales on a banjo, move the batter around the well in a whirlpool. Continue moving the fingers steadily around the bowl as a rotary mixer would, like a centrifuge. The batter will gently pull in the packed flour. After a few rotations, it will have pulled in sufficient flour to make a very wet dough in the center of the bowl, cradled by the rest of the flour.

Re-flour both hands in the remaining flour and scrape the wet mess off the gooey hand back into the dough. Re-flour both hands and slide under the dough, turning it completely over in the remaining flour, with the wet portion of the flour at the bottom of the dough and the top portion completely floured.

Re-flouring hands as needed, pinch off an egg-sized portion of the dough sufficient for a 1 1/2-inch biscuit. The portion pulled from the dough will be wet. Dip it into the flour so the total exterior of the dough is now floured. Cup one hand, making sure the palm is floured, and move the dough on top of the palm. Use the palm of the second hand to smooth the top of the dough with pinkie and thumb to keep it round. Using a metal spatula if necessary, move biscuit to an iron skillet or small baking sheet. Repeat with subsequent biscuits, nestling close to each other to keep upright.

When pan is full and dough is completely used, dump any flour remaining in the bowl onto a piece of waxed paper. Scrape out the bowl if necessary to remove any stubborn bits. Sift the flour back into the flour bag or back into the bowl, discarding any pieces of dough left in the sifter and cover flour with a clean tea towel to use the next day.

Bake the biscuits on the top rack of the oven for a total of 10 to 14 minutes, until light golden brown. After 6 minutes, rotate the pan in the oven so that the front of the pan is now turned to the back, and check to see if the bottoms are browning too quickly. If so, slide another baking pan underneath to add insulation and retard browning. Continue baking another 4 to 8 minutes, until the biscuits are light golden brown. When they are done, remove from the oven and lightly brush the tops with butter. Turn out upside down on a plate to cool slightly. Serve hot, right side up.

ANGEL OR BRIDEGROOM'S BISCUITS

Makes 30 to 40 (2-inch) Biscuits

THESE WERE OFTEN CALLED BRIDE'S BISCUITS, *as even the most inept bride could make them. Nowadays, it might be the groom who makes the first breakfast, so we've changed the name just a little to accommodate the broader number of first-time bakers. The secret to this recipe is the combination of yeast and self-rising ingredients, ensuring the biscuits will rise and be soft and tender. Actually, these are rolls of sorts—don't tell the groom though. Just brag on the biscuits.*

1 package active dry yeast
1/4 cup granulated sugar
3 tablespoons warm water (110–115 degrees)
5–6 cups commercial or homemade self-rising flour (page 451)
1 teaspoon baking soda
1/2 teaspoon salt
1/2 cup shortening, room temperature
1/2 cup butter, room temperature
2 cups buttermilk, room temperature
Butter, softened or melted, for finishing

Dissolve the yeast and sugar in warm water in a small bowl and set aside.

Fork-sift or whisk 5 cups of self-rising flour (reserving 1 cup), baking soda, and salt in a large bowl, preferably wider than it is deep. Break the shortening and butter into pieces and scatter over the flour. Work in by rubbing fingers with the fat and flour as if snapping thumb and fingers together (or use two forks or knives, or a pastry cutter) until the mixture looks well crumbled.

Make a deep hollow in the center of the flour with the back of one hand. Stir the yeast mixture into the buttermilk and pour this mixture into the hollow, stirring with a long wooden spoon. Add flour as needed to make a very damp, shaggy dough.

Flour a clean work surface and turn the dough out onto the flour. With floured hands, knead the dough by folding in half, pushing out, refolding, and turning the dough clockwise until the dough is tender (like a baby's bottom), about 10 minutes. Add flour as necessary to make a supple dough. There are three options at this point: 1) shape now, 2) for an even lighter biscuit, move to an oiled plastic bag and let rise until doubled in size, then punch down and proceed to shape, or 3) refrigerate up to 1 week and use as desired. When ready to use, divide dough in half to shape easily.

Roll dough out into a 1/3- to 1/2-inch-thick round. Fold in half and roll or pat out again until 2/3 to 1 inch thick. Repeat with second half as desired. For each biscuit, dip a 2-inch biscuit cutter into the reserved flour and cut out the biscuits, starting at the outside edge and cutting very close together, being careful not to twist the cutter. Move the biscuits to an oiled baking sheet. Let double at room temperature, about 30 minutes.

Preheat oven to 400 degrees. Bake the biscuits on the middle rack of the oven for a total of 10 to 14 minutes, until light golden brown. After 6 minutes, rotate the pan in the oven so that the front of the pan is now turned to the back. Check to see if the bottoms are burning too quickly. If so, slide another baking sheet underneath to add insulation and retard browning. Continue baking another 6 to 9 minutes, until light golden brown. When the biscuits are done, remove from the oven and lightly brush the tops with softened or melted butter. Turn the biscuits out upside down on a plate to cool slightly. (If an angel-like touch is desired, sprinkle with flour.) Serve hot, right side up.

SWEET POTATO OR PUMPKIN BISCUITS

Makes 18 (2-inch) biscuits

SOME THINK THIS IS THEIR FAVORITE BISCUIT *because it is so moist. It has a special glow somehow, boasting that it would be better with any filling, whether sandwiched with ham or other savory filling, or sweet and brushed with icing.*

2 1/4 cups commercial or homemade self-rising flour (page 451), divided
1/4 teaspoon ground cinnamon, optional
1/4 teaspoon ground nutmeg, optional
1/3 cup chilled shortening or lard, cut into 1/2-inch pieces
1 cup mashed cooked sweet potato or pumpkin purée
1/4 cup milk, optional

Icing

1/2 cup confectioners' sugar
2 tablespoons buttermilk or milk

Preheat oven to 450 degrees.

Select the baking pan by determining if a soft or crisp exterior is desired. For a soft exterior, use an 8- or 9-inch cake pan, pizza pan, or ovenproof skillet where the biscuits will nestle together snugly, creating the soft exterior while baking. For a crisp exterior, select a baking sheet or other baking pan where the biscuits may be placed wider apart, allowing air to circulate and create a crisper exterior; brush selected pan with butter.

Fork-sift or whisk 2 cups of flour, cinnamon, and nutmeg in a large bowl, preferably wider than deeper, and set aside the remaining 1/4 cup flour. Scatter fat over the flour and work in by rubbing fingers with the lard and flour as if snapping thumb and fingers together (or use two forks or knives, or a pastry cutter) until the mixture looks well crumbled, with no pieces larger than a pebble. Shake the bowl occasionally to allow the larger pieces of fat to bounce to the top of the flour, revealing the largest lumps that still need rubbing. The quicker, the better. If this method takes longer than 5 minutes, move the bowl to the refrigerator for 5 minutes to re-chill the fat.

Make a deep hollow in the center of the flour with the back of your hand. Scoop the sweet potatoes into the hollow and stir with a rubber spatula or large metal spoon, using broad circular strokes to quickly pull the flour into the sweet potatoes. Mix just until the dry ingredients are moistened and the sticky dough begins to pull away from the sides of the bowl. If too dry, add 1 to 4 tablespoons milk.

Lightly sprinkle a plastic sheet, a board, or other clean surface with some of the reserved flour. Turn the dough out onto the board and sprinkle the top lightly with flour. With floured hands, fold the dough in half and pat it into a 1/3- to 1/2-inch-thick round, using a little additional flour only if needed. Flour again if necessary and fold the dough in half a second time. If the dough is still clumpy, pat and fold a third time. Pat dough into a 1/2-inch-thick round for normal biscuits, a 3/4-inch-thick round for tall biscuits, or a 1-inch-thick round for giant biscuits. Brush off any visible flour from the top. For each biscuit, dip a 2-inch biscuit cutter into the reserved flour and cut out the biscuits, starting at the outside edge and cutting very close together, being careful not to twist the cutter. The scraps may be combined to make additional biscuits, although they will be tougher. For hand shaping and other variations, see pages 468–69.

Using a metal spatula if necessary, move the biscuits to the pan or baking sheet. Bake the biscuits on the top rack of the oven for a total of 12 to 14 minutes, depending on thickness, until light golden brown. After 6 minutes, rotate the pan in the oven so that the front of the pan is now turned to the back, and check to see if the bottoms are browning too quickly. If so, slide another baking pan underneath to add insulation and retard browning. Continue baking another 6 to 8 minutes, until the biscuits are light golden brown.

Meanwhile, whisk the confectioners' sugar and buttermilk until smooth to make an icing. When the biscuits are done, remove from oven and slide them onto a rack over a piece of waxed paper. Drizzle the icing over the warm biscuits. Discard the paper with the excess icing. Serve biscuits hot right away.

Variations:

- To make a savory biscuit, omit the optional spices and icing.
- For bacon biscuits, add 1/2 cup crumbled cooked bacon before adding the sweet potatoes.

BEATEN BISCUITS

Makes 50 (1 1/4-inch) biscuits

INITIALLY, THESE BISCUITS *(sometimes called "ham biscuits") were designed to be stored for a long time, like hardtack. They were beaten and folded 1001 times with wooden boards, rolling pins, or bats. The goal was an absolutely smooth dough that blistered and snapped as it was beaten. Rudimentary machines were developed to do this job, usually wooden stands holding rollers similar to wringer washers, and a hand crank. A special cutter with "stickers" punched holes in the tops of the biscuits.*

In 1975, I devised the food processor method of "beating" biscuits. The first time I tried it, I burned out the motor of my food processor. I learned to avoid very firm doughs. If the machine slows down, turn it off and feel the base to be sure it is still cool. It is better to make two or three smaller batches than to double the quantity of flour, unless a large machine is available.

3 1/4 cups all-purpose flour, divided
1 teaspoon salt
1 teaspoon granulated sugar
1 teaspoon baking powder
1 cup chilled shortening, cut into 1/2-inch pieces
3/4 cup milk, divided

Preheat oven to 350 degrees.

Pulse together 3 cups of the flour, salt, sugar, and baking powder in a food processor fitted with the knife or dough blade. Set aside the remaining 1/4 cup of flour. Scatter the chilled shortening pieces over the flour mixture and pulse until mixture is well crumbled, with no piece larger than a pebble. Add 1/2 cup milk and pulse briefly to incorporate into a very damp, shaggy dough. If it is dry or crumbly, add more milk. If it is too wet, add more flour. "Beat" in the food processor a few minutes until it is smooth, removing it if the food processor starts to whine or stagger; then turn out onto a floured board. Beat the dough briefly on the counter with a rolling pin, fold over, and beat again. Repeat until it "snaps"—how long depends on the dough when it comes out of the processor. When it's ready, the dough should "snap" when you hit it and feel very smooth, supple, and still damp but not sticky. Roll out to 1/2 inch thick.

Fold the dough in half to make the biscuits easier to split later. Roll out to 1/2 inch thick again. Starting from the outside edge of the dough and working toward the center, avoiding the fold, cut small rounds with a 1 1/4-inch biscuit cutter. Combine the scraps, fold over, and roll if necessary. Cut out the rest of the dough, rolling and folding scraps as necessary. Pierce the top of each round with the tines of a fork in three neat rows. Move the biscuits to a lightly greased baking sheet. Bake for 30 minutes, until crisp and, preferably, still white or only lightly dappled with brown. They should open easily when split with a fork. They will keep for weeks tightly covered in a tin or in the freezer. Split open before serving.

CORNBREAD

If biscuits are for holding ham or being slathered with butter and jam, cornbread is the sturdy standby with flavor to boot. Cornmeal is a staple bequeathed by the Native Americans, and breads made from it are perfect for dunking in potlikker and buttermilk alike.

LIGHT AND TENDER CORNBREAD

Serves 6 to 8

IN THIS RECIPE, *we mix both cornmeal mix and self-rising flour, which gives a tremendous boost to the cornbread, making it very light and tender but not dry. It's perfect for splitting and sandwiching with cooked greens, lady peas, butter beans, or other juicy vegetables. Of course, it can sop up those juices from the bowl when no one is looking.*

1 1/2 tablespoons bacon drippings or oil, cook's preference
1 cup self-rising cornmeal mix (below)
1/2 cup self-rising flour (page 451)
1 large egg, beaten to mix
1 cup milk

Preheat oven to 500 degrees.

Add the drippings or oil to a 9-inch iron skillet or 9-inch-square heavy pan and heat in the oven for 5 minutes.

Meanwhile, whisk together the cornmeal mix, flour, egg, and milk in a large bowl.

Remove the hot pan from the oven and pour the hot fat or oil into the cornmeal mixture. It will sizzle. Stir. Pour the entire cornmeal mixture into the hot pan and bake for 15 minutes. Remove from the oven, cool briefly on a rack, cover with a plate, upend, and cut into wedges or squares.

CORNMEAL MIX

Cornmeal mix is cornmeal mixed with leavening. It can be substituted much the same way as self-rising flour is substituted for flour and leaveners in making biscuits. Of course, cooks with time and a vast capacity for ingredients express disdain, using only cornmeal. But I keep it on hand.

STUFFED CORNBREAD

Serves 6

THIS RECIPE FROM JACK-OF-ALL-TRADES REBECCA LANG—*talented cookbook writer, cooking teacher, wife, and mother, who also does videos for Southern Living—is one of my favorite recipes from her book* Quick-Fix Southern. *She says, and I agree, it is beautiful and tastes fantastic. It can be cut into small wedges for pickup party food or served as a side dish, light entrée, or with soup. I'm tempted to call it go-anywhere, all-purpose stuffed cornbread. Rebecca uses white cornmeal, but I'm partial to yellow. Sometimes. Actually, any cornmeal will do, because in one county, they may primarily use white, the next primarily yellow, and now, of all things, there are cornmeals for sale that mix the two. And then there is blue cornmeal!*

1 (8.5-ounce) jar sun-dried tomatoes, packed in oil
1 cup cornmeal
3/4 cup all-purpose flour
2 teaspoons baking powder
1 teaspoon baking soda
1/2 teaspoon salt
1 cup milk
1 large egg
1 teaspoon finely chopped fresh rosemary
2 ounces goat cheese, crumbled

Drain the sun-dried tomatoes over a small mixing bowl, reserving the oil, and chop the tomatoes. Add 2 tablespoons of the reserved oil to a 10-inch cast-iron skillet. Move the skillet to the oven as it preheats to 425 degrees. Reserve the remaining oil for another use.

Whisk the cornmeal, flour, baking powder, baking soda, and salt in a medium mixing bowl. Lightly whisk the milk and egg in a small mixing bowl then stir into the cornmeal mixture.

Remove the heated skillet from the oven and pour the hot oil into the batter. It will sizzle and bubble immediately. Stir to incorporate the oil with the batter.

Pour half the batter into the hot skillet. Sprinkle tomatoes, rosemary, and goat cheese stuffing evenly over the batter. Pour the remaining half of batter over the stuffing without spreading. It will not cover it completely.

Bake for 18 to 20 minutes, or until golden brown. Cool briefly on a rack.

Variation: If only dried tomatoes are available, soak 10 minutes in boiling water to cover, drain, and chop the tomatoes. Add 2 tablespoons preferred oil to the pan.

SKILLET CORNBREAD WITH BACON DRIPPINGS

Serves 6 to 8

I WENT TO A COOKING CLASS *in Williamsburg, Virginia, where a version of this light, cakey cornbread of John Taylor's was taught. John lived in the Lowcountry of South Carolina much of his life and wrote a pivotal cookbook,* Hoppin' John's Lowcountry Cooking.

1 tablespoon bacon drippings
1 large egg
2 cups buttermilk
1 3/4 cups white or yellow cornmeal
1 teaspoon baking powder
1 teaspoon salt
1 teaspoon baking soda

Add bacon drippings to a 9- or 10-inch cast-iron skillet and move to a cold oven. Heat oven to 450 degrees.

Whisk the egg with the buttermilk. Beat the cornmeal into the batter, which should be thin. Mix together the baking powder, salt, and baking soda.

When the oven has preheated and the skillet is "smoking hot," beat the baking powder mixture into the batter. Pour the batter into the sizzling hot pan. Return to the oven to bake for 15 to 20 minutes, or until the top just begins to brown. Cool briefly on a rack and serve.

Variation: In another of John Taylor's cornbread recipes, he substitutes and browns butter in the pan. The brown butter gives the bread a slightly nutty taste, and it is as yummy as his bacon drippings cornbread.

BUTTERMILK CORNSTICKS OR CORNBREAD

Makes 6 to 8

BUTTERMILK IS FOUND IN MANY CORNBREAD RECIPES, *contributing a pleasant, slightly acidic underlying flavor. Cornbread and "clabber," as buttermilk is colloquially called, is a favorite rainy-night supper or late-night snack. The debate is one of the imponderable questions in Southern life: Is the buttermilk poured over the cornbread or is the bread crumbled into the buttermilk?*

Another imponderable is whether cornbread should have a crisp or a soft outside. When the pan and fat are heated first and then the batter poured in, there will be a crisp exterior. When the pan is room temperature and the fat is cold, the exterior will be soft. Rather than get into the debate, we have included a soft-outside cornbread in this chapter as well.

5 tablespoons melted unsalted butter, bacon drippings, or oil, divided
1 cup white or yellow cornmeal
1 cup all-purpose flour
1 1/2 teaspoons baking powder
1 teaspoon salt
1/2 teaspoon baking soda
1 cup buttermilk
2 large eggs

Preheat oven to 425 degrees.

Divide 2 tablespoons of melted fat among the wells of a well-seasoned cast-iron cornstick mold and move it to the oven.

Toss the cornmeal, flour, baking powder, salt, and baking soda together on a piece of waxed paper. Lightly beat the buttermilk and eggs in a small bowl. Add 3 tablespoons of melted butter into the buttermilk mixture. Fold into the dry ingredients without overmixing.

Remove the mold from the oven, pour batter into each well of the hot pan, filling 3/4 full, and bake in the middle of the oven until the tops are golden brown, 12 to 15 minutes. If necessary, run a knife around the outside edge of each cornstick to turn out. Best served warm.

If making ahead, turn out onto a rack to prevent softening the crisp crusts. May be frozen up to a month. It will crisp up slightly when reheated, but there's nothing like the crispy crust of just-baked bread.

Variations:

- To make cracklin cornbread, use Cracklins (page 613), or brown 2 ounces diced fatback. Remove with a slotted spoon and add to the batter. Proceed as above.
- To make buttermilk cornbread, heat an 8-inch well-seasoned skillet with 2 tablespoons of butter in a 425-degree oven. Add the batter and bake 20 to 25 minutes, until the top of the cornbread is lightly browned, the bottom is crusty brown, and a toothpick comes out clean. Turn out upside down onto a plate and serve warm.

Cornmeal should be kept refrigerated or frozen unless it is used up in a short period of time. It attracts critters, and the meal can turn rancid in hot weather over time, as no preservatives are used.

CORNBREAD CROUTONS

Erin Simpson made these croutons out of leftover cornbread. Preheat oven to 400 degrees. Cut leftover cornbread into 1-inch cubes. Move to a baking sheet lined with foil or parchment paper. Bake 10 minutes, or until the croutons are browned and crisp. Store in an airtight container for up to a week or freeze for up to a month. Use to top soups or salads, or snack on them.

BEER CORNBREAD MUFFINS

Makes 12 muffins

THESE TINY, TASTY LITTLE MUFFINS *are perfect for a brunch or lunch buffet. They can be made ahead and frozen or kept a day in a tightly covered container at room temperature. The beer gives a satisfying yeasty flavor.*

2 cups white or yellow cornmeal
1 cup commercial or homemade self-rising flour (page 451)
1 tablespoon baking powder
1 teaspoon salt
1 tablespoon granulated sugar, optional
1/4 cup unsalted butter, melted
2 large eggs, beaten
8 ounces beer or nonalcoholic beer
1/2 cup buttermilk
1 cup shredded Cheddar cheese

Preheat oven to 400 degrees. Oil a 12-cup muffin tin and set aside.

Sift together the cornmeal, flour, baking powder, salt, and sugar. Mix together the butter, eggs, beer, buttermilk, and cheese in a large bowl. Add the dry ingredients to the wet and stir until just mixed.

Divide the batter among the 12 muffin cups, filling each about two-thirds full. Bake 20 to 25 minutes, or until they are light golden brown and a wooden skewer inserted near the center comes out clean.

Cool in the tins on a wire rack for 10 minutes. Turn muffins out onto the wire rack to cool, or serve warm.

SOUR MILK

Buttermilk originally was the butterless liquid remaining after fat had been separated out of cream in order to make butter, and it had a light sour flavor. Buttermilk was the milk most often drunk on farms, as the best milk was sold off.

Clabber was milk, primarily fresh buttermilk, which was left unrefrigerated and turned sour in the South's heat. Clabber was common, and it was useful for baking, adding acid that aided in leavening, and it had a piquant, tart flavor.

Over time, buttermilk was preferred by many over sweet milk and, like the French *crème fraîche,* became a desirable product. The milk's natural bacteria produced acid that soured and curdled, or "clabbered." The milk protein was inhibited when the milk was refrigerated, so the desired consistency and flavor could be reproduced consistently for drinking and baking. True buttermilk is only produced by unpasteurized milk, as the heating process of pasteurizing kills the bacteria.

Today's buttermilk is cultured, with special lactic acid added to create and enhance a sour, or tart, flavor, but it is nowhere near the same consistency and flavor of true clabber or buttermilk. There are various "recipes" for turning pasteurized milk into soured milk:

1. Add 1 tablespoon of lemon juice per cup of pasteurized milk and let sit until curdled, making a sour milk that has a bit of a tang and a thick consistency.
2. Mix 1 part fresh yogurt (which has a live culture) or sour cream with 8 parts slightly heated pasteurized milk (as one would when making a mock *crème fraîche*), stir, lightly cover, and leave at room temperature overnight or up to 2 days to let it thicken and develop a sour taste; then refrigerate until ready to use. It has a paler taste than true buttermilk and is "bumpier."
3. Add fresh milk to a jar of clabber, causing the fresh milk to clabber as well, so re-clabbering isn't necessary.

DORI'S PEACH CORNMEAL MUFFINS

Makes 12

THIS RECIPE IS ADAPTED *from Dori Sanders'* Country Cooking *and is unique. I would be startled at the combination of peaches and cornmeal had I not visited Dori at her family's peach farm. A human dynamo, she works planting and pruning and picking and selling at the farm stand while writing award-winning novels and cookbooks. Whatever you can do with peaches, Dori can do, so why not cornmeal muffins? They are a fabulous surprise. And served with Peach Butter (page 645), they are a dazzling treat for the most hard-hearted Yankee who doesn't like cornbread. The choice of fresh or frozen peaches is mine—after all, I don't live on a peach farm!*

- 1/2 cup unsalted butter
- 1/2 cup granulated sugar
- 1 large egg, beaten to mix
- 1 cup all-purpose flour
- 1/2 cup white cornmeal
- 1/8 teaspoon salt
- 1 1/2 teaspoons baking powder
- 1/2 cup milk
- 1 cup finely chopped fresh or frozen and defrosted peaches (about 2 medium)

Preheat oven to 350 degrees. Oil a 12-muffin pan and set aside.

Beat the butter and sugar together until light, using a mixer or by hand. Add the egg and beat again until light in color.

Mix together the flour, cornmeal, salt, and baking powder onto a piece of parchment or waxed paper. Funnel half this dry mixture into the butter mixture, add half the milk, and stir well until just combined; then add the second half of each, stirring after each addition until just combined. Add the fresh chopped peaches and stir to blend.

Fill each muffin cup two-thirds full with the batter and bake 20 to 25 minutes, until golden. Cool for 5 minutes on a wire rack, carefully remove from muffin tins, and allow to cool completely—unless you want to serve hot with Peach Butter.

Variation: Dori adds 1/8 teaspoon ground nutmeg; I leave it out sometimes and add ground cinnamon or ginger or other good spices.

CYNTHIA'S SNACKING SOUR CREAM CORNBREAD

Serves 6 to 8

CYNTHIA FELL IN LOVE WITH THIS CORNBREAD *while we were taping* New Southern Cooking. *She's been making it the twenty-five plus years since that time and insisted we put it in here. In fact, it is her daughter Rachel's favorite comfort food. Oh—and it has soft sides. Cynthia unabashedly uses self-rising cornmeal mix.*

- 2 large eggs
- 1/2 cup oil, cook's preference
- 1 cup sour cream
- 1 (7-ounce) can creamed corn
- 1 cup self-rising cornmeal mix

Preheat oven to 375 degrees. Oil an 8-inch square baking pan.

Beat together the eggs, oil, sour cream, and corn in a large bowl. Add the cornmeal mix and beat until smooth.

Pour into the prepared pan and bake 30 to 40 minutes, until a knife inserted in the center comes out clean. Remove from oven, cool slightly, cut into squares, and serve from the pan.

YEAST BREADS

Yeast bread is both fascinating and quixotic to make. The breads made in the South were as varied as the settlers. The English favored softer rolls, the Germans darker grains, and the Italians artisan breads, particularly in the community bakeries as in Charleston. Yeast bread was primarily made from wheat because of its gluten, but grits, rice, and other substitutes were used as needed.

The South's early European heritage initially elevated the status of kneaded yeast breads, popular perhaps because of their tightly regulated texture, which forms a platform for butter, cheese, and meat. It was usual to make a sponge first. Now we incorporate a portion of the yeast into the flour and liquid, distributing them equally throughout the bread to develop the flour's gluten and texture. Most of the recipes for yeast breads in this book are kneaded and tight-grained, but there are a couple of no-knead artisan breads to get novices started.

Artisan breads are rough in shape and form, but for those with time to let the dough "knead" itself, these are easy.

While using hands is the tried and true method of kneading, machines now make kneading much easier, and we certainly want to make things easy.

My grandmother lived on a farm and baked loaves of bread twice a week until after my grandfather died, when she and her three children under seven years of age had to leave the farm. When we visited her as children, she went to the bakery every Sunday after church, waiting in line to pick up fresh sliced bread. She always insisted on fresh bread and real butter, even during the war, teaching us that it was better to go without than to compromise on bread and butter. Although she was from a line of bakers—both my grandmother's and my grandfather's families—the art died in the move to the city, and my mother never learned. When I learned to knead, I felt a satisfaction I had never known before—as if it was part of my heritage, a gift from above.

Ingredients

Yeast—Yeast is a natural leavening—an organism that grows everywhere. Since yeast occurs naturally, it is possible to make yeast bread from flour and water left exposed to air for a sufficient period of time to develop the natural yeast. This results in a loose or artisan bread with large air pockets. Its long rising time as it gathers wild yeast cells from the air increases its flavor. An example of this is in the No-knead Artisan Bread recipe on page 485.

Always, always, always check the "use by" date on the package of the yeast, and if unsure of the expiration, "proof" the yeast (page 483), no matter what kind it is.

Yeast cakes are solid blocks of compressed fresh yeast, once sold in 2-ounce blocks to supermarkets and specialty stores and in 1- to 2-pound blocks to commercial bakeries. It lasts in the refrigerator up to 2 weeks. Divide them into ounce cubes, wrap well, and store up to 1 year in the freezer. They defrost quickly but must used immediately. One (2½-teaspoon) package of active dry yeast equals 0.6 ounces of fresh yeast.

There are two main kinds of commercially sold dry yeast. They are distinct, but in a pinch they can be substituted for each other.

Active dry yeast—Made of dry yeast granules, each package has an expiration date and storing instructions. I refrigerate mine. Active dry yeast should be dissolved in water between 105 and 115 degrees. If the yeast is old or near the expiration date, proof the yeast (page 483) by leaving it in the liquid until it foams, "proving" the yeast is alive. Too hot a temperature kills the yeast and too cold results in a sluggish rise. Hot liquid added to a mixture of flour and yeast can be over 130 degrees, because the flour deflects the high heat so the liquid will not be that hot when it hits the yeast. Follow package directions when in doubt. Contrary to logic, additional yeast does not make a bread rise any higher—there is a maximum amount of air any dough can hold—and can make the dough taste more "fermented" or "beery."

RapidRise or instant yeast—Made of very fine dry yeast granules, each package has an expiration date and storing instructions. I refrigerate mine. These instant, rapid- and quick-rising yeasts are highly active strains of yeast that replace active dry yeast in equal measure. Used according to package directions, these yeasts reduce bread-making time by about half. These steps call for adding the yeast directly to a portion of the dry ingredients. Liquids are heated to a very warm temperature (125 to 130 degrees) and added to the dry ingredients. Many recipes for these yeasts need a short resting period and only one rising. Check package directions and adapt the recipe if speed is crucial. (When in doubt, this too can be proofed if necessary.)

Instant yeast is also sold in a block form preferred by the commercial bakers who use it religiously. It is a sister to RapidRise—same components but a different yeast flavor.

Any yeast can be substituted for any other. Although it is best to use specific package directions, they can all be adapted to another method if temperature is kept in mind. Remember, 115 degrees is ideal for active dry yeast; 125 to 130 degrees for instant yeast. Active dry needs to be dissolved, or proofed, first; instant prefers to be mixed in with the other ingredients.

The ingredient ratios for yeast breads are 1 part liquid (water or milk, primarily) to 2½ to 3½ parts flour.

Salt—Salt gives bread flavor and retards the growth of yeast sufficiently to ensure an even rise. (When I was chef of a restaurant in Majorca, all the available bread was unsalted. It was a joyous occasion when we crossed the water over to Spain and I had my first toast with salt in it after months without.) We use about 1 to 1½ teaspoons of salt per 3 cups of flour.

Sugar—Sugar adds flavor and tenderness. Yeast eats sugar. If no sugar is called for in the recipe, yeast will eat the available sugar in the flour. As long as the sugar is in evidence, the yeast will grow and be happy. When no sugar is available, the bread will collapse. Use between 1 teaspoon and 1 tablespoon of sugar per 3 cups of flour.

Liquid—The traditional liquid is water, preferably one that is not chlorinated and has no distinct taste that will dominate the bread. Milk makes a more tender dough and aids in browning, as does cream. Buttermilk and "sour milk" are frequently seen in older recipes.

Scalding Milk

When milk was only available unpasteurized, scalding milk to kill any bacteria was common. Many modern bakers still scald milk because it enhances the activity of the yeast (as adding cold milk would slow down the rise) and deactivates the whey proteins that inhibit gluten development. To scald milk, heat until small bubbles form around the edge of the container, reaching about 115 degrees.

Techniques

Proofing Yeast—To proof yeast is to prove it is alive. Stir approximately 1 tablespoon of active or quick rising yeast to ¼ to ½ cup of water warmed to between 105 and 115 degrees. A little sugar will speed it up. Within a few minutes of being in a warm spot, the yeast should start bubbling and growing a light froth on top. That proves it is living and active and is ready to use. Left alone, it will grow to the top of a cup, for instance, producing giant bubbles. Proofed yeast is scooped out with a rubber spatula and added to the flour along with the rest of the warm liquid.

Dissolving yeast—Proofing is not necessary when the yeast packet is fresh. Stir the yeast into ⅓ to ½ cup warm water. It should lose its graininess and become a thick fluid.

Kneading the dough—*Kneading* is a broad term that defines a method of handling to produce a smooth dough that traps the gases formed by leaveners (primarily yeast) in a network of stretched and expanded gluten strands. It can take up to 30 minutes by hand. The hand process involves folding and stretching the dough vigorously.

Make a soft and shaggy, slightly sticky dough by stirring together all of the liquid and an initial quantity of flour, yeast, and all of the salt and sugar. A wet dough is always better than a stiff dry dough. It is then turned out onto a floured surface. To knead by hand, using the heel of the hand, push out from the center of the dough, then fold and push out, fold over toward you and push it out again. Rotate the dough and repeat the process for up to 10 minutes. Pull in more flour only if the dough becomes too sticky to manipulate. Hand kneading is embraced by many as a near-spiritual experience, or as a way to "let off steam" for those who have a grievance.

A 6-cup heavy-duty stand mixer is optimum for kneading dough. A larger mixer is inconvenient in most home kitchens, while a smaller one won't always do the best job and the motor may burn out. I prefer a KitchenAid mixer, but other companies also make machines that do a good job. It usually takes 8 to 10 minutes of kneading with a dough hook to achieve a good 2-loaf dough, less time for 1 loaf.

A sturdy food processor (I prefer a Cuisinart or KitchenAid) also kneads dough. It takes about 1 to 2 minutes to knead a 2½–3-cup bread dough in the food processor. More flour than that requires a larger-than-standard food processor.

The final result of kneading is a soft dough that feels like a tender baby's bottom. It will bounce back when touched gently with a finger. One can add too much flour and not knead enough, or add too little flour and knead the right amount. There is a symbiotic relationship the kneader finds with the dough after practice that may not be found with the first few attempts at making bread. I try to remind new bakers that to practice making bread, piecrust, or biscuits is a personal experience that need not be shared with the world any more than hitting one's first round of golf balls—which, by the way, cost a lot more! A wet dough is always better than a dry one.

Letting the dough rise—I let all my yeast doughs rise in an oiled plastic ziplock bag set inside a large glass batter bowl, leaving the zipper open a few inches. It is easy to see when the dough has doubled and reduces cleanup.

A warm space next to a window or oven is usually the best place for dough to rise. To speed up rising, move the bowl of covered dough into a pan of water heated to 140 degrees. Doughs can be refrigerated, covered, up to a couple of days. The cold slows down the rising process. Remove the dough from the refrigerator, shape, and let double. A cold dough will take up to twice as long to double. Freezing dough is possible but tricky, and I don't do it.

Shaping the dough—Shape loaf bread using both hands to smooth and stretch the surface of the loaf, finishing with a tuck-under motion at the sides. For a tight crumb, make the dough into a rectangle, and roll into a loaf. Move loaf seam side down in the prepared loaf pan, tucked under at the sides if needed.

To shape rolls, use a knife or flour scraper to divide the dough into equal portions. (Some bakers weigh each piece to achieve equal sizes.) The goal of shaping a roll is to stretch the top of the roll to give it an even crust and to seal the bottom to prevent the roll from opening up while baking. Rolling a piece of dough on a barely floured or oiled surface using a lightly floured hand achieves both. Drop the dough onto the counter and, using a circular motion against the countertop, roll it under the palm of one hand using a slight downward pressure. As the top becomes smooth, change the position of the hand to cup the roll from the side, using fingers to smooth the sides and tuck under the roll.

Crisping breads—A pan of hot water, sprays, or mists added to the oven will help crisp the exterior of breads and rolls. Those that will benefit from crisping will be noted in the recipe, as many Southern breads are meant to be served soft. Another method is to bake in a preheated covered pan, as in the No-Knead Artisan Bread (facing page). If the bread tends to brown more on the bottom, then bake with 2 baking sheets—one under the other, stacked together—to conduct the heat more evenly and to give the product time to brown on top as well as on the bottom. If one part of the bread bakes faster than the other, rotate the pan halfway through the baking time. Many bakers prefer a baking stone. Ideally, of course, one would have one's own brick oven, but this is only a dream for most home cooks.

Testing for doneness—The internal temperature of breads and rolls should register 195 degrees on an instant-read thermometer inserted diagonally into the loaf. A loaf of bread will sound hollow when tapped on the bottom if done.

BASIC NO-KNEAD ARTISAN BREAD

Makes 1 loaf

THIS ADAPTATION OF JIM LEAHY'S NO-KNEAD BREAD *takes only five hours from start to finish resulting in a crusty bread. This I can do! The blessing of these breads is that they give you plenty of time to do other things, and what could be better than making soup. This technique can be adapted to any bread. For a crusty one, preheat the pan and lid. Otherwise, bake in an uncovered pan. There are several other bread books dedicated to this method, such as Nancy Baggett's* Kneadlessly Simple: Fabulous, Fuss-Free, No-Knead Breads.

3 cups bread or all-purpose flour
1 package active dry or instant yeast
1 1/2 teaspoons salt
1 1/2 cups room-temperature water
Oil as needed

Stir together flour, yeast, and salt in a bowl. Stir in water to barely combine the ingredients. Do not knead. Dump the roughly mixed contents into an oiled plastic bag and leave for about 4 to 8 hours in a warm room (70 degrees). It will become a risen dough. If necessary, it may go into the refrigerator (in the bag) overnight or up to 2 days. Bring to room temperature before baking.

Meanwhile, put a 6- to 8-quart heavy covered pot (cast-iron, enamel, oven-safe glass, or ceramic) in the oven. Immediately preheat the oven to 450 degrees. Lightly oil or flour a clean board or counter; slide the dough out of the bag and move it to the board. Gently fold in half. Return to the oiled plastic bag for another 30 minutes. Moving quickly and carefully, remove the very hot pot from the oven and close the door of the oven to keep it hot. Using a hot pad or oven mitts, remove the lid and set aside carefully. Quickly and gently pick up the dough and set it in the middle of the hot pot. Lightly shake the pot to make the dough rest evenly in the pan. (It will readjust itself just a bit in the oven.) Cover with hot lid, return to the hot oven, and bake 30 minutes; remove lid and bake uncovered another 15 to 30 minutes, until browned. The bread is done when the internal temperature reaches 195 degrees on an instant-read thermometer. Remove bread from the pan and cool on a rack.

When cool, the bread will last up to 4 days or may be frozen up to 3 months. Whether fresh or frozen, to re-crisp crust, reheat in a 400-degree oven 10 to 15 minutes. (It toasts beautifully.)

Variations: For 2 loaves, put 2 (3- to 4-quart) heavy covered pots (or covered paté or loaf pans) in the oven. Divide the dough in half quickly, place in the two pans, and cover, as with one loaf.

Sprinkle with flour for a rough-baked finish.

MAKING CRUSTY BREADS

The lidded heavy pot creates an oven that gives a crisp dough. Although any covered heatproof pan can be used, I think Le Creuset enameled cast-iron pots are superb. I've used several sizes and shapes, including the covered paté pan, all to good effect. For smaller sizes, I've halved the risen dough.

Another method of making crusty bread follows on page 486—creating steam in the oven as opposed to the pot.

MAKING PATENT YEAST

Put half a pound of fresh hops into a gallon of water and boil it away to two quarts, then strain it and make it a thin batter with flour; add half a pint of good yeast, and when well fermented, pour it in a bowl and work in as much cornmeal as will make it the consistency of biscuit dough; set it to rise, and when quite light, make it into little cakes, which must be dried in the shade, turning them very frequently; keep them securely from damp and dust. Persons who live in towns, and can procure brewer's yeast, will save trouble by using it; take one quart of it, add a quart of water, and proceed as before directed.

—*The Virginia House-Wife,* 1824

FOOD PROCESSOR QUICK-RISE CRUSTY BREAD

Makes 1 loaf

The food processor is the easiest and fastest way to make a yeast bread. *With a bit of kneading by hand after the dough is pulled together in the food processor, it produces an excellent product—in some ways, better than only hand kneading or kneading in a mixer.*

This is a simple, traditional, crusty bread with the most basic of ingredients, adapted to using the quick-rise technique for rapid-rise yeast, rising only once after a 10-minute rest. Flour and water-only bread makes great toast and rusks (twice-baked breads) and will freeze up to 3 months. Alas, it becomes stale quickly and readily takes on freezer odors and tastes, so wrap carefully.

1 tablespoon cornmeal for the pan
2 1/2–3 1/2 cups bread flour, divided
1 package instant or active dry yeast
1 teaspoon salt
1 1/2 teaspoons granulated sugar
1 cup hot water (130 degrees)
1 large egg, beaten, mixed with 1 tablespoon water

Sprinkle a baking sheet with cornmeal. This gives it a touch of flavor and acts like ball bearings to prevent sticking.

Pulse together 2 1/4 cups of the flour, yeast, salt, and sugar with the knife or plastic blade of a food processor. Add the hot water. Process to make a soft dough, adding 1/4 cup flour at a time of the remaining flour if needed. This will take about 1 minute. Remove from the food processor carefully, avoiding the blade, and move to a floured surface. Knead the dough (page 483) by pushing, folding over, and pushing again, adding flour only if needed, until the wet dough has absorbed only enough flour to come easily off hands and board without sticking but is still pliable and soft to the touch like a baby's bottom, about 3 or 4 minutes. It should bounce back lightly when touched with two fingers.

Cover, still on the board, with plastic wrap or a tea towel. Let rest 10 minutes. Roll out on the board to a rectangle about 10 x 5 inches. Roll into a cylinder 10 inches long, starting at one side and working to the other. Pull the ends slightly into points.

Move to the baking sheet. Let rise on the pan until double, in a warm but not hot place.

Meanwhile, preheat oven to 400 degrees. Slash the top of the loaf with a sharp knife. Brush with the egg wash (egg plus water). Bake on the middle rack of the oven with a small cake pan of boiling water on the bottom rack to make a crisp crust. Bake 25 to 30 minutes, until crisp and the bottom sounds hollow when tapped. The bread is done when the internal temperature registers 195 degrees on an instant-read thermometer inserted diagonally at the end or side. Remove and cool on a wire rack.

Sprinkle with flour for a rough-baked finish. When cool, the bread will last up to 4 days or may be frozen up to 3 months. Whether fresh or frozen, to recrisp crust, reheat in a 400-degree oven 10 to 15 minutes. (It also toasts beautifully.)

Variation: Olive Bread
Add 1 cup pitted kalamata or niçoise olives and 1 to 2 tablespoons rosemary or other herbs to the dough after adding the first 1/4 cup of flour.

Variation: Focaccia
To shape into a focaccia, pat the rested olive-filled dough out to fill an oiled jelly roll pan. Let double in the pan, about 30 minutes. Drizzle with olive oil. Bake for 20 to 30 minutes, until it registers 195 degrees.

Variation: Two Loaves
Divide the dough in two after the 10-minute resting period, and shape into 2 loaves. Bake several inches apart. Bake for a shorter period of time, checking for doneness after 30 minutes.

Variation: Tomato Basil Bread
Top toasted bread with chopped tomatoes drizzled with oil and chopped basil.

FENNEL FLOWER LOAF

Fennel is almost a weed in the South. It reseeds abundantly and naturally. There is also an indigenous wild fennel. One plant will have twenty baby plants in no time. The seeds, with their slight licorice flavor, make a tasty addition to this bread. The bread makes a savory toast as well as croutons.

Add $1/2$ teaspoon fennel seeds to any dough with about 3 cups of flour. Shape the rested dough into a smooth ball about 8 inches in diameter. Move to an oiled baking sheet. Make a hole the size of a small can through the center of the dough. Oil the outside of an empty small metal can and place in the hole while the dough rises. Cut a circle $1/4$ inch deep in the dough, 1 inch from the can. With the tip of a sharp knife, make slashes from the circle to the edge, scalloping the edges to form the petals of a flower. Bake with the can in place.

BAKER'S BREAD (*PAIN DE BOULANGER*)

Makes 5 loaves

CREOLE BREADS ARE A SOURCE OF PRIDE IN NEW ORLEANS, *and this recipe from* The Picayune's Creole Cook Book, *1954 edition, is described by the authors as having "exquisite lightness, white and tender, of an even, porous character, with a thin, crisp crust, and, best of all, is just such a bread as is required in our climate. Made into toast, it is most delightful of all breads, no homemade light bread or baker's bread in any other part of the United States standing comparison with it."*

1 cake of compressed yeast
1 1/2 ounces of salt
2 pints of water
Flour sufficient to make a smooth dough

Allow one ounce of compressed yeast to one quart of lukewarm water, and mix well in a wooden bread trough. Then add flour enough to make a nice smooth dough of medium degree, not too stiff, nor yet too soft. Work it well, and then let it stand for about five hours in a warm place, so as to rise well. When it doubles in size (you can tell this by watching the sides of the dough), add two teaspoonfuls of salt dissolved in two teaspoonfuls of water before adding it.

Work this well, and then throw dough on the table, cut and mold the dough into loaves of whatever length is desired, and take a smooth stick and press lightly down across the loaf about two inches from the edge. The bakers put the loaves into the oven without setting in a pan. Watch carefully, and see that the oven is at 360 degrees. Breads should be in the oven about ten minutes before it begins to brown.

—*The Picayune's Creole Cook Book*

THE TOAST TEST

To know one's oven, spread pieces of bread on a baking sheet. Bake in a 350- or 400-degree oven. Remove, note the pattern, and place pans accordingly.

BEGINNER'S LOAF FOOD PROCESSOR BREAD

Makes 1 loaf

THIS IS VERY SIMILAR TO THE CRUSTY BREAD RECIPE, *except fat—either shortening or butter—is added, and the liquid is divided between milk and water. To make a more tender dough, the total liquid can be milk, and the fat increased. This recipe can also be adapted to hand kneading or a stand mixer, kneading for a longer time.*

1 package active dry or instant yeast
3 cups bread flour, divided
1 1/2 teaspoons salt
1 tablespoon granulated sugar
1 tablespoon shortening or butter
1/2 cup hot milk
1/2 cup hot water (130 degrees)
1 large egg mixed with
 1 tablespoon water
Pinch salt

Oil a 9 x 5-inch loaf pan. Line with 2 pieces of parchment or waxed paper—one cut to the width of the pan and the other to the length of the pan plus 4 inches of overhang to use as handles to lift the loaf from the pan.

Pulse together the yeast, 2 cups of flour, salt, and sugar in a food processor fitted with the metal or plastic blade. Pulse in the shortening or butter, followed by the milk and the water. Add 1/4 cup flour and pulse again; repeat, adding 1/4 cup of flour at a time until a soft dough is formed. Process up to 1 minute total, stopping if the machine slows down and checking the dough for consistency. If wet, add another 1/4 cup of flour as needed. If very dry, add a very little water or milk. The dough should be soft, pliable, and slightly sticky. Remove from the processor carefully, avoiding the blade, and move to a floured surface. Knead by pushing, folding over, and pushing again, adding flour when sticky, until pliable and smooth as a baby's bottom, about 3-4 minutes on the board. The dough should bounce back when touched lightly with two fingers. Let rest on the counter, covered with plastic wrap or a tea towel, or move to an oiled plastic bag to rest 10 minutes.

Press the dough into a rectangle 8 inches long by 5 inches wide. Using the heels of the hands, roll the dough beginning on one of the 8-inch sides. Move to the prepared pan, seam side down. Let rise at room temperature until double in size.

When ready to bake, preheat oven to 350 degrees. Brush the top of the loaf with the egg wash. Bake 35 to 40 minutes, until a rich golden brown. The bread is done when the internal temperature registers 195 degrees on an instant-read thermometer inserted diagonally at the end. Cool slightly on a rack. Lift the bread out of the pans, remove the paper, and let cool a bit longer on a rack.

Variation: Raisin Cinnamon Bread
Add 1 tablespoon cinnamon to the flour mixture and proceed as above. Soak 1/2 cup raisins in hot water to cover for 10 minutes. Drain. Add to dough when kneading on the counter. Bake as above. Omit the egg wash and glaze with Creamy Glaze (page 493).

Variation: Country Ham and Cheese Bread
After the rise, punch down the dough and knead in 1 cup grated Cheddar cheese and 2 cups minced country ham, blanched for 2 minutes, drained, and patted dry. Proceed as above.

SHAPING AND BAKING DOUGH FOR ROLLS

To shape, divide in half and pull off dough in egg-sized pieces. Drop each dough piece onto the counter and roll under the palm of one hand with a circular motion against the countertop, using a slight downward pressure. As the top becomes smooth, change the position of the hand to cup the roll from the side, using fingers to smooth the sides and tuck under the roll. Move them to an oiled baking sheet and leave egg-sized spaces in between. Let rise until doubled, about 1/2 hour.

When ready to bake, preheat oven to 425 degrees. Brush dough pieces with water to give them a crisp crust. Cut a cross on top of each piece with a sharp knife. Bake 20 minutes, until nicely browned. The rolls are done when the internal temperature registers 195 degrees on an instant-read thermometer inserted diagonally into one roll. Remove to a rack to cool.

ADAPTING BREAD RECIPES FOR THE FOOD PROCESSOR

Any bread may be adapted for making in the food processor. Take care the food processor bowl is of a sufficient size to knead the total amount of ingredients, or divide into batches. A good limit for a regular-sized food processor is 3 to 3½ cups.

If the machine slows down while kneading, it is usually because the dough is too wet. Add more flour before proceeding. Avoid processing for more than 1 minute in all once the liquid and flour are combined. Overprocessing can prevent a good rise. Once a soft dough is formed, remove it and knead for the last 1 or 2 minutes on a floured board. If any ingredient is needed—say, more liquid—or if an ingredient has been inadvertently omitted, tear the dough into small pieces and put the dough pieces and the omitted ingredient into the food processor and process until incorporated. (To add yeast, sugar, or salt, dissolve in a little liquid first to ensure even distribution.) It will look messy for a while, but it will pull together. It may not be perfect, but it will be better than tossing it away.

WHITE LOAF BREAD

Makes 2 loaves (or 60 finger rolls)

HOMEMADE LOAF BREAD *is still a staple on the Southern table. There are times when tender white bread is the only bread that will do. For pimento cheese or peanut butter sandwiches, for instance, and for the first tomato sandwich of the season, it would be a sacrilege to use any other kind. This loaf rises beautifully, its golden crust towering out of the pan, to make giant slices of bread. Note that different types of flour require different amounts.*

2 packages active dry yeast
1½ tablespoons granulated sugar
½ cup warm water (105–115 degrees)
¾ cup milk
2 teaspoons salt
½ cup unsalted butter, room temperature
3 large eggs, lightly beaten
6½–9 cups soft-wheat all-purpose flour, divided, or 5–7 cups bread flour
¼ cup butter, melted

Oil 2 (9 x 5-inch) loaf pans. Line with 2 pieces of parchment or waxed paper—one cut to the width of the pan and the other to the length of the pan plus 4 inches of overhang to use as handles to lift the baked loaf from the pan.

Dissolve the yeast and sugar in the warm water in a large bowl or the bowl of a stand mixer.

Scald the milk by heating it until small bubbles appear around the edge of the pan. Add salt and ½ cup butter to the milk. The mixture should be less than 115 degrees.

Stir the milk mixture into the yeast mixture. Stir in the eggs. Stir in 5 cups of the all-purpose or 3 cups of bread flour. Beat until smooth, adding enough additional flour as needed to form a soft, pliable dough that is slightly sticky. Knead on a floured board, or in a mixer or processor, adding flour as needed, until pliable and smooth as a baby's bottom, about 4 minutes. Knead 2 minutes more on the board. The dough should bounce back when lightly touched. Move to an oiled plastic ziplock bag.

Let rise in a warm place until the dough has doubled, about 1 hour. Insert two fingers into the dough. If the holes they make don't come back, it has risen sufficiently. Punch down the dough and knead it lightly.

Divide the dough in two, form into ovals approximately the length of the pans, and move 1 loaf into each prepared pan. Let rise again, covered, until doubled.

When ready to bake, preheat oven to 375 degrees. Brush the loaves with melted butter. Bake 30 minutes, or until the bread comes away easily from the pans. The bread is done when the internal temperature registers 195 degrees on an instant-read thermometer. Cool briefly in the pans. Lift the bread out of the pans, remove the paper, and let cool on a rack.

SALLY LUNN BREAD

Makes 2 loaves

WHEN DETERMINING WHICH SALLY LUNN RECIPE TO USE, *we decided to start all over and test a number of them. We finally settled on one from* Southern Cooking *by Mrs. S. R. Dull, for years the food editor for the Atlanta newspaper. This adapted recipe makes a scrumptious bread—perfect for butter and jam, delicious for accompanying tea, and lovely for wedding sandwiches. The extra rising stages may take more time, but they give this bread an unmistakable yeasty flavor that is hard to resist. Like a brioche, it is nearly a cake. Were Marie Antoinette Southern, she would have said, "Let them eat Sally Lunn bread" (rather than the cake-like brioche to which she referred), and she might have lived. At any time, the dough may be refrigerated covered for up to 2 days to retard the rising. Bring the dough back to room temperature before proceeding.*

1 package active dry yeast
2 tablespoons granulated sugar
1/4 cup warm water (105–115 degrees)
2 cups milk
2 tablespoons unsalted butter, melted
2 teaspoons salt
3 large eggs, lightly beaten
4–5 cups bread flour, divided

Oil 2 (9 x 5-inch) loaf pans. Line with 2 pieces of parchment or waxed paper—one cut to the width of the pan and the other to the length of the pan plus 4 inches of overhang to use as handles to lift the baked loaf from the pan.

Dissolve the yeast and sugar in the warm water in a large bowl or the bowl of a stand mixer. Scald the milk by heating it almost to the boil (small simmering bubbles will appear around the edge of the pan). Add the butter and salt to the milk. The mixture should be less than 115 degrees.

Stir the milk mixture into the yeast mixture. Add eggs. Mix in 4 cups of bread flour. Add 1/4 cup flour at a time, stirring, as needed to make a shaggy dough that holds together but is not dry. Move to an oiled plastic ziplock bag or cover in an oiled bowl.

When dough has doubled, stir or punch down the dough. Let rise again and punch down again. This several-hours process takes the place of kneading (see Basic No-Knead Artisan Bread, page 485).

When the dough has doubled the third and final time in the bag, scoop the dough into 2 oiled loaf pans and let double in size, which will take about 1 hour.

When ready to bake, preheat oven to 400 degrees. After moving the pans to the oven, turn the oven down to 350 degrees and bake from 45 minutes to 1 hour, according to the depth of the loaves. The bread is done when the internal temperature registers 195 degrees on an instant-read thermometer. The loaves should be brown and well cooked, with a thick crust. Remove the pans from the oven and move to a wire rack to cool 10 minutes. Lift the bread out of the pans, remove the paper, and let cool on a rack.

Variations:

- Small Sally Lunns: Divide dough into 24 pieces and put into greased muffin molds to make individual Sally Lunns. The small Sally Lunns will require 25 to 30 minutes of cooking time.
- Bake in an oiled tube pan to make one large loaf. Bake 1 to 1 1/2 hours, depending on pan size, checking with thermometer as above.
- Speedy Sally Lunn: Knead with the dough hook about 7 minutes or in a large food processor for 2 to 3 minutes and let rise one time only in an oiled plastic ziplock bag before the final shaping and rising.

GRANDMOTHER KREISER'S POWDER-PUFF DINNER ROLLS

Makes 20 to 24 rolls

THIS GRANDMOTHER KREISER *was really my great-uncle Harry's wife. She indulged Harry, who was rail thin, so she always added two tablespoons more sugar than the recipe needed and brushed a sugar-egg wash on them, both of which can be omitted. Remember, though, that the extra sugar in the dough also adds tenderness. These rolls, his daughter told me, are light enough to powder your face. (This is something women used to do with the fluffy round of fabric called a "puff" that was kept with loose face powder in a round container. No lady would appear with a shiny un-powdered nose indicating she was not well groomed or had "worked outdoors." This was to be done privately—never out in public. Hence the "powder room" became a euphemism for the "ladies room." Large makeup brushes have largely taken over that function these days, which is a shame, as no one would ever say "soft as a makeup brush.") The egg and sugar will cause the bread to brown more rapidly, so take care to check the temperature as needed.*

1 package active dry yeast
2–4 tablespoons granulated sugar, divided
1/4 cup warm water (105–115 degrees)
3/4 cup fresh milk or reconstituted powdered milk (mixed according to package directions)
3 tablespoons unsalted butter
1 tablespoon salt
1 large egg, lightly beaten
3–4 cups bread flour, divided
3 tablespoons fresh milk or reconstituted powdered milk, mixed according to package directions
2 tablespoons granulated sugar, optional

Preheat oven to 350 degrees. Lightly oil a 9 x 13-inch baking sheet, or line with parchment paper.

Dissolve the yeast and 1 tablespoon of sugar in the warm water.

Scald the milk by heating it almost to the boil (small simmering bubbles will appear around the edge of the pan). Move to a large bowl or the bowl of a stand mixer. Add the remaining sugar, butter, and salt to the milk. The mixture should be less than 115 degrees.

Stir in the lightly beaten egg and the yeast mixture. Stir in 2 1/2 cups of flour. Beat until smooth, adding enough additional flour as needed to form a soft, pliable dough that is slightly sticky.

Turn out onto a floured board and knead, or knead in the mixer, adding flour in 1/4-cup increments as needed until pliable and smooth as a baby's bottom, about 4 minutes. Knead 2 minutes more on the board. The dough should bounce back when lightly touched. Move to an oiled plastic ziplock bag.

Let rest in a warm place until the dough has doubled, about 1 hour. Insert 2 fingers into the dough. If the holes they make don't come back, it has risen sufficiently. Punch down the dough, and knead it lightly.

To shape, divide the dough in half. Pinch off small pieces of dough or cut the dough into 10 to 12 equal pieces. Drop each dough piece onto the counter and roll under the palm of one hand with a circular motion against the countertop, using slight downward pressure. As the top becomes smooth, change the position of the hand to cup the roll from the side, using fingers to smooth the sides and tuck under the roll. Nestle them cozily touching each on the baking sheet, and let double again. Bake 15 minutes.

Meanwhile, make a milk wash by mixing together the milk and sugar.

Remove the rolls from the oven, brush with the milk wash, and return them to the oven for another 5 to 10 minutes. The rolls are done when the internal temperature registers 195 degrees on an instant-read thermometer inserted diagonally into the edge of one of the rolls. Cool on a rack briefly. Turn upside down on the rack and let the rolls cool out of the pan. The rolls freeze well wrapped for up to 3 months.

continued

continuation from previous page

Variation: Grandmother Kreiser's Savory Ring

Here is the same recipe with some added strong flavors and put together in a pull-apart ring. Less salt is used due to the bacon.

Preheat oven to 350 degrees. Oil a 10-inch angel food or tube cake pan.

Thoroughly mix 2 tablespoons sesame seeds, 1 tablespoon chopped fresh basil, and 1/2 cup grated Parmesan cheese in a small bowl. Dust the bottom and sides of the pan with 1/3 of the seed/cheese mixture. Continue as above, using only 2 teaspoons salt, through the end of the first rise.

Divide the dough into 20 balls. Put 10 of them in the bottom of the pan, making sure that they touch. Melt the remaining butter and drizzle 6 tablespoons onto the dough. Sprinkle with the crumbled bacon and half of the remaining seed/cheese mixture. Add the remaining bread dough balls, making sure that they are again touching. Drizzle with the rest of the butter, and sprinkle with remaining seed/cheese mixture.

Bake 20 minutes, or until golden brown. Cover with foil and bake 15 to 20 minutes more, or until bread is no longer doughy and the internal temperature registers 195 degrees on an instant-read thermometer inserted diagonally into the side of one of the rolls. Remove the bread from the pan onto a wire rack. Brush with 1 tablespoon melted butter. These can be served either inverted or baked side up.

FRUIT, SEED, AND NUT BREAD

Makes 1 loaf

I CRAVE THIS BREAD FOR WINTER BREAKFASTS *or afternoon snacks, sliced and toasted and buttered. The condiments can be varied or omitted, but the total amount should be roughly 1/2 cup loosely packed.*

- 1 package active dry yeast
- 1 tablespoon sorghum or molasses
- 1 cup warm water (105–115 degrees)
- 2 1/2–3 cups bread flour, divided
- 1 tablespoon cocoa powder, optional
- 1 1/2 teaspoons ground cinnamon, optional
- 2 teaspoons salt
- 1/4 cup bran cereal
- 2 tablespoons currants or raisins, optional
- 2 tablespoons roughly chopped sunflower seeds, optional
- 2 tablespoons roughly chopped pine nuts, optional
- 2 tablespoons roughly chopped pecans, walnuts, hazelnuts, or almonds, optional
- 1 egg, beaten with 1 tablespoon water

Oil a baking sheet and set aside.

Dissolve the yeast and the sorghum or molasses in the warm water in a large bowl or in the bowl of a stand mixer. Stir together 2 cups of bread flour, optional cocoa powder and/or cinnamon, salt, and bran cereal and add to the yeast mixture. Beat until smooth, adding enough additional flour as needed to form a soft, pliable dough that is slightly sticky.

Turn out onto a floured board and knead, or knead in the mixer, adding flour as needed until pliable and smooth as a baby's bottom, about 4 minutes. Knead 2 minutes more on the board. The dough should bounce back when lightly touched. Knead in the currants, sunflower seeds, pine nuts, and pecans. Move to an oiled plastic ziplock bag.

Rest in a warm place until the dough has doubled, about 1 hour. Insert 2 fingers into the dough. If the holes they make don't come back, it has risen sufficiently. Punch down the dough, and knead it lightly. Form the dough into a round and move to the prepared pan. Let rise again until doubled.

When ready to bake, preheat oven to 350 degrees. Brush the loaf with the egg wash and bake 1 to 1 1/2 hours, or until the bread sounds hollow when tapped on the bottom. The bread is done when the internal temperature of the bread registers 195 degrees on an instant-read thermometer inserted diagonally into the side of the loaf, or when a toothpick inserted in the center comes out clean. Remove from the pan and let cool on a rack.

PECAN AND CURRANT OR APPLE RING

Serves 8

THE SOUTHERN SWEET TOOTH ASSERTS ITSELF HERE, *not to mention it is so pretty that no one can resist. Kelly Skelly, one of our dedicated interns, revised this coffee cake recipe.*

Sweet Dough

1 package active dry yeast
1 teaspoon granulated sugar
1/2 cup warm water (105–115 degrees)
1/2 cup buttermilk
1/4 cup light or dark brown sugar
1/2 cup unsalted butter
1/2 teaspoon salt
1 teaspoon vanilla extract
3 1/2–4 1/2 cups bread flour, divided
Grated rind of 1 lemon, no white attached

Filling

1 cup currants or chopped apples
3/4 cup chopped pecans
5 tablespoons black sesame seeds or poppy seeds
1/2 cup unsalted butter, room temperature
1/2 cup light or dark brown sugar
1 teaspoon ground cinnamon
1/2 teaspoon grated nutmeg
1/4 cup all-purpose flour

Creamy Glaze

1 cup confectioners' sugar, sifted
2 tablespoons unsalted butter, softened
3/4 teaspoon vanilla extract
2–3 tablespoons heavy cream, divided

Lightly oil a baking sheet and set aside.

Dissolve the yeast and granulated sugar in the warm water in a large bowl or in the bowl of a stand mixer. Scald the buttermilk by heating it almost to the boil (small simmering bubbles will appear around the edge of the pan). Add the brown sugar, butter, salt, and vanilla to the milk. The mixture should be less than 115 degrees.

Stir the milk mixture into the yeast mixture. Stir in 2 cups of bread flour and lemon rind. Beat until smooth, adding enough additional flour as needed to form a soft, pliable dough that is slightly sticky. Turn out onto a floured board and knead, or knead in the mixer, adding flour as needed, until pliable and smooth as a baby's bottom, about 4 minutes. Knead 2 minutes more on the board. The dough should bounce back when lightly touched. Move to an oiled plastic ziplock bag.

Let rest in a warm place until the dough has doubled, about 1 hour. Insert 2 fingers into the dough. If the holes they make don't come back, it has risen sufficiently. Punch down the dough, and knead it lightly. The dough may be refrigerated at this point.

Meanwhile, toss the filling ingredients together in a bowl.

Turn out the dough onto a floured board and roll into a rectangle 10 inches wide by 16 inches long. Spread the filling to within 1 inch of the edges of the rectangle. Roll up lengthwise, pinching the seam to seal. Shape the dough into a ring, joining the ends of the ring securely.

Move to the prepared baking sheet. Insert an oiled ramekin in the center of the ring to keep the ring open during baking. Slash the ring in 10 spokes almost to the center and twist each cut section clockwise, exposing the filling. Let rise again until doubled, about 45 minutes to 1 hour.

When ready to bake, preheat oven to 375 degrees. Bake the ring for 25 to 30 minutes, or until golden. The ring is done when the internal temperature of the bread registers 195 degrees on an instant-read thermometer inserted diagonally into the center of the bread. Remove from the oven, remove center ramekin, and cool on a rack.

Mix together the confectioners' sugar, butter, vanilla, and 1 tablespoon of heavy cream, stirring until smooth and thick but still pourable; add additional cream to thin the glaze, if necessary. Drizzle onto cooled ring and serve at once.

BRIOCHE ROLLS

Makes 10

THE RICHEST AND MOST CAKE-*like of fashionable yeast breads, the dough is traditionally baked in fluted brioche molds. Knead this in a food processor, although it may be adapted to a stand mixer. The rolls freeze up to three months if well wrapped, so consider making a double batch. They make ideal accompaniments to eggs and impress breakfast, brunch, and weekend guests with their lightness. They're also wonderful sliced and buttered as French toast, or toasted and served with butter and jam.*

1 package active dry yeast
1/3 cup granulated sugar, divided
1/4 cup warm water (105–115 degrees)
2 1/3 cups bread flour
1 1/2 teaspoons salt
3/4 cup unsalted butter, cool but not hard chilled
3 large eggs
1 egg yolk, beaten, mixed with 2 tablespoons water

Oil and flour 10 small fluted (1/3-cup) brioche or muffin tins or 1 (3-cup) brioche or loaf pan.

Dissolve the yeast and a pinch of sugar in the warm water.

Mix together the flour, salt, and remaining sugar in a food processor or stand mixer. Beat in the cool butter until it resembles coarse meal. Add the yeast mixture. Beat in the eggs, one at a time. Continue to beat until the dough is shiny and glossy, and forms long, slick strings that have an adhesive quality. If the food processor turns off automatically, the dough is ready.

Move to an oiled plastic ziplock bag and turn to coat. Seal and let rise in a warm place until tripled, about 1 to 1 1/2 hours. Punch the dough down. Refrigerate in the bag 8 hours or up to 3 days.

Take two-thirds of the now cold, spongy dough and, working quickly, form it into 10 balls. Drop each dough ball onto the counter and roll under the palm of one hand with a circular motion against the countertop, using a slight downward pressure. As the top becomes smooth, change the position of the hand to cup the roll from the side, using fingers to smooth the sides and tuck under the roll; each ball will fill a brioche tin two-thirds full.

Cut a 1/2-inch-deep cross in the center of each ball. With the remaining dough, form 10 small pear-shaped knobs. Fit the pointed ends of the knobs into the center holes, making sure to press firmly in place. For the brioche or loaf pan, roll dough to the shape of the pan and move to the prepared pan. Let rise uncovered in a warm place until the dough has doubled, about 45 minutes.

When ready to bake, preheat oven to 375 degrees.

Brush the dough with the egg wash. Bake on middle rack of oven until nicely browned, about 15 to 20 minutes for the small tins or 30 to 40 minutes for the large pan. The bread is done when the internal temperature registers 195 degrees on an instant-read thermometer inserted diagonally into the side of one roll. Cool slightly before removing from tins and cool further on a rack. Keep in an airtight container.

To speed up the process, the kneaded dough may be moved to the oiled plastic ziplock bag and chilled in the refrigerator for 3 hours. Oil and flour the brioche tins. When the dough is chilled, shape as described above. Brush all over with the glaze. Let double. Bake about 10 minutes, or until brown. Serve with jam and butter if desired.

RICH CLOVERLEAF ROLLS

Makes 12 rolls

USING EGGS AND BUTTER *makes a very rich dough, almost like a brioche (facing). If speed is of the essence, add another package of yeast and a bit more water to dissolve the yeast. An egg replaces 2 ounces of liquid in this recipe.*

1 package active dry yeast
1/4 cup granulated sugar, divided
1/4 cup warm water (105–115 degrees)
1/2 cup milk
1/4 cup unsalted butter, melted
1 tablespoon salt
2 large eggs, lightly beaten
2 1/2–3 cups bread flour, divided
Melted butter, optional, for brushing

Oil 2 (12-cup) muffin tins and set aside.

Dissolve the yeast and 1 tablespoon of sugar in the warm water in a large bowl or in the bowl of a stand mixer.

Scald the milk by heating it almost to the boil (small simmering bubbles will appear around the edge of the pan). Add the remaining sugar, butter, and salt to the milk. The mixture should be less than 115 degrees.

Stir the milk mixture into the yeast mixture. Stir in the eggs. Stir in 2 1/2 cups of bread flour. Beat until smooth, adding enough additional flour as needed to form a soft, pliable dough that is slightly sticky.

Turn out onto a floured board and knead, or knead in the mixer, adding flour as needed until pliable and smooth as a baby's bottom, about 4 minutes. Knead 2 minutes more on the board. The dough should bounce back when lightly touched. Move to an oiled plastic ziplock bag.

Rest in a warm place until the dough has doubled, about 1 hour. Insert 2 fingers into the dough. If the holes they make don't come back, it has risen sufficiently. Punch down the dough and knead it lightly. The dough may be refrigerated at this point.

To shape into cloverleafs, divide the dough into fourths. Divide each fourth into 9 (1-inch) balls. Roll the balls lightly to smooth the top. Place 3 balls in each oiled muffin cup. They should fit easily. Let rise until doubled.

When ready to bake, preheat oven to 400 degrees. Bake 10 to 12 minutes, until golden brown. The rolls are done when the internal temperature of the bread registers 195 degrees on an instant-read thermometer inserted diagonally into one roll.

Remove the rolls from the oven. Remove them from the pan and cool on a rack. Brush the tops with butter if desired. The rolls freeze well wrapped for up to 3 months. Reheat in the oven for 5 to 10 minutes at 350 degrees.

Variation: Baps

Recipes for baps—as much buns as rolls—may be found in many old Southern cookbooks, derived from old English cookbooks. I served them in my restaurant for dinner, making them day after day. I think I could make them in my sleep. They freeze very well and are best served hot. For a heavier, sturdier bun, as for a barbecue pork sandwich, use bread flour and make them larger. I prefer using a Southern soft-wheat flour in this recipe.

Use the exact ingredients as above except omit eggs and substitute 2 1/2 –3 1/2 cups all-purpose flour for the bread flour. Shape as on page 488 (Beginner's Loaf). Dust with flour and bake at 350 degrees for 20 to 25 minutes, or until lightly browned on top and cooked through. Brush with butter.

SWEET BEIGNETS

Makes 1$\frac{1}{2}$ dozen

As any traveler to New Orleans knows, *Café du Monde is the place for beignets and coffee. Brought to the Crescent City in the late 1700s, beignets have been a staple in rural home kitchens for 200 years. On baking day, a small amount of bread dough was reserved then stretched flat by hand before frying. Some say the hand-stretched dough tastes better; others say the evaporated milk makes the difference,. But we guess you can fry just about any dough, toss it in confectioners' sugar, and be content whether it puffs or not. Ideally, the dough puffs up, leaving a gracious plenty of air inside. If the dough is more like a doughnut, next time roll it thinner.*

1 package active dry yeast
1/4 cup granulated sugar
3/4 cup warm water (105–115 degrees)
1 large egg, slightly beaten
3/4 teaspoon salt
1/2 cup evaporated milk or half-and-half
3 1/2 cups bread flour
Shortening or vegetable oil for deep-frying
1 1/2–2 cups confectioners' sugar

Dissolve the yeast and granulated sugar in the warm water in a large bowl or in the bowl of a stand mixer.

Beat the eggs, salt, and milk together in a separate bowl. Stir the egg mixture into the yeast mixture. Stir in 3 cups of bread flour. Beat until smooth, adding enough additional flour as needed to form a soft, pliable dough that is slightly sticky.

Turn out onto a floured board and knead, or knead in the mixer, adding flour as needed, until pliable and smooth as a baby's bottom, about 4 minutes. Knead 2 minutes more on the board. The dough should bounce back when lightly touched. Move to an oiled plastic ziplock bag. Let rise in a warm place for at least 2 hours.

Heat oil in a deep-sided skillet to 350 degrees, making sure the oil does not come more than halfway up the pan. It should be deep enough that it comes a bit more than halfway up the finished beignet.

Add the confectioners' sugar to a paper or plastic bag and set aside.

Roll the dough out on a lightly floured board to about 1/4 inch thick and cut into 2- to 3-inch squares. (Tip: making a test piece is always a good idea. Fry 1 beignet, remove, drain, and taste. If it is more like a doughnut than a puffed-up creation full of air, roll the dough thinner if possible.) Deep-fry dough pieces in batches until they become golden. Turn halfway through, and cook on the second side. Turn again as necessary. After beignets are fried, drain them for a few seconds on paper towels and then toss them into the bag of confectioners' sugar. Hold bag closed and shake to coat evenly. Serve hot. (But no one turns them down cold.)

This recipe doubles easily. No need to add a second package of yeast, however.

GARLIC CROÛTES

Makes 48 pieces

THESE HOMEMADE TOASTS, *much like thick Melba toasts, are a wonderful snack as well as a good accompaniment to soup. They keep very well in a sealed container for weeks, and they can be frozen.*

2–3 garlic cloves, finely chopped
1/4–1/2 cup Perfumed Olive Oil (page 671)
24 slices French bread (about 1/2 inch thick)

Preheat oven to 400 degrees.

Mix the garlic with the oil and let stand 30 minutes. Lightly brush the slices with the flavored oil and bake for 15 to 20 minutes, turning as necessary until golden brown. The croûtes freeze in an airtight container. Crisp in the oven before serving.

Variation: Rusks

To make rusks (twice-baked bread) from French bread, slice thinly and move to a pan in a 200-degree oven until crisp but not brown, about 1 hour, depending on original freshness of the bread.

Variation: Homemade Croutons

Cut French bread—leftovers are fine—into cubes, leaving the crust on. Toss the cubes with herbed olive oil or melted butter and then with salt and pepper.

Bake croutons at 325 degrees until baked through, about 5 minutes. Turn them if necessary. The size of the cubes determines how long they bake.

Variation: Tiny Croutons

Very tiny diced croutons are now seen in restaurants and are a delight. Cook dice in hot olive oil in a frying pan on the stovetop, watching very carefully.

Variation: Toast Points

These are toothsome served with soup or a spread. Make them ahead and freeze, reheating if needed. Brush with melted butter or oil and sprinkle with coarse salt, garlic, or grated Parmesan before baking if desired.

Remove the crusts from 2 loaves of thinly sliced sandwich bread. Cut each slice into 4 triangles. Move the triangles to an ungreased baking sheet and bake in a 325-degree preheated oven until lightly browned, about 10 to 20 minutes, turning once. Makes 100 to 120 toast points.

PASTRIES & PIES

A good pie, including its crust, lingers in the mind long after the last crumb disappears. It should be the thing of dreams and memories, flakes on the tongue cradling the tastiest of ingredients. Getting there is a step-by-step process, and understanding these steps can make baking a joy. Take a little time to read the chapter rather than rushing into the first crust.

Learning to make a piecrust was easy when a busy kitchen made several pies a week, with children watching to see how it was done and learning from seeing. Novices should "practice" by taking a cool morning and making several piecrusts in a row, making notes about what works, and not counting on making a finished product for a soon-to-come meal. After all, golfers practice putting and driving, so why shouldn't a novice pie baker practice? Learning will save money later, since pies use are elegant packages for what otherwise might be wasted scraps of food, as in quiches, and maximizing bruised fruit.

PIECRUST BASICS

Heat is the enemy of piecrust making, whether from the temperature of the room, hands, or proximity of the ingredients to a running dishwasher, stovetop, or oven. Therefore, piecrusts are best made before anything else, even the filling. Starting with a cool room makes a big difference. For that reason, the historic time to make piecrusts was in the early morning or late evening. For those with sun beaming into their kitchens, this is still a good idea.

Most pie bakers agree that all the ingredients should be as cold as possible, as cold retards the development of gluten, making a piecrust more tender and flaky. Some cooks freeze both the fat and the flour. Frozen shortening and lard are still a bit pliable when frozen, but butter is too difficult to incorporate unless a food processor is used (page 509). Making piecrust is a snap in the food processor.

I grew up during WWII, when butter was rationed. If lard wasn't made at home by rendering pork fat, it was hard to come by. My mother kept cans on the stovetop to gather any fat possible, from chicken fat to the rare bacon fat. Lard begins to melt between 97 and 113 degrees (the purer the lard, the higher the melting temperature), while butter puddles and melts at 98 degrees. So in 105-degree temperatures, before air-conditioning, lard was a real boon!

Along came shortening—another blessing to pie makers. It was nearly as light as lard, brought no porky flavor, and required no rendering. It was more than an adequate substitute for lard, particularly if the cook didn't slaughter her own pig.

Still, pork products and shortenings have gotten a bad name, like so many other products, even though the saturated fat has been considerably reduced in shortening with a changed formula. If it were eliminated from all foods except home pie baking, its deleterious effect would be negligible.

PIECRUST INGREDIENTS

Flour—There is no doubt that all-purpose flour, preferably a low-gluten Southern brand, is a superior flour for making piecrusts. See page 451 for more information. Flours absorb moisture from the air differently, so flour can rarely be measured exactly. Keep extra flour handy in a flour shaker, and be prepared to add more water to make a dough roll out smoothly rather than crumble. Once the water is added to a portion of the dough, the dough should be worked as little as possible, as water develops the gluten in flour and toughens the dough.

Sifting, or lightening, is not necessary for most modern flours unless they are old or lumpy. Whisking is the modern method of "sifting," first in the container and then in the bowl with any other dry ingredients, such as salt or sugar.

Fat—Using lard or shortening is best for beginning pie makers, as they make a lighter, more tender crust. Butter makes for a more flavorful and flaky crust but it is crisper and can be less tender. Practice using different fats. After each dough is formed, roll it out, cut off a small strip, and bake it and the other practice crust strips. See which one is best—flaky, crumbly, whatever suits your taste. Taste them, and if they are good, use them. If they are not, toss them out with no qualms at all, as a golfer would a bad golf ball.

There is a much better chance of making a good crust, whether with hands or in a food processor, if the fat is added in two stages. First work half of the fat cut into 1/4-inch pieces into the flour until it looks like crumbled blue cheese, which causes tenderness throughout; secondly, work in the remaining fat, cut into 1/2-inch pieces, until these pieces of butter are the size of kernels of corn. These

Originally, pies were flour and water "doughs" devised for wrapping around other foods to keep them from burning and to keep them moist in a wood oven or fireplace. The crust around the four-and-twenty blackbirds was not meant to be eaten, nor were any of the earlier ones.

A clever cook realized that, with the addition of a little fat, not only could a pie be eaten but the fat would enhance the food in it as well. Nowadays, a good piecrust is an integral part of a pie and should complement the filling, both in texture and taste—one reason there are so many types of crusts. Other reasons include type of flour and fat used, and temperature at which the crust is baked. Until the advent of air-conditioning in the 1950s, it was crazy-making to attempt piecrust in the Deep South in the middle of summer.

contribute flakiness (page 504). By the time the second fat is incorporated, the first is about the size of cornmeal. This is easily done in the food processor, but learning by hand to recognize each step is a better resource for the cook. This two-step procedure produces a tender as well as flaky crust.

Liquid—Once water is added to a portion of the dough, the dough should be worked as little as possible, as water develops the gluten in flour and toughens the dough.

Adding more liquid rather than less will make the dough easier to handle, particularly for the novice. Gentle handling of the dough once the water is added prevents toughness. For this reason, our Very Beginner's Piecrust (pages 504–6) divides the flour/fat into portions to which the liquid is added rather than sprinkling the whole mass and running the risk of overworking the entire quantity of dough. Adding a dash of lemon juice or vinegar to the water will make the crust more tender. Adding ice to the measuring cup of water will help keep the water cold and still allow the water to be easily added to the dough in spoonfuls. A friend says putting water with ice in a martini shaker is an easy method for measuring out the desired amount of cold water.

PIECRUST EQUIPMENT

Pie Pans—In trying to be exact about pie pan size, we found some treacherous discrepancies—no two of my glass pie pans measured the same. Some would be 9 inches at the top, but only 7 inches at the bottom. Others had quite different measures. This was also true of some pretty ceramic dishes. Tart pans have straight sides, so the top and bottom measure the same. It helps to set glass and ceramic pie pans on top of metal baking sheets in the oven, as the metal conducts heat to the bottom of the glass, helping it brown and speeding cooking a bit.

Metal pie pans make a better crust because they conduct the heat faster. That said, the darker the pan the darker the crust, which can be a mixed blessing. If using dark pans, reduce the oven temperature by 25 degrees. With the exception of double-crust, deep-dish, and meringue pies, I would rather use metal tart pans with removable bottoms, because the tarts or pies can be removed and stand alone, making them prettier and easier to cut and serve.

A pastry cutter and/or forks, a flour shaker, a pastry brush, and a pastry scraper are all helpful when rolling out the dough. Rolling pins vary widely according to personal preference. A short stubby rolling pin will not be as easy to use as one that is longer than the width of the finished dough.

SELECTING A PIECRUST RECIPE

The pie recipes in this section give the baker instructions to use a specific piecrust recipe or select another favorite.

For the first-time pie baker: you must follow the detailed instructions in the Very Beginner's Piecrust. Note: that recipe yields a pie dough suitable for all pies in this book. Following is an annotated list of all the piecrust recipes in the book:

Very Beginner's Piecrust (page 504)—for the true beginner, with detailed instructions, suitable for all pie recipes.

Basic Piecrust (page 507)—suitable for all pie recipes.

Double-Crust Piecrust (page 508)—suitable for all double-crust pies, although every piecrust recipe in this book can be made into a double-crust pie simply by doubling the ingredients.

Food Processor Piecrust (page 509)—a basic piecrust made in the food processor, easy once the baker is familiar with how the dough should look, and suitable for all pie recipes.

Mixer Piecrust (page 510)—a basic piecrust made in an electric stand mixer, easy once the baker is familiar with how the dough should look, and suitable for all pie recipes.

Sweet Piecrust (page 511)—a rich, sweet "short" crust, very easy to make, used most often for tarts or tassies.

Very Versatile Cream Cheese Dough (page 512)—a sweet crust, easily made in the food processor, and suitable for all pie recipes where a sweet, flaky, browned crust is desired.

Cookie Crusts (page 513)—perhaps the easiest of all crusts, and most suited to sweet pies.

Pecan Crust (page 514)—an easy-to-make sweet "short" crust containing chopped pecans, suitable for many pies, in particular the Caramel Cream Pecan Crust Pie (page 527).

PIECRUST TECHNIQUES

Working the dough—Cut the fat into the flour either with a snapping motion of thumb and finger, or with two knives or forks, or with a pastry cutter. Overworking the fat and flour will cause the gluten strands to shorten, as in a cookie or short-crust dough. It is natural for a beginner to overwork the dough. A method that works well is to add some liquid to a portion of the ingredients, push it aside, add liquid to another portion, etc., until all portions are moistened, then gathering together all the portions and flattening into a round of dough. The standard method of sprinkling the ingredients with water before working it in is more difficult for the novice cook.

Shaping and resting the dough—Once the fat, flour, and liquid are combined to make dough, form it into the shape that will be needed for the final pie—usually a round. Pull the dough together, shape it into a ball with two hands moving around the outside edge of the dough to turn it on the counter, then press it into a 6-inch or larger disc. The bottom of the dough is smoothed by the counter; the top by patting it lightly. The thinner the disc, the faster the dough will chill, the more the gluten will relax, and the easier it will be to roll out. A thick ball is difficult to press down, takes longer to chill, and is harder to roll. Wrap the dough in plastic wrap or slide it into a plastic bag. Note the time and date, in case you want to save it for another day. Refrigerate at least 30 minutes to relax any gluten that may have developed. The longer this dough rests, the more it will relax, up to several days.

Rolling the dough—Flouring or not flouring when rolling the dough depends on the heat of the kitchen, the type of surface, and the wetness of the dough. Many times, novices assume a sticky piecrust is wet, when, in fact, that is a sign the dough is too hot, the fat has melted, or the dough has been overworked. The temptation is to add more flour and wind up with a mess. If not sure whether the dough has enough liquid, take a small piece and push it gently on a floured work surface. If it releases easily, it is just a little wet. If it comes off in pieces, the chances are the fat has been overworked and not enough liquid was added. Rolling out the dough between sheets of plastic wrap or in a large plastic bag helps, and chilling it before and after rolling even more so. There are even pastry cloths and plastic sheets—some with circles drawn on—that are great aids in pie rolling. Whatever works is fine!

Use a long, wide rolling pin, longer than the diameter of the ultimate round. (I use one with no handle.) This will allow long, sweeping strokes rather than a series of small strokes, which takes more time and overworks the dough.

Keep a flour shaker filled with all-purpose flour and a pastry brush handy. Sprinkle the counter with flour and move the disc to the counter. If the dough is sticky, sprinkle flour on top of the dough. Brush the top of the dough lightly with the pastry brush to remove any excess but leaving on any flour that is clinging. Sprinkle the rolling pin with flour and lightly rub it all over. Move the rolling pin to the center of the unwrapped disc. Roll forward from the middle, preferably in one stroke, to the edge but not over the edge. Pick up and return the rolling pin to the middle of the disc and roll backwards to the edge. Pick up the dough. If it sticks, use a pastry scraper to help lift it off the counter. Sprinkle the counter with flour as necessary, and move the dough clockwise a quarter of a circle to keep the dough round. Continue this way until the dough has a diameter 2 inches larger than the pie pan, moving and turning the dough a quarter of a circle in clockwise fashion each time after each rolling; this prevents the dough from sticking to the counter and keeps it in a rough circle.

Filling the pie pan—Lightly wrap the dough around the rolling pin and move it to the pie pan. Unroll carefully into the pan, or fold the dough in quarters then settle it around the bottom and sides of the pan, extending it over

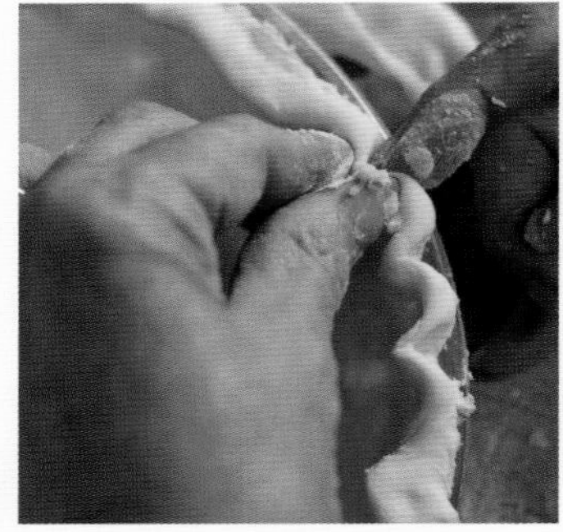

the rim. If it is not centered properly, slide a hand under the dough and move it carefully. Gently lift the dough so it is banked against the sides without stretching. Use a sharp knife, slanting upward from below, or a good scissors, and trim the excess dough from around the outside of the pan to leave a 3/4- to 1-inch overhang of dough. Fold the extra inch of dough under itself on the rim of the pan. Run a fingernail underneath it to be sure it is not stuck on the edge. Refrigerate for at least 1 hour or freeze for 20 to 30 minutes. (When the cold crust is moved to the hot oven, the flour sets and steam helps the cold fat to explode, creating flakiness.)

Decorating the edges—The simplest decoration is to take two fingers or a fork, floured if necessary, and press quickly around the edge. Fluting the rim of the pie is another option. Pinch thumb and pointing figure together to form a V on the inside of the piecrust's rim. Push in with the forefinger of the other hand, making an indentation enabling the dough to "stand up" on the rim. Continue around the pie. Other edges include pressing the pastry-covered rim with the tines of a fork, or cutting out pieces of dough into shapes such as leaves, hearts, etc., to decorate the top and edge of the pie.

Gather and roll scraps of pastry, layering together. Wrap and refrigerate in case patching is needed or decorations are desired. (Wadding the dough into a ball will make it tougher, and the patch will be uneven.) If not needed, these are fine to be rolled out, cut into strips, sprinkled with sugar and/or cinnamon, and baked for snacks.

Chill any decorated scraps before baking and watch carefully in the oven, as they cook quickly due to their size.

Patching cracks—If the dough crumbles and cracks, it needs more water. Water is hard to add, so try rolling the dough between plastic wrap, pushing together as much as possible. If it still is too dry, a food processor comes in handy. Tear the dough into large pieces, place in a food processor with a metal blade or pastry blade, and add 1 or 2 tablespoons of water. Process quickly. Pull the dough into a ball and then pat into a round disc. This dough must rest an hour in the refrigerator, or preferably overnight. After all, it has had a hard time!

Cracks that develop while rolling can be patched with stray pieces of dough. Brush the area around the crack with water and affix the stray piece of dough over the crack; press to seal. The cracked pastry bakes along with the rest of the pie. No one will notice!

Patch a cracked already-baked piecrust in the same manner and return it to the oven for 10 to 15 minutes, covering any brown areas with foil to prevent overcooking.

Prebaking piecrust—Prebaking enhances all pie dough, as it prevents the crust from becoming soggy. *There are two types of prebaking:* one is to prebake the crust completely for a filling that needs no further cooking; the other type of prebaking is to cook the crust to the point where it is thoroughly set and on its way to browning, then to add the filling and return it to the oven. Prebaking unfilled dough is done at higher temperatures than is safe for custard and other delicate fillings. The prebaked crust allows the custard fillings to keep their soft textures without curdling but finish baking at a lower temperature. If the crust becomes brown when filled, cover with foil to prevent further browning of the edges, or turn down the oven heat—or both.

There are several methods of pre-baking. Prick the bottom of the crust all over with a fork or other piercing mechanism. Weigh down the crust to prevent it from bubbling up. Crumble a piece of parchment or waxed paper, or buttered aluminum foil, open it up completely over the crust and up the sides. Fill the paper with a mixture of dry ingredients, usually a combination of rice and beans, commercial pie weights of ceramic or metal, or even clean copper pennies. Store the weights, whatever they may be, in an ovenproof bag (similar to what is sold to roast a turkey or chicken) so the whole bag can be settled in and no parchment will be needed.

Resting the piecrust—After lining the pie pan, wrap tightly and refrigerate for at least 30 minutes before baking. Resting and chilling dough makes it more tender and less elastic. Freezing does not let the gluten rest, as it suspends it, but if frozen before going into a hot oven, the butter won't melt before the flour sets. The colder the shaped piecrust is when it goes into the oven the better, so the flour sets before the butter melts.

Piecrusts can be frozen at this point. Alas, freezing doesn't rest the gluten; it suspends it, so it does nothing for the tenderness. But it certainly does keep the butter from melting before the flour sets. Avoid using a pie dish that cannot take the temperature extremes of moving from freezer to oven.

Shaping free-form tarts—Free-form tarts are baked flat on a rimmed baking sheet instead of inside a tart pan. They may be cut or shaped into any design, but circles and rectangles are most common. As with any crust, these perform better when chilled or frozen before placing into the hot oven. Bake before or after adding filling, depending on the filling. To build up the sides of the tart, brush one rim of the dough lightly with water and gently press strips of dough on top. Decorate the strips and rim as with any pie.

USING STORE-BOUGHT CRUSTS

There are piecrusts on the market that are worth a try for a cook who doesn't make piecrust frequently enough to feel confident. The kind currently available that works the best is sold in elongated packages with two crusts rolled inside. Bring them to room temperature before unrolling and shaping further. They vary in quality, but all are superior to the frozen crusts in flimsy tins and the boxed mixes to which water is added. Diligent searching in gourmet stores can sometimes result in finding all-butter piecrusts for sale, which are nearly like homemade. Be sure to follow package directions.

VERY BEGINNER'S PIECRUST (*PÂTE BRISÉE*)

Makes 1 (9-inch) piecrust

BEGINNERS NEED ALL THE HELP THEY CAN GET *when making their first piecrust. I've done so many dumb things, like rolling out a piecrust on top of a going dishwasher spewing out heat and steam, that I am making sure this includes all the tricks of the trade. A more experienced piecrust baker may skip this; but for those making a piecrust for the first time or two, read all the tips and the pie making basics on pages 499–503 first, before moving to this recipe. No one was born knowing how to make a piecrust, so try to do this at a calm, leisurely time, preferably when the kitchen is cool.*

This recipe is unique in two ways. First, it divides the fat into two different-sized cubes. The first portion is well incorporated and adds tenderness. The second portion is less incorporated so remains larger and adds flakiness. The second unique method is dividing the both flour and ice water into four portions, adding a portion of water to each portion of flour, removing what is dampened, then gathering all the damp dough into a ball and patting it smooth.

For answers about which types of fats and flours to use, see page 499 before proceeding. Beginners should use shortening or lard for their first crusts; after that, a mixture of half shortening and half butter is my favorite combination.

Water and over manipulation (overworking) are enemies of piecrust, as they encourage too much development of gluten. A high ratio of fat to flour is used in mixing this dough so that extra flour may be added when rolling and shaping the dough.

1¼ cups all-purpose flour, preferably soft-wheat
½ teaspoon salt
½ cup cold shortening, lard, and/or unsalted butter, divided
6–8 tablespoons cold water, preferably iced, divided
1 large egg mixed with 1 tablespoon water, to glaze

Before measuring the flour, whisk a portion of flour in its container with a wire whisk or fork to lighten. Take a large spoon and scoop up the flour from the container and slide it into a dry measuring cup. When full, level off any excess flour with the back of a knife and move the flour to a wide bowl. A wide bowl allows for a light hand when working in the fat rather than a bowl with a small diameter and high sides, which encourages overworking. Whisk the flour and salt together in the bowl to distribute the salt evenly.

Cut half of the fat into ¼-inch cubes and the second half into ½-inch cubes. (This can be done ahead and the fat refrigerated until ready to use.) Add the ¼-inch cubes of fat to the flour. Cut fat into the flour in one of several ways. 1) Grasp a small portion of the flour mixture and, holding it an inch or so above the rest of the flour, rub it between the third finger and the thumb in a snapping motion, repeating until the fat is broken up into fine pieces resembling oatmeal. 2) Use two knives or forks to make broad crisscross cutting motions in the bowl to "chop" the ¼-inch cubes or fat until they look like oatmeal or grits. Quickly add the ½-inch cubes and rub or cut in as above until the larger pieces are the size of corn kernels and the smaller the size of cornmeal. Shake the bowl occasionally to enable the larger pieces of fat to bounce to the top.

Push the flour to the sides of the bowl, leaving an empty well in the center, revealing a small part of the bottom of the bowl. Dump a fourth of the cold water into the well. Using the fingers of one hand, a rubber or metal spatula, or a fork, stir a fourth of the flour into the well, making little clumps. Push the clumps together to make a rough, lumpy dough. If they won't cling together, add a bit more water. It is better to add too much water than not enough, as a dry dough cracks and is harder to handle. Remove the wet, rough mass and set aside wherever convenient on plastic wrap or a board, or slide up the side of the wide bowl until needed. Repeat, using a third of the remaining flour and water each time; mix each portion in the well, then the next, until all flour is used, removing or sliding up the side of the bowl to store briefly.

Gather all four portions of dough together into a mound and quickly dab it around the bowl to gather any loose pieces of dough. Move the dough to a clean, lightly floured board. Make a ball from the dough; flatten and fold onto itself two times. Cupping the dough with both hands, rotate the dough a few times to slightly smooth the still rough dough and flatten the bottom of the dough and the sides into a disc. Pat the top smooth, making a 6- or 8-inch-wide or wider disc. The thinner the disc, the easier the dough will come to room temperature. Wrap carefully or insert into a plastic ziplock bag and refrigerate at least 30 minutes or up to 5 days to rest the dough.

Sprinkle a cool counter surface with flour. (A novice will need more flour than a practiced pie maker.) Unwrap the dough and center on the lightly floured surface. Alternatively, roll it between two sheets of plastic wrap or in a large plastic bag. Push dough slightly with one finger to see if it is pliable. If too cold, the dough will crack. Check every few minutes until the dough becomes pliable enough to roll but is still cool. Flour a rolling pin (if using plastic wrap or bag, no flour is needed), and begin rolling the dough by placing the rolling pin in the middle of the disc and lightly rolling forward. Avoid pressing the rolling pin down into the dough. Stop rolling just before the edge of the dough. Lift and move the rolling pin back to the middle of the dough and roll backwards to the edge. If the dough develops cracks, push the cracks together with a finger. The dough is still too cold, let sit a few minutes more.

If any dough sticks to the rolling pin or board, scrape off any stuck portions, and sprinkle the rolling pin, surface, and dough with flour. Brush off any excess flour with a pastry brush. Pick up the dough slightly, flour the counter, and rotate the dough a quarter turn to the right. If necessary, re-flour the counter or pin. Move the rolling pin to the middle of the dough and roll forward and backward as before. Moving the dough will keep it from sticking. Start in the center each time after turning to keep the dough round. Move as quickly as possible. Avoid rolling the pin over the edges to keep the edges and center the same depth. Turn again. Proceed this way until the dough is about 1/8 inch thick and 2 inches larger than the total diameter of the pan plus the depth of its sides. If it is not in a rough circle, cut off ungainly pieces and add on to form a rough circle.

Move the dough to the pie pan by lightly wrapping the dough around the rolling pin and moving it an inch or so above the pie pan. (If using a tart pan with a removable bottom, surround the bottom and sides of the tart pan tightly with foil to prevent any filling from leaking out while baking.) Unroll carefully into the pan and settle it around the bottom and sides of the pan, extending it over the rim. If it is not centered properly, slide a hand under the dough and move it carefully. Gently lift the dough so it is banked against the sides without stretching. Take a floured knuckle and press the sides down to the bottom to be sure there is no air under the crust and the dough is not stretched in such a way that it will bounce back or slide later.

Holding the pan up in the air, use a sharp knife, slanting upward, or good scissors, and trim the excess

dough from around the outside of the pan to leave a 1-inch overhang of dough. Fold the extra dough under itself on of the pie pan. Decorate the edge as desired (page 502 and shown at right).

Chill the dough-filled pie pan 30 minutes or preferably several hours, or up to 5 days. Wrap the dough with plastic wrap or refrigerate in a plastic bag. Layer the scraps and roll together without wadding the dough into a ball.

When ready to prebake, preheat oven to 375 degrees. Gently prick the bottom of the dough in the pie pan with a fork several times. This allows for the expansion of the dough.

Crumple a 12-inch piece of parchment, waxed paper, or aluminum foil; reopen, smooth out, and spread in the bottom and sides of the pie shell, extending past the rim. Pour about 2 cups of raw rice, beans, or baking weights onto the paper, taking care to avoid spilling any of it onto the piecrust itself rather than the paper. Spread out on top of the paper to weigh down the bottom crust and push some of the rice or beans up the sides to stop the sides of the dough from sliding while baking. A roasting bag, as used for roasting chicken, is an ideal substitute for the paper. It can be filled with rice and beans or weights, put on the crust, removed, and reused at a later time.

Move the pie pan to a rimmed pizza pan or rimmed baking sheet and bake on the middle rack of the 375-degree oven. Bake 15 minutes. (The paper will not stick when the crust is done but may if the crust is still raw.) When done, scoop out the rice or beans using a measuring cup, cool, and store them for use in another crust. Remove the paper carefully to avoid breaking of the crust. If this does happen, brush the crack lightly with water and press a small piece of the reserved layered dough over the crack.

Mix the egg and water together with a fork and brush over the bottom of the crust. Return the pie to the oven 6 to 8 minutes more to seal the crust. If the crust puffs up while baking, prick gently with a fork. Any holes or cracks can be patched with the reserved scraps of dough. If no scraps are available, dampen the area with a little water and push together as best as possible. Cover the edges of the dough with aluminum foil as needed to prevent over-browning when returning to the oven for final baking. If the filling is pre-cooked or needs no further cooking, return the crust to the oven for another 5 or 10 minutes, until lightly brown on the bottom and a bit darker on the edges. If the filling needs further cooking, check regularly to be sure the crust is not browning too much. Reduce the oven temperature if needed.

BASIC PIECRUST

Makes 1 (9-inch) piecrust

Once all the rules of making piecrusts *are absorbed, it is easy to move to this abbreviated version of instructions and use it as a basic recipe. Be sure to refer back to the previous recipe if any problems happen. My favorite combination of fats is half shortening and half butter, always cold, with the shortening in 1/4-inch cubes and butter in 1/2-inch cubes. The combination of the two gives tenderness and flakiness.*

1 1/4 cups all-purpose flour, preferably soft-wheat
1/2 teaspoon salt
1/2 cup cold shortening, lard, and/or unsalted butter, divided
6 tablespoons cold water, preferably iced, divided
1 large egg mixed with 1 tablespoon water, to glaze

Before measuring the flour, whisk a portion of flour in its container with a wire whisk or fork to lighten. Take a large spoon and scoop up the flour from the container and slide it into a dry measuring cup. When full, level off any excess flour with the back of a knife and move to a wide bowl. Add the salt and whisk again.

Cut the first half of the desired fat into 1/4-inch pieces and the second half into 1/2-inch pieces. Keep refrigerated until needed.

Add the 1/4-inch pieces of fat to the flour, lift a portion, and snap between two fingers, or make a crisscross cutting motion in the bowl with two knives or forks, or use a pastry cutter to manipulate it until the mixture looks like oatmeal or grits. Add the second half of the fat and repeat the same directions until the mixture has some large lumps that look like corn kernels and some that are smaller, like cornmeal.

Hollow out a well in the bottom of the bowl deep enough to reveal a small part of the bottom of the bowl, and pour in 2 tablespoons of water. Stir one-third of the flour into the water in the well until it holds together in little clumps when pressed. Remove the clumps to the counter. Divide remaining mixture and liquid in two and repeat the process with each portion. If there is any flour remaining in the bowl, scoop it out and add to one of the portions. Pull all the dough together on the counter, including dumping in any stray bits left in the bowl, to make a rough dough. Push down to flatten. Fold over twice and then shape into a ball. Flatten to make a large disc, about 8 inches in diameter. Wrap in plastic or place in a plastic bag and refrigerate at least 30 minutes or up to 5 days.

Roll out the pastry (pages 501–2) and line a pie or tart pan with the dough. If using a tart pan with a removable bottom, surround the bottom of the pan with foil to prevent the filling from leaking out while baking. Decorate edges as desired. Chill 30 minutes or more, or freeze if desired.

When ready to use, preheat oven to 375 degrees. Gently prick the bottom of the dough in the pie pan.

Crumple a piece of parchment, waxed paper, or aluminum foil; reopen, smooth out, and place into the piecrust; fill with raw rice and beans and prebake 15 minutes, covering edges as necessary to prevent burning. A roasting bag, as used for roasting chicken, is an ideal substitute for the paper. It can be filled with rice and beans or weights, put on the crust, removed, and reused at a later time. Remove from oven, scoop out rice and beans, remove paper, brush bottom with egg glaze, and return to the oven for 6 to 8 minutes, until the bottom is dry and the piecrust is lightly browned. This produces a completely baked pie crust. Remove from oven, cool on a rack, and fill as desired.

Cold is the piecrust's best friend. All the ingredients should be as cold as possible—fat, flour, and water, and the room cool, too. Work away from the oven heat. Once the dough is made into a disc, wrapping and chilling relaxes the gluten strands in the dough, making it tender. Bring back to room temperature so it won't crack from the cold, and roll into the proper size round. Only refrigerate at this point if hard too handle (sticking, etc.) Fill pie pan. Chill the pastry-lined pan to relax the dough further and to insure the fat is cold going into the hot oven.

DOUBLE-CRUST PIECRUST

Makes 2 (9-inch) piecrusts

A STEAMING, GLISTENING DOUBLE-CRUST PIE *being removed from the oven is an iconic image of American cooking. Here in this recipe we use exactly double the ingredients of a single-crust pie dough, as we prefer having the extra dough for decorating—or patching, if needed. Plus, the extra dough baked with a sprinkle of cinnamon and sugar is a nice reward for any cook's helpers.*

2 1/2 cups all-purpose flour, preferably soft-wheat
1 teaspoon salt
1 cup cold shortening, lard, and/or unsalted butter, divided
12 tablespoons cold water, preferably iced, divided

Make dough using directions on pages 504–6.

Divide finished dough into two discs for rolling; make one portion slightly larger and use that for the top crust. Wrap in plastic or place in a plastic ziplock bag and refrigerate at least 30 minutes or up to 5 days.

Roll out both discs into circles (pages 501–2). The bottom crust should roll out to 2 inches larger than the pie pan, and the top crust 3 inches larger. Add the larger crust to the pie pan and fill according to recipe. After filling the bottom crust with the desired mixture, lightly moisten the rim of the bottom crust with water. Cut a circular strip from around the outside of the second round and press it onto the entire rim of the bottom crust. You may have to do this in sections. Moisten the strip. The top crust adheres to this, which prevents everything sliding into the pan. To move the top crust, fold in half once then fold in half again. Place the point carefully in the center atop the filling. Unfold carefully without stretching. Press the outside edge of the top crust onto the moistened strips. Go around the whole crust pressing the rim firmly. Decorate the edges as desired and remove any excess dough with a sharp knife. Cut decorative slits in the top crust and bake according to recipe.

Variation: For a sweet crust, add 1 tablespoon or up to 4 tablespoons sugar, preferably confectioners'.

Double-crust pies are usually filled without prebaking, although in some cases, particularly deep-dish apple pies, prebaking of the bottom crust only may be done, following the directions for a single-crust recipe. For those rare cases, prebake the bottom crust only if necessary to ensure it will be thoroughly baked at the same time that the filling is done, and not partly raw. Remove the pie weights then fill and follow recipe, adding top crust.

FOOD PROCESSOR PIECRUST

Makes 1 (9-inch) piecrust

IN MANY WAYS, *a food processor crust is the easiest crust to make. Take care not to overprocess the dough at any of the stages. All the ingredients should be very cold, as room-temperature ingredients will over-incorporate. An all-butter crust is more easily mastered in a food processor than by hand. We suggest starting with half shortening and half butter, and then moving on to all butter and seeing which is preferred.*

1 1/4 cups all-purpose flour, preferably soft-wheat
1/2 teaspoon salt
1/2 cup frozen shortening, lard, and/or unsalted butter, divided
5–6 tablespoons cold water, preferably iced
1 large egg mixed with 1 tablespoon water, to glaze

Before measuring the flour, whisk a portion of flour in its container with a wire whisk or fork to lighten. Take a large spoon and scoop up the flour from the container and slide it into a dry measuring cup. When full, level off any excess flour with the back of a knife. Add to the food processor along with the salt and pulse 3 or 4 times, until mixed. Divide the fat into two sections, and cut one half into 1/4-inch cubes and the other into 1/2-inch cubes. Add half of the frozen fat and pulse until the size of cornmeal. Add the remainder of the fat and pulse until the mixture looks like oatmeal or grits. Add 5 tablespoons water all at once and pulse quickly until little clumps are formed that stay together when pinched. Add more water if they do not. Resist the temptation to run the processor too long, allowing a ball of dough to form. This will produce a tough piecrust.

Taking care to avoid the metal blade, pull the clumps out onto a floured board and form into a ball; flatten out and fold two times, then form into a round and flatten into an 8-inch disc. Place in a plastic ziplock bag or wrap in plastic and refrigerate at least 30 minutes or up to 5 days.

Roll out the pastry (pages 501–2) and line a pie or tart pan with the dough. If using a tart pan with a removable bottom, surround the bottom and sides of the tart pan tightly with foil to prevent any filling from leaking out while baking. Decorate edges as desired. Chill 30 minutes or more, or freeze if desired. When ready to use, preheat oven to 375 degrees. Crumple a piece of parchment, waxed paper, or aluminum foil; reopen, smooth out, and place into the piecrust; fill with raw rice and beans and bake 15 minutes, covering edges as necessary to prevent burning. A roasting bag, as used for roasting chicken, is an ideal substitute for the paper. It can be filled with rice and beans or weights, put on the crust, removed, and reused at a later time. Remove from oven, scoop out rice and beans, remove paper, brush bottom with egg glaze, and return to the oven for 6 to 8 minutes, or until completely baked. Remove from oven, cool on a rack, and fill as desired.

MIXER PIECRUST

Makes 1 (9-inch) piecrust

A LARGE STAND MIXER IS BEST *for making mixer piecrusts. Small electric hand mixers tend to get the fat stuck in the beaters and seem more frustrating than speedy.*

1 1/4 cups all-purpose flour, preferably soft-wheat
1/2 teaspoon salt
1/2 cup cold shortening, lard, and/or unsalted butter, divided
6 tablespoons cold water, preferably iced, divided
1 large egg mixed with 1 tablespoon water, to glaze

Before measuring the flour, whisk a portion of flour in its container with a wire whisk or fork to lighten. Take a large spoon and scoop up the flour from the container and slide it into a dry measuring cup. When full, level off any excess flour with the back of a knife and move to the mixer bowl. Add the salt and mix with the paddle blade until well mixed.

Cut the first half of the fat into 1/4-inch pieces and the second half into 1/2-inch pieces. Add first half of the fat and mix until the size of oatmeal or grits, preferably with a paddle blade. Add the second half and mix until the mixture has some large lumps that look like corn kernels and some that are smaller, like cornmeal. Add the water and mix quickly until little clumps are formed that stay together when pinched; add more water if they do not. Pull the clumps out onto a floured board and form into a ball; flatten out and fold two times, then make into a round and flatten into an 8-inch disc. Move to a plastic ziplock bag or wrap in plastic for at least 30 minutes or up to 5 days.

Roll out the pastry (page 501) and line a pie or tart pan with the dough. If using a tart pan with a removable bottom, surround the bottom of the pan with foil to prevent the filling from leaking out while baking. Decorate edges as desired. Chill 30 minutes or more, freezing if desired.

When ready to use, preheat oven to 375 degrees. Crumple a piece of parchment, waxed paper, or aluminum foil; reopen, smooth out, and place into the piecrust; fill with raw rice and beans and prebake 15 minutes, covering edges as necessary to prevent burning. A roasting bag, as used for roasting chicken, is an ideal substitute for the paper. It can be filled with rice and beans or weights, put on the crust, removed, and reused at a later time.

Remove from oven, scoop out rice and beans, remove paper, brush bottom with egg glaze, and return to the oven for 6 to 8 minutes, or until completely baked. Remove from oven, cool on a rack, and fill as desired.

SWEET PIECRUST (*PÂTÉ SUCRÉE*)

Makes 1 (9-inch) piecrust

SPECIFICALLY DESIGNED FOR FRUIT PIES, pâté sucrée *means "sweet pastry" in French. The dough produces a sweet, buttery "short" dough, more like a cookie dough than a flaky piecrust. It is nearly impossible to make incorrectly. Since no water is added, overworking the fat is no problem, as short gluten strands are desired. The egg yolks are a fatty protein, adding richness and color to the crust. This can be made in the food processor or a mixer with equal success. The edges of a* pâté sucrée *pie are rarely decorated. Completely prebake before filling. This can be made in the food processor or mixer with equal success.*

1 cup all-purpose flour, preferably soft-wheat
1/4 cup unsalted butter, at room temperature
1/3 cup granulated sugar
2 egg yolks, beaten to mix
1/4 teaspoon vanilla extract
1 large egg mixed with 1 tablespoon water, to glaze

Before measuring the flour, whisk a portion of flour in its container with a wire whisk or fork to lighten. Take a large spoon and scoop up the flour from the container and slide it into a dry measuring cup. When full, level off any excess flour with the back of a knife and move to a counter or flat surface. Push the flour away from the center to make an empty place. Add the butter, sugar, mixed egg yolks, and vanilla. Mix these together roughly. Pull in the flour a bit at a time, pressing the whole mixture together until a dough forms. Turn out onto a lightly floured counter and form into a ball. Press the ball out to be a smooth, flat disc, about 8 inches in diameter. (Don't worry if it sticks.) Wrap well with plastic wrap or place in a large plastic bag, and refrigerate for 1 to 2 hours.

Remove the dough from the refrigerator. Press occasionally until soft enough to manipulate. Unwrap dough and move to a lightly floured surface, between two sheets of plastic wrap or into a large plastic bag. Roll or press out enough to line bottom and sides of a pie or tart pan with the dough. Do not worry if it breaks or crumbles when moving to the pan. Since it has no water, it can be pressed in if necessary. If using a tart pan with a removable bottom, surround the bottom of the pan with foil to prevent the filling from leaking out while baking. Chill 30 minutes or more or freeze if necessary.

When ready to use, preheat oven to 350 degrees. Crumple a piece of parchment, waxed paper, or aluminum foil; reopen, smooth out, and place into the piecrust; fill with raw rice and beans and prebake 15 minutes, covering edges as necessary to prevent burning. Remove from oven, scoop out rice and beans, remove paper, and brush bottom with egg glaze. Reduce the heat to 300 degrees and return to the oven for 6 to 8 minutes, or until completely baked. Remove from oven, cool on a rack, and fill as desired.

Variation: Food Processor Version

Process flour 3 or 4 times in a food processor. Add butter, sugar, egg, and vanilla and pulse until a smooth dough is formed; remove carefully and proceed as above.

Variation: Mixer Version

Measure the flour into a wide bowl. Beat in the butter, sugar, egg, and vanilla until incorporated into a dough. Remove and proceed as above.

VERY VERSATILE CREAM CHEESE DOUGH

Makes 1 (9-inch) piecrust or 30 to 40 tassies

THIS IS A MIRACLE DOUGH. *Anyone can make it, although it is easiest made in a food processor or mixer. It is flaky and tender and browns beautifully. All this is due to the cream cheese, which emulsifies, adds color, tenderizes, and is pretty indestructible. Its only moment of trickiness is rolling it out, as it wants to stick and pull apart. Sticking and pulling apart doesn't hurt the dough, as it can be pushed back together, but it is a bit scary when it first happens. Rolling the dough between pieces of plastic wrap or in a large plastic bag may ease the anxiety.*

1 cup all-purpose flour, preferably soft-wheat
1 (3-ounce) package cream cheese, cut into 4 pieces and chilled
1/2 cup unsalted butter, cut into 1/2-inch cubes and frozen
1 large egg mixed with 1 tablespoon water, to glaze

Before measuring the flour, whisk a portion of flour in its container with a wire whisk or fork to lighten. Take a large spoon and scoop up the flour from the container and slide it into a dry measuring cup. When full, level off any excess flour with the back of a knife. Add the flour to the bowl of a food processor.

Add the butter and pulse until the size of oatmeal or grits. Add the cream cheese and pulse quickly until it becomes dough. Scrape out the dough between two pieces of plastic wrap or onto a large plastic bag. Press dough into a smooth, flat disc, about 8 inches in diameter. Move the dough to a clean plastic bag or wrap in plastic, and refrigerate at least 30 minutes or up to 5 days. If making tassies, follow directions on page 520.

Roll out the pastry into a 1/8-inch-thick round between two pieces of plastic wrap or in a large plastic bag. If using a tart pan with a removable bottom, surround the bottom and sides of the tart pan tightly with foil to prevent any filling from leaking out while baking. Remove the top sheet of plastic wrap or slit the bag and flip the dough into a pie or tart pan. Remove second sheet. Decorate edges as desired. Chill 30 minutes or more, or freeze if desired.

When ready to use, preheat oven to 350 degrees. Crumple a piece of parchment, waxed paper, or aluminum foil; reopen, smooth out, and place into the piecrust; fill with raw rice and beans and prebake 15 minutes, covering edges as necessary to prevent burning. A roasting bag, as used for roasting chicken, is an ideal substitute for the paper. It can be filled with rice and beans or weights, put on the crust, removed, and reused at a later time.

Remove from oven, scoop out rice and beans, remove paper, and brush bottom with egg glaze. Reduce the heat to 300 degrees and return to the oven for 6 to 8 minutes, or until completely baked. Remove from oven, cool on a rack, and fill as desired.

CREAM CHEESE DOUGH WITH VINEGAR

Makes 1 (9-inch) piecrust

Rose Levy Beranbaum, *author of the* Cake Bible *and* The Pie and Pastry Bible, *said she "loved the word* pie, *particularly the way Southern Women said it.* Paaah, *sort of like a sigh." She developed this cream cheese dough recipe where the acid helps produce a more tender crust. This crust is just a little bit more difficult to work with, so abide by the instructions for using plastic wrap or a large plastic bag (facing). As always, keep pie dough cold.*

1 1/3 cups pastry or bleached all-purpose flour, preferably soft-wheat
1/8 teaspoon baking powder
1/8 teaspoon salt
8 tablespoons unsalted butter, cut into 1/2-inch cubes and frozen
1 (3-ounce) package cream cheese, cut into 4 pieces and chilled
2 tablespoons heavy cream
2 teaspoons cider vinegar
1 large egg mixed with 1 tablespoon water, to glaze

Use the directions for Cream Cheese Dough (facing), adding the baking powder and salt with the flour in the food processor and pulse 3 or 4 times to combine. After pulsing in the fats, pulse in the cream and vinegar and continue with the recipe directions facing.

COOKIE CRUSTS

Makes 1 (8- or 9-inch) crust

Gingersnaps, chocolate and vanilla wafers, *butter cookies, and shortbreads were among the first cookie crusts I ever made. Certainly they are the easiest, impossible to ruin and, let's face it, yummy. Use this in place of other short crusts or nut crusts.*

1 1/2 cups crushed graham crackers, gingersnaps, vanilla or chocolate wafers, or butter cookies
6 tablespoons unsalted butter, melted
1/4 cup granulated sugar

Crush cookies inside a plastic bag using a rolling pin. Move to a bowl. Add butter and sugar, and blend together. If using a tart pan with a removable bottom, surround the bottom of the pan with foil to prevent the filling from leaking out while baking. Pour into a 9-inch tart pan or pie pan. Smooth out the mixture evenly and press up the sides of the pan. Chill in the freezer for 5 to 10 minutes, or until set.

When ready to bake, preheat oven to 350 degrees. Bake for 10 minutes. Cool on a rack to room temperature. Fill as desired.

Variations:

- Add 1/4 cup chopped pecans.
- For an absolutely splendid crust, add 2 chopped dry figs to the butter and sugar before pressing into the tart pan or pie pan.

Store-bought pre-ground cookie crumbs tend to taste stale and are more finely ground than when done by hand or in a food processor. If using store-bought, use 1 to 2 tablespoons less per measured cup.

PECAN CRUST

Makes 1 (9-inch) piecrust

THIS VERSATILE CRUST *is at home in either a pie pan or a tart pan and is the base used for the sinful Caramel Cream Pecan Crust Pie on page 527. It is one of those pies I dream about and yearn for.*

- 1/2 cup plus 2 tablespoons unsalted butter, at room temperature
- 1/2 cup granulated sugar
- 1 1/3–1 1/2 cups all-purpose flour, preferably soft-wheat
- 1/4 teaspoon salt
- 1 1/4 cups chopped pecans, divided

Beat the butter and sugar together until light, using a food processor or electric hand mixer. Sift the flour with the salt onto a piece of waxed paper.

Chop half the pecans more finely, keeping them larger than a crumb. Add both the finely chopped and roughly chopped pecans to the flour mixture. Pulse once or stir this into the butter-sugar mixture, pulling it all together to make the dough. Shape into a round and flatten. Place between two pieces of plastic wrap or in a large plastic bag. Roll out into a 1/8-thick round of approximately 11 inches. (If the dough is sticking miserably, add some flour and start again. Extra handling will not hurt this short crust dough.)

Chill the dough 30 minutes, or until firm. (It may be refrigerated several days or frozen.) If using a tart pan with a removable bottom, surround the bottom of the pan with foil to prevent the filling from leaking out while baking. Remove the top sheet of plastic wrap or slit the bag and flip the dough into a 9-inch tart pan. Push the dough onto the sides of the pan, pushing together any cracked places in the dough. Check carefully to see if there are any holes; if so, patch them. Save any leftover dough for patching later if necessary. Chill another 30 minutes.

When ready to bake, preheat oven to 350 degrees. Move the pan to a rimmed baking sheet and bake 10 minutes. Remove when still soft and pastry has turned light brown. There should be just a faint scent of cooking pecans in the air; more than that indicates the crust is overcooked. Check for cracks and patch if necessary with the leftover dough.

The crust may be made ahead to this point, kept a day or two at room temperature, or frozen up to 3 months, carefully wrapped. Leftover dough can be cut into small shapes and baked as cookies.

A short crust is a near cookie-like crust having a much higher fat-to-flour ratio than a traditional piecrust. The crust is dense, buttery, and flavorful.

PHYLLO CUPS

Makes 24 cups

THE PHYLLO CUPS SOLD COMMERCIALLY ARE PERFECTLY ACCEPTABLE, *but they do not have the buttery goodness of these. Either make a small batch like this, or double the amount and work with a friend to use a whole package of dough with plenty to freeze. Fill with anything that will fit—savory or sweet. Any phyllo sheets remaining are difficult to reuse if dried out. Usually it is better to discard them.*

4 sheets phyllo dough, thawed according to package directions

1 stick butter, melted

Preheat oven to 325 degrees. Lightly butter the cups of a mini muffin pan.

Unfold room-temperature phyllo dough and move to a baking pan. Cover with a slightly damp (not wet) light cloth, such as a sturdy paper towel or light tea towel. Brush a large rimmed baking sheet with butter and move 1 phyllo sheet on top of the buttered pan. Cover remaining stack of phyllo with the damp cloth and keep it covered while working. Brush phyllo with butter and layer another phyllo sheet on top and press down. Repeat layering and buttering until 4 sheets are buttered.

Cut phyllo stack of 4 sheets into 24 equal squares by cutting into 4 even vertical strips and then cutting each strip horizontally, resulting in 6 even pieces approximately 2¼ inches square. Press 4 layers of squares into each mini muffin pan cup and bake until golden brown and crisp, 15 to 17 minutes. Allow to cool. Repeat process with remaining phyllo dough, melting more butter as necessary. Freeze cups in a sturdy, airtight container up to 3 months. They defrost instantly and may or may not be reheated.

Variations:

- For savory cups, fill with Basic Chicken Salad (page 96), Pimento Cheese (page 57), or Chunky Eggplant Spread (page 52).
- For sweet cups, fill with whipped heavy cream and berries, or Fig Jam (page 646).

RAPID PUFF PASTRY

Makes 1 pound

Found in many Southern cookbooks, *including Thomas Jefferson's and Mary Randolph's, puff pastry (in French* pâté feuilletée, *as differed from cream puff pastry,* pâté a choux*) is a flaky pastry that has 1,000 layers, which is the basis of many sophisticated dishes, such as* mille-feuilles, *or Napoleons. Comprised initially of a dough that is folded in three (or four for some recipes) layers, turned, re-rolled, and refolded, each layer increases exponentially. It takes some care and practice, as well as a cool room. Two kinds of flour are used to make this tender, pliable dough.*

- 3/4 pound (2 3/4 cup, plus 1 tablespoon) bread flour
- 1/4 pound (1 cup) all-purpose soft-wheat flour or cake flour (page 454)
- 1 teaspoon salt
- 1 pound unsalted butter, cold
- 1 cup ice water
- Flour for rolling (either kind)
- 1 egg mixed with 1–2 tablespoons water, to glaze

Before measuring the flour, whisk a portion of flour in its container with a wire whisk or fork to lighten. Take a large spoon and scoop up the flour from the container and slide it into a dry measuring cup. When full, level off any excess flour with the back of a knife and move with the salt to a wooden board, marble slab, or large wide bowl. Cut the butter into 1/2-inch squares. (This can be done ahead and butter kept refrigerated until needed.) Toss briefly with some of the salted flour.

Work the butter into the flour with a pastry scraper, an electric hand mixer, or hands until the flour coats the butter pieces, squeezing them until they are the size of large lima or fava beans.

Move the dough to a board or slab and make a well in the middle of the flour. Without causing any to run onto the floor, add the water starting from the back of the circle of dough, using hands or a pastry scraper to mix together and make a messy clump. Push the clump aside, re-form the circle of flour, add more liquid to the back of the circle of flour, and proceed making little clumps until all the water is used up. Pull the clumps together along with any flour left on the board, and flatten out into a rectangle as much as possible. (It will look terribly messy. Don't worry.) Set it aside on a piece of waxed paper while thoroughly scraping the board clean.

Lightly turn the rough-looking dough out onto the clean surface. Dust the dough and a rolling pin with flour. Brush off any excess. Push or roll the dough out into a rectangle at least 15 inches long and about 8 inches wide. Pick up the dough to be sure it isn't sticking. Dust the surface with flour and place the dough back on it. Don't worry if the dough is crumbly.

Fold the dough over in thirds like a business letter: first fold the bottom up to one-third the way from the top, then fold the top down to cover it. Turn the dough so that the long open side is to the right (I view this as a book with the folded side being the spine and the three unfolded sections forming the pages). Have a flour shaker, pastry brush, and pastry scraper (even a metal spatula will do) at hand. Press down on each of the edges of the "book" so that all the layers will roll in unison. With the "spine" of the book on the left, press down at intervals, forming a series of ridges, making sure that all the layers are pressed together and moving simultaneously. If the butter seems to be coming through, shake flour over, brush off any that does not adhere, and continue.

Return to the bottom, and roll forward between the ridges. At the top, stop short of the end so the rolling pin

> Puff pastry is traditionally equal amounts of flour and butter by weight, half as much water and some salt. The method is more complicated than this one, hence this is called "rapid" when it may not seem so at all. Although my cooking teacher said this was "the most difficult pastry in the world," I find it easy now, and can make a batch of it in less than half an hour of my time, plus resting and chilling time. Oddly enough, the famed Chef Escoffier said it should be made and baked within an hour, which just goes to show that no one knows everything!

does not roll over the edge, causing the top layer to slide out farther than the rest. Get the pastry as long as possible, preferably 15 inches. Move aside. Sprinkle the work surface again with flour and return the dough. (Any time the butter seems to melt in the dough, wrap and refrigerate until cold enough to proceed.) With a floured rolling pin, make slight ridges every few inches to press the dough out as long as possible. Sprinkle the dough with flour, brush it off, and scrape and flour the pin again if necessary. Roll between the ridges until it is a 15 x 8-inch rectangle, stopping short of the edges to avoid rolling over them, which creates an uneven dough. Fold then turn as directed above. Ridge and roll three more times. After the fourth fold and turn, wrap in plastic wrap and let rest in the refrigerator at least 1 hour, or up to 2 days.

Remove the dough from the refrigerator and let sit at room temperature until it is easy to roll but not soft (usually 15 minutes). Give the dough two more rolls, folds, and turns, making a total of six turns, then divide in half. Refrigerate one half. Roll the second half 1/8 inch thick. Repeat with the second half, refrigerating any dough not in use.

Make a test pastry. Use a pizza cutter to cut a small rectangular box 1/8 inch thick and about 2 inches wide by 1 inch. This is called a *feuilletée*. Refrigerate the remainder. Measure the thickness of the small box of dough. If it is 1/4 inch thick rather than the previously rolled 1/8 inch thick, the dough has bounced back and is not at its optimum elasticity. If possible, all the dough should rest, covered, in the refrigerator several hours or overnight.

Preheat oven to 400 degrees. Heat a small pan or rimmed baking sheet lined with parchment paper.

Brush the test piece (preferably 1/8 inch thick or up to 1/4 inch thick if further resting is not an option) with the egg glaze, taking care to avoid getting the glaze over the edges. Place the dough on the preheated pan and cook 10 minutes at 400 degrees. Turn the oven down to 350 degrees. Remove from the oven to a cooling rack when browned to the color of a pecan shell. When cool enough to handle, split the layers in two, and examine the middle portion. Ideally it will be dry. If there is a great deal of "wet appearing" pastry in the center, remove it and throw away, keeping the rest. Put the bottom portion of the *feuilletée* on a plate, fill, and replace the top. If the dough did not rise sufficiently to fill, it may be necessary to use one rectangle of finished dough for the bottom and another as the top, as the dough is not rising sufficiently.

Using the information from this test pastry, or *feuilletée,* roll the remaining dough to the desired thickness, usually close to 1/8 inch. If it bounces back to 1/4 inch, let it rest, tightly covered, in the refrigerator up to 3 days. (If the dough turns a grayish color, the gray is oxidation and disappears once baked.)

Puff pastry may be shaped and refrigerated or frozen. Bake the pastry when cold, preferably frozen, the same way as the test piece above.

Variation: Feuilletées

Cut all the dough into 1/8- or 1/4-inch-thick rectangles approximately 3 x 4 inches. Move to a baking sheet about 1/2 inch apart. Freeze. Remove when frozen, move to a plastic bag, and freeze. When ready to serve, preheat the oven to 400 degrees and heat a baking sheet. Brush still frozen *feuilletée(s)* with the egg glaze. Add the *feuilletée(s)* to the hot sheet. Reduce heat to 350 degrees. Bake *feuilletée(s)* until brown and crisp. Remove. Serve topped with lemon curd, whipped cream, jam, or a savory filling, like chicken salad. To fill, split pastry and fill between two layers, or use two pastries. There are many other shapes and fillings.

Variation: Jalousie

Cut dough into two matching 1/8-inch thick rectangles of any size. Spread a modest layer of raspberry or favorite jam onto one rectangle, leaving a 1/4-inch rim all around. In the center of the other rectangle, make a few horizontal slits, to look like slats in a window blind. Move the slit rectangle on top of the jam, and press the edges of the two rectangles together. Refrigerate or freeze. When ready to use, move the frozen pastry onto a baking sheet. Glaze and bake as above, until brown and crisp.

These directions include baking a test piece of dough. This is a good idea for any pastry. After all, why should anyone be humiliated by serving something they have not even tasted that then turns out to be less than satisfactory? A test piece of dough will enable the baker to know the taste, texture and suitability of the dough for the shapes desired.

NATHALIE'S CREAM PUFFS

Makes 20 puffs, depending on size

In French this is called pâté a choux, *either because it looks like a baby cabbage (*choux*) or because someone thought it sounded like* chaud (for hot). *Nearly every European nation has a version of this dough, which can be baked, fried, boiled, or mixed with other foods to make another product altogether. A version was in Martha Washington's cookbook as well as Thomas Jefferson's. I invented this version thirty years ago and have used it ever since. It makes a roux first, then adds the liquid, stirs until thoroughly cooked, and then beats in the eggs to incorporate air. It's a handy dough to master, as usually the ingredients are readily available and inexpensive. The recipe doubles easily, and the cooked puffs freeze well in a sturdy airtight container. Weighing the bread flour is crucial.*

6 tablespoons unsalted butter
5 3/4 ounces bread flour
1 teaspoon salt
1 tablespoon granulated sugar, optional
1 cup water
4 large eggs
2 egg whites
1 egg yolk mixed with 1 teaspoon water, for glaze

Melt the butter in a heavy 8- to 10-inch frying pan. Whisk together the flour, salt, and optional sugar. Stir into the melted butter over medium heat until the butter and flour come together. Continue to stir until the butter-flour mixture is smooth. Add the water and continue stirring until the mixture comes together. At first it will be paste-colored. When it resembles well-buttered mashed potatoes, with no streaks of white, indicating the flour has been sufficiently cooked , remove from the heat. In a frying pan this should take about 5 minutes.

Cool slightly. Move the paste to a food processor fitted with the metal blade. Mix the eggs and egg whites together; then add the eggs 1/4 cup at a time to the dough, beating after each addition. (This can also be done with an electric hand mixer or a sturdy spoon.) Continue to beat until the dough is glossy and drops slowly from a spoon. At this point, add cheese if desired, and any other flavorings as desired. The mixture may be made ahead to this point and refrigerated tightly covered for several days. Bring back to room temperature before baking.

Preheat oven to 350 degrees.

Line a rimmed baking sheet with parchment or waxed paper. Use a small amount of the dough to hold down the four corners of the paper. Snip a small corner off one end of a plastic or pastry bag. (Using a pastry tube makes a more polished end product but is not crucial.) Prop the bag in a glass or other object able to hold it while filling the bag. Fill the bag one-half to two-thirds full. Gather the rest of the bag up and twist or seal tightly.

Pressing from the tops and sides of the bag, pipe the pastry into nearly identical rounds or other shapes onto the parchment paper. The pastries may vary in size and shape from baking sheet to baking sheet, but those on each sheet should be consistent. Brush puffs with egg glaze and lightly press a fork on top to flatten top of puff. Bake one pan at a time until medium brown,

about 30 minutes, with no paste-colored streaks showing. Remove from oven, insert a needle, skewer, or small knife tip and pierce a hole in the side or bottom of each pastry. Return to oven. Reduce heat to 325 and bake 10 minutes more. Test by removing one puff and setting aside to cool.* Return the batch to the oven as needed, continuing to test. Adjust baking time for remaining pastry. Remove and cool briefly on a rimmed baking sheet before moving to a rack. The puffs may be kept covered a day or so at room temperature or frozen. Recrisp in a 350-degree oven for about 4 to 5 minutes before filling if they have become soggy. Fill as desired before serving.

To fill, insert a pastry tip into the previously cut hole and pipe in a smooth mixture, or split the puff in half horizontally, remove any undercooked centers, and fill with desired mixture. Replace the top and serve.

**Most novices tend to under bake the dough. Before the pan is returned to the oven, set one puff aside. As it cools, it will become softer. If it is not thoroughly cooked, it will become very soft and collapse to the touch. This indicates it was not cooked thoroughly. Return to the oven. After 10 minutes, remove another puff and repeat the test.*

Variations: Sweet and Savory Cream Puff Varieties

- For sweet puffs, add 1 tablespoon granulated sugar to the dough before baking. Bake quarter-sized, split, and fill with whipped heavy cream, custard, or lemon curd. Sprinkle with confectioners' sugar or dip in caramel.
- For a savory version of a cream puff, add 3/4 cup grated Gruyère cheese to the dough. Pipe dime-sized puffs and bake for a shorter time, to serve alone or to add to soups. Bake quarter-sized, split, and fill with chicken salad or other savory fillings.

Both sweet and savory cream puffs accommodate a variety of fillings, from custard and sauces to tasty chopped items such as berries, nuts, or olives. These ingredients can also be added to the batter, as can cocoa or curry powder, when making small puffs as tasty little bites.

PECAN TASSIES

Makes 30 to 40 tassies

TASSIES ARE TINY TARTS, *typically served at parties such as showers. Cream cheese dough is ideal to work with, as it is easily pushed into the tiny tins, but just about any pie dough will work for tarts. Pecans have a certain affection for bourbon, but vanilla is also a good addition. They are a busy cook's secret weapon since they freeze so well.*

1 recipe Very Versatile Cream Cheese Dough (page 512)
1 large egg
1/2 cup packed light or dark brown sugar (use 3/4 cup for a sweeter filling)
1 tablespoon unsalted butter
1 teaspoon bourbon extract, bourbon, or vanilla extract
1/8 teaspoon salt
2/3 cup chopped pecans, divided

Divide the dough into 30 equal balls. Chill the balls for 30 minutes.

Move the balls to 30 tiny, lightly greased, fluted mini tart pans or miniature muffin cups placed on a rimmed baking sheet. Press the dough with fingertips or a tart tamper (a wooden dowel which comes with different-sized rounded ends) against the bottoms and sides. Place the baking sheets with the lined pans in the refrigerator to chill while preparing the filling. If any tassies crack after refrigeration, press a small amount of dough onto the crack to cover.

Preheat oven to 325 degrees. Beat together the egg, brown sugar, butter, extract, and salt in a mixing bowl until all the lumps are gone. Place half the pecans into the dough-lined pans and carefully spoon in the egg mixture, taking care to keep the filling below the sides of the dough, thus preventing it from slipping under the dough and caramelizing, making it difficult to remove the tassie. Dot with the remaining pecans. Bake 25 minutes, or until the filling is set. Cool 5 minutes on a rack, but be sure to remove the tassies from the pans while they are still warm.

If tassies are reluctant to come out of the pan, insert a small thin knife between the tassie and the pan and give the tassie a boost.

These will keep several days closely wrapped or 3 months in the freezer. They defrost quickly at room temperature or heat on a rimmed baking sheet while still frozen.

Variation: Chocolate Pecan Tassies

Add 1/3 cup chocolate chips to the recipe, putting half into the tins with half of the pecans. Dot the filled tins with the remaining half of the chips and nuts.

FRUIT TARTS

Makes 1 (9-inch) flan ring or 30 mini tarts

USE YOUR FAVORITE PIE DOUGH *and add 1 1/2 tablespoons granulated sugar to the dry ingredients, or use a* pâté sucrée *recipe* (page 511) *if you prefer a cookie-like crust.*

Pastry

1 piecrust dough

1 large egg mixed with 1 tablespoon water, to glaze

Filling

3/4 cup apricot or currant jam*

1 tablespoon water

1/2 teaspoon fresh lemon juice

2–2 1/2 cups assorted fruits (such as small strawberries, red and green grapes, kiwi, or raspberries), sliced

To make a large tart, roll out the dough between two sheets of plastic wrap or in a large plastic bag until 10 inches in diameter; then remove top layer of plastic wrap or pull out of the plastic bag. Gently flip the dough over into the flan ring. Remove the second sheet of plastic wrap, if using. Gently settle the dough into the ring without stretching, and trim off the excess dough. If it cracks or is difficult, push it together.

Chill the shaped dough on the baking sheet for at least 15 minutes.

When ready to use, preheat oven to 350 degrees. Crumple a piece of parchment, waxed paper, or aluminum foil; reopen, smooth out, and place into the piecrust; fill with raw rice and beans and prebake 20 minutes, covering edges as necessary to prevent burning. Remove from oven, scoop out rice and beans, remove paper, brush bottom with egg-white glaze, and return to the oven for 10 minutes, or until completely baked. Remove from oven, and cool on a rack.

Heat the jam with water and lemon juice until it reaches the consistency of syrup. Strain.

To glaze, dip a pastry brush into the hot liquid and brush the cooled pastry. Move to a serving plate with a doily and arrange the fruit alternately in the precooked shells; glaze with more jam.

**Use the apricot glaze for light-colored fruit and the currant glaze for red or dark-colored fruit.*

Variation: To make mini tarts, divide dough into 30 pieces. Press into individual tart shells or a mini muffin tin. Move tin to a rimmed baking sheet to bake.

ELEGANT CHOCOLATE PECAN TARTS

Makes 4 (4-inch) round tarts

THESE ARE HEAVENLY SERVED WITH A CUP OF COFFEE *or a glass of bourbon in front of a fireplace in the middle of winter. The short crust pastry in these tarts is sturdy enough to hold the filling but still melts in the mouth. Different from pecan tassies, which use brown sugar, these use corn syrup. To measure corn or cane syrup, molasses or sorghum, lightly grease or oil a liquid measuring cup first so the syrup will slide in and out easily and the measure will be more accurate.*

- 1 recipe Very Versatile Cream Cheese Dough (page 512), prepared through chilling in a disc
- 1/3 cup dark corn syrup or sorghum syrup
- 1/4 cup granulated sugar
- 1/4 cup unsalted butter
- 1/4 cup semisweet chocolate chips
- 2 large eggs
- 1 cup coarsely chopped pecans
- 2 tablespoons all-purpose flour
- 1/2 teaspoon bourbon or vanilla extract
- Pecan halves, optional
- Chocolate curls, optional

After chilling the dough, divide it among four 3/4-inch-deep by 4-inch-round fluted tart pans with removable bottoms or six smaller ones; press evenly over the bottoms and up the sides of the pans. Refrigerate the tart shells 30 minutes, then freeze 30 minutes or until needed.

When ready to bake, preheat oven to 350 degrees. For the filling, stir the corn syrup or sorghum and sugar together in a small saucepan; cook over medium heat until the sugar dissolves and the mixture boils. Remove from heat and stir in the butter and chocolate chips until melted and smooth; set aside to cool slightly.

With a whisk or fork, beat the eggs in a large bowl until frothy; add the chocolate mixture in a slow, steady stream, beating constantly. Stir in the pecans, flour, and extract.

Pour the filling into the prepared tart shells and bake until the filling is set in the center and slightly puffed, 25 to 30 minutes.

Move the pans to wire racks and cool slightly. Remove the sides of the tart pans while still slightly warm and release the tarts carefully from the pans, both sides and bottoms.

Serve plain or decorated with chocolate curls, made with a vegetable peeler, and pecan halves.

LEMON AND BERRY PIE

Makes 1 (9-inch) pie

LAST-MINUTE SUMMER DESSERTS *are easy with prebaked piecrusts and lemon curd already stashed in the refrigerator. All our piecrusts are delightful with this filling. Store-bought crusts work too.*

- 1 recipe piecrust, prepared through prebaking, selecting from pages 504–11
- 1 pint berries (strawberries, raspberries, or blueberries)*
- 1 recipe Lemon Curd (page 618)
- 2 cups heavy cream, whipped

Set prebaked crust aside to cool.

Fill the prebaked piecrust with two-thirds of the berries. Mix Lemon Curd with enough of the whipped cream to make a tasty filling, and scoop into the piecrust with a large spatula or spoon. Sprinkle with the remaining berries and serve within a few hours.

**If berries are too tart, gently toss them with confectioners' sugar to taste.*

LEMON MERINGUE PIE

Makes 1 (9-inch) pie

LEMON MERINGUE PIE *is an enormous favorite of ours, particularly when we have trees full of lemons. A good bite encompasses a tender but not mushy crust, a lemony but not too tart custard filling, and a cloud-like meringue. The crust and the lemon filling (actually a cornstarch pudding) are precooked before topping with meringue. It is only the meringue that actually gets cooked in the shell. This recipe demands obedience until it is mastered because every step depends on another. If feeling a bit slap-dash, just make a Lemon Curd (page 618), put it in a pre-baked piecrust or tarts, and save this for another day. Cookie crusts are also suitable for this pie.*

My first "job" as a cook was as a volunteer in an international student house when the cook was sick. I used her large commercial-sized can of lemon filling from under the sink and graham cracker pie crusts. Later, with higher standards, I was unsatisfied with beads on the meringue from overcooking (causing the sugar to boil) and water in the bottom of the pie from the meringue weeping at being undercooked. A hot filling and a low oven solve both problems.

1 recipe piecrust or Graham Cracker Crust (page 544), prebaked

Lemon Pie Filling

3/4 cup granulated sugar
1/4 cup cornstarch
1/8 teaspoon salt
1 tablespoon finely grated lemon rind, no white attached
1/2 cup fresh lemon juice
1 1/2 cups water
6 large egg yolks
2 tablespoons unsalted butter

Meringue

4 large egg whites
1/4 teaspoon cream of tartar
1/2 teaspoon vanilla extract
1/2 cup granulated sugar

Set prebaked piecrust aside to cool.

When ready to bake the filling, preheat oven to 350 degrees. Move the oven rack to the middle of the oven.

For the Lemon Pie Filling, whisk together sugar, cornstarch, salt, lemon rind, and lemon juice in a medium saucepan. Gradually stir in the water with a rubber spatula until the liquid and dry ingredients are smooth and lump free. Bring slowly to a simmer, stirring with a rubber spatula, until it is translucent and lightly bubbling. Slide off heat, keeping it warm. Lightly beat the egg yolks in a separate bowl. Whisk a few spoonfuls of the hot cornstarch mixture into the eggs. Lightly whisk this egg yolk mixture, followed by the butter, into the still warm cornstarch mixture. Return to the heat and continue to whisk until lightly bubbling and at a full boil. Reduce heat as needed and continue cooking, stirring with the rubber spatula 1 to 2 minutes to thicken. Slide off the heat and cover the surface with plastic paper to prevent a skin from forming. Work quickly to make the Meringue, as the filling should still be warm when it is topped with the Meringue.

For the Meringue, start slowly beating the egg whites in a clean bowl with the cream of tartar and vanilla extract, preferably using a stand mixer or wire whisk. Gradually increase the speed and beat until soft peaks form, about 1 minute. Add the sugar, 1 tablespoon at a time, beating until the mixture forms glossy, stiff peaks. (If unsure, tip the bowl slightly. The whites should cling to the bowl without sliding.)

Move the prebaked crust to a rimmed baking sheet. Remove the plastic from the lemon mixture. If it is not warm, carefully stir with a rubber spatula over low heat until hot. If there are still lumps, don't try to get them out, as it will probably thin the sauce. Pour the still warm filling into the prebaked crust. The warm filling will help finish cooking the crust. Lightly spread some of the meringue evenly on top with a stiff rubber spatula, so it clings to the edges of the piecrust, and then moving quickly to the center. Add the remainder of the meringue mixture evenly, making pretty swirls with the stiff rubber spatula or the back of a large metal spoon. Bake the pie topped with meringue for 20 minutes, just until the meringue tips begin to brown. Cool on a rack, and let cool completely before cutting or it will get watery. The meringue also needs to continue cooking on top of the lemon mixture, out of the oven, until both are cool together. Because the cornstarch binds very lightly, it is easy for this pie to get watery once it is cut into. Don't worry if it does, it is still good. Use a bit of paper towel to clean up the dish.

Variation: Lemon-Lime Pie

Use juice and rind of 1/2 lemon and 1/2 lime. Add 1 to 2 slices of finely chopped candied ginger if desired.

CORNMEAL LEMON CHESS PIE

Makes 1 (9-inch) pie

I HAVE MANY MEMORIES OF THIS CLASSIC RECIPE. *One was during President Clinton's inauguration when the Senate wives were having a function for Hillary and one of the wives called me and asked for my favorite recipe. This is the one I proudly sent.*

1 piecrust, prebaked
2 cups granulated sugar
1 tablespoon all-purpose flour, preferably soft-wheat
1 tablespoon cornmeal
3 large eggs
1/4 cup unsalted butter, melted
1/4 cup milk
Juice and grated rind of 1 lemon, no white attached
1 teaspoon vanilla extract

Set the prebaked piecrust aside to cool.

When ready to bake the pie, preheat oven to 350 degrees.

Toss the sugar together with the flour and cornmeal on a piece of parchment or waxed paper. Whisk the eggs in a large bowl until mixed, preferably with a stand mixer. Add the sugar mixture and whisk until light and lemon-colored. Add butter, milk, lemon juice and rind, and vanilla; mix well.

Move the prebaked pie shell to a rimmed baking sheet. Pour the mixture into the pie shell and bake 30 to 40 minutes, or until firm. Cover the edges of the prebaked crust with aluminum foil as needed to prevent over-browning. Remove to a wire rack to cool, and serve at room temperature or chill until serving.

Variation: Make small tarts with the pastry dough, fill, and bake until the filling is just firm, slightly less time than for the pie.

CHOCOLATE CHESS PIE

Makes 1 (9-inch) pie

RICH, DECADENT, AND ROMANTIC *are just a few of the adjectives to describe this pie.*

1 piecrust, prebaked
1/2 cup granulated sugar
4 large eggs
6 tablespoons unsalted butter, melted
3/4 cup heavy cream, divided
4 ounces semisweet chocolate chips, melted
2 tablespoons confectioners' sugar
1 teaspoon vanilla extract

Set the prebaked piecrust aside to cool.

When ready to bake the pie, preheat oven to 325 degrees.

Beat the sugar and the eggs together until light. Beat in the butter, 1/4 cup cream, and chocolate.

Move the prebaked piecrust to a rimmed baking sheet. Pour the mixture into the crust. Bake until set, 30 to 35 minutes. Cover the edges of the prebaked crust with aluminum foil as needed to prevent over-browning. Remove from the oven and cool the pie in the pan on a wire rack until room temperature; then chill.

Whip the remaining cream with the confectioners' sugar and vanilla. Just before serving, top the pie with the whipped cream.

CHOCOLATE PEANUT BUTTER PIE

Makes 1 (9-inch) pie

My assistant Michelle Hammond and I *were craving a peanut butter mousse pie, without much luck. So we started to look at each element of the pie as its own recipe that when combined would create a rich and decadent dessert. A crisp, chocolaty crust with a rich, creamy mousse filling and topped with a glossy ganache, this pie is sure to satisfy any sweet tooth. It might be tempting to skip the step of making the ganache and just use a store-bought frosting, but please resist this urge, as consistency is key, and a store-bought topping will not spread properly over the mousse filling. The peanut butter mousse is also tasty enough to be served on its own with a little shaved chocolate. Because graham crackers are a staple in the house, we used them, but chocolate graham crackers or chocolate wafers would be good substitutes, with or without the added peanuts and chocolate in the crust. Unfortunately, store-bought pre-ground crumbs are frequently stale.*

Peanut-Chocolate-Graham Cracker Crust

1/2 cup semisweet chocolate chips
3 tablespoons granulated sugar
1 tablespoon roasted (unsalted or lightly salted) peanuts
10 sheets (double crackers) graham crackers (about 5 ounces)
7 tablespoons unsalted butter, melted

Peanut Butter Filling

2 tablespoons unsalted butter
1/3 cup plus 2 tablespoons packed light brown sugar
1/2 cup heavy whipping cream, divided
1 (3-ounce) package cream cheese, room temperature
1/3 cup creamy peanut butter
1 teaspoon vanilla extract

Chocolate Ganache Topping

1 cup semi-sweet chocolate morsels
1/2 cup heavy whipping cream
2 tablespoons chopped peanuts for garnish (optional)

Preheat oven to 350 degrees.

For the crust, process the chocolate chips with the sugar, peanuts, and graham crackers until ground to small crumbs in the bowl of a food processor fitted with the metal blade. Add the melted butter and pulse or stir until mixed. Press 2 cups of the mixture into a 9-inch pie pan and reserve the rest for another use. Move the crust into the preheated oven and bake for 8 to 10 minutes. Remove from the oven and set aside to cool.

For the filling, melt the butter with 1/3 cup of the brown sugar and 1/4 cup of the cream in a small pan. Heat until the butter is melted and the sugar is dissolved. Transfer this mixture to a large bowl and allow to cool to room temperature.

Whip the remaining 1/4 cup of the cream with the remaining brown sugar in another bowl and set aside.

When the brown sugar-butter mixture has cooled, beat in the cream cheese, peanut butter, and vanilla extract with an electric hand mixer until smooth. Fold in the whipped cream. Carefully spoon the filling into the chilled crust. Chill until firm, about 1 hour.

For the ganache topping, add chocolate morsels and heavy whipping cream to a microwave-safe bowl. Microwave for 30 seconds, remove bowl from microwave, stir, and continue the process until the chocolate has melted smoothly into the whipping cream. (There will be enough ganache to cover the pie and any extra may be reserved for a later use.) Allow the ganache to cool slightly. Carefully spoon the chocolate topping over the chilled pie, smooth, and top with chopped peanuts if desired. Chill until ready to serve.

SUSAN'S COCONUT CUSTARD PIE

Makes 1 (9-inch) pie

COCONUTS WERE USED AS BALLAST *in ships that came to the South. An enterprising man, Mr. Baker, started a company grating and selling them in addition to marketing the whole coconuts. They became a treasured food, integrated into pies, cakes, and other foods.*

This recipe is one that Susan Rice fixes regularly in her 1830 Edisto Island, South Carolina, home.

1 piecrust, prebaked
6 tablespoons unsalted butter
3 large eggs, lightly beaten
1/4 cup buttermilk
1/2 cup granulated sugar
1 1/2 teaspoons vanilla extract
1 cup unsweetened coconut flakes

Set the prebaked piecrust aside to cool.

When ready to bake the pie, preheat oven to 350 degrees.

Melt the butter in a medium saucepan. Lightly whisk together the eggs, buttermilk, sugar, vanilla, and coconut; add to the melted butter.

Move the prebaked crust to a rimmed baking sheet. Pour the mixture into the prebaked piecrust. Bake for 10 minutes; reduce the heat to 300 degrees and bake for 35 minutes, or until the middle is set. Cover the piecrust edges with foil if they begin to brown too quickly. Remove from the oven and cool the pie in the pan on a wire rack. Serve room temperature or chill until serving.

HOME-STYLE BUTTERMILK PIE

Makes 1 (9-inch) pie

THIS TRULY SOUTHERN PIE *is a melt-in-your-mouth custard—smooth and silky with a very slight tang. It is possible to use reconstituted powdered buttermilk in this.*

1 piecrust, prebaked
1/2 cup unsalted butter, melted
3 large eggs
3/4 cup buttermilk
1/2 teaspoon vanilla extract
2 tablespoons all-purpose flour, preferably soft-wheat
1 3/4 cups granulated sugar
1/2 teaspoon salt

Set the prebaked piecrust aside to cool.

When ready to bake the pie, preheat oven to 325 degrees.

Whisk the butter and eggs together until thoroughly mixed. Add the buttermilk and vanilla, and mix well. Sift the flour, sugar, and salt onto a piece of parchment or waxed paper, and then stir the flour mixture into the liquid.

Move the pie pan with the prebaked crust to a rimmed baking sheet. Ladle the filling into the piecrust and bake until set and lightly browned, 40 to 45 minutes. Cover the edges of the prebaked crust with aluminum foil as needed to prevent over-browning. Remove from the oven and cool in the pan on a wire rack. Serve warm, at room temperature, or chilled.

CARAMEL CREAM PECAN CRUST PIE

Makes 1 (9-inch) pie

THIS FEATURES PECANS IN THE CRUST, *filled with rich custard much like Italian panna cotta, only caramel-flavored. The finished pie dough is tricky to serve out of a traditional glass or metal pie pan, so a tart pan with a removable bottom is the best one to use. Be sure to wait until the custard is nearly set before pouring into the crust to prevent leaking. This crust can be used in place of some of the other sweet and short crusts.*

1 Pecan Crust (page 514), prepared through prebaking
1/4 cup granulated sugar
1 cup water
2 1/4 cups heavy cream, divided
1 package powdered gelatin

Preheat oven to 375 degrees.

Heat sugar with water in a heavy pan over low heat without boiling until sugar is dissolved. Turn up the heat, bring to the boil, and boil until the water is greatly evaporated and the syrup is making large bubbles. Watch carefully as it turns deep amber, taking care it doesn't burn. (*See* Caramel Sauce, page 628.)

Cover hands with a towel or oven mitt and tip the pan to see how deep the color is in the thickest part of the pan. If it is too pale, the dessert will not be flavored sufficiently. When a deep amber color is achieved, cool slightly. (Do not let harden.) Cover hands again with towel or oven mitt and add 1 cup heavy cream to the mixture. It may bubble up. Stir well. If the mixture seems uneven, put back over the heat, stirring to mix the cream and caramel thoroughly. It should be uniform in color.

Meanwhile, add 1/4 cup cream to a small pot or metal measuring cup. Sprinkle the gelatin on top and stir lightly to make sure it is distributed. After the gelatin becomes absorbed into the cream and thickens, heat gently until melted, with no granules remaining. Do not boil.

Stir gelatin into the warm caramel mixture, followed by the remaining cup of cream, making sure there are no lumps of gelatin and that the caramel is evenly distributed throughout. Refrigerate 10 to 15 minutes. When cool but not set, stir and gently pour into the piecrust. Refrigerate at least 30 minutes, or until set. When ready to serve, remove the tart by putting the pan on top of a large jar, and pulling down the exterior ring of the pan. If the tart sticks, run a knife around the inside of the ring.

Variation: Add 1 cup lightly toasted pecan halves or pieces to the pie, decorating the top in a spiral or in rows.

PUMPKIN-CHOCOLATE CHEESECAKE PIE

Makes 1 (9-inch) pie

ALTHOUGH THIS CAKE PROCLAIMS CHOCOLATE, *it may be left out if desired.* Better Homes and Gardens, *from which I adapted this recipe, recommends chopping the chocolate into small pieces to prevent it sinking into the cheesecake. This cake freezes for 3 months, tightly wrapped.*

1 piecrust, prebaked
12 ounces cream cheese, softened
1/4 cup granulated sugar
1 large egg, lightly beaten
3/4–1 cup finely chopped semisweet chocolate or miniature chocolate pieces, optional, divided
1 (15-ounce) can pumpkin purée
2/3 cup packed light or dark brown sugar
2 teaspoons pumpkin pie spice
4 large eggs, lightly beaten
3/4 cup half-and-half or light cream

Set the prebaked piecrust aside to cool.

When ready to bake the pie, preheat oven to 375 degrees.

Use a mixer or food processor to beat the cream cheese, sugar, and egg on low speed until smooth. Spread the cream cheese mixture in the cooled pastry shell. Sprinkle with 3/4 cup chopped chocolate if desired.

Mix together the pumpkin, brown sugar, and spice in a bowl. Stir in the eggs. Gradually stir in the half-and-half. Slowly pour pumpkin mixture onto the cream cheese layer.

Cover the edges of the prebaked crust with aluminum foil as needed to prevent over-browning. Bake 60 to 65 minutes, or until a knife inserted near the center comes out clean. Cool on a wire rack. Cover and refrigerate within 2 hours.

LULEN'S GRATED APPLE PIE

Makes 1 (9-inch) pie

LULEN WAS A YOUNG TEENAGER *when her parents were transferred out of the country and she came to live with me so she could pursue her dance career and college. It seemed to me that she mostly ate yogurt; but she wanted to learn to cook, and pies were on the top of her list. This was the first pie she cooked, and she still makes it, many years later. The food processor works very well to grate the apples. Because the pie takes so long to cook, the piecrust doesn't need prebaking (that also keeps it "beginner simple"), although it's always a bit better if it is.* *See page 540 for apple choice and baking information.*

1 piecrust
2/3 cup granulated sugar
1 tablespoon all-purpose flour
2 teaspoons ground cinnamon
1/4 teaspoon salt
4 1/2 cups tart apples, peeled, cored, and coarsely grated
1 large egg, lightly beaten
1/3 cup unsalted butter, melted
1 cup chopped pecans

Fill the pan with the piecrust. Prebake if desired.

When ready to bake the pie, preheat oven to 400 degrees. Mix together the sugar, flour, cinnamon, salt, and apples; then combine with the egg and butter.

Move the pie pan to a rimmed baking sheet. Pour the filling into the piecrust and sprinkle with pecans. Place on the top or upper-middle rack of the oven and bake for 10 minutes; then lower the heat to 350 degrees and bake for another 45 to 50 minutes. Cover the edges of the crust with aluminum foil as needed to prevent over-browning. Cool the pie in the pan on a wire rack. Serve warm or cold.

CLASSIC PUMPKIN PIE

Makes 1 (9-inch) pie

THE EASIEST WAY TO MAKE PUMPKIN PIE *is from commercially made purées. There are now organic pumpkin purées, pumpkin pie mix, and other fillings available in jars and cans. A large regular "Halloween" pumpkin is grown for goblins and candles, not for pie, and is sinuous and grainy. There is, however, a type of pumpkin available—a sugar pumpkin—that is an ideal size for making the pumpkin purée needed for a pie, if the baker so chooses (see box). Frankly, I use the commercial purée, but not the pumpkin pie mix. An unbaked piecrust may be used, but may make for a soggy pie.*

1 piecrust, prebaked
2 large eggs
1/2 cup packed light or dark brown sugar
1/4 cup granulated sugar
1/2 teaspoon salt
1–2 teaspoons ground cinnamon
1/2–1 teaspoon ground ginger
1/4 teaspoon ground nutmeg
1/4 teaspoon ground cloves
2 cups pumpkin purée (not pumpkin pie filling)
1 1/2 cups heavy cream or evaporated milk
1 cup heavy cream whipped with 6 tablespoons sugar and 1 teaspoon vanilla extract

Set prebaked piecrust aside to cool.

When ready to bake, preheat oven to 350 degrees.

Beat the eggs with an electric hand mixer. Measure the brown sugar, granulated sugar, salt, cinnamon, ginger, nutmeg, and cloves on a large piece of parchment or waxed paper and mix together thoroughly. Mix together the pumpkin purée and the cream. Add the spice and sugar mixture to it, stir well, and add to the eggs, beating.

Move the prebaked piecrust to a rimmed baking sheet and carefully pour in the filling. Bake 45 minutes, and remove from oven to insert a knife carefully in the center to see if it comes out clean. If not, return to the oven for 15 minutes, until a knife inserted in the center comes out clean. There should be a wobble to the filling; if overbaked, the filling will crack. Cover the edges of the prebaked crust with aluminum foil as needed to prevent over-browning. Cool the pie to room temperature in the pan on a wire rack, and refrigerate until chilled and set, about 4 hours. Serve cold with whipped cream.

MAKING PUMPKIN PURÉE

Cut out the stem from a small- to medium-sized sugar pumpkin. Use a large spoon to scrape out the inside pulp and seeds. Save the seeds for another purpose if desired, and discard the stringy pulp.

Cut the pumpkin, skin on, into large pieces. Cook in the microwave until soft, or place in a steamer basket and steam in a saucepan with several inches of water until soft. Scoop the "meat" from the skin. Purée the soft pumpkin in a food processor or put through a food mill until smooth.

MELT-IN-YOUR-MOUTH SWEET POTATO PIE

Makes 1 (9-inch) pie

THE SWEET POTATO—A TUBEROUS ROOT VEGETABLE WITH EDIBLE GREENS—*is one of more than 1,000 species of its family. We think of it as Southern, although at one time it was grown in the North. The sweet potato and pumpkin are both hard-times staples in the South and can be found substituting for each other in traditional pies, similarly spiced. These pies have a lush, custardy flavor and texture.*

A perfect foil for a tender crust, this pie can stand alone but is usually served with whipped cream. The recipe was developed by Ray Overton, a longtime assistant of mine who now is a cookbook author and teacher.

1 piecrust, prebaked
3 large eggs, separated
2 cups canned sweet potatoes, drained and mashed
3/4 cup packed light or dark brown sugar
1/2 cup unsalted butter, softened
1 teaspoon ground cinnamon
1/2 teaspoon freshly ground nutmeg
1/2 teaspoon ground cloves
1/2–1 teaspoon ground ginger
1/2 teaspoon salt
1 1/2 cups heavy cream or evaporated milk

Whipped Cream

1/2 cup heavy cream
6 tablespoons granulated sugar
1 teaspoon vanilla extract

Set prebaked piecrust aside to cool.

When ready to bake, preheat oven to 400 degrees.

Beat the egg yolks with an electric hand mixer in a large bowl until light, about 3 to 4 minutes. Beat in the sweet potatoes. Measure the brown sugar, butter, cinnamon, nutmeg, cloves, ginger, and salt onto a piece of parchment or waxed paper and thoroughly mix. Beat them into the egg mixture until light, about 3 to 4 minutes. Add the cream and beat until just combined.

Whisk the egg whites in a clean bowl until they form soft peaks, about 2 minutes. Fold a dollop of the egg white into the potato mixture to soften, and then fold the potato mixture into the egg whites.

Move the prebaked piecrust in the dish to a rimmed baking sheet. Pour the filling into the piecrust. Bake for 10 minutes; then reduce the heat to 350 degrees and continue baking for an additional 45 to 50 minutes, until a fork lightly inserted in the center of the pie comes out clean. Cover the edges of the crust with foil if browning too quickly. Cool the pie in the pan on a wire rack.

For topping, whip cream and sugar until a consistency you like; stir in vanilla. Serve pie with whipped cream.

Variations:

- Evaporated milk and half-and-half are frequently substituted for the cream.
- When whipping the cream, whip an additional 1/2 cup of heavy cream with sugar to taste. Add chopped candied ginger to taste. Serve atop or along with the pie.
- Use fresh sweet potatoes. Pierce two large sweet potatoes lightly with a fork and bake directly on the oven rack at 450 degrees until soft. Scoop out the flesh and beat briefly with a whisk or mixer until smooth.

TRADITIONAL PECAN PIE

Makes 1 (9-inch) pie

PECAN PIE IS ICONIC *in the South and our most favorite of the pies. Pecans usually fall from the trees near the holidays, so we usually think of it as a holiday pie. The crust should be secondary to the filling, melting in the mouth. Pecan pies vary in the sweeteners they use—sugar and/or corn syrup—and the flavoring liquids added—bourbon, buttermilk, and vanilla, for example. The color of the corn syrup and the color of the sugar will partially determine the color of the pie. Pecan halves are more expensive and make a more "important" looking pie. Pecan pieces, while less expensive, make a jumbled looking pie, so avoid them if possible. Arranging the pecans in the pie is time-consuming but produces an absolutely stunning effect. A tart pan with a removable bottom makes the most beautiful presentation.*

1 piecrust, prebaked
4 large eggs
2/3 cup sugar (granulated, light brown, or dark brown)
1/3 cup unsalted butter, melted
1 cup light or dark corn syrup
1/2 teaspoon salt
1 1/2 cups pecan halves or broken pieces

Set aside the prebaked piecrust to cool.

When ready to bake, preheat oven to 350 degrees.

Whisk the eggs together and beat in the sugar, butter, corn syrup, and salt with an electric hand mixer.

Move the pie pan to a rimmed baking sheet. Pour the filling into the piecrust. Add the pecans, laying them on top, preferably in a decorative pattern of spirals or rows. Bake 40 to 60 minutes, until a fork lightly inserted in the center of the pie comes out clean, checking after 30 minutes, rotating the pan 180 degrees in the oven as needed if the pie is cooking unevenly. Cover the edges of the crust with foil if browning too quickly.

Cool the pie to room temperature in the pan on a wire rack. Refrigerate approximately 2 hours, until set. Reheat and serve warm if desired.

To freeze: After refrigerating the pie for 2 hours, freeze unwrapped for approximately 2 hours, or until frozen. Remove the pie and wrap well, date it, and return to the freezer. Freeze for up to 3 months. Thaw in the refrigerator for 30 minutes. Reheat before serving if desired.

Variations:

- For Bourbon or Brandy or Rum Pecan Pie, decrease sugar to 1/4 cup and add 1/4 cup liquor.
- Add some grated orange rind.
- The sugar may be reduced by half to yield a less sweet pie.
- Add un-melted chocolate chips to the filling.
- Use Sweet Piecrust (page 511) and serve with Caramel Cream Sauce (page 628).

Every convection oven is different. Many of them create "waves" on the cooking liquid, moving the contents enough to cause variations on the top of the pie. Unless you know your convection oven will not do this, do not use the convection part of your oven for Traditional Pecan Pie.

CHOCOLATE PECAN PIE

Makes 1 (9-inch) pie

A PECAN PIE *is a caramel pie with pecans. Add chocolate and it becomes a seductive, melt-in-your-mouth dessert.*

- 1 piecrust, prebaked
- 1/2 cup light or dark corn syrup
- 1/2 cup unsalted butter, melted
- 1/4 cup semisweet chocolate chips
- 3 large eggs
- 1/2 teaspoon vanilla extract
- 1 1/2 cups pecan halves

Set aside the prebaked piecrust to cool.

When ready to bake, preheat oven to 350 degrees.

Stir the corn syrup, butter, and chocolate chips over medium heat until melted and smooth. Whisk the eggs together quickly in a large bowl until just combined and lightly frothy; add the chocolate mixture in a slow, steady stream, beating constantly. Stir in the vanilla extract.

Move the prebaked piecrust to a rimmed baking sheet and carefully pour in the filling. Decorate with the pecan halves. Bake 40 to 60 minutes, until a fork inserted lightly in the center comes out clean, checking after 40 minutes. Cover the crust with foil if browning too quickly.

Cool the pie in the pan on a wire rack. Serve with chocolate curls or a sprinkling of confectioners' sugar.

Variation: Brown the butter first; then add the corn syrup and chocolate and stir until melted.

PEACH-PECAN PIE

Makes 1 (9-inch) pie

I ADAPTED THIS *from Grace Hartley's* Southern Cookbook *in the 1980s and have been using it ever since. It uses a crunchy nut crumb topping, which is also nice on streusels.*

- 1 piecrust, prebaked
- 1/4 cup unsalted butter, softened
- 1/2 cup granulated sugar
- 2 tablespoons all-purpose flour
- 1/2 cup corn syrup
- 1/4 teaspoon salt
- 3 large eggs
- 1 1/2 cups diced ripe or frozen peaches, drained

Topping

- 1/4 cup all-purpose flour
- 1/3 cup packed light or dark brown sugar
- 3 tablespoons unsalted butter, softened
- 1 1/2 cups pecans, coarsely chopped

Set the prebaked piecrust aside to cool.

When ready to bake, preheat oven to 375 degrees.

For the filling, beat the butter, sugar, and flour together in a large bowl with an electric hand mixer or whisk until light. Beat in the corn syrup and salt, then the eggs one at a time. Add the peaches. Move the prepared piecrust to a rimmed baking sheet and carefully pour in the filling.

For the topping, toss the flour and sugar together. Work in the butter with a fork until crumbly, and then mix in the pecans. Sprinkle over the filling.

Bake in the oven for 35 minutes, or until firm in the center. Cover the edges of the prebaked crust with aluminum foil as needed to prevent over-browning. Cool the pie in the pan on a wire rack. Serve warm or cold.

PEACHES 'N' CREAM PIE

Makes 1 (9-inch) pie

THIS LIGHT CUSTARD PIE *from my book* New Southern Cooking *is ridiculously easy to make with store-bought crust and frozen peaches.*

1 piecrust, prebaked
3/4 cup granulated sugar
1/2 cup all-purpose flour
2 cups fresh or frozen peach wedges, defrosted
1 cup heavy cream

Set the prebaked piecrust aside to cool, or place a store-bought crust in the pan.

When ready to bake, preheat oven to 350 degrees.

Toss the sugar and flour together in a medium bowl, and then toss the peaches in the sugar mixture until the sugar is evenly distributed.

Move the pie pan to a rimmed baking sheet. Pour the peach mixture into the prebaked piecrust. Pour the heavy cream over the top. Move the peaches around a bit with a fork so that the cream completely covers the peaches. Bake 45 to 50 minutes, until a fork inserted in the center comes out clean. Cover the edges of the prebaked crust with aluminum foil as needed to prevent over-browning. Serve hot, or cool the pie on a wire rack. May be made ahead of time and frozen up to 2 months.

Variation: Add 1 to 2 tablespoons finely chopped candied ginger.

DOUBLE-CRUST BLUEBERRY PIE

Makes 1 (9-inch) double-crust pie

Blueberry pie is one of the first pies of summer, *made from blueberries arriving from Florida as early as late May. Frozen and thawed blueberries are as usable as fresh ones in this recipe, adding a bit more liquid. Either way, since this is not a deep dish pie crust, the pie slices and presents very well. If using a deep dish pie, serve traditionally, with a spoon.*

- 1 recipe Double-Crust Piecrust (page 508), prepared through rolling out discs
- 4 cups fresh blueberries or frozen blueberries, thawed
- 1/3–1/2 cup granulated sugar
- 3 tablespoons cornstarch
- 1 large egg mixed with 1 tablespoon water, to glaze

Line a shallow 9-inch pie pan with the smaller crust and move the larger crust onto a rimmed baking sheet. Refrigerate both until needed.

When ready to bake, preheat oven to 400 degrees and move rack to the center of the oven.

Wash blueberries and pick out any stems. Toss blueberries in a large bowl with sugar and cornstarch. Set aside.

Move pie pan with the chilled crust to a rimmed baking sheet. Pour the filling into the crust. Lightly moisten the rim of the crust with water. Cut a 1-inch strip around the outside of the second piecrust and press it onto the rim of the bottom crust. Moisten the strip with water. Place the top crust over the filling and crimp the edge decoratively to seal. Brush the top crust with the egg glaze. Cut 4 to 5 slits in the top of the piecrust to allow steam to escape.

Bake for 20 minutes, reduce oven temperature to 350 degrees, and bake for another 40 minutes, until crust is nicely browned, covering edges or any dark portion with foil if necessary. Cool the pie in the pan on a wire rack. This pie slices nicely at room temperature and is heavenly with whipped cream or ice cream.

Variation: Single-Crust Blueberry Pie

Prepare pie as directed but with 1 (9-inch) Very Beginner's Piecrust (page 504), or 1 cookie crust, preferably gingersnap. Bake as directed above, covering rim with foil if necessary. Remove pie from oven and gently stir pie filling immediately to bring the glossy blueberries to the top and to integrate any white cornstarch spots. Cool the pie in the pan on a wire rack.

FREE-FORM BLUEBERRY CORNMEAL CROUSTADES

Makes 4

CROUSTADE IS A FANCY NAME FOR A PIECRUST. *I tend to think of it as more rustic, shaped as a container for a filling, without a top crust. The blueberries are thickened with cornmeal. If the sugar is not sufficient to sweeten the blueberries, add more to taste, but be judicious, as too much can make the filling watery. Michelle Avenel Hammond developed this recipe once when we had extra blueberries.*

1 recipe Double-Crust Piecrust (page 508), prepared through mixing
2 cups blueberries
1/2 cup granulated sugar
1–2 tablespoons cornmeal
1 tablespoon grated lemon or orange rind, no white attached
1 large egg mixed with 1 tablespoon water, to glaze

Preheat oven to 375 degrees.

Roll the piecrust out into a square, 1/8 inch thick. Chill 30 minutes. Remove from refrigerator to a floured surface. Using a sharp knife, cut the dough in four equal portions, and move the pieces separately to a rimmed baking sheet. Toss the clean blueberries with the sugar and cornmeal. Add half the rind and taste. Add remaining rind as needed to add citrus flavor, but not too much as to dominate the blueberries. It will be runny-looking.

Use a large spoon to move a fourth of the mixture into the center of one of the squares. Leaving a 1-inch border around the square, spread the mixture over the square evenly. (If the amount seems excessive for the size of the square, remove some of the mixture.) Fold the 1-inch border up over the blueberry mixture on each side to make a rim to contain the mixture. Repeat with the other three squares. Refrigerate at least 15 minutes, or as necessary to chill the dough.

Move the baking sheet to the hot oven and bake the croustades for 20 minutes. Remove from the oven, brush the edges with the glaze, reduce the oven temperature to 350, and bake an additional 10 to 20 minutes, as needed to color the crust a light golden brown. Remove the pan to a wire rack. The blueberry mixture will thicken as it cools. Serve at room temperature.

Variations:

- Substitute chopped candied ginger for the citrus rind.
- Serve with whipped cream.
- Roll each portion of dough into a circle and proceed as above.

FREE-FORM TARTS

Makes 1 tart

FREE-FORM TARTS ARE NOT DEPENDENT *on a particular pan or dish, which makes them very handy at vacation homes or when variable amounts of fruit are available. They may be formed into shapes of all types and sizes, from peach or pear shaped to rectangles. Fruit fillings are usually uncooked, but cooked fillings may be used as well if not runny.*

1 unbaked piecrust
2–3 cups blueberries or raspberries whole, and/or sliced strawberries, peaches, plums, or figs
1/4–1/2 cup granulated, or packed light brown or dark brown sugar
1–2 tablespoons fresh lemon juice
1/2 cup apricot jam (for red fruits use strained strawberry or raspberry jam)

Roll out the dough to about 1/8 inch thick on a floured surface. Put your rolling pin lightly on the dough and roll the dough over the pin for moving; move to a rimmed baking sheet and gently unfold the dough onto the baking sheet. Cut out the design of your choice, either by hand or with a pattern.

Cut a 1/2-inch-wide strip of dough to use as a rim if needed. Brush the outer 1/2-inch edge of the dough with water. Lightly press the strip of dough onto the moistened part to seal. Decorate if desired. Roll any scraps out into a rose, bow, or pattern of your choice, or cut into shapes for the top of the tart. Chill the crust and the scraps until needed, for 30 minutes or up to 5 days.

When ready to bake, preheat oven to 375 degrees.

Fill the chilled form with crumpled parchment paper, waxed paper, and rice or beans (prebaking, page 503), then bake for 20 minutes. Scoop out rice or beans and remove paper.

Slice and arrange the fruit in the form, overlapping them slightly to account for shrinkage, either in vertical rows or in a pattern. Sprinkle with sugar to taste. Bake 20 to 30 minutes, or until the fruit is soft.

To make the glaze, mix the lemon juice and jam, bring to the boil, and strain. Brush the hot glaze onto the fruit. Cool the tart on a wire rack. Serve it lukewarm or at room temperature.

Variations:

- Sprinkle the fruit with finely chopped ginger.
- Spread a custard or other base under the fruit. Prebake crust completely, top with the custard or other base as desired, and lightly arrange uncooked fresh fruit onto the crust. Glaze as above.
- Serve with optional Caramel Cream Sauce (page 628).
- Free-form tarts may also be savory.

FREE-FORM APPLE TART

Makes 1 tart

WHEN APPLES ARE AT THEIR PEAK, *there is nothing better than a free-form tart of crisp, thinly rolled pastry topped with a swirl of apples and brown sugar and burnished with a glaze of strained jam. Substitute pears for the apples if desired.*

1 unbaked Basic Piecrust (page 507)
2–3 Golden Delicious or Granny Smith apples, peeled, cored, and sliced
1/4–1/2 cup packed light or dark brown sugar
1/4 cup raisins or currants, plumped in water
1–2 tablespoons fresh lemon juice mixed with 1/2 cup apricot jam, for glaze
1 recipe Caramel Cream Sauce (page 628), optional

Roll out the dough to about 1/8 inch thick on a floured surface then place on a cookie sheet. Cut out the design of your choice, either by hand or with a pattern. (A traditional shape is a 10-inch circle or a rectangle, but alternate shapes include a Christmas tree, Christmas ball, turkey, pear, or an apple.)

Cut a 1/2-inch-wide strip of dough from around the outside of the dough to use as a rim. Brush the outer 1/2-inch edge of the dough with water. Put the strip of dough on the moistened part and press lightly to seal. Leave the edge as it is, or decorate it. Roll any scraps out into a rose, bow, or other shape. Chill.

When ready to bake, preheat oven to 375 degrees.

Crumple a piece of parchment or waxed paper, smooth out, and place into the piecrust; fill with rice or beans and prebake 20 minutes (prebaking, page 503), covering edges as necessary to prevent burning. Bake any scrap shapes on a baking sheet at the same time. Remove from oven, scoop out rice or beans, and remove paper.

Arrange apples on the form, overlapping them slightly to account for shrinkage. To make a spiral pattern, overlap apple slices, starting from the outside rim, with the rounded edges towards the outside rim and spiraling to the center in one layer. Sprinkle with brown sugar to taste. Sprinkle the raisins down the center to look like apple seeds. Bake 20 to 30 minutes, or until the fruit is soft.

To make the glaze, mix the lemon juice and jam, bring to the boil, and strain. Brush the hot glaze onto the apples. Decorate tart with any shaped pieces and glaze those also. Cool the tart on a wire rack. Serve it lukewarm or at room temperature. Serve with Caramel Cream Sauce.

PEACH PIE

Makes 1 (9-inch) double-crust pie

THIS RECIPE CAME VIA MY FORMER STUDENT REBECCA LANG, *from a friend of ours, Angie Mosier, who is a baker and food stylist from Atlanta. I have always imagined that peach pies were a rarity in the South until air-conditioning, because the peaches all came at one time in hot weather and had to be "put up" if they weren't used right away. Making piecrust at peach time was an arduous task, because it had to be made in the cool of morning, just when the homemaker was getting breakfast for the family.*

When slicing into this delectable pie, don't be surprised by the gap between the filling and the top crust. This happens when a pie is baked at high heat, because the crust sets before the fruit in the filling has cooked down.

1 unbaked (9-inch) Double-Crust Piecrust (page 508)
8 large ripe but firm peaches (3 1/2 pounds)
3/4 cup granulated sugar
1 1/2 tablespoons fresh lemon juice
1/4 cup plus 1 tablespoon all-purpose flour, preferably soft-wheat
1 1/2 tablespoons unsalted butter, thinly sliced
1 egg yolk mixed with 2 tablespoons water, to glaze
Whipped Cream (page 530), for serving

Line a 9-inch pie pan with the smaller crust and move the larger crust to a rimmed baking sheet. Refrigerate both until needed.

Bring a large saucepan of water to the boil, and fill a large bowl with ice water. Using a sharp knife, mark a shallow X in the bottom of each peach. Blanch the peaches in the boiling water for about 1 minute, until the skins begin to loosen. Using a slotted spoon, transfer the peaches to the ice water to cool.

Drain and peel the peaches and cut them into 3/4-inch wedges. Transfer peaches to a large bowl. Add the sugar, lemon juice, and flour; toss well and let stand for 5 minutes.

When ready to bake, preheat oven to 400 degrees. Move pie pan with the chilled crust to a rimmed baking sheet. Pour the peaches and their juices into the chilled pie shell, and scatter the butter slices on top. Lightly moisten the rim of the crust with water. Cut a 1-inch strip around the outside of the second piecrust and press it onto the rim of the bottom crust. Moisten the strip with water. Place the top crust over the filling and crimp the edge decoratively to seal. Brush the top crust with the egg glaze. Cut 4 to 5 slits in the top of the piecrust to allow steam to escape.

Bake for 30 minutes. Reduce the oven temperature to 375 degrees, cover the edge of the pie with foil, and bake for about 40 minutes longer, until the filling is bubbly and the crust is deeply golden on the top and bottom. Cool the pie in the pan on a wire rack. Serve with Whipped Cream.

SUNDANCE RIVERA'S PEACH PIE

Makes 1 (9-inch) double-crust pie

UNLIKELY AS HIS NAME IS—*he was named for Sundance (in the movie* Butch Cassidy and the Sundance Kid*) and first baseman Carlos Rivera—he was an excellent cook and assistant. This pie can be made year-round, thanks to frozen peaches.*

- 1 unbaked (9-inch) Double-Crust Piecrust (page 508)
- 1 large egg
- 2 tablespoons all-purpose flour
- 1 cup granulated sugar
- 5 tablespoons unsalted butter, melted
- Pinch of salt
- 6 medium peaches, peeled and cut off the stone into wedges
- 1 egg yolk mixed with 2 tablespoons water, to glaze

Line a 9-inch pie pan with one crust and move the other crust to a rimmed baking sheet. Refrigerate both until needed.

When ready to bake, preheat oven to 350 degrees.

Whisk together the egg, flour, sugar, butter, and salt in a bowl. Move the pie pan to a rimmed baking sheet. Add the peach wedges to the pie pan. Ladle the egg mixture over the peaches.

Lightly moisten the rim of the bottom crust with water. Cut a strip off the outside of the second round and press it onto the rim of the bottom crust. Moisten the strip with water. Place the top crust over the filling and crimp the edge decoratively to seal. Brush the top crust with the egg glaze. Cut 4 to 5 slits in the top of the piecrust to allow steam to escape. Bake for 1 hour, until the crust is nicely browned. Cool the pie in the pan on a wire rack.

CARAMEL BROWN SUGAR PIE

Makes 1 (9-inch) double-crust pie

CARAMEL IS FOUND EVERYWHERE IN SOUTHERN SWEETS, *including cakes and pies. This recipe adds brown sugar to custard and is temptingly good.*

- 1 unbaked (9-inch) Double-Crust Piecrust (page 508)
- 1/4 cup unsalted butter, room temperature
- 6 tablespoons all-purpose flour, preferably soft-wheat
- 1/2 cup heavy cream
- 2 cups firmly packed light or dark brown sugar
- 2 large eggs, lightly beaten
- 2 teaspoons vanilla extract
- 1 cup fresh or frozen peaches or berries for garnish, optional

Line a 9-inch pie pan with the smaller crust and move the larger crust to a rimmed baking sheet. Refrigerate both until needed.

When ready to bake, preheat oven to 375 degrees.

Stir the butter with the flour in a heavy saucepan over low heat to make a smooth paste. Whisk in the cream and sugar. Bring to the boil, reduce the heat, and simmer the filling until it thickens, about 3 minutes, whisking constantly. Add a small portion of the warm liquid to the eggs, and then lightly whisk the eggs back into the pan. Stir in the vanilla.

Move the pie pan to a rimmed baking sheet and strain the filling into the lined pie pan. Lightly moisten the rim of the crust with water. Cut a strip off the outside of the second round and press it onto the rim of the bottom crust. Moisten the strip with water. Place the top crust over the filling and crimp the edge decoratively to seal. Cut 4 to 5 slits in the top of the piecrust to allow steam to escape. Bake until the crust is nicely browned and the filling is set, 45 minutes to 1 hour. Cool the pie in the pan on a wire rack.

Serve with fresh peaches or berries, if using.

CLASSIC CINNAMON-APPLE DOUBLE-CRUST PIE

Makes 1 (9-inch) double-crust pie

THIS IS THE KIND OF PIE *we dream about our mothers making when we need comfort and love. I have always thought of it as American and Southern, partly because of the phrase "As American as Apple Pie." When I went to London for culinary school, our first quiz included a question on apple pie and England—which I failed, as I never thought of it as being an English dessert.*

1 unbaked (9-inch) Double-Crust Piecrust (page 508)
6–8 Granny Smith apples (about 2 pounds), peeled, cored, and sliced 1 inch thick
1 tablespoon fresh lemon juice
1 tablespoon bourbon, optional
1/4 cup granulated sugar, or to taste, depending on the tartness of the apples
2 teaspoons ground cinnamon, or to taste
1/2 teaspoon ground cloves
Pinch salt
2–3 tablespoons unsalted butter, divided
2–3 tablespoons milk

Line a 9-inch pie pan with one crust and move the other crust to a rimmed baking sheet. Refrigerate both until needed.

When ready to bake, preheat oven to 450 degrees.

Toss the apples with the lemon juice and bourbon, if using, in a large bowl. Alternate mixing in the sugar, cinnamon, and cloves, tossing to coat evenly. Add a pinch of salt.

Move the pie pan to a rimmed baking sheet. Pour half the mixture into the chilled unbaked piecrust and dot with half the butter. Add the rest of the apple mixture and dot with the remaining butter.

Lightly moisten the rim of the crust with water. Cut a 1 1/2-inch strip off the outside of the second round and press it onto the rim of the bottom crust. Moisten the strip with water. Place the top crust over the filling and crimp the edge decoratively to seal. Brush the top crust with the milk. Cut 4 to 5 slits in the top to allow steam to escape. Bake for 10 minutes, reduce the oven temperature to 375 degrees, and continue baking another 45 to 50 minutes, until the crust is nicely browned. Cool the pie in the pan on a wire rack.

WHAT MAKES APPLE PIES TRICKY?

Apple pies are a bit tricky because apple varieties have different qualities of sweetness and exude different amounts of water. This makes the product of cooked apples slightly different each time. I don't mind a crust that towers above a shrunken filling, or a slightly runny filling, but others do. If you are one of those, precook the apples and seasonings in a heavy pan until the juices are extracted and somewhat reduced. Or try a different type of apple. I am used to Golden Delicious and Gala apples, as they grow abundantly in the Georgia mountains, as well as Granny Smith for when I want a tart apple. A mixture of Granny Smith and McIntosh apples is a good combination as well but will need 2 tablespoons flour to thicken the juice; add with the sugar.

Buying apples—Flick an unblemished apple with your finger. It should be firm.

RASPBERRY-MINT PIE

Makes 1 (9-inch) double-crust pie

OUR MOUNTAIN REGIONS IN THE SOUTH *are particularly nurturing to raspberries, yielding plump berries bursting with flavor. After eating the berries of the season with cream, I get a craving for the rich, deep tones of cooked raspberries in a pie.*

- 1 unbaked Double-Crust Piecrust (page 508)
- 1½ cups granulated sugar
- 3 tablespoons cornstarch
- ½ teaspoon salt
- 5 cups fresh raspberries
- 2 heaping tablespoons finely chopped fresh mint
- 2 tablespoons unsalted butter
- 1 large egg mixed with 1 tablespoon water, to glaze

Line a 9-inch pie pan with one crust and move the other crust to a rimmed baking sheet. Refrigerate both until needed.

When ready to bake, preheat oven to 375 degrees.

Toss the sugar, cornstarch, and salt in a bowl until well combined. Gently toss in the berries and mint. Lightly spoon the mixture into the unbaked bottom piecrust. Dot with butter.

Lightly moisten the rim of the crust with water. Cut a strip off the outside of the second round and press it onto the rim of the bottom crust. Moisten the strip with water.

Place the top crust over the filling and crimp the edge decoratively to seal. Brush crust with the egg glaze then cut 4 to 5 slits in the top to allow steam to escape. Bake until the crust is nicely browned, about 40 to 50 minutes. Cool the pie in the pan on a wire rack. Serve slightly warm or at room temperature.

Treat raspberries very gently. Do not wash them until ready to use, as they are highly perishable and may mold.

Tossing raspberries and other "weepy" fruit with cornstarch before baking helps prevent a soggy bottom crust.

KEY LIME PIE

Makes 1 (9-inch) pie

KEY LIME PIE IS REALLY AN EASY RECIPE. *It calls for a graham cracker crust and sweetened condensed milk. The original juice used was from Key limes, but this recipe is for the more common Persian lime. Beating the yolks with the rind makes the mixture greener. One caveat: do not use green food dye lest you show your ignorance of the Key lime.*

- 1 (9-inch) Graham Cracker Crust (page 544)
- 1 (14-ounce) can sweetened condensed milk
- 4 large eggs, separated with 1 white reserved
- 1 1/2 tablespoons grated lime rind, no white attached
- 1/2 cup lime juice
- 1 cup heavy cream
- 1/4–1/3 cup granulated sugar
- 1/2 lime, thinly sliced and dipped in sugar

Prepare graham cracker crust in a 9-inch pie pan and chill.

When ready to bake, preheat oven to 350 degrees.

Whisk together the condensed milk, egg yolks, lime rind, and lime juice in a large bowl. Beat the reserved egg white in a clean bowl until stiff. Fold the egg white into the milk mixture. Move the prepared crust to a rimmed baking sheet. Turn the filling into the prepared crust and bake for 10 to 15 minutes. The filling will be loosey-goosey. Cool the pie on a rack and chill before serving. Top with sweetened whipped cream if desired.

KEY LIMES

Key limes have been in short supply since the majority of their groves were destroyed by weather events in the twentieth century, especially Hurricane Andrew in 1992. I had a beau whose family had a Key lime tree, however, and he insisted they were superior in every way to the common Persian lime, a hardier species. Cynthia and I went to Homestead, Florida, and located a rare Key lime tree in the mid-1980s and brought back the limes. We also purchased Haitian limes, a smaller variety than Key limes. We tested all three types. Persian limes are not as acidic as the other two, so they make a softer custard. Baking the custard firmed it up to the consistency of the Key lime. Haitian limes, also round and tart, are now being called "Key" limes. Both Haitian and Key require more limes for a pie. In my opinion, it is not worth the time or trouble to squeeze and seed either Key or Haitian limes. There is a bottled juice, but I don't use that either.

LEMON-LIME MERINGUE PIE

Makes 1 (9-inch) pie

Lemon meringue pie with lime— *it's especially ethereal. I do love the ease of graham cracker crusts, as well as their flavor. Read the Lemon Meringue Pie recipe instructions for more detail (page 523).*

1 (9-inch) Cookie Crust (page 513), made with graham crackers

Filling

1 cup granulated sugar
1/2 cup cornstarch
1/4 teaspoon salt
1 cup water
5 egg yolks
2 tablespoons unsalted butter
1/4 cup fresh lemon juice
1/4 cup lime juice
1 tablespoon grated lemon rind, no white attached
1 tablespoon grated lime rind, no white attached

Meringue

6 egg whites
1/2 teaspoon cream of tartar
1/2 cup granulated sugar

Prepare Graham Cracker Crust in a 9-inch pie pan and chill.

When ready to bake, preheat oven to 350 degrees.

For the filling, whisk together the sugar, cornstarch, and salt in a medium saucepan. Gradually stir in the water until well mixed. Cook over medium-high heat, whisking until thick. Reduce the heat and cook, stirring or whisking, for another 2 minutes. Remove from heat and quickly beat in the egg yolks one at a time. Return to heat and cook, stirring constantly, for 2 more minutes. The sauce should be very thick. Add the butter, juices, and rinds to the hot mixture. Allow to cool slightly before pouring into the crust.

For the meringue, combine the egg whites and cream of tartar in a mixing bowl and beat to soft peaks. Gradually add the sugar 1 tablespoon at a time, beating until the mixture forms stiff peaks. Spread the meringue over the still warm filling, being sure to spread it all the way to the outside of the crust to seal in the filling and prevent shrinkage. Bake until the meringue is golden brown, 15 minutes. Cool before serving.

WORKING WITH CORNSTARCH

Cornstarch is tricky. Because I don't have many recipes using it, I always have to review its rules before starting: 1 tablespoon will thicken about 1 1/2 to 2 cups liquid. Use a heavy pan, and make sure that as it cooks the mixture is constantly stirred with a rubber spatula, bringing the hot outside into the cold center. Cornstarch has two cookings—one when it begins to thicken over low heat, the other when it is brought to a full boil for 1 minute. After this, it cannot be moved or stirred, as it will liquefy.

NANA'S BANANA CREAM PIE

1 (9-inch, deep dish) pie

CYNTHIA'S MATERNAL GRANDMOTHER *had just a few culinary specialties, and this banana cream pie is a standout from Cynthia's childhood. A prebaked pastry crust may be substituted.*

Graham Cracker Crust
1 1/2 cups graham cracker crumbs
2 teaspoons granulated sugar
1/2 cup melted butter

Banana Cream Pie Filling
2 medium bananas, cut into 1/2-inch slices
3/4 cup granulated sugar
5 tablespoons cornstarch
1/4 teaspoon salt
3 cups milk
4 egg yolks
1/4 cup butter
2 teaspoons vanilla extract

Meringue
5 egg whites
8 tablespoons granulated sugar

Preheat oven to 350 degrees.

To make the graham cracker crust, toss together the crumbs, sugar, and butter. Press into a deep 9-inch pie pan. Bake 15 minutes. Let cool.

For the filling, arrange the banana slices in the crust. Whisk the sugar, cornstarch, and salt together in a heavy saucepan. Stir together until there are no lumps. Mix together the milk and egg yolks and stir into the sugar-cornstarch mixture until smooth, whisking if necessary. Move the pan over medium heat and stir constantly until the custard comes to the boil, taking care to scrape the bottom and sides. Reduce the heat to simmer and cook, stirring, until thick, about 3 minutes. Avoid scorching. Remove from the heat and beat in the butter and vanilla. Strain out any brown lumps. Taste to be sure it is not scorched. Pour the custard over the bananas. Cool 20 minutes at room temperature, covered with plastic wrap to prevent a skin from forming.

Meanwhile, make the meringue by beating the egg whites until they form firm peaks. Fold in the sugar and beat again, if necessary, to peaks. Spread the meringue over the custard, all the way to the crust. Bake 12 to 15 minutes, until the meringue is golden brown. Cool to room temperature. Refrigerate if not serving within a couple of hours, but serve at room temperature.

MISS MARY'S DATE AND SODA CRACKER PIE

Makes 1 (9-inch) pie

THIS NO-CRUST PIE RECIPE *came from an early-twentieth-century handwritten receipt book of Victoria Mooney's grandmother from Griffin, Georgia. It was a very typical pie of the day—some people even made their own soda crackers, which are much like our saltines today.*

12 dates or figs, chopped
1/2 cup finely chopped pecans
12 soda crackers, rolled into fine crumbs
1/2 teaspoon baking powder
3/4 cup granulated sugar, divided
3 egg whites
1/2–1 teaspoon almond extract
1 cup heavy cream, whipped with optional 2 teaspoons sugar

Preheat oven to 325 degrees.

Mix the fruit, nuts, crackers, baking powder, and 1/4 cup of sugar in a bowl.

Whisk the egg whites in a clean bowl until soft peaks form; slowly add the rest of the sugar, beating until stiff. Add almond extract to the egg whites.

Fold a small portion of the whites into the cracker mixture and then fold the cracker mixture into the remaining whites. Place a 9-inch glass pie pan on a rimmed baking sheet. Spread the filling into the pan and bake 40 to 45 minutes. Cool the pie in the pan on a wire rack. Serve with whipped cream.

FRIED FRUIT PIES

Makes 6 pies

FRIED PIES—THE SOUTH'S FAVORITE HAND-HELD PIE—*probably originated with leftover biscuit dough and leftover cooked dried fruit. Fresh fruit can be used, but great care must be taken to be sure it is not too juicy. So, too, can pie crust dough be used, but this is seen more in fast-food restaurants than in homes. Some like slices of fruit, others chopped. Much depends on the quality of the fruit.*

Filling

1 (7-ounce) package dried peaches, figs, or apples, roughly chopped
1 cup water
1/2 cup granulated sugar

Dough

2 1/4 cups commercial or homemade self-rising flour (page 451), divided
1/4 cup chilled shortening or butter, roughly cut into 1/2-inch pieces
1 cup milk or buttermilk, divided
2–4 cups vegetable oil or shortening for frying
Confectioners' sugar for finishing

Put the fruit and water in a medium-size heavy saucepan and let stand for 1 hour or overnight. Cook over low heat until thick enough to cling to a spoon, about 45 minutes. Stir in the sugar.

Fork-sift or whisk 2 cups of flour in a large bowl, preferably wider than it is deep, and set aside the remaining 1/4 cup of flour. Scatter the shortening over the flour and work in by rubbing fingers with the shortening and flour as if snapping thumb and fingers together (or use two forks or knives, or a pastry cutter) until the mixture looks like well-crumbled feta cheese, with no piece larger than a pea. Shake the bowl occasionally to allow the larger pieces of fat to bounce to the top of the flour, revealing the largest lumps that still need rubbing. If this method took longer than 5 minutes, place the bowl in the refrigerator for 5 minutes to rechill the fat.

Make a deep hollow in the center of the flour with the back of your hand. Pour 3/4 cup of milk or buttermilk into the hollow, reserving 1/4 cup, and stir with a rubber spatula or large metal spoon, using broad circular strokes to quickly pull the flour into the milk. Mix just until the dry ingredients are moistened and the sticky dough begins to pull away from the sides of the bowl. If there is some flour remaining on the bottom and sides of the bowl, stir in 1 to 4 tablespoons of reserved milk, just enough to incorporate the remaining flour into the shaggy, wettish dough. If the dough is too wet, use more flour when shaping.

Lightly sprinkle a board or other clean surface with some of the reserved flour. Turn the dough out onto the board and sprinkle the top lightly with flour. With floured hands, fold the dough in half, and pat dough out into a round. Pinch off a piece of dough about the size of a small egg. Roll and flatten it into a 5-inch circle. Center about 2 tablespoons of the fruit mixture on the bottom half of the pastry round, about 1/2 inch from the edge. Fold the top half of the pastry over the fruit, forming a half circle. Trim to within 1/4 inch of the filling. Press the edges together with the tines of a fork and prick the top of the pastry in several places. The pies may be made ahead to this point and refrigerated several hours before frying.

When ready to fry, heat enough oil or shortening in a large heavy skillet to reach a depth of 1/8 inch when melted. When the oil is 325 degrees F, add the pies, one at a time, prettiest side down. The fat should come about halfway up the pies when all the pies are added and still be sizzling around the edges of the pies. Cook until golden brown. Turn and fry the second side until golden brown, adding more shortening if needed. Drain briefly on a paper towel. Sprinkle with confectioners' sugar.

Variation: Savory Fried Pies

To change a sweet fried pie to a savory one, handy for a picnic or a packed lunch, add a few more ingredients to the pie. For an apple and sausage fried pie, reduce the amount of apple and add a tablespoon or two of fried and drained sausage before sealing and frying. For a fried peach pie, reduce the amount of peaches and add pepper jelly and a bit of country ham cut into small strips.

Variation: Sweet Fried Pies

Add candied ginger, cinnamon, or other pie spices; substitute brown sugar for granulated.

CAKES

Cakes have been a big part of the Southern experience. The South's long-time rural nature, with eggs and milk readily available, encouraged cake baking, especially in the winter and during the holidays. Recipes, primarily but not exclusively English in origin, were passed on to homemakers through books and printed in handwritten journals. African American cooks, who learned the recipes from white homemakers using rudimental instructions, frequently excelled and became the baking experts.

It used to be that children learned hands-on how to make cakes, as they pulled up kitchen stools and watched the bakers in their homes brush the cake pans with grease, saw how they floured the pans, helped beat the batter with a fork on a platter (I did it!), learning how every step looked, how the cake felt when it came out of the oven, how to ice it, and even how to cut it.

Our grandmothers knew their ovens so well they could test the heat by sticking their hands briefly inside to determine the temperature. Now, with only a piece of paper called a recipe as a guide, we expect our first cakes to miraculously emerge from the oven a perfect color, tender, light, and succulent.

Our grandmothers knew when to substitute butter for shortening and what kind of flour to use. They also knew which pans to use, preferring light-colored ones with butter cakes (which might get too brown with dark pans). They developed the skill to adjust to the equipment they had, partly because they knew their own pans and ingredients so well.

I'm a laissez-faire cook. My natural inclination is far from measuring accurately and doing every step carefully. A little of this, a little of that, is my modus operandi. I love spontaneity in the kitchen. Cynthia too, was a self-described terrible baker, with little patience for the exactness required for measuring ingredients. (She's come a long way!) Even so, we've learned that if we follow the steps, taking them one by one, we can be great bakers.

Baking is one area where the techniques must be learned first, and spontaneity then follows through changing spices, adding ingredients, and even experimenting with the amount of eggs, liquid, sugar, or butter. Mastering a basic cake is important to novice cooks. Because I'm not a natural baker, I hope to make every step of this clear with techniques and theories garnered. Before getting started, please read about ingredients. If I can make a baker out of Cynthia, I can make a baker out of anyone.

I've gotten a lot of help over the years from cookbooks such as Carole Walter's *Great Cakes,* Damon Lee Fowler's *Southern Baking,* James Peterson's *Baking,* Nancie McDermott's *Southern Cakes,* Rose Levy Beranbaum's *The Cake Bible,* and others we have referred to throughout.

There are many different cake varieties. So many, in fact, that the experts even classify them differently from each other. There are many varieties found in other regions of the United States, but Southern cakes fall into three broad types: Cobblers, Dump Cakes, or Batter Cakes (pages 550–60); Butter Cakes (pages 561–67); and Foam Cakes (pages 568–78).

EQUIPMENT FOR CAKE MAKING

Oven—Knowing one's oven is a key to baking. Test the oven by the "toast test" (page 487) to show the hot spots in the oven and which layers must be rotated to cook evenly. It is a good habit to adjust the racks and preheat the oven when starting a recipe, even though it might take a while to prepare the batter. Forgetting and putting the cake into a cold oven can be disastrous.

Stand mixers—Use a heavy-duty stand mixer, if possible, when making a cake with more than 3 eggs. It's difficult to use an electric hand mixer for one with a very thick batter or more than 3 eggs. The best kind of mixer has a revolving rotary whisk that beats air into the batter. With a spatula, scrape the sides of the bowl frequently while mixing. An electric hand mixer is handy for small batches as well as sometimes filling in a part of the recipe, as in the Daffodil Cake. Having two mixing bowls for the stand mixer is the best way to save time and get the best product. An electric hand mixer rarely beats egg whites satisfactorily unless the cook is very skilled.

Pans and linings—Metal cake pans with straight sides are worth the investment. Many cooks are tempted by the glories of nonstick, but these dark pans absorb more heat. Reduce the baking temperature by 25 degrees if using nonstick. Novelty pans are inconsistent. All pans need to be "greased" using melted lard or shortening, room-temperature butter (which gives a thicker protective coating than melted butter), or oil. Lining the pans with parchment or waxed paper is also a boon when trying to turn cakes out of the pan. The paper gives the cake something to hold on to so it doesn't crumble when released.

To line a pan, draw a circle on waxed paper, using the bottom of the pan as a guide. Or fold a piece of parchment or waxed paper in half, then quarters, then eighths to look like a pie wedge. Place the tip end in the center of the baking pan and mark where the edge of the paper meets the pan. Cut the paper at that edge. Unfold and use to line the pan. If using a loaf pan, line with two perpendicular pieces of parchment or waxed paper, each with a four inch overhang added to use as handles to lift the loaf from the pan. Cut one to the width of the pan and the other to the length of the pan. For the finest finish, brush the grease on the bottom and sides of the pan, flour the bottom and sides of pan, upend and tap on pan to remove excess flour. Then put in the paper, and repeat, greasing and flouring the paper. Parchment is a superior liner to waxed paper, but if only waxed paper is available, it is preferable to nothing. There are many commercial liners available as well. When substituting another liner, follow manufacturer's directions.

Racks—A cooling rack allows air to move underneath the pan. This cools the cake, preventing sweat on the bottom and providing easy release. If no rack is available, move to a cool stovetop ring or use a folded tea towel under the pan to absorb some of the heat.

INGREDIENTS

All ingredients for baking cakes should be at room temperature. Room temperature should be 70 degrees.

Eggs—All eggs for baking should be large Grade A eggs. One egg is 2 ounces. One white is a bit more than 1 liquid ounce, the yolk a bit less. There is a lot of discussion about which eggs are better for baking, fresh or several days old. Both work, but several days old is considered better, though not crucial. Eggs contract in size as they age, so avoid weeks-old ones.

Before refrigeration, women like MaMa Dupree of Americus, Georgia, kept eggs on a cool closet shelf, to be used weeks later, unafraid of the contamination more prevalent with mass production. We recommend all eggs be kept refrigerated until 20 minutes before using, for optimum performance in baking.

Since it is easier to separate eggs when they are cold, separate first, then let separated eggs come to room temperature, about 20 minutes, for maximum volume. (The air bubbles in cold eggs don't expand as much; see page 272.)

Extra whites can be refrigerated, tightly covered, for a week or so, or they can be frozen. An easy way to separate the frozen ones is to freeze them in ice cube trays and then pop them out into a freezer container so they can be removed one at a time. (Always mark the container clearly to avoid them winding up in someone's drink.) They defrost quickly.

Beat any extra yolks with a fork and refrigerate covered for a day or two, at the most, to add to omelets, dressings, custards, and the like.

Butter—Unsalted butter is best for cakes, as it has a clean, fresh taste. Butter should be at room temperature, or around 70 to 72 degrees Fahrenheit. Warmer than that, it may melt. Cut butter into 1-inch pieces when it is cold and then let it get to room temperature. To speed it up, use a cheese slicer or microplane grater to cut the butter into thin slices. Melted butter does not perform the same way, so resist defrosting it in the microwave.

"Creaming" butter, a confusing terminology I try to avoid, means to beat butter until it is has the ripple and color of cream. This allows it to absorb air and adds to the cake's texture. In very old cookbooks, it is called "rubbing." Now, we say "beat until light and fluffy" for the same result.

Flour—Use a low gluten soft-wheat all-purpose, such as a Southern flour or cake flour, if possible. Otherwise, use a national brand all-purpose flour. Most Southern flour and cake flour is pre-sifted and technically does not need further sifting. Self-rising flour should always be whisked in the package to be sure it is well combined before measuring. See further "Sifting" under Techniques (facing).

> Rather than dirty a bowl, I measure dry ingredients onto a piece of waxed paper. It is easier to funnel into a mixer from the paper.

Sugar—These recipes are designed for cane sugar. Beet sugar performs differently. Many bakers use extra-fine granulated sugar. To make extra-fine sugar, resulting in a lighter cake, measure granulated sugar first and then process it in a food processor until fine before adding to the batter. In this book, this procedure is not necessary for recipes calling for plain granulated sugar.

Dark and light brown sugars stay moist when stored with a slice of apple for moisture exchange. If the sugar has clumped, a brief period in the microwave or in the food processor usually speeds recovery. Otherwise, put it through a large strainer and discard the lumps or use for another purpose. When measuring, always pack brown sugar tightly into the container.

Milk—Milk should be at room temperature (70–72 degrees Fahrenheit) for most cakes. A few recipes heat it to a simmer, the point when bubbles appear around the edge of the pan.

Baking soda—This leavening reacts with an acid to give lift to baked goods. Measure carefully, as too much baking soda will result in a metallic taste.

Baking powder—Baking powder is a combination of

> European cakes are traditionally basted with a sugar syrup (sometimes flavored with a favorite alcohol) to moisten. Thus they appear tender and stay moist longer. Coconut cake is typically basted with sugar syrup.

One-fourth teaspoon baking soda is equal in leavening power to 1 teaspoon baking powder. To test for freshness, see page 453.

baking soda, a dry acid, and cornstarch and produces two leavening actions. The first occurs when the powder comes in contact with liquid, and the second when the powder comes in contact with heat. Thus it is "double-acting." Use nonaluminum baking powders such as Argo, Rumford, Bakewell Cream, and Red Star. Others, such as Calumet and Clabber Girl, contain aluminum and add a slight metallic taste to the cake. Once opened, a can of baking powder usually remains fresh for about six months.

Cornstarch—Sometimes added to cakes to lighten their texture, cornstarch is used most often as a thickener for fruit pies and sauces.

Nuts—Store nuts in the freezer if possible. Always taste nuts before using in case they have become rancid. When grinding finely, take care to stop before they are oily. Toasted nuts have much more flavor than untoasted. Nuts are called for in various sizes, depending on the recipe—sometimes they are used as a flour, as in the pecan roll, and sometimes for crunch and flavor additions, as in a filling. They chop more easily when dusted with flour.

Salt—Added to enhance the flavors of the cake, salt also adds a bit of lightness. The recipes in this book use table salt unless otherwise specified.

Flavorings—Use the best vanilla extract available. Many grocery store varieties are not top quality and are more expensive per ounce, as they come in small containers. It is cumbersome to extract seeds from fresh vanilla beans and use them in a cake, but boiled icings are very accommodating to vanilla beans. I make my own extract with bourbon and vanilla beans. Although an initial expense, as it requires purchasing the beans in bulk, the extract lasts several years.

TECHNIQUES

Sifting—Flour does not sell as quickly in grocery stores as it used to, so it tends to pack. Whisk the flour in the container before measuring. Take a large spoon or ladle, and spoon out the flour into a dry measuring cup until full. Sweep excess off by running the back of a knife or a metal spatula blade across the top. If it is the first ingredient going into a mixer, whisk it a few times (professional bakers whisk flour in the mixer bowl for 30 seconds) before adding other ingredients. If measuring onto parchment or waxed paper to be funneled in later, put the flour in a large strainer and tap the side lightly until it is on the paper. A triple sifter—the kind that hand rotates a sifting mechanism—is a nuisance to store, and ingredients can become lodged in the sifter, altering the measured ingredient.

Testing for doneness—Although different types of cakes vary slightly, a cake is usually cooked when it reaches an internal temperature of 190 to 195 degrees and springs back when touched lightly and/or when a toothpick, skewer, or fork inserted into the middle of the cake comes out clean.

Inverting a cake—To remove a cake from the pan, hold a small sharp knife next to the inside of the pan and move it carefully around the circumference to separate the cake from the pan. Place a platter larger than the pan upside down on top of the pan and flip both together. The cake will now be on the plate. Peel the paper off gently, starting at one side and moving to the other without jerking. If it breaks, or leaves bumps, and it is a layer cake, use this as the middle layer; if it is a single layer cake, cover as best as possible with icing, powdered sugar, etc.

Multiple-layered cakes—The thinner the layer, the more difficult it is to cut horizontally. There are two popular ways of converting a two- or three-layer cake into more layers. The first is slicing a thick layer horizontally to make 2 or more layers. The best specialty gadget is made of thin wire, designed to cut layers horizontally. Another, more rudimental, method is to evenly insert toothpicks around thicker layers to use as a guide for slicing. Use a serrated knife and cut into the round, turning the cake while cutting, going 1 inch deep all around. Go back and cut another inch toward the middle, all around the layer, until the two halves are separated. This is much easier than starting on one side and sawing through to the other, which produces uneven layers.

The other way of making a layer cake is to bake the batter in more pans, dividing the batter as desired. It is necessary to keep a good eye on thinner layers to prevent browning. Take care to have air circulating around the cake layers and to avoid crowding. When this happens, the bottoms of cakes on the lowest rack and the tops of cakes on the top rack burn because the air can't circulate. Rotate or change positions of pans partway through the cooking time so they cook evenly.

The amount of icing should be increased to nearly double for each layer added. It is better, however, to have too much icing than too little. Keep the icing between layers at a minimum so the cake layers don't slide.

Filling a cake—If a cake recipe calls for a filling to be placed between the layers, parcel it out carefully. Too much will cause the layers to slide; too little will rob the cake of flavor. Select and ice the top layer first to make sure it has enough icing then divide the filling among the remaining layers.

Freezing a cake— If planning to freeze an iced cake, use a cake round under the bottom layer before icing to keep the bottom from crumbling. Stick toothpicks in the cake to prevent the icing from sticking to the wrapper. Wrap tightly around the toothpicks with plastic wrap and then freezer foil, or put in a cake holder that can go in the freezer.

Icing a cake—I think it is charming for home cakes to have a dome, declaring they are "homemade." When necessary, even out domes or overbrowned layers with a sharp serrated knife. If they aren't burned, keep the trimmings and make them into crumbs for decorating or into cutouts to keep children (and the cook) happy until it is time to eat the cake.

The tops of cakes will frequently crumb. Cake bakers usually remove this crumb with a pastry brush before icing. Move the prettiest layer to a rack set over waxed paper to catch icing drippings. Ice the cake layer by ladling or spooning a portion of the icing into the middle of the cake. Use a long spatula to spread, starting in the middle and working out to the sides. Wait to ice the sides until the cake is assembled. Keep the drippings in case more icing is needed for the bottom and middle layers. (It can't be used for the sides, as it will have cake crumbs in it.)

Divide the remaining icing onto the number of layers left to ice, remembering to save some for the sides. Choose the least desirable layer as the bottom layer. Any broken layer should be in the middle. After the bottom layer is determined, move it to a cardboard cake round. If using a cake plate, make spokes with 5 x 3-inch strips of parchment or waxed paper on the serving plate, extending slightly, to catch the icing from dripping onto the plate. Ice as above, remembering that too much icing on the bottom two layers will cause the cake to slide.

Ice middle layer on a cake rack, then move on top of bottom layer. Top with the pretty layer, which is already iced. Spread icing over the sides if there is sufficient remaining. Slide out the strips of paper and tidy up the plate.

If icing is too stiff to spread smoothly, recheck the recipe to determine if ingredients were measured carefully, and adjust as needed. If it is simply too cold to spread, warm it quickly and carefully over low heat or in the microwave. If the icing is runny, chill slightly first, then try to add some of the thickest ingredient to make it firmer.

COBBLERS, DUMP CAKES, OR BATTER CAKES

These cakes became popular in the mid-1800s in England and the United States after the invention of baking powder. The technique, as the name implies, is simple: dump all the ingredients into one bowl or container and stir. They host a variety of ingredients, from Coca-Cola and marshmallows to grated carrot and fruits for cobbler variations. Some use butter; some use oil. The cakes usually use less egg, with the leavening being baking powder. This was particularly important in hard times, such as during and after wars and the Depression, when eggs and butter were expensive and difficult to come by.

Dump cakes are most popular when completely made in one pan, from mixing to baking to serving. The first printed article using the name "dump cake" was in the *Christian Science Monitor* in 1921. Cake mix manufacturers took them up with varied success, at one time reputedly including pans that were too small, causing big messes in the oven. It's a wonder these cake mixes survived.

COBBLERS

Cobblers have been made since at least the mid-1800s, getting their name from the top, which looks like cobbled streets. There are many kinds of Southern cobblers. Some call for piecrusts, others for batters. Some use eggs as leavening, others use self-rising flour. With no bottom crust and just a topping over the fruit, they are sometimes called the "lazy girl's pie."

While many regions use a biscuit topping over the fruit, the South does the typical cobbler with self-rising flour, where the batter is poured into hot butter in a pan (usually not a pie dish), then fruit and juices are poured over. The batter grows through the fruit, gathering some of its flavor and staying like a soft cake, leaving buttery crisp bottom edges.

Cobbler Cousins

Crisps and crumbles—are cooked with the fruit mixture on the bottom and a crumb topping of flour, ground nuts, bread or cookie or graham cracker crumbs, or ground or whole breakfast cereal (oats, for example).

Betty or Brown Betty—consists of a cooked fruit, usually apples but sometimes pears, layered between buttered crumbs or bread.

Grunt or slump—are terms for a cobbler in New England that is cooked on top of the stove.

Buckle—is a batter cake with blueberries or other fruit added in a single layer. The topping is similar to a streusel.

Pandowdy—is a deep-dish fruit dessert that is most commonly made with apples sweetened with sorghum, molasses, syrup, or brown sugar. The topping may be a type of biscuit or fried bread. The crust is sometimes "broken up" during baking and pushed down into the fruit to allow the juices to come through.

Bird's-nest pudding—is an apple pudding where the apple cores have been replaced by sugar. The crust creates a bowl around the apples.

Sonker—is a deep-dish fruit or sweet potato pie or cobbler, most likely unique to North Carolina.

Streusel—is from a German word meaning "something scattered or sprinkled" and refers to a crumb topping that is baked on top of muffins, breads, and cakes.

QUICK 'N' EASY CINNAMON APPLE COBBLER

Serves 4 to 6

As my intern Joseph Dweck *was growing up, he remembers going to his best friend's house and smelling a fragrant home-baked apple cobbler on occasion. To this day, smelling one takes him back, remembering tasting it fresh out of the oven. A treasured family recipe, this cobbler is a comforting old-fashioned dessert. It travels well and slices nicely, so it's perfect for picnics or tailgate parties. Use another favorite fruit to wow any number of people.*

8 tablespoons unsalted butter, divided
2 cups thinly sliced apples
1 teaspoon ground cinnamon
1 cup self-rising flour
1 cup granulated sugar, divided
1 cup milk

Melt 6 tablespoons of butter in an 8 x 10-inch baking dish in the oven while the oven preheats to 375 degrees.

Melt the remaining butter in a medium-sized skillet over medium-high heat. Add the apples, cinnamon, and 2 tablespoons sugar. Sauté the apples until they are light golden brown. Set aside.

Meanwhile, mix the flour, the remaining sugar, and milk in a medium bowl. Remove the pan with the melted butter from the oven and pour the flour mixture into it. The butter may sizzle while rising to the top of the batter. Spread the apples on top and return to the oven. Bake for about 30 to 35 minutes, or until light golden brown on top.

LAZY GIRL PEACH BATTER COBBLER

Serves 4 to 6

THIS WAS NAMED *by my dear friend Keri Whitley of Social Circle, Georgia. After I'd been making it as peach cobbler for many years, she said, "It really is for lazy girls." Really, it is for anyone smart enough to know it is as memorable as it is easy. The fruit ends up surrounded by the buttery cake formed by the batter. This cobbler is on country buffets all over the South, served in small dishes, perhaps with a bit of vanilla ice cream. It will serve more, but frankly, my husband and I can eat one by ourselves.*

1 cup granulated, light, or dark brown sugar, divided
2 cups sliced peaches
1/2 cup unsalted butter
1 cup self-rising flour
1 cup whole milk

Sprinkle 1/4 cup of sugar over the peaches and let sit while melting the butter in a 8 x 11-inch baking pan or decorative oven-to-table dish in the oven as it preheats to 350 degrees. (The butter crisps the edges, so I say "the bigger the dish, the better." If you prefer a deeper cobbler, a smaller pan may be used.)

Whisk together the flour, milk, and remaining sugar. It can be just a bit lumpy. When the butter is melted, remove the hot pan and pour the batter into the bottom of the pan. Don't worry if the batter puffs up a bit on the sides. Sprinkle the peaches over the top of the batter.

Bake for 45 minutes, or until the batter has risen around the fruit, the top is light brown, and the sides are darker brown. Serve hot. It can be made ahead and refrigerated or frozen. Reheat before serving.

Variations:

- Blueberries, raspberries, and/or sliced strawberries are equally mouthwatering substitutions. To gild the lily, serve with ice cream or whipped cream.
- Add 1 tablespoon chopped candied ginger, 1 tablespoon chopped fresh mint leaves, or 1 1/2 teaspoons ground cinnamon.

Variation: Upsy-Daisy Cobbler

When we were small, "upsy daisy" was what my father said when he would toss one of us into the air and turn us upside down. Well, that is what this cobbler does! Use an 11-inch nonstick or well-seasoned iron skillet for a thinner, tart-like cake. For a thicker cake, use a smaller well-seasoned 9-inch iron or nonstick skillet. After cooking, cool slightly, cover with a large flat cake plate, invert, and the cake should come out easily. If not, peer under and pry off a bit with a blunt knife.

Variation: Upside-Down Apple Cobbler

I learned this from David Hagedorm at the *Washington Post*.

Melt the butter in a 9-inch iron or nonstick skillet while preheating the oven. Use brown sugar. Toss half the sugar with 2 1/2 cups thinly sliced tart apples. Mix the remaining sugar with the self-rising flour and milk. Remove the pan from the oven. Quickly arrange some of the sliced apples in a spiral pattern around the bottom of the pan. Pour the batter into the still hot pan. Top with the remaining apples. Cook as above. When a fork comes out clean, remove from the oven. Cool slightly on a rack. Top with a plate, invert the pan, give a shake, and the cake should come out onto the plate.

MRS. DULL'S SIMPLE APPLE CAKE

Makes 1 (9-inch) round cake

GEORGIA'S HENRIETTA DULL, *in her book* Southern Cooking, *first published in 1928, included a recipe for this simple apple cake. From that book, the recipe was purloined and renamed far and wide. In Charleston, it was served in the Huguenot Tavern, and thus included in* Charleston Receipts *as Huguenot Torte. In Missouri, it was served by Bess Truman as "Ozark Pudding," and she brought it with her to Washington, D.C. Methinks it is neither Charlestonian nor Ozarkian, but Georgian, given that Mrs. Dull's book predates the other events. The range of this cake's popularity attests to its ease of preparation and depth of flavor.*

- 1/2 cup all-purpose or cake flour, divided
- 2 teaspoons baking powder
- 1/2 teaspoon salt
- 2 large eggs
- 1 cup packed light or dark brown sugar
- 2 teaspoons vanilla extract
- 1 cup chopped pecans, plus more for garnish if desired
- 1 cup chopped peeled apples

Position rack in the center of the oven and preheat to 350 degrees. Butter a 9-inch pie plate.

Sift 1/4 cup flour, baking powder, and salt together onto a piece of waxed paper and set aside.

Beat the eggs and sugar with an electric hand mixer until light. Stir in flour mixture and vanilla, and blend quickly and well with the mixer. Toss the nuts and apples in the remaining flour and stir into the batter.

Spoon batter into the pie plate and bake for 35 minutes. Sprinkle more nuts over the top if desired, and serve warm or room temperature with ice cream or whipped cream.

HOME-STYLE PEACH CAKE

Makes 1 (9 x 13 x 2-inch) cake

THE SOUTH IS FAMOUS FOR PEOPLE *who eat dessert every night. So every home cook needs a repertoire of quick desserts like this one and the Lazy Girl Cobbler (facing).*

- 2 cups sliced peaches, fresh or frozen
- 1 tablespoon fresh lemon juice
- 1 cup light or dark brown sugar, divided
- 1 teaspoon ground ginger
- 1/2 cup unsalted butter, melted
- 2 large eggs, lightly beaten
- 1/4 cup sour cream
- 1 teaspoon vanilla extract
- 1 cup all-purpose or cake flour
- 1 tablespoon granulated sugar

Position rack in the center of the oven and preheat to 350 degrees. Lightly butter a 9 x 13-inch baking dish or pan.

Cut the peach slices in half and toss with the lemon juice, 1/4 cup brown sugar, and ginger. Pour into the prepared baking dish.

Mix together the butter, remaining 3/4 cup brown sugar, eggs, sour cream, and vanilla in another bowl until just blended. Fold in the flour, making sure the ingredients are all incorporated, and spread the batter evenly over the peaches. Sprinkle with granulated sugar and bake the cake until the top is golden and crusty around the edges, about 30 minutes. Cool the baking dish slightly on a wire rack before cutting into squares and serving.

Variation: Instead of peaches, substitute 2 cups fresh or canned pineapple, peeled, cored, and cut into 1-inch chunks.

PECAN APPLE CAKE WITH CARAMEL TOPPING

Makes 1 (8-inch) round cake

WHEN WE FIRST STARTED CONVERTING *the machine shop warehouse for my restaurant, Nathalie's, at Mount Pleasant Village, Georgia, Grace Reeves, who lived in a trailer on the property, brought us an apple cake. My brother, husband, and I loved it, eating it all ourselves in a day, although it would normally have fed a nice-sized group. Grace was from the mountains of Georgia and always brought back apples when she went home to visit her family. Somehow, I never got her recipe, but this recipe, adapted from one of Abby Mandel's, reminds me of it. It remains moist and tasty for several days and freezes beautifully. We debated many times about adding the caramel on top of the apples, as it hides the beautiful apples on top. But every man we know wants the caramel on top and could care less about seeing the apples. Hence, this is the final version.*

- 1/2 cup plus 2 tablespoons unsalted butter, divided
- 1 1/2 cups granulated sugar, divided
- 1/2 teaspoon ground cinnamon
- 1/2 teaspoon ground ginger
- 1 1/2 cups all-purpose or cake flour, divided
- 4 tart apples, such as Granny Smith, peeled, cored, and halved
- 2 large eggs
- 1/3 cup milk
- 2 tablespoons bourbon or rum
- 2 teaspoons vanilla extract
- 2 teaspoons baking powder
- 1 teaspoon baking soda
- 1/2 teaspoon salt
- 2 tablespoons finely chopped pecans

Position the rack in the center of the oven and preheat to 350 degrees. Wrap foil around the outside of an 8 x 3 1/4-inch springform pan to prevent leakage.

Melt 2 tablespoons butter and brush the insides of the pan. Line the bottom of the pan with parchment or waxed paper and brush the paper with butter.

Mix together 1/2 cup sugar, cinnamon, ginger, and 1/4 cup flour, and sprinkle this sandy mixture evenly over the bottom of the pan.

Halve, core, and slice three of the apples into 1/4-inch wedges. Starting at the outside edge of the pan, arrange a ring of apple slices, slightly overlapping and pointing to the center. Fill in the center with another circle of apples, with some overlap occurring. Layer any remaining apple slices evenly, overlapping to prevent the batter from escaping.

Cut the two remaining apple halves into quarters. Pulse a few times in the food processor to chop roughly, or chop roughly by hand into 1/2-inch or smaller pieces, and set aside. In the same bowl, pulse the remaining 1/2 cup butter and the remaining 1 cup sugar in the food processor or beat together in a stand mixer until light. Add eggs, milk, bourbon, and vanilla, and pulse or beat to combine. The batter will look curdled. Whisk or sift together the remaining 1 1/4 cups flour with the baking powder, baking soda, and salt. Add to the batter along with the chopped apples and chopped nuts, pulsing or beating only until the flour is completely incorporated and the apples and nuts integrated into the batter. Pour the batter over the apples and spread evenly.

Place the pan on a foil-lined rimmed baking sheet and bake in the middle of the oven about 70 minutes, until the internal temperature of the cake reaches 190 to 195 degrees or a toothpick inserted in the cake comes out clean. Cover with a piece of foil if the top begins to brown. Let the cake rest in the pan on a rack for 5 minutes. Go around the pan with a long knife to gently separate the sides of the cake from the pan. Invert the cake on the rack, leaving the pan on for another 10 minutes so the cinnamon mixture melts around the apples. Remove the pan, lifting it up carefully. Peel off the paper, showing the inviting caramel and the apples peeking through. This cake slices easiest with a long knife, and a small wedge goes a long way. But, then, everyone wants seconds or thirds anyway.

HUMMINGBIRD CAKE

Makes 1 (9-inch) round 3-layer cake

MY OLD FRIEND HELEN MOORE *of* The Charlotte Observer *discovered this cake's origins were Jamaican, where it is called "Doctor Bird Cake," named after a local bird. After being published as "Hummingbird Cake" in* Southern Living *magazine in 1978, it quickly became a regional favorite, showing up at church parties and funerals. Perhaps it is the name as well as the ease of preparation. It is a type of dump cake—made with oil in one bowl—and is very light. The added fruit makes us feel virtuous and, of course, adds a different texture and flavor. This is a wetter, looser batter than many other cakes. A cream cheese icing is traditional, familiar to those making carrot cake and some coconut cakes.*

3 cups all-purpose or cake flour
2 cups granulated sugar
1 teaspoon baking soda
1 teaspoon ground cinnamon
1/2 teaspoon salt
3 large eggs, lightly beaten
3/4 cup oil, cook's preference
1 3/4 cups mashed bananas (about 2)
1 (8-ounce) can crushed pineapple with juice
1 cup chopped pecans
2 teaspoons vanilla extract
1 recipe Cream Cheese Icing (page 585) or other favorite

Position rack in the center of the oven and preheat to 350 degrees. Butter and flour three 9-inch round cake pans. Line the bottoms of the pans with parchment or waxed paper. Butter and flour the paper.

Whisk the flour, sugar, baking soda, cinnamon, and salt together in the bowl of a stand mixer. Add the eggs and oil, and beat until the entire mixture is moist. Stir in the bananas, pineapple with juice, pecans, and vanilla. Pour the batter evenly into the prepared pans. Tap the pans once against the counter to remove any air bubbles then smooth the top of the batter.

Bake 25 to 30 minutes, until a toothpick inserted in the middle comes out clean. The internal temperature of the cake should be 190 to 195 degrees on an instant-read thermometer.

Move the pans to a wire rack to cool for 10 minutes. Carefully run a knife around the inside edge of the cake pans to loosen the cake. Turn the pans out upside down onto the wire rack and peel off the waxed paper. The cakes may be made ahead to this point. (Well-wrapped, they will freeze up to 4 months.)

Always select and ice the prettiest layer first for the top, to be sure it gets sufficient icing. Icing directions are on page 550.

Variation: Top iced cake with 1/2 cup chopped pecans.

FIG CAKE

Makes 1 (9-inch) 2-layer cake

Figs add a unique richness and fullness *to a cake's flavor. I love this in the middle of the fall or winter—it makes me feel warm and cozy. Because we don't drink enough buttermilk to warrant its being kept fresh in the house, I use powdered buttermilk most of the time, and find it works well. Follow package directions for substitution.*

2 cups all-purpose or cake flour
1 cup granulated sugar
1 teaspoon baking soda
1 teaspoon salt
1 teaspoon ground cinnamon
1/2 teaspoon ground cloves
1/2 teaspoon ground nutmeg
3 large eggs, lightly beaten
1 cup oil, cook's preference
1/2 cup buttermilk
1 teaspoon vanilla extract
1 1/2 cups fig preserves, homemade or store bought
1/2 cup applesauce
1 cup chopped pecans, toasted
1 recipe Cream Cheese Icing (page 585) or other favorite

Position rack in the center of the oven and preheat to 350 degrees. Butter and flour two 9-inch round cake pans. Line the bottoms of the pans with parchment or waxed paper. Butter and flour the paper.

Toss the flour, sugar, baking soda, salt, cinnamon, cloves, and nutmeg together in the bowl of a stand mixer. Add the eggs, oil, buttermilk, and vanilla, and beat until the entire mixture is moist. Fold in the fig preserves, applesauce, and pecans. Pour the batter evenly into the prepared pans. Tap the pans once against the counter to remove any air bubbles and smooth the top of the batter.

Bake 35 to 40 minutes, until a toothpick inserted in the middle comes out clean. The internal temperature of the cake should be 190 to 195 degrees on an instant-read thermometer.

Move the pans to a wire rack to cool for 10 minutes. Carefully run a knife around the inside edge of the cake pans to loosen the cake. Turn the cake pans upside down onto the wire rack and carefully remove the waxed paper. The cakes may be made ahead to this point. (Well-wrapped, they will freeze up to 4 months.)

Always select and ice the prettiest layer first for the top, to be sure it gets sufficient icing. Icing directions are on page 550.

CHOCOLATE BUTTERMILK CAKE

Makes 1 (8-inch) round 3-layer cake or 1 (13 x 9 x 2-inch) cake

THIS IS A CELEBRATORY CAKE, *suited for a birthday or other special occasion. The only caveat is that once you've made it, it will be called for over and over again. This dump cake is the simplest kind to make: nothing is beaten more than 2 minutes. It is prettier made into a layer cake but serves easily from a 13 x 9 x 2-inch pan.*

2 cups all-purpose or cake flour
2 cups granulated sugar
1/2 cup unsweetened cocoa powder
1 teaspoon baking soda
1/2 teaspoon salt
3/4 cup oil, cook's preference
1/2 cup buttermilk
2 large eggs, lightly beaten
2 teaspoons vanilla extract
1 cup boiling water
1 recipe Rich Chocolate Icing (page 583) or other favorite

Position rack in the center of the oven and preheat to 350 degrees. Butter and flour three 8-inch round or one 13 x 9 x 2-inch pan. Line the bottom(s) with parchment or waxed paper. Butter and flour the paper.

Sift the flour, sugar, cocoa powder, baking soda, and salt in a large mixing bowl. Beat in the oil, buttermilk, eggs, and vanilla with an electric hand mixer, starting on low and increasing to medium-high for 2 more minutes. Stir in the boiling water until blended. The batter will be thin. Pour the batter evenly into the prepared pans. Tap the pans once against the counter to remove any air bubbles then smooth the top of the batter.

Bake 30 to 35 minutes, until a toothpick inserted near the center comes out clean. The internal temperature of the cake should be 190 to 195 degrees on an instant-read thermometer.

Move the pans to a wire rack to cool for 10 minutes. Carefully run a knife around the inside edge of the cakes to loosen. Turn the cakes out onto the rack and remove the waxed paper. The cakes may be made ahead to this point. (Well-wrapped, they will freeze up to 2 months.) Always select and ice the prettiest layer first for the top, to be sure it gets sufficient icing. Icing directions are on page 550.

COCOA POWDERS

There are two commonly available cocoa powders. One is Dutch process cocoa powder, which is treated with an alkali to reduce its acids. Being neutral, it is used in baking recipes where there are other acids to activate any leavens. The other is natural unsweetened cocoa powder, which is bitter and sharp tasting, giving baked goods a deep chocolate flavor. It has not been neutralized, so it is frequently the acid component used in baking to activate the leavens. The most popular brands are Hershey's and Ghirardelli.

When substituting one for the other in baking, follow these guidelines:

If the recipe calls for Dutch Process Cocoa, use 1/8 teaspoon baking soda per 3 tablespoons unsweetened cocoa powder.

If the recipe calls for unsweetened cocoa powder, use exact measure and omit any baking soda in the recipe.

Hot chocolate mix isn't an effective substitution, as it contains sugar and milk powders, which alter the balance of the recipe ingredients. Use it in a pinch, reducing the sugar called for in the recipe, but with no guarantee of success.

COCA-COLA CAKE

Makes 1 (9 x 11-inch) cake

THIS CAKE COMBINES *all the things Southern children love—Coca-Cola, nuts, and marshmallows, making it super sweet. It is a hit at church and covered-dish suppers, where children of all ages have generous servings from the pan. The recipe is from a church friend, Judi Walz.*

2 cups all-purpose or cake flour
2 cups granulated sugar
1 cup unsalted butter, softened
1 cup Coca-Cola
3 tablespoons cocoa powder
1/2 cup buttermilk
1 teaspoon baking soda
2 large eggs, lightly beaten
1 teaspoon vanilla extract
1 1/2 cups miniature marshmallows
1 recipe Coca-Cola Icing (below)

Position rack in the center of the oven and preheat to 350 degrees. Butter a 9 x 11-inch cake pan.

Sift the flour and sugar together into a large mixing bowl. Bring the butter, Coca-Cola, cocoa, and buttermilk to the boil in a saucepan. Pour the Coca-Cola mixture over the flour mixture. Add the baking soda, eggs, vanilla, and marshmallows, and mix well with an electric hand mixer.

Pour the batter into the buttered pan. Tap the pan once against the counter to remove any air bubbles then smooth the top of the batter.

Bake 45 minutes, until a toothpick inserted in the center comes out clean. The internal temperature of the cake should be 190 to 195 degrees on an instant-read thermometer. Let the cake cool on a rack for 10 minutes.

Note: For more servings, the cake can be baked in a 9 x 13-inch sheet cake pan, decreasing the baking time by 10 to 12 minutes. Increase icing by at least half to compensate for the extra surface.

COCA-COLA ICING

Makes 4 to 5 cups

COOKING WITH COCA-COLA *is second nature to most Southerners. This recipe came from a friend who was an Atlanta native and, out of loyalty, has never drunk any other cola. It is debilitatingly sweet—making a cake lover's knees weak.*

1/2 cup unsalted butter, softened
3 tablespoons cocoa powder
6 tablespoons Coca-Cola
3 1/2 cups confectioners' sugar, sifted
1 cup chopped pecans
1 teaspoon vanilla extract

Heat the butter, cocoa, and Coca-Cola in a saucepan and bring to the boil. Remove from the heat and fold in the sugar, pecans, and vanilla.

See page 550 for how to ice a cake.

Variation: For a two-layer cake, omit the second-layer step.

Variation: Cocoa Icing
Sift 3 1/2 cups of confectioners' sugar and 1/3 cup cocoa powder together on a sheet of waxed paper. Beat together 1 cup melted butter, 1 teaspoon vanilla extract, and 1 cup chopped pecans in a bowl. Add the sugar mixture and beat until smooth. Spread the icing over the cake.

PEACH OR PINEAPPLE UPSIDE-DOWN CAKE **Makes 1 (9-inch) round cake**

UPSIDE-DOWN CAKE *is a good cake for an aspiring baker to try, as it is so easy. Freestone peaches make a prettier presentation, as they are easily removed from the pit. Substitute fresh pineapple or see the variations.*

- 4 ripe freestone peaches, or 1 (8-ounce) can pineapple slices, with juice
- 1/3 cup plus 2 tablespoons unsalted butter, divided
- 1/2 cup light or dark brown sugar
- 4 pitted Bing cherries, halved
- 3/4 cup granulated sugar
- 2 teaspoons vanilla extract
- 1 large egg
- 1 1/2 cups all-purpose or cake flour
- 2 1/2 teaspoons baking powder
- 1/4 teaspoon salt

Position rack in the center of the oven and preheat to 350 degrees. Butter a 9-inch round cake pan or a 10-inch iron skillet.

Peel the peaches and cut them in half, twisting them from the stone and reserving any juices; set aside. Or drain the pineapple, reserving juice. Remove 1 tablespoon juice and add to the brown sugar. Measure the rest of the juice and add enough water to make 2/3 cup; set aside.

Cut a piece of parchment or waxed paper to fit the pan. Move the parchment to the pan. Thickly butter the parchment paper with the 2 tablespoons of butter. Sprinkle the parchment paper with the brown sugar and 1 tablespoon of the fruit juice. Arrange peaches cut side down, or arrange pineapple slices in the pan, placing cherry halves as desired in the center of the fruit.

Beat the remaining 1/3 cup butter in a bowl with an electric hand mixer, adding the sugar and vanilla, until well blended. Add the egg and beat for 1 minute more. Sift together the flour, baking powder, and salt. Add a third of the flour mixture to the sugar and butter mixture, beat briefly, then add half of the fruit juice; beat. Then add the second third of the flour and beat before and after adding the remaining juice. Finish by adding the last portion of the dry ingredients; beat well. Spread the batter in the pan.

Bake for 30 to 40 minutes, until a toothpick inserted in the middle comes out clean. Cool the cake in the pan 5 minutes on a rack and then invert onto a plate.

Variation: Fig Upside-Down Cake

Use fresh figs, or pour boiling water to cover over 6 dried figs in a small bow; let sit for 15 minutes to reconstitute and drain. Remove stems. Melt 2 tablespoons butter with 1/4 cup light or dark brown sugar and 1/4 cup orange marmalade. Pour into prepared pan. Top with the figs (split if large) and 1/4 cup chopped pecans. Continue with the recipe above, beginning with beating the remaining 1/3 cup butter.

Variation: Caramelize (page 66) fresh pineapple rounds or peaches before adding to the cake pan.

OLD-FASHIONED GINGERBREAD WITH PEACH SAUCE

Makes 1 (9 x 13-inch) cake

I YEARN FOR THIS CAKE, *which brings back the memory of a time when I baked it in a fireplace and the aroma of the spices permeated the room. The Peach Sauce melts on the gingerbread, and all combine to make a totally gratifying experience.*

1/2 cup granulated sugar
1/2 cup unsalted butter
1 large egg
1 cup sorghum or molasses
2 cups self-rising flour
2 teaspoons ground ginger
1/2 teaspoon ground cinnamon
1/2 cup buttermilk
1/2 cup bourbon or apple juice
1 teaspoon brandy flavoring
1 recipe Peach Sauce (below)

Position rack in the center of the oven and preheat to 350 degrees. Butter a 9 x 13-inch baking dish or pan and line with parchment or waxed paper. Butter the paper.

Beat the sugar and butter together with an electric hand mixer until light. Add the egg and sorghum or molasses, and beat well to mix.

Sift the dry ingredients together onto a piece of waxed paper.

In a separate bowl, combine the buttermilk, bourbon or apple juice, and brandy flavoring. Alternately add the flour mixture and milk to the egg mixture, beating after each addition, beginning and ending with the dry ingredients. After the last addition, beat until smooth. Pour into the prepared pan and bake on the middle rack for 30 minutes, until a toothpick inserted in the center comes out clean. The internal temperature of the cake should be 190 to 195 degrees on an instant-read thermometer. Remove from oven and let cool on a wire rack 10 minutes. Remove the cake from the pan, invert, peel off the paper, and let cool on a rack slightly Serve warm or at room temperature topped with Peach Sauce.

Variation: Use Cane Syrup Icing (page 582).

PEACH SAUCE

Makes 1 1/2 cups

DELICIOUSLY *light, this is the basis for a cold French sabayon sauce. It can be modified by using white wine, Grand Marnier, Cointreau, Limoncello, or fruit juices.*

4 egg yolks
1/4 cup granulated sugar
1/3 cup peach juice, peach brandy, or peach schnapps
1 cup heavy cream, whipped

Lightly whisk the egg yolks with the sugar in a heavy saucepan, bain-marie, or double boiler.

Heat the peach juice or liqueur in a small saucepan, but do not boil. Slowly pour the heated juice into the eggs, stirring constantly. Stir the egg mixture with a rubber spatula over low heat until thick but still able to fall easily from a spoon, 5 to 10 minutes, making sure to scrape the sides and bottom occasionally. The temperature should register approximately 170 degrees, but it is not a disaster if the mixture simmers at the edges of the pan; strain out any bits of cooked egg.

Cover tightly and refrigerate. Fold in whipped cream before serving.

BUTTER CAKES

These cakes contain a fat such as butter or shortening, with leavening of baking powder or baking soda, alone or with eggs as well. Think white or yellow cakes and some pound cakes. The two most important butter cakes are the Classic Pound Cake and its derivation, the 1-2-3-4 Cake (the work horse of the family). There are many variations of both with a diversity of ingredients, but all use the same basic technique. (Just to make things confusing, some pound cakes have only eggs as leavening, omitting the baking powder or soda.)

LEMON POPPY SEED POUND CAKE

Makes 1 (9 x 5 x 3-inch) loaf

THIS CLASSIC POUND CAKE, *adapted from a recipe of Rose Levy Beranbaum's, is enhanced by the sugar syrup used to lavishly baste it. It is necessary to make the cake a day ahead. Pour the syrup on while the cake is still warm so it permeates the cake. Wrap it tightly, and leave it to moisten throughout and prevent crumbling.*

2 1/4 cups all-purpose or cake flour
1 cup plus 2 tablespoons granulated sugar
1 teaspoon salt
1 tablespoon grated lemon rind, no white attached
4 tablespoons black poppy seed
1 1/4 cups plus 1 tablespoon unsalted butter, softened
5 large eggs, lightly beaten
1 tablespoon vanilla extract

Sauce
3/4 cup granulated sugar
3/4 cup fresh lemon juice

Position rack in the center of the oven and preheat to 350 degrees. Butter and flour a 9 x 5 x 3-inch loaf pan. Line with 2 pieces of parchment or waxed paper, one cut to the width of the pan and the other to the length of the pan plus 4 inches of overhang to use as handles to lift the loaf from the pan. Butter and flour the paper.

Sift together the flour, sugar, and salt into a large mixing bowl. Add the lemon rind, poppy seed, and butter, a third of the beaten eggs, and the vanilla. Using an electric hand mixer or with the paddle blade of a stand mixer, mix on low speed until moist. Increase the speed and beat for 1 minute. Add another third of the eggs, scraping down the sides of the bowl, and beat for 30 seconds. Scrape down the sides of the bowl again and add the remaining eggs, beating for another 30 seconds. Pour the batter into the prepared pan. Tap the pan slightly on the counter to remove any air bubbles.

Bake 60 to 75 minutes, until a toothpick inserted in the center of the cake comes out clean. The internal temperature of the cake should be 190 to 195 degrees on an instant-read thermometer.

Meanwhile, make the syrup. Stir the sugar and lemon juice in a small pan over low heat until the sugar is dissolved and the syrup is clear.

Remove the cake pan from the oven and poke the top of the cake with a fork in several places. Brush the top of the cake with the syrup and let soak into the sides and bottom of the cake. Cool slightly in the pan before removing the cake to a rack to finish cooling. Wrap tightly with foil or plastic wrap and let rest a day before serving. This cake keeps nearly a week at room temperature or in the refrigerator. It freezes well when wrapped thoroughly.

Variations:

- Substitute sesame seed for the poppy seed.
- Use orange rind in place of the lemon rind and make an orange syrup, substituting orange juice and Grand Marnier for the lemon juice or bring a larger quantity of orange juice to the boil and boil until the flavor is concentrated.
- Substitute Courvoisier, brandy, Drambuie, or other liquor for the lemon juice in the syrup.

OLD-FASHIONED POUND CAKE

Makes 1 (10-inch) tube pan or Bundt pan or 2 (5 x 3-inch) loaf pans

Pound cake—the mother of butter cake—*is a good cook's secret weapon. Brought to the South in pre-Revolutionary days, their origin is believed to be English. Traditional pound cakes containing equal weights of flour, butter, sugar, and eggs have a thick batter and do not contain liquid, baking powder, or baking soda. A stand mixer—the sturdier the better—is an enormous modern-day asset. Imagine doing all this beating by hand with a wooden spoon! For very powerful mixers a paddle blade is best. Tapping the pan is important with a pound cake as it should be free of big air holes.*

Rosewater, an alternate for vanilla extract here, was a great favorite of colonials, including Thomas Jefferson, and was made locally as well as imported. Our tester said this was the best pound cake she's ever had!

It's natural for a pound cake to crack on the top. If a prettier top is desired, check the cake after 40 minutes and make a 1/4-inch-deep slit down the length of the crack using a sharp knife. Pound cakes stay fresh a long time.

3 cups plus 2 tablespoons all-purpose or cake flour
1 teaspoon salt
1 1/2 cups unsalted butter, softened
1 1/2 cups granulated sugar
6 large eggs, lightly beaten, room temperature
1 1/2–2 teaspoons vanilla extract or rosewater
Confectioners' sugar

Position rack in the lower third of the oven and preheat to 325 degrees. Butter and flour a 10-inch tube Bundt pan or 2 (9 x 5 x 3-inch) loaf pans. Line with parchment or waxed paper (facing). Butter and flour the paper.

Using a whisk or fork, mix the flour and salt together in a bowl for about 30 seconds to thoroughly combine the ingredients, or tap flour and salt into a strainer over a sheet of waxed paper. Set aside.

Cut the butter into 1-inch pieces and add to the bowl of a stand mixer, and beat on low speed until soft. Increase the speed and whisk for 1 or 2 minutes, until it looks like lightly whipped cream.

Add the sugar 1 tablespoon at a time, starting on slow and increasing speed until well whipped, about 7 or 8 minutes. Scrape down the sides of the bowl as necessary throughout the batter process. Reduce mixer speed to medium.

Slowly add half the eggs, 1 or 2 tablespoons at a time, until they are incorporated. (If the batter curdles, it is still usable; just try to add the eggs slower the next time the cake is made.) Add the vanilla and beat 30 seconds more. Reduce speed to medium-low.

Add the dry ingredients in three parts, alternately with the remaining eggs, mixing for 20 seconds after each addition, continuing to scrape the bowl as needed. The batter should be smooth and creamy.

Spoon or ladle the batter into the prepared pan or pans, filling the pan two-third full; smooth the top. Give the pan a light tap on the counter. Bake in the preheated oven for 85 to 90 minutes, or until the cake is golden brown on top and begins to come away from the sides of the pan, and a toothpick inserted into the center of the cake comes out clean. The internal temperature of the cake should be 190 to 195 degrees on an instant-read thermometer.

Remove the cake from the oven. Cool on a wire rack 10 minutes. Invert the pan to remove the cake. Cool the cake top side up or resting on its side. Remove the parchment after cooling and dust the top with confectioners' sugar. It freezes well.

To serve, slice the cake thinly—less than 1/2 inch—with a serrated knife. Leftover pound cake is good toasted or brushed with butter and heated in a 400-degree oven until brown. And, of course, it goes well with sauces like Lemon Curd (page 618).

Variation: For a lighter cake, separate eggs. Add the yolks as in the original recipe above. Beat the egg whites until stiff but not dry, and fold into the batter.

Variation: Chocolate Pound Cake
Fold in 12 ounces of melted chocolate and 1 cup chopped pecans before pouring batter into pan. Drizzle baked cake with extra chocolate and top with extra pecans.

CREAM CHEESE–BROWN SUGAR POUND CAKE

Makes 1 (10-inch) round cake or 2 (9 x 5 x 3-inch) loaves

Unusual for its use of cream cheese, *combined with brown sugar and buttermilk, this has strayed far from a traditional pound cake, yet it is still ideal for serving with tea or berries and cream. It toasts well for breakfast. Equal amounts of sour cream can be substituted for the cream cheese if necessary. Cream cheese adds moisture to cakes.*

1 (8-ounce) package cream cheese, softened
1/2 cup unsalted butter, softened
1 1/2 cups granulated sugar
1 cup light or dark brown sugar
6 large eggs
3 cups all-purpose or cake flour
1/2 teaspoon baking powder
1/2 teaspoon baking soda
1/2 teaspoon salt
1 cup fresh or reconstituted powdered buttermilk
1 tablespoon vanilla extract

Position rack in the center of the oven and preheat to 325 degrees. Butter and flour a 10-inch tube pan, Bundt pan or 2 (9 x 5 x 3-inch) loaf pans. Line with parchment or waxed paper (right). Brush the pan bottom and sides with butter, add flour, remove excess. Butter and flour the paper.

Beat the cream cheese, butter, granulated sugar, and brown sugar with an electric hand mixer until light, about 3 minutes. Add eggs one at a time, beating for 1 minute after each addition.

Sift the flour, baking powder, baking soda, and salt onto a piece of waxed paper.

Combine the buttermilk and vanilla in a small measuring cup.

Add a third of the flour mixture at a time, alternating with half the buttermilk mixture, to the butter-egg mixture, beginning and ending with the flour. Pour into the prepared pan. Give the pan a light tap on the counter.

Bake 60 to 75 minutes, until a wooden toothpick inserted into the center comes out clean. The internal temperature of the cake should be 190 to 195 degrees on an instant-read thermometer. Cool in the pan for 10 minutes on a wire rack. Remove from the pan and cool completely. Remove the paper. Freezes well, tightly wrapped, for 3 months.

REMOVING AIR BUBBLES

Over-whisking and using an electric whisk creates air bubbles. To remove any big bubbles, hold the batter-filled cake pan with two hands and tap the bottom of the pan on the countertop. Another method is to cut through the batter with a long knife or spatula. Tube and Bundt pans need to be cut through with a knife.

LINING A LOAF OR TUBE PAN

Take 2 pieces of parchment or waxed paper, one cut to the width of the pan and the other to the length of the pan plus 4 inches of overhang to use as handles to lift the loaf from the pan. To line a tube pan, make a pattern of the bottom of the pan on the paper, fold in quarters and cut to unfold into a circle. Estimate the size of the funnel if there is one, and cut a circle to fit, not worrying if it is exact.

MINI CHOCOLATE POUND CAKES

Makes 8 to 10 (6 x 2½-inch) rectangle pans or 1 (10-inch) round cake

It is my firm belief *one can never have too much chocolate, and that chocolate and pecans convey riches of the Southern purse and earth. This, then, is an ideal gift for extremely special people. It seems that no two miniature loaf pans are the same size; hence the variation in number of loaves made. A little trick is to make a note of the cup measurement of each pan and write it on the bottom of the pan in indelible ink. This helps enormously when making holiday gifts, for instance.*

1½ cups unsalted butter, softened
2½ cups granulated sugar
6 large eggs
3 cups all-purpose or cake flour
1½ teaspoons baking powder
1 teaspoon salt
1 cup milk
12 ounces chocolate chips, melted
1 cup chopped pecans
1 recipe Chocolate Sauce (page 636), optional

Position rack in the center of the oven and preheat to 325 degrees. Butter and flour ten mini pans (6 x 2½ inches) or one 10-inch tube pan. Line with parchment or waxed paper (page 563). Butter and flour the paper.

Cut the butter into 1-inch pieces and add to a bowl for use with a stand mixer or an electric hand mixer, and beat on low speed until soft. Increase the speed and whisk for 1 or 2 minutes, until it looks like lightly whipped cream. Add the sugar 1 tablespoon at a time, starting on slow and increasing speed until well whipped, about 7 or 8 minutes. Add the eggs one at a time, beating 1 minute after each addition.

Sift the flour with the baking powder and salt onto a piece of waxed paper. Add a third of the flour mixture and half of the milk to the butter mixture; repeat, ending with the flour. Stir in the melted chocolate, blend well, and add the pecans if using.

Pour the batter into the prepared cake pans, give them a light tap on the counter, and bake 25 to 30 minutes (75 minutes for the tube pan), until a toothpick inserted in the middle comes out clean. The internal temperature of the cake should be 190 to 195 degrees on an instant-read thermometer.

When the cakes are done, cool them in the pan for 15 minutes, then move the pans to a wire rack to cool completely. Carefully run a knife around the inside edge of the cake pans to loosen the cake. When cool, turn the cake pans upside down over pieces of waxed paper. Remove the pans and peel off the paper.

The cakes may be made ahead to this point. Well-wrapped, they will freeze up to 2 months. For a festive look, drizzle with Chocolate Sauce. If giving as a gift, pack the sauce separately or omit it.

Variation: Bourbon Chocolate Pound Cake
Substitute ¼ cup bourbon mixed with ¾ cup milk for the milk in this recipe. Top with Bourbon Hard Sauce Icing (page 584) if desired.

ORANGE CAKE

Makes 1 (9-inch) round 2-layer cake

This cake is a deceptively easy, ambrosial cake. *For an elegant presentation, pipe extra icing evenly along the edges of the cake and garnish with sliced oranges. A thin layer of icing is put over the cake when chilled, trapping any loose crumbs. Additional icing is added for a clean presentation.*

- 1 cup unsalted butter, softened
- 2 cups granulated sugar
- 4 large eggs
- 3 cups all-purpose or cake flour
- 3 teaspoons baking powder
- 1/4 teaspoon salt
- 1 cup fresh orange juice
- Orange wedges, for garnish
- 1 recipe Lazy Orange Buttercream Icing (page 583) or other favorite

Position rack in the center of the oven and preheat to 350 degrees. Butter two 9-inch cake pans and line the bottoms with parchment or waxed paper. Butter the paper.

Cut the butter into 1-inch pieces and add to the bowl of a stand mixer, and beat on low speed until soft. Increase the speed and whisk for 1 or 2 minutes, until it looks like lightly whipped cream. Add the sugar 1 tablespoon at a time, starting on slow and increasing speed until well whipped, about 7 or 8 minutes. Add the eggs one at a time, beating after each addition.

Sift together the flour, baking powder, and salt onto a piece of waxed paper. Add a third of the flour mixture and half of the orange juice to the butter mixture, beating to incorporate. Repeat, finishing with the flour. Beat until all ingredients are well incorporated and a smooth batter is formed. Pour the batter equally into the prepared pans. Tap the pans once against the counter to remove any air bubbles and smooth the top of the batter.

Bake for 30 minutes, until a toothpick inserted in the center comes out clean. The internal temperature of the cake should be 190 to 195 degrees on an instant-read thermometer. Cool the cakes in the pans on a wire rack for 10 minutes. Turn out the layers onto the rack. Peel off the paper.

Always select and ice the prettiest layer first for the top, to be sure it gets sufficient icing. Follow icing directions on page 550.

PLAIN 1-2-3-4 CAKE

Makes 1 (9-inch) round 3-layer cake

THE 1-2-3-4 CAKE *is an offshoot of the pound cake, most likely measured originally by weight but measured with traditional dry measuring cups since the latter half of the twentieth century. The name of this cake came from its proportions: one portion of butter, two of sugar, three of flour, and four of eggs. The secret to its rise comes from the beating of the butter, just as in a pound cake, as there is no other leavening. There are many variations of this cake, with the ratio of the ingredients changing, as well as the addition of leavening and liquid. This heavy batter is best beaten in a stand mixer but may be whisked or beaten by hand (although an arduous task). Select an icing from the recipes starting on page 579 or use a family favorite.*

1 cup unsalted butter, softened
2 cups granulated sugar
4 large eggs
1 teaspoon vanilla extract
3 cups all-purpose or cake flour
1 teaspoon salt
1 recipe icing (pages 579–85), cook's choice

Position rack in the center of the oven and preheat to 350 degrees. Butter and flour three 9-inch round cake pans. Line the bottoms of the pans with parchment or waxed paper cut to fit. Butter and flour the paper.

Cut the butter into 1-inch pieces and add to the bowl of a stand mixer, and beat on low speed until soft. Increase the speed and beat for 1 or 2 minutes, until it looks like lightly whipped cream. Add the sugar 1 tablespoon at a time, starting on slow and increasing speed until well whipped, about 7 or 8 minutes. Mix the eggs and vanilla together in a measuring cup or small bowl and add a fourth at a time, beating 1 minute after each addition. It may look curdled, but all will be well.

Sift together the flour and salt onto a piece of waxed paper. Move the batter to a wide bowl if necessary. Pour the flour mixture on top of the batter. Fold in the flour by using a rubber spatula or metal spoon to cut through the batter, scraping down to the bottom of the bowl and coming back up through the batter in a figure-eight motion. When the flour is incorporated, divide the batter equally among the prepared pans, tap the pans lightly against the counter and smooth the top of the batter.

Bake 25 minutes, until a toothpick inserted in the middle comes out clean. The internal temperature of the cake should be 190 to 195 degrees on an instant-read thermometer.

Move the pans to a wire rack to cool for 10 minutes. Carefully run a knife around the inside edge of the cake pans to loosen the cake. Turn the cakes out upside down onto the wire rack and peel off the waxed paper. The cakes may be made ahead to this point. Well-wrapped, they will freeze up to 4 months.

Always select and ice the prettiest layer first for the top, to be sure it gets sufficient icing. Select an icing and follow icing directions on page 550.

Variation: Substitute various flavorings for the vanilla—grated orange and/or lemon rind or extract; a couple tablespoons of liquor, such as bourbon or Grand Marnier; or spices such as cinnamon, ginger, or crystallized ginger.

UPDATED 1-2-3-4 CAKE

Makes 1 (9-inch) round 3-layer cake or two (9-inch) square layers

Damon Lee Fowler's variation *of a 1-2-3-4 cake, from* New Southern Baking, *uses ingredients that could be added once baking soda was developed. He adds more butter, a liquid, and a leavening (baking powder) to help make the cake rise. He also uses unbleached all-purpose flour, which has higher gluten content than bleached. (I find, however, that bleached all-purpose flour, preferably cake flour or low-gluten Southern flour, makes a more tender cake). Select an icing from the recipes starting on page 579 or use a family favorite.*

1 1/2 cups unsalted butter, softened
2 cups granulated sugar
4 large eggs
1 teaspoon vanilla extract

3 cups all-purpose or cake flour
2 teaspoons baking powder
1 teaspoon salt
1 cup milk

1 recipe icing (pages 579–85), cook's choice

Position rack in the center of the oven and preheat to 350 degrees. Butter and flour three 9-inch round cake pans. Line the bottom of the pans with parchment or waxed paper. Butter and flour the paper.

Cut the butter into 1-inch pieces and add to the bowl of a stand mixer, and beat on low speed until soft. Increase the speed and whisk for 1 or 2 minutes, until it looks like lightly whipped cream. Add the sugar 1 tablespoon at a time, starting on slow and increasing speed until well whipped, about 7 or 8 minutes. Mix the eggs and vanilla together in a measuring cup or small bowl and add a fourth at a time, beating 1 minute after each addition. It may look curdled, but all will be well.

Sift together the flour, baking powder, and salt onto a piece of waxed paper. Add a third of the flour mixture to the batter and beat to incorporate; then add half the milk and beat to incorporate. Repeat with flour and milk, ending with flour and beating about 1 minute, only enough to incorporate the flour. When the flour is incorporated, divide the batter equally among the prepared pans, tap the pans once against the counter to remove any air bubbles and smooth the tops.

Bake 25 minutes, until a toothpick inserted in the middle comes out clean. If using two square pans, they will take a little longer. The internal temperature of the cake should be 190 to 195 degrees on an instant-read thermometer.

Move the pans to a wire rack to cool for 10 minutes. Carefully run a knife around the inside of the pans to loosen the cake. Turn the cakes out upside down onto the wire rack and peel off the waxed paper. The cakes may be made ahead to this point. Well-wrapped, they will freeze up to 4 months.

Always select and ice the prettiest layer first for the top, to be sure it gets sufficient icing. Select an icing and follow icing directions on page 550.

FOAM CAKES

These cakes are light and delicate, with a high proportion of eggs to flour. Air beaten into egg whites or whole eggs provides the sole source of leavening. Angel food cakes, meringue cakes, sponge cakes, and chiffon cakes fall into this category. The busty, large, and impressive chiffon cakes date back to 1944, when they were developed to use oil rather than hard shortening or butter, most likely as a response to the rationing enforced in World War II and the new processing methods developed for cooking oils. Sunshine and Daffodil Cakes are included here, although they could also be called sponge cakes, as they combine techniques. These cakes are delicate, so many stand alone without icing or are served with a spooned-on sauce. Angel food cakes are pulled apart with forks rather than cut with cake knives, for instance.

MRS. LANE'S PRIZE CAKE

Makes 1 (9-inch) round 3-layer cake

THIS CLASSIC SOUTHERN HOLIDAY CAKE RECIPE *was first printed in Mrs. Emma Rylander Lane's cookbook* Some Good Things to Eat, *which she self-published in 1898. In the novel* To Kill a Mockingbird, *the character Maudie Atkinson bakes a Lane cake to welcome a relative to the Finch home. The character Scout notes the alcohol content of the cake saying, "Miss Maudie Atkinson baked a Lane cake so loaded with shinny [liquor] it made me tight." The recipe has lasted in popularity for more than 100 years, but there have been many liberties taken with both the filling and the icing. Be sure to note the variations.*

Cake

1 cup unsalted butter, softened
2 cups granulated sugar
2 teaspoons vanilla extract
3 1/4 cups all-purpose or cake flour
3 1/2 teaspoons baking powder
1/2 teaspoon salt
1 cup milk
6 large egg whites
1/4 teaspoon cream of tartar

Filling

1/2 cup unsalted butter, softened
1 cup granulated sugar
1/3 cup water
8 large egg yolks, lightly beaten
1 cup chopped raisins
3/4 cup chopped pecans
1/3 cup bourbon or orange juice
1 teaspoon vanilla extract
1/2 teaspoon salt
1 recipe Meringue Icing (page 581) or other favorite

Position rack in the center of the oven and preheat to 350 degrees. Butter and flour three 9-inch round cake pans and line the bottoms with parchment or waxed paper. Butter and flour the paper.

Cut the butter into 1-inch pieces and add to the bowl of a stand mixer, and beat on low speed until soft. Increase the speed and whisk for 1 or 2 minutes, until it looks like lightly whipped cream. Add the sugar 1 tablespoon at a time, starting on slow and increasing speed until well whipped, about 7 or 8 minutes. Stir in the vanilla.

In a separate bowl, sift together the flour, baking powder, and salt onto a piece of waxed paper.

Add a third of the flour mixture to the butter mixture and beat, then half the milk and beat; repeat, ending with flour and beating after each addition only enough to fold in the flour.

Use a clean mixing bowl and the wire whisk attachment to beat the egg whites and cream of tartar, starting on low speed then on medium speed until they break up and are foamy. Increase the speed to high and beat until they are shiny and stand up in peaks, taking care not to overbeat, scraping the insides of the bowl regularly. Using a metal spoon or spatula, fold a large dollop of the whites into the batter, and then gently fold this lightened mixture into the whites only until incorporated.

Divide the batter evenly among the prepared pans. Tap the pans once against the counter to remove any air bubbles and smooth the top of the batter. Bake until pale brown, 20 to 25 minutes, and a toothpick inserted in the middle comes out clean. The internal temperature of the cake should be 190 to 195 degrees on an instant-read thermometer.

Move the pans to a wire rack to cool for 10 minutes. Carefully run a knife around the inside edge of the cake pans to loosen the cake. Turn the cakes out onto the rack and peel off the waxed paper. The cakes may be made ahead to this point. Well-wrapped, they will freeze up to 2 months. In preparation for the filling and icing, move one layer to a plate lined with 3 x 5-inch strips of waxed paper.

To prepare the filling, heat the butter with the sugar and water in a medium saucepan until the butter is melted and the sugar is dissolved. Increase the heat and cook to the soft-ball stage (240 degrees), stirring if necessary to dissolve the sugar. Use a candy thermometer to accurately judge the soft-ball stage. Stir some of this hot mixture into the egg yolks then move the egg yolks to the saucepan.

Carefully cook the mixture over medium heat, stirring, until thickened and 160 degrees, about 12 to 15 minutes more. Remove from the heat. Stir in the raisins, pecans, bourbon or orange juice, vanilla, and salt. Cover and allow to cool to room temperature. This may be refrigerated several days. Spread the filling between layers, leaving 1 to 2 inches at the edge so it doesn't squoosh out when the cakes are put together. Follow instructions for icing on page 550.

Variations:

- Add 1/2 cup flaked coconut to the cake batter.
- Add 1/2 cup pitted and chopped fresh Bing cherries to the cake batter.

LADY BALTIMORE CAKE

Best known for his Wild West classic *The Virginian,* author Owen Wister first mentioned the Lady Baltimore Cake in his 1906 novel titled *Lady Baltimore,* inspiring his readers to avidly search for such a cake. It seems that Mr. Wister's fictional hero had been served a slice of this luscious cake by the fictional character modeled on Miss Alicia Rhett Mayberry of Charleston. It is identical, however, to a Lane Cake, with orange juice and rind substituted for the flavorings and water for the milk. When made with a yellow cake and slightly different ingredients, it is known as a Lord Baltimore Cake.

COCONUT CAKE

Makes 1 (9-inch) round 3-layer cake

COCONUT CAKE IS SO POPULAR *that Nancie McDermott has five variations in her cake book,* Southern Cakes. *I've culled through mine, testing and retesting, and here is my favorite of all time. It takes a little trick each from Kate Almand's, Elise Griffin's, and Grace Reeves' cakes, among others that have never been printed.*

This light, moist butter cake is tender throughout. There's a choice of icings here, and there are even more out there in the "Southern Universe" of cake baking. But this is my darling, no matter which frosting. Fresh coconut is best, but use what you have. Kudos to Kate for making the coconut sugar syrup!*

Coconut Cake

3 cups all-purpose or cake flour
2 teaspoons baking powder
1 teaspoon salt
1 cup unsalted butter, softened
2 cups granulated sugar
4 large eggs, separated
2 teaspoons vanilla extract
1 cup milk, divided
1/2 cup grated or shredded coconut

Coconut Syrup

1 cup granulated sugar
1 cup water
1/2 cup grated or shredded coconut

1 recipe Meringue Icing (page 581) or other favorite
4 cups shredded coconut for icing

Position rack in the center of the oven and preheat to 350 degrees. Butter and flour three 9-inch round cake pans. Line the bottom of the pans with parchment or waxed paper. Butter and flour the paper.

Sift together the flour, baking powder, and salt onto a piece of waxed paper. Cut the butter into 1-inch pieces and add to a bowl for use with a stand mixer or an electric hand mixer, and beat on low speed until soft. Increase the speed and whisk for 1 or 2 minutes, until it looks like lightly whipped cream. Add the sugar 1 tablespoon at a time, starting on slow and increasing speed until well whipped, about 7 or 8 minutes. Add the egg yolks one at a time, beating well after each addition. Stir the vanilla into the milk. Add a third of the flour mixture to the sugar and butter mixture, then half the milk, repeat, ending with the flour and beating only enough to fold in the flour after each addition.

Use a clean mixing bowl to whisk the egg whites, starting on low speed then on medium speed until they break up and are foamy. Increase the speed to high and beat until they are shiny and stand up in peaks, taking care not to overbeat, and scraping the insides of the bowl regularly. Using a metal spoon or spatula, fold a large dollop of the whites into the batter, then gently fold this lightened mixture into the whites only until incorporated. Fold in the coconut.

Divide the batter evenly among the prepared pans. Tap the pans once against the counter to remove any air bubbles and smooth the top of the batter. Bake until pale brown, 20 to 25 minutes, until a toothpick inserted in the middle comes out clean. The internal temperature of the cake should be 190 to 195 degrees on an instant-read thermometer.

Move the pans to a wire rack to cool for 10 minutes. Carefully run a knife around the inside edge of the cake pans to loosen the cake. Turn the cakes out onto the rack and peel off the waxed paper.

Meanwhile, or up to a week in advance, make the Coconut Syrup. Heat the sugar and water in a heavy saucepan until the sugar is completely dissolved. Bring to the boil and boil 1 minute. Add the coconut and let steep. Refrigerate covered. When ready to use, reheat slightly and strain to remove the coconut. Using a large spoon or a squeeze bottle, lightly drizzle the tops of the cakes with the syrup. The cakes may be made ahead to this point. Well-wrapped, they will freeze up to 2 months.

See page 550 for how to ice a cake.

**To extract flesh from a coconut, either put the coconut in a 350 oven for about 10 minutes, until it cracks, or take it out on the back steps and pound with a hammer until it cracks. Pry flesh away from the hard shell using something like a nut pick or sturdy knife. Shred in food processor or by hand.*

Variation: Toast the shredded coconut before using.

CLASSIC CARAMEL CAKE

Makes 1 (9-inch) round 3-layer cake or 1 (9 x 13 x 2-inch) 2-layer cake

THIS WAS ONCE MADE ALL OVER THE UNITED STATES, *but since the 1930s, the South has claimed it as its own. Three or four layers may be made from the same batter. If four layers are made, however, reduce the cooking time and either be very stingy with the icing or double the caramel mixture to have a surfeit.*

The Burnt Sugar Icing is traditionally made in an iron skillet. Only a small amount of sugar is caramelized for the icing, but it flavors the whole mixture, giving the icing a grainy texture from the un-dissolved sugar. Some people prefer it that way. Heavy cream (my favorite) or half-and-half is preferred for the higher fat content that will prevent curdling. Use a candy thermometer to accurately judge the soft-ball stage. Some recipes have said that once the icing is prepared, there are only 20 seconds to get it on the cake! Actually, it may be kept warm by keeping the bowl of icing in a pan of hot water, or it can be microwaved to reheat, checking in 10- to 20-second increments to make sure it does not overcook. For best results, the icing should be spreadable, like plain peanut butter. A thermometer, whether instant-read or candy, makes any sugar work easier. Sugar work is much more difficult on a rainy day because of the relationship between sugar and humidity.

1 1/2 cups unsalted butter, softened
2 cups granulated sugar
5 large eggs
3 cups all-purpose or cake flour
1/4 teaspoon salt
1/2 teaspoon baking powder
1 1/4 cups milk
1 teaspoon vanilla extract
1 recipe Caramel Icing (page 580) or other favorite

Position rack in the center of the oven and preheat to 325 degrees. Butter and flour three 9-inch cake pans or two 9 x 13-inch pans. Line the bottoms with parchment or waxed paper. Butter and flour the paper.

Cut the butter into 1-inch pieces and add to the bowl of a stand mixer, and beat on low speed until soft. Increase the speed and whisk for 1 or 2 minutes, until it looks like lightly whipped cream. Add the sugar 1 tablespoon at a time, starting on slow and increasing speed until well whipped, about 7 or 8 minutes. Beat in the eggs one at a time, beating after each addition.

Sift together the dry ingredients onto a large piece of waxed paper. Add a third of the flour mixture into the egg mixture and beat to incorporate, then half the milk and beat; repeat, ending with flour. Add the vanilla extract and beat until smooth. Pour the batter evenly into the cake pans. Tap the pans once against the counter to remove any air bubbles and smooth the top of the batter.

Bake 35 to 45 minutes, until a toothpick inserted in the middle comes out clean. The internal temperature of the cake should be 190 to 195 degrees on an instant-read thermometer.

Move the pans to a wire rack to cool completely. Carefully run a knife around the inside of the pans to loosen the cakes. Turn the pans upside down over pieces of waxed paper. Remove the pans and peel off the paper. The cakes may be made ahead to this point. Well-wrapped, they will freeze up to 2 months.

Ice with either Caramel Icing or Quick Caramel Icing (both page 580), and follow icing directions on page 550.

Variation: Decorate the top and sides with pecan halves.

Variation: Orange Caramel Cake

Substitute 8 ounces sour cream for the milk and use orange extract instead of vanilla extract. Add 1/2 cup orange juice and 2 teaspoons grated orange rind, no white attached, to the icing ingredients when bringing them to a simmer.

CARAMEL SNACK CAKE

Makes 1 (9 x 13 x 2-inch) cake

THIS RECIPE, *adapted from Nancie McDermott's* Southern Cakes, *adds a portion of caramel syrup to the cake, lightening it and carrying the flavor throughout. It's an easier process than a layer cake and makes a great snack cake.*

3 cups all-purpose or cake flour
1 tablespoon baking powder
1/2 teaspoon salt
1 teaspoon vanilla extract
1 cup milk
1 cup unsalted butter, softened
1 3/4 cups granulated sugar
4 large eggs
1/2 cup Caramel Syrup (below)
1 recipe Burnt Sugar Icing (page 581) or other favorite

Position rack in the center of the oven and preheat to 350 degrees. Butter and flour a 9 x 13-inch rectangular baking pan. Line the bottom of the pan with parchment or waxed paper. Butter and flour the paper.

Sift together the flour, baking powder, and salt onto a sheet of waxed paper. Add the vanilla to the milk.

Cut the butter into 1-inch pieces and add to the bowl of a stand mixer, and beat on low speed until soft. Increase the speed and whisk for 1 or 2 minutes, until it looks like lightly whipped cream. Add the sugar 1 tablespoon at a time, starting on slow and increasing speed until well whipped, about 7 or 8 minutes. Add the eggs one by one, beating well after each addition. Pour in 1/2 cup Caramel Syrup and beat well. Add a third of the flour mixture, and then half the milk, beating after each addition just long enough to make the flour or milk disappear into the batter. Mix in another third of the flour, the rest of the milk, and then the last of the flour in the same way.

Pour the batter into the pan. Tap the pans once against the counter to remove any air bubbles and smooth the top of the batter. Bake for 20 to 25 minutes, until the cake is golden brown, springs back when touched gently in the center, and begins to pull away from the sides of the pan. The internal temperature of the cake should be 190 to 195 degrees on an instant-read thermometer. Cool in the pan on wire racks for 15 minutes.

Ice with Burnt Sugar Icing, following icing directions on page 550.

CARAMEL SYRUP

Makes 1 cup

1 cup granulated sugar
1/2 cup water
1/2 cup boiling water

To make the syrup, add sugar and water to a heavy saucepan with a broad bottom and high sides. Dissolve sugar over medium-low heat, stirring occasionally until it turns into a clear brown caramel. Carefully add the boiling water, pouring it down the side of the pan. The syrup will foam and bubble up. Continue cooking and stirring until the caramel is thinned to form a tea-colored syrup. Set aside.

SOUTHERN BELLE CAKE

Makes 1 (9-inch) round 3-layer cake

THIS FOAM CAKE, *adapted from a recipe in* Martha Meade's Recipes from the Old South, *makes good use of our Southern oranges, in season from before Christmas to March, depending on the region. Mace is the outside covering of the nutmeg. Pale brown in color, a little of it adds an underlying flavor in the cake.*

Cake

2¼ cups self-rising flour
½ teaspoon mace
1 cup unsalted butter, softened
1½ cups granulated sugar
4 large eggs, separated
⅔ cup orange juice
Grated rind of 1 orange, no white attached

Filling

1 cup granulated sugar
4 tablespoons all-purpose flour
1 teaspoon salt
½ cup fresh orange juice
1 teaspoon fresh lemon juice
4 tablespoons grated orange rind, no white attached
2 large eggs, lightly beaten
2 tablespoons unsalted butter

Icing

1½ cups heavy cream, whipped with sugar to taste
½ teaspoon mace

Position rack in the center of the oven and preheat to 350 degrees. Butter and flour the bottoms and sides of three 9-inch cake pans. Line the bottom of the pans with parchment or waxed paper. Butter and flour the paper.

Sift the flour with the mace onto a piece of waxed paper. Cut the butter into 1-inch pieces and add to a bowl for use with a stand mixer or an electric hand mixer, and beat on low speed until soft. Increase the speed and whisk for 1 or 2 minutes, until it looks like lightly whipped cream. Add the sugar 1 tablespoon at a time, starting on slow and increasing speed until well whipped, about 7 or 8 minutes. Add the egg yolks one at a time, beating after each addition. Add the flour, orange juice, and orange rind, and continue beating until smooth.

In a separate, clean mixing bowl, whisk the egg whites until stiff and glossy. Using a metal spoon or rubber spatula, fold 1 large spoonful of the whites into the batter, then fold the lightened batter into the whites. Pour the batter evenly into the prepared cake pans. Tap the pans once against the counter to remove any air bubbles and smooth the top of the batter.

Bake 30 minutes, or until a toothpick inserted in the middle comes out clean. The internal temperature of the cake should be 190 to 195 degrees on an instant-read thermometer. Cool in the pans 5 minutes. Invert the cakes onto a rack, peel off the waxed paper, and let cool completely. Move the cakes to a plate lined with strips of waxed paper to catch drips.

To make the filling, sift the sugar, flour, and salt together in a large nonaluminum saucepan over low heat. Add the orange and lemon juices and the orange rind, and mix well. Add the eggs and butter, and stir until thick and smooth, about 10 minutes.

To finish, spread the orange filling between the layers and on top of the cake. Cover the sides with the sweetened whipped cream mixed with mace. Remove the paper strips. Refrigerate the cake if not serving it immediately.

ORANGE OR LEMON DAFFODIL CAKE

Makes 1 (10-inch) tube cake

TO DUPLICATE SPRING, *this deep yellow-and-white cake heralds the first flower of the year. I was told it was "Southern" when I first made it, as it was in a White Lily flour cookbook from Knoxville, Tennessee. I was shocked when I recently found it in a 1973 Betty Crocker Cookbook, but then realized it too had followed the course of Caramel Cake and others; they were in the national mainstream, but were sweet enough to please the Southern palate and so became standards here.*

- 1 3/4 cups plus 2 tablespoons superfine granulated sugar, divided
- 1 1/4 cups plus 2 tablespoons all purpose or cake flour, divided
- 1 3/4 cups egg whites (12–14 large eggs)
- 1 1/2 teaspoons cream of tartar
- 1/4 teaspoon salt
- 1 1/2 teaspoons orange or lemon extract
- 1 tablespoon Grand Marnier or Limoncello, optional
- 5 large egg yolks
- 3 tablespoons grated fresh orange rind, no white attached, divided
- 1 recipe Hot Lemon or Orange Glaze (page 579)

Position rack in the lower third of the oven and preheat to 325 degrees. Butter and flour a 10-inch tube pan (page 563).

Divide the sugar into 1 cup, 3/4 cup, and 2 tablespoon portions.

Sift 1 1/4 cups flour and 3/4 cup sugar together onto a piece of waxed paper and set aside.

Whisk the egg whites, cream of tartar, and salt in the bowl of a stand mixer until soft peaks form, taking care not to overbeat. From the 1 cup of sugar, slowly add about 2 to 3 tablespoons at a time, continuing to beat until stiff, glossy peaks form and the entire cup of sugar is added. (This may take nearly 10 minutes.)

Sift about a fourth of the flour-sugar mixture over the egg whites; gently fold, using a rubber spatula, sweeping down to the bottom of the bowl and pulling back up in a figure-eight motion. Repeat with remaining flour mixture, a fourth at a time. Add the orange or lemon extract and 2 tablespoons of the freshly grated rind with the last addition of the flour mixture. Remove a third of the entire meringue batter to a clean bowl and set aside for a few minutes.

Quickly beat the egg yolks and liquor, if using, with the 2 remaining tablespoons of cake flour and sugar with an electric hand mixer until thick and pale yellow. Fold the remaining 1 tablespoon grated rind into the egg yolk mixture. Pour egg yolk mixture over reserved third of the batter and fold just until blended, using a figure-eight motion. (It is better to under-fold than to over-fold.)

Scoop up the yellow batter with an ice cream scoop and gently drop into an ungreased angel food pan or other pan with a center tube. Repeat with the egg white batter, and alternate until the tube pan is full. Run a knife gently through batter to eliminate air pockets and to swirl the two batters slightly.

Bake in lower third of preheated 375-degree oven for 35 to 40 minutes, until a toothpick inserted in the batter comes out clean and there is a slight bounce when the cake is touched lightly. The internal temperature of the cake should be 190 to 195 degrees on an instant-read thermometer.

Remove the cake from the oven. Invert the cake in its pan to cool, using a bottle through the neck of the tube to hold it up off the floor or resting on top of the inverted tube if it is steady.

When completely cool, remove from pan by running a thin knife up and down between cake and pan to loosen. Remove paper. Drizzle with hot Lemon or Orange Glaze. Slice with a bread knife to serve.

MISSISSIPPI MUD CAKE

Makes 1 (9 x 13 x 2-inch) cake

Ever popular, this cake is luscious and easily transported. *Once one has lived in Mississippi, one understands how aptly this cake is named. There are places in the state where the heat bakes the mud until it cracks. There are also oases such as Oxford and Jackson, and the creeks, rivers, and lakes around the Natchez Trace that are green much of the year.*

- 1 cup unsalted butter, softened
- 2 cups granulated sugar
- 4 large eggs
- 1 1/2 cups all-purpose or cake flour
- 1/2 cup cocoa powder
- 1/4 teaspoon salt
- 1 tablespoon vanilla extract
- 1 cup pecans, chopped
- 1 recipe Cocoa Icing (page 558) or other favorite

Position the rack in the center of the oven and preheat to 350 degrees. Butter a 9 x 13-inch pan. Fit a piece of parchment or waxed paper to the bottom of the pan. Butter the paper.

Cut the butter into 1-inch pieces and add to a bowl for use with a stand mixer or an electric hand mixer, and beat on low speed until soft. Increase the speed and whisk for 1 or 2 minutes, until it looks like lightly whipped cream. Add the sugar a tablespoon at a time, starting on slow and increasing speed until well whipped, about 7 or 8 minutes. Add the eggs one at a time, beating after each addition. Sift the flour, cocoa, and salt onto a piece of waxed paper. Add to the bowl and beat again. Add the vanilla and nuts and quickly beat.

Pour the batter into the pan and bake for 20 to 25 minutes, until a toothpick inserted in the middle comes out clean. Remove from the oven and cool on a rack. When cool, remove from the pan, invert on a plate and peel off the paper. Spread the icing on the cake.

Variation: To serve from the pan, which is better for carrying to picnics and church suppers, use a nonstick pan and do not line it with paper. Do not remove the cake from the pan. Ice the cake in the pan.

WHITE FRUITCAKE

Makes 2 ($4^1/_2$ x $8^1/_2$-inch) loaves

AN EDITOR OF MINE *at* Atlanta Magazine *gave this recipe to me long ago when I made a sour face about fruitcakes. It was his grandmother's, and after I tested and tasted it, I fell in love with it. This one will be eaten, not re-gifted.*

2½ cups golden raisins
1 cup dried apricots, quartered
1 cup chopped crystallized ginger
2¾ cups all-purpose or cake flour, divided
1 cup unsalted butter, room temperature
1 cup granulated sugar
5 large eggs
1 tablespoon vanilla extract
1 teaspoon almond extract
1 teaspoon lemon extract
1 teaspoon baking powder
½ teaspoon salt
2 cups chopped toasted pecans
2 teaspoons grated lemon rind, no white attached
2 teaspoons grated orange rind, no white attached

Position rack in the center of the oven and preheat to 250 degrees. Butter and flour two 4½ x 8½-inch loaf pans. Line with 2 pieces of parchment or waxed paper, one cut to the width of the pan and the other to the length of the pan plus 4 inches of overhang to use as handles to lift the loaf from the pan. Butter and flour the paper.

Toss the raisins, apricots, and ginger in ¼ cup of flour to coat, and set aside.

Cut the butter into 1-inch pieces and add to a bowl for use with a stand mixer or an electric hand mixer, and beat on low speed until soft. Increase the speed and whisk for 1 or 2 minutes, until it looks like lightly whipped cream. Add the sugar 1 tablespoon at a time, starting on slow and increasing speed until well whipped, about 7 or 8 minutes. Mix the eggs and all extracts together in a small bowl; then add to butter mixture a fourth at a time, beating 1 minute after each addition. It may look curdled, but all will be well.

Sift the remaining flour with the baking powder and salt onto a piece of waxed paper. Add half the flour mixture to the batter, beat well and then add the remaining flour mixture and beat. When the flour is incorporated, fold in the nuts and dried fruit. Fold in the grated rinds. Divide the batter between the prepared pans. Tap each pan once against the counter to remove any air bubbles and smooth the top.

Bake 2 hours, until a toothpick inserted in the middle comes out clean. Move the pan to a wire rack to cool for 10 minutes. Carefully run a knife around the inside of the pans to loosen the cakes. Turn the cakes out upside down onto the wire rack and remove the waxed paper.

Well-wrapped, these will freeze up to 4 months.

MOLTEN CHOCOLATE CAKES

Makes 6 mini cakes

CHOCOLATE CAKES THAT RELEASE MELTED CHOCOLATE *in a lava-like flow have been popular since the mid-1970s. They will keep their place as long as chocoholics live in the South.*

5 tablespoons unsalted butter
14 ounces semisweet chocolate chips
2 tablespoons granulated sugar, divided
2 large eggs
1 tablespoon all-purpose or cake flour
1/4 teaspoon salt

Position rack in the center of the oven and preheat to 375 degrees. Butter a 6-cup regular-size muffin tin and set aside.

Melt the butter, chocolate chips, and 1 tablespoon of the sugar together in a saucepan over low heat, in a microwave, or over simmering water, stirring until the chocolate has melted and the mixture is smooth. Remove from the heat and let cool until the mixture is thick, about 5 minutes.

Whisk together the eggs and the remaining tablespoon of sugar in a bowl or with an electric hand mixer until pale and doubled in volume. Sift the flour and salt into the egg mixture and whisk until combined and there are no lumps. Add the chocolate 1 cup at a time, and mix until all is incorporated and the mixture is smooth. Spoon the batter into the muffin tin, filling each cup about three-fourths full.

Bake the cakes for about 18 to 20 minutes, or until the tops are spongy when pressed. Run a knife around the edge of each cake and turn out onto a wire rack to cool. If making ahead, reheat 5 minutes in a 375-degree oven.

STACK CAKE

Makes 1 (8- or 9-inch) stack

RARELY SEEN NOWADAYS, *"stack cakes" were community cakes. Each homemaker brought a layer of cake, usually made from biscuit dough, and the cakes were layered together with a filling, usually something like peach butter or applesauce. This Appalachian recipe has been in Fred Sauceman's wife Jill's family for nearly 100 years. Her grandmother, Nevada Derting, used a pie pan with a scalloped edge to cut out the rounds and often baked her layers in an iron skillet.*

1 pound dried tart apples
1/2 cup sorghum
1/2 cup sugar
1/2 cup buttermilk
1 egg
1 teaspoon baking soda
1 teaspoon baking powder
1/2 teaspoon salt
1/3 cup shortening
Approximately 4 1/2 cups flour, plus enough for flouring the board when rolling out each layer

Cover dried apples with water and cook over medium-low heat until most of the water is absorbed and the apples break up when stirred. If apples are not soft enough to break up, add more water and keep cooking. If desired, add 1 tablespoon or so of sugar to taste. Cool and run apples through a sieve to produce a smooth sauce.

Meanwhile, combine the remaining ingredients. Dough should be the consistency of stiff cookie dough. Separate dough into 5 to 7 balls. Roll out each ball of dough to 1/8- or 1/4-inch thickness. Cut into 8- or 9-inch rounds. Prick each layer with a fork, making a nice design. Sprinkle individual layers with granulated sugar and bake on a greased cookie sheet at 400 degrees until golden brown (about 5 to 8 minutes, depending on thickness). Cool and place the first layer on a cake plate. Spread a coating of cooked applesauce over the layer, within half an inch of the edge. Stack the other layers, alternating cake and applesauce and ending with a cake layer on top. Save the layer with the prettiest design for the top. Store, covered, in a cool place for several days before serving.

CHEESECAKE WITH CHOCOLATE CRUST

Makes 1 (9-inch) round cake

THREE PEOPLE TEST EVERY ONE OF OUR RECIPES IN ADDITION TO US. *They're usually interns fresh out of cooking school or college. Along the way, we each learn from each other. In this case, Ashley Strickland told me this tip to keep cheesecake from cracking: run the knife around the inside edge of the cake pan right after removing it from the oven. This stops the sides from holding it taut while it is settling, which is what causes the crack. If you notice a cheesecake cracking earlier in the baking, quickly remove it from the oven, run the knife around the inside edge of the cake pan, and return it to the oven. Make a note on the recipe of the approximate time to repeat this whenever baking the cake.*

18 small chocolate cookies, such as Oreos or wafers
1/4 cup unsalted butter, melted
2 (8-ounce) packages cream cheese, room temperature
2 large eggs, lightly beaten
2/3 cup plus 3 tablespoons granulated sugar, divided
1 vanilla bean, split and seeds scraped, or 2 teaspoons vanilla extract
1 1/2 cups sour cream

Position rack in the center of the oven and preheat to 350 degrees. Wrap a layer of aluminum foil around the bottom and sides of a 9-inch springform pan.

To make the crust, crush the cookies in a plastic bag with a rolling pin and mix with the butter, preferably with the paddle attachment of a mixer, or pulse in the food processor until gathered together lightly. Press the mixture into the bottom and up the sides of the springform pan to form an even crust. Refrigerate while preparing the filling.

Beat the cream cheese until smooth and creamy. Add the eggs, 2/3 cup sugar, and the seeds from the vanilla bean; beat until well incorporated and there are no lumps, scraping the bowl occasionally. Pour onto the prepared crust and bake for 25 minutes, until firm. Remove from the oven and let sit for 5 minutes.

Increase the oven temperature to 450 degrees.

Meanwhile, combine the sour cream with the remaining 3 tablespoons sugar. Spread evenly over the top of the cheesecake, and bake for an additional 7 to 10 minutes, or until the top is golden.

Remove from the oven and run a knife around the edges to prevent it from cracking. Release from the springform pan and cool on a wire rack. Refrigerate overnight. Use a knife dipped in hot water and quickly dried to slice the cake.

Variation: Substitute graham cracker crumbs for the chocolate wafers. Gingersnaps also make a great crust.

GLAZES AND ICINGS

A few cakes can stand alone, unadorned by any other flavoring or decoration. But like most of us, a little sweetening doesn't hurt. A glaze or an icing can make a cake. And usually does.

BROWN SUGAR GLAZE

Makes 1 1/3 cups

THIS IS A HANDY AND EASY GLAZE *for a sheet cake or an extra layer of cake from the freezer. Reheat cake gently before glazing. I've even had a few friends who used it to dress up a store-bought cake. Don't tell anyone.*

1 cup light or dark brown sugar
1/3 cup unsalted butter, softened
1 teaspoon vanilla extract
2 tablespoons milk

Stir the sugar, butter, vanilla, and milk together in a heavy saucepan over medium heat. Bring to a gentle boil, stirring frequently, and cook for 3 to 5 minutes, until slightly thickened. Spoon the glaze over a hot cake and then let cake cool completely before slicing.

HOT LEMON OR ORANGE GLAZE

Makes 1 1/2 cups

THIS CLEAR SAUCE *is good with a host of desserts, including fresh fruit.*

1/2 cup granulated sugar
2 tablespoons cornstarch
1 cup water
2 teaspoons grated fresh orange or lemon rind, no white attached
2 tablespoons fresh orange or lemon juice, Grand Marnier, or Limoncello
1 tablespoon unsalted butter

Heat sugar, cornstarch, and water over medium heat until smooth and thickened; bring to the boil and boil 1 minute. Add the rind, juice, and butter; stir and heat until warm.

CARAMEL ICING

Makes 3½ to 4 cups

THIS CLASSIC RECIPE *should be in every cook's repertoire. An easier version appears below.*

3¼ cups granulated sugar, divided
¼ cup boiling water
½ cup unsalted butter, softened
¼ teaspoon baking soda
1 teaspoon vanilla extract
1½ cups cream, half-and-half, or milk, divided

Stir ¼ cup of the sugar with the boiling water in a small pot. Heat over low heat until the sugar is dissolved, then proceed to cook until it turns a deep copper-amber color, watching carefully and swirling the pot over the heat as necessary to distribute the color evenly. A small portion may appear burnt—don't worry unless the whole mixture seems burnt and has a burnt odor. If the whole mixture seems burnt, discard and start over.

Meanwhile, on low heat, dissolve the remaining 3 cups sugar with the butter, baking soda, vanilla, and 1 cup cream or milk in a large heavy pan or Dutch oven. When dissolved, bring to a simmer, just until little bubbles appear around the outside of the pan. Take care not to let it boil over.

Cover both hands with oven mitts or cloths to protect them from caramel splashes. Add a small portion of the cream or milk mixture to the caramel and bring to the boil to dissolve; pour it into the simmering milk mixture. If necessary to remove all the caramel from the pan, repeat this step. Bring the mixture to the boil and boil rapidly to the soft-ball stage (240 degrees on a candy thermometer), stirring constantly.

Carefully remove the pan from the heat and place in a large roasting pan filled with enough cold water to stop the caramel from cooking. Transfer the caramel cream quickly to the bowl of a stand mixer, preferably heavy duty, and beat until very thick and creamy. It should look and spread like peanut butter. If necessary, add a bit more of the cream to make spreadable. If it is too cold to spread, place the bowl in a pan of hot water to warm up, and add a bit more cream if necessary. May be briefly warmed in the microwave as well, if transferred out of the metal bowl.

Spread the icing on the cake. See page 550 for how to ice a cake.

QUICK CARAMEL ICING

Makes 4 cups

THIS RECIPE CAME FROM JONETTE SAWYER, *the mother of an apprentice. A version of this recipe that lacked clear instructions had been passed down for generations by her in-laws. This recipe is the product of years of experimentation and adjustment.*

½ cup unsalted butter
3 cups light or dark brown sugar
¾ cup evaporated milk
⅛ teaspoon baking powder

Stir the butter, brown sugar, and evaporated milk in a heavy saucepan over low heat until combined. Bring to the boil, and boil until caramel reaches the soft-ball stage (240 degrees on a candy thermometer). Remove from heat and pour the mixture into the bowl of a stand mixer. Allow to cool slightly. Add baking powder and beat until thick and creamy. Ice cake immediately, before the icing cools.

See page 550 for how to ice a cake.

CARAMEL ICINGS

Making caramel for icings is a bit of a skill. Take time to study all the guidelines on page 629. And always be respectful of caramelizing to avoid bad burns.

BURNT SUGAR ICING

Makes 3 to 4 cups

BURNT SUGAR IS ANOTHER NAME FOR CARAMEL ICING, *this one using Caramel Syrup, which can be made in advance and brought to a warm temperature before proceeding.*

3¾ cups confectioners' sugar, sifted
½ cup Caramel Syrup (page 572)
¼ cup unsalted butter, softened
½ teaspoon vanilla extract
2–3 tablespoons cream or milk

To make the icing, mix together the confectioners' sugar, Caramel Syrup, butter, and vanilla. Beat with a mixer at medium speed for 2 to 3 minutes, scraping down the bowl now and then to bring the ingredients together. Add 2 tablespoons cream or milk and continue beating until the icing is like peanut butter—thick, soft, smooth, and easy to spread. Add a little more sugar if it is thin, and a little more cream if it seems too thick.

See page 550 for how to ice a cake.

MERINGUE ICING

Makes 3 to 4 cups

MAKING *Meringue* ICING, ALSO CALLED BOILED ICING, *is an art and a skill. Once learned and understood, however, it is valuable to have in one's repertoire and becomes a snap. The icing tastes immeasurably better on the cake than when licked off a spoon, where it doesn't have the same personality. This icing is perfect on our Coconut Cake (page 570). Since the whites are cooked by the sugar syrup it is safe to leave unrefrigerated.*

1 cup granulated sugar
Pinch salt
½ cup water
3 large egg whites
1 teaspoon vanilla extract

Heat the sugar, salt, and water in a heavy saucepan. Cook over low heat until the sugar is dissolved, then increase heat to high. Bring to the boil and boil until the syrup reaches 225 degrees, using a thermometer. This will be a signal to start beating the whites, so the whites and syrup are close in finishing time. Continue cooking while beating egg whites in a separate bowl.

Begin beating the egg whites to soft peaks in a clean, heavy-duty stand mixer bowl. Once again, use a candy thermometer to make sure the syrup is the right temperature to cook the egg whites. When the syrup reaches 240 degrees, add it to the egg whites in a slow stream, beating continually. Continue to beat until the egg whites are glossy and in soft peaks and the mixture is cool. Stop beating if the whites begin to look clumpy or rocky and dry. Beat in the vanilla.

See page 550 for how to ice a cake.

SORGHUM OR CANE SYRUP ICING

Makes 1 1/2 cups

THIS GIVES AN OLD-TIME FLAVOR *to a simple confectioners' sugar icing. Some people have been known to give it a shot of bourbon in lieu of the sorghum or cane—it's an old-time flavor, too.*

1/4 cup unsalted butter, softened
2 cups sifted confectioners' sugar, divided
1 teaspoon vanilla extract
1/2 teaspoon salt
2 tablespoons pure sorghum, cane syrup, or maple syrup

Beat the butter with an electric hand mixer until light. Add half the confectioners' sugar, vanilla extract, and salt, beating at medium speed until smooth. Add remaining sugar and syrup, and beat until smooth and creamy.

See page 550 for how to ice a cake.

SORGHUM AND CANE HERITAGE

A Jesuit priest planted the first crop of sugar cane in Louisiana in 1751, and then it spread to other sandy soils in Texas, Florida, Georgia, and coastal South Carolina. Sugar was an expensive commodity and grew only in the lower South. Sorghum, also a grass-like sugar cane, grew in the upper South, with Kentucky and Tennessee producing the largest yields in years past. During the Civil War, the isolated mountain areas relied on processing the sorghum as their only source of sweetener.

Both crops were harvested in the fall and processed the same way: the stalks were mashed between rollers (called "crushers") in a mule-driven mill, and the liquid extracted, heated, and poured down a 12-foot-long pan with a built-in maze, causing the juice to run very slowly down the pan over a low fire in a serpentine fashion. By the time it reached the end, which took about an hour, it had reached syrup consistency.

Cane- and sorghum-growing communities had a Syrup Master, who owned the mill and each season turned an acre of harvest into 300 gallons of syrup over two or three days. The cook occasionally used a wooden spatula to aid the flow of the boiling juice. Seven to ten gallons of raw juice was boiled down to one gallon of syrup. All refuse and waste from the raw juice rose to the top while the juice was cooking. This waste was removed by the cook with a "skimmer" made of a fine wire sieve attached to a long wooden handle. These by-products and skimmings were stored and fed to cattle and hogs; the ingredients in the skimmings helped to fatten hogs quickly and also brought a shine to their coats.

RICH CHOCOLATE ICING

Makes 3 to 4 cups

THIS ICING, CALLED A GANACHE, *is especially elegant and rich. It lasts up to a month in the refrigerator. Leftover ganache will freeze; beat well when defrosted and re-fluff. Chilled, it can be rolled to make chocolate truffles or sandwich meringues. Melted, it becomes a thick sauce. Reheat gently to pour over ice cream or cream puffs.*

- 1 pound semisweet chocolate, chopped or grated
- 2 cups heavy cream
- 1 teaspoon vanilla extract

To make icing, melt the chocolate with the cream in a heavy saucepan over medium-low heat, stirring constantly. Transfer the chocolate mixture to a bowl, add the vanilla, stir to blend, and cool in the refrigerator about 1 hour. Remove from the refrigerator and beat on high with an electric hand mixer until mixture becomes thick and fluffy, about 1 to 2 minutes. Store covered in the refrigerator.

See page 550 for how to ice a cake.

LAZY ORANGE BUTTERCREAM ICING

Makes 10 to 11 cups

THE ICING IS CALLED A LAZY BUTTERCREAM, *as it does not require a sugar syrup. It will last a week or two in the refrigerator. Leftovers are good on cupcakes, muffins, or pound cake.*

- 1 cup unsalted butter, softened
- 9 cups confectioners' sugar
- 1 (8-ounce) package cream cheese, room temperature
- 3/4 cup fresh orange juice
- 2 tablespoons grated orange rind, no white attached

Beat all ingredients until smooth. Spread an even layer over the bottom layer of the cake and move the prettiest layer on top, forming two layers. Spread a thin layer of icing over the entire cake to form a crumb coating, and refrigerate until firm.

Remove the cake and continue icing over the crumb coating. Remove the waxed paper strips. Pipe any extra icing around the edges of the cake and garnish with orange wedges.

BOURBON HARD SAUCE ICING

Makes 4 to 5 cups

IT WOULD BE HARD *to say what wouldn't be better served with this icing than fruit cake.*

1 (8-ounce) package cream cheese, softened
1/2 cup butter, softened
3 1/2 cups confectioners' sugar, divided
1/4 cup bourbon, divided, optional
1 teaspoon vanilla extract

Beat cream cheese and butter together with 1 cup of the confectioners' sugar. Beat well and add another cup of sugar, followed by half of the bourbon. Beat well and add remaining bourbon, sugar, and vanilla. Beat well until smooth. Keeps up to 3 days at room temperature, up to 3 weeks refrigerated, or up to 6 months frozen. Soften and stir, or beat until smooth before using.

See page 550 for how to ice a cake.

Variation: Substitute grated orange rind, no white attached, for bourbon.

BROWNED BUTTER ICING

Makes 1 1/2 cups

THE FLAVOR OF BROWNED BUTTER *is rich enough to carry a simple icing and make it special. This would be enough for a two- or three-layer cake.*

6 tablespoons unsalted butter
3 cups confectioners' sugar, sifted
1 1/2 teaspoons vanilla extract
3–4 tablespoons milk, divided

Melt the butter in a small saucepan over medium heat. Stir constantly as the butter foams and then turns golden brown; do not let it burn. Set aside to cool.

Beat together the confectioners' sugar, vanilla, and cooled browned butter in a medium bowl with an electric hand mixer until combined, scraping the sides frequently. Add 2 tablespoons of milk and beat until the icing is smooth. Use a bit more milk as necessary until the icing is smooth and spreadable.

See page 550 for how to ice a cake.

CREAM CHEESE ICING

Makes 4 to 5 cups

IF A BOILED OR OTHER ICING SEEMS DAUNTING, *fall back on cream cheese icing. Leftover cream cheese icing, good for cupcakes or muffins, stores for several weeks in the refrigerator covered tightly.*

1 (8-ounce) package cream cheese, softened
1/2 cup unsalted butter, softened
1 teaspoon vanilla extract
1 (1-pound) box confectioners' sugar, or 3 3/4 cups
Heavy cream

Beat the cream cheese, butter, and vanilla with an electric hand mixer on medium speed until smooth. Reduce speed to low, and slowly add confectioners' sugar until frosting is thick. Thin it with heavy cream if it is not spreadable.

See page 550 for how to ice a cake.

Any leftover icing makes a special treat dolloped into a hulled strawberry.

Variations:

- For a two-layer cake, omit the second-layer step.
- Add 1 tablespoon grated orange or lemon rind, no white attached.

Variation: Coconut Cream Cheese Icing

Add 1 1/2 cups coconut with the confectioners' sugar.

SOUTHERN WHISKEY SAUCE

Makes 1 2/3 cups

JOY OF COOKING CALLS THIS SAUCE *the original American hot dessert sauce, saying it was one of the earliest brought from England. It is a milk-less kind of butter custard that can be boiled without curdling. It must be boiled to thicken. To bring back a separated or crystallized sauce, whisk in a bit of hot water, as with hollandaise. It accompanies bread and biscuit puddings, fruit cakes, and other wintry desserts splendidly.*

8 tablespoons unsalted butter
1 cup granulated sugar
1/4 cup bourbon
2 tablespoons water
1/4 teaspoon freshly grated or ground nutmeg
1/8 teaspoon salt
1 large egg

Melt the butter over low heat in a small, heavy saucepan. Stir in the sugar, bourbon, water, nutmeg, and salt. Continue stirring until the sugar dissolves. Remove from heat.

Allow the mixture to cool about 5 minutes. Thoroughly whisk the egg into the sugar mixture. Return to medium heat and bring to the boil. Cook until thickened, about 1 minute, stirring gently. Serve immediately or let cool, cover, and refrigerate up to 3 days. To serve, reheat over low heat. If sauce separates, whisk in a little hot water.

MEMORABLE SWEETS

The burning question when planning a meal is "What shall we have for dessert?"—meaning, what shall we have that will make people lie in bed at night wishing they had more.

Some desserts float on the tongue, like a Cold Lemon Soufflé (page 605). Others, like the Chocolate Pecan Torte (page 612), are so densely chocolate that old ladies put slices in their purses to smuggle home. Pecan rolls light as air, wrapped around whipped cream, vie with rich, grainy fudge as part of Southern culture.

Whipping egg whites is an art leading to the best and most seductive of desserts. When I was a girl, I was so enamored of meringues that when I stayed home from school I would make them. Some were little clouds of crispness. Others slid off the pan in gloppy messes. Our step-by-step directions will make masters of all, leading to islands of air, coddled in the custards that soothe and beckon us.

Some of these recipes have only been in the South since the advent of air-conditioning. We are as susceptible to chocolate as anyone and have gathered here a few recipes, like chocolate chip cookies, that bear no Southern claim except longevity of usage and general practice. Forgive us.

In a land where manners are supreme, it is not acceptable to lick your plate. Instead, we must be more discreet—as in finger-licking good.

COOKIES

Tucked with love into a lunch box, served warm from the oven, or gift-wrapped for the holiday cookie swap, it's always the perfect time for a cookie. Once the basics of cookie making are mastered, the variations become endless, and taking a favorite family recipe from just fine to fabulous is easy.

Ingredients

For more in-depth ingredient information, see Cakes (page 546) and Breads (page 540). Unless otherwise stated, cookie ingredients should be at room temperature.

Fats—Cookies are made with butter, margarine, or shortening. The fat determines the spread of a cookie—more fat produces a flatter cookie and less fat produces a puffier cookie. Cookies made with butter spread more than those made with shortening.

Flour—Most cookie recipes call for all-purpose flour. To decrease the spread of a cookie, substitute a portion of bread flour for the all-purpose flour.

Baking powder and baking soda—Baking powder keeps a cookie lighter in color and a bit puffier. Baking soda also allows the cookies to brown in the oven.

Sugar—White sugar makes a crisper cookie than brown sugar or honey. Cookies made with brown sugar will absorb moisture after baking, helping to ensure that they stay chewy. Most chocolate chip cookie recipes contain both brown and white sugars. Using a little less sugar can make for a puffier cookie.

Eggs—Egg yolks help the dough bind together and make a rich-tasting dough. Egg whites make drier, more cake-like cookies. Whole eggs are sometimes the only liquid in cookie dough.

Cookie Techniques

Beating the fat and sugar together until light in color, fluffy, and smooth is an important step. Use an electric hand mixer if at all possible; this beats air into the dough. Eggs are added to the dough and are beaten in just enough to incorporate them into the mix.

Chilling the dough—This is perhaps the most overlooked technique in baking cookies. Allowing the dough to rest in the refrigerator for 12, 24, or even 36 hours is best. Not only will the flavors marry, but the dough will relax and be easier to handle. Chilling is a must with rolled cookies cut out with cutters, as those doughs need to hold their shape and have clear-cut edges. Chilling is less critical with drop cookies, but resting the dough greatly improves their flavor.

Piping cookies—To make a pastry bag at home, put a plastic ziplock bag in a measuring cup and fold open the bag over the top edge of the cup; fill the bag with the batter. Barely cut off one of the corners. Test the bag to make sure the hole isn't too big and the cookies are coming out at the size needed. Get a rhythm going when piping the cookies onto the sheet; it makes it easier to have a consistent cookie size and shape.

Making cookie cups and baskets—Almost any thin cookie can be shaped while still warm. Oil the exterior of a small bowl and turn it rim down on the counter. Once the cookie is cool enough to handle, drape it over the bottom of the bowl and let it cool enough to harden; then remove. Work quickly. If the cookies harden before you get them draped over the bowl, return them to the oven to reheat enough to be pliable.

Equipment for Cookie Baking

Different baking sheets and ovens produce different results. The best pans for baking cookies are light-colored rimmed aluminum baking sheets. These produce even browning on the bottom of the cookies. Insulated baking sheets work well, although sometimes they don't allow enough browning on the bottom, and the dough has a tendency to spread more. Nonstick, as well as other rimmed baking sheets with a dark finish, will usually brown a cookie too fast. Reduce the baking temperature by 25 degrees if using a nonstick pan. If a multipurpose pan is desired, a jelly roll pan can be ideal.

To make cookie removal and cleanup easier, invest in parchment paper or silicone baking mats. The entire sheet can be lifted off of the pan and onto a wire rack for cooling. Simply load a fresh sheet of paper with more dough, move to the hot cookie sheet, and move immediately to the oven. Placing dough directly onto a

continued

continuation from previous page

hot pan will cause the cookie to spread prematurely.

If cookies tend to burn, slide another cookie sheet underneath. Rotate the pan in the oven halfway through the baking time if there are hot spots in the oven.

Ovens differ, as do pans. Baking sheets should go into the oven from front to back, not side to side, to give the maximum room for air circulation. Two pans should be placed on two racks, neither touching the sides of the oven, and staggered in the oven so they are not immediately above and below each other (which causes the cookies underneath to brown too much on the bottom and the cookies on the top to brown too much on the top.)

Two pans should be rotated front to back. Change shelves halfway through baking time.

PECAN COOKIES

Makes 30 cookies

THESE BUTTERY PECAN COOKIES *are those that find their way into dreams. They are marvelous by themselves but also work fabulously sandwiched with peaches, mangos, or strawberries, and whipped cream.*

10 tablespoons unsalted butter
1/2 cup granulated sugar
1 1/2 cups all-purpose flour
1/3 teaspoon salt
1 1/4 cups finely chopped toasted pecans

Beat the butter and sugar together with an electric hand mixer until light in color, fluffy, and smooth.

Whisk the flour with the salt, add the pecans, and stir into the butter mixture to make an even dough.

Divide the dough into 3 or 4 equal portions. Roll out each piece between 2 pieces of parchment or waxed paper until slightly less than 1/8 inch thick. Chill 30 minutes, or until firm. Alternatively, roll each portion into a 3-inch-thick log. Chill. Slice into 1/8-inch rounds and move to rimmed baking sheets and proceed as below.

When ready to bake, preheat oven to 375 degrees. Line 2 rimmed baking sheets with parchment paper or a silicone baking mat. Remove the top sheet of paper from the dough and cut the dough into 3-inch rounds with a cookie cutter. Reroll scraps, cut out, and add cold cookies to the prepared cookie sheets. Bake 10 minutes, or until the edges begin to brown, rotating the pan 180 degrees halfway through baking time. The cookies will be soft even though done, hardening as they cool. When they are nearly hard, remove to racks to cool.

When cool, store in an airtight container or cookie jar at room temperature, or wrap well in an airtight container and freeze up to 3 months.

Variation: Whip 1 cup heavy cream with 1 teaspoon peach brandy or schnapps and 3 teaspoons granulated sugar. Slice 1 to 2 cups peaches. Thirty minutes before serving, sandwich a portion of the whipped cream and a slice or two of peaches between 2 cookie rounds and move to the refrigerator. Immediately before serving, decorate the top with additional whipped cream or sprinkle with confectioners' sugar.

Variation: Peach Torte

For a glamorous torte, divide the Pecan Cookie dough into 3 equal pieces and roll or pat into flat rounds. Place each round between 2 sheets of parchment paper and chill 30 minutes, or until firm. Remove top layer of paper and turn a round upside down on the baking sheet. Remove remaining paper and bake 10 minutes at 375 degrees, or until edges begin to brown. Be careful not to overbake. The rounds will still be soft when done and will harden as they cool. While still warm, score one of the rounds in pie-shaped wedges with a knife, being careful not to cut all the way through. This will be the top round and will facilitate cutting the dessert when assembled. Move the rounds to racks to cool and harden.

Move one round to a serving platter and top with 1 cup sliced peaches and half the whipped cream. Add another round and top again with 1 cup sliced peaches and remaining whipped cream. Top with reserved scored round.

PECAN CRESCENTS

Makes 60 crescents

THESE MELT IN THE MOUTH *as well as being crisp enough to satisfy a craving for crunch. They are particularly welcome as a gift or on a holiday party table.*

1 cup unsalted butter, softened
1/4 cup granulated sugar
2 teaspoons vanilla extract
1 teaspoon almond extract
Pinch of salt
2 cups all-purpose flour
1 1/2 cups finely ground pecans
Confectioners' sugar, sifted

Beat the butter, sugar, extracts, and salt with an electric hand mixer until light in color, fluffy, and smooth. Beat in the flour and then the pecans, scraping down the sides of the bowl to incorporate everything well. Chill the dough from 30 minutes up to 2 days.

When ready to bake, preheat oven to 325 degrees. Line a rimmed baking sheet with parchment paper or a silicone baking mat.

Scoop the dough into 1-inch balls with the large end of a melon baller and roll them into crescent shapes. Place the crescents 1 1/4 inches apart on the prepared sheet. Bake one sheet at a time, rotating pan 180 degrees halfway through baking time, and bake until very lightly browned on the bottom, about 10 to 15 minutes. The tops do not brown. Cool the crescents briefly in the pan on a wire rack.

Gently roll the crescents in the confectioners' sugar. When fully cooled, store the crescents in an airtight container between layers of waxed paper, or wrap well in an airtight container and freeze up to 3 months.

SHORTBREAD COOKIES

Makes 4 dozen cookies

SCOTLAND GAVE US THESE—*crumbly, butter cookies made from a simple dough. Shortbread refers to the shortness of the gluten strands due to the buttery content of the dough.*

1 cup unsalted butter, softened
3/4 cup confectioners' sugar
1/2 teaspoon vanilla extract
1/2 teaspoon almond extract
2 cups all-purpose flour
1/4 teaspoon baking powder
1/8 teaspoon salt

Beat butter and sugar in an electric hand mixer until light in color, fluffy, and smooth. Stir in vanilla and almond extracts.

Whisk together the flour, baking powder, and salt on a sheet of waxed paper. Gradually add the flour mixture to the butter mixture, beating on low until blended.

Remove dough from mixer to waxed paper. Shape dough into 2 (7-inch) logs. Wrap in parchment or waxed paper and refrigerate 4 hours, or move logs to a freezer container, without touching each other, and freeze.

When ready to bake, preheat oven to 350 degrees. Line 2 rimmed baking sheets with parchment paper or a silicone baking mat.

Remove as many logs as desired from the refrigerator or freezer. If frozen, allow to stand at room temperature for 10 minutes. Slice each log into 24 slices. Move slices 1 inch apart on baking sheets. Bake 10 to 12 minutes, until edges of cookies begin to turn golden, rotating the pan 180 degrees halfway through baking time. Remove baking sheets and cookies to a wire rack to cool.

When cool, store in an airtight container or a cookie jar at room temperature, or wrap well in an airtight container and freeze up to 3 months.

Variations:

- Stir in 1 cup finely chopped pecans.
- Use dough as a piecrust. Pat out the dough 1/4 inch thick in a tart pan with a removable bottom. Bake as above. Serve topped with sliced peaches, mangos, or figs and whipped cream.

LACY PECAN COOKIES

Makes 48 (3-inch) rounds or 36 (4-inch) rounds

LACE COOKIES CAN BE GIANT DISCS *sufficient to make a child think of the moon, or discreet rounds. Either way, they are brittle, thin, and nearly sheer enough to read through. The skilled may drape them over rolling pins until cool to make tuile shapes: shape on the back of small bowls to make cups; mold over cone shapes to make ice cream cones; or shape around the handle of a spoon to form a tube. Any or all of these may be eaten alone or topped with mascarpone, whipped cream, lemon curd, or berries. Flours vary, so if the first batch of cookies baked spread more than desired, add a bit more flour.*

2 cups pecans
2 cups all-purpose flour, divided
1/2 cup granulated sugar
1/2 cup light brown sugar
1/2 teaspoon salt
1 cup light corn syrup
1 cup unsalted butter, room temperature
1/2 teaspoon bourbon or vanilla extract

Preheat oven to 350 degrees. Line 2 or more rimmed baking sheets with parchment paper or silicone baking mats.

Toast the pecans on a baking sheet until golden, about 10 minutes. Chop into pea-sized pieces. Toss with 1 3/4 cup of the flour on a piece of parchment or waxed paper.

Add the sugars, salt, corn syrup, and butter to a heavy saucepan. Cook over moderately low heat, stirring constantly, until the butter is melted and the ingredients are dissolved and incorporated. Stir in the flour-and-pecan mixture, add the bourbon or vanilla, and mix well. Cool slightly. It should be like thick honey. Add remaining flour if too thin.

Drop the batter by tablespoons onto the prepared pans, leaving at least 3 inches between the cookies; each sheet will hold only 4. If a round shape is desired as opposed to free-form, push lightly into a round. The smoothest presentation will be to use a small ice cream scoop that holds about a tablespoon of batter.

Bake one sheet at a time, rotating 180 degrees halfway through baking time, until the cookies are golden and most of the bubbling has stopped, 6 to 8 minutes.

Remove the baking sheet from the oven and cool 2 to 3 minutes, until the cookies are just firm enough to move. Ease the cookie off with a spatula and move to a rack to cool. Continue with the remaining batter in the same manner. If the baked cookies become too firm to remove from the baking sheet, return them to the oven until warm and softened enough to move.

If making shapes, mold the still warm cookies onto an oiled rolling pin or the back of oiled custard cups, pressing gently. Cool completely before moving. When cool, store in an airtight container or cookie jar at room temperature, or wrap well in an airtight container and freeze up to 3 months.

Variations:
Add 2 tablespoons white or black benne (sesame) seeds or 1 to 2 teaspoons grated orange or lemon rind.

BLACK BENNE (SESAME) SEEDS

Black benne seeds are not traditional for Benne Seed Wafers but can give them a unique spicy flavor. The same goes with using a variety of sugars. Dark brown sugar gives the cookies a heavier molasses-like flavor, and white sugar gives them a lighter flavor and color.

BENNE SEED WAFERS

Makes 50 to 75 cookies

SESAME SEEDS ARE NOW MAINLY IMPORTED FROM INDIA, *but they were thought to have been originally brought to the Lowcountry with the West African slaves, who called them "benne." The benne seeds of that time were quite different in flavor from today's. (I'm growing some in my garden.) They were used in ancient Roman cooking for various purposes like oils and wine, and were, of course, added to doughs. These thin, crispy cookies are not only light and toothsome, but the benne seeds in them are thought to bring good luck.*

- 6 tablespoons unsalted butter, room temperature
- 3/4 cup light or dark brown sugar
- 2 large egg whites, room temperature
- 5 tablespoons all-purpose flour
- 1/8 teaspoon baking powder
- 1/8 teaspoon salt
- 1/2 teaspoon vanilla extract
- 1/2 cup toasted white or black benne (sesame) seeds (facing)

Preheat oven to 325 degrees. Line 2 rimmed baking sheets with parchment paper or silicone baking mats.

Beat the butter and sugar with an electric hand mixer until light in color, fluffy, and smooth. Add egg whites one at a time, incorporating them into the batter with the mixer at a low speed.

Mix together flour, baking powder, and salt, and sift into the batter, mixing until smooth. Add the vanilla and beat at medium speed. Fold in the benne seeds.

Fill a pastry bag with the batter and pipe the cookies onto prepared pans, about 1/2 teaspoon each (the size of a dime) and about 1 1/2 to 2 inches apart. Bake 8 to 10 minutes, rotating the pans 180 degrees halfway through baking time. Move pans to a rack to cool briefly, and then move the cookies to a wire rack to cool completely.

When cool, store in an airtight container or cookie jar at room temperature, or wrap well in an airtight container and freeze up to 3 months.

TOASTING BENNE (SESAME) SEEDS

Preheat oven to 350 degrees. Pour the amount of seeds needed onto a rimmed baking sheet that has been lined with parchment paper or a silicone baking mat. Toast the seeds in the oven until their color has changed from off-white to light brown. If they aren't toasting fast enough, move them under the broiler, but watch them carefully to ensure they don't over-toast or burn.

BEGINNER'S LEMON BARS

Makes about 36 bars

WHETHER FOR WEDDINGS, FUNERALS, CHURCH SUPPERS, OR PICNICS, *lemon bars are always popular. I love making them because I know they'll be a hit. For those who are preparing to take their first steps to making pies and custards, this is a no-fail recipe. The "short" crust—really a cookie crust—pats out and the lemon custard goes on top. Take special care to grate just the yellow rind of the lemon with no white pith attached.*

- 2½ cups all-purpose flour, divided
- 1 cup unsalted butter, softened
- ½ cup confectioners' sugar
- 2 cups granulated sugar
- ½ cup fresh lemon juice
- 4 large eggs
- Grated rind of 1 lemon, no white attached, optional
- Confectioners' sugar for finishing

Preheat oven to 350 degrees. Oil a 9 x 13-inch baking dish.

Mix together 2¼ cups of the flour, butter, and confectioners' sugar in a large bowl until a soft dough forms. Remove and press dough into prepared pan. Bake 20 to 25 minutes, or until lightly browned. Remove from oven.

Beat the granulated sugar, lemon juice, remaining ¼ cup flour, eggs, and optional lemon rind until well mixed. Pour over hot crust. Return to the oven and bake an additional 20 minutes, or until set.

Cool on a wire rack then cut into bars. The center will be soft like a custard or pie filling. Sift confectioners' sugar over the top and then remove bars from the pan. Separate with parchment or waxed paper if layering to store. These will keep a couple of days, covered at room temperature, refrigerated up to 1 week, or wrapped well in an airtight container and frozen up to 3 months.

FOOD PROCESSOR FLORENTINE LACE COOKIES

Makes 65 to 70 cookies

THESE COOKIES ARE BEAUTIFUL *with their stained glass window colors and are lacy light. They are particularly suited to holiday giving. If possible, search for high-quality candied fruit.*

Crust

- 1½ cups all-purpose flour
- ½ cup confectioners' sugar
- ½ cup unsalted butter, cut into pieces
- 2 teaspoons vanilla extract
- 2 tablespoons heavy cream

Topping

- ¾ cup unsalted butter
- ½ cup granulated sugar
- ¼ cup whipping cream
- ½ cup chopped candied red cherries
- ½ cup chopped candied pineapple
- ½ cup sliced blanched almonds
- 2 tablespoons grated orange rind, no white attached
- ½ cup semisweet chocolate pieces, melted

Preheat oven to 375 degrees. Line a 15 x 10-inch jelly-roll pan with foil.

Make the dough by pulsing together the flour and confectioners' sugar in the bowl of a food processor fitted with a metal blade. Add the butter and pulse until well blended. With the motor running, add the vanilla and cream through the feed tube, and process until the dough begins to form a ball. Remove the dough, press into the foil-lined pan, and refrigerate while preparing the topping.

To make the topping, cook the butter, sugar, and cream in a medium saucepan over medium heat until the mixture comes to the boil, stirring often. Boil 1 to 2 minutes and then add the cherries, pineapple, almonds, and orange rind. Spread the mixture evenly over the chilled crust. Bake until golden, 15 to 20 minutes. Allow to cool in the pan.

While still slightly warm, use a fork to drizzle the chocolate over the crust. When cooled, cut into 5 lengthwise strips and then cut each strip into about 13 triangles. Store in the refrigerator, or wrap well in an airtight container and freeze up to 3 months.

MORAVIAN GINGER SNAPS

Makes 100 cookies (1 1/2 pounds)

One of the real treats in visiting Salem, North Carolina, *is seeing all the heirloom plants, as well as savoring just-baked thin cookies that come right out of the same oven they were baked in during colonial times. It's worth a trip to see the architecture but also just to stand there and smell these cookies baking.*

These wafer-thin gingersnaps are popular at Christmas and are fabulous with soft white cheeses such as triple-cream (crème) cheese, mascarpone, Brie, and Montrachet. The dough should be rolled wafer thin to duplicate the originals from this 1776 Moravian recipe. But if the cookies end up as thick as gingersnaps, they will still be quickly gobbled up.

1/2 cup light or dark brown sugar
1 cup molasses, preferably unsulfured*
1/4 cup shortening or lard, melted
1/4 cup unsalted butter, melted
1/2 tablespoon ground cinnamon
3/4 teaspoon ground cloves
1/2 tablespoon ground ginger
1/4 teaspoon baking soda
1/4 teaspoon salt
2 1/2–3 cups all-purpose flour, divided
Flour for shaping

Mix the sugar and molasses in a large bowl. Add the shortening and butter. Sift together the cinnamon, cloves, ginger, soda, and salt with 3 tablespoons of the flour. Stir into the molasses mixture.

Stir in a third of the flour with a wooden spoon and then add the second third. Turn out onto a board sprinkled with the remaining flour and knead into the dough until a heavy dough is formed. Divide in half and shape each half into a disc. Alternatively, roll each portion into a 3-inch-thick log. Tightly wrap each in a plastic bag. Let stand at least overnight at room temperature to mature, or preferably several days refrigerated. It will be much easier to roll after it has mellowed several days.

When ready to bake, preheat oven to 350 degrees. Line 2 rimmed baking sheets with parchment paper or silicone baking mats. Remove dough from the refrigerator and bring to room temperature before trying to roll it out. Add flour as needed to form a damp, but not sticky, flexible dough. Spread plastic wrap or parchment paper on the counter. Pat the dough out on the wrap or paper and top with another sheet of wrap.

Roll as thinly as possible—1/16 to 1/32 of an inch—using a heavy rolling pin (the very patient might prefer rolling these in a pasta machine; it works, but I'm not sure it is easier). Cut into shapes and use a metal spatula to move the cookies to a prepared pan. Bake until lightly browned, about 8 minutes, rotating the pan 180 degrees halfway through baking time. (The pans should be alternated, facing front to rear in the oven, not horizontally one on one top of the other. The air needs to circulate around them or the bottom pan will burn and the top will not be done.)

Cool on the pan on a rack for several minutes. Remove cookies with a spatula to a wire rack and cool until crisp. Repeat with the rest of the dough. If the cookies tended to brown around the edges, turn down the oven temperature for the remaining batches. Wrap tightly and store in a tin or freeze up to 3 months. Pack in an airtight container so they don't soften. Re-crisp on a rimmed baking sheet in a 250-degree oven as necessary.

**Sometimes sold in health food stores.*

Variation: An alternate method of cutting the dough is to divide and roll it into four logs. After refrigerating for several days, the cold dough can be thinly sliced into cookies and baked.

CHOCOLATE CHIP OR KISS COOKIES

Makes about 2 dozen (3½-inch) cookies

Chocolate chip and kiss cookies are staples *in any household with children of every age. I use chocolate kisses when I have anyone willing to take the aluminum foil off of them. One day we toured the Hershey's factory for a segment on my television show and decided to use the kisses in a chocolate chip cookie, chopping half of them and leaving the rest whole. (This is a good way to use leftovers at Christmas or Easter once the holiday has passed.) Wow! Unforgettable!*

2½ cups all-purpose flour
1 teaspoon baking soda
1 teaspoon salt
¼ teaspoon ground cinnamon
1 cup unsalted butter, softened
1 cup light or dark brown sugar
1 cup granulated sugar
2 large eggs
2 teaspoons vanilla extract
2 cups (16 ounces) semisweet chocolate chips or kisses, divided
1½ cups chopped pecans

Preheat oven to 375 degrees.

Whisk together the flour, baking soda, salt, and cinnamon; set aside.

Beat the butter and sugars with an electric hand mixer until light in color, fluffy, and smooth. Beat in the eggs, and vanilla. Stir in flour mixture.

If using kisses, chop 1 cup. Stir in all the chocolate chips or both the chopped and whole kisses and the nuts. Drop heaping tablespoonfuls of the mixture onto an ungreased rimmed baking sheet, 2 inches apart. Bake in a hot oven 8 to 10 minutes, rotating the pan 180 degrees halfway through baking time. Cool on a wire rack.

When cool, store in an airtight container or cookie jar at room temperature, or wrap well in an airtight container and freeze up to 3 months.

Variations:

- For chewy, melt-in-your-mouth cookies, decrease temperature to 325 degrees and bake 10 to 13 minutes.
- Use ½ cup grated coconut and 1 cup chopped macadamia nuts in place of the 1½ cups chopped pecans. Bake as directed.

CHARLESTON CHEWIES

Makes 20 to 30 squares

These bar cookies are really a cross between the famous candy and a cookie, *they are chewy and yummy! Great care must be taken to bake them lightly, without a deep color or tough top.*

1 pound light or dark brown sugar (or half each)
1/2 cup unsalted butter, melted
2 large eggs
1 teaspoon vanilla extract
2 cups all-purpose flour
1 teaspoon baking powder
1/2 teaspoon salt
1 1/2 cups chopped pecans
Confectioners' sugar for decoration

Preheat oven to 350 degrees. Butter and lightly flour a 9 x 13-inch baking pan.

Beat the sugar and butter with an electric hand mixer in a pan over low heat, until the sugar is melted. Remove from heat. Beat in the eggs and vanilla.

Mix flour with baking powder and salt. Stir into the butter mixture. Stir in the pecans. Turn mixture into the prepared baking pan.

Bake for 20 minutes, or until a toothpick inserted in the center comes out clean. Cool in the pan on a rack. Sprinkle with confectioners' sugar and cut into small squares as desired. When cool, store in an airtight container or cookie jar at room temperature, or wrap well in an airtight container and freeze up to 3 months.

MERINGUES

Egg whites and sugar are the most magical combination of ingredients. With them in the house, a myriad of forms and shapes can be created, crisp or melting, dappled with brown or pale as snow. In short, together they form meringue, whether to top a pie crust, to sandwich with whipped cream or fill with berries, or to pop into one's month for a crisp, sugary treat. We use the word interchangeably to describe each of these, but first we will tackle the namesake.

Meringues are foamy egg whites and sugar, beaten until in peaks and dried in the oven crisp but still white. They melt in the mouth when eaten. Drying them removes their moisture. In humid places, such as much of the South, making them is a challenge. Southerners have grown to love them when the result is a pale brown, lightly caramelized meringue. Many of us even think they taste better that way, like a marshmallow lightly caramelized in a campfire.

The perfect way to make a beautifully whipped egg white is by hand in a copper bowl, using a balloon whisk. The copper contains an ingredient that stabilizes the egg whites, and the balloon whisk enables wide sweeps of the bowl, resulting in high peaks of beauty. It also requires a strong tennis arm and is impractical—but better than in the days when a large platter was used to hold the whites, and a fork was drawn from end to end of the platter to incorporate the air, an arduous effort.

Today, using an electric hand mixer in a wide bowl and running the mixer around the bowl, turning the bowl as the mixer whirls around, and finishing off the last bit with a balloon whisk will produce a fairly good meringue. The more the whisk is shaped like a balloon, with many wires, the better. Good bakers, however, try to secure a large stand mixer with a rotating wire whisk that emulates hand beating. After the meringues form a light peak, they too are best finished off with a hand whisk.

There are three basic methods of making meringues—traditional, Swiss and Italian—delineated by temperature of the mixture, the method of beating, and the ease of preparation. All require a bowl free of fat of any sort, particularly egg yolk. (See page 272 to learn how to separate eggs.) Room-temperature egg whites give more volume than refrigerator cold ones. The fresher the better, but not noticeably so to the home cook. They may each be formed into the same shapes.

Ingredients are usually twice as much sugar as egg white, an acid stabilizer such as cream of tartar, lemon juice or vinegar, and a flavor addition such as vanilla, liqueur, etc. Nuts are a common variation.

Meringues don't like to sit around before being cooked, so move as rapidly as possible to shape and dry them. Making large batches at a time requires more oven space, so avoid doubling the recipe until the oven capacity is determined. Making another batch is easier than dealing with egg whites that have sat out for an hour or two waiting for the oven.

Under-beating egg whites will make them droopy. Overbeating, which makes the egg whites look rocky, will cause the bubbles to break and release their moisture. Eggs are inexpensive and it is worth practicing a bit, if possible, to get a perfect peak of meringue that clings to the bowl or whisk when turned upside down carefully.

Free of cholesterol (unless adding a filling such as whipped cream or ice cream), meringues really are one of the easiest of all desserts to make.

When they are completely dry, the meringues keep covered in an airtight container or frozen. Serve with Peach Butter (page 645), Lemon Curd (page 618), fresh berries and whipped cream or yogurt, or sprinkle with shaved chocolate or cocoa. Or eat as is.

BASIC TECHNIQUES

We have tried to include everything in this chapter that a fledgling but enterprising cook would want to conquer that we hadn't covered elsewhere—whipping egg whites for meringues; making caramel syrup and pecans; dealing with chocolate; making roulades, or meringue rolls.

TRADITIONAL SIMPLE MERINGUES

Makes 30 to 35

SINCE THE RATIO OF 2 PORTIONS OF SUGAR *to 1 portion of egg white is the same no matter how many eggs are whipped, the recipe works as well with larger or smaller amounts.*

4 egg whites, room temperature
1/4 teaspoon cream of tartar
1/2 teaspoon salt
1 cup granulated sugar

Preheat oven to 200 degrees.

Oil and flour one or two rimmed baking sheets. Line with parchment or waxed paper, and oil and flour the paper. (This makes cleanup *much* easier.) The pans should be no longer than the length from the front of the oven when the door is closed to the back. If the pans are larger and only fit across the oven, halve the recipe, using just one pan rather than setting the pans one directly under the other or letting the meringue mixture sit more than an hour while the first batch dries.

Beat the egg whites in a large bowl using a stand mixer fitted with a rotary whisk, or with a balloon whisk or electric hand mixer, starting slowly and increasing speed until they are "foamy." Add the cream of tartar and salt, then continue beating, gradually increasing the speed (it gets easier to beat as the pockets of air form) just until soft peaks form and the egg whites barely slide in the bowl when tipped. Avoid letting them get "rocky" looking and over-beaten.

Beat in half the sugar, 1 tablespoon at a time and continue to beat until the meringue is very stiff and shiny. Sprinkle the rest of the sugar on top and fold in with a metal spoon or rubber spatula, using a figure-eight motion to go down to the bottom of the pan and back up again, rotating the bowl after each "eight." If the meringue deflates, beat further by hand with a balloon whisk to make firm peaks. Shape and bake as on page 599.

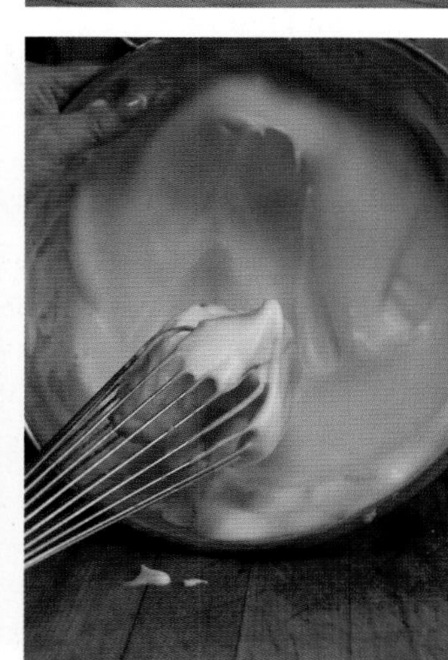

Leftover and crumbled meringue mixed with whipped cream and a sauce or purée, such as lemon curd or raspberry purée, can be served as is or chilled and frozen in a plastic-lined loaf pan. Freeze, remove, and slice to serve.

SWISS MERINGUES

Makes 30 to 35

THIS PRODUCES A MORE STABLE MERINGUE *as a result of cooking the egg white to 120 degrees before baking, and a "brighter white" meringue. I find measuring the sugar onto a piece of waxed or parchment paper makes it easy to add with one hand while beating with the other. Use same ingredients as page 597.*

Whisk the egg whites in a large bowl using a stand mixer with a rotary whisk or with a balloon whisk or electric hand mixer, starting slowly, until they are foamy. Add the cream of tartar and the salt and continue, gradually increasing speed, until they form very soft peaks and barely slide in the bowl. Move the bowl over a pan of simmering water and slowly and steadily whisk in the sugar. Add the vanilla. Continue whisking until the mixture forms a glossy stiff peak and does not slide in the bowl, about 5 minutes by mixer, longer by hand. The mixture will register 120 degrees on a thermometer. If beaten too long, it looks rocky and starts to separate. Remove from the heat and continue whisking until the meringue is cool. Shape and bake as on page 599.

ITALIAN MERINGUES

Makes 40 (1-inch)

IN THESE MERINGUES, *a sugar syrup is made and poured into the egg whites as they are beating. This takes absolutely no chance the whites will undercook, as they are, as with the Swiss above, already cooked. The difficulty is making the sugar syrup simultaneously while whisking the eggs if one is not using a stand mixer. If it is easier to make a sugar syrup ahead of time, then heat it to add to the egg whites, by all means do this.*

The addition of butter makes this a Classic Butter Cream and Chocolate Butter Cream.

Beat the 4 egg whites in a large bowl with a stand mixer fitted with a rotary whisk, or with a balloon whisk or electric hand mixer, until they are foamy. Add the cream of tartar and the salt, increase the speed gradually until they are in soft peaks.

Meanwhile, make the sugar syrup by dissolving one cup of sugar over low heat in a pan with 1 cup of water. When totally clear, turn up the heat and bring to the boil, and boil until the mixture is at the soft-ball stage (238 degrees on a candy thermometer).

Reduce the beating speed of the meringues and slowly drizzle the boiling syrup into the egg whites, taking care to avoid dribbling on the beater where the syrup will harden, increasing the speed until the syrup is completely added. Beat until the meringue forms stiff shiny peaks and cool. Proceed to shape and bake (facing), or make into a sauce or filling, in the variation.

Variation: Butter Cream and Chocolate Butter Cream

Beat in a large bowl half as much unsalted butter as sugar (for the above recipe, 1/2 a cup butter) until it is very pale, soft, and fluffy. Fold 1 to 1 1/2 cups of Italian meringue into the butter, using a figure-eight motion. Flavor with orange zest, melted chocolate (about 4 tablespoons, melted), chocolate liqueur, vanilla, etc.

CREAM OF TARTAR

Cream of tartar, a mildly acidic salt, is used as a stabilizer when beating egg whites, particularly in Italian meringues. In her excellent book *Bakewise,* Shirley Corriher points out that it is absolutely necessary to use cream of tartar with cooked meringues and not to overbeat the egg whites so they will keep their shape without cracking. For detailed information on the egg protein, read her book.

MERINGUE SHAPES

Shaping meringues—To make cloud shapes, dump a spoonful of meringue onto the paper, make a little depression with the back of the spoon that will be deep enough to hold cream and berries and repeat to fill the pan. Different-sized spoons will produce different-sized meringues that require adjustments in time of baking. Bake (dry) 1 to 3 hours at 200 degrees to dry the meringues.

To make rounds to sandwich with fillings like whipped cream or lemon curd, with or without fruit, draw circles on the paper. Spoon the meringue into the rounds evenly so they will stack when dried.

To pipe the meringue, cut a small slit in one corner of a plastic bag or use a plastic or pastry bag with a tip. Position the bag in a sturdy mug or glass, and fold the bag down around the outside of the container. Scoop the meringue from the bowl into the bag until it is half full. Pull up the surrounding part of the bag and twist the meringue-free top to keep the meringue from gushing out. Hold the twisted part of the bag with the dominant hand, and position the fingers of the other hand at the bottom tip, avoiding putting a hand (which is hot and will melt the sugar) on the side of the bag. Push from the top.

For traditional kiss-sized meringues, guide the bag with the fingers to the top of the pan, push gently from the top of the bag onto the pan and make a small round, lift the bag, pulling up the bag to make a point on the top of the meringue, and stop pushing.

To make larger, "two-bump" meringues, push from the top onto the pan, making a much larger bottom round. Pull up slightly, releasing, then push down again, making a second smaller bump, and pull up to make a point on the top.

Baking meringues—Put the first tray into a preheated 200-degree oven on the top shelf vertically without touching the sides of the oven. Fill the second tray, as above, and move down a rack and to the other side of the oven, staggering the pans so the air can circulate around them. This will prevent the meringues on the top and bottom rows from overbrowning when the heat hits and can't circulate.

Meringue baskets—Using a pastry bag fitted with a round tip, pipe 3-inch rounds of meringue onto prepared pans. Go back and pipe a ring on top of the outside edge of the basket bottoms, building the side of the basket (or shape mounds with 2 tablespoons, or pipe into mounds; see Traditional Simple Meringues, page 597). Bake until firm and ivory-colored, 1 to 2 hours. If the meringues are to be filled with whipped cream, ice cream, or a favorite yogurt, turn them over when almost cooked, crack the center of the base to hollow the shell, and continue baking until dry.

Meringue mushrooms—For this special treat, draw small circles on paper, and pipe three-fourths of the meringue into the circles, leaving round on top. With the remaining mixture, pipe little straight sticks, or stems. Bake as above. When ready to use, take a small knife and make a tiny hole in the flat bottom of the mushroom top. Insert the stem in the hole.

Making meringues ahead—Meringues and nut meringues (page 600) are best made without the pressure of time, as they have their own minds and dry out according to the humidity of the day. They freeze well, separated by layers of parchment or waxed paper in a tightly sealed container. They may also last a few days, tightly sealed, at room temperature, depending on humidity. Remember, they are fragile and must be stored in a sturdy container that will protect them.

KNOW THE OVEN

Many ovens do not have an easily regulated low-temperature setting. The first time making meringues, leave the oven light on and keep checking, and adjust the time according to the idiosyncrasies of the oven.

STICKY MERINGUE RESCUES

If time necessitates, leave meringues in the turned-off oven overnight and continue to bake the next day. They are divine even if caramelized.

Another method is to remove them from the oven and pop the baking sheet into the freezer. When frozen, move to an airtight container. They are remarkable and do "stiffen up" in the freezer. Serve frozen if need be, or dry a bit more in a low oven. Usually they are just fine as is.

PAVLOVA

Makes 1 (9-inch) round

Both Australia and New Zealand *claim the honor of creating this airy, cream-filled fruit-bedazzled dessert, which has been named for the famous Russian ballerina Anna Pavlova (1885–1931).*

- 3 egg whites
- 3/4 cup sugar
- 1 tablespoon cornstarch
- 1 1/2 teaspoons white vinegar or 1/4 teaspoon cream of tartar
- 1 teaspoon vanilla
- 1 cup heavy cream, whipped until it holds firm peaks
- Sugar
- 3 cups sliced fresh tropical fruit in season (strawberries, bananas, kiwis, peaches, papayas, mangos, or pineapple)

Preheat oven to 250 degrees. Grease and flour an 9-inch pie plate or line a rimmed baking sheet with parchment, and draw a 9-inch circle, using the plate as your guide.

Whip egg whites until they hold stiff peaks. Beat in sugar, 1 teaspoon at a time, until the mixture is stiff and shiny. Then beat in the cornstarch, vinegar, and vanilla. Fill the plate with the meringue mixture, hollowing out the center slightly. Or mound mixture in center of circle. Spread meringue out to cover circle, and then make a depression in the center. Bake for 1 1/4 to 1 1/2 hours, or until the meringue is very light brown. Cool slightly then unmold and cool completely. (It may collapse slightly.) Just before serving, add sugar to taste to the whipped cream, add half the fruit, and fill the center of the Pavlova with it. Pile the remaining fruit on top.

NUT MERINGUE

Makes 12 (2-inch) baskets or 3 (8-inch) circles for layering

The key to this impressive nut meringue dessert *is long, slow cooking. Who would guess something so incredible would be so easy? Take care to finely chop the nuts rather than grind into a paste, or they will be oily. Be sure to weigh the nuts if possible. With the addition of the nuts comes the addition of cornstarch and a dash of salt.*

- 1 cup granulated sugar
- 4 ounces (about 3/4 cup) ground toasted pecans or hazelnuts, blanched almonds, or a combination
- 1 tablespoon cornstarch
- 4 egg whites
- 1/8 teaspoon salt
- 1/4 teaspoon cream of tartar
- 1 teaspoon vanilla extract

Prepare pans and oven as above.

Stir sugar, nuts, and cornstarch together in a bowl.

Beat the egg whites until foamy with a wire whisk or electric hand mixer. Add the salt and cream of tartar, and continue beating until stiff and glossy. Add the vanilla extract. Sprinkle the sugar-nut-cornstarch mixture on top of the egg whites one-third at a time, folding in a figure-eight motion, avoiding over-folding. Work quickly—don't take longer than a minute for the whole process.

Shape and bake as baskets (page 599) or rounds (as in Pavlova above). Check after 1 hour and recheck every 30 minutes. They are done when they are lightly colored and when a corner of the paper can easily be peeled off the bottom of the meringues. Remove them carefully onto racks and cool. They will not seem totally "done," but they do crisp up as they cool. Be careful, because they crack and break. If they crack, you can cover them with whipped cream. (I've seen cracked ones pictured in gourmet magazines, so it is no tragedy.)

FLOATING ISLANDS

Serves 8

THESE DELICATE, SNOWY PUFFS, *called* oeufs à la neige *in classic French cooking, float on a cool custard and are traditionally topped with streams of golden caramel. They incite exclamations of praise! I found recipes for them in all sorts of Southern colonial cookbooks.*

Meringue Puffs
3 egg whites
1/4 teaspoon cream of tartar
Pinch of salt
1/2 cup granulated sugar

Custard
1 recipe Crème Anglaise (page 619)

1/2 cup Caramel Syrup (page 572), hot or at room temperature

Beat the whites with the cream of tartar and salt by hand or with an electric hand mixer until shiny and glossy. Fold in the sugar.

Meanwhile, heat a deep sauté pan of water to a temperature of 170 to 200 degrees. Using an ice-cream scoop or 2 large metal spoons, form ovals of whites, using a finger to get the "egg" as round as possible. Gently drop the "egg" into the water. Poach until the "eggs" turn over when prodded gently. Poach on the second side, lift out with a slotted spoon or spatula onto parchment or waxed paper, and drain.

Meanwhile, pour the chilled Crème Anglaise into a serving dish with a rim. Gently arrange the little islands on the sauce. Refrigerate while preparing the caramel.

Using a fork or whisk, drizzle the hot caramel over the "eggs."

Variations:

- Instead of poaching the "eggs" in water, try poaching them in milk. It gives them a better flavor.
- Instead of using caramel over the "eggs," heat some jam with a small amount of water and drizzle over the eggs and Crème Anglaise.

CLOUD ROLL

Serves 6 to 8

THIS LEMON-FLAVORED AND -FILLED EGG-WHITE MERINGUE SOUFFLÉ *is baked on a rimmed baking sheet and is used to hold a sauce, berries, or whipped cream. A cloud-like dessert reminiscent of an angel food cake, it freezes for up to a month when well wrapped. The lemon or pineapple curd may be made weeks in advance and may also be used for many other recipe fillings.*

Meringue Soufflé

8 large egg whites
1½ cups granulated sugar, divided
1 tablespoon fresh lemon juice
1–2 teaspoons grated lemon rind, no white attached
1 teaspoon vanilla extract
2 tablespoons cornstarch

Filling

½ cup heavy cream
2–3 cups Lemon Curd (page 618) or pineapple curd
Confectioners' sugar

Preheat oven to 325 degrees. Line a 15 x 10½-inch rimmed baking sheet with parchment paper or a silicone mat and set aside. (If parchment paper is not available, oil a sheet of waxed paper.)

Beat the egg whites with half the sugar in stand mixer, preferably with a rotary whisk, or by hand just until stiff peaks form and the egg whites barely slide in the bowl when tipped. Continue to beat until the meringue is very stiff and shiny. Avoid letting them get rocky-looking and overbeaten. Sprinkle the rest of the sugar on top and fold it in with a metal spoon or rubber spatula, using figure-eight motion to go down to the bottom of the bowl and back up again, rotating the bowl between the "eights."

Fold in the lemon juice, lemon rind, vanilla, and cornstarch, mixing just enough to incorporate without deflating the egg whites. Ladle or spoon the meringue mixture onto the parchment paper and spread evenly with a spatula. Bake in the middle of the oven for 20 minutes, or until the top is light brown. Remove and cool on a rack.

Meanwhile, whip the cream to soft peaks. Add to lemon or pineapple curd to taste, making 2 to 3 cups of filling.

After the meringue has cooled, run a knife around the edge. Spread a piece of parchment or waxed paper slightly longer than the pan on the work surface. Sprinkle lightly with confectioners' sugar. Flip the roll still in the pan over so the lightly browned surface is on the sugared paper. Remove any clinging baking paper. Trim off any very dark or crisp edges. Spread the roll with the desired filling. Lift up the edge of the floured paper to propel the dessert into a spiraled, filled roll. The dessert may be rolled vertically or horizontally. A horizontal roll will result in a thicker roll for 6 larger servings. A vertical roll will serve 8 people with smaller servings. Roll as tightly as possible without breaking it. Move the edge of the paper onto the platter and lift up for the final roll, centering the roll with hands if necessary. Slice into 1-inch-thick pieces and serve. This may be made ahead, filled, and served up to 8 hours later with optimum results. Any leftover roll will still be relished by the family.

CHOCOLATE ROLL

Serves 6 to 8

THIS FLAT, FLOURLESS SOUFFLÉ ROLL *is nearly indestructible. So indestructible, in fact, that I would double the recipe for my restaurant. It's easy, but here are some caveats. Expect it to crack like a log. If a smooth look is desired, roll it inside out. The size of pan is important: too large and it will be dry; too small and it will be too soft and too deep to roll. This recipe doubles easily and may be refrigerated or frozen unfilled. It can be found in many Junior League Cookbooks throughout the South. Serve alone or with Caramel Cream Sauce (page 628) or Chocolate Sauce (page 636).*

Chocolate Roll

6 ounces semisweet chocolate, chips or chopped

1/4 cup water

5 large eggs, separated

1 cup granulated sugar

1/2 teaspoon cream of tartar

Filling

1 1/2 cups heavy cream

1/4 cup confectioners' sugar

1 teaspoon vanilla extract or bourbon, optional

Confectioners' sugar for garnish

Position rack in the center of the oven and preheat to 350 degrees. Line a 7 1/2 x 15 1/2-inch jelly roll pan with parchment or waxed paper slightly extending over the edges. If using waxed paper, oil the pan and the paper or spray with nonstick spray.

Melt the chocolate with the water in a heavy pan over low heat or in the microwave.

Beat the egg yolks vigorously with the sugar until light.

In a clean bowl, beat the egg whites and cream of tartar until they form stiff but not rocky peaks.

Fold the melted chocolate into the yolk mixture. Add a dollop of the white mixture to the yolks to soften, and then fold the heavier chocolate mixture into the lighter whites until incorporated. Spread out in the pan, smooth the top, and bake until a toothpick comes out clean, about 15 minutes. Remove and let cool thoroughly.

Meanwhile, whip the cream with the confectioners' sugar and vanilla or bourbon into stiff peaks, taking care not to overbeat.

Sprinkle another sheet of waxed paper with confectioners' sugar. Flip the pan over so the lightly browned surface is on the sugared paper, and remove the pan. Tear off the baked-on paper in strips. Trim off any very dark or crisp edges.

Spread the whipped cream over the entire chocolate soufflé. Lift up the sugared paper and use the paper to propel the soufflé into a spiraled, filled roll, rolling from one end to the other lengthwise for 6 people, and horizontally to make a longer roll if serving more. Roll as tightly as possible without breaking it. Move the edge of the paper onto the platter and lift up for the final roll, centering the roll with hands if necessary. Sprinkle with confectioners' sugar and pipe remaining cream in rosettes on cake.

Slice into 1-inch-thick pieces and serve. This may be made ahead, filled, and served up to 8 hours later for optimum results. Any leftover rolls are "family" good for a day or two or frozen.

Variations:

- Add chopped pecans or whipped cream to the batter.
- Add orange extract rather than vanilla; add grated orange rind to the batter and the cream.

PECAN ROLL WITH CHOCOLATE SAUCE

Serves 6 to 8

The origin of recipes fascinates me, *particularly in the South, where recipes cling to cooks and vice versa. In this case, I thought my student, now friend, Cathy Forrester had learned this from me. Not at all! The recipe was firmly ensconced in her grandmother's hand-written notebooks. She had served the roll with a chocolate sauce to legions of Charleston's elite. Read Cathy's* At Home Charleston *for more charming stories and recipes.*

6 large eggs, separated
3/4 cup granulated sugar
1 1/2 cups finely chopped pecans
1 tablespoon baking powder
1/3 cup confectioners' sugar
2 cups heavy cream, whipped and sweetened with 1/4 cup granulated sugar
1 recipe Chocolate Sauce (page 636)

Position rack in the center of the oven and preheat to 350 degrees. Line a 10 1/2 x 15 1/2-inch jelly roll pan with parchment paper slightly extending over the edges or a silicone mat can be substituted. If using waxed paper, oil the pan and the paper or spray with nonstick spray.

Beat the egg yolks vigorously with the sugar in a stand mixer until very light. In a clean bowl, beat the egg whites until they form stiff but not rocky peaks. Add the pecans and baking powder to the yolk mixture. Add a dollop of the whites to the yolks to soften, then fold this mixture into the egg whites. Spread out in pan, smooth the top, and bake until a toothpick comes out clean, about 20 minutes. Remove and let cool thoroughly.

Sprinkle another sheet of paper with confectioners' sugar. Flip the pan over so the lightly browned surface is on the sugared paper, and remove the pan. Tear off the baked-on paper in strips. Trim off any very dark or crisp edges. Spread the roll with the sweetened whipped cream. Lift the paper and roll, as with a jelly roll, rolling from one end to the other, lengthwise for 6 people or horizontally to make 8 or more smaller servings.

Move the edge of the paper onto the platter and lift up for the final roll—centering the roll with hands if necessary. Cover with Chocolate Sauce.

Variation: Chocolate Gravy

As a lighter option for Chocolate Sauce, try this recipe.

Stir 1/4 cup butter, 1/4 cup cocoa, 1/4 cup granulated sugar, and 1/4 cup milk or water together in a small heavy pot over medium heat. Continue stirring until the ingredients are melted together. Turn up the heat slightly, bring to a simmer, and carefully simmer until the sauce becomes the thickness of gravy.

COLD LEMON SOUFFLÉ OR MOUSSE

Serves 6 to 8

THE RECIPE BREAKS DOWN INTO DISTINCT PARTS, *so you need to separate the eggs when cold, grate the lemon rind, and juice the lemons before starting. Each part of the soufflé—base, partially whipped cream, and egg whites—needs the same texture so they may be folded together easily. Tender, light, and memorable, this is worth every bit of effort for a special occasion. It is called a soufflé because it has the appearance of a soufflé when set, but it is really a mousse. It may also be set in an oiled mold, bowl, or other container, which also makes it a mousse. This dish includes uncooked eggs (see page 609).*

1 1/2 tablespoons unflavored gelatin
1/4 cup water
4 egg yolks, room temperature
1 cup granulated sugar
3 tablespoons finely grated lemon rind, no white attached
3/4 cup fresh lemon juice
6 egg whites, room temperature
1 cup heavy cream, lightly whipped
1/2 cup heavy cream for decoration, optional

Oil a 4-cup soufflé dish. Attach a paper collar (page 281).

Sprinkle the gelatin over the water in a small pan or metal cup and let it become sponge-like, about 5 minutes.

Beat the egg yolks, sugar, and lemon rind with an electric hand mixer until thick and pale in color, about 4 minutes.

Meanwhile, bring the lemon juice to a simmer in a small pan. Slowly add the lemon juice to the egg yolk mixture, stirring constantly. Beat the mixture on medium speed until it reaches the ribbon stage, about 10 minutes.

Carefully melt the gelatin and water mixture over medium heat until it dissolves. Do not allow it to boil or burn. Stir into the egg yolk mixture.

Beat the egg whites in a clean bowl, using a clean whisk, until stiff peaks form and they cling to the bowl. Set aside.

Move the bowl holding the egg yolk mixture into a pan partially filled with ice (ice bath) to thicken the mixture. Stir constantly about 6 to 8 minutes, cleaning sides and bottom of bowl, as gelatin is attracted to cold, until it has thickened and leaves a "trail." If the egg yolk mixture is not thickening, add more ice to the pan.

Remove egg yolk mixture from the ice. Check to be sure there are no clumps of gelatin. Add a dollop of egg yolk mixture to the whites, and carefully fold in the beaten egg whites and lightly whipped cream. Pour into the prepared soufflé dish. The mixture should come halfway up the collar. Refrigerate until firm, about 2 hours.

Beat the remaining 1/2 cup of heavy cream by hand or with an electric hand mixer until stiff peaks form. Carefully remove the collar from the soufflé. Spread whipped cream or pipe rosettes over the top.

BAKED LEMON SOUFFLÉ-PUDDING

Serves 6 to 8

THIS WELL-LOVED RECIPE *is both a pudding and a soufflé—it will rise somewhat like a soufflé and will separate, with the whites coming to the top and the bottom being a bit pudding-like. It is a combination of gossamer lightness and creamy comfort.*

The tricky part is finding the right dish. The completely incorporated mixture before baking is about 1¾ quarts, depending on volume gotten from the eggs. The result is prettier if it comes to the top of the dish; a medium 8-inch dish is ideal. A less wide dish may be used but will take longer to cook, as it will have to be deeper to hold the same amount. Individual molds can also be made; they may take less time and are equally luscious. Timing will vary considerably according to size and thickness of the dish. For using individual molds, the best way to be sure of timing is to bake an extra ramekin ahead of time.

Consider your first soufflé-pudding a practice one—it will be superb and no one will be sorry they ate it; in fact, they will want more. Make a note on the recipe about pan size capacity and diameter and also mark the bottom of the dish. The pudding may be combined ahead of time and cooked later, or it may be cooked ahead of time and reheated. It is even satisfying as a stone-cold snack from the refrigerator.

1 cup granulated sugar, divided
2 tablespoons grated lemon rind, no white attached
6 tablespoons softened unsalted butter, at room temperature
5 large eggs, separated
⅓ cup all-purpose flour
5 tablespoons strained fresh lemon juice
1¾ cups warm whole milk, heated in microwave
½ cups confectioners' sugar, optional

Preheat oven to 350 degrees. Butter an 8-inch 2-quart casserole, or 8 individual ramekins.

Set aside 2 tablespoons of sugar and toss remaining sugar with the grated lemon rind.

Beat the butter in a mixing bowl until the butter lightens. Gradually beat in the sugar-and-lemon zest mixture with an electric hand mixer, beating until the mixture is fluffy looking. Beat in the egg yolks one by one, and then the flour and lemon juice. Pour in the milk a little at a time, continuing to beat.

Whisk the egg whites in a separate clean bowl until they begin to stiffen, add the remaining 2 tablespoons sugar, and continue beating until the whites are stiff, hold their shape, and cling to the bowl.

Gently fold a dollop of the whites into the batter. Pour the batter over the rest of the egg whites and fold together, using a figure-eight motion with a metal spoon or rubber spatula. Gently pour into a buttered dish. The pudding can be made several hours ahead to this point and left at room temperature. Avoid refrigerating it, as it is best to start cooking from room temperature.

Place a clean tea towel in the bottom of a large shallow baking pan. Move the filled baking dish (soufflé dish, ramekins, or springform pan wrapped in aluminum foil to prevent leakage) to the pan lined with the tea towel and pour boiling hot water into the pan until the water reaches halfway up the side of the baking dish. Carefully move this water bath and baking dish to the preheated oven. Using boiling hot water decreases the time it takes to heat the pan water back to 212 degrees. The soufflés are done when light brown and just beginning to pull away from the sides. Check after 30 minutes and cook another 10 minutes if needed.

Sprinkle with confectioners' sugar if desired and serve hot, using any bottom soupiness as a sauce.

Variations:

- For a more cake-like pudding, add 1 egg white to the base and use only 4 egg whites for the soufflé top.
- For a softer pudding, add ¼ cup more milk to the egg mixture and bake until barely brown.

HOT CHOCOLATE SOUFFLÉ

Serves 4 to 6

CHOCOLATE SOUFFLÉS ARE NOT DIFFICULT TO MAKE *or magical, but they seem that way to the uninitiated. Guests are always thrilled by them.* *See pages 280–81 for more soufflé information.*

2½ tablespoons unsalted butter, divided
5½ tablespoons sugar, divided
1 tablespoon cornstarch
½ cup milk
½ cup semisweet chocolate bits
4 egg yolks
6 egg whites
Confectioners' sugar

Preheat oven to 350 degrees. Butter a 1½-quart soufflé dish and dust it with sugar. Wrap a buttered and crumbed parchment or waxed paper collar around the outside of the dish if extending the capacity of the dish is desired.

Whisk the cornstarch and milk together in a heavy pan and stir over medium-high heat until smooth. Move the pan off the heat and add the chocolate, 2 tablespoons butter, and 3 tablespoons sugar. Stir until the butter and chocolate are melted, moving the pan back over low heat if necessary. Remove from the heat and stir in the egg yolks one at a time. This base may be prepared ahead to this point and covered with plastic wrap.

Whisk the egg whites until soft peaks form. Fold in 2 tablespoons sugar and beat to stiff, shiny peaks. Stir 3 or 4 tablespoons of the egg white mixture into the soufflé base to lighten it, and then fold this mixture into the egg whites. Pour the mixture into the prepared soufflé dish. Smooth the surface with a spatula. May be prepared ahead to this point. Refrigerate if holding more than 1 hour. Bring back to room temperature before cooking.

A half hour before serving, place the soufflé on a metal pan in the lower third of the hot oven. Bake for 25 minutes for a soft center or 30 to 35 minutes for a firmer one. Sprinkle with confectioners' sugar and serve immediately.

Variation:

- Serve with Chocolate Sauce (page 636).
- Serve with sweetened whipped cream.
- Coat the soufflé dish with crumbs from chocolate wafer cookies rather than sugar.

CHOCOLATE DESSERTS

When I was a girl, chocolate was a winter treat, something to be found in one's Christmas stocking. It was impossible to get home in the summer with a bar of chocolate without it melting. It would sometimes even melt on the kitchen shelf. After air-conditioning, chocolate found a year-round place in the Southern recipe book. Community cookbooks have long been a reflection of this, and many of these recipes can be found there.

Chocolate is made by roasting, crushing, and refining cacao beans along with sugar. Usually, some additional ingredients, like lecithin, cocoa butter, and vanilla, are added to alter the flavor and texture. If a chocolate is labeled with a percentage (like 70%), this refers to the percentage of the chocolate that comes from cacao beans. Dark chocolate is usually at least 50% cacao.

Milk chocolate is similar, but some type of dehydrated milk is added. This milk softens the chocolate and adds flavors that may be buttery, cheesy, or creamy. Milk chocolate usually has a smaller cacao percentage than dark chocolate, and may be as little as 10 percent.

Melting and tempering—Tempering is necessary to keep the cocoa butter from coming to the surface. By and large the home cook doesn't need to temper chocolate, as we use chocolate chips or blocks of commercial chocolate that have already been tempered sufficiently.

To melt chocolate, cut chocolate into small pieces or chips and heat on a heatproof plate over a pot of simmering water, or in the microwave, a double boiler or in a bowl in a hot water bath. Always melt more than needed. When melted, remove from the heat and stir while cooling.

To temper, once the chocolate (above) has been stirred and cooled to 140 degrees, add a few pieces of unmelted chocolate, stirring, to continue the cooling-down process. This takes about 10 minutes. Remove with a spoon any chocolate that is not smooth and melted. Test it on any cool surface until it reaches 70 degrees, when it is ready to use.

Blooming Chocolate

Chocolate may turn gray ("bloom") if it is old, most likely due to the temperature, or possibly to the friction of small pieces rubbing together. Don't worry, it will melt just fine.

THE PERFECT BROWNIE

Makes 16 squares

Cynthia Graubart's dear friend *Catherine Fliegel is a wonderful cook known widely for her fabulous baking. She wrote this recipe after years of refining and it is truly the perfect brownie. Don't skimp on the cocoa powder—buy the best.*

1½ cups unsalted butter
1 cup unsweetened cocoa powder
1¾ cup light or dark brown sugar
Pinch of salt
2 teaspoons vanilla extract
3 large eggs
1 cup all-purpose flour

Preheat oven to 375 degrees. Oil an 8-inch square baking pan and set aside.

Melt the butter in a saucepan over medium heat. Remove from heat and stir in cocoa powder, brown sugar, salt, vanilla, and eggs until well mixed and smooth. Stir in flour. Pour the batter into the prepared baking pan.

Bake for 30 minutes. Bake only until the top starts to look a little dry—the center will be moist. Do not overbake. Remove from oven to a wire rack to cool. Completely cooled brownies are easier to cut, but it's hard to wait that long.

SIMPLE CHOCOLATE MOUSSE

Makes 6 (4-ounce) servings

This is a basic chocolate mousse recipe. *The tricks are in avoiding overbeating the egg white and in folding them in. Any concern about mixing water with chocolate does not apply in this recipe, as the amount of water is enough to prevent the chocolate from seizing.*

8 ounces semisweet chocolate bits
4 tablespoons water
1/2–1 teaspoon rum or vanilla extract
1 1/2 tablespoons unsalted butter
4 large eggs, separated
1/2 cup whipped and sweetened heavy cream for garnish

Melt the chocolate and water together over low to medium heat in a medium pan or in a microwave. Do not let boil. Let cool slightly and stir in the extract and butter. Stir in the egg yolks one at a time, stirring well after each addition.

Whisk the egg whites until stiff peaks form. Fold a dollop of the egg whites into the chocolate mixture with a rubber spatula or metal spoon, and then lightly fold the chocolate mixture into the egg whites using a figure-eight motion. There may be a few specks of egg white left, but most should be incorporated.

Ladle or pour into small pots or a glass bowl. Cover and chill overnight. Serve with a rosette of whipped cream piped on top. May be made several days in advance and refrigerated or frozen.

Variation: For a sweeter mousse, try using 4 ounces of milk chocolate and 4 ounces of semisweet.

Variation: Chocolate-Orange Mousse
Add 1 tablespoon grated orange rind, and substitute orange liqueur for the rum or vanilla extract.

RISKS OF UNCOOKED EGGS

When foods include uncooked eggs, they run a risk of being tainted with salmonella or other bacteria, which can lead to food poisoning. This risk is of most concern to small children, older people, pregnant women, and anyone with a compromised immune system. If there are health and safety concerns, do not consume undercooked eggs. Using pasteurized eggs is an option you may prefer.

FOUR FAILSAFE CHOCOLATE DESSERTS

I owe many recipes to living in England and learning the symbiotic relationship between our two cultures. When I left the London Cordon Bleu in 1971, degree in hand, four of their chocolate desserts became indispensable: Chocolate Pecan Torte; Chocolate Snowball; Chocolate Roulade and Chocolate Mousse. I used them over and over as chef of a restaurant in Majorca and owner-chef of my own restaurant, and in cooking classes from then until now. I have included them in this book because I think they are important fall-back desserts for anyone who loves chocolate and wants a signature dish that is easily assembled and reliable time after time without pitfalls. Each uses different techniques for essentially the same ingredients—eggs, chocolate, sugar, and little if any flour.

CHOCOLATE SNOWBALLS

Serves 6 to 8

Our snow is as light as this layer of snowy white whipping cream. *Covering a dense chocolate ball as big as a glass bowl, it is as easy to serve and cut as a cake and even easier to make using a food processor or mixer. Having arrived in the South from the North, this recipe is here to stay. The recipe doubles easily, making one gigantic ball or two dinner party–sized ones.*

1 (10-ounce) package semisweet chocolate chips
1/2 cup water
1 cup granulated sugar
1 cup unsalted butter, room temperature
4 large eggs
1 tablespoon vanilla extract, optional
1 cup heavy cream
2 tablespoons granulated sugar
1 teaspoon vanilla extract
Chocolate Shards or leaves for garnish (facing)

Preheat oven to 350 degrees. Line a 5-cup ovenproof bowl with a double thickness of foil.

Melt the chocolate with the water and sugar over low heat or in the microwave; cool slightly. Transfer the chocolate mixture to a mixing bowl or food processor bowl fitted with the metal blade. Beat in the butter, add the eggs one by one, followed by the vanilla, beating after each addition.

Pour the mixture into the foil-lined mold. Bake 1 hour, or until a thick crust has formed on top. It will still be soft and slightly wet under the crust.

Remove from oven. It will collapse. Cool completely. Cover tightly and refrigerate until solid, 2 to 3 hours or overnight, or freeze. This can be done several days in advance.

When ready to serve, whip the cream, sugar, and vanilla until stiff (see method below), and move to a piping bag with a star tip. Remove the snowball from the bowl and peel off the foil. Place on a serving dish, flat side down.

Pipe rosettes of whipped cream over the entire surface until no chocolate shows. Chill until served. Garnish with chocolate leaves if desired. Slice in wedges to serve. Leftovers freeze well, tightly wrapped—good enough for family anyway.

Variation: To double the recipe, bake 1 1/2 to 2 hours.

WHIPPING CREAM IN A FOOD PROCESSOR

For better results when piping or decorating, whip cream in the food processor. Use the metal blade, add the very cold heavy cream, sugar, and flavoring, and process about 30 seconds, checking frequently to avoid overprocessing.

The food processor does not produce as much volume as beating by hand or with a mixer, but the cream pipes more easily and does not weep as readily. To avoid weeping, spoon the whipped cream into a piece of cheesecloth or a fine sieve and let drain a few hours before using.

STORING A DESSERT WITH CREAM

To store a cream-decorated dessert, cover it with a large glass dome or plastic cake cover and place it in a larger, airtight container. Alternatively, poke long skewers into the dessert and lightly wrap the whole thing with plastic wrap. It looks like a crazy beehive, but it works.

CHOCOLATE SHARDS

Makes 10 ounces

THIS QUICK DELIGHT IS PERFECT *after a heavy or filling meal, when just a taste of sweetness is needed to cap off your dinner. This should be made several hours or several days ahead.*

1 (10-ounce) package semisweet chocolate chips

Melt the chocolate over low heat in a saucepan or in a measuring cup in the microwave, stirring so the chocolate does not scorch. Let cool for 5 minutes and then spread the chocolate about 1/8 inch thick on parchment, waxed paper, or aluminum foil. Allow to harden; break into irregular pieces and serve alone in a pretty silver bowl or use as a garnish for ice cream, custards, or fresh berries, or for a Chocolate Snowball (facing).

To make chocolate leaves, wash and thoroughly dry several rose or thick-veined leaves. With a small brush, "paint" the chocolate onto the underside of the leaf. Allow to harden and then gently remove the leaf from the chocolate.

MOTHER'S CHOCOLATE CREAM FUDGE

Makes 16 (1 1/2-inch) squares

THIS IS A MOUTH-WATERING OLD-FASHIONED FUDGE, *ever so slightly grainy, as it should be. It will be gone before you know it. Mother told me she got this recipe from a 1930 cookbook her mother gave her and it is the recipe my sister and I made when we were little girls. Everyone who eats it has a story to tell about someone special who made this for them when they were young. The original recipe called for nut meats—an old-time term for chopped nuts. The corn syrup prevents over-crystallization and over-graininess. This is a case where an electric hand mixer or immersion blender does better than a stand mixer.*

3 cups granulated sugar
1/4 cup light corn syrup
3 (1-ounce) squares unsweetened chocolate
1/4 teaspoon salt
1 cup evaporated milk
1 teaspoon vanilla extract
1/2 cup roughly chopped pecans or walnuts, optional

Butter an 8-inch square pan. Heat the sugar, corn syrup, chocolate, salt, and milk in a heavy pan, stirring constantly. Bring to the boil, and boil to the soft-ball stage (238 degrees on a candy thermometer), or drop a little of the liquid into cold water to see if it forms a soft ball.

Cool until lukewarm, add the vanilla and nuts, and beat with an electric hand mixer or immersion blender until creamy. Pour into prepared pan. When cool, cut into 1 1/2-inch squares. Store in an airtight container, or wrap well in an airtight container and freeze up to 3 months.

CHOCOLATE PECAN TORTE

Makes 1 (9-inch) torte

THIS FLOURLESS CHOCOLATE TORTE *has been made in the South at least since I started serving it in my restaurant in Social Circle, Georgia, in the early 1970s, which makes it semi-Southern, I suppose. It is one of those always good, always praised desserts. Finely ground pecan meal, or pecan flour, is available commercially and is much less expensive than grinding pieces of pecans. Otherwise, use a food processor to grind very finely.*

Panko or dry breadcrumbs
6 ounces semisweet chocolate bits
3/4 cups unsalted butter, room temperature
3/4 cup granulated sugar
6 large eggs, separated
1 1/4 cup finely ground pecans

Preheat oven to 375 degrees. Butter a 9 x 2 1/2 x 3-inch springform pan. Cut a piece of parchment or waxed paper and fit it to the bottom of the pan; dust with panko or breadcrumbs.

Melt chocolate slowly in a double boiler over low heat, or in a glass dish in the microwave. Cool slightly.

Beat the butter with an electric hand mixer until light. Add the sugar and beat another 2 or 3 minutes, until fluffy. Add egg yolks one at a time, beating after each addition until thoroughly incorporated. Slowly beat in chocolate followed by ground pecans.

Meanwhile, beat the egg whites in a clean bowl until firm peaks form. Fold a dollop of the egg whites into the chocolate mixture to lighten it a bit. Pour this mixture onto the egg whites and fold in. (It is easier to fold heavier mixtures into lighter ones than lighter into the heavier.)

Fill the prepared springform pan with the mixture and place the pan on a rimmed baking sheet. Bake in the oven for 20 minutes then reduce heat to 350 degrees. Check after another 30 minutes; the cake should be soft and moist in the center but firm on the exterior. Return to the oven and bake another 15 or 20 minutes as needed, checking occasionally. It will be a bit damp in the center when checked with a toothpick.

Remove the pan from the oven and set it on a wet folded towel. Let stand 25 minutes. Remove sides of springform pan. Place a baking rack over the top of the cake, invert, and remove the bottom of the pan and the paper. Invert again on serving plate. Edge 4 long pieces of waxed paper underneath the cake to catch any drippings from the icing. Spread the top of the cake with the Chocolate Ganache Icing, starting from the middle and working toward the outside; cover top and sides. After 5 minutes, pull out waxed paper and discard. Chill, and serve thin wedges.

CHOCOLATE GANACHE ICING

8 ounces semisweet chocolate bits
1/2 cup heavy cream

To make the icing, heat the cream in a heavy saucepan until tiny bubbles arise around the exterior. Add the chocolate bits and heat until the chocolate appears to be melting, about 1 minute. When chocolate is melted, remove from heat and whisk until cool. Transfer to a small bowl or put pan over ice to cool. When it reaches room temperature (about 15 minutes or so), stir again to be sure it is smooth.

FRUIT DESSERTS

These sweet reflections of local goodness beckon in the mind as the seasons change. Of course, a little sugar and cream is "good enough," but a little more effort produces heaven.

BAKED TROPICAL FRUIT

Serves 4

BANANAS FOSTER INSPIRED THIS EASY-TO-PREPARE DESSERT, *which is significantly lower in fat than the original recipe. Even if the fruit is not perfectly ripe, it will be enhanced sufficiently by the caramelized brown sugar. A dollop of vanilla frozen yogurt is a nice addition to keep the calorie count low; otherwise, serve with ice cream or a bit of heavy cream.*

1 pineapple, peeled, cored, cut into 1-inch chunks
2 bananas, peeled, cut into 1-inch chunks
1/4 cup flaked unsweetened coconut
1/4 cup sliced almonds
1/4 cup light or dark brown sugar
1/2 teaspoon ground cinnamon
Grated rind of 1 orange, no white attached
2 tablespoons rum, or 1 teaspoon rum extract
2 tablespoons orange juice

Preheat the broiler.

Mix all ingredients together in a large bowl, tossing to coat completely. Pour into a shallow broiler-proof dish, and broil 4 to 6 inches from the heat until the sugar and juices begin to caramelize, about 3 to 4 minutes. Serve hot or at room temperature.

WATERMELON BASKET WITH FRESH BERRIES

Serves 8

WHAT FUN! *This makes any summer meal festive and glamorous, with very little effort.*

1 small watermelon
10 mint sprigs
½ pint strawberries, hulled
½ pint blueberries
Grated orange rind, no white attached, optional
Citrus Sabayon Sauce (below)

Draw and cut out a paper design (such as a scalloped edge) to use as a guide for cutting the watermelon into a basket. Draw and cut out another design for the handle if desired. (Brown paper bags are ideal for this purpose.) Carefully place the design pattern over the watermelon and cut the melon to match it, cutting all the way through to the center. Slowly lift off the top then scoop out all the watermelon flesh with a melon-ball scoop, leaving about ½ inch of the fruit intact to line the basket. Chop the melon flesh into bite-sized pieces, removing seeds as needed.

Set aside the prettiest sprigs of mint for garnish. Chop the rest and toss with the watermelon, strawberries, and blueberries; chill the fruit in a plastic ziplock bag or in the watermelon basket; wrap the basket in plastic wrap or foil, and chill until serving time. Remove the chilled fruit and watermelon shell from the refrigerator, top with Citrus Sabayon Sauce, and garnish with mint sprigs and orange rind.

Variation: Cantaloupe Salad Bowl

We cut cantaloupe into cubes as soon as it ripens, looking for those with the softest stem ends and the fullest aroma, even if there is a soft spot or two. Refrigerated, covered, we snack on it all week. For dessert, sprinkle the cubes with mint or lemon thyme. To serve in the cantaloupe shell, cut the cantaloupe into 6 or 8 wedges and scoop off the flesh. Move the rind wedges to a large bowl. Return the scooped flesh to the rinds in a mound, and sprinkle with fresh herbs if desired.

CITRUS SABAYON SAUCE

Makes 2 cups

WHETHER SERVED COLD *over melon or warm over a green vegetable such as asparagus, this citrus sabayon sauce is simply divine.*

⅔ cup fresh orange juice
⅓ cup fresh lemon juice
½ cup granulated sugar
6 egg yolks, lightly beaten
1½ cups heavy cream, whipped

Heat the orange and lemon juices and sugar in a heavy saucepan over low heat to dissolve the sugar. When dissolved, bring the syrup to the boil and remove from the heat.

Meanwhile, put the egg yolks in another heavy saucepan and whisk slightly with a wire whisk or electric hand mixer. Whisking constantly, pour the citrus syrup into the egg yolks in a slow, steady stream, and cook without boiling until the sauce is thick, light, and smooth—about 160 to 180 degrees. Chill and then fold in the whipped cream.

PEACH FOOL

Serves 4 to 6

FOOLS, LIKE FLUMMERIES, *are English bits of fluff that worked their way into the American repertoire. They bring to mind long, sunny summer days when the evening meal is served while it is still light outside. They are perfect for special backyard entertaining, particularly when the grass is green and the flowers are special. Frozen peaches, especially those home-frozen in season, may be used, in which case chilling is not always necessary.*

3 ripe peaches, peeled and pitted
1/4 cup granulated sugar
2/3 cup heavy cream
2 tablespoons chopped pecans

Purée the peaches with the sugar in a food processor or blender. Strain the purée if it needs to be smoother.

Whip the cream until it leaves a thick trail, about the same consistency as the purée; avoid overbeating. Fold it into the fruit. Spoon into four stemmed glasses or individual containers, cover with plastic wrap, and chill for 30 minutes. If the containers are freezer-proof, move them briefly to the freezer if necessary to chill rapidly. Garnish with nuts before serving.

STRAWBERRY-PEACH CRISP

Serves 6 to 8

SOME YEARS THE TAIL END OF THE STRAWBERRY SEASON *meets the peach season. This crisp topping is our sole nod to whole wheat flour. It is simple and enhances the fruit.*

2 cups sliced strawberries
2 cups sliced peaches
1 tablespoon fresh lemon juice
3/4 cup granulated sugar
1/4 cup whole-wheat flour
1/2 teaspoon ground cinnamon
Pinch freshly grated nutmeg

Topping
1 cup whole-wheat flour
3/4 cup light or dark brown sugar
1/2 cup quick oats
1/2 cup unsalted butter, melted
1/2 teaspoon ground cinnamon

Preheat oven to 375 degrees.

Mix the strawberries, peaches, lemon juice, sugar, flour, cinnamon, and nutmeg in an 8-inch square baking dish.

Make the topping by tossing together the flour, sugar, oats, butter, and cinnamon.

Sprinkle the topping mixture over the strawberry-peach filling. Bake for 35 minutes, or until the top is golden brown and crisp. Serve with ice cream or whipped cream.

ROASTED STRAWBERRIES

Makes 1 pint

Roasting brings out the full flavor of the strawberries. *Eat alone or add to ice cream, use for strawberry short cakes or cobblers, or add to salads.*

1 pound fresh strawberries

½ cup granulated sugar

Preheat oven to 450 degrees. Line a rimmed baking sheet with parchment or waxed paper.

Slice strawberries in half, or in quarters if large. Toss with sugar. Spread out in one layer on prepared baking sheet. Move to the middle rack of the oven and roast 10 to 20 minutes, stirring every 5 minutes, until the berries are soft and the juices appear thickened. Cool briefly in the pan, and then scrape into a bowl, including the juices. Chill in the refrigerator.

Variations:

- Add 2 teaspoons balsamic vinegar to strawberries before tossing with sugar.
- Add a pinch of freshly ground black pepper to strawberries before tossing with sugar.

SUMMER PUDDING

Serves 6

English in origin, *this is a mightily glorified bread and jam served with whipped cream. Beloved for a dinner party or buffet, no wonder it claims popularity in the South, long the berry capital of the United Sates.*

8 cups mixed berries (raspberries, strawberries, and/or blueberries), divided
1 cup granulated sugar
½ cup unsalted butter, room temperature
10–15 slices firm-textured white bread, crusts removed
Whipped heavy cream or mascarpone cheese, optional

Reserve 1 cup of berries for garnish. Bring 7 cups berries and the sugar to the boil in a saucepan. Reduce heat, cover, and simmer slowly until the fruit has released its juices, about 10 minutes, resulting in about 3 cups of berries and juice. Set aside to cool slightly.

Meanwhile, spread a light layer of butter on each slice of bread.

Butter a 1½-quart soufflé dish. Line the dish tightly with the bread slices, buttered side inside, cutting to fit as necessary. Do not overlap the slices—it should appear like a seamless cloth.

Pour the cooked berries into the bread-lined dish. (The berries should fill about three-quarters of the bowl.) Top the berries with additional bread slices, covering the berries completely. Spread plastic wrap directly on top of the bread and place a slightly smaller plate directly on the plastic wrap. Add a 2- to 3-pound weight (such as a can) on top. Refrigerate overnight or up to 3 days.

To serve, remove the weight and plate, and run a knife around the edges of the pudding to loosen. Invert the pudding onto a serving plate. Top with the remaining berries. If there is any juice remaining in the bowl, pour it over the pudding until every bit of the bread is stained. Serve with sweetened whipped cream or mascarpone if desired.

Variation: Substitute 1 to 2 cups of buttered biscuits torn or cut into ½-inch pieces for the bread.

Weighting down compacts the ingredients, in this case the cooked berries and bread, flattening and making for tidier serving.

APPLE CHARLOTTE

Serves 2 to 4

THIS IS A DREAMY COMBINATION *of creamy soft apple inside a crisp, buttery bread shell. A traditional charlotte mold is fun to use, but a soufflé dish works well.*

5 or 6 Golden Delicious apples,* peeled, halved, and cored
1/4–1/2 cup granulated sugar
1/2 cup unsalted butter, divided
8 slices bread, crusts trimmed

Preheat oven to 350 degrees. Butter a soufflé dish or charlotte mold.

Cut the apples into 3/4-inch chunks. Move to a saucepan with sugar and 2 tablespoons butter. Cover and cook over low heat until apple chunks are tender, checking occasionally. Add water as needed.

Meanwhile, melt remaining butter on low heat. Cut two slices of bread into large circles, hearts or other design to fit the top and the bottom and set aside, saving trimmings. Cut the remaining slices of bread into rectangular "sticks" slightly higher than the height of the mold. Brush both sides of bread with melted butter, being careful not to leave any unbuttered patches. To form the mold, put one of the decorative circles in the bottom of the dish. Fill in with any patches of bread so the bottom is a layer of bread. Line the mold with the sticks of buttered bread.

Pour the apple mixture into the charlotte mold. Top with the second decorative circle of bread. Bake 1 hour. Remove the charlotte mold from the oven, cool to room temperature, and refrigerate until thoroughly chilled, about 2 hours. Carefully run a knife around the insides of the dish to loosen the bread from the dish. Even up stick edges if necessary. Place a dish on top of the mold, invert mold and dish and give a firm shake. It should unmold easily. If not, put a hot towel on the mold to loosen slightly. Serve cold.

**Experiment with other varieties of cooking apples.*

Variations:
- Sauté bread until light brown before lining mold.
- Serve with custard, ice cream, or sweetened whipped cream.
- Substitute a thick homemade applesauce for the apples.
- Add Applejack or other apple liqueur to apple mixture.

CUSTARD DESSERTS

My sweet tooth grows with the temperature. The hotter it is, the more I want a jolt of pure sugar and the less I want to bake, even with air-conditioning. What on earth did they do in colonial days, I wonder. There were taste-tempting recipes for sweets in *Martha Washington's Booke of Cookery, Two Hundred Years of Charleston Cooking, Carolina Housewife,* and even *The Compleat Housewife.* If they could cook in the heat, so can I.

Custards dominated the list of desserts. Fruit and chocolate mousses held their own. Syllabubs and fools—wine or liqueur foams to be spooned from chilled glasses—gelatin desserts (called isinglass), and puddings of rice and tapioca beckoned. If it weren't for the long hoop skirts, I'd wish to go back in time.

There are rules for these delicate egg-laden desserts. Although most of these desserts exceed the required minimum 140 degrees for egg safety, if you are serving the elderly or children, you may prefer pasteurized eggs. Eggs heated over 180 degrees will "cook" and will need to be strained out of a delicate sauce.

LEMON CURD (LEMON CHEESE)

Makes 2½ cups

THIS RECIPE EMERGES *in old and modern French, English, and Southern recipes. Thomas Jefferson's and Martha Washington's recipe collections show its use as well. The curd itself is delicious as a filling for cakes, meringues, tarts, and pies.*

Like mayonnaise, it will last a long time in the refrigerator when it has a high degree of acid (a low pH). Once it is mixed with something that changes the acidity, it will not last as long. Since citrus acidity varies and the home cook has no real idea of its strength, some care should be taken. Usually it may be kept up to a month, tightly sealed in the refrigerator. Peculiarly, egg yolks do not like sugar sitting on top of them without any agitation from spoon or whisk. The sugar tends to "cook" the egg yolk.

5 large egg yolks
1 cup granulated sugar
½ cup unsalted butter, softened
½ cup fresh lemon juice
3 tablespoons lemon rind, no white attached

Lightly whisk the egg yolks in a heavy saucepan or bowl, or in a bain-marie, or double boiler. Whisk in the sugar and butter, then the lemon juice.

Stir the egg mixture with a rubber spatula over low heat until thick but still falling easily from a spoon, 5 to 10 minutes, making sure to scrape the sides and bottom occasionally. The temperature should register approximately 170 degrees. (If the mixture simmers at the edges of the pan, quickly strain; it will be usable if smooth and no egg bits remain.)

Add the rind to the egg mixture. Taste for flavor and add more juice or rind if necessary and available. Remove from the heat and cool. Store in the refrigerator in a tightly covered jar.

Variations:

- To lighten, fold in whipped cream, mascarpone, or meringue before serving.
- Lime, orange, and other citrus juices, as well as cooked caramelized pineapple, are wonderful variations. Adjust the amount of juice as needed, keeping in mind that acid is necessary for thickening the mixture and to lower the pH.

CRÈME ANGLAISE

Makes 3 cups

CUSTARDS ARE A COMBINATION *of milk or cream and eggs. There are two kinds: stirred (stovetop, like this one) and baked. Crème Anglaise is very basic light custard sauce that becomes ice cream when frozen; with the addition of gelatin, it becomes a* bavarois; *with chocolate, it's a chocolate sauce; and with butter, it's a rich butter cream. The English were famous for their boiled custards; hence, the French named this dish "English Cream." Vanilla bean truly enhances this custard, but feel free to use what's available.*

1 vanilla bean, optional
1½–2½ cups milk, divided
4 egg yolks
½ cup granulated sugar
¼ cup well-chilled heavy cream, optional
2 teaspoons vanilla extract, optional

Scrape the seeds from the vanilla bean and add both bean and seeds to 1½ cups of the milk. Heat until small bubbles form at the edges of the pan. Rinse the bean pod and reserve for another purpose.

Whisk the yolks in a heavy pan, add the sugar, and whisk until thick.

Slowly beat the hot milk into the yolk mixture. Turn on the heat under the pan and cook for a few minutes over medium heat, stirring with a wooden spoon until the mixture coats a metal spoon like a sheer fabric—about 160 to 180 degrees on an instant-read thermometer. Don't overcook or the eggs will be scrambled. Immediately pour the sauce through a fine strainer into another bowl set over ice if concerned about cooling it down rapidly so the eggs are stopped cooking. Add the vanilla extract, if using instead of the vanilla bean. For a thinner sauce, add the remaining 1 cup milk and/or optional cream. Refrigerate covered with plastic wrap.

Variations:

- Flavor with orange liqueur, Madeira, sherry, or other liquid.
- Substitute cinnamon stick, cardamom pods, or other spices for the vanilla bean.

STRAINING A CUSTARD

Not all egg dishes need straining, but there are two reasons for straining "boiled" custards: 1) to remove the chalazae, or "stringy" part of the egg whites, and 2) to remove any overcooked eggs lurking on the bottom and sides of the pan. Straining cools down the custard as well as removes the less desirable bits and the bean pod.

LEFTOVER VANILLA BEANS

Once a bean has been used and lost its oomph, cut it up a bit and add to a few cups sugar in a closed container. After a month or two you will have a vanilla sugar.

PEACH OR MANGO AND CREAM CUSTARD WITH CARAMEL PECAN TOPPING

Serves 6

THIS IS A RECIPE ANN BYRN AND I *made up that I've revised over a period of years. I've learned many tricks along the way—using a tea towel to insulate, for instance, and adding water as needed. Plan ahead, as the custards need to be refrigerated overnight. The peaches and mangos can be caramelized as performed in the Peach or Mango Omelet (page 277).*

Custard

2 cups heavy cream
4 large egg yolks
4 1/2 tablespoons granulated sugar, divided
1 teaspoon vanilla extract
1/2 cup sliced peaches or mangos, fresh or frozen, reserving slices for garnish

Topping

1 cup granulated sugar, divided
1/2 cup water
1 tablespoon light corn syrup
1 cup pecan pieces, finely ground

Preheat oven to 325 degrees.

Slowly heat the cream until there are bubbles around the side of a heavy saucepan, taking care not to burn it.

Beat the egg yolks with a wooden spoon or whisk in a large bowl, gradually adding 2 tablespoons sugar. Stir several tablespoons of hot cream into the egg mixture to raise its temperature while cooling the remaining cream slightly. Add the remaining cream, stirring constantly.

Purée the peaches in a food processor or blender with the remaining sugar. (This can be done ahead of time.) Add the vanilla and the puréed fruit to the cream mixture, stirring until just blended.

Ladle into 6 small custard cups, filling three-fourths full; do not overfill. Make 6 rounds of parchment or waxed paper to create tops for the custards. Butter each one lightly on one side and put buttered side down on the custards. This will prevent a skin from forming. Fold a tea towel on the bottom of a large roasting pan and place the custard cups on top of the towel. Pour boiling water into the pan so that it reaches halfway up the sides, being careful not to get any water in the custard. Bake uncovered until the custard barely moves when shaken, about 30 minutes, and registers approximately 180 degrees on an instant-read thermometer. The water bath keeps the custard from overcooking, as long as the water in the pan does not boil or evaporate, while the tea towel insulates the bottom of the custard from the bottom of the hot pan. (If the water evaporates, add more.)

Meanwhile, prepare the topping. Melt the sugar with water and corn syrup in a heavy pan. When the sugar has dissolved, bring the syrup to the boil and boil steadily until it turns a golden caramel color. Remove carefully from the heat, being careful not to spill it. Pour onto a greased rimmed baking sheet and set aside to harden. When hard, pulse in a food processor or by hand to make caramel crumbs. Stir in the pecan pieces and keep in a covered jar until ready to use.

Remove the pan with the custard cups from the oven. Sprinkle each custard with some of the topping and run under the broiler for 2 to 3 minutes, watching carefully, until the topping is browned; or carefully brown custards with a torch. Remove the custard cups from the pan and refrigerate overnight. Serve cold. Garnish with fruit slice just before serving. Pass extra caramel and pecan topping at the table.

Note: To make more like a crème brûlée, sprinkle the custard with brown sugar and use a propane torch or broil just before serving. In this case, move the cool custards to an ice bath to prevent breaking the dishes or overcooking while browning.

PEACH GINGER FLAN

Serves 8 to 10

FLAN—THE SPANISH WORD FOR A THICKER AND DENSER CUSTARD *than the French crème caramel—needs a long, slow cooking time in a bain-marie. It is important to keep the water below the boiling point so little "pock marks" won't mar the custard at the bottom and sides. This custard is flavored with peaches. We use canned because they are sweetened and cooked, but fresh sweetened and cooked will also work.*

1 cup canned peach halves (one 17-ounce can)
1 1/2 cups granulated sugar, divided
1 tablespoon light corn syrup
1/3 cup water
2 2/3 cups milk
Rind of 1 lemon, peel off strips with vegetable peeler, no white attached
3 large whole eggs, beaten to mix
5 large egg yolks, beaten to mix
2 1/2 teaspoons vanilla extract
1/4 cup chopped candied ginger

Preheat oven to 325 degrees and move the oven rack to the center of the oven. Select a soufflé or other baking dish where the custard will fill the dish within an inch or so of the rim. Much fuller than that increases the odds the custard will crack when turning out onto the serving plate.

Drain the peach halves. Purée the solids in a food processor or blender until smooth and set aside.

Dissolve 1 cup sugar with the corn syrup and water in a heavy pan over low heat without boiling. When dissolved, brush the insides of the pan with a wet pastry brush to remove the sugar crystals. Turn up the heat, bring to the boil, and boil until the liquid turns a golden caramel color, about 10 minutes. (For more about working with caramel, see page 629.)

Meanwhile, warm a 1 1/2-quart ovenproof soufflé or other heatproof dish in the oven for 15 minutes (this makes it easier to move the hot caramel around the dish. Using oven mitts, remove the dish from the oven, pour in the hot caramel, and tilt the dish from side to side to coat the bottom and lower sides with the caramel.

Add the milk and lemon strips to the original caramel pan and heat until small bubbles form around the side. This flavors the flan further by removing any caramel clinging to the pan. (It also makes it easier to clean the pan.)

Gently whisk together the eggs, yolks, and remaining 1/2 cup sugar. Pour the hot milk into the egg mixture all at once, stirring constantly. Strain the mixture into another bowl and stir in the vanilla, peach purée, and candied ginger. Pour or ladle the custard carefully into the prepared soufflé dish; it will foam if not poured slowly. Make a round of parchment or waxed paper to create a top for the custard. Butter lightly and put buttered side down on the custard. This will prevent a skin from forming on the top.

Fold a tea towel and put in the bottom of a large roasting pan; place the soufflé dish on top of the towel. Pour boiling water into the pan so that it reaches halfway up the sides of the dish, being careful not to get any water in the dish. Place the roasting pan in the center of the oven and cook approximately 1 3/4 to 2 hours, or until the custard is set and a knife inserted in the center comes out clean. Do not let the water boil, as the boiling will overcook the custard and make holes in it; if necessary, add cold water to the pan to prevent bubbling.

Remove the pan from the oven; remove the soufflé dish from the pan. Cool slightly then cover and refrigerate at least 3 hours.

When the flan has chilled completely, run a knife around the edge, then pull the custard lightly away from the sides. Place a shallow serving plate on top and then invert the dish to unmold the flan. The caramel forms a topping and sauce. If there is still a good deal of caramel in the bottom of the dish, heat briefly in the microwave or add a little boiling water to melt the caramel. Spoon over soufflé. Serve chilled.

Variation: Substitute apricots for the peaches.

Candied ginger may be found in the spice section of the grocery store or in Asian grocery stores in boxes, where it is much less expensive.

GRITS PUDDING

Serves 6

GRITS PUDDING *is every bit as comforting and adaptable as rice pudding. My grandchildren call it "nummy," their word for "yummy."*

- 1/2 cup grits cooked in 3 cups milk
- 1 tablespoon unsalted butter
- 1/2 cup granulated sugar
- 2 cups heavy cream
- 4 large eggs, beaten
- 1 teaspoon vanilla extract, optional
- 1 tablespoon ground cinnamon, optional

Preheat oven to 325 degrees. Butter a 4-cup soufflé dish.

Stir the cooked grits with butter, remove from heat, and cool slightly.

Stir in the sugar, cream, eggs, vanilla and optional cinnamon. Pour into the prepared dish and bake until set and a knife inserted in the center comes out clean, about 45 minutes. Do not worry if it becomes light brown on top and forms a skin, as this almost tastes like caramelized sugar; but don't let it burn or boil.

PEACH AND GRITS PARFAIT

Serves 6

AFTER THE PUBLICATION *of* Nathalie Dupree's Shrimp and Grits Cookbook, *this was so popular that I was requested to teach it again and again. It's sophisticated and delectable.*

- 2 cups milk
- 1 vanilla bean, or 1 teaspoon vanilla extract
- 1/2 cup plus 2 tablespoons granulated sugar
- 3 tablespoons unsalted butter
- 1 cup grits
- 4 cups hot water
- 6 ripe peaches

Pour the milk into a heavy-bottomed saucepan over medium heat. If using the vanilla bean, split it in half and scrape the seeds into the milk. Add the vanilla bean and sugar to the milk. Stir and bring to a simmer, remove from heat, and let stand for 30 minutes. Remove the vanilla bean. If using vanilla extract, add now.

Melt the butter in a large heavy-bottomed saucepan over medium-high heat. Add the grits and stir for 5 minutes. Whisk in the hot water. Reduce the heat to low and cook, stirring frequently, until the grits have thickened—up to 30 minutes, depending on the type of grits.

Reheat the milk and whisk it into the grits. Cook the grits over low heat, stirring frequently, until thickened, from 20 to 30 minutes. Remove from the heat, pour into a bowl, cool, and refrigerate until chilled.

Slice the peaches just before assembling the parfaits. Layer peach slices, grits, and Berry Sauce into parfait or wine glasses and serve.

BERRY SAUCE

- 1 pint fresh raspberries or strawberries
- 1/4 cup granulated sugar
- 1/2 teaspoon fresh lemon juice

Heat the Berry Sauce ingredients in a heavy-bottomed saucepan over medium-low heat, stirring occasionally, until the berry juices flow and the mixture thickens. Remove from the heat, cool to room temperature, and refrigerate until chilled.

TRADITIONAL RICE PUDDING

Serves 6

Given rice's importance *as a Southern crop, rice pudding has a long legacy. It is found in many English as well as antebellum cookbooks, including all manner of ingredients from cinnamon and raisins to cardamom, lemon rind, and other flavorings. Traditionally, it was made with the popular rice of the time, short- or medium-grain rice. Now, just about any rice will do, although, of course, if you can get Carolina Gold, an heirloom rice, by all means do. Long-grain rice—basmati, popcorn, jasmine, and some other varieties—all have unique flavors and are worth experimenting with.*

The pudding may also be cooked from raw rice or cooked rice of any size, varying the liquid and cooking time as needed. It is particularly helpful as a way to use up leftover rice and is oh, so soothing to those suffering from a cold, whether served hot or cold. My husband Jack grew up eating rice with milk and raisins for breakfast.

2 cups cooked rice, cooked in water or milk

4–5 cups whole milk or half-and-half, divided
1/2 cup granulated sugar
1/4 teaspoon salt

1 vanilla bean, split, or 1/2 teaspoon vanilla extract
Ground cinnamon, optional

Add the cooked rice to 4 cups milk, sugar, and salt, adding the vanilla bean if using. Bring to the boil, reduce heat to a slow simmer, and cook for 30 to 40 minutes, stirring frequently down to the bottom of the pan.

When the rice begins to "blurp," take special care to stir until rice is meltingly tender and a bit looser than cooked oatmeal or grits, about 5 minutes more. Reduce heat if necessary. If the pudding is solid rather than smooth and velvety, add enough of the remaining milk or half-and-half to moisten.

Remove from the heat and discard the vanilla bean. If not using the vanilla bean, stir in the vanilla extract at this point. Spoon into a large bowl or individual serving dishes and serve warm, at room temperature, or cold. If not serving right away, lightly push plastic wrap directly on top to prevent the pudding from forming a skin. When ready to serve, top with a dash of cinnamon if desired. This will last up to 1 week refrigerated.

Variations:

- Serve with Butterscotch Sauce (page 636) or Butterscotch Liquor Sauce with Thyme (page 636).
- Add 1/4 to 1/3 tablespoon ground cinnamon and 1/2 cup currants or raisins with the rice.
- Add the grated rind of 1 orange, and/or 1 lemon and/or 1 lime, no white attached, to the rice, sugar, milk, and salt at the initial cooking process.
- Use whipping cream in place of the cooking milk for sheer decadence.

When deciding how much rice to use in a recipe, remember that 3/4 cup of raw long-grain rice cooked with 2 cups of water will yield 3 times as much cooked rice—about 2 1/4 cups.

RICE CUSTARD PUDDING

Serves 8 to 10

THE ULTIMATE COMFORT FOOD, *this has more body than the traditional pudding and is creamy and voluptuous. The puddings are delightful served with sliced peaches, strawberries, raspberries, or other fruit, sugared as necessary. For a more upscale presentation, serve in stemmed wine goblets.*

1 recipe Traditional Rice Pudding (page 623), warm
2 large eggs
1/3 cup granulated sugar
1 cup heavy cream
1/2 cup chopped toasted pecans, optional
1/2 cup grated chocolate, optional
Fresh fruit, optional

Cool the pudding slightly in the pan.

Lightly whisk the eggs with the sugar in a medium bowl, mix half the pudding with the eggs, and then return this portion to the pan with the remaining pudding.

Taking care not to boil, cook over low heat, stirring constantly until the pudding starts to thicken, about 5 minutes. Remove from heat and lightly push plastic wrap on top of the pudding to prevent a skin from forming. Refrigerate until cool.

Whip the cream until it stands in firm, soft peaks. Fold the cream into the cool pudding, using a figure-eight motion.

Spoon into a serving bowl or into individual goblets or bowls. Serve right away, or push down plastic wrap directly on top of the pudding to prevent a skin from forming.

When ready to serve, sprinkle with pecans, chocolate, fruit, or other desired flavoring. Will last up to 4 days refrigerated.

Variation: Brûlée the pudding as in the Peach or Mango and Cream Custard (page 620).

As Nathalie was beginning to shoot her second TV series in January of 1990, I was on maternity leave, home with my six-week-old son. Although several replacements were interviewed, the studio selected someone I emphatically declared was unsuitable, whom, of course, they hired (because he was a man, in my opinion). Needless to say, the first week of January arrived and indeed the new producer couldn't handle the job. I could not resist the distress call to come in and save the day, so I did, with baby in tow. I was still nursing, so I hired a nanny to bring my son in midday for a few hours for a couple of feedings. The only thing that kept me going was the warm, aromatic, and seductive rice pudding one of the kitchen staff cooks, Will, made for me every single day. I believe that dish was singularly responsible for my son's robust growth and my sanity! It is one of my fondest memories from those years, and I cannot eat rice pudding without thinking of it.

—Cynthia

BAKED RICE PUDDING

Serves 6

BAKED RICE PUDDING *has a different texture than stovetop-cooked rice pudding. It is sturdier and can be unmolded successfully. The time and temperature can be changed easily—going up to 350 degrees and cooking for 45 to 50 minutes, or lowering the temperature to 300 degrees or less and cooking longer. Timing is dependent on the size and thickness of the baking dish. The raisins or currants will plump up as they are cooked, so they need not be soaked before baking.*

- 2 large eggs
- 1/3 cup granulated sugar
- 1/4 teaspoon salt
- 2–3 tablespoons finely grated lemon or orange rind, no white attached
- 1/2 cup dried currants or raisins, optional
- 1/3 teaspoon ground cinnamon, optional
- 1 1/2 cups cooked white rice
- 1 1/2 cups whole milk or half-and-half
- 1 teaspoon vanilla extract
- 1 cup heavy cream, whipped

Preheat oven to 325 degrees.

Whisk the eggs briefly with the sugar and salt in a large bowl until thoroughly mixed. Add the grated rind, currants, and cinnamon. Stir in the rice.

Meanwhile, bring the milk to a simmer in the microwave or on top of the stove. Stir the milk thoroughly into the rice mixture. Add the vanilla extract.

Spoon into a buttered 5-cup mold or 6 individual ramekins. Line the bottom of a sided roasting pan with a kitchen towel. Move the mold(s) to the pan, adding boiling water to come halfway up the sides of the dish(es). Bake until a knife inserted in the center comes out clean, about 1 hour and 15 minutes for the 5-cup mold, less for the smaller ramekins, checking after 1 hour. Add water to the pan as necessary to prevent the water from evaporating or boiling. If the cinnamon or other spice rises to the top of the pudding in the first half hour, carefully stir, cover with a piece of buttered parchment or waxed paper, and return to the oven.

Remove the pan and mold(s), and allow to cool in the water bath about 30 minutes. Remove from the water bath and serve immediately, or at room temperature or chilled. Serve with the whipped cream.

This pudding may be made up to 3 days ahead, covered directly with plastic wrap to prevent a skin from forming, and then refrigerated. To serve warm, reheat in a water bath as above at 300 degrees for 15 to 20 minutes. To unmold, move a knife around the inside of the dish(es) to loosen. Upend a plate on top of the mold, flip, and give the mold a firm shake. If it separates, it should push together fairly easily. It is easier to unmold without the solids of currants or raisins.

SUGAR WORK

Sugar work is one of the most fun and dazzling adventures in the kitchen. It takes a little patience and calm, and it is important to remember that if it burns a bit all that is necessary to clean a pan is to add water and boil it for a little while.

SUGAR SYRUP

Makes 1 3/4 cups

Also called Simple Syrup, *this is a beginning syrup, good for ice tea, for moistening cake layers, for making butter cream icing, and as the basis for moving on to making caramel. It can be made thicker or thinner by adding water or some other liquid. Although it is perfectly easy to make a sugar syrup with just sugar and water, cream of tartar and corn syrup as well as acids like lemon and orange juice stabilize the syrup. Only add one or the other. Substitute bourbon or rum in place of some or all of the liquid.*

1 cup granulated sugar
1 cup water
1/4 teaspoon cream of tartar (optional)
1 tablespoon corn syrup (optional)

Heat the sugar and water over low heat until the sugar is dissolved, stirring as necessary. Brush the inside of the pan with a wet pastry brush to wash down any crystals, remove the brush, and bring up to the boil. Boil until the desired thickness. Remove pan from heat and cool uncovered. Will last a couple of weeks tightly covered at room temperature or indefinitely (six months or so) in the refrigerator.

Variations: Substitute honey for the sugar.

DANGER

Hot sugar and sugar syrups can cause terrible burns, so using oven mitts and cloths is crucial. When sugars cool and harden on the skin surface, it is their rigidity that causes the skin to come off so painfully. If this happens, a less onerous result can be achieved by immersing the burned spot in warm water, which melts off the sugar rather than hardening it. Then treat as any burn.

If the syrup boils before the sugar is dissolved, crystallization will occur. The same thing will happen if, once the sugar is dissolved and begins to boil, a spoon, the sides of the pan, or other objects with grains of sugar attached cause undissolved sugar to drop into the boiling liquid. For this reason, some like to cover the pan, letting the resulting steam wash down the sides. Because covering the pan can cause inattention, I use a cup of water and a pastry brush. Brush down the insides of the pan with the wet pastry brush before bringing the mixture to the boil, and return the spoon to the cup of water in between stirrings.

Stirring or not stirring is debatable with sugar syrups. Adopt a comfortable method and stick to it. One of the dangers of stirring or whisking once the sugar is dissolved is reusing an implement that retains sugar crystals, setting off a "chain reaction" and causing partial crystallization. If stirring feels crucial, be sure to use a clean implement each time, rinsing it off between insertions.

CANDIED ORANGES

Makes 30 slices

FAIR WARNING: THESE CANDIED ORANGES WILL DISAPPEAR UNDER YOUR NOSE! *Dip them in chocolate and the sophisticated taste becomes classic. When simmering the orange slices in the sugar syrup, be sure not to let them boil, as the rough boil will destroy the interior of the orange and cause it to separate from the rind. Use these on top of whipped cream on a tart, or chop and sprinkle on anything with orange in it.*

3 cups granulated sugar
3 cups water
3 tablespoons corn syrup
3 oranges, sliced thinly into 10 slices per orange

Heat sugar, water, and corn syrup in a large saucepan over medium heat until liquid becomes translucent and all is dissolved, making a sugar syrup. Add the sliced oranges, bring to the boil, reduce heat to low, and simmer gently for up to 2 hours, or until liquid is the consistency of molasses and the oranges are tender and candied. Remove oranges with a slotted spoon to a rimmed baking sheet lined with parchment or waxed paper. Let stand several hours, or layer, separated by plastic wrap, in a tight container. Refrigerate, tightly sealed.

CANDIED CITRUS RIND

Makes 2 cups

USE VARIOUS CITRUS, AS BELOW, OR JUST ONE TYPE. *Serve whole or chop and use in cakes, fruit cakes, and any time you would use candied ginger.*

1 large orange with thick skin
1 lemon
1 lime
1½ cups granulated sugar, divided
2 tablespoons corn syrup

Using a knife or vegetable peeler, remove rind from the orange, lemon, and lime, trying not to get any of the white. Add the peels to a 3-quart pot of cold water, making sure the water completely covers the rind. Bring the water to the boil for about 30 seconds. Drain in a colander and rinse the rind under cold water. Return rind to the clean pot and cover with cold water. Repeat the boiling and rinsing process.

After rinsing the rind the second time in cold water, add rind to a clean pot along with 4 cups water, ¾ cup of the sugar, and the corn syrup. Cook over low heat until the sugar is dissolved. Bring to a gentle boil and cook for 1 to 1½ hours. When done, the rind should be transparent, and there should be just enough syrup to coat all the pieces.

Spread the remaining sugar on a cookie sheet and roll the rind in the sugar. Allow to dry on a wire rack for 1 hour or more.

Turn the pieces over with tongs and make sure they are dry before storing. Allow to sit if they are not completely dry. Store in the refrigerator.

CRYSTALLIZING MINT LEAVES

Brush clean dry leaves with egg white; roll in granulated sugar and dry on a rack. Leaves keep nearly a day, not much more.

CARAMEL SAUCE

Makes 1 to 2 cups

*T*HERE ARE TWO SPECIFIC KINDS OF SUGAR *caramelization—dry and wet. Some people find it very easy to melt sugar in a pan and stir it until it caramelizes. Others like adding some liquid, from an equal amount to a fraction of the amount of sugar, making a sugar syrup. The liquid is boiled out and the sugar caramelizes. Although it takes longer to remove all the liquid, it is a safer and easier method of caramelizing. The result is a hard caramel.*

Liquid can be added back into the hard caramel, as in this case, to make a sauce. After practicing a time or two with the full complement of water, reduce the amount of initial water to what is comfortable to the cook, or remove it entirely. (It doesn't affect a home sugar syrup or caramel to add water in varying quantities.)

It is a good habit to partially fill a larger pan, such as a roasting pan, with cold water and have it near the stove. If the caramel browns too quickly, it can be slowed down or stopped altogether by immediately putting the pan in the water.

1 cup granulated sugar, or a mixture of brown and granulated sugar, brown sugar, or honey
1/4 cup white corn syrup
2 cups water, divided

Heat the sugar in a saucepan with the corn syrup and 1 cup water over low heat, without boiling, stirring once or twice if necessary, to completely dissolve the sugar in the water. (There may be a little "sugar scum" on top, but the sugar on the bottom should be dissolved.) If there are sugar crystals on the sides, brush down the sides of the pan with some water.

Once the sugar is completely dissolved, bring to the boil. This is the sugar syrup. Boil steadily until large bubbles form on the surface. Watch closely as the caramel turns from bursting bubbles to little bubbles then caramel. Cover hands or use an oven mitt, and tip the pan once it begins to color so the sugar is uniformly colored. When it turns amber, remove from the heat. It will continue to bubble. If it becomes as dark as mahogany, carefully move it to the pan of water to cool it down immediately and stop the cooking. (Be careful of the bubbling water and sugar.) This is now a "caramel." Left alone to cool, it will harden.

To continue making the sauce, wipe the of the pot if necessary and return to the heat, adding the remaining cup of water. Return to the boil. If part of the caramel syrup has solidified, stir with a clean wooden spoon so the caramel will be evenly distributed. Bring back to the boil, and boil until reduced by one-fourth and slightly syrupy. Cool, pour into another container, and chill. This will last several weeks covered in the refrigerator.

Variations:

- *Caramel Cream Sauce*—Add heavy cream in place of the last cup of water. It will boil up, but not over, in a large-enough pan. It makes a much richer, creamier sauce. Butter can also be added, and also a few roasted pecans if pouring over ice cream.
- *Ginger-Caramel Sauce*—Thinly slice 1/4 pound fresh or candied ginger by hand or in a food processor. When the sugar is completely dissolved, add the desired amount of ginger. Strain if desired.
- *Orange-Lemon Caramel Sauce*—Add 1 to 2 tablespoons fresh lemon or orange juice, or 1 tablespoon Limoncello, Grand Marnier, or Cointreau to the finished sauce. To add shine, mix in 2 tablespoons unsalted butter cut into small pieces.

CARAMELIZATION

It's hard for anyone to forget their first toasted marshmallow, particularly if it was done over a campfire. The exterior turns brown, the insides melt, and when popped into the mouth, there is an exquisite taste of nutty, gooey sweetness that is the essence of caramelizing. It's also when we learn about the colors sugar can take and the results. Some like a flaming, charred marshmallow, with a dark, crisp, leaf-like wrapping and very hot goo inside. Others are careful to turn the marshmallow slowly over the flame, wanting a pale brown, and still others want a darker but not charred result. Whatever the fancy, the marshmallows are caramelized.

Caramelization is the oxidation of sugars at high temperatures, which produces the rich, complex flavors and colors of caramel. Even experts don't understand completely the complex chemical reactions, so that is all anyone needs to know unless they want to become a professional candy maker or baker. Sugar syrups must lose all their water to brown and develop the rich, complex flavor we love. As with the marshmallow, the final result depends on the palate and patience of the cook.

ORANGES IN CARAMEL SAUCE

Serves 6

I LEARNED THIS AT THE LONDON CORDON BLEU *and have used it ever since. It is a simple and refreshing dessert, bathing orange slices in a cooling caramel sauce. A cookie or two on the plate wouldn't hurt a bit. I justify this recipe's presence in this book by the oranges grown in the South, and their natural affinity for caramel.*

6 oranges

1 recipe Caramel Sauce (facing)

Before peeling the oranges, grate the rind, leaving no white attached to the rind, using a grater or a microplane, or peel strips with a potato peeler and slice into thin julienne strips. Remove the remaining rind and slice the oranges into rounds; remove the seeds.

Pour Caramel Sauce as needed over the oranges up to a day before serving. Sprinkle on the grated or julienned orange peel. Cover with plastic wrap. This is particularly pretty served in a glass bowl.

Variations: Add candied ginger and/or candied orange peel rather than the grated rind, or add candied ginger to the caramel sauce.

MICROWAVING CARAMEL

Although sugar can be caramelized in the microwave, author Harold McGee states that a "different spectrum of flavors is produced" using that method (see *On Food and Cooking, Revised Edition*). It can be very dangerous because glass or plastic producers don't guarantee their products at such a high heat, which could cause terrible burns by damaging the product and causing leakage. So don't do it!

CANDIED LEMON SLICES

THESE MAKE DECADENT SLICES *to accompany pound cakes, ice creams, and other desserts. Or to eat standing up at the refrigerator when no one is looking. 1 or 2 lemons*

1 cup granulated sugar
1 cup water

Prepare an ice-water bath and set aside.

Using a mandoline or sharp knife, cut the lemon into 1/8-inch-thick slices. Discard the seeds and ends of the rind.

Bring a 2-quart saucepan of water to a rolling boil. Remove from the heat and add lemon slices. Stir until softened. Remove the lemon slices with a slotted spoon or skimmer and immediately place in the ice bath prepared earlier. Drain the lemons when cool.

Heat sugar and water in a medium 7- to 8-inch skillet until sugar is dissolved and the liquid is translucent. Bring to the boil, and when clear and bubbling, reduce heat to low. Add lemon slices, arranging them so they are not lying on top of one another. Simmer until rinds are translucent, about 1 hour. Remove the slices with a slotted spoon. Transfer to a rimmed baking sheet lined with parchment. Let stand several hours, or layer, separated by plastic wrap, in a tight container.

DIVINITY

Makes 2 1/2 dozen pieces

SWEET, SWEET DIVINITY IS DIVINE *and makes its appearance at weddings and lavish occasions. According to cookbook author Steven Schmidt, this candy—like its counterpart, Sea Foam—dates back to the 1900s. Both were popular all over the United States, but both became known as Southern. This recipe can be doubled easily.*

It is best to make the candy on a sunny, dry day; use 1 tablespoon less water on humid days. Divinity freezes well and will keep for days if tightly covered. Use a stand mixer for best results.

2 1/2 cups granulated sugar
2 tablespoons corn syrup
1/2 cup water
3 egg whites
1 teaspoon vanilla extract
1/2 cup chopped pecans

Heat the sugar, corn syrup, and water in a heavy saucepan over low heat until the sugar is dissolved. Brush down any sugar crystals with a brush dipped in water. Continue cooking without stirring to the hard-ball stage, 260 degrees.

Beat the egg whites in a stand mixer until stiff peaks form. Pour the hot sugar syrup over the egg whites in a steady stream, beating constantly. Add the vanilla and beat until the mixture holds its shape and loses its glossy sheen, about 10 minutes. Fold in the chopped nuts.

Drop the candy by tablespoons onto racks covered with waxed paper and allow to dry at room temperature. The candy should hold its shape. Store in an airtight container or freeze.

CHARLESTON PRALINES

Makes 2 1/2 dozen

LEGEND HAS IT THAT CLÉMENT LASSAGNE, *personal chef to Monsieur Marshal du Plessis-Praslin of France, in 1636 created the praline, which is now a firm fixture in New Orleans, Charleston, and other coastal areas. It is ironic that this is where they reign, because the humidity in those areas increases the difficulty of sugar work. Although there are dire warnings about doing sugar work in humid areas, it is not impossible, even on rainy days. Don't be daunted by this recipe: if the pralines don't harden, freeze them and they will harden and be delightful, too.*

1 1/2 cups granulated sugar
1 1/2 cups light or dark brown sugar
1 cup evaporated milk
1/4 cup unsalted butter
2 cups pecan halves, toasted
1 teaspoon vanilla extract

Dissolve sugars in the milk in a large heavy pan over low heat, taking care not to boil before the sugars are dissolved. If the sugar is not dissolved before it boils, the pralines will be grainy, but they will still be delicious.

When dissolved, turn up the heat and bring to the boil. Cook over medium heat for 11 minutes, or until a candy thermometer registers 228 degrees (thread stage). Stir in butter and pecans; cook, stirring constantly, until candy thermometer reaches 238 degrees (soft-ball stage).

Remove from heat and stir in vanilla. Beat with a wooden spoon 1 to 2 minutes, or until mixture begins to thicken. Quickly drop by heaping tablespoons onto buttered waxed paper or parchment paper; it will spread a bit and then become firm. If still runny and it doesn't harden, scoop up and put the candy into a clean pan, bring up to 236 degrees again, and repeat as above. Store in an airtight container at room temperature or freeze. Once frozen, pralines seem to stay hard—or maybe it just seems that way, as I eat them straight from the freezer.

DIFFERENCE AMONG SUGARS

Each sugar produces a different result with preferences open to the cook. Although cane sugar and beet sugar are chemically the same, makers of jam, marmalade, and candy insist that they don't behave the same and much prefer cane sugar. Beet sugar is very tricky. Also, many makers of fine candy and pastry disdain brown sugar, calling it harsh. Brown sugar also varies according to region of the world. Finally, sugar workers and candy makers have some specialty sugars that make their work easier and finer.

Variation: That said, if there is a problem the first time, my friend Teresa Taylor says to create a new dessert by folding them into softened vanilla ice cream. If they're too soft, scrape up the mixture, chill it, and roll into 1-inch balls. Dip the balls into melted chocolate to make truffles.

Variation: Martha Foose ran a fabulous bakery in Oxford, Mississippi, when my husband and I lived there. I would try to get there regularly to eat her croissants and tempting goodies. We both moved away but have stayed in touch, primarily because we have very similar philosophies of life and food. In her marvelous book, *Screen Doors and Sweet Tea,* she adds crumbled crisp bacon slices along with the pecans, approximately four to each cup of sugar.

Variation: White Pecan Pralines
Unlike the traditional Charleston Pralines, these pralines of Chuck Lee's are made with only white granulated sugar, which gives them a beautiful pale color and a lighter flavor than those made with brown sugar. These are seen frequently at weddings and ladies luncheons.

SUPER-THIN PECAN BRITTLE

Fills about 1 gallon-size plastic ziplock bag

BRITTLE IS USUALLY *a thick caramel with nuts in it. This brittle has a lacy, delicate texture.*

One of the benefits of being a teacher is learning from one's students and interns. One intern, Meri, taught another intern and me the method of rolling out the brittle with a rolling pin and pulling it while it is still warm to create a thin, crisp brittle that melts in the mouth instead of sticking in the teeth! How thin the brittle becomes all depends on the sensitivity of the fingertips. Since Chuck and Meri are bakers with "asbestos hands," they started stretching the brittle while it was still fairly warm, resulting in a thinner brittle. Thinner is better, but don't risk burns if it feels too hot to handle. Buttered or oiled fingers or latex gloves will help keep the brittle from sticking to the skin and hardening, causing the skin to peel off painfully. Humidity will affect sugar, so avoid rainy days or the brittle won't set up properly.

3 cups granulated sugar
1 cup light corn syrup
1/2 cup water

3 cups pecan halves, toasted and roughly chopped into peanut-sized pieces

1 tablespoon baking soda
1/4 cup unsalted butter
1 teaspoon vanilla extract

Butter three jelly-roll pans or silicone baking mats. If no thermometer is available, set aside a small bowl of ice water for testing.

Heat the sugar, corn syrup, and water in an 8- to 10-cup saucepan over moderate heat without boiling until the sugar dissolves. Bring to the boil, stirring if needed and using a clean spoon, until the mixture is golden brown and reaches 310 degrees on a candy thermometer, or until a little of the hot syrup turns hard when dropped into ice water. Add the pecans.

Remove pan from the heat, add baking soda, butter, and vanilla, and stir until the butter melts and the mixture foams. Quickly pour onto the buttered jelly-roll pans before the mixture has a chance to foam out of the pot. Don't worry if it's not divided quite evenly between the pans. Spread quickly with a buttered spatula. Top with a buttered silicone baking mat or buttered waxed paper, and use a rolling pin on top of the mat to roll out thinly.

As the mixture begins to harden and cool, pick it up around the edges with buttered or oiled fingers or latex gloves, and pull and stretch it as thinly as possible. When hardened, crack into bite-sized pieces with fingers. Store the brittle carefully in an airtight container. To clean the pot quickly and easily, fill with water and bring to the boil. The sugar will dissolve.

Variation: Substitute peanuts, pistachios, almonds, or other nuts for the pecans.

ICE CREAM

The way ice cream was made, even from the time of Thomas Jefferson and George Washington, was to fill the container of a hand-crank (and later, electric) ice cream churn with a custard of eggs, sugar, and cream that had been cooked over low heat, cooled, and flavored to suit the whole crowd—usually peach, strawberry, chocolate or vanilla. And then the laborious work began. The suspense was intense, particularly among the children. The imprecise ratio of salt and ice made for a hit-and-miss product, sometimes too icy and at other times too soupy. Modern machines have made ice cream making at home more predictable. It's nearly as easy as using a slow cooker for a meal: place the ingredients in the container, set it, and forget it.

PLAIN VANILLA ICE CREAM

Makes 1 3/4 quarts

THIS ICE CREAM *can be made in any number of other flavors. It was hard to choose our favorite from the ones below, and we would make them all again were it not for the calories. It is remarkable how much flavor and freshness the herbs add. I really wouldn't have believed it. Since it is not a custard and contains no eggs, it is safe for all ages.*

1 1/2 cups whole milk
1 1/8 cups granulated sugar
3 cups heavy cream
1/2–1 1/2 teaspoons vanilla extract

Beat the milk and granulated sugar in a bowl with an electric hand mixer for 1 or 2 minutes, until the sugar is dissolved. Stir in the cream and 1/2 teaspoon vanilla. Taste and add more vanilla as needed. Pour the mixture into an ice cream machine, and let it mix about 20 to 25 minutes, until thick. The ice cream will have a soft cream texture. Move to an airtight container and freeze about 2 hours to mellow and harden. Remove from freezer about 15 minutes before serving.

Variations:

- To use fresh vanilla bean instead of vanilla extract, heat the cream with a split vanilla bean and let cool to infuse. Remove bean from ice cream when half frozen. The ice cream will have beautiful black specks.
- *Banana*—substitute light or dark brown sugar for granulated sugar if desired. Add 3 very soft bananas, smooshed with fingers into small pieces. Add 1 slice candied ginger finely chopped, or 1/4 to 1/3 cup chopped chocolate if desired.
- *Chocolate and Orange*—add grated rind of 1 navel orange, no white attached, and 2 to 4 ounces of chopped chocolate.
- *Thyme or Lemon Balm*—add 1/3 cup finely chopped herbs, or to taste.
- *Benne Seed*—Add 3 tablespoons roasted benne or sesame seeds. Omit vanilla extract.

FROZEN CARAMEL MOUSSE ICE CREAM

Serves 6 to 8

THIS RECIPE HAS BEEN IN MY REPERTOIRE *for thirty years. I admit, however, that it took many attempts to get the recipe this perfect. It is a smooth-as-silk and melt-in-your mouth ice cream. It doesn't require churning and can be used as a base for many other recipes. There are some techniques that definitely need to be followed here, so, as a refresher, refer to page 629 for caramel tips.*

6 egg yolks
1 cup granulated sugar
1 cup water, divided
2½ cups heavy cream
1 teaspoon vanilla extract
Fresh fruit, optional

Beat the egg yolks with an electric hand mixer until they are thick and pale.

Meanwhile, heat the sugar and ½ cup water in a small heavy saucepan over low heat until the sugar is dissolved. Use a wet brush to sweep down any sugar crystals that collect on the side of the pan. When the sugar has dissolved, turn up the heat and boil steadily until sugar turns to a golden brown caramel (330 to 360 degrees).

As the sugar browns, bring remaining ½ cup water to the boil separately. Carefully pour the hot water down the inside of the pan cooking the caramel mixture. The addition of the boiling water may cause the hot syrup to splatter, so keep hand covered with a tea towel or oven mitt. Stir until water is incorporated.

While beating the egg yolks continually, add the caramel syrup in a steady stream. Continue to beat until the mixture is light and creamy. Set this bowl over another bowl filled with ice cubes, and continue to beat while the mixture thickens and cools. Set aside.

Whip the cream and vanilla into soft peaks; save some for decoration. Fold the rest of the whipped cream into the cooled caramel mixture. Spoon into little mousse pots or a freezer-proof serving bowl and freeze at least 2½ hours before serving. May be wrapped tightly and frozen several weeks ahead.

When ready to serve, leave bowl at room temperature until a knife can be run around the bowl to release the ice cream. Place a serving dish on top of the bowl and flip the bowl and the ice cream onto the serving dish, remove the bowl. Decorate the top with the reserved whipped cream and a few slices of fresh fruit.

Variation: Fig Caramel Ice Cream
Purée 2 cups quartered fresh figs in a blender until smooth. Fold figs into the egg yolk mixture. Continue as above.

Variation: Add candied ginger.

LEMON CURD ICE CREAM

Makes 1¾ quart

I'M ALWAYS ASKED IF LEMON CURD FREEZES. *Clearly the answer is "yes," as my intern Hayley showed in this recipe of hers. The lemon curd base serves as a custard.*

1 recipe Lemon Curd (page 618)
1 cup milk
1½ cups heavy cream

Bring the Lemon Curd to room temperature in a large bowl.

Heat the milk. Add the milk to the Lemon Curd and whisk to combine. Move the bowl to the refrigerator to cool to room temperature, or leave overnight.

Once it has cooled, whisk in the cream. Pour the resulting custard into an ice cream machine and churn for 20 minutes. Transfer to a container and allow to mellow and harden in the freezer about 2 hours. Remove from freezer 15 minutes before serving.

BUTTERSCOTCH ICE CREAM

Makes 1 1/2 quarts

DID WE LOVE THIS? *Yes! Would we make it again? Yes! In other words, a splendid dessert, by intern Julia Regner.*

6 egg yolks
2 cups heavy cream
6 tablespoons unsalted butter
1 cup light or dark brown sugar
1/4 teaspoon salt
2 cups whole milk
1 teaspoon vanilla extract

Whisk the egg yolks until well blended. Set aside.

Pour the cream into a metal bowl set in a larger bowl of ice. Have a sieve ready to strain mixture into the bowl.

Melt the butter in a medium-heavy saucepan. Add the brown sugar and salt. Stir until the sugar completely melts. Slowly add the milk, stirring to incorporate. It will foam up initially, so make sure your pan is deep enough. Heat until all of the sugar is completely dissolved. Do not let boil or the mixture may curdle.

Slowly pour half of the milk-and-sugar mixture into the eggs, whisking constantly to incorporate. Then add the warmed egg mixture back into the saucepan with the remaining milk-and-sugar mixture. Stir the mixture constantly over medium heat with a wooden spoon or heatproof rubber spatula, scraping the bottom as you stir, until the mixture thickens and coats a metal spoon and registers about 180 degrees, about 5 to 7 minutes. Do not boil.

Pour the custard through the sieve to catch any cooked eggs; discard the cooked eggs. Stir the custard into the cream. Stir the custard into the bowl of cream sitting over ice. Add vanilla and stir until cool. Chill mixture thoroughly in the refrigerator, at least 1 hour or overnight.

Pour the custard mixture into an ice cream machine and churn until soft, about 20 minutes. Move to an airtight container and freeze at least 2 hours to mellow and harden. Let sit at room temperature about 15 minutes, until easy to serve.

Variation: Before freezing, add 4 slices Caramelized Bacon (page 413), finely chopped.

LEMON MINT ICE

Serves 2 to 4

AMAZINGLY REFRESHING BETWEEN COURSES OR ON FRUIT AS A DESSERT. *Make this up to a week in advance and freeze, ready to serve. Mint and lemon balm really like a shady spot in my garden where there is plenty of water.*

1 1/4 cups water
3/4 cup granulated sugar
Grated rind of 2 large lemons, no white attached
12 mint or lemon balm leaves, finely chopped
Juice of 2 lemons, strained
1 egg white
Crystallized mint leaves (page 627), optional

Heat the water and sugar in a heavy saucepan until sugar is dissolved and liquid is clear. Add the lemon rind (making sure no white part has been included) and the mint. Bring to the boil and boil 10 minutes. Remove from heat and cool. Add lemon juice and taste for flavor. Add more rind and juice if necessary.

Beat the egg white until stiff, then add to lemon mixture. Pour into a prepared ice cream freezer and freeze until stiff. Remove from freezer and let stand 10 to 15 minutes. Serve in pretty cups or wine glasses, or in variation below. Garnish with 2 or 3 crystallized mint leaves if desired.

Variation: Serve in hollowed orange, grapefruit, or lime halves that have been dusted with sugar.

BUTTERSCOTCH SAUCE

Makes 1 cup

I grew up with butterscotch sauce *and then kind of forgot about it. All of a sudden, I began craving it again. The apple cider vinegar in this variation gives it a special zip.*

- 1/2 cup unsalted butter
- 1 cup light or dark brown sugar
- 1 cup heavy cream
- 1 teaspoon vanilla extract
- 2 teaspoons apple cider vinegar
- 1/2 teaspoon salt

Heat the butter and sugar together in a heavy saucepan over medium heat until the sugar has melted completely and the mixture has a thick, frothy, lava-like appearance.

Remove the pot from the heat and whisk in the cream until thoroughly incorporated. Let cool for 10 minutes; add the vanilla, vinegar, and salt. Serve immediately, hot or cold. Refrigerate covered up to 2 weeks (or as long as the cream stays fresh). It can be reheated before serving.

Variation: Butterscotch Liquor Sauce with Thyme
Melt 1/2 cup butter in a saucepan with 2 large sprigs of fresh thyme. Add 1 cup light or dark brown sugar, stirring occasionally until smooth, about 5 minutes. Remove from heat and whisk in 1/3 cup Scotch. Return to heat and whisk in 1/3 cup heavy cream until smooth and glossy. Remove thyme sprigs and season to taste with salt.

CHOCOLATE SAUCE

Makes 1 1/4 cups

This is a foolproof sauce, *the base of which is a Chocolate Ganache (page 612). Better chocolate makes better sauce.*

- 1 cup heavy cream
- 1/2 cup semisweet chocolate chips or small pieces

Heat the cream in a heavy pan or in the microwave until hot but not boiling. When hot, add the chocolate and continue to cook over low heat until the chocolate is melted and smooth. Serve hot or set aside until needed. It will harden when cool. Keep in the refrigerator covered for several weeks. Reheat over low heat or in the microwave.

ORANGE-LEMON SAUCE

Makes 2 cups

Magnificent over fresh fruit, *this sauce can also adorn a hot biscuit or a slice of angel food cake.*

- 2/3 cup fresh orange juice
- 2/3 cup fresh lemon juice
- 1/2 cup granulated sugar
- 6 egg yolks
- 1 1/2 cups heavy cream, whipped

Dissolve the sugar in the orange and lemon juices in a small heavy pan over medium heat to make a syrup. Bring the mixture to the boil and remove from the heat.

Move the egg yolks to another heavy pan over low heat, and pour the sugar mixture (now a syrup) into the egg yolks in a slow, steady stream, whisking constantly. Cook, whisking constantly, until mixture begins to thicken and becomes light and smooth.

Remove to a bowl and chill. When cold, fold in the whipped cream.

APRICOT-AND-PINEAPPLE FILLING

Makes 4 cups

I TRY TO WORK FRUIT IN WITH EVERY MEAL, *if not every course. But there are also fruits that begin to reach their prime before we have time to eat them. I love this with fresh fruit, but using dried or frozen fruit or mixing both types, which is what I normally have to do, is a very good compromise. Use to sandwich meringues, fill cream puffs, or spread between cake layers.*

- 5 fresh or frozen apricots
- 1/2 cup pineapple, preferably fresh
- 2/3 cup granulated sugar
- 5 egg yolks
- 1/2 cup unsalted butter
- 3 tablespoons peach brandy, Cointreau, or Grand Marnier

Peel and pit the fresh fruit. Purée in a food processor or blender until smooth. Add the pineapple, sugar, and egg yolks, and purée again.

Melt the butter in a heavy saucepan. Add the puréed mixture. Cook, stirring constantly over low heat until thick. Add the liqueur. Cool, cover, and refrigerate.

Variation: Substitute approximately 2 peaches for the apricots.

Lightly whisk the egg yolks with the sugar in a heavy saucepan, bain-marie, or double boiler.

RASPBERRY CREAM

Serves 4 to 6

THIS RECIPE OF THOMAS JEFFERSON'S *in Damon Lee Fowler's* Dining at Monticello *is such an easy thing to make. This was written in an era when heavy cream had a thicker consistency than these days, so I suggest whipping the cream. I confess, I always keep heavy cream in the refrigerator; it lasts a month or more and is ever so handy when a quick dessert is needed. Butter cookies or meringues make a nice accompaniment.*

- 1/2 cup raspberry preserves
- 2 cups heavy cream, lightly whipped

To remove any raspberry seeds, heat the preserves enough to pass through a strainer. Cool to room temperature.

Whisk the room-temperature preserves in a medium bowl. Gradually whisk in the whipped cream, a little at a time at first, until the cream is smooth and evenly colored rich pink.

Cover and chill in the refrigerator. To serve as a dessert cream on its own, spoon into small sherbet glasses and chill thoroughly.

Heavy cream is 36 percent fat. The fat enables it to be beaten easier and to hold longer.

Whipping cream has less fat, 30 percent, so is more difficult to whip.

CONDIMENTS, SAVORY SAUCES, & MARINADES

Condiments are preparations or sauces used to enhance the enjoyment of a food, and in a broad sense include preserved foods, all sauces, and marinades. Eating would be pretty dull without them.

My refrigerator, pantry shelf, and freezer are full of odd little jars and containers that hold magic to enhance our meals. In the freezer, curried dried fruit beckons, ready to be put on any meat; a batch of marinara sauce is ready to be defrosted and heated at the last minute to go over some pasta or with some mussels; some leftover White Butter Sauce is nearby in a plastic bag. Tomato conserve shines beautifully through a glass container on the refrigerator top shelf, and several small plastic containers of hot pepper jelly are stacked up next to the jars of marmalade and refrigerator strawberry preserves. In short, all of them do the same thing—add flavor to something already cooked, or in the process of being cooked. Marinades add flavor and perhaps tenderness before cooking and are frequently boiled up to make a sauce as well.

PRESERVED CONDIMENTS

Gleaming jars filled with brightly colored vegetables and jewel-toned fruits are a common sight in Southern pantries. Lucky is the hostess who receives "put up" delights as a gift. Even better, though, is to stock up when the garden is overflowing with its bounty. The names are generalized, with no real consistency except in the mind of the cook.

Pickles—whole vegetables or large chunks, preserved in a mixture of vinegar and salt, with a host of spice options.

Relishes—a close cousin to pickles and are made with similar vegetables (and some fruits), but they are chopped fine before putting into vinegar. Relishes are easily confused with chutneys. Not surprising, as chutneys can be savory and relishes can be sweet.

Chutneys—chunky and often contain sugar. They are usually strongly spiced. Relishes are often more crunchy than chutneys.

Fruit butters—less sweet than jams or preserves and are an easy place to start for the novice in condiments. Fruit butter is made by cooking whole fruit and puréeing or passing it through a food mill. The resulting pulp is then cooked further with sugar and sometimes spices until it is thick and spreadable. When made without sugar, fruit butters are called spreads.

Jams—typically made with small fruits, like berries, and cooked with sugar and pectin until thick. Jam has an even, thick consistency but is not strained and should not be runny. Made without additional pectin, these jams are called "refrigerator" or "freezer" jams, as their shelf life is short, about 3 weeks in the refrigerator. Savory jams, such as onion or tomato, are popular in the South and are also called conserves.

Preserves—have the consistency of chunky jam.

Jellies—clear, solid spreads usually made from fruit. Fruit (or vegetables) are cooked down with pectin and an acid (usually lemon juice), and strained to produce the clear jelly.

Marmalades—usually made with citrus fruits. The primary consistency is like jam and includes pieces of the rind.

Conserves—traditionally whole fruits but also include cut-up tomatoes and sliced onions stewed in sugar. The cooking time is shorter than with jam, so the resulting product is softer-set than a jam. Some conserves are a mix of fruits, and some contain dried fruits or nuts. The best-known savory conserve in the South is tomato conserve, also called tomato jam.

REFRIGERATOR PRESERVES VS. HOME CANNED PRESERVES

Canning is a whole process on its own. It is important that the jars and lids are sterile and the filled containers are processed correctly. These condiment recipes are presented as "refrigerator" items, with a shelf life of about 2 to 3 weeks, even if they are packed in sterile jars. Label them as refrigerator products. The adage "When in doubt, throw it out" applies here. If any develop an off smell or taste, discard them.

There are excellent books written on traditional canning, and the recipes contained in them use the proper proportions of acids, sugars, and pectins to achieve delicious and safe results. Our recipes here are not meant to be prepared for long-term or shelf storage. They are just the start for a creative mind.

REFRIGERATOR CUCUMBER PICKLES

Makes 2 to 3 cups

"Pickling" cucumbers, traditionally 3 to 4 inches in size, *are most common for sterile pickling. The cucumbers with the most "warts" are best, as these are still young and have fewer seeds. We used garden cucumbers, as this is what was available in local grocery stores. The resulting refrigerator pickles were a pleasure, and completely eaten within a few days, not weeks!*

1/2 cup water
1 cup apple cider vinegar
1 teaspoon salt
5 garlic cloves
3 cups (about 2) sliced cucumbers

Heat the water, vinegar, salt, and garlic in a heavy pan until it comes to the boil. Remove from the heat and let it sit for 5 minutes. Meanwhile, add the cucumbers plus the garlic from the boiled mixture to one or more containers, such as glass jars or plastic containers, packing each tightly. Slowly pour the slightly cooled mixture over the cucumbers into the container.

Refrigerate the pickles for 24 hours, but they are best served after 3 days. These will keep for 2-3 weeks in the refrigerator.

Variation: Herb-Laced Cucumbers
Interlace cucumbers and garlic with about 3/4 cups chopped fennel frond, thyme, or lemon balm while filling the containers.

Variation: Spiced Cucumbers
Experimenting with spices is exciting when pickles are ho-hum. This is just a hint of the spices that like pickles: coriander, cumin, cardamom, and fennel seeds. Immediately after the water, vinegar, salt, and garlic come to the boil, add 1/4 teaspoon mustard seeds, 1/2 teaspoon ground turmeric, and 1/4 teaspoon celery seed to the liquid.

Variation: Pickled Okra
Substitute an equal amount of okra for the cucumbers. Experiment with the herbs and spices listed above.

MARGARET ANN'S DRIED CURRIED FRUIT

Serves 8

THERE WAS A TIME WHEN CURRIED FRUIT, *served every Thanksgiving on many Southern tables, was made with canned fruit. Logical, as everyone canned their own fruits in season and, thus, these were what was available for fall and winter meals. When excellent dried fruits, such as cherries, blueberries, and cranberries, became widely available, my then-assistant Margaret Ann Surber suggested we modify the age-old recipe and use dried fruit. What a difference this makes! It becomes nearly a chutney, a perfect accompaniment for the meal and even better the next day on a cold turkey sandwich.*

2 pounds mixed dried fruit (apricots, apples, cherries, blueberries, cranberries, plums, figs, peaches, raisins, peaches)
1/2 cup dry sherry, Madeira wine, or apple cider
1/2 cup butter
1/2 cup light or dark brown sugar
4 teaspoons curry powder
1 teaspoon ground cumin
1 cup chicken stock or broth

Chop fruit to desired size. Soak the fruit in the sherry overnight; the fruit will absorb most of the liquid.

Preheat oven to 350 degrees. Melt the butter in a skillet; stir in the brown sugar, curry powder, and cumin, and cook briefly. Mix in the fruit and stock. Move to a buttered 9 x 13-inch or 1-quart ovenproof casserole. Bake for 45 minutes to 1 hour, stirring every 10 to 15 minutes to prevent burning. Serve warm, cold, or at room temperature. May be refrigerated, covered, for several weeks, or frozen.

Variations:

- Double the ingredients, and use a large Dutch oven for the increased quantity.
- While soaking any of the dried fruit, defrost frozen pineapples, mangos, peaches, mixed berries, apricots, or plums as desired to make approximately six cups total of defrosted and soaked and plumped dried fruit. Proceed as above, substituting the juices of the defrosted fruit for the chicken broth.

CRANBERRY RELISH

Serves 10 to 12

ALAS, CRANBERRIES ARE ONE THING WE CANNOT GROW *in the South. The most sensible thing to do is to purchase them when they are in the store and freeze them just as they are. Pull them out when holidays arrive. I was particularly delighted with this very typical relish when French visitors oohed and ahhed about it! This can be refrigerated or frozen.*

1 cup granulated sugar
1 cup water
Chopped rind of 1 orange, no white attached
1 (12-ounce) package fresh or defrosted cranberries

Bring the sugar and water to the boil in a 1-quart saucepan. Add the orange rind and cranberries, return to the boil, reduce heat, and simmer 15 minutes. Remove from the heat. Cool and store in the refrigerator in clean, airtight containers and use within 2 to 3 weeks.

Serve the traditional way with turkey or other poultry.

Variation: Cranberry-Blueberry Relish
In summer, simmer a jar of this cranberry relish with 1/2 to 1 cup blueberries and 1/2 to 1 teaspoon cinnamon, and serve over hot biscuits.

MEYER LEMON RELISH

Makes 1 cup

MY NEIGHBOR PEG MOORE *adapted this from an old recipe and finds it good with chicken, fish, and shellfish. I'm particularly grateful in the years when my Meyer lemon tree bursts with more lemons than I can possibly use.*

A Meyer lemon is about the size of an orange, with juice milder than a traditional lemon. To substitute for 1 traditional lemon, use 1 1/2 Meyer lemons. Taste and add more lemon as desired. Sprinkle with a little sugar if needed.

1 large shallot, finely chopped
1 tablespoon white wine vinegar or fresh lemon juice
Salt
1 large Meyer lemon
1/2 cup olive oil
2 tablespoons chopped parsley
1 tablespoon chopped chervil or chives
Freshly ground black pepper

Soak diced shallot with vinegar and a pinch of salt in a medium bowl for 10 or 15 minutes.

Cut the lemon into 8 wedges. Remove the seeds and central core from each piece. Cut each wedge in half lengthwise. Slice the wedges crosswise into thin slivers to make about 1/2 cup. Add to the shallot. Stir in the olive oil, parsley, chervil, and pepper. Taste and adjust the seasoning.

Cover and refrigerate up to several days until needed. Serve cold or at room temperature.

Lemons freeze easily. Pop into freezer singly and when frozen, combine in a plastic ziplock bag with other lemons. Pull out as needed.

GRILLED ONION RELISH

Makes 4 cups

Simple grilled fish or meats *become spectacular with this slightly tart addition. It is also tasty spread on crackers or toast as a starter. The onions may be grilled or baked. Grilling them adds a smoky flavor, while baking gives a richer, fuller onion taste. When possible, use sweet Vidalias. The natural sugars in the onions caramelize, adding a whole new dimension.*

2 tablespoons oil, cook's preference
2 tablespoons Dijon mustard
6 large onions, peeled and cut in half
2 tablespoons chopped fresh rosemary
1 teaspoon fennel seeds
1/2 cup chopped fennel bulb (optional)
1/4 cup red wine or sherry vinegar
1 teaspoon granulated sugar, optional
Salt
Freshly ground black pepper
1/2 cup chopped pecans, toasted (optional)

Whisk the oil and mustard together and brush onto the onions. Cook on a grill over medium-high heat until the onions begin to soften and char slightly, about 20 minutes, turning every 5 minutes or so. Alternatively, preheat oven to 400 degrees and bake the onions in a single layer on a rimmed baking sheet lined with foil for about 20 to 25 minutes, turning once. With either method, sprinkle the onions with the rosemary after the initial turning.

Coarsely chop the cooked onions, move to a bowl, and add the fennel seeds, chopped fennel, vinegar, and sugar. Season to taste with salt and pepper. Add pecans if desired.

Cover and refrigerate 4 hours before serving for flavors to develop. Serve at room temperature. It will last several weeks in the refrigerator.

Variation: Use half white and half red onions or shallots.

CORN RELISH

Makes 3 pints

This condiment is a clever way to use up *abundant fresh corn and bell peppers when they are at a reasonable price. While it happily stands alone as an accompaniment to meats, fish, or vegetables, it is also good mixed with tomatoes chopped shortly before serving.*

1/4 cup granulated sugar
1 teaspoon salt
6 ears fresh corn, kernels cut from the cob
2 tablespoons butter or oil, cook's preference
1/2 jalapeño pepper, finely chopped, optional
1 yellow or orange bell pepper, chopped
1 red bell pepper, chopped
1 red onion, chopped
1 tablespoon celery seed
2 teaspoons mustard seed
1 teaspoon freshly ground black pepper
3/4 cup apple cider vinegar

Sprinkle the sugar and salt over the corn kernels.

Heat the butter or oil in a large skillet and quickly sauté the jalapeño and bell peppers with the onion until softened, about 5 minutes.

Add the corn mixture to the skillet and cook for 2 to 3 minutes. Add the remaining ingredients and bring to the boil. Remove from heat.

Cool and move to airtight containers, storing in the refrigerator up to 2 to 3 weeks.

REFRIGERATOR GREEN TOMATO RELISH

Makes 10 cups

THE SOURNESS OF TOMATOES *that come too early or late to ripen is a special treat for those of us who enjoy a bit of a pucker every once in a while. Serve with just about anything, particularly meats.*

2 cups apple cider vinegar
1 cup granulated sugar
1 1/2 teaspoons whole allspice berries
1 1/2 teaspoons whole celery seeds
2 or 3 bay leaves
2 large red bell peppers, cored, seeded, and cut into strips
2 large Vidalia onions, sliced or chopped
5 pounds green tomatoes, cut into 6 wedges each

Bring all ingredients except tomatoes to the boil, stirring occasionally. Reduce heat and cook 15 minutes, stirring frequently, until mixture thickens.

Add tomatoes, bring to the boil, reduce heat, and cook 15 more minutes. Cool and move to airtight containers, storing in the refrigerator up to 2 to 3 weeks.

TOMATO CONSERVE OR PRESERVE

Makes 1 quart

ALSO CALLED TOMATO JAM, *this probable forerunner of ketchup may be purchased store-bought, but the homemade version is so much more enchanting that I had to start making my own. It is served atop vegetables of all sorts—beans and peas, greens, zucchini, eggplant, and others—as well as added to sauces such as White Butter Sauce (page 656). Its earthy, deep red color adds dimension wherever it goes. One woman wrote me recently that she also serves it with collards in a sandwich.*

8 pounds fresh tomatoes, skinned, quartered, and seeded, or 4 (28-ounce) cans of tomatoes with juice
2 cups apple cider vinegar
1–1 1/2 cups granulated sugar, divided
Salt
Freshly ground black pepper

Bring the tomatoes, vinegar, 1 cup sugar, and salt and pepper to taste to the boil in a heavy saucepan. Reduce heat and simmer until the mixture is thick enough to cling to a spoon, about 1 1/2-2 hours, stirring so it does not burn. Taste and add some of the remaining sugar if desired. Cool and move to airtight containers, storing in the refrigerator up to 2 to 3 weeks, or freeze for later use.

Use fresh ripe heirloom tomatoes when possible. Fresh vegetables do not come out of the ground in a uniform manner, although the grocery store varieties may look that way. Never make conserve with the pale pink tomatoes that march like identical soldiers in a box. They are tasteless and not worth the effort. If using canned tomatoes, use the finest available, avoiding cheaper store brands.

FRUIT BUTTERS & SPREADS

Fruit butters and spreads are quick answers to real questions—whether at breakfast, lunch, dinner, or snack times in particular.

PEACH BUTTER

Makes 4 pints

THIS IS ASTONISHING AS A SPREAD *for buttered biscuits, toasted biscuits, pancakes, or waffles. It is also a good filling to sandwich between small meringues or butter cookies, and is superb served with peach cobbler or other peach desserts.*

5 pounds peaches (about 14)
1 cup water
3½ cups granulated sugar
2 tablespoons fruit liqueur or peach brandy, optional
1 tablespoon candied ginger, optional

Simmer the peaches in a pot of water until the skins are easy to remove, about 30 seconds. Remove the peaches, reserving the cooking liquid. Peel and pit the peaches. Cut into large pieces and purée, using an immersion blender, food processor, or blender. Measure the purée and add reserved cooking liquid if necessary to make about 8½ cups total.

Add the peaches and juice to the sugar in a heavy pan and cook uncovered over low heat about 3 hours, until thick, stirring occasionally. Taste and add liqueur or brandy and cook a few minutes more. Add the ginger if desired.

Remove from the heat. Cool and move to airtight containers, storing in the refrigerator up to 2 to 3 weeks, or freeze until ready to use.

FIG JAM OR BUTTER

Makes about 1 1/2 cups

At first, my figs *come out on the tree a few at a time, and we relish them. Then comes a big rush, when we must pick a quantity every day, poking far under the tree branches to find the ones hidden away, fighting the birds and squirrels for the ones on top. When we have too many to eat before they over-ripen, we throw them into a pot and cook them. Their volume is greatly reduced during the cooking process, and it always makes me a little wistful until I taste the condensed and focused flavor of the jam. This goes very well with biscuits or other breakfast breads and makes a great surprise gift for family, friends, and neighbors.*

- 4 cups halved figs
- 1/2 cup water
- 2 tablespoons honey
- 1/4 cup red or white wine vinegar or sherry
- 3 teaspoons chopped candied ginger
- 1/8 teaspoon salt
- 2 tablespoons unsalted butter, softened

Move all ingredients except butter to a pot. Simmer uncovered for about 45 minutes, or until the figs are soft.

Purée the mixture using an immersion blender, food processor, or blender. Add butter, and stir until well-blended. Cool and move to airtight containers, storing in the refrigerator up to 2 to 3 weeks.

BAKED FIGS AND FENNEL

Makes 1 1/2 cups

I am a glutton when it comes to both figs *and fennel. I never give away my homegrown figs, and when they are gone, I purchase any figs I see. I use fennel in everything, from fish and figs to salads and zucchini. This condiment is glorious to serve with any meat. Or steal down to the refrigerator in the middle of the night and spread it on a sandwich with cheese and other leftover bits and pieces.*

- 6 large ripe figs, quartered, or 12 small ripe figs, halved, stems removed
- 2 cups sliced fennel (about 4 small fennel bulbs)
- 2 tablespoons oil, cook's preference
- 1/4 cup sherry vinegar
- 2 tablespoons light or dark brown sugar
- Salt
- Freshly ground black pepper

Preheat oven to 400 degrees. Line a baking pan with parchment paper or foil. Move the figs and fennel to the pan.

Whisk together the oil, vinegar, and sugar. Season to taste with salt and pepper. Pour over the fennel and figs, and bake for 20 minutes, until tender and browned.

Move fennel and figs to a large platter and drizzle with the pan juices. This may be made ahead and refrigerated. Reheat or serve cold as a spread.

EASY REFRIGERATOR STRAWBERRY JAM

Makes 3 cups

THERE WAS A TIME WHEN THE LAND *surrounding Charleston, South Carolina, was the strawberry capital of the East Coast. The strawberries came out here before anywhere else and were shipped up in trains with blocks of ice. Then came refrigeration, and Florida became the mecca for growing strawberries. After the mid-1960s, Gainesville, Florida, became the boundary line of Southern foodies for what they considered the land of Southern food.*

This recipe doesn't require any pectin, making it easy to throw together without another trip to the store.

2 pounds fresh strawberries, hulled

4 cups granulated sugar

1/4 cup fresh lemon juice

Place two saucers in the freezer for testing the jam.

Crush the strawberries in batches to make 4 cups of mashed berries. Stir the strawberries, sugar, and lemon juice together in a heavy pan over low heat until the sugar is dissolved.

Turn up the heat to high, and bring the mixture to the boil. Boil, stirring often, until the mixture reaches 220 degrees. Spoon a little of the mixture onto one of the saucers from the freezer and return it to the freezer briefly to cool down; then push the mixture with your finger until it "crinkles," or leaves a soft trail. If it is not thick enough to leave a trail, bring the fruit back to the boil and test again in a few minutes on the second plate. If it doesn't run together, it is ready. Cool and move to airtight containers, storing in the refrigerator up to 2 to 3 weeks.

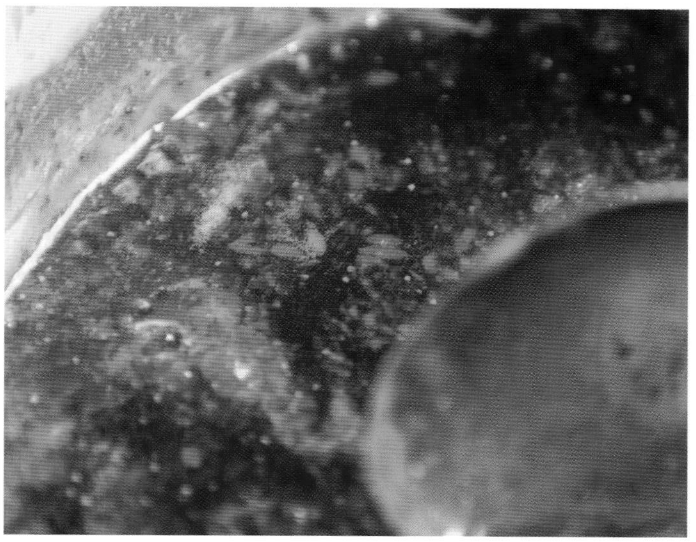

ONION JAM

Makes 1 quart

THIS THICK CONSERVE IS SWEET ENOUGH *to spread on bread but is a fabulous condiment on meats and vegetables. This technique calls for sweating the onions, covered, over low heat to extrude their juices before adding the other ingredients. This is very different from the Grilled Onion Relish (page 643) but can be used much the same way.*

4 tablespoons unsalted butter
5 pounds yellow onions, thinly sliced
3/4 cup granulated sugar

1 cup red wine vinegar
1 cup red wine
1/4 cup dry sherry, optional

1 1/2 teaspoons freshly ground black pepper

Melt the butter in a large heavy pot with a lid. Add the onions, cover, and cook over low heat for at least 30 minutes, taking care they do not burn. The onions will create their own juice.

Uncover and stir in rest of the ingredients. Bring to the boil, quickly reduce heat, cover, and cook over a low heat at least 30 minutes, checking occasionally and stirring if necessary, until the mixture thickens like jam.

Cool and move to airtight containers, storing in the refrigerator up to 2 to 3 weeks, or freeze for later use.

HOT PEPPER JELLY

Makes about 8 cups

PEPPER JELLY CAN BE MADE WITH ANY KIND OF PEPPER. *The pepper jelly I first made was from a pepper shaped much like a horn, called "cow horn pepper"—a misnomer that should have perhaps been called "bull horn pepper." Three or four times the size of a Tabasco or jalapeño pepper, it made a mildly hot jelly. Now the market is flooded with pepper jellies made from every kind of pepper—some of which are a bit too hot for me, like the feisty Scotch Bonnet—including bell peppers, which are hardly suitable for a region where homemade hot sauce made from hot peppers and vinegar used to sit on every kitchen table for sprinkling on food during the meal.*

1 cup seeded and coarsely chopped hot peppers, red, green, and/or yellow
1 medium onion, chopped
1½ cups apple cider vinegar
5 cups granulated sugar
1 pouch liquid pectin

Process the peppers, onion, and vinegar in a food processor or blender until the vegetables are very finely chopped. Add to the sugar in a heavy nonaluminum pot. Bring to the boil and boil for 1 minute, remove from the heat, and stir in the pectin. Return to the heat, bring to the boil, and boil 1 minute longer.

Let the jelly sit for 5 minutes before skimming off the foam. Pour into clean containers, and keep refrigerated. Turn the jars upside down occasionally to keep the peppers mixed until the jelly is cool and set.

Variation: Pepper jelly is used as a sweet-hot condiment for nearly everything. It sparks up pork, ham, or goat or cream cheese as a starter, or can be dolloped on a piece of chicken nestled in a biscuit. It is also used to glaze or accompany chicken and pork, or is melted as a sauce, as with country ham.

MANAGING PEPPER HEAT

As a general rule, the smaller the pepper the hotter, with the exception, perhaps, of the Spanish padrone pepper or its cousin the Japanese shishito pepper. The hottest part of a pepper is the membrane nearest the stem end, which sits inside next to the interior of the skin where it first transfers its hotness. It is important to remove the membrane and seeds judiciously, using plastic gloves or bags to protect the hands and, later, the eyes and mouth from residual heat. If there is just a small quantity of peppers, the tip of a peeler will aid by sliding it right up the halved pepper, removing seeds and part of the interior. A larger quantity goes faster by pushing a finger up the middle. Keep the peppers covered with a lid, towel, or waxed paper while working in batches, to keep the air free of the burning aromas. Once the pepper jelly is finished, it is so good that the pain is forgotten.

MARMALADE

Making orange marmalade in Charleston is quite a different thing from making it in Spain or England, where I learned the process. For one thing, we don't grow the preferred Seville oranges. We use Valencia (Florida) or other thin-skinned Florida or South Carolina oranges, even those with a brushing of green on their skins. Of course, the skin of these oranges has not been softened by riding in the bottom of a big ship as ballast, as was once done.

I read a number of cookbooks while trying to determine the best method. My favorite was the *Grand Diplome,* an American version of a London Cordon Bleu series. It was the only one to suggest reducing the amount of sugar, if using Valencia oranges rather than Seville.

The pith (the white part) of the orange may be left on or scraped off. I leave it on. Taking it off is arduous and makes the marmalade overly sweet. If the pith is removed, it must be added to the cheesecloth along with the seeds. This cheesecloth sack adds the necessary pectin to gel the marmalade.

Many recipes called for boiling the oranges whole before slicing them and continuing to cook them. It is much easier to slice the oranges first, soak them overnight to soften them, and then cook them with the sugar.

The sugar, as in any sugar syrup, needs to be dissolved before the mixture starts to boil to prevent crystallization. Use a wide heavy pan. I used an old copper jelly-making pan and thought it would be too big, but in fact it was just right.

Marmalade thickens as it cools, so don't overcook.

ORANGE-LEMON MARMALADE

Makes 4 to 6 cups

MY PHYSICIAN, WHO ALSO PLAYS BRIDGE WITH MY HUSBAND, *loves marmalade jam and has an orange tree that produces an abundance of oranges, so he supplies these unnamed oranges and I make the marmalade. Sometimes I mix them with lemons from my tree. This also works just fine with most oranges, but the tarter the orange, the better. There is plenty of acid in this, so it can be safely eaten for some time if kept in the refrigerator.*

- 4 Valencia oranges
- 1 medium-large lemon
- Sugar, as needed

Wash and sterilize jars in boiling water or in the dishwasher.

Slice the oranges and lemon in half, and then slice each one into 1/8-inch-thick slices. Cut a large square of cheesecloth. Save the seeds and move them, along with any pith or odd trimmings, to the cheesecloth and tie with a long cotton string, discarding only the cores.

Chop the remaining fruit. Move to a nonaluminum container with a lid. Soak the lemons, oranges, and cheesecloth in 4 to 5 cups water for 24 hours.

To prepare the marmalade, place 2 saucers in the freezer for testing purposes. Measure the fruit and water. Add 3/4 cup of sugar for every cup of fruit and water, along with the cheesecloth and seeds, and move to a wide, heavy, nonaluminum-lined pan.

Brush down the sides of the pans with a pastry brush dipped in water to prevent sugar crystals. Bring to the boil and boil steadily 20 to 30 minutes, until citrus is a light copper color or thermometer registers 218 to 220 degrees. Spoon a little of the mixture onto one of the saucers from the freezer and return it to the freezer briefly to cool down; then push the mixture with your finger until it "crinkles," or leaves a soft trail. If it is not thick enough to leave a trail, bring the fruit back to the boil and test again in a few minutes on the second plate.

When ready, gently squeeze the remaining liquid from the cheesecloth using the side of the pan, and discard the bag. Allow the marmalade to rest for 20 minutes.

Heat the clean jars in a 350-degree oven for approximately 5 minutes. Use a funnel and ladle to help pour the marmalade into the jars. Seal according to proper canning methods while the jars are still warm. Allow to cool and then label. Turn jars upside down and right side up every hour or so until cool to distribute fruit evenly.

Variations: Spread on bread, Sally Lunn (page 490), a biscuit, or baked pork or chicken.

SAUCES

If there is a better description of sauces than Irma Rombauer's in the *Joy of Cooking*, I don't know it. She calls them the "old dowagers who try to dominate sauciety." It is indeed hard to get away from their caste system. There is a lack of boundaries, however, as they cross over each other and nothing is as exacting as the "sauciety" would like it to be, even more so here than in the rigid system of the French Mother sauces.

Sauces enhance and embellish the plainest of foods, whether jumping in the mouth or caressing the tongue. There are those who want every meat to be sauced and others who love simple pan juices. I tend to omit rich sauces when serving just family but frequently use them when making a company meal special. I keep refrigerated and frozen bits of sauces around, adding them to other sauces to combine them—adding a tablespoon of hollandaise sauce, for instance, to a bit of leftover white sauce rather than wasting either. What looks peculiar on its own, such as a frozen cube of basil sauce, changes an entire meal when added to leftover White Butter Sauce.

Pan sauce—The most basic sauce is a pan sauce (page 667) without any additional thickenings, using the luscious juices from the pan and their natural viscosity to thicken. To make a pan sauce, remove food and fat from the pan and keep warm. Leave the bits and pieces of meats and vegetables in the bottom of the pain, as well as any liquid. Taste the fat-free liquid. If it tastes "thin," bring it to the boil, stirring to get the unburned goodness off the bottom and sides (deglazing page 357) and boil briefly until it thickens (called thickening by reduction). If it is too thick, add a bit of water, stock, milk, cream, lemon juice, wine, dry vermouth, sherry, Madeira, bourbon or other liquor, juice, or other appropriate liquid to thin and flavor, and stir as above. Bring to the boil, taste again, and season with salt and pepper as desired.

Glace de viande—Further thickening of a pan sauce may come from the juices of meats and fowls (such as roast beef, turkey, or chicken). They frequently form a thick sauce that will jell when cold. (Its technical name is *glace de viande*—roughly translated as "glaze of the meat.") This special treat should be used as the base for another gravy or sauce. Add a bit of water to thin out, and the resulting juice (called a demi-glaze or half-glaze) makes a sauce on its own. (See turkey recipe on page 374; roasted chicken recipe on page 366.) In good sauces, every bit of flavor is retained, every nutrient saved, making something else better.

Flour-thickened sauces—These are the next basic type of sauce. They are thickened primarily by mixing flour with butter or oil. Stirring the flour and fat in the liquid over heat until it comes to the boil is necessary so the starch granules can swell and thicken. A hot liquid may be added to a cold roux and brought up to the boil, stirring, or a cold liquid may be added to a hot roux and stirred until it comes up to the boil. The easiest way is to heat the fat, stir in the flour to make a roux (page 655), cook lightly, add a room-temperature or cold liquid, bring to the boil, and thoroughly cook the flour while stirring. (Professional chefs whisk in boiling or hot liquid to cook the flour, and strain if there are lumps.) The color of the fat or roux changes the flavor, as does the color of the liquid, going from white sauce to brown or creole sauce.

Browned flour and roux may be made in quantities and refrigerated or frozen, to be used in portions as needed. Browned flour has less thickening power than the flour in other roux (page 655 for pictures of roux).

Ratio of flour to liquid for thickening—1 1/2 tablespoons of fat and 1 1/2 to 2 tablespoons of flour to 1 cup of liquid makes a medium-thick sauce. To make a thick sauce, use 3 tablespoons of flour.

Butter and oil sauces—These sauces vary as well. Pesto, for instance, is a simple oil sauce. Butter sauces range from melted white to brown butter by itself, to white butter sauces, to butter added at the end of a sauce to give it a shine and a bit of thickness. Butter is added to a warm, not boiling, liquid so it will keep its thickness. As a rule of thumb, butter sauces will separate if boiled unless emulsified (page 102).

Egg-based emulsified sauces—These include mayonnaise (a cold oil-based sauce) and hollandaise (a hot butter sauce). Whisk the eggs thoroughly with a little liquid until they thicken, turn pale yellow, and begin to cling to the whisk a bit. Whisk in the fat, slowly at first, until the incorporated mixture clings to the whisk and the bottom of the bowl or pan can be seen between whisking. Then another bit of fat may be added and whisked in. After there is enough air whisked in for the fat to have a place to go, add the fat more quickly. If it is thin or starts to separate, a little water may help. If that doesn't work, and the whole thing is a mess, start with a clean bowl and, if possible, another egg and liquid or some commercial mayonnaise, and whisk the curdled mixture slowly into the thickened mixture. If no egg is available, whisk a small quantity of the curdled mixture in the clean bowl until it is emulsified and then add the remaining curdled mixture slowly as above.

Heating helps thicken an egg and butter sauce, such as a hollandaise, but may also evaporate the liquid, causing the sauce to separate. A little water will bring it back. If the temperature is too high, the eggs will scramble (egg yolks cook at 180 degrees). In this case, straining may help but not always. It will taste good, but whether or not to use it in this state is something only the cook can decide. Don't discard, however; repurpose it by calling it something else—like "grated egg-butter-lemon sauce."

Tomato sauces—These are certainly an important part of Southern cuisine.

Prepared sauces—Sauces are also part of other sauces—soy sauce, Worcestershire sauce, and other prepared sauces are part of other sauces just as much as tomato sauce or hollandaise might be added to a white sauce.

Marinades—Marinades such as the Mint-Mustard Sauce (page 447) with the boned leg of lamb are frequently treated as a reduced sauce as well, only needing boiling to ensure the uncooked food does not contaminate the cooked food.

Don't take sauces too seriously—they can usually be fixed.

Thickeners

Cornstarch slurry—1 tablespoon cornstarch equals 2 tablespoons flour (use half as much corn starch as flour). To thicken, mix an equal amount of cornstarch with an equal amount or more of cold water; this is called a slurry. Mix until smooth before adding to hot liquid. Boil gently 2 minutes. One tablespoon will thicken 1 1/2 to 2 cups liquid. When cooking dessert sauces, particularly those that become clear due to the cornstarch, use a *bain-marie* (water bath) or double boiler until the raw taste of the cornstarch disappears. Overbeating thins cornstarch-based sauces.

Arrowroot—One of the lightest of the thickeners, it should be served within 10 minutes of using; it will neither reheat nor hold and doesn't need to be boiled to thicken. This is good in a pinch when thickening needs to be done quickly, or when a delicate egg sauce needs a bit more thickening. The ratio is 2 1/2 teaspoons arrowroot to 1 cup liquid.

Egg thickeners—Eggs (usually yolks) are a light thickener, called a liaison, or a temporary thickening that will not take too much heat. Add some of the warm—not hot—liquid to the yolks to help the eggs warm up, swell, and thicken, and then add the egg mixture to the deglazed and reduced liquid in the pan. Bring carefully up to about 180 degrees. (If there is already flour in the mixture, it can go up to 210 degrees.) The ratio is 3 egg yolks to thicken 1 cup liquid.

Odds and ends—Jams, jellies, conserves, tomato sauce, mayonnaise, heavy cream, cheese, vegetable and fruit purées, and many other oddities may be used to thicken pan juices.

Kneaded butter *(beurre manié)*—Knead butter and flour together. Add slowly on the back of a spoon, rubbing against the hot sides of the pan until they melt in and the sauce thickens.

Butter—Swirl the pan of nearly finished sauce while adding dots of butter at the last minute to give a gloss and thicken a sauce. Pour right away without any further stirring or whisking.

TWO TRICKY THICKENERS

1. Mixing fat and flour together, adding around the edge of a pan of hot liquid, and boiling ever so briefly to cook the flour.
2. Adding hot liquid to lightly whisked eggs, then returning this liquid to the pot as in the first method is called "a liaison of eggs," as it is not a permanent arrangement. Too much heat breaks it and not enough heat thins it, hence, a liaison, not a marriage.

HOLLANDAISE SAUCE

Makes 1 cup

A HOLLANDAISE IS AN EMULSIFIED SAUCE, *as is béarnaise, white butter sauce, and mayonnaise. The water and lemon keep the sauce light and aid in emulsifying the egg and oil. This is an unorthodox manner of making a hollandaise, but it works for my students every time. Rather than using a metal double boiler pan, which invariably heats up too much or too little, I use a glass heatproof bowl set into a pan of simmering water. (This is a variation of a bain-marie, or water bath.) The trick is to ignore the pan of water and concentrate on the temperature of the egg mixture, preferably using an instant-read thermometer. The glass helps slow the cooking and lets the cook see what's happening in the bowl. The defining temperature is 170 degrees, although a sauce may be thickened satisfactorily at 160 degrees on occasion. At any rate, the temperature must be kept below boiling yet be hot enough to cook the egg yolks and let them swell. For more information on emulsions,* *see page 102.*

4 egg yolks
Juice of 1 lemon, divided
1 tablespoon water
Boiling water
8 tablespoons butter, cut into 1/4-inch pieces
Salt
1/8 teaspoon ground hot red pepper

Move a heavy glass heatproof bowl containing the egg yolks, 2 tablespoons lemon juice, and 1 tablespoon water into a frying pan that has 2 inches of simmering water in the bottom (a bain-marie). Whisk the yolk mixture steadily for 5 minutes, or until thick, keeping the mixture in the bowl under 180 degrees, preferably at 160 degrees. (The water may be boiling as long as the mixture is not too hot. Do not let the water evaporate.) Slowly add the butter piece by piece, whisking after each addition, still keeping under 180 degrees. Season to taste with salt and hot red pepper.

If the sauce doesn't thicken, turn up the heat, but be sure the temperature of the sauce remains below 180 degrees. If the sauce separates, add water to bring it back. (If the eggs for a hollandaise heat over 180 degrees, they will be scrambled. Try straining the sauce quickly to see if it can cool and to catch any hardened egg. If still scrambled, call it a scrambled egg sauce or start over.) The hollandaise may be made up to 1 hour ahead of time and kept in the bain-marie, covered with waxed paper or plastic wrap to prevent it forming a skin. It may also be refrigerated and reheated carefully in the bain-marie.

Variations:

- For Red Pepper Hollandaise, add 1 red bell pepper (roasted, peeled, chopped, and drained of juices) to the hollandaise just before serving.
- For Herbed Hollandaise, add 1 tablespoon fresh chopped dill, thyme, or tarragon.
- For Gingered Hollandaise, add 1 tablespoon minced fresh ginger.
- For Mustard Hollandaise, add 2 to 3 tablespoons Dijon mustard.
- Add 1/2 cup dry white wine to a small saucepan and boil until reduced to 1 to 2 tablespoons liquid. Substitute this for the lemon juice. Proceed with other variations if desired.
- For Béarnaise Sauce, substitute 1 chopped shallot cooked in 1/3 cup of white wine vinegar until reduced to 1 tablespoon. Add chopped tarragon to taste. Strain if desired. This is often served with French fried potatoes in Louisiana.

MENDING A HOLLANDAISE SAUCE

To bring back a separated hollandaise, first add 1 to 2 tablespoons water. It may be separating because there is not enough liquid or because it did not get hot enough.

If it still does not come back, move a small portion of the curdled mixture and 2 tablespoons water or lemon juice to a clean, heavy pan. Whisk until smooth, and then add the remaining curdled mixture, little by little.

Alternatively, start with a fresh egg yolk, whisk until thick, and then slowly add the curdled mixture.

REHEATING HOLLANDAISE AND BUTTER SAUCES

Experienced cooks can reheat hollandaise and other butter sauces easily because they know the temperatures of their stovetops. Commercial stoves have an "apron" that is not as hot as the rest of the stove, and many times the sauce may be held there during service. However, in this day of salmonella worries, it is best to hold the hollandaise no more than an hour at a lukewarm temperature.

If the sauce must be made ahead of time, practice refrigerating and reheating it. Reheat in a bain-marie, whisking the whole time, until it reaches at least 160 degrees. Have at hand a white sauce (pages 654–55), and if the hollandaise sauce melts and separates, unwilling to come together no matter how much you whisk it, spoon the broken sauce slowly into the white sauce. It will still be a nice sauce, although perhaps not as light as possible. Either way, whether serving as melted lemon butter or lemon white sauce, change the name to suit the situation and don't apologize.

SLAKING

Slake by whisking 4 portions of liquid into 2 portions of flour or 1 of cornstarch, corn flour, arrowroot, tapioca, or other thickening agents until smooth. Add a bit of the hot liquid from the pan to the whisked mixture, making sure it is smooth, and pour the whole flour or cornstarch mixture into the pan juices. Return to the boil. Boil as necessary, no more than 2 minutes for cornstarch. If thickening with arrowroot, sour cream, or yogurt, watch very carefully when heating, and avoid boiling. If it is clear at the time the food is removed that the remaining liquid is never going to be thick enough, taste then leave enough of the fat in the pan to mix with flour to make a roux that will thicken the liquid and make a pan gravy. Heat the fat, add the flour, and stir until smooth (see Roux, page 655). Add any of the above liquids, stirring the bottom.

WHITE SAUCE

Makes 1 cup

THIS CLASSIC SAUCE, *called* béchamel *in French cooking and also known as white gravy, is useful to coat vegetables, fish, chicken, and meat. It is also the base for soufflés and other dishes; hence, it is known as a "mother" sauce. As subsequent ingredients are added (such as cheese, curry, or onions), the name of the sauce changes.*

When a white sauce or gravy is made in a pan in which something has been cooked that renders fat, such as sausage, turkey, or chicken, remove any pan juices and set aside, leaving 2 tablespoons of fat in place of the butter in this recipe. Stir the flour into the fat, followed by the milk. The pan juices may be added back in for more flavor but will thin the sauce. If the bits in the pan are brown, this sauce will become more of a bronze color, as the roux will be brown (facing).

2 tablespoons butter
2 tablespoons flour
1 cup strained Flavored Milk (page 657)
Salt to taste

Melt the butter in a heavy saucepan. Add the flour and stir briefly until smooth. This is a "blond" roux and may be made in advance, even in large quantities. Add the milk all at once. Stir with a wooden spoon until the mixture boils and is smooth. If lumps remain, strain. To prevent a skin forming, cover the sauce with a piece of plastic wrap.

Note: Chefs and other professionals frequently add hot liquid to a hot roux. I find it easier to have roux and liquid at alternate temperatures—i.e., a hot roux with a cold liquid or a cold roux with a hot liquid—so the flour doesn't cook immediately and lump. As cooks gain experience, more leeway can be taken.

Variation: Dijon Sauce
Whisk in 2 or 3 tablespoons Dijon mustard to the white sauce, to taste.

Variation: Curried Béchamel
Add 1 teaspoon to 1 tablespoon curry powder to the white sauce.

Variation: Mornay Sauce
Add $1/2$ cup grated cheese, such as sharp white Cheddar or Gruyère. Add a small bit of Dijon mustard; it will bring out the cheese flavor.

Variation: Cream Gravy
Leave 2 tablespoons of fat from meat or pan drippings in a skillet, or add to a pan and heat. Stir 2 tablespoons flour into the fat a few minutes, until nearly nut-colored. Add 1 cup milk or cream and stir over heat until it boils down and is thick. Serve with potatoes, tomatoes, biscuits, or cornbread. It will wilt crisp meat or chicken, so put it on the side. Season well with freshly ground black pepper.

Variation: Onion Sauce
A plain sauce becomes an onion sauce (in French, *soubise*) with the addition of soft and translucent onions. Add sliced apples or pears for yet another variation.

Melt 2 tablespoons butter in a saucepan and add 1 chopped onion. Cover onion with a piece of parchment or waxed paper to encourage it to "sweat," and put out light moisture. Cook over low heat until the onion is soft and translucent. Let the onions turn caramel-colored and a totally different sauce ensues. Add to the white sauce.

Variation: Turnip Green Sauce
Boil 2 chopped shallots with the juice of 1 lemon until the liquid is nearly gone. Add 2 cups heavy cream and 4 tablespoons butter, and boil until thick, about 5 minutes. Add $1\frac{1}{2}$ pounds blanched and chopped turnip greens (well-drained).

When the first asparagus comes out of the ground, it tastes so of spring we are happy to let it have full attention on the plate. But as the season wears on and we eat it day after day, sauces come to mind. Hm. How about a hollandaise? Or melting butter sauce and tossing the asparagus in it over the heat? Or would the butter sauce be better if a little tomato conserve was added to it and it was put over the accompanying chicken? Or should the chicken be topped with hot pepper jelly? Whether made at the last minute or lingering in the refrigerator or freezer, these preparations bring further tastes of the South, and combine to make our cuisine one of the best.

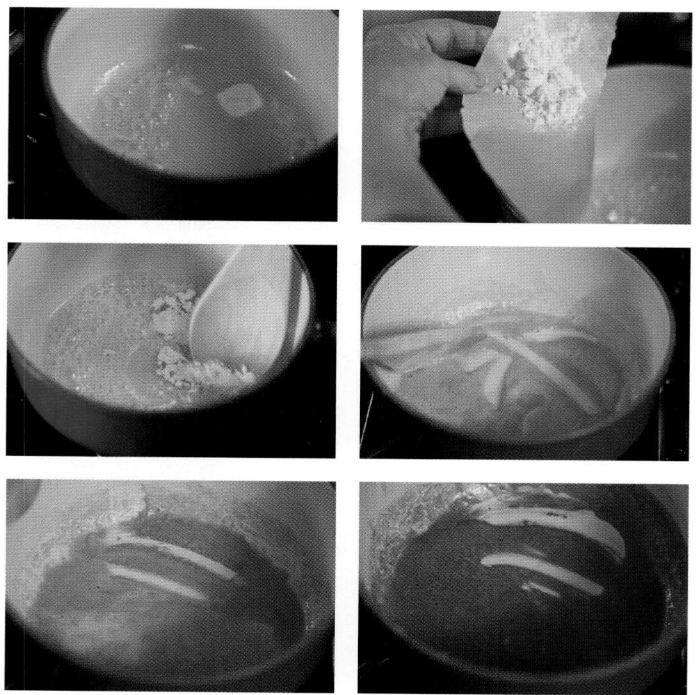

ROUX

When the combination of fat and flour changes color, the flavor of the sauce changes. The first stage is white; the next stage is light tan; the next is the color of a pecan; and then dark, nearly burned, for the roux used in Creole and Cajun cooking.

The term *roux* can be confusing, as it means different things to different people. A roux in this recipe, as well as in many Louisiana and Mississippi recipes, means a mahogany brown roux of fat and flour. These roux are also sold commercially, as is browned flour that some people use with butter or oil. In French and other cooking, a roux is melted fat with flour added. It may be white (*blanc*), blonde (*blond*), brown (*brun*) or nutty brown (*noisette*).

WHITE BUTTER SAUCE

Makes $1^1/_2$ cups

A WHITE BUTTER SAUCE *(*beurre blanc *in French) is a versatile and sophisticated sauce with vegetables, seafood, eggs, poultry, or meat. It's also a very good substitute for hollandaise and béarnaise, both of which require eggs. This sauce became popular in the South in the early 1970s. While the thought of attempting to make a butter sauce can be daunting to some, it's worth the attempt. Even a failed white butter sauce will taste scrumptious stirred into vegetables, rice, or grains. Although it has no eggs, it is still an emulsified sauce.*

The main thing to remember when making this sauce is to be careful not to overheat it. While heat is needed to melt the cold butter, too much heat—as in rapidly boiling water—may cause the sauce to break, or separate into oil and liquid. A little practice will make perfect—finding the right pan and heat may take a few tries. Restaurant cooks use the "apron" of their stovetops, which maintains an even heat, to keep white sauce warm. Even if the sauce breaks, it is usable and may even be "saved" according to the directions below. And, of course, if a sauce breaks, call it a melted butter.

2/3 cup fresh lemon juice (or other acid, see variation below)
2 tablespoons minced shallots
1 1/2 cups butter, cut into 1-inch pieces
Salt
Freshly ground black pepper

Combine lemon juice and shallots in a small to medium-sized saucepan. Bring to the boil and boil until the liquid is reduced to 2 tablespoons. If it is less than that, add water.

Turn heat to low and whisk in butter one piece at a time. If what looks like oil appears in the otherwise creamy yellow sauce, remove the pot from the heat and set it over ice, or add a little water or crushed ice to the sauce. Cooling it just a little might save the sauce from breaking. Season to taste with salt and pepper.

If the sauce is too tart, add a little water, more butter, or granulated sugar to correct. Serve right away, or cover the top with plastic wrap to prevent a skin from forming, and leave at room temperature or refrigerate.

Many times the temperature of the food will be sufficient to reheat it. To reheat the sauce on the stove, add a little of the cold sauce to a small saucepan over low heat. Whisk sauce until it thickens, adding additional small portions of cold sauce to the pan, whisking continuously, until the entire sauce is reheated.

Variations:

- Add small pieces of Caramelized Pineapple (page 66), to the completed sauce for a tropical fruit flavor. For a more subtle fruit flavor, add peeled and chopped fresh peaches.
- A spoonful or so of Tomato Conserve (page 644) added to the completed sauce provides sweetness and color.
- Adding a bit of Hot Pepper Jelly (page 648) will liven it up.
- Red butter sauce is made with red wine. Other acids may be used in place of the lemon juice. Try using 1/2 cup dry white wine, or 2 tablespoons white wine vinegar, or a combination.
- Add 1 to 3 chopped garlic cloves with the shallots.
- Add 1 tablespoon grated or chopped fresh ginger to the lemon juice and vinegar.

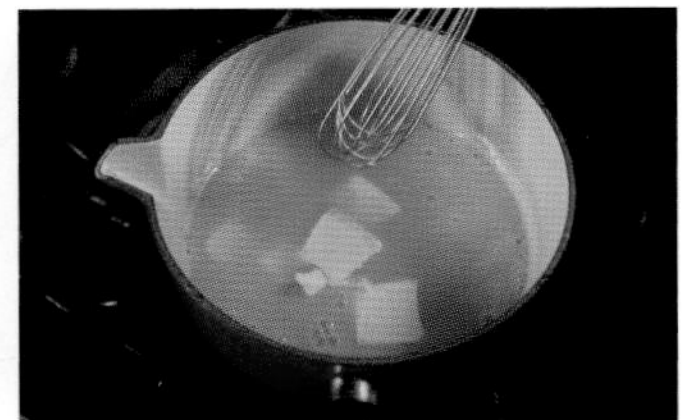
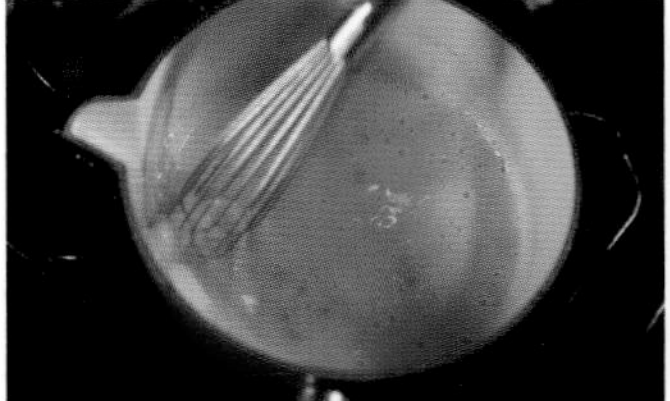

KEEPING WHITE BUTTER SAUCE

A white butter sauce is great to have on hand and can be kept in the refrigerator or frozen. While it's possible for the sauce to stay together in the refrigerator, it is more difficult to keep it together in the freezer. Fortunately, it is still usable. To use it frozen, or if the whole thing melts into a mess, toss hot vegetables or other ingredients into enough of the sauce to coat lightly; miraculously they will gleam and are mouthwatering.

FLAVORED MILK

Makes 1 to 2 cups

ANY TIME MILK IS USED IN A SAVORY RECIPE—*from a white sauce to a quiche or soufflé—it is worth taking a little extra effort to flavor the milk. It enhances the end product immensely. Add bits and pieces as in a brown stock, using anything in the refrigerator that would enhance the flavor. Even onion and carrot peels can be used to flavor the milk. Do take care with celery leaf, as it is very strong and can dominate.*

1–2 cups milk
1 slice onion
1 slice celery
1 slice carrot
1 slice fennel bulb
Peppercorns as desired
Thyme, parsley stalk, as desired

Heat milk in a saucepan or a glass measuring cup in the microwave with any of or all of the ingredients until warm and nearly at a simmer. Remove from heat and sit 1/2 hour at room temperature or more in the fridge. Strain before using.

CREOLE BROWN FISH SAUCE

Makes 2 1/2 cups

THIS IS CALLED BROWN FISH SAUCE *because it calls for either a traditional brown stock like canned beef bouillon or is made from browning fish bones and vegetables. The finishing step makes it a full-bodied, glossy, rich sauce.*

13 tablespoons butter, cut into pieces, divided
5 tablespoons all-purpose flour
1 cup fish stock or brown stock (page 113) or broth
2 tablespoons chopped fresh parsley
1 tablespoon Worcestershire sauce
Juice of 1/2 lemon

Melt 5 tablespoons of the butter and cook until it turns a rich brown color. Stir in flour and cook until pecan brown. Pour in the stock and bring to the boil, stirring constantly. Reduce heat to a simmer.

To finish the sauce, whisk in the remaining butter, parsley, and Worcestershire sauce, and without boiling, cook until the butter is completely absorbed into the sauce. Add lemon juice and whisk again until smooth.

PEPPER JELLY SAUCE

Makes about 1 1/2 cups

RED HOT PEPPER JELLY *is used frequently as a sauce, either by itself or added to onion sauce or other cream or chicken stock sauces.*

1 tablespoon oil, cook's preference
2 tablespoons butter
1 pound onions, sliced lengthwise
1 cup heavy cream, or 1/2–1 cup chicken stock or broth
1/2 cup Hot Pepper Jelly (page 648)
Salt
Freshly ground black pepper

Heat the oil and butter; add the onions and cook until soft and browned, about 15 minutes.

Stir in the cream or stock and bring to the boil; then reduce heat, add the jelly, and stir until melted. Bring to the boil and boil until somewhat reduced, about 2 minutes. Season to taste with salt and pepper.

May be made ahead and reheated carefully over low heat while stirring. Serve with roasted pork or chicken.

RED BELL PEPPER DIP OR SAUCE

Makes 3 to 4 cups

Onion dip was once a standard party *and chip dip in the South. Now it is replaced with fresh dips and sauces like this one. Three roasted red peppers yield approximately 1 cup of purée. Vary the amounts of herbs as needed.*

2 whole garlic heads
5 tablespoons olive oil, divided
4 roasted red bell peppers, chopped
1 pound soft goat cheese
1/2 cup finely chopped fresh basil
1 tablespoon finely chopped fresh thyme
2 tablespoons finely chopped fresh rosemary
1/4 teaspoon ground hot red pepper
Salt
Freshly ground black pepper

Preheat oven to 325 degrees.

Peel off the paper layer around the garlic heads and break the heads into cloves. Toss the unpeeled cloves with 1 tablespoon olive oil and bake on a well-oiled rimmed baking sheet for 45 minutes. Remove when soft. Cool, and pop the garlic out of their peels.

Process the garlic, bell peppers, and cheese in a blender or food processor until smooth.

Add the remaining oil, basil, thyme, rosemary, and hot red pepper. Season to taste with salt and pepper.

Cover and chill. Keep refrigerated until ready to serve. Store up to 1 week in the refrigerator.

COCKTAIL SAUCE

Makes 4 cups

My husband loves making this, *as he will not eat plain cooked shrimp without it, just as I won't eat them without melted butter. This sauce is good on any seafood.*

4 cups ketchup (or 2 cups ketchup and 2 cups chili sauce)
2 tablespoons Dijon mustard
6 tablespoons horseradish
2 tablespoons fresh lemon juice
3 tablespoons red wine vinegar
Salt
Freshly ground black pepper

Pour the ketchup into a large bowl. Whisk in the mustard, horseradish, lemon juice, and vinegar. Season to taste with salt and pepper. Chill at least 2 hours before serving.

TARTAR SAUCE

Makes 1 cup

For many, it is impossible to eat fried fish *without tartar sauce. Homemade or commercial mayonnaise can be used.*

1 cup mayonnaise
1/4 cup finely chopped red onion
2 tablespoons finely chopped capers
1 teaspoon Dijon mustard

Scoop the mayonnaise into a small bowl. Stir in the red onion, capers, and mustard. Refrigerate several hours before using.

Variation: Spicy Tartar Sauce
Add 1 to 2 finely chopped jalapeño peppers and a dash of hot sauce to the tartar sauce.

CREOLE RÉMOULADE SAUCE

Makes 2 cups

I learned this recipe *in Commander's Palace Restaurant in New Orleans when I worked briefly in the kitchen with Chef Paul Prudhomme. It is the Creole alternative to a French* rémoulade *sauce, a derivative of mayonnaise, and is used for a variety of purposes. Creole mustard is not crucial but much preferred and may be purchased in upscale markets or on-line.*

1 1/2 cups mayonnaise (page 103)
1/4–1/2 cup prepared mustard, preferably Creole
2 tablespoons paprika
1 teaspoon ground hot red pepper
1 teaspoon salt
1/2 cup white vinegar
1 cup finely chopped green onions
Dash of hot sauce
1/2 cup finely chopped celery
1/2 cup finely chopped fresh parsley
1/2 cup ketchup
2 garlic cloves, chopped

Whisk or blend together the mayonnaise, 1/4 cup mustard, paprika, hot red pepper, salt, vinegar, green onions, hot sauce, celery, parsley, ketchup, and garlic. Stir in the lemon juice. Taste. Add 1/4 cup more mustard if desired. Cover and chill, preferably 4 hours, before serving. Serve over cold cooked shrimp (page 327).

FENNEL SAUCE

Makes 2 cups

Fennel in particular *loves to accompany fish and pork, and so does this sauce.*

1/3 cup chopped fennel fronds
1 cup of vermouth
1 cup heavy cream
1 cup butter

Boil fennel fronds in a saucepan with vermouth. Reduce the liquid to a glaze, taking care not to evaporate completely. Add heavy cream and bring to the boil, reducing to 1/2 cup. Remove from heat. Add butter, whisking well until incorporated. Strain into a sauceboat and serve immediately.

Pass the sauce, pouring 1 spoonful on top of each fish and its juices, or in Moist Fish in Pouches (page 302), open the pouches and top each with a tablespoon or so.

NORMAN'S RÉMOULADE

Makes about 1/2 cup

CYNTHIA TAUGHT HER SON, NORMAN, *to cook as he was growing up, but just before he left for his freshman year of college in France, the teaching intensified out of necessity. Culinary directions constituted a large part of their telephone and Skype calls. Norman tends to make this sauce a little differently every time. Definitely use a preferred mustard; he uses spicy Dijon. Spoon over crab cakes, any unmolested fish dish, or favorite grilled or roasted green vegetables. Norman loves it on artichokes and green or white asparagus. In fact, he says, "If you love the tangy taste as much as I do, you can put it on almost anything. I'd dip a grilled cheese sandwich in it."*

1/2 cup mayonnaise
1 tablespoon fresh lemon juice or white wine vinegar
1/2 teaspoon garlic powder
1 heaping teaspoon Dijon mustard
Dash of Worcestershire sauce
Few drops of Tabasco or favorite hot sauce

Scoop the mayonnaise into a small bowl. Stir in the lemon juice, garlic powder to taste, mustard, Worcestershire, and hot sauce to taste. If the flavor is lacking, add a heaping teaspoon of cocktail sauce. Refrigerate a couple of hours before using to intensify the flavors.

PEANUT SAUCE OR DIP

Makes 1 cup

THIS PEANUT SAUCE, *also a dip, was developed for cold pork tenderloin but is good with any cold pork, as well as chicken.*

2 tablespoons finely chopped fresh ginger
2 garlic cloves, chopped
1/3 cup red wine vinegar
1/3 cup creamy peanut butter
1 teaspoon hot red pepper flakes, optional
1/3–1/2 cup soy sauce

Combine the ginger, garlic, red wine vinegar, peanut butter, pepper, and soy sauce in a food processor or blender. Process until well blended and refrigerate.

GINGER PEANUT SAUCE

Makes 1 1/2 cups

THIS DIPPING SAUCE *can be made in minutes in a blender or food processor. It's good for vegetables, chicken wings, and anything that likes to be dipped.*

1 cup creamy peanut butter
1 tablespoon chopped ginger
1/4 cup fresh lemon juice
1 tablespoon soy sauce
2 tablespoons water

Combine the peanut butter, ginger, lemon juice, soy sauce, and water in a food processor or blender. Purée until smooth.

TOMATO SAUCE

Makes 5 cups

THIS IS MY HOMEMADE TOMATO SAUCE. *I use a neutral oil, such as peanut, and let the tomatoes shine. It's always a good idea to use the best canned tomatoes available. A little sugar takes out any tinny taste.*

- 1/4 cup oil, cook's preference
- 2 small onions, chopped
- 2 garlic cloves, chopped
- 2 (28-ounce) cans plum tomatoes with juice, seeded and chopped
- 1/4 cup tomato paste
- 1 teaspoon–1 tablespoon each of chopped fresh oregano, basil, and thyme
- 1 tablespoon granulated sugar, optional
- Salt
- Freshly ground black pepper

Heat the oil in a heavy saucepan. Add onions and cook until soft. Add garlic and cook briefly. Stir in tomatoes, tomato paste, and herbs. Bring to the boil. Taste and add sugar if needed. Season to taste with salt and pepper. Reduce to a simmer and cook partially covered for 20 to 30 minutes, stirring occasionally.

If the sauce gets too thick, thin down with water or tomato juice. If too watery, simmer enough to reduce liquid. Purée using an immersion blender, food processor, or blender, or work through a sieve if a smooth sauce is desired. Will keep in the refrigerator covered for several weeks. Or freeze for up to 3 months.

TOMATO GRAVY

Few older recipe books even printed recipes for tomato gravy, but it lives in the memories of those who grew up with warm spoonfuls on biscuits, rice, chicken, or chops.

Heat 2 to 3 tablespoons bacon fat in a frying pan. Add 1 cup chopped onion. Sauté 5 minutes over medium-high heat. Add 1 chopped garlic clove and stir 1 minute. Add 1 tablespoon flour and stir until the flour just begins to brown, 2 to 3 minutes. Stir in 1 cup chopped peeled and seeded fresh tomatoes (or canned). Season to taste with salt and freshly ground black pepper. Cook 5 minutes, stirring well. Add 1 cup half-and-half. Reduce heat to low, and stir frequently while simmering 5 more minutes. Serve immediately.

MARINARA SAUCE

Makes 6 cups

MARINARA IS AN UPTOWN NAME *for fancying up tomato sauces. Like a tomato sauce, it is good with seafood, meat, pasta, or vegetables, and I use it interchangeably with tomato sauce.*

- 1/2 cup oil, cook's preference
- 3 medium onions, chopped
- 6 garlic cloves, chopped
- 3/4 cup red wine vinegar
- 1/4 cup red wine
- 4 pounds tomatoes, chopped, or 2 (28-ounce) cans chopped tomatoes with juice
- 3 tablespoons chopped fresh herbs such as basil, thyme, or oregano
- Salt
- Freshly ground black pepper
- Sugar

Heat oil in a large heavy pot. Add onions, and cook until soft. Add garlic and cook a few minutes more. Add vinegar and wine and bring to the boil. Reduce heat and simmer until most of the liquid is cooked away.

Add tomatoes and simmer partially covered about 45 minutes, stirring as needed and making sure it does not burn on the bottom. Add herbs 10 minutes before finishing. Season to taste with salt, pepper, and sugar.

Refrigerate covered up to several weeks, or freeze up to 3 months. Serve hot or cold.

SOUTHERN BASIL SAUCE

Makes 3/4 cup

THIS IS MY ALL-PURPOSE, *use-anytime version of a pesto sauce without the pine nuts, which become rancid very quickly in the South's heat. I make it up in batches and keep it refrigerated or frozen. Toss a spoonful into soups, mayonnaise, or other sauces or vinaigrettes; toss with hot rice or pasta.*

It is amazing how a cup of whole basil leaves shrinks. When chopped, the amount is next to nothing. Herbs and their flowers may both be used, but the stems are rarely used. At the end of the season, gather all the basil leaves and its flowers from the garden, chop them, and add garlic and olive oil. Freeze, as below. Add cheese as needed.

1 cup fresh basil leaves
1 garlic clove
1/4–1/2 cup olive oil
1/2 cup freshly grated Parmesan cheese

Chop the basil leaves with the garlic in a food processor. With the processor running, slowly drip oil into the basil in a steady stream. Add the cheese. Process until well combined.

If not using immediately, move sauce to an airtight container and cover the surface of the sauce with a thin layer of oil. The sauce can also be stored by freezing in an ice tray, then popping the sauce cubes into a freezer container; use a cube at a time as needed.

Variation: Sometimes I substitute butter for the oil in this sauce.

HONEY MUSTARD SAUCE

Makes 1/3 cup

ANY SANDWICH *is elevated with this sauce.*

1/3 cup mayonnaise
3 tablespoons whole-grain or Dijon mustard
2 tablespoons honey
1 tablespoon grated orange rind, no white included

Whisk together mayonnaise, mustard, honey, and orange rind. Use right away or cover and refrigerate.

SWEET BARBECUE SAUCE

Makes 4 cups

Enjoy this sweet sauce *with grilled beef or pork. Add it very close to the end of cooking, as it will burn due to the chili sauce and syrup. It has a rich, full, dominating flavor, so use it judiciously.*

2 tablespoons butter
2 medium onions, finely chopped
5 garlic cloves, finely chopped
2 cups tomato or chili sauce
½ cup dark corn syrup
½ cup red wine vinegar
4 tablespoons soy sauce
Juice of 2 lemons
3 tablespoons chopped fresh marjoram or thyme
Freshly ground black pepper

Heat the butter in a medium saucepan; add the onions and cook until soft. Add the garlic and cook briefly. For a smooth sauce, purée the onions and garlic before proceeding. Stir in the tomato sauce, corn syrup, vinegar, soy sauce, lemon juice, and marjoram. Season to taste with pepper.

May be made ahead, covered, and refrigerated. Freezes up to 3 months.

TART BARBECUE BASTING SAUCE

Makes 6 cups

It is a good basting sauce, *as it will not burn.*

4–6 tablespoons oil, cook's preference
2 tablespoons chopped fresh ginger
2 medium onions, chopped
4 tablespoons chili powder
4 garlic cloves, chopped
2 (12-ounce) cans beer
1 cup tomato juice
½ cup Worcestershire sauce
Juice of 1 lemon or lime
3 tablespoons paprika
5 tablespoons Dijon mustard
2 tablespoons chopped fresh basil, thyme, or parsley
Salt
Freshly ground black pepper

Heat the olive oil in a saucepan; add ginger, onions, chili powder, and garlic, and cook until soft.

Add the beer, tomato juice, Worcestershire sauce, lemon or lime juice, paprika, mustard, and herbs. Bring to the boil and then simmer briefly. Season to taste with salt and pepper.

The sauce keeps several days in the refrigerator, covered.

A slice of fresh ginger the size of a quarter makes about 1 tablespoon chopped ginger.

GEORGIA PEACH BARBECUE SAUCE

Makes 3½ cups

CANNED PEACH PRESERVES *are the basis for this sauce. It is excellent for ribs, steaks, or chicken.*

½ cup light or dark brown sugar
1 tablespoon onion salt
2 teaspoons freshly ground black pepper
1 teaspoon garlic powder
1 teaspoon ground ginger
¼ teaspoon ground cloves
¼ teaspoon ground mace
⅓ cup white vinegar
2 cups tomato ketchup
1 cup puréed peach preserves
2 tablespoons Worcestershire sauce
2 tablespoons honey
4 tablespoons butter, cut in ½-inch cubes, well chilled

Purée the sugar, onion salt, pepper, garlic powder, ginger, cloves, mace, vinegar, ketchup, peach preserves, Worcestershire, and honey in a food processor or blender until smooth. Move purée to a saucepan and bring to the boil, stirring to dissolve the sugar. Reduce the heat and simmer for 25 minutes, stirring occasionally. Gradually stir in the cubes of butter until the sauce is smooth.

VINEGAR-BASED BARBECUE SAUCE

Makes 4 cups

GOOD FOR BASTING, *this sauce is popular in parts of North Carolina, South Carolina, and a few spots in Georgia.*

3 cups cider vinegar
1 cup tomato sauce or ketchup
½–1 cup light or dark brown sugar
1 teaspoon–½ cup hot sauce or red pepper flakes
Salt
Freshly ground black pepper
Chopped garlic, optional
Chopped onion, optional
Herbs and spices, optional

Mix the vinegar, tomato sauce or ketchup, sugar to taste, and hot sauce or pepper flakes to taste, erring on the side of caution with the hot sauce. Season to taste with salt and pepper. Bring to the boil in a pan, reduce heat, and cook 10 minutes. Customize this recipe using the optional ingredients if desired.

VIDALIA ONION AND VINEGAR SAUCE

Makes 2 to 3 cups

THIS IS A STRONG, TASTY SAUCE, *and few things other than beef can stand up to it. It is good accompaniment for beef tenderloin and is tasty as well on a chuck roast or sirloin tip.*

1/2 cup plus 3 tablespoons butter
1/2 cup all-purpose flour
2 cups brown stock or broth
Salt
Freshly ground black pepper
3 medium onions, sliced
1/2 cup dry white wine
1/2 cup red wine vinegar

Melt 1/2 cup of butter in a large saucepan. Remove the pan from the heat and add flour to make a roux, stirring constantly. When smooth, place over moderate heat and stir until the flour and butter are browned. Remove from the heat, add stock or broth, and salt and pepper to taste. Place back on the heat and stir 3 to 4 minutes. This base sauce may be kept warm until needed for up to 30 minutes, or it may be cooled and refrigerated or frozen.

Melt the 3 tablespoons of butter in a heavy frying pan and add the onions. Cook over moderately low heat about 20 minutes, stirring constantly, until a rich brown. Add wine and vinegar. Bring to the boil and cook over high heat until the liquid has nearly evaporated, about 3 minutes. Add the base sauce to the onion-and-vinegar mixture, and bring back to the boil. Cook about 5 minutes. Season to taste with salt and pepper.

For a smooth sauce, discard the onions and strain remaining sauce through a sieve.

FIG AND BOURBON SAUCE

Makes 1 pint

AFTER DRIED FIGS *soak up honey and bourbon or brandy, they cause ahs and ohs. This is a real boon in the middle of the winter served with meat or game.*

1 cup apple cider
2/3 cup bourbon
1 tablespoon light or dark brown sugar
10 ounces dried figs, chopped

Combine apple cider, bourbon, and brown sugar in a small saucepan. Stir in figs and let stand 10 minutes.

Bring the fig mixture to a simmer over low heat and cook 10 minutes, until figs are soft. Move figs to a bowl using a slotted spoon.

Return the saucepan to the heat and simmer until the liquid is reduced by half. Pour liquid over figs. Serve warm or at room temperature.

Variation: Figs in Bourbon or Brandy

Cover figs with a mixture of 2 parts honey and 1 part bourbon or brandy in a sterile container. Refrigerate 2 months before serving; keeps a very long time.

MUSCADINE SAUCE

Makes 1 cup

MUSCADINES ARE NATIVE WILD AMERICAN GRAPES, *ranging in color from flecked bronze to dark purple-black. They have a strong, sweet wine flavor much like a Concord grape. With big seeds in the center and a very tough skin, one has to love them to be willing to peel and seed them. Which I do. This sauce goes well with game such as duck and venison, as well as red meats.*

4 cups muscadines, peeled and seeded
1 teaspoon oil, cook's preference
1/2 cup chopped onion
1 garlic clove, chopped

Purée the seeded and skinned muscadines using a food processor or blender. Heat the oil in a large sauce pan, add the onion and cook until translucent. Add the garlic and cook briefly. Add muscadine purée and simmer about 5 minutes, until mixture becomes slightly thick. (Thin with water if necessary.) May be made in advance up to several days and refrigerated covered or frozen. Serve hot or cold.

Variations:

- Chop the muscadines finely in a food processor before peeling and rub through a strainer rather than peeling first. Remove pits before puréeing.
- Add cinnamon, cloves, or other seasonings associated with game condiments.

PEELING AND PIPPING MUSCADINES AND SCUPPERNONGS

Drop the grapes into boiling water. Leave about 10 seconds. Test one to see if it peels easily. If so, drain and then run cold water over the grapes. Slip off peels and cut in half. Pull out seeds with a grape-pipper gadget or the rounded side of an unfolded paper clip as a hook. Take care the paper clip is discarded and does not get mixed with any food.

All grapes freeze. Move whole or seeded muscadines or scuppernongs to a rimmed baking sheet and freeze until solid. Transfer to a plastic ziplock bag and store frozen until needed.

BROWNED BUTTER SAUCE

Makes 1/2 cup

Browned butter has a rich, *full, toasted-nut flavor.*

4–6 tablespoons butter

Add butter to a clean pan, heat over medium heat, swirling the pan until the butter foams and turns a golden brown, giving off an aroma like browning pecans. Pour over any fish or vegetables.

Variation: Add 2 tablespoons lemon juice for fish or chicken, but not for green vegetables, as the acid will turn the green vegetables gray.

TYPICAL PAN SAUCE

Makes 1/2 cup

Probably the most important of the home cook's sauces, *it uses a stock to "deglaze" the pan, which is to remove the goodness, before boiling it down to reduce and thicken. This is a gracious plenty, and the volume may be reduced when just a small bit of sauce is needed for a family meal.*

1/2 cup stock, white or red wine, or dry port

Remove the steaks, chops, or chicken from the frying pan. Add the liquid, bring to the boil, and scrape the bottom of the pan to get all the good bits loosened. Reduce the heat to a simmer and cook until the volume is reduced by half. Spoon over the steaks, chops, or chicken.

Variation: Add 1 to 2 teaspoons chopped herbs, such as parsley, basil, thyme, oregano, or tarragon.

Variation: Heavy Cream Sauce
Add 1 cup heavy cream to the reduced liquid. Return to the boil, and cook until reduced in volume by half.

MUSTARD SAUCE FOR STEAKS AND CHOPS

Makes 1 cup

My grandson must have a sauce on everything to be happy, *even the finest steak. This is quick and easy, and is enough for the whole family. It can be made ahead several days and freezes well.*

2 cups chicken stock
3 tablespoons Dijon mustard
2–3 tablespoons butter or heavy cream
Salt
Freshly ground black pepper

Bring chicken stock to the boil in a frying pan. Boil until the volume is reduced to 1 cup. Whisk in the mustard and butter or cream. Season to taste with salt and pepper. Pour over cooked steaks or chops. Refrigerate of freeze.

Variation: Add 1 tablespoon chopped fresh tarragon.

SALSA

Makes 1 cup

SALSA, THE SPANISH WORD FOR "SAUCE," *has become as common as ketchup in the South.*

- 4 ripe plum tomatoes, seeded and chopped
- 1/3 cup red onion, finely diced
- 1 jalapeño pepper or other small hot pepper, seeded and finely diced
- 1/3 cup chopped cilantro
- 1 1/2 tablespoons olive oil
- Juice of 1 lime
- Salt
- Freshly ground black pepper

Mix the tomatoes, onion, jalapeno, cilantro to taste, olive oil, and lime juice together in a medium bowl. Season to taste with salt and pepper.

PEACH AND CUCUMBER SALSA

Makes 3 cups

WE CAME UP WITH THIS ONE DAY *when we needed something to give pizzazz to a simple baked fish. Pow! Indeed!*

- 2 cups diced peeled pitted peaches
- 2 medium cucumbers, diced
- 1 medium red bell pepper, seeded and diced
- 1/3 cup chopped fresh cilantro
- 2 tablespoons fresh lime juice
- 2 tablespoons peach or apricot preserves
- 1 teaspoon chopped canned chipotle chilies, optional
- Salt
- Freshly ground black pepper

Mix the peaches, cucumbers, bell pepper, cilantro, lime juice, preserves, and chilies together in a bowl. Season to taste with salt and pepper.

Refrigerate covered until ready to serve. Serve cold or at room temperature with tortilla chips or crackers.

LIME CUCUMBER SALSA

Makes 1 cup

THIS IS A THROW-TOGETHER SALSA *for the middle of the summer, when something is needed on the table to freshen up cold meats or even leftovers. All of a sudden everything seems new again.*

- 1 large cucumber, finely chopped
- 1 garlic clove, finely chopped
- 3 green onions, sliced
- 2 tablespoons chopped fresh cilantro
- 2 tablespoons fresh lime juice
- 2 tablespoons olive oil
- 1 teaspoon grated lime rind, no white attached, finely chopped
- 1/2 teaspoon salt
- 1/4 teaspoon freshly ground black pepper

Mix the cucumber, garlic, onions, cilantro, lime juice, olive oil, rind, salt, and pepper in a medium bowl. Refrigerate covered until ready to use. Serve cold or at room temperature.

FLAVORED BUTTER

Makes 1/2 cup

BOTH IN MY FORMER RESTAURANTS *and now at home, flavored butters are handy. Start with a small amount and try just a pat on bread, a steak or chop, or rice or pasta. If it is scrumptious, make more or your own variation.*

1/2 cup butter, softened

Mix butter and other ingredients until thoroughly distributed in the butter.

Variation: Herb Butter
Add 2 tablespoons chopped herbs.

Variation: Norman's Compound Butter with Lime and Cilantro
Add 2 tablespoons cilantro, the grated rind of 1/2 lime (no white attached) and the juice of 1/2 lime.

Variation: Orange-Honey Butter
Best on biscuits, this sweet variation is even good on rice pudding.

Add 1 teaspoon grated orange rind (no white attached) and 2 tablespoons honey.

PACKAGING HOMEMADE FLAVORED BUTTERS

There are many ways to package homemade flavored butters.

- Roll into a log using a plastic bag or plastic wrap, and freeze. This gives the butter the longest shelf life and allows the cook to cut off rounds of different sizes according to the use.
- Scoop the butter into a ramekin or other serving dish.
- Cut the corner off of a plastic bag, inserting a piping tip and making roses or other shapes that make pretty presentations for the table.

Always cover as tightly as possible, as butter may take on the taste of the refrigerator or freezer. Taste stored butters before serving.

CREOLE SEASONING

Makes 1 cup

CREOLE SEASONINGS ARE AS VARIED *as Creole cooks. I make a batch of this, use some, and store the rest tightly covered in the refrigerator. Rather than using an expensive unknown store-bought variety, adjust these seasonings to your taste, and you'll know what you have.*

1 tablespoon dried oregano
1 tablespoon salt
3 garlic cloves, crushed with 1 tablespoon salt (page 204)
2 tablespoons freshly ground black pepper
2 tablespoons ground hot red pepper
1 tablespoon dried thyme
2 tablespoons paprika

Mix the oregano, salt, garlic, peppers, thyme, and paprika together in a small bowl. Store tightly wrapped in the refrigerator.

JAMAICAN JERK SEASONING

Makes 2 to 3 tablespoons

THE CARIBBEAN HAS A MODEST INFLUENCE *to this day in the South, but I truly did not hear of "jerk" seasoning until the 1980s.*

2 teaspoons onion powder
1 teaspoon granulated sugar
1 teaspoon ground thyme
1 teaspoon salt
1/2 teaspoon ground allspice
1/4 teaspoon ground cinnamon
1/4 teaspoon ground nutmeg
1/4 teaspoon ground hot red pepper
1/4 teaspoon ground cumin

Mix together the onion powder, sugar, thyme, salt, allspice, cinnamon, nutmeg, hot red pepper, and cumin together in a small bowl. Store in an airtight container.

PERFUMED OLIVE OIL

Makes 2 cups

THIS OLIVE OIL MAKES ALL THE DIFFERENCE *in the world, adding a subtle flavor to salads or to soups as a final drizzle. One caveat: this oil should be kept refrigerated, and the garlic should be thoroughly strained out before storing.*

2 cups olive oil
6 heads garlic, broken into cloves
6 cups basil, thyme, rosemary, or other fresh herbs (include some stems), divided

Pour the olive oil into a roasting pan. Add the garlic and half the herbs. On the stovetop, heat slowly and carefully until just below the boiling point. Remove from the heat; stir in the rest of the herbs and leave to infuse for 1 hour. Strain well. The oil keeps up to 1 month covered. It must be refrigerated.

Variation: Substitute 1 teaspoon red pepper flakes for the herbs.

PRESERVED GINGER

Makes 1/4 pound

"HANDS" OF GINGER *are too large to be used up quickly by the home cook. Storing ginger in dry sherry preserves the ginger as well as flavors the sherry. (Vodka works too!) Ginger grows easily in my garden. I use the attached greens in salads and marinades as well.*

1/4 pound fresh ginger
1/2 cup dry sherry or vodka

Cut fresh ginger, peeled or unpeeled, into chunks and move to a jar. Pour dry sherry or vodka over ginger and cover tightly. The preserved ginger can be used in place of fresh ginger, and the sherry will add a little pick-up to some dishes when needed.

MARINADES

There is hardly a cut of meat that doesn't benefit from a marinade. These are some of our favorites. Combine the ingredients for each in a plastic ziplock bag. Add meat and refrigerate 30 minutes or up to overnight.

GARLIC-THYME-WINE MARINADE

6 garlic cloves, chopped
2 tablespoons olive oil
2 tablespoons fresh thyme leaves
1/2 cup red wine
Salt
Freshly ground black pepper

GARLIC-WINE MARINADE

3 garlic cloves, chopped
5 sprigs fresh thyme
1/2 medium onion, sliced
1/2 cup red or white wine
1 tablespoon granulated sugar
3 tablespoons olive oil

SPICY LIME MARINADE

1 teaspoon salt
1/2 cup lime juice
1/2 cup red currant jelly
1/4 teaspoon ground allspice
1 garlic clove, chopped
2 tablespoons chopped fresh cilantro
1/4 cup chopped seeded jalapeños

SOY SAUCE MARINADE

1/2 cup oil, cook's preference
1/2 cup soy sauce
1/3 cup red wine vinegar
1/4 cup fresh lemon juice
3 tablespoons Worcestershire sauce
1 tablespoon freshly ground black pepper
2 tablespoons Dijon mustard
1 onion, sliced
2 garlic cloves, chopped

RUBS

Rubs are dry herb-and-spice mixtures rubbed onto meats and poultry to give them more flavor. Rub the meat or poultry generously with any of the following recipes. Let sit, or cook right away. Here are some of our favorites. Increase the volume for large meats or to make enough to store for another day.

ALL-PURPOSE RUB

4 tablespoons granulated sugar
4 tablespoons salt
1 tablespoon paprika
2 tablespoons dry mustard powder
1/2 teaspoon freshly ground black pepper
1/4 teaspoon dried oregano
1/4 teaspoon dried thyme

SPICY RUB

3/4 cup paprika
1/4 cup freshly ground black pepper
1/4 cup light or dark brown sugar
2 tablespoons chili powder
2 tablespoons garlic powder
2 tablespoons onion powder
1 tablespoon salt
2 teaspoons ground hot red pepper

SMOKY RUB

2 tablespoons salt
2 tablespoons ground coriander
2 tablespoons ground cinnamon
1 tablespoon ground cumin
1 tablespoon ground nutmeg
1 tablespoon freshly ground black pepper

INDEX

C

D

F

H

I

J

K

L

N

O

V

W

Y

Z

BIBLIOGRAPHY

Abala, Ken. *Beans: A History*. Oxford, UK: Berg Publishers, 2007.

Aidells, Bruce, and Denis Kelly. *The Complete Meat Cookbook: A Juicy and Authoritative Guide to Selecting, Seasoning, and Cooking Today's Beef, Pork, Lamb, and Veal*. New York: Houghton Mifflin, 1998.

Anderson, Brett. *Cornbread Nation 6: The Best of Southern Food Writing*. Athens: University of Georgia, 2012.

Baker, Jack D. *Cherokee Cookbook*. Fayetteville, AR: Indian Heritage Association, 1971.

Baking Illustrated: A Best Recipe Classic. Brookline, MA: America's Test Kitchen, 2004.

Bass, A. L. Tommie, and J. K. Crellin. *Plain Southern Eating from the Reminiscences of A. L. Tommie Bass, Herbalist*. Durham, NC: Duke University Press, 1988.

Beard, James. *James Beard's American Cookery*. Boston: Little, Brown, 1972.

Bell, Malcolm, Jr. "Romantic Wines of Madeira." *The Georgia Historical Quarterly 38*, (December 1954): 322–36.

Better Homes and Gardens Cookbook. Des Moines, IA: Meredith Publishing Co., 1950.

Bjornskov, Elizabeth. *The Complete Book of American Fish and Shellfish Cookery*. New York: Alfred A. Knopf, 1984.

Brown, Marion. *Southern Cook Book*. Chapel Hill, NC: University of North Carolina Press, 1968.

Burn, Billie. *Stirrin' the Pots on Daufuskie*. Hilton Head, SC: Impressions Print, 1985.

Cajun Cuisine. Lafayette, LA: Beau Bayou Publishing Company, 1985.

Caldwell, Anne Foster. *Anne Foster Caldwell's Book of Southern and Creole Home Cooking.* Nashville: Benson Printing, 1929.

Caldwell, Betty Rye. *From the Tennessean . . . Betty's Best Recipes!* Nashville: Favorite Recipes Press, 1982.

Carney, Judith Ann., and Richard Nicholas Rosomoff. *In the Shadow of Slavery: Africa's Botanical Legacy in the Atlantic World*. Berkeley: University of California, 2009.

Junior Assembly of Anderson. *Carolina Cuisine: A Collection of Recipes*. Anderson, SC: Hallux, 1969.

Castle, Sheri. *The New Southern Garden Cookbook: Enjoying the Best from Homegrown Gardens, Farmers' Markets, Roadside Stands, & CSA Farm Boxes*. Chapel Hill: University of North Carolina, 2011.

Charleston Hospitality: Recipes from Johnson & Wales University at Charleston. Charleston, SC: Broad Street Printing, 1992.

Charleston Receipts. Charleston, SC: The League, 1950.

Charleston Receipts Repeats: Recipes. Charleston, SC: League, 1986.

Chase, Leah. *The Dooky Chase Cookbook*. Gretna: Pelican Pub., 1990.

Child, Julia. *From Julia Child's Kitchen*. New York: Alfred A Knopf, 1970.

Child, Julia, Simone Beck, and Louisette Bertholle. *Mastering the Art of French Cooking, Volume I.* New York: Alfred A. Knopf, 1961.

Child, Julia and Simone Beck. *Mastering the Art of French Cooking, Volume II.* New York: Alfred A. Knopf, 1970.

Child, Lydia Maria. *The American Frugal Housewife.* Cambridge, MA: A George Dawson Book, 1832.

Christ Church Cook Book. Savannah, GA: Kennickell Printing Co., 1956.

Claiborne, Craig. *Craig Claiborne's Southern Cooking*. New York: Times Books, 1987.

Clark, Arthur. *Bayou Cuisine; Its Tradition and Transition.* Indianola, MS: St. Stephen's Episcopal Church, 1970.

Collard Greens, Watermelons and "Miss" Charlotte's Pie: A cookbook. Swansboro, NC: Swansboro United Methodist Women, 1993.

Conway, Linda Glick. *Party Receipts.* New York, NY: Algonquin, 1993.

Corbitt, Helen. *Helen Corbitt's Cookbook*. Boston: Houghton Mifflin, 1957.

Corriher, Shirley O. *BakeWise: The Hows and Whys of Successful Baking with Over 200 Magnificent Recipes*. New York: Scribner, 2008.

Corriher, Shirley O. *Cookwise: The Hows and Whys of Successful Cooking*. New York: William Morrow, 1997.

Cossart, Noël. *Madeira: The Island Vineyard*. London: Christie's Wine Publication, 1984.

Cunningham, Marion, and Fannie Merritt Farmer. *The Fannie Farmer Cookbook*. New York: Knopf, 1990.

Dabney, Joseph Earl. *Smokehouse Ham, Spoon Bread & Scuppernong Wine: The Folklore and Art of Southern Appalachian Cooking*. Nashville, TN: Cumberland House, 1998.

Dalsass, Diana. *Miss Mary's Down-home Cooking*. New York and Scarborough, Ontario: NAL Books, 1984.

DeBolt, Margaret Wayt. *Savannah Sampler Cookbook*. Norfolk, VA: Donning Company, 1978.

Deihl, Craig. *Cypress*. Layton, UT: Wyrick, 2007.

DeWitt, Dave. *The Founding Foodies: How Washington, Jefferson, and Franklin Revolutionized American Cuisine.* Naperville, IL: Sourcebooks, Inc., 2010.

Down Home in High Style. Dothan, AL: Houston Academy Library Committee, 1980.

Dull, Mrs. S.R. *Southern Cooking*. Atlanta: The Ruralist Press, 1928.

Dupree, Nathalie. *Cooking of the South*. New York: Irena Chalmers Cookbooks, 1982.

———. *Nathalie Dupree Cooks Everyday Meals from a Well-Stocked Pantry: Strategies for Shopping Less and Eating Better.* New York: Clarkson Potter, 1995.

———. *Nathalie Dupree Cooks Quick Meals for Busy Days.* New York: Clarkson Potter, 1996.

———. *Nathalie Dupree Cooks for Family and Friends.* New York: Morrow, 1991.

———. *Nathalie Dupree's Comfortable Entertaining: At Home with Ease & Grace.* New York: Viking, 1998.

———. *Nathalie Dupree's Matters of Taste.* New York: Knopf, 1990.

———. *Nathalie Dupree's Southern Memories: Recipes and Reminiscences*. New York: Clarkson Potter, 1993.

Dupree, Nathalie, and Cynthia Graubart. *Southern Biscuits*, Layton, UT: Gibbs Smith, 2011.

Dupree, Nathalie, and Marion Sullivan. *Nathalie Dupree's Shrimp & Grits Cookbook.* Charleston SC: Wyrick, 2006.

Dyer, Ceil. *The Carter Family Favorites Cookbook*. New York: Delacorte E. Friede, 1977.

Edge, John T., ed. *The New Encyclopedia of Southern Culture, Volume 7: Foodways.* Chapel Hill: University of North Carolina, 2007.

Edisto Island Yacht Club. *Creekside Cooking*. Morris, 2011.

Egerton, John. *Cornbread Nation 1: The Best of Southern Food Writing*. Chapel Hill: Published in Association with the Southern Foodways Alliance, Center for the Study of Southern Culture, University of Mississippi, by the University of North Carolina, 2002.

Egerton, John. *Side Orders: Small Helpings of Southern Cookery & Culture*. Atlanta: Peachtree, 1990.

———. *Southern Food at Home, on the Road, in History*. New York: Alfred A. Knopf, 1987.

———. *Southern Food at Home, on the Road, in History*. Chapel Hill: University of North Carolina, 1993.

Ellis, Merle. *Cutting-up in the Kitchen*. San Francisco: Chronicle Books, 1975.

Episcopal Churchwomen and Friends of Christ Episcopal Church. *Pass the Plate*. New Bern, NC: 1981.

Eustis, Célestine, and Louis Szathmáry. *Cooking in Old Créole Days*. New York: Arno, 1973.

Exum, Helen McDonald. *Helen Exum's Chattanooga Cook Book*. Chattanooga, TN.: Chattanooga News-Free Press, 1970.

Feibleman, Peter S. *American Cooking: Creole and Acadian*. New York: Time-Life Books, 1971.

Foley, Joan, and Joe Foley. *The Chesapeake Bay Fish & Fowl Cookbook: A Collection of Old and New Recipes from Maryland's Eastern Shore*. New York: Macmillan, 1981.

Folse, John D. *The Encyclopedia of Cajun & Creole Cuisine*. Gonzales, LA: Chef John Folse & Pub., 2004.

Food Editors of *Farm Journal*. *Farm Journal's Picnic & Barbecue Cookbook*. New York: Greenwich House, 1982.

Foose, Martha. *Screen Doors and Sweet Tea: Recipes and Tales from a Southern Cook.* New York: Clarkson Potter, 2008.

Fowler, Damon Lee. *Damon Lee Fowler's New Southern Baking: Classic Flavors for Today's Cook*. New York: Simon & Schuster, 2005.

———. *Damon Lee Fowler's New Southern Kitchen Traditional Flavors for Contemporary Cooks*. New York: Simon & Schuster, 2002.

———. *Dining at Monticello: In Good Taste and Abundance*. Charlottesville, VA: Thomas Jefferson Foundation, 2005.

———. *The Savannah Cookbook*. Layton, UT: Gibbs Smith, 2008.

Four Great Southern Cooks. Atlanta: Dubose Publishing, 1980.

Fox, Minerva Carr, and Alvin Langoon. Coburn. *The Blue Grass Cookbook*. New York: Fox, Duffield, 1904.

Gibson, Belinda Ellis, and Julie Maples. *White Lily Sunday Best Baking: Over a Century of Secrets from the White Lily Kitchen*. Atlanta: Longstreet, 1998.

Gillette, F. L., and Hugo Ziemann. *The Presidential Cookbook: Adapted from the White House Cook Book*. Akron, OH: Saalfield, 1914.

———. *The White House Cookbook: A Comprehensive Cyclopedia of Information for the Home*. New York: Saalfield, 1916.

Gleaners Class. *Favorite Recipes of the Red River Valley*. Shreveport, LA: First Methodist Church, 1968.

Glenn, Camille. *The Heritage of Southern Cooking*. New York: Workman Pub., 1986.

Goldstein, Jonathan, ed. *Georgia's East Asian Connection, 1733–1983*, vol 22. Carrolton, GA: West Georgia College Studies on Social Sciences, 1983.

The Good Housekeeping Cookbook. New York: Rinehart and Company, 1944.

Goolsby, Sam. *Cedar Creek Game Cookbook*. Monticello, GA: Cedar Creek Hunting Lodge, 1975.

Graubart, Cynthia Stevens, and Catherine Fliegel. *The One-Armed Cook: Quick And Easy Recipes, Smart Meal Plans, And Savvy Advice For New (And Not So New) Moms*. Des Moines, IA: Meredith, 2004.

Greene, Bert. *Honest American Fare*. Chicago: Contemporary Books, 1923.

Gutierrez, Sandra A. *The New Southern-Latino Table: Recipes That Bring Together the Bold and Beloved Flavors of Latin America & the American South*. Chapel Hill: University of North Carolina, 2011.

Hanley, Rosemary and Peter. *America's Best Recipes. State Fair Blue Ribbon Winners.* Boston and Toronto: Little, Brown, 1983.

Hartley, Grace. *Grace Hartley's Southern Cookbook*. New York: Doubleday, 1976.

Harris, Jessica B. *Iron Pots and Wooden Spoons: Africa's Gifts to New World Cooking*. New York, NY: Simon & Schuster, 1999.

Head Table Cooks: A Collection of Favorite Recipes from Around the World. Fort Valley, GA: Society, 1982.

Hearn, Lafcadio. *Creole Cook Book*. New Orleans, LA: Pelican Publishing House, 1967.

Herbst, Sharon Tyler, and Ron Herbst. *The Deluxe Food Lover's Companion*. Hauppauge, NY: Barrons Educational Series, 2009.

Herbst, Sharon Tyler. *The New Food Lover's Companion: Comprehensive Definitions of over 4000 Food, Wine and Culinary Terms*. New York: Barron's, 1995.

Hess, Karen, and Samuel G. Stoney. *The Carolina Rice Kitchen: The African Connection*. Columbia, SC: University of South Carolina, 1992.

Hess, John L. and Karen. *The Taste of America*. New York: Grossman Publishers, 1977.

Hill, A. P., and Damon Lee Fowler. *Mrs. Hill's Southern Practical Cookery and Receipt Book*. Columbia, SC: University of South Carolina, 1995.

Hooker, Richard J. *A Colonial Plantation Cookbook: The Receipt Book of Harriott Pinckney Horry, 1770.* Columbia, SC: University of South Carolina Press, 1984.

Huguenin, Mary Vereen, and Anne Montague Stoney. *Charleston Receipts*. Charleston, SC: Walker, Evans & Cogswell Company, 1950.

Hurt, Caroline Darden., and Joan Hundley. *The Smithfield Cookbook*. Hampton, VA: Multi-Print, 1978.

Jefferson, Thomas, and Robert C. Baron. *The Garden and Farm Books of Thomas Jefferson*. Golden, CO: Fulcrum, 1987.

Jenkins, Charlotte, William P. Baldwin, Jonathan Green, and Mic Smith. *Gullah Cuisine: by Land and by Sea*. Charleston, SC: Evening Post Pub., 2010.

Jones, Evan. *American Food: The Gastronomic Story*, 2nd ed. New York: Random House, 1981.

Junior Charity League of Monroe, Louisiana. *The Cotton Country Collection*. Memphis, TN, 1972.

Junior League of Atlanta. *Atlanta Cooknotes*. Atlanta: Stein Printing Co., 1982.

Junior League of Augusta, Georgia. *Tea-time at the Masters*. Augusta, GA, 1977.

Junior League of Baton Rouge. *River Road Recipes*. Baton Rouge, LA, 1981.

Junior League of Charleston. *Charleston Receipts*. Charleston, SC, 1950.

Junior League of Columbia. *Putting on the Grits*. Columbia, SC, 1984.

Junior League of DeKalb County, Georgia. *Puttin' on the Peachtree*. Memphis, TN: Wimmer Brothers Books, 1979.

Junior League of Fayetteville. *The Carolina Collection*. Fayetteville, NC: Kansas City Press, 1978.

Junior League of Greenville. *300 Years of Carolina Cooking*. Greenville, SC, 1970.

Junior League of Hampton Roads. *Virginia Hospitality*. Hampton Roads, VA, 1975.

Junior League of Jackson. *Southern Sideboards*. Jackson, MS, 1978.

Junior League of Lynchburg, Virginia. *Good Cookin' from the Heart of Virginia*. Lynchburg, VA, 1985.

Junior League of Norfolk-Virginia Beach. *Toast to Tidewater: Celebrating Virginia's Finest Food & Beverages*. Norfolk, VA, 2004.

Junior League of Richmond. *Virginia Seasons: New Recipes from the Old Dominion*. Richmond, VA, 1984.

Junior League of Savannah. *Southern Style*. Savannah, GA, 1908.

Junior League of Shreveport. *A Cook's Tour of Shreveport*. Shreveport, LA, 1964.

Junior League of Tuscaloosa, Alabama. *Winning Seasons*. Tuscaloosa, AL, 1979.

Junior Service League of Americus, Georgia. *Something Southern: A Collection of Recipes*. Americus, GA, 1976.

Junior Women's Club of Smithfield. *The Smithfield Cookbook*. Hampton, VA: Multi-Print, 1978.

Kamman, Madeleine. *New Making of a Cook: the Art, Techniques, and Science of Good Cooking*. New York: Morrow, 1997.

Kimball, Marie Goebel. *Thomas Jefferson's Cook Book*. Charlottesville: University of Virginia, 1976.

King, Daisy. *Miss Daisy's Healthy Southern Cooking*. Nashville, TN: Cumberland House, 2004.

Knowles, Laura Thornton. *Southern Recipes Tested by Myself*. New York: George H. Doran, 1913.

Lady, Of Charleston., and Sarah Rutledge. *The Carolina Housewife: or, House and Home*. Charleston, SC: W.R. Babcock, 1851.

Lane, Emma Rylander. *Some Good Things to Eat*. 1989. Reprint, Clayton, AL: The Clayton Record, 1976.

Lang, Rebecca D. *Quick-fix Southern: Homemade Hospitality in 30 Minutes or Less*. Kansas City, MO: Andrews McMeel Pub., 2011.

LeClercq, Anne Sinkler Whaley, and Emily Wharton Sinkler. *An Antebellum Plantation Household: including the South Carolina Low Country Receipts and Remedies of Emily Wharton Sinkler*. Columbia, SC: University of South Carolina, 1996.

Lee, Matt, and Ted Lee. *The Lee Bros. Southern Cookbook: Stories and Recipes for Southerners and Would-be Southerners*. New York: W.W. Norton, 2006.

Leslie, Eliza. *Directions for Cookery: In Its Various Branches*. Philadelphia: Carey & Hart, 1838.

Lewis, Edna. *The Taste of Country Cooking*. New York: Alfred A. Knopf, 1982.

Lewis, Edna, and Mary Goodbody. *In Pursuit of Flavor*. New York: Knopf, 1988.

Lewis, Edna, and Scott Peacock. *The Gift of Southern Cooking: Recipes and Revelations from Two Great Southern Cooks*. New York: Alfred A. Knopf, 2003.

Lewis, Nelly Custis, and Patricia Brady. *Nelly Custis Lewis's Housekeeping Book*. New Orleans, LA: Historic New Orleans Collection, 1982.

Lundy, Ronni. *Butter Beans to Blackberries: Recipes from the Southern Garden*. New York: North Point, 1999.

———. *Shuck Beans, Stack Cakes, and Honest Fried Chicken: the Heart and Soul of Southern Country Kitchens: Seasoned with Memories and Melodies from Country Music Stars*. New York: Atlantic Monthly, 1991.

Lupo, Margaret. *Southern Cooking from Mary Mac's Tea Room*. Atlanta: Marmac Publishing Co., 1983.

Marriott, Norman G., and Herbert W. Ockerman. *The Ultimate Guide to*

Country Ham: An American Delicacy. Radford, VA: Brightside, 2004.

Marshall, Lillian Berstrom. *Cooking Across the South*. Birmingham, AL: Oxmoor House, 1980.

———. *Southern Living Illustrated Cookbook*. Birmingham, AL.: Oxmoor House, 1976.

Maynard, Gloria C. *Caterin' to Charleston*. Charleston, SC: Merritt Publishing Co., 1981.

McCullough, Glenn, ed. *Georgia Receipts*, Atlanta: Georgia Press Association, 1971.

McDermott, Nancie. *Southern Cakes Sweet and Irresistible Recipes for Everyday Celebrations*. San Francisco: Chronicle Books, 2007.

———. *Southern Pies: A Gracious Plenty of Pie Recipes, from Lemon Chess to Chocolate Pecan*. San Francisco: Chronicle Books, 2010.

McGee, Harold. *The Curious Cook: More Kitchen Science and Lore*. San Francisco: North Point, 1990.

———. *On Food and Cooking: the Science and Lore of the Kitchen*. New York: Scribner, 1984.

McRee, Patsie. *The Kitchen and the Cotton Patch*. Atlanta: Cullom & Ghertner, 1948.

Meade, Martha L. *Recipes from the Old South*. New York: Holt, Rinehart & Winston, 1981.

Monroe, Betty. *Huntsville Heritage Cookbook*. Huntsville, AL: Grace Club Auxiliary, 1967.

Montpelier Hospitality: History, Traditions and Recipes. Montpelier Station, VA: Montpelier Foundation, 2002.

Morrison, Sally. *Cross Creek Kitchens: Seasonal Recipes and Reflections*. Gainesville, FL: Triad Pub., 1983.

National Fisheries Institute. *Galley Greats, Fish and Seafood*. Washington, DC: 1981.

The National Society of the Colonial Dames of America in the State of Georgia. *Georgia Heritage, Treasured Recipes*. Atlanta, 1979.

Neal, Bill. *Biscuits, Spoonbread, and Sweet Potato Pie*. New York: Knopf, 1990.

Neal, Bill. *Southern Cooking*. Chapel Hill, NC, and London: University of North Carolina Press, 1985.

The New Good Housekeeping Cookbook. New York: Hearst, 1999.

Newnan Junior Service League. *A Taste of Georgia*. Newnan, GA, 1977.

Oliver, Sandra L. *Food in Colonial and Federal America*. Westport, CT: Greenwood, 2005.

The Original Picayune Creole Cook Book. New Orleans: Times-Picayune Pub., 1945.

Owens, Janis. *Cracker Kitchen: A Cookbook in Celebration of Cornbread-Fed, Down Home Family Stories and Cuisine*. New York, NY: Scribner, 2009.

Paddleford, Clementine, Kelly Alexander, and Molly O'Neill. *The Great American Cookbook: 500 Time-Tested Recipes: Favorite Foods from Every State!* New York: Rizzoli, 2011.

Page, Linda Garland. *The Foxfire Book of Appalachian Cookery*. New York: Gramercy, 2001.

Pass the Plate: the Collection from Christ Church. New Bern, NC: Episcopal Churchwomen and Friends of Christ Episcopal Church, 1981.

Payne, Susan Carlisle. *The Southern Living Cookbook*. Birmingham, AL: Oxmoor House, 1987.

Peterson, James. *Baking*. Berkeley: Berkeley: Ten Speed Press, 2009.

———. *Fish & Shellfish*. New York: Morrow, 1996.

———. *Sauces: Classical and Contemporary Sauce Making*. Hoboken, NJ: Wiley, 2008.

———. *Vegetables*. New York: Morrow, 1998.

Phillips, Anne Byrn. *Cooking in the New South*. Atlanta: Peachtree Publishers, 1984.

Prudhomme, Paul. *Chef Paul Prudhomme's Louisiana Kitchen*. New York: William Morrow & Co., 1984.

Randolph, Mary. *The Virginia House-wife*. Karen Hess (ed.). Columbia SC: University of South Carolina Press, 1984.

Randolph, Mary, Henry Stone, and Henry Stone. *The Virginia house-wife: Method is the soul of management, Second edition, with amendments and additions*. Washington [D.C.]: Printed by Way & Gideon, Ninth Street, near Pennsylvania Avenue, 1825.

Rattray, Diana. *The About.com Guide to Southern Cooking: All You Need to Prepare 225 Delicious Home Cooked Favorites*. Avon, MA: Adams Media, 2006.

Ravenel, Rose P., and Elizabeth Ravenel Harrigan. *Charleston Recollections and Receipts: Rose P. Ravenel's Cookbook/ [edited by Elizabeth Ravenel Harrigan]*. Sewanee, TN: E.R. Harrigan, 1983.

Rawlings, Marjorie Kinnan, *Cross Creek Cookery*. New York: Charles Scribner's Sons, 1942.

Rhett, Blanche S., and Gay Lettier. *Two Hundred Yearts of Charleston Cooking*. Columbia, SC: University of South Carolina Press, 1976.

Robinson, Sallie Ann., and Gregory Wrenn. Smith. *Gullah home cooking the Daufuskie way: Smokin' Joe Butter Beans, Ol' 'Fuskie Fried Crab Rice, Sticky-Bush Blackberry Dumpling, and Other Sea Island Favorites*. Chapel Hill: The University of North Carolina Press, 2003.

Rombauer, Irma Von Starkloff, and Marion Rombauer. Becker. *Joy of Cooking*. Indianapolis: Bobbs-Merrill, 1946 and 1964.

Root, Waverly. *Food*. New York: Simon & Schuster, 1980.

Rudisill, Marie, and Sook Faulk. *Sook's Cookbook: Memories and Traditional Receipts from the Deep South*. Atlanta: Longstreet, 1989.

Ruhlman, Michael. *Ratio: The simple codes behind the craft of everyday cooking*. New York, NY: Scribner, 2009.

Rutledge, Sarah. *The South Carolina Housewife*. Columbia, SC: University of South Carolina Press, 1979.

The St. James' 40th Anniversary Cookbook. Mount Vernon: Congregation of St. James' Episcopal Church, 1998.

Sanders, Dori. *Dori Sanders' Country Cooking Recipes and Stories from the Family Farm Stand*. Chapel Hill, N.C: Algonquin Books of Chapel Hill, 1995.

Sanders, Zoe D. *Entertaining at the College of Charleston*. Charleston, SC: College of Charleston Foundation, 1998.

Schultz, Philip Stephen. *Cooking with Fire and Smoke*. New York: Simon & Schuster, 1986.

Scott, Pearlie B. *Southern Recipes: a Collection of the South's Favorite Recipes*. Nashville, TN: Music City Art, 1992.

Shell, Ella Jo, and John Shell. *Recipes from Our Front Porch: Hemlock Inn, Bryson City, North Carolina*. Bryson City, NC: E. J. & J. Shell, 1982.

Smalls, Alexander, and Hettie Jones. *Grace the Table: Stories and Recipes from My Southern Revival*. New York: Harper Collins Publishers, 1997

Smith, Andrew F. *The Oxford Companion to American Food and Drink*. Oxford: Oxford UP, 2007.

———. *The Oxford Encyclopedia of Food and Drink in America*. Oxford: Oxford UP, 2004.

Smith, Bill. *Seasoned in the South: Recipes from Crook's Corner and from Home*. Chapel Hill, NC: Algonquin of Chapel Hill, 2005.

Smith, E. *The Compleat Housewife, or, Accomplish'd Gentlewoman's Companion*. London: Printed for J. Pemberton, 1729.

Social Circle United Methodist Church. *Sesquicentennial Cookbook*. Social Circle, GA: Cookbook Publishers, 1979.

Southern Heritage Cookbook Library. Birmingham, AL: Oxmoor House, 1983.

Southern Living 1983 Annual Recipes. Birmingham, AL: Oxmoor House, 1983.

Stamps, Martha Phelps. *The New Southern Basics: Traditional Southern Food for Today*. Nashville, TN: Cumberland House, 1997.

Stitt, Frank. *Frank Stitt's Southern Table: Recipes and Gracious Traditions from Highlands Bar and Grill*. New York: Artisan, 2004.

Symphony League of Jackson, Mississippi. *The Jackson Cookbook*. Jackson, MS, 1971.

Swainsboro United Methodist Women. *Collards, Watermelon and "Miss" Charlotte's Pie*. Swainsboro: Swainsboro United Methodist Women, 1993.

Talmadge, Betty. *Lovejoy Plantation Cookbook*. Atlanta: Peachtree Publishers, 1970.

Talmadge, Betty, Jean Robitscher, and Carolyn Carter. *How to Cook a Pig and Other Back-to-the-Farm Recipes*. New York: Simon & Schuster, 1977.

Tannahill, Reay. *Food in History*. New York: Stein and Day, 1973.

Taylor, John Martin. *Hoppin' John's Lowcountry Cooking: Recipes and Ruminations from Charleston & the Carolina Coastal Plain*. New York: Bantam, 1992.

———. *The New Southern Cook: Two Hundred Recipes from the South's Best Chefs and Home Cooks*. New York: Bantam, 1995.

Thoroughbred Fare Cookbook of Aiken, Inc. *Thoroughbred Fare*. Aiken, SC, 1984.

Thornton, P., and P. Thornton. *The Southern Gardener and Receipt Book: Containing Directions for Gardening; a Collection of Valuable Receipts for Cookery, the Preservation of Fruits and Other Articles of Household Consumption, and for the Cure of Diseases*. Camden, SC: Printed for the Author, 1840.

Thurman, Sue Bailey, and Anne Bower. *The Historical Cookbook of the American Negro*. Boston: Beacon, 2000.

Tuckahoe Tidbits. Lenexa, KS: Cookbook, 1999.

Villas, James, and Martha Pearl. Villas. *My Mother's Southern Desserts*. New York: Morrow, 1998.

———. *The Glory of Southern Cooking*. New York: Wiley, 2007.

———. *Pig: King of the Southern Table*. Hoboken, NJ: John Wiley, 2010.

Voltz, Jeanne A. *Barbecued Ribs and Other Great Feeds*. New York: Alfred A. Knopf, 1985.

————. *The Flavor of the South*. New York: Gramercy Publishing Company, 1983.

Vashti Auxiliary. *Pines and Plantations*. Thomasville, GA, 1976.

Walter, Carole, and Rodica Prato. *Great Pies & Tarts*. New York: C. Potter, 1998.

Walter, Carole. *Great Cakes*. New York: Ballantine, 1991.

Walter, Eugene. *American Cooking: Southern Style*. New York: Time-Life Books, 1971.

Washington, Martha. *Martha Washington's Booke of Cookery*. Karen Hess (ed.), New York: Columbia University Press, 1981.

White Lily Foods Company. *Great Baking with White Lily Flour*. Des Moines, Iowa: Meredith Corporation, 1982.

Willan, Anne. *La Varenne Practique: The Complete Illustrated Cooking Course, Techniques, Ingredients, and Tools of Modern Cuisine*. New York: Crown, 1996.

Williams, Susan. *The McClellanville Coast Cookbook*. McClellanville, SC: McClellanville Arts Council, 1992.

The Williamsburg Cookbook. Williamsburg, VA: Colonial Williamsburg Foundation, 1971.

Williamson, CiCi. *The Best of Virginia Farms Cookbook & Tour Book: Recipes, People, Places*. Atlanta: CI, 2003.

Willis, Virginia. *Basic to Brilliant, Y'all: 150 Refined Southern Recipes and Ways to Dress Them up for Company*. Berkeley: Ten Speed, 2011.

———. *Bon Appétit, Y'all: Recipes and Stories from Three Generations of Southern Cooking*. Berkeley: Ten Speed, 2008.

Wilson, Mrs. Henry Lumpkin. *The Atlanta Exposition Cookbook*. Athens, GA: University of Georgia Press, 1984.

Wilson, Henry Lumpkin. *Tested Recipe Cook Book*. Atlanta: Foote & Davies, 1895.

The Women's Ministries of First Assembly of God. *Country Cookbook*. Collierville, TN: Fundcraft Publishing, 1984.

METRIC CONVERSION CHART

Volume Measurements

U.S.	Metric
1 teaspoon	5 ml
1 tablespoon	15 ml
1/4 cup	60 ml
1/3 cup	75 ml
1/2 cup	125 ml
2/3 cup	150 ml
3/4 cup	175 ml
1 cup	250 ml

Weight Measurements

U.S.	Metric
1/2 ounce	15 g
1 ounce	30 g
3 ounces	90 g
4 ounces	115 g
8 ounces	225 g
12 ounces	350 g
1 pound	450 g
2 1/4 pounds	1 kg

Temperature Conversion

Fahrenheit	Celsius
250	120
300	150
325	160
350	180
375	190
400	200
425	220
450	230